THE OXFORD HANDBO

JOHN BUNYAN

Praise for *The Oxford Handbook of John Bunyan*

'This beautifully produced volume is coherent, wide-ranging, and full of delights. It brings together a global roster of Bunyan experts from the United Kingdom, United States, Canada, France, Japan, and Israel who write with confidence on topics that they have pursued throughout their careers. Contributors cite each other's work frequently, creating a strong sense of respect for foregoing scholarship and creating a dynamic of long-running conversations being picked up and pursued. A volume could not contain more expertise than this.'
Tessa Whitehouse, *XVII–XVIII: Revue de la Société d'études anglo-américaines des XVIIe et XVIIIe siècles*

'With an impressive range of high-quality contributions from the best scholars in the field, *The Oxford Handbook of John Bunyan* was always likely to become the most important single volume guide to this hugely significant puritan writer for a generation; what cannot have been foreknown (although it must have been pre-planned at length) is the sheer delight with which the reader peruses this elegantly constructed and beautifully readable account of the order and structure of Bunyan's mental and physical worlds.'
Mark Burden, *The Seventeenth Century*

'[The book] is an extensive resource that will be consulted by people seeking an informative yet focussed introduction to the man, his works, his times, and his influence.'
Stephen Copson, *Baptist Quarterly*

'This is the ideal book for all Bunyan enthusiasts both within and without the churches … the editors are to be congratulated not only on a wide-ranging choice of essay topics … Oxford University Press has produced a handsome volume which would be welcome on most book lovers' shelves.'
Alan Argent, *Congregational History Society Magazine*

'a landmark of scholarship on Bunyan.'
David Parry, *Bunyan Studies: A Journal of Reformation and Nonconformist Culture*

Winner of the International John Bunyan Society's Richard L. Greaves Prize

THE OXFORD HANDBOOK OF

JOHN BUNYAN

Edited by
MICHAEL DAVIES
and
W. R. OWENS

Great Clarendon Street, Oxford, OX2 6DP,
United Kingdom

Oxford University Press is a department of the University of Oxford.
It furthers the University's objective of excellence in research, scholarship,
and education by publishing worldwide. Oxford is a registered trade mark of
Oxford University Press in the UK and in certain other countries

© the several contributors 2018

The moral rights of the authors have been asserted

First published in 2018
First published in paperback in 2021

All rights reserved. No part of this publication may be reproduced, stored in
a retrieval system, or transmitted, in any form or by any means, without the
prior permission in writing of Oxford University Press, or as expressly permitted
by law, by licence or under terms agreed with the appropriate reprographics
rights organization. Enquiries concerning reproduction outside the scope of the
above should be sent to the Rights Department, Oxford University Press, at the
address above

You must not circulate this work in any other form
and you must impose this same condition on any acquirer

Published in the United States of America by Oxford University Press
198 Madison Avenue, New York, NY 10016, United States of America

British Library Cataloguing in Publication Data

Data available

Library of Congress Cataloging in Publication Data

Data available

ISBN 978-0-19-958130-6 (Hbk.)
ISBN 978-0-19-285568-8 (Pbk.)

Links to third party websites are provided by Oxford in good faith and
for information only. Oxford disclaims any responsibility for the materials
contained in any third party website referenced in this work.

Acknowledgements

This book has been a long time coming, and a number of debts have accrued while awaiting its arrival. Thanks are owed, first and foremost, to the volume's many contributors, who have been anticipating its appearance for longer than could reasonably be expected. Michael Davies would like to express enormous gratitude to Bob Owens, who joined him as co-editor, both for working so hard to see the volume into completion and for making a hard climb so productive and enjoyable. His support, friendship, and continual 'Good Chear' are always deeply appreciated. A no less sincere note of thanks is also owed to various friends and colleagues whose help and support—particularly in bringing to light Bunyan-related phenomena over the last few years—should not go unacknowledged: Alex Broadhead, Dinah Birch, Paul Baines, and David Salter. We would like to thank at Oxford University Press Jacqueline Norton, both for commissioning this *Oxford Handbook* and for her invaluable guidance and support throughout, and Aimee Wright, for her unfailing assistance and good spirit in bringing the book to press. Last, though never least, thanks are owed, as ever, to Carina Vitti and Patti Owens for their own enduring patience, help, and support.

It seems fitting, and gives us pleasure, to dedicate the collective endeavours of this *Handbook* to the members of the International John Bunyan Society who have done so much to help 'Bunyan Studies' to flourish over the last three decades, and who will no doubt continue to do so. The collection is also dedicated to the memory of Nick Davis: friend, colleague, Senior Lecturer in English at the University of Liverpool, and indefatigable generator of sympathetic electricity.

M. D. & W. R. O.

Contents

List of Figures — xi
List of Tables — xiii
Abbreviations — xv
Notes on Contributors — xvii
Bunyan's Life: Some Significant Dates — xxv

    Introduction: Bunyan's Presence — 1
    MICHAEL DAVIES

PART I CONTEXTS

1. Bunyan's Life, Bunyan's Lives — 21
   MICHAEL A. MULLETT

2. Bunyan's England: The Trials and Triumphs of Restoration Dissent — 36
   JOHN COFFEY

3. Bunyan and the Bedford Congregation — 53
   ANNE DUNAN-PAGE

4. Bunyan's Theology and Religious Context — 69
   DEWEY D. WALLACE, JR

5. Bunyan and the Word — 86
   ALISON SEARLE

6. Bunyan's Reading — 101
   ROGER POOLEY

7. Bunyan and Gender — 117
   MARGARET J. M. EZELL

8. 'Come ye out from among them, and be ye separate': Bunyan and the Writing of Dissent — 133
   N. H. KEEBLE

9. Bunyan's Partners in Print 149
   KATHLEEN LYNCH

PART II WORKS

10. Early Works: Bunyan in the 1650s 171
    DAVID WALKER

11. Bunyan in Prison: Writings from the 1660s 186
    DAVID GAY

12. *Grace Abounding to the Chief of Sinners* (1666) 204
    NIGEL SMITH

13. 'The Desired Countrey': Bunyan's Writings on the Church in the 1670s 220
    KEN SIMPSON

14. *The Pilgrim's Progress* (1678): Chasing Apollyon's Tale 241
    MICHAEL DAVIES

15. *The Life and Death of Mr. Badman* (1680) 258
    KATSUHIRO ENGETSU

16. *The Holy War* (1682) 275
    NANCY ROSENFELD

17. Piety and Radicalism: Bunyan's Writings of the 1680s 290
    ARLETTE ZINCK

18. *The Pilgrim's Progress, Part II* (1684) 308
    MARGARET OLOFSON THICKSTUN

19. 'Truth in Meeter': Bunyan's Poetry and Dissenting Poetics 325
    ELIZABETH CLARKE

20. Bunyan's Posthumously Published Works 343
    W. R. OWENS

PART III DIRECTIONS IN CRITICISM

21. Bunyan, Emblem, and Allegory 361
    JEREMY TAMBLING

22. Bunyan and Romance — NICK DAVIS — 379

23. The Prose Style of John Bunyan — MARY ANN LUND — 397

24. The Language of *The Pilgrim's Progress* — JULIE COLEMAN — 413

25. 'Nor do thou go to work without my Key': Reading Bunyan Out to the Edges — MAXINE HANCOCK — 434

26. Bunyan and the Historians — TAMSIN SPARGO — 453

27. Bunyan Unbound: Prison and the Place of Creativity — VERA J. CAMDEN — 470

28. Bunyan, Poststructuralism, and Postmodernism — STUART SIM — 487

29. Bunyan, Theory, and Theology: A Case for Post-Secular Criticism — LORI BRANCH — 502

PART IV JOURNEYS

30. Bunyan and the Early Novel — CYNTHIA WALL — 521

31. *The Pilgrim's Progress* in the Evangelical Revival — ISABEL RIVERS — 537

32. Bunyan and the Romantics — JONATHON SHEARS — 555

33. Bunyan and the Victorians — VINCENT NEWEY — 573

34. Bunyan and America — JOEL D. S. RASMUSSEN — 590

35. Bunyan: Class and Englishness 608
    GARY DAY

36. Wayfaring Images: The Pilgrim's Pictorial Progress 624
    NATHALIE COLLÉ

37. Bunyan for Children 650
    SHANNON MURRAY

38. Bunyan and Empire 665
    SYLVIA BROWN

Index 683

List of Figures

9.1	'Catalogue-Table of Mr. Bunyan's Books', in *The Works of that Eminent Servant of Christ, Mr. John Bunyan* (1692). (By permission of the Folger Shakespeare Library [shelf mark B5479].)	150
9.2	'*Advertisement from the Bookseller*', in *The Pilgrim's Progress* (1680). (By permission of the Folger Shakespeare Library [shelf mark 207–14q].)	159
9.3	Frontispiece portrait of Bunyan, in *The Works of that Eminent Servant of Christ, Mr. John Bunyan* (1692). (By permission of the Folger Shakespeare Library [shelf mark B5479].)	164
25.1	Opening page of Proverbs, in a 1649 edition of *The Holy Bible*. (Image courtesy of Bruce Peel Special Collections, University of Alberta.)	437
25.2	Pages from the 1679 edition of *The Pilgrim's Progress*. (Image courtesy of Bruce Peel Special Collections, University of Alberta.)	446
36.1	*The Sleeping Portrait*, frontispiece, Robert White engraver, *The Pilgrim's Progress*, 3rd edn (London: Nathaniel Ponder, 1679). (© The British Library Board. All Rights Reserved (C.70.aa.3).)	626
36.2	*The Death of Faithful at Vanity Fair*, woodcut reproduction of one of the original illustrations for *The Pilgrim's Progress*, anonymous engraver, *The Pilgrim's Progress*, 7th edn (London: Nathaniel Ponder, 1681). (© The British Library Board. All Rights Reserved (C.59.a.32).)	627
36.3	Title page of a chapbook version of *The Pilgrim's Progress* (Glasgow: Orr and Sons, n.d.). (© The British Library Board. All Rights Reserved (4408.bb.25.12).)	629
36.4	Illustrated page of a chapbook version of *The Pilgrim's Progress* (Glasgow: Orr and Sons, n.d.). (© The British Library Board. All Rights Reserved (4408.bb.25.12).)	631
36.5	*Christian and Hopeful Reaching the Celestial City*, portfolio illustration of *The Pilgrim's Progress* by Thomas Stothard, engraver, and Joseph Strutt, printmaker (sepia print) (London: John Thane, [1788]). (© John Bunyan Library, Bedford Central Library, Bedford, England.)	632
36.6	*Evangelist Points the Way*, postcard illustration of *The Pilgrim's Progress* by Harold Copping (London: The Religious Tract Society, [c.1903]). (From the author's private collection.)	633

36.7 'Slough of Despond', *The Moving Panorama of Pilgrim's Progress*, 1851. (© Collection of the Dyer Library/Saco Museum, Saco, Maine, USA.) 634

36.8 'Christiana, her Children and Secret', *The Moving Panorama of Pilgrim's Progress*, 1851. (© Collection of the Dyer Library/Saco Museum, Saco, Maine, USA.) 635

36.9 'John Bunyan in Prison', stained-glass window, Bunyan Meeting Church, Bedford. Photograph by David Stubbs. (© By kind permission of the Trustees of Bunyan Meeting, Bedford, England.) 639

36.10 '*Evangelist Points the Way*', stained-glass window, Bunyan Meeting Church, Bedford. Photograph by David Stubbs. (© By kind permission of the Trustees of Bunyan Meeting, Bedford, England.) 640

36.11 *Evangelist Points the Way*, illustration by Harold Copping in *The Pilgrim's Progress* (London: The Religious Tract Society, [*c.*1903–1904]). (From the author's private collection.) 641

36.12 *Christian's Fight with Apollyon*, pear-wood sculpture by Joseph Parker. (© By kind permission of the Trustees of Bunyan Meeting, Bedford, England.) 642

36.13 *Christian's Combat with Apollyon*, illustration drawn by H. C. Selous and M. Paolo Priolo and engraved by L. Chapon, in *The Pilgrim's Progress* (London, Paris, New York, & Melbourne: Cassell & Company, 1902). (From the author's private collection.) 643

36.14 Bronze doors representing scenes from *The Pilgrim's Progress* at the entrance of the Bunyan Meeting Church, Bedford. (© By kind permission of the Trustees of Bunyan Meeting, Bedford, England.) 644

36.15 'Bunyan's Dream/*The Pilgrim's Progress*', needlework/tapestry by Edward Bawden. (© By kind permission of the Trustees, Cecil Higgins Art Gallery, Bedford, England, and the Estate of Edward Bawden.) 645

36.16 'Bunyan's Dream/*The Pilgrim's Progress*', watercolour by Edward Bawden. (© By kind permission of the Trustees, Cecil Higgins Art Gallery, Bedford, England, and the Estate of Edward Bawden.) 645

36.17 *Hopeful Had Much Ado to Keep his Brother's Head Above Water*, book sculpture by Justin Rowe. (© By kind permission of Justin Rowe, Cambridge, England.) 647

36.18 *Hopeful Had Much Ado to Keep his Brother's Head Above Water*, book sculpture by Justin Rowe, showcased. (© By kind permission of Justin Rowe, Cambridge, England.) 647

List of Tables

24.1	Strong verb paradigms in *The Pilgrim's Progress*	422
24.2	Bunyan's use of *my/mine* and *thy/thine* as possessive determiners	424
24.3	Bunyan's use of *thou* and *you* as singular subjects before selected auxiliary verbs	426
24.4	Bunyan's use of *thou* and *you* forms for singular addressees	428
24.5	Subject–verb inversion after *then*	428
24.6	The use of *did* (only) in *The Pilgrim's Progress*	429
24.7	*Have* contraction	430
24.8	Third-person singular present tenses in *The Pilgrim's Progress*	432

Abbreviations

Bunyan's Works

CB   H. G. Tibbutt (ed.), *The Minutes of the First Independent Church (now Bunyan Meeting) at Bedford, 1656–1766*, Publications of the Bedfordshire Historical Record Society 55 (Bedfordshire Historical Record Society, 1976)

GA   *Grace Abounding to the Chief of Sinners*, ed. Roger Sharrock (Oxford: Clarendon Press, 1962)

HW   *The Holy War*, ed. Roger Sharrock and James F. Forrest (Oxford: Clarendon Press, 1980)

MB   *The Life and Death of Mr. Badman*, ed. Roger Sharrock and James F. Forrest (Oxford: Clarendon Press, 1988)

MW   *The Miscellaneous Works of John Bunyan*, gen. ed. Roger Sharrock, 13 vols (Oxford: Clarendon Press, 1976–94)

PP   *The Pilgrim's Progress*, ed. James Blanton Wharey; 2nd edn, rev. Roger Sharrock (Oxford: Clarendon Press, 1960; corrected reprint, 1967)

Works About Bunyan

Greaves, *Glimpses*   Richard L. Greaves, *Glimpses of Glory: John Bunyan and English Dissent* (Stanford, CA: Stanford University Press, 2002)

Hill, *Bunyan*   Christopher Hill, *A Turbulent, Seditious, and Factious People: John Bunyan and his Church 1628–1688* (Oxford: Clarendon Press, 1988); published in the USA as *A Tinker and a Poor Man: John Bunyan and his Church, 1628–1688* (New York: Alfred A. Knopf, 1989)

Journals

BQ	*Baptist Quarterly*
BS	*Bunyan Studies*
ELH	*English Literary History*
ELR	*English Literary Renaissance*
PMLA	*Publications of the Modern Language Association of America*
RES	*Review of English Studies*
SEL	*Studies in English Literature, 1500–1900*
SP	*Studies in Philology*

Reference Works

ODNB   *Oxford Dictionary of National Biography*, ed. H. C. G. Matthew and Brian Harrison, 60 vols (Oxford: Oxford University Press, 2004); now online at: http://www.oxforddnb.com/

OED   *Oxford English Dictionary*, 2nd edn, prepared by J. A. Simpson and E. S. C. Weiner, 20 vols (Oxford: Clarendon Press, 1989); now online at: http://www.oed.com/

Publication Details

All pre-1800 works are published in London, unless otherwise stated, and details of publishers are not usually included.

Notes on Contributors

Lori Branch is Associate Professor of English at the University of Iowa. Among her publications is *Rituals of Spontaneity: Sentiment and Secularism from Free Prayer to Wordsworth* (2006); she is also editor of the monograph series 'Literature, Religion, and Postsecular Studies' for Ohio State University Press. Her books-in-progress are *The Violation of God: Masculinity and Secularism in Enlightenment* and *Postsecular Reason*.

Sylvia Brown is Professor of English at the University of Alberta, Canada. Among her publications are edited books on *Women's Writing in Stuart England* (1999), *Women, Gender and Radical Religion in Early Modern Europe* (2007), *N. H., The Ladies Dictionary (1694)* (2010), and *Marginated: Seventeenth-Century Printed Books and the Traces of their Readers* (2010). She is editing the manuscript life of the Presbyterian minister Christopher Love, and a volume of the letters of Richard Baxter (1661–1670).

Vera J. Camden is Professor of English at Kent State University, and Clinical Assistant Professor of Psychiatry at Case Western Reserve University. She is Training and Supervising Analyst at the Cleveland Psychoanalytic Center, and Geographic Rule Supervising Analyst for the Institute for Psychoanalytic Education, NYU Medical School. She has edited *Compromise Formations: Current Directions in Psychoanalytic Criticism* (1989), *The Narrative of the Persecutions of Agnes Beaumont* (1992), and *Trauma and Transformation: The Political Progress of John Bunyan* (2008).

Elizabeth Clarke is Emeritus Professor of English at the University of Warwick. Among her publications are *Theory and Theology in George Herbert's Poetry* (1997), *Gendered Writing in Early Modern England* (ed. with Danielle Clarke, 2000), and *Politics, Religion and the Song of Songs in Seventeenth-Century England* (2011). Her most recent publication, *John Nichols's 'The Progresses and Public Processions of Queen Elizabeth I'*, 5 vols (ed. with Elizabeth Goldring, Faith Eales, and Jayne Elisabeth Archer, 2014) won the Modern Language Association (MLA) Prize for a Scholarly Edition in 2015.

John Coffey is Professor of Early Modern History at the University of Leicester. His books include intellectual biographies of Samuel Rutherford and John Goodwin, *Persecution and Toleration in Protestant England, 1558–1689* (2000), *Exodus and Liberation: Deliverance Politics from John Calvin to Martin Luther King Jr* (2014), and *The Cambridge Companion to Puritanism* (co-ed., 2008). He is editor of the *Oxford History of Protestant Dissenting Traditions*, vol. 1: *The Post-Reformation Era, c.1559–c.1689* (2020), and co-editor of *Reliquiæ Baxterianæ* (2020), both from Oxford University Press.

Julie Coleman was Professor of English Language and Pro-Vice Chancellor at the University of Leicester until 2018. She is the founder of the International Society for Historical Lexicology and Lexicography. Among her publications are four volumes of her *History of Cant and Slang Dictionaries, 1567–1984* (2004–10), *The Life of Slang* (2010), and an edited volume, *Global English Slang: Methodologies and Perspectives* (2014).

Nathalie Collé is Senior Lecturer in English Literature at Université de Lorraine in Nancy, France. She is co-editor of *Left Out: Texts and Ur-Texts* (2009), *The Lives of the Book* (2010), and volumes in the Book Practices and Textual Itineraries series: *Tracing the Contours of Literary Works* (2011), *Contemporary Textual Aesthetics* (2013), *Textual Practices in the Digital Age* (2014), *From Text(s) to Book(s)* (2015), and *Illustration and Intermedial Avenues* (2017).

Michael Davies is Senior Lecturer in English at the University of Liverpool. Among his publications is *Graceful Reading: Theology and Narrative in the Works of John Bunyan* (2002). He is co-editor of *Literature and Authenticity, 1780–1900* (2011), and is currently preparing a critical edition of *The Bunyan Church Book, 1656–1710* for Oxford University Press.

†Nick Davis was Senior Lecturer in English at the University of Liverpool until his untimely death in June 2017. Among his publications are *Stories of Chaos: Reason and its Displacement in Early Modern Narrative* (1999), *Six Things to Do with Narrative* (2007), *Early Modern English Writing and the Privatization of Experience* (2013), and *Narrative Space* (2013). He also co-edited the Cambridge Scholars monograph series Texts and Embodiments in Perspective.

Gary Day recently retired as Principal Lecturer in English at De Montfort University, Leicester. He is the editor of a number of books, most recently, with Jack Lynch, *The Wiley Encyclopedia of British Literature 1660–1789* (2015). He is also the author of *Re-Reading Leavis: Culture and Literary Criticism* (1996), *Class* (2001), *Literary Criticism: A New History* (2008), *Modernist Literature 1890–1950* (2010), and *The Story of Drama: Tragedy, Comedy and Sacrifice from the Greeks to the Present* (2016).

Anne Dunan-Page is Professor of Early-Modern British Studies at Aix-Marseille Université and Director of the Research Centre on the Anglophone World (Laboratoire d'Études et de Recherche sur le Monde Anglophone (LERMA, E.A. 853)). Her books include *Grace Overwhelming: John Bunyan, 'The Pilgrim's Progress' and the Extremes of the Baptist Mind* (2006), *L'Expérience puritaine. Vies et récits de dissidents* (2017), (ed.) *Roger L'Estrange and the Making of Restoration Culture* (with Beth Lynch, 2008), and (ed.) *The Cambridge Companion to Bunyan* (2010). She is currently co-editing the correspondence of Sir Thomas Browne for the Oxford University Press Complete Works.

Katsuhiro Engetsu is Professor of English at Doshisha University in Japan. In addition to translating Roger Sharrock's *John Bunyan* and Christopher Hill's *Collected Essays* into Japanese, he has written extensively on early modern British literature in both Japanese and English. He has contributed chapters to *Milton and the Terms of Liberty* (2002), *The*

Cambridge Companion to John Dryden (2004), and *A Concise Companion to Milton* (2007).

Margaret J. M. Ezell is Distinguished Professor of English and the John and Sara Lindsey Chair of Liberal Arts at Texas A&M University. She is the author of *The Patriarch's Wife: Literary Evidence and the History of the Family* (1987), *Writing Women's Literary History* (1992), *Social Authorship and the Advent of Print* (1999), and, most recently, *The Oxford English Literary History*, vol. 5: 1645–1714: *The Later Seventeenth Century* (2017).

David Gay is Professor of English Literature at the University of Alberta, Canada. He is the author of *The Endless Kingdom: Milton's Scriptural Society* (2002) and co-editor of *Awakening Words: John Bunyan and the Language of Community* (2000). His latest book is *Gifts and Graces: Prayer, Poetry, and Polemic from Lancelot Andrewes to John Bunyan* (University of Toronto Press, 2021).

Maxine Hancock is Professor Emerita of Interdisciplinary Studies and Spiritual Theology at Regent College, Vancouver, Canada. She is the author of *The Key in the Window: Marginal Notes in Bunyan's Narratives* (2001) and of articles in *Bunyan Studies*, *The Seventeenth Century*, and *The Recorder*. She is also co-author with Ehud Ben Zvi and Richard Beinert of *Readings in Biblical Hebrew: An Intermediate Textbook* (1993).

N. H. Keeble is Professor Emeritus at the University of Stirling. His publications include *Richard Baxter: Puritan Man of Letters* (1982), *The Literary Culture of Nonconformity in Later Seventeenth-Century England* (1987), *The Restoration: England in the 1660s* (2002), and a two-volume *Calendar of the Correspondence of Richard Baxter* (1991; with Geoffrey F. Nuttall). He is general and contributing editor of the Oxford University Press edition of Richard Baxter's *Reliquiæ Baxterianæ* (2020; with John Coffey, Tim Cooper, and Thomas Charlton).

Mary Ann Lund is Associate Professor in English at the University of Leicester. She is the editor of *The Oxford Edition of the Sermons of John Donne*, vol. 12: *Sermons Preached at St Paul's Cathedral, 1626* (2017), and the author of *Melancholy, Medicine and Religion in Early Modern England: Reading 'The Anatomy of Melancholy'* (2010). She is currently editing volume 13 of *The Oxford Edition of the Sermons of John Donne*.

Kathleen Lynch is Executive Director of the Folger Institute at the Folger Shakespeare Library in Washington, DC. She has written on devotional literature and autobiographical narrative with attention to the intersecting histories of regulation of religion and the press. Her book, *Protestant Autobiography in the Seventeenth-Century Anglophone World* (2012) was awarded the Richard L. Greaves Prize by the International John Bunyan Society in 2013.

Michael A. Mullett is Emeritus Professor of Religious and Cultural History at the University of Lancaster. His books include *Radical Religious Movements in Early Modern Europe* (1980), *Sources for the History of English Nonconformity, 1660–1830* (1991), *John*

Bunyan in Context (1996), *Catholics in Britain and Ireland, 1558–1829* (1998), *The Catholic Reformation* (1999), *Martin Luther* (2004; 2nd edn, 2015), *English Catholicism 1680–1830* (6 vols, 2006), *Historical Dictionary of the Reformation and Counter-Reformation* (2010), and *John Calvin* (2011).

Shannon Murray is Professor of English at the University of Prince Edward Island, Canada, where she teaches early modern and children's literature. A Canadian 3M National Teaching Fellow, she has published and presented on John Bunyan, on John Milton, on the Polish children's writer, Janusz Korczak, and on learning communities and teaching for creativity in higher education. She is also a published children's author.

†Vincent Newey was Emeritus Professor of English at the University of Leicester. Editor of *The Pilgrim's Progress: Critical and Historical Views* (1980) and author of *Cowper's Poetry: A Critical Study and Reassessment* (1982) and *The Scriptures of Charles Dickens: Novels of Ideology, Novels of the Self* (2004), he was also joint general editor of 'The Nineteenth Century' series for Ashgate, and co-editor of *The Cowper and Newton Journal*. He died in May 2020.

W. R. Owens is Emeritus Professor of English Literature at the Open University, and Visiting Professor at the University of Bedfordshire. His publications include volumes 12 and 13 of *The Miscellaneous Works of John Bunyan* (1994), editions of *Grace Abounding* (1987) and *The Pilgrim's Progress* (2003), *The Canonisation of Daniel Defoe* (co-author, 1988), *A Critical Bibliography of Daniel Defoe* (co-author, 1998), *The Works of Daniel Defoe* (joint general editor, 44 volumes, 2000–09), and an edition of *The Gospels: Authorized King James Version* (2011).

Roger Pooley is Honorary Research Fellow in Humanities, Keele University. Among his publications are *The Green Knight: Selected Poetry and Prose of George Gascoigne* (ed., 1982), *The Lord of the Journey: A Reader in Christian Spirituality* (co-ed., 1986), *English Prose of the Seventeenth Century, 1590–1700* (1993), *The Discerning Reader: Christian Perspectives on Literature and Theory* (co-ed., 1995), and the Penguin Classics edition of *The Pilgrim's Progress* (2008).

Joel D. S. Rasmussen is Associate Professor of Nineteenth-Century Christian Thought at the University of Oxford, and Tutorial Fellow of Mansfield College, Oxford. He is the author of *Between Irony and Witness: Kierkegaard's Poetics of Faith, Hope, and Love* (2005), one of the editors of *Kierkegaard's Journals and Notebooks* (2007–), co-editor of *William James and the Transatlantic Conversation: Pragmatism, Pluralism, and Philosophy of Religion* (2014), and co-editor of *The Oxford Handbook of Nineteenth-Century Christian Thought* (2017).

Isabel Rivers is Professor of Eighteenth-Century English Literature and Culture at Queen Mary University of London. Her books include *Reason, Grace, and Sentiment: A Study of the Language of Religion and Ethics in England, 1660–1780* (2 vols, 1991, 2000), (ed.) *Books and their Readers in Eighteenth-Century England* (1982), (ed.) *Books and their Readers in Eighteenth-Century England: New Essays* (2001), and *Vanity Fair and* the Celestial City: Dissenting, Methodist, and Evangelical Literary Culture in England, 1720–1800 (2018). She directs the Dissenting Academies Project: <http://www.qmulreligionandliterature.co.uk/research/the-dissenting-academies-project/>.

Nancy Rosenfeld is Senior Teacher (Emerita) in the Department of English Studies and in the Humanities program at the Max Stern College of Jezreel Valley, Israel. She is the author of *The Human Satan in Seventeenth-Century English Literature: From Milton to Rochester* (2008), and of *John Bunyan's Imaginary Writings in Context* (2018), as well as articles on Milton, Bunyan, Rochester, and Keats. A secondary research interest is the British soldier-poets of the First World War, and she has published on both Robert Graves and Siegfried Sassoon.

Alison Searle is Associate Professor of Textual Studies at the University of Leeds. She is the author of *'The Eyes of Your Heart': Literary and Theological Trajectories of Imagining Biblically* (2008), co-general editor of *The Complete Correspondence of Richard Baxter* (forthcoming from Oxford University Press), and editor of James Shirley's *The Sisters* (also forthcoming from Oxford University Press). Other recent publications examine the performance of religious nonconformity in early modern Britain.

Jonathon Shears is Senior Lecturer in English at Keele University. His books include *The Romantic Legacy of* Paradise Lost (2009), *Reading, Writing and the Influence of Harold Bloom* (2010), *Literary Bric-à-Brac and the Victorians* (2013), *Byron's Temperament: Essays in Body and Mind* (2016), and *The Great Exhibition, 1851: A Sourcebook* (2017). He has recently published *The Hangover: A Literary and Cultural History* (2020) and is co-editing *The Oxford Handbook of Lord Byron*.

Stuart Sim was Professor of Critical Theory and Long Eighteenth-Century English Literature at Northumbria University until his retirement in 2013. His books include *Negotiations with Paradox: Narrative Practice and Narrative Form in Bunyan and Defoe* (1990), *Bunyan and Authority* (co-authored, 2000), *John Bunyan and his England, 1628–88* (co-ed., 1990), *Reception, Appropriation, Recollection: Bunyan's Pilgrim's Progress* (co-ed., 2007), and, more recently, *Fifty Key Postmodern Thinkers* (2013), *A Philosophy of Pessimism* (2015), and *The Edinburgh Companion to Critical Theory* (ed., 2016).

Ken Simpson taught in the Department of English and Modern Languages at Thompson Rivers University, Kamloops, Canada. Among his publications are *Spiritual Architecture and Paradise Regained: Milton's Literary Ecclesiology* (2007) and an edited collection, *Texting Bunyan: Essays on Attribution, Influence and Appropriation* (2010).

Nigel Smith is William and Annie S. Paton Foundation Professor of Ancient and Modern Literature at Princeton University. His books include *Andrew Marvell: The Chameleon* (2010), *Is Milton Better than Shakespeare?* (2008), *Literature and Revolution in England, 1640–1660* (1994), and *Perfection Proclaimed: Language and Literature in English Radical Religion 1640–1660* (1989). He has edited *George Fox: The Journal* (1998), Andrew Marvell's *Poems* (2003), the Ranter pamphlets (1983; rev. 2014), and, with Laurent Curelly, *Radical Voices, Radical Ways: Articulating and Disseminating Radicalism in Seventeenth- and Eighteenth-Century Britain* (2016).

Tamsin Spargo was Reader in Cultural History at Liverpool John Moores University and Visiting Professor in English at the University of Malaya, before her retirement. Her books include *The Writing of John Bunyan* (1997), *Foucault and Queer Theory* (1999), *Reading the Past: Literature and History* (2000), *Wanted Man: The Forgotten Story of an American Outlaw* (2004), *Free to Write: Prison Voices Past and Present* (2013), and *John Bunyan* (Writers and their Work series, 2016). She has published articles on nonconformist culture, theories of history, and post-secular thinking.

Jeremy Tambling was Professor of Literature at Manchester University, and is Honorary Professor of Comparative Literature at the University of Hong Kong. Author of several books which engage with critical theory, most recently *Hölderlin and the Poetry of Tragedy* (2014), he also works on Dante and on nineteenth-century literature, as with *Dickens' Novels as Poetry: Allegory and the Literature of the City* (2014). His book *Allegory* appeared in the Routledge 'New Critical Idiom' series in 2010. His most recent book is *Histories of the Devil* (2017).

Margaret Olofson Thickstun is Jane Watson Irwin Professor of Literature at Hamilton College, USA. Her publications include *Fictions of the Feminine: Puritan Doctrine and the Representation of Women* (1988), *Milton's Paradise Lost: Moral Education* (2007), *Milton's Rival Hermeneutics* (co-edited with Richard J. DuRocher, 2012), and *Witness, Warning, and Prophecy: Quaker Women's Writing 1655–1700* (co-edited with Teresa Feroli, 2018).

David Walker is Professor of Seventeenth-Century English Literature at Northumbria University. Among his publications are *Bunyan and Authority: The Rhetoric of Dissent and the Legitimation Crisis in Seventeenth-Century England* (with Stuart Sim, 2000); *The Discourse of Sovereignty from Hobbes to Fielding* (with Stuart Sim, 2003); *British Satire, 1785–1840*, vol. 2: *Longer Satires* (ed., 2003); *Depression and Melancholy 1600–1800*, vol. 1: *Religious Writings* (ed. with Anita O'Connell, 2012).

Cynthia Wall is the William R. Kenan, Jr. Professor of English at the University of Virginia. She is the author of *The Prose of Things: Transformations of Description in the Eighteenth Century* (2006) and *The Literary and Cultural Spaces of Restoration London* (1998). She has edited *The Pilgrim's Progress* (2009), Defoe's *A Journal of the Plague Year* (2003), and Pope's *The Rape of the Lock* (1998). Her latest book is *Grammars of Approach: Landscape, Narrative, and the Linguistic Picturesque* (2019).

†Dewey D. Wallace, Jr was Professor Emeritus of Religion at The George Washington University, USA. His books include *Puritans and Predestination: Grace in English Protestant Theology, 1525–1695* (1982), *The Spirituality of the Later English Puritans: An Anthology* (edited and annotated texts, 1987), and *Shapers of English Calvinism, 1660–1714: Variety, Persistence, and Transformation* (2011). He died in February 2021.

Arlette Zinck is Associate Professor of English Literature and Dean of the Faculty of Arts at The King's University in Edmonton, Alberta, Canada. Her publications on Bunyan include a co-edited volume of essays, *Awakening Words: John Bunyan and the Language of Community* (2000), a co-authored article, 'Baxter, Bunyan, and a Puritan Reframing of Ageing', *Bunyan Studies*, 14 (2010), and 'Dating the Spiritual Warfare Broadsheet', in *Texting Bunyan: Attribution, Appropriation, and Influence*, ed. Ken Simpson (2010).

Bunyan's Life: Some Significant Dates

1628   Born at Elstow in Bedfordshire (baptized 30 November), first of three children of Thomas Bunyan, a brazier, and his second wife, Margaret Bentley.

1630s   Attends local school for a short period. Upon leaving, follows father's trade and becomes a brazier (or 'tinker').

1642   First Civil War begins.

1644   Mother and sister Margaret die (in June and July); father remarries within two months. (November) Bunyan is mustered in the Parliamentary forces stationed in the garrison town of Newport Pagnell, Buckinghamshire.

1647   Demobilized and returns to Elstow.

1649   Marries first wife and sets up house in Elstow. Her name is unknown, but, according to Bunyan in *Grace Abounding*, her father 'was counted godly', and she brought as her dowry two religious books: Arthur Dent's *The Plaine Mans Path-Way to Heaven* (1601) and Lewis Bayly's *The Practise of Pietie* (1612). Trial and execution of Charles I. Abolition of the monarchy and House of Lords. England proclaimed a free commonwealth. Bunyan undergoes a spiritual crisis lasting for nearly three years. Receives counsel from John Gifford, pastor of the Independent congregation in Bedford.

1650   First child, Mary, born blind (baptized 20 July); three other children follow. Experiences a spiritual awakening after listening to 'three or four poor women' in Bedford talking about their faith. Starts attending John Gifford's congregation in Bedford (and eventually becomes full member by 1655).

1655   Moves to live in Bedford, and begins to preach, first to the Bedford church and then more widely in the locality.

1656   Involved in controversy with Quakers, and as a result his first work, *Some Gospel-Truths Opened*, is published.

1657   *A Vindication of Some Gospel-Truths Opened* is published.

1658   First wife dies. Oliver Cromwell dies; his son Richard becomes Lord Protector. One of Bunyan's most popular sermon treatises, *A Few Sighs from Hell*, is published.

1659   Marries second wife, Elizabeth; three children are born of this marriage. *The Doctrine of the Law and Grace Unfolded* is published. Richard Cromwell's Protectorate collapses.

1660   Charles II returns to England and is restored to the throne. Trial and execution of regicides. In November, Bunyan is arrested for preaching illegally at

	Lower Samsell, is taken to Harlington Manor for questioning, then held in custody in Bedford. Wife gives birth prematurely to a baby, who dies shortly afterwards.
1661	Fifth Monarchist uprising in London is crushed. Election of 'Cavalier' Parliament. Widespread persecution of Dissenters begins. Bunyan is tried in Bedford and sentenced initially to three months' imprisonment. Continued refusal to give undertaking to stop preaching leads to Bunyan remaining in jail for twelve years. In August, Elizabeth Bunyan appeals for his release at the assizes, to no avail. Bunyan supports family by making shoelaces, and continues to write. His first prison book, a poem entitled *Profitable Meditations*, is published.
1662	*I Will Pray with the Spirit*, an attack on the use of the Book of Common Prayer, is published. Act of Uniformity leads to the ejection of over 1,000 clergy from Church of England.
1663	*Christian Behaviour* is published, and another poem, *Prison Meditations*.
1665	Two poems, *One Thing Is Needful* and *Ebal and Gerizzim*, a millenarian treatise, *The Holy City*, and a sermon treatise, *The Resurrection of the Dead*, are published.
1666	Spiritual autobiography, *Grace Abounding to the Chief of Sinners*, is published.
1667	Milton publishes *Paradise Lost*.
1670	Persecution of Dissenters worsens. Members of Bedford congregation are arrested.
1671	On 21 December, Bunyan is elected pastor of the Bedford congregation. Milton publishes *Paradise Regained* and *Samson Agonistes*.
1672	Following a royal pardon, Bunyan is released from prison in March. In May he is licensed to preach. Congregation purchases barn in Bedford as a meeting place. *A Defence of the Doctrine of Justification, by Faith* and *A Confession of my Faith, and A Reason of my Practice in Worship* are published.
1673	*Differences in Judgment about Water-Baptism, No Bar to Communion* (arising from dispute with some London Baptists), is published, as well as a sermon, *The Barren Fig-Tree*.
1674	*Peaceable Principles and True* published, answering attacks by Baptist leaders, Thomas Paul and Henry Danvers.
1675	Doctrinal catechism, *Instruction for the Ignorant*, and a sermon, *Light for Them that Sit in Darkness*, published.
1676	Two sermon treatises, *Saved by Grace* and *The Strait Gate*, are published. Bunyan's father dies.
1677	Imprisoned again during the first six months of the year.
1678	*The Pilgrim's Progress* and *Come, & Welcome, to Jesus Christ* are published.
1679	*A Treatise of the Fear of God* published. 'Cavalier' Parliament is dissolved. Censorship lapses with expiry of the Licensing Act. Beginning of the 'Exclusion Crisis' (the attempt to exclude James, Duke of York, from the succession because he is a Roman Catholic).

1680	*The Life and Death of Mr. Badman* is published.
1681	Persecution of Dissenters is intensified, and continues until 1684.
1682	*The Holy War* and *The Greatness of the Soul* published. T. S. publishes his own (unauthorized) 'second part' of *The Pilgrim's Progress*.
1683	*A Case of Conscience* (attacking separate meetings by women) is published. Rye House Plot is followed by execution of leading Whigs.
1684	*The Pilgrim's Progress, Second Part* is published, as are *Seasonable Counsel, or Advice to Sufferers*; *A Holy Life*; and *A Caution to Stir up to Watch against Sin*.
1685	Bunyan makes over all his property to his wife, in fear of further persecution. *A Discourse upon the Pharisee and the Publicane* and *Questions about the Nature and Perpetuity of the Seventh-Day-Sabbath* published. Death of Charles II and accession of James II. Monmouth's rising defeated at Sedgemoor. Revocation of Edict of Nantes and arrival of Huguenot refugees in England.
1686	*A Book for Boys and Girls* published.
1687	James II issues Declaration of Indulgence granting freedom of worship to Dissenters.
1688	Five works published: *The Advocateship of Jesus Christ*; *The Jerusalem Sinner Saved*; *A Discourse of the Building […] of the House of God*; *The Water of Life*; and *Solomon's Temple Spiritualized*. Bunyan dies (31 August) from fever contracted while riding from Reading to London in heavy rain. Buried (2 September) in Bunhill Fields, Finsbury. James II reissues Declaration of Indulgence. Trial and acquittal of seven bishops for their opposition to the Declaration. William of Orange lands at Torbay; James flees to France.
1689	Two works are published posthumously: *The Acceptable Sacrifice* and *Last Sermon*. William and Mary proclaimed king and queen. Toleration Act grants freedom of worship to Protestant Dissenters, but not civil rights.
1691	Elizabeth Bunyan (Bunyan's second wife) dies.
1692	Charles Doe publishes, in folio, *The Works of that Eminent Servant of Christ, Mr. John Bunyan*, including twelve previously unpublished pieces: *An Exposition on the Ten First Chapters of Genesis*; *Of Justification by an Imputed Righteousness*; *Paul's Departure and Crown*; *Of the Trinity and a Christian*; *Of the Law and a Christian*; *Israel's Hope Encouraged*; *The Desire of the Righteous Granted*; *The Saints Privilege and Profit*; *Christ a Compleat Saviour*; *The Saints Knowledge of Christ's Love*; *Of the House of the Forest of Lebanon*; *Of Antichrist, and his Ruine*.
1698	*The Heavenly Foot-man* is published by Charles Doe.

INTRODUCTION
Bunyan's Presence

MICHAEL DAVIES

In 1946 the great seventeenth-century Nonconformist preacher and writer John Bunyan made his debut as a star of the silver screen, having been given a small but significant walk-on part in Michael Powell and Emeric Pressburger's Second World War 'classic', *A Matter of Life and Death* (released in the United States under the somewhat softened title, *Stairway to Heaven*). Bunyan's appearance occurs at a crucial point in the film's plot. A young English airman and poet, Peter Carter (played by the inimitable David Niven), was destined to die on the night of 2 May 1945, shortly before the cessation of war in Europe, when returning from an Allied raid over Germany. Owing entirely to a celestial error, however, he survives, only then to fall in love with June (Kim Hunter), an American servicewoman stationed in England with whom Carter had been in radio contact just moments before leaping, parachute-less, from his doomed Lancaster bomber. Despite repeated visits from Conductor 71 (Marius Goring), the guide responsible for escorting him into the next world, Carter refuses to leave Earth, arguing that, through no fault of his own, his circumstances have now changed (he has fallen in love) and so he should be allowed to live on. To decide the case, an appeal court is established in heaven. The trial for Carter's life or death takes place at the film's climax, concurrently with emergency surgery for a head injury: a detail that provides a medical explanation for various unworldly occurrences that may (or may not) be hallucinations. It is just before the hearing begins that John Bunyan enters the frame, accompanying into heaven the man who will act as Carter's advocate, Dr Frank Reeves (Roger Livesey). Dressed in seventeenth-century garb, and looking exactly as he does in some early engraved portraits, Bunyan signs Dr Reeves over to Conductor 71 so that the trial may commence. Touching him lightly on the shoulder, Bunyan says to Reeves, 'Be of good cheer, friend', and then leaves. 'One of the best in the service', Conductor 71 observes with admiration, though he struggles momentarily to recall his name: 'John, uhh … ?', he says airily, to which Reeves replies, 'Bunyan! Yes, of course.'

Although Bunyan's career as a movie star was short-lived (in *A Matter of Life and Death* he remains on screen for no longer than thirty seconds), nevertheless this cameo has a lasting resonance. On one level, it invites us to meditate upon Bunyan's presence, not only in this particular film but elsewhere—in literature, history, art, culture, politics—over the three centuries since he lived, and why that presence is both so important and so enduring. We might assume, for instance, that his sudden appearance in *A Matter of Life and Death* is no more than whimsy: part of the film's idiosyncratic playfulness.[1] Yet Powell and Pressburger had long held a serious interest in Bunyan, having planned at one stage to adapt *The Pilgrim's Progress* for the big screen. *A Matter of Life and Death*, then, like their previous films, *A Canterbury Tale* (1944) and *I Know Where I'm Going!* (1945), employs a Bunyanesque 'journey-of-life' plot, while invoking too values that transcend the merely material or materialistic. Peter Carter becomes, then, a traveller quite literally caught between two worlds (the physical and the spiritual, the seen and the unseen, Technicolor and monochrome) but who finds himself for love unwilling just yet to complete his pilgrimage from this realm to the next.

Bunyan's presence is also essential to the film's politics. Originally commissioned by the Ministry of Information as a propaganda piece, required to revive strained Anglo-American relations at the end of the war, *A Matter of Life and Death* becomes instead a cinematic essay on the inherent rights of ordinary men and women, in the defence of which the Second World War had ostensibly been fought. As Carter's situation exemplifies, these rights include protection from arbitrary arrest and detention, as well as the guarantee of an open and fair trial by jury: basic principles of justice inscribed within *habeas corpus*. Bunyan's appearance in the film, occurring immediately before Carter's climactic trial takes place, provides its audience with a timely reminder of how liberty, justice, and democracy are allegedly shared, upheld, and promoted by both Britain and the United States. What better example could be found to represent this heritage, one rooted in the 'inalienable rights' of the ordinary individual, as the film's trial concludes, than that of John Bunyan: the tinker of Bedford and author of *The Pilgrim's Progress* who famously suffered over twelve years in prison in the name of religious liberty, and whose literary and cultural presence is recognized equally on both sides of the Atlantic?[2] The words that Bunyan speaks in *A Matter of Life and Death* become all the more poignant, as well as politically weighted, in this context. For while his encouragement for Dr Reeves to 'Be of good cheer' echoes Hopeful's cry to Christian when crossing the River of Death in *The Pilgrim's Progress* (*PP*, 157–58), itself an echo of Scripture (Mark 10:49, Matthew 9:2, Acts 23:11), these are also the words that Bunyan himself spoke just before his own arrest and imprisonment for preaching in Lower Samsell, Bedfordshire, on 12 November 1660: 'Come, be of good cheer', he said to an anxious friend, 'let us not be daunted, our cause is good' (*GA*, 105). Such is the implicit epigraph of Peter Carter's case in *A Matter of Life and Death*, in which he becomes another Bunyan: the 'uncommon man', as the film's denouement puts it, ready to fight 'the system' in the name of individual rights and liberties.

---

[1] For a more detailed account of the following discussion, see Michael Davies, 'The Relevant Pilgrim: John Bunyan in *A Matter of Life and Death*', in W. R. Owens and Stuart Sim (eds.), *Reception, Appropriation, Recollection: Bunyan's Pilgrim's Progress* (Bern: Peter Lang, 2007), 185–211.

[2] See, further, Chapter 34 in this volume.

It is worth taking time to register the rich significance of Bunyan's presence in *A Matter of Life and Death* in part because it offers a salutary reminder of how galvanizing the invocation of his name can prove at key points in history. In this case, Bunyan is brought back to life by Powell and Pressburger not just to fulfil the film's original propagandist brief: to create a bridge between the otherwise quite disparate worlds of Britain and the USA in 1946. Its aim too, we might surmise, is to issue a timely warning to those Western democracies about to embark on a new, much colder global war: even the most benevolent government (in this case, that of heaven itself) can become authoritarian, tyrannical even, as soon as it disregards human rights and civil liberties. In these terms, Powell and Pressburger's deployment of Bunyan in *A Matter of Life and Death* invites a revision of his importance as a writer for a post-1945 world. For, as the author and committed pacifist, Vera Brittain, would echo in her biography of Bunyan, first published in 1950 but begun shortly after *A Matter of Life and Death* was released, Bunyan's relevance could now be said to lie not so much in his fame as a 'father' of the English novel nor in the fact that *The Pilgrim's Progress* had, for better and for worse, been shipped around the globe.[3] Rather, Bunyan could be seen as a forerunner of the modern conscience: a writer whose life, imprisonment, and suffering for his Nonconformist principles could speak directly to pacifism, conscientious objection, and to peaceful political transformation in a world now on the threshold of nuclear destruction.[4]

The years immediately following the end of the Second World War saw, then, a radical reshaping of Bunyan as a writer. He could now be hailed as 'universal' not just because his most famous work, *The Pilgrim's Progress*, had long been almost universally available, but, more importantly, because he could be upheld as representing the historical struggle for those rights and liberties that should be acknowledged as fundamental to human existence. The Universal Declaration of Human Rights was issued by the United Nations in 1948, we should remember, as a direct result of the atrocities and holocausts (military, genocidal, and atomic) that had been committed around the world over the previous fifty years. The mid-century Bunyan of Vera Brittain's timely book and of Powell and Pressburger's prescient film is, to some degree, a Bunyan for this Declaration: a champion of rights, a sufferer for conscience, a hero for our time.

To begin any discussion of Bunyan's presence in these terms—that is, as a figure who can speak to contemporary concerns over human rights, social justice, and civil liberties—is, in some sense, deliberately to shake off some of the well-worn myths that have long encircled Bunyan's fame. To assert his continuing relevance we need to do more than reiterate the notions that his importance rests on his status as the creator of a book long held to be second only to the King James Bible as the most popular and widely circulated in the English language, or that he in some sense helped to sire the English novel while serving at the same time to civilize the colonized peoples of the British

---

[3] See, further, Isabel Hofmeyr, 'How Bunyan Became English: Missionaries, Translation, and the Discipline of English Literature', *Journal of British Studies*, 41 (2002), 84–119.

[4] See Vera Brittain, *In the Steps of John Bunyan* (London: Rich and Cowan, 1950), 15–16, 266–7, 415–18.

empire: all views with problems that have duly been identified and interrogated.[5] Yet, the fact that Bunyan's presence in history, literature, and culture can often turn dynamically on key issues of politics, liberty, and revolutionary change also allows us to locate Bunyan in a very different tradition of 'Englishness': that which Peter Ackroyd has termed an 'English Music', by which he means 'not only music itself' (that of Henry Purcell and Vaughan Williams, for example), but also 'English history, English literature and English painting'.[6] If John Bunyan has a presence within and a relevance to the contemporary world, then it is because, as Ackroyd notes, he stands not only as a visionary writer in his own right, one whose profoundest imaginative achievement and source of influence remains *The Pilgrim's Progress*, but also within a long line of visionaries, all of whom invest in their work some form of revolutionary ethos: from William Langland to William Blake, and beyond. 'We draw half our strength and inspiration from the writers of the past', Ackroyd can concede, Bunyan included, for it is '[f]rom their example' that 'we learn that the history of the English imagination is the history of adaptation and assimilation', in which 'Englishness' becomes something outward-looking and inclusive: 'the principle of diversity itself', in fact, whereby 'heterogeneity becomes the form and type of art.' What Ackroyd describes as 'the territorial imperative' of such 'art'—'by means of which a local area can influence or guide all those who inhabit it'—can thus be 'transposed' in Bunyan's case to include not just 'the nation' but the world.[7]

BUNYAN: POPULAR, UNPOPULAR

As many critics and scholars have shown when assessing his legacy, John Bunyan was hard-wired long ago into the kind of imaginative and political consciousness to which Ackroyd refers, whether as a major literary influence or as a significant historical and religious figure, and on a global scale. Few other writers can be said to have had such an extensive reach or such a unique and profound impact upon the minds and lives of others.[8] Yet there are problems with seeing Bunyan in such unambiguously heroic—or

---

[5] See, for example, Tamsin Spargo, *The Writing of John Bunyan* (Aldershot: Ashgate, 1997); Isabel Hofmeyr, *The Portable Bunyan: A Transnational History of The Pilgrim's Progress* (Princeton, NJ: Princeton University Press, 2004).

[6] Peter Ackroyd, *English Music* (London: Penguin, 1993), 21. For Bunyan's presence, see esp. 17–18, 23–47.

[7] Peter Ackroyd, *Albion: The Origins of the English Imagination* (London: Chatto & Windus, 2002), 448–49; on Bunyan see esp. 47–51, 164, 302–04, 307.

[8] On Bunyan's literary and historical reception since the Restoration, see James F. Forrest and Richard Greaves, *John Bunyan: A Reference Guide* (Boston, MA: G. K. Hall & Co., 1982), ix–xvii; Richard Greaves, 'Bunyan through the Centuries: Some Reflections', *English Studies*, 64 (1983), 113–21; N. H. Keeble, '"Of him thousands daily Sing and talk": Bunyan and His Reputation', in N. H. Keeble (ed.), *John Bunyan: Conventicle and Parnassus* (Oxford: Oxford University Press, 1988), 241–63; W. R. Owens, 'The Reception of *The Pilgrim's Progress* in England', in M. van Os and G. J. Schutte (eds.), *Bunyan in England and Abroad* (Amsterdam: Vrije Universiteit University Press, 1990), 91–104; Hill, *Bunyan*,

perhaps even politically sentimental—terms as those outlined so far. Writers such as Ackroyd and, more recently Alan Moore, have continued to nurture a sense of Bunyan the visionary artist, but it is hard to say how widely their views might be held. After all, Bunyan has long proved a divisive and controversial rather than a unifying or harmonizing presence. In the 1960s, for example, the left-wing historian E. P. Thompson famously heralded *The Pilgrim's Progress* as one of two books upon which a political consciousness distinctive to the English working class can be said to have been founded (the other being Thomas Paine's *Rights of Man* (1791)): an assertion that centres Bunyan in England's class warfare. Thompson bases this claim, in part, upon the sheer ubiquity of Bunyan's allegory in the popular print cultures of eighteenth- and nineteenth-century England: a sign of the persistence of the radical Dissenting tradition.[9] If, as we are often told, a household possessed any books at all during the years prior to, during, and following the Industrial Revolution, until the middle of the twentieth century quite possibly, one of them would almost certainly have been a copy of *The Pilgrim's Progress*. Bunyan was, in other words, popular.

Yet, 'popularity' is a complex concept. Thompson himself held no illusions about what he regarded as 'the obvious negatives' that Bunyan's faith and its 'imagery' communicate: 'the unction, the temporal submissiveness, the egocentric pursuit of personal salvation', 'the forbidding Puritan joylessness'. It is not Bunyan or his religion per se but the 'slumbering Radicalism' that *The Pilgrim's Progress* awakened in others that Thompson is keen to extol.[10] Moreover, while the widespread ownership of the unlettered Bunyan's most famous book may only have reinforced a lack of esteem among the more refined literati, Bunyan has never sat entirely comfortably within what is usually termed 'popular culture'. Commentators have long hailed him as a writer of and for 'the people', regarding him as a representative of a populist 'folk tradition' and of a 'plebeian culture': 'our greatest working class imaginative writer'.[11] Yet, Bunyan's own 'Puritan' values and religious beliefs, the products of his radical religious conversion during the English Revolution, stand in stark opposition to some aspects of what an English 'folk' culture still includes, particularly in its more 'festive' manifestations. After all, for 'Puritans' like Bunyan, traditionally celebratory (and now overwhelmingly commercial) occasions,

---

348–80; Greaves, *Glimpses*, 601–34; Ken Simpson, 'Introduction', in Ken Simpson (guest editor), 'Reading Bunyan's Readers: New Essays on the Reception of *The Pilgrim's Progress*', a special group of essays in *1650–1850: Ideas, Aesthetics, and Inquiries in the Early Modern Era*, 13 (2006), 167–74; Owens and Sim (eds.), *Reception, Appropriation, Recollection*, 15–23; Tamsin Spargo, *John Bunyan* (Tavistock: Northcote House/British Council, 2016), 1–5, 79–89. On Bunyan's reception beyond the English-speaking world, see Auguste Sann, *Bunyan in Deutschland* (Giessen: Wilhelm Schmitz, 1951); Kazuko Nishimura, 'John Bunyan's Reception in Japan', *BS*, 1:2 (1989), 49–62; G. J. Schutte, J. B. H. Alblas, A. Th. van Deursen, and T. Brienen, *Bunyan in Nederland* (Houten: Den Hertog, 1989); Hofmeyr, *The Portable Bunyan*; Gennady Kosyakov, 'Bunyan in Russian Literature', *BS*, 14 (2010), 96–103.

[9] E. P. Thompson, *The Making of the English Working Class*, rev. edn (London: Penguin, 1991), 34–9.
[10] Thompson, *Making of the English Working Class*, 37, 33–4.
[11] Roger Sharrock, 'Bunyan Studies Today: An Evaluation', in Van Os and Schutte (eds.), *Bunyan in England and Abroad*, 45–57 (50); Keeble, '"Of him thousands daily Sing and talk"', 263; Hill, *Bunyan*, 348–57, 365–66, 373, 377.

such as Christmas, were notably shunned as being shamefully pagan and ungodly: festive holidays that have little 'holy' about them.[12] Even the traditional English calendar, with its non-Christian weekday and month names, was to be avoided, being replaced for some (Bunyan included) by a numerical style based on the Scriptures: in godly fashion, Wednesday thus became 'the fourth day' of the week, May 'the third month' of the year (with March being the first), and so on.[13] As Chapter 15 in this volume illuminates, Bunyan hardly looked with much warmth either upon the alehouse culture of late seventeenth-century England. There is plenty of saintly singing in Bunyan's writings, but the pleasures of dancing, drinking, or flirting at fairs remained forms of festive fellowship strictly prohibited for the 'saved'.

Bunyan's religious identity, one that would no doubt be seen today as fundamentalist,[14] makes him hard to assimilate, then, within an English festive culture that Puritanism sought comprehensively to reform in the seventeenth century.[15] The hangover induced by this clash of seventeenth-century worlds can still be felt today. Indeed, if there is a single aspect of Bunyan's literary and historical standing which still gives readers difficulty, it is his particular mode of religious belief: one often seen (not entirely fairly, as I have suggested elsewhere) as dogmatic and narrow-minded because typically badged Calvinist and comfortless, predestinarian and 'Puritan'.[16] In apparently assigning the faithful few to salvation and the majority of humankind to eternal perdition, as well as for its allegedly unbending 'joylessness', to borrow Thompson's phrasing, Bunyan's religion might be regarded by some as no better than the seventeenth-century equivalent of today's hard-line Christian Evangelicalism or, as some TV historians have supposed, the intolerant fanaticism of the Taliban: impossible either way to accommodate within a modern, liberal, humanist-secular Western intellectual tradition.[17] One

---

[12] Christopher Durston, 'Lords of Misrule: The Puritan War on Christmas 1642–60', *History Today*, 35: 12 (December 1985), 7–14; Ronald Hutton, *The Rise and Fall of Merry England: The Ritual Year, 1400–1700* (Oxford: Oxford University Press, 1994).

[13] See, further, Michael Davies, 'When Was Bunyan Elected Pastor? Fixing a Date in the Bedford Church Book', *BS*, 18 (2014), 7–41 (9–13).

[14] Bunyan has been described as 'the most popular of all long-eighteenth-century authors' and 'history's most loquaciously speculative fundamentalist': Kevin L. Cope, 'Foreword', in *1650–1850: Ideas, Aesthetics, and Inquiries in the Early Modern Era*, 13 (2006), xiii–xvi (xvi). See also Stuart Sim, 'Bunyan and His Fundamentalist Readers', in Owens and Sim (eds.), *Reception, Appropriation, Recollection*, 213–28.

[15] See, for example, Christopher Durston, 'Puritan Rule and the Failure of Cultural Revolution, 1645–1660', in Christopher Durston and Jacqueline Eales (eds.), *The Culture of English Puritanism, 1560–1700* (Basingstoke: Macmillan, 1996), 210–33. For a more positive account of seventeenth-century 'Puritan' culture, see Bernard Capp, *England's Culture Wars: Puritan Reformation and its Enemies in the Interregnum, 1649–1660* (Oxford: Oxford University Press, 2012).

[16] See Michael Davies, *Graceful Reading: Theology and Narrative in the Works of John Bunyan* (Oxford: Oxford University Press, 2002), 1–80.

[17] See Tristram Hunt, 'Britain's Very Own Taliban', *New Statesman* (17 December 2001), available at http://www.newstatesman.com/node/194286, accessed 5 September 2017. Hunt draws on Simon Schama's description of Cromwell's major-generals as 'the Protestant Taliban on horseback': *A History of Britain*, BBC television documentary, series 2, episode 2 ('Revolutions'), first broadcast 15 May 2001. On the relationship between Bunyan's church and Major-General William Boteler, appointed to

critic has recently cheered the supposed disappearance of *The Pilgrim's Progress* from our contemporary literary landscape precisely on this basis. Bunyan's allegory, Steven Moore avers, is 'about a religious nut' whose brain has been 'addled by Bible-study' and who 'abandons his wife and children' in order to wander through 'a Christian theme park' for 'the grand prize' of 'a shiny gold suit'. What he regards as its 'goofy religiosity' and 'Christian hokum' leaves Moore with no choice but to wish it sunk into oblivion with a rather sour, but no doubt sincere, 'Good riddance.'[18]

While courting controversial reactions was ever the case with Bunyan, it is not hard to see that there are some deep-seated contradictions inherent within his literary and historical reputation. Bunyan has always been one of the most 'popular' English authors, yet one who writes from a position largely antithetical to and condemnatory of certain aspects of a 'popular culture', whether defined in festive or commercial terms. He is the great English Calvinist preacher, a product of Cromwell's Puritan Revolution, yet a writer whose powerful imagination produced some of English literature's most enchanting, enduring, and influential works. Unsurprisingly, these kinds of fracture points and divisions have long been reflected in Bunyan's reception, the terms of which have become almost as famous as his own writings. Following Samuel Taylor Coleridge's dictum, we may still wonder whom should we admire most when reading *The Pilgrim's Progress*: the Bunyan of Parnassus (the writer inspired with a unique literary imagination), or the Bunyan of the conventicle (the convinced 'Puritan' pastor)? Equally, whom or what should we celebrate: Bunyan the revolutionary (possibly republican) preacher of the 1650s, Bunyan the heroic Restoration Nonconformist and prisoner of conscience, or Bunyan the dogmatic 'Puritan' whose fundamentalism points to values that will remain for some permanently beyond the pale? Should we regard Bunyan as left wing, or right wing? A champion of toleration, or fundamentally intolerant? Was he theologically conservative, or a religious radical? Such have been, and remain still, our terms of engagement when it comes to reading Bunyan's writings, making Bunyan himself a battleground of sorts: the 'Mansoul' in an ongoing cultural psychomachia still being fought on the fields of literature and history, politics and religion.

---

impose godly rule upon Bedfordshire in the mid-1650s, see Michael Davies, 'The Silencing of God's Dear Ministers: John Bunyan and his Church in 1662', in N. H. Keeble (ed.) *'Settling the Peace of the Church': 1662 Revisited* (Oxford: Oxford University Press, 2014), 85–113. Kevin Cope has observed that what he regards as Bunyan's relatively 'modest position among eighteenth-century scholars' could be due to the latter 'fearing the evangelicalism that plays so large a role in contemporary American cultural politics': 'Foreword', xvi. In November 2016, the contemporary British author, Mark Haddon, described *The Pilgrim's Progress* as one of the 'founding texts of that literalistic fundamentalist Christianity that causes great and genuine suffering in parts of the modern world still'. What made it 'readable' for Haddon was that it is open to 'multiple', even 'contradictory' interpretations, allowing him to see it as an allegory of mental illness: a 'psychotic fugue'. BBC Radio 4, 'Front Row', Mark Haddon interviewed by John Wilson: broadcast on 4 November 2016: http://www.bbc.co.uk/programmes/p04f67l8, accessed 1 September 2017.

[18] Steven Moore, *The Novel: An Alternative History, 1600–1800* (New York and London: Bloomsbury, 2013), 596. Moore is equally dismissive of *The Life and Death of Mr. Badman*, and of Bunyan's verse: 597, 621 n. 83.

A different yet related question, of course, is one also posed with some regularity: who still reads Bunyan? The answer to this question, however, is rarely positive, usually pointing to an allegedly ever-diminishing audience. As its phenomenal publication history makes manifest, *The Pilgrim's Progress* was once found everywhere: from the dwellings of poor eighteenth-century English textile workers and the ships of nineteenth-century African missionaries to the backpacks of soldiers fighting in the trenches of the First World War. Today, by contrast, or so we are often told, it can be difficult to identify much dedication to it beyond the realms of evangelical Christianity and the academy: constituencies that, in themselves, are hardly insignificant. Richard Greaves, for example, has pointed to a survey of American teenagers undertaken in the late 1980s to confirm that Bunyan's common readers have been dwindling in number, and supposedly for quite some time.[19] In the early 1930s, the critic Q. D. Leavis could likewise lament that '[i]t is now impossible to count on even an educated person's knowing his [or her] Bunyan'.[20] Much the same point was made in a survey of 1886, which reported: 'Now it is to be feared that very few working men or women read the *Pilgrim's Progress*.'[21] Current examples can be found that appear to keep alive this story of vanishing readers. In 2006, for instance, the Labour Education Secretary, Alan Johnson, ruffled feathers by insisting that although, as one newspaper noted, '[f]ew read *The Pilgrim's Progress* today', it should still keep its place within the UK's National Curriculum for schools: a decision deemed unusual enough to warrant comment in the national press.[22]

If such a tale of woe were to be believed, then we would have to ask: where can Bunyan be said to be present? One answer to this question is, of course, in academia. As several commentators have proposed, Bunyan's purportedly diminishing 'popularity' has been met by a counterbalancing rise in scholarly devotion shown to him by literary specialists and historians. Moreover, the watershed for this alleged transformation in Bunyan's fortunes has been identified by Richard Greaves and James F. Forrest as the Second World War. As they have hazarded to suggest, 'World War II probably precipitated a decline in the popularity of Bunyan with the masses' simply because, they assume, 'traditional values' were so 'severely shaken in the post-war decades'. 'Apart from evangelicals', they remark, 'the jaded post-war generations caught between continuing international crises

---

[19] Greaves, *Glimpses*, 622–23.
[20] Q. D. Leavis, *Fiction and the Reading Public* (London: Peregrine Books, 1979; first published Chatto & Windus, 1932), 229 n.1.
[21] David Vincent, *Literary and Popular Culture: England, 1750-1914* (Cambridge: Cambridge University Press, 1989), 179, cited by Greaves, *Glimpses*, 622.
[22] 'In Praise of ... John Bunyan', *The Guardian* (14 August 2006), available at https://www.theguardian.com/commentisfree/2006/aug/14/historybooks.comment, accessed 1 September 2017. Curiously, *The Pilgrim's Progress* is not among books that Johnson lists as having encountered as a child: see Alan Johnson, *This Boy: A Memoir of a Childhood* (London: Bantam Press, 2013), 59–61, 117–18, 228–29, 249–51.

and economic dislocation on the one hand and pervasive materialism on the other, have found Bunyan of relatively little interest.'[23]

This myth of Bunyan's disappearance from among 'the masses' as a phenomenon concurrent with his post-war emergence as 'the darling of the universities' would,[24] of course, necessarily turn Bunyan's cinematic presence in *A Matter of Life and Death* from being a herald of his popular resurgence after 1945—a resurgence bolstered by the subsequent publication of Brittain's biography in 1950 and the premiere of Vaughan Williams's operatic adaptation of *The Pilgrim's Progress* in 1951—into a death-knell of valediction. Yet this can hardly be the case. There can be no doubt that the professional foundations of what would become known today as 'Bunyan studies' were being laid at precisely the time when Powell and Pressburger were making their Bunyan-related masterpiece. For it was exactly at this point that a young English scholar, Roger Sharrock, published two major articles on Bunyan,[25] thereby inaugurating an academic career that would revolutionize the modern study of Bunyan: in effect, creating the contemporary landscape of Bunyan scholarship as we know it today. Yet, this development need hardly be seen in contradistinction to or in some sense as a compensation for an alleged decline in Bunyan's previously 'record-breaking popularity'.[26] For, as Ann Rigney has argued, literary scholarship in itself can act as a powerful 'counter-force' to the processes of cultural 'amnesia' that might otherwise threaten the 'popularity' of a writer such as Bunyan. Because critics and scholars 're-inscribe books so that they become readable—in the sense of worth reading—again', their work (and, of course, their teaching too) carries the potential to counter the kinds of 'erosion' into 'illegibility' that can be 'brought about by cultural change', and thereby 're-awaken the interest of the next generation'.[27]

It is this 'counter-amnesiac force' that can be seen emerging in Roger Sharrock's life-long work on Bunyan,[28] and in the interest it would help to inspire in others. Crucially, Sharrock went on to establish the standard critical editions of *The Pilgrim's Progress* (1960) and of Bunyan's spiritual autobiography, *Grace Abounding to the Chief of Sinners* (1962), both for Oxford University Press, alongside an ever-popular Penguin Classics edition of *The Pilgrim's Progress* (1965): one that remained in print, and must therefore have been bought and read by countless numbers both within and outwith academia,

---

[23] Forrest and Greaves, *John Bunyan: A Reference Guide*, xii–xv. See also Sharrock, 'Bunyan Studies Today', 47–8; Richard Greaves, 'Tercentenary Reflections', in Richard Greaves, *John Bunyan and English Nonconformity* (London: Hambledon Press, 1992), 193–206 (193); Greaves, *Glimpses*, 623–4; Spargo, *John Bunyan*, 79–85.

[24] Forrest and Greaves, *John Bunyan: A Reference Guide*, xvii.

[25] 'Bunyan and the English Emblem Writers', *RES*, 21 (1945), 105–16, and 'Spiritual Autobiography in *The Pilgrim's Progress*', *RES*, 24 (1948), 102–20.

[26] Cope, 'Foreword', xvi.

[27] Ann Rigney, *The Afterlives of Walter Scott: Memory on the Move* (Oxford: Oxford University Press, 2012), 221, 224–25.

[28] Rigney, *Afterlives*, 225.

for over forty years. Overseeing too the subsequent publication of the thirteen-volume edition of Bunyan's *Miscellaneous Works* (also for Oxford University Press), it is owing to Sharrock and his team of editors that we now have a scholarly text of Bunyan's complete oeuvre: a confirmation of Bunyan's status within the established canon of English literary and religious authors, and the culmination of his living popularity among readers, both erudite and 'common', secular and religious, that stretches back centuries.

GLIMPSES OF BUNYAN

It is to Sharrock, then, along with other notable critics and historians researching, writing, and publishing on Bunyan and his contemporaries throughout the decades immediately following the Second World War, and on both sides of the Atlantic (Henri Talon, Richard Greaves, James Forrest, Christopher Hill, Geoffrey Nuttall, to name just a handful), that we owe the origins of what has become, by the beginning of the twentieth-first century, a thriving scholarly concern: the multinational industry of Bunyan studies. The representatives of this cooperative venture, as this *Oxford Handbook* demonstrates, hail from around the globe, and their work has flourished over the last thirty years, having been nurtured individually by some key influential scholars (N. H. Keeble, Nigel Smith, Vincent Newey, and W. R. Owens, among others) and collectively, by both the International John Bunyan Society and the journal, *Bunyan Studies*.

Of course, on the basis of such well-established, worldwide scholarly activity, it might seem foolhardy to attempt to refute the narrative that has been constructed by Richard Greaves and others: that in the latter half of the twentieth century Bunyan's presence migrated irreversibly from the lives of ordinary people to the libraries of academics and their students. Yet to let this idea remain unchallenged would be seriously remiss. For, on the one hand, the 'popular' versus 'academic' distinction establishes something of a false dichotomy, one that imagines that these worlds can never overlap, speak to, or influence one another in ways that they clearly do. On the other, to rework one of Ann Rigney's formulations, it places Bunyan in danger of being remembered now largely for having been forgotten.[29] Would it be either accurate or helpful, then, to suggest that Bunyan's presence has largely vanished from the world beyond academia? The answer to this question must, of course, be a resounding: 'No'. To demonstrate why this is the case, however, we need to gauge Bunyan's contemporary status in a way other than simply surveying those who may or may not have read *The Pilgrim's Progress*. Rather than trying to count readers, and in anticipation too of a more detailed account of the publication, distribution, and readership patterns of Bunyan's books, we can turn instead to what this discussion has been pointing towards all along: Bunyan's 'presence'—that is, his place both in the contemporary world and within the literary and historical heritage

---

[29] Rigney, *Afterlives*, 10.

that informs it, through 'a study of reception that goes beyond the matter of literary value' and even 'beyond the medium of writing' to reveal 'the multiple appropriations' of Bunyan's life and work across a range of 'cultural spheres, media, and constituencies'.[30]

One way to do this, as Kirsty Milne has recently shown in her own study of Bunyan, is to consider Bunyan's presence in terms of 'cultural memory', and by way of the 'resonance' and 'portability' of his writings.[31] Such an approach engages with Bunyan as 'a shared cultural resource', Milne has argued, and as 'common intellectual property' to be negotiated both individually and collectively, rather than in the more traditional terms of literary adaptation, appropriation, and commentary typically associated with 'reception' studies. It can even include those who 'are not strictly readers at all' but those who may have 'formed an idea of a text without having actually read it'.[32] It is in these terms, then, that Milne has pursued 'Bunyan's runaway metaphor'[33] of 'Vanity Fair' from its original location in *The Pilgrim's Progress* through its numerous literary and cultural transformations over the centuries that have followed. Much the same could be done with what I am describing here as Bunyan's 'presence', and on numerous counts. For there can be no doubt that Bunyan is still with us. As his thirty-second appearance in *A Matter of Life and Death* demonstrates, however, his is a presence most often experienced most intensely in the glimpse: that fleeting and momentary, often fragmentary but no less potent, reminder of his living force.

On an obvious level, for instance, and whether we are aware of it or not, Bunyan is present in the phrasing of an everyday language: one can become caught in a 'slough of despond', or conversely be relieved of a burden that has, as it were, rolled from one's shoulders. 'House Beautiful', like 'Vanity Fair', is another of those 'runaway metaphors', taking on a life of its own far beyond *The Pilgrim's Progress*, whether in a Rudyard Kipling short story, 'They' (1904), or that veritable oracle of interior design and decoration, *House Beautiful* magazine. Likewise, Bunyan's Apollyon or even his famous 'hymn', 'Who would true Valour see' (better known as 'To Be a Pilgrim'), could easily command full-length studies in their own right in terms of their cultural and political 'portability' since first appearing in 1678 and 1684 respectively. And we can sense Bunyan's presence all too palpably in the titles of myriad other works (paintings, films, novels, autobiographies, pop music albums, literary criticism), whether they have any direct bearing on Bunyan's allegory or not: *A Rake's Progress, A Harlot's Progress, Plebeians Progress, Pacifist's Progress, Private's Progress*, even (and quite deliberately) *Pilgrims Progress*.

More profound engagements with Bunyan's presence can be recognized beyond direct quotation, subtle allusion, or outright adaptation. *The Pilgrim's Progress* occupies an important place, for example, in nineteenth-century English and American literature as a

---

[30] Rigney, *Afterlives*, 12.
[31] Kirsty Milne, *At Vanity Fair: From Bunyan to Thackeray* (Cambridge: Cambridge University Press, 2015), 3, 7, 10, 13–14; Wai Chee Dimmock, 'A Theory of Resonance', *PMLA*, 112 (1997), 1060–71; Ann Rigney, 'Portable Monuments: Literature, Cultural Memory, and the Case of Jeanie Deans', *Poetics Today*, 25 (2004), 361–96, and *Afterlives*, 1–48, esp. 6–7, 9, 17–20.
[32] Milne, *At Vanity Fair*, 10–11, 137.
[33] Milne, *At Vanity Fair*, 2.

fact of material life, organizing our responses to certain texts as an object of realism as well as a narrative model or an intertextual opening. We glimpse well-thumbed copies of it in Gabriel Oak's modest library in *Far from the Madding Crowd* (1874) and in the childhood lives of the redoubtable heroines of *Ruth* (1853) and *The Mill on the Floss* (1860). As both Joel Rasmussen and Margaret Thickstun in Chapters 34 and 18 of this volume remind us, it is remembered fondly by Louisa May Alcott's 'little women', and handled thoughtfully by Mark Twain's Huckleberry Finn. Yet we feel its presence too in the narratives of African American slaves, such as William and Ellen Craft.[34] It is there among the heaped belongings of those wretched economic migrants fleeing the dustbowl of Depression in *The Grapes of Wrath* (1939), just as it is present as a fact, a real thing, in the homes of British working-class autodidacts who, with Benjamin Franklin, found within its pages a gateway to the greater intellectual adventure of reading.[35] And Bunyan can be glimpsed in other material forms: as a statue in Bedford (sculpted by Joseph Edgar Boehm, erected in 1874), as a painting in London's National Portrait Gallery (by Thomas Sadler, from around 1684), and in commemorative windows and murals found not only in the Bunyan Meeting Free Church in Bedford, but also in Anglican cathedrals and churches.[36] Visitors to Bunyan's home town of Bedford can sense the 'percolation' of his life and work into 'everyday lives' by cruising the Great Ouse aboard 'The John Bunyan' boat, or even by imbibing Bunyan's presence in a pub named The Pilgrim's Progress.[37]

That Bunyan himself would have been profoundly unamused at being commemorated in the stained-glass art of the 'Antichristian' national church that once persecuted him or likewise in having modern alehouses named in his honour is, in terms of a 'memorial dynamics', neither here nor there. Such is the way that the cultural 'resonance' of authors and their texts functions in their transmission through the centuries. For better and for worse, it is 'discontinuity' as much as 'continuity' that prevails in the travelling of literary works, their characters, and their authors through time and space, resulting in their continual decomposition and re-composition as they are 'relocated' and 'reactivated' in different contexts.[38] In Bunyan's case this can involve what Milne describes as the inevitable and at times 'spectacular' 'loss of control over his original text': a text which is subject to 'persistent unraveling', resulting in both 'gains' and 'losses' as *The Pilgrim's Progress* is unmade and remade in different forms across various media.[39]

---

[34] William and Ellen Craft, *Running a Thousand Miles for Freedom* (London: William Tweedie, 1860), 74. See, further, Philip Gould, 'The Rise, Development, and Circulation of the Slave Narrative', in Audrey Fisch (ed.), *The Cambridge Companion to the African American Slave Narrative* (Cambridge: Cambridge University Press, 2007), 11–27 (20–1) and, in the same volume, Kerry Sinanan, 'The Slave Narrative and the Literature of Abolition', 61–80 (63).

[35] See Jonathan Rose, *The Intellectual Life of the British Working Classes* (New Haven, CT, and London: Yale University Press, 2001); Benjamin Franklin, *Autobiography and Other Writings* (Oxford: Oxford University Press, 1993), 13.

[36] See, further, Chapter 36 in this volume.

[37] Rigney, *Afterlives*, 6.

[38] Rigney, 'Portable Monuments', 361, 383, 385–89.

[39] Milne, *At Vanity Fair*, 137; Dimmock, 'Resonance', 1061–2, 1065. See also Rigney, *Afterlives*, 1–17.

Yet Bunyan's presence can be felt in ways that are far from either haplessly ironic or hopelessly discontinuous. In 2012, for example, the year that Vaughan Williams's *The Pilgrim's Progress* was revived by English National Opera in London to rave reviews, Rachel Joyce's best-selling Man Booker-longlisted novel, *The Unlikely Pilgrimage of Harold Fry*, returned Bunyan to its readers through an epigraph that quotes Bunyan's famous pilgrim song, 'Who would true Valour see': an appropriate beginning for another story of a man who walks away from his wife and home without saying why.[40] By contrast, Alan Moore's *Jerusalem* (2016) has reactivated Bunyan's presence in a more experimental way. In this immense novel, both Bunyan and the realm of 'Mansoul' stand at the centre and the circumference of Moore's kaleidoscopic social, historical, and imaginative vision. At once fantastical and realist, cosmic and yet concertedly local, *Jerusalem* deals with the fortunes, past and present, of Moore's home town of Northampton, on whose streets Bunyan is resurrected, at one point, to converse with John Clare and Samuel Beckett. Moore's point in returning Bunyan to our attention is to acknowledge the 'levelling moral apocalypse' of a writer who represented in his own time 'that new and dangerous breed, the literate commoner': one who 'insisted that plain English was a holy tongue, a language with which to express the sacred' and who demonstrated that 'art and literature' could arise from the 'earnestness' and 'visionary passion' of the common people.[41] Perhaps for different reasons, 2016 also saw the release of a concept album, *The Similitude of a Dream*, by the prog rock group, The Neal Morse Band, based on *The Pilgrim's Progress* and including tracks suitably titled 'City of Destruction', 'The Slough', and 'The Man in the Iron Cage'. Likewise, the award-winning Terrence Malick's *Knight of Cups* (USA: Dogwood Films, 2015), a meditative, episodic journey through the hedonistic life of a Hollywood scriptwriter (played by Christian Bale), who wanders through the wilderness of a materially and sensually replete but spiritually empty world of present-day Los Angeles, signals its cinematic intentions with a key opening aural epigraph: Sir John Gielgud's reading of the words that begin *The Pilgrim's Progress*.

Although these examples offer us no more than shards of Bunyan's image and splinters of his writings—forms of 'intermedial sampling and recycling', as Rigney puts it—they show that Bunyan surrounds us, and that *The Pilgrim's Progress* is not only still being read, meditated upon, and mediated for us but that it remains too part of the fabric of a contemporary 'popular'—perhaps even 'post-popular'—culture.[42] It can be

---

[40] The novel appears to have been developed from Joyce's radio play, 'To Be a Pilgrim': first broadcast on BBC Radio 4, 11 July 2007.

[41] Alan Moore, *Jerusalem*, pbk edn, 3 vols (London: Knockabout, 2016), 3: 73, 80–1, and see also 184–95, 301–02, 311; 2: 243–44. Volume 2 in this edition is given the title *Mansoul*.

[42] Rigney, *Afterlives*, 13. Richard Burt uses 'post-popular' when considering how 'mass media' can transform an author's 'status and reproduction', the writer becoming 'a nodal point whose position and presence, when recognized, are relative to the media in which he appears': see 'Shakespeare, "Glo-calization", Race, and the Small Screens of Post-Popular Culture', in Richard Burt and Lynda E. Boose (eds.), *Shakespeare, The Movie, II: Popularizing the Plays on Film, TV, Video, and DVD* (London: Routledge, 2003), 14–36 (17). On 'post-popular' as 'the recirculation of past popular cultures in new circuits of popularity', see C. Parfitt-Brown, 'The Problem of Popularity: The Cancan between the French and

glimpsed in books, films, magazines; heard in music and radio broadcasts; or found as 'No. 1' in a literary list of 'The 100 Best Novels'.[43] It is even on the street. No one traversing Southampton Row in Holborn, London, in the early months of 2015 could have failed to notice, at the corner of Catton Street, a billboard bearing a massive facsimile of the frontispiece to the first (1678) edition of *The Pilgrim's Progress*.[44] Placed there during the cleaning of Richard Garbe's sculpture of Bunyan (*c*.1901), part of the conversion of the Baptist Church House into a luxury boutique hotel, the billboard, like the sculpture it temporarily replaced, reminds us that Bunyan is still very much here, before our eyes as well as in our ears. He lives in our world, often confronting us in curious juxtapositions of colliding cultural values. In Bedford, then, one may drink in The Pilgrim's Progress without, perhaps, ever thinking to drink in the genius of Bunyan's allegory, while in London a statue of Bunyan erected at the former headquarters of the Baptist Church is now destined to adorn the facade of L'Oscar: an exclusive designer hotel at the heart of the ever-thriving Vanity Fair of England's capital.[45]

With such strident examples in mind it is difficult to concur with Kirsty Milne that Bunyan is one of those writers 'who have fallen spectacularly out of fashion', 'whose power has vanished', and 'whose story is unsuited to our times'.[46] Moreover, while Steven Moore would no doubt be delighted to see Milne join a growing list of commentators who remark routinely upon the supposed retreat of *The Pilgrim's Progress* from the world, his own wish to issue it a permanent 'Good riddance' remains as impotent as it is futile. We cannot bid farewell either to Bunyan or to *The Pilgrim's Progress* because they remain so recurrent, so foundational, so resonant that nothing can dislodge them from their firmly embedded, indeed enmeshed, places within 'cultural memory'. For if we are to appreciate the novels of George Eliot and Thomas Hardy, or to understand the histories of class struggle in Britain and of colonialism and post-colonialism around the world, or if we wish simply to recognize the value of literacy and the power of reading as points of entry into the life of intellectual endeavour, then we must remember Bunyan, and admit his presence.

Far from evaporating, the glimpses of Bunyan that invite us to trace his relevance in the world seem not to be diminishing but proliferating. It is our duty to pursue these glimpses and fragments for the wider vistas of discovery to which they point, in order

---

Digital Revolutions', in Sherril Dodds and Susan C. Cook (eds.), *Bodies of Sound: Studies across Popular Music and Dance* (Farnham: Ashgate, 2013), 9–24 (23–4).

[43] Robert McCrum, 'The 100 Best Novels: No 1—The Pilgrim's Progress by John Bunyan (1678)', *The Guardian* (23 September 2013): https://www.theguardian.com/books/2013/sep/23/100-best-novels-pilgrims-progress accessed 12 September 2017; Robert McCrum, *The 100 Best Novels in English*, new edn (Cambridge: Galileo Publishers, 2016).

[44] I owe thanks to Jane Giscombe at Dr Williams's Library, London, for drawing my attention to this billboard. See http://embracebuildingwraps.co.uk/gallery/southampton-row/ and http://ahamm.co.uk/john-bunyan-the-pilgrim%27s-progress-hoarding-billboard-holborn/, both accessed 9 September 2017.

[45] See, further, the contractor's website: https://www.mclarengroup.com/casestudies/2-6-southampton-row/ and http://www.planningresolution.co.uk/project/loscar/ accessed 11 September 2017.

[46] Milne, *At Vanity Fair*, 3, 137–38.

to make better sense both of Bunyan's resonance and of the profound effects that it has had, and continues to have, upon us. In Bunyan's case, such an endeavour is all the more complex and exciting because his writings cross so many lines of interdisciplinary enquiry. As a writer of allegory he is as open to investigation by literary theorists as he is by theologians, just as Bunyan the polemical religious controversialist is as much the subject of historians of seventeenth-century religion as he is of feminist literary critics. The Calvinist preacher is as revered as the archetypal class warrior and the political rebel. Will we ever be able to keep up with a writer so nimble and mobile, so adaptable to his constantly changing environments? As the critic and intellectual historian Stefan Collini has remarked, for both common readers and specialists alike, Bunyan must remain 'the great unclassifiable': 'great', in part, precisely because 'unclassifiable'; inimitable because illimitable.[47]

The Oxford Handbook of John Bunyan

Bunyan's supposed terminal decline as a cultural and literary force should be considered, then, a myth to be interrogated like any other: a death the reports of which have been somewhat prone to exaggeration. In actuality, the situation is much more complex, not least because, though Bunyan's inscription within various forms of 'cultural memory' remains indelible, we might register his presence more intensely at certain times than at others. As E. P. Thompson observed of eighteenth- and nineteenth-century revolutionary politics, when 'the context is hopeful and mass agitations arise', then 'the active energies' of England's Dissenting tradition become most apparent: 'Christian does battle with Apollyon in the real world' at such times. By contrast, in 'times of defeat and man's apathy, quietism is in the ascendant', reinforcing a sense of political 'fatalism': at such moments, 'Christian suffers in the Valley of Humiliation'.[48] This kind of pattern, rooted in Thompson's sense of Bunyan's 'ambivalence' as a writer whose message is always both religiously conservative and at the same time socially radical, can be discerned elsewhere. Always loved in a crisis, it seems, it was during the Industrial Revolution and the formation of an English proletarian class that Bunyan likewise emerged in the 'ascendant', just as he would rise to cultural prominence once again during the First World War and, as we have seen, in the immediate aftermath of the Second World War. This routine of picking Bunyan up when he is most needed—whether in the form of a postcard sent to a hostage held in Beirut in the late 1980s, or in a poem composed on the election of the USA's first African American president in 2008, or in a compassionate reflection upon

---

[47] Stefan Collini, *Common Reading: Critics, Historians, Publics* (Oxford: Oxford University Press, 2008), 250.
[48] Thompson, *Making of the English Working Class*, 37.

the terrorist outrage committed in Barcelona on 17 August 2017[49]—may help to explain why Bunyan's presence appears to come to the fore in moments of crisis or transition, nationally and globally: because both his life and his writings allow us to confront values and ideals that demand to be challenged and reassessed in times of conflict and change, whether in terms of conscience, anti-materialism, compassion, or revolution.

Bunyan remains, then, not just formidably present but also a formidable presence, haunting our ways of reading, thinking, and living in key ways at key times, ghosting our world, leaving us with the distinct impression that he has not quite finished with us yet, nor we with him. It is within its 'custodianship' of this cultural inheritance, as Rigney puts it, that the academic study of both Bunyan's writings and milieus—whether historical or literary, theoretical or theological—has long dedicated its efforts and ambitions.[50] *The Oxford Handbook of John Bunyan* is, in this respect, no different: its purpose is both to register and to examine the importance of Bunyan's presence in a series of ways, motivated by aims and objectives individual to each chapter and its contributor. The composite aim of this volume, however, is to assist its readers in considering Bunyan's presence afresh across a range of disciplines and through a spectrum of scholarly specialisms. Where Part I, 'Contexts', deals with the historical Bunyan in relation to various aspects of his life, background, and work—from the basics of his biography and the books he read to the nature of his church at Bedford, his theology, and his relationship to the religious, literary, and social cultures of seventeenth-century Dissent—Part II considers Bunyan's output as a writer comprehensively: from his earliest printed tracts to his posthumously published works, in prose as well in the poetry that he produced throughout his authorial career. While offering individual discussion of each of his major narrative and allegorical texts, the chapters in 'Works' also consider Bunyan's oeuvre in its entirety, treating Bunyan the religious controversialist and polemical preacher with as much care and detail as Bunyan the allegorist and master of imaginative prose.

The chapters of Parts I and II inform our understanding of Bunyan and his works within the contexts of the later seventeenth century, allowing us to absorb the Bunyan of the conventicle with as much energy and conviction as would typically be granted to appreciating the Bunyan of Parnassus. These chapters address Bunyan's place, his presence, within the worlds of the English Revolution and the Restoration, and they centre Bunyan at the heart

---

[49] See Terry Waite, *Taken on Trust* (London: Hodder & Stoughton, 1993), 262–63, 266, 360, and Tamsin Spargo, 'The Purloined Postcard: Waiting for Bunyan', *Textual Practice*, 8 (1994), 79–96. On the poem 'Pilgrim's Progress' by Nigerian writer Tolu Ogunlesi, written to mark Barack Obama's election victory in November 2008, see Isabel Hofmeyr, 'Bunyan: Colonial, Postcolonial', in Anne Dunan-Page, *The Cambridge Companion to John Bunyan* (Cambridge: Cambridge University Press, 2010) 162–76 (162). The poem is available in a special issue of *Wasifiri*, 24 (2009), 126, and online, https://toluogunlesi.wordpress.com/2013/01/26/poetry-pilgrims-progress-for-barack-obama/, accessed 5 September 2017. For John Bell's Bunyan-inflected reflections on the Barcelona attack, first broadcast on 18 August 2017 for BBC Radio 4's 'Thought for the Day', a feature of the 'Today' programme, see http://www.bbc.co.uk/programmes/p05cpl6v#play, accessed 5 September 2017.

[50] Rigney, *Afterlives*, 225–26.

of their respective maelstroms: religious and political, persecutory and controversial, literary and radical. Parts III and IV, by contrast, turn to Bunyan's literary presence, though again in quite distinct ways. Part III, 'Directions in Criticism', engages with Bunyan across a number of critical concerns, traditional and novel, generic and theoretical. While some chapters deal with Bunyan's relationship to and his employment of allegory, romance, language, and style, others consider Bunyan in terms of literary theory: from historicist and psychoanalytic criticism to postmodernism and the post-secular. By contrast, Part IV, 'Journeys', tackles some of the ways in which Bunyan's literary presence, and especially that of *The Pilgrim's Progress*, has been felt throughout the world since the late seventeenth century. These chapters assess Bunyan's place within and his influence upon key literary periods and their distinctive developments, from the eighteenth-century novel to the Evangelical Revival, and from the Romantics to the Victorians. They also focus on Bunyan's presence within children's literature and American literary culture, in the writing of 'empire' and the concepts of 'class' and 'Englishness'.

Structured in this way, *The Oxford Handbook of John Bunyan* seeks to provide its readers with a collection unparalleled in range, depth, and scope, negotiating as it does the kinds of interdisciplinary approaches that Bunyan naturally invites: from literary theory to church history, and from linguistics to post-colonial criticism. Such is the extent of Bunyan's presence. However, although this *Handbook* seeks to offer a comprehensive series of tightly focused accounts of Bunyan's life and writings, their contexts and 'journeys', it is far from exhaustive. Without hoping to capture anything like the 'complete' Bunyan, the very incompleteness of this volume invites other presences, other resonances, to be felt, traced, and glimpsed. One way to do this is to pursue the kind of study undertaken by Kirsty Milne, which examines the ongoing portability of Bunyan's 'runaway' texts in art, literature, and culture. Alternatively, we could follow Isabel Hofmeyr and Margaret Sönser Breen, whose ground-breaking research directs us to read *The Pilgrim's Progress* as a book that continues to travel along 'transnational pathways of circulation' and with 'academic currents' that 'draw on and reconfigure older traditions' of reading and thinking. Their scholarship has been reactivating *The Pilgrim's Progress* in relation to a range of African writers and 'long-standing African interpretations of the text', on the one hand, and, on the other, as an allegory in productive dialogue with gay and lesbian writers, and feminist and queer studies. In such cases, a 'reading praxis' emerges that, as Breen has aptly put it, 'opens up new possibilities for appreciating the richness of Bunyan's text—and, perhaps, appreciating anew the richness of its narrative subversiveness'.[51]

---

[51] Hofmeyr, 'Bunyan: Colonial, Postcolonial', 168–69, and *The Portable Bunyan*, 191–213. See also Chapter 38 in this volume. Margaret Sönser Breen, 'The Pilgrim's Art of Failure and Belonging: Dialogues between Bunyan and Queer Studies', *BS*, 18 (2014), 61–77 (74–5), and see also '*Desert of the Heart*: Jane Rule's Puritan Outing', in Tracy Fessenden, Nicholas F. Radel, and Magdalena J. Zaborowska (eds.), *The Puritan Origins of American Sex: Religion, Sexuality, and National Identity in American Literature* (New York and London: Routledge, 2001), 235–52, and *Narratives of Queer Desire: Deserts of the Heart* (Basingstoke: Palgrave, 2009).

Bunyan's presence—always travelling, always on the move—at all times has invited new engagements, new responses, and new perspectives. It continues to do so now. For to read Bunyan, to glimpse the manifold and heterogeneous points of contact that his life and writings ask us to discover, is to embark upon 'a journey propelled by an expansive sense of belonging, whereby', as Breen has so generously remarked, 'no one gets left behind'—least of all John Bunyan.[52]

---

[52] Breen, 'The Pilgrim's Art', 75.

PART I
CONTEXTS

CHAPTER 1

BUNYAN'S LIFE, BUNYAN'S LIVES

MICHAEL A. MULLETT

ONE way of reading Bunyan's life is to see Bunyan's lives as a five-part sequence. In such an ordering, we may identify an initial phase, made up of a group of sub-stages. These consisted of what he later recalled as a disorderly youth; then, in the mid-1640s, a period of military service in the Parliamentarian army during the first English Civil War, followed by marriage in the late 1640s, which brought him, through his first wife, into the ambit of Puritan piety and its literature; there then took place a religious conversion, which he later came to discount as being only superficial. The second phase, which is difficult by its very nature to date, but occupied a period between the late 1640s and 1650s was made up of the spiritual crisis recorded in his autobiography, *Grace Abounding to the Chief of Sinners*, published in 1666; the resolution of that trauma shaped the remainder of Bunyan's life. Phase three saw his inclusion within institutional Puritanism through his joining the Independent or Congregational church in his town of Bedford, which led into a first period of authorship and church ministry over the years 1656 to 1660. In the fourth stage, from 1660 to 1672, Bunyan was a prisoner as a religious dissident under the repressive conditions of the restored monarchy of Charles II. The fifth and final stage witnessed Bunyan's increasing prominence as an author and Dissenting minister from 1672 to his death in 1688.

Alongside these five subdivisions of Bunyan's life, we shall also be tracing a binary divide between, on the one hand, a recorded existence, which was for much of the time characterized by privacy, interiority, and solitude, and, on the other, a career made up of life and action taking place in the public sphere. Much of the focus of this introductory chapter will be on Bunyan's self-representation in his autobiography, *Grace Abounding*, the first of many accounts of Bunyan's life, and one that records the events and ordeals that formed the mature man. In common with other writings about its subject, this narration is shaped by preconceptions implanted in the mind of the writer. We begin, then, with a review of *Grace Abounding*'s indications of its subject's social origins, in order to be aware of literary conventions used—not to distort the record of a life, but to present it in terms of conformity with prior expectations held.

Origins, Background, Education, and Early Career

The first of these literary conventions was a long-standing assumption, rooted in Judaeo-Christian tradition, that God's servants would be recruited from the ranks of the lowly. It may have been in line with such assumptions that both Martin Luther and John Calvin, for example, represented their origins in terms of a lower social status than their families actually enjoyed. Bunyan too—and more dramatically than Luther and Calvin—represented his background as base and deprived: 'For my descent then, it was [...] of a low and inconsiderable generation; my fathers house being of that rank that is meanest, and most despised of all the families in the Land' (*GA*, 5). In the course of a polemical encounter in the 1670s, Bunyan accused an opponent of disdaining 'my *low* descent among men' (*MW*, 4: 195). Now, the objective facts that we can reconstruct are that Bunyan's grandfather operated as a 'petty chapman'—a self-employed and skilled tradesman. His father, Thomas Bunyan (d. 1676), lived in his own house in Elstow, Bedfordshire, and left property in his will.[1] Of old and once substantial yeoman farming stock, albeit slipping down the social scale, the Bunyans still had a long way to descend before they hit the bottom line. That line would have placed them amongst 'the meanest, and most despised of all the families'—the homeless, the workless, the vagrants, the criminal underworld of an early Stuart England that knew real social distress and acute economic recession.

Bunyan's family did not belong within that underclass. Yet when he represented them as such, his very language reflected expectations about the lowliness of God's servants which are rooted in Christian Scripture. Thus, where Bunyan spoke of not being able to boast of 'Noble blood, or of a High-born state according to the flesh' (*GA*, 5), he was consciously modelling his language on that of St Paul, who, in 1 Corinthians 1:26, had reminded his auditors that 'not many wise men after the flesh, not many mighty, not many noble are called'. The higher truth, then, was that the Almighty went to work to transform base human metals into higher currencies. In this way, John Bunyan, reinvented as emerging out of the lowest of the low, was able to 'magnifie the Heavenly Majesty' (*GA*, 5). Bunyan's first biographer, Charles Doe, captured this line of thought, citing 1 Corinthians 1:26, and confirming Bunyan's 'Mean and Despicable' background:

> [F]or tho' his Original and Birth was but Poor and Despised, yet it pleased God to chuse him before many others to be an Instrument for the bringing of many Souls

---

[1] Greaves, *Glimpses*, 4.

unto God [...] that the Grace of God that was given to him, may be the more exceedingly magnified.²

Linked to Bunyan's depiction of his family's straitened circumstances was a recollection of the meagre education he received. It was Bunyan himself who composed his educational curriculum vitae made up of disadvantage: 'I never went to school to *Aristotle* or *Plato*, but was brought up at my fathers house, in a very mean condition, among a company of poor Countrey-men' (*MW*, 2: 16). Notwithstanding their 'meanness and inconsiderableness', his parents 'put me to School, to learn both to Read and Write [...] though to my shame [...] I did soon loose that little I learned' (*GA*, 5).

Beyond Bunyan's own recollections, the theme of under-education became a key ingredient in images of him presented by others, creating a miasma which settled and becomes difficult to dispel when we try to assess his actual academic attainment. According to Henry Danvers, in his writings on baptism Bunyan displayed 'egregious Ignorance' and 'Self-condemnation'.³ This was an exaggerated reiteration, albeit from a hostile point of view, of a commonplace made about Bunyan from around the time of his first appearance in public life. The Baptist minister Henry Denne was an early entry into the field of myth construction in patronizingly stereotyping Bunyan as a '*Tinker*' who '*strives to mend Souls as well as Kettles and Pans*' and as one of those '*men full of faith and of the Holy Ghost*' who, precisely because of their lack of formal qualifications, were best equipped '*to preach to* [...] *unbelieving heathens*'.⁴ The cliché became ingrained: it was repeated in 1692 by the author of a 'Continuation of Mr. Bunyan's Life', who described how, when Bunyan 'used his Talent' to preach to London Dissenting congregations to whom he 'had been misrepresented, upon the account of his Education', they 'were convinced of his Worth and Knowledge in Sacred Things' (*GA*, 171).

Yet the facts about Bunyan's education may be more complex than the *idées fixes* sometimes deployed to represent it. To start with, young Bunyan may have attended a grammar school in Bedfordshire—on a level above that of the local elementary school. If he did not learn some Latin, it is difficult to explain the fact that the Latin phrase *ad infinitum* makes an appearance in *The Pilgrim's Progress* (*PP*, 1). As an author, Bunyan handled the intricacies of Calvinist theology with great dexterity and, especially in his theological writings, wrote a scholarly English prose. For such reasons, Bunyan scholars have exercised considerable industry in revealing him as a well-read man. Sources that he encountered included a translation of Martin Luther's commentary on the Epistle to the Galatians; work by the leading literary figure in English Calvinism, William Perkins; and the 1603 *A Plain and Familiar Exposition of the Ten Commandements*, partly by the

---

² Charles Doe, 'The Life and Death of Mr. John Bunyan' (1698), in *The Pilgrim's Progress*, ed. Cynthia Wall (New York and London: W. W. Norton, 2009), 263.

³ See 'A Brief Answer to Mr. *Bunyan* about Communion with Persons Unbaptized', in H[enry] D[anvers], *A Treatise of Baptism* (1673), 45 (separately paginated 'Post-script').

⁴ Hen[ry] Denne, *The Quaker No Papist* (1659), sig. A2r–v.

Cambridge scholar John Dod. In addition, there is evidence that he studied *St. Paul's Catechism* (1687), authored by the General Baptist Thomas Grantham.[5]

There is no point in over-rectifying the account to depict a Bunyan far better educated than he was and is sometimes made out to be. He really was a 'tinker' by trade. He had no university education, may have been a largely autodidactic and adult learner, and took part in an exclusively English-language literary culture. However, if, on the other hand, Bunyan was rather better schooled than he and others have claimed him to be, that too was part of a purpose, one of depicting the Almighty as his tutor. According to this version, God filled in the *tabula rasa* of his being. After he had lost 'that little I learned, even almost utterly […] the Lord did work his gracious work of conversion upon my Soul' (*GA*, 5).

Unimpeded by academic pretensions, Bunyan was thus as putty in God's hands for the radical transformation of a life. Once again, though, expectation can be seen to have dictated the shape of narration. Indeed, the ideal of Christian personal history may be viewed as a process made up of repentance, spiritual rebirth, conversion, and newness of life. St Francis of Assisi, Luther, Calvin, Loyola, George Fox, and John Wesley are only a few of the great figures in the history of Christianity whose life histories were marked by renovation. As an autobiographical essay, Bunyan's *Grace Abounding* must also be understood within a Christian literature of narrations of personal rebirth that goes back to St Paul and St Augustine. *Grace Abounding* must be a key source in our exploration of Bunyan's life, recounting as it does the formation of the minister, preacher, and, above all, author that we know. However, it will not function as a complete or rounded or even entirely factual account of a life lived, but as 'A Brief Relation of the exceeding mercy of God in Christ, to his poor Servant *John Bunyan*' (*GA*, 5).

Military Service, Marriage, and 'Conversion'

Grace Abounding can be seen as a kind of sermon, serving, as Richard Greaves writes, 'as de facto credentials to demonstrate [Bunyan's] qualifications to preach'.[6] Its message was to be applied to others in such a way that it operated primarily as a *spiritual* autobiography, in which external, including political and military, events were incidental and invoked only to illustrate the central truth of this extended homily. Of his role in the Civil Wars, we can hardly rely on Bunyan himself to give us an intelligible historical account. It is true that painstaking historians' work has been carried out so as to disinter Bunyan's actual military role between 1644 and 1647. As a result of such research,

---

[5] Richard Greaves, *John Bunyan and English Nonconformity* (London: Hambledon Press, 1992), 40. See, further, Chapter 6 in this volume.

[6] Greaves, *John Bunyan and English Nonconformity*, 38.

we know from army recruitment records that from 30 November 1644 to 8 March 1645 he was enlisted in a unit of Parliament's New Model Army and stationed at Newport Pagnell in Buckinghamshire; from 21 April 1645 to, probably, September 1646 he served in the same army in a company commanded by a Major Robert Bolton.

Even so, the impression we have so far is that as a young—sixteen-year-old—conscript, he may have been commandeered into Parliament's forces more by the weight of political and military dominance prevailing in his part of the world than by any mature personal conviction of the rightness of the cause of Parliament and 'godly' religion. His own reminiscences of a youth dominated by the 'lusts and fruits of the flesh', amidst 'the vileness of my companions', at an age when 'the thoughts of Religion was very grievous to me' (GA, 7), do not indicate an adolescent driven by the religious convictions that had led to the formation of the New Model Army. It is true that in June 1647 he offered himself for service in a company commanded by a Captain Charles O'Hara, part of a regiment destined for service in Ireland, a battle zone where the ideological and religious collision between the forces arrayed in the British Civil Wars was at its most intense. However, in the month after Bunyan volunteered for service in Ireland, Parliament broke up the regiment posted for the Irish campaign and the youth's career as a trooper was over, leaving him with a knapsack of military metaphors to be brought out for later writings such as *The Holy War* (1682).[7]

It is, of course, possible to speculate that the hectic flow of religious discourse in the New Model Army may have influenced the adolescent Bunyan. But it is just the point that piecing together such influences, filling in those tantalizing gaps, must be a matter of speculation, since Bunyan himself provided only minimal information on that period of his life. Of course, to recall in any detail active service with the army that had been the chief force in bringing down the monarchy and Church of England in the course of the 1640s would hardly have been a wise move on the part of a prisoner at the hands of a restored version of that political system in the 1660s. But any such consideration apart, Bunyan's fragmentary recollection of his military service was included in his narration not to fill a gap in his biography but rather to illustrate a point. What that point was can best be understood when we consider the passage about the war in the context of a group of recounted incidents which, taken together, led to an inescapable conclusion.

Bunyan's initial phase, he recalled, was that of an unsupervised village boy and youth living a bucolic life. His recall of it depicts him as Satan's captive, albeit prodded with pricks of conscience: he is 'filled with all unrighteousness [...] all manner of vice and ungodliness'. This was an essentially literary projection, confirming Bunyan's status as 'the chief of Sinners'. When it came to actual evil deeds, there was little of substance, apart from 'cursing, swearing, lying and blaspheming the holy name of God'. However, a series of four near-fatal accidents in Bunyan's boyhood and adolescence—including two near-drownings and a dangerous encounter with a snake in the Bedfordshire

---

[7] Richard Greaves, 'John Bunyan', *ODNB*; Anne Laurence, 'Bunyan and the Parliamentary Army', in Anne Laurence, W. R. Owens, and Stuart Sim (eds.), *John Bunyan and his England, 1628–1688* (London: Hambledon Press, 1990), 17–29.

countryside—came to take on a higher meaning. A wartime episode is written up with a combination of dreamy vagueness over time and place and horrifying immediacy over the outcome:

> [W]hen I was a Souldier, I with others were drawn to go out to such a place to besiege it; but when I was just ready to go, one of the company desired to go in my room, to which, when I had consented he took my place; and coming to the siege, as he stood Sentinel, he was shot into the head with a Musket bullet and died. (*GA*, 6–8)

The occurrence during that unidentified siege came as the grim culmination of the set of incidents in Bunyan's early life which formed a sequential drama in four acts that manifested to Bunyan God's mercy towards him. Those four near-death experiences were 'Judgements', yet 'mixed with mercy': 'mercy yet preserved me alive' and 'God [had] been mercifull to me' (*GA*, 7–8). The series of mercies also foreshadowed the even greater one of God's subsequent pouring out to Bunyan his grace abounding. Above all, the incident of the siege was to be understood in the light of Providence's benevolence to him. Old men forget, but aging Bunyan conserved the memory of the sentry shot in his place—not so much as a wartime adventure but as a moral, forming his consciousness of himself as a firebrand plucked out of the burning. As Doe recalled, 'This was a deliverance that Mr. *Bunyan* would often mention, but never without Thanksgiving to God.'[8]

Persisting in his bad language, demobilized Bunyan was a young man who 'sinned still' but whose sinfulness could be represented as largely verbal: 'cursing and swearing […] I swore and cursed at that most fearful rate […] *the ungodliest Fellow for swearing* […] this wicked way of swearing […] I knew not how to speak unless I put an Oath before, and another behind, to make my words have authority' (*GA*, 11–12). Bunyan was to become pre-eminently a man of words, a preacher, and an author on a prolific scale, from his anti-Quaker polemic *Some Gospel-Truths Opened* (1656) to his death in 1688, and, posthumously, beyond it. And it is as a man of speech that he now emerges in his autobiography, desperate to give 'authority' to his words. Words were indeed to be his stock-in-trade. In the 1650s the process of his religious conversion was to be triggered by pious discourse he heard in Bedford, and in his subsequent spiritual crisis it was to be words of Scripture that were first to impede and then to promote his attainment of peace of mind, shaping the mature paradigm of Bunyan's life. However, in his pre-converted state, Bunyan, given over to cursing and swearing, was speaking the wrong words.

In the wake of this impiety there followed a stage of religious devotion that was, however, purely external, in the sense that it was centred on the church as an institution and as a location for rituals and for pre-packed liturgical expressions: 'I fell in very eagerly with the Religion of the times, to wit, to go to Church twice a day, and […] there

---

[8] Doe, 'Life and Death of Mr. John Bunyan', 269.

should very devoutly both say and sing as others did' (*GA*, 8–9). The chronology Bunyan gives indicates that his ritualist period came about following his marriage to a woman of 'godly' background which, in turn, came after his army service: 'Presently after this, I changed my condition into a married state' (*GA*, 8). That sequence would take us to a point in time no earlier than July 1647, when Bunyan was released from military service, in a period when the formulary of Anglican worship, the Book of Common Prayer, had been abolished by Parliament's authority in March 1645, to be replaced by the Directory of Worship, a structured text of congregational prayer approved by the Westminster Assembly of Divines, with its Presbyterian ascendancy.

Bunyan's later deprecation in *Grace Abounding* of his purely mechanical stage of piety was entirely consistent with a view of worship which was to remain integral to his churchmanship for the remainder of his life. At his trial as a religious dissident in January 1661 Bunyan rejected the use of the liturgy of the Book of Common Prayer whose restitution to the heart of public worship in England was crucial to the Restoration settlement of 1660–62. On that occasion, Bunyan took part in a debate on the Prayer Book, in an exchange with the judge Sir John Kelyng, a drafter of the 1662 Act of Uniformity which officially reinstated the use of the Book of Common Prayer. In the debate, Bunyan faulted the Book of Common Prayer for its absence of spontaneity in worship:

> Keel. He said, we were commanded to pray.
> Bun. I said, but not by the Common Prayer-book.
> Keel. He said, how then?
> Bun. I said with the spirit. As the Apostle saith, *I will pray with the spirit and with understanding*. I. Cor. xiv. 15. (*GA*, 114)

This was a curtain-raiser to an extended treatment of the subject of prayer which Bunyan was to deliver in an early work, *I Will Pray with the Spirit* (1662). In part, in *I Will Pray* Bunyan excoriated the Prayer Book for its alleged Catholic antecedents—'the Scraps and Fragments of the devices of some Popes, some Friars' (*MW*, 2: 239). However, this propagandist assault on the Book of Common Prayer was really beside the point, in the sense that it was the inherent nature of the kind of worship—unspontaneous and prescribed—of which the Prayer Book was an archetype that aroused Bunyan's ire, and did so because it was the diametrical opposite of what prayer should be. What that was, was made perfectly clear in *I Will Pray*. Prayer, being conducted 'between God and the Soul in secret', arose from God's initiative working upon the passive believer (*MW*, 2: 257). Prayer was induced in the individual 'by God's spirit' (*MW*, 2: 246). In his discourse with Kelyng, and in the treatise *I Will Pray*, in which he argued that real prayer was 'a sincere, sensible [sensitive], affectionate [affective] pouring out of the heart or soul to God' (*MW*, 2: 241), Bunyan evolved a durable theory of worship, one that would have led to a repudiation of the Westminster Directory little less than of the Book of Common Prayer.[9] It was an attitude to prayer that would

---

[9] See Michael A. Mullett, *John Bunyan in Context* (Keele: Keele University Press, 1996), 151–58.

remain constant with Bunyan, as, for instance, when he reverted briefly to the topic in his treatise *Instruction for the Ignorant* (1675). Indeed, to the end of his days, Bunyan held to the line on this subject, having taken it up as a result of the relearning he had undergone in his earlier years.

Crisis and Conversion

The account of Bunyan's infatuation with the formal 'Religion of the times' gives way in *Grace Abounding* to the narration of a spell of about a year of 'some outward Reformation'. It was because this was a stage of piety, albeit, as it transpired, of external and wordy piety, that Bunyan's 'holy' interval was dangerous and had to be renounced, so that he could be stripped down to the bare bones of his utter human unworthiness, and then be rebuilt from scratch. In this phase, Bunyan's self-made sanctity was focused on words—'some outward Reformation, both in my words and life' (*GA*, 12). As a seemingly reformed character, he totally replenished his verbal repertoire, cleaned up his vocabulary, and did 'from this time forward [...] leave my swearing'. He was spoken of approvingly as being godly and 'was now a brisk talker [...] in the matters of Religion' (*GA*, 12, 14). He was, however, a kind of early prototype of his vainly verbose character of Talkative in *The Pilgrim's Progress*, the orator of godliness who comes in for some exceptionally sharp condemnation because his religion is purely verbal.

The situation was complicated by the fact that words in themselves were neither good nor ill. It was as a glib gabbler of godly garrulity that at some point in the 1650s, going about his tinker's business, Bunyan chanced to eavesdrop upon three or four saintly women of Bedford conversing, on a level of authenticity 'far above' his own pious prattle,

> about a new birth, the work of God on their hearts, also how they were convinced of their miserable state by nature [...] how God had visited their souls with his love in the Lord Jesus, and with what words and promises they had been refreshed, comforted and supported against the temptations of the Devil; [...] they also discoursed of their own wretchedness of heart [...] and did contemn [...] their own righteousness, as filthy, and insufficient to do them any good. (*GA*, 14)

This converse in a Bedford backstreet was a breakthrough encounter for Bunyan, initiating the long and painful mechanism of conversion, the process that was to shape the remainder of his life. This accidental meeting also came to define what was to be his enduring sense of Christianity as essentially experiential and inward. As such, it could not be confined by prepared texts of prayers, whether Church of England, Presbyterian, or whatever. Words were valuable coin but they must not be counterfeit, or borrowed from others, or from ages past. The 'gathered' churches themselves required of would-be entrants personal testimonies of spiritual travail preceding admission, and *Grace Abounding* may be considered in part as a rich and extended variant of this genre. However, the rules of discernment applied by experienced members of congregations who were knowledgeable in such matters demanded that such evidences must be true and sincere—as were the words of the Bedford women.

Rejection of formalism and the demand for spontaneity and immediacy were reflected in a quest for heartfelt authenticity in both prayer and witness which was to shape the whole of the mature Bunyan's sense of the church, producing in him a rejection of externality, ritual, and ordinances. Especially from 1672 onwards, Bunyan was to rise to prominence as a leading builder of the English 'gathered' congregations in a crucial period of their reconstruction over years of repression for English Nonconformity during the post-Restoration decades. A prominent pastor amongst the Dissenting churches, Bunyan was to stand out as a creative ecclesiastical politician. However, a politician should have a policy and Bunyan's manifesto for his church—the avoidance of conflict over what he, at least, defined as lesser matters—arose from a conviction, formed relatively early on in his career and bequeathed to him by his first pastor at Bedford, John Gifford, that the Christian life was in the first place an interior and spiritual one. His trilogy of the early 1670s on the nature and composition of the Church was made up of the works *A Confession of my Faith, and A Reason of My Practice* (1672), *Differences in Judgment about Water-Baptism, No Bar to Communion* (1673), and *Peaceable Principles and True* (1674). In these ecclesiological treatises, Bunyan set out his criterion for church membership. It was based, not on the established 'Anabaptist' benchmark, going back to the sixteenth-century Reformation, of believers' baptism, administered by water in adulthood, nor should disagreements on that issue prevent participation in the Lord's Supper. Rather, the qualifying test for church membership was 'faith and holiness'. The 'shadowish, or figurative ordinances', including baptism itself, were as nothing in discerning qualifications for inclusion of persons in the Church, which required instead 'a faithful relation, of [their] faith and holyness' (*MW*, 4: 160). This approach to the defining composition of the true church, which set him radically at odds with leading 'orthodox' Baptists, can be seen to have been formed by Bunyan's earlier exposure to formative influences. These included John Gifford, the minister of the Bedford congregation that Bunyan entered in the 1650s, who vigorously counselled against making divisions over the issue of baptism, and William Dell, the Cambridge theologian who, in the 1640s and 1650s, taught a spiritualized baptismal doctrine. However, it was the powerful impact of the Bedford women's discourse on him that left Bunyan with his lasting appreciation of the nature of the saints as essentially people of heartfelt and genuine inner processes, 'Faith, experience, and conversation' (*MW*, 4: 165).[10]

---

[10] See, further, Mullett, *John Bunyan in Context*, 176–81; Anne Dunan-Page, *Grace Overwhelming: John Bunyan, The Pilgrim's Progress and the Extremes of the Baptist Mind* (Bern: Peter Lang, 2006), 56.

Ministry and Doctrine

Bunyan's virtually uninterrupted imprisonment for twelve years from 1660 onwards obviously precluded his full involvement in the pastorate of his church in Bedford, but in December 1671 he was elected to 'the pastorall office or eldership' (*CB*, 71) in that church and went on to a position as a leading national figure amongst the Dissenting congregations. This all amounted to a vigorously public and political life, but in order to live it out, Bunyan had had first to come through and then to overcome the intense and introverted self-concern of which *Grace Abounding* is the chronicle. There is, then, a sharp contrast in Bunyan's life between his public roles and the private drama that formed him for them. *Grace Abounding* is the narration of a solitary agony that its author had to undergo, a struggle that saw him as self-obsessed, probably endangering his sanity but in the end leaving him tempered and equipped for those later stages in the public sphere.

The beginnings of an acute crisis followed hard on Bunyan's false pious period. The overheard discourse of the godly women of Bedford presented to their hearer, Bunyan, in a nutshell the Calvinist agenda of redemption. The 'righteousness' on which Bunyan prided himself up to that point was 'filthy'—a Puritan term for our imagined virtue, derived from Isaiah 64:6—since the inherent state of humans 'by nature' was miserable and it was God who went to work on their hearts. According to the Reformation doctrine of justification by faith, as developed by Calvin, those justified must first be full of wrongdoing, as are all human beings in the condition of inherited original sin. As Calvin had written: 'As all mankind are, in the sight of God, lost sinners […] Christ is their only righteousness', for when the 'whole human race perished in the person of Adam', collapsing into 'our foulness and dishonour', God 'appeared as Redeemer in the person of his only begotten Son […] the office enjoined upon Christ by the Father.'[11] In the posthumously published *Of Justification by an Imputed Righteousness* (1692), Bunyan set out the classic Luthero-Calvinist doctrine of justification of sinners through an external righteousness that had to be credited to us for the very reason that '*There is none righteous, no not one*' (citing Romans 3:10). Therefore, the 'Righteousness that Justifieth us, was performed long ago by the Person of Christ […]. He is said to have purged our Sins by *HIMSELF*' (*MW*, 12: 296, 329). It was sinfulness that set up both the opportunity and the necessity for redemption, and Bunyan saw himself as replete with it, for he was the 'chief of sinners' and therefore in a condition of extreme singularity. His plenitude of sin, the precondition of his being rescued from it and justified, was summed up in his obsessive temptation to 'sell Christ', the ultimate, unpardonable sin, that of Judas Iscariot: he was on the precipice of repeating a hitherto unique offence.[12] The polar oscillations of

---

[11] *Reply by John Calvin to Letter by Cardinal Sadolet to the Senate and People of Geneva* (1539), in *John Calvin: Tracts and Treatises on the Reformation of the Church*, ed. Thomas F. Torrrance, tr. Henry Beveridge, 3 vols (Grand Rapids, MI: Wm B. Eerdmans, 1958), 1: 42; John Calvin, *Institutes of the Christian Religion*, ed. John T. McNeill, tr. Ford Lewis Battles, 2 vols (Philadelphia, PA: Westminster Press, 1960), 1: 340–41, 494.

[12] See Vera J. Camden, 'Blasphemy and the Problem of the Self in *Grace Abounding*', *BS*, 1 (1989), 14–15.

his condition, following the overheard Bedford discourse, were made up of guilt, desperation, flashes of joy and peace, and the assistance he received from Gifford. Yet it is the sheer solitude in which Bunyan dealt with this depression that strikes us most forcibly—haunting him even in the most elementary tasks, undermining his work in his trade, taking him from his meals to confront it alone, walking in the fields, in lone internal dialogue with a terrible 'Tempter', Satan.

The spell of his misery in virtual solitude included the years of his marriage to a wife who, clearly, could do nothing to alleviate his plight, while his introverted obsessions and compulsions threatened derangement. As we have seen, he was a man haunted by words, and words, above all biblical words, made all the difference to his mental state and depression. If words of comfort occurred to him that lifted his mood, they needed to be located in Scripture and it was his phenomenal recall of the Bible that enabled Bunyan to find a form of words, in Hebrews 12:22, 24, by means of which he was able to begin to restore his own psychic health. However, it is significant that, once this alternation out of depression took place, he applied himself to the Bedford church, for he now 'longed for the company of some of Gods people, that I might have imparted unto them what God had shewed me' (*GA*, 82).

Preaching, Authorship, Church, and State

This, then, was the major caesura in Bunyan's life between his, first, solitary and, next, his public *personae*. In the latter phase, his work, increasingly directed outside of himself, can be subdivided into the public endeavours of preaching, published authorship, ecclesiastical administration, and political counselling.

Preaching, Bunyan recalled, began at the invitation of leading members of the Bedford church 'after I had been about five or six years awakened, and helped [...] to see both the want and worth of Jesus Christ our Lord' (*GA*, 83). From that point on, it was Bunyan's very success in the work of preaching that further lifted his spirits, giving him 'staid peace and comfort thorow Christ' (*GA*, 86). The tenor of his preaching also shifted, evidently, from his own recollections, lightening up and stressing the process of conversion. Its content was Reformation doctrine, justification by faith alone without the works of the law. However, a kind of corollary to that premise, predestination, was not to the fore. Instead, the content of Bunyan's preaching was finding a place for a voluntarism that may seem at odds with the absolute decree of predestination.

Bunyan remained a preacher and indeed one of his last actions, before his death at the end of August 1688, was delivery of a sermon at a meeting in London. However, if we turn now to a further aspect of his public work, authorship, we shall see in how in practice Bunyan muted the principles of predestinarian Calvinism to which he subscribed in order to find a place for human initiative. It is important to point out that Bunyan's work in this sphere was didactic in the sense that it was intended to stimulate good conduct. In this way, while Bunyan signed up to a kind of theoretical Calvinism in terms of the Reformation doctrine of vicarious justification, in practical terms he advocated a strenuous pursuit of virtue and obedience to God's law. The disparity is present in his earliest published work, the anti-Quaker polemic *Some Gospel-Truths Opened* (1656), in which the sinner is not '*profited by the works of the Law* [...] *salvation was* [...] *fully, and completely wrought out for poor sinners by the man Christ Jesus*', while at the same time the reader is shown 'the way' to have heaven and escape hell and to 'strive' and 'labour' for saving faith (*MW*, 1: 15, 17, 99).

A further early literary outcome of his ministry was the explanatory treatise *The Doctrine of the Law and Grace Unfolded* (1659), which Greaves rightly describes as Bunyan's 'principal exposition of covenant theology' (*MW*, 2: xxii). Expressing the intellectual position that its author had consolidated in published debates against Quakers, who were seen as teaching the redemptive role of good works, *Law and Grace* is, at least on the face of it, an orthodox Calvinist tractate. It sets out that our redemption is secured from outside of ourselves as the passive beneficiaries of an agreement between the Father and the Son to save us by the latter's sacrifice. That said, we are also aware of Bunyan's acceptance, for practical and hortatory purposes, of moral initiatives by human beings, inevitably connoting the exercise of human free volition: 'if thou wouldest be saved thou mayest come to Christ'. Even justification itself is made to appear a matter of willing it for oneself: 'if thou wouldest be justified'. If there is here a contradiction between determinist premises and voluntarist homiletics, Bunyan's tasks as a moral preacher, resolved to impel his hearers to 'stir thee up to mend thy pace towards heaven', enforced that conflict (*MW*, 2: 223, 226).[13]

So the dualism between pastoral moralism and classical Calvinism created a creative tension that remained present in Bunyan's work as a teaching author. Thus, in *The Strait Gate* (1676), with its constant reiteration of that strenuous verb 'strive', readers are urged 'not only to talk of, or to wish for, but to understand how we shall, & to seek that we may be effectualy saved' (*MW*, 5: 72). Perhaps we can resolve any evident discrepancy between these two positions on theory and practice, or determinist Reformation theology versus Christian behaviour and choice, with reference to a group of works which Bunyan, above all, intended to popularize his messages, by incorporating them in popular fiction. Thus, in the two parts of *The Pilgrim's Progress* (1678, 1684) the very metaphor of journey assumes a positive Christian life of effort in the direction of goodness and holiness. While in *Part I* the character of Talkative satirizes the Puritan 'professor' whose Reformation doctrines are technically correct while his conduct is out of order, in *The Life and Death of Mr. Badman* (1680), published between the two parts of *The Pilgrim's Progress*, the central character is predestined both to evil and damnation. That saints 'strive' to attain what is theirs is Bunyan the preacher's message, alongside the hopelessness of reprobation.

---

[13] See, further, Mullett, *John Bunyan in Context*, 137–46.

As an ecclesiastical administrator, Bunyan played a leading role in paving the way for the remarkable success on the part of Bedfordshire congregations in surviving a time of danger. Even during his imprisonment, Bunyan had been able to take a part in coordinating the administration of the Bedford church, and from his release onwards he worked with ministerial colleagues to build organizational structures amongst Dissenting churches, including the setting up of a panel of preachers. Such practical efforts helped to counter the effects of the harsh penal laws of post-Restoration England, while, as a result of such work, local 'gathered' churches, both Baptist and Congregational, were able to respond positively to the prospects for toleration opened up by Charles II's March 1672 Declaration of Indulgence to Nonçonformists.[14] In the longer term, Bunyan's work as the coordinator of a ministerial strategy for his church in Bedfordshire paid off in the remarkable demographic strength of Dissent in the region well into the eighteenth century.

Beyond the limited sphere of his home territory, from 1672 Bunyan was to play an increasing part in church life nationally. The year 1672 was critical in this process because it followed his call to the ministry in December 1671, and it saw Charles II's initiative in opening up toleration to Protestant Dissenters. Under the provisions of the royal Declaration, Bunyan extended his preaching operations to the East Midland town of Leicester in October 1672, the prelude to his development of a widening arc of public appearances, ranging into the deeply Puritan counties of southern East Anglia—Cambridgeshire, Essex, and Suffolk.[15] Then, as the so-called Bishop Bunyan, he was increasingly called up for ministry in the headquarters of English Dissent, London.

In considering John Bunyan's public profile in the 1670s and 1680s, we should review briefly his work as a political thinker and strategist. It is in this area that the contrast in Bunyan's life between its essential privacy before his conversion and its public nature subsequently is most apparent. Before the major divide in his life took place, Bunyan showed no awareness of the political world revolving around his inner traumas; after his transformation, he emerged as fully engaged with the *polis* as a major thinker and writer on political questions of the day. His first contribution, *A Few Sighs from Hell* (1658), delivers an apocalyptically charged denunciation of a predatory ruling class. Apocalyptic themes are again to the fore in the post-Restoration work *The Holy City, or, the New Jerusalem* (1665). In this book, Bunyan was drawing away from a revolutionary sense of the implications of the apocalypse, which he believed was imminent: though kings had persecuted the saints of God, the setting up of His kingdom posed no threat to them. Indeed, the breakthrough in Bunyan's development as a political thinker was the emergence of his post-Restoration royalism. It was following his arrest that Bunyan set out his enduring political credo: 'I look upon it as my duty to behave myself under the King's government, both as becomes a man and a christian; and if an occasion was offered me, I should willingly manifest my loyalty to my Prince, both by word and deed' (*GA*, 120).

---

[14] Greaves, *John Bunyan and English Nonconformity*, 71–87.
[15] Greaves, *John Bunyan and English Nonconformity*, 89–99.

Though these sentiments were genuine, personal loyalty to the Stuart kings of the period 1660–88 also made much tactical sense for a leading spokesman on behalf of organized Nonconformity such as Bunyan. This was because of a major tension in the nation's political life throughout the decades between the Restoration in 1660 and the Revolution of 1688–89. During those years the two royal brothers, Charles II and his successor in 1685, the openly Catholic James II, were bent on securing toleration for England's Christian religious minorities. The four royal Declarations of Indulgence of 1662, 1672, 1687, and 1688—the last of which was largely instrumental in costing James II his throne—were expressive of that commitment. Opposing both kings was an intransigent lay and clerical Cavalier-Anglican and, from 1681 onwards, Tory, ascendancy determined to protect the privileged position of the Church of England through the maintenance of the penal laws designed to that effect. It was becoming widely apparent that the collective self-interest of organized Dissent in seeking the alleviation of the discriminatory laws against it lay in a close political alliance with the Stuart monarchy. Bunyan's important contribution was to harness the Puritan apocalyptic tradition to an ardent attachment to the Stuart Crown. In this task, the vital work was the millenarian tract *Of Antichrist, and his Ruine* (probably written around 1683), with its message of personal loyalty to the monarch, renewed, for example, in *Seasonable Counsel* (1684): 'let the King have verily a place in your Hearts, and with Heart and Mouth give God Thanks for him […] Pray for the long Life of the King' (*MW*, 13: 488–89). The emergence of John Bunyan as quintessentially a public figure was encapsulated in his work in the political forum.

The review of aspects of the life and work of John Bunyan, in this introductory chapter and in the chapters that follow, reveals a towering figure in the history of Protestantism in the English-speaking world and, beyond that, in the global history of Christianity. As a spiritual autobiographer he brought candour and intimacy to an exploration of the human condition that deepens our understanding of our own humanity, both in its dungeons of misery and in its capacity for rescue and even redemption. As a prisoner of conscience, simply unable to silence his own preacher's voice, Bunyan teaches lasting lessons of courage and fortitude, while as a church leader he delivered in his day practical guidance on how the repression of freedom may be countered. As a man of, and from, the people, simply and eloquently speaking his gospel truths to all sorts and conditions of men and women, John Bunyan has inspired and continues to inspire generations of people of all races and tongues aspiring to a life of the spirit. The 'Puritan' beliefs and way of life Bunyan espoused may have become for many bywords for narrowness and negativity, but in the Bedford tinker they achieve a level of greatness.

Suggested Reading

Dunan-Page, Anne, *Grace Overwhelming: John Bunyan, The Pilgrim's Progress and the Extremes of the Baptist Mind* (Bern: Peter Lang, 2006).

Gay, David, James G. Randal, and Arlette Zinck, *Awakening Words: John Bunyan and the Language of Community* (Newark, DE: University of Delaware Press, 2000).

Greaves, Richard, *John Bunyan and English Nonconformity* (London: Hambledon Press, 1992).

Greaves, Richard L., *Glimpses of Glory: John Bunyan and English Dissent* (Stanford, CA: Stanford University Press, 2002).

Hill, Christopher, *A Turbulent, Seditious, and Factious People: John Bunyan and his Church* (Oxford: Clarendon Press, 1988).

Keeble, N. H., *The Literary Culture of Nonconformity in Late Seventeenth-Century England* (Leicester: Leicester University Press, 1987).

Keeble, N. H. (ed.), *John Bunyan: Conventicle and Parnassus* (Oxford: Clarendon Press, 1988).

Laurence, Anne, W. R. Owens, and Stuart Sim (eds.), *John Bunyan and his England, 1628–1688* (London: Hambledon Press, 1990).

Mullett, Michael A., *John Bunyan in Context* (Keele: Keele University Press, 1996).

Owens, W. R. and Stuart Sim (eds.), *Reception, Appropriation, Recollection: Bunyan's Pilgrim's Progress* (Bern: Peter Lang, 2007).

CHAPTER 2

BUNYAN'S ENGLAND
The Trials and Triumphs of Restoration Dissent

JOHN COFFEY

READERS of Bunyan acquire a stark impression of Restoration England. Bunyan stood in the martyrological tradition and he depicted himself as a suffering saint, a prisoner for Christ.[1] His world was sharply divided between the godly and the godless, Dissenters and Anglicans, martyrs and persecutors. In the eighteenth and nineteenth centuries, Dissenting historiography consolidated this 'cult of heroic victimhood'.[2] Baptists and Congregationalists recalled Bunyan's twelve-year ordeal in Bedford jail; the Society of Friends viewed the Restoration through the prism of Joseph Besse's *A Collection of the Sufferings of the People Called Quakers* (1753); Presbyterians and Independents treasured the memorials of their ejected ministers constructed by Edmund Calamy.

In this chapter I will argue that the martyrological tradition both captures and obscures the truth about Bunyan's England and Restoration Dissent. In the first half, I will consider what Gerald Cragg called 'the Great Persecution'.[3] We will find that there was ample reason for Bunyan's lachrymose portrayal of his times. Restoration England witnessed a persecution of Protestant minorities by a Protestant state, which, in its scale and aggression, was without precedent or parallel in post-Reformation Europe. The sufferings of Dissent and the bitterness of ecclesiastical conflict were all too real. In the second half of the chapter, however, I will add some vital nuances. Dissent was a dynamic religious, intellectual, literary, and political presence; the binary division between Anglican and Dissenter was often blurred; the Church of England was internally divided as were the Nonconformist minorities; and there was much support for comprehension

---

[1] See John R. Knott, *Discourses of Martyrdom in English Literature, 1563–1694* (Cambridge: Cambridge University Press, 1993), ch. 6.

[2] Sharon Achinstein, *Literature and Dissent in Milton's England* (Cambridge: Cambridge University Press, 2003), 19.

[3] Gerald Cragg, *Puritanism in the Period of the Great Persecution, 1660–1688* (Cambridge: Cambridge University Press, 1957).

and indulgence. Bunyan's Dissenters may have been a minority, but the culture wars in which they fought were more evenly balanced than we often think. Bunyan's England could be a hostile environment for the godly, but it could also prove surprisingly fertile ground. Restoration Dissent had its triumphs as well as its trials.

The Trials of Dissent

The Restoration looked especially terrible to Dissenters because of what had preceded it. During the Puritan Revolution, the godly had enjoyed political and religious hegemony.[4] Puritans had formed the core of the Parliamentary party at Westminster, the spearhead of the cause in the localities, and its shock troops in the army. Their clergy had delivered scores of thunderous sermons before MPs and peers, who in their turn had passed a tranche of godly legislation against heresy, blasphemy, adultery, horse-racing, Sunday sports, and other assorted evils. Episcopacy had been abolished, the Book of Common Prayer outlawed, and over 2,000 anti-Puritan clergy purged from their livings. Of course, in the eyes of moderate Puritans (those now called Presbyterians), parliamentarianism had lost the plot. The work of the Westminster Assembly, both a parliamentary committee and a clerical synod, had been shelved. The Assembly's staunchly Calvinist Confession of Faith, its non-liturgical Directory of Worship, its presbyterial Form of Church Government, and its Larger and Shorter Catechisms, had been officially adopted by the Church of Scotland, but in England they had become a dead letter because of the rise of the Independents, backed by the New Model Army. Presbyterians were horrified when Oliver Cromwell and his faction put the king on trial and then had him executed outside Whitehall Palace in January 1649. For men like Richard Baxter, this was a coup by 'the Sectarian Party' who had abandoned traditional Protestant politics for republicanism and toleration.[5]

Bunyan had fought for Parliament in the First Civil War, but only in the 1650s did he firmly attach himself to radical Puritanism, undergoing believers' baptism and joining John Gifford's Congregational church in Bedford. With its policy of open communion, the church brought together Baptists and Congregationalists, two groups now flourishing across England and even making inroads into Scotland and Ireland thanks to New Model Army soldiers. Congregationalist clergy like John Owen and Thomas Goodwin were among Cromwell's closest advisors, and they did much to shape the Cromwellian religious establishment. Some Calvinistic Baptists held parish livings in the state church, and several open-communion Baptists, including John Tombes and Henry Jessey, even sat on the national committee of Triers which examined candidates for the parish ministry. In parishes all over the land, Puritan preachers were riding high.

---

[4] Bernard Capp, *England's Culture Wars: Puritan Reformation and its Enemies, 1649–1660* (Oxford: Oxford University Press, 2012).

[5] Richard Baxter, *Reliquiæ Baxterianæ*, ed. Matthew Sylvester (1696), Part I, 64, 74, 102.

Richard Baxter, no friend to Cromwell, admitted that at 'no Age since the Gospel came into this Land' had there been such freedom and advantages for preaching. 'Godliness', he recalled wistfully in 1664, 'had Countenance and Reputation also, as well as Liberty'; 'it became a matter of Reputation and Honour to be Godly', which 'abundantly furthered the Successes of the Ministry'.[6]

The achievements of the Cromwellian era made the Restoration settlement all the more galling. For Baptists and Quakers it was an unmitigated disaster from the outset. The anarchic politics of 1659 fed the backlash of 1660, when panic about 'fanatics' and 'sectaries' was rife. The crisis was exacerbated by the armed uprising of the Fifth Monarchist, Thomas Venner, in January 1661. In the alarm that followed, Baptists and especially Quakers were imprisoned en masse. What was more surprising was the exclusion of the Presbyterians from the re-established Church of England. They had opposed the regicide and played a major role in the restoration of the monarchy, and they expected to have a hand in shaping the new national church. But the tide was running against them. Aggrieved Royalists saw Independents and sectaries as the spawn of the Presbyterians. Associating Puritanism with rebellion, they embraced an exclusivist 'Anglican' identity, whose markers were episcopal hierarchy and conformity to the Book of Common Prayer.[7] When Edward Hyde, the Earl of Clarendon, addressed both Houses at the dissolution of the Convention Parliament in December 1660, he praised the English Church as 'the best and the best-reformed church in the Christian World'. It had been 'buried so many years, by the boisterous hands of profane and sacrilegious persons'; now, God had 'miraculously [...] raised it from the grave'.[8]

The Royalist gentry who packed the 'Cavalier' Parliament in 1661 were even more vehemently anti-Puritan than Clarendon. In 1660, Charles II had hoped that the Declaration of Breda (April), the Act of Indemnity and Oblivion (August), and the Worcester House Declaration (October), would lead to a generous settlement. But the new MPs were determined to reassert the central place of bishops and liturgy in the life of the English Church, and to exclude the godly militants who had abolished both in the 1640s. Parliament now enacted a raft of legislation, later misleadingly known as 'the Clarendon Code'. The Corporation Act of 1661 was designed to undo the political ascendancy of the Puritans during 'the late Troubles'.[9] All civil magistrates now had to swear the Oaths of Allegiance and Supremacy, declare their abhorrence of rebellion, renounce the Solemn League and Covenant, and take 'the Sacrament of the Lord's Supper according to the rites of the Church of England'. The Act of Uniformity (1662) turned from the Puritan laity to the Puritan clergy. Deploring the growth of 'schisms'

---

[6] Baxter, *Reliquiæ Baxterianæ*, Part I, 86–7.

[7] Anne Whiteman, 'The Restoration of the Church of England', in Geoffrey Nuttall and Owen Chadwick (eds.), *From Uniformity to Unity, 1662–1962* (London: SPCK, 1962), ch. 1; N. H. Keeble (ed.), *'Settling the Peace of the Church': 1662 Revisited* (Oxford: Oxford University Press, 2014).

[8] John Kenyon (ed.), *The Stuart Constitution: Documents and Commentary*, 2nd edn (Cambridge: Cambridge University Press, 1986), 347.

[9] Kenyon (ed.), *Stuart Constitution*, 351.

during 'the late unhappy troubles', it required all clergy, lecturers, and schoolmasters to renounce the Covenant, subscribe to all of the Thirty-Nine Articles, acquire episcopal ordination, and declare 'unfeigned assent and consent to all and everything contained and prescribed' by the newly revised Book of Common Prayer. Those who failed to comply would 'ipso facto be deprived' of their benefices.[10] Many Puritan clergy found it impossible to conform. Hundreds had already been forced from their livings by returning incumbents or angry parishioners in 1660–62; hundreds more now preached farewell sermons on 'Black Bartholomew's Day'. In all, around 2,000 Puritan clergy were ejected, almost a fifth of the total ministry. Their farewell sermons often contained bitter (if coded) attacks on their persecutors, oppositional gestures relayed in popular printed editions calculated to inflame a sense of injustice.[11]

Three other pieces of legislation aimed to close down the religious marketplace that had developed under Cromwell, and eradicate conventicles outside the established church. The Quaker Act (1662) targeted Quakers, 'Anabaptists', and 'schismatics', but the first Conventicle Act (1664) was broader in scope, catching Presbyterians and Congregationalists in its net. It was now illegal for any adult to attend a religious meeting of five or more people outside the household without using the Book of Common Prayer. Those found guilty of attending Nonconformist worship would be fined £5 (or suffer three months' imprisonment) for the first offence; £10 (or six months' imprisonment) for the second; and £100 (or transportation) for the third. When the Act expired in 1669, it was quickly replaced by a Second Conventicle Act (1670), which imposed crippling fines on those found guilty of hosting or preaching to illegal meetings, and promised informants one-third of the proceeds collected from fines. Finally, the Five Mile Act (1665) banned ejected clergy from coming within five miles of their former parish or any corporate town.

These Acts set the tone for the Restoration era. Far from healing the nation's divisions, the religious settlement exacerbated them, and ensured that the politics of religion would dominate the era. The centre had failed to hold. This owed much to the rise of a hard-line conformist faction led by Archbishop Sheldon which insisted on *jure divino* episcopacy, denied the validity of presbyterial ordination, kept its distance from Europe's Reformed churches, rejected Calvinist theology, exulted in the uniqueness of the English Church, and associated Puritanism with rebellion and regicide. High church defenders of uniformity, including Sir Roger L'Estrange, Samuel Parker, Thomas Long, and Henry Dodwell, took up the arguments used by St Augustine to justify the use of force against Donatist schismatics in the early fifth century. Toleration was dismissed as a 'sectarian' policy, and episcopal divines liked to point out that it had been denounced by the Presbyterians themselves. Even the young John Locke, later renowned

---

[10] Kenyon (ed.), *Stuart Constitution*, 353–56.
[11] See A. G. Matthews (ed.), *Calamy Revised* (Oxford: Clarendon Press, 1934); David Appleby, *Black Bartholomew's Day: Preaching, Polemic and Restoration Nonconformity* (Manchester: Manchester University Press, 2007).

as a tolerationist, defended the imposition of religious uniformity in his manuscript work, 'Two Tracts on Government' (1660–62).

Locke was measured in tone, but many Anglican clerics were vitriolic. As Mark Goldie observes, 'Scarcely a tremor of embarrassment disturbed the voices of divines who called for "a holy violence", "a vigorous and seasonable execution of penal laws" against "fanatic vermin" whose conventicles troubled the land.' Samuel Parker fulminated that the Dissenters were '*Zealots*', '*Brain-Sick People*', '*Madmen*', '*Seditious Preachers*', '*Vermin*' guilty of spreading '*Religious Lunacies*'.[12] Angry words and penal laws were backed up by active repression. The most common penalty was fiscal. The Second Conventicle Act provided financial incentives for informers who reported on illegal Nonconformist activities. Dissenters were frequently condemned on unreliable evidence, having been denied a fair trial. The Presbyterian minister John Howe complained that informers were guilty of 'multitudes of Perjury', leading to 'Convictions made without a Jury, and without any Hearing of the Persons accused; Penalties inflicted; Goods rifled; Estates seized and imbezl'd; Houses broken up'. Sheep, cows, horses, pigs, and wool were confiscated, along with pewter, pans, pots, sheets, pillowcases, and even clothes. In 1684, a Baptist pastor in Dorset was deprived of 'four hundred sheep, twenty cows, seven horses, six or seven hogs', 'all the hay, corn, and wool of the last year's produce', and his malt and hops.[13]

To avoid prosecution, Dissenters resorted to clandestine gatherings. They met in private houses, woods, fields, moors, caves, and barns. John Flavell, one of the most celebrated Dissenting authors and preachers, held services on a rock in Kingsbridge estuary at low tide. The Baptists at Broadmead in Bristol walked to meetings in plain clothes to avoid detection, set guards to warn of the approach of informers, and built a trapdoor so their preacher could escape in an emergency. When they assembled in the woods, they were caught and pursued, with one member drowning in a vain attempt to flee across the River Avon. Others met very early in the morning or very late at night, or broke up into small groups, with their pastor visiting each one in turn.[14]

No Dissenter was executed for conventicling, but many lived in fear for their lives. When Bunyan mentally prepared himself for the gallows (*GA*, 100), he was not indulging in the fantasies of a would-be martyr: he had been imprisoned under the Elizabethan Act against 'seditious sectaries' (1593), which stipulated that repeat offenders could be put to death. In 1664, twelve General Baptists received capital sentences according to the Act, only to be saved by a royal pardon. In 1682, a Quaker merchant in Bristol was

---

[12] Mark Goldie, 'The Theory of Religious Intolerance in Restoration England', in Ole Peter Grell, Nicholas Tyacke, and Jonathan Israel (eds.), *From Persecution to Toleration: The Glorious Revolution and Religion in England* (Oxford: Oxford University Press, 1991), 331–68 (330); Samuel Parker, *A Discourse of Ecclesiastical Politie* (1670), iii, iv, l–li.

[13] Michael R. Watts, *The Dissenters: From the Reformation to the French Revolution* (Oxford: Clarendon Press, 1978), 231–32; John Marshall, *John Locke, Toleration, and Early Enlightenment Culture* (Cambridge: Cambridge University Press, 2006), 96–7, 104–05.

[14] Watts, *Dissenters*, 230–31; Marshall, *John Locke*, 98–9.

condemned to death under the same Act, and reprieved only when William Penn interceded with his friend the Duke of York.[15]

While the state stopped short of using the death penalty against Dissenters, hundreds did perish in Restoration jails. Over the course of the Restoration era, as many as 10,000 Quakers may have endured a spell in prison. Nor was jail reserved for the sects alone. In 1682, at the start of the Tory Reaction, fifty-two Presbyterians were consigned to Bristol jail together with eight-six Quakers, 'almost stifled' with up to thirty in a single room. Over 200 of the ejected clergy served time in Restoration prisons, including Richard Baxter. Conditions in Restoration jails varied considerably. Bunyan and Baxter were fortunate, using their time inside to write, but others were exposed to desperate overcrowding, cold, filth, and disease. Among the Quaker leaders who met their deaths in prison were Richard Hubberthorne, Edward Burrough, and Francis Howgill, young men who had played a key role in creating the national movement. Altogether around 450 Quakers died as a result of their sufferings.[16]

There were also numerous incidents involving physical attacks and intimidation by mobs, gangs, or soldiers. The Quakers' books of 'Sufferings' recorded many cases, but every Nonconformist denomination could testify to violent assaults. In 1660, the Baptist meeting house in the heart of the City of London was attacked by a 'rude multitude', with 'all the doors, seats, windows, galleries, and floors etc. to the value of about 200 pounds carried away'. Following the Second Conventicle Act of 1670, the king ordered the pews and pulpits in Dissenting meeting houses to be destroyed, and a number of churches were pulled down in London, Bristol, and elsewhere. During 'the Tory revenge' from 1682 to 1686, many meeting houses were torn down or nailed up, and even more Dissenting meetings were broken up.[17] London Dissenters were terrorized by the notorious Hilton gang, a group of more than forty disreputable informants with authorization from the king himself. In the space of two years, they exacted fines of more than £40,000 and took out warrants against scores of meeting houses, publicizing their activities in a dedicated newspaper, the *Conventicle Courant*. Their victims included eminent Dissenters—the Presbyterians Richard Baxter, Vincent Alsop, Matthew Sylvester; the Independent Stephen Lobb; and the Quakers George Fox and William Penn. 'Dissenters feared that nothing less than their total destruction was intended.'[18]

As they set their own sufferings into a broader, European context, Nonconformists saw themselves as victims of a wave of 'popish' persecution sweeping the Continent. Since the early seventeenth century, Protestants had been losing the territorial battle as

---

[15] Marshall, *John Locke*, 96; Tim Harris, *Restoration: Charles II and his Kingdoms* (London: Allen Lane, 2005), 302.

[16] William C. Braithwaite, *The Second Period of Quakerism*, 2nd edn (Cambridge: Cambridge University Press, 1961), 114–15; Cragg, *Puritanism*, ch. 4; Watts, *Dissenters*, 234–38; Achinstein, *Literature and Dissent*, ch. 3; Marshall, *John Locke*, 100–1.

[17] Marshall, *John Locke*, 102, 112–13.

[18] Mark Goldie, 'The Hilton Gang and the Purge of London in the 1680s', in H. Nenner (ed.), *Politics and the Political Imagination in Later Stuart Britain* (Rochester: University of Rochester Press, 1997), 43–73 (44).

re-catholicization took hold in large swathes of Central and Eastern Europe. The fear of popery was to fuel the Exclusion Crisis of the late 1670s, when the Whigs attempted to exclude the Catholic James Duke of York from succession to the throne; in the conspiracy theories of Titus Oates, anti-popery reached irrational levels of paranoia. But there was plenty of evidence that militant Catholicism was on the march. The 1680s has been described as 'one of the most religiously repressive decades in European history'.[19] In 1685, the persecution of the French Huguenots culminated in the Revocation of the Edict of Nantes, as Protestants were given a choice between conversion and expulsion. Around 200,000 went into exile, at the same time as a Catholic king, James II, assumed the English throne. The future of European Protestantism seemed to hang in the balance, alarming Anglicans and Dissenters alike. No wonder, then, that Bunyan and his fellow Dissenters saw themselves as caught up in an apocalyptic struggle between pure Reformed religion and the popish Antichrist.[20]

The experience of persecution left many of the godly profoundly alienated from the established church. Under the early Stuarts, Puritan clergy had often been Nonconformists, but very few had become separatists. During the Cromwellian era, Puritans had been at the heart of the nation's religious establishment. Now even the Presbyterians were estranged. While older clergy (the so-called 'Dons' like Baxter, William Bates, and Thomas Manton) still longed to be reincorporated into the Church, the younger 'Ducklings' such as Samuel Annesley and Vincent Alsop became more willing to consider setting up separate congregations. Even Baxter himself seemed to have 'turned his back upon the ideal of the "National Church"' during the politico-religious crisis between 1678 and 1683.[21] Quakers had always been implacably opposed to parish churches, as were most Baptists, but now Congregationalists too turned separatist. John Owen argued strenuously against participating in Anglican services, and he showed little interest in comprehension, working instead for the toleration of gathered churches. Puritanism had once been a movement within the Church; now it was largely beyond it. Church and Dissent were drifting apart.

The alienation of Dissenters was frequently expressed in violent rhetoric, but a militant minority went further, actively conspiring against the Stuart regime.[22] Despite the fiasco of Venner's rising in 1661, there were a series of further plots, starting with

[19] Marshall, *John Locke*, 17.

[20] W. R. Owens, '"Antichrist must be Pulled Down": Bunyan and the Millennium', in Anne Laurence, W. R. Owens, and Stuart Sim (eds.), *John Bunyan and his England, 1628–1688* (London: Hambledon Press, 1990), 77–94.

[21] C. G. Bolan, Jeremy Goring, H. L. Short, and Roger Thomas, *The English Presbyterians: From Elizabethan Puritanism to Modern Unitarianism* (London: George Allen & Unwin, 1968), 98–101; William Lamont, *Richard Baxter and the Millennium: Protestant Imperialism and the English Revolution* (London: Croom Helm, 1979), 243–53.

[22] See Achinstein, *Literature and Dissent*, ch. 4: 'Violence'; the trilogy by Richard Greaves: *Deliver Us from Evil: The Radical Underground in Britain, 1660–1663* (New York: Oxford University Press, 1986); *Enemies under his Feet: Radicals and Nonconformists in Britain, 1664–1677* (Stanford, CA: Stanford University Press, 1990); *Secrets of the Kingdom: British Radicals from the Popish Plot to the Revolution of 1688–89* (Stanford, CA: Stanford University Press, 1992); and Greaves, 'John Owen', *ODNB*.

the Northern Rising (1663) and culminating in the Rye House Plot (1683) and the Monmouth Rebellion (1685). One of Bunyan's printers, Francis Smith, was up to his neck in oppositional conspiracies, and by 1682, John Owen was rearticulating a doctrine of active resistance led by authorized magistrates. Owen's associate, Robert Ferguson, was closely linked to the Rye House plotters, among whom were three Baptist and ex-Cromwellian army officers. Owen himself was hauled in for questioning after the plot to assassinate the king and his heir was foiled, and he seems to have had advance knowledge of the Monmouth Rising, in which Dissenters, including Baptist and Presbyterian pastors, were implicated. In this episode at least, numerous Dissenters were literally at war with the Restoration state.

The Triumphs of Dissent

Yet there was more to Bunyan's England than polarization and persecution. To begin with, Restoration Nonconformity was a major phenomenon, far larger than the tiny sects of Elizabethan and early Stuart England. Before 1640, there had been no more than a few hundred Baptists; by 1660, they counted around 25,000 adherents, gathered in 250 substantial congregations. Quakers had arisen from nothing to perhaps 60,000 by the Restoration. The gathered churches of the Congregationalists approached the same size. Together, these groups amounted to almost 3 per cent of the population.[23] As for the Presbyterians, they were larger than all the other Dissenting groups put together. At a conservative estimate, at least 6 per cent of the population—approximately 300,000 people—identified with the major Dissenting groupings. Given the sheer scale of Dissent, and the stature of some of its clergy, it was hard to dismiss as a lunatic fringe, even harder to eradicate.

Moreover, Dissenters were not content to operate in survival mode. Within a year or two of the Restoration, London Dissenters had begun to build their own meeting houses; one designed for Samuel Annesley could accommodate 800 people, while Nonconformists also met in warehouses, the halls of City companies, gentry houses, and country barns. The Quakers erected perhaps twenty meeting places before 1670, over sixty in the following decade, and at least twenty in 1687–89. In Essex, Quaker numbers almost doubled between 1660 and 1684; by that time, they may have constituted 7 per cent of the population of Colchester.[24] In London, following the Plague of 1665 and

---

[23] John Morrill, 'The Puritan Revolution', in John Coffey and Paul Lim (eds.), *The Cambridge Companion to Puritanism* (Cambridge: Cambridge University Press, 2008), 67–88 (77–9); Joel Halcomb, 'A Social History of Congregational Religious Practice during the English Revolution' (PhD thesis, University of Cambridge, 2009).

[24] David L. Wykes, 'James II's Declaration of Indulgence of 1687 and the Early Organization of Dissent', *Midland History*, 16 (1991), 86–102 (89–92); Adrian Davies, *The Quakers in English Society, 1655–1725* (Oxford: Oxford University Press, 2000), 156–58.

the Great Fire of 1666, Presbyterians and Congregationalists 'did keep their Meetings very openly, and prepared large Rooms, and some of them plain Chappels, with Pulpits, Seats, and Galleries for the reception of as many as could come'. According to Richard Baxter, 'many of the Citizens went to those Meetings called private, more, than went to the publick Parish Churches'.[25]

The literary culture of Nonconformity thrived.[26] The trials of these years prompted a remarkable surge of creativity, as Dissenting writers produced works that would attain classic status. To *The Pilgrim's Progress* and *The Holy War*, we should add the late, great works of John Milton. We can hear the voice of Dissent in the speeches of Abdiel and Michael in *Paradise Lost* (1667), the Son in *Paradise Regained*, and Samson in *Samson Agonistes* (1671). Less celebrated Dissenters developed children's literature, poetics, and hymnody, preparing the ground for Isaac Watts. The clergy revamped Reformed theology for a new era: John Owen continued to produce major treatises and commentaries; John Flavell reached a wider audience with his imaginatively packaged practical divinity; Peter Sterry invested Reformed divinity with a Neoplatonist mysticism learned from the Greek Fathers; Joseph Alleine promoted an urgent, evangelical Calvinism in his immensely popular tract, *An Alarme to Unconverted Sinners* (1671); Richard Baxter and John Howe responded to contemporary irreligion with works of apologetics and natural theology. A number of Nonconformist texts became best-sellers; reaching far beyond Dissent, they found an eager audience among conformists.

Indeed, the boundary between 'Anglicanism' and 'Dissent' was 'highly porous'. As Mark Goldie explains, 'many, perhaps most, of the ejected ministers were careful to maintain their loyalty to the national Church', while 'the great majority of the Dissenting laity were likewise partial conformists'.[27] The Presbyterian clergy regularly attended parish worship and scheduled their own meetings so as not to clash with the official Prayer Book services. Unlike the Episcopalians of the 1650s, they were extremely reluctant to ordain new clergy, clinging to the hope that they would soon be accommodated within the national church.[28] The Puritan gentry also straddled the divide between Church and Dissent, frequently attending parish worship on Sunday morning and hearing ejected pastors in the afternoon. Although they felt under siege during the Restoration, their patronage was a major source of support for the Nonconformist clerical leadership, and they often employed ejected ministers as domestic chaplains or family tutors. While most Baptists and some Independents shared Bunyan's separatism during the Restoration, others (like Philip Nye) were prepared to defend attendance

---

[25] Baxter, *Reliquiæ Baxterianæ*, Part III, 19.

[26] For what follows, see N. H. Keeble, *The Literary Culture of Nonconformity in Later Seventeenth-Century England* (Leicester: Leicester University Press, 1987); Achinstein, *Literature and Dissent*; Dewey D. Wallace, Jr, *Shapers of English Calvinism, 1660–1714* (Oxford: Oxford University Press, 2011).

[27] Mark Goldie, *Roger Morrice and the Puritan Whigs* (Woodbridge: Boydell Press, 2016), 229–30.

[28] Compare Kenneth Fincham and Stephen Taylor, 'Episcopal Ordinations and Ordinands in England, 1646–1660', *English Historical Review*, 125 (2011), 319–44 with David L. Wykes, 'The Minister's Calling: The Preparation and Qualification of Candidates for the Presbyterian Ministry in England, 1660–1689', *Nederlands Archief voor Kerkgeschiedenis*, 82 (2004), 271–80.

at parish sermons. John Tombes, the ejected Baptist, 'came constantly' to Edward Fowler's parish church in Salisbury, 'heard common prayer and received the sacrament kneeling'. When Fowler became vicar of one of London's largest parishes, St Giles Cripplegate, he had numerous Dissenting parishioners, some of whom were elected to the parish vestry.[29]

Among the established clergy were Puritan incumbents who survived the Great Ejection. John Spurr has suggested that the events of 1660–62 'severed a broad-based parish puritanism leaving half of the ministers and their followers within the restored church and half outside'.[30] This may exaggerate the size of the Puritan clerical remnant, but among the godly clergy who conformed were some respected figures, including a number of Westminster Assembly divines: John Conant and Simon Ford in Northamptonshire, the Hebraist John Lightfoot, Edward Reynolds who accepted a bishopric, and the mathematician John Wallis. In the Puritan heartland of East Anglia, the godly conformists included the diarist Ralph Josselin and William Gurnall, author of the Puritan classic, *The Christian in Complete Armour* (1655–62). Lincolnshire had 'many learned Pious Able and Worthy Conformists' who maintained the ethos of moderate Puritanism. One of them, John Rastrick, wrote a memoir which recorded his deep admiration for the writings of Richard Baxter. Despite growing unease with the established church, he ministered within it from 1671 to 1687, when he finally resigned his cure and became a Presbyterian.[31]

The Church also had a resilient strain of conformist Calvinism, inspired by earlier Reformed archbishops like Thomas Cranmer, Edmund Grindal, John Whitgift, George Abbott, and James Ussher, as well as by eminent Jacobean bishops such as George Downame and John Davenant. Calvinist divinity retained its dominance at the University of Oxford, and leading conformist Calvinists included George Morley (d.1684), Bishop of Winchester; Henry Compton (d.1713), Bishop of Oxford and then London; Thomas Barlow (d.1691), Lady Margaret Professor of Divinity at Oxford and later Bishop of Lincoln; Robert South (1634–1716), Canon of Christ Church; and Edward Reynolds (1599–1676), Bishop of Norwich.[32] While these figures were not equally sympathetic to the plight of Nonconformists, they did share theological common ground with John Owen and John Bunyan.

The so-called Latitudinarians, who emerged as another distinct tendency within the Restoration Church, also sought to build bridges with the Dissenters.[33] They were

---

[29] Trevor Cliffe, *The Puritan Gentry Besieged 1650–1700* (London: Routledge, 2002); Mark Goldie and John Spurr, 'Politics and the Restoration Parish: Edward Fowler and the Struggle for St Giles Cripplegate', *English Historical Review*, 432 (1994), 572–96 (574, 591–95).

[30] John Spurr, *English Puritanism, 1603–1689* (London: Macmillan, 1998), 131.

[31] Andrew Cambers (ed.), *The Life of John Rastrick, 1650–1727* (Cambridge: Cambridge University Press, 2010), 97–8. For Rastrick's frequent references to Baxter, see Index.

[32] Stephen Hampton, *Anti-Arminians: The Anglican Reformed Tradition from Charles II to George I* (Oxford: Oxford University Press, 2008); Wallace, *Shapers of English Calvinism*, ch. 6.

[33] John Spurr, '"Latitudinarianism" and the Restoration Church', *Historical Journal*, 31 (1988), 61–82; William Spellman, *The Latitudinarians and the Church of England, 1660–1700* (Athens, GA: University of Georgia Press, 1993).

influenced by the Cambridge Platonists Benjamin Whichcote, Ralph Cudworth, and Henry More, three philosophical theologians who belonged to the Cromwellian establishment in the 1650s and conformed to the Restoration Church. Among the younger Latitudinarian clergy were men who had held university fellowships or parish livings under Puritan rule: Simon Patrick, the likely author of *A Brief Account of the New Sect of Latitude-Men* (1662); John Tillotson, a fellow of Clare College, Cambridge, in the 1650s and a future archbishop of Canterbury; John Wilkins, who had married the sister of Oliver Cromwell and was a founder of the Royal Society; Edward Stillingfleet; and Edward Fowler. These clergy had firm support from devout laymen such as the lawyer Sir Matthew Hale, a Puritan turned Latitudinarian. Hale had listened sympathetically to Elizabeth Bunyan in 1661, and he became a close friend of Baxter, including the Dissenting pastor in his will.

After the failure of the Savoy Conference and the passing of the Clarendon Code, the first major push for comprehension came in 1668. Hale drafted a bill and the campaign was orchestrated by John Wilkins, soon to become Bishop of Chester. The scheme was sunk by parliamentary opposition, and it also divided Dissenters. While Baxter and the older Presbyterians were enthusiastic, John Owen was not. He feared that comprehension might reincorporate the Presbyterians and so leave Congregationalists and Baptists badly exposed. But there were further drives for comprehension in the mid-1670s (when leading Presbyterians entered negotiations with the bishops) and in 1680. During the reign of James II and again in 1689, hopes of comprehension revived, only to be dashed. Yet they reveal considerable sympathy within the Church for moderate Nonconformists.[34]

Such mutual respect was expressed in other ways. At the funeral of the eminent Presbyterian, Thomas Manton, in Stoke Newington in 1677, Nonconformist pastors walked side by side with their conformist brethren.[35] The Welsh Trust—which perpetuated the Cromwellian project of propagating the gospel and educating the poor in 'the dark corners of the land'—had an ecumenical membership, with Anglicans such as Tillotson, Whichcote, and Stillingfleet sitting alongside the Presbyterians Baxter and Sir Edward Harley.[36] The Company for the Propagation of the Gospel in New England sponsored the labours of the Puritan missionary John Eliot, and funded his translations into Algonquian both of the Bible and of books by Baxter and Joseph Alleine. The governor of the Company for a quarter of a century after 1662 was the scientist Robert Boyle, a devout layman who maintained good relations with Presbyterians (like Baxter and John Howe) and Anglicans (such as Barlow, Wilkins, and Stillingfleet). At the Restoration, Boyle had persuaded Barlow and Sir Peter Pett to write treatises in favour of toleration, and he deplored the persecution of Dissenters. His distinguished siblings—Roger (Lord Broghill), Mary (Countess of Warwick), and Katherine

---

[34] Goldie, *Roger Morrice and the Puritan Whigs*, 238–46.
[35] Achinstein, *Literature and Dissent*, 30–1.
[36] Goldie and Spurr, 'Politics and the Restoration Parish', 583–84.

(Viscountess Ranelagh)—also epitomize the survival of the Puritan ethos among aristocratic 'Anglicans'.[37]

In matters of theology too, there was a great deal of traffic between Anglicans and Dissenters. Latitudinarians turned away from Reformed orthodoxy towards Arminian theology, but the revolt against strict Calvinism was also apparent among Dissenters. During the 1650s, the most vigorous English proponent of Arminianism had been the London Puritan divine, John Goodwin, an ardent defender of the regicide. After the Restoration, Goodwin was implacably hostile to the established church, but his Arminian protégé, the former Baptist William Allen, became a respected Anglican theologian. While few Dissenters were prepared to embrace Arminianism, Presbyterians often gravitated towards the 'middle way' theology worked out by Richard Baxter, which softened the doctrine of predestination, and emphasized the role of good works in a sinner's justification. Fowler admired Baxter as one of the 'orthodox divines of the Church of England', and the two men exchanged letters bemoaning the errors of antinomians (like Bunyan). Indeed, Baxter's correspondence network included a wide range of Anglican divines, including Edward Stillingfleet, Henry More, Joseph Glanvill, and two future archbishops of Canterbury, John Tillotson and Thomas Tenison.[38]

The Congregationalist John Owen was more hostile to the Arminian drift of Anglican theology, being a high Calvinist and an admirer of Bunyan. As a former Vice-Chancellor of Oxford University, Owen was very well connected. He maintained amicable relations with Restoration bishops like Wilkins and Barlow, and with leading nobles including the Earl of Orrery, the Earl of Anglesey, Lord Wharton, and the second Duke of Buckingham. He had face-to-face meetings with both the king and the Duke of York, and when he was laid to rest at Bunhill Fields (the Nonconformist burial ground) in 1683, the procession was attended 'by near a hundred Noblemens, Gentlemens and Citizens Coaches with six Horse each, and a great number of Gentlemen in mourning on horseback'.[39]

Within the political nation, the Anglican exclusivism of the Restoration settlement was arguably as controversial and contested as the Puritan Reformation of the 1640s and 1650s. In both cases, militant minorities were trying to reshape church and state according to their own powerful vision. And in both cases, they faced an uphill struggle. For much of the Restoration era, in fact, the cause of Anglican uniformity suffered from a lack of royal support. Charles II's court was notorious for its libertinism, and insofar as he had sincere religious sympathies, he leaned towards the Roman Catholicism of his mother. His brother, James Duke of York, had converted by 1673, when the Test Act

---

[37] Michael Hunter, *Boyle: Between God and Science* (New Haven, CT: Yale University Press, 2009), 20–2, 123, 129–31, 166, 200, passim; Michael Hunter, 'Robert Boyle', *ODNB*.

[38] Goldie and Spurr, 'Politics and the Restoration Parish', 583; N. H. Keeble and Geoffrey Nuttall (eds.), *Calendar of the Correspondence of Richard Baxter*, 2 vols (Oxford: Oxford University Press, 1991), 2: 1660–96.

[39] Tim Cooper, *John Owen, Richard Baxter and the Formation of Nonconformity* (Farnham: Ashgate, 2011), 272, 282.

exposed him as a Catholic. Neither man was consistent in matters of religious policy, but both made serious attempts to introduce toleration. In the Declaration of Breda (1660), Charles had promised 'liberty to tender consciences', and despite being thwarted by the Cavalier Parliament, he favoured toleration for Dissenters until the Exclusion Crisis in the latter part of his reign.

In 1662, Charles II had issued a Declaration of Indulgence, only to be forced to withdraw it due to parliamentary opposition. In 1672, his second Declaration of Indulgence was more successful. Its preamble declared that there had been 'very little fruit of all those forcible courses', and it announced an immediate suspension of all penal laws against both Protestant Nonconformists and Catholic recusants. While the latter were only allowed to hold services in private, Protestant Dissenters could apply for licences for their ministers and their places of worship. Altogether 1,610 preachers—including Bunyan and several other leading members of his church—took out licences (939 as Presbyterians, 458 as Congregationalists or Independents, and 210 as Baptists), and many Nonconformist householders had their homes licensed. In some places, Bedford being one of them, Dissenters even erected meeting houses and chapels. Although the Declaration was overturned within a year by the Cavalier Parliament, it had provided Dissent with a vital boost for the likes of Bunyan, who would be among the almost 500 imprisoned Dissenters pardoned in 1672 by the king.[40]

Between 1674 and 1678, under the influence of the Earl of Danby, the king made a strategic alliance with the 'Church Party', and he would turn emphatically against Dissent as a result of the Exclusion Crisis. But by 1687, James II was determined to woo Nonconformists, turning for advice to the Quaker William Penn and seeking to build a coalition of Catholics and Dissenters against Tory Anglicanism. That project proved a catastrophic failure as the king alienated powerful interests, but his two Declarations of Indulgence in 1687 and 1688 did end the years of persecution, and introduced the era of toleration.[41] There was considerable elite support for toleration or comprehension or for a combination of the two. Charles II's Council of State included a surprising number of former Parliamentarians and ex-Cromwellians. Even in the Cavalier Parliament, it has been estimated that over a third of the 859 MPs had some sympathy for Dissent. Many MPs maintained dual loyalties to both the Church and the Puritan tradition.[42]

---

[40] G. Lyon Turner (ed.), *Original Records of Early Nonconformity under Persecution and Indulgence*, 3 vols (London: T. F. Unwin, 1911–14); Frank Bate, *The Declaration of Indulgence, 1672: A Study in the Rise of Organised Dissent* (London: Archibald Constable, 1908); Greaves, *Glimpses*, 286–91.

[41] Scott Sowerby, '"Of Different Complexions": Religious Diversity and National Identity in James II's Toleration Campaign', *English Historical Review*, 124 (2009), 29–52; Gary DeKrey, 'Reformation and "Arbitrary Government": London Dissenters and James II's Polity of Toleration, 1687–88', in Jason McElligott (ed.), *Fear, Exclusion and Revolution: Roger Morrice and Britain in the 1680s* (Farnham: Ashgate, 2006), 13–31.

[42] George Southcombe and Grant Tapsell (eds.), *Restoration Politics, Religion and Culture: Britain and Ireland, 1660–1714* (Basingstoke: Palgrave, 2009), 28, 185 n.34. For a list of sympathetic MPs, see Mark Goldie (ed.), *The Ent'ring Book of Roger Morrice*, 6 vols (Woodbridge: Boydell & Brewer, 2007), 1: 507–10.

The leading Puritan politician of this era was the veteran MP, Denzil Holles. Back in the 1640s, he had been at the head of the political Presbyterians at Westminster, where he was an implacable foe of Oliver Cromwell. At the Restoration, Holles was awarded a peerage, and in 1666 he was sent as ambassador to the court of Louis XIV. In the mid-1670s, he emerged as one of the leaders of the 'Country party', a group of dissident peers and MPs opposed to the absolutist and high church politics of the Earl of Danby. Holles had always been a communicant member of the established church, but he was determined to protect Dissenters from persecution. His third wife was a patron of Richard Baxter, and under the Declaration of Indulgence in 1672, he himself had applied for fourteen licences for Nonconformist worship and Presbyterian ministers. Together with Lord Wharton and Sir John Maynard, Holles was one of the leaders of the 'Puritan Whigs', a powerful faction in Restoration politics united around a clear agenda:

> sympathy for Dissent, antipathy to the authority of the church hierarchy, a desire to relax the terms of the Clarendon Code and to pass a bill for Comprehension, hostility to Danby's administration, suspicion of the crown's independence and of standing armies, a wish to see the dissolution of the Cavalier Parliament and the calling of 'frequent parliaments', energetic pressing of prosecutions against papists, and support for the exclusion of the duke of York, or for limitation of the crown's power should he succeed to the throne.[43]

Holles and the Puritan Whigs were allied with Anthony Ashley Cooper, first Earl of Shaftesbury. Shaftesbury had sat on Cromwell's Council of State, and while he was no Puritan, he actively promoted toleration during his time as one of the king's chief ministers in the 'Cabal' of 1667 to 1673, and again in the years of the Exclusion Crisis (1678–81) in which he played a central part.[44] It was after joining Shaftesbury's household in 1667 that John Locke began writing papers in defence of the Nonconformists, culminating in his seminal work, *A Letter concerning Toleration* (published in 1689).

Dissenters had powerful allies within the nation's political and intellectual elite. In localities across England, however, Nonconformists also enjoyed a measure of protection. In Gloucester, Bishop Nicolson was initially willing to connive at the preaching of ejected ministers and even held friendly conferences with Quakers. When he became alarmed at the strength and persistence of Nonconformity, he found many justices and civil officers unwilling to assist in its suppression, so that the law was in danger of becoming 'a dead letter'.[45] Quaker books of suffering recounted increasing evidence of public sympathy by the 1670s. Parish officers were often reluctant to act against the Friends, and in some cases even paid their fines. Quakers themselves had access to good legal advice, and resourcefully defended themselves from persecution. In towns, Nonconformists could be

---

[43] Goldie, *Roger Morrice and the Puritan Whigs*, 191.

[44] John Spurr (ed.), *Anthony Ashley Cooper, First Earl of Shaftesbury 1621–1683* (Farnham: Ashgate, 2011).

[45] David L. Wykes, 'They "assemble in greater numbers and [with] more daring than formerly": The Bishop of Gloucester and Nonconformity in the late 1660s', *Southern History*, 17 (1995), 24–39 (26–8).

a major force. In Coventry, almost half of the mayors and 37 per cent of municipal office holders between 1660 and 1687 were Dissenters or Dissenting sympathizers. Dorchester in the West Country—an old Puritan stronghold—had as many as seven Nonconformist or partially conformist mayors between 1671 and 1682. In the capital, Whigs were ascendant by 1680—among them, they could count the mayor, both sheriffs, the majority of the common council, and the City electorate. Even in 1681, jury panels proved remarkably understanding towards radical Whig activists as well as Nonconformists. When the king ordered the suppression of Dissenting conventicles in December 1682, thousands flocked to the meeting houses to protect Nonconformist ministers. The Hilton gang suffered attacks from angry parishioners and Presbyterian apprentices, and was repeatedly frustrated by parish magistrates reluctant to divide the community and by juries committed to the principle of a fair trial. Despite their best efforts, they were unable to bridge 'the yawning gap between enactment and enforcement'.[46]

Even the so-called sectaries were often integrated into parish life. At the Restoration, Quakers had toned down their verbal assault on the 'steeple-houses'. They established a network of monthly and quarterly meetings in 1667, and from the mid-1670s began a systematic campaign to win allies and use the legal system to prevent persecution. At a local level, some became parish officials, serving as overseers of the poor, surveyors of highways, and even parish constables. In Essex, 80 per cent of Quaker wills between 1660 and 1700 were witnessed by people who did not belong to the Society of Friends. Like the Quakers, the Baptists practised endogamous marriage, thus setting themselves apart from their neighbours. Yet they were married in parish churches, and retained many lines of connection with their neighbours. In Fenstanton, Huntingdonshire, Edmund Mayle was a licensed teacher and host of Baptist meetings, but he was also the village's chief scribe, who witnessed more wills than anyone else, drew up lists of goods for probate entries, and sat as a juror on a manorial court. Dissenters did experience persecution, but they remained part of the local community. According to Bill Stevenson, both Quakers and Baptists 'enjoyed significant degrees of social acceptance in Bedfordshire, Buckinghamshire, Cambridgeshire, Hertfordshire, and Huntingdonshire'.[47] Apart from their Nonconformity, the vast majority of Dissenters conducted themselves as model citizens, eschewing plots and armed resistance. In 1660, the Quakers issued their famous 'peace testimony' (*A Declaration from the Harmless and Innocent People of God called Quakers*), and Bunyan himself denounced would-be rebels in *Seasonable Counsel, or Advice to Sufferers*, written at the height of the Tory revenge in 1684.

By 1689, the political elite had come to the view that Dissenters were at least tolerable. Under William of Orange, England would imitate the pluralist path of the Dutch republic rather than the confessional uniformity of Louis XIV's France. The so-called

---

[46] Harris, *Restoration*, 193–96; Goldie, 'The Hilton Gang', 51–4, 67–8.

[47] Bill Stevenson, 'The Social Integration of Post-Restoration Dissenters', in Margaret Spufford (ed.), *The World of Rural Dissenters, 1520–1725* (Cambridge: Cambridge University Press, 1995), 360–87 (369); Davies, *The Quakers in English Society*, ch. 14.

Toleration Act of 1689 did not actually mention toleration—it offered a mere suspension of the penal legislation, unaccompanied by any ringing endorsement of liberty of conscience. It excluded anti-Trinitarians, Catholics, and atheists. It left moderate Dissenters—the Presbyterians—outside the established church, their dreams of comprehension in ruins. And it confirmed that all Dissenters would be second-class citizens, ineligible for public office unless they took communion with the established church. Nevertheless, for all its limitations, it was a major achievement for Dissenters and their friends in Parliament. The Act applied not merely to Presbyterians or Congregationalists, but to 'Anabaptists' and 'Quakers'. It allowed them to register thousands of licensed meeting houses. By 1715, there were at least 400,000 Dissenters in England and Wales, gathered in some 2,000 congregations. They had a disproportionate presence and influence in towns and cities, not least in the capital, where Presbyterians were even elected to the office of Lord Mayor. Dissenting academies flourished. It would have been hard to predict such an outcome in the dark days of the 1660s or the early 1680s. Amidst adversity, Dissent had not merely survived, it had thrived.

Conclusion

Bunyan's Restoration world is boldly rendered. It is a world of stark opposition between conformists and Dissenters, persecutors and martyrs, an opposition mapped onto biblical dichotomies between Cain and Abel, Christ and Antichrist. As Neil Keeble observes in Chapter 8 of this volume, Bunyan is fiercely at odds with many aspects of Restoration culture—its materialism, courtly fashions, sexual profligacy, and oppression of the godly. When reading Bunyan, we are reminded that Restoration England was 'a persecuting society', bitterly divided by the politics of religion.

Yet conflict and coercion were not the whole story. If Dissent was a counter-culture, it was also thoroughly indigenous. The lines between Dissenters and their neighbours often blurred. The Bedford Church Book indicates that members of Bunyan's own congregation frequently failed to maintain their separateness, returning to the parish churches or succumbing to the ways of the world (*CB*, passim). Bunyan's martyrological account of his own imprisonment is disrupted by the admission that his jailor bent the rules, allowing him to make a trip to London in 1661 where he preached against the Book of Common Prayer (*GA*, 129). Dissenters enjoyed a good deal of public sympathy, and they had substantial patrons and powerful allies. They were subjected to the last great campaign to enforce religious uniformity in England, but that campaign failed. Bunyan's England was more receptive to his message than he himself admitted. Indeed, he was the product of a deeply Protestant nation, a nation in which Calvinist divinity and Puritan piety had sunk deep roots. Like the seed of the Sower in Christ's parable, Bunyan's writings would fall on hard, rocky, and thorny ground, but they would also take in root in good soil, producing a rich crop.

Suggested Reading

Achinstein, Sharon, *Literature and Dissent in Milton's England* (Cambridge: Cambridge University Press, 2003).

Cragg, Gerald, *Puritanism in the Period of the Great Persecution, 1660–1688* (Cambridge: Cambridge University Press, 1957).

Davies, Adrian, *The Quakers in English Society, 1655–1725* (Oxford: Oxford University Press, 2000).

Goldie, Mark, *Roger Morrice and the Puritan Whigs* (Woodbridge: Boydell Press, 2016).

Harris, Tim, Paul Seaward, and Mark Goldie (eds.), *The Politics of Religion in Restoration England* (Oxford: Wiley-Blackwell, 1994).

Keeble, N. H., *The Literary Culture of Nonconformity in Later Seventeenth-Century England* (Leicester: Leicester University Press, 1987).

Keeble, N. H. (ed.), *'Settling the Peace of the Church': 1662 Revisited* (Oxford: Oxford University Press, 2014).

Southcombe, George and Grant Tapsall (eds.), *Restoration Politics, Religion and Culture* (Basingstoke: Palgrave Macmillan, 2010).

Spufford, Margaret (ed.), *The World of Rural Dissenters, 1525–1725* (Cambridge: Cambridge University Press, 1995).

Wallace, Jr, Dewey D., *Shapers of English Calvinism, 1660–1714* (Oxford: Oxford University Press, 2011).

CHAPTER 3

BUNYAN AND THE BEDFORD CONGREGATION

ANNE DUNAN-PAGE

THE GATHERED CHURCH

IN the early 1650s, John Bunyan joined a 'Congregation of Christ'—or gathered church—in Bedford. As that term may seem somewhat abstract, we can borrow a more immediately telling phrase used about a similar community at Bristol: a gathered church was a church with a chimney in it.[1] This was worship in a context of hearth and home. The beginnings usually lay with small groups of parishioners, who met in a private house to pray, to review sermon notes, to read the Scriptures, to fast or eat together, and sometimes simply to edify one other by godly conference. As their spiritual life matured and deepened, they might decide to assemble in a more formal manner modelled upon the practice of the first Christians as recorded in the New Testament. It was hospitality and neighbourliness that mattered.[2] The members wanted a church where all could meet in the same place and know each other well. Following Matthew 18:20 ('For where two or three are gathered together in my name, there am I in the midst of them'), they considered that a very small number of people, usually between three and seven, could form a congregation.[3] A gathered church was therefore born indoors, without either priest or sacrament, but with a handful of people, with bread, drink, prayer, and godly conversation. The Bedford church owed its existence to such an idea of communion:

---

[1] *The Records of a Church of Christ in Bristol, 1640–1687*, ed. Roger Hayden (Bristol: Bristol Record Society, 1974), 86.

[2] See Adam Sills, 'Mr. Bunyan's Neighborhood and the Geography of Dissent', *ELH*, 70 (2003), 67–87.

[3] William Bartlet, *Ichnographia: Or a Model of the Primitive Congregational Way* (1647), 34; Thomas Goodwin, *Of the Constitution, Right Order, and Government of the Churches of Christ* (1696), Book VI, 241; John Williams, *The Divine Institution, Order and Government of a Visible Church of Christ* (1701), 4.

> [T]here hath of a long time bene persons godly, who in former times, (even while they remained without all forme and order as to visible church communion according to the Testament of Christ) were very zealous according to their light, not onely to edify themselves, but also to propagate the Gospell, and help it forward, both by purse and presence, keeping alwayes a door open and a table furnished and free. (*CB*, 15)

A gathered church was 'a free society or communion of visible Saints, embodyed and knit together by a voluntary consent, to worship God, according to his Word, making up one ordinary congregation, with power of Government within it selfe only', 'a company of Saints Assembling together in one place, built by a special covenant into one Distinct Body […] to enjoy constant Fellowship with Christ in all his Ways and Ordinances'.[4] There would be much to comment upon in such expositions of Congregational polity. At the core of Congregationalist principles that inspired the gathering of a church like Bedford lay the consent of 'visible' saints who had entered into fellowship with God and each other, and the autonomy of congregations on questions of government and discipline.

Bunyan probably never knew the Jacobean and Caroline conferences that nurtured the more formally organized Congregational churches of the 1640s and 1650s.[5] What he did know, however, when he joined the Bedford church, was the ecclesiastical settlement of the Cromwellian years, when a Congregational minister could hold a parochial living. Two of his predecessors, John Gifford and John Burton, had accepted the living of the parish church of St John's, Bedford.[6] These men were not 'separatists' or 'sectarians', let alone 'Anabaptists', but rather 'parochial' or 'non-separating' Congregationalists willing to operate within a national system. Even though they felt (as did Presbyterians) that the sacrament should be restricted to worthy believers, they considered parish churches to be true churches. Twenty years later, however, members of the Bedford congregation would be admonished for their 'evill in goeing to hear the nationall ministers' (*CB*, 80), while others were sharply questioned about their 'seperation from the Church of England' (*CB*, 108). Interregnum parochial Congregationalism had given birth to separated Dissent.

The degree of commitment shown by Interregnum Congregational ministers to the parish has long been a matter of contention.[7] Practical arrangements varied from place

---

[4] Bartlet, *Ichnographia*, 30; Goodwin, *Constitution*, 256.

[5] See, for instance, Patrick Collinson, 'The English Conventicle', in W. J. Sheils and Diana Wood (eds.), *Voluntary Religion* (Oxford: Basil Blackwell, 1986), 223–59; Alec Ryrie, 'Congregations, Conventicles, and the Nature of Early Scottish Protestantism', *Past & Present*, 91 (2006), 45–76.

[6] John Brown, *John Bunyan: His Life, Times, and Work*, rev. Frank Mott Harrison (London, Glasgow, and Birmingham: Hulbert, 1928), 66–90; Greaves, *Glimpses*, 61–7.

[7] Murray Tolmie, *The Triumph of the Saints: The Separate Churches of London 1616–1649* (Cambridge: Cambridge University Press, 1977), 85–119. For a recent reappraisal, see Joel Halcomb, 'A Social History of Congregational Religious Practice during the Puritan Revolution' (PhD thesis, University of Cambridge, 2009). For the pre-revolutionary context, see Stephen Brachlow, *The Communion of Saints: Radical Puritan and Separatist Ecclesiology, 1570–1625* (Oxford: Oxford University Press, 1988).

to place and cohabitation was not always peaceful.[8] Members of a gathered congregation could hear their minister's sermon on Sunday, among the parishioners, and then hold separate meetings to deal with the internal affairs of their congregation, and to receive the sacraments. The ministers, at times, found themselves in an untenable position. Separatists accused them of meeting in impure buildings, Presbyterians charged them with being separatists, and parishioners claimed they looked after their own congregations and were therefore unfit recipients of their tithes.[9]

At the Restoration, the gathered churches were forced to worship outdoors or to return to the enclosed spaces that had nurtured their tentative beginnings. In Bedford, this is recorded in late August 1660 (*CB*, 36). Congregationalists had never truly left these domestic settings, for the churches had met in the houses of their members throughout the 1640s and the 1650s. The difference was that by the 1660s these meetings became illegal 'conventicles': a diminutive and disparaging form of the Latin *conventus*. The first Conventicle Act (1664) specified that the owners of a 'House, Outhouse, Barne, or Roome Yard or Backside Woods or Grounds' allowing meetings to be held on their premises would be punished.[10] Bunyan, like many of his contemporaries, must therefore have joined worship in many different outdoor and indoor locations. His was a generation that might hear the Word of God as much in the chancel of a cathedral as in the front room of a godly widow. It is not surprising that the churches of his fictional and pastoral works are at once temples and cottages, palaces and inns. They were modelled on the meeting *houses* of the Dissenting tradition, a term that survived the erection of legally tolerated chapels which were themselves inspired by domestic architecture.

In 1688, Bunyan published *A Discourse of the Building, Nature, Excellency and Government of the House of God*. His intentions here were practical; he wanted to provide a versified church order. The 'house' is described as both a public and a private space, certainly not as a 'temple' only. It is a fortress, a palace, a stately home, but also a hospital, an inn, and an almshouse. 'Call this [...] what you *will*' is one of Bunyan's opening phrases (*MW*, 6: ll. 18–20, 275). The nature of the building matters less than its materials: God's elect or 'living stones', a metaphor used time and again in Congregational literature.[11] Singled out among 'living stones', were 'foundation stones', the name given

---

[8] See Geoffrey Nuttall, *Visible Saints: The Congregational Way 1640–1660* (Oxford: Basil Blackwell, 1957), 22–40, 134–37; Tolmie, *Triumph of the Saints*, 111–16; Susan Hardman Moore, *Pilgrims: New World Settlers and the Call of Home* (New Haven, CT, and London: Yale University Press, 2007), 123–42; Ellen S. More, 'Congregationalism and the Social Order: John Goodwin's Gathered Church, 1640–1660', *Journal of Ecclesiastical History*, 38 (1987), 210–35; Francis J. Bremer, *Congregational Communion: Clerical Friendship in the Anglo-American Puritan Community, 1610–1692* (Boston, MA: Northeastern University Press, 1994).

[9] More, 'Congregationalism and the Social Order', 222–23; and on tithes, Nuttall, *Visible Saints*, 138–41.

[10] 'Charles II, 1664: An Act to Prevent and Suppress Seditious Conventicles', in *Statutes of the Realm*: vol. 5, *1628–80*, ed. John Raithby (London: Dawsons of Pall Mall, 1819), 516–20 (518).

[11] Bartlet, *Ichnographia*, 31; John Owen, *The True Nature of a Gospel Church and its Government* (1689), a2^r; Benjamin Keach, *The Glory of a True Church, and its Discipline Display'd* (1697), 6.

to founding members such as the twelve men and women of the Bedford congregation (*CB*, 17, 63).

Such a shift of emphasis from material to spiritual stones might suggest an indifference to the physical construction and situation of the house of God. At the Restoration, after all, the multiplication of clandestine and ever-changing places of worship, together with a distrust of the legally established 'steeple-house', meant that people, not spaces, were given pre-eminence. The Church existed where the elect existed, even where no permanent, let alone dignified, buildings could be found. Although this was undoubtedly true, physical displacement also had the opposite effect. Historical circumstances had given Dissenters a heightened sense of place. The ideal Congregational space represented by Palace Beautiful in *The Pilgrim's Progress* is primitive, modelled on the New Testament (*PP*, 45–56). It is a domestic and homely place (more 'house' than 'palace', despite its porter's lodge, chambers, study, and armoury) whose inhabitants meet at nightfall to converse and eat supper. There, Christian could read not only the 'Acts' of his noble predecessors but also the 'Records of the House', the minutes or book of that gathered church (*PP*, 53–4).[12] The culture of the conventicles allowed the Dissenting congregations to revert to their original—indeed truly natural—mode of worship. The clergy, informers, and judges who pushed Dissent underground failed to remember that private worship behind closed doors was the original locus of Dissenting life and that it could become its strength again.

The Restoration also forced the Dissenters to reconsider their form of worship when no regular meetings could be held, when ministers were imprisoned, when letters replaced the spoken word, and baptisms were administered in the middle of the night.[13] But, even then, it did not entirely extinguish the experience of a Dissenting 'church' after generations of Puritans had explained (parting company with Calvin on this point) 'the soteriological significance of ecclesiology'.[14] Church meetings were held, conversion narratives were heard, baptisms were performed, and sentences of excommunication pronounced, all in the midst of the harshest persecutions. In the following pages we will witness the paramount attention that was given to church life by Bunyan and his fellow believers, following them from the Cromwellian era through the Restoration to the first decades of the eighteenth century: from St John's parish church to the barn that stood in the orchard of the cordwainer Josias Ruffhead, and to their first erected chapel in 1707. A convincing story could be assembled from Bunyan's works of fiction, but this one will be recounted from a document perhaps as extraordinary in Dissenting culture as *The Pilgrim's Progress*: the minutes of the Bedford congregation that were kept from 1656 onwards.

---

[12] See Robert Archer, 'Like Flowers in the Garden: John Bunyan and his Concept of the Church', *BQ*, 36 (1996), 280–93.

[13] H. G. Tibbutt (ed.), *Some Early Nonconformist Church Books* (Bedford: Bedfordshire Historical Record Society, 1972), 28.

[14] Brachlow, *Communion of Saints*, 35.

The Bedford Church Minutes

The tall folio that provides the evidence for this chapter, today in the John Bunyan Museum (Bunyan Meeting, Bedford), was published in facsimile in 1928, with an introduction by G. B. Harrison. It was transcribed and edited by H. G. Tibbutt in 1976, and a new edition is being prepared by Michael Davies.[15] The records of meetings begin in 1656, though entries for the years 1656–71 have evidently been copied from an earlier and no longer extant source, with a retrospective narrative of the foundation of the church in 1650 and an epistle from its first pastor, John Gifford, written just before his death in September 1655, also having been inscribed at the beginning. It is clear from this document that the saints who intended to gather a church were never reluctant to seek help from other congregations and ministers, to correspond with each other, to send messengers to gather information, or to require the presence of neighbouring elders. Guidance was at hand on most aspects of ecclesiology but one: the way the church should keep and preserve its records. As a result, historians today are confronted with a wide variety of documents that pass under the name of 'Church Books' or 'Church Records'.

The Bedford manuscript, entitled 'A Booke Containing a Record of the Acts of a Congregation of Christ, in and about Bedford', is referred to internally as 'the church booke' (*CB*, 34, 85). 'Acts' was an important term, redolent of apostolic times and emphasizing the nature of a gathered church as a voluntary association taking autonomous actions. In large metropolitan congregations, there is evidence that three, and sometimes four, separate documents could be kept at the same time: an account book, a minute book to record the decisions of the monthly assemblies, a church book in which important events or controversies were transcribed, and a register of members. In smaller congregations, one book might fulfil all of these functions. The fact that the Bedford manuscript has no section dedicated to its finances suggests that a separate account book was in use, which has unfortunately not survived. The extant manuscript contains, for the most part, the minutes of the church meetings and registers of members. In that sense, the term 'Church Book', the abbreviated title given by Harrison, and the one by which the document has come to be known in Bunyan scholarship, is slightly misleading.

Until recently, scholars have been reluctant to broach these documents, being understandably suspicious of their incompleteness, their partiality, and the uneven geographical distribution of what happens to survive.[16] The Bedford book is nevertheless a point of entry for studying Bunyan's career as the minister of a gathered church and also indeed for the criticism of his writings, as Davies has so eloquently shown.[17] It is very important

---

[15] See *The Church Book of Bunyan Meeting, 1650–1821*, intro. G. B. Harrison (London and Toronto: Dent, 1928); and *CB*.

[16] James F. Cooper, *Tenacious of their Liberties: The Congregationalists in Colonial Massachusetts* (New York and Oxford: Oxford University Press, 1999); Halcomb, 'Social History'.

[17] Michael Davies, 'Spirit in the Letters: John Bunyan's Congregational Epistles', *The Seventeenth Century*, 24 (2009), 323–60.

to emphasize here that the autonomy of each congregation does not invalidate any remarks we might wish to make about the way each one fitted into a Congregational polity. The Bedford manuscript is often representative of other surviving church records, even though its depth of detail and patient transcription of information over more than 200 folios make it one of the fullest in existence.[18] The reinscription into a new book of entries recorded between 1656 and 1671 occurs just a few months before Bunyan was elected. Perhaps it was Bunyan himself who insisted on this more systematic and organized record-keeping, in the light of his Restoration efforts to maintain and encourage membership.[19]

Visible Saints

One of the most controversial aspects of Congregational ecclesiology was the admission and ejection of members. For Congregationalists, admittance to the Church was subordinated to a long process that included a spiritual examination of a prospective member by the whole church and an enquiry into his or her 'conversation'. When a church was formally gathered, the founding members, who had known each other for many years, did not always need further testimonies of their spiritual worth. In some cases, on the very day they did relate their 'awakening' or 'conversion' again, but there is no trace of this in the Bedford minutes. The Bedford church originally began through the willingness of its first brothers and sisters simply to enter into a covenant with God and each other:

> The manner of their putting themselves into the state of a Church of Christ was:—after much prayer and waiting upon God and consulting one with another, by the Word, they, upon the day appointed for this solemne worke, being met, after prayer and seeking God as before, with one consent they joyntly first gave themselves to the Lord, and one to another by the will of God. (*CB*, 17)

These original members of the Bedford church were guided by John Gifford, who was immediately chosen as their pastor, but also by 'other ministers' of the 'Congregationall

---

[18] For recent scholarly work on church records, see Mark Burden, Michael Davies, Anne Dunan-Page, and Joel Halcomb, *An Inventory of Puritan and Dissenting Records, 1640–1714* (2016), available at http://www.qmulreligionandliterature.co.uk/online-publications/dissenting-records, accessed 9 January 2018. See also Michael Davies, Anne Dunan-Page, and Joel Halcomb (eds.), 'Dissenting Hands', special issue *BS*, 20 (2016); Anne Dunan-Page, *L'Expérience puritaine. Vies et récits de dissidents (XVIIe–XVIIIe siècle)* (Paris: Éditions du Cerf, 2017); and Michael Davies, Anne Dunan-Page, and Joel Halcomb (eds.), *Church Life: Pastors, Congregations, and the Experience of Dissent in Seventeenth-Century England* (Oxford: Oxford University Press, 2019).

[19] On Bunyan's election, see Michael Davies, 'When was Bunyan Elected Pastor? Fixing a Date in the Bedford Church Book', *BS*, 18 (2014), 7–41.

way', with whom Gifford had met, and by 'members of other societyes' (*CB*, 17), although no messengers from other churches seem to have been present, as was often the case at the gathering of a new church.

As soon as the church was gathered, the founding members and their pastor established the criteria to determine admission: 'faith in Christ and holines of life, without respect to this or that circumstance or opinion in outward and circumstantiall things' (*CB*, 17). This was both typical and innovative. It was typical, because the Bedford congregation required that prospective applicants should give a testimony of their 'faith in Christ' before the church, while their conduct was duly scrutinized; it was innovative, because agreeing to display a spirit of tolerance on 'circumstanciall' matters—baptism being a case in point—was turned into a condition for joining the church. 'Open communion' was not a mere idea or principle in Bedford, but a founding article of the church, and one that determined its membership. It was still compulsory to abide by it in 1697: 'Twas then agreed on also that all persons for the future that are admitted to fellowship do explicitely declare their approbation of, and do give up themselves upon, the stated principle of the Church, *viz*:—faith in Christ and holiness of life, though there be different apprehensions in circumstantialls or externalls' (*CB*, 111).

The founding members had neither a written covenant nor even a confession of faith, another fairly untypical move for a Congregational church. The drafting of a confession was proposed only in the summer of 1672, but it had to be postponed, Bunyan being still in prison:

> It was also agreed that a brief confession of faith be drawne up by the elders and gifted brethren of the congregation, against the next meeting: that after the Churche's approbation thereof it may be propounded to all that shall hereafter give up themselves to the Lord and us by the will of God, and their unfeigned consent thereto required. (*CB*, 73)

It is unclear whether such a document was ever written, but the fact that it was being discussed soon after Bunyan had composed *A Confession of my Faith, and A Reason of my Practice* (1672) to vindicate open communion can hardly be a coincidence.

The lack of both a written covenant and a confession of faith can perhaps be explained by the extraordinary status acquired by another document: John Gifford's deathbed epistle to the church (*CB*, 18–21). It summarized its spirit and gave advice on church discipline and government. The letter also provided practical and spiritual guidance, rendering other documents unnecessary. It was still read at church meetings some forty years after it was drafted, where a covenant would normally have served this function: 'The Church principle as 'tis in the account of the Churche's first gathering, and Dr. Gifford's epistle to the Church, was read and by the Church still approved, and agreed to be maint[ained] as what is agreeable to God's word' (*CB*, 108).

Once criteria of admission had been agreed, how did the Bedford congregation choose its members? First, an applicant had to manifest a 'desire' to join the church—a step deemed important enough to be mentioned in the minutes. Then, he or she was heard during private visits. If everybody was satisfied, the person was 'propounded' to the whole church. For a whole month, church members had the opportunity to make enquiries into the life of the applicant and the slightest 'uneasiness' or 'unsatisfaction' or 'objection' could halt the procedure, until it was resolved. The interval between being 'propounded' and appearing before the church could nevertheless be extended. In 1697, a sister was admitted 'who for years past stood propounded but could not attend a Church meeting to be received' (CB, 111). It took two years for Ann Muns, who had 'two bastards', to show repentance and be finally accepted, 'giving in a very satisfactory experience' (CB, 137). Conversely, there were cases in which members were propounded and received at the same meeting, or not propounded at all, but this measure remained exceptional. In November 1694, Alice Clarck 'was propounded and received into our fellowship both at the same meeting, not as a president for others, but because she feared she might be hindred her duty if her husband heard it' (CB, 101). Later, there were cases of pregnant women who were exempt from having to deliver their 'experiences' before the church, as they were so close to giving birth (CB, 124, 127, 132). On 26 June 1695, 'Josua Read of Cloph[ill] was received, though not before propounded, it being the request of his mother then present and he very well known to the Church; but this is not to be afterwards a praesident for other person' (CB, 105). The minutes failed to record the precise nature of such motherly concern.

If nothing unfavourable was reported once the candidate had been propounded, he or she came before the church to deliver a conversion narrative, or 'an acc[ount of] the work of grace' (CB, 22), or an 'experience' (CB, 25). Exemptions were sought—but not often—and apparently always by women. Mrs Whitebread, for instance, was exempted 'because of the great distress she lay under at her speaking to the Church' (CB, 129). A Mrs Freeman pleaded physical infirmities: 'Twas then also concluded that Mrs Freeman who stands propounded for communion, have libertie to speake her experience to some brethren in private, she not being able to speak before the Church by reason of her fitts, but not as a president for future practices' (CB, 114). Other candidates failed to convince the assembly and were told to wait (CB, 22). The church ensured that they were properly looked after in the interval, 'to incourage them to farther waitinge, and indeavour the prevention of any temptation' (CB, 24), but deferral could lead to complaints and grudges, as in the case of Hester Brace, whose mother was exhorted 'not to conceive prejudice against any on her daughter's being refused for the present' (CB, 146). There is no real indication that the church lowered its standards of admission under persecution; people were still asked to wait when they were not considered to be ready (CB, 40). If the relation were deemed satisfactory, the candidate was finally received into fellowship after a collective decision.

In Bedford, the visits that members paid to prospective applicants were often gendered: women visited women and men visited men. This was not a standard procedure among gathered churches. When the minutes open, in April 1656, visits are mentioned but the 'propounding' stage seems to have been omitted; brothers and sisters apparently had the power to invite an applicant to the next church meeting to deliver his or her experience, after one, two, or three visits. Not all churches would have admitted such private screening by lay members, and this seems to have ended abruptly in the latter part of 1657. From then on, the records mention that members were 'propounded' before being allowed before the church. For the first two years of the minutes, 1656 and 1657, the pastor John Burton is mentioned only once in relation to the visits. It seems curious that a pastor would almost systematically delegate this important work to ordinary members and refrain entirely from participating in the admission process. It should not be forgotten, however, that Gifford's epistle had recommended that a pastor should be on trial for one or two years before his election (CB, 21). Perhaps Burton was on trial only, until late 1657 (although he was appointed to the St John's living in January 1656). A meeting in August of the same year nominated other 'officers necessary for the congregation'. Bunyan was one of them, though he would be exempted from serving as a deacon at this time on account of his preaching activities (CB, 28).

A second point concerns the audience for the conversion narratives that applicants were required to give. Polemical tracts from the 1640s reveal that narratives were originally given in New England on Sundays, when not only members of the church, but also children and outsiders to the community, were present.[20] Listeners could then learn how to frame a suitable account by listening to those of others. In Bedford, a narrative could indeed be heard on the Lord's Day, at least after the Restoration (CB, 111, 120, 123), but it was not the church's regular practice. Most members were heard during the monthly church meetings which, in theory, were accessible only to church members. There is, however, a late entry that points out into another direction. On 26 February 1707, five newcomers were admitted but 'Samuell Hensman, before propounded, his speaking his experience was defered till next meeting because many members were dissatisfyed with him, and there was such an appearance of strangers at this Church meeting that 'twas not thought convenient to enter upon the debate about him' (CB, 133). This crucial entry provides evidence for the way the congregation had evolved in the early eighteenth century. First of all, meetings dealing with the internal affairs of the church in general, and cases of discipline in particular, had been opened to non-members, at an unspecified date, but before 1707, when the church was worshipping and holding its meetings in a brand-new chapel. Second, the church was becoming increasingly sensitive to issues of privacy. It would take another decade to resolve the matter. On 3 September, 1718, 'it was resolved not to admit any person to our Church meetings, for Church business, but Church members, or transient members, or those propounded' (CB, 146). Bedford was closing its door to 'strangers' with the effect that its eighteenth-century applicants for membership cannot have had access to first-hand testimonies of experiences. If Bedford was typical of a general move towards increased privacy, then the evangelical conversion narratives of the eighteenth century could hardly have been studied, so to speak, within the walls of the meeting houses.[21]

---

[20] See, for instance, Thomas Lechford, *Plain Dealing: Or, Newes from New-England* (1642).

[21] For the opposite hypothesis, see Bruce D. Hindmarsh, *The Evangelical Conversion Narrative: Spiritual Autobiography in Early Modern England* (Oxford: Oxford University Press, 2005), 293.

The admission procedures described so far were followed for anyone not already a member of a gathered church. If an existing member of another congregation wished to join, however, a dismission was required from that congregation, usually in the form of a testimonial letter. Most churches considered that this was a sufficient qualification for membership. Bedford, however, insisted that even these people should deliver a conversion narrative when they arrived. Conversely, some members of the Bedford church asked for a recommendation when they changed residence. The churches to which they were entrusted give an idea of the Bedford network: in London, the congregations of Henry Jessey, George Cockayne, John Owen, Anthony Palmer, George Griffith, John Simpson, Richard Taylor, Matthew Meade, John Nesbitt, and Robert Trail. Some of these were directly consulted at various times, for instance to find an assistant to the ailing Burton (*CB*, 34, 66) or a replacement for Bunyan (*CB*, 91).

In nearby areas, Bedford was in contact with the church of Stephen Hawthorne at Stevington and had entered into association with those of John Donne (the ejected rector of Pertenhall) at Keysoe, William Wheeler at Cranfield, and John Gibbs at Newport Pagnell (*CB*, 31, 35). These churches were to be consulted in case of difficulties, to assist in preaching, to help administer the sacrament, or to give advice on the choice of a pastor, and could be asked to spare a gifted brother to assist, for example, with preaching. As in all such associations, messengers met, discussed church affairs, and couched their proceedings in writing: an entry for March 1659 refers to 'the 8th proposall of our agreement with other congregations adjacent' (*CB*, 33).[22] Bedford was also at the centre of a cluster of satellite 'meetings' in villages and hamlets from which it drew members, all 'upheld by the congregation' (*CB*, 86). In 1672, licences were sought for no less than eleven such locations in Bedfordshire, Hertfordshire, and Cambridgeshire.[23] Some, such as those at Gamlingay and Blunham, would eventually 'inchurch by themselves', with Bedford's approval, respectively in 1710 and 1734 (*CB*, 134–35, 155).

All these London and Bedfordshire churches were Congregational. There is no indication that the church was willing to dismiss members to Baptist churches that did not practise open communion or even to churches 'whose principles and practices, in matters of faith and worshippe, we as yet are strangers to' (*CB*, 66). For instance, in May 1674 a letter was dispatched to the congregation of the late Henry Jessey to ensure that the church was still practising open communion and could therefore receive one member of the Bedford church, now a London resident, named Martha Cumberland (*CB*, 77, 79). Martha had been given a choice between the congregations of George Cockayne, Anthony Palmer, and John Owen, but had declined. Bedford feared she might have adopted closed-communion views. The letter, signed by Bunyan, was respectful of John

---

[22] See B. R. White, 'The Fellowship of Believers: Bunyan and Puritanism', in N. H. Keeble (ed.), *John Bunyan: Conventicle and Parnassus* (Oxford: Clarendon Press, 1988), 1–19.

[23] Blunham, Goldington, Oakley, Kempston, Cardington, Stagsden, Haynes, Maulden, Edworth, Gamlingay, Toft, and Ashwell. See Brown, *John Bunyan*, 210–38; Richard L. Greaves, 'The Organizational Response of Nonconformity to Repression and Indulgence: The Case of Bedfordshire', *Church History*, 44 (1975), 472–84; Geoffrey F. Nuttall, 'Church Life in Bunyan's Bedfordshire', *BQ*, 26 (1976), 305–13.

Gifford's tolerance over baptism, and yet it effectively forbade a member to join with the congregation of her choice. As I have suggested elsewhere, if Bunyan was labelled an 'Anabaptist' it had more to do with polemics than with church practice.[24] Not only was he not a strict Baptist himself (he had his children baptized as infants) but he was clearly reluctant to recommend members to closed-communion Baptist churches.

Bedford's Officers

The 'embodying' of a church preceded the election of its officers. Most churches were originally gathered without a minister; if necessary, they could function without one for weeks, months, or even years. This was indeed mentioned in John Gifford's epistle: the church ought to continue as a church, if their 'teacher at any time be laide aside' (*CB*, 21). It is not always easy, though, to determine the role of officers in Bedford, due to the church's idiosyncratic use of its terms and their variation over time. Congregational polity distinguished between the offices of 'pastor', 'teacher', 'elders', and 'deacons', but without attributing pre-eminence to either pastor or teacher.[25] In Bedford, John Gifford had used 'overseer', 'teacher', and 'pastor' indiscriminately (*CB*, 18, 21), and John Burton was referred to as a 'teacher' (*CB*, 38), although he clearly fulfilled the functions of a 'pastor' as well. In January 1659, as his health declined, the congregation appointed two 'elders', John Whiteman and John Grew (*CB*, 32), and it was suggested that an 'assistant' should be found with the help of London ministers (*CB*, 34). Samuel Fenne and John Whiteman were referred to as 'overseers', 'pastors', 'elders', 'ministers', and even 'bishops', the latter term being normally favoured by Baptists (*CB*, 50). Bunyan was elected 'to the pastorall office or eldership' (*CB*, 71). Similarly, the first mention of Bunyan's successor, Ebenezer Chandler, is both as 'pastor and elder' (*CB*, 90).

Election preceded the ordination of officers, which normally comprised fasting, praying, and the laying on of hands of the eldership. Yet this is not a point on which the Bedford minutes give much information. The founding members, we are told, simply 'made choyce' of Gifford without neighbouring elders being present, while Burton's election is not even mentioned, and Samuel Fenne and John Whiteman's appointments are simply alluded to (*CB*, 17, 38–9). Likewise, Bunyan is described as having been given 'the right hand of fellowship' (Galatians 2:9), whereas Chandler was 'elected and sett apart to the work and office of pastor' (*CB*, 94). In practice, moreover, the management

---

[24] Anne Dunan-Page, *Grace Overwhelming: John Bunyan, The Pilgrim's Progress and the Extremes of the Baptist Mind* (Bern: Peter Lang, 2006), 47–100.

[25] The Savoy Declaration, in *The Creeds and Platforms of Congregationalism*, ed. Williston Walker, intro. Elizabeth C. Nordbeck (1893; rpr. New York: Pilgrim Press, 1991), 340–408 (404); James M. Renihan, *Edification and Beauty: The Practical Ecclesiology of the English Particular Baptists, 1675–1705* (Milton Keynes: Paternoster, 2008), 88–117; Halcomb, 'Social History', 63; Bartlet, *Ichnographia* 62–4; Goodwin, *Constitution*, 279–90.

of the Bedford congregation was mostly in the hands of a single person named overseer, bishop, teacher, pastor, elder, or pastor *and* elder—when there was one. The only exception was between 1663 and 1681. In December 1663, the haberdasher Samuel Fenne and the yeoman John Whiteman were jointly elected as 'pastors and elders' (*CB*, 38). In May 1674, in connection with Martha Cumberland's affair (as mentioned), Bedford received a letter from the congregation of the late Henry Jessey, addressed 'To the church of Christ in Bedford wherof our beloved Samuell Fenn is pastor' (*CB*, 79), Whiteman having died in 1672. Either the news of Bunyan's election in December 1671 must have taken considerable time to reach the capital or the congregation deliberately omitted his name.[26] The latter is a distinct possibility. After all, Bunyan had recently appended Jessey's principles to his *Differences in Judgment about Water-Baptism, No Bar to Communion* (1673)—and yet now questioned this London church's faithfulness to their former minister's spiritual legacy.

It may well be that Bunyan's appointment to the Bedford pastorate was not as straightforward as it seems with hindsight. It is true that William Whitbread, in a letter to the congregation, had mentioned his dissatisfaction with the dual leadership of Fenne and Whiteman (*CB*, 47) and Michael Davies has shown that the correspondence inserted in the Church Book might have served as a campaign to promote Bunyan's qualifications to the pastorate.[27] And yet such isolated complaints (Whitbread repented in October 1671) would not have been sufficient to challenge the co-pastors' leadership, especially since it was in perfect agreement with Congregational polity. The appointment of Bunyan was a somewhat strenuous affair. It took no less than five meetings, in three different places, to prepare it, and much 'conference' and 'prayer' so 'that [the church's] way in that respect may be cleared up to them' (*CB*, 70). We do not know how Fenne and Whiteman took it or, more importantly, how their roles were altered after the new appointment. In May 1672, they both applied for licences to teach in satellite meetings, at Cardington and Haynes, respectively. Somewhat conveniently, Whiteman died soon afterwards, but that leaves open the possibility that Bedford had three 'pastors or elders', at least for a few months. Fenne lived until November 1681, being described at his death as 'one of the elders of this congregation' (*CB*, 86). Just before, he and Bunyan had signed a letter of admonition to Sister Hawthorne as 'elders' (*CB*, 85).[28] Whatever happened in the Bedford congregation in the winter and spring of 1671–72, Whiteman and Fenne must have consented to enter into an unusual pastoral triumvirate, granting pre-eminence to Bunyan as soon as he was released from prison.

Samuel Fenne died on 12 November 1681. The church used a similar phrase, citing God's 'heavie hand', as it would for Bunyan seven years later (*CB*, 86, 89), and appointed in both cases the holding of a day of humiliation. Fenne's death led directly to a reorganization of the internal affairs of the church, among which the institution of the office of 'ruleing elders', whose 'qualifications' were considered 'in order to choyce and

---

[26] On the date of the election, see Davies, 'When was Bunyan Elected Pastor?'
[27] Davies, 'Spirit in the Letters', 340.
[28] Greaves, 'Organizational Response', 478.

apointment of som to that work in this congregation' (*CB*, 87). It seems that Bunyan was unwilling to repeat the experience of a decade of shared pastoral leadership: he became the sole overseer of the congregation while ruling elders assisted in matters concerning discipline. This is what he would later theorize in *A Discourse of* [...] *the House of God*, where he distinguished between 'overseers', 'rulers', 'deacons', and 'widows'. The overseer, a 'Distributor of the word of Grace' (*MW*, 6: l. 397, 286), was meant to exhort, preach sound doctrine, administer the sacraments, and exercise a cure of souls. The ruling elders were to enforce appropriate discipline and keep schisms and contentions at bay (*MW*, 6: ll. 514–31, 289–90). Deacons were in charge of charitable works, while widows were supposed to instruct '*Younger Women*' and visit the sick (*MW*, 6: ll. 580, 586, 291).

Although Bunyan explicitly recognized the role of widows in print, the Bedford congregation does not seem to have had 'widows', but it did have elected deacons in charge of the finances. There were at least three of them during Bunyan's pastorate. 'Gifted' brothers whose 'call' to preach had been endorsed by the church were also vital to maintain the circuits of satellite meetings in the area, and, at the same 1681 meeting, it was decided they should all meet once every six weeks. More complex was the identity and role of the 'principall' brethren (sometimes also named elders) because—unlike pastors, ruling elders, and deacons—these were not formally elected by the church. Such brethren are mentioned for the first time in July 1658, when it was decided that they would meet to prepare the church's meetings and set the affairs in 'order and readiness' (*CB*, 30). In London, though not explicitly in Bedford, there were concerns that they instituted an oligarchy of eminent members who would use their private meetings to steer the general assembly, in direct opposition to the Congregational principle of open discussion of the church's affairs (at least among male members).[29] It is clear that they continued to operate in the Bedford church during the Restoration, but whether they were ever elected officially as ruling elders remains uncertain (*CB*, 50, 67, 70).

Absentees and Lewd Livers

Discipline within the Bedford church was always a key concern, and the minutes dedicate a great deal of attention to the activities of the congregation's 'disorderly walkers', as such church records often describe them. 'Scandalous livers', however, could easily be identified and, in that sense, caused fewer problems than did brothers or sisters who had become disaffected with the church and stopped attending the Lord's Supper and meetings. Even if attendance at the latter was not compulsory, it was expected that members would show an acceptable degree of commitment. 'Generall' meetings were also held (in the 1650s, quarterly; after the Restoration, yearly) to which everybody was supposed to

---

[29] Renihan, *Edification*, 81; Murdina D. MacDonald, 'London Calvinistic Baptists 1689–1729: Tensions within a Community under Toleration' (DPhil thesis, University of Oxford, 1982), 109–31.

come 'without any delay or excuse' (*CB*, 35). These meetings were specifically designated to 'inspect the state of the Church' (*CB*, 136), and yet some members still failed to turn up. It therefore became necessary to remind everybody, at regular intervals, that an interest in the collective management of church affairs, as well as participation in the sacraments and 'performing with other spiritual services as tend to their mutual edification', was not optional.[30] In October 1656, it was decided that two brethren would visit the members 'to certify us how they doe in body and soule, and to stirre them up to come' (*CB*, 23). Two years later, in order to facilitate the work of its visitors, the Congregation was divided into several districts: brothers were appointed for Bedford, Kempston, Houghton Conquest, Wilshamstead, Elstow, Cardington, Oakley, Stevington, and Radwell, to which were later added 'Fensom' and Haynes (*CB*, 30, 38). After 1688, they were visiting 'Bedford and adjacent places', 'Cotten End, and thereabouts', 'Bletsoe and round him [sic]', and 'Gamlingay and those parts' (*CB*, 104).

Those visits maintained a vital link between members who lived far apart, to give comfort to the sick and to those 'complaining of lowness in their spiritts' (*CB*, 128), such as Sister Chamberlaine, who was visited 'in a very sad condition by reason of temptation' (*CB*, 33). They were also used to keep a tally of membership. One of the first measures taken by Ebenezer Chandler, elected pastor in 1691, was 'an inspection how those members stand that are under the senshures of the Church, or have at any time been admonished, and to know what there offences are and who do absent from the Church meeting' (*CB*, 95 and 101). Because of the gathered churches' insistence on godly fellowship and strict watchfulness, it has often been supposed that members must have been kept under strict control. In fact, loosened spiritual bonds, unrecorded changes of residence, and series of unanswered admonitions all meant that the officers rarely had a clear idea of the precise size of their flock, hence the need for visitations. In 1694, it was recommended that a visit should finally be paid to Oliver Dix who had been 'withdrawn' from the church, without ever leaving it, for the last thirty-three years (*CB*, 100). What exactly Dix thought about his relation to the church can only be a matter of conjecture. Like some others before and after him, he may have quietly slipped back to parish worship, avoiding his former companions, without reflecting unduly upon his role as a member of a Dissenting brotherhood.

Such cases of absenteeism are carefully recorded in the Bedford volume alongside more colourful or tragic forms of misdemeanour: playing at cards (or shuffleboard, quoits, or nine pins), drunkenness, adultery, 'carnal' marriages, ancillary elopement, 'light unbecoming actions about stool ball and the may pole' (*CB*, 124), attempted suicide, wife-beating, getting into debt, Sabbath-breaking, and prophesying. Recorded cases of such crimes swelled at the Restoration and beyond, but it is impossible to determine whether the Bedford church had become stricter and more systematic in its exercise of discipline or whether the minutes began to be kept, on that particular point, with greater care and regularity. Doctrinal or ecclesiological errors were also a source

---

[30] Savoy Declaration, 397.

of anxiety, such as insisting on adult baptism, refusing to sing hymns, asserting that 'the soul was perfect' (*CB*, 159), 'going to the Moravians' (*CB*, 175), or simply hearing 'nationall' ministers (*CB*, 40, 51, 56, 63, 115).

In cases of 'passive' absenteeism or 'active' wrongdoing, the procedure was identical. The person was admonished once or twice in private, and then asked to come and explain himself or herself before the whole church. Some excommunications were nevertheless judged too sudden (*CB*, 148). In one instance, it was considered that two brothers might be excommunicated 'forthwith' for drunkenness, but the 'more ordinary way' was to give a warning (*CB*, 116). Members were naturally sensitive to due procedure. A 'private' offence would normally be dealt with first in private, a 'public' offence before the whole church. Some, then, took upon themselves to remind the church of the nature of a 'public' offence. In 1694, John Hensman interrupted the proceedings of the assembly on the grounds that his disciplinary appearance before the church, on account of running into debt, was disorderly, 'alledging that noe faults deserve publick dealing but gross enormityes and haresyes' (*CB*, 99, 101). If little or no repentance was shown, the person would be 'withdrawn from', meaning that he or she could still come to hear sermons and participate in public events but was barred from the communion table. After a period of time which could vary considerably from case to case, a sentence of excommunication was officially pronounced, entered in the minutes, and notified, in person, to those concerned. It should be noted that the church's censures did not spare its main officers. In August, 1669, Edward Coventon (the husband of one of the founding members) and William Wallis were removed from the church's diaconate on account of their negligence.

It has sometimes been supposed, given the apparent rigidity of moral standards and the obligation of members to keep watch upon each other, that gathered churches were as quick to sever themselves from backsliders as they were slow in admitting visible saints. Nothing could be further from the truth. The community was aware that excommunication was a last resort, delivered only when everything else had failed, and then only after protracted debate. It was also reversible. Cases were scrupulously examined, witnesses were heard, the offender was given every opportunity to repent, and the church prayed and fasted regularly for the return of the prodigal (*CB*, 39). The nature of the offence, and its supposed gravity, mattered far less than a willingness to confess and acknowledge one's sins before God, the church, and oneself (*CB*, 149).

Marrying outside the faith was a case in point. In theory, this was strictly forbidden, but when the deed was done, no remedy could be found, unless the church was willing to excommunicate the offender. This rarely happened and expedients were found. An ungodly wife or husband could prove to be 'gracious' (*CB*, 120); a misguided wife might confess she had acted rashly. Acknowledgement of wrongdoing and repentance might be sufficient to assuage the ire of the pastor (*CB*, 115–16, 128), especially if the newly-wed was happy to resume his or her place within the community (*CB*, 176). Mary Gates, after months of admonition, came to plead her cause after she had been repeatedly seen in the parish church with her 'carnall' husband: 'and for her going to Church 'twas to please her husband only, and that because he threatened otherwise to leave her and her children' (*CB*, 128).

Conclusion

A full history of the Bedford congregation in the seventeenth and eighteenth centuries is still to be written. In the space available here, it has been impossible to dwell on topics that would require an entirely separate treatment, such as the role of the Bedford sisters or hymn singing. Neither has it been possible to provide a systematic comparison with other Congregational churches. It has been possible, however, to reconstruct the breadth of John Bunyan's activities. His days were filled with visiting the sick and the spiritually afflicted, with stirring up the lukewarm, admonishing youngsters who had fallen in love around the maypole, notifying the excommunicated, listening to conversion narratives, investigating those churches elsewhere that might welcome his own members, drafting recommendation letters, or organizing meetings. Such documents as the Bedford minutes deserve a more comprehensive treatment than they have hitherto received. The relationships between ordinary members and the elders, the shifting notion of a communal 'identity' within the Bedford church of visible saints who were also parents, husbands, wives, tradesmen, and villagers, the tension between the autonomous congregations, the pre- and post-Toleration changes in Congregational ecclesiology—these are all topics which a study of John Bunyan's congregation and its records may help to illuminate.

Suggested Reading

Brachlow, Stephen, *The Communion of Saints: Radical Puritan and Separatist Ecclesiology, 1570–1625* (Oxford: Oxford University Press, 1988).

Burden, Mark, Michael Davies, Anne Dunan-Page, and Joel Halcomb, *An Inventory of Puritan and Dissenting Records, 1640–1714* (2016), available at http://www.qmulreligionandliterature.co.uk/online-publications/dissenting-records, accessed 9 January 2018.

Cooper, James F., *Tenacious of their Liberties: The Congregationalists in Colonial Massachusetts* (New York and Oxford: Oxford University Press, 1999).

Davies, Michael, 'When was Bunyan Elected Pastor? Fixing a Date in the Bedford Church Book', *BS*, 18 (2014), 7–41.

Davies, Michael, Anne Dunan-Page, and Joel Halcomb (eds.), 'Dissenting Hands', special issue *BS*, 20 (2016).

Greaves, Richard L., 'The Organizational Response of Nonconformity to Repression and Indulgence: The Case of Bedfordshire', *Church History*, 44 (1975), 472–84.

Halcomb, Joel, 'A Social History of Congregational Religious Practice during the Puritan Revolution' (PhD thesis, University of Cambridge, 2009).

MacDonald, Murdina D., 'London Calvinistic Baptists 1689–1729: Tensions within a Community under Toleration' (DPhil thesis, University of Oxford, 1982).

More, Ellen S., 'Congregationalism and the Social Order: John Goodwin's Gathered Church, 1640–1660', *Journal of Ecclesiastical History*, 38 (1987), 210–35.

Nuttall, Geoffrey F., *Visible Saints: The Congregational Way 1640–1660* (Oxford: Basil Blackwell, 1957).

CHAPTER 4

BUNYAN'S THEOLOGY AND RELIGIOUS CONTEXT

DEWEY D. WALLACE, JR

UNDERSTANDING John Bunyan's theology and relating it to the religious context of England in the second half of the seventeenth century is crucial for the interpretation of his classic writings. Two remarks by Samuel Taylor Coleridge help focus this task. First is Coleridge's familiar remark separating Bunyan as a literary figure (the Bunyan of Parnassus) from the preacher and theological author (the Bunyan of the conventicle), to the detriment of the latter.[1] Many who have studied Bunyan have felt that while his imaginative narratives rose to the level of literary greatness, they could be separated from the dreary Calvinistic sermons and treatises that flowed from his pen and that were of interest only to his fellow Dissenters. But abetted by the editing and publication of his *Miscellaneous Works* and by the recognition of his ties to radical currents of seventeenth-century English religiosity, the climate of opinion has changed, so that it is now widely acknowledged that Bunyan's literary works cannot properly be understood apart from awareness of his religious and theological context and commitments. Most Bunyan scholars now agree that his autobiography and fictions are integrally related not only to the general cast of his religious outlook but also to some of his most precise theological formulations, though few would go so far as Richard Dutton, who calls *The Pilgrim's Progress* a 'Calvinist tract'.[2]

---

[1] Roberta Florence Brinkley (ed.), *Coleridge on the Seventeenth Century* (Durham, NC: Duke University Press, 1955), 475–76.

[2] A. Richard Dutton, '"Interesting but Tough": Reading *The Pilgrim's Progress*', SEL, 18 (1978), 439–56 (439). See also Greaves, *Glimpses*, 230, 261; Kathleen M. Swaim, *Pilgrim's Progress, Puritan Progress: Discourses and Contexts* (Urbana: University of Illinois Press, 1993), 16; Michael Davies, *Graceful Reading: Theology and Narrative in the Works of John Bunyan* (Oxford: Oxford University Press, 2002), 4, 20–1, 170, 181, 323; Monica Furlong, *Puritan's Progress: A Study of John Bunyan* (London: Hodder & Stoughton, 1975), 108; Galen K. Johnson, *Prisoner of Conscience: John Bunyan on Self, Community and Christian Faith* (Carlisle: Paternoster Press, 2003), 127–28, 168.

To acknowledge that Bunyan's literary works are articulations of his theology is not necessarily to affirm that those theological writings are not unpleasantly Calvinistic. However, to help grant his theology a more sympathetic investigation, another Coleridge quotation, not about Bunyan, is apropos: 'If ever book was calculated to drive men to despair, it is Bishop Jeremy Taylor's on Repentance. It first opened my eyes to Arminianism, and that Calvinism is practically a far, far more soothing and consoling system.'[3] That Bunyan's Calvinist theology was to him a theology of comfort and intended for the comfort of others who felt themselves hopelessly lost souls is important for understanding his thought and writings. It was because Bunyan felt that his opponents undermined the possibility of comfort for sinful human beings that he so ferociously assaulted them.

Bunyan is commonly designated a Calvinist, and accordingly it should be noted that the term Calvinism is shorthand for Reformed theology, a theology that had roots in Ulrich Zwingli, Martin Bucer, and others besides John Calvin; however, by the later seventeenth century, Calvinism as a term was widely used and often acknowledged by its protagonists—though, ironically, not by Bunyan, one of its most ardent supporters, who, in a rare mention of Calvin, denied that he followed him or any other source besides Scripture (*MW*, 4: 38).

Bunyan was not a university-trained theologian, treating in orderly fashion the major topics of Christian doctrine; his writings were occasional and homiletic, called forth to answer an opponent, respond to a situation in his Bedford congregation, or exhort people to faith and piety. Nonetheless, he offered opinions on most major Christian doctrines, and in his writings on soteriology (doctrine of salvation) provided lengthy and sophisticated treatments of his views, following the traditional schemes of Reformed theologians, covenant, and *ordo salutis* (order of salvation). Thus it is appropriate to unpack his theological teaching using the scheme of the typical body of divinity. In a chapter as brief as this, however, it is not possible to detail the shifting emphases and contributions of particular treatises that shaped Bunyan's developing theology.

Bunyan's Sources and Method

Bunyan made few references to his theological sources, playing down what he had read in order to present himself as unschooled in Plato and Aristotle or dependent on libraries, drawing only on the Bible, with the use of a concordance (*MW*, 2: 16; 3: 71–2; 7: 9; 8: 51). His biblical wordplay indicates his deployment of a concordance and his treatment of biblical texts evidence his exegetical labours. But other evidence points to much else that he read and heard: while in the Parliamentary army he listened to

---

[3] Samuel Taylor Coleridge, *Notes on English Divines*, ed. Derwent Coleridge, 2 vols (London: Edward Moxon, 1853), 2: 38.

Calvinist preachers and radical sectarians alike; through marriage he came into possession of two standard works of Reformed piety, Bishop Lewis Bayly's *The Practise of Pietie* (3rd edn, 1613) and Arthur Dent's *The Plaine Mans Path-Way to Heaven* (1601); in *Grace Abounding* he described the impact Luther's *Commentary on Galatians* (1535; 1575) had upon him; and in the fellowship of the Bedford meeting he was nourished by lively theological instruction and discussion, especially that of its pastors, John Gifford, 'whose doctrine [...] was much for my stability' (*GA*, 37), and later John Burton, who declared that Bunyan had not come from an earthly university, but from 'the heavenly University, the Church of Christ' (*MW*, 1: 11).

Later, Bunyan had contacts with such London Independents as George Cockayne, Thomas Goodwin, and John Owen. Owen, the most important English Calvinist theologian of the second half of the seventeenth century, spoke highly of Bunyan's preaching. It is likely that Bunyan discussed theology with Owen and read some of Owen's writings.[4] Bunyan was familiar with the Westminster Confession of Faith, probably in its revision by Owen and the Independents in the Savoy Confession of 1658. Bunyan referred to John Foxe's *Acts and Monuments* (*MW*, 7: 163), and from it quoted John Wyclif.[5] He also knew writings of earlier Puritan authors such as John Dod and William Perkins, as well as of contemporaries such as Henry Jessey and Benjamin Keach, and had used biblical commentaries. He also read the books of opponents, including Quakers and Edward Fowler (*MW*, 4: 353).[6]

Bunyan asserted the insufficiency for salvation of knowledge of God through the light of nature or conscience; but agreed with Calvin that it shows there is a God to whom worship is due and that all have sinned by breaking God's moral law (*MW*, 4: 337; 1: 55–7; 8: 13). For Bunyan, Scripture contained 'the words of God' and 'the way of salvation' (*MW*, 4: 152). But in his early experience he found the Bible a series of random pronouncements that puzzled him, as appears in *Grace Abounding*, where 'isolated texts, alternately arousing hopes and fears [...] displace each other in his consciousness', until he discovered a hermeneutic able to order it coherently or see it as a whole.[7] His hermeneutic had three interpretive principles: less clear passages should be interpreted by clearer ones; valid scriptural interpretation required the guidance of the Holy Spirit; and a pattern of covenants bound together the whole of Scripture. His concordance helped him with the first; the illumination by the Holy Spirit and the fellowship of the

---

[4] Greaves, *Glimpses*, 150, 226, 315, 347; Francis J. Bremer, *Congregational Communion: Clerical Friendship in the Anglo-American Puritan Community, 1610–1692* (Boston, MA: Northeastern University Press, 1994), 233, 239; Michael A. Mullett, *John Bunyan in Context* (Keele: Keele University Press, 1996), 107–08.

[5] N. H. Keeble, *The Literary Culture of Nonconformity in Later Seventeenth-Century England* (Leicester: Leicester University Press, 1987), 5.

[6] Greaves, *Glimpses*, 105, 176, 521, 603–06. See also Chapter 6 in this volume.

[7] John R. Knott, Jr, '"Thou Must live upon my Word": Bunyan and the Bible', in N. H. Keeble (ed.), *John Bunyan: Conventicle and Parnassus* (Oxford: Clarendon Press, 1988), 153–70 (158–59); Davies, *Graceful Reading*, 123–25.

godly with the second; and typological interpretation that tied together Old and New Testaments, law and grace, with the third.

Protestant confessions of faith and bodies of divinity often began with the nature and attributes of God. Bunyan's *A Confession of my Faith, and A Reason of my Practice* (1672) began by listing many of the divine attributes typical of such doctrinal exposition: 'Almighty, Eternal, Invisible, Incomprehensible', perfect in 'power, wisdom, justice, truth, holyness, mercy, love' (*MW*, 4: 137; 12: 99–100). Elsewhere Bunyan interpreted the attribute of incomprehensibility to mean that language used in Scripture about God is limiting, because it is human, analogical, and has to be accommodated to human weakness ('he condescends to our capacities', *MW*, 13: 367–68); such accommodation was important in Calvin's theological method and biblical hermeneutic.

Soteriology

When dealing with the doctrine of the Trinity, Bunyan approached the soteriological heart of his theology. He called this doctrine the 'ground and fundamental of all' and defined it in the conventional terminology of three subsistences, even referring to the double procession of the Holy Spirit from Father and Son (*MW*, 4: 137; 12: 100–04, 405). Bunyan also employed the theological motif of perichoresis, the intertwining of the three persons in all divine workings; this put soteriology into the heart of his Trinitarianism, as in the salvation of sinners each person 'putteth forth his grace' (*MW*, 8: 82, 165, 326). Bunyan's orthodoxy regarding the Trinity has been questioned, but this judgement is extrapolated from a broadsheet diagram rather than from Bunyan's doctrinal exposition. His friendship with the meticulously orthodox Owen probably would have precluded heterodoxy on such a point.[8]

Bunyan's primary interest was the relation of the Triune God to humanity, beginning with creation. God created time and then chaos, or 'First Matter', out of which the Earth and its inhabitants were shaped (*MW*, 12: 104–05). The immortal human soul was created the noblest part of a person, and 'acteth' the body to which it is joined (*MW*, 9: 144–51, 156; 163–66). Although God desires communion with human souls, they have been 'infected' with sin by the fall of Adam and Eve, and pass it on to their progeny. This sin is a transgression of the law of God, both the law of nature and the revealed law of the Ten Commandments, and all—'Heathens, Turks, Jews, Atheists'—have a conscience convicting them of sin. Fallen souls will be the object of God's eternal wrath unless redeemed from this fate (*MW*, 1: 168; 9: 169, 190–91, 204–5; 8: 13).

Essential to Bunyan's understanding of salvation was the Chalcedonian Christology of Christ's two natures, human and divine, joined in one person in the incarnation. He

---

[8] Gordon Campbell, 'Fishing in Other Men's Waters: Bunyan and the Theologians', in Keeble (ed.), *Bunyan: Conventicle and Parnassus*, 137–51 (144–46); W. R. Owens, 'Introduction', *MW*, 12: xxvi–xxvii.

emphasized the real physicality of the incarnate Son, echoing the ancient opponents of Gnostic docetism in his writings against the Quakers, whose spiritualizing of Christ he took as denying real incarnation (*MW*, 2: 189; 4: 139; 8: 54–5). Bunyan insisted that Christ was 'flesh of our flesh' (*MW*, 13: 165), that his physical body was 'actually' buried (*MW*, 1: 44–8, 65, 68), that he rose from the dead as 'flesh and bones' to redeem believers who will also rise in the flesh, and that Christ ascended to heaven in that same body, in which he shall also return (*MW*, 1: 73, 75, 82, 106–07, 114–15). He stressed this fleshliness by frequent use of the phrase 'the man Jesus', and by many references to Jesus as the son of Mary who took flesh from her (*MW*, 1: 132, 136, 140–42, 161, 200, 212; 2: 180, 188–90; 8: 81–2), perhaps an unwitting reprise of the patristic emphasis on the Virgin Mary as important for two-nature Christology.

But the divine nature of Christ was also essential for Bunyan's soteriology, which centred on Christ as mediator in his atoning death. Christ as a truly human and truly divine 'God–Man' can redeem sinners who owe God recompense for their sins, since in his human nature he becomes the indebted sinner to make recompense while in his divinity he can pay the infinite debt owed by sin against an infinite God that only God can pay (*MW*, 8: 88). Bunyan thought this was the only way redemption could have come about (*MW*, 4: 38; 12: 293), disagreeing with the high Calvinist Thomas Goodwin who thought that in his sovereign will sin could have been forgiven in other ways had God so chosen.[9] For Bunyan, the death of Christ was necessary to satisfy divine justice, which, after the fall required the punishment of sinners to remain inviolable—God saves sinners out of his mercy, but through Christ's death it is done through law and justice (*MW*, 1: 52; 8: 76–7, 84, 210; 13: 69–70). Atonement was also necessary to avert the wrath of God, as Christ is substituted for sinners and suffers the wrath, curse, and forsakenness of God due to them. For Christ, the pain of his abandoned soul was greater than that of the physical body on the cross, his soul suffering 'the pains and torments of the damned in hell'. Following the high Calvinist theologians of his time such as Owen, Bunyan accentuated the agonies of Christ as the very pains due the worst of sinful humanity—he was made sin for sinful humanity, and the 'revenging Hand of God' had to 'fall upon him' as he bore the sins of all and all at once (*MW*, 2: 106–07, 145; 8: 78, 85–95, 99–101, 105; 13: 370–77). This atonement 'effectually obtained' forgiveness for 'all that shall be saved', as Bunyan affirmed a limited atonement only for those whom God elected to salvation (*MW*, 4: 40; 1: 105; 12: 289).

For Bunyan, the atonement purchased the righteousness of Christ, and God the Father imputed that righteousness to unrighteous sinners. Imputation was a central theme of Bunyan's message: sinners have no hope of salvation by their works, but only by their escape from the curse and wrath of God through the imputation to them of Christ's righteousness. By this imputation, God 'forgets' and no longer sees the sinfulness of the elect as the redeemed stand accepted by God from eternity (*MW*, 2: 86; 3: 263; 12: 387; 4: 71; 8: 174, 298; 10: 172; 13: 276; 5: 159). Bunyan devoted a treatise to this theme,

---

[9] Richard L. Greaves, *John Bunyan* (Grand Rapids, MI: Eerdmans, 1969), 36–7.

Of Justification by an Imputed Righteousness (1692) and stressed it in his *A Defence of the Doctrine of Justification, by Faith* (1672), an attack upon the treatment of that doctrine by Edward Fowler, a Church of England vicar in Bedfordshire, later made a bishop (*MW*, 4: 35, 71). Bunyan shared this emphasis with such high Calvinist theologians as Thomas Goodwin and John Owen.

According to Bunyan, Christ supplemented his high priestly office of atonement by his intercession that followed upon his ascension into heaven, where, at the right hand of God the Father, he 'abideth a Priest continually', pleading that the righteousness earned by his death be imputed to the elect. Thus Christ must not only die, but 'ever live to make intercession for us' (*MW*, 1: 80–2, 173; 2: 114–15; 4: 141; 13: 165, 223). He also pleads that the sins of believers committed after conversion be forgiven and the graces received by them 'be maintained and supplied'; for the final salvation of believers Christ must continually intercede for them (*MW*, 2: 116; 13: 258, 277, 326).

Law and Covenant

Bunyan developed his soteriology as it pertained to the human side of the process in two ways, both important to the theology of English Calvinists and Reformed theologians elsewhere: the covenant and the order of salvation, both of which have sequence, historical in the case of the first and theological-pastoral in the case of the second. One of his earliest theological treatises, *The Doctrine of the Law and Grace Unfolded* (1659), outlined his covenant theology. Bunyan thought most persons erroneously expected to be saved by obeying the laws of God because they were ignorant of the covenants. His prefatory epistle to *The Doctrine of the Law and Grace Unfolded* asserts that a proper understanding of the covenants would lead to salvation. All are either under the covenant of works, which requires complete obedience to the law of God, or the covenant of grace, under which all efforts at righteousness should be abandoned and the imputed righteousness of Christ accepted. Truly understanding the first is to be driven from the covenant of works to the covenant of grace, by becoming aware of one's sinful state—Bunyan said of his own case, God 'did open the glass of his Law to me', making sin 'manifest' and 'abound' (*MW*, 2: 157, 48). But the covenant of grace makes persons aware that there is a saviour: 'Reckon thyself […] the biggest sinner in the world', Bunyan exhorts his reader, 'let the guilt of it seize on thy heart, then also go in that case and condition to Jesus Christ, and plunge thyself into his Merits, and the vertue of his Blood; and after that thou shalt speak of the things of the Law, and of the Gospel, experimentally' (*MW*, 2: 14).

To be under the covenant of works is to be a sinner under the curse and wrath of God; to be under the covenant of grace is to be a forgiven sinner. The covenant of works can be recognized in the conscience, was delivered to Adam, and presented clearly in the Mosaic Law (*MW*, 2: 24–7). The covenant of grace did not first appear with Christ, but was prefigured by Adam, Noah, Abraham, and even Moses, and prophesied by Isaiah,

Jeremiah, and others, down to 'Old Simeon' (*MW*, 1: 33–5; 12: 252–54). This covenant is not a contract, but a testament, in which the God who promises it fulfils the conditions; there are no conditions on the human side. Under this covenant of grace, the redeemed are 'dead to the law' insofar as it is a covenant of works (*MW*, 4: 115). For Bunyan, 'the Christian's task throughout life is to inquire into himself and discern his relationship to the covenants'.[10] In affirming this two-covenant scheme Bunyan was following the path of high Calvinist theology; many Reformed theologians before and after Bunyan maintained a theology of one covenant, that of grace, administered differently under law and gospel.[11]

Bunyan further took the covenant of grace back into eternity in company with some Reformed theologians as a covenant between God the Father and God the Son, an agreement to save sinners by grace alone through atonement made before time, the contractual element being between Father and Son, as Christ agreed to make atonement for sinful humanity (*MW*, 2: 88, 90–1; 8: 245, 247; 13: 225, 324; *HW*, 32). Some Calvinist theologians thought of this as a third covenant, the covenant of redemption, distinct from the covenant of grace, but Bunyan seems to conflate the two.[12] This tripling, or doubling, of the covenants was important to high Calvinist theologians intent on maximizing grace, because it preserved grace from being legalized by connecting the moral law (natural and biblical) with a non-salvific covenant of works, thus further separating law and gospel. It matched double predestination with doubled covenants. But it also had the consequence of seeming to lead to Antinomian conclusions.[13]

A puzzling question remains: Does the law apply to believers who are under the covenant of grace? Reformed theologians taught three uses of the law: as civil restraint of evildoers; as begetting recognition of sin; and as a guide to believers. Did Bunyan acknowledge such a third use? And if not, was he Antinomian? Bunyan is tantalizing on this question as he frequently used the phrase 'the Law, as it is a Covenant of Works', the terminology of the Westminster and Savoy Confessions, and also referred to a 'new law', a 'law of grace', and 'the Law of Faith', that makes believers 'truly Holy in heart'. 'Justified persons are dead to the law, as a Covenant of Works', 'that they might live to another' (*MW*, 4: 78, 115, 120). There are enough references in Bunyan to something like the third use of the law to establish that he concurred with this Reformed theme. The law given at Sinai, which Bunyan usually considered as condemning, was in its 'second giving' (after the tablets had been broken and Moses returned with them again) coupled with

---

[10] Greaves, *Bunyan*, 97–111; Richard A. Muller, 'Covenant and Conscience in English Reformed Theology: Three Variations on a Seventeenth-Century Theme', *Westminster Theological Journal*, 42 (1980), 308–34 (325).

[11] Michael McGiffert, 'Grace and Works: The Rise and Division of Covenant Divinity in Elizabethan Puritanism', *Harvard Theological Review*, 75 (1982), 463–502.

[12] Pieter de Vries, *John Bunyan on the Order of Salvation* (New York: Peter Lang, 1994), 99; Greaves, *Bunyan*, 103–04.

[13] Michael McGiffert, 'The Perkinsian Moment of Federal Theology', *Calvin Theological Journal*, 29 (1994), 117–48 (135); Michael McGiffert, 'From Moses to Adam: The Making of the Covenant of Works', *Sixteenth Century Journal*, 19 (1988), 131–56 (153); McGiffert, 'Grace and Works', 465–68, 485.

the proclamation of God's grace so that it could be received 'after a gospel manner'. What had been the 'fiery law' that the sinner could not 'endure', the believer could now by the 'inward man delight and walk in', while unable to 'abide' the notion that it could 'take the work of its salvation out of Christs hand'. This is the moral law 'gospellized' as the 'Royal Law', the 'Perfect Law' of the Epistle of James, and is 'righteousness in the joy and peace of the holy Ghost', fulfilled by love, a rule of 'faith and moral precept', and 'directory' for those in Christ (*MW*, 2: 174, 155–56; 4: 115, 166–67; 12: 411).

Bunyan says that Christ has 'given us such Laws and Rules as are helpful and healthful to the soul' (*MW*, 13: 431). Thus the moral law as known by nature and given to Moses has been newly contextualized by the Gospel and the covenant of grace; but unbelievers are still and always under the covenant of works while believers, even in their obedience to God, are under the covenant of grace. Some of Bunyan's remarks suggest that given with the Gospel was a new and better law, not just a different understanding of the Mosaic Law—a point disputed by some Reformed theologians who understood the third use of the law to be recognition of the original natural and Mosaic Law as a pattern for believers under the covenant of grace. In giving a legal aspect to the covenant of grace Bunyan differed from many Antinomians, although some acknowledged a legal aspect if it was clear that this was an entirely different law, which Bunyan sometimes does imply. Richard Greaves's assertion that for Bunyan the covenant of grace had a legal aspect is perhaps even an understatement.[14]

Order of Salvation

Bunyan also articulated his soteriology as an order of salvation. Reformed theologians, bodies of divinity, and various confessions of faith differed in the sequence of this order, but generally they included the same basic elements. In his brief *A Confession of my Faith* under the title 'How Christ is Made Ours' Bunyan laid out these elements as justification, faith, election, effectual calling, repentance, and sanctification (*MW*, 4: 143–51). Other writings arranged the order differently, and developed additional elements of the order, including conversion after effectual calling and perseverance, assurance, and glorification after sanctification. Pieter de Vries has described the order of salvation as the 'Salient theme in Bunyan's theology', and has argued that *Grace Abounding* and *The Pilgrim's Progress* can be understood as orders of salvation in autobiographical and allegorical narrative. The former has been referred to as an 'actually lived' order of salvation.[15]

Bunyan's discussion of justification in *A Confession of my Faith* relates it to the imputation of Christ's righteousness to believers, for Bunyan the basis of both the covenant of

---

[14] Greaves, *Bunyan*, 111–16.
[15] De Vries, *Bunyan*, xi; Davies, *Graceful Reading*, 103.

grace and the order of salvation. Justification is first of all justification before God, who has imputed the righteousness of Christ to sinners, forgiving their sins, and pronouncing them just and 'dead to the Law'. One can be justified in this sense without knowing it (*MW*, 4: 115; 10: 194–95) and from eternity (*MW*, 4: 115; 8: 171; 10: 194–95). In 1653 Owen endorsed a book that taught justification from eternity, though he later stepped away from this view; many Antinomians held it, and moderate Calvinists like Richard Baxter strongly rejected it, regarding Bunyan as Antinomian.[16] But although speaking of justification from eternity, in keeping with his focus on the spiritual life Bunyan treated it more often as it was in the human 'Understanding and Conscience', where it followed faith and was the recognition of sinfulness and of the application of the imputation of Christ's righteousness to oneself (*MW*, 10: 195; 4: 144–45).[17]

Justification as it followed faith was, for Bunyan, justification by a faith that was neither notional nor historical, but a trusting and believing that one's sins are forgiven, not for any condition fulfilled on the believer's part, 'but meerly for the mans sake, that did hang on Mount Calvary, between two Theeves, some sixteen hundred years ago', thereby providing satisfaction for sins even before they had been committed. Thus the faith of believers acknowledges that they are 'accepted of him already', by Grace through faith, and is a gift of God's love, recognized by believers soon after they become aware of the wrath and condemnation of God under the curse of the law (*MW*, 2: 77–81; 12: 334; 4: 41).

In *A Confession of my Faith* Bunyan ended his discussion of faith by declaring that it was 'effectually wrought in none, but those which before the world, were appointed unto Glory', leading to consideration of God's eternal election of some to salvation. This places predestination in a soteriological context, as Calvin did in his *Institutes of the Christian Religion* (1536). In *A Mapp Shewing the Order and Causes of Salvation and Damnation* (?1663), which may have been influenced by William Perkins's *A Golden Chaine* (1590; 1591),[18] Bunyan placed predestination at the beginning of the order, though below the covenants of grace and works (*MW*, 4: 145; 12: 420–23). However, Bunyan did not emphasize predestination as much as many high Calvinists did, although it lurks in the background of his writings: the elect are chosen by God's grace; written in God's book; given in covenant by God the Father to the Son. In *The Holy War*, 'Election-doubters' were among the enemies of Mansoul (*MW*, 4: 15; 3: 273; 8: 245; *HW*, 186, 240–41).

Nonetheless, predestination was important to Bunyan as the guarantee of the freeness of God's grace. Furthermore, Bunyan seems to have held the more moderate, infralapsarian view of predestination whereby it followed (not temporally, but logically) the fall of Adam.[19] He commonly used the term 'election', the redemptive side of predestination and the phrase, characteristic of moderate Calvinists, of election in Christ (*MW*, 4: 75, 146; 12: 287). He also cautioned against worrying whether or not one was elected to salvation, offering the advice typical of Calvinist writers: ask whether you have faith in

---

[16] Greaves, *Glimpses*, 109, 286.
[17] Greaves, *Bunyan*, 81–2; Greaves, *Glimpses*, 532–33, 551; De Vries, *Bunyan*, 150–51.
[18] Greaves, *Glimpses*, 173.
[19] Greaves, *Glimpses*, 272; Greaves, *Bunyan*, 52.

Christ; if so, believe you are among the elect. Avoid 'prying overmuch into God's secret decrees' (*MW*, 2: 214–15; 5: 156).

Bunyan sometimes referred to reprobation, or predestination to damnation, the parallel term to election, but it is now generally agreed that the treatise *Reprobation Asserted* (?1674), once thought to be his, is not by him.[20] His allegory *The Life and Death of Mr. Badman* (1680) is often regarded as a narrative of reprobation, as *The Pilgrim's Progress* (1678; 1684) is of election. When Bunyan referred to reprobation, he did not discuss an eternal decree of damnation, but the sins of which the reprobate were guilty. Mr Badman is spoken of as choosing an evil life; reprobates 'sport themselves in sin' and are damned, not 'because they were not elected, but because they sinned'. 'No sin, but the sin of final impenitence, can prove a Man a Reprobate.' In hell they will see they deserved damnation, having refused every offer of grace (*MB*, 43–44; *MW*, 4: 138; 11: 57; 3: 281–82).

Bunyan's commitment to the doctrine of predestination stands alongside his frequent and urgent exhortations for sinners to 'awake' and 'Flye in all haste to Jesus Christ' (*MW*, 5: 120, 2: 17; 12: 348). It has been noted that there is in *The Pilgrim's Progress* the appearance of free choice even though Bunyan was a predestinarian.[21] *A Few Sighs from Hell* (1658) exhorted to belief and conversion while assuming predestination. At many points where Bunyan invites sinners to come to Christ he tips his hand to the predestinarianism that lurks within the offer. Richard Greaves has coined the term 'pastoral Arminianism' to describe this phenomenon in Bunyan,[22] but Bunyan is not exceptional among Reformed spiritual writers in this regard: apart from a few rigid supralapsarians and some hyper-Calvinists, works of Calvinist piety are filled with pleading requests for sinners to come to Christ. There is nothing un-Calvinist in this insofar as Reformed theologians thought that God worked through the 'means' of secondary causality, including the operation of the human will, as Bunyan noted when he stated that election does not pre-empt 'the means which are of God appointed to bring us to Christ' (*MW*, 4: 147). In his own case, Bunyan declared that 'The Lord won over my heart to some desire after the means', including hearing the Word preached (*MW*, 2: 157).

Bunyan, like other Calvinists, reconciled predestination and exhortations to choose Christ through an Augustinian understanding of freedom as voluntary necessity, God never forcing the will and the will freely acceding to its predestined end. Fallen humanity, in bondage to sin, freely wills sin; with the intervention of grace, by 'a voluntary act of the will' the believer wills what God wills (*MW*, 9: 124–25). The believer is urged to cry to God that he would 'inflame thy Will' with spiritual matters (*MW*, 5: 164). Bunyan in *A Discourse upon the Pharisee and the Publicane* (1685) maintained that fallen humanity can not only choose and do evil, but also will salvation, with power to pursue the will, but only in the wrong way of the covenant of works, not by faith in Christ. Thus persons have will and power to become self-righteous Pharisees, but not to enter into the 'Mysteries of the Gospel' without the gift of grace. The point was repeated

---

[20] Greaves, *Glimpses*, 617.
[21] Hill, *Bunyan*, 209; Furlong, *Puritan's Progress*, 144.
[22] Greaves, *Glimpses*, 110.

in the posthumous *Mr. John Bunyan's Last Sermon* (1689) where he denied he was a 'Free-willer' but argued that 'Carnal Men' have both a 'Will to be Vile' and a 'Will to be Saved'—even if fruitless (*MW*, 10: 162–63; 12: 88). Thus in Bunyan's theology there is a dialectical relationship between absolute divine decree and the voluntary action of the human will.

In *Come, & Welcome, to Jesus Christ* (1678), willing, choosing, and striving are conformed to God's electing grace. Those who experience their will 'coming' to Christ should recognize it as both God's work within them and also their own striving, however feebly. In *The Strait Gate* (1676) Bunyan repeats the verb 'strive' as he exhorts his readers to enter the narrow gate of salvation (*MW*, 8: 255, 273, 283, 292, 352; 5: 76). In *The Heavenly Foot-man* (1698) he urges those coming to Christ to cast off slothfulness and run the race of salvation: 'They that will have Heaven, they must run for it' (*MW*, 5: 140, 148, 150). Bunyan insisted that such exhortations were for sinners, including thieves and murderers (*MW*, 8: 295)—no amount of self-righteous respectability privileged those summoned to faith; on the contrary self-righteousness is the greatest barrier to faith, whereas recognition of flagitious wickedness brings one closer to faith. This is the theme of *A Discourse upon the Pharisee and the Publicane*, in which the Publican is 'a notorious sinner' while the Pharisee appeared to be 'very good' (*MW*, 10: 122–23), and it is apparent too in Bunyan's title *Good News for the Vilest of Men* (1688), where he invites 'the worst to come to Christ', for 'I have been Vile myself, but have obtained Mercy' (*MW*, 11: 7). For Bunyan, a 'broken heart prizes Christ' (*MW*, 12: 60), and is more likely found among the poor than the rich (*MW*, 5: 177). One of Bunyan's deepest grievances against Edward Fowler was Fowler's claim that 'It is not possible a Wicked Man should have God's Pardon', which is precisely what Bunyan claimed the Gospel was all about (*MW*, 4: 69).

In *A Confession of my Faith* Bunyan placed effectual calling after election, defining it as the work of the Holy Spirit, who accompanies the gospel with the power of 'electing love' by 'quickening' and 'awakening' the soul and adopting the believer as a child of God. This calling 'implants' repentance as a response to the gospel, and produces faith, hope, and love. By repentance, the believer turns his heart to 'God in Christ' and away from sin and the devil (*MW*, 4: 147–50; 8: 205; 7: 204). Although not ordinarily items in the order of salvation but steps in the morphology of the spiritual life, conversion and union with Christ follow effectual calling and repentance. One of the most important developments in Puritan spirituality was a focus on the believer's experience of conversion that could be identified as to time and place, and understood as the sinner's reception of a new heart and new birth (*MW*, 1: 91; 4: 30; 2: 242; 8: 192; 10: 69; 12: 89). Conversion united the believer's soul with Christ in a mystical union about which Bunyan, like other Puritan authors, waxed rapturous (*MW*, 2: 242; 4: 35, 64, 140). Bunyan observed of himself that 'God led me into something of the mystery of union with Christ' (*GA*, 86).

Effectual calling, according to Bunyan's *A Confession of my Faith* (*MW*, 4: 111), carried the promise of sanctification, giving 'sanctifying vertue' and 'a principle of Grace' to the redeemed soul. Sometimes he spoke of this principle as the Holy Spirit 'in the hearts of the converted' (*MW*, 4: 94, 149; 10: 181; 8: 84). Sanctification entailed holiness of life produced by grace and made believers 'truly Holy in heart' (*MW*, 4: 120). This holiness was not the mere morality proclaimed by his opponent Fowler, which Bunyan thought no better than that of heathen philosophers (*MW*, 3: 15; 13: 79–80, 87; 4: 120); the true holiness of believers in Christ went beyond natural goodness, and was one of the purposes of God's election of the redeemed and of Christ's dying for them (*MW*, 4: 63). But the holiness of believers did not mean they were free of sin (*MW*, 9: 292–93; 12: 143). Bunyan found comfort in recalling that great saints in the Bible, such as David and Solomon, were not without sin (*MW*, 11: 28). For Bunyan, 'sinful infirmities' even attended the godly in their good works (*MW*, 12: 387).

These good works, according to Bunyan, flowed from the faith, sanctification, and holiness of the redeemed (*MW*, 12: 371–72). Indeed, 'whoever pretends to Sanctification, if he shews not the Fruits thereof by a Holy Life' is deceived (*MW*, 13: 115). Those who professed faith but had no good works declared they were children of the devil (*MW*, 9: 338). The good works of the redeemed also show their redemption to others (*MW*, 9: 251). Among these good works Bunyan included compassion for the poor and 'castout', and generosity in 'Alms-giving' (*MW*, 12: 384; 13: 279). Believers should remember that they were not born to serve themselves, but to have hearts 'tenderly affected with the welfare and prosperity of all things' and that 'seek the good of all' (*MW*, 12: 384–85; 13: 279; 10: 5). This ruled out extreme Antinomians who rejected emphasis on good works as dark and legal. Bunyan thought those who maintained that 'the Doctrine of the Gospel is a licentious Doctrine' 'have not tasted of the vertue of the Blood of Jesus Christ' nor known his love, but turn the grace of God into 'wantonness' (*MW*, 2: 200; 7: 208). Bunyan's insistence that in heavenly beatitude the saints will be rewarded proportionately for their good works might also be seen as separating him from the Antinomian impulse (*MW*, 3: 57; 12: 386–90).

In the order of salvation, perseverance followed sanctification, by which believers were protected by God from falling away. Bunyan thought perseverance to the end was what salvation meant (*MW*, 13: 267; *HW*, 246). Thus, however much the world and the devil worked against them, those for whom Christ shed his blood have been predestined, justified, and shall be preserved to glorification (*MW*, 2: 199). Glorification, or the heavenly rest, brought the order of salvation to its final point. Just as believers were to glorify and enjoy God in their lives, in the heavenly rest they will be glorified and always have 'a burning flame of love to God and his Son Jesus Christ' (*MW*, 8: 84, 180). There believers will be rewarded and enthroned (*MW*, 3: 237, 242; 13: 283). Puritan piety stressed heavenly mindedness as an aspect of the devout life, and Bunyan used the expression and encouraged the godly to desire heaven (*MW*, 3: 280; 13: 17–18, 136).

Divine Grace was, for Bunyan, the moving force behind the steps of the order of salvation. Grace alone saves: it chooses, justifies, calls, sanctifies, preserves, and brings to glory (*MW*, 13: 187; 3: 179–80). Bunyan defined grace as 'the free love of God in Christ to sinners, by vertue of the new Covenant, in delivering them from the power of sin, from the curse and condemning power of the Old Covenant' (*MW*, 2: 84–5), and considered it rooted in the love of God, a love 'essential' to the divine being and quite beyond mere human love (*MW*, 8: 77; 13: 249, 366–67). This 'amazing Grace' (*MW*, 11: 20;

HW, 45) flowed from the Triune God through atonement and imputation and the steps of the order of salvation. Bunyan followed Protestant theology in defining grace as both forensic, a declaration of free pardon, and an animating principle of regeneration from which good works flowed (*MW*, 3: 11, 53). As Greaves has asserted, 'Grace is the keystone of Bunyan's theology';[23] but to grace 'comfort' should be added, as Bunyan found comfort in the message of salvation by grace alone, and invited others to partake of that comfort.

That Bunyan presented the Christian faith as comforting brings the thread of this chapter back to Coleridge's remark about Jeremy Taylor. As Coleridge recognized, Arminianism, or any theology that required conditions, however minimal, to be fulfilled by the believer, cannot comfort those who have experienced Bunyan's kind of despairing helplessness. This puts Bunyan's opponents in perspective: the reason for attacking Fowler, Arminians, Quakers, Socinians, Roman Catholics, and others was that he felt they denied comfort to helpless sinners. This also puts his theological emphases in perspective: election to eternal life apart from merit renders predestination, often tagged as anything but comforting, an ultimately comforting doctrine, grounding salvation in an eternal gift of God, as are justification by the imputation of Christ's righteousness, the belief that Christ at the right hand of the Father continually intercedes for believers (*MW*, 13: 265), and the maximization of the sufferings of a very human as well as divine Christ for sinners in an atoning death. Having arrived at the understanding that salvation was by grace, and that its acceptance rather than the fulfilling of any conditions was the gospel, Bunyan aimed to dispense to others the comfort he found in this doctrine. He found the parable of the Pharisee and the Publican 'very comfortable' (*MW*, 10: 113–14) and hoped that the 'fancies' of *The Pilgrim's Progress* might be '*to the Helpless, Comforters*' (*PP*, 7). The gospel, Bunyan declared, is 'Glad Tidings of good things' (*MW*, 4: 81).

Nothing was more central to comfort in the daily life of believers than achieving assurance of salvation. The search for assurance as developed by many Puritans has been regarded as a return to legalistic introspection and a departure from the earlier Reformation Protestant view that assurance came primarily simply through believing.[24] Bunyan reverted to that earlier stance that assurance was a concomitant of faith, possible only for those who have been effectually called and have confidence in the covenant of grace (*MW*, 2: 147, 186, 215; 3: xxi, 11; 11: 88–9).[25] His fellow travelling with some Antinomians on this point is an indication that he, like they, was fearful that a punctilious search for assurance might relapse to dependence on good works for justification. Thus for all Bunyan's stress on sanctification and good works, he did not treat these

---

[23] Greaves, *Glimpses*, 582.

[24] Dwight Bozeman, *The Precisianist Strain: Disciplinary Religion and Antinomian Backlash in Puritanism to 1638* (Chapel Hill: University of North Carolina Press, 2004), 125, 139; Michael P. Winship, 'Weak Christians, Backsliders, and Carnal Gospelers: Assurance of Salvation and the Pastoral Origins of Puritan Practical Divinity in the 1580s', *Church History*, 70 (2001), 462–81.

[25] Davies, *Graceful Reading*, 28; De Vries, *Bunyan*, 193–98.

as sources of assurance, although he conceded that, according to James 2:18, while justification before God was by grace alone, there was a justification before men and women by works (*MW*, 3: 9). Bunyan did think that one might find assurance in the desire to do good works and in the pleasure the 'Soul finds in God', but these are assurances through faith rather than works (*MW*, 13: 124–26). However, assurance, an inner conscious witness of the Holy Spirit, might not be given immediately with faith—those feeble in faith might still have many doubts (*MW*, 10: 182–83).

Bunyan's Ecclesiology

Bunyan's ideas about church, worship, and sacraments combined his commitment to a religion of grace with his sectarian Puritan/Dissenter outlook. The visible church should be a local and voluntary community of believers who desired to walk together in 'church-fellowship' (*MW*, 4: 164; 13: 130). The requirement for acceptance into fellowship was 'a discovery' of someone's faith and holiness, only the profane being excluded as a 'mixed communion polluteth the ordinances of God'. It cannot be known who might be a hypocrite and one should not speculate concerning who was elected (*MW*, 4: 154, 157, 162). The church is for the comfort of sinners, a 'Hospital of sick, wounded, and afflicted People, with Christ as physician' (*MW*, 12: 336).

According to Bunyan, the godly should gather regularly for worship, but to insist on any particular day as essential such as the emergent Seventh-Day Baptists did, was unwarranted legalism, though strong reasons suggested the appropriateness of the first day of the week (*MW*, 4: 335–40, 361–63). Christ appointed two 'shadowish, or figurative ordinances', water baptism and the supper of the Lord, both of which were aids of faith useful to a congregation, and 'love-tokens' of God, but not among the 'fundamentals of our Christianity' (*MW*, 4: 160, 163). Bunyan rejected the usual Protestant parallel of baptism with circumcision (*MW*, 4: 163) as an entry into the community of faith, and therefore rejected the connection of baptism and covenant, a commonplace of Reformed theology. 'Christ is my righteousness, not water', he declared, and approved admittance to church fellowship without baptism—the Lord's Supper, initiated by Christ, was a duty more incumbent upon the church (*MW*, 4: 215, 202–03).

Bunyan wrote occasionally of feeding on Christ and of the water of grace washing away sin, but context shows these remarks unrelated to sacraments (*MW*, 7: 187; 2: 215). Attempts to interpret Bunyan as more traditionally sacramental overlook his ties to the radical Reformation.[26] He joined and eventually led the Bedford meeting, which, under Gifford, practised adult believers' baptism, but did not require it, a position attacked by strict Baptists.[27] In *Peaceable Principles and True* (1674) Bunyan rejected such 'factious'

---

[26] Johnson, *Prisoner*, 156–57.
[27] Greaves, *Glimpses*, 273–75; Joseph D. Ban, 'Was John Bunyan a Baptist?', *BQ*, 30 (1984), 367–76.

titles as 'Anabaptist, Independents, Presbyterians' (*MW*, 4: 270). He even sounded like the Quakers when he declared that the heart of baptism is spiritual belief in Christ, water being only 'the outward shew' (*MW*, 4: 171–72). Bunyan's reservations about these rites were based on their potential for legalism and works-righteousness, his reason also for his bitter strictures against the clergy and worship of the Church of England, which he had, according to *Grace Abounding*, once tried as a route to salvation, only to find a soul-destroying legalism like that of the Pharisee in the parable (*MW*, 2: 239, 247, 249, 273; 10: 143).

Bunyan was also akin to the radical Reformation in his conviction that the true church was a suffering church (*MW*, 10: 93–4; 13: 494), an opinion rooted in his reading of Foxe and the precarious situation of Bunyan and his fellow worshippers, but also a retrieval of the tradition of Waldensians and Anabaptists. Like other Protestants, he thought the 'primitive church' had fallen into the apostasy of the 'Romish Babel' (*MW*, 12: 275–77). Like many advanced Puritans, he thought that later believers saw with greater clarity than had those during the earlier Reformation (*MW*, 3: 154). Bunyan sometimes vented apocalyptic and millenarian hopes like those of radicals on the Puritan fringe such as the Fifth Monarchists, but he did not favour revolutionary plots or violence against the government. He found comfort for believers in his eschatological hope for the end of persecution and the punishment of persecutors (*MW*, 13: 494, 499).[28]

Conclusions

A consistent, identifiable, and fairly sophisticated Reformed or Calvinist theology focused on soteriology and practical piety undergirds Bunyan's writings, constituting an operative, if not systematic, body of divinity upon which he drew as occasion warranted. His mixture of doctrine and spirituality was characteristic of Puritan and Dissenter sermons and treatises. His theology reflected the wider heritage of the Calvinist tradition as well as some of the special emphases of English Puritan spiritual and doctrinal instruction as they had developed by his time. Bunyan reveals a theological acumen drawn from the Dissenting Calvinist world he inhabited. This does not mean he either read or was interested in Calvin, although the absence of references to Calvin is not particularly significant: few seventeenth-century Calvinists cited Calvin with any frequency. He can also be identified as an evangelical Calvinist intent on summoning sinners to faith, conversion, and a holy life by insisting that there was hope for them if they acknowledged their sin and relied on God's grace alone. He strove to convey comfort and assurance to troubled believers so that they might avoid the spiritual pitfalls into which he had himself fallen. His relatively moderate tone on predestination reflected an

---

[28] Greaves, *Glimpses*, 90–93, 137–39, 558–59; Mullett, *Bunyan in Context*, 92.

eagerness to call to conversion, as did his use of that doctrine to comfort believers that they were safely in God's hands.

Other aspects of his theology, if not his infralapsarian treatment of predestination, suggest his commitment to high Calvinism of the sort represented by John Owen and Thomas Goodwin. Like them he emphasized a double covenant theology and a covenant of redemption sealed in eternity, the extremity of the sufferings of Christ in his atoning death, including their identity with those of damned sinners, the imputation of Christ's righteousness to sinners, and holiness as possible only by grace, as distinct from natural virtue. Bunyan as a high Calvinist could affirm that 'we do nothing for salvation' (*MW*, 2: 82). But at two points Bunyan stepped away from the most extreme forms of Calvinism. By the end of his career a hyper-Calvinism that rejected unguarded calls to sinners to repent as a consequence of their predestinarianism had appeared. Bunyan was far from this, with his repeated invitations to sinners to believe. Antinomian Calvinists earlier in the century in England had protested against legalism and in a few respects Bunyan agreed with them: he accepted justification from eternity, thought that God did not see sin in believers, and did not rely on good works for assurance of salvation. But at crucial points Bunyan veered away from Antinomianism: cautious in dealing with the place of obedience to the law in believers, he nonetheless accepted a version of the third use of the law and was adamantly opposed to those who declared that true believers might sin without restraint, a view perhaps held by Ranters, but not by Calvinistic Antinomians.[29]

Antinomianism raises the question of Bunyan's relation to Luther, whose repudiation of the law inspired English Antinomians such as John Eaton and Tobias Crisp. Bunyan's reading of Luther—whose commentary on Galatians he valued above all other books except the Bible—was a key moment in his religious understanding (*GA*, 40–1). However, to describe Bunyan as Lutheran in his theology is an exaggeration: Luther inspired him and abetted his escape from legalism, but, immersed as he was in the theology of the Bedford meeting and of his Puritan and Dissenting heritage, Bunyan read Luther in a Calvinist context and put the inspiration he received from him at the service of a high Calvinist double-covenant theology.[30] Luther did not elaborate a covenant theology, and far from agreeing with Luther that the biblical book of James was an 'epistle of straw', Bunyan thought it laid out the godly life as a 'Perfect Law' (*MW*, 4: 166).

Description of Bunyan's theology enables his placement in the ecclesiastical setting of later seventeenth-century England, although he warned against party labels, even 'Anabaptist', though acknowledging 'I go under that name myself' (*MW*, 5: 153). Bunyan recognized his roots in the earlier Puritans, considering that the name the 'godly' went by 'in times past' (*MB*, 144). Among the various Dissenting descendants

---

[29] Greaves, *Bunyan*, 158; Greaves, *Glimpses*, 532–33; Davies, *Graceful Reading*, 30–4; Roger Pooley, 'Bunyan and the Antinomians', in Vera J. Camden (ed.), *The Political Progress of John Bunyan* (Stanford, CA: Stanford University Press, 2008), 120–34; De Vries, *Bunyan*, 160.

[30] Vera J. Camden, '"Most Fit for a Wounded Conscience": The Place of Luther's Commentary on Galatians in *Grace Abounding*', *Renaissance Quarterly*, 50 (1997), 819–49.

of the earlier Puritans Bunyan straddled the boundary separating the Independents (Congregationalists) from the Particular, or Calvinistic, Baptists, two parties who blended high Calvinist theology and warm, grace-centred piety, and who were also committed to a separatist model of the church as a gathered community. This was precisely where the Bedford meeting stood.[31] He was critical both of stricter Baptists and of moderate Presbyterians, such as Baxter (*MW*, 4: 284), and, aware that the Church of England had once been closer to his own theology, scorned its apologist Fowler for departing from the Thirty-Nine Articles (*MW*, 4: 123). With the 'Popish Plot' and the accession of James II, Bunyan feared the danger of Roman Catholicism. He deplored Socinianism as a departure from true Christianity and expressed alarm at the increasing atheism and godlessness of his time (*MW*, 4: 120; 10: 135; *HW*, 118; *MB*, 85–6). As such, Bunyan's literary works can only be understood fully in the light of his theology and religious context.

Suggested Reading

Davies, Michael, *Graceful Reading: Theology and Narrative in the Works of John Bunyan* (Oxford: Oxford University Press, 2002).
de Vries, Pieter, *John Bunyan on the Order of Salvation* (New York: Peter Lang, 1994).
Furlong, Monica, *Puritan's Progress: A Study of John Bunyan* (London: Hodder & Stoughton, 1975).
Greaves, Richard L., *John Bunyan* (Grand Rapids, MI: Eerdmans, 1969).
Greaves, Richard L., *Glimpses of Glory: John Bunyan and English Dissent* (Stanford, CA: Stanford University Press, 2002).
Johnson, Galen K., *Prisoner of Conscience: John Bunyan on Self, Community and Christian Faith* (Carlisle: Paternoster Press, 2003).
Mullett, Michael A., *John Bunyan in Context* (Keele: Keele University Press, 1996).
Wallace, Dewey D., Jr, *Puritans and Predestination: Grace in English Protestant Theology, 1525–1695* (Chapel Hill: University of North Carolina Press, 1982).

---

[31] Bremer, *Congregational Communion*, 238–39.

CHAPTER 5

BUNYAN AND THE WORD

ALISON SEARLE

IN a very real sense one can claim that the Bible authored the convicted, converted, imprisoned, and impassioned pastor John Bunyan and all his writings in numerous genres. Bunyan's emphasis on the centrality of Scripture in convincing him of sin, awakening his soul, and reconstructing his entire consciousness through the saving and sanctifying work of the Holy Spirit, was far from unique in seventeenth-century England. It is entirely typical of the Puritanism that was politically dominant during the Commonwealth and which formed a powerful, but suppressed, opposition subculture following the Restoration of the monarchy (1660) and the Act of Uniformity (1662). This chapter traces the diverse ways in which John Bunyan engaged with Scripture and its impact upon his life and writings. I will first examine the manner in which he read the Bible: understanding Bunyan's scriptural hermeneutic is crucial to coming to terms with his request that readers of *The Pilgrim's Progress* lay the book together with their head and heart. Secondly, I will consider how Bunyan appropriates and is appropriated by Scripture as he writes across a variety of genres, including, for example, his use of typology, allusion, prescription, admonition, eschatology, proverbs, prophecy, metaphor, and emblems. Whilst many of these methods of engaging with Scripture are characteristic of Protestants of the hotter sort, Bunyan's intense imagination, pithy prose style, and effectiveness as a preacher distinguish his writings in quality, though not in kind, from most of those produced by his fellow Nonconformists. I will focus on two key themes—marriage and pilgrimage—in order to explore the various ways Bunyan uses the Bible in his fictional writings, sermons, letters, and theological works (didactic and controversial).

How Bunyan Read the Bible

Bunyan offers a distinctively biblical account of his inspiration as an author in the 'Apology' that prefaces *The Pilgrim's Progress, Part I* (1678). As he was writing of '*the*

Way' he '[f]ell suddenly into an Allegory' and 'having now my Method by the end; / Still as I pull'd it came; and so I penned / It down' (PP, 1–2). Envisaging himself as a passive receptacle he notes that his method is modelled on Scripture: the Old Testament set forth God's laws in '*Types, Shadows and Metaphors*'; the prophets used '*Metaphors / To set forth Truth*'; so did '*Christ, his Apostles too*' (PP, 4). Bunyan's experience of passive reception as a writer becomes the paradigm for his ideal reader and leads him to make a bold claim for the authority of his own words: '*Would'st read thy self* [...] *know whether thou art blest or not* [...]? *O then come hither, / And lay my Book, thy Head and Heart together*' (PP, 7). Bunyan did not reach this position with ease; his retrospective account of his hard-won progress towards this assumption of pastoral authority is provided in his autobiography *Grace Abounding to the Chief of Sinners* (1666). Specifically addressed to those whom 'God hath counted him worthy to beget to Faith, by his Ministry in the Word', Bunyan—like his biblical predecessors Samson, Moses, David, and Paul—relates '*the very beginnings of Grace*' in his own soul (GA, 2–3). He urges them:

> *Remember also the Word, the Word, I say, upon which the Lord hath caused you to hope: If you have sinned against light; if you are tempted to blaspheme; if you are down in despair, if you think God fights against you, or if heaven is hid from your eyes; remember 'twas thus with your father*, but out of them all the Lord delivered me. (GA, 3)

Here he outlines the pain and cost of his own struggle to embody a hermeneutic that enabled him to apply Scripture positively, rather than corrosively, to his soul. This also underwrites the key turn in his spiritual experience (a process that took several years)—from introspection to pastoral initiative—and which is mirrored in the two parts of *The Pilgrim's Progress*.

The changing contours of John Bunyan's approach to the written Word of God are vividly set out in his autobiography. As he began to awaken to the concerns of religion, though not of true sanctifying grace, Bunyan records:

> I fell in company with one poor man that made profession of Religion; who, as I then thought, did talk pleasantly of the Scriptures, and of the matters of Religion: wherefore falling into some love and liking to what he said, I betook me to my Bible, and began to take great pleasure in reading, but especially with the historical part thereof: for, as for *Pauls* Epistles, and Scriptures of that nature, I could not away with them, being as yet but ignorant either of the corruptions of my nature, or of the want and worth of Jesus Christ to save me. (GA, 12)

However, when Bunyan overheard the conversation of 'three or four poor women' in Bedford, who 'spake as if joy did make them speak [...] with such pleasantness of Scripture language, and with such appearance of grace in all they said, that they were to me as if they had found a new world', he realized that there was something missing in his own experience of reading Scripture (GA, 14–15). Being providentially kept, as he records it, from the errors of the Ranters, he notes: 'The Bible was precious to me in those days' (*GA*, 17). Bunyan

> began to look into the Bible with new eyes, and read as I never did before; and especially the Epistles of the Apostle S. *Paul* were sweet and pleasant to me: and indeed, I was then never out of the Bible, either by reading or meditation, still crying out to God, that I might know the truth, and way to Heaven and Glory. (*GA*, 17)

Despite the newly experimental quality of his reading experience, and his growing taste for the letters of Paul, Bunyan had not developed a comprehensive hermeneutic that enabled him to interpret Scripture as a whole. Rather, he was battered by apparently conflicting verses, incapable of drawing any certain conclusions from the nature of his own experience: Was his faith in Christ genuine? Did he pray correctly? Was he elected to salvation? Had the day of grace passed him by? Had he committed the unpardonable sin? However, Bunyan gradually gained a greater knowledge of Scripture and a more personal experience of God's love; he also situated himself in a community of like-minded readers. As he recounts it, this enabled him to focus more on the beauty and sufficiency of Jesus Christ. He was less vulnerable to the threatening and interpretative challenges of individual texts which seized upon him, sending him into ecstasy or despair. Bunyan notes, for example, how an unknown verse 'fell with weight upon my spirit, *Look at the generations of old, and see, did ever any trust in God and were confounded?*' This encourages him and he decides to '*Begin at the beginning of Genesis, and read to the end of the Revelations, and see if* [he] *can find that there was any that ever trusted in the Lord, and was Confounded.*' He goes to his Bible and finds 'it [...] so fresh [...] that I was as if it talked with me'. Ironically, though he 'continued above a year', he could not find the relevant verse until 'casting my eye into the Apocrypha-Books, I found it in *Ecclesiasticus* 2. 10'. He had learnt, however, to read individual verses in their specific context and interpret them in the light of the Bible's overarching storyline.

Bunyan was daunted to discover, in this instance, that his key verse was in an apocryphal, rather than canonical, book of the Bible. However, he explains that

> by this time I had got more experience of the love and kindness of God, it troubled me the less; especially when I considered, that though it was not in those Texts that we call holy and Canonical, yet forasmuch as this sentence was the sum and substance of many of the promises, it was my duty to take the comfort of it, and I bless God for that word, for it was of God to me. (*GA*, 21–2)

Driven by his desperate sense of guilt and unsettled by the many different ways in which Scripture was read in the 1650s by religious radicals, such as the Quakers and Ranters, Bunyan undertook a 'narrow search of the Scriptures'. '[T]hrough their light and testimony', he was 'not only enlightened, but greatly confirmed and comforted in the truth'. He learnt to see in the Bible 'the blood of Christ' which 'again, and again, and again' took off his guilt 'sweetly, according to the Scriptures' (*GA*, 39).

This hard-won understanding of how to read the Bible informed Bunyan's pastoral care, the fictional worlds he imagined, his evangelical fervency, and didactic instruction: it is set out at length in his exegesis of the parable of Dives and Lazarus in *A Few Sighs from Hell* (1658; *MW*, 1: 348–82). Michael Davies has observed:

> The kind of hermeneutics that Bunyan brings to Scripture acts as a blueprint for his reading of all things (and for our reading of his texts) because, in holding the key to the promises of salvation, it demands something deeply unworldly, experiential, and faithful from one's understanding […]. The principal means by which Bunyan enacts this kind of a spiritual hermeneutics is through elaborate typological readings of Old Testament passages and events or, in the case of *Solomon's Temple Spiritualized* (1688), even whole buildings and objects.[1]

Though he provides a colourful and highly individualistic dramatization of his encounter with Scripture, Bunyan's way of reading was deeply influenced by the historical development of hermeneutics in the various ecclesiastical traditions of Western Christendom. Though there was a movement away from the fourfold system of biblical exegesis that had prevailed during the medieval period as a result of the sixteenth-century Protestant Reformation, in favour of the literal and historical meaning of the text, and though the Puritans, including Bunyan, were deeply indebted to the scriptural hermeneutic outlined by the likes of John Wyclif, Martin Luther, and John Calvin, their strong predilection towards typology renders the distinction—between Catholic and Protestant ways of reading Scripture—somewhat tenuous.

Typology views a person, object, or event outlined in Old Testament history as a prefiguring of some person or thing revealed in the new dispensation inaugurated by the gospel. Writers and preachers in the New Testament initiated this approach to the Old Testament Scriptures. Jesus, for example, identifies John the Baptist as the Elijah that was to come (Matthew 11:13–14); the image of the rough and strident Israelite prophet thus becomes key to the gospel definition of John. The Apostle Paul likewise articulates this hermeneutic when writing to the church at Corinth about the historical record of God's dealings with the Israelites: 'Now all these things happened unto them for ensamples: and they are written for our admonition, upon whom the ends of the world are come' (1 Corinthians 10:11). Typology, as Davies notes, is a peculiarly adaptable method of reading, and the Puritans, including Bunyan, applied scriptural events in this way in order to interpret their own individual experience, that of their Church, and their nation (England, Ireland, Scotland, and the North American colonies in particular). Its attraction for radical Protestants, such as Bunyan, was twofold: there was scriptural precedent for the practice; and it enabled all events, personal and corporate, to be understood as chapters unfolding within the metanarrative recorded in the Bible.

---

[1] Michael Davies, *Graceful Reading: Theology and Narrative in the Works of John Bunyan* (Oxford: Oxford University Press, 2002), 70–2.

Bunyan frequently claimed that the Bible was the sole source of his authority, inspiration, and instruction as a pastor, writer, and theologian. He states, for instance, in *The Doctrine of the Law and Grace Unfolded* (1659):

> I never went to School to *Aristotle* or *Plato*, but was brought up at my fathers house, in a very mean condition [...]. But if thou do finde a parcel of plain, yet sound, true, and home sayings, attribute that to the Lord Jesus, his gifts and abilities, which he hath bestowed upon such a poor Creature, as I am, and have been. (*MW*, 2: 16)

He writes similarly in 1675: '*I have not writ at venture, nor borrowed my Doctrine from Libraries. I depend upon the sayings of no man: I found it in the Scriptures of Truth, among the true sayings of God*' (*MW*, 8: 51). His claim is somewhat tendentious. Though Bunyan never attended university, his writings evidence his reading of commentaries and controversial works by earlier theologians, such as Martin Luther, and his contemporaries, like Edward Fowler. However, there is no doubt that it was Bunyan's vivid and visceral engagement with Scripture that primarily shaped his imagination and worldview as a whole. Richard Greaves has demonstrated that Bunyan accessed the Bible in several English translations, including the Authorized and Geneva Bibles: 'the extensive marginalia in the latter provided a running commentary in its own right'. Greaves speculates that Bunyan's 'pronounced interest in typology' meant that he had probably read works by William Guild, Thomas Taylor, or John Everard on the subject.[2]

Produced by English Protestants who had fled to Switzerland to escape persecution, the Geneva Bible (1560) was respected for its excellent scholarship, but Elizabeth I and James I regarded its paratextual material as objectionable, even inflammatory. Despite this, it continued to be the translation of choice for several generations of English Protestants. It was eventually overtaken in popular usage by the version that has come to be known as the King James Bible, because it was translated by a team of scholars during the reign of James I and first published in 1611. The King James Bible was printed without the marginalia included in the Geneva Bible and was placed in all English parishes in an attempt to foster uniformity within the state church. Despite being familiar with several versions, as Greaves indicates, scholarly consensus suggests that the King James Bible was the biblical text that Bunyan cites most often,[3] though he definitely knew and referred to the Geneva Bible as well (*MW*, 12: xxxvi–vii; 13: 533–34). Bunyan was a biblical literalist and, to some extent, an autodidact, but his reading of Scripture was inevitably informed by the work of various translators, theologians, and commentators.

---

[2] Greaves, *Glimpses*, 604–05. See also Chapter 6 in this volume.

[3] Hannibal Hamlin, 'Bunyan's Biblical Progresses', in Hannibal Hamlin and Norman W. Jones (eds.), *The King James Bible after 400 Years* (Cambridge: Cambridge University Press, 2010), 202–18 (212); Michael Davies, 'The Wilderness of the Word: John Bunyan and the Book in Christian's Hand', *BS*, 15 (2011), 26–52; W. R. Owens, 'John Bunyan and the Bible', in Anne Dunan-Page (ed.), *The Cambridge Companion to Bunyan* (Cambridge: Cambridge University Press, 2010), 39–50.

Marriage

Bunyan's exegetical and symbolic uses of marriage demonstrate the complexity of his approach to Scripture.[4] It can function, for example, in an eschatological sense, as in the marriage supper of the Lamb (Revelation 21); in a typological sense, representing God's relationship with Israel, or the Church's relationship with Christ; in a prescriptive and admonitory sense, as illustrated by the cases of conscience and discipline that are recorded in the Bedford Church Book; or in an illustrative, even proverbial, sense, as Mr Badman's two marriages and the discussion of Mercie's relationship with Mr Brisk in *The Pilgrim's Progress, Part II* (1684) demonstrate. I will briefly examine some of the uses of marriage in Bunyan's writings across a variety of genres, before focusing on his detailed fictional treatment of marriage in *The Life and Death of Mr. Badman* (1680).

In *The Advocateship of Jesus Christ* (1688) Bunyan extends Paul's allegorical use of marriage—illustrating the difference between the Old and New Covenants, or Law and Grace (Romans 7:1–4)—to demonstrate the third privilege of the office of Jesus Christ as the believer's advocate, namely, that Satan cannot plead their former guilt against them. For, as 'a Woman, a Widow, that oweth a Sum of Money', cannot be prosecuted for debt if she remarries, because 'she is not who she was, she is delivered from that State by her Marriage', so the believer is delivered by Christ from 'what the Law can claim' (*MW*, 11: 163). In *Christian Behaviour* (1663), Bunyan interrogates his reader at one point—'Hast thou a Wife?' If so, Bunyan asks, is she one who believes, or not? If she is a true Christian, the husband is required to thank God for her (Proverbs 12:4; 31:10; 1 Corinthians 11:7). He is to love her both as his own flesh (Ephesians 5:29) and as a fellow heir of the kingdom of heaven (1 Peter 3:7). Finally, in addition to these prescriptive elements, the believing couple are to image forth the relationship between Christ and the Church (Ephesians 5:28, 29), which Bunyan underscores by referring to '*Solomon* and *Pharaoh*'s Daughter', who 'had the art of thus doing, as you may see in the Book of *Canticles*'. If a woman is not a believer, however, her husband is to walk lovingly with her and seek to save her soul (*MW*, 3: 26–8).

In *Come, & Welcome, to Jesus Christ* (1678) Bunyan uses marriage analogically. Just as a man gives his daughter, 'first in order to marriage, and this respects the time past; and he giveth her again on the day appointed, in marriage', so the Father gave all the elect to Jesus 'before the world was' and 'he giveth them again to him, in the day of their espousals' (*MW*, 8: 248). Bunyan's biblical justification for this analogical reading is

---

[4] It is important to note the way Bunyan used early modern English translations of the Hebrew and Greek Scriptures to construct his understanding of marriage. Naomi Tadmor has argued that English translations from the Hebrew played a significant role in synthesizing a variety of terms that created 'a discourse pertaining to monogamous Christian unions' in seventeenth-century England. This demonstrates in a very tangible way how Bunyan and many of his contemporaries were authored by the early modern English Bible, before they even started to write themselves. See Naomi Tadmor, *The Social Universe of the English Bible* (Cambridge: Cambridge University Press, 2010), 81.

Psalm 45:14: '*She shall be brought unto the King, in raiment of needle work.* That is, in the righteousness of Christ' (*MW*, 8: 248). In *A Confession of my Faith, and A Reason of my Practice* (1672) Bunyan conflates the allegorical or typological and the didactic in his treatment of marriage. He emphasizes the importance of abstaining from communion or fellowship with individuals who are openly profane and, in order to justify this practice biblically, he refers both to the union of the sons of God with the daughters of men, which resulted in the Flood (Genesis 6 and 7), and to God's command to the Israelites to refrain from intermarrying with Gentiles (Numbers 25:1–5; Joshua 22:17; Deuteronomy 7:1, 2, 6; 12; 32:16, 19; Psalm 106:30, 40; Nehemiah 1:26). Solomon's decision to marry many foreign women supplies the clinching example (*MW*, 4: 158).

By contrast, in *The Holy City* (1665), marriage functions eschatologically. The bride on her wedding day is used to symbolize both the heavenly Jerusalem and the individual believer in their perfected state:

> [T]his City at her appearing is said to be adorned and prepared, as a Bride is for her Husband; which we all know is the most perfect and compleatest Attire that is possible to be got: And therefore it is again, that at the coming of the Lord, those that go in with him to the Marriage, are said to be *ready beforehand*, Rev. 21. 2. Matth. 25. 10. (*MW*, 3: 126)

The same biblical passages inform the conclusion of *The Pilgrim's Progress, Part I*, in which Christian and Hopeful are met by a Heavenly Host near the gate of the city with 'a great shout, saying, *Blessed are they that are called to the Marriage Supper of the Lamb*', for which Bunyan provides a marginal reference to Revelation 19 (*PP*, 160). In Part II, the references to marriage demonstrate Bunyan's deepened pastoral experience and his concern for the spiritual health of those under his care. Christiana's fellow pilgrim, Mercie, is courted by Mr Brisk—'A man of some breeding, and that pretended to Religion; but a man that stuck very close to the World' (*PP*, 226). After consultation with 'the Maidens that were of the House', she discovered that 'he was a very busie Young-Man, [...] but was as they feared, a stranger to the Power of that which was good' (*PP*, 227). Mercie therefore resolves to have nothing to do with him, '*for I purpose never to have a clog to my Soul*' (*PP*, 227). She later marries a godly husband, Christiana's son, Matthew, and there is the clear implication that they have children who are raised in the context of a community of believers (*PP*, 260–61, 269, 277, 287).

Bunyan's most detailed biblical examination of marriage, however, occurs in his didactic allegory, *The Life and Death of Mr. Badman*. This work demonstrates the multiple ways in which Scripture was used to develop a prescriptive approach to marriage in Bunyan's congregation during the Restoration. The pastoral application of the Bible to particular cases of conscience can be fleshed out further by an analysis of the Bedford Church Book. Thomas Luxon has argued that Bunyan's writings do not celebrate the model of companionate marriage promoted by other Puritans such as William Gouge. Instead, Bunyan presents subjection as the first duty of a Christian wife. She is also to refrain from wandering and gossiping, to keep at home, master her tongue, dress modestly, and manage the home in her husband's absence. Never, Luxon claims, does Bunyan 'encourage [the wife] to become a fitter companion by endeavoring to approach her husband's level, to regard herself as his spiritual equal and companion; in fact he does quite the opposite'. Nor is there anything in Bunyan's printed writings about marital sex, though sex itself is referred to often in connection with Mr Badman's adulteries.[5] In these terms, Bunyan's construction of human marriage could be seen as primarily negative (as a preventative to sin) and defined as earthly (and therefore temporary and, in a sense, dispensable). The eschatological dimension that Bunyan recognizes in Scripture's depiction of marriage encourages him to disparage the present in the light of the future, rather than sanctifying the present as a sign of the future.

This does not necessarily imply that Bunyan's view of marriage is entirely antifeminist or misogynistic. *The Pilgrim's Progress, Part II*, which is widely held to reflect his changing view of the communal dimensions of the Christian life as a result of his pastoral experience, presents a far more positive portrait of marriage and procreation amongst the second generation of believers than does the relationship between Christian and Christiana in *Part I* (PP, 260–61, 269, 277, 287).[6] Likewise, Bunyan depicts two kinds of marriage in *The Life and Death of Mr. Badman*. Although neither is ideal, nevertheless the primary purpose of these portraits is pastoral rather than misogynistic, and is driven by Bunyan's resolution to apply Scripture to every aspect of life—spiritual, moral, and practical. Bunyan's determination to demonstrate the problems inherent in mixed marriages (the union of a believer with an unbeliever, in Badman's first marriage) and in self-centred lust (the union of a philanderer and a whore, in his second) is a reflection of his biblically informed concern for vulnerable young people and his appreciation of the implications of self-centred indulgence in a relationship as intimate as marriage.

Badman's first wife, then, is a godly woman who possesses a reasonable competence—the main object of Badman's ambition. She is also an orphan, and therefore unprotected by those most likely to have her interests (spiritual and worldly) at heart. She is indicted in the narrative for her failure to seek godly counsel and to make sufficient enquiries as to Badman's character and business before marrying him. However, Wiseman does note that 'As to his Person, there she was fittest to judge,

---

[5] Thomas H. Luxon, 'One Soul versus One Flesh: Friendship, Marriage, and the Puritan Self', in Vera J. Camden (ed.), *Trauma and Transformation: The Political Progress of John Bunyan* (Stanford, CA: Stanford University Press, 2008), 81–99 (85). Michael Davies also notes Bunyan's failure to discuss marital sex and his abstention from the Puritan celebration of sex in marriage; see 'Bunyan's Bawdy: Sex and Sexual Wordplay in the Writings of John Bunyan', in Camden (ed.), *Trauma and Transformation*, 100–19 (108–09).

[6] N. H. Keeble, '"Here is her glory, even to be under him": The Feminine in the Thought and Work of John Bunyan', in Anne Laurence, W. R. Owens, and Stuart Sim (eds.), *John Bunyan and his England, 1628-88* (London: Hambledon Press, 1990), 131–47; Galen K. Johnson, *Prisoner of Conscience: John Bunyan on Self, Community and Christian Faith* (Carlisle: Paternoster Press, 2003), 143–54. Tasmin Spargo has explored Bunyan's careful attempts to restrict the role of women within his congregation and, to some extent, within his texts, as a way of underwriting his own pastoral authority and helping to establish the respectability and good order of Nonconformists in a period of renewed persecution; see *The Writing of John Bunyan* (Aldershot: Ashgate, 1997), 68–95.

because she was to be the person pleased, but as to his Godliness, there the Word was the fittest Judge, and they who could best understand it, because God was therein to be pleased' (*MB*, 73). The element of physical attraction in this marriage is important; the primary decision-maker here is to be the woman herself. However, failure rightly to discern, assess, and evaluate the character of the man under consideration is also critical.

Here, then, the future Mrs Badman, however godly she may be, is held up as a deterrent. But this first wife's erroneous decision-making and her vulnerability both to the shrewd hypocrisy of Mr Badman and to his external show of godliness are still depicted with sympathy and understanding. Bunyan is not simply presenting an *exemplum*, like the monument to Lot's wife that Christian and Hopeful encounter in *The Pilgrim's Progress* (*PP*, 108–09); he is demonstrating the pain incurred by a young woman who, without family support, is susceptible to the solicitations of a plausible fortune hunter. Through the words of Attentive (Wiseman's dialogue partner and audience in *Mr. Badman*) Bunyan also outlines the conjugal opportunity that this first wife has and which conveys something of his ideal of a Christian, if not a companionate or equal, marriage:

> *It is a deadly thing, I see, to be unequally yoaked with Unbelievers. If this woman had had a good Husband, how happily might they have lived together! Such a one would have prayed for her, taught her, and also would have encouraged her in the Faith, and ways of God.* (*MB*, 72)[7]

There is also the strong suggestion in the narrative that if she had not committed the error of entering into a mixed marriage more than one of her seven children would have been wholeheartedly godly.

Mr Badman's second marriage depicts not the sorrow that comes to those unequally yoked in biblical terms, but rather the self-induced punishment of those who live for their own lusts, rejecting the fidelity and integrity essential to maintaining a healthy relationship. Wiseman recounts how Badman and his second wife 'would fight and fly at each other [...] like Cats and Dogs' living 'in a most sad and hellish manner'. Badman comes to regret the death of his first wife, not out 'of love that he had to her Godliness [...] but for that she used always to keep home', whereas his second wife 'would go abroad' and be 'a Whore of her body'; the first 'loved to keep things together', but the second would whirl things 'about as well as he'; the first was 'silent when he chid' or

---

[7] In some respects Mrs Badman's dilemma mirrors that of Agnes Beaumont, 'a devout daughter who attempts to negotiate a position of dutiful obedience to two opposing fathers, her biological father and her spiritual father, Bunyan. Her mother is dead, her father refuses to allow her to attend a meeting at which Bunyan is to preach—she has work to do, looking after her father. To obey her father would be to deny her duty to her divine father, God, figured to her in Bunyan'; Spargo, *Writing of John Bunyan*, 87. On the scandal created by Beaumont (and Bunyan) in the Bedford church, see Greaves, *Glimpses*, 309–12. See also Elspeth Graham, 'Authority, Resistance and Loss: Gendered Difference in the Writings of John Bunyan and Hannah Allen', in Laurence, Owens, and Sim (eds.), *John Bunyan and his England*, 115–30.

'abused her', the second 'would give him word for word, blow for blow, curse for curse' (*MB*, 146–47). This is poetic justice: Badman has met his match. Whilst his first wife is held up as an ideal for her patience under injustice, it is obvious that both Mr Badman and his second wife have failed to do as they ought: their marriage is consequently a self-determined hell. But the ideal is implied through the negative archetype: a union of peace, love, and mutual edification that may be hierarchical, but not necessarily misogynistic.

The cases of discipline recorded in the Bedford Church Book likewise demonstrate that in Bunyan's congregation pastoral concerns over mixed marriages were rooted both in actual experience and in a determination to ensure that all aspects of life in the church were shaped by biblical moral imperatives. However, real-life situations could be even more complex than the down-to-earth fictional descriptions that characterize Bunyan's pseudo-novel *Mr. Badman*. What did a pastor and congregation do, for example, if a believer who has entered into a mixed marriage does not regret her decision and respond repentantly to biblical correction, as does the first Mrs Badman? Moving from the realm of fictional narrative to pastoral practice and congregational discipline entails recognizing the complexities of such relationships. Despite what Beth Lynch has described as the 'sheer inquisitorial energy that Bunyan's congregation invested in monitoring, interrogating, and punishing errant individuals',[8] discipline in such cases was only effective if the individual concerned—like Mr Badman's first wife—eventually concurred with the congregation's judgement. The Church Book records, for example, the admonition of one woman, Mary Gates, on 27 April 1698, who 'had married a carnall man', even though 'she was (besides the strict prohibition of the word of God) charged to the contrary by her parents and told of the greatness of the evil by our brother Chandler [the pastor] and by him earnestly pressed to decline it' (*CB*, 115–16). On 3 January 1699, it is further recorded that Mary Gates was now frequently attending Church of England services despite being under admonition, more messengers having been sent to her by this point. These messengers reported back to the church on 31 January 'that they had been with Mary Gates, but found her very senceless under her sins; 'twas concluded to exercise some patience towards her' (*CB*, 121). Gathered congregations had to ameliorate their passion for biblical discipline, then, with an awareness of their embattled minority position in a state that continued to mistrust them, despite the provisions of the Act of Toleration (1689).

Bunyan's treatment of marriage demonstrates the manner in which the Bible dominated every aspect of his life and thought. Despite his humble background as a tinker, he absorbed the complex and multilayered scriptural hermeneutic that dominated godly circles in mid-seventeenth-century England. However, his commitment to the Word of God went further than this. As his didactic writings and the records of meetings at his gathered congregation in Bedford demonstrate, he held the Bible to be sufficient

---

[8] Beth Lynch, *John Bunyan and the Language of Conviction* (Cambridge: D. S. Brewer, 2004), 112.

for all matters of practice, as well as of faith, according to the Reformed doctrine of *sola scriptura*: by the Word alone. Consequently, it shaped Bunyan's own walk as a believer, and it also informed his pastoral care over the decades in which he ministered to Dissenters in both Bedford and beyond.

Pilgrimage

In Bunyan's works pilgrimage operates as a narrative structure; as a hermeneutic approach to life and writing; as a sermon *topos*; as an imaginative experience; as a way of understanding time in relation to eternity through typological readings of the Old and New Testaments; as a means of distinguishing between the godly and the unrighteous; and as a help in understanding the biblical doctrine of sanctification. Bunyan's decision to represent life as a journey is not unique to *The Pilgrim's Progress*, then, nor is it in and of itself a specifically biblical concept. However, his appropriation of the biblical usage of the terms 'way' and 'race', imaginatively fused together in his central figure of the Christian as a pilgrim, juxtaposed alongside the unremittingly eschatological orientation of his tale, transforms the universal narrative motif of the pilgrimage or quest into an unmistakably biblical journey.[9]

Bunyan's use of the term 'Way' to describe the spiritual pilgrimage of the believer from the City of Destruction to the Celestial City is drawn directly from the earliest references to Christians in the New Testament, as people of 'the way'. For instance, Saul 'breathing out threatenings and slaughter against the disciples of the Lord, went unto the high priest, and desired of him letters to Damascus to the synagogues, that if he found any of this way, whether they were men or women, he might bring them bound unto Jerusalem' (Acts 9:1–2). In Ephesus, 'there arose no small stir about that way' (Acts 19:23). The Apostle Paul picks up the same term in his defence in Jerusalem: 'I persecuted this way unto the death' (Acts 22:4), and before the Roman governor, Felix: 'this I confess unto thee, that after the way which they call heresy, so worship I the God of my fathers, believing all things which are written in the law and in the prophets' (Acts 24:14). Felix himself is described as 'having more perfect knowledge of that way' (Acts 24:22). In the 'Apology' prefacing his most famous work, Bunyan states that he was '*writing of the Way / And Race of Saints*' (*PP*, 1) when he suddenly fell into an allegory. Indeed, the term 'way' occurs over two hundred times in *The Pilgrim's Progress, Part I* and over one hundred times in *Part II*.

---

[9] For an analysis of how the concept of a literal pilgrimage was transformed into a metaphorical, literary motif that was eagerly adopted by zealous Protestants, see N. H. Keeble, '"To be a pilgrim": Constructing the Protestant Life in Early Modern England', in Colin Morris and Peter Roberts (eds.), *Pilgrimage: The English Experience from Becket to Bunyan* (Cambridge: Cambridge University Press, 2002), 238–56.

In the instance cited—'*the Way / And Race of Saints*'—the biblical echo is enriched by a reference to the Epistle to the Hebrews, where the author admonishes:

> let us lay aside every weight, and the sin which doth so easily beset us, and let us run with patience the race that is set before us, looking unto Jesus the author and finisher of our faith; who for the joy that was set before him endured the cross, despising the shame, and is set down at the right hand of the throne of God. (12:1–2)

This biblical image of the pilgrimage as a journey that is to be run by the determined athlete shapes Bunyan's narrative at several levels. Jesus is the model, mediator, and ultimate goal or reward of the pilgrims: literally, 'the way, the truth, and the life' (John 14:6). The journey they pursue is arduous and filled with obstacles, yet there is an engaged audience consisting of those who have gone before, or who travel alongside the pilgrims, testifying to the nature and truth of God's word.

Bunyan found pilgrimage, like warfare, a congenial unifying motif that enabled him to fuse his personal experience as a Christian, his role as a pastor, and his imaginative engagement with the Bible into a dynamic and powerful allegorical narrative. The typological hermeneutic he employed was crucial to this artistic achievement. Christian's journey is informed, for example, by the Old Testament types of Israel's exodus from Egypt under the leadership of Moses and Abraham's journey from pagan Ur to the Promised Land. Christian's journey also maps out Bunyan's theological understanding of the process of individual salvation and sanctification, as derived from his reading of the New Testament, particularly Paul's epistles. The pilgrimage undertaken by Christian's wife, Christiana, their children, and the various other individuals that they collect in *The Pilgrim's Progress, Part II* is an imaginative representation of the gathered church on their collective pilgrimage to the New Jerusalem. *The Life and Death of Mr. Badman*, by contrast, fleshes out the journey of a reprobate actively pursuing the broad way to damnation and who, throughout his life, avoids reading Scripture, mocking rather than 'reverencing the Word' (*MB*, 39–40, 126–28).

Mr Badman offers, in this sense, a fuller, more grossly corporeal portrait of characters like Talkative and Ignorance in *The Pilgrim's Progress*. Though respectful of faith and religion in a way that Badman is not, nevertheless Ignorance, chillingly, holds to an incorrect view of how one can be saved (according to Bunyan's theological reading of Scripture), and after Christian and Hopeful have been accepted into the Celestial City with rejoicing, the narrator comments:

> I […] saw *Ignorance* come up to the River side: but he soon got over, and that without half that difficulty which the other two men met with. For it happened, that there was then in that place one *Vain-hope* a Ferry-man, that with his Boat helped him over […]. When he was come up to the Gate […] they asked him for his Certificate, that they might go in and shew it to the King. So he fumbled in his bosom for one, and found none. […] Then they took him up, and carried him through the air to the door that I saw in the side of the Hill, and put him in there. Then I saw that there was a way to Hell, even from the Gates of Heaven, as well as from the City of *Destruction*. (*PP*, 162–63)

This final image in *The Pilgrim's Progress, Part I* demonstrates that Bunyan was committed to maintaining his theological reading of Scripture uncompromisingly, even when envisaging the pilgrimage of the believer in fictional form. Failure appropriately to seek and receive the Bible's offer of salvation through Christ led to damnation, even if one had reached the very gates of heaven itself.

It can be typical of critical readings of Bunyan's work to examine his writings in other genres—theological, devotional, and controversial—as mere precedents or source materials that help to illuminate his 'true literary' achievements—*The Pilgrim's Progress, Grace Abounding,* and, at a stretch, *The Holy War*. The difficulty with adopting this approach in a chapter on Bunyan's relationship with the Bible, however, is that it anachronistically projects contemporary preferences for the literary and artistic over the theological and didactic in its reading of Bunyan's oeuvre. In Samuel Taylor Coleridge's famous formulation, it privileges the inspired writer of 'Parnassus' over the preacher of the 'conventicle'. For many of Bunyan's contemporaries, though, it was his imaginative fiction, *The Pilgrim's Progress*, that was suspect and not, for example, his devotional works, or his critical interventions in controversies over baptism and the identity of his church. I would, therefore, like to conclude this section on Bunyan's use of pilgrimage by analysing its occurrence in two treatises directed specifically towards professed believers who were in danger of hypocrisy, formalism, or practising merely outward piety, both of which have a direct bearing on the biblical shape of *The Pilgrim's Progress*: *The Heavenly Foot-man* (1698) and *The Strait Gate* (1676).[10]

The Strait Gate is a treatise based on the well-known exhortation of Jesus, 'Enter ye in at the strait gate: for wide is the gate, and broad is the way, that leadeth to destruction, and many there be that go in thereat: Because strait is the gate, and narrow is the way that leadeth unto life, and few there be that find it' (Matthew 7:13–14). Here, in seminal form, is the concept of the Christian life as an arduous pilgrimage on which one must embark and ultimately complete if salvation and heaven are to be enjoyed at last. Bunyan's focus throughout this treatise is on the image of the gate, rather than the journey, particularly the duty to examine oneself in order to prove that one is neither a hypocrite, nor a formalist, so that entrance into heaven following the Day of Judgement is assured. Bunyan's key concern, communicated here in the epistle to the reader, is to ensure that his representation of the 'gate of *heaven*' is neither 'too wide' nor '*too narrow*'; '*I have here presented thee with as true a measure of it as by the word of God I can: reade me, therefore, yea, reade me and compare me with the* bible; *and if thou findest my doctrine, and that book of God concur; embrace it, as thou wilt answer the contrary in the day of Judgment*' (*MW*, 5: 69).

The Heavenly Foot-man, by contrast, concentrates on and develops the image of the journey (as the title suggests) and draws its inspiration primarily from two texts: a typological reading of the Old Testament narrative detailing the flight of Lot

---

[10] Graham Midgley, 'Introduction', *MW*, 5: xvi, xxxviii–xxxix.

and his family from Sodom (Genesis 19:17) and the exhortation of Paul to the church in Corinth, 'So run, that ye may obtain' (1 Corinthians 9:24). It is possible that this is the treatise detailing *'the Way / And Race of Saints'* that Bunyan was working on when he *'Fell suddenly into an Allegory / About their Journey and the way to Glory'*, culminating in his most famous work, *The Pilgrim's Progress*.[11] However, it is arguable that we get closer to Bunyan's heart and literary intentions in the direct closing exhortation of this treatise, than we do when he is attempting to bait the most difficult fish in his more developed allegorical treatment of the biblical concept of pilgrimage:

> Well then, *Sinner*, what sayst thou? Where is thy Heart? Wilt thou Run? Art thou resolved to Strip? Or art thou not? Think quickly Man, it is no dallying in this matter. Confer not with Flesh and Blood, look up to Heaven, and see how thou likest it; also to Hell, […] and accordingly Devote thy self. If thou dost not know the way, *inquire at the Word of God*. If thou wantest Company, cry for God's Spirit, if thou wantest Incouragement, entertain the *Promises*: But be sure thou begin betimes, *get into the way*, Run apace, and hold out to the *end*. And the Lord give thee a prosperous Journey. (*MW*, 5: 178)

This is Bunyan the minister of the Word aiming to pierce his reader's heart by a direct, personal address, vividly applying Scripture through urgent rhetorical questions. Both evidence his unshaken conviction that the Word and Spirit of God are essential if pilgrims are to complete the journey safely by starting off on the right way, running speedily, and continuing until the end.

For Bunyan, the Word of God was most emphatically not the subjective and volatile 'inner light' of either the Quakers or any others on the more radical wing of the Puritan Revolution, but neither did his strongly held conviction that every word of the canonical Scriptures was literally inspired by God result in the bibliolatry of later conservative Christian proponents of the doctrine of inerrancy. Rather, Bunyan's imagination was saturated in and gripped by the storyline, types, and similes of Scripture; his conscience was captivated by its moral imperatives; and his pragmatic approach to its application resulted in a personal and congregational discipline that attempted to implement these doctrines in every part of life—including marriage and pilgrimage. This ideological and imaginative commitment to the Bible produced both a life and corpus of work that attempted to see the Word made flesh in seventeenth-century England—a mini-incarnation modelled on the divine prototype: 'And the Word was made flesh, and dwelt among us, (and we beheld his glory, the glory as of the only begotten of the Father,) full of grace and truth' (John 1:14).

---

[11] Midgley suggests that this treatise was probably composed *c*.1671 or earlier and therefore was written at about the same time as *The Strait Gate* and possibly *The Pilgrim's Progress, Part I*; 'Introduction', *MW*, 5: 134. Greaves argues for a composition date between December 1667 and February 1668; *Glimpses*, 211.

Suggested Reading

Austin, Michael, 'The Figural Logic of the Sequel and the Unity of *The Pilgrim's Progress*', *SP*, 102 (2005), 484–509.

Branch, Lori, '"As Blood is Forced Out of Flesh": Spontaneity and the Wounds of Exchange in *Grace Abounding* and *The Pilgrim's Progress*', *ELH*, 74 (2007), 271–99.

Davies, Michael, *Graceful Reading: Theology and Narrative in the Works of John Bunyan* (Oxford: Oxford University Press, 2002).

Dunan-Page, Anne, *Grace Overwhelming: John Bunyan, The Pilgrim's Progress and the Extremes of the Baptist Mind* (Bern: Peter Lang, 2008).

Hamlin, Hannibal, 'Bunyan's Biblical Progresses', in Hannibal Hamlin and Norman W. Jones (eds.), *The King James Bible after 400 Years* (Cambridge: Cambridge University Press, 2010), 202–18.

Hindmarsh, Bruce, *The Evangelical Conversion Narrative: Spiritual Autobiography in Early Modern England* (Oxford: Oxford University Press, 2008).

Johnson, B. A., 'Falling into Allegory: The "Apology" to *The Pilgrim's Progress* and Bunyan's Scriptural Methodology', in R. G. Collmer (ed.), *Bunyan in Our Time* (Kent, OH: Kent State University Press, 1989), 113–37.

Keeble, N. H., '"To be a pilgrim": Constructing the Protestant Life in Early Modern England', in Colin Morris and Peter Roberts (eds.), *Pilgrimage: The English Experience from Becket to Bunyan* (Cambridge: Cambridge University Press, 2002), 238–56.

Lynch, Beth, *John Bunyan and the Language of Conviction* (Cambridge: D. S. Brewer, 2004).

Tadmor, Naomi, *The Social Universe of the English Bible* (Cambridge: Cambridge University Press, 2010).

CHAPTER 6

BUNYAN'S READING

ROGER POOLEY

It would be difficult to overstate Bunyan's indebtedness to the Bible above any other book, though he does it himself when he states in his preface to *Solomon's Temple Spiritualized* (1688) that the Bible and a concordance 'are my only library in my writings' (*MW*, 7: 9). It is a polemical point more than a true confession: he is joining with the other 'mechanick preachers' from the 1640s and 1650s who, like Samuel How in *The Sufficiencie of the Spirits Teaching, without Humane Learning* (1640), assert that the message of the Bible is plain to all who are led by the Holy Spirit, and that a university degree is unnecessary to qualify one as a preacher of the Word of God. In saying this, Bunyan is also separating himself from Christian writers and preachers in the Restoration whose arguments are as likely to come from classical or patristic sources as the Bible. When it comes to authority—in the early modern sense of the word, of a text that can be cited as authoritative—only the Bible, and the Spirit that inspires its writers and readers, will do. Bunyan knew the Bible extremely well, as Chapter 5 in this volume explains, not only the sweep of the major themes—in which he was indebted to a Pauline perspective on how Law and Grace, Old Testament and Gospel fit together—but, as is clear through his deployment of it, on a verse-by-verse basis.

The mention of Bunyan's using a concordance points to his habit of piling up verses from various parts of the Bible to reinforce a point. Open almost any page of his nonfictional works, and the reader will find a paragraph that concludes with an array of biblical citations—so, for example, in a paragraph on the soul dwelling once more in the body in *The Resurrection of the Dead* (?1665), there are references to verses from Exodus, Acts, Daniel, Matthew, Luke, and Colossians (*MW*, 3: 222). Bunyan was not unusual among Puritan and Reformed writers in doing this. Most important, though, is the sheer visceral impact of the Bible on him, described in his spiritual autobiography, *Grace Abounding to the Chief of Sinners* (1666) using the language of physical force. We might say that the Bible mastered him before he mastered it.

The primacy of Scripture in his writing doesn't mean that Bunyan read nothing else; indeed, we can draw up a fair-sized reading list simply from the open acknowledgements in his writing. As we shall see, some are books he regrets having read, like the cheap romances he absorbed as an unconverted young man, though it is arguable that they had a continuing influence on his writing, as Chapter 22 demonstrates. Others, like Luther's commentary on Galatians, had a profound effect on his spiritual development. There are also the books he contends against in polemic, from the Quakers that first drew him into print, to the Anglican Edward Fowler in the 1670s; and beyond those, there is a penumbra of books of which there is some evidence that he read them.[1]

As Andrew Cambers has argued, 'reading was vital to the practice of Puritanism'.[2] If Puritan piety was largely centred on the Word, this Word was not just the Bible itself but manuals of piety and accounts of spiritual experience, ranging from autobiography to the history of Christian martyrs in John Foxe's *Acts and Monuments* (first published in 1563). The practices of reading such texts would range from solitary private reading, such as the norm today, to reading aloud in gatherings of family and others. Of course, there is an exclusive side to this; just as Puritan belief encouraged and spread literacy and regular reading, so it drew a circle to include books that were thought to be edifying and to exclude frivolity and anything that might lead the believer astray.

Books were important for Bunyan. He wrote sixty of them, after all, and read others, some of them very substantial, assiduously. But he was also a powerful preacher, yet we know almost nothing of the preaching that he heard and from which he learnt. Other than his valedictory epistle to the Bedford congregation, penned before his death in 1655 and copied into the Bedford Church Book, nothing has survived of the teaching of John Gifford, his first pastor in Bedford, but it may well be that sermons and conversation were at least as important in Bunyan's Christian formation as the printed sources we can more readily access.

Early Reading

Bunyan's unredeemed reading as a young man, before his conversion experience, was limited to entertainment. In *A Few Sighs from Hell* (1658) he appears to confess at one point that when he was 'in the world' (meaning not on the way to the Heavenly City) he preferred 'a Ballad, a Newsbook, *George* on horseback, or *Bevis* of *Southampton*' to the Scriptures (*MW*, 1: 333). He is referring here to a whole area of popular print, responding to, and playing its part in creating a broader literate reading public which continued to expand in Bunyan's lifetime, and of which the young Bunyan, with his basic schooling, was literate enough to take advantage.[3] It is worth considering each of the categories of print that he mentions here in turn: ballads, newsbooks, and popular romances.

---

[1] See Greaves, *Glimpses*, 603–07.
[2] Andrew Cambers, *Godly Reading: Print, Manuscript and Puritanism in England, 1580–1720* (Cambridge: Cambridge University Press, 2011), 7.
[3] See Margaret Spufford, *Small Books and Pleasant Histories: Popular Fiction and its Readership in Seventeenth-Century England* (Cambridge: Cambridge University Press, 1985).

The ballads that were available in print were mostly 'broadsides', printed on a single 'broad' sheet of paper. There was a great variety of them, in subject matter and quality. They included accounts of contemporary events as well as what we would call 'traditional' folksong materials and topical verses set to well-known tunes. Did they constitute Bunyan's introduction to poetry? They certainly fit with what we know of Bunyan's interest in music. The musical instruments he appears to have made—the metal violin and the flute made out of a chair leg, now in the Bunyan Meeting Museum in Bedford—are part of the evidence. The musical notation in *A Book for Boys and Girls* (1686) shows that Bunyan might well have had the facility to read music and even to compose it (*MW*, 6: 234, 238). The fact that he appears to have written music as well as played it, even at a time when the gathered church in Bedford did not sing hymns, counters the popular stereotype of Puritanism as anti-art.[4] It is true, though, that many of the popular printed ballads that Bunyan admits to liking once, written to be sung to an already existing tune, are not much concerned with spiritual matters. For example, 'The Batchelors Delight', an undated ballad thought to have been published between 1640 and 1660, is to be sung 'to the tune of the Kings delight'. It includes a flippantly misogynist verse on Adam and Eve, a rather coarser version of Marvell's 'Two paradises were in one / To live in paradise alone' from 'The Garden':

> Whilst Adam was a Batchelor,
>   in Eden he did tarry.
> It is an Eden upon earth,
>   to live and never marry.[5]

The picture Bunyan paints of his unrepentant youth in *Grace Abounding* is certainly reinforced by the language and tone of many of these ballads (see *GA*, 6–8).

Bunyan's early interest in reading newsbooks perhaps gives the lie to the caricature of the unpolitical Bunyan, or perhaps it was an early introduction to the strange (to us) tales that function as illustrations of God's providence and judgement in some of his books. Newsbooks were small pamphlets, usually twenty-four pages long, sometimes shorter, with the same mixture of hard political and military news with sensationalism and propaganda that we find in the popular press four centuries later. Some of the earlier newsbooks were translations of foreign news stories; others confined themselves to stories from home. However, there was a big change in the 1640s, when topical news about the growing crisis began to appear on a regular basis. As Joad Raymond has demonstrated, 'The newsbook soon transformed from a plain and non-controversial narration of parliamentary proceedings into a bitter and aggressive instrument of literary and political faction.'[6] *Mercurius Civicus*, for example, was founded in 1643 to counter the

---

[4] This point was well made in Percy Scholes, *The Puritans and Music in England and New England* (Oxford: Oxford University Press, 1934).

[5] Anon., 'The Batchelors Delight' (London, n.d.), broadsheet.

[6] Joad Raymond, *The Invention of the Newspaper: English Newsbooks 1641–1649* (Oxford: Clarendon Press, 1996), 13.

pro-Royalist *Mercurius Aulicus*. But which of them might Bunyan have read? Some may have circulated in the army, while Bunyan was serving in the Newport Pagnell garrison. This is where, if anywhere, he would have been party to the political debates about the progress and purposes of the Civil War.

Equally, newsbooks, like the tabloid press in our own time, contained many accounts of spectacular happenings, though (unlike in their modern counterparts) these are often explained by the workings of Providence. This may have given Bunyan a taste for the stories of remarkable occurrences he used in *The Life and Death of Mr. Badman* (1680), many of them gathered from Samuel Clarke's *A Mirrour or Looking-Glass both for Saints, and Sinners* (1646; 2nd edn, 'much enlarged', 1654). Clarke's compilation is one of the few examples of Bunyan using a source book other than the Bible in a sustained fashion for his writing; and while the stories he cites are sometimes spectacularly improbable (to a modern reader, at least), they are not presented as fictions within his own fictions (*MB*, 56, 134, 146). As Alexandra Walsham has pointed out, compilations such as Clarke's also reinforced an anti-Catholic providentialism which had a political and polemical purpose throughout the seventeenth century.[7] The figure of Giant Pope in *The Pilgrim's Progress* indicates that Bunyan felt that way, too, even if he had shared Bedford jail with recusants as well as sectaries like himself.

'*George* on horseback' almost certainly refers to the first section of Richard Johnson's *The Seven Champions of Christendom*, first published in 1596–97 and often reprinted throughout the seventeenth century and beyond.[8] The whole collection covers the patron saints of seven countries in Western Europe (counting Scotland, Ireland, and Wales as separate countries). Johnson moves the genre of the saint's life into chivalric romance, and in that respect he creates a popular parallel to Edmund Spenser's verse epic *The Faerie Queene* (1590; 1596). Like Redcrosse, the hero of the first book of *The Faerie Queene*, George is a knight errant, avoiding the charms of the enchantress Kalib, slaying a dragon, of course (which is fiery like Bunyan's Apollyon, but not much like him in other respects), and travelling through the Middle East. His Christianity is largely defined, like that of many crusaders, historic and fictional, by his not being Muslim—nothing more positive than that. As Naomi Conn Liebler notes, 'Johnson's St. George is in many respects no saint. He is as often petulant, self-absorbed, frightened, and cruel as he is courageous and steadfast. He is, in other words, quite ordinary.'[9] She illustrates this by referring to his despair and self-pity while in prison. The point is well made, though we might also think of it as a (possibly unconscious) source for the episode of Doubting

---

[7] Alexandra Walsham, *Providence in Early Modern England* (Oxford: Oxford University Press, 1999), esp. ch. 5.

[8] See Richard Johnson, *The Seven Champions of Christendom*, ed. Jennifer Fellows (Aldershot: Ashgate, 2003). See also Chapter 22 in this volume.

[9] Naomi Conn Liebler, 'Bully St. George: Richard Johnson's *Seven Champions of Christendom* and the Creation of the Bourgeois National Hero', in Naomi Conn Liebler (ed.), *Early Modern Prose Fiction: The Cultural Politics of Reading* (New York and London: Routledge, 2007), 123.

Castle and Giant Despair in *The Pilgrim's Progress*, and even more than that. After all, it features an ordinary hero in a landscape which veers between the exotic, the fabulous, and the mundane.

While Bunyan may have been understandably dismissive of his early reading as one more demonstration of his unredeemed life before his conversion, it doesn't mean this reading was unimportant. It is more likely that it was part of his formation as a storyteller; it is part of the reason why his narrative style in his major allegorical works, while deeply infused with biblical images and concepts, doesn't read like that of a biblical narrative. Instead, it has the stamp of popular story, even folk literature. Although it could be argued that Bunyan could have been drawing on oral tradition, it seems more likely that popular print was the medium he felt at home in, even before his conviction and conversion drove him to read the Bible and other religious texts with intense, hungry concentration.

POPULAR RELIGIOUS BOOKS: BAYLY AND DENT

In *Grace Abounding* Bunyan does not refer to his first wife by name, but he does tell us that she brought with her as a kind of dowry two books of popular devotion: Lewis Bayly's *The Practise of Pietie* (3rd edn, 1613) and Arthur Dent's *The Plaine Mans Path-Way to Heaven* (1601) (*GA*, 8). These were pocket-sized volumes, often reprinted: religious 'best sellers' in C. John Somerville's perspective.[10]

Bayly's book went through some sixty-nine editions before 1743 (the first and second editions have not survived, but the third came out in 1613). It is still there, as an emblem of piety and chastity, in the 1736 engraving of William Hogarth's 'Before'. As the heroine fights off her amorous suitor, her dressing-table drawer falls open, and in it we can see the title page of Bayly's book. Although he was at times prominent in the Church of England—chaplain to Prince Henry and later King Charles, Prebendary of Lichfield, and eventually Bishop of Bangor in North Wales—Bayly remained Calvinist, and had some Puritan sympathies, with his opposition to stage plays, and his criticism of the Book of Sports.[11]

'Piety' sounds, well, pious, but what did it mean for Bayly, and what might it have meant for Bunyan? Although the book has a strongly practical orientation, its version of piety stresses an inward focus. A sentence like this has affinities with the spiritual and psychological world of *Grace Abounding*: '*without Piety there is* no internall comfort to *bee found* in Conscience, nor externall peace *to bee looked for in* the World, nor

---

[10] C. John Sommerville, *Popular Religion in Restoration England* (Gainesville, FL: University Press of Florida, 1977), ch. 3.
[11] J. Gwynfor Jones and Vivienne Larminie, 'Lewis Bayly', *ODNB*.

any eternall happines *to be hoped for in* Heaven'. The opening chapters of the book are a series of meditations, on the nature of God, for example, and on '*the miseries of a man in life & death, that is not reconciled to God in Christ*' and '*of the blessed state both in life and death, of a Man that is reconciled to God in Christ*'.[12] Much of the rest of the book consists of ways of ordering the day, with prayers for morning and evening, advice on keeping the Sabbath holy, preparing to take communion, and so on. Bunyan was hostile to set prayers, and wrote against the re-imposition of the Prayer Book in 1662 in *I Will Pray with the Spirit*, and so might only have followed Bayly during his period of ultimately fruitless religious observance. However, he might have appreciated Bayly's household rules, and seems to have adapted some of them for *Christian Behaviour* (1663), and he may also have been influenced by Bayly's scheme for reading the whole Bible in a year.[13] Equally, we may want to see Bayly's ordered, conformist piety as an example of the kind of formal religion that Bunyan was first seduced by and then rejected. But these are speculations; Bunyan does not say anything about the book.

Dent's book was similarly popular, running through twenty-five editions from its first publication in 1601 to 1640. It was aimed at ordinary people like the young John Bunyan and his wife, rather than scholars and theologians. Dent was a Cambridge graduate who became minister of South Shoebury in Essex, and he may well have picked up on the usefulness of the dialogue form from one of his fellow ministers in Essex, George Gifford, whose *Country Divinity* (1581) featured arguments between Zelotes and Atheos.[14] The title page of Dent's book explains that in it 'every man may clearely see, whether he shall be saved or damned'. That question is what drives Bunyan's search for certainty in *Grace Abounding*, and it is the principal question that the English Calvinist theologians thought people should ask. It is the ultimate case of conscience for a Puritan: How do you know you are saved?[15]

The Plaine Mans Path-Way is written throughout as a dialogue, and although the four characters have Greek names, Dent's learning is not on display, and the emphasis is on accessibility. The principal speaker is Theologus, a divine, and his sympathetic listener is Philagathus, '*an honest man*'. They have a similar relationship to that of Mr Wiseman and Mr Attentive in *The Life and Death of Mr. Badman*, Bunyan's own extended dialogue. The other two are described by Philagathus as follows: 'They be a couple of neighbours of the next Parish, the one of them is called Asunetus, who in very deed is a very ignorant man in Gods matters: and the other is called Antilegon, a notable Atheist, and caviller against all goodnesse.' 'Asunetos' means 'foolish' in Greek, and the name Antilegon obviously

---

[12] Lewis Bayly, *The Practice of Pietie* (1630), 'Epistle Dedicatorie', 59–102, 103–71.

[13] See W. R. Owens, 'Modes of Bible Reading in Early Modern England', in Shafquat Towheed and W. R. Owens (eds.), *The History of Reading*, vol. 1: *International Perspectives, c.1500–1990* (Basingstoke: Palgrave Macmillan, 2011), 32–45 (38).

[14] See Brett Usher, 'Arthur Dent', *ODNB*.

[15] See, for example, William Perkins, *A Case of Conscience the Greatest that Ever was, How a Man may Know, Whether He Be the Child of God or No* (1592); William Ames, *Conscience with the Power and Cases Thereof* (1639).

signifies an opponent of the Word of God. They are on their way to buy a cow, but they are happy to stop for two or three hours to discuss 'matters of religion'.[16] As Christopher Haigh notes, 'that is what men and women did: they often talked about religion, because they cared about religion and because religion was unavoidable'.[17] The whole of Haigh's book is of interest here, because he structures his analysis of post-Reformation England according to the four characters in Dent's book, along with a Catholic priest to fill out an obvious gap in the picture.

To begin with, Dent lets Philagathus question Theologus in a manner that is close to catechizing—except that the teaching relationship is reversed. There is a certain crispness to the exchange:

> *Phila.* Cannot a man will and desire that which is good, before he be borne again?
> *Theol.* No more then a dead man can desire the good things of this life. For mans will is not free to consent unto good, til it be inlarged by grace.[18]

The Reformed theology at work here is precisely that which Bunyan himself adopted, after his conversion. Yet Dent's book is of considerable importance to Bunyan's formation as a writer as well as a Christian. Writing '*Dialogue-wise*' (*PP*, 6) is a key feature of Bunyan's style, not just in the fictional works, but in enlivening sermon-treatises and controversial works as well. However, he writes in *Grace Abounding* of Dent's and Bayly's books that, 'though they did not reach my heart to awaken it about my sad and sinful state, yet they did beget within me some desires to Religion' (*GA*, 8). It seems odd, in view of the considerable emphasis on sinfulness in the early pages of *The Plaine Mans Path-Way*, that they were not 'awakening' texts for him. Perhaps he skipped them, or followed Dent's own advice to the enquirer not to be put off by those earlier pages a little too readily. Or he did not find its fierce Calvinism persuasive. Whatever the case, twenty years later, in beginning *The Pilgrim's Progress*, Bunyan seems to have remembered something of Dent's ability to catch the tone of the objector to Puritan Christianity. Here is a typical example of Theologus dealing with Asunetus:

> *Asune.* Tush, tush: what needes all this adoe? If a man say his Lords prayer, his tenne Commandements, and his beleefe, and keepe them, and say no bodie no harm, nor doe no bodie no harme, and doo as hee would bee done to, to have a good faith to Godward, and be a man of Gods beliefe, no doubt he shall be saved, without all this running to sermons, and pratling of the scriptures.
> *Theol.* Now you powre it out in deed: you think you have spoken wisely. But alas you have bewraied your great ignorance.[19]

---

[16] Arthur Dent, *The Plaine Mans Path-Way to Heaven* (1601), 1, 2.
[17] Christopher Haigh, *The Plain Man's Pathways to Heaven: Kinds of Christianity in Post-Reformation England* (Oxford: Oxford University Press, 2007), 5.
[18] Dent, *The Plaine Mans Path-Way*, 13.
[19] Dent, *The Plaine Mans Path-Way*, 25–6.

As the dialogue progresses, however, even Asunetus becomes convinced. The genius of Bunyan's versions of such figures, though, is that the opponents are tragically and comically fixed in their views, and remain unconvinced by the truth. He doesn't credit easy conversions. Nonetheless, he seems to have taken from Dent the ability to catch the authentic voice of opposition to his own viewpoint, and set it up for criticism within the dialogue form. In his more systematic use of dialogue in *Mr. Badman*, however, the relation of Wiseman and Attentive is much closer to that of Theologus and Philagathus than anything in *The Pilgrim's Progress*.

Luther's Commentary on Galatians

The third Christian book Bunyan mentions in *Grace Abounding* is Martin Luther's commentary on Galatians, and he gives it the most explicit and positive recommendation of all. He stresses the providential character of it falling into his hand, and the fact that it was so old that it almost fell apart, and 'the which, when I had but a little way perused, I found my condition in his experience, so largely and profoundly handled, as if his Book had been written out of my heart'. Luther's text, Bunyan found, dealt with the temptations of blasphemy and despair that he was struggling with at the time; though without expanding much more, he writes, 'I do prefer this book of Mr. *Luther* upon the *Galathians*, (excepting the Holy Bible) before all the books that ever I have seen, as most fit for a wounded Conscience' (*GA*, 40–1).

Given the age of the copy Bunyan read, it seems likely that it was one of the Elizabethan copies of *A Commentarie of M. Doctor Martin Luther upon the Epistle of S. Paule to the Galathians*, first printed by Thomas Vautroullier in 1575, and reissued well into the seventeenth century. Before we get to Luther's own preface, there is a commendation 'To all afflicted consciences which grone for salvation and wrastle under the crosse for the kingdom of Christ', which precisely addresses Bunyan's anxieties at the time. The notion of looking to something as apparently dry and academic as a biblical commentary in a moment of spiritual crisis may seem odd to a modern reader; but this anonymous opening summary of the book immediately answers that objection:

> [T]hou mayst see and behold the admirable glory of the Lord and all the riches of heaven, thy salvation freely and onely by faith in Christe, his love and grace toward thee so opened, thy victory and conquest in him so proved, the wrath of God so pacified, his lawe satisfied, the full kingdome of life set open, death, hell and hell gates, be they never so strong, with all the power of sinne, flesh and the world vanquished, thy conscience discharged, all feares and terrours removed.[20]

---

[20] *A Commentarie of M. Doctor Martin Luther upon the Epistle of S. Paul to the Galathians* (1575), sig. Aii.

So even before Bunyan got as far as Luther's words he had picked up something of the message of the Reformation about salvation by faith as a work of God's grace. But this was never merely an intellectually generated switch of doctrines, for reader or writer, or an offshoot of anti-clericalism; it was an answer to Bunyan's deepest fears about his eternal salvation.

The contrast between the Law and the Gospel, as a theological and indeed psychological concept, is central to Bunyan's understanding of the latter. It is there in his early *The Doctrine of the Law and Grace Unfolded* (1659), the key to understanding Bunyan's theology, as well as in his own story as recounted in *Grace Abounding*, and in episodes like Christian's diversion to Mount Sinai in *The Pilgrim's Progress*. He found it in John Gifford's teaching, as his brief tribute to him attests (*GA*, 25, 37). He found it in Luther: 'Wherefore the afflicted and troubled conscience hath no remedy against desperation and eternall death, unlesse it take holde of the forgevenesse of sinnes by grace, freely offered in Christe Jesus: that is to say, this passive righteousnesse of Faith.'[21] The word 'passive' is interesting, because it is at the heart of the Reformation understanding of how God's grace works for the believer, whether we call it Calvinist or Lutheran. There is a lot of striving around this still centre, but it shows, for example, why, despite all the hard travelling and difficult choosing that Christian does in *The Pilgrim's Progress*, he loses his burden at the cross without any activity on his part. He sees the cross, and the burden falls off.

Luther had other lessons for Bunyan. Paul's Epistle to the Galatians has a crux passage on the use of allegory in biblical interpretation. In chapter 4, verse 24, Paul identifies Hagar and Sarah, the slave and the wife by whom Abraham had sons, as an allegory of the two covenants, of Law and Grace. Luther makes the following general point:

> Allegories doe not strongly prove and perswade in Divinitie, but as certaine pictures they beuttifie and sette out the matter. For if *Paule* had not proved the righteousness of Faith against the righteousness of workes by strong and pithie arguments, he should have little prevailed by this allegorie. But because he had fortified his cause before with invincible arguments taken of experience, of the example of Abraham, the testimonies of the Scripture, and similitudes: now, in the ende of his disputation he addeth an allegorie, to geve a beautie to all the rest. For it is a seemely thing sometime to adde an allegorie when the foundation is well laide and the matter thorowly proved.[22]

This is interesting in a number of ways. It affirms a common rule of biblical interpretation that allegory does not prove anything; it only illustrates what is already proved. Bunyan follows this rule in his expository works, even in such a radically allegorizing work as *Solomon's Temple Spiritualized*. But it also might help to explain why he has such an anxious time in deciding to publish an allegory, as he explains in the 'Author's

---

[21] Luther, *A Commentarie [...] upon [...] Galathians*, fols 4v–5r.
[22] Luther, *A Commentarie [...] upon [...] Galathians*, fol. 206v.

Apology' to *The Pilgrim's Progress*. Allegory, according to Paul as expounded by Luther, is an ornament, not a method of proof.[23]

Most of all, Luther's commentary provided Bunyan with the spiritual comfort that he needed at a time of crisis. But it also provided him with his central theological idea, the distinction between Law and Grace; and it might also have given him something of a rule of how to employ allegory within a biblical framework. Luther's influence on Bunyan through the Galatians commentary has been acknowledged and explored in a number of studies. Theology, writing, and psychological insight (and relief) have all been acknowledged.[24] Although Bunyan might also have been influenced indirectly through Luther's English followers, his theology is usually and correctly identified with the British brand of Calvinism of the kind found in the writings of William Perkins. Bunyan's *Mapp Shewing the Order and Causes of Salvation and Damnation* (?1663) is often compared to William Perkins's more abstract 'Table Declaring the Order of the Causes of Salvation and Damnation' in *A Golden Chaine* (1590; 1591), and if Bunyan had read this book, he would also have come across a number of other Reformed ideas, both Lutheran and Calvinist in basis.

In one of his other books, Perkins argues that the way a person dies is no guide to their eternal salvation. If someone dies in a troubled fashion, it may simply be the effect of their fatal illness; and a peaceful death may conceal an indifference to sin. 'For indeed a man may die like a lambe, and yet go to hell: and one dying in exceeding torments and strange behaviours of the body, may go to heaven', writes Perkins.[25] So Mr Badman dies peacefully, and it is viewed as a fearful, tragic end. Bunyan's Wiseman comments:

> [T]he common people conclude, that if a man dyes quietly, and as they call it, like a Lamb, he is certainly gone to Heaven: when alas, if a wicked man dyes quietly, if a man that has all his dayes lived in notorious sin, dyeth quietly; his quiet dying is so far off from being a sign of his being saved, that it is an uncontrollable proof of his damnation. (*MB*, 161)

'Like a lamb' is too general and colloquial a phrase to be reliable evidence of Bunyan's indebtedness to Perkins, but the passage as a whole is an indication that he is solidly within that Puritan tradition of practical divinity in such matters.[26]

---

[23] See Daniel V. Runyon, 'Luther's Influence on Bunyan's Use of Allegory', *BS*, 14 (2010), 76–84.

[24] See particularly Michael A. Mullett, *John Bunyan in Context* (Keele: Keele University Press, 1996), 35–6, 129–30; Vera J. Camden, '"Most Fit for a Wounded Conscience": The Place of Luther's *Commentary on Galatians* in *Grace Abounding*', *Renaissance Quarterly*, 50 (1997), 819–49; Dayton Haskin, 'Bunyan, Luther, and the Struggle with Belatedness in *Grace Abounding*', *University of Toronto Quarterly*, 50 (1981), 300–13; David Parry, 'John Bunyan and Edwin Sandys on Luther's Galatians Commentary', *Notes & Queries*, 61 (2014), 377–80.

[25] William Perkins, *A Salve for a Sicke Man, or, A Treatise Containing the Nature, Differences, and Kindes of Death* (Cambridge, 1595), 17; discussed in Christopher P. Vogt, *Patience, Compassion, Hope, and the Christian Art of Dying Well* (Lanham, MD: Rowman & Littlefield, 2004), ch. 2.

[26] The possible link between Bunyan and Perkins on the dangers of taking 'dying like a lamb' as evidence of salvation is noted by David Parry, '"A Divine Kind of Rhetoric": Puritanism and Persuasion in Early Modern England' (PhD thesis, University of Cambridge, 2011), 207.

Francis Spira

Bunyan's continuing concern with the role of fear, and the right kind of godly fear as opposed to a slavish fear in the Christian life, is also clear in his reading. In *Grace Abounding* he describes his desperate concern at one stage in his fraught conversion experience that he had committed the unpardonable sin (*GA*, 49–50). There are two principal biblical sources for this notion: one is the comment of Jesus, as reported in the synoptic gospels, that whoever sins against the Holy Ghost shall not be forgiven (Matthew 21:31–2, Mark 3: 8–9, Luke 12:10), and the other is Hebrews 6:4–8, where the issue appears to be apostasy, going back on being a Christian. At this point Bunyan discovered the case of Francis Spira, in Nathaniel Bacon's *A Relation of the Fearfull Estate of Francis Spira, in the Year, 1548* (1638, and reprinted several times). Although the sentence he actually quotes, '*Man knows the beginning of sin, but who bounds the issues thereof?*' (*GA*, 55), is a comment by Bacon, rather than part of his translation of the eyewitness accounts, Bunyan clearly finds a scary echo of his own despair in Spira. Francesco Spiera was an Italian lawyer, practising in the Veneto, and by his own admission very keen on the money that profession brought him. That confession led him to a conversion experience, and to Lutheran Christianity. But almost immediately he began to have doubts and recanted in front of the Papal Legate in Venice, only to hear a 'direful voice' accusing him: '*thou hast broken thy vow, hence Apostate, beare with me the sentence of thy eternall damnation*'. His friends try to persuade him of God's mercy, but he rebuts them: '*My sinne* (said he) *is greater than the mercy of God*.'[27]

The case of Spira, as well as the wider issue of early modern atheism, became a central example for Calvinist psychotheology. An earlier version of the story appears to have influenced Marlowe's *Dr Faustus*.[28] For Bunyan it continued to resonate. In *The Greatness of the Soul* (1682) he puts Spira in biblical company: 'Behold *Spira* in his book, *Cain* in his guilt, and *Saul* with the Witch of *Endor*, and you shall see men ripened, men inlarged and greatned in their fancies, imaginations and apprehensions [...] about their Loss, their misery, and their woe, and their Hells' (*MW*, 9: 167) He also refers to Spira in *The Barren Fig-Tree* (1673) and *The Heavenly Foot-man* (1698) (*MW*, 5: 58, 151, 173). However, Bunyan responds to the story most creatively in the figure of the Man in the Iron Cage in *The Pilgrim's Progress*. Christian sees him in the House of the Interpreter, quite early in his pilgrimage. The marginal note encourages us to see the Iron Cage as a figure of despair, and the man's history parallels Spira's history, in that he 'was once a fair and flourishing Professor' but then, he confesses, 'I have grieved the Spirit, and he is gone' (*PP*, 34). Christian's questioning is similar to those who visited Spira in his despair

---

[27] Nathaniel Bacon, *A Relation of the Fearfull Estate of Francis Spira, in the Year 1548* (1649), 20–1, 28.
[28] Daniel Gates, 'Unpardonable Sins: The Hazards of Performative Language in the Tragic Cases of Francesco Spiera and *Doctor Faustus*', *Comparative Drama*, 38 (2004), 59–81; for a wider perspective, see Kenneth Sheppard, 'Atheism, Apostasy, and the Afterlives of Francis Spira in Early Modern England', *The Seventeenth Century*, 27 (2012), 410–34.

after recanting, urging the mercy of Christ which the man in the cage rejects because he knows that he cannot repent.

DID BUNYAN READ AND ANNOTATE ISAAC AMBROSE?

At this relatively early stage in his growth as a Christian, Bunyan may also have read some of the works of the Lancashire preacher, Isaac Ambrose.[29] A volume containing three of Ambrose's works, all published in 1650 and bound together—*Prima, The First Things; The Doctrine & Directions*; and *Ultima, The Last Things*—may possibly have been owned by Bunyan, and there is a trail of evidence leading back into the mid-eighteenth century that he annotated the first ninety or so pages of *Prima*. Some of these marginal notes were cut out and given as souvenirs to friends by a later owner of the volume, Olinthus Gregory. One was given to the Liverpool Baptist minister and autograph collector Thomas Raffles, and is now with his collection in the John Rylands Library in Manchester. In a letter to Raffles of 20 April 1837, Gregory says that

> Since I gave one of these scraps to Mr. Proudfit[?], and sent one, by him, to my friend Dr. Sprague, I have had so many applications that the book is almost ruined on account of its numerous indentations. […] I have every reason to believe that the writing is really Bunyan's. The original owner of the book testifies it to be such. I have shown it to Mr. Hillyard of Bedford, and have compared it with Bunyan's writing in the church book at Bedford—and cannot but think that the similarity is great.[30]

Not everyone agrees. T. J. Brown compares the writing of the Rylands fragment with that of Bunyan's Deed of Gift and the extant signatures, as well as some entries supposed to be in Bunyan's hand in the Bedford Church Book, and concludes that it cannot be by Bunyan.[31]

The book itself (minus the cut-out souvenirs), was presented to the Firestone Library, Princeton University, in 1968.[32] In a blog article, Stephen Ferguson sets out a provenance for the book going back to 1768, but the eighty years from Bunyan's death until then remain unaccounted for. However, there is one further teasing piece of evidence to

---

[29] For Ambrose, see Roger Pooley, 'Isaac Ambrose', *ODNB*.
[30] Timothy D. Whelan (ed.), *Baptist Autographs in the John Rylands University Library of Manchester, 1741–1845* (Macon, GA: Mercer University Press, 2009), 20.
[31] T. J. Brown, 'English Literary Autographs XXXIII: John Bunyan 1628–1688', *The Book Collector*, 9 (1960), 53–5.
[32] See Stephen Ferguson, '"A Relic of John Bunyan (?)": The Mystery Continues', 2012, available at https://blogs.princeton.edu/rarebooks/page/3/, accessed March 2015. I am very grateful to Stephen Ferguson and his colleagues for sending me a scan of the volume.

consider. Pasted on the back of the title page is a slip of paper with a printer's ornament and a signature, 'J. Bunyan', which is very different from the marginal annotations, but which matches some of the other extant Bunyan signatures quite well.[33]

If the Ambrose volume did belong to Bunyan, and preserves a record of how he read a book, as opposed to being a disputed footnote in the burgeoning field of early modern marginalia studies, a few provisional conclusions can be made.[34] There are several kinds of annotation: some pages are annotated quite densely, so there is not much marginal space left, others barely at all. Sometimes the notes do no more than suggest additional biblical references. Sometimes they comment further, usually in a supportive manner (using a little capital L shape in the text so that the textual reference is precise). For example, on page 66, where a section on 'The promises procuring a relying on Christ' begins, at the sentence '*I am* (sayest thou) *a most vile, unworthy, wicked wretch*' there is a little L after the parenthesis, and the marginal comment reads 'therfore more welcom to Christ'. Other sentences may be underlined, with or without a comment. Earlier, on page four, a series of words are underlined to point up the sequence of Ambrose's ideas about God's attributes in a long sentence: 'his Justice [...] his truth [...] his patience [...] his holiness'. It is the kind of thing a preacher might do, looking out for a series of headings to structure his own discourse. And it is selective: he misses out 'anger' and 'power', not aspects of God from which Bunyan would normally shy away.

There is another, idiosyncratic mode of annotation. Starting on page 11, a page which has some bits already cut out, the annotator introduces a little circular sign with a cross inside it, the function of which he describes: 'here my soul diligently enquire w[ha]t is thy state & if I find any thing I can claime to note thus'. This he does for a few pages, for example against 'the affections must be renewed' (page 15), inserting the comment 'bless the Lord oh my soul for his tenderness'. The reader of *Prima*, whether Bunyan or someone else, is clearly a deeply engaged one, actively involved in applying to the text to his own spiritual state, swapping biblical references, and maybe looking for other applications as well.

A more reliable guide to Bunyan's reading habits can be found in his treatment of books with which he disagreed. He began his writing career as a controversialist, attacking the Quakers in *Some Gospel-Truths Opened* (1656). This followed various encounters and oral debates in Bedfordshire between members of Bunyan's church and leading Quakers. One of them, Edward Burrough, responded to Bunyan's book in *The True Faith of the Gospel of Peace* (also 1656), which Bunyan in turn responded to in *A Vindication of the Book Called, Some Gospel-Truths Opened* (1657), published like its predecessor in London as well as Newport Pagnell. He did not respond to Burrough's further reply, *Truth (the Strongest of all) Witnessed Forth* (1657).[35]

---

[33] Roger Pooley, 'Bunyan's Annotations of Isaac Ambrose (Allegedly): A Question', *The Recorder*, 23 (2017), 23–4.

[34] For an introduction and bibliography, see William H. Sherman, *Used Books: Marking Readers in Renaissance England* (Philadelphia, PA: University of Pennsylvania Press, 2008), particularly Part II, 'Reading and Religion'.

[35] See Chapter 10 in this volume.

Other books Bunyan argued against directly were also linked to the pressures on his Bedfordshire congregation. The Anglican clergyman Edward Fowler was part of a new movement in the Church of England, sometimes called Latitudinarian, and had been made rector of Northill in Bedfordshire in 1656. His second book, *The Design of Christianity*, was published in 1671, and was criticized by Bunyan in 1672, in *A Defence of the Doctrine of Justification, by Faith*. This shows a rather different kind of reader to the one revealed in *Some Gospel-Truths Opened*. Bunyan's response to Burrough was derived almost as much from discussions with him as from the books, and he responds to Burrough's rather freewheeling, incantatory style with a firm, even earthy insistence on the incarnation of Christ ('the Son of Mary' is his constant refrain). *A Vindication* is still a response to what Burrough and his Quaker friends have said as much as to the book. Writing against Fowler, however, Bunyan summarizes his arguments in a neat preface (he calls it a 'Premonition to the Reader') with page references for each of Fowler's points. The actual argument has been well discussed by Isabel Rivers; the point here is to notice that Bunyan has become a more experienced and systematic reader as well as writer in the intervening sixteen years.[36]

Foxe's *Acts and Monuments*

In *A Few Sighs from Hell* (1658) Bunyan warns 'there is a time coming, O ye surly dogged persecutors of the Saints, that they shall slight you as much as ever you slighted them' (*MW*, 1: 284). Even at the height of the Commonwealth, the separatist churches like Bunyan's never had an easy ride, and Bunyan's strength and faith were about to be tested further. But he was already reading John Foxe's *Acts and Monuments* (first published in English in 1563), and refers to it in *A Few Sighs* (*MW*, 1: 358). Foxe's 'original idea, of using martyrology as a line upon which to hang a history of the conflict between the True Church and the False' helped form Bunyan's already sensitive and combative distinctions between Christians, whether in his earliest writings against the Quakers, or his general wariness of superficial Christianity.[37] This in turn finds its way into *The Pilgrim's Progress* and *The Holy War* (1682), with their mockery of religious hypocrites—though one might argue that Bunyan could have got this directly from the Gospels, where Jesus is harder on Pharisaic religiousness than on those rejected as sinners. The division between true and fake Christians is essential to Bunyan's thinking about himself, his opponents, even his own church.

---

[36] Isabel Rivers, *Reason, Grace and Sentiment: A Study of the Language of Religion and Ethics in England, 1660–1780*, vol. 1, *Whichcote to Wesley* (Cambridge: Cambridge University Press, 1991), chs 2 and 3.

[37] David Loades, 'The Early Reception', in *John Foxe's The Acts and Monuments Online*, para. 3, available at http://www.johnfoxe.org/index.php?realm=more&gototype=modern&type=essay&book=essay7, accessed 10 January 2018.

In this way of looking at the world, the ideological impact of Foxe was substantial; Bunyan's early reading of it aligns him with a wide Protestant, anti-Catholic consensus about the heroism of true believers. It shows his hunger for learning: *Acts and Monuments* is a big book, whichever of the available editions he used (probably those of 1632 or 1641 which both run to three folio volumes), and an expensive one. But Bunyan does not come across as a lonely, eccentric autodidact, because his learning aligns so strongly with the Reformed consensus, Lutheran and Calvinist. For such a combative, fissiparous movement, 'consensus' may seem to be the wrong word. But Bunyan did not move from one sect to another, unlike so many of his radical contemporaries. And Foxe is quite catholic (with a very small 'c') in compiling his list of heroic martyrs of the true, invisible church. As John Knott points out, Bunyan gets from Foxe a sense of how a church under persecution might behave: combining patient suffering with bold speaking.[38]

Bunyan clearly knew the *Acts and Monuments* well and frequently refers to it in his writings. The posthumously published *A Discourse of the House of the Forest of Lebanon* (1692) includes a long quotation from Foxe, a transcription of a letter from the Italian martyr Pomponius Algerius, emphasizing the spiritual comfort he had in prison: 'The Place is sharp and tedious to them that be guilty; but to the innocent and guiltless it is *mellifluous*' (*MW*, 7: 159–60). Bunyan's identification with imprisonment for the truth is clear enough from his spiritual autobiography. It is not a great speculative leap to see how important Foxe's account of the often persecuted true church is to Bunyan remaining steadfast during twelve years' imprisonment.

Foxe also supplies Bunyan, or more precisely the illustrations to *The Pilgrim's Progress*, with some of its iconography. In the fifth edition of the first part, a woodcut of the martyrdom of Faithful appears for the first time. The *Acts and Monuments* includes a number of woodcuts illustrating the burning of 'heretics', and the bottom half of the woodcut of Faithful's martyrdom has echoes of these in its depiction of the man bound to the stake with flames swirling up, and the axe-heads of the soldiers round about. The link between Faithful's martyrdom and Foxe is convincingly argued by John Knott; and he also points out the influence of instances of martyrdom in the early church, something that occupies Foxe at the beginning of his vast collection, although New Testament sources are equally at work in Bunyan's imagery.[39] Faithful is accused of treason, an accusation which is common enough in Foxe's accounts, particularly among the Reformation martyrs. The accusation of treason triggers the death penalty, of course, which may account for its particular terror. Although the deaths at the end of the second part of *The Pilgrim's Progress* are not those of martyrs in Foxe's sense, they do make use of the trope of the final words of the martyrs. Laurence Saunders, one of the Marian martyrs, calls out 'Welcome Life' in the woodcut of his death in *Acts and Monuments*; Bunyan gives the

---

[38] John Knott, *Discourses of Martyrdom in English Literature, 1563–1694* (Cambridge: Cambridge University Press, 1993), especially ch. 6, 'Bunyan and the Language of Martyrdom'.

[39] Knott, *Discourses of Martyrdom*, 25.

same words to Mr Ready-to-halt as he passes through the River of Death.[40] Earlier on in *Part II*, Gaius gives an account of the early church martyrs which is indebted to Foxe's redaction of Eusebius (*PP*, 260, 349).

Conclusion

Bunyan's use of some of the books in his library may have been quite uncritical, but of others, such as the works of the early Quakers, or the (loosely speaking) Latitudinarian divine Edward Fowler that he attacked, he was systematically and destructively critical in the common seventeenth-century manner. His reading ranges from broadsides, tracts, and pamphlets to works of substance, such as Foxe's massive ecclesiastical history. We can see that books stirred him; they informed him, fed his imagination, satisfied his emotional needs, and helped turn a poorly educated man into an articulate preacher and author, one of the great writers of prose fiction.

Suggested Reading

Cambers, Andrew, *Godly Reading: Print, Manuscript and Puritanism in England, 1580–1720* (Cambridge: Cambridge University Press, 2011).
Greaves, Richard L., *Glimpses of Glory: John Bunyan and English Dissent* (Stanford, CA: Stanford University Press, 2002).
Green, Ian, *Print and Protestantism in Early Modern England* (Oxford: Oxford University Press, 2000).
Rivers, Isabel, *Reason, Grace and Sentiment: A Study of the Language of Religion and Ethics in England, 1660–1780*, vol. 1: *Whichcote to Wesley* (Cambridge: Cambridge University Press, 1991), chs 1–3.
Ryrie, Alec, 'The Protestant and the Word', in Alec Ryrie, *Being Protestant in Reformation Britain* (Oxford: Oxford University Press, 2013), 259–314.
Spufford, Margaret, *Small Books and Pleasant Histories: Popular Fiction and its Readership in Seventeenth-Century England* (Cambridge: Cambridge University Press, 1985).

---

[40] See Thomas S. Freeman, 'A Library in Three Volumes: Foxe's "Book of Martyrs" in the Writings of John Bunyan', *BS*, 5 (1994), 47–57 (52–3).

CHAPTER 7

BUNYAN AND GENDER

MARGARET J. M. EZELL

Bunyan's writings, in particular the two parts of *The Pilgrim's Progress*, have always invited the critical reader to focus on gender issues. However, there has been little consensus as to what his writings reveal about Bunyan's attitudes towards the women in his congregation, in his writings, or in his conceptualization of a spiritual life. On the one hand, he suggests throughout *The Pilgrim's Progress, Part II* that women are unable to undergo the trial of a Christian life unaided, while on the other, he equally vehemently asserts that it is an error to believe that men are spiritually superior to women or that women are lesser in the sight of God, even if they do 'bear about with them the badge of their inferiority' (*MW*, 4: 326). What emerges consistently in Bunyan's texts, in which such seemingly contradictory views are frequently asserted in close proximity, is his insistence on gender difference based on biological sex and his rejection of a concept of humans as ever being free of gendered roles, as troublesome as he seems to have found the embodied forms. Writing initially during periods in which conventional hierarchies within the family and the church were being aggressively challenged by sectarian prophets and preachers, and subsequently during times in which definitions of masculinity, femininity, and sexuality were dramatically performed, Bunyan and his writings were immersed in a world in which gender roles and sexual bodies mattered.

As a minister, Bunyan understood that attention must be given to the literal bodies of his congregation and their behaviour, even while attempting to awaken and animate their souls. Part of his duty to his congregation was to encourage godly living, and for Bunyan, godly living required recognition of hierarchy and one's place within it according to gendered terms as well as social ones.

> *It is amiable, and pleasant to* God, *when* Christians *keep their Rank, Relation and Station, doing all as become their Quality and Calling. When Christians stand every one in their places, and do the work of their* Relations, *then they are like the flowers in the Garden,* that stand *and grow where the Gardner hath* planted them. (*MW*, 3: 10)

Bunyan published this statement in praise of stability and hierarchy in domestic and social relations and between the sexes in 1663 while imprisoned in Bedford. Outside of those confines, however, the conventional understandings of rank, relation, and station were all under intense pressure, in particular from issues relating to gender and sexuality. If one considers Bunyan not only as a provincial minister and 'mechanic preacher', but also as part of larger contemporary controversies about gender and sexuality during the Restoration, his attacks on lewd attire and wanton behaviour, about the nature of the feminine as opposed to the female, and about the proper roles of the man take on further resonance and complexity.

Bodies

[Women] are not builded to manage such Worship. (*MW*, 4: 306)

As historians and critics have pointed out, women sectarians as authors and prophets during the 1650s and 1660s openly challenged societal expectations about women's roles in the congregation, and, indirectly, within the family. Bunyan was clearly familiar with women of this type, as can be seen in his denunciation of contemporary women prophets in *A Case of Conscience Resolved* (1683) as well as his earliest writings, such as *Some Gospel-Truths Opened* (1656), in which he warns spiritually vulnerable readers not to be misled by charismatic sects such as the Ranters and Quakers. It is most clearly seen in his rebuttal of Quaker writers such as George Fox and Margaret Fell, who, in arguing for the authority of women to preach and speak in church, cited the examples of women of the Old Testament, including Deborah and Miriam. Bunyan challenges his congregation and readers to recall not only such anomalous, extraordinary women, but also to remember that while Miriam was a woman who is explicitly referred to as a prophetess in the Bible and who did lead the Israelite women in song praising the Lord, she was also the woman whose criticism of Moses's marriage to a Cushite woman angered the Lord and who was punished with leprosy (Numbers 12:6–10). 'Remember what God did to Miriam', he concludes, 'and be afraid' (*MW*, 4: 329).

Bunyan was also an early opponent of the Quakers on several issues regarding the corporeal versus the spiritual, which has relevance to his understanding of gender issues. In his exchanges with Edward Burrough and George Fox, Bunyan contends that they do not respect the human embodiment of Christ, that Christ became a physical human male who was born of a human female body. His attack in the late 1650s on the Quaker 'Widow Morlin' in his defence of Margaret Pryor, who had charged her with witchcraft, likewise suggests that he viewed Quakers as even possessing the powers through witchcraft to alter human embodiment, to change a woman's body into that of an animal.[1]

---

[1] Margaret J. M. Ezell, 'Bunyan's Women, Women's Bunyan', in Vera J. Camden (ed.), *Trauma and Transformation: The Political Progress of John Bunyan* (Stanford, CA: Stanford University Press, 2008), 63–80 (70–3).

At the same period in his life, Bunyan was attacking Quaker belief concerning the resurrection of Christ. In *Some Gospel-Truths Opened*, he argued that at the resurrection Christ would appear again in 'the body of flesh wherewith he was crucified', his male body that walked, talked, and ate (*MW*, 1: 46):

> *Did he leave the body behind him, which was born of the Virgin Mary, which walked up and down with his disciples in the world, was afterward hanged upon the Cross, buried, rose again from the dead, with which body he did eat, drink, and likewise walk with his Disciples after his resurrection from the dead, and did bid his Disciple see if he were not flesh and bones, yea, or no?* (*MW*, 1: 115)

Christ rose, Bunyan asserts repeatedly, 'that very man, whom the Jewes did crucifie between two theeves' (*MW*, 1: 68). The proof of his resurrection was the corporeal male body, a physical Christ who invites doubting Thomas to touch him and who eats the honeycomb brought by the disciples. 'Was that Jesus, that was born of the Virgin *Mary*, a real man of flesh and bones, after his resurrection from the dead, out of *Josephs* Sepulcher, yea, or no? for the Scripture saith he was', concludes Bunyan in his final questions to the Quakers: 'if you say he hath no body, but the Church, the Saints, Then I ask, what that was that was taken down from the Cross, and laid into *Josephs* Sepulcher' (*MW*, 1: 114, 115).

Furthermore, in this human male body he would judge the human sinners when they were physically resurrected from their graves in their male and female bodies. As Nigel Smith has pointed out, Bunyan, in his later writings such as *The Greatness of the Soul* (1682), urges his readers to consider the ways in which the body after death will be reunited with the soul and will be the vehicle through which the soul will feel the physical torments of hell: the damned will see themselves in hell, 'and this will be a torment to their body, there is bodily torment, as I said, ministred to the body by the senses of the body' (*MW*, 9: 209). In *The Resurrection of the Dead* (?1665), Bunyan had explicitly described how the 'Body ariseth as to the nature of it; the self-same nature', and 'at our rising, we shall not change our *nature*, but our *glory*' (*MW*, 3: 217, 218). Against such assertions of the corporeal reality of the resurrection, Quakers such as Burrough and Fox argued that Christ had risen spiritually and had entered into the believer and that Bunyan's insistence on the physical nature of the resurrection and of heaven itself left him mired in 'Carnal sottishness'.[2] In his rebuttal of Bunyan's *Vindication*, Fox charges Bunyan with overvaluing the 'creature' and ignoring the inward light which is Christ in every person. Using a dialogue format, the 'priest' speaks for Bunyan and is answered by Fox:

> *Pr.* He saith, *The Lord Jesus Christ is afar off in his bodily presence. Ans.* And yet he saith, *the Lord is at hand*. And the Apostle saith, *he was in them*. And Christ said, *he would dwell with them*.

---

[2] Edward Burrough, *The Memorable Works of a Son of Thunder and Consolation* (1672), 147, 306–07. See also Greaves, *Glimpses*, 76–81; Nigel Smith, 'Bunyan and the Language of the Body', in Anne Laurence, W. R. Owens, and Stuart Sim (eds.), *John Bunyan and his England, 1628–88* (London: Hambledon Press, 1990), 161–74.

As to Bunyan's assertion that Christ will return to the Mount of Olives in his physical body to judge the resurrected bodies of the sinners, Fox charges that this clearly places Bunyan in the company of 'false Prophets, who bid people look for him beyond the Sea, *look here, be there*: But who are come to Christ the light, the life, they need not go forth'.[3]

Bunyan's emphasis on acknowledging the biblical physical body, male and female, and the reuniting of that male or female body with the individual soul after resurrection would place him at odds with the Quaker doctrine expressed by Margaret Fell and William Penn, among others, that in Christ 'is neither male nor female' (Galatians 4:28) and that souls have no gender. While souls may not have genders, they do, in Bunyan's view, inhabit gendered, sexual bodies and, in Bunyan's understanding, do not, as in Andrew Marvell's 'The Garden', leave the body to exist outside it.

Bunyan's resistance to the erasure or the dismissal of the human body, male and female, in religious discourse is in part pragmatic. Much of Bunyan's writing was didactic rather than controversial in nature, aimed at his congregation and those readers struggling to understand their place in the spiritual realm while toiling in the physical world; it is in these texts that Bunyan addresses most directly issues that affected men and those that affected women, as well as considering the needs of children of both sexes. As Michael Davies has argued, Bunyan's attitudes towards human sex and sexuality link them unequivocally to sin; furthermore, 'if you are a man, Bunyan implies [...] sexual sin and the temptation of desires that "hang in thy flesh", will constantly be "lying at thee"'.[4] In matters of daily social intercourse, Bunyan was well aware that bodies, male and female, are important, and that a Christian in the material world would be forced to deal with issues involving not only the appropriate roles and behaviours of men and women but also the ways in which sexual bodies can subvert hierarchy and social convention.

The Restoration was a period of flamboyant display of the body, from actresses on stage, to public performances of libertine sexuality and the spread of cheap pornographic literature. Transgressive sexuality was sometimes explicitly linked to religious practices, often in an intentionally shocking manner. Writing in London in 1663, the same year as Bunyan published *Christian Behaviour*, Samuel Pepys frequently noted in his diary with a mingled horror and fascination the chaotic behaviour exhibited by members of court, male and female: how, for example, favourites of Charles II such as Sir Charles Sedley cavorted naked on the balcony of the appropriately named Cock Inn in front of an enormous and outraged crowd below, 'preaching a mountebanke sermon from that pulpit' and 'acting all the postures of lust and buggery that could be imagined'.[5] That same year, Barbara Palmer, Countess of Castlemaine, Charles II's most powerful and flagrant mistress, was being painted with her eldest son (an

---

[3] George Fox, *The Great Mistery of the Great Whore Unfolded* (1659), 8, 9.
[4] Michael Davies, 'Bunyan's Bawdy', in Camden (ed.), *Trauma and Transformation*, 110–19 (106, 110).
[5] *The Diary of Samuel Pepys*, ed. Robert Latham and William Matthews (London: University of California Press, 1971), 4: 209–10.

illegitimate child of the king) by the court painter Sir Peter Lely in the traditional posture of Madonna and child, with rather more *décolleté* than is conventional in religious art.[6] The intoxicating and infuriating flouting of sexual decorum involving blasphemous religious signifiers must have been deeply shocking to average Englishmen and women, those making up the angry crowd in the street, but the elite status of these sexual performers placed them above the civil laws which attempted to control such behaviour.

Popular entertainments, however, shadowed those of the elite. Theatre managers such as Thomas Killigrew exploited audiences' interest in women's bodies on stage by offering in 1664 and 1672 an all-female cast for a revival of his bawdy farce, *The Parson's Wedding*, which Samuel Pepys described as 'an obscene, loose play' in which a hypocritical Puritan minister is tricked into marrying a prostitute. In addition to the entertainment provided by women portraying men, characters with familiar names including Lady Wild, Mrs Pleasant, and Mrs Wanton discuss men, sex, and marriage. The men in the play, including Mr Sadd and Mr Jolly, seek to exploit Lady Love-all, who is described as 'an old Stallion hunting Widow'. Mrs Wanton, described in the cast of characters as 'The *Captains* Livery Punk, Married to the *Parson* by Confederacy', instructs the other women of the necessity of female control in a relationship, especially in marriage:

> *Baud.* Any thing that may get Rule; I love to wear the Breeches.
> *Wanton.* So do we all, Wench; Empire? 'tis all our aim; and I'll put my ranting *Roger* in a Cage but I'll tame him; he loves already, which is an excellent Ring in a fools nose, and thou shalt hear him sing.—
> Happy onely is that Family, that shewes A Cock that's silent, and a Hen that crowes.[7]

Bunyan's lusty ladies are likewise confident in their places in the world and every bit as potent in their ability to turn the heads of godly men. Madame Wanton who tempts Faithful in *The Pilgrim's Progress, Part I* was nearly successful in snaring her pilgrim, promising him 'all carnal and fleshly content'. So powerful are her charms that even though he shut his eyes to avoid being bewitched by her looks, he nevertheless tells Christian, 'Nay, I know not whether I did wholly escape her, or no' (*PP*, 68, 69). Madame Wanton reappears in *Part II* as one of Christiana's neighbours, who discuss the foolishness of her going on pilgrimage. In a scene paralleled in the unruly parties of Killigrew's whores, Mrs Light-mind remarks that:

> I was Yesterday at Madam *Wantons*, where we were as merry as the Maids. For who do you think should be there, but I, and Mrs. *Love-the-flesh*, and three or four more,

---

[6] Catharine MacLeod, '"Good but not Like": Peter Lely, Portrait Practice, and the Creation of a Court Look', in Catharine MacLeod and Julia Marciari Alexander (eds.), *Painted Ladies: Women at the Court of Charles II* (London: National Portrait Gallery, 2001), 50–61.
[7] Thomas Killigrew, *The Parson's Wedding*, in Thomas Killigrew, *Comedies and Tragedies* (1664), 93.

> with Mr. *Lechery*, Mrs. *Filth*, and some others. So there we had Musick and dancing, and what else was meet to fill up the pleasure. (*PP*, 185)

The most famous of Bunyan's emblematic whores is Madame Bubble, who brings Stand-fast to his knees in *Part II*:

> There was one in very pleasant Attire, *but old*, that presented her self unto me, and offered me three things, to wit, her *Body*, her *Purse*, and her *Bed*. […] Well, I repulsed her once and twice, but she put by my Repulses, and smiled. Then I began to be angry, but she mattered that nothing at all. Then she made Offers again, and said, If I would be ruled by her, she would make me great and happy. For, said she, I am the Mistriss of the World, and men are made happy by me. (*PP*, 300–01)

In the context of the period during which Bunyan wrote this passage, it is difficult not to think here of Barbara Palmer, Countess of Castlemaine, with her long string of lovers after Charles II, assisting in the careers of such young men as Henry Killigrew, the future admiral, and John Churchill, the future Duke of Marlborough, with whom she consorted between 1671 and 1675 and gave £5,000 of the king's money.[8] Great-heart is able to explain the significance of Madame Bubble to the other pilgrims: 'this is she that maintaineth in their Splendor, all those that are the Enemies of Pilgrims', and she is 'a bold and impudent Slut'. She is furthermore characterized as one of the elite, who 'loveth Banqueting and Feasting' and she has 'given it out in some places, that she is a Goddess, and therefore some do Worship her. She has her times and open places of Feasting, and […] she will promise to some Crowns, and Kingdoms, if they will but take her Advice' (*PP*, 302).

The figure of the powerful courtesan who can offer men not only sex but also wealth and promotion is matched in the period's literature by the sexually confident prostitute who outsmarts gullible men, especially hypocritical Puritan ministers. The mass popular culture of the period has been described as being 'saturated with anti-republican pornographic pamphlets', such as *The Wandering Whore* series (1660) and *Select City Quaeries* (1660).[9] This material, which was produced in cheap pamphlets and broadsides, was not targeted at the elite members of Charles's court, but 'quite likely the citizens, citizen's wives, artisans, and working poor who lived and worked in the neighborhoods where booksellers operated—the very people whom pornographic satires were most eager to vilify as "private whores, cuckolds, and cuckold-makers"'.[10] Even relatively formulaic broadside ballads such as 'The Maid's Lament' conventionally, during the 1670s and

---

[8] John B. Hattendorf, 'John Churchill, First Duke of Marlborough', *ODNB*. Madame Bubble was also associated with Louise de Kéroualle, Duchess of Portsmouth, in an early biography of her; see Henri Forneron, *Louise de Kéroualle, Duchess of Portsmouth, 1649–1734*, 3rd edn (London: Swan Sonnenschein, Lowrey, 1888), viii.

[9] Melissa M. Mowry, *The Bawdy Politic in Stuart England, 1660–1714* (Aldershot: Ashgate, 2004), 10.

[10] Mowry, *Bawdy Politic*, 12.

1680s, feature crude woodcuts of ladies with long bare necks and court hairstyles exposing vast expanses of bosom.

Bunyan was clearly aware not only of the ways in which men and women of all social classes fell into sexual misconduct, including ministers, but also of the ways in which the behaviours and fashions of the elite would filter through society. As Wiseman and Attentive in *The Life and Death of Mr. Badman* (1680) discuss, 'uncleanness' is 'one of the most reigning sins in our day':

> ATTEN. *So they say, and that too among those that one would think had more wit, even among the great ones.*
> Wise. The more is the pity: for usually Examples that are set by them that are great and chief, spread sooner, and more universally, then do the sins of other men; yea, and when such men are at the head in transgressing, sin walks with a bold face through the Land. (*MB*, 49)

Badman himself observed of the times that '*Who would keep a Cow of their own, that can have a quart of milk for a penny?* Meaning, Who would be at the charge to have a Wife, that can have a Whore when he listeth?' (*MB*, 145).

Sectarian preachers were frequently accused of improper relationships with women in their congregations; some like Laurence Clarkson freely acknowledged it, declaring that 'I was still careful for moneys for my wife, onely my body was given to other women.'[11] Bunyan himself was accused of sexual misconduct: 'that which was reported with the boldest confidence, was, that I had my *Misses*, my *Whores*, my *Bastards*, yea, *two wives at once*, and the like', and he was no stranger to any of those terms (*GA*, 93). Mr Badman's infamy towards his pious wife whom he had married for her portion is confirmed by his relationship with lewd women: his true nature is revealed after his marriage when he begins again to frequent prostitutes and even bring them back to his house and 'wo be to his wife when they were gone, if she did not entertain them with all varieties possible, and also carry it lovingly to them' (*MB*, 70).

Bunyan famously defended himself in his spiritual autobiography, *Grace Abounding to the Chief of Sinners* (1666), from all charges of inappropriate behaviour with the opposite sex, declaring that 'if all the Fornicators and Adulterers in *England* were hang'd by the Neck till they be dead, *John Bunyan*, the object of their Envie, would be still alive and well' (*GA*, 94). The incident with Agnes Beaumont in 1674 makes it abundantly clear that it was not due to a lack of interest in him by women. Beaumont herself records her pride at being seen in such a familiar pose with this famous preacher. 'But to speak the truth I had not gone far behind him', she confesses, 'but my heart was puffed up with pride, and I began to have high thoughts of myself, and proud to think I should ride behind such a man as he was; and I was pleased anybody did look after me as I rode along.'[12] 'I know

---

[11] Laurence Clarkson, *The Lost Sheep Found* (1660), 26.
[12] *The Narrative of the Persecutions of Agnes Beaumont*, ed. Vera Camden (Lansing, MI: Colleague's Press, 1992), 43–4.

not', Bunyan asserted, 'whether there be such a thing as a woman breathing under the Copes of the whole Heaven but by their apparel, their Children, or by common Fame, except my Wife' (*GA*, 94), and he was notably reluctant to let Agnes ride behind him. This caution proved to have good cause, as her scandalized neighbours and scorned suitor used the event to charge her with involvement in her father's death.

As commentators have noted, Bunyan's claim to be oblivious to women's bodies is simply not borne out in his writings. Women's bodies, especially exposed female flesh, are dangerous to men, and Bunyan, in *Christian Behaviour* (1663), highlights this in the section 'Of Adultery or Uncleanness', seeing the second as being 'a very predominate and master *Sin*, easie to overtake the sinner, as being one of the first that is ready to offer it self at all occasions' (*MW* 3: 50). Uncleanness, as opposed to actual fornication, is 'committed unawares to many, even so soon as a man hath but looked upon a woman'. It is 'a very taking *sin*, it is natural above all sins to mankind; and as it is most natural, so it wants not tempting occasions, having object for to look on in every corner'. Uncleanness can be committed by both men and women, as revealed in three ways: the '*wanton eye*', '*wanton* and *immodest talk*', and 'adorning themselves in *light* and *wanton Apparel*'. 'If those that give way to a wanton eye, wanton words, and immodest apparel, be not *Whores*, &c. in their hearts, I know not what to say', he concludes (*MW*, 3: 50-1). Both men and women, Bunyan warns, risk uncleanness in their choice of attire: 'the attire of an Harlot is too frequently in our day the attire of Professors', he charges, and indeed it is one of the duties of the master of a family to keep his household 'temperate in all things, in Apparel, in Language, that they be not Gluttons, nor Drunkards' (*MW*, 3: 51, 26).

During the Restoration, as represented in almost every media, however, the new fashions drew attention to the body, male and female, in disturbing ways. Court portraits of Charles II in his regalia with his regal sceptre, such as those by John Michael Wright and Sir Peter Lely, notoriously emphasize not only his relaxed carriage of kingly power but also his athleticism and shapely legs. Lely's famous series of paintings of the women of the court, 'the Windsor Beauties', are notable for their display of the female form, much of it lushly spilling out of their loose and casual attire; such images had a wide circulation through the growing popularity of purchasable engraved prints. Mr Wiseman observes that such court fashions had even permeated Sunday worship, where women attended with painted faced and 'their naked shoulders, and Paps hanging out like a Cows bag' (*MB*, 125). On stage, the new plays written for the new commercial theatres delighted in displaying actress's limbs in breeches parts, and one critic has credited the period with the invention of 'the bosom as letterbox', the stage business of concealing letters in a lady's décolletage.[13]

As sexually provocative as the new fashions of the 1660s were, critics have argued that during the Restoration the robust 'masculinity' that had imbued representations of Cromwell in power was replaced by a seeming return to the 'femininity' characterizing Charles I and the Royalists. This shift in representation, it is argued, resulted in a

---

[13] J. L. Styan, *Restoration Comedy in Performance* (Cambridge: Cambridge University Press, 1986), 92.

destabilization of gender norms, a radical proliferation of gender possibilities, and even the short-lived celebration of the bisexual libertines who used Charles II's court as their stage.[14] The very fashions worn by men during the Restoration, some cultural historians have argued, made the male body equal to that of the female form in terms of theatrical display, highlighting what would come to be considered, by the end of the century, feminine gestures:

> [T]he lace on his sleeves required him to hold his arms away from his body, and toying with his cane or flourishing his handkerchief gave his hands thus poised something to do; the weight of his coat required a swinging stride that came close to a swagger, or, with the shorter steps of a fop, a mincing walk [...].When standing, his weight would fall on the back leg, and, tensing the calf muscles of the other, he would always seem to be posing to display his well-turned 'parts'.[15]

This description corresponds well to the fop character which becomes a conventional male type in the comedies of the 1670s, such as Sir Fopling Flutter in Etherege's *The Man of Mode* (1676). Notably, however, although absorbed in his 'equipage' and attire, his speech deliberately affected, and his posture mincing, the seeming embodiment of the feminine man, Sir Fopling is depicted as attracted to and attractive to women, not men. It is the rake protagonist Dorimant, who seeks to have sex with every good-looking woman he meets, who also greets his male friend Medley with a kiss of such intimacy that the orange-woman bawd who observes it spits and describes the behaviour as 'filthy'. Historians of sexuality have argued that during this period such conduct was not perceived as 'homosexual' in a modern sense but instead as male hypersexuality. John Wilmot, Earl of Rochester, captured this excessive male desire in his poetic satire of an elderly rake looking back on his conquests in 'The Disabled Debauchee': 'Nor shall our Love-fits *Cloris* be forgot, / When each the well-look'd Link-boy strove t'enjoy; / And the best Kiss was the deciding Lot, / Whether the Boy Fuck'd you, or I the Boy.'[16] Bunyan, as critics have noticed, for all his condemnation of fornication and adultery, does not single out homosexual conduct. He ranks the sins of Sodom as being 'very great' and describes them in *Instructions for the Ignorant* (1675) as being 'such sins as may not be spoken of without blushing' (*MW*, 8: 15–16). Yet when in *The Pilgrim's Progress* Christian and Hopeful reach the site of the destroyed Sodom, their attention is less on the nature of its sins than the fate of Lot's wife. 'The sin of Sodom', Barry Burg argues, 'looms neither particularly large nor particularly repugnant to either Bunyan or to his pilgrim.'[17]

---

[14] See Randolph Trumbach, 'The Birth of the Queen: Sodomy and the Emergence of Gender Equality in Modern Culture, 1660–1750', in Robert Shoemaker and Mary Vincent (eds.), *Gender and History in Western Europe* (London: Arnold, 1998), 161–73; Jeremy Webster, *Performing Libertinism in Charles II's Court: Politics, Drama, Sexuality* (Basingstoke: Palgrave Macmillan, 2005), ch. 1.

[15] Styan, *Restoration Comedy*, 65.

[16] *The Works of John Wilmot, Earl of Rochester*, ed. Harold Love (Oxford: Oxford University Press, 1999), 45.

[17] Barry R. Burg, *Sodomy and the Pirate Tradition: English Sea Rovers in the Seventeenth-Century Caribbean*, 2nd edn (New York: New York University Press, 1995), 32.

While few would care (or dare) match the extravagant sexual performances of the courtier rakes and their women associates, the challenges posed by their actions and fashions to conventional codes of social conduct, morality, and sexual expression were disruptive to notions of hierarchical gender roles. 'Uncleanness' generated by highly sexualized fashion and behaviour was, for Bunyan the minister, a characteristic sin of his times, one through which women and men in their carnality could destroy each other. His strictures on Christian decorum within the family and the duty to control unruly bodies, thoughts, and acts by the minister and father are his defences against such dangers. While Bunyan seems to have strongly resisted any understanding of the spiritual that erased the sexed human body, and to have strongly argued too for the necessity of hierarchy in all relationships, nevertheless his writings prompt us still to ask, how fixed was the performance of gender roles for Bunyan?

Roles

The Lord doth put no *difference betwixt* Male *and* Female, as to the communications of his Saving Graces. (*MW*, 4: 295)

The duty of godly men to control the bodies and speech of their families as well as of themselves is a recurring theme in Bunyan's fictions as well as in his guides to Christian living. As early as the nineteenth century, critics reading Bunyan frequently addressed the gendered hierarchical aspects of his writings. Sir Walter Scott, in reviewing Robert Southey's life of Bunyan, describes the relationship of the two parts of *The Pilgrim's Progress* as representing archetypal male and female characteristics: Christian 'a man, and a bold one, is represented as enduring his fatigues, trials, and combats, by his own stout courage, under the blessing of Heaven', and Christiana and Mercie 'are supported in the path of duty, notwithstanding the natural feebleness and timidity of their nature' by the manly Great-heart, 'by whose strength and valour their lack of both is supplied, and the dangers and distresses of the way repelled and overcome'.[18] John Brown declared in 1886 that the women in *Part II* were perhaps modelled on Bunyan's two wives, and that this provided the counterpart for 'religious life in man [...] as it shows itself in woman'.[19] In the twentieth century, several generations of critics were likewise in agreement over the manliness of Christian and his author, but declared that Bunyan himself was not particularly interested in women as a group and that 'women play a very small part in Bunyan's voluminous writings'.[20]

---

[18] Sir Walter Scott, 'Southey's Life of John Bunyan', in *The Miscellaneous Prose Works of Sir Walter Scott*, 28 vols (Edinburgh: Robert Cadell, 1835), 18: 109.

[19] John Brown, *John Bunyan: His Life, Times, and Work*, rev. Frank Mott Harrison (London: Hulbert, 1928), 259–60.

[20] Hill, *Bunyan*, 302.

The critical and historical view of the relative insignificance of women in Bunyan's world and of the manly nature of Christian pilgrimage was considerably challenged with the recovery in the 1980s and 1990s of the writings of contemporary women prophets, preachers, and autobiographical authors. These included texts by women such as the Fifth Monarchist Anna Trapnel, a leading figure of the Quakers, Margaret Fell, and an admirer of Bunyan, Agnes Beaumont. The recovery of such texts and such female voices complicated the study of women's place in Bunyan's writings: influential feminist studies of those decades found in Bunyan's writings not so much an avoidance of dealing with women or the feminine as a determined suppression of it.

Many of these studies focused fresh attention on the psychology of the man and the times. Monica Furlong's early psychoanalytic interpretation argued that Bunyan's Puritanism and subsequent Oedipal anxieties necessitated the repression of his desires for women, resulting in their absence from his writings such as *The Holy War* (1682), the story of a town under siege that she claims (incorrectly) contains not a single woman.[21] Tamsin Spargo has argued with conviction that, for Bunyan, those women who contested patriarchy must be silenced: the claims by female prophets and preachers to be delivering the Word of God and speaking with godly authority, Spargo says, would have imperilled the 'secure masculine identity of God'.[22] Critics such as Thomas Luxon and Michael Mullet have likewise highlighted the extent to which Bunyan seems constantly to position women as the 'Other' and therefore to have excluded them from full participation not only in his writings but also in his church, possibly to the point of denying that women as a group had either minds or souls.[23] Certainly Bunyan's *A Case of Conscience Resolved*, in which he argues against women of his congregation holding separate meetings, adheres firmly to St Paul's command that women should not speak in church, and preferably not much elsewhere. N. H. Keeble, in an early essay, drew attention to the importance godly women played in Bunyan's own conversion experience and the bravery of Elizabeth Bunyan, his second wife, in attempting to persuade the justices to free her husband, but nevertheless concluded that Bunyan 'welcomes women on pilgrimage, but he welcomes them not as fellow-wayfarers [...] but as persons in need of especially solicitous ministerial care

---

[21] Monica Furlong, *Puritan's Progress: A Study of John Bunyan* (London: Hodder & Stoughton, 1975), 177–79; this reading is strongly disputed by Robert J. McKelvey, *Histories that Mansoul and her Wars Anatomize: The Drama of Redemption in John Bunyan's Holy War* (Göttingen: Vandenhoeck & Ruprecht, 2011), 148–49.

[22] Tamsin Spargo, 'Contra-Dictions: Women as Figures of Exclusion and Resistance in John Bunyan and Agnes Beaumont's Narratives', in Kate Chedgzoy, Melanie Hansen, and Suzanne Trill (eds.), *Voicing Women: Gender and Sexuality in Early Modern Writing* (Pittsburgh, PA: Duquesne University Press, 1997), 173–84 (174), and Tamsin Spargo, *The Writing of John Bunyan* (Aldershot: Ashgate, 1997), 34–6, 95.

[23] Thomas H. Luxon, 'One Soul versus One Flesh: Friendship, Marriage, and the Puritan Self', in Camden (ed.), *Trauma and Transformation*, 81–99; Michael A. Mullett, *John Bunyan in Context* (Keele: Keele University Press, 1996), 246–48.

and guidance' and that his 'imaginative sympathy for women is never so intense as to jeopardize patriarchy'.[24]

More recently, however, critics have returned to scrutinize this portrait of Bunyan as a man of his times, whose treatment of women both in his congregation and in his writings was bound by his rigid understanding of the biblical role of women. This new direction in Bunyan studies explores Bunyan's embrace of femininity, if not of actual women, arguing that his understanding of human interaction with the divine is a fundamentally gendered one. Margaret Thickstun has directed readers' attention to Bunyan's appropriation of the feminine as a metaphor, arguing that 'Bunyan is more interested in the female experience of marital subordination as a metaphor for male spirituality than he is in either marriage or female spirituality for its own sake'.[25] In a 2003/04 special issue of *Bunyan Studies*, 'Feminine Authority, Agency, and Identity in Bunyan's England', contributors 'wade into the murky waters of gender as figured in Bunyan's writings and those of his contemporaries', and emerge '[finding] a version of the "reproductive" Puritan text'.[26] Here, Jean Graham and Sylvia Brown focus attention on the gendering of discourse and textuality. Brown argues that Bunyan is part of a larger Puritan sensibility of the female-gendered 'reproductive' text, able to give birth to other texts and to nurse others, a view of textuality having more in common with the dynamic postmodern text. Graham complements this argument with her analysis of Bunyan's distrust of human speech in general, while recognizing the human relationship with God as one in which God is male and the true believer (whether man or woman) is female.[27] Rather than ignoring, repressing, or excluding women and the feminine, these more recent studies find these to be the binding, infusing metaphors in Bunyan's writings. Vera Camden argues that 'his saturation in women's ways and women's words' enables the transformative experience that shaped Bunyan's growth as a both a writer and minister.[28]

The celebration of the feminine as it is manifest in Bunyan's writings raises the question of how he can embrace the feminine while seemingly rejecting the female and pays less attention to whether his depiction of masculinity might be likewise complex. The seeming contradictions on matters of gender, however, might also be understood as an issue relating to performative gender and the distinction between sexual embodiment and socialized behaviour, both male and female. This returns us to Bunyan's

---

[24] N. H. Keeble, '"Here is her Glory, even to be under Him": The Feminine in the Thought and Work of John Bunyan', in Anne Laurence, W. R. Owens, and Stuart Sim (eds.), *John Bunyan and his England, 1628–88* (London: Hambledon Press, 1990), 131–48 (147).

[25] Margaret Thickstun, *Fictions of the Feminine: Puritan Doctrine and the Representation of Women* (Ithaca, NY, and London: Cornell University Press, 1988), 88.

[26] Vera J. Camden and Kimberly S. Hill, 'Introduction', BS, 11 (2003/04), 5–7.

[27] Sylvia Brown, 'The Reproductive Word: Gender and Textuality in the Writings of John Bunyan', BS, 11 (2003/04), 23–45 (23–6); Jean Graham, '"Tell All Men": Bunyan and the Gendering of Discourse', BS, 11 (2003/04), 8–22. See also Margaret Sönser Breen, 'The Pilgrim's Art of Failure and Belonging: Dialogues between Bunyan and Queer Studies', BS, 18 (2014), 61–77 for a reading of *Part II* as engaging in queer temporality, with Christiana as the pilgrim figure who 'never looks back' (72).

[28] Vera J. Camden, 'John Bunyan and the Goodwives of Bedford', in Anne Dunan-Page (ed.), *The Cambridge Companion to Bunyan* (Cambridge: Cambridge University Press, 2010), 51–64 (62).

insistence on adhering to what is 'appropriate' in terms of place and action. *Christian Behaviour*, for example, sets out very clearly and plainly the social roles of men and women as master and mistress of a household. God expects 'faithful deportment' from every member of the family (*MW*, 3: 22). The father acts as a pastor in his family, being sound in his own doctrine and exemplary in his behaviour, exhorting all members of the family to increased faith, but he also must '*rule his own house*' (*MW*, 3: 23). In addition to encouraging godliness in the family as a unit, the father must provide through his livelihood food and clothing for his household without becoming too involved in the trades of the world. Towards his wife, his behaviour must depend on whether she is a believer or not. If she, too, is godly, the husband should love her in Christian love, as she is part of his flesh and bone and a partner in receiving God's grace. This leads Bunyan to the common metaphor of the husband's relationship with his wife being like that of Christ to the Church: '*For the husband is the head of the wife, even as Christ is the head of the Church; and He is the Saviour of the Body*', and this 'is one of God's chief ends in instituting Marriage'. '*He that loveth his Wife, loveth himself*', Bunyan asserts, and therefore the man must 'bear with their weaknesses, help their infirmities, & honour them as the weaker vessels, and as being of a frailer constitution'. A man who does not do so is behaving 'contrary to the Rule' (*MW*, 3: 27).

A wife, Bunyan stresses, 'is bound by the Law to her Husband'. However, his emphasis is on her 'carriage' as a wife towards her husband. She should 'look upon him as her head and lord' and she should therefore 'be subject to him': '*that the wife, if she walk with her husband as becomes her, she shall preach the Obedience of the Church to her husband. Therefore, as the Church is subject to Christ, so let the wives be to their own husband in every thing*.' In the performance of this work, the wife must avoid gossiping, wandering, and '*brangling* [squabbling]': it is 'odious either in maids or wives, to be like Parrats, not bridling their tongue'. 'Do you think it is seemly', Bunyan asks, 'for the Church to parrat it against her Husband?' Worse is 'to see a *woman* so much as once in all her life-time, to offer to over-top her husband; she ought in every thing to be in subjection to him', charges Bunyan. 'And indeed here is her glory, even to be under him, as the Church is under Christ.' He then moves from the abstract and metaphorical back to the practical, warning against '*immodest apparel*' and '*a wanton gate* [gait]' which will serve as a bad example, inciting lust and lasciviousness abroad and offending the godly husband at home. He concludes this section with a significant qualification: 'do not think that by the subjection I have here mentioned, that I do intend women should be their husbands slaves. Women are their husbands yoak-fellows, their *flesh* and their *bones*' and indeed, 'the wife is master next her husband, and is to rule all in his absence': 'in his presence she is to guide the house' (*MW*, 3: 32–4).

The patterns of behaviour set out in *Christian Behaviour* resonate throughout Bunyan's *The Life and Death of Mr. Badman* in the behaviours of Badman's two wives, one pious and the other not. Badman forbids his pious wife to attend sermons or even to read godly books; he spends all the money that she brought as her portion and does not provide for his family. As Chapter 5 in this volume illustrates, this woman's lot serves as a warning to others to be cautious in their marriages for, as Attentive states, '*things are past with this poor woman, and cannot be called back, let others beware, by her misfortunes, les they also fall into her distress*' (*MB*, 73). She is at least rewarded, however, with a comfortable death, a 'soul full of Grace, an heart full of comfort, and by her death ended a life full of trouble' (*MB*, 144). Badman's second wife, however, is a creature straight out of Killigrew's play and the *Wandering Whore*. After getting him drunk,

> she was so cunning as to get a promise of marriage of him, and so held him to it, and forced him to marry her. And she, as the saying is, was as good as he, at all his vile and ranting tricks: she had her companions as well as he had his, and she would meet them too at the Tavern and Ale-house, more commonly than he was aware of. To be plain, she was a very Whore. (*MB*, 145)

While his first wife kept herself at home and never chided him, his second 'would give him word for word, blow for blow, curse for curse' (*MB*, 147).

The men and women of *The Pilgrim's Progress* continue to demonstrate the patterns of behaviour laid out in *Christian Behaviour*, but unlike Mr Badman and his second wife, who dwell in the physical carnal body and cannot seem to escape from it, Bunyan's pilgrims are men and women in their nature and also, where needed and where appropriate, feminine and masculine in behaviour and carriage. As noted, critics have highlighted how, if the relationship between the believer and God is like that of the Church to Christ, then even the male pilgrim must play the woman in that in his conversion and subsequent wayfaring he must take on the role of feminine subjection otherwise enjoined to wives. Likewise, it would appear from the actions of Christiana and Mercie that when women are on their own, as stated in *Christian Behaviour*, they have the capacity to 'rule' all. They, too, must perform masculinity, in other words, playing the man and taking on masculine roles: leaving the home, journeying abroad, and asking for answers. While Christian when confronted by the demon Apollyon must stand his ground and fight, in contrast, he and Faithful do not fight back when they are reviled and attacked in Vanity Fair, where the inhabitants 'beat them pitifully, and hanged Irons upon them, and led them in Chaines up and down the *fair*, for an example'. Like Badman's first wife, they 'received the ignominy and shame that was cast upon them, with so much meekness and patience' that they won some to their side and although Faithful's body suffers terribly, he, too, has that good death (*PP*, 91–2). Similarly, as Christian and Hopeful near the Celestial City, they fall ill, but it is from desire to submit to a masculine embrace: 'here they lay by it a while, crying out because of their pangs, *If you see my Beloved, tell him that I am sick of love*' (*PP*, 155). When Christian falters at the final river and almost drowns, it is not an act of manly strength or will that gets him to the other side, but instead a feminine reliance on Christ. 'Oh I see him again! and he tells me, *When thou passest through the waters, I will be with thee, and through the Rivers, they shall not overflow thee*' (*PP*, 158)—the strong male figure of Christ assisting the faltering and feeble Christian.

Christiana and Mercie in *Part II* likewise display both the behaviour and actions of the good wife but also the behaviour of the good husband as required. The start of their pilgrimage comes with a recognition from Christiana that 'her unbecoming behaviour towards her Husband' was one reason that the bond between them had been broken: 'all her unkind, unnatural, and ungodly Carriages to her dear Friend' (PP, 177). As the mistress of the house without her husband there, she makes the decision for herself that she and her children will also now go on pilgrimage. Her neighbours remind her of the trials faced by Christian—'*if he, tho' a man, was so hard put to it, what cast thou being but a poor Woman do?*'—and declare that for the sake of her children she must not cast herself away. Her response is to embrace the challenge: 'for that you tell me of all these Troubles that I am like to meet with in the way, they are so far off from being to me a discouragement, that they shew I am in the right'. She concludes by briskly turning away the gossiping and fearful Mrs Timorous, saying 'since you cam not to my House, *in Gods name* [...] I pray you to be gon, and not to disquiet me further' (PP, 182–83). In the same way that the male pilgrims encounter ungodly men and women who remain firm in their roles of bad men/bad women, Christiana is mocked by her carnal neighbours at a gossipy party.

As with Christian's journey, there are physically frightening, dangerous trials to be faced by the women, but when confronted with them they demonstrate those traits assigned to the master of the house. When Christiana, Mercie, and the children arrive at the wicket gate, they are all frightened by the mastiff; however, Christiana continues to knock at the gate until the Keeper arrives and when she is permitted with the children through the gate, she makes a forthright intercession for Mercie, left on the other side. When the women are accosted on the road by two men who attempt to assault them, Christiana commands them to 'stand back', and when the men lay hands on them, the women fight: 'Christiana waxing very wroth, spurned at them with her feet' (PP, 194). Christiana will likewise persistently demand attention when they arrive at the house of the Interpreter; once inside, the women are shown by him the Significant Rooms and Christiana, 'a Woman quick of apprehension', does not need to have all explained to her (PP, 200). There are some physical challenges, however, they cannot overcome unaided. After the assault, their male Reliever suggests that it would be good for them to have a guide, to which Christiana admits 'we were so taken with our present blessing, that Dangers to come were forgotten by us' (PP, 196). Their chaperon Great-heart, however, does not accompany them inside when the women arrive at the Porter's Lodge of House Beautiful: instead, he leaves them, and the women must again boldly declare who they are and what their purpose is.

As critics have noted, *The Pilgrim's Progress, Part II* is as much about a Christian community assisting each other in a carnal world as it is about women's spiritual experiences. In fact, one might argue, there is no difference in the men's and women's pilgrimage in that each must play the appropriate role in the appropriate relationship, as created by God. For the male believer, this is to enact the feminine submissive role to his bridegroom Christ; for women, who already play that role in domestic life, it is to take on the masculine qualities demanded of them when the occasion requires, without always relying on a human male guide to make crucial spiritual decisions about seeking salvation. Such an explanation of the significance of performing gender in Bunyan's writings helps us to understand his loathing of unlicensed sexual behaviour. His ranking of adultery and fornication as sins equal to murder, his repeated criticism of women's attire that draws attention to breasts and incites the ever-ready lustful responses in males: these are all behaviours which confine the individual to the part played out by the biological self. Bunyan had no desire to deny the carnal nature of the body. Yet, at the same time, he was able to imagine the male worshipper embracing the feminine role in relation to the divine, and the female communicant boldly asking, with conviction and courage, 'what shall I do to be saved?'

Suggested Reading

Camden, Vera J. (ed.), *Trauma and Transformation: The Political Progress of John Bunyan* (Stanford, CA: Stanford University Press, 2008).

Camden, Vera J. and Kimberly S. Hill (eds.), 'Feminine Authority, Agency, and Identity in Bunyan's England', special issue *BS*, 11 (2003/04).

Greaves, Richard L., *Glimpses of Glory: John Bunyan and English Dissent* (Stanford, CA: Stanford University Press, 2002).

Laurence, Anne, W. R. Owens, and Stuart Sim (eds.), *John Bunyan and his England, 1628–88* (London: Hambledon Press, 1990).

Mowry, Melissa M., *The Bawdy Politic in Stuart England, 1660–1714* (Aldershot: Ashgate, 2004).

Mullett, Michael A., *John Bunyan in Context* (Keele: Keele University Press, 1996).

Spargo, Tamsin, *The Writing of John Bunyan* (Aldershot: Ashgate, 1997).

Thickstun, Margaret, *Fictions of the Feminine: Puritan Doctrine and the Representation of Women* (Ithaca, NY, and London: Cornell University Press, 1988).

Trumbach, Randolph, 'The Birth of the Queen: Sodomy and the Emergence of Gender Equality in Modern Culture, 1660–1750', in Robert Shoemaker and Mary Vincent (eds.), *Gender and History in Western Europe* (London: Arnold, 1998), 161–73.

Webster, Jeremy, *Performing Libertinism in Charles II's Court: Politics, Drama, Sexuality* (Basingstoke: Palgrave Macmillan, 2005).

CHAPTER 8

'COME YE OUT FROM AMONG THEM, AND BE YE SEPARATE'

Bunyan and the Writing of Dissent

N. H. KEEBLE

'Taken from You in Presence'

'As I walk'd through the wilderness of this world, I lighted on a certain place, where was a Denn': in what is perhaps the most readily recognizable opening to any text in English, the reader, like the narrator, is seemingly removed from the clamour and business of the everyday and eased into an allegorical world of wonders as gently as falling asleep—'And I laid me down in that place to sleep: And as I slept I dreamed a Dream.' This reassuringly untroubled transition into the fictional is, however, rudely disturbed by the margin's disconcerting gloss on 'Denn': 'The Gaol' (*PP*, 8). *The Pilgrim's Progress* (1678) opens in prison: it is the work of an author penalized and incarcerated as a dangerously insubordinate, if not seditious, subject who posed a threat to the religious and political stability of the newly restored Stuart regime and to the re-established episcopal Church of England.[1] It is an imprisoned man's dream of liberty:

> For though men keep my outward man
> Within their Locks and Bars,
> Yet by the Faith of Christ I can
> Mount higher than the Stars. (*MW*, 6: 43)

---

[1] On the penal religious legislation of the Restoration and its consequence, see G. R. Cragg, *Puritanism in the Period of the Great Persecution 1660–88* (Cambridge: Cambridge University Press, 1957); N. H. Keeble, *The Literary Culture of Nonconformity in Later Seventeenth-Century England* (Leicester: Leicester University Press, 1987), 25–78. See also Chapter 2 in this volume. On the process by which the Church of England was re-established and Nonconformity created, see N. H. Keeble (ed.), *'Settling the Peace of the Church': 1662 Revisited* (Oxford: Oxford University Press, 2014).

No comment or explanation is offered, nor, by 1678, the year of the publication of *The Pilgrim's Progress*, was any needed: the fame of 'Bishop Bunyan' was extensive throughout London, Bedfordshire, and the surrounding counties,[2] and the circumstances of his imprisonment widely known. He was, in Sharon Achinstein's phrase, a 'celebrity prisoner'.[3] Indeed, far from disguising his circumstances, for nearly twenty years Bunyan had been calling public attention to his prisoner status. At the Restoration, he had four published titles to his name, but with his arrest in November 1660 and subsequent twelve-year imprisonment his rate of output greatly increased: incarceration impelled him to write.[4] As the Puritan leader Richard Baxter, himself later imprisoned for Nonconformity, tellingly noted, '*Preachers* may be silenced or banished, when *Books* may be at hand.'[5] For Bunyan, separated from his people by imprisonment, writing was the one way he could continue his preaching ministry. '*Taken from you in presence*' and unable in person to '*perform that duty that from God doth lie upon me, to you-ward*', through print he could yet address not only his congregation but also the wider community (*GA*, 1).

His precedent lay in the epistles St Paul wrote from captivity in Rome, which in Bunyan's time were thought to include the epistles (1 Timothy and Hebrews) that provided him with the titles for *Grace Abounding to the Chief of Sinners* (1666) and *The Pilgrim's Progress*.[6] As Paul, although imprisoned, continued undaunted to preach the gospel through writing and to extol the power of divine grace, so the title page of *Christian Behaviour* (1663) describes Bunyan as 'a Prisoner of *Hope*' (*MW*, 3: 5). *Prison Meditations* (1663) was written 'in Prison' by 'JOHN BUNYAN, a Prisoner' (*MW*, 6: 39, 42). 'Upon a certain *First day*, I being together with my Brethren, in our Prison-Chamber, they expected that, according to our Custom, something should be spoken out of the Word'; it 'being my turn to speak', Bunyan preached what became *The Holy City* (1665; *MW*, 3: 69). He addressed the prefatory 'Premonition to the Reader' to *A Defence of the Doctrine of Justification, by Faith* (1672) 'From Prison' (*MW*, 4: 10), and in the preface to *A Confession of my Faith, and A Reason of my Practice* (1672), he speaks of his '*long tryalls*', his '*almost twelve years imprisonment*' and signs himself 'Thine in Bonds' (*MW*, 4: 135, 136).

---

[2] For the nickname 'Bishop Bunyan' see [George Cockayne?], 'The Continuation of Mr Bunyan's Life', first printed in the seventh edition of *Grace Abounding* (1692) and included in John Bunyan, *Grace Abounding to the Chief of Sinners*, ed. W. R. Owens (Harmondsworth: Penguin, 1987), 114.

[3] Sharon Achinstein, *Literature and Dissent in Milton's England* (Cambridge: Cambridge University Press, 2003), 61.

[4] For Bunyan's arrest and imprisonment, see Greaves, *Glimpses*, 127–72.

[5] Richard Baxter, *A Christian Directory* (1673), Part 1, 60. On the use of writing and print to maintain contact within the Nonconformist community, see Keeble, *Literary Culture*, 78–92.

[6] 1 Timothy 1:14–15: 'the grace of our Lord was exceeding abundant […] Christ Jesus came into the world to save sinners; of whom I am the chief'; Hebrews 11:13: 'These all died in faith […] and confessed that they were strangers and pilgrims on the earth.' See, further, Margaret Thickstun, 'The Preface to *Grace Abounding* as Pauline Epistle', *Notes and Queries*, 230 (1985), 180–82.

Grace Abounding too will relate what its author 'hath met with in Prison' and 'was written by his own hand there' (*GA*, xliv); it is '*from* the Lions Dens', from the prison where '*I stick between the Teeth of the Lions in the Wilderness*' that Bunyan addresses its prefatory epistle to the reader. Lions signify here, as they do in *The Pilgrim's Progress*, the cruelties of persecution (*GA*, 1; *PP*, 45–6, 218–19). After his release from prison in 1672, Bunyan was still liable to prosecution for failing to attend the parish church and for holding conventicles: that is, religious gatherings not conducted according to the rites of the Book of Common Prayer. On at least one occasion he appears to have had to leave Bedfordshire to avoid court proceedings: in the prefatory epistle to the catechetical *Instruction for the Ignorant* (1675) addressed to his gathered Bedford church, he describes himself as '*being driven from you in presence, not affection*' and signs himself '*Yours, to serve by any Ministry (when I can)*' (*MW*, 8: 7).[7]

This is all biographically accurate, but its reiteration by Bunyan in generically diverse works whose business is not autobiographical—poetry, practical divinity, theological exposition, controversy, and allegory—points to a significance for Bunyan's authorial self-presentation that goes well beyond a wish to keep the record straight. In 1678, years after his imprisonment and when he was the long-serving pastor of the Bedford congregation, this identity still mattered sufficiently for him to add that marginal gloss on 'Denn' to the opening sentence of *The Pilgrim's Progress*. This was to be the text that would establish his national—and international—reputation: the renowned Bunyan of his final years, 'the author of *The Pilgrim's Progress*' advertised by his later title pages, remains the man who had been in prison. The importance of this self-construction for Bunyan takes us back to Paul. Paul described himself in his epistles as 'the prisoner of Jesus Christ', 'the prisoner of the Lord' (Ephesians 3:1, 4:1; Philemon 1:9). By repeatedly and explicitly locating his texts in jail, Bunyan associates his work with Paul's ministry. This gives resolution and assertiveness to his literary and ministerial persona; he assumes something of the Apostle's authority to preach. From the account in Acts 23–4 of the charges preferred by the Jews against Paul before Felix, Roman procurator of Judaea, Bunyan infers that '*an hypocritical people, will persecute the power of those truths in others, which themselves in words profess*', pointedly adding 'I am this day, and for this very thing persecuted by them' (*MW*, 3: 204). As he takes the role of Paul, so the Restoration authorities are cast in the role of the persecuting Romans. Bunyan is not merely, and audaciously, claiming his readers' attention despite his marginalized status and official disapprobation; he implicitly adduces that condemnation as proof of his integrity and of his authority to preach and to write.[8]

---

[7] On Bunyan's release from prison, this episode of withdrawal from Bedfordshire, and his second imprisonment, see Greaves, *Glimpses*, 286–88, 313–14, 338, 340, 341, 342–43, 344–45.

[8] On Nonconformist prison writing, including Bunyan's, see Kathleen Lynch, 'Into Jail and into Print: John Bunyan Writes the Godly Self', and Rivkah Zim, 'Writing behind Bars: Literary Contexts and the Authority of Carceral Experience', *The Huntington Library Quarterly*, 72 (2009), 273–90, 291–311; Kathleen Lynch, *Protestant Autobiography in the Seventeenth-Century Anglophone World* (Oxford: Oxford University Press, 2012), 179–232; Achinstein, *Literature and Dissent*, 59–83; Keeble, *Literary Culture*, 187–214.

By so insisting on the circumstances of his texts' production Bunyan, like other Nonconformist authors, associates his experiential authority with a validating tradition of Christian witness stretching from Paul through the early Christian martyrs to his own day. Biblical instruction (notably Luke 6:22: 'Blessed are they that are persecuted for righteousness' sake, for theirs is the Kingdom of Heaven'), the accounts of the persecutions of Christians in John Foxe's *Acts and Monuments* (first published in English, 1563),[9] and their own persecution, taught Puritans and Nonconformists that suffering is a defining characteristic of Christian experience. There is barely a Nonconformist writer of note who was not at some time arrested, imprisoned, fined, bound over, pursued, or persecuted. Although not in prison, Milton was 'fallen on evil days […] In darkness, and with dangers compassed round, / And solitude' when he wrote his three great Restoration poems.[10] No wonder that in Nonconformist writing the Christian demeanour is almost by definition adversarial and the Christian condition oppressed. In Book 12 of *Paradise Lost*, Michael foretells that the Apostles will be succeeded by 'grievous wolves' who will 'force the spirit of grace it self, and bind / His consort liberty', with the result that 'heavy persecution' will fall on 'all who in the worship persevere / Of spirit and truth'.[11] In an inescapable reference to the plight of Nonconformists in the 1660s, the Chorus in *Samson Agonistes* is dismayed at the suffering of God's chosen, dragged before 'unjust tribunals, under change of times, / And condemnation of the ungrateful multitude'.[12] Just so, Evangelist, echoing Acts 14:22, warns Christian and Faithful that they 'must through many tribulations enter into the Kingdom of Heaven' and that 'bonds and afflictions' await them (*PP*, 87).

The Independent leader and admirer of Bunyan, John Owen, wrote that '*Every circumstance in suffering shall add to the glory of the Sufferer*; and those who suffer here for Christ without witness, as many have done to Death in Prisons and Dungeons, have yet an *all-seeing witness* to give Testimony in due Season.'[13] That 'the people of God are a suffering people' (*MW*, 10: 95) is, argues Bunyan's *Seasonable Counsel: Or, Advice to Sufferers* (1684), to be welcomed. The persecuted should, like Paul, rejoice in their afflictions as occasions for God's sustaining grace (*MW*, 10: 22, citing 2 Corinthians 12:9 and Romans 8:37–9):

---

[9] Bunyan refers to Foxe more frequently than to any other author (for examples, see Greaves, *Glimpses*, index *s.v.* Foxe).

[10] Milton, *Paradise Lost*, ed. Alastair Fowler, rev. 2nd edn (Harlow: Pearson Longman, 2007), 7: 26–8.

[11] Milton, *Paradise Lost*, 12: 508–35.

[12] Milton, *Samson Agonistes*, in *Milton: Complete Shorter Poems*, ed. John Carey, rev. 2nd edn (Harlow: Pearson Longman, 2006), ll. 695–96.

[13] John Owen, *A Continuation of the Exposition of the Epistle of Paul the Apostle to the Hebrews* (1684), 16, quoted in Achinstein, *Literature and Dissent*, 75. On Bunyan and Owen, see Greaves, *Glimpses*, 226, 315, 344–47, and for the anecdote that Owen told Charles II 'he would willingly exchange his learning for the tinker's power of touching men's hearts', see John Brown, *John Bunyan: His Life, Times and Work*, rev. Frank Mott Harrison (London, Glasgow, and Birmingham: Hulbert, 1928), 366.

The hotter the rage and fury of men are against righteous ways, the more those that love righteousness, grow therein. For they are concerned for it, not to hide it, but to make it spangle; not to extinguish it, but to greaten it, and to shew the excellency of it in all its features and in all its comely proportion. [...] A man when he suffereth for Christ, is set upon an *Hill*, upon a *Stage*, as in a *Theatre*, to play a part for God in the World. [...] God himself looks on. (*MW*, 10: 62)

'The best Christians are found in the worst of times' (*MW*, 10: 36) for, in Milton's words, 'that which purifies us is trial'.[14] 'Prison is the furnace, thy graces are the Silver and Gold, wherefore as the Silver and Gold are refined by the fire [...] so the Christian [...] is by his sufferings refined and made more righteous' (*MW*, 10: 61). 'Goals [*sic*] are Christ his Schools / In them we learn to dye' (*MW*, 6: 45). Bunyan's authority to teach, and to write, lies not in formal qualifications or state approval but in the education he has received in such schools.[15]

'My Kingdom Is Not of This World'

What Bunyan learned in those schools was not compromise but a strengthened commitment to the Nonconformist Christian way for which he suffered. Throughout his writings this is distinguished, often in withering terms, from the values and practices of those who condemned him: the social, political, and religious elites of the restored Stuart government and the re-established episcopal Church of England. The account of the arrest, trial, and martyrdom of Faithful at Vanity Fair (*PP*, 88–97) draws on Bunyan's own experience of Restoration courts and prisons and it represents the experience of social harassment, penal persecution, and state repression known to his Nonconformist readers. Beyond this, though, it expresses a satirical contempt for social superiors and their time-serving hypocrisy. Unbiased testimony is not to be expected from witnesses named Envy, Superstition, and Pickthank, nor impartial assessment of the facts by jurors named Mr Blindman, Mr No-good, Mr Malice, Mr Love-lust, nor fair administration of justice from Lord Hategood. The Restoration *beau monde* is bitterly satirized in Vanity Fair's materialism and acquisitiveness, and in the preoccupation of its citizens with status, fashion, and self-adornment. It is damned, too, in the figure of Mr Badman, who, eager to get on in life, as a youth adopts the habit of 'Swearing and Cursing' as 'a Badge of Honour', the mark of 'a mans Fellow' and very 'Gentleman-like' (*MB*, 27).

---

[14] *The Complete Prose Works of John Milton*, gen. ed. Don M. Wolfe, 8 vols (New Haven, CT, and London: Yale University Press, 1953–82), 2: 515.

[15] See, on this theme, John R. Knott, *Discourses of Martyrdom in English Literature 1563–1694* (Cambridge: Cambridge University Press, 1993); Keeble, *Literary Culture*, 187–214; Greaves, *Glimpses*, 493–98.

This is a theme recurrent in Nonconformist writing, including that of the Quakers Bunyan so detested, notably William Penn's *No Cross, No Crown* (1669; enlarged 1682), which scorns 'Sumptuous apparel, rich unguents, delicate washes, stately furniture, costly cookery, and such diversions as balls, masques, music-meetings, plays, romances, &c., which are the delights and entertainments of the times' as antithetical to 'the holy path that Jesus and his true disciples and flowers trod to glory'.[16] These pleasures are embodied in Bunyan's 'Gentlewoman' Madame Bubble, who 'laugheth Poor Pilgrims to scorn, but highly commends the Rich', who 'loveth Banqueting, and Feasting', who 'will cast out of her Purse, Gold like Dust, in some places, and to some Persons', and who would draw true Christians '*into many foolish and hurtful Lusts, which drown men in Destruction and Perdition*' (*PP*, 301–02). In *The Life and Death of Mr. Badman* (1680), Mr Wiseman is dismayed at the sway courtly fashions have over even church members: he has seen them 'so deckt and bedaubed with their Fangles and Toyes' that he has 'wondred with what face such painted persons' could attend worship 'without swounding'; 'what can be the end of those that are proud, in the decking of themselves after their antick manner? why are they for going with their Bulls-foretops, with their naked shoulders, and Paps hanging out like a Cows bag?' (*MB*, 122, 125).

In short, in Bunyan's writings, fashionable carriage, wealth, and social privilege are almost invariably signs of moral turpitude: Giant Despair owns a castle and a great estate barred to trespassers; By-ends is 'a Gentleman of good Quality' from '*Fair-speech*', 'a *Wealthy place*', where he has 'very many rich Kindred'; Mercie's suitor Mr Brisk is 'a man of some breeding' but merely 'pretended to Religion' (*PP*, 98–9, 113, 226); in the story of infanticide told by Mr Wiseman to Mr Attentive, the mother is a 'young Lady' and the murderous father of the illegitimate child 'a brave young Gallant', a 'Gentleman' (*MB*, 52–3). Bunyan finds it readily understandable that in the parable of Dives and Lazarus 'the ungodly [are] held forth under the notion of a rich man', for 'to see how the great ones of the world will go strutting up and down the streets sometimes, it makes me wonder'; by contrast, God's own people 'are most commonly of the poorer sort', 'for the most part, a poor, despised, contemptible people' (*MW*, 1: 252, 253–54, 255).[17]

Bunyan speaks for, and to, these despised people, who, in his texts, are far from contemptible: 'Nor shall thou want Dignity tho' thou art but a *private* Christian. Every Christian man is made a King by Christ' (*MW*, 10: 33). This is a main reason why, as they advert to his imprisonment, so his texts also insist on his own commoner status. Bunyan is no elite commentator upon the religious practices of the poor from a position of privilege such as bishops enjoyed but is himself one who shares their impoverishment and disadvantage. He presents himself as a Bedfordshire tinker, 'of a low and inconsiderable generation' from one of the 'meanest and most despised of all the families in the Land' with no social or educational advantages, unable 'as others, to boast of Noble blood, or

---

[16] William Penn, *No Cross, No Crown*, ed. Norman Penney (1930; rrp. York: William Sessions, 1981), 213, quoted in Keeble, *Literary Culture*, 219, where see 215–29 for a discussion of this emphasis in Nonconformist writing.

[17] For further such readings of Bunyan, see Hill, *Bunyan*, 125–30, 212–21, 243–50.

of a High-born state'. Although his parents 'put me to School, to learn both to Read and to Write [...] I did soon loose that little I learned, even almost utterly' (*GA*, 5).[18] His first three publications carried commendatory prefaces by ministerial colleagues which anticipated, and turned to advantage, the objection that Bunyan lacked the cultural resources to set up as a preacher or writer of books: 'Reader, in this book thou wilt not meet with high-flown aerie notions [...] but the sound, plain, common [...] truths of the Gospel' delivered 'not by humane art, but by the spirit of Christ' (*MW*, 1: 10, 12).

Paul's claim to preach 'not with enticing words of man's wisdom, but in demonstration of the Spirit' (1 Corinthians 2:1–5), alluded to here, informed Bunyan's self-fashioning as a writer whose authority lies not in academic distinction but in experiential authenticity and divine inspiration: he 'never endeavoured to, nor durst make use of other men's lines, *Rom.* 15. 18' for he 'found by experience, that what was taught me by the Word and Spirit of Christ, could be spoken, maintained, and stood to, by the soundest and best established Conscience' (*GA*, 87–8). Unlike 'carnal Priests' who 'tickle the ears of their hearers with vain Philosophy', he 'never went to School to *Aristotle* or *Plato*, but was brought up at my fathers house, in a very mean condition, among a company of poor Countrey-men' (*MW*, 1: 345; 2: 16). He '*has not writ at a venture, nor borrowed my Doctrine from Libraries. I depend upon the sayings of no man: I found it in the Scriptures of Truth, among the true sayings of God*', nor has he 'fished in other mens *Waters*, my Bible and Concordance are my only Library in my writings' (*MW*, 8: 51; 7: 9). He does not clutter his margins with 'a Cloud of Sentences from the Learned FATHERS, that have according to their Wisdom (possibly) handled these Matters long before me' because 'I have them not, nor have not read them': 'I prefer the BIBLE before them; and having that still with me, I count my self far better furnished than if I had (without it) all the Libraries of the two Universities' (*MW*, 3: 71–2).[19]

Bunyan's literary persona is, then, that of a socially insignificant and culturally impoverished man at the mercy of an authoritarian regime. He has no prospects as this world goes; but, and this is the wonder of his gospel, the Restoration world is powerless to deny him (and those like him) access to unlimited prospects far beyond its ken. The aspirations he articulates for the underprivileged and disadvantaged look beyond the grubby world of later Stuart politics, the sexual profligacy and materialism of its culture. *The Pilgrim's Progress* casts a sharp eye over the contemporary world, but its sights are set on another. After the crushing political disappointment of 1660–62, John 18:36 ('My kingdom is not of this world') provides its theme, as it does for such other late Puritan works as Milton's *Paradise Regain'd* (1671) and George Fox's *Journal* (1696).[20] Its allegorical vehicles were ready-made to Bunyan's hands.

---

[18] In fact, Bunyan rather overstated the case: see Greaves, *Glimpses*, 3–4, and Chapter 1 in this volume.

[19] Again, Bunyan rather overstated the case. He may have attended a grammar school (Greaves, *Glimpses*, 4–6) and he had read rather more widely than he admits, see Gordon Campbell, ' "Fishing in Other Men's Waters": Bunyan and the Theologians', in N. H. Keeble (ed.), *John Bunyan: Conventicle and Parnassus* (Oxford: Clarendon Press, 1988), 137–51; Greaves, *Glimpses*, 603–07; and Chapters 1 and 6 in this volume.

[20] See on this theme, Keeble, *Literary Culture*, 187–214.

In conceiving and representing the Christian life, the Puritan and Nonconformist imagination drew on the narratives of the many migrations through which, in the Old Testament, God guides his chosen people Israel, and on the Bible's many metaphorical deployments of wayfaring, culminating in the great dominical assertion of John 14:6 ('I am the way'). Its preferred images and narrative patterns derive from journeying and itinerancy—witness, for example, *The Travels of True Godliness* (1683) by the Baptist Benjamin Keach, as well as *The Pilgrim's Progress*. The key to Bunyan's representation of the Christian life as a journey lies in particular in chapter 11 of the Epistle to the Hebrews. Its image of the faithful as nomadic 'strangers and pilgrims on the earth' who 'seek a country', 'that is, an heavenly' (11: 13–16), structures *The Pilgrim's Progress*.[21] It is with these very words that Christian and Faithful describe themselves as foreigners in transit through Vanity Fair (*PP*, 90); though they, like all 'Pilgrims […] must needs go thorow [Vanity] *Fair*', they have no intention of settling there (*PP*, 89). In scorning Nonconformists as 'Outlandish-men' (*PP*, 90), Restoration society tacitly recognized the Dissenting values of those 'adventurers for the other World', who strove to live '*as a Citizen of Heaven, and a Pilgrim on Earth*', as the Presbyterian Nonconformist Thomas Gouge instructed London apprentices in *The Young Man's Guide through the Wilderness of this World to the Heavenly Canaan* (1670).[22]

'A Harmless Man'

As strangers in, rather than natives of, the world brought into being by the Restoration, Bunyan and other Nonconformists professed to have little interest in its transformation save through the conversion of individuals and personal reformation of manners. They were careful to distance themselves from radical enthusiasm and rebellious republican thinking and adopted a stance of political passivity. In his autobiography, Richard Baxter wrote that 'As for the divine Government by the Saints […] I dare not expect such great matters upon Earth, lest I encroach upon the Priviledge of Heaven, and tempt my own Affections downwards, and forget that our Kingdom is not of this World.'[23] In a similar vein, Bunyan characterizes himself as 'one of the old-fashioned Professors, that *covet to fear God, and honour the King*' (*MW*, 13: 489). In *Seasonable Counsel: Or, Advice to Sufferers* (1684), far from arguing for retaliation, revolution, or sedition, he insists that '*a Christian must be a harmless man*', demonstrating '*Faith and Patience*, in persecution'.

---

[21] See, further, Brainerd P. Stranahan, 'Bunyan and the Epistle to the Hebrews', *SP*, 79 (1982), 279–96; N. H. Keeble, '"To be a pilgrim": Constructing the Protestant Life in Early Modern England', in Colin Morris and Peter Roberts (eds.), *Pilgrimage: The English Experience from Becket to Bunyan* (Cambridge: Cambridge University Press, 2002), 238–56.

[22] Thomas Gouge, *The Young Man's Guide through the Wilderness of this World to the Heavenly Canaan* (1670), 37, 70.

[23] Richard Baxter, *Reliquiæ Baxterianæ* (1696), Part 2, 297, §402.

'Let us mind our own business, and leave the Magistrate to his work': 'We are bid [...] to give thanks to God for all men, *for Kings, and for all that are in authority*' and should 'say and do always that that should render thee a good neighbour, a good Christian, and a faithful subject'; 'it becomes all godly men to study to be quiet, to mind their own business' (*MW*, 10: 5, 6, 33, 35, 98). Bunyan insists that the proper response to adversity, including persecution, is not retaliation but patience: '*Revenge* is of the flesh; [...] it proceeds from [...] unwillingness to suffer, from too much love to carnal ease [...]. It also flows from a fearful cowardly spirit' (*MW*, 10: 100). 'Living by Faith, makes a Man exercise Patience and Quietness under all his Afflictions; [...] *Faith* lodgeth the Soul with Christ. [...] Therefore it were no shame to him, to wear a Chain for his Name and Sake' (*MW*, 12: 342).

Nevertheless, resistance, even if passive, against those who would coerce conscience is Bunyan's great theme, as it is of Nonconformist writing in general. To advocate patience under suffering was to recommend submissiveness, not submission. Bunyan's twelve-year imprisonment, when to agree to stop preaching would have secured his release, is sufficient testimony to his resolve. He rejected retaliation, but he was far from compliant, refusing absolutely any compromise with the persecuting authorities, being quite capable of open and explicit denunciation of Church of England clergymen as frequenters of 'alehouses' who led 'cursed, drunken, whorish, and abominable Lives' (*MW*, 2: 240) and opining that 'God sometimes visits Prisons more / Than lordly palaces' (*MW*, 6: 46). More obliquely, his 'similitudes' could be devastatingly suggestive. Within the general allegorical representation of worldliness in Vanity Fair may be detected by attentive readers 'a precise portrait of the drunken, jeering, conformist culture' of Restoration London,[24] and of its preoccupations in the 'Merchandize sold' at the Fair: 'Houses, Lands, [...] Places, Honours, Preferments, Titles, [...] Lusts, Pleasures, [...] Whores, Bauds, [...] Silver, Gold [...]'; and, still more subversively, an all but treasonable allusion to Charles II in its lord, Beelzebub, 'the Prince of this Town, with all the Rablement [of] his Attendants [...] more fit for a being in Hell, then in this Town and Countrey' (*PP*, 88, 95).

No wonder the restored regime was nervous about the dissemination of such dissent, however other-worldly its professed aims. At the Restoration, the Licensing Act (1662) re-established the apparatus of press control and pre-publication censorship that had been developed since the time of Henry VIII by governments who, seeing in print publication a threat to their authority, sought to restrain and control the output of the press in an attempt to silence oppositional opinion.[25] In addition, laws on defamation,

---

[24] James Grantham Turner, 'From Revolution to Restoration in English Literary Culture', in David Loewenstein and Janelle Mueller (eds.), *The Cambridge History of Early Modern Literature* (Cambridge: Cambridge University Press, 2002), 790.

[25] This apparatus is reproduced in Geoff Kemp and Jason McElligott (eds.), *Censorship and the Press, 1580–1720*, 4 vols (London: Pickering & Chatto, 2009) and discussed in Frederick Siebert, *Freedom of the Press in England, 1476–1776* (Urbana: University of Illinois Press, 1952); Cyndia Clegg's three volumes on *Press Censorship* in Elizabethan, Jacobean, and Caroline England (Cambridge: Cambridge University

libel, slander, sedition, and treason could intimidate the outspoken. Very substantial fines and terms of imprisonment, and even banishment or execution—such as Bunyan himself feared (*GA*, 95–101)—were risked by printers who produced, booksellers who disseminated, and authors who wrote unlicensed texts or texts judged to be subversive. Nonconformist publishing was a collaborative enterprise requiring from printers, booksellers, and other tradesmen a shared commitment with the author to challenge and outwit the agents of the state. These networks, operating in Restoration London in defiance of the authorities, included the publishers and printers of Bunyan's works.[26]

Puritan, Whig, and Nonconformist writers, including Bunyan, adopted a number of expedients to circumvent the restraining authority of the censor. Manuscript circulation was one such stratagem. Heterodox works, such as Milton's theological treatise *De Doctrina Christiana*, and satirical works, such as Andrew Marvell's Restoration verse satires, might circulate in manuscript and not be put into print. *The Pilgrim's Progress*, begun probably in 1668 and completed by 1671, was circulated in manuscript among friends in this way before its publication in 1678 (*PP*, 2); the seven-year delay was perhaps due in part to apprehensions about its reception by the authorities.[27] Bunyan's much more directly inflammatory *Relation of his Imprisonment* remained in manuscript until 1765 (*GA*, xxiii–xxv) and his contentious, millenarian *Of Antichrist, and his Ruine* (1692), with its praise of Tudor but not Stuart monarchs, its criticism of the established church and condemnation of Roman Catholicism (at a time when the heir to the throne was a known Catholic), its promotion of liberty of conscience and denunciation of persecutors, was only published posthumously (*MW*, 13: 424–26, 439–41, 493–94, 497–98). This was one of fifteen (perhaps sixteen[28]) works in manuscript at Bunyan's death, their number suggesting he withheld works from the press rather than risk their publication; certainly, the censor was hardly likely to pass the explicit association of 'Absolute Monarchy' with the persecuting tyranny of Nimrod in Bunyan's *An Exposition on the Ten First Chapters of Genesis* (*MW*, 12: 267–69).

To evade the censor in printed works, Nonconformist writers might, as we have seen Bunyan doing, imply meanings that could be denied by an author under interrogation. They also often resorted to anonymous and unlicensed publication. Indeed, the cat-and-mouse game with the censors and the authorities could become part of the rhetorical strategy of the texts themselves. In his printed but unlicensed and anonymous prose satires *The Rehearsal Transpros'd* (1672) and *Mr. Smirke* (1676), Marvell ridicules the impotency of the censors and the absurdities of the system they attempt to operate:

Press, 1997, 2001, 2008); Keeble, *Literary Culture*, 93–126; Christopher Hill, 'Censorship and English Literature', in his *Writing and Revolution in 17th Century England* (Brighton: Harvester Press, 1985), 32–71; Joad Raymond, *Pamphlets and Pamphleteering in Early Modern Britain* (Cambridge: Cambridge University Press, 2003), 66–71, 196–201; Martin Dzelzainis, *The Flower in the Panther: Print and Censorship in England 1662–1695* (Oxford: Oxford University Press, in preparation).

[26] See, further, Chapter 9 in this volume.
[27] Greaves, *Glimpses*, 211, 216–18, 226.
[28] Whether the posthumous *Last Sermon* (1689) was printed from Bunyan's own copy or from an auditor's notes is not known; see, further, Chapter 20 in this volume.

the imprint of the former mockingly called attention to its illegal status: 'Printed for the Assigns of *John Calvin* and *Theodore Beza*.'[29] To our knowledge, Bunyan never published anonymously, but he, like other authors, often resorted to unlicensed publication. Only eight first editions of the forty or so titles published during his lifetime appear to have been properly licensed,[30] including the two parts of *The Pilgrim's Progress*, but neither *Badman* nor *The Holy War* (1682), both of which might be readily construed as deeply critical of the social values and political practices of the Restoration. Indeed, in *The Holy War* Bunyan himself had a tilt at the licensing authorities in the figure of Mr Filth, almost certainly a caricature of Roger L'Estrange, the Surveyor of the Press (*HW*, 31, 257n.).[31]

'My Strength Is Made Perfect in Weakness'

Although not overtly politically subversive, Bunyan's works, like those of other Nonconformists, are hence fiercely oppositional texts, maintaining in the hostile Restoration world their commitment to outlawed Puritan perspectives and aspirations. This, indeed, was fundamental to the Independent Dissenting tradition from which Bunyan's church derived, inspired as it was by 2 Corinthians 6:17: 'Wherefore come ye out from among them, and be ye separate, saith the Lord, and touch not the unclean thing.' Independency's emphasis on the autonomy of individual gathered churches exercising the right to choose their own pastor, to admit church members, and to administer discipline, created a powerful sense of a covenanted community deliberately withdrawn from, and at odds with, the world and its ways.[32] This was an ethos strengthened by the experience of persecution and the ethic of self-sufficient communal support it engendered.

This Dissent was far more comprehensive than the theological, liturgical, and ecclesiological issues through which it was articulated. It saw the world in a way fundamentally opposed to the materialism, libertinism, mannered social preoccupations, and witty cynicism of an England (and especially London) that took its cue from Charles II and his court. As well as being religious—or rather, because it was religious—it was also

---

[29] Annabel Patterson, with Martin Dzelzainis, Nicholas von Maltzahn, and N. H. Keeble (eds.), *The Prose Works of Andrew Marvell*, 2 vols (New Haven, CT: Yale University Press, 2003), 1: 4–6; 2: 51–2, 56.

[30] Greaves, *Glimpses*, 637–41.

[31] On the activities of L'Estrange in pursuing Nonconformist printers and writers, see Keeble, *Literary Culture*, 102–10, and for his contribution more generally, Anne Dunan-Page and Beth Lynch (eds.), *Roger L'Estrange and the Making of Restoration Culture* (Aldershot: Ashgate, 2008).

[32] As an 'open communion' gathered church, its covenanted membership was far more important to the culture of the Bedford church than the practice of adult baptism which was not required of its members in 1673, when its pastor, Bunyan, published *Differences in Judgment about Water-Baptism*,

social, literary, and cultural. Bunyan's writings, like those of other Nonconformists, are marked by a moral earnestness, an intense subjectivity and psychological particularity, a zealous engagement with issues of conscience, colloquially direct address, and a domestically based realism quite unlike the salacious and witty drawing-room (and bedroom) antics of the comedies of manners, the exoticism and melodrama of the heroic dramas, the amorous intrigues of the *nouvelles galantes* and secret histories of court liaisons, and the decorously stylized romances of Madeleine de Scudéry so admired by the prevailing culture of the Restoration, and quite different, too, from the prudent and poised moralism of such Episcopalian Latitudinarians as Edward Fowler and the future Archbishop of Canterbury, John Tillotson.[33]

Although Bunyan did engage with tricky soteriological issues in his treatise *The Doctrine of the Law and Grace Unfolded* (1659), and he was more than once diverted into controversial divinity, his genius was homiletic, moral, and casuistical, engaging with the actual challenges faced by believers. He quickly followed *Law and Grace* with *Christian Behaviour* (1663) 'touching Good Works' (*MW*, 3: 9), and he would later publish *A Holy Life, the Beauty of Christianity* (1683) in which he argued that faith that does not eventuate in moral improvement and active charity is merely vacuous hypocrisy. The fate of overconfident Ignorance trusting to works and good intentions in *The Pilgrim's Progress* should not blind us to Christian's assertion in discrediting Talkative that 'The Soul of Religion is the practick part' (*PP*, 79). 'It was never the will of God that bare *speculation* should be the end of his *Revelation* or of *our belief*. Divinity is an *Affective practical* Science' asserted Baxter.[34] The Puritan and Nonconformist classics are exercises in what would now be called psychological analysis and counselling, remarkable for their clear-sighted address to fallible human nature and the conditions of human life. These treatises have no concept of the 'spiritual' or 'religious' life separate from everyday business, social, and family dealings. 'In the using of your Trades and Callings in your Houses and Shops', wrote Gouge, 'you must manage all things as those that do not make mens practices but Gods precepts the rule of your [...] dealings.'[35] Bunyan's great works may be allegories but, like his non-fictional works, they contextualize the life of faith in the actual world of the reader's (and author's) domestic and commercial experience conveyed by a circumstantially accurate realism rendered through the conversational immediacy and apparently uncontrived directness of a '*plain and simple*' style (*GA*, 3) that

---

No Bar to Communion (*MW*, 4: 189–264). See, further, Anne Dunan-Page, *Grace Overwhelming: John Bunyan, The Pilgrim's Progress and the Extremes of the Baptist Mind* (Bern: Peter Lang, 2006), 47–76; B. R. White, 'The Fellowship of Believers: Bunyan and Puritanism', in Keeble (ed.), *Bunyan: Conventicle and Parnassus*, 1–19. For early Congregational Church practices, see Geoffrey F. Nuttall, *Visible Saints: The Congregational Way 1640–1660*, 2nd edn (Oswestry: Quinta Press, 2001). See also Chapter 3 in this volume.

[33] The definitive account of this distinction is Isabel Rivers, *Reason, Grace and Sentiment: A Study of the Language of Religion and Ethics in England 1660–1780*, vol. 1 (Cambridge: Cambridge University Press, 1991), 25–163.

[34] Richard Baxter, *Directions for Weak Distempered Christians* (1669), Part 1, 97–8.

[35] Gouge, *Young Man's Guide*, sigs A4–A4v.

eschewed carefully turned periods for 'a parcel of plain, yet sound, true and home sayings' (*MW*, 2: 16).[36]

Conscience is the guide and touchstone to which these works of practical divinity insistently turn in advising readers how to manage, and respond to, everyday dilemmas, challenges, and fears. Bunyan's steady refusal to contravene his convictions in order to secure his release from prison was, in this respect, an enacted sermon on the primacy of conscience. Such uncompromising individualism champions conscience above worldly authorities and always prefers inwardness and experiential immediacy to formalism and convention. Milton's God, the 'Spirit, that dost prefer / Before all temples the upright heart and pure',[37] is more concerned with personal integrity than with compliant conformity to tradition or authority. Personal attentiveness to inner experiential (or, as the seventeenth-century term was, *experimental*) Christianity was encouraged by the practice in gathered churches, including Bunyan's Bedford church (see *MW*, 4: 162, 165), of requiring from prospective members accounts of their conversion experiences,[38] and by the duty of self-scrutiny to analyse spiritual progress promoted by Nonconformist writers, including Bunyan (e.g. *MW*, 9: 332–36), in order to achieve assurance of grace and to ensure sincerity in Christian profession. Baxter's titles *The Vain Religion of the Formal Hypocrite* (1660) and *The Mischiefs of Self-Ignorance* (1662) make the point.

These practices lay behind the development of spiritual autobiography as a distinct genre of Puritan writing, of which there is no more intense or harrowing example than the '*Relation of the work of God upon my Own Soul*' in *Grace Abounding* (*GA*, 1–2).[39] 'It is', wrote Bunyan, '*profitable for Christians to be often calling to mind the very beginnings of Grace with their Souls*' and he noted that '*It was* Pauls *accustomed manner* [...] *to open* [...] *the manner of his Conversion*' to others, particularly his critics and accusers. Just so, Bunyan's '*Relation of the work of God upon my Own Soul*' in *Grace Abounding* is, at least in part, a defence of his ministry in response to its legal condemnation on the experientially authentic grounds that 'I preached what I felt, what I smartingly did feel, even that under which my poor Soul did groan and tremble to astonishment' (*GA*, 2, 85). Bunyan's pilgrims are inveterately curious about each other, keen whenever they meet to '*talk with you of all the things that have happened to you in your Pilgrimage*' that '*perhaps we may better our selves thereby*' (*PP*, 47, 66–8). They are in the habit of rehearsing their own autobiographical histories precisely so that they may compare, and learn from, others' personal experiences and the ways they have remained true to their consciences in the face of a hostile world.

---

[36] On Bunyan's style, see, further, Chapter 23 in this volume.

[37] Milton, *Paradise Lost*, 1: 17–18.

[38] On the practice and its literature, see Nuttall, *Visible Saints*, 109–16; Patricia Caldwell, *The Puritan Conversion Narrative: The Beginnings of American Expression* (Cambridge: Cambridge University Press, 1983); Lynch, *Protestant Autobiography*, 121–78.

[39] Owen Watkins, *The Puritan Experience* (London: Routledge & Kegan Paul, 1972); D. Bruce Hindmarsh, *Spiritual Autobiography in Early Modern England* (Oxford: Clarendon Press, 2005). On the genre's contribution to the development of the novel, see G. A. Starr, *Defoe and Spiritual Autobiography* (Princeton, NJ: Princeton University Press, 1965).

Just so, '*To prevent drowsiness*' as they cross the Inchanted Ground, Christian proposes to Hopeful that they '*fall into good discourse*', to which Hopeful responds, closely questioned by Christian, with a full account of his conversion and subsequent spiritual experiences. This example of '*Saints fellowship*' which, '*if it be manag'd well / Keeps them awake, and that in spite of hell*' is tellingly juxtaposed with the self-ignorance of Ignorance who rejoins the pilgrims at the end of Hopeful's account, but unwillingly, for he 'take[s] [...] pleasure in walking alone' and 'trusts his own heart', resenting Christian's encouragements to him to look inward and examine his true motives and proclivities (*PP*, 136–49). Unlike the complacently (and tragically) confident Ignorance, the true pilgrim is spiritually alert and morally engaged at all times: '*Departing from iniquity*', wrote Bunyan, 'is not a work of an hour, or a day, or a week, or a month, or a year: *But it's a work will last thee thy life time*' (*MW*, 9: 276). This point was often made by associating with the figures of the journey and the pilgrimage the Pauline image of the race for the prize or crown of salvation.[40] It was with this image that Milton had famously scorned the notion of religious retreat from the world: he could not praise 'a fugitive and cloister'd vertue, unexercis'd and unbreath'd, that slinks [...] out of the race, where that immortall garland is to be run for, not without dust and heat'.[41]

Although the journey is the controlling metaphor of *The Pilgrim's Progress*, Bunyan's allegory draws also upon another store of imagery: combat. Its climactic moments and exemplary figures are martial: Christian in his Pauline armour of faith (Ephesians 6:11–13) confronting Apollyon; Valiant-for-truth fighting so vigorously with his '*right* Jerusalem *blade*' that his sword cleaves to his hand with blood; Great-heart the giant slayer (*PP*, 56–60, 290–91, 295). In such moments, Bunyan draws on popular story and chivalric romance, rather than recollections of his own Civil War experience, but, beset by doubts and misgivings, prone to fits of despair, walking a weary road, his hero bears less resemblance than we might at first think to the questing knight errant of medieval chivalry. Milton, mocking the 'long and tedious havoc' of medieval and Renaissance chivalric romance and asserting that he is 'Not sedulous by nature to indite / Wars, hitherto the only argument / Heroic deemed', proposes as 'more heroic' than traditional epic subjects 'the better fortitude / Of patience and heroic martyrdom' exercised by those apparently weak. This was to repudiate an ideal that had inspired Europe for two millennia.

In *Paradise Lost*, then, Michael denigrates the heroic code as the worship of brute force, and traditional heroes as 'Destroyers rightlier called and plagues of men.'[42] It is to Satan that Milton gives the 'heroic' virtues; in *Paradise Regain'd*, the Son of Man is a pacifist. Like Milton, Bunyan too appeals to 2 Corinthians 12:9 ('My grace is sufficient for thee; for my strength is made perfect in weakness') as, addressing his gospel to the socially insignificant and personally unremarkable, he substitutes for an elitist model an ideal attainable by every reader in the context of their daily lives. The 'better fortitude' that *Paradise Lost* defines in terms of self-denial rather than self-assertion, of trust

---

[40] See, for example, 1 Corinthians 9:24; Galatians 5:7; Philippians 2:16; Hebrews 12:1.
[41] Milton, *Prose Works*, 2: 515.
[42] Milton, *Paradise Lost*, 9: 14, 26–41; 12: 561–71; 11: 689–97.

rather than aggression, is not restricted to a privileged armigerous class;[43] no more is the model of Christian fortitude represented in Bunyan's character of Christian. It is his very ordinariness that is the key at once to his pastoral effectiveness as an exemplar and to the psychological persuasiveness of his depiction. Christian heroism is enacted not in the biblical or mythical past by exceptional and ferocious figures but in humdrum and daily toil by the anxious, weary, and preoccupied.[44]

Nor, as of old, is this Christian hero embarked on a solitary quest. Although he turns his back on family and friends, Bunyan's Christian is not alone; he has companions along the way, and at the Palace Beautiful joins a gathered church, admitted after an account of his spiritual experiences (*PP*, 47–52). This sense of community is still more evident in *The Pilgrim's Progress, Part II* (1684), written not in prison in the 1660s but probably in the early 1680s after years of pastoral experience ministering to a persecuted congregation. Two things are striking about this community. First, although there is unquestionably an anti-feminist prejudice in Bunyan,[45] as in virtually all early modern traditions, his Christian ideal is not gender-specific. Loving relations between man and wife—the 'sum of earthly bliss' in Milton's words—are taken by Bunyan to be definitive of the Christian life (*MW*, 3: 26–7, 34), as they are by Milton, whose Eve is created not as an afterthought but as the completion and perfection of a paradise in which, without her, Adam is discontented: 'In solitude / What happiness?' Marriage and sexual relations are essential features of the divine conception of human nature and of happiness in a paradise in which 'The happier Eden' is the experience of Adam and Eve 'Imparadised in one another's arms.'[46] There is no patience with Roman Catholic notions of asceticism and abstinence. 'Who bids abstain / But our destroyer, foe to God and man?' asks the narrator in *Paradise Lost*. The Independent and republican Lucy Hutchinson has only scorn for the 'superstitious prince' Edward the Confessor 'who was sainted for his ungodly chastity,'[47] and for Bunyan '*Nunnish*' is an insult (*MW*, 4: 307). Within marriage, although the husband is undoubtedly the master of the family, women are their husbands' 'yoak-fellows' not 'slaves' (*MW*, 3: 34), with a responsibility to exercise their own judgement. In *The Pilgrim's Progress, Part II* the female protagonist Christiana is required to take the initiative and, with whatever qualifications,[48] to make her own way.

---

[43] Milton, *Paradise Lost*, 12: 561–87.

[44] There is, nevertheless, a good deal of violence, belligerency, and fear in Bunyan and in Nonconformist writing; see Achinstein, *Literature and Dissent*, 84–114; Dunan-Page, *Grace Overwhelming*, 195–234.

[45] A case in point is Bunyan's refusal in *A Case of Conscience Resolved* (1683) to allow women a separate meeting, on the grounds, chiefly, that Eve's weakness 'over-threw [...] the reputation of Women for ever' (*MW*, 4: 305).

[46] Milton, *Paradise Lost*, 8: 364–65; 4: 506–07, 748–49; 8: 522.

[47] Milton, *Paradise Lost*, 4: 748–49; Lucy Hutchinson, *Memoirs of the Life of Colonel Hutchinson*, ed. N. H. Keeble (London: Dent, 1995), 5.

[48] On matters of gender in Bunyan, see Vera Camden and Kimberly Hill (eds.), 'Feminine Authority, Agency and Identity in Bunyan's England', special issue *BS* 11 (2003/04); N. H. Keeble, '"Here is her glory, even to be under him": The Feminine in the Thought and Work of John Bunyan', in Anne Laurence, W. R. Owens, and Stuart Sim (eds.), *John Bunyan and his England, 1628–1688* (London: Hambledon Press,

Secondly, the socially, physically, and mentally disadvantaged and disabled attach themselves to Christiana and Great-heart (in a clear representation of a gathered church) and, incapable though they are, yet succeed in reaching the Celestial City. The Shepherds of the Delectable Mountains greet the pilgrim band in *Part II* with the words 'This is a comfortable Company, you are welcome to us, for we have for the *Feeble*, as for the *Strong*; our Prince has an Eye to what is done to the least of these' (*PP*, 284). To those afraid that their 'natural *weakness* and *timorousness*' will let them down, Bunyan replies that God 'can make the most soft spirited man, as hard as an Adamant, harder than Flint, yea, harder than the northern Steel': '*Timorous* Peter, *fearful* Peter, he could make as bold as a Lyon' (*MW*, 10: 19, 20). Salvation is available to Christiana, to family and friends, and to a gathering of pilgrims far less independent than Christian, through engagements and encounters that are as much domestic and neighbourly as adventurous. The sense of community here, of interdependence and inclusiveness regardless of status, marks the final dissent of Bunyan and of Nonconformist writing, from the exclusivity and elitism of prevailing Restoration culture.

Suggested Reading

Achinstein, Sharon, *Literature and Dissent in Milton's England* (Cambridge: Cambridge University Press, 2003).

Coffey, John (ed.), *The Oxford History of Protestant Dissenting Traditions*, vol. 1: *The Post-Reformation Era, c.1559–c.1689* (Oxford: Oxford University Press, 2020).

Cragg, G. R., *Puritanism in the Period of the Great Persecution 1660–88* (Cambridge: Cambridge University Press, 1957).

Greaves, Richard L., *Glimpses of Glory: John Bunyan and English Dissent* (Stanford, CA: Stanford University Press, 2002).

Keeble, N. H., *The Literary Culture of Nonconformity in Later Seventeenth-Century England* (Leicester: Leicester University Press, 1987).

Keeble, N. H. (ed.), *'Settling the Peace of the Church': 1662 Revisited* (Oxford: Oxford University Press, 2014).

Lynch, Kathleen, *Protestant Autobiography in the Seventeenth-Century Anglophone World* (Oxford: Oxford University Press, 2012).

Watts, Michael R., *The Dissenters: From the Reformation to the French Revolution* (Oxford: Clarendon Press, 1978).

1990), 131–47; Tamsin Spargo, *The Writing of John Bunyan* (Aldershot: Ashgate, 1997), 71–95; Kathleen Swaim, *Pilgrim's Progress, Puritan Progress* (Urbana and Chicago, IL: University of Illinois Press, 1993), 160–97; Margaret Olofson Thickstun, *Fictions of the Feminine: Puritan Doctrine and the Representation of Women* (Ithaca, NY: Cornell University Press, 1988), 87–104; and Chapters 7 and 18 in this volume.

CHAPTER 9

BUNYAN'S PARTNERS IN PRINT

KATHLEEN LYNCH

CHARLES DOE, who edited the first (incomplete) *Works* of John Bunyan in 1692, saw a neat symmetry in the list he compiled of sixty titles for Bunyan's sixty years (see Figure 9.1). Others have corrected Doe's count. But Bunyan's oeuvre was a substantial one, and Doe was Bunyan's first bibliographer. There are various ways to divide Bunyan's works. Doe distinguished between printed works and those left in manuscript. Another division, cutting across the first, was the set of texts that Doe printed as the first volume of the collected works and those he promised for future volumes. Yet another division lies behind that one, and it stymied Doe. That division could be made according to which stationers held which copy privileges in Bunyan's works. Several of the stationers who published Bunyan had colourful nicknames, including Elephant Smith and Bunyan Ponder. We may think of them as Bunyan's publishers. Doe's dilemma encourages us to switch the possessive around. What if we think, instead, of Smith's Bunyan, Ponder's Bunyan, and so on? One reason to do so is to get a clearer view of the conditions and regulations of the printing trade in the time before authorial copyrights. Another is to get a different perspective on the culture of exemplarity that so advanced the status of John Bunyan.[1]

Doe worked with the bookseller William Marshall on the first Bunyan collection, and it was clear that the two saw the product as a folio from the start. The subscriptions' proposal that Marshall prepared bespeaks a prudent business plan. The book was to cost ten shillings in sheets. The two would collect five shillings on every order in advance and five shillings on delivery. They would print only when they had secured commitments from three hundred subscribers. In the event, they had four hundred subscribers, solicited from across a network of Dissenters across the country. As W. R. Owens has noted, it was a bold move to produce a folio volume of Bunyan's work. Owens further notes how

---

[1] See Tamsin Spargo, *The Writing of John Bunyan* (Aldershot: Ashgate, 1997).

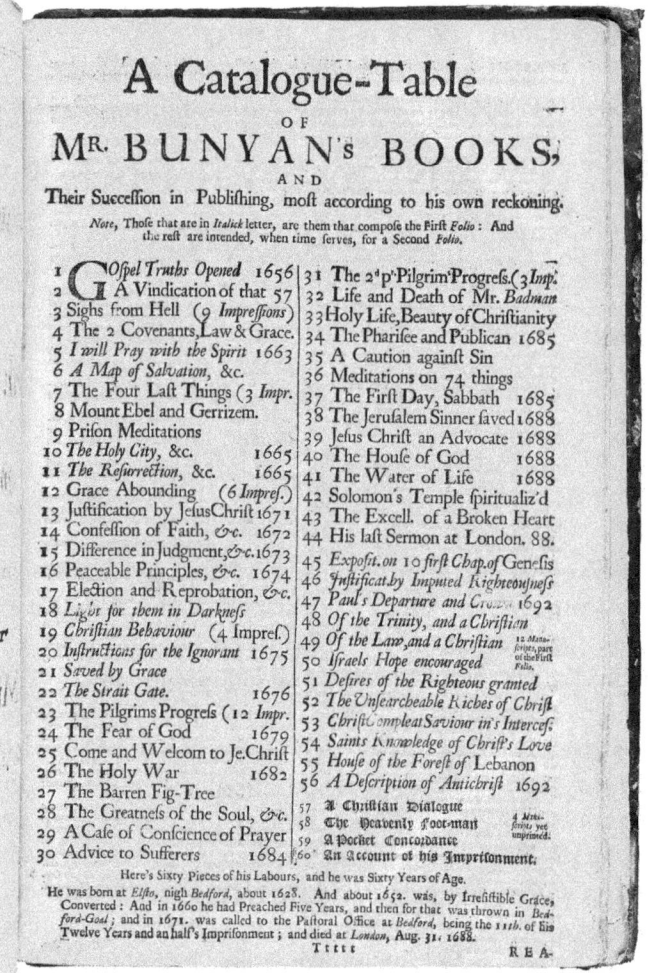

FIGURE 9.1 'Catalogue-Table of Mr. Bunyan's Books', in *The Works of that Eminent Servant of Christ, Mr. John Bunyan* (1692).

(By permission of the Folger Shakespeare Library [shelf mark B5479].)

much Doe and Marshall wanted to position Bunyan in the company of learned clergymen, who were also receiving the kind of folio treatment that preserves an oeuvre and consolidates an author's reputation.[2] Yet none of the ten manuscripts printed for the first time in *The Works of that Eminent Servant of Christ* or the ten 'Books formerly Printed',

---

[2] W. R. Owens, 'Reading the Bibliographical Codes: Bunyan's Publication in Folio', in N. H. Keeble (ed.), *John Bunyan: Reading Dissenting Writing* (Bern: Peter Lang, 2002), 59–77. For a contemporary assessment of Doe, see Anne Dunan-Page, 'Charles Doe and the Publication of John Bunyan's Folio (1692)', *Notes and Queries*, 57 (2010), 508–11. Of particular relevance to this chapter is the charge that Doe's bookselling ventures are inappropriately venal.

as it was phrased on the title page, have added much to Bunyan's reputation as an author. Doe and Marshall stressed the value of Bunyan's 'Christian Ministerial Labours', and they delivered the engraved portrait that they promised in the prospectus. They even absorbed sixpence of the one shilling and sixpence more that the book cost to print than was advertised. They did everything that was conventionally to be done to create a lasting monument to John Bunyan.[3] All that was missing were the significant texts. For much as Doe may have wanted to collect John Bunyan's *Works*, he could only work with the texts to which he could secure the rights to publish, and those were the works consigned by later generations to the category of miscellaneous.

Doe styled himself the Struggler. His palpable sense of the difficulty of making an appropriate monument to the great man's memory reveals the difference between the two partners in the folio enterprise. It is the difference between the professional and the amateur. Marshall let the subscribers cover the costs of printing, as he tested the market for new works by the author of *The Pilgrim's Progress* (which is how he promoted Bunyan in the subscription prospectus). Doe was the disciple, the true believer, struggling indeed to complete a biography, compile an index, and construct a bibliography. He may have been responsible for the miscalculation of sheets, which brought up the cost of the printed book. He was in over his head. It is perhaps not a surprise that, when fifteen years later, plans for a second volume were resuscitated by Marshall, when he took out an advertisement for subscribers, Doe countered with his own advertisement, blasting Marshall's claims to new titles, and asserting his own 'better' claims to titles, including, this time, *The Pilgrim's Progress*.[4] Nothing came of either of their trial balloons, though the long textual history of Bunyan's works was just beginning.

This chapter examines the realities of publishing that Charles Doe seemed to hope he could wish away, the infrastructure of the book trade, and its copyrights at the end of the seventeenth century.[5] Doe was not a member of the Stationers' Company, which enjoyed a monopoly on printing. At the time that Doe was struggling with these issues, they were all about to wash away with the lapsing of the Printing Act in 1695. But during both Bunyan's lifetime and when Doe was publishing his *Works*, the relationship between members of the book trade and authors was such that the stationers—those responsible for publishing (that is, printing and selling) books—were the ones rewarded with copy rights for their investments. The activities of printing, bookselling, and binding were all encompassed in the Stationers' Company, a London-based trade company, incorporated in 1557. Members of the company thereby enjoyed a monopoly on the printed book industry. But they also had to adhere to regulations aimed at controlling the circulation

---

[3] On the absence of a conventional burial monument, in the context of the moral duty of remembrance so central to Bunyan's work, see Sharon Achinstein, 'Bunyan and the Politics of Remembrance', in Vera J. Camden (ed.), *Trauma and Transformation: The Political Progress of John Bunyan* (Stanford, CA: Stanford University Press, 2008), 135–52.

[4] Owens, 'Reading the Bibliographical Codes', 75–6, quotes Doe's advertisement in full.

[5] See Michael Treadwell, 'The Stationers and the Printing Acts at the End of the Seventeenth Century', in John Barnard, D. F. McKenzie, and Maureen Bell (eds.), *The Cambridge History of the Book in Britain, Vol. 4: 1557–1695* (Cambridge: Cambridge University Press, 2002), 755–76.

of ideas. A series of proclamations and Acts established the terms and limits of the privilege. The consequences of violating those terms could include loss of equipment, the imposition of fines, and even imprisonment for non-compliance with statutory regulations. In the second half of the seventeenth century, the business of publishing was increasingly motivated by ideational affiliation as much as by economic remuneration. Those ideational affiliations also made stationers targets for exemplary punishments.

In bringing several of Bunyan's associates among the book and print trade more to the foreground, we may articulate terms by which they may better figure in a model of distributed knowledge. We can illuminate stages in Bunyan's writing career and public life by mapping them onto the impositions and lapses of printing regulations. By trying to discern stationers' motivations through their investments, we can also see the ways in which the genres Bunyan worked in and the audiences he reached out to intersected at some points and diverged at others. The strategic inclusion of illustrative materials at various stages and in particular genres may also illuminate the circulation of his works, not simply in terms of production, but as indicators of community formation and the development of new reading publics at the end of the seventeenth century.

A Public Ministry

John Bunyan first came into print controverting points of doctrine with others, mostly Quakers. His was a voice from the provinces, where the contest for the hearts and minds of the godly was fiercely waged. Shortly after his admission into the gathered church at Bedford led by John Gifford, Bunyan was preaching and also appearing in print. *Some Gospel-Truths Opened* (1656), like his next three books, was published in London by John Wright 'the younger', or by an 'M. Wright'. Each had a separate imprint for Matthias Cowley, a bookseller in Newport Pagnell, Buckinghamshire.[6] The fact that Bunyan's work had a separate local imprint is indicative of the distribution networks by which the products of the book trade reached across the country. The trade was limited by statute to members of the Stationers' Company of London (with exceptions for the universities of Oxford and Cambridge). The geographies of distributive knowledge networks remain understudied, but Bunyan's early work illustrates the provincial reach of the London-centric book trade. Bunyan's first three books had prefaces by local Nonconformist ministers, each of whom testified to Bunyan's godliness. But in 1660, just a few short years after his public ministerial life had commenced, the provincial itinerant polemicist who is represented in these early works was imprisoned for illegal preaching.

Imprisonment only spread Bunyan's fame and influence. His person was (mostly) removed from the streets of Bedford, but his voice was amplified through print. This was

---

[6] There is no extant copy of *A Few Sighs from Hell* (1658) with the Newport Pagnell imprint, but the pattern seems clear enough.

achieved largely through the offices of Francis Smith, his principal publisher from 1661 to 1676. Smith was a leading member of London's Baptist community, and the Bedford meeting had Baptist tendencies. Smith's career as a bookseller illustrates the ways in which stationers were advancing ideological points of view in the mid-seventeenth century. He was every bit as much an exemplary victim of religious persecution as John Bunyan, though Smith saw fit to use the promotional tools of his trade to expose the systemic corruption that sustained that persecution, while Bunyan became the clear voice of conscientious victimhood. Smith was widely known by his nickname, Elephant Smith, for the sign of his bookshop, the Elephant and Castle (which he apparently hung at several different locations in the course of his career). His most historically resonant achievement was to fight back against the prosecutions for seditious libel that he endured during the years of the Exclusion Crisis. He embraced the court challenges that Bunyan shied away from, using the courtroom as a forum in which to advocate legal protections for the liberty of conscience that he and Bunyan both fervently sought in their private worship.

Francis Smith

Smith's career started out conventionally enough. He was apprenticed to Thomas Hazard in 1647 and freed of the Stationers' Company in 1654. His first imprints from that year are two works of religious polemic issued together. One taunted the by then disestablished Church of England with a gesture of one-upmanship by promising *The True Gospel-Faith* […] *Collected into* Thirty *Articles* (emphasis added); the other cautioned against 'those grand Impostors called Quakers'. George Thomason dated his purchase of them 26 October 1654, an act that almost seals Smith's formal entrance into the polemical arena that was the book trade in the years of Civil War and revolution, after the collapse of the Privy Council and the expiration of the 1637 Printing Act. Smith comes into his own as a stationer, then, with a clear religious agenda at the very time that pamphlet literature was flourishing and sectarian polemic was rife, positioning himself as a spokesperson for Baptists.

How representative a member of the Stationers' Company was Francis Smith? One way of addressing that question is by looking at his record of entry of copy privilege in the Stationers' Register. This was a requirement of the trade. In theory, entrance in the register allowed for orderly claims to be made, and contested if need be, within the company. With its provision for licensing, or the securing of ecclesiastical permission, entrance also fulfilled the regulatory interests of the state. Smith did not enter his earliest titles in the Register, but from 1656 through September 1660, he entered ten books, about a third of the number he published. These are mostly works of religious polemic, including one authored by himself: *Symptoms of Growth and Decay to Godliness* (24 February 1659/60), for which he rather excessively listed four licensers under the rubric 'Imprimatur'. He also entered *An Introduction of the First Grounds or Rudiments of*

Arithmetique (7 September 1660), perhaps a bid for a steady moneymaker. When considering percentages of entrance in the Register, most scholars accepted a fairly low percentage as indicative of stationers' practices. Either a claim was well enough established through production, or the title promised little enough return in profit, that the payment of a fee and the requirement of a pre-publication review by censors did not seem worth the trouble. It is also the case that Smith's religious views were tolerated in the interregnum. Indeed, the Baptists and other sects practised openly in the years of the Commonwealth and the Protectorate.

If Smith's actions seem characteristic of the company as a whole in those early years, however, the pattern was soon broken. As early as 1659, Smith was attracting attention as a religious radical. With the Restoration, his entries in the Stationers' Register stop abruptly. Though this is not direct evidence of radical beliefs, it is an indirect indicator that his work would not pass under the new censorship regime. He fanned the flames of worries about the political loyalties of Nonconformists by co-publishing with Livewell Chapman Henry Jessey's *The Lord's Loud Call to England* (1660), which reported some natural disasters as God's judgements on the nation. In the same year he may have tried to temper that judgement by publishing *The Humble Apology of some Commonly called Anabaptists* (from his new shop 'at the sign of the Elephant and Castle without Temple-Bar'). The *Apology* loudly asserted the Baptists' loyalty to the king and their distance from the abortive rebellions of the Fifth Monarchist Thomas Venner and others. But it was a hard sell for Nonconformists to distance themselves from political rebels in the months immediately after the Restoration, and Smith notably failed to establish that distance convincingly. He complained years later of how he was falsely accused of taking part in Venner's uprising, and of having arms in his house:

> upon which I was ten times *Searched by that Lawless Company,* my Goods *Torn and Stole, Chests, Trunkes and Closet Doors broke open, and a Carbine* put three times to my *Brest to Shoot me.*[7]

Smith may not have had arms in his house, but he did have a weapon in the ideological war. That was the press, and he understood as well as anyone its power to disseminate news and influence public opinion. In partnership with Elizabeth Calvert, he published *Mirabilis Annus, or, The Year of Prodigies and Wonders* (1661). For that he was imprisoned. As reported in the Calendar of State Papers Domestic, he stonewalled his examiners, claiming that he had never heard of the book, contributed to it, read it, or distributed it. Henry Jessey, who had also been arrested for his assumed involvement in the publication, denied any knowledge, though he admitted collecting notes of 'remarkable events' and that someone had shown him a copy of the printed work.

There were no legal protections against self-incrimination, but Smith and Jessey had some measure of protection in the very difficulty of ascribing ownership of, or

---

[7] Francis Smith, *An Account of the Injurious Proceedings of Sir George Jeffreys K$^{nt.}$* [. . .] *against Francis Smith* [1681], 8.

responsibility for, printed texts. From the perspective of its governmental overseers, the fact that it was so hard to identify the responsible parties was one of the essential dangers of the press. It could be especially hard to identify publishers. Their capital investments did not leave material traces on the printed sheets. This accounted for the government's use of coercion to make the Stationers' Company police its members. From his earliest run-ins with the law, it is clear that Smith was not afraid to challenge his accusers with the burden of proof, or to bring the abusive treatment of prisoners, including himself, to the attention of possible champions. This kind of tenacious opposition on the part of some members of the book trade led to the appointment of Sir Roger L'Estrange as Surveyor of the Press once the Printing Act was reintroduced in 1662. Adding to the welter of competing claims to authority over the book trade, the 1662 Act was the first statutory (or parliamentary) Act regulating the press. But the king appointed the surveyor, and several times the king stacked the court of the Stationers' Company with his own printers and binders.

At this time and in this context, Smith started publishing Bunyan. Richard Greaves speculates that Bunyan's wife could have been the one who first presented Smith with the manuscript of *Profitable Meditations* (1661) when she travelled to London to petition the Earl of Bedford for her husband's release from imprisonment.[8] It is a nice thought, and Elizabeth Bunyan certainly demonstrated tenacity in seeking legal recourse for her husband's treatment in the early months of his imprisonment. However the arrangements were made, Bunyan's relationship with Smith was forged in the context of their shared showcase persecutions. The relationship outlasted Bunyan's prolonged imprisonment and ensured that his name and his case were kept alive as an example of conscientious fortitude.

By the time he was working with Smith, Bunyan's texts no longer needed the endorsement of a better-known preacher. Several titles even stressed his unjust imprisonment. For example, the title page of *Christian Behaviour* (1663) promoted its author as 'a Prisoner of Hope', and Bunyan's verse *Prison Meditations* appeared first in this work. *I Will Pray with the Spirit* (2nd edn, 1663) was announced as 'Printed for the Author'— contemporary wording for self-published works. In this case, however, as an impoverished prisoner, deprived of his trade as a tinker because he would not abandon his profession of preaching, it is hard to believe that Bunyan was laying out any money for the publication of a book. Rather, it was more plausibly published as a charitable benefit to Bunyan.

Within Protestant English culture, Smith was dedicated to giving voice to the oppressed. In pamphlets like *A True and Impartial Narrative of some Illegal and Arbitrary Proceedings* [...] *against Innocent and Peaceable Nonconformists in* [...] *Bedford* (1670), he provided detailed cases of injustices done against Nonconformists, several of whom were members of Bunyan's church.[9] Many of Smith's Baptist pamphlets were signed by

---

[8] Greaves, *Glimpses*, 147.
[9] See, further, Kathleen Lynch, ' "Her Name Agnes": The Verifications of Agnes Beaumont's Narrative Ventures', *ELH*, 67 (2000), 71–98 (81–4).

leaders of the congregations (including himself). When, much later, he was writing his own first-person testimony of persecution, *An Account of the Injurious Proceedings* [...] *against Francis Smith, Bookseller* (1681), he listed by name the members of the London grand jury who exonerated him. Given that Smith was John Bunyan's champion throughout the latter's years of imprisonment, it must have stung him to have missed out on the opportunity to publish first, and thereby profit fully from, Bunyan's spiritual autobiography, *Grace Abounding to the Chief of Sinners* (1666). The bookseller George Larkin, who was just setting himself up in business, got that chance instead.[10] This may have been because, according to Smith's own retrospective account, he had fled London's outbreak of plague in 1665 and then was overwhelmed in 1666 by a seizure of his unlicensed books, including 'Mr. *Bunyans*'. The bulk of those books were subsequently lost in the Great Fire, 'to my real dammage above Fifty Pounds'.[11] By the third edition of *Grace Abounding* (?1672), however, Smith had taken over its publication from Larkin, and he continued to publish it until Nathaniel Ponder acquired it, with a fifth edition appearing under the latter's imprint in 1680. The only copy privilege that Smith entered in the Stationers' Register for a work by Bunyan was *A Few Sighs from Hell*, at the time he published the fourth edition in 1674.[12] *A Few Sighs from Hell* was the best-selling title by Bunyan to have been published by Smith. It went through seven editions in Bunyan's lifetime. Increasingly mired in his own legal troubles, however, Smith published no new titles by Bunyan after *The Strait Gate* and *Saved by Grace* in 1676.

Smith's reasons for publishing unlicensed books during the Restoration, such as those that had either been seized in 1666 or lost in the Great Fire, were circular: he had to publish them without licences because he couldn't secure these. He charged the authorities with prejudice against Bunyan and other of his authors, though their books were 'neither against Church nor State'.[13] However, at this time, and under the increasingly harsh measures of the Restoration's penal legislation against Nonconformists (sometimes referred to as the 'Clarendon Code'), the burden of proof lay on Smith. His antagonists, though, were not limited to the governmental regulators; he also made enemies in the company. The most egregious example had to do with Henry Danvers's *A Treatise of Baptism* (1673), which took up again the cause of Baptists. As he told the story, Smith 'had the second Impression' underway (the first impression having been licensed) when the king's bookbinder, Samuel Mearne, and other officers of the company, entered his house, searched the premises, and seized the sheets then in press.[14] At the same time,

---

[10] George Larkin has been a shadowy figure in the annals of the book trade. Turned informer by L'Estrange, he was ostracized by the Stationers' Company. He came back into the business of printing Bunyan only in the last year of Bunyan's life. See Martin Dzelzainis, 'Managing the Later Stuart Press, 1662–1696', in Lorna Hutson (ed.), *The Oxford Handbook of English Law and Literature, 1500–1700* (Oxford: Oxford University Press, 2017).

[11] Smith, *An Account of the Injurious Proceedings*, 11.

[12] Smith had published *A Few Sighs from Hell* since its second edition in the early years of Bunyan's imprisonment.

[13] Smith, *An Account of the Injurious Proceedings*, 11.

[14] Smith, *An Account of the Injurious Proceedings*, 14 (misnumbered 18).

Mearne countenanced the reprinting of the book on other presses for other stationers. It may have been at this time that Smith first caught the sympathetic ear of the then Lord Chancellor Shaftesbury. He aired his grievances to a committee of the House of Lords, and Charles himself approved the restitution of his pirated copies.

By the years of the Exclusion Crisis, Smith was turning to a more directly political agenda. As Timothy Crist has argued, he may also have been taking active steps to prepare to increase his output as soon as the Printing Act of 1662 lapsed in 1679. He mortgaged his £40 share of the Stationers' Company English Stock to another stationer in November 1678, Crist surmises to raise capital.[15] This was an opportunistic step, leveraging corporate profits to capitalize individual initiative. His own, individual trade interests were high among the rights that Smith had taken it upon himself to advance. The king was also taking steps to deal with the lapse of the Act. He secured the position of Company Warden for Samuel Mearne, and he turned to the courts to pursue charges of seditious libel against members of the opposition press. In the next few years, Smith was repeatedly arrested, facing trials before Lord Chief Justice Scroggs and appearing before the Privy Council. Just as he was becoming a key figure within the formation of a Whig opposition, he was also becoming a target for the king's attempts to fight back against the exclusionist policies of Parliament.

It all came to a head when Smith published the Earl of Shaftesbury's *A Speech Lately Made by a Noble Peer of the Realm* (1681), in which Shaftesbury vehemently objected to 'the *Prorogations*, the *Dissolutions*, the Cutting *short* of *Parliaments*, not suffering them to *have time* or opportunity *to look into any thing*'. Shaftesbury argued against popery and arbitrary government, challenging Charles to 'first shew that he is *intirely ours*, that he *Weds* the *Interest* and the *Religion* of the *Nation*' before receiving any assurances of money or parliamentary support.[16] Shortly thereafter, Smith also published *An Account of the Injurious Proceedings*. What began as a first-person account of the prosecution by the London Recorder, Sir George Jeffreys, became an outraged indictment of abuses of the many legal procedures against Smith over his twenty-year career. As were Shaftesbury's actions at this time, Smith's rehearsal of grievances in public was provocation of the highest order. It was issued from the very centre of political struggle in the endgame of the Exclusion Crisis. If one makes allowances for the anti-Catholic hysteria behind the exclusionists' campaign, Smith's self-defence could also be said to be as pointed a defence of political principle, the rule of law, and the public interest as had theretofore been made in print. By the end of the year, after the execution of Stephen College, the author of *A Ra-Ree Show* (1681), a libellous ballad, Smith, its publisher, fled to the Netherlands, where Shaftesbury had also earlier fled. Smith returned two years later, whereupon he was immediately arrested and tried (again by Jeffreys) for publication of the libel. Smith's last act was characteristic, if pathetic. He was pilloried and fined £500. Unable to raise money or security for his release, he remained in prison for four

---

[15] Timothy Crist, 'Government Control of the Press after the Expiration of the Printing Act in 1679', *Publishing History*, 5 (1979), 49–77 (51–2).

[16] *A Speech Lately Made by a Noble Peer of the Realm* (1681), [2].

years, until pardoned by James II. What followed was also characteristic for the indomitable Smith. He took his sign to Pope's Head Alley and re-established his business.[17]

If Smith's Bunyan is the exemplary victim of religious persecution, Bunyan's Smith is an early champion of the individual's rights that were only beginning to be articulated as such. It may be that we need to look at the two approaches together to see more clearly pacifism and protest as two faces of a single objective. The critical goal here is not to collapse the intersecting circles of politics and religion into one, as so easily happens. Rather, opening up our investigations of John Bunyan to his associates in the world of publishing may grant us a better, fuller view of shifting individual and communal identities within Restoration Nonconformity. Had Bunyan's letters from jail been published in print at the time they were written, for instance, we would certainly have a sharper view of his principled victimhood at the start of the Restoration. But those letters remained in manuscript for another century, which is one of the factors that has kept Bunyan distanced from Smith in our understanding of their shared experiences of persecution—the one squarely in the realm of religious confession, and the other in the realm of direct political activism.

What else might we learn from Smith's example? That the book trade was in crisis, beset with competing regulators, and also pressured by conflicting interests within the company: forces that set printers against booksellers and encouraged individual stationers to begin to put their own interests before the company's. We also see in Smith a new political role, that of the promoter of religious freedom, of political rights. Finally, we see the increasing visibility of the courts as a forum for the resolution of political problems. Charles II had his reasons to turn to the courts. So did Francis Smith and the other stationers tried for seditious libel with him. Smith took full advantage of the opportunity to speak his truth. He brought into the courtroom an already fully developed notion of the significance of first-person witnessing, gained in the Nonconformist meeting house. The discourses of testimony as deployed in the meeting house and the courthouse were not one and the same, but each inflected the other.

Nathaniel Ponder

Bunyan had a second extended relationship with a publisher, and it, too, was one that resonates in the history of rights—in this case intellectual property—and of the steps taken to apportion and protect it. Nathaniel Ponder published *The Pilgrim's Progress* (1678), possibly on the recommendation of John Owen, the leading Independent minister.[18] Francis Smith thereby lost out on the greatest profits to be had in Bunyan's bestselling work. By contrast, Ponder gained a nickname—Bunyan Ponder—that gives us

---

[17] See Beth Lynch, 'Francis Smith', *ODNB*.

[18] On Ponder's confessional affiliations, see Beth Lynch, 'Nathaniel Ponder', *ODNB*; see also Frank Mott Harrison, 'Nathaniel Ponder: The Publisher of *The Pilgrim's Progress*', *The Library*, 4th ser., 15 (1934), 257–94.

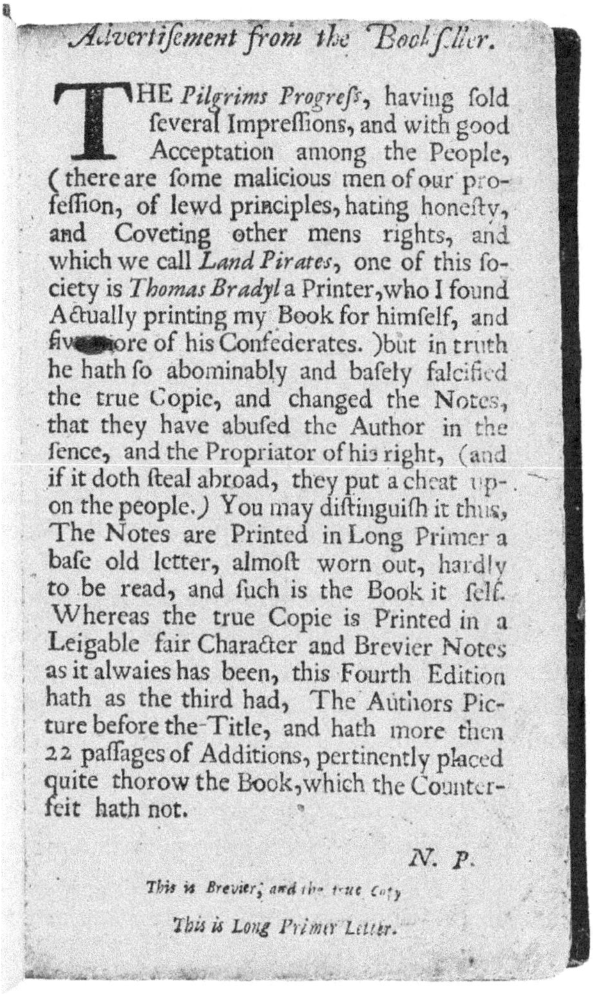

Advertiſement from the Bookſeller.

THE *Pilgrims Progreſs*, having ſold ſeveral Impreſſions, and with good Acceptation among the People, (there are ſome malicious men of our profeſſion, of lewd principles, hating honeſty, and Coveting other mens rights, and which we call *Land Pirates*, one of this ſociety is *Thomas Bradyl* a Printer, who I found Actually printing my Book for himſelf, and five more of his Confederates.) but in truth he hath ſo abominably and baſely falcified the true Copie, and changed the Notes, that they have abuſed the Author in the ſence, and the Propriator of his right, (and if it doth ſteal abroad, they put a cheat upon the people.) You may diſtinguiſh it thus, The Notes are Printed in Long Primer a baſe old letter, almoſt worn out, hardly to be read, and ſuch is the Book it ſelf. Whereas the true Copie is Printed in a Leigable fair Character and Brevier Notes as it alwaies has been, this Fourth Edition hath as the third had, The Authors Picture before the Title, and hath more then 22 paſſages of Additions, pertinently placed quite thorow the Book, which the Counterfeit hath not.

N. P.

This is Brevier, and the true Copy

This is Long Primer Letter.

FIGURE 9.2 *'Advertisement from the Bookseller'*, in *The Pilgrim's Progress* (1680).

(By permission of the Folger Shakespeare Library [shelf mark 207–14q].)

a glimpse into a commercial association that for us has overtones of name branding. Ponder entered *The Pilgrim's Progress* in the Stationers' Register on 22 December 1677. An entry in the Stationers' Term Catalogue specified the price as 1s 6d bound. He published two editions in 1678, a third in 1679, and eleven by 1688, the year of Bunyan's death. That same year, Ponder published *The Water of Life*, a third edition of *Mr. Badman*, and the sixth edition of *Grace Abounding*. Ponder was cornering the market on Bunyan.

That the market for Bunyan had grown—by leaps and bounds—is clear in the addition of a statement warning against spurious editions of *The Pilgrim's Progress* that Ponder added as early as the fourth edition (1680) (see Figure 9.2).[19] In a verse preface

[19] To prove the inferiority of the type used in the pirated edition, Ponder printed a line in comparison with the 'Leigable fair Character' of his own brevier (see *PP*, xlix).

to *The Pilgrim's Progress, Part II* (1684), Bunyan himself worries that there have been so many imitations that people won't recognize this work as his own:

> '*Tis true, some have of late, to Counterfeit*
> My *Pilgrim, to their own, my Title set;*
> *Yea others, half my Name and Title too;*
> *Have stitched to their Book, to make them do;*
> *But yet they by their* Features *do declare*
> *Themselves not mine to be, whose ere they are.* (*PP*, 168)

On the verso of the title page of that work, Bunyan asserted Ponder's property rights: 'I appoint Mr. *Nathaniel* Ponder, But no other to Print this Book.' This was an act more symbolic than dispositive. There was not yet in place a copyright statute that asserted authorial rights over their writings. Yet the system of Stationers' copy privileges with which Ponder had taken pains to comply no longer had any efficacy. The Licensing Act of 1662 had lapsed in 1679, and it would limp along until its final collapse in 1695.

The trail of false imprints, plagiarisms, and misleading titles is dense, but it leaves no doubt how vulnerable Bunyan and Ponder were to knock-offs.[20] Bunyan had also acquired an authorial identity that now had to be protected in the marketplace, something that comes to inform the paratextual material found in subsequent works (see *HW*, 251; *PP*, 167–73). The financial implications of those fraudulent editions and unauthorized continuations are clear in a trail of records that cumulatively detail Ponder's unremitting efforts to protect his investments. As early as 1679, he sued the printer Thomas Braddyll for printing more copies of *The Pilgrim's Progress* than he had been hired to and then holding on to the balance to sell himself.[21] Hard as he worked to protect his investment in Bunyan's works, Ponder could not escape the precariousness of the book trade, with its small profit margins and unprincipled competitors. A decade later, Ponder was in the King's Bench prison for debt—even after putting into print Bunyan's massive output of works in 1688, before and shortly following his death. Another decade on, shortly before he died in poverty at the age of fifty-nine, Ponder was posting an advertisement in a London newsbook to be elected one of London's bridge-masters. That was a post that John Strype described as having 'sometimes been a good Relief for some honest Citizen fallen to decay'.[22] Perhaps the fullest picture we get of Ponder's dire straits, as well as of the perilous state of the book trade in general, is through the depositions for a Chancery

---

[20] Albert B. Cook III, 'John Bunyan and John Dunton: A Case of Plagiarism', *The Papers of the Bibliographical Society of America*, 71 (1977), 11–28; Natasha Simonova, *Early Modern Authorship and Prose Continuations: Adaptation and Ownership from Sidney to Richardson* (Basingstoke: Palgrave Macmillan, 2015), 106–23.

[21] Many of the legal entanglements of Ponder's career are described in Harrison, 'Nathaniel Ponder'. See also, David Stoker, 'William Proctor, Nathaniel Ponder, and the Financing of *Pilgrim's Progress*', *The Library*, 4 (2003), 64–9.

[22] Margaret Dowling, 'Nathaniel Ponder', *The Library*, 4th ser., 17 (1936–37), 109–10.

case that Ponder brought in 1691 against Edmund Dixon, a goldsmith and pawnbroker from Cheapside. Ponder's charge was that Dixon had taken his stock under the pretence of securing it and then auctioned it off and pocketed the proceeds.

As Giles Mandelbrote explains in his study of the organization of book auctions at the end of the century, 'the numbers of sales were being swelled by disposals of unwanted stock and unsaleable books in a climate of financial instability, political uncertainty and disruption of foreign trade by war […]. The figures [peaked] between about 1689 and 1692, when Ponder's was only one of numerous trade bankruptcies.'[23] David Stoker's reading of the ledgers of William Proctor, a wealthy stationer, make it clear that Ponder was deeply indebted to Proctor as well, and that Proctor financed the publication of several editions of *The Pilgrim's Progress* to recover the outstanding debts at Ponder's death.[24] In a dispiriting way, there may be nothing special about Nathaniel Ponder's financial troubles. His experience simply underscores the uncertain profitability of the book trade, especially once the Printing Act began to experience a series of lapses towards the end of the century, and the company lost the ability to protect its monopoly privileges.

In the 1691 Chancery case depositions, the following (partial list of) works by Bunyan are among the books catalogued as having been removed from Ponder's home:

> 560 Bunyans called The Doctrine of Law and Grace in 8o [i.e. octavo] [1685]
> 40 Bunyan on the Fear of God in 8o [1679]
> 690 Bunyans water of life in 8o [1688]
> 680 A booke for Boyes and Girles by Jo. Bunyan in 8o [1686]
> 330 bookes of Bunyan called Mr Badmans life in 12o [i.e. duodecimo] [1688]
> 2500 Bunyans Grace abounding [1688]
> 544 Bunyan on the sabath in 12o [1685]
> 600 Bunyan on the foure last things in 12o [1683].[25]

No copies of *The Pilgrim's Progress* are listed in the auction. Did they hold their value on the open market in a way other titles by Bunyan did not? Were they dealt with in some other fashion? In any event, there remained a large inventory of works by Bunyan in Ponder's possession, too many to be absorbed into the market at any one time. Despite Ponder's assurances in his 1691 deposition that his stock had a value of £900 'between Bookseller and Bookseller', the organizer of the auction testified that the proceeds had barely covered Ponder's £91 debt to Dixon and the auctioneer's expenses.[26]

---

[23] Giles Mandelbrote, 'The Organization of Book Auctions in Late Seventeenth-Century London', in R. Myers, M. Harris, and G. Mandelbrote (eds.), *Under the Hammer: Book Auctions since the Seventeenth Century* (New Castle, DE: Oak Knoll Press, 2001), 15–50 (20).

[24] Stoker, 'William Proctor', 67–9.

[25] Mandelbrote, 'Organization of Book Auctions', appendix, 'Nathaniel Ponder's Stock in 1688', 39. The dates in square brackets were provided by Mandelbrote.

[26] Mandelbrote, 'Organization of Book Auctions', 16, 18.

The staggering number of copies of *Grace Abounding* in this cache is particularly notable. This is higher by a thousand than the number we typically assume to be included in any one edition.[27] Presumably, they had just been printed—and the high number of copies could be another indication of Ponder's hopes for sales in the year of Bunyan's death. This was also an edition that had some pretensions to completeness, at least from the perspective of Bunyan's life. It announced the text as expanded, added a biographical report on the last years of Bunyan's life, and contained a portrait of the author. It aimed, in other words, to pre-empt such competitors as the Doe and Marshall project.

'Many Persons Desired to Have It Illustrated with Pictures'

Among the contributions that Ponder made to the presentation of Bunyan-as-author was the illustration of *The Pilgrim's Progress*, having first added an author portrait of Bunyan as a frontispiece engraving to the third edition (1679).[28] This image, by Robert White, is unusual both for what it signals about Bunyan's marketability as an author, and because it was not the (by then) typical or formulaic author portrait: head-and-shoulders, engraved in an oval frame. Rather, we are presented with Bunyan in a scene, eyes closed, resting on an elbow, propped on top of a 'denn', presumably dreaming the allegory to which this scene acts as a visual preface. A woodcut of the martyrdom of Faithful further embellished the fifth edition (1680). Also on offer with the latter edition was a suite of thirteen copper engravings, available for a shilling extra, sold either with the book or separately.[29] A customer could choose the desired price point. As Chapter 36 in this volume, by Nathalie Collé, demonstrates, the rich iconographical tradition of illustrating *The Pilgrim's Progress* was only beginning to be explored. These histories introduced a whole new set of agents and agendas into the transmission of *The Pilgrim's Progress*. They have at least one foot in Nathaniel Ponder's restless attempts to distinguish and authenticate the editions coming from his press.

Collé has discerned, in fact, a twofold significant relationship important to consider here: that of image to text and of image to book.[30] In the first of those relationships, Collé stresses the many readers' accounts that highlight their close association with the

---

[27] The numbers of editions described by Stoker are also remarkably high: 8,000 for *The Pilgrim's Progress, Part I*; 5,000 for *Part II*.

[28] See Figure 36.1, Chapter 36 in this volume.

[29] Frank M. Harrison, 'Editions, Versions, Illustrations, and Imitations of *The Pilgrim's Progress*', in John Brown, *John Bunyan: His Life, Times, and Work*, rev. Frank Mott Harrison (London: Hulbert, 1928), 439–67.

[30] Nathalie Collé-Bak, 'The Role of Illustrations in the Reception of *The Pilgrim's Progress*', in W. R. Owens and Stuart Sim (eds.), *Reception, Appropriation, Recollection: Bunyan's Pilgrim's Progress* (Bern: Peter Lang, 2007), 81–97 (89–90).

illustrations of one or another edition of the work, especially in the nineteenth century. The associations of the story with the pictures that Collé finds in English culture have been confirmed, amplified, and indeed complicated by many examples of African missionary editions that Isabel Hofmeyr has also detailed in *The Portable Bunyan* (2004). These diverse examples, drawn from a long textual tradition, move the book forward in history, into new engagements with ever more diverse audiences, and with illustrations playing an ever more prominent role in conveying the allegorical story.

It is worth stressing that the early illustrations also send somewhat mixed signals both in terms of market positioning and the setting of readerly expectations. This is so even within the fifth (1680) edition of *The Pilgrim's Progress*. The engraved allegorical frontispiece scene of the dreaming author first published in 1679 alluded to different interpretative traditions, drew on the resources of very different players, and had a different price point from the woodcut of Faithful's death at Vanity Fair that was printed as a matter of course with the text in the fifth edition.[31] The most available point of reference for that woodcut would, of course, be the various martyrdom scenes found in John Foxe's ever-popular *Book of Martyrs* (first published in English in 1563). Yet, Robert White's mode of engraving was less populist and more upmarket. White was a leading English publisher of prints as well as an engraver of them.[32] By being drawn and then engraved by White for *The Pilgrim's Progress*'s frontispiece, Bunyan moves closer to a recognized pantheon of English authors, and indeed persons of noteworthiness. White's oeuvre includes a series of royal portraits, beginning with one of Charles II (1679), continuing to James II as Duke of York (1682), and then Mary of Modena as queen (1686). Pepys, who also collected prints, commissioned a bookplate from White.[33] White also often engraved after his own drawings, usually made from life and sometimes in black lead or crayon.[34] His pencil sketch of Bunyan on vellum, the source for so many of the early representations that followed in print, is extant at the British Museum. The line that extends from a sketch drawn from life to an engraved portrait was a chain of custody that would also signify authenticity. Indeed, White asserted such a claim in a warning against counterfeits that he engraved under a portrait of Titus Oates for a 1679 broadsheet (around the same time he drew Bunyan). 'This is the true Originall taken from the Life done for HEN: BROME and RIC: CHISWELL. All others are counterfeit.' This original drawing is also extant.[35] We encounter a more complicated chain in the case of his pencil portrait of Bunyan. As Anne Dunan-Page has remarked, 'within a year of its execution, the original drawing of Robert White was engraved by four different artists, used by four

---

[31] On the iconography of the 'sleeping portrait', see Anne Dunan-Page, *Grace Overwhelming: John Bunyan, The Pilgrim's Progress, and the Extremes of the Baptist Mind* (New York: Peter Lang, 2006), 128–41.

[32] On White, see Antony Griffiths, *The Print in Stuart Britain 1603–1689* (London: British Museum Press, 1998), and Antony Griffiths, 'Robert White', *ODNB*.

[33] Griffiths, *Print in Stuart Britain*, 203–07.

[34] Griffiths, *Print in Stuart Britain*, 25, 28, 176.

[35] Griffiths, *Print in Stuart Britain*, 281.

FIGURE 9.3 Frontispiece portrait of Bunyan, in *The Works of that Eminent Servant of Christ, Mr. John Bunyan* (1692).

(By permission of the Folger Shakespeare Library [shelf mark B5479].)

publishers, and had appeared in four different works'. The frontispiece portrait engraved by White's student John Sturt for the *Works* (1692) is one derivative—as well as a collectable, available for purchase independent of the volume (see Figure 9.3).[36] The salient point to bear in mind about publishers of engravings is that they owned the copperplates; they therefore had rights of property to protect, as well as stationers.[37] Given the

---

[36] Anne Dunan-Page, '"The Portraiture of John Bunyan" Revisited: Robert White and Images of the Author', *BS*, 13 (2008), 7–39.

[37] See Malcolm Jones on the uses of evidence from the Stationers' Register in the study of the English engraving trade, in *The Print in Early Modern England: An Historical Oversight* (New Haven, CT: Yale University Press, 2010), xi.

circulation of plates and copies among the publishers that Dunan-Page traces, however, the only thing clear is that there was a great deal of flux in relations among engravers and stationers as well as among stationers at this time.

The one engraving of Bunyan's works that seems to have been intended as a standalone broadside from inception was *A Mapp Shewing the Order & Causes of Salvation & Damnation* (?1663).[38] Yet even this sheet illustrates the muddy lines that separated attached engravings in printed books and the detached, stand-alone broadsheets. The *Mapp* is listed in Doe's edition as having been previously published, but there are no extant copies of the first edition, presumed to be a product of Bunyan's prison years, only of the single fold-out sheet bound with the *Works* (1692). There is also evidence that the sheet was sold alone at that time, for sixpence.[39] This single-sheet engraving moves Bunyan into the realm of the schematic print of godly instruction. Such a print may well have been intended for domestic use. The *Mapp* gives the theology of predestination a rigorously symmetrical form, and it also presents an overarching view of the stages in reprobation and salvation by which one might gauge the state of one's own actions (and teleological destination).

Such broadsides speak to a continuing call for visual imagery in a text-centric religious culture. For instance, William Perkins had included a 'Survey, or Table declaring the order of the causes of Salvation and Damnation' in *A Golden Chaine* (1591).[40] These schematic representations of a spiritual journey have a place in the tradition of printed godly tables that Tessa Watt has examined. Importantly, she stressed their mnemonic function—not so much to impart new information as to provide repeated reminders, perhaps even to be used as 'a daily exercise reinforcing essential truths'.[41] Later, more representational depictions of the dangers and temptations of the devotional life would draw directly on the stages of Christian's journey in *The Pilgrim's Progress*.[42] As no engraver is credited on the 1692 *Mapp*, presumably this was not the work of an engraver-publisher. Or perhaps the plate had been sold after the first edition, and the original publisher's name excised. John Bunyan's rights of authorship are asserted with the engraved phrase 'by *John Bunyan Author of the Pilgrim's Progress*', and the stationer, William Marshall, made clear his rights of property by specifying that the sheet was engraved 'for' him and that it could be bought at his bookshop, whether wholesale or retail, 'at the Bible in Newgate Street'.

---

[38] The *Mapp* is reproduced in *MW*, 12: 418–23.

[39] Edward Arber, *The Term Catalogues, 1668–1709*, 3 vols (London: privately printed, 1903–06), 2: 368, 3: 195. See also Jones, *The Print in Early Modern England*, 52, where he notes advertisements in the newsbooks, *The Flying Post, or, The Post Master* (15–18 June 1700).

[40] See Gordon Campbell, 'The Source of Bunyan's *Mapp of Salvation*', *Journal of the Warburg and Courtauld Institutes*, 44 (1981), 240–41; P. J. H. Titlestad, 'From Beza to Bunyan: The Pilgrim Road Mapped?' *BS*, 13 (2008/09), 64–81.

[41] Tessa Watt, *Cheap Print and Popular Piety* (Cambridge: Cambridge University Press, 1991), 252–53.

[42] Sheila O'Connell, *The Popular Print in England* (London: British Museum Press, 1999), 71, fig. 4.5; colour plate II b.

The various illustrations of John Bunyan's works considered here thus take us up and down the socio-economic scale of his readership and confirm the broad cultural impact of a work such as *The Pilgrim's Progress*. On the one hand, these illustrations reach back to the chapbooks, the cheapest products of the press that circulated at levels below the yeomanry. The clearest connection between the chapbook tradition and the early illustrated editions of *The Pilgrim's Progress* is that of an early pirated edition extant in Pepys's collection of chapbooks at Magdalene Library, Cambridge.[43] Yet, on the other, the engraved author portraits and allegorical scenes described give us a more aspirational view of Bunyan's position vis-à-vis learned clerics and professional writers.

Conclusion

The foregoing survey of practices and agents involved in the print publication of John Bunyan's texts gives us a fresh perspective on *The Pilgrim's Progress*—tantalizingly or even insistently unsettled between the book of divine revelation and a book of fiction. As Kevin Seidel has recently argued, a new common reader was thus implied (if we may hearken back to Wolfgang Iser's terms). That reader was moving, uneasily perhaps, along with Bunyan, down certain 'channels already carved out by the circulation of the scriptures in late seventeenth-century England'. As Seidel describes them, these channels were partly literary, partly legal, and partly domestic.[44]

It has been the aim of this chapter to understand better the means and mechanisms by which such discursive channels were dug, maintained, sometimes crossed, and then re-established or diverted. A delta may be a richer metaphor for the ways discourses of truthfulness and authenticity travelled across lines of devotion, trade, legal practice, and political activism. Bunyan's books provide an especially useful case study of the confluences of interests that are mediated by a text. Bunyan's discourse of religious confession is put in touch with discourses of truthful testimony, as in Smith's trials for seditious libel and property rights. The questions of authority that dogged Bunyan throughout his preaching career are transmuted into questions of authenticity in Ponder's lawsuits against counterfeit printing. Almost in spite of himself, Bunyan's texts, especially *The Pilgrim's Progress*, came to supplant the very scriptural exemplars he hoped to reinforce.

Scholarship in the area of book history encourages us to bring Bunyan's partners in print more fully into our accounts of his development as an author and the means by which he is remembered. The treatment of copyrights as a privilege of trade company membership in this period has sometimes led scholars to draw battle lines between bookseller and author. Those competing interests are real enough. But that is not the whole story—especially at the end of the century, with the book trade in crisis, beset

---

[43] See Kirsty Milne, '"The Miracles They Wrought": A Chapbook Reading of *The Pilgrim's Progress*, with an Edited Transcript of *The Pilgrim's Progress to the Other World* (1684)', *BS*, 13 (2008/09), 40–63.

[44] Kevin Seidel, '*Pilgrim's Progress* and the Book', *ELH*, 77 (2010), 509–34 (512).

with competing regulators, and also pressured too by conflicting interests within the company. Internal conflicts set printers against booksellers and encouraged individual stationers to begin to put their own interests before the company's. In the case of Francis Smith we can see that there were different collectives, whose interests stationers may have felt more obliged to advance. Joseph Loewenstein talks about stationers having a branding effect on interest groups, and Tim Harris describes Smith as a 'publicist' for the Whigs, in his promotion of religious freedom and political rights.[45] I am not sure that is a strong enough word for Smith's activity. Or perhaps our sense of that activity has been degraded. Either way, the problem remains—how do we apportion out agencies? How do we bring knowledge networks and communal identities into our understanding of early modern authorship? Focusing on a wider cast of strong actors operating in a resonant historical moment—in this case, by situating Bunyan amongst the Dissenting voices and Dissenting agendas of his partners in print—may offer us a way towards the answers to such questions.

Suggested Reading

Achinstein, Sharon, 'Bunyan and the Politics of Remembrance', in Vera J. Camden (ed.), *Trauma and Transformation: The Political Progress of John Bunyan* (Stanford, CA: Stanford University Press, 2008), 135–52.

Collé-Bak, Nathalie, 'The Role of Illustrations in the Reception of *The Pilgrim's Progress*', in W. R. Owens and Stuart Sim (eds.), *Reception, Appropriation, Recollection: Bunyan's Pilgrim's Progress* (Bern: Peter Lang, 2007), 81–97.

Crist, Timothy, 'Government Control of the Press after the Expiration of the Printing Act in 1679', *Publishing History*, 5 (1979), 49–77.

Dunan-Page, Anne, '"The Portraiture of John Bunyan" Revisited: Robert White and Images of the Author', *BS*, 13 (2008/09), 7–39.

Owens, W. R., 'Reading the Bibliographical Codes: Bunyan's Publication in Folio', in N. H. Keeble (ed.), *John Bunyan: Reading Dissenting Writing* (Bern: Peter Lang, 2002), 59–77.

Seidel, Kevin, '*Pilgrim's Progress* and the Book', *ELH*, 77 (2010), 509–34.

Simonova, Natasha, *Early Modern Authorship and Prose Continuations: Adaptation and Ownership from Sidney to Richardson* (Basingstoke: Palgrave Macmillan, 2015).

Smith, Nigel. 'Non-Conformist Voices and Books', in John Barnard, D. F. McKenzie, and Maureen Bell (eds.), *The Cambridge History of the Book in Britain, Vol. 4: 1557–1695* (Cambridge: Cambridge University Press, 2002), 410–12.

Treadwell, Michael, 'The Stationers and the Printing Acts at the End of the Seventeenth Century', in John Barnard, D. F. McKenzie, and Maureen Bell (eds.), *The Cambridge History of the Book in Britain, Vol. 4: 1557–1695* (Cambridge: Cambridge University Press, 2002), 755–76.

---

[45] Joseph Loewenstein, *The Author's Due: Printing and the Prehistory of Copyright* (Chicago: University of Chicago Press, 2002); Tim Harris, *Restoration: Charles II and his Kingdoms* (London: Penguin Books, 2005), 142–44.

PART II
WORKS

CHAPTER 10

EARLY WORKS

Bunyan in the 1650s

DAVID WALKER

THE 1650s—the decade in which Bunyan made his debut in print—is one of the most significant in all of English history, framed as it is by the trial and execution of Charles I in 1649, and the restoration of his eldest son to the monarchy in 1660. The former event shocked all Europe, with its judicial execution of an anointed monarch; while the latter, after the death of Oliver Cromwell in 1658, and the failure of successive regimes in the following two years, surprised and delighted some, but disappointed others who had regarded it as the most unlikely of outcomes. Between 1649 and 1660 lies the English republic, with its rule by the Rump Parliament and then by the first and second Protectorates: of Oliver Cromwell from 1653 to 1658, and of his son Richard, from 1658 to 1659.

The decade is captured at key points by Andrew Marvell's brilliant triptych of poems: 'An Horatian Ode upon Cromwell's Return from Ireland', 'The First Anniversary of the Government under His Highness the Lord Protector', and 'A Poem on the Death of His Late Highness the Lord Protector'. Although the references are not always explicit, 'The First Anniversary' testifies to the unstable state of the nation at mid-point in the decade, which saw 'republican hostility to the Protectorate [and] assassination attempts by Royalists and some disaffected republicans on Cromwell's life', as well as the emergence of a vigorous Quaker movement.[1] As we shall see, the spread of the Quakers initiated and then exercised Bunyan's literary and polemical skills in the 1650s. It is also a great decade of English political prose, the highlights of which are Milton's republican writings, Marchamont Nedham's *The Case of the Commonwealth Stated* (1650), Thomas Hobbes's *Leviathan* (1651), James Harrington's *Oceana* (1656), and Richard

---

[1] Nigel Smith, *Andrew Marvell: The Chameleon* (New Haven, CT, and London: Yale University Press, 2010), 126. For the poems, see Nigel Smith (ed.), *The Poems of Andrew Marvell* (London: Pearson Longman, 2007). Smith dates the three Cromwell poems, respectively, at June–July 1650, December 1654–January 1655, and September 1658–January 1659.

Baxter's *The Holy Commonwealth* (1659). The English republic was brand new, unprecedented, and, for many contemporaries, unwelcome. So too was the proliferation of new religious sects, some of them wild and wonderful in their novelty. There was little new in them, however, in their cry against an incomplete Reformation. From its beginning, the Reformation in Europe had a tendency to splinter, leading to the 'Birth of Protestantisms'.[2] In their refrain, seventeenth-century English Nonconformists and sectaries were singing from an old hymn sheet. Consequently, as George Southcombe has recently remarked, religious Nonconformity 'was thus both an old and a new thing'.[3]

Radical Religion in the 1650s

Bunyan formed his faith in the crucible of the Civil War and its aftermath. Influenced by radical preachers employed as army chaplains in the 1640s, he embraced Independent (or Congregational) and Baptist ideas when, in 1653, he joined the Bedford congregation led by John Gifford. A 'Kentish man, a great Royalist and an officer in the King's army' during the Civil War, Gifford had been a confirmed sinner and had his personal demons to slay.[4] After experiencing conversion, Gifford, with his military background, was uniquely placed to offer Bunyan counsel. He was keen to oppose heresies, as he saw them, and his influence is palpable in Bunyan's earliest works: the writings against the heterodox beliefs of Quakers, and the critique of social injustice that is so prominent a part of *A Few Sighs from Hell* (1658). As well as providing spiritual guidance, Gifford has been credited with inspiring Bunyan's views on equality, ecumenism, and fellowship in church affairs.[5] And it is to Gifford that Bunyan turns when his faith is at its most tenuous in the early days of his own conversion. In *Grace Abounding to the Chief of Sinners* (1666), Bunyan relates that after a protracted period of spiritual doubt and anxiety he turned to his congregation and confided his thoughts to 'those poor people in *Bedford*'. They in turn informed Gifford, who took him under his wing and to whom Bunyan revealed 'something of the vanity and inward wretchedness of my wicked heart' (*GA*, 25). As *Grace Abounding* testifies, Bunyan's despair in the 1650s was pronounced, and he feared that the temptation to sin would be too strong for him to withstand. As his anxieties about salvation deepened, so too did his reliance on Gifford: 'At this time [. . .] I sat under the Ministry of holy Mr. *Gifford*, whose Doctrine, by God's grace, was much for my stability' (*GA*, 37). As Richard Greaves puts it, Gifford 'instructed Bunyan

---

[2] Diarmaid MacCulloch, *Reformation: Europe's House Divided, 1490–1700* (London: Allen Lane, 2003), 172–79; Euan Cameron, *The European Reformation*, 2nd edn (Oxford: Oxford University Press, 2012), 109–13.

[3] George Southcombe (ed.), *English Nonconformist Poetry, 1660–1700*, 3 vols (London: Pickering & Chatto, 2012), 1: xii.

[4] Joseph Ivimey, *A History of the English Baptists*, 2 vols (London: Sutton, 1814), 2: 19. See also Tamsin Spargo, 'John Gifford', *ODNB*.

[5] Hill, *Bunyan*, 90–1, 235.

in how to withstand temptation by crying mightily to God rather than trusting others. For Bunyan's soul this lesson was like rain on parched earth, and he prayed for confirmation of divine mercy.'[6]

Following his conversion, Bunyan quickly became intimately involved with the revolutionary godly movement as a preacher. At some point from the mid-1650s, having relocated with his wife from Elstow to Bedford, Bunyan was sought out by the congregation 'to take in hand in one of the Meetings to speak a word of Exhortation unto them' (*GA*, 83). He also 'began to accompany others on teaching missions outside Bedford during which he privately spoke words of admonition to the people' (*MW*, 1: xv). From the beginning, then, Bunyan nailed his colours to the mast, defending his beliefs, and entering wholeheartedly and fearlessly into disputation whenever he deemed it necessary. His position was courageous and confident. To associate oneself with Baptist practices on any level in the seventeenth century—such as believers' baptism or 'anabaptism' (meaning, to be baptized again)—was to embrace notoriety: 'Like many religious terms from the early modern period, "Baptists" was first a term of derision and only later a mark of honour'.[7] Baptists were habitually labelled as 'Anabaptists' and analogies with the Radical Reformation that took place in Münster in the 1530s were regularly made. Early modern pamphlets often defamed the English Baptists by reminding their readers of the horrors of the Münster experiment. As J. F. McGregor has remarked, for well over a century the memory of the Münster Anabaptists and their 'mentally deranged' leader Jan Beukels ('John of Leyden') 'remained potent images of anarchy; vivid examples of the dangers of popular heresy and justification for the stern suppression of all its manifestations'. In his control of Münster, Beukels 'lost all connection with reality', 'lived a life of luxury, took sixteen wives and proclaimed himself king of the world'. When the city fell, it did so in a bloodbath, with ringleaders being 'tortured to death'.[8]

In the 1640s, then, and in the wake of the proliferation of sects, conservative—often Presbyterian—pamphleteers wrote violently against those of the Baptist faith. Pre-eminent among these critics were Thomas Edwards, the author of *Gangraena; or A Catalogue and Discovery of Many of the Errours, Blasphemies and Pernicious Practices of the Sectaries of this Time Vented and Acted in England in these Four Last Years* (1646), and Daniel Featley, author of *The Dippers Dipt; or, The Anabaptists Duck'd and Plung'd Over Head and Eares* (1645). Edwards was a Presbyterian controversialist with strong

---

[6] Greaves, *Glimpses*, 47.

[7] Mark Bell, 'Freedom to Form: The Development of Baptist Movements during the English Revolution', in Christopher Durston and Judith Maltby (eds.), *Religion in Revolutionary England* (Manchester: Manchester University Press, 2006), 181–201 (181).

[8] J. F. McGregor, 'The Baptists: Fount of all Heresy', in J. F. McGregor and Barry Reay (eds.), *Radical Religion in the English Revolution* (Oxford: Oxford University Press, 1984), 23–63 (25). See also Eric Ives, *The Reformation Experience: Living through the Turbulent 16th Century* (Oxford: Lion, 2012), 108. Texts from the 1640s that collapsed the distinction between Münster Anabaptists, and English Baptists for polemical purposes include: *A Short History of the Anabaptists of High and Low Germany* (1642); *A Warning for England, Especially for London in the Famous History of the Frantic Anabaptists, their Wild Preachings and their Practices in Germany* (1642).

anti-sectarian views. *Gangraena* is unequivocal in its condemnation of MPs who stand idly by while '*Heresie, Schism, Disorder*' go unchecked and '*Seekers, Anabaptists, Antinomians, Brownists, Libertines, and other Sects*' are allowed to flourish. '*You have […] done Worthily against Papists, Prelates and scandalous Ministers*' but '*With this Reformation have we not a Deformation, and worse things come in upon us then ever we had before?*'[9] Edwards has been described as a vainglorious, controversial, and ultimately disappointed author. This does not, however, detract from the importance of his most significant work: '[i]n its time—its brief time in 1646 and 1647—*Gangraena* was the most famous book in a revolutionary era in which printed texts played a crucial role.'[10]

The Baptists in seventeenth-century England, therefore, were always vulnerable to the popular and scandalous associations drawn between themselves and their German 'antecedents'. By the time of the Restoration, however, they were among the most powerful and numerous of those 'organised groups of Protestants' that 'took permanent shape outside the established national Church'.[11] The unprecedented religious radicalism of the twenty-year period that preceded the Restoration significantly enabled the growth and consolidation of the movement, so much so that in the words of one historian, the English Revolution provided Baptists with their 'breakout moment'.[12] Yet there were more than Baptists with whom to contend. Edwards in particular has mapped the extent to which the godly were fragmenting in the wake of the Civil War. His *Gangraena* 'enumerated 16 sects, 70 pernicious practices and no less than 176 different errors'. 'Having set out to erect the new Jerusalem, conservative Puritans now found themselves looking at a new Babel.'[13]

Bunyan and the Ranters

Conservative anger at the spread of heretical sects and Independency more generally fuelled a considerable pamphlet literature in the 1640s and 1650s. The main target of this anger proved to be the Ranters, a sect that (initially at least) attracted and repelled Bunyan in almost equal measure. We rely on *Grace Abounding* for Bunyan's views on the events of the years leading up to his first publication in 1656. In his description of his conversion and how he stood fast against temptation, Bunyan describes 'how he met

---

[9] Thomas Edwards, *Gangraena* (1646), sig. A4r. See also Stuart Sim and David Walker, *Bunyan and Authority: The Rhetoric of Dissent and the Legitimation Crisis in Seventeenth-Century England* (Bern: Peter Lang, 2000), 36; Greaves, *Glimpses*, 23.

[10] Ann Hughes, *Gangraena and the Struggle for the English Revolution* (Oxford: Oxford University Press, 2004), 2.

[11] MacCulloch, *Reformation*, 525.

[12] Bell, 'Freedom to Form', 182.

[13] John Coffey, *Persecution and Toleration in Protestant England, 1558–1689* (Harlow: Pearson Education, 2000), 144.

with some *Ranters* books that were put forth by some of our Country men'. Unable to comprehend the rightness or otherwise of Ranter doctrine Bunyan turns to prayer in the hope that he might see revealed '*Truth from Errour*', and to facilitate this he throws himself upon the mercy of God: '*Lord, I lay my Soul, in this matter, only at thy foot, let me not be deceived, I humbly beseech thee*'. At this point, he is given a timely and illustrative example of a friend who has succumbed to Ranterism, 'and to all manner of filthiness, especially Uncleanness'. Worse, this 'one religious intimate Companion' denies 'that there was a God, Angel, or Spirit, and would laugh at all exhortations to sobriety'. Not satisfied with this, the newly minted Ranter brags that he has 'gone through all Religions and could never light on the right till now' (*GA*, 16).

As this example testifies—and there were many others in the mid-seventeenth century doing something very similar—religious affiliation can be highly fluid and apt to change quickly and dramatically. By the time he came to write *Heights in Depths* in 1651, by which time he had turned Ranter, Joseph Salmon, for instance, had passed through the ranks of the Presbyterians, the Independents, and the Baptists, all of which he ultimately rejected: 'all my former enjoyments being nothing in appearance to that glory that now rested on my spirit'.[14] Bunyan's outrage at his friend's Ranterism in *Grace Abounding* leads him to turn with renewed vigour to the Bible and to read 'as I never did before' (*GA*, 17). Later, in *A Few Sighs from Hell*, he would explain that the Bible must be read as a totality: 'Have a care, that thou own the whole Scripture, and not own one part, and neglect another.' If we are to be saved by 'Christ's blood from the guilt of sin', we must be free from bondage 'to the filth of sin'. To do otherwise is to have one's 'understanding' and 'will' bewitched by the devil, and in such a case, the sinner is warned, 'thou wilt Ranter-like turn the Grace of God into wantonness, and bring upon thy soul double, if not treble damnation' (*MW*, 1: 380, 381–82).

The Ranters appear to be the benchmark amongst Bunyan's contemporaries for the worst excesses of antinomianism. As such they attracted a welter of criticism not only from conservative critics, but from all points on the Nonconformist spectrum.[15] According to Bunyan, however, they were also popular. In *Grace Abounding* he discusses the extent to which on his travels he had encountered Ranter converts whilst in pursuit of his 'Calling [. . .] in the Countrey'. In doing so he also demonstrates the attractiveness of antinomian beliefs and the charismatic Ranters who attracted the gullible to their ranks. The people to whom he refers, he suggests, should have more sense. Despite being 'strict in Religion formerly, yet were [they] also swept away by these Ranters'. For their part, Ranters condemn Bunyan for being 'legal and dark', pretending, he says, that 'they only had attained to perfection and could do what they would and not sin' (*GA*, 17). Ranter rhetoric was seductive to many. As Nigel Smith argues, Ranters deployed 'a deeply expressive language, a performance which attempts to render the inner light

---

[14] Joseph Salmon, *Heights in Depths* (1651), in Nigel Smith (ed.), *A Collection of Ranter Writings* (London: Junction Books, 1983), 208.

[15] A useful selection of anti-Ranter pamphlets can be found in an appendix to J. C. Davis, *Fear, Myth and History: The Ranters and the Historians* (Cambridge: Cambridge University Press, 1986), 138–203.

in words'.[16] They were highly articulate and linguistically far from being an uneducated rabble. As the example of Bunyan suggests, such language was often enormously attractive as well as being blasphemous. Accordingly, it could not be ignored.

The proliferation of sects in the 1640s accelerated further in the 1650s and was remarked upon by contemporaries at the time and during the Restoration. These sects fiercely contested their beliefs in print and indulged in pamphlet wars of considerable viciousness.[17] Bunyan cut his polemical teeth in dispute with the Ranters and Quakers, not least because they tempted him. As we shall see, in his anti-Quaker texts Bunyan engaged aggressively in debate with the Quakers about the body and the spirit, biblical literalism, and plain style. More obliquely, we can also discern an engagement in these texts with contemporary politics in the shape of millenarian thought and the prospect of 'King Oliver's' coronation. In other writings of the 1650s, Bunyan widens his scope. In his exposition of the biblical story of Dives and Lazarus elaborated in *A Few Sighs from Hell*, we see him engaging in a socio-economic critique of mid-seventeenth-century England, and in *The Doctrine of the Law and Grace Unfolded* (1659) we have the most impressive of his contributions to the burgeoning literature in the seventeenth century expounding covenant theology.

Bunyan and the Quakers

Antipathy between Baptists and Quakers was particularly fierce nationally during the 1650s. As Beth Lynch has noted, this was more than usually the case in Bedfordshire, where, by the late 1650s, it 'was particularly volatile', with Bunyan becoming 'embroiled in very public disputes with local Quakers'. George Fox himself in 1655 'was moved [by] the Lord to go into' the county of Bedfordshire to speak to a gathering at the house of the recently converted John Crook. There he met with like-minded believers who accepted wholeheartedly his assertion of the paramount importance of the light within, even over Scripture. In 1658 Quakers 'converged' at Crook's house 'for the first yearly general meeting'. Disputations between Quakers and Baptists took place across the county. Bunyan debated publicly with them on several occasions in 1656 before he put pen to paper. The first recorded instance took place on 12 April 1656 in Pavenham, and this was

---

[16] Smith (ed.), *A Collection of Ranter Writings*, 8; see also, Nicholas McDowell, *The English Radical Imagination: Culture, Religion, and Revolution* (Oxford: Oxford University Press, 2003), ch. 4.

[17] The classic treatment of sects in the mid-seventeenth century is Christopher Hill, *The World Turned Upside Down: Radical Ideas during the English Revolution* (1972; London: Penguin, 1991); more recently, see Ann Hughes, 'Religion 1640–1660', in Barry Coward (ed.), *A Companion to Stuart Britain* (Oxford: Blackwell, 2009), 350–73. On how religious dispute was disseminated in print, see Joad Raymond, *Pamphlets and Pamphleteering in Early Modern Britain* (Cambridge: Cambridge University Press, 2003).

followed on 23 May by a further disputation in St Paul's, Bedford. There were further debates in October 1656 and January 1657.[18]

A central point of contention was that while adherents of both groups held firmly 'that the Bible issued from the Spirit', the Quakers emphasized the Spirit's superiority over the Baptists' reverence for 'scriptural authority'. Bunyan's earliest published literary response to Quaker doctrine was *Some Gospel-Truths Opened according to the Scriptures* (1656), a comprehensive attack on the Quakers that foregrounded the sufficiency of Scripture. In line with the confrontational nature of much polemical writing in the period, the tone of this initial attack was bellicose to say the least, owing something perhaps to the generally militaristic context of the years 1640–50. Not surprisingly, the Quakers did not allow Bunyan's attack on them go unchallenged. A young Quaker polemicist, Edward Burrough, was stimulated to write a response to *Some Gospel-Truths Opened* entitled *The True Faith of the Gospel of Peace Contended For* (1656), to which in turn Bunyan responded with *A Vindication of* [...] *Some Gospel-Truths Opened* (1657). The debate thus became a back-and-forth literary battle, as was characteristic of sectarian disputation in the seventeenth century. In this particular case, it seems that Burrough had the last word. He wrote a riposte to Bunyan's *A Vindication*, entitled *Truth (the Strongest of all) Witnessed Forth* (1657), to which Bunyan made no reply. A couple of years later, in *The Great Mistery of the Great Whore Unfolded* (1659), George Fox crafted 'a scathing retrospective attack on Bunyan's two pamphlets', but once again, Bunyan offered no response.[19]

In *Some Gospel-Truths Opened*, Bunyan removes himself aggressively from the beliefs of the Quakers. He attacks them as both deceived and deceivers: 'I say again and again, look to your selves, that you receive no Christ but Gods Christ: for he is like to be deceived that will believe everything that calls itself a Christ. *For many*, saith he, *shal come in my name, and shall deceive many*, Matth. 24. 5' (*MW*, 1: 47). In *A Vindication of* [...] *Some Gospel-Truths*, he inflames this invective further by conflating Familists, Quakers, and Ranters, considering them as one and asking rhetorically 'what harme [does it do] to joyne a *Dog* and a *Wolfe* together?' Quakers and Ranters are indistinguishable in that the 'thredbare' alehouse doctrines of the latter have been re-established by the Quakers, who have 'set a new glosse upon them again, by an outward legall holinesse, or righteousness' (*MW*, 1: xxvii–xxviii, 138–39).

The deployment of invective as a literary device by contemporaries in debates of this kind was generated often enough by the competitive urge to recruit whenever and wherever possible to one's sect in what was a relatively open market. It follows from this that Bunyan was not only seeking to disabuse Quakers of their mistaken faith; he was also, in the nature of things, displaying to the reader the credence of his own beliefs and demonstrating their superiority. Given the startling number of sects and positions

---

[18] Beth Lynch, *John Bunyan and the Language of Conviction* (Cambridge: D. S. Brewer, 2004), 15; Greaves, *Glimpses*, 75–6. See also T. L. Underwood, *Primitivism, Radicalism, and the Lamb's War: The Baptist–Quaker Conflict in Seventeenth-Century England* (Oxford: Oxford University Press, 1997), 24.

[19] Lynch, *John Bunyan and the Language of Conviction*, 15.

that were available to the seeker after spiritual truth in the 1650s, aggressive defences in print were common, heightened somewhat by the relevant freedom sects enjoyed in being able to articulate their views in print. The 1650s are rightly celebrated for the toleration extended to Nonconformists. As scholars have pointed out, Oliver Cromwell countenanced religious diversity as long as it did not interfere with the smooth running of the state. However, within that very broad statement significant qualification must be made. Roman Catholics and Socinians were naturally beyond the pale.[20] The latter, in particular, wrote one contemporary, forgot the nature of the Calvinist deity and supposed 'an indulgent God, content with anything'.[21] Yet the general temper of government policy towards Protestants was benign. Bernard Capp draws attention to an 'often overlooked' order of 10 October 1653 by the Barebones Parliament 'for a public Declaration "giving fitting liberty to all that fear God"'. Capp also notes the award of appropriate 'land and material' granted by Parliament to 'a group of separatists in Barking Essex' for the erection of the 'country's first custom-built nonconformist meeting house'.[22]

Arguments about toleration from within Puritanism in the 1650s made distinctions between toleration and liberty of conscience: 'there was a basic difference between allowing people to believe what they liked and permitting beliefs which were consciably held. Liberty of conscience would allow doctrines which did not breach fundamental truths whose acceptance was central to salvation.'[23] It is precisely on these grounds—the Quaker denial, as he sees it, of incontrovertible truths regarding salvation—that Bunyan finds their views repellent. Their respective positions are irreconcilable. The Quakers believed that 'the Bible is not the word of God'. They believed that 'the Spirit of God dwells in every person'. They did not believe 'in the resurrection of the bodies of the dead', or that the Jesus who died on the cross 'ascended into heaven', or that he would 'one day return to earth in the Second Coming'.[24] For Bunyan, these differences are fundamental and impossible to resolve.

In the prefatory address, 'To the Reader', in *A Vindication of the Book Called, Some Gospel-Truths Opened*, Bunyan makes it clear that his motivation to write is derived from the Holy Spirit: *'it hath pleased the Lord to work in my soul by his holy Spirit, and hath transplanted in me some measure from darknesse to light'*. Thus equipped, he can discern *'the seeming legal-holiness of others, together with their damnable doctrine; which have, notwithstanding their professions, made shipwrack of the Faith, both to themselves*

---

[20] On Socinians, see Sarah Mortimer, *Reason and Religion in the English Revolution: The Challenge of Socinianism* (Cambridge: Cambridge University Press, 2010).

[21] Samuel Gott, *An Essay on the True Happiness of Man* (1650), 267, cited in Blair Worden, *God's Instruments: Political Conduct in the England of Oliver Cromwell* (Oxford: Oxford University Press, 2012), 67.

[22] Bernard Capp, *England's Culture Wars: Puritan Reformation and its Enemies in the Interregnum, 1649–1660* (Oxford: Oxford University Press, 2012), 28.

[23] Worden, *God's Instruments*, 71.

[24] Robert G. Collmer, 'John Bunyan', in Andrew W. Hass, David Jasper, and Elisabeth Jay (eds.), *The Oxford Handbook of English Literature and Theology* (Oxford: Oxford University Press, 2007), 575–89 (580).

and their followers' (*MW*, 1: 123). In *Some Gospel-Truths Opened*, he repeatedly seeks to establish the truth of his arguments by recourse to the Bible: 'And therefore that Christ is very God, I shall first prove by plain texts of Scripture. 2. From the testimony of God, Angels, and men, witnessed by the Scriptures. 3. By several Arguments drawn from Scripture, which will prove the same clearly' (*MW*, 1: 48).[25] Although they participated vigorously in the polemical war of words, the Quakers did not privilege print to anywhere near the same extent as other sects. This occasionally extended to the Bible itself, something they saw as no more 'than the literary account of individual experience'. In his initial response to Bunyan's *Some Gospel-Truths Opened*, Edward Burrough 'charges the teachers of this generation' that the Gospel they revere is a mediated text far removed from the original Scripture, and is 'not the Gospel which the saints preached'. Printers, stationers, schools, and universities have polluted the text.[26]

For a scriptural literalist of Bunyan's persuasion, and in common with many other Protestants of his time, this challenge to the authority of the Bible was a step too far. In a catalogue of the errors of the Quakers that Bunyan includes in *Grace Abounding*, the very first one is 'That the holy Scriptures [are] not the Word of God.' Other travesties include that 'every man in the world had the spirit of Christ' and grace and faith, and that Christ's sacrifice was meaningless and 'did not satisfy divine justice for the sins of the people'. The Quaker belief in universal spiritual enlightenment was in direct opposition to Bunyan's belief in the imputation of Christ's righteousness. The Quakers fomented so many 'more vile and abominable things' that Bunyan felt 'driven' to the Scriptures to contend with them, by which he was 'greatly confirmed and comforted in the truth' that the 'blood of Christ' takes off 'the guilt of sin' (*GA*, 39). Among Bunyan's complaints about Quaker doctrine was that the physicality of Christ was denied and also the truth of his resurrection (*GA*, 38–9). In *Some Gospel-Truths* and *A Vindication*, Bunyan's response to this denial was to point out relentlessly to his readers the Quaker rejection of Scripture's validity.

In both of his anti-Quaker tracts, Bunyan makes central his belief in a physical Christ. He ridicules the Quaker belief in an inner light that stands free of Scripture's warrant (*MW*, 1: 20). His response to Burrough in *A Vindication* is direct and uncompromising: 'you say that Christ is crucified within, dead within, risen and ascended within, which also you have no word of Scripture to prove' (*MW*, 1: 176). His primary concern in these works is to point out to his readers two cardinal errors, referred to by Greaves as 'satanic fabrications', namely, 'that salvation is not completely undertaken for sinners by Christ and that the inner light which all people have can lead them to the kingdom

---

[25] For differing accounts and emphases regarding Bunyan's confrontational literary dialogue with the Quakers during the Cromwellian Protectorate, see Sim and Walker, *Bunyan and Authority*, ch. 3; Greaves, *Glimpses*, 75–88; Lynch, *John Bunyan and the Language of Conviction*, 11–33; and Robert J. McKelvey, *Histories that Mansoul and her Wars Anatomize: The Drama of Redemption in John Bunyan's Holy War* (Oakville, CT: Vandenhoeck & Ruprecht, 2011), 32–8.

[26] Sim and Walker, *Bunyan and Authority*, 56; Edward Burrough, *Truth Defended: or, Certain Accusations Answered* (1656), 9.

of God'.²⁷ Although Quakers believed in the efficacy of Scripture, they did not do so to the same extent as the Baptists. In *A Paper Sent Forth* (1654), Fox informs his reader that 'the letter is a declaration of the Gospel, and many have the letter, but not Christ; but we having received the Gospel know them to be no ministers of it and therefore do deny them'.²⁸ Both groups believed that the Word and the Spirit worked in conjunction, with the Quakers supporting the latter over the former. Bunyan, on the other hand, believed that the Holy Spirit was the guide, and Scripture the rule.²⁹

A FEW SIGHS FROM HELL

A Few Sighs from Hell (1658) is 'a treatise developed from a sermon (or perhaps from a course of sermons) which [Bunyan] preached on the story of Dives and Lazarus found in Luke xvi. 19–31' (*MW*, 1: xxxvi). In this parable, Jesus portrays starkly the contrast between a rich man (traditionally called Dives) who 'was clothed in purple and fine linen, and fared sumptuously every day', and a beggar, named Lazarus, who had only 'crumbs which fell from the rich man's table: moreover the dogs came and licked his sores'. But when they both die, the rich man is taken down into hellfire, whereas Lazarus is 'carried by the angels into Abraham's bosom'. The sermon origins of Bunyan's treatise are observable in its many divisions and subdivisions, and in its drawing out of 'uses' and 'applications'. After the prefatory material, the main body of the treatise falls under three headings: 'The Scripture and its Purpose;' the 'Commentary on the Scripture', which is divided into eleven subsections; and finally 'Use and Application', which is divided into four subsections (*MW*, 1: xxxvi–xxxvii).

Given its subject matter and its roots in the exposition of the parable from Luke 16, *A Few Sighs from Hell* is often read as an early expression of Bunyan's views on the inequity of socio-economic relations in the seventeenth century. In a more specifically contemporary context, this text from the 1650s takes its place alongside other works written in the mid-seventeenth century that were socially, politically, and economically aware, such as those written by the Digger leader Gerrard Winstanley, and the Leveller writers, William Walwyn, Richard Overton, and John Lilburne. In their own distinctive ways all of these men share with Bunyan the same radical sympathy for the poor and oppressed. So, for example, in *A Whisper in the Eare, of Mr Thomas Edwards, Minister*, Walwyn advertises himself as 'one that truly and heartily love[s] mankind', and one, moreover, who grieves to see anyone 'afflicted, molested, or punished'. In responding to the intolerant bigotry of the Presbyterian Edwards, Walwyn posits the view that all men are deserving and require equal consideration when it comes to receiving justice. He would

---

[27] Greaves, *Glimpses*, 77.
[28] George Fox, *A Paper Sent Forth from Them that are Scornfully called Quakers* (1654), in A. C. Ward (ed.), *A Miscellany of Tracts and Pamphlets* (Oxford: Oxford University Press, 1927), 343–59 (347).
[29] Underwood, *Primitivism, Radicalism, and the Lamb's War*, 25.

strengthen the weak, inform the ignorant, and be clement in his judgements on the 'vicious' and the 'cruel'. He is an enemy to no man but an inveterate foe of 'injustice, oppression, innovation' and 'arbitrary power'.[30]

Leveller writing abounds with such rhetoric. *An Agreement of the People* (1647), a printed output of the Putney Debates, explicitly calls for equality before the law irrespective of 'tenure, estate, charter, degree, birth or place'. The laws of the land 'must be good and not evidently destructive to the safety and well-being of the people'.[31] Economic and social power in Leveller writing confers no especial privilege. There is little in prose such as this to endear itself to writers such as Thomas Edwards, or to Presbyterians more generally. For readers like Bunyan, however, as Christopher Hill has argued, there might be much to admire.[32]

In *A Few Sighs from Hell*, Bunyan follows his biblical text in associating the beggar with the godly and the rich man with the damned. More particularly, in his exposition of Luke 16:22–3, when Jesus tells his hearers that death comes equally to all men, good or bad, Bunyan makes it clear that after death rewards and punishments will be appropriately conferred. Whereas Lazarus is welcomed into Abraham's bosom, the rich man is in hell, 'being in torment' (v. 23). In Bunyan's text, what comes after death for the unregenerate is grim indeed. They will be carried forth by 'Angels of darkness from their death-beds to hell, there to be reserved to the judgement of the great day, when both body and soul shall meet, and be united together again, and made capable to undergo the uttermost vengeance of the Almighty to all eternity' (*MW*, 1: 259, 260). Further references to the unremitting agony awaiting the unregenerate are found throughout the sermon. The lesson of this Scripture obviously had a place close to Bunyan's heart, given its recurrence in the House of the Interpreter in a passage added to the second edition of *The Pilgrim's Progress* (1678). In his dialogue with the Interpreter regarding the superiority of patience over passion, Christian observes that 'Patience *has the best Wisdom* [...] *because he stays* [i.e. waits] *for the best things. And also because he will have the glory of* His, *when the other had nothing but Raggs*'. The Interpreter responds in agreement and illustrates his point with an appropriate example from Scripture: 'therefore it is said of *Dives, In thy life thou receivedst thy good things; and likewise* Lazarus *evil things; but now he is comforted and thou art tormented*' (*PP*, 31–2). Having your best things last is to be in the best of all possible worlds.

In 1658 Bunyan was thirty years of age, and 'at thirty', states Richard Greaves, he was 'a man of some bitterness, but he channeled his rage into a vivid description of the fate that awaited the ungodly in a hell which was undeniably material'.[33] Bunyan would have had

---

[30] William Walwyn, *A Whisper in the Eare of Mr Thomas Edwards, Minister* (1646), in Jack R. McMichael and Barbara Taft (eds.), *The Writings of William Walwyn* (Athens, GA: University of Georgia Press, 1989), 173–87 (175–76).

[31] *An Agreement of the People*, in Geoffrey Robertson and Philip Baker (eds.), *The Levellers: The Putney Debates* (London: Verso, 2007), 52–6 (54).

[32] Hill, *Bunyan*, 87–9.

[33] Greaves, *Glimpses*, 101.

his prejudices fed by his occupation as an itinerant tinker, as he would have observed the 'poverty and the wretched living conditions of the poor', and by his reading of Arthur Dent's *The Plaine Mans Path-Way to Heaven* (1601), a text that denounced the rich as 'bloudsuckers, for you sucke the bloud of many poore men, women, and children: you eate it, you drinke it, you have it served in at your sumptuous tables every day' (*MW*, 1: xliii, xlv). In his preoccupation with the fate of the body and the soul in *A Few Sighs from Hell*, Bunyan prepares the reader for the fullest expression of the fate of sinners in the 1659 publication, *The Doctrine of the Law and Grace Unfolded*.

The Doctrine of the Law and Grace Unfolded

Bunyan suffered significant spiritual trauma in the 1650s, but the end of the decade witnessed his emergence from this trauma equipped with a renewed sense of confidence in his faith and his vocation. By the time *The Doctrine of the Law and Grace Unfolded* was published in 1659, the agonies and anxieties that Bunyan had experienced earlier in the decade seem to have passed (*MW*, 2: xv). The political agonies and anxieties of the country, however, were at fever pitch. Oliver Cromwell died in 1658 and the succession of his son, Richard, as Protector proved to be a short-lived affair. Throughout the 1650s 'Cromwell and his supporters had steadily multiplied varieties of enemy', and as the debates surrounding what shape the Commonwealth should take became more heated, the printing presses were in overdrive as various positions were advocated or attacked, promoted, or defended.[34] Expositions on an appropriate form of government came from a significant number of diverse sources stressing different perspectives. Milton was particularly busy. *A Treatise of Civil Power* and *Considerations Touching the Likeliest Means to Remove Hirelings Out of the Church* appeared in 1659, and in February 1660 came the first edition of *The Readie and Easie Way to Establish a Free Commonwealth*, quickly followed a few months later by a second edition.[35] The return of the king was imminent. Lest we be unaware of the dangers that lie therein, we are given an appropriate warning: 'if we return to kingship, and soon repent, as undoubtedly we shall', says Milton, we will be faced with the return of the old regime, 'which must necessarily proceed from king and bishop united inseparably in one interest'.[36] Harrington in 1658

---

[34] Ronald Hutton, *The Restoration: A Political and Religious History of England and Wales, 1658–1667* (Oxford: Clarendon Press, 1987), 14.

[35] Pamphlets in defence of the Good Old Cause were legion and include the following: *An Invocation to the Officers of the Army* (1659); *To the Right Honourable Lord Fleetwood [. . .] in Support of the Good Old Cause* (1659); *A Declaration of the Faithful Soldiers of the Army [. . .] Showing their Resolution to Stand by the Good Old Cause* (1659).

[36] John Milton, *The Readie and Easie Way to Establish a Free Commonwealth* (1660), in Don M. Wolfe (gen. ed.), *Complete Prose Works of John Milton*, 8 vols (New Haven, CT and London: Yale University Press, 1953–82), 7: 357.

published *The Prerogative of Popular Government* in which 'the first Preliminary of *Oceana*' is 'enlarged, interpreted, and vindicated'. In 'The Epistle Dedicatory', he maintains that it is every man's right 'to vindicate the reason of popular government', and the 'voice of the people is the voice of God'.[37]

From another perspective the exponents of religious radicalism were vocal in their defence of liberty of conscience. They were also antagonistic towards support for a state church, whatever form it might take, especially if it persecuted those who chose not to worship within it. A resurgent Presbyterianism was once more articulating its hatred for those who did not subscribe to its tenets, with all sectarians being captured by the term 'Anabaptist' to signify them as the harbingers of anarchy and religious excess. The term became 'a generic label that covered all those sectarians both actual and imagined, who sought to strip the parochial clergy of their state sponsorship'.[38]

Unlike Milton's prose works from these years, and Harrington's writings on the Rota Club, popular government, and, of course, *Oceana*, Bunyan's *The Doctrine of the Law and Grace Unfolded* is not per se a political pamphlet crying out for the preservation of the Good Old Cause; nor is it a work of republican political theory. The lack of direct critical engagement with the politics of the day in *The Doctrine of the Law and Grace Unfolded*, however, should not be construed as unqualified compliance. Rather than meet the issues of the day head-on, Bunyan is subtle in his criticism. His principal concern is for the elect and their fate in uncertain times. In this respect the politics of the text is implied in its use of the language of Lutheran and Calvinist eschatology. In his 1535 *Commentary on Galatians*, with its exhortation to the godly to remain faithful in the face of pressure, Luther echoes Paul's Epistle to the Galatians. Similarly, in *The Doctrine of the Law and Grace Unfolded* Bunyan makes much use of Paul's text (*MW*, 2: 15, 32, 37, 56, 74). Elsewhere I have described this tendency of Bunyan to criticize obliquely in *The Doctrine of the Law and Grace Unfolded* as 'a politics of the will', a means of maintaining spiritual consistency without resorting to, or encouraging explicitly, outright rebellion. For Bunyan, as he would later put it in *The Heavenly Foot-man* (1698), '*the Will is all* [...]. Get thy *Will tipt* with the Heavenly Grace, and resolution against all discouragements, and then thou goest *full speed* for Heaven.' To fail in this regard is to '*fall short*' of salvation (*MW*, 5: 165).[39] Bunyan's mission in *The Doctrine of the Law and Grace Unfolded* is to provide the elect with the means to be saved. 'I am yours', he writes, 'though not to serve your lusts and filthy minds, yet to reprove, instruct, and according to that proportion of faith and knowledge which God hath given me, to declare unto you the way of life and salvation' (*MW*, 2: 19).

---

[37] James Harrington, *The Prerogative of Popular Government* (1658), in J. G. A. Pocock (ed.), *The Political Works of James Harrington* (Cambridge: Cambridge University Press, 2010), 390, 391.

[38] Gary De Krey, *London and the Restoration, 1659–1683* (Cambridge: Cambridge University Press, 2009), 55.

[39] David Walker, ' "Heaven is prepared for whoever will accept of it": Politics of the Will in Bunyan's *The Doctrine of the Law and Grace Unfolded*', *Prose Studies*, 21 (1998), 19–31 (21).

Central to this work is an exposition of covenant theology based upon Bunyan's experiences to date. It is in *The Doctrine of the Law and Grace Unfolded* that Bunyan draws upon the 'sermons and pastoral activities' of the 1650s to consider which covenant his readers and listeners might lie under. In this sense, in its structure and composition, it is a work of practical theology. The treatise 'follows a common method of sermon construction' whereby the biblical text is opened, articulated, and where 'finally the application or "uses" of this material' are delineated.[40] The structure is explicitly '*laid down*' by Bunyan on the page immediately preceding the formal opening of the text (*MW*, 2: 20).

In setting out his ideas on covenant theology, Bunyan was participating in what had become a significant and extensive area of debate among eminent Puritan scholars and writers, of whom the most influential was the sixteenth-century Calvinist theologian, William Perkins. Covenant theology was concerned with the nature of the relationship of God to human beings. The idea was that there were two covenants. The first was the 'Covenant of Works', which God established with Adam in the Garden of Eden, and subsequently restated in the Ten Commandments. Because of original sin, human beings were unable to obey God's Law and keep the Covenant of Works. However, God had established a second covenant, the 'Covenant of Grace', by which Christ took upon himself the sins of the world, and thus provided a means of salvation for the elect, those chosen by God from all eternity.[41] When he writes of those living under the Covenant of Works, Bunyan is keen to point out just how little mercy they might expect to receive. He illustrates his point by a comparative analysis of the law of man and the Law of God, using liberally the language of secular law and the contemporary courtroom. To sin, even once against the Law of God means that forgiveness is unobtainable and damnation inevitable. Pardon cannot be achieved and the prisoner cannot be released unless 'full and compleat satisfaction' is given in blood, by the offender, or by proxy: '*For without shedding of blood there is no remission*, Hebrews 9. 22.' There is no way out of this 'except some one do give a full and compleat satisfaction to it for him, and bring the Prisoner into another Covenant, (to wit) the Covenant of Grace, which is more easie, and soul-refreshing, and sin-pardoning' (*MW*, 2: 37–9). Thus, Christ's sacrifice on the cross redeems the elect from damnation. Those not under the Covenant of Grace can never have 'assurance' that their sins will be pardoned. Neither can they hope for eternal life in the hereafter: 'because they are under that administration, upon whose souls God doth not smile'. Whereas the godly do shine in the light of 'Jesus Christ, the Lord of life and consolation', the unrighteous despair, 'for they have his frowns, his rebukes, his threatnings, and with much severity they must be dealt withall' (*MW*, 2: 46).

As *The Doctrine of the Law and Grace Unfolded* reaches its conclusion, Bunyan returns to the redemptive figure of Christ: 'Canst thou hear of Christ, his bloody sweat, and death, and not be taken with it, and not be grieved for it, and also converted by

---

[40] Greaves, *Glimpses*, 104.
[41] See Richard L. Greaves, 'Bunyan and Covenant Thought in the Seventeenth Century', *Church History*, 36 (1967), 46–67; Richard L. Greaves, *John Bunyan* (Abingdon: Sutton Courtenay Press, 1969), ch. 4; Hill, *Bunyan*, ch. 15. See also Chapter 4 in this volume.

it?' For those not willing to listen, an appalling fate awaits 'to bring thee down with a vengeance into hell fire, devouring fire, the lake of fire, eternall, everlasting fire; Oh! To make thee swim and roul up and down in the flames of the furnace of fire' (*MW*, 2: 226). It would not be long after writing this, of course, that Bunyan's familiarity with a courtroom would be greatly enhanced, and not in a positive way. The restored Church of England, in tandem with the Cavalier Parliament, almost immediately made life more difficult for Nonconformists of all stripes. Bunyan's faith would be sorely tested in the intensely persecutory context of the later seventeenth century. The experience he gained from writing the works he produced in the highly contested decade of the 1650s would serve him well in the trials and tribulations ahead.

Suggested Reading

Capp, Bernard, *England's Culture Wars: Puritan Reformation and its Enemies in the Interregnum, 1649-1660* (Oxford: Oxford University Press, 2012).

Greaves, Richard L., *Glimpses of Glory: John Bunyan and English Dissent* (Stanford, CA: Stanford University Press, 2002).

Hill, Christopher, *The World Turned Upside Down: Radical Ideas in the English Revolution* (1972; London: Penguin, 1991).

Lynch, Beth, *John Bunyan and the Language of Conviction* (Cambridge: D. S. Brewer, 2004).

MacCulloch, Diarmaid, *Reformation: Europe's House Divided, 1490-1700* (London: Allen Lane, 2003).

McDowell, Nicholas, *The English Radical Imagination: Culture, Religion, and Revolution* (Oxford: Oxford University Press, 2003).

McGregor, J. F., 'The Baptists: Fount of all Heresy', in J. F. McGregor and Barry Reay (eds.), *Radical Religion in the English Revolution* (Oxford: Oxford University Press, 1984), 23–63.

Sim, Stuart and David Walker, *Bunyan and Authority: The Rhetoric of Dissent and the Legitimation Crisis in Seventeenth-Century England* (Bern: Peter Lang, 2000).

Walker, David, '"Heaven is prepared for whosoever will accept of it": Politics of the Will in Bunyan's *Doctrine of the Law and Grace Unfolded* (1659)', *Prose Studies*, 21 (1998), 19–31.

Worden, Blair, *God's Instruments: Political Conduct in the England of Oliver Cromwell* (Oxford: Oxford University Press, 2012).

CHAPTER 11

BUNYAN IN PRISON

Writings from the 1660s

DAVID GAY

THE year 1660 marks both the beginning of a decade and a major event in English history: the restoration of the monarchy. The return of Charles II raised hopes among his supporters for the reunion of a divided body politic under the symbolic head of a visible sovereign. Public pageants and rituals promoted a sense of providential order in Charles's return. However, that sense of order had still to address the reality of diverse religious sects in England. Despite the king's gestures to religious toleration in the Declaration of Breda, issued on 4 April 1660, the restored regime steadily forced religious conformity in the early years of the decade. Under old statutes and new laws, the penalties for defiance included fines, exile, execution, and imprisonment.

Punishment became, as Laura Lunger Knoppers suggests, the 'dark twin' of Restoration 'celebratory pomp'.[1] John Milton's *Samson Agonistes* (1671) illustrates well the relationship between pageant and punishment. Milton, briefly imprisoned in November 1660, depicts Samson in prison on a day proclaimed for the public celebration of his defeat. The day turns from triumph to tragedy for the Philistines when Samson destroys the temple of Dagon, transforming humiliation into vindication for himself and his followers. This prison poem explores Samson's movement from painful, isolated self-analysis to public, defiant self-confidence, while raising challenging questions about the relation of faith to action in its violent outcome. The poem represents prison as a confined space of physical and psychological punishment that could also be a formative site of faith, memory, and expectation. In fact, prison became just such a formative space for hundreds of members of minority religious communities throughout the decade.

---

[1] Laura Lunger Knoppers, *Historicizing Milton: Spectacle, Power and Poetry in Restoration England* (Athens, GA: University of Georgia Press, 1994), 1.

Bunyan, a non-violent religious leader, also represents his spiritual formation in prison as both anxious self-reflection and heightened purpose. In both aspects, he wrote to affirm followers whose faith could be shaken by the scorn of a persecuting regime. The introspective spiritual record of *Grace Abounding to the Chief of Sinners* (1666) complements the confident ministerial leadership of Bunyan's other prison writings of the 1660s. Just as *Grace Abounding* validates the intense spiritual struggles of Dissenting readers, the prison writings instruct and support those pressured by the censure of the state and troubled by the millenarian expectations of some violent groups. For Bunyan, these pressures called for patience, discernment, and scepticism, not violent action. In a time of persecution, prison is a focal point for this complex spiritual epistemology.

Like Milton, Bunyan remembered Samson in addressing this audience:

> *I have sent you here enclosed a drop of that honey, that I have taken out of the Carcase of a Lyon,* Judg. 14. 5, 6, 7, 8. *I have eaten thereof my self also, and am much refreshed thereby. (Temptations when we meet them at first, are as the* Lyon *that roared upon* Sampson: *but if we overcome them, the next time we see them, we shall finde a Nest of Honey within them.) The Philistians understand me not.* (GA, 1)

Here, in the preface to *Grace Abounding*, scriptural allusion creates a circumspect discourse that assures Bunyan's readers of God's concern. Temptation could mean accepting release from prison in exchange for religious conformity. The 'Philistians' are the magistrates offering this bargain. This 'Samsonian moment', in Sharon Achinstein's apt phrase, uses Samson's riddle to 'give readers an experience of active resistance through reading'.[2] Writing, reading, and interpretation become modes of genuine action: they support Bunyan's readers inside and outside of prison. The body of the lion and the drop of honey make a fit emblem of the prison and the writings Bunyan produced there.

VOICING DISSENT: *I WILL PRAY WITH THE SPIRIT*

The circumstances of Bunyan's arrest, trial, and imprisonment are well documented. The Nonconforming Bedford congregation in which Bunyan rose to a position of leadership met without hindrance for most of 1660. By November 1660, Richard Greaves observes, 'Bunyan and his pastoral colleagues had no compelling reason to anticipate severe punishment if they continued to preach.'[3] Bunyan knew that Francis Wingate, a local Justice of the Peace, had issued a warrant for his arrest if he should preach at a meeting at Lower

---

[2] Sharon Achinstein, 'Honey from the Lion's Carcass: Bunyan, Allegory, and the Samsonian Moment', in David Gay, James G. Randall, and Arlette Zinck (eds.), *Awakening Words: John Bunyan and the Language of Community* (Newark, DE: University of Delaware Press, 2000), 68–80 (78).

[3] Greaves, *Glimpses*, 131–32.

Samsell on 12 November, but he nevertheless did so, and constables duly took him into custody. As Michael Mullett notes, an Act passed in 1593 under Elizabeth I and renewed under Charles I provided grounds for his arrest by requiring people to attend authorized parish worship and by banning religious meetings in conventicles. Bunyan could have avoided prison through conformity to the Church of England and the renunciation of his ministry. As Mullett puts it, Wingate 'left the outcome of the situation entirely within [Bunyan's] hands: by refusing the conditions for bail, he *chose* to go to prison'.[4]

Bunyan's subsequent interview with Dr William Lindale was more heated than his meeting with Wingate. As Greaves remarks, Bunyan and Lindale 'traded biblical verses as if they were weapons', with Bunyan's citations asserting his vocation to preach while suggesting that Lindale typified 'the priests and Pharisees whose hands were stained with Christ's blood'. This exchange marks 'a transition from the relatively limited question of Bunyan's right to preach' to the 'much broader insistence of each disputant that the other's church was false'.[5] This transition from precise legal manoeuvring to broad Reformation polemic reveals Bunyan's determination to lead his community from prison. He asserts:

> I was not at all daunted, but rather glad, and saw evidently that the Lord had heard me, for before I went down to the justice, I begged of God, that if I might do more good by being at liberty than in prison, that then I might be set at liberty: But if not, his will be done; for I was not altogether without hopes, but that my imprisonment might be an awakening to the Saints in the country, therefore I could not tell well which to chuse. Only I in that manner did commit the thing to God. And verily at my return, I did meet my God sweetly in the prison again, comforting of me and satisfying of me that it was his will and mind that I should be there. (*GA*, 113)

Inevitably, Bunyan's trial at the quarter sessions of January 1661 became a debate over true and false religion. His indictment states that he had 'devilishly and perniciously abstained from coming to church to hear divine service, and is a common upholder of several unlawful meetings and conventicles'. Bunyan answered that he was, in fact, a 'common frequenter of the church of God' (*GA*, 114). 'Church' here signifies Bunyan's congregation, and not the 'church' of the indictment. The subject of valid prayer soon arose as a central issue. Bunyan's adversary in this debate was Justice Kelyng, who had prosecuted the regicides Francis Hacker and William Heveningham in October 1660, would prosecute Sir Henry Vane in June 1662, and would help to frame the Act of Uniformity that imposed set forms of liturgy prescribed in the Book of Common Prayer on the Church. This Act precipitated a major crisis of Nonconformity through the ejection of some two thousand ministers on 24 August 1662, known as 'Black Bartholomew's

---

[4] Michael A. Mullett, *John Bunyan in Context* (Pittsburgh, PA: Duquesne University Press, 1997), 74, 75.

[5] Greaves, *Glimpses*, 133.

Day'. Kelyng may be the model for Lord Hategood in the trial scene at Vanity Fair in *The Pilgrim's Progress* (1678).[6]

Bunyan challenged the authority of the Book of Common Prayer. The status of this work reflected the history of the times. Parliament abolished it in 1645 and replaced it with the less popular Directory of Public Worship. John Gauden and others defended the Book of Common Prayer on behalf of Charles I in *Eikon Basilike* (1649); Milton opposed the suffocating nature of set forms of prayer in *Eikonoklastes* (1649). Proponents of conformity welcomed the return of the Prayer Book after 1660, commissioning a revision published in 1662; nevertheless, attacks on the Book of Common Prayer continued in works such as Vavasor Powell's *Common-Prayer-Book No Divine Service* (1660).[7] Bunyan rejected the Prayer Book as a human invention without divine authority. At his trial, Justice Kelyng argued that even scriptural prayers use other men's words. Christ, after all, taught his disciples the Lord's Prayer. Underestimating Bunyan, Kelyng misrepresented facts by claiming that the Book of Common Prayer 'hath been ever since the Apostles time' (GA, 117). Undeterred, Bunyan argued credibly and forcefully with his judges.

The argument between Bunyan and Kelyng produced Bunyan's first prison treatise, *I Will Pray with the Spirit,* [...] *or, A Discourse Touching Prayer*, first published in 1662 and reissued in a second edition in 1663. N. H. Keeble calls the treatise 'an openly oppositional text' that 'contrasts the sincerity of true spirituality with the hollow formalism of liturgies and prescribed rites'. Consigned to prison, Bunyan clarified his determination to 'dissent from, and stand against, prevailing ideology'.[8] Bunyan's central text is 1 Corinthians 14:15, 'I will pray with the Spirit, and with understanding.' In describing genuine prayer, Bunyan safeguards the voice of the Spirit from all forms of speech and writing that appropriate it to prevailing ideology. As Lori Branch insightfully argues, this mistrust of invention, or a fear that 'words themselves can be bare or naked, disconnected from substantive reality', leads to emotion, 'particularly a "feeling of misery" which forces words spontaneously from the heart', as the source of validation, or the 'true substance or the sign and seal of words in prayer'. In Branch's analysis, emotion becomes a 'sort of currency in which all true prayer traded'; it merges with the mercantile discourses of value and reward that Bunyan and others both reflect and internalize in a mode of spirituality underwritten by the divine contract of the atonement.[9]

Emotion is a sign of authentic prayer, yet that authenticity paradoxically entails a kind of spiritual bankruptcy: 'the soul will spend itself to nothing, as it were, rather than it will go without that good desired, even communion and solace with Christ. And hence it is, that the Saints have spent their strengths, and lost their lives, rather than go without the blessing' (MW, 2: 239–40). The soul in prayer, moreover, sees the world as vain or

---

[6] See Stuart Handley, 'Sir John Kelyng', *ODNB*.
[7] Greaves, *Glimpses*, 152.
[8] N. H. Keeble, *The Restoration: England in the 1660s* (Oxford: Blackwell, 2002), 134–35.
[9] Lori Branch, *Rituals of Spontaneity: Sentiment and Secularism from Free Prayer to Wordsworth* (Waco, TX: Baylor University Press, 2006), 45, 48.

empty in the manner of Ecclesiastes: 'the Soul that thus prayeth indeed, sees an emptiness in all things *under heaven*; That in *God* alone there is rest and satisfaction for the Soul' (*MW*, 2: 240). 'Right *Prayer* sees nothing substantial, or worth the looking after, but *God*' (*MW*, 2: 241). Right prayer carries a 'mighty *vehemency* in it', while the language of prayer books and public ritual is empty: many 'are very great strangers to a sincere, sensible, and *affectionate* pouring out their hearts or souls to God; but even content themselves with a little lip-labour, & bodily exercise, mumbling over a few imaginary Prayers' (*MW*, 2: 239).

The first section of the treatise—'What PRAYER is'—begins by representing 'right' prayer in the individual, and ends by bringing the individual into relationship with God in the three persons of the Trinity. The individual comes to God as a member of Christ 'so that God looks on that man as part of Christ, part of his Body, flesh and bones, united to him by election, conversion, illumination'; moreover, 'by vertue of this union, also, is the holy Spirit, conveyed in to him' (*MW*, 2: 242). This incorporation is manifested in a godly community residing within a 'crooked and perverse Nation': 'For God, and Christ, and his People, are so linked together, that if the Good of one be prayed for, to wit, the Church, the glory of God, and advancement of Christ must needs be included' (*MW*, 2: 244).

Part 2 of the treatise—'What it is to pray with the Spirit'—explains that when 'the Spirit gets into the heart then there is Prayer indeed, and not till then' (*MW*, 2: 257). Bunyan notes that Paul and the Apostles chose not to produce a prayer book, a rejoinder to Justice Kelyng's claim for the antiquity of the Book of Common Prayer. Without the Spirit, Bunyan replies, 'though we had a thousand *Common-Prayer-Books*, yet we know not what we should pray for as we ought' (*MW*, 2: 248). The Book of Common Prayer is 'none of God's Ordinances; but a thing since the Scriptures were written, patched together, one piece at one time, and another at another; a meer humane invention and institution', which God forbids (*MW*, 2: 249). Moreover, the Prayer Book is an instrument of blasphemy and hypocrisy because it compels the ungodly to pray through it. Ironically, the ungodly are 'counted the only honest men, and all because, with their blasphemous throats and hypocritical hearts, they will come to Church and say, *Our Father*' while Dissenters 'must be looked upon to be the only Enemies of God and the Nation' (*MW*, 2: 253). Bunyan sees no positive function for the Prayer Book; it is a device for the compulsion of individual conscience and the formation of a false church.

Part 1 emphasizes the internal characteristics of sincere prayer; Parts 2 and 3—'What it is to Pray with the Spirit, and with the Understanding also'—address external temptations that compromise prayer with blasphemy and hypocrisy. Conformity is one such temptation. Prayer in the Spirit requires a condition of unknowing. Bunyan echoes Paul in Romans 8:26–7: '*We know not what we should pray for as we ought; but the Spirit it self maketh intercession for us, with groanings which cannot be uttered. And he that searcheth the heart, knoweth the meaning of the Spirit, because he maketh intercession for the Saints according to the will of God*' (*MW*, 2: 246). Paul's rapture (2 Corinthians 12:4) supports the inexpressible nature of true prayer: 'Consider first the person speaking, even *Paul*, and in his person all the Apostles. We Apostles, we extraordinary Officers, the wise Master-Builders, that have some of us been caught up into *Paradise*, I Cor. 3. 10. 2 Cor.

12. 4. *We know not what we should pray for*' (*MW*, 2: 246). Paul writes of 'a man who was caught up into Paradise, and hears unspeakable words which it is not lawful for a man to utter. Of such a one will I glory, yet of myself I will not glory, but in mine infirmities' (2 Corinthians 12:2–5). The word 'infirmities' echoes Romans 8:26, 'the Spirit also helpeth our infirmities'. Paul gives Bunyan a model for distinguishing genuine prayer from both exceptional private experiences such as rapture and the public uniformity of scripted common prayer. Hence, in Part 3, Bunyan emphasizes empathetic communication that edifies the Church through the use of the 'Mother tongue', protecting his attack on the Book of Common Prayer from the imputation of sectarian religious fervour.

Bunyan uses the trope of prayer as a spiritual weapon in his major allegories. Christian turns to 'a weapon called All-Prayer' when he passes through the Valley of the Shadow of Death in *The Pilgrim's Progress* (*PP*, 63). In *The Holy War* (1682), Emanuel provides a weapon for the defence of the town of Mansoul against Diabolus: 'There was also an instrument invented by *Emanuel*, that was to throw stones from the Castle of *Mansoul*, out at *Mouth-gate*' (*HW*, 117). This nameless instrument is arguably prayer.[10] Bunyan transforms the intense polemical thrust of *I Will Pray with the Spirit* into combat metaphors in these episodes. He also represents an interplay of sacred and profane voices in his allegories to acknowledge the pressures Dissenting readers faced. He writes for an audience susceptible to invective and coercion voiced by conformist ideology. The rejection of human inventions that appropriate the Spirit to that ideology also gives the Spirit room to validate individual prayer. Moreover, reversals of perspective polarize the sacred and profane by viewing false religious practices through the lens of the Spirit. This polemical dynamic ultimately redeems the prison itself by making it a space where the reception of the Spirit is possible.

Prison Conditions: Bunyan the Poet

Sharon Achinstein shows how the sufferings of Dissenters focus on the 'psychological needs of victims to regain esteem'. Bunyan was an astute manager of this process, both in making the prison part of the narrative of his own spiritual formation and in defining esteem through the distinction between true and false religious practices for his followers. As Achinstein remarks, Bunyan was one of a number of 'celebrity prisoners' who were able to minister from prison. Prison conditions, however, were harsh:

> Present were the dangers of maltreatment, physical abuse, loneliness, harassment, humiliation, starvation, gaol-fever, plague, or small-pox. Families as well as

---

[10] See David Gay, 'The Name of the Prayer in *The Holy War*', *BS*, 19 (2015), 98–117; James F. Forrest, 'Milton and the Divine Art of Weaponry: That Two-Handed Engine and Bunyan's "Nameless Terrible Instrument at Mouthgate"', *Milton Studies*, 16 (1982), 131–40; for a contrary view, see Daniel V. Runyon, *John Bunyan's Master Story: The Holy War as Battle Allegory in Religious and Biblical Context* (New York: Mellon, 2007), 152–55, 178–79.

individuals suffered: bouts in prison could mean the loss of a household's income. The psychological consequences of imprisonment were debilitating: the loss of public presence, social esteem, and personal agency. John Bunyan, an exceptionally long prison-sitter himself, well understood the psychology of suffering behind bars.[11]

Bunyan enjoyed occasional furloughs from August 1661 to April 1662 during the early phase of his imprisonment.[12] He used these opportunities to preach, notably against the Book of Common Prayer in autumn 1661, and his furloughs were revoked.[13] He earned some money by making shoelaces in Bedford jail, but felt the burden his imprisonment had placed on his wife and children, particularly his blind daughter, Mary. The option of release through conformity was a source of great emotional strain.

Prisons became crowded, particularly when the Conventicle Act of 1664 brought new prosecutions of Nonconformists. As J. Sears McGee observes, 'the resultant crowding was physically unhealthy but spiritually a boon', providing Bunyan with the opportunity to preach, counsel, and minister inside the prison walls. Moreover, the transient nature of the prison population allowed for covert communication with the outside world when prisoners affected by Bunyan's message were released. As McGee remarks, the turnover in prisoners 'made Bedford gaol the nerve centre for Nonconformity in the region' (*MW*, 3: xvi). For Bunyan, prison time was not always the oppressive tedium of ordinary time; rather, he believed that God could meet and employ him 'sweetly in the prison', 'satisfying of me that it was his will and mind that I should be there' (*GA*, 113). Bunyan expressed this conviction in poetry: *Profitable Meditations* (1661), *Prison Meditations* (1663), *One Thing is Needful* (?1665), and *Ebal and Gerizzim* (?1665). Graham Midgley notes that 'Bunyan turned his pen to poetry throughout his life, and his poems are distributed fairly regularly among his prose treatises and his sermons', suggesting further that poetry might have provided some 'relief from the intellectual and structural demands of his longer prose allegories or the close argument and theological technicalities of his treatises' (*MW*, 6: xv). Greaves argues that the prison poems 'reveal his indebtedness to the ballads, broadside, and chapbooks beloved by commoners', though with a focus on religious themes after his conversion, and with the influence of poetic texts such as metrical psalms.[14]

The function of poems in the later allegories may also illustrate their role in Bunyan's prison writing. In *The Pilgrim's Progress*, hymns and poems summarize insights during pauses in the narrative by providing a character's interpretive response to a prior episode. In *Profitable Meditations*, Bunyan explores this reading activity.

---

[11] Sharon Achinstein, *Literature and Dissent in Milton's England* (Cambridge: Cambridge University Press, 2003), 60, 61.
[12] Beth Lynch, *John Bunyan and the Language of Conviction* (London: D. S. Brewer, 2004), 35.
[13] Greaves, *Glimpses*, 150–52.
[14] Greaves, *Glimpses*, 147. See also Chapter 19 in this volume.

Meditation is prominent in seventeenth-century poetry. Donne's Holy Sonnets, for example, offer discrete meditations on specific scenes from biblical narratives or religious doctrines such as the fall or the Last Judgement. Similarly, Bunyan's meditations abide within a larger narrative structure: the poem's nine sections explore fallen human nature, the sufferings of Christ, temptation, death, and judgement. At the same time, Bunyan's numbered quatrains present a sequence of autonomous aphorisms that challenge readers to pause and meditate on each topic. That of XVIII is one example:

> The pains he bore were more than we can think,
> Which by his bloody sweat and wounds we see:
> For he the Cup of Gods Wrath up did drink,
> That he us bondslaves by it might set free. (*MW*, 6: 7)

The quatrain composes the image of Christ's passion while placing it beyond human comprehension, much as Bunyan places genuine prayer beyond human invention. Bunyan construes the doctrine of atonement from the image. He then adds marginal citations to Luke, Matthew, and Galatians, supporting the meditation through a conference of biblical places. Part of a larger narrative of Christ's sufferings, the quatrain is sufficient in itself for meditation.

Bunyan's motive in writing *Profitable Meditations* was also practical. The volume could 'raise money for his family, to pay his jailer, and perhaps to acquire funds for a legal appeal'.[15] At the same time, the book fulfilled his need to persuade people to 'close with Christ'. The first three sections of *Profitable Meditations* instruct readers in the soteriological scheme that leads from conviction of sin to the merits of Christ's sufferings to the formation of the church of visible saints who are justified by faith. While Bunyan's precepts apply to many life situations, persecution and imprisonment give some a special poignancy. That of XXXIX is an example:

> Now then, if Jesus Christ stands, so shall I;
> For he is my Compleatness all the day:
> I'le look no further, here I'le live and dye;
> Come Death or Judgment, *CHRIST* will nev'r decay. (*MW*, 6: 11)

These lines point to two of the four 'last things'—death and judgement—as well as to Bunyan's anxiety over the possibility of execution. The fourth section—*A Discourse between Satan and the Tempted Soul*—introduces two more of the four last things, heaven and hell, in an interrogation by a sceptical Satan: 'But where's thine Evidence for Heav'n? thou fool! / How canst thou tell the work of Grace is true?' (*MW*, 6: 12). The section amplifies the questions of the judges at Bunyan's trial, and the temptation to renounce his convictions and conform.

---

[15] Greaves, *Glimpses*, 147.

Subsequent sections intensify the Calvinist polarities of saints and sinners, elect and reprobate. Christ engages in dialogue with a sinner and a doubting soul, and Death speaks with a sinner and a saint before the final judgement and the consequences of heaven or hell. The final section before the conclusion is a discourse '*between a* Saint in Heaven *and a* Sinner in Hell: *alluding to the* 16th *of* Luke'. Luke 16 includes the parable of Dives and Lazarus, which presents the afterlife as a radical inversion of worldly structures of power and privilege. Bunyan's portrait of the sinner in this discourse, as in his earlier treatment of the same parable in *A Few Sighs from Hell* (1658), is particularly vivid, in keeping with his purpose of raising the fear of judgement in his reader. The decree of reprobation does not compromise free will; the sinner rejects grace deliberately: 'The fault was mine, his Grace I did refuse' (*MW*, 6: 34). The dialogue anticipates the more elaborate analysis of Calvinist premises in Bunyan's allegories, such as the relation of Law and Grace, and the role of free will in the lifelong process of sanctification.

Prison Meditations (1665) affirms the transformation of suffering through divine grace. Bunyan contrasts spiritual and physical space:

> For though men keep my outward man
>   Within their Locks and Bars,
> Yet by the Faith of Christ I can
>   Mount higher than the Stars. (*MW*, 6: 43)

The jail becomes a vantage point, being 'a Hill, / From whence we plainly see / Beyond this World' (*MW*, 6: 47). Stanza 36 begins with a Shakespearean comparison of the world to a stage:

> Here we can see how all men play
>   Their parts, as on a Stage,
> How good men suffer for God's way,
>   And bad men at them rage. (*MW*, 6: 47)

Stanza 15 vocalizes the authoritarian invective that was oppressive to Dissenters:

> You Heretick, Deceiver, come
>   To Prison you must go,
> You preach abroad, and keep not home,
>   You are the Churches foe. (*MW*, 6: 44)

In fact, Bunyan maintained his sense of the true church in prison. His shift to the plural pronoun affirms jail can be a seminary:

> Though they say then, that we are Fools
>   Because we here do lye,
> I answer, Goals are Christ his Schools,
>   In them we learn to dye. (*MW*, 6: 45)

Bunyan concludes *Prison Meditations* with a defiant challenge to 'carnal' men and 'carnal policy':

> Know then true Valour there doth dwell
>   Where Men engage for God,
> Against the Devil, Death and Hell,
>   And bear the Wickeds rod. (*MW*, 6: 50)

Like Milton, Bunyan equates spiritual warfare with patient suffering. Prison valour, exemplary in a persecuting nation, anticipates the now famous hymn from *The Pilgrim's Progress, Part II*: 'Who would True Valour See' (*PP*, 295).

First published in the Doe Folio of 1692, Bunyan's *Mapp Shewing the Order and Causes of Salvation and Damnation* is among Bunyan's prison works, dating from 1663 or 1664.[16] The design of the *Mapp* is symmetrical, with a straight path indicating 'the way into and out of this world' leading from the Holy Trinity at the top of the page to the outcomes of heaven or hell at the bottom. Similar 'maps' in William Perkins's *A Golden Chaine: or, The Description of Theologie* (Cambridge, 1591) and Theodore Beza's *Tractationes Theologicae* (Geneva, 1570) are possible sources for Bunyan's *Mapp*. The order and causes of salvation or damnation are laid out in pathways of twenty-four circles, indicating the influence of Ramist analysis, though with variations noted by Gordon Campbell: the *Mapp* requires reading from top to bottom rather than from left to right, it encloses scriptural texts within its various circles, and it contains more visual decoration that Perkins's more austere presentation. As Campbell argues, 'these changes can be understood as indicative of the differences between Elizabethan Puritanism and post-Restoration sectarianism'. In particular, the use of scriptural citations marks Bunyan's effort 'to make his theology Biblical rather than systematic or abstract'.[17]

The *Mapp* also reflects Bunyan's pastoral concerns in his prison writings. His next poem, *One Thing is Needful* (?1665), complements the *Mapp* with a discourse on the four last things: death, judgement, heaven, and hell. The poem emphasizes fear of death and judgement to affirm the urgency of self-examination and repentance. Death is the great leveller, eradicating the difference between freedom and imprisonment:

> *Death* favours none, he lays at all,
> Of all sorts and degree:
> Both Old and Young, both great and small,
> Rich, Poor, and bound, and free. (*MW*, 6: 66)

---

[16] Greaves, *Glimpses*, 173. The *Mapp* is reproduced in *MW*, 12: 418–23.

[17] Gordon Campbell, 'The Source of Bunyan's *Mapp of Salvation*', *Journal of the Warburg and Courtauld Institutes*, 44 (1981), 240–41 (241). See also P. J. H. Titlestad, 'From Beza to Bunyan: The Pilgrim Road Mapped?' *BS*, 13 (2008/09), 64–81.

Heaven holds white-robed saints walking in 'righteousness, / With shining Crowns of Gold' (*MW*, 6: 84) in communion with the angels, prophets, and martyrs. Hell, in contrast, intensifies the hopelessness of prison:

> Which Prison with its locks and bars,
> Of Gods lasting decree,
> Will hold them fast; O how this marrs
> All thought of being free.
>
> Out at these brazen bars they may
> The Saints in glory see;
> But this will not their grief allay,
> But to them torment bee. (*MW*, 6: 93)

Bunyan found hope in prison, but could imagine absolute despair and alienation for the reprobate. His confidence in divine justice allows him to chart reprobation in *The Mapp*. Yet, as John Knott argues, limiting these images of punishment to the severity of Calvinist reprobation risks 'dissolving the social ground of Bunyan's frequently satiric vision'. Bunyan understood the 'cultural violence' that meted out public punishments to Dissenters. As Knott suggests, in Bunyan's imaginative world, 'violence against the reprobate and the enemies of God cannot be separated readily from instances of violence that Bunyan uses to express the struggles of the soul and of the Christian community on the path to the New Jerusalem'.[18] Prison, with its psychological torments, is an aspect of this violence.

Bunyan introduces *Ebal and Gerizzim* (?1665), his final poem of the decade, as an 'after-word' to *One Thing is Needful*, which examined 'the Four last Things' (*MW*, 6: 105). The title refers to the dichotomy of blessing and curse:

> Behold, I set before you this day a blessing and a curse; A blessing, if ye obey the commandments of the LORD your God, which I command you this day: And a curse, if ye will not obey the commandments of the LORD your God, but turn aside out of the way which I command you this day, to go after other gods, which ye have not known. And it shall come to pass, when the LORD thy God hath brought thee in unto the land whither thou goest to possess it, that thou shalt put the blessing upon mount Gerizim, and the curse upon mount Ebal. (Deuteronomy 11:26–9)

'From Mount *Gerizzim*' addresses the 'amazing love' of God and the nature of sanctification through the imputed righteousness of Christ (*MW*, 6: 105). 'From Mount *Ebal*' explains

> How God doth curse that soul that shall appear
> An unbelieving man, a graceless wretch,

---

[18] John Knott, 'Bunyan and the Cry of Blood', in Gay, Randall, and Zinck (eds.), *Awakening Words*, 51–67 (53, 54).

> Because he doth continue in the breach
> Of *Moses* Law, and also doth neglect
> To close with Jesus; him God will reject. (*MW*, 6: 123)

Bunyan's attention to the role of the Law again reveals its importance to the development of his theology and his understanding of persecution. If the latter conditioned the resistance Bunyan shared with other Dissenting groups, the former defined his sense of difference from them. As Roger Pooley argues, 'release from the burden of the Law', evident in Christian's encounter with Mr Legality in *The Pilgrim's Progress, Part I*, is central to Bunyan's 'pastoral theology'. The 'radical' antinomianism Bunyan saw in the Ranters diminishes the soteriological sequence in which the Law has its place: 'Alas, our God is a consuming fire / So is his Law, by which he doth require / That thou submit to him' (*MW*, 6: 124). God's Law evokes 'Godly fear', which Pooley contrasts with 'slavish fear' in Bunyan's 'psychotheology'. Godly fear entails conviction of sin and submission to the divine will; slavish fear is the fear of the persecuting state that can destroy the relationship with God. Hence, 'Justice discovers its antipathy / Against prophaneness and malignity' (*MW*, 6: 125). These theological assertions are framed by a world of persecution, giving theology 'immense potential in the political realm'. As Pooley notes, the interrogation of persecution requires a careful articulation of the relation of Law and Grace: 'once your conscience has recognized that you are free from the penalty for breaking the law of the Old Testament, in what ways might that free you to be independent and selective in your approach to the laws of your own country?'[19] Bunyan's exploration of this question is implicit throughout his prison poetry and in the prose works to which we now turn.

THE TRIPTYCH OF TIME: DURATION, MILLENARIANISM, RESURRECTION

Prison imposes two terrible conditions on people: the restriction of space and the extension of time. We have seen how Bunyan transformed space as the prison became a school of faith. Time changes from hellish tedium through meaningful work. Bunyan's prison writings explore the supersession of temporal alienation by providential time frames. The three aspects of time that Bunyan addresses are duration, or the duties of the Christian in ordinary time; millenarianism, or the intervention of Providence in historical time; and resurrection, or the Christian triumph over time.

Christian Behaviour (1663) considers time in its first aspect. As Greaves suggests, Bunyan perhaps considered this guide to Christian conduct as his final testament to his

---

[19] Roger Pooley, 'Bunyan and the Antinomians', in Vera J. Camden (ed.), *Trauma and Transformation: The Political Progress of John Bunyan* (Stanford, CA: Stanford University Press, 2008), 120–34 (129).

followers, since the uncertain duration of his imprisonment could have ended with exile or execution. Addressing new converts, Bunyan evokes temporal urgency in 'his belief that a time would come when the day of grace will be past, a fear that had once filled him with dread and despair when he thought such a season had already arrived for him'.[20] The inscrutability of Providence warns potential converts against procrastination. Yet *Christian Behaviour* is also a guide to a godly life in time. Central to this expression is the right understanding of the relationship between faith and works, a vexing issue that entails Bunyan's disagreements with other sects, notably, as McGee suggests, Ranters, who seemed to deny 'any distinction between good and evil works', and Quakers, who, Bunyan feared, assumed that 'moral perfection was possible', based on the inner light of Christ (*MW*, 3: xxii).

Citing Titus 3:7–8, Bunyan asserts, '*Good works do flow from Faith*' (*MW*, 3: 12). Faith depends on a regenerate heart through the operation of divine grace, without which good works are impossible. Thus, faith expressed in good works demonstrates grace to the unregenerate, whether for their conversion or condemnation. Faith becomes 'a prevailing argument to the sinner' (*MW*, 3: 14). The 'way to provoke others to *Good Works*, is constantly (in the evidence and demonstration of the Spirit) to shew them the certainty of their being by Grace made heirs of *Eternal Life*' (*MW*, 3: 11). This function of the faithful raises awareness of the true nature of time, since good works require a sense of 'right Time':

> Every work is not to be done at the same time, every time not being convenient for such a work: *There is a time for all things; and every thing is beautiful in its time, Eccles. 3. 1–11*. There is a *time* to pray, a *time* to hear; a *time* to read; a *time* to confer; a *time* to meditate; a *time* to do, and a *time* to suffer. Now, to be hearing when we should be preaching, and doing, that is, yeelding active obedience to that under which we ought to suffer, is not good. Christ was very wary, that both his doings and sufferings were rightly timed. (*MW*, 3: 19)

This paraphrase of Ecclesiastes implies that time is not finally in the control of persecutors. It also recalls Bunyan's reason for being in prison: his objection to the Book of Common Prayer with its regulation of time, prayer, and authority; moreover, good works as the 'evidence and demonstration of the Spirit' recall his oppositional tone in *I Will Pray with the Spirit*. Bunyan defends his converts against charges of heresy and blasphemy in his treatment of prayer, and against sedition and treason in his treatment of Christian obedience. The balance of *Christian Behaviour* emulates Paul's view of the duties of fathers, wives, children, and servants as divine appointments that distinguish conformity from 'active obedience'. Following Christ's example, the faithful must perceive that 'doings and sufferings' should be 'rightly timed'.

The question of right timing in the conduct of the individual Christian expands into the dimension of history in *The Holy City* (1665), with its focus on millenarianism, or

---

[20] Greaves, *Glimpses*, 162.

the expectation that before Judgement Day, Christ and the saints who comprise the true church will reign on earth for one thousand years. The scriptural basis for millenarian expectations is Revelation 20:1–6, according to which Satan is bound for a thousand years, while the saints reign on earth, but is then loosed 'for a season' until the final consummation of history. As W. R. Owens argues, belief in a future millennium was not prominent in the sixteenth century: 'the early English reformers agreed with their European counterparts in condemning millenarianism as a dangerous heresy which could easily be used as justification for moral anarchism and social revolution'. This changed in the seventeenth century, when commentaries on Revelation by Thomas Brightman and Joseph Mede, combined with millenarian sentiments in other publications, intensified expectation of an imminent millennium.[21]

Civil war and regicide fuelled millenarian fervour, leading to the rise of Fifth Monarchists who contemplated violence in preparing for the reign of Christ. Thomas Venner, whom Greaves describes as a 'misguided millenarian zealot', joined others in planning an insurrection against Cromwell during the winter of 1656–57.[22] Arrested and jailed until 1659, Venner planned another uprising in January 1661, this time against Charles II. Some contemporary accounts set his followers at five hundred, but fifty is a more realistic estimate.[23] Government forces crushed this second insurrection and executed Venner. His action offered a pretext for a broader persecution of Nonconformists. As John Coffey points out, 'more than 4000 Quakers and Baptists were arrested and imprisoned in the space of a few weeks'.[24] These events, combined with the failure of a negotiated policy of religious toleration and the subsequent refusal of the Cavalier Parliament to 'tolerate any dissent from, or diminution of, the episcopal ideal',[25] led to the passage of new laws comprising the 'Clarendon Code', which supplemented the Elizabethan statutes that provided for Bunyan's first arrest. These laws would keep Bunyan in prison for twelve years.

As Greaves observes, prison had taken a heavy psychological toll on Bunyan by the middle of the 1660s.[26] Bunyan reveals his state of mind in the conception of *The Holy City*. His fellow prisoners needed an encouraging sermon, 'but at that time I felt my self (it being my turn to speak) so empty, spiritless, and barren, that I thought I should not have been able to speak among them so much as five words of Truth, with Life and Evidence' (*MW*, 3: 69). Despite Bunyan's productivity as a prison writer, we cannot discount the strain of prison life, compounded by worry for his family. In addition, the uncertain outcome of imprisonment was a terrible burden for prisoners. Observing how prison influenced the depiction of the Man in the Iron Cage

---

[21] W. R. Owens, 'John Bunyan and English Millenarianism', in Gay, Randall, and Zinck (eds.), *Awakening Words*, 81–96 (81–2).
[22] Richard L. Greaves, 'Thomas Venner', *ODNB*.
[23] Keeble, *Restoration*, 116.
[24] John Coffey, *Persecution and Toleration in Protestant England: 1558–1689* (Harlow: Pearson, 2000), 167.
[25] Keeble, *Restoration*, 116.
[26] Greaves, *Glimpses*, 174–76.

in *The Pilgrim's Progress*, Anne Dunan-Page notes Bunyan's fear 'that his love for his family might prove stronger than his ability to bear his punishment'.[27] At the same time, Bunyan's articulation of his dryness of spirit in the preface to *The Holy City* may show his sceptical view of overt millenarian demonstrations such as the Venner rebellion. By revealing his state of depression, Bunyan contrasts naïve millenarianism, a potentially fanatical form of presumption in its expectation of an immediate, visible outcome, and textual millenarianism, a more mature perspective that grounds the millennium in a temporality of deferral, calling for patient hope through the exercise of reading and interpretation.

Bunyan's preface identifies four types of readers: the godly reader, the learned reader, the captious or 'wrangling' reader, and the 'Mother of Harlots', or the figure of Rome–Babylon that is the antagonist of the New Jerusalem in Bunyan's central text, the Book of Revelation. Bunyan compares his treatise to a banquet of 'Milk and Meat' unsuitable for the 'voluptuous Palate' of the demonic mother. Food imagery in the preface connects the sharing and reading of the Word to liturgy, including a type of Eucharist. He informs the godly reader that his eye fell 'providentially' on Revelation 21:11, which compares the light of the Holy City to Jasper. Revived by the passage, he carries his 'Meditations to the Lord JESUS for a Blessing, which he did forthwith grant according to his Grace; and helping me to set before my Brethren, we did all eat, and were well refreshed' (*MW*, 3: 69–70). This exegetical meal then expands into the full written treatise.

Bunyan cautions his readers not to expect too much from his reading:

> I shall not meddle where I see nothing, neither shall I hide from you that which at present I conceive to be wrapt up therein: onely you must not from me look for much inlargement, though I shall endeavor to speak as much in few words, as my Understanding and Capacity will enable me, through the help of Christ. (*MW*, 3: 75)

This is a caution against the naïve, at times violent, millenarian expectations often generated by readers of the Book of Revelation. Bunyan grounds his approach in 'John's qualification', or the guidance of the Spirit in reading. His method is typological rather than literal: the Spirit carried John to a high mountain which

> signifieth the *Lord Christ*, on which the Soul must be placed, as on a mighty Hill, whereby he may be able (his Eyes being anointed with spiritual Eye-salve) to see over the tops of those mighty Corruptions, Temptations, and spiritual Enemies, that like high and mighty Towers are built by the wicked one, to keep the view of Gods things from the sight of our Souls: wherefore Christ is called, *The Mountain of the Lords House*, or that on which the House of God is placed. (*MW*, 3: 77–8)

---

[27] Anne Dunan-Page, *Grace Overwhelming: John Bunyan, The Pilgrim's Progress and the Extremes of the Baptist Mind* (Bern: Peter Lang, 2006), 206–07.

As in the apocalyptic vision Michael gives to Adam at the end of *Paradise Lost* (1667; 1674), the extension of perspective in space approximates deferral in the dimension of time. The vision of the saints rises above the structures of persecution.

Architectural features and spaces of the Holy City lead Bunyan to read the history of the structure as a history of the true church. The phases of its construction in time are '*Altar-work, Temple-work, and City-work*' (*MW*, 3: 134). The 'Altar-men' who repaired the altar prior to the building of the temple are types who 'figure-out for us our famous and holy Worthies', particularly Reformers such as '*Wickliff, Hus, Luther, Melancton, Calvin*, and the blessed Martyrs in Q. *Maries* dayes' (*MW*, 3: 134). Temple workers, typified by Zerubbabel and Joshua, are '*a select company of visible Believers*' who are '*for building up one another an holy Temple in the Lord*'. The godly are 'separate and distinct from that confused heap of rubbish and carnal Gospelers, that every where like Locusts and Maggots craul up and down the Nations' (*MW*, 3: 135). City work preserves true worshippers 'in the purest order', but their security is not assured until the work is complete. When the city is finished,

> there will be great peace; yet all the time that these things are doing, before they be done, let the work-men look for *opposition, taunts, underminers*, and a thousand tricks for the hindrance of it; *For the street of the City shall be built, and the Wall, even in troublous times*. (*MW*, 3: 136)

Bunyan defers the millennium in order to orient and strengthen his readers in a 'troublous' era. His emphasis on figurative architecture and interpretation as forms of edification indicates the maturity of his apocalyptic thinking.

Bunyan expected a millennium in which doctrinal differences among sects would disappear; however, this expectation does not reveal a conciliatory attitude to the errors he saw in others. Bunyan's convictions deepened with the price they exacted. He was confident in the endurance of his own gospel precepts. This certainty is the focus of the final text in his triptych of time: *The Resurrection of the Dead* (?1665). Where *The Holy City* allowed for deferral, this treatise confronts the finality of the end of time, affirming, on its title page, the 'truth of the *Resurrection* of the *Bodies*' according to 'Gods Word', and the reality of 'the finall Conclusion of the whole World' (*MW*, 3: 201). Bunyan's sectarian adversaries included the Ranters and the Quakers, who, Bunyan believed, misrepresented the resurrection to their followers.[28] To deny the resurrection of the dead is to 'open a Floud-gate to all manner of impiety'. To say that the resurrection has already occurred, meaning it 'is past either with him or any Christian', leads 'directly to the destruction and overthrow of the faith of them that hear him' (*MW*, 3: 214). More prominent than this polemical agenda is the experience of trial and incarceration that demanded vindication. As Greaves observes, for Bunyan's 'incarceration to have meaning, the dead must

---

[28] Greaves, *Glimpses*, 192. See also T. L. Underwood, '"For then I should be a Ranter or a Quaker": John Bunyan and Radical Religion', in Gay, Randall, and Zinck (eds.), *Awakening Words*, 127–40.

be resurrected. Shorn of this belief, he would have no purpose in his imprisonment and no reason to cause his family to struggle in his absence.'[29]

Bunyan begins with Acts 24:14–15, in which Paul affirms the resurrection. The context of this affirmation is Paul's arrest, trial, and imprisonment, paralleling Bunyan's condition:

> You see here, that *Paul*, being upon his Arraignment, accused of many things, by some that were violent for his blood; and being licensed to speak for himself by the then *Heathen* Magistrate; he doth in few words tell them, that as touching the Crimes wherewith they charged him, he was utterly faultless. (*MW*, 3: 204)

Paul asserts that the just and unjust will rise, requiring a final judgement. This judgement intensifies Bunyan's Calvinist views and the certitude of his own election. The reprobate 'standing upon their tryal' will hear and see 'such dreadful things, both written and witnessed against every one of them' (*MW*, 3: 271). Bunyan depicts the full horror of their hopeless pleas: 'how gastly they look, and how now the brinish tears flow down like Rivers from their eyes, ever re-doubling their Petition' (*MW*, 3: 272). The elect, once persecuted, are now affirmed. Christ observes 'how patiently they took all crosses, afflictions, persecutions, and necessities for the Kingdome of Heavens sake; how they indured burning, starving, stoning, hanging, and a thousand calamities' (*MW*, 3: 279). Bunyan evokes scenes and language familiar to Dissenters, but transposes them to the heavenly court: 'now [the wicked] shall see, that there was never any Quarter-Sessions, nor general Goal-delivery more publickly foretold of, then this day' (*MW*, 3: 282). At the same time, Bunyan can cite Matthew 25:36, commending those who supported prisoners of conscience by noting that Christ, the judge, was the world's prisoner (*MW*, 3: 279). These contrasting scenes produce what Keeble calls a 'lexical reversal', whereby the condition of worldly persecution is reversed in the sight of God. Those 'who err are no longer the Dissenters, but those who stand against the Dissenters'.[30] While Bunyan's triptych of time emphasizes duty, suffering, and endurance in the course of time, the radical inversion of circumstance represented in this lexical reversal of Dissent is a crucial component of the meaning Bunyan gives to imprisonment.

Conclusion

Laws passed to restrain writers like Bunyan also galvanized a dynamic literary culture. Bunyan was one of many religious leaders who suffered imprisonment after the Restoration. Many such leaders wrote for their followers and fellow prisoners. Bunyan alone became one of the most read authors in English literature. We cannot speculate on

---

[29] Greaves, *Glimpses*, 192.
[30] Keeble, *Restoration*, 134.

the kind of writer Bunyan might have been without his prison experience, nor should we imagine that such suffering was somehow salutary and necessary.[31] We can consider that for Bunyan, as for later writers such as Dietrich Bonhoeffer and Martin Luther King, prison was a defining experience. Much attention has been given to the relationship between *Grace Abounding* and Bunyan's fictional writings. How do the other prison works we have surveyed anticipate his literary achievement? They do so in several ways. The polemical urgency of *I Will Pray with the Spirit* shows Bunyan's determination to protect the integrity, not only of religious precepts, but of the godly voice in Restoration England. The confident assertions of the prison poems show that imaginative space cannot be limited by physical incarceration; this sense of imaginative space surely shaped the narrative framework of *The Pilgrim's Progress, Part I*, in which the dreamer finds himself in the 'Denn' of a Restoration 'Gaol' (*PP*, 8). The visionary depictions of the New Jerusalem and the Last Judgement construct ultimate parameters of space and time inseparable from the local settings of prisons or cities and the unique life journeys that unfold within them, giving rise to the coordination of local and universal histories in *The Holy War*. Above all, Bunyan discovered that reading and writing do not simply drive away the time: they transform time by becoming modes of leadership, communion, action, and resistance.

Suggested Reading

Achinstein, Sharon, *Literature and Dissent in Milton's England* (Cambridge: Cambridge University Press, 2003).

Branch, Lori, *Rituals of Spontaneity: Sentiment and Secularism from Free Prayer to Wordsworth* (Waco, TX: Baylor University Press, 2006).

Coffey, John, *Persecution and Toleration in Protestant England: 1558–1689* (Harlow: Pearson, 2000).

Greaves, Richard, *Glimpses of Glory: John Bunyan and English Dissent* (Stanford, CA: Stanford University Press, 2002).

Keeble, N. H., *The Restoration: England in the 1660s* (Oxford: Blackwell, 2002).

Owens, W. R., 'John Bunyan and English Millenarianism', in David Gay, James G. Randall, and Arlette Zinck (eds.), *Awakening Words: John Bunyan and the Language of Community*, (Newark, DE: University of Delaware Press, 2000), 81–96.

Pooley, Roger, 'Bunyan and the Antinomians', in Vera J. Camden (ed.), *Trauma and Transformation: The Political Progress of John Bunyan* (Stanford, CA: Stanford University Press, 2008), 120–34.

---

[31] See, further, Chapter 27 in this volume.

CHAPTER 12

GRACE ABOUNDING TO THE CHIEF OF SINNERS (1666)

NIGEL SMITH

IN THE BEGINNING: INCARCERATION

Grace Abounding to the Chief of Sinners: or, A Brief and Faithful Relation of the Exceeding Mercy of God in Christ, to his Poor Servant John Bunyan was first published in 1666. Bunyan was in prison at the time, held under the legislation of the Cavalier Parliament against Dissenters. Despite Charles II's promise in the Declaration of Breda of 1660 to maintain religious toleration, the Anglican majority in Parliament had ensured the imposition of the 1664 Conventicle Act that made meetings of Dissenters for worship illegal and imposed fines, imprisonment, and other penalties on those who participated in or who harboured meetings. The year 1666 was possibly the most confident year of this policy, sometimes known as the 'Clarendon Code', after the king's chief minister, Edward Hyde, Earl of Clarendon. But the combination of plague, the Great Fire of London, and compromise and embarrassment in the war with the Dutch, would lead to Clarendon's departure from office and exile by the end of 1667. The years of the late 1660s and the very early 1670s would hold out greater hope for the Dissenters and their supporters that a toleration policy might be established. Nonetheless, *Grace Abounding* was conceived, written, and appeared at a gloomy moment.

The work itself is broken down in its first edition into five sections. The preface is an explanation of the context of imprisonment and why the book is being published. Since Bunyan cannot fulfil his role as a preacher because he is imprisoned, *Grace Abounding* is a witness to his continuing faith and his desire to make that faith work on his fellow Christians for their own salvation:

> *I being taken from you in presence, and so tied up, that I cannot perform that duty that from God doth lie upon me, to you-ward, for your further edifying and building up in Faith and Holiness, &c. yet that you may see my Soul hath fatherly care and desire after*

> *your spiritual and everlasting welfare; I now once again, as from the top of* Shenir *and* Hermon, *so from* the Lions Dens, *and from the Mountains of the Leopards (Song 4.8.) do look yet after you all, greatly longing to see your safe arrival into* THE *desired haven.* (GA, 1).

'Look […] after you' is classic Bunyan, implying a spontaneity of expression and composition, as if it came directly in conversation. The phrase seems to mean both 'taking care of' and quite literally 'looking at' his flock, as if he could see them, or could see them in his mind's eye, from prison. 'Haven' suggests 'Heaven', and note how the choice of italics and upper case letters in the compositing works to support these emphases.

The use of Scripture is also characteristic. Bunyan begins with a simile drawn from the Song of Solomon 4:8, '*I now once again, as from the top of* Shenir *and* Hermon, *so from* the Lions Dens, *and from the Mountains of the Leopards*', but in the next paragraph accelerates to inhabit part of an entire biblical narrative—the story of Samson in the Book of Judges—and where Bunyan, the persecuted minister, becomes Samson, the prisoner of the Philistines and resourceful Nazarite:

> *I have sent you here enclosed a drop of that honey, that I have taken out of the Carcase of a Lyon* (Judg. 14. 5, 6, 7, 8). *I have eaten thereof my self also, and am much refreshed thereby. (Temptations when we meet them at first, are as the* Lyon *that roared upon* Sampson; *but if we overcome them, the next time we see them, we shall finde a Nest of Honey within them.*) (GA, 1)

At another level the metaphor of food is equally significant. Bunyan himself cannot be swallowed by the lions (he 'sticks' in their teeth), while the 'thirsting' of his congregation after the Lord, and their signs of humility, are welcome 'food' to the imprisoned minister, just as the testimony that is *Grace Abounding* will be honey to the flock. These two powerful elements are followed by a much more predictable reference to the persecuted English godly as the Israelites travelling through affliction in the wilderness.

There then comes the key element that the book is a work of 'remembrance'. Not least in the absence of the minister, but in any case: '*It is profitable for Christians to be often calling to mind the very beginnings of Grace with their Souls*' (GA, 2). In all these memories, the centrality of St Paul's experience is very clear for Bunyan:

> *It was* Pauls *accustomed manner,* Acts 22. *and that when tried for his life,* Acts 24. *even to open before his Judges, the manner of his Conversion: He would think of that day and that hour, in the which he first did meet with Grace: for he found it support unto him. When God had brought the children of* Israel *thorow the* Red Sea, *far into the wilderness; yet they must turn quite about thither again, to remember the drowning of their enemies there,* Num. 14.25. *for though they sang his praise before, yet they soon forgat his works,* Psal. 106. 11, 12. (GA, 2)

Diligent, unceasing search for sins, and for the signs that faith pitched against those sins and was met by God's grace, will provide the assurance the believer-reader needs to overcome the overwhelming sense of one's own sinfulness.[1] Memory guides one into the life record, and the harder one looks, the more one will find evidence of saving grace, howsoever at first the chance might seem unlikely. But one might not, and there is always the possibility, for some, of despair being justified, like the case of Ignorance in *The Pilgrim's Progress* (1678). The preface closes by reminding the reader of the painful yet necessary existential reality of this conclusion, even in the most mundane of settings: that in experience God is absolutely everywhere and working on each of us:

> *Have you forgot the Close, the Milk-house, the Stable, the Barn, and the like, where* God *did visit your Soul? Remember also the Word, the Word, I say, upon which the Lord hath caused you to hope: If you have sinned against light, if you are tempted to blaspheme, if you are down in despair, if you think* God *fights against you, or if heaven is hid from your eyes; remember 'twas thus with your father,* but out of them all the Lord delivered me. (GA, 3)

Experience

Then begins the narrative itself. It is here that we should pause to consider the nature of this second and most substantial part of the work. Bunyan is using as a surrogate preaching device the genre that is second only to the sermon in Puritan literary tradition: the conversion account or 'experimental narrative'. The theology of 'experiment' or experience, formulated most forcefully by the Cambridge divine William Perkins in the 1590s, and influential in old and New England through the seventeenth century, is that the believer must examine her or his experiences, as they were accessible through memory and as logic was able to analyse them.[2] Life experience as well as the Bible is 'great evidence'. The result of the analysis would be a measurement of how God had worked upon the individual, how sin had been recognized, how repentance had been made, and how conversion had occurred. The ongoing threat from sin in all of its temptations and how the believer struggled with that would make up the rest of the content of the 'experimental narrative'.

Within Congregational or 'Independent' churches the conversion narrative became a required statement of how a believer came to be saved, made at the same time as such

---

[1] This central quality of unceasing, obsessive unease makes Bunyan's conversion finally very different from St Paul's; and also very different from St Augustine's in the kind of identified sin (blasphemy rather than improper sex). See Michael Davies, '*Grace Abounding to the Chief of Sinners*: John Bunyan and Spiritual Autobiography', in Anne Dunan-Page (ed.), *The Cambridge Companion to Bunyan* (Cambridge: Cambridge University Press, 2010), 67–79 (69).

[2] See G. F. Nuttall, *Visible Saints: The Congregational Way, 1640–1660* (Oxford: Basil Blackwell, 1957); Edmund S. Morgan, *Visible Saints: The History of a Puritan Idea* (New York: New York University Press, 1963); Patricia Caldwell, *The Puritan Conversion Narrative: The Beginnings of American Expression* (Cambridge: Cambridge University Press, 1983).

believers made a confession of faith, the formal statement of theological profession of a given congregation. The conversion narrative was thus an act of authorship made by a great many godly believers from the 1630s onwards. Since many of these people were of humble origins, it was an ascent for them into authorship from the realms of marginal literacy or in some cases initial illiteracy. By the mid-seventeenth century, several confident Independent congregations began to publish collections of conversion narratives as a printed sign of their regenerate nature. Remembered dream visions are a crucial feature of this genre, like the dream Bunyan has of the Bedford women 'on the Sunny side of some high Mountain, there refreshing themselves with the pleasant beams of the Sun, while I was shivering and shrinking in the cold, afflicted with frost, snow, and dark clouds' (GA, 19),[3] but in which the speaker was eventually able to pass through the very narrow gap in the separating wall—a version of the biblical 'strait gate' (Matthew 7:13–14) and the 'wicket gate' of *The Pilgrim's Progress*—and join the women inside, much to his own comfort.[4] As is equally typical of a conversion narrative, this dream is then explained by a voice from outside the text:

> Now this Mountain and Wall, &c. was thus made out to me; the Mountain signified the Church of the living God; the Sun that shone thereon, the comfortable shining of his mercifull face on them that were therein: the wall I thought was the Word that did make separation between the Christians and the world: and the gap which was in this wall, I thought was Jesus Christ, who is the way to God the Father. (GA, 20)

The conversion narrative is a cultural phenomenon of enormous significance in literary history, enabling the modern novel (Daniel Defoe's *Moll Flanders* (1722) is a fictive conversion narrative) and giving a generic framework for many other kinds of expression that would otherwise have none: such as slave and captivity narratives.[5] Bunyan's was a Congregational or Independent 'gathered' church, which in some ways resembled a Baptist meeting in that adult baptism was practised as a sign of belief, repentance, and conversion, but was not a requirement for admission and membership (and so is often referred to as an 'open communion' church). As a Congregational church, only a confession of faith and experience was required on admission, as the Bedford Church Book shows (e.g. *CB*, 23). I suspect Bunyan prepared an original *Grace Abounding*, perhaps resembling the brief account of 'the Authors experience' that appears in *The Doctrine of the Law and Grace Unfolded* (1659; *MW*, 2: 156–60), and delivered it in front of his church before greatly extending this narrative while in

---

[3] I say 'Bunyan' but, of course, acknowledge that the speaking first-person voice of John Bunyan in *Grace Abounding* is a constructed persona.

[4] See Nigel Smith, *Perfection Proclaimed: Language and Literature in English Radical Religion 1640–1660* (Oxford: Clarendon Press, 1989), ch. 2.

[5] See, for example, Olaudah Equiano, *The Interesting Narrative of the Life of Olaudah Equiano, or Gustavus Vassa, the African: Written by himself*, 2 vols (1789); Mary Rowlandson, *The Sovereignty & Goodness of God [...] being a Narrative of the Captivity and Restauration of Mrs. Mary Rowlandson* (Cambridge, MA, 1682).

prison in the first half of the 1660s. The conversion narratives published in the 1650s often stop, as they would be expected to do, at the point at which the gathered church is joined. By contrast, Bunyan extrapolates through time, offering an account of his trials and temptations long after he has become a member of the Bedford congregation, being driven to do so by his ministerial as opposed to merely confessional mission. That, coupled with his acute sense of the ongoing claims of original sin, makes *Grace Abounding* distinctive.

Style, Structure, and Sin

Bunyan declares his literary intention at the end of his preface with a very important statement concerning style:

> *I could also have stepped into a stile much higher then this in which I have here discoursed, and could have adorned all things more then here I have seemed to do: but I dare not:* God *did not play in convincing of me; the* Devil *did not play in tempting of me; neither did I play when I sunk as into a bottomless pit, when* the pangs of hell caught hold upon me: *wherefore I may not play in my relating of them, but be plain and simple, and lay down the thing as it was.* (GA, 3–4)

'Plain style' means many things in this period, from theology and politics to science writing (what was then called natural philosophy); here Bunyan makes a plea for unadorned writing as the basis for the utter seriousness of the experimental arena. The claim also implies that Bunyan knows well what 'adorned' style means: a significant subject for another chapter. Bunyan had been publishing for over a decade by 1666. While the very first writings of his that we have (of 1656) are stylistically awkward, it is notable that he not only has a clear literary plan here, and a very Puritan one at that, but his literary capacity is also very considerable, howsoever the subject matter is interiorized in the most personal of ways: *Grace Abounding* drips with memorable quotations. It may be plain, but it is far from plain reading.

The narrative is structured as numbered paragraphs. This in itself suggests that Bunyan had spent time refining an original conversion document, now lost, that was once perhaps a more continuous and shorter text. Over the course of its six editions in Bunyan's lifetime (of which no copies of the second and fourth editions survive) phrases and several paragraphs (some very important) were added, altered, or expanded, which again gives the sense not of a fixed text but of one in a permanent and ongoing state of development: a mirror to Bunyan's unsettled mind. Paragraphs 12–14, added in the third edition, summarize with intensity a further set of Providences, demonstrating that God 'did not utterly leave' Bunyan even if he continued a sinner, including the oft-cited episode when, as a New Model Army soldier, Bunyan has his place as a siege sentinel taken by another who was 'shot into the head with a Musket bullet and died' (*GA*, 8). The investigation of conscience never stops for the living, and Bunyan's revisions reflected his growing grasp of literary convention, 'correct' English, and of the need for clarity.

In general, Bunyan is at pains to make himself look respectable, and less of a 1650s sectary (in the third edition, paragraphs 43–5 and 161 are introduced, for example, to show how he resisted the calls both to swearing and to free love that were to be encountered in Ranter pamphlets of the early 1650s), without sacrificing the sense of immediacy in his writing.[6] He was also keen to distance himself from apparent Quaker views of the Bible's inferiority to the Spirit and their alleged attacks on the historical reality of Jesus. The interpolations of *Grace Abounding*'s third edition play up the careful biblical scholar as opposed to the sectary who hears voices in his head: references to more biblical texts are added. But in the ongoing process of revision some errors were perpetuated or were introduced for the first time. Moreover, the small enhancements of stylistic assurance do in some instances detract from the power and spontaneity of the first edition. An emphasis on politeness dilutes the stylistic impact in favour of refinement, and one wonders whether Bunyan himself can have been responsible: the fifth edition turns 'God *did not play in convincing of me; the* Devil *did not play in tempting of me*' into 'God *did not play in tempting of me.*' Even 'stunned' for 'stounded' in the sixth edition diminishes Bunyan's rustic authenticity. Too much ministerial identity is not good for the authentic presence of a struggling believer.

Both the text's standard edition and most other modern editions uphold the primacy of the first edition of 1666. The third edition of 1672–74 contains the greatest number of changes, but the fifth (1680) is also significant as it adds a twelve-paragraph conclusion to the life narrative: a defence of Bunyan's integrity against local charges that he had committed adultery with Agnes Beaumont (and conspired to murder her father), and that he was 'a Witch, a Jesuit, a Highway-man, and the like' (*GA*, 93). There was a further hint of Ranterism in the charges. One point to raise here is a familiar one in Bunyan scholarship. *The Pilgrim's Progress, Part I* appears to be an allegory of that which is literally represented in *Grace Abounding* and there are several crossover points. Does the elastic nature of *Grace Abounding* have implications for the structure of *The Pilgrim's Progress*, or how the allegory should be read?

The life story told in *Grace Abounding* is not merely concerned with the dimensions of grace. Bunyan sees his predicament as a fusion of the life of the soul and life in the world. In order to prove that 'the goodness and bounty of God towards me, may be the more advanced and magnified' (*GA*, 5), Bunyan will relate that he comes from a very low part of the social scale. He clearly felt deeply abject, shamed by deprivation into a profound sense of social inferiority, which he had interiorized to the extent of being awed and humbled in the presence of social superiors, be they aristocrats, gentry, or priests. It is significant that by 1666 he could write of this in terms of at least a moderately educated person, someone of the middling sort who understood the social scale very well,

---

[6] See Thomas N. Corns, 'Bunyan's *Grace Abounding* and the Dynamics of Restoration Nonconformity', in Neil Rhodes (ed.), *English Renaissance Prose: History, Language, and Politics* (Tempe, AZ: Medieval and Renaissance Texts and Studies, 1997), 259–70.

speaking of 'my pedigree, and manner of bringing up' (*GA*, 5). 'For my descent then, it was, as is well known by many, of a low and inconsiderable generation; my fathers house being of that rank that is meanest, and most despised of all the families in the Land' (*GA*, 5) is a famous sentence. Against it Bunyan notes that his real 'nobility' is to 'magnifie the Heavenly Majesty' (*GA*, 5).

The Bunyans had been Bedfordshire yeoman farmers and his immediate family had declined even from that standing, thereby sharpening the abjection. Nonetheless his parents were able to have him schooled in basic literacy and numeracy, though, as he confessed, 'I did soon loose that little I learned, even almost utterly' (*GA*, 5). As a young teenager, he was just ripe, as he describes it, to be 'captive to the devil' in a surfeit of unedifying 'cursing, swearing, lying and blaspheming the holy Name of God' (*GA*, 6). Sometimes Bunyan makes this version of himself sound almost like a Ranter, the religious contemporaries who used swearing to manifest their particular sense of holiness: 'there cursing and swearing, and playing the Mad-man' (*GA*, 11). Such a wholly 'natural' youth could carry on like this for many years, even as God, so Bunyan understands it, began to make his displeasure felt to the young man in terrifying nightmares. But the contents of these dream visions were of devils, so we might presume he then thought they were of demonic origin, or does Bunyan mean that God uses the devil always for his own, higher purposes and therefore Satan cannot win, except, of course, that he will finally have the damned in his kingdom of darkness?

We soon learn that Bunyan is urgently looking for signs that he will be saved, and this continues even after his conversion, for that is the only way that one might be able to learn that one is not damned. Bunyan's writing is ultimately full of assurance but it is also faithful to that famously central element of the Calvinism that infected his contemporaries: God has the power and the right to predestine someone to salvation or to damnation before they are born. It is not a matter of the individual's freedom of will. You could think you believed, and be known and acknowledged as a great 'professor', but still you might turn out to be damned: 'I was kept from considering that sin would damn me, what Religion soever I followed, unless I was found in Christ' (*GA*, 9). And if you know you are a sinner, and have no hope in the next life, you may as well continue to sin. Or to know sin, you have to sin and sin greatly, so that Bunyan's speaker commits at one point, from an orthodox Calvinist viewpoint, the Antinomian heresy:

> I found within me a great desire to take my fill of sin, still studdying what sin was set to be committed, that I might taste the sweetness of it; and I made as much haste as I could to fill my belly with its delicates, lest I should die before I had my desire. (*GA*, 11)

It is not a happy scenario. Later on, when well acquainted with a sense of assurance that came from a deep familiarity with the Bible, the speaker still records periods of severe doubt, including even the existence of God (*GA*, 31).

Indeed, when we read on we learn that the young Bunyan thought he was damned, and that he would burn in hell:

These things, I say, when I was but a childe, about nine or ten years old, did so distress my Soul, that then [...] I was often much cast down and afflicted in my mind therewith, yet could I not let go my sins: yea, I was so overcome with despair of Life and Heaven, that then I should often wish, either that there had been no Hell, or that I had been a Devil; supposing they were onely tormentors; that if it must needs be, that I indeed went thither, I might be rather a tormentor, then tormented my self. (*GA*, 6)

To be 'a Devil' was to avoid the torment, as the young Bunyan thought. He represents himself at this time as a very recognizable figure: a forward village youth—'the very ring-leader of all the Youth that kept me company, into all manner of vice and ungodliness' (*GA*, 7)—even to the extent of falling foul of the law as well as the higher law of eternal justice. The village gang leader was, so his later self judges, a kind of atheist as well as a hard drinker, so that he palpably recoiled from pious books and their readers. He claims even to have offered a conjuration against God:

Then I said unto God, Depart from me, for I desire not the knowledge of thy ways, Job 21. 14, 15. I was now void of all good consideration; Heaven and Hell were both out of sight and minde; and as for Saving and Damning, they were least in my thoughts. (*GA*, 7)

Note that past present construction 'I was now': a strong feature of the conversion narrative, and an important element in the free indirect discourse that would come with the novel. The sentence also contains a proverb, a predecessor of the modern 'out of sight, out of mind'.

Abjection in the eyes of God, or the need to make such a gesture of worthlessness, makes Bunyan's sense of sin huge, but he also says when he encountered sinfulness in others, especially when registered in disgusting behaviour, he was appalled. In other words, despite his protests to the contrary, he had a fairly normal view of acceptable behaviour, relatively uninflected by his religiosity.

Books, the Book, and Godliness

The issue of books becomes apparent in the eleventh paragraph where Bunyan discusses his marriage, which union you might think was more about books than wives. Both he and his wife were from poor families and had very few possessions—fewer than we would think would make life bearable. But her father was a Puritan and he left her two famous books, both of which passed through many editions, Arthur Dent's *The Plaine Mans Path-Way to Heaven* (1601) and Lewis Bayly's *The Practise of Pietie* (3rd edn, 1613) (*GA*, 8). It is from here that Bunyan began to have some connection with godly ways, these being standard works of piety for Puritans of all kinds. The Bunyans read them and John gained a sense of an obligation to religious duty, even if his God was not such a benevolent figure as we find in the pages of Arthur Dent. He started going to church 'twice a day, and that too with the foremost, and there should very devoutly both say and sing as others did; yet retaining my wicked life' (*GA*, 8–9). The 'wicked life' involved, as he later saw it, superstition and, in particular, the love of priestly authority. I used to think that this was part of Bunyan's social abjection, but now I think that Bunyan was awed by priestly authority because he wanted that authority. He presents it as an awing by and then a desire for sacerdotal authority: 'I could have layn down at their feet, and have been trampled upon by them; their Name, their Garb, and Work, did so intoxicate and bewitch me' (*GA*, 9). He claims that he swore, in the sense of using oaths, in order to have 'authority'. Class difference can incite the desire for the trappings of the other superior class.

Into the third edition Bunyan inserted the three paragraphs (129–31; *GA*, 40–1) that recall how, when feeling that his salvation was certain, he consulted a tattered copy of Luther's commentary on Galatians. He treated it as a conversion narrative, 'some ancient Godly man's Experience', and was delighted by its authenticity and how closely he thought it matched his own experience. Unlike most contemporary experimental discourse, where men wrote only of other men's experiences (that is, they 'faked it', so that the genre had become merely conventional, devoid of authenticity), Bunyan felt Luther wrote 'out of my heart', as if he were living in Bunyan's time, or was Bunyan, even though he lived over a hundred years previously. It was in Luther that Bunyan saw the specific point of Christ's role in man's salvation; he was, he said, surprised to find Luther condemning the 'law of Moses' as well as blasphemy and desperation, but he learned from it. Luther was talking about the difference between the 'letter' and the 'spirit' and for Bunyan this was a crucial moment.[7]

It was not reading, or conversation, or parental advice, that finally changed Bunyan, but preaching, in a sermon transmitting biblical authority:

> But one day, (amongst all the Sermons our Parson made) his subject was, to treat of the Sabbath day, and of the evil of breaking that, either with labour, sports, or otherwise: (now I was, notwithstanding my Religion, one that took much delight in all manner of vice, and especially that was the Day that I did solace my self therewith). Wherefore I fell in my conscience under his Sermon, thinking and believing that he made that Sermon on purpose to shew me my evil-doing. (*GA*, 9–10)

It is this moment that Bunyan claims as the point where he began properly to realize the guilt that must be associated with sin, and that it would require a massive rejection of what he understood to be former pleasures, a radical reorientation of the self. Even before dinner that day, the impact of the sermon began to wear off and by the end of the meal he had forgotten it, the instance of food nicely and implicitly representing the

---

[7] See Vera J. Camden, '"Most Fit for a Wounded Conscience": The Place of Luther's "Commentary on Galatians" in *Grace Abounding*', *Renaissance Quarterly*, 50 (1997), 819–49.

hold of natural over spiritual man. But the guilty awareness of always-present sin returns through a process of psychological transformation: a traumatic sense of division between a tortured self suffering in the present and a formerly happy yet sinful self. Famously, this awareness in Bunyan is recorded in a game of 'cat':[8]

> [A]s I was in the midst of a game at Cat, and having struck it one blow from the hole; just as I was about to strike it the second time, a voice did suddenly dart from Heaven into my Soul, which said, *Wilt thou leave thy sins, and go to Heaven? or have thy sins, and go to Hell?* At this I was put to an exceeding maze; wherefore leaving my Cat upon the ground, I looked up to Heaven, and was as if I had with the eyes of my understanding, seen the Lord Jesus looking down upon me, as being very hotly displeased with me, and as if he did severely threaten me with some grievous punishment for these, and other my ungodly practices. (*GA*, 10)

Having heard the voice of God in the form of the Bible quoted and interpreted in the sermon, Bunyan is now shattered by a split consciousness as a surely related voice 'did suddenly dart from Heaven into my Soul'. As Bunyan construes the moment, Jesus has looked down upon him in anger and has spoken. So begins the great string of anxiety in the text, intimating that this moment had come far too late: '*it was now too late for me to look after Heaven; for Christ would not forgive me, nor pardon my transgressions*' (*GA*, 10).

Still, the speaker, after reforming his life subsequent to this experience through an outward religious conformity, claims he did not know Christ even though he presented himself as one of the godly. Perhaps he would have regarded himself as one of the 'formal' Christians, who laid too much store in the external dimensions of worship. But when he met the group of women in Bedford, he realized they had access to something higher and were in a state of joy achieved by a transformed inner state:

> Upon a day, the good Providence of God did cast me to *Bedford*, to work on my calling; and in one of the streets of that town, I came where there was three or four poor women sitting at a door in the Sun, and talking about the things of God; and being now willing to hear them discourse, I drew near to hear what they said; for I was now a brisk talker also my self in the matters of Religion: but now I may say, *I heard, but I understood not*; for they were far above out of my reach, for their talk was about a new birth, the work of God on their hearts, also how they were convinced of their miserable state by nature: they talked how God had visited their souls with his love in the Lord Jesus, and with what words and promises they had been refreshed, comforted, and supported against the temptations of the Devil. (*GA*, 14)

---

[8] Cat, short for tipcat, was 'A game in which the wooden cat or tip-cat is struck or "tipped" at one end with a stick so as to spring up, and then knocked to a distance by the same player' ('tipcat', *OED* n²; 'cat' n¹ 10b).

This looks very much like a part of the Bedford church, or that congregation in the making. They used Scripture language, there was 'such appearance of grace in all they said', so that the speaker feels he has 'found a new world' (*GA*, 15). Although he again returned to his regular ways, he could not go for long without joining these people, and discovered that he had an openness ('a very great softness and tenderness of heart' (*GA*, 15)) that enabled him to reflect on the Scriptures they discussed.

The Scripture now answers the deprivations of sin, and the anxiety that the believer has manifested about it. It is significant that what Bunyan represents as a medicinal instrument, a salve, at this point is not the Bible but the mind, cast as a horseleech, incessantly sucking the blood of the vein of the horse. Bleeding was a regular part of early modern medicine but the urgency contained in the image is still, to a modern viewpoint, rather alarming, more as we imagine today the voice of a demanding child: 'my mind was now so turned, that it lay like a Horseleach at the vein, still crying out, *Give, give*; Prov. 30. 15. Yea, it was so fixed on Eternity' (*GA*, 15). This begins the further and agonizing search for whether Bunyan's speaker has faith, but something significant has changed: he has the ability to argue with the voice of Satan. This is made to seem part and parcel of a logic that belongs both to the speaker and to Providence so that he reasons himself away from temptations even if he does not quite understand why at the time:

> One day as I was betwixt *Elstow* and *Bedford*, the Temptation was hot upon me to try if I had Faith by doing of some miracle; which miracle at that time was this, I must say to the puddles that were in the horse pads, *Be dry*; and to the dry places, *Be you the puddles*: and truly, one time I was a going to say so indeed; but just as I was about to speak, this thought came into my minde, *But go under yonder Hedge, and pray first, that God would make you able*: but when I had concluded to pray, this came hot upon me, That if I prayed and came again and tried to do it, and yet did nothing notwithstanding, then besure I had no Faith, but was a Cast-away and lost: Nay, thought I, if it be so, I will never try yet, but will stay a little longer. (*GA*, 18–19)

It is a confession of a state of ignorance that is likened to his inability to 'know how to begin and accomplish that rare and curious piece of Art' (*GA*, 18), which is another definition of superior human accomplishment, along with nobility and priesthood. And yet earlier Bunyan has delivered a piece of art that is also entirely spontaneous: the voice that interrupts during the game of 'cat' leaves him in a 'maze', a remarkable pun, referring both to a state of amazement and to an apt description of the network of indecipherable pathways that the speaker finds himself in as time passes.

Another voice tells Bunyan to read the Bible from end to end, and this is done, with no evidence of any trusting believer who was betrayed being found. It is the description of the Bible here that remains so arresting: 'it was so fresh, and with such strength and comfort on my spirit, that I was as if it talked with me' (*GA*, 21). Ever for finding doubts about the state of his own salvation, he internalizes the Bible in his memory with such familiarity that it appears to burst into consciousness often just at the right time:

> But when I had been long vexed with this fear, and was scarce able to take one step more, just about the same place where I received my other encouragement, these words broke in upon my mind, *Compell them to come in, that my house may be filled, and yet there is roome*, Luke 14. 22, 23. These words, but especially them, *And yet there is roome*, were sweet words to me; for, truly, I thought that by them I saw that there was place enough in Heaven for me, and moreover, that when the Lord Jesus did speak these words, he then did think of me. (*GA*, 22–3)

Bunyan's experience and the narrative in which it is captured are like an elastic band: he seems to move further away from a sense of assurance only to have the presence of Scripture pull him back. Even then 'certainty' comes with quotations accompanied by a simile: 'I was as if'. The periods of doubt lasted for as long as a year, and even to the extent of fearing that he had committed the unpardonable sin of blaspheming against the Holy Ghost. Bunyan's claim is that biblical texts were sent to him as warnings, even though he did not at the time understand this. These textual visitations were sometimes personified:

> [A]bout a week or fortnight after this, I was much followed by this Scripture, *Simon, Simon, behold, Satan hath desired to have you*, Luk. 22.31. And sometimes it would sound so loud within me, yea, and as it were call so strongly after me, that once above all the rest, I turned my head over my shoulder, thinking verily that some man had behind me called to me, being at a great distance. (*GA*, 30)

No less a physical incarnation is Satan, who also comes to Bunyan with temptations. Somehow, according to his testimony, Bunyan was able to keep calling for God's help.

To Bunyan's imagination Scripture words trigger a visual representation of life. Today we would call this cinematic, and Bunyan thinks of it as a visually perceivable narrative: 'me thought I was as if I had seen him born, as if I had seen him grow up, as if I had seen him walk thorow this world' (*GA*, 38). This vividness is coupled with sensitivity to a notion of the acceleration of lived awareness of experience. When things get tough, the motion of life speeds up:

> [O]ne morning, as I did lie in my Bed, I was, as at other times, most fiercely assaulted with this temptation, to *sell and part with Christ*; the wicked suggestion still running in my mind, *Sell him, sell him, sell him, sell him*, as fast as a man could speak; against which also in my mind, as at other times I answered, No, no, not for thousands, thousands, thousands, at least twenty times together; but at last, after much striving even until I was almost out of breath, I felt this thought pass through my heart, *Let him go if he will!* and I thought also that I felt my heart freely consent thereto. Oh, the diligence of Satan! Oh, the desperateness of mans heart! [...] Now was the battel won, and down I fell, as a Bird that is shot from the top of a Tree. (*GA*, 43)

Even while texts of Scripture and the words of the devil are being agonizingly parsed, there is often a sense of the present physical world: Bunyan is in inner turmoil but he is sitting on this or that bench, by this or that hedge. The world of rural and provincial Bedfordshire becomes the source for a series of sharply defined images, often violent in nature:

> I did liken my self in this condition unto the case of some Child that was fallen into a Mill-pit, who though it could make some shift to scrable and spraul in the water, yet because it could find neither hold for hand nor foot, therefore at last it must die in that condition. (*GA*, 62)

Drowning comes more than once: 'for now, though I could not suck that comfort and sweetness from the Promise, as I had done at other times, yet, like to a man asinking, I should catch at all I saw: formerly I thought I might not meddle with the Promise, unless I felt its comfort' (*GA*, 77). It is but a small step to Bunyan's making of allegory, and as Michael Davies shows, it is present too in Bunyan's controversial and theological writing.[9]

Eventually the life story leads to a very proper Protestant statement of Christ's role in human redemption. The text from Hebrews 13:8 leads Bunyan to see Christ's role through his sacrifice in making possible human righteousness and sanctification before God. This would be a plain theological statement were it not for the force of joy in both the tone and rhythm of a sentence cast in a typically arresting image, sourced once again from Bunyan's sense of social difference:

> 'Twas glorious to me to see his exaltation, and the worth and prevalencie of all his benefits, and that because of this; Now I could look from my self to him, and should reckon that all those Graces of God that now were green in me, were yet but like those crack'd-Groats and Four-pence-half-pennies that rich men carry in their Purses, when their Gold is in their Trunks at home: O I saw my Gold was in my Trunk at home! In Christ my Lord and Saviour! (*GA*, 73)

In this way, Jesus is the 'common or publick person, in whom all the whole Body of his Elect are always to be considered and reckoned' (*GA*, 73). Bunyan also identifies the reason for the torment he experiences after his conversion, first, in his failure to pray for God's help with future temptations. That seems formal too, but his second reason is both experimental and theological at once. When pleading that his pregnant wife might be relieved of pain, he couched his prayer conditionally: '*Lord, if thou wilt now remove this sad affliction from my Wife, and cause that she be troubled no more therewith this night* [. . .] *then I shall know that thou canst discern the most secret thoughts of the heart*' (*GA*, 75). The 'if' is an importunate challenge of God's power and Bunyan imagines that he was then punished for his lack of trust (*GA*, 76).

---

[9] Michael Davies, *Graceful Reading: Theology and Narrative in the Works of John Bunyan* (Oxford: Oxford University Press, 2002), 166–70.

Vocation

The final section of *Grace Abounding* is a record of Bunyan's call to the ministry. Strictly speaking, it is outside of the conversion narrative's concerns, and is signalled as a separate section. It maps onto *The Pilgrim's Progress, Part II* (1684). Bunyan found that although according to his testimony he was very inexperienced and halting in speech, he could move fellow believers when they asked him to address them. He found too that he was moved to preach. Preaching is a retransmission of the experimental, and Bunyan claims that it was crucial to begin by reminding his congregation of their sin: 'I preached what I felt, what I smartingly did feel, even that under which my poor Soul did groan and tremble to astonishment' (*GA*, 85). The guilt made him tremble as he entered the pulpit and returned as soon as he finished preaching. But after preaching union with Christ for five years, Bunyan was arrested and imprisoned. He drew attention to himself with his efficacy, thereby 'the Doctors and Priests of the Countrey' (*GA*, 87) preached or published against him. He must have been a sitting target. He also recognizes that preaching is an art, although typically he denies his own powers as preacher-artist in order to point up Jesus as the true player of Bunyan, who is merely 'the Cymbal':

> Just thus I saw it was and will be with them who have Gifts, but want saving-Grace; they are in the hand of Christ, as the Cymbal in the hand of *David*; and as *David* could, with the Cymbal make that mirth in the service of God, as to elevate the hearts of the Worshippers; so Christ can use these gifted men, as with them to affect the Souls of his People in his Church, yet when he hath done all hang them by, as lifeless, though sounding *Cymbals*. (*GA*, 91)

Yet even gifted preaching and great skill with words are not as important as a simple modicum of faith: 'a little Grace, a little Love, a little of the true Fear of God' (*GA*, 91).

This gives a humble but reassuring message, as we might expect from a ministerial statement. The tone changes, however, when we enter the brief captivity narrative at the very end. During five and a half years of imprisonment, the fears and doubts come after Bunyan with no less intensity, unsurprisingly. Once isolated from his pastoral role, the great fear that he will simply die privately without witness (and hence not be counted a martyr or even part of any fellowship) looms large. Even though he had prepared himself for this deprivation, had found Scriptures to support him, and had imaginatively confronted the fact that he would become as dead to his familiar world, family, and friends, this great fear tormented him. Being parted from his family was 'as the pulling the flesh from my bones' (*GA*, 98) but there was a Scripture to rely on, as there was at the thought that he might be treated with violence. Thinking early in his imprisonment that he might be hanged changes from a literal fear to a large figurative concern with the condition in which he would die alone:

> I thought with my self, that in the condition I now was in, I was not fit to die, neither indeed did think I could if I should be called to it: besides, I thought with myself, if I should make a scrabling shift to clamber up the Ladder, yet I should either with quaking or other symptoms of faintings, give occasion to the enemy to reproach the way of God and his People, for their timerousness: this therefore lay with great trouble upon me, for methought I was ashamed to die with a pale face, and tottering knees, for such a Cause as this. (*GA*, 100)

The reassurance that arrives from Psalm 44:12 does not quite alleviate the unsettledness of perpetual doubt after every certainty reached, and the very image of the gallows is simply most gloomily arresting: the common man's icon of a harsh fate at the hands of a brutal and uncaring ruling elite.

It is perhaps no surprise, then, that *Grace Abounding*'s brief six-point conclusion is not all that joyous, but addresses the toughness required of the faithful: never to question the truth of the New Testament; to remember that a sense of the presence of God, including from the Bible, might disappear as quickly as it appears; to recognize that the human spirit is beset with doubts of God's existence, rejections of Christ's love, inadequate prayer; to beware of a readiness to complain without appreciating what one has; and to know that original sin will taint all human action, however well intentioned. It is a further shock still to find that in consequence God exhorts his faithful to endure psychological stress in acknowledging their ongoing self-abhorrence and lack of trustworthiness, and to learn too that inherent righteousness, though God-given, is insufficient, meaning that Jesus must not merely be turned to, he must be absolutely 'fled' to. *Grace Abounding* concludes, then, where *The Pilgrim's Progress, Part I* begins—with Christian fleeing down the road as fast as he can from his wife, children, and neighbours in order to find the wicket gate and the way to grace. The call to believe exacted a high price.

Grace Abounding is remarkable for the intensity and anxiety with which it presents the making of a Nonconformist Puritan believer and minister. Few who have read it will forget the incessant fear of inadequacy, failure, and punishment, even as assurance is also delivered, incrementally and finally. The reason for this is that as a narrative it belongs to a genre, the conversion narrative, that privileged the authentic, and hence the unconventional: that which 'could not be made up'. At the same time, and even though published conversion narratives themselves were often editorially fashioned, Bunyan wanted to make his conversion narrative serve a more than experimental context. He wanted it to function as a sermon, to be his preached word when, through imprisonment, he could not preach. In this context, he worked hard, and through successive editions, to make the text as rhetorically effective as possible without losing its sincerity. He was also determined to make it theologically accurate, consistent with his beliefs as he understood them, reconciling experience with theology. In these goals, in the third as well as in the first edition, he was eminently successful. *Grace Abounding* is one of those books you cannot put down, and without it, there could have been no *Pilgrim's Progress*.

SUGGESTED READING

Branch, Lori, *Rituals of Spontaneity: Sentiment and Secularism from Free Prayer to Wordsworth* (Waco, TX: Baylor University Press, 2006), ch. 2.

Davies, Michael, *Graceful Reading: Theology and Narrative in the Works of John Bunyan* (Oxford: Oxford University Press, 2002), chs 2 and 3.

Luxon, Thomas, *Literal Figures: Puritan Allegory and the Reformation Crisis in Representation* (Chicago: University of Chicago Press, 1995).

Lynch, Beth, *John Bunyan and the Language of Conviction* (Cambridge: D. S. Brewer, 2004), 64–76.

Lynch, Kathleen, *Protestant Autobiography in the Seventeenth-Century Anglophone World* (Oxford and New York: Oxford University Press, 2012), ch. 4.

Newey, Vincent, '"With the eyes of my understanding": Bunyan, Experience and Acts of Interpretation', in N. H. Keeble (ed.), *John Bunyan: Conventicle and Parnassus* (Oxford: Clarendon Press, 1988), 189–216.

Stachniewski, John, *The Persecutory Imagination: English Puritanism and the Literature of Religious Despair* (Oxford: Clarendon Press, 1991), ch. 3.

Ward, Graham, 'To Be a Reader: Bunyan's Struggle with the Language of Scripture in *Grace Abounding to the Chief of Sinners*', *Literature and Theology*, 4 (1990), 29–49.

CHAPTER 13

'THE DESIRED COUNTREY'

Bunyan's Writings on the Church in the 1670s

KEN SIMPSON

SINCE the early 1990s, historians have rewritten the Restoration, and the 1670s in particular, as a period of crisis in which 'instability was the norm'.[1] While foreign policy involving Charles II's French alliances and a third Dutch war, constitutional conflicts between the Crown and Parliament over succession and prerogative, political strife over the king's 'supply', and the emergence of entrenched parties all contributed to this decade of destabilization, religious diversity and the toleration of 'tender consciences' proved to be the most intractable and recurrent source of conflict. Gary De Krey argues that 'the debate about liberty of conscience, a debate that had been central to the English revolution' emerged from 1667–72 as the first of a series of crises of religious ideology, but, as he also suggests, the crisis of toleration for Nonconformists predates the 1670s and also underlies the Exclusion Crisis of 1679–81.[2]

Richard Greaves also subscribes to the 'seismographic' model of Restoration historiography and like De Krey attributes to the 'debate about liberty of conscience' most of the crises that disrupted the Restoration landscape, even though in his account the number of crises grows from three to five: in 1658–64, 1667–73, 1678–83, 1685, and 1689.[3] Greaves proves that, in addition to his choice to remain in prison rather than conform to the practices of the Church of England prescribed by law, Bunyan was an active participant

---

[1] Richard L. Greaves, 'Great Scott! The Restoration in Turmoil, or, Restoration Crises and the Emergence of Party', *Albion*, 25 (1993), 605–18 (605). For a summary of the historiography, see Tim Harris, 'Introduction: Revising the Restoration', in Tim Harris, Paul Seaward, and Mark Goldie (eds.), *The Politics of Religion in Restoration England* (Oxford: Blackwell, 1990), 1–28.

[2] Gary S. De Krey, 'Rethinking the Restoration: Dissenting Cases for Conscience, 1667–1672', *The Historical Journal*, 38 (1995), 53–83 (53); Gary S. De Krey, 'Reformation in the Restoration Crisis, 1679–1682', in Richard Strier and Donna Hamilton (eds.), *Religion, Literature, and Politics in Post-Reformation England* (Cambridge: Cambridge University Press, 1996), 231–52 (231).

[3] Greaves, 'Great Scott!', 605.

in the toleration debates in *The Pilgrim's Progress*.⁴ Although he largely ignores Bunyan's prose of the 1670s, Greaves successfully answers De Krey's challenge to contextualize Bunyan's works within the seismographic convulsions of the Restoration caused by the failure to accommodate or comprehend Nonconformists within the state church or to tolerate or indulge them outside of it.⁵

By accepting the political terms of the toleration debate, however, Greaves, like De Krey, tells only half the story of the struggle of Bunyan and the gathered church of Bedford to worship with liberty of conscience. There is, of course, no doubt that Bunyan and other members of his church, like Nonconformists elsewhere in the country, suffered persecution under the laws governing religious practice during the Restoration, and the personal, professional, and material loss felt by Nonconformists should not be underestimated. Bunyan himself was arrested in November 1660 and spent much of the next twelve years in prison for violating the Elizabethan Act to Retain the Queen Majesty's Subjects in their Due Obedience (35 Eliz., c.1, 1593). After the Declaration of Indulgence was cancelled in 1673, he faced new forms of persecution, from having his licence to preach revoked and a warrant for his arrest issued to being forced into hiding and imprisoned on at least two occasions during the 1670s.⁶ *A True and Impartial Narrative of some Illegal and Arbitrary Proceedings […] against Several Innocent and Peaceable Nonconformists in and near the Town of Bedford* (1670) records the actions taken against Bunyan's church under the second Conventicle Act (22 Car. II, c.1, 1670), in which those meeting at John Fenne's house for 'Religious Exercise' were fined and the preacher, Nehemiah Cox, imprisoned 'for words he spoke against the Church of England'.⁷ This narrative of persecution and resilience, however, is only half the story because it does not tell us *why* Bunyan and his church resisted assimilation by the Church of England in favour of toleration and liberty of conscience.

To answer this question it is necessary to acknowledge that for Bunyan the universal, invisible, triumphant church of everlasting glory to which gathered saints were predestined was more important—because it was the goal of Christian life—than the particular, visible church on Earth: the militant body of believers, that is, which struggled against anti-Christian forces in the world, including anti-tolerationists in Restoration England. The full title of Bunyan's most famous work makes clear the distinction between the visible, militant church in its state of struggle and the invisible, triumphant church in its state of glory. Christian's 'dangerous journey', representative of the imperfect 'progress' of the militant church in its temporal, horizontal dimension, occurs in 'this world', while 'the Desired Countrey', or the invisible church in its eternal, vertical

---

⁴ Richard L. Greaves, '"Let Truth Be Free": John Bunyan and the Restoration Crisis of 1667–1673', *Albion*, 28 (1996), 587–605 (590, 599–605).

⁵ De Krey, 'Rethinking the Restoration', 83.

⁶ Greaves, *Glimpses*, 131–32, 313–14, 341–42, 218. I follow Greaves for the dating of Bunyan's works (637–41).

⁷ *A True and Impartial Narrative* (1670), A2.

dimension, occurs in the world 'which is to come' (*PP*, facing xxxvi). If faith is the shape of desire fulfilled, then the shape of Bunyan's faith is the imagined community of the invisible church, 'the Desired Countrey' described in the closing scenes of both parts of *The Pilgrim's Progress*.

For Bunyan, the visible church refers to a particular congregation or communion of saints that gathers voluntarily to worship according to Scripture. Only those who publicly profess the grace of faith initiated by the Holy Spirit—the 'visible saints by calling'—are members, distinguishing the gathered, Independent church from the Church of England, whose members are joined by law, sacramental grace, and Scripture guided by tradition. The particular, visible church, such as the one in Bedford that Bunyan was called to lead in 1671 (*CB*, 71), is in a militant condition of struggle not only because of its own imperfections—some members profess faith but do not actually possess it, while others fail to live up to moral standards that properly reflect the true faith represented in the New Testament—but also in relation to the state and other visible churches, whether Protestant or Catholic. This is the feature of the church that concerns De Krey and other historians of the Restoration Crisis and to which Bunyan devoted so much of his life and work. The visible church lacks purpose without the invisible church, however, since only its members—the elect known only to God—participate in the church's triumphant state at the end of time. Worship in a scripturally faithful gathered church is required, but it is not a guarantee of election and of invisible church membership.

The particular, visible church of gathered saints, then, is not coterminous with the universal, invisible church, but following Scripture with the guidance of the Holy Spirit, separating from the national church, and placing authority for discipline, worship, and governance in the congregation and its leaders, are signs of membership in the invisible, triumphant church. The invisible church corresponds in some ways to what Benedict Anderson refers to as the imagined community in the development of nationalism: a community that while not empirically observable or simultaneously present makes concrete action—in this case, participation in the visible church—possible and meaningful in the face of persecution and intolerance.[8] As much as Bunyan and his church lived in a material present—resisting the Church of England, maintaining discipline among themselves, worshipping and teaching according to Scripture, supporting other Independent churches, and engaging in debate—they also lived proleptically, anticipating and imagining in the present a future community in God's presence. Bunyan rarely lost sight of what he considered 'the great and chief design of God':

> Remember Man, if the grace of God hath taken hold of thy Soul, thou art a Man of another World, and indeed, a Subject of another and more noble Kingdom, the

---

[8] Benedict Anderson, *Imagined Communities*, 2nd edn (London and New York: Verso, 2006), 6–7, 12–18, 22–46.

Kingdom of God which is the Kingdom of the Gospel, of grace, of faith and righteousness, and the Kingdom of Heaven hereafter. (*MW*, 12: 371)

The unstable relationship between the visible and invisible church in Bunyan's thought and practice is evident in almost everything he wrote in the 1670s, including *The Pilgrim's Progress*. Even though invisible church membership was ultimately known only by God, good standing in a gathered church of visible saints was a sign of election, and this led to the need to defend the congregation from challenges to the principle upon which the Bedford church, under John Gifford's leadership, and later Bunyan's, was founded: 'that union with Christ is the foundation of all saintes' communion, and not any ordinances of Christ, or any judgement or opinion about externalls', whether 'baptisme, laying on of hands, anoynting with oyle', or the singing of 'psalmes' (*CB*, 19). Justification by faith, based on the careful examination of conscience and the sincere search of Scripture, might have underpinned Bunyan's defence of toleration and sustained the church during persecution, but it also led to the excommunication of members who failed to live up to the standard of visible sainthood and the condemnation of those Christians whose doctrine was contrary to 'union with Christ'.

The distinction between things necessary for salvation, such as belief in the 'union with Christ', and those things indifferent to salvation, such as the 'ordinances' and 'externals' identified by Gifford in a valedictory letter to his congregation, written just before his death in 1655 and subsequently copied into the Bedford Church Book (*CB*, 18–21), underlies the church's doctrine of toleration and church unity, but it was a distinction easier to defend in theory than practice since many Nonconformists also believed that God revealed in the Bible specific worship and discipline practices. On the grounds of theological and doctrinal essentials Bunyan could justify the exclusion of Catholics, Anglicans, and Quakers from the invisible church and still claim he should be free to worship in a visible church according to conscience without being forced to join the state church or suffer violence, imprisonment, exile, fines, or loss of property for failing to do so. At the same time, tolerance should be extended to other Protestants who differed in the use of 'ordinances', sacraments, or 'externals', but who were united in doctrine and 'the truth of the worke of grace in their heartes' (*CB*, 24). With other senior brethren, Bunyan was appointed by the church in September 1658 to find ways towards the 'continuing of unity and preventing of differences among the congregations [...] and ourselves', and 'to consider of some things that may conduce to love and unity amongst us all' (*CB*, 31). While the distinction between things necessary for and things indifferent to salvation informed the limits of toleration and church unity, it also determined invisible church membership since some details of worship, government, and discipline in the visible church were prescribed in Scripture, turning some 'externals' (such as baptism) into essentials while others could be tolerated and considered indifferent to salvation.

Doctrinal Works: The Essentials of Faith

Bunyan's first and most important doctrinal and theological work of the 1670s, *A Confession of my Faith, and A Reason of my Practice* (1672), inscribes these tensions between essentials and externals in and among the visible churches and between the flawed earthly church and the glorified elect community. Indeed, the tract attempts to negotiate conflicts left undeveloped in Gifford's original letter to the Bedford church and points forward to theological and pastoral issues that Bunyan would return to throughout the decade. Probably written in late 1671, while Bunyan was imprisoned under the second Conventicle Act, and published before the Declaration of Indulgence (15 March 1672), the tract is evidence of Bunyan's call for toleration of Nonconformists by Anglican authorities, even as he excludes his persecutors from the invisible church, and for toleration among Nonconformists, especially those who excluded visible saints because they did not practise adult baptism as a necessary ritual of church membership.[9]

In the tract's prefatory letter, Bunyan asserts that he incites neither 'heresie' nor 'rebellion' and remains 'an obedient Subject', even after nearly twelve years of imprisonment. Nevertheless, he is compelled to remain in prison rather than ignore his conscience and abandon his 'faith and principles' since they are based on 'the word of God alone' (*MW*, 4: 135–36). Part of the tract, especially the section, 'Of Magistracy', is addressed to Anglican authorities to assure them that toleration and liberty of conscience will not lead to disorder in the state or church.[10] At the same time, he briefly outlines doctrines such as the justification of sinners by the imputation of Christ's righteousness and rejects communion with the 'open prophane, and ungodly', despite its common practice in Anglican parishes, because it 'polluteth [God's] ordinances [...] prophaneth his holiness [...] defileth his people; and provoketh the Lord to severe, and terrible judgments' (*MW*, 4: 140–45, 159).

Over half of the tract presents a defence of the Bedford church's open-communion principles and its willingness to admit visible saints even if they have not been baptized as part of the admission process. But it also addresses practical matters. Bunyan might have thought it necessary to outline his principles in response to his calling to the ministry by the congregation on 21 December 1671 (*CB*, 71).[11] 'A brief confession of faith' to which all members could give 'their unfeigned consent' was requested by the congregation on 25 June 1672 (*CB*, 73), even though the proposal seems to have

---

[9] Greaves, *Glimpses*, 271–72.

[10] See De Krey, 'Rethinking the Restoration', 56–60. Note, however, that Bunyan's argument for toleration is not political but ecclesiological, and doesn't fit any of the four categories of tolerationist thought described by De Krey.

[11] Michael Davies, 'When was Bunyan Elected Pastor? Fixing a Date in the Bedford Church Book', *BS*, 18 (2014), 7–41 (29).

been tabled due to Bunyan's absence on 29 August 1672 (*CB*, 74). As he complains in *Differences in Judgment about Water-Baptism, No Bar to Communion* (1673), leaders of closed-communion Baptist churches had recently revived earlier 'assaults' on Bunyan and other members to leave the Bedford church, so Bunyan set out 'to settle the Brethren, and to arm them against the attempts' (*MW*, 4: 193, 196–97, 247). The admission of members of the Bedford church to other churches became an increasing problem as they either ignored the church's recommendation to join other open-communion churches, or at least those tolerant of the practice (such as the congregations led by Cokayne, Simpson, Jessey, Rogers, Griffith, Palmer, or Owen in London). Others were turned away from closed-communion churches perhaps because of the Bedford church's position on baptism (*CB*, 31, 34, 66, 79, 80).[12] Despite the measured tone of most of the *Confession*, then, Bunyan was interceding in a highly charged practical and theological controversy that had clear implications for the 'eternall condition' (*CB*, 66) of his church's members.

Observing the distinction between essentials of faith and 'externals' that were 'things indifferent' to salvation, Bunyan divides his work between the confession of faith and his 'practice in worship', which he assumes should be tolerated as long as it is based on Scripture (*MW*, 4: 137–53, 153–87). The confession unfolds, with logical simplicity, the theological implications of the biblical representation of God's transcendent sovereignty and human sinfulness. Since human beings are incapable of justifying themselves before God and acquiring righteousness due to original and specific sin, they are utterly and completely dependent on faith in God's offer of free grace in Christ's sacrifice and on Christ's imputation, or symbolic transfer, of justifying righteousness to human beings. Saving faith itself is a result of God's calling, since faith arising from human nature would be flawed, and those who acquire this faith have been appointed to do so 'before the foundation of the world' (*MW*, 4: 145).

Bunyan's worship follows as closely as possible his belief in salvation by faith in the free gift of grace enacted in Christ's crucifixion and resurrection. Since 'heaven and eternal happiness' are dependent on this doctrine alone and since membership in the invisible church, or election, is a mystery 'and known to none but God', church admission must be based on the visible signs of grace and conversion, which consist in a declaration of faith to the church, repentance, and 'holyness of life' rather than the performance of rituals such as baptism, which 'are not the fundamentals of our Christianity' (*MW*, 4: 175, 164, 154, 160). Besides, argues Bunyan, baptism as an initiating ordinance of visible church membership is not scriptural in typological or historical readings, even though, like the Lord's Supper, it is 'of excellent use to the Church' in representing 'the death, and resurrection of Christ' (*MW*, 4: 160). Rejecting visible saints for not conforming to externals also confuses and weakens other members, sows disunity rather than love, emphasizes carnal divisiveness rather than gospel spirituality, and degrades the church in the eyes of those not yet converted (*MW*, 4: 181, 178, 177, 179–80, 186).

---

[12] See T. L. Underwood, 'Introduction', in *MW*, 4: xvii–lv (xxviii–xxix).

Perhaps anticipating how the 'brethren of the Baptized way' will respond, in this section of the treatise Bunyan chooses a dialogue format in which he imagines his opponents posing questions to which he responds. The tone becomes accusatory and severe at times, lecturing his opponents that 'Tis possible to commit Idolatry, even with Gods own appointments' and that 'Sathan abuseth it [baptism], and wrenched [. . .] out of its place [. . .] that which was ordained of God for the edification of believers' (*MW*, 4: 160, 181). The brethren of 'the Baptized way' provide a 'Prop to Antichrist' (*MW*, 4: 183) when they demand rigid conformity to their forms of worship, rather than recognizing the law of love among those who acknowledge the fundamentals of faith in every other way.

Polemical Works: The Baptism Controversy

The opposition anticipated by Bunyan in *A Confession of my Faith* came in the form of two polemical works aimed directly at his defence of the Bedford church's practice of welcoming visible saints to worship regardless of baptism: Thomas Paul's *Some Serious Reflections on that Part of Mr. Bunion's Confession of Faith: Touching Church Communion with Unbaptized Persons* (1673) and John Denne's *Truth Outweighing Error* (1673).[13] The occasional truculence directed towards closed-communion Baptists in *A Confession of my Faith* is replaced by consistently pointed, methodical animadversions in *Differences in Judgment about Water-Baptism, No Bar to Communion*, which targets Paul's *Some Serious Reflections*. After defending both himself against personal attacks about his 'low descent' and his church against aggressive proselytizing by 'the rigid Brethren' who exclude 'visible saints' on the grounds that baptism is an initiating ordinance (*MW*, 4: 195–98), Bunyan refutes Paul's ten objections to his position, presents fourteen objections of his own to Paul's arguments, answers specific questions raised by Paul, and concludes by citing a work by Henry Jessey, a revered Nonconformist of the previous generation, that supports his position.

Bunyan argues that his opponents should tolerate those practices in worship that are based on Scripture, as long as the 'essentials'—that members show evidence of conversion and continue to manifest holiness of life—are present. Love, repeats Bunyan, should be observed in matters of conscience when fellow Nonconformists have searched the Scriptures only to arrive at forms of worship that differ from those of others. To do otherwise is to mistake the sign or the external nature of a practice such as baptism for what the sign signifies, and thereby to violate Jesus's central teaching. As moderate as this may sound, however, he makes it clear that proper worship in this world is not an indifferent matter and will have some influence on admission to the invisible church.

---

[13] See Greaves, *Glimpses*, 292–93.

'*Rigid* and Church-disquieting-Principles are not fit for any Age and state of the Church' (*MW*, 4: 195), he asserts, and the 'harsh, and unchristian surmises' of his opponents will be resolved on Judgement Day (*MW*, 4: 227).

Peaceable Principles and True (1674), Bunyan's last controversial work on 'externals', rehearses arguments already outlined in his previous works on baptism. He continues to present himself as an irenic moderate, claiming the title 'Christian' rather than one of the 'Factious Titles' adopted by '*Anabaptists, Independents, Presbyterians*, or the like' (*MW*, 4: 270), and often alluding to the unfair or misinformed attacks of William Kiffin, Thomas Paul, John Denne, and Henry Danvers to maintain this persona. At the same time, his conviction that what is prescribed in Scripture for the church does affect eternal life and, therefore, is not open to toleration emerges in two passages that reveal the fault lines on which his ecclesiology is built. In the first passage he dismantles the argument for toleration and liberty of conscience advanced by Thomas Paul, who claims Baptists are 'for liberty for all according to their light' but forbid communion with anyone who, 'abiding by his own light', does not agree that baptism is a rite of church membership (*MW*, 4: 272). Bunyan does not admit, of course, that the same argument could be made against him.

More importantly, the second passage confirms the link between the church and Bunyan's view of toleration. In the process of retracting his claim that baptism is an initiating ordinance for the particular church, Paul, according to Bunyan, never denies that it makes 'a Believer a member of the universal, orderly, Church-visible', revealing his opponent's confusion about the nature of the church and the role of free conscience. Baptism could never initiate someone into the universal and visible church at the same time, Bunyan argues, since the universal church includes 'that vast Body already in Heaven, and a great part as yet (perhaps) unborn' which 'remains always to the best mans eye invisible', the '(perhaps)' revealing the gap in knowledge that must separate the invisible, universal church from the visible, particular one. What the writer implies, Bunyan suggests, is that his own church is the universal church, and baptism is required to enter it; therefore, it should be required of everyone. Even if we accept Paul's 'unheard-of fictitious Church', those who are visible saints become visible members of Christ's body prior to being baptized, confirming Bunyan's view that baptism 'neither makes him a Member, nor visible Member, of the Body of Jesus Christ' (*MW*, 4: 273, 274).

As these examples from *Peaceable Principles and True* show, the heat of the baptism controversy refined Bunyan's thinking about the church, even if contradictions in the practice of toleration, originating in the conflict between things essential for eternal life in the invisible church and things indifferent in the visible one, never disappeared. What began as a pastoral initiative in *A Confession of my Faith, and A Reason of my Practice* 'to present to publick view the *warrantableness* of our Holy-Communion, and the *unreasonableness* of their [the closed-communion Baptists] seeking to break us to pieces' (*MW*, 4: 286) ended with the two parties agreeing to disagree, although they did not quite ignore each other and probably suspected the other's salvation was in question. Bunyan performed his communal identity in the process of defending his church from external attacks and internal dissension while pointing towards the invisible church. Arguments about 'things indifferent', however, virtually disappeared from his prose after 1674, while works on fundamentals of doctrine, both controversial and pastoral, preoccupied him from the beginning to the end of the decade.

POLEMICAL WORKS: THE DOCTRINE OF JUSTIFICATION

Even before he published his *A Confession of my Faith* (1672) Bunyan set his sights on fundamentals of doctrine and theology in *A Defence of the Doctrine of Justification, by Faith* (1672), a polemical work written in jail, targeting Edward Fowler's *The Design of Christianity* (1671), a book containing 'open Blasphemy, (such as endangereth the Souls of thousands)' (*MW*, 4: 11). If the practice of baptism as an initiating ordinance was a 'thing indifferent' in theory, although not always in practice, there was for Bunyan no such ambiguity about belief in the doctrine of justification: it was an essential of faith without which invisible church membership was impossible. Indeed, the doctrine is so central to Bunyan's construction of the community of eternal life that his prose of the 1670s can be seen as an attempt to clarify in a variety of ways its pastoral and devotional implications. For Bunyan, 'to be Justified is [...] the beginning of Eternal Life in [Christ]' (*MW*, 4: 72). As a result, the doctrine, discipline, and worship of the church must rest on this foundation.

A Defence of the Doctrine of Justification, by Faith clearly demonstrates that toleration does not extend to violations of fundamentals of faith. Bunyan begins by describing the two principles that underlay Fowler's book: that human beings are capable of righteousness by exercising reason, and that it was the purpose of Christ to promote this holiness in his life and gospel. He then proceeds to expose over and over again Fowler's ignorance of justification and its corollary doctrines: that human nature is radically flawed and, therefore, incapable of righteousness; that Christ's purpose, through his crucifixion, was to impute righteousness to human beings, thereby justifying them in God's eyes; and that faith in this work of Christ, the essence of the Gospel, was made possible by the activity of the Holy Spirit in transforming the individual. There is little common ground: Fowler's doctrine represents the Law, human arrogance, and works while Bunyan's represents the Gospel, God's sovereignty, and faith. The barbed, uncompromising language makes clear Bunyan's belief that Fowler's doctrine is 'but the abuse of Christ, of Scripture, and Reason; it is but a wresting and corrupting of the Word of God, both to your own destruction, and them that believe you' (*MW*, 4: 35). Bunyan's polemic concludes with a short section in which he discredits Fowler, first by associating him with both Catholic and Quaker doctrines, since both ignore Scripture as Fowler does, and then by showing that he even contradicts 'the Articles of the Church of *England*', the church he claims to defend (*MW*, 4: 123).

Bunyan's other approach is to suggest the unworthiness of Fowler's doctrine by emphasizing the shortcomings of his character and his church. He implies that the 'Unstable Weathercock Spirit' of clergymen like Fowler, once a Presbyterian and now a 'glorious Latitudinarian' of the Church of England, causes the weak to lose faith and gives 'advantage to the Adversary' (*MW*, 4: 83, 102). Conformist ministers have abandoned their former faith for 'Love of filthy Lucre, and the pampering [of] their idle Carcasses' in the established church, revealing the 'feigned good Conscience they had' before the Restoration. Fowler's view of fundamentals, which amounts to the need for everyone to adapt to the religion of the time and to 'tolerate that which is plainly forbidden' in doctrine and worship, will encourage others to 'hop from Presbiterianism, to a Prelatical Mode' as the customs and fashions of the time suit them (*MW*, 4: 82, 102, 101). At the same time, Fowler's inversion of fundamentals and indifferent things leads to his support of 'the power to persecute Non-conformists': further evidence of his 'devilish design to promote Paganism, against Christianity' (*MW*, 4: 106). Writing his defence of justification while suffering persecution under the second Conventicle Act, and determined to overcome intolerance with 'truth, and patience' (*MW*, 4: 106), Bunyan suggests that the limits of toleration are God's, not man's, since the limits are defined by scriptural doctrines that lead to eternal life rather than by customs and morals that require conformity to the national church within the established political order. The same point is made in *The Pilgrim's Progress* (1678), when By-ends claims 'liberty' only to be rebuked by Christian (*PP*, 100).

DOCTRINAL SERMONS: JUSTIFICATION AND GRACE

Turning from polemics to doctrinal sermons on fundamentals such as the doctrine of justification and salvation by grace alone, it is easy to see why Bunyan was such a popular preacher. Combining careful biblical exegeses, precise and uncomplicated theological distinctions, and predictable patterns of organization with colloquial diction, metaphors drawn from everyday life, and rhythmic immediacy, the sermons—even when written down and expanded after their delivery—are strikingly vibrant in ways the polemical works can never be. This is not to say that the sermons completely escape the indignant, dogmatic tone of some sections of the controversial tracts. In 1675, freed from prison temporarily but no doubt disheartened by both the king's withdrawal of the Declaration of Indulgence and a renewed warrant for his arrest, Bunyan published *Light for Them that Sit in Darkness*, in which the doctrines of justification and Christ's imputed righteousness are again unfolded, occasionally erupting with the same venom that more frequently marks *A Defence of the Doctrine of Justification, by Faith*.[14] Here,

---

[14] Greaves, *Glimpses*, 313–15; *MW*, 8: xix.

however, he addresses '*the Godly themselves*' and the possibility that, in a state of spiritual darkness, they could be swayed by the '*Fables, Seducing-Spirits, and Doctrines of Devils through the Intoxications of Delusions, and the Witchcrafts of false Preachers*' (*MW*, 8: 49).[15] The false preachers hold the same views of justification as Edward Fowler and the Latitudinarians of the Church of England: they reject that Christ's purpose was to take upon himself the sin of the world in order to redeem and justify believers, and that 'Holiness, to which is annexed eternal Life' derives from faith in what Christ has purchased through his blood, not from the human effort to attain moral perfection (*MW*, 8: 90, 134). In a passage that looks ahead to *The Pilgrim's Progress* (*PP*, 38), Bunyan proclaims with overpowering emotion that only utter and complete dependence on the cross will suffice:

> Wouldest thou know Sinner, what thou art; *look up to the Cross*, and behold a Weeping, Bleeding, Dying Jesus: nothing could do but that, nothing could save thee but his Blood. […] What a thing is Sin, that it should sink all that bear its burden, yea it sunk the Son of God himself […] had he not been able to take it on his Back, *and bear it away*. […] If thy Righteousness can save thee, then Christ died in vain. […] BLOOD! BLOOD, the sound of *Blood*, abaseth all the Glory of [man's righteousness]. (*MW*, 8: 151–53)

More often, though, the focus in this sermon is on 'the Doctrine of the Person, and Doings and Sufferings of Christ with the true cause thereof', with the aim of reiterating the doctrine of justification that will lead to the invisible church, rather than tearing down the doctrines of the 'crafty Children of darkness', in spite of the impression left by the prefatory letter that this will be a vituperative, combative work throughout (*MW*, 8: 50).

Even though Acts 13:23 is the focus of *Light for Them that Sit in Darkness*, the reference to Galatians 3:13 on the title page is also worth noting, since it pinpoints what the doctrinal emphasis will be: '*Christ hath redeemed us from the Curse of the Law, being made a Curse for us*.' Bunyan's careful unfolding of Paul's words as they apply to the passage from Acts leads to a precise analysis of the nature of Jesus as the saviour promised by God literally and typologically in the Old Testament and revealed in the flesh in the New, before he concludes that believers cannot save themselves but are dependent on Christ for salvation (*MW*, 8: 53–78). Bunyan seizes the opportunity to urge those who 'dare not think upon God, nor the Sins which they have committed', whether out of fear or despair, to 'Turn again, hearken; the Heart of God is much set upon Mercy, from the beginning of the World he resolved and promised, ay, and sware we should have a Saviour' (*MW*, 8: 64). Unfortunately, reassuring pastoral moments like this are rare as Bunyan focuses instead on tedious details about seemingly uncontroversial doctrines:

---

[15] Greaves, *Glimpses*, 319.

Quest. 3. *What it was for him to come to be a Saviour.*

For the further handling of this Question I must shew:
1. What it is *to be* a Saviour.
2. What it is *to come* to be a Saviour.
3. What it is for *Jesus to come to be a Saviour*. (*MW*, 8: 75)

Bunyan's overall strategy should be kept in mind, however, since by linking doctrines and textual exegeses with which everyone can agree to contentious doctrines of justification and Christ's imputed righteousness, he implies that by rejecting the latter his opponents also reject the fundamental beliefs of Christian faith, including the mystery of the incarnation and Christ's office of redemption. Indeed, immediately following his analysis of Paul's reference to 'a Saviour', Bunyan explains *how* Jesus performed his work as saviour: clearly the most important implication of the text given the length of this section (*MW*, 8: 78–147). Alluding to the quotation from Galatians on the title page, Bunyan asserts that Christ 'bore the Curse due to our Sins' (*MW*, 8: 78), making believers righteous or justified in God's eyes by transference. This is why Jesus had to become fully human but remain sinless, and how he 'hath paid full price to God for Sinners, and obtained Eternal Redemption for them' (*MW*, 8: 127). When Bunyan refutes objections to the doctrine here, he clearly still has Fowler and other Latitudinarian members of the Church of England in mind, for his condemnation of the righteousness and holiness acquired by human effort associated with the social and political conformity of 'Sir Johns', like Fowler in *A Defence of the Doctrine of Justification, by Faith*, is repeated here and recurs in his portraits of Worldly-Wiseman, By-ends, and Ignorance in *The Pilgrim's Progress*. The doctrines of human sufficiency are '*Anathematised of God, and shall stand so, till the Coming of the Lord Jesus*' (*MW*, 8: 160). As a fundamental of faith, the doctrine of justification can be used, according to Bunyan, as a means of identifying who will enjoy eternal life in the invisible church and who will be condemned, clearly marking the limits of toleration.

In *Saved by Grace: Or, A Discourse of the Grace of God* (?1676), Bunyan approaches the doctrine of justification from a more visionary perspective, providing his listeners with a glimpse of the invisible church: 'Heaven is the place for the saved to enjoy their Salvation in [. . .], There is *Mount Sion, the heavenly Jerusalem, the general Assembly, and the Church of the first born*' (*MW*, 8: 177). The state of blessedness includes the harmony of body and soul, the perfection of the 'Will and Affections' leading to 'a burning flame of love to God', and the gathering of the innocent, symbolized by their white raiment (*MW*, 8: 180–81). To be saved, however, it is first necessary to be convicted of sin; it is impossible to be saved without first asking, as Christian does in *The Pilgrim's Progress* (*PP*, 8, 9), 'what shall we do? That is, *Do to be saved?* Acts 2. 37', and then listening to those '*who hath warned thee to flee from the wrath to come*' (*MW*, 8: 169–70). The extent of sin is such that salvation could only come from grace—consisting of the Father's free choice of the elect '*before the World began*' (*MW*, 8: 171), the Son's righteousness imputed to sinners, and the Holy Spirit's illumination—and never from merit or works. God's effort in saving both ordinary people who transgress 'many times; may I not say, sometimes, many hundred times a day' and saints who receive 'Millions of pardons from God' are further evidence of God's mercy, the human need for grace, and 'the only remedy against despairing thoughts, at the apprehension of our own unworthiness' (*MW*, 8: 208, 221).

For Bunyan, the doctrines of salvation by grace and justification by faith ensure that there will always be 'progress from this world to that which is to come' as long as the ministry of writing and preaching keeps alive the biblical vision of the invisible church and assures the visible church that God's grace will never be withdrawn, even though members will stumble badly. It is the latter concern that is addressed in these pastoral works, for if Bunyan's doctrinal and controversial works of the 1670s set the terms for church membership on the grounds of what doctrines are essential and what differences in practice should be tolerated, his pastoral works concentrate on how the congregation might respond emotionally, imaginatively, and spiritually to these doctrines.

Politics and the Pastoral Sermons

Bunyan's pastoral sermons, whether delivered to the Bedford congregation, gatherings in surrounding counties, or churches in London, address more immediately than the doctrinal sermons or controversial tracts the spiritual needs of his listeners and readers. This does not mean that the doctrinal sermons are without direct appeals to what Bunyan imagines the audience's emotional and spiritual responses to doctrine will be. In *Saved by Grace*, for example, his expository and exegetical method unfolds the doctrine of salvation by grace alone, but swerves from this purpose and method to prompt his auditors, at the most opportune moment in the development of the topic, to consider their 'Hypocrisies, Pride, Unbelief, hardness of Heart, Deadness [. . .] doubts and fears of Damnation', before asking them simply and pointedly, 'But what will God do now? Will he take this advantage to destroy the Sinner? No. Will he let him alone in his Apostasie? No. What then? Why he will seek this man out, till he finds him, and bring him home to himself again' (*MW*, 8: 205, 207). The conversational rhythm of Bunyan's dialogue concentrates the abstract theological doctrine, like a shard of glass, to a point of intense immediacy, but his sense of timing and pace, as he intuits when to interrupt the textual explication to probe the consequences of the doctrine in the hearts of his listeners, is impressive as well. It is no wonder, then, that the sermons that focus on the spiritual conditions of the audience, not in passing, as in the doctrinal sermons, but continuously and insistently, are among Bunyan's most admired in both style and psychological insight.[16] Imagery, diction, and speech rhythms drawn from the Bible and the

---

[16] See Graham Midgley, 'Introduction', in *MW*, 5: xxii–xxx.

everyday experience of his listeners are used to create vivid, compelling psychological dramas designed to strengthen the church in its condition of living ahead of itself for eternal life.

At the same time, the sermons that map the inner territory of Bunyan's listeners are also inseparable from the struggles of the visible church to define the limits of toleration based on what is necessary for salvation, especially as the Declaration of Indulgence was rescinded in 1673, the Test Acts of 1673 and 1678 were passed, licences to preach were revoked in 1675, persecution of Nonconformists was renewed, and fear of Roman Catholic influence on the king and Parliament intensified throughout the decade, reaching a climax during the Popish Plot (1678–79) and the Exclusion Crisis (1679–81). Preached and then expanded for print following the withdrawal of the Declaration of Indulgence, *The Barren Fig-Tree* (1673) suggests that a true church consists not of a national institution maintained by the use of force, and barren of toleration, but of a voluntary gathering of visible saints whose good works are the fruit of faith. Bunyan also appears to have Fowler and the Church of England in mind when he condemns those 'whose heart is estranged from Communion with the Holy Ghost, whose fruit groweth *from themselves*, from their Parts, Gifts, Strength of wit, natural or moral Principles' (*MW*, 5: 22).

In the year preceding the publication of *The Strait Gate* (1676), the Church of England renewed attempts to enforce church attendance. Bunyan was charged with illegal preaching under the second Conventicle Act, and was excommunicated for not attending his parish church, St Cuthbert's, or receiving the Eucharist.[17] Bunyan's sermons seem to respond to these conditions. Entry through the 'strait gate' of the invisible church includes conditions, such as spiritual rebirth and 'Gospel-holyness' (*MW*, 5: 100) that correspond to criteria for gathered church membership, while his condemnations of the 'covetous' and 'wanton' professor and the *'temporizing Latitudinarian'* whose 'religion is always like the times, turning this way and that way, like the cock on the steeple' (*MW*, 5: 124–26), recall similar anti-Anglican rebukes in the doctrinal and controversial works of the 1670s as well as satirical portraits of wealthy Anglicans like By-ends in *The Pilgrim's Progress*, who never strive 'against Wind and Tide' unlike 'the stricter sort' of Nonconformist visible saints (*PP*, 99).

The recurrence of fear as a theme in *A Treatise of the Fear of God* (1679) and, to a lesser extent, *Come, & Welcome, to Jesus Christ* (1678), and the praise of patient suffering for the gospel in *Paul's Departure and Crown* (possibly written around 1678–79 but published only in 1692), might also represent deliberate interventions in the religious politics of the last years of the decade. Fear of a Catholic sovereign during the Popish Plot and Exclusion Crisis and the persecution of Nonconformists were also challenges faced by Dissent as a whole in its pursuit of toleration. Bunyan's main concern in these works, however, is the spiritual preparedness of his listeners to enter the invisible church, a sign of which was active participation in the visible, militant church on Earth.

---

[17] Greaves, 'Introduction', *MW*, 8: xxii.

Pastoral Sermons: Hypocrisy

The theological basis of *The Barren Fig-Tree* (1673) is Bunyan's belief that 'A man must be good, else he can bring forth no good fruit; he must have righteousness imputed, that he may stand good in God's sight from the curse of his Law' (*MW*, 5: 24). Rather than expounding the theological relationship between grace and works, however, Bunyan here creates the character of the hypocrite, the 'Fruitless Professor' or 'Cumber-ground', who appears religious and may even attend church, but who is actually without grace (*MW*, 5: 9). His purpose is to underline the connection between visible sainthood and the invisible church. Referring to the character directly allows him to create the fiction that the professor isn't present, while forcing his readers and listeners at the same time to examine whether their faith has led to good works and visible sainthood: 'Barren *Fig-tree*, fruitless Professor, Hast thou heard all these things? Hast thou considered that this *Fig-tree* is not acknowledged of God to be his, but is denied to be of his Planting? [...] Barren *Fig-tree*, fruitless Christian, do not thine ears tingle?' (*MW*, 5: 18). The spiritual and emotional implications of the doctrine of imputed grace are made clear. Complacency and hypocrisy will result in disciplinary action from the visible church and exclusion from the invisible church, for as Bunyan warns his readers, alluding to Luke 13:6–9:

> [W]hich way soever God dealeth with thee, *O thou barren Fig-tree*, whether by himself immediately, or by his Church, it amounts to one and the same. For if timely Repentance prevent not, *The end of that Soul is damnation*. They are blasted, and withered, and gathered by men, Gods enemies, and at last being cast into the fire, *burning must be their end*. (*MW*, 5: 36)

Even though holiness of life and the performance of good works are criteria of visible church membership, and visible church membership in good standing is a sign of the mystical, invisible church, Bunyan stresses the lack of contiguity between the visible and invisible church: it is one thing to be in the church and another to be of it '& to belong to that Kingdom, that is prepared for the Saint' (*MW*, 5: 15). Exploiting this uncertainty, Bunyan compels his listeners to see themselves, at least to some extent, as 'fruitless professors', leading to fear and doubt, self-examination, and renewed commitment to acts of faith that mark the presence of the true church as a gathering of visible saints.

In Bunyan's explication of Jesus' parable, the vineyard is the church, the fig tree is the member of the church, the fruit is evidence of visible sainthood, the lord of the vineyard is God the Father, and the dresser of the vineyard, who shows mercy to the barren fig tree by offering opportunities to repent, is Jesus. These simple, vivid images are powerful enough to provoke the process of self-assessment and psychological drama in which Bunyan wants his listeners to participate, but they are also combined with incisive character sketches and brief narratives designed to move his audience to action. In his discussion of the signs of being past grace, for example, Bunyan uses allegorical narrative and dialogue to account for God's numerous attempts to save the fruitless professor from damnation, laying bare the roots of the barren fig tree in fear, self-delusion, and the need for social acceptance: things felt by all of his auditors at one time or another. Having threatened and pardoned the sinner twice, God 'will take up his ax again, and will put him under a more heart-searching Ministry, a Ministry that will search him, and turn him over and over' just as Bunyan does in his sermon, but to no avail: the fruitless professor will 'wrangle'; he 'wags and is wanton' and, like Talkative in *The Pilgrim's Progress* (*PP*, 77–85), he believes 'the glory of the Gospel consisteth in talk and shew' (*MW*, 5: 53–4).

Pastoral Sermons: Complacency

While it lacks the cohesiveness of *The Barren Fig-Tree*, probably due to the limitations of its central image, *The Strait Gate* illustrates more severely the 'heart-searching Ministry' that Bunyan practised in the earlier sermon, exposing the self-deception and hypocrisy of visible church members who profess faith but who 'will come short of eternal life' (*MW*, 5: 69). Although the gate of heaven is 'wide enough for all them that are the truly gracious, and sincere lovers of Jesus Christ', few will be saved, and many a 'high professor', even some 'that are famous in the congregation of Saints', including Baptists, Formalists, Latitudinarians, Socinians, and Quakers, will be excluded from the invisible church of eternal glory for their lack of election, conversion, faith, gospel holiness, and perseverance (*MW*, 5: 76, 69, 92, 125–27, 100–01). Bunyan insists that his text '*calls for sharpness,* [and] *so do the times*'; his purpose is to rouse his listeners to '*strive to enter in*' at the gate rather than to 'content themselves with a profession that is never like to bring them thither' (*MW*, 5: 69, 86). Thus, he anticipates the spiritual and emotional consequences of his doctrine of imputed grace: not only does he address the uncomfortable fact that many who think they are elect are not, once again dividing the visible from the invisible church (*MW*, 5: 109–11), but his emphasis on striving also acknowledges that sloth and complacency are spiritual flaws to which congregations of visible saints are especially vulnerable, a theme explored in more detail in *The Heavenly Foot-man* (published posthumously in 1698) and in the imagery of sleeping, running, and striving throughout *The Pilgrim's Progress* (*PP*, 43–4, 136–37, 144–45).

Perseverance in grace is ultimately God's work, and this might lead to passivity and sloth, but 'God worketh together with his children' (*MW*, 5: 101) to inspire the striving to live God's Word that characterizes gospel holiness and visible sainthood. If only a few are saved, listeners might be discouraged from striving at all, especially those who are convicted of sin without the necessary reassurance of grace; nevertheless, Bunyan also advises,

> let not this thought, *few shall be saved*, weaken thy heart, but let it cause thee to mend thy pace, to mend thy crys, to look well to thy grounds for heaven; let it make thee fly

faster from sin, to Christ, let it keep thee awake and out of carnal security, and thou maist be saved. (*MW*, 5: 124)

In *The Strait Gate* the note of sympathy for those feeling discouragement, despair, and fear as a result of the doctrines of imputed righteousness and invisible church membership is quite brief. Yet Bunyan must have realized the need of his congregations for direction and reassurance since of the three pastoral sermons published or written after *The Strait Gate* between 1676 and 1680, each addresses fear.

Pastoral Sermons: Fear

As its title suggests, *A Treatise of the Fear of God* (1679) approaches its subject systematically, including in its scope much more than an analysis of fear in the hearts of those who are unsure about election and the doctrine of Christ's imputed righteousness. Bunyan's emphasis is clearly on godly or righteous fear, but the pastoral function of righteous fear within the treatise is to comfort and motivate those whose godly fear is temporary by convincing them that fear, correctly understood, is a sign of grace. He reminds his readers that there are many '*temptations, difficulties*, snares, traps, trials and troubles that the people of God pass through in the world', and that even after the 'spirit of adoption' has been received 'a Christian shall [...] again be in as *great* fears, for he may have *worse* than he had at first', but 'fear of the Lord is the *pulse* of the soul' and just as the pulse can be intermittent and yet not lead to death, so fears continue without leading to damnation (*MW*, 9: 124, 35, 127).

Many fears must be sent by Satan, Bunyan avers, since God's promise of grace through the spirit of adoption is immutable. Fears of this kind must be distinguished from 'Fatherly chastisements' when God withdraws the 'comfort of their adoption' to correct and test the sinner's understanding of godly fear (*MW*, 9: 44–5), as Hopeful explains in response to Christian's 'hearty fears that he should die in that River' (*PP*, 157, 158). If, after examining the kinds of fear they are experiencing, people must still ask, 'How shall I know that I fear God?', Bunyan's answer is simply to assert that 'sincere desires to fear God, flow from grace already in the soul', a response that converts epistemological and spiritual uncertainty into a striking statement of pastoral comfort and reassurance (*MW*, 9: 127, 128). Unlike temporal or natural desire, which manifests an absence that might not be fulfilled, sincere spiritual desire '*to be good, to believe, to love, to hope, and fear God, doth flow from the nature of grace itself*' (*MW*, 9: 128). Alluding to Hebrews 11:16, Bunyan promises his readers that the desire to fear God is a sign of invisible church membership:

True, *desires* are *lower*, than *higher* acts of grace, but God will not look over desires: *But now they DESIRE a better Country, that is an heavenly; wherefore God is not ashamed to be called their God, for he hath prepared for them a City.* Mark, they desire a *Country*, and they shall have a *City*. (*MW*, 9: 128)

Thus, even 'one of the most troublesome Pilgrims', Mr Fearing, from the town of Stupidity, who had a '*Slow of Dispond* in his Mind' as a result of 'his Fear [...] about his Acceptance at last', successfully enters the Celestial City (*PP*, 249, 251, 253).

Pastoral Sermons: The Invisible Church and Desire Fulfilled

Come, & Welcome, to Jesus Christ, published in 1678, a year before *A Treatise of the Fear of God*, also addresses fear as a spiritual condition of Bunyan's theology of justification, but emphasizes Jesus's comfort of the flawed elect rather than acceptable and unacceptable kinds of fear. More sympathetic to the everyday struggles of believers than *The Barren Fig-Tree* or *The Strait Gate*, *Come, & Welcome* argues that the invisible church, as the perfect form of collective desire promised in the New Testament, is within the reach of all who sincerely desire it. Bunyan asks his reader, 'Well, will things that are less satisfie thy Soul? will a less thing than Heaven, than Glory, and Eternal life, answer thy desires?' (*MW*, 8: 350). Desire might account for the form of the invisible church, but it also accounts for the fear of losing it, for as Bunyan observes, 'strong *Desires* to *have*, are attended with strong *Fears* of *missing*. What a Man most sets his Heart upon, and what his Desires are most after, he (oft-times) most fears, he shall not obtain' (*MW*, 8: 345). Like a young man '*Sick of Love*', 'the Soul at first Coming to Jesus Christ' often torments itself with fears of unworthiness and rejection, but the knowledge that fear arises from desire, not rejection, will lead to a stronger belief that 'Coming-Souls [...] will also get safe into Christ's Bosom' and attain eternal life (*MW*, 8: 345–47).

In the initial stage of his explication of John 6:37 Bunyan stresses the Father's role in choosing, before the creation of the world, the elect who will come to Christ and enjoy eternal life (*MW*, 8: 247). Coming to Christ is synonymous with '*a sound Sense of the absolute want that a man hath of* [Christ] *for his Justification and Salvation*', a desire that 'hath no dependence upon our own will' (*MW*, 8: 255, 274). The underlying theological doctrines of election and justification, however, crucial as they are in determining invisible church membership, are less important in this sermon than the assurance given to readers that fears of exclusion from the church of glory are unfounded. Bunyan reiterates throughout the explication that all of those who depend on Christ's merits for their salvation 'will in no wise be cast out', but his acute analysis of the psychological realities of his audience, rooted in his disciplinary and pastoral work in Bedford, is what sets this work apart from others.

To underline that his purpose is to address the emotional struggles of his readers rather than to pursue doctrinal issues, Bunyan interrupts his explication twice to answer objections posed by a fictional believer whose fears stifle the joy that the doctrine should inspire. The objector's first fear is that he believes for the wrong reason, but Bunyan assures him that believing in order to attain eternal life 'is a lawful, and good coming to Jesus Christ' (*MW*, 8: 260). He goes on to assure his readers through this dialogue that other worries, arising from falling to temptation after beginning to come to Christ or being slow, indifferent, or late in turning to Christ, limit believers but are not enough to exclude them from the invisible church, although he is quick to warn, possibly with antinomians in mind, to 'let no Man turn this Grace of God into Wantonness; my design is now to encourage the coming Soul' (*MW*, 8: 270).

In the second set of objections, Bunyan allays his readers' fears by insisting on the unconditional nature of election, God's 'big-bellied promise', in some cases answering objections related to extreme forms of obstinacy, spiritual blindness, and idolatry by turning the 'shall come' of his text into an allegorical name reminiscent of *The Pilgrim's Progress*: 'Object. 1. *But they are dead, dead in Trespasses and Sins, how shall they then come? Answ. Why? Shall-come can raise them from this Death*' (*MW*, 8: 278). Bunyan's most sustained analysis of spiritual fear and God's abounding love, however, comes in the observations and applications of the text. In spite of God's promise to 'in no wise cast out' any believer, Bunyan observes 'how prone poor man is, to give way, when truly awakned, to despondings, and heart-misgiveings […] between the time of his first setting out, and that of his coming to his Father' (*MW*, 8: 342). Such fears arise from seven different causes, and in each case Bunyan urges readers who suffer 'the hideous Roarings of the Devil' (*MW*, 8: 351) to focus on the sincerity of Jesus's promise to save everyone who comes to him. Some are complacent, proud, slothful, or presumptuous, and others might be tempted in order to teach others, but all will be saved if they come to Christ (*MW*, 8: 360–62). After briefly applying the doctrine to those who will not come to Christ, Bunyan concludes by underlining two important implications of his text: that his readers must examine themselves to discover if they have accepted Christ and that Christ is a God of love and forgiveness who 'despiseth not any', so they have every reason to be joyful (*MW*, 8: 388).

The popularity of *Come, & Welcome, to Jesus Christ* might have been due to its close attention to the spiritual conditions of its audience and its hopeful, encouraging message about the doctrines of election and justification.[18] Yet Bunyan's narrative and exegetical skill is evident throughout as well. Direct references to his audience and himself as well as to contemporary politics and the perceptions that others have of visible saints ensure that the reader is engaged throughout this work in a personal drama being performed upon an inner stage (*MW*, 8: 239, 263, 264, 283, 336). Forms of dialogue also encourage the reader to imagine and be moved by the psychological conflicts probed by Bunyan: extended question and answer formats, short, abrupt, almost catechetical exchanges between Christ and the sinner, and impassioned conversations between imagined characters and the author all create the dramatic immediacy that his pastoral

---

[18] The text was published in six editions between 1678 and 1688. See *MW*, 8: 231–38.

purpose demands and that is lacking in the drier, more strictly exegetical and doctrinal sermons (*MW*, 8: 259–73, 340, 344–45).

Bunyan's flair for allegory and parable is demonstrated throughout *Come, & Welcome* as well. His narrative exegesis of the Prodigal Son parable (*MW*, 8: 301, 341–42, 389–90) is carefully realized as he supplements the text with pertinent character motivations. Likewise, his parable of the physician is imaginatively extended from Scripture, but he also invents his own parables and characters, such as the prince and the maidservant, the conceited man, and the lover (*MW*, 8: 348, 349–50, 359, 344–47). Finally, in addition to allegorical figures, Bunyan uses simple, accessible images, most derived from Scripture, to create vivid illustrations of his ideas. The struggling sinner 'Flings and Tumbles like a Wild Bull in a net' (*MW*, 8: 358). Discouraging thoughts, like cold weather, encourage sluggishness, he notes, while God's promises, like spring, are invigorating: 'You see how little the *Bee* and *Flye* do play in the Air in Winter; why, the cold hinders them from doing it; but when the Wind and Sun is warm, who so busie as they?' (*MW*, 8: 267). In style and theme, then, *Come, & Welcome, to Jesus Christ* represents Bunyan's best work of the decade: all of his talents are devoted to convincing his uncertain audience that the eternal glory of the invisible church is theirs.

Conclusion

These pastoral works, while they reflect Bunyan's direct engagement with members of the visible church, and to a lesser extent with the defence of the tolerationist cause during the 1670s, are also inseparable from the imagined community of the invisible church. In vivid parables and inner dramas, Bunyan explores the spiritual conditions created by the doctrines of justification and imputed righteousness, belief in which was the only essential criterion of salvation and invisible church membership. Fear, doubt, and complacency but also the joyfulness of Christ's assurances and the solace of church fellowship are addressed in order to sustain readers and listeners in the interval between the resurrection and the heavenly city, between remembrance and desire.

Bunyan's doctrinal works on essentials of faith and things indifferent to salvation, in both polemical and theological modes, register more directly the tremors caused by conflicts between the liberty and toleration claimed by Nonconformists and the authority claimed by the Crown and Parliament to enforce uniform Anglican worship. Even here, however, the struggle of visible churches for toleration and 'liberty of conscience' cannot be separated from its purpose, especially for gathered, Independent churches such as Bunyan's: to prepare for the invisible church. De Krey and Greaves rightly emphasize the important role played by religious ideology in destabilizing the Restoration, but in limiting their explanation to the political dimensions of the visible church, important nuances and arguments can be overlooked, and the contributions of Protestantism to the development of tolerationist theory can be too easily dismissed. While De Krey and Greaves avoid this latter shortcoming, the same cannot be said for

Anderson, Habermas, and Israel, who all define modernity and its foundational values, including toleration, in secular terms, framing seventeenth-century religious debates as transitional stages in the slow emergence of nationalism, the bourgeois public sphere, or the liberal democratic values promoted by the 'radical enlightenment', respectively.[19] Bunyan's prose of the 1670s, however, shows that an alternative view of toleration is possible, in which the imagined invisible church plays a formative role.

Suggested Reading

Bloch, Ernst, *The Principle of Hope*, tr. Neville Plaice, Stephen Plaice, and Paul Knight, 3 vols (Cambridge, MA: MIT Press, 1986; repr. 1995).

Keeble, Neil, *The Literary Culture of Nonconformity in Later Seventeenth-Century England* (Athens, GA: University of Georgia Press, 1987).

Knott, John R., 'Bunyan and the Holy Community', *SP*, 80 (1983), 200–25.

Lake, Peter and Steven Pincus (eds.), *The Politics of the Public Sphere in Early Modern England* (Manchester: Manchester University Press, 2007).

Moltman, Jürgen, *The Theology of Hope: On the Ground and the Implications of a Christian Eschatology*, tr. James W. Leitch (London: SCM, 1967).

Nuttall, Geoffrey, *The Holy Spirit in Puritan Faith and Experience* (1946; repr. Chicago and London: University of Chicago Press, 1997).

Nuttall, Geoffrey, *Visible Saints: The Congregational Way 1640–1660*, 2nd edn (Weston Rhyn: Quinta Press, 2001).

Spurr, John, *The Restoration Church of England, 1646–1687* (New Haven, CT: Yale University Press, 1991).

Torrance, T. F., *Kingdom and Church: A Study in the Theology of the Reformation* (Edinburgh: Oliver & Boyd, 1956).

Tyacke, Nicholas, 'The "Rise of Puritanism" and the Legalizing of Dissent', in Ole Peter Grell, Jonathan I. Israel, and Nicholas Tyacke (eds.), *From Persecution to Toleration: The Glorious Revolution and Religion in England* (Oxford: Clarendon Press, 1991), 17–49.

---

[19] See Anderson, *Imagined Communities*, 11, 23, 37–43; Jürgen Habermas, *The Structural Transformation of the Public Sphere: An Inquiry into a Category of Bourgeois Society*, tr. Thomas Burger and Frederick Lawrence (Cambridge, MA: MIT Press, 1989), 11, 27, 52, 265; and Jonathan Israel, *Enlightenment Contested: Philosophy, Modernity, and the Emancipation of Man, 1670–1752* (Oxford: Oxford University Press, 2006), vii, 11, 63–155.

CHAPTER 14

THE PILGRIM'S PROGRESS (1678)

Chasing Apollyon's Tale

MICHAEL DAVIES

On our left a steep and shell-pocked bank, over which the moon is peeping. To our right and below us is the river stretching across a vista of broken stumps, running water and shell pools, to the skeleton gleaming white of another village on the far bank. If only an artist could paint the grim scene now while the hand of war and death is still hovering over it. In our steel helmets and chain visors we somehow recall *Pilgrim's Progress*, armoured figures passing through the valley of the shadow. On—for Apollyon's talons are over near.[1]

THESE words were written by Christian Creswell Carver, a young Royal Field Artillery officer from Harborne, Birmingham, in a letter sent to his brother on 14 March 1917 from that most dreadful arena of conflict, the Somme. Why it is that this lieutenant—who died in action, aged 20, just a few months after composing these lines—would 're-call' in this 'grim' nocturnal 'scene' John Bunyan's *The Pilgrim's Progress* (1678), a book first published almost two hundred and fifty years before the First World War began, has been explored by Paul Fussell. How could British soldiers, Fussell asks, communicate to those at home anything of what they had seen and suffered in this catastrophe? How could they 'describe the indescribable'? One answer would be to 'recall' *The Pilgrim's Progress*, the imaginative resources of which offered a way for combatants to convey this war's 'utter incredibility' and to overcome its sheer 'incommunicability'. Like Christian Creswell Carver, whose first name carries special resonance in this respect, other British soldiers and officers, in their letters and memoirs, would likewise turn to Bunyan's

---

[1] *War Letters of Fallen Englishmen*, ed. Laurence Housman; foreword Jay Winter (Philadelphia, PA: University of Pennsylvania Press, 2002), 68–9. Paul Fussell silently emends the phrase 'over near' to 'ever near' when quoting from this letter in *The Great War and Modern Memory* (Oxford: Oxford University Press, 2000), 141.

allegory in order to express the misery of No Man's Land as a 'Slough of Despond' and to recount their deadly travails as a daily trudge through 'the Valley of the Shadow of Death'.[2]

If *The Pilgrim's Progress* served to provide a language of experience that could be shared between those fighting the Great War and their correspondents at home, then this must be due, in some part, to its legendary ubiquity. A palpable hit at its first publication in 1678, with Bunyan seeing into press two further editions, with significant 'Additions', within its first year, it has never been out of print, famously having been translated into almost every language and read around the globe. Given that few books could be said to have had such an extensive reach, or such a pervasive and sustained influence upon the imaginations of so many other writers and their works, it can hardly surprise us to see such a rich array of allusions to *The Pilgrim's Progress* emerging in letters and memoirs of the 1914–18 war. At this point, almost everyone in Britain—whether they had actually read it or not and whether they actually liked it or not—would at least have known about Bunyan's allegory. When, in 1904, Wilfrid Owen's father presented *The Pilgrim's Progress* as a gift to Owen's mother, reading it aloud to his children in the evenings at their home in Birkenhead, such experiences would not, presumably, have been unusual at that time. As Fussell puts it, 'Everybody had been raised on it.'[3] No wonder this ill-fated soldier-poet would also 'recall' Bunyan's allegory when describing the battlefield as 'like the eternal place of gnashing teeth': 'the Slough of Despond', Owen would write, 'could be contained in one of its crater-holes'.[4]

I start with this brief meditation on the important place occupied by *The Pilgrim's Progress* in the literary records of the Great War not just because I am writing at a time when the centenary of this tragic conflict is being commemorated widely both in Europe and across the world, but because it offers an opportunity to reflect upon the sustained longevity of Bunyan's '*little Book*' (PP, 1). My aim, however, is not to survey the reception history of Bunyan's most famous work, nor to track the astonishing journeys it has undertaken since its first appearance in the late seventeenth century. Rather, the purpose of this chapter is to consider, more simply, what it is about this religious allegory—both in terms of the story that it tells and the way that Bunyan has crafted its telling—that makes it so richly available to readers who, over time and in innumerable ways, have sought to have their own experiences, whether religious or not, either recognized or tested or confirmed through the simple (though, at times, far from straightforward) business of reading and recalling it.

Any appreciation of why *The Pilgrim's Progress* has endured must begin, however, with the simple recognition that it is one of the great literary works of endurance: of perseverance, pressing on, pulling through in the knowledge that, as Lieutenant Carver

---

[2] Fussell, *The Great War*, 137–44; *War Letters*, 69.
[3] Fussell, *The Great War*, 137–38.
[4] John Stallworthy, *Wilfrid Owen* (1974; Oxford: Oxford University Press, 1998), 30, 158.

puts it, 'Apollyon's talons' are always too close for comfort ('over near'). It is, then, a work supremely about struggling: whether forward, through crises or past obstacles, or with and over difficulties, whether they be enemies or dilemmas, temptations or humiliations, or that most subtle and dangerous of all opponents, oneself. Regardless of how assured Christian's entry into the Celestial City may seem, the story that *The Pilgrim's Progress* tells is never one of assured triumphalism or easy victory. It is, rather, one of hard-fought and hard-won conflicts, in which the book's hero often suffers terribly as a result of his own failings and mistakes, but who is sustained, in the end, by both fellowship and faith. It is a book, in other words, about hope and fear, courage and trembling, comfort and despair: matters with which any soldier fighting in the trenches of the First World War might easily identify. It is about seeking for 'Grace': faith, that is, in the limitless accommodation of human errors and fallings-away by an unlimited capacity to forgive and to restore. Yet, it is also about mental fight: those interior struggles rooted in conscience and the experience of suffering, written by a man who, by the time *The Pilgrim's Progress* appeared, had known almost two decades of religious persecution, and over twelve years' imprisonment, for his commitment to his Nonconformist cause.

Where better, then, to taste something of the enduring quality of *The Pilgrim's Progress* as a literary masterpiece—to begin to unlock the profound power of Bunyan's writing, its almost unparalleled imaginative effectiveness, as well as its ability to speak both to and beyond Bunyan's own historical and theological contexts—than to address the episode to which Christian Creswell Carver alludes in his letter from the Somme of 14 March 1917: his namesake's fearsome battle with Apollyon.

'HIS NAME IS *APOLLYON*'

How Christian meets Apollyon requires a brief summary of a deceptively simple plot. A narrator, having 'wandered through the Wilderness of this World', has 'lighted' on a 'Denn' that a marginal note (from the third (1679) edition onwards) glosses as Bunyan's 'Gaol'. There, we are told, he slept and 'dreamed a Dream', in which a nameless '*Man cloathed with Raggs*' is seen standing with '*a Book in his hand, and a great burden upon his Back*'. While reading this book, he 'wept and trembled', we are told, before issuing 'a lamentable cry; saying, *what shall I do?*' (*PP*, 8). An inhabitant of the City of Destruction, the man in question—whom we shall come to know as Christian—has been struck by the conviction that his own good works (in the terms dictated by Bunyan's covenant theology) cannot preserve him from the wrath of God. So what shall he do? Needing both to escape the justice of God's judgement and to be released from the terrible burden upon his back (his guilt over sins that otherwise condemn him to destruction), Evangelist provides the necessary directions, setting Christian on his way to the Celestial City via the all-important Wicket-gate (the 'strait gate' of Matthew 7:13–14 and Luke 13:24): that is, towards a faith in salvation by grace, the complete forgiveness of sins, provided only by Christ in his death on the cross. The great Reformation idea of being saved by grace and justified by faith, not works, thus becomes, from the outset, the key theological point of the allegory, suitably reiterated by Bunyan throughout: whether at Interpreter's House, or in the accounts of Faithful's and Hopeful's religious conversions, or in Christian's conversations with graceless wayfarers, such as Talkative and Ignorance (*PP*, 28–37, 66–85, 123–24, 137–49).[5]

Christian thus flees home, wife, and children—fingers in ears, 'crying, Life, Life, Eternal Life'—and bolts towards the heavenly refuge (*PP*, 9–10). Losing his burden before the cross, where he receives the 'Roll' that guarantees his entry into heaven (*PP*, 38), Christian goes on to meet a series of bystanders and fellow travellers, good and bad, both on the road and in havens of rest or places of torment. Such folk either encourage Christian and his companions—first Faithful, then Hopeful—to continue along the way (such as Interpreter, the staff at Palace Beautiful, and the shepherds of the Delectable Mountains), or to abandon it (such as Mr Worldly-Wiseman, Giant Despair, and, of course, Apollyon). While Faithful takes the express route via his martyrdom at Vanity Fair, Christian and Hopeful reach the Celestial City only after facing their final obstacle, the River of Death, which they cross together before submitting their 'Certificates' at the heavenly gate, walking in to receive their 'Crowns' and 'Harps' and 'Raiment [...] that shone like Gold' (*PP*, 161–62).

In what sounds like a sequential board game of some kind—the 'Game of (Eternal) Life', perhaps, or a soteriological round of snakes-and-ladders, where one's steady progress can be upset at any moment by a sudden sliding backwards to the start (or worse, in Mr Ignorance's case)—this apparently simple narrative is obviously reminiscent of other stories, other structures. The 'journey-of-life' motif, for example, has myriad possible sources and analogues, including works that Bunyan certainly knew—Arthur Dent's *The Plaine Mans Path-Way to Heaven* (1601), for example (*GA*, 8)—and others he may have known, such as John Welles's *The Soules Progresse to the Celestiall Canaan, or Heavenly Jerusalem* (1639) and Simon Patrick's *Parable of the Pilgrim* (1666). The immediate inspiration for *The Pilgrim's Progress*, however, appears to have been closer to home: Bunyan's *The Heavenly Foot-man* (1698). This is more than likely the work '*of the Way / And Race of Saints*' that Bunyan was writing when, according to his 'Author's Apology' to *The Pilgrim's Progress*, he '*Fell suddenly into an Allegory*' (*PP*, 1). Published posthumously a decade after Bunyan died, though evidently written at least twenty years before then, and offering an exhortatory explication of 1 Corinthians 9:24, 'So run, that ye may obtain', it is in *The Heavenly Foot-man* that the genesis of *The Pilgrim's Progress* can be discerned. Here, Bunyan encourages his reader to 'Flee to the City of Refuge' and 'Run in a Race' in order to obtain the 'Prize' that is 'Heaven' via the '*way*' of Christ's '*Righteousness*'. It is a 'Journey', Bunyan explains, involving 'many a dirty step,

---

[5] On Bunyan's covenant theology, see Chapter 4 in this volume; *MW*, 2: xxi–xxxvii; Richard Greaves, *John Bunyan* (Abingdon: Sutton Courtenay Press, 1969), 97–121; Greaves, *Glimpses*, 103–15; Michael Davies, *Graceful Reading: Theology and Narrative in the Works of John Bunyan* (Oxford: Oxford University Press, 2002), 17–80.

many a high Hill', with 'Briers and Quagmires', and 'many Crooked lanes and by-paths' to tempt the unwary (*MW*, 5: 148, 150–55, 161–66). Like us, Christian and Hopeful would certainly recognize their travelling in these terms: they are, says Christian, just 'such footmen' (*PP*, 131).

Yet, in the allegory, we encounter much more than just an extended version of this earlier tract. On the one hand, the form of *The Pilgrim's Progress* appears to look back to a rich literary heritage: that of William Langland's allegorical dream vision, *Piers Plowman* (c.1370), for example, as well as of chivalric romance stretching from the Gawain poet to Edmund Spenser's *The Faerie Queene* (1590; 1596) and Richard Johnson's *The Seven Champions of Christendom* (1596). On the other, and in a not unconnected way, it is obviously a 'road' story. Episodic and linear, albeit taking in some interesting narrative swirls and switchbacks at times, we are likely to be reminded in *The Pilgrim's Progress* not just of the wandering tales of folklore and legend, but also of more contemporary versions (and sometimes inversions) of its basic 'progressive' narrative form: from L. Frank Baum's children's classic, *The Wonderful Wizard of Oz* (1900), with its step-by-step adventure to the Emerald City, to Cormac McCarthy's journey into a terrifying post-apocalyptic future in *The Road* (2006).

It is within this context of familiar narrative structures and motifs that Christian engages with Apollyon. Having left Palace Beautiful—an allegorical representation of the true (that is, 'gathered') church, where he receives refreshment, instruction, and a breastplate with helmet, sword, and shield to match—Christian presses on to the Valley of Humiliation. There, he spies 'a foul Fiend coming over the field to meet him' whose 'name is Apollyon': a 'Monster […] hidious to behold', 'cloathed with scales like a Fish' yet with 'Wings like a Dragon' and 'feet like a Bear, and out of his belly came Fire and Smoak, and his mouth', we are told, 'was as the mouth of a Lion'. Fixing on Christian 'a disdainful countenance', this diabolical mishmash of mismatched body parts recognizes the pilgrim as one of his own '*Subjects*', albeit one who has '*ran away from thy King*' [sic]: '*be content to go back*', this surprisingly eloquent beast coolly recommends (*PP*, 56–7). As Christian refuses to do so, claiming that he must 'serve and honour' another 'Prince', the true 'King' from whose 'High-way, the way of Holiness' he will not be moved (*PP*, 58–9), Apollyon resorts to force. The face-off that ensues is one of the most exciting episodes in the entire allegory, and arguably it remains one of the most memorable fights in English literature. It is worthwhile quoting at length (with Bunyan's marginal notes indicated in square brackets):

> Then *Apollyon* strodled quite over the whole breadth of the way, and said, I am void of fear in this matter, prepare thyself to dye, for I swear by my Infernal Den, that thou shalt go no further, here will I spill thy soul: and with that he threw a flaming Dart at his brest; but *Christian* had a Shield in his hand, with which he caught it, and so prevented the danger of that. Then did *Christian* draw, for he saw 'twas time to bestir him; and *Apollyon* as fast made at him, throwing Darts as thick as hail; by the which, notwithstanding all that *Christian* could do to avoid it, *Apollyon wounded him in his *head*, his *hand*, and *foot* [**Christian wounded in his understanding, faith and conversation*]; this made *Christian* give a little back: *Apollyon* therefore followed

his work amain, and *Christian* again took courage, and resisted as manfully as he could. This sore Combat lasted for above half a day, even till *Christian* was almost quite spent. For you must know, that *Christian*, by reason of his wounds, must needs grow weaker and weaker.

Then *Apollyon*, espying his opportunity, began to gather up close to *Christian*, and wrestling with him, gave him a dreadful fall; [Apollyon *casteth down to the ground* Christian] and with that, *Christian's* Sword flew out of his hand. Then said *Apollion, I am sure of thee now*; and with that he had almost prest him to death; so that *Christian* began to despair of life. But as God would have it, while *Apollyon* was fetching of his last blow, thereby to make a full end of this good Man, [Christians *victory over* Apollyon] *Christian* nimbly reached out his hand for his Sword, and caught it, saying, **Rejoyce not against me, O mine Enemy! when I fall, I shall arise* [*Mich. 7. 8]; and with that, gave him a deadly thrust, which made him give back, as one that had received his mortal wound: *Christian* perceiving that, made at him again, saying, **Nay, in all these things we are more then Conquerours, through him that loved us* [*Rom. 8. 37]. And with that [James 4. 7], *Apollyon* spread forth his Dragons wings, and sped him away, that *Christian* saw him no more. (*PP*, 59–60)

Aside from an opening challenge made all the more obnoxiously pugnacious by that remarkable word 'strodled'—a Bedfordshire variant standardized to 'strad[d]led' from the second (1678) edition onwards—what first strikes us when reading this passage is how masterfully Bunyan controls the energized movement of its action. For a Nonconformist preacher who, by the time that *The Pilgrim's Progress* appeared, had published only one other narrative work, *Grace Abounding to the Chief of Sinners* (1666), Bunyan displays a surprisingly professional understanding of the imaginative mode in which he is now immersed, commanding our suspense with consummate skill. On one level, we experience this 'sore Combat'—the breathless cut-and-thrust of battle, the parry of blow for blow—through the dynamic arrangement of balancing clauses that choreograph the dance of this fight artfully upon the page: 'Then did *Christian* draw […], and *Apollyon* as fast made at him'; '*Apollyon* wounded him' and '*Christian* gave a little back'; '*Apollyon* […] followed his work' but '*Christian* […] resisted'. On another level, Bunyan is internal to the conventions of the medium into which his allegory has suddenly slipped: that of the adventure story, the ripping yarn, in which the villain, Macbeth-like, vaunts his imminent victory with wicked relish, saying 'prepare thy self to dye', 'here will I spill thy soul'. Our hero, meanwhile, having weakened at a fatal moment, finds his weapon—as ever in such situations—flying 'out of his hand'. Preparing 'to make a full end' of our 'good Man', his nemesis sneers gloatingly, as all good villains must, '*I am sure of thee now*'—only for our hero, somehow, to catch up his weapon again 'nimbly' and deliver the final 'deadly thrust'.

Bunyan's twenty-first-century readers will have encountered this kind of storytelling before, in countless fictive and cinematic forms, from the 'Western' and the 'James Bond'-style spy thriller to the likes of *Star Wars*. That Bunyan is able to tell the tale of Christian's fight with Apollyon so capably may well be a reflection, then, of his familiarity with (and former enjoyment of) early modern equivalents of such popular narrative forms. For Bunyan, however, seventeenth-century pulp fiction—chapbook romances, for example, recounting the 'old fables' of '[Saint] *George* on horseback, or *Bevis* of *Southampton*'—are not what 'visible saints' (godly members of churches such as Bunyan's) should be reading (*MW*, 1: 333; and see *MB*, 39–40; *HW*, 31–2).[6] This fact may account for some of the unease Bunyan reports having initially experienced over whether to publish a book written '*in such a stile as this*' (*PP*, 2). Yet it is from just this kind of material that some of the most salient and memorable, as well as theologically important, episodes within *The Pilgrim's Progress* appear to be made: the capture of the pilgrims by Giant Despair within the darkly Gothic dungeons of Doubting Castle, for instance, or their crossing of that perennial folktale territory, the 'Inchanted Ground'. In these terms, Christian's encounter with Apollyon appears to be little more than the legend of St George reloaded, with Apollyon featuring as the terrible dragon and the armour-clad Christian (often depicted by illustrators in full crusader's kit, the red cross of St George emblazoned upon his shield) taking on the role of knight errant, as if having just stepped from the pages of an Arthurian tale.

In *The Pilgrim's Progress*, though, Bunyan's storytelling is never quite as straightforward as it seems, and we are never quite reading what we think we are reading. There are two obvious reasons for this. The first is that our engagement with an episode such as Christian-versus-Apollyon depends not just upon our ability to recognize the way it fulfils certain narrative expectations, but also upon our capacity to perceive *The Pilgrim's Progress*'s investment in the Bible as its principal source. First and foremost, what Bunyan displays in *The Pilgrim's Progress* is a scriptural art: one in which, as we read, we are taken not just through a tale of spiritual progress, an *ordo salutis* that traces the stages of conversion from conviction of sin to perseverance in faith—an allegorical version, that is, of Bunyan's *Grace Abounding*—but also through the pages of the Bible. As one scholar has put it, '*Pilgrim's Progress* is all Bible, all of the time.'[7] This fact alone makes our experience of reading it significantly different—and differently demanding—from that of almost any other work of fiction in English.

We are meant to recognize in Apollyon, then, no straightforward monster of popular fiction but instead, as his Greek name (meaning 'the Destroyer') signals, the demon-king released from 'the bottomless pit' in the New Testament's book of Revelation (9:1–11), whence his name is taken. His fiendish form is, in fact, the result of some careful textual patchworking, Bunyan having stitched features of Leviathan in Job 41 (its 'scales', for instance) onto the Beast of Revelation 13. Yet Christian's appearance is no less determined by Scripture than Apollyon's. Emerging Bible in hand when first we meet him, his costume throughout has been carefully selected from a capsule wardrobe of scriptural quotations. The 'Raggs' he wears at the beginning are those of Isaiah 64:6, and the 'Raiment' in which he is transformed by the 'three shining ones' is lifted from Zechariah 3:4 (*PP*, 1, 38). By the time he faces Apollyon, Christian has changed into the notably

---

[6] On Bunyan and romance, see Chapter 22 in this volume.
[7] Hannibal Hamlin, 'Bunyan's Biblical Progresses', in Hannibal Hamlin and Norman W. Jones (eds.), *The King James Bible after 400 Years* (Cambridge: Cambridge University Press, 2010), 202–18 (207).

Pauline outfit of 'the whole armour of God' presented to him at Palace Beautiful: 'the breastplate of righteousness', 'the shield of faith', 'the helmet of salvation', and, of course, 'the sword of the Spirit, which is the word of God' (Ephesians 6:13–18). Significantly, Christian's moment of despair comes only when he loses touch with this all-important 'Word-sword', while his 'nimbly' reaching out to grasp it again results in a crucial moment of redress, not only in the return of Christian's strength but also in the redoubling of the Bible's power upon the page. Our resurgent Word-warrior roars his way to victory with two explosive scriptural blasts, twinned from the Old and New Testaments: '*Rejoyce not against me, O mine Enemy!*' (Micah 7:8) and '*Nay, in all these things we are more than Conquerours*' (Romans 8:37). In doing so, his weapon doubles before our eyes, transforming into yet another text. It becomes, as Bob Owens has pointed out, 'the word of God' of Hebrews 4:12: 'quick, and powerful, and sharper than any two-edged sword'.[8]

Curiously, Bunyan places the organizing principle of this episode in a biblical quotation that goes unvoiced in the narrative itself. When the wounded Apollyon flees the field, a lone reference appears in the margin, rather like the hand that comes unbidden to Christian with 'some of the leaves of the Tree of Life', imprinting something instructive upon the page: simply, 'James 4. 7' (*PP*, 60). This scriptural link is important for us to open, for it provides the homiletic conclusion to the skirmish we have just witnessed: 'Submit yourselves therefore to God. Resist the devil, and he will fly from you.' If we know the Geneva or King James translations of the New Testament well enough to recall without hesitation the words of James 4:7, this quotation may well come to mind with a sudden and intimate immediacy as our eyes fall across it, in the way that Bunyan describes biblical quotations coming to (and falling upon) him in *Grace Abounding*. If not, then we may have to stop reading *The Pilgrim's Progress* altogether, setting it aside in order to take up and search the book in which this reference originally appears: the Bible. Such is the trick in Apollyon's tale.

'INTO AN ALLEGORY'

In asking us to put down *The Pilgrim's Progress* and pick up the Scriptures, Christian's clash with Apollyon becomes a scene of conflict over reading itself. Here, popular fiction wrestles 'up close' with biblical instruction for dominance on the page, just as the marginal notes tussle for attention against the gravitational pull of the 'main' story, tapping us on the shoulder as we read, breaking our concentration by telling us what's happening even as it occurs, and commenting knowingly on the actors, as in the note that bids Talkative, at one point, '*A good riddance*' (*PP*, 85).[9] How is it best, then, to interpret the episode we have just read: as another adventuresome tale of derring-do, or

---

[8] W. R. Owens, 'John Bunyan and the Bible', in Anne Dunan-Page (ed.), *The Cambridge Companion to Bunyan* (Cambridge: Cambridge University Press, 2010), 39–50 (49–50).

[9] On Bunyan's use of marginal notes, see Chapter 25 in this volume.

as an unerring exposition of James 4:7? Are we in danger of merely '*playing with the out-side of* Bunyan's '*Dream*', as the verse 'Conclusion' warns us (*PP*, 164), if we enjoy it simply as a story? Yet what kind of fiction invites us to close the book we are reading in order to find in another the key that will unlock its significance? Such is the complex biblical art of *The Pilgrim's Progress*. Like an immersive virtual world, everything we see rendered imaginatively upon its pages—its landscapes, conversations, and people, as lifelike as they appear to be at times—is constructed from the informational building-blocks of Scripture. This is a text programmed, as it were, in biblical 'code'. Reading *The Pilgrim's Progress* can, then, be like walking through the Bible itself: artfully rearranged and homiletically expounded; disguised as fiction but revealed as '*Truth*' by characters who encounter scriptural quotations as objects to be held or beheld and who, like figures in Puritan guidebooks, address us '*Dialogue-wise*' (*PP*, 6), at times as imitations of humanity and at others as animated concordances.

That Bunyan asks us to look beyond the surface of his text to read the code out of which it has been composed, often by rendering that code visible upon the page for us plainly to see, also points to the second way in which Christian's confrontation with Apollyon, and indeed *The Pilgrim's Progress* as a whole, are always more complicated than at first appears. For to be required to see Christian's sword as something other than a sword—because, in reality, it is 'the sword of the Spirit', which in turn is really 'the Word of God'—is to be invited to step into the vertiginous world of allegory and of allegorical interpretation. In such a world—by definition—nothing is ever as it seems. In allegory, categories of the real—that which is physical or spiritual, visible or invisible, literal or figurative—can swap places, or even occupy more than one representational space and meaning at a time, often with dizzying effects. An allegorical '*Method*' that works like this—employing the '*Dark Figures*' of '*Similitude*' and of '*Types, Shadows, and Metaphors*' as the media through which Bunyan will tell his story of Christian salvation—is designed to induce psycho-active effects (*PP*, 2, 4–5). Reading *The Pilgrim's Progress* can be mind-bending. This book, Bunyan states, will allow us to 'Dream, and yet not sleep'; to 'loose thy self' in its labyrinth and yet 'find thy self again without a charm'. Most importantly, Bunyan's '*Allegories*' expect the reader, through the delicate business of laying his '*Book, thy Head and thy Heart together*', to '*read thy self*', even though, he warns, '*thou knows't not what*' you might be reading at times (*PP*, 4, 6–7).

Christian's encounter with Apollyon presents a good example of one of those times. Can we be sure that we 'know' what we are reading here? After all, the way that Bunyan presents this contest is as a superlatively physical event: the blasting of Apollyon's 'Darts', the blows and thrusts, the wounding and the up-close wrestling, all of this is experienced bodily by figures engaged in actual combat. Yet, even while the language reinforces this sense of heavy kinetic activity, Bunyan asks us to see the action as entirely non-physical, indeed metaphysical. For the struggle with Apollyon is, of course, inward and interior, spiritual and mental, not corporeal. No body-blow is delivered; no visible wound is received. Apollyon's are the 'fiery darts of the wicked' of Ephesians 6:16, 'quenched' by Christian's 'shield of faith', and his sword, as we know, is not material but spiritual: the Word of God. Everything is happening, then, 'inside': everything we 'see' is invisible. Yet because the central conceit of battling for survival is developed so extensively it is easy to forget, as we read on, that this is anything other than a straightforward fight: that it is, in fact, taking place 'within' Christian, and that when our hero is hurt 'in his head, his hand and foot', what is actually being '*wounded*', as the helpful marginal hand informs us, is his '*understanding, faith and conversation*' (*PP*, 59).

While it may seem no more than obvious to point out that in the head-spinning world of allegory there is literally (or do we mean figuratively?) more going on than meets the eye, it is important nevertheless to draw out how such a scene works to upset our interpretative instincts. Like Christian when Apollyon begins to 'gather up close' to him, allegory likewise can throw us. Is, for instance, Christian's struggle with Apollyon a literal battle, to be read figuratively (i.e. as spiritual and internal), or a figurative fracas to be read literally (i.e. again, strangely enough, as spiritual and internal)? What would be the difference? To ask such questions is to begin to unlock the conceptual complexity of Bunyan's allegorical project, because in the metaphorically encoded world of *The Pilgrim's Progress* the mêlée we witness between Christian and Apollyon is both literal and figurative; both physical and metaphysical. Either/or categories break down in this '*Method*' as 'physical-psychical-spiritual distinctions' dissolve: a process given further imaginative richness by Bunyan's employment of the dream-narrative device which permits disembodied hands and celestial chariots to break into the narrative frame with ease (*PP*, 60, 97).[10] The 'reality' of what we see in Christian's clash with Apollyon, and everywhere else in *The Pilgrim's Progress*, thus flickers beneath the gaze, making us hesitate between dual frames of reference: literal and figurative, surreal and diurnal, spiritual and physical, magical and truthful. These boundaries keep crossing and dissolving throughout, playfully yet meaningfully drawing attention to how this allegory's excluded middles—neither either/or, but both/and—encode its '*Truth within a Fable*' (*PP*, 7).

To approach *The Pilgrim's Progress* in this way is simply to be reminded, of course, that allegory is never simply 'a way of writing' but also 'a mode of reading'.[11] Indeed, as a traditional hermeneutic method, interpreting by allegory offered Bunyan and his contemporaries a helpful (and also necessary) way of reading the Old and the New Testaments 'as one and the same', as Bunyan puts it, by translating obscure or 'dark' passages into 'Types, Figures and Similitudes' in order to reveal their 'Gospel' significance. Scriptural interpretation for Bunyan thus involves the ability to convert or 'Gospellize' (*MW*, 12: 276) as types and allegories those parts of the Bible which, when first encountered, can be difficult to comprehend and which must be 'spiritualized': 'we may, yea,

---

[10] John Stachniewski, *The Persecutory Imagination: English Puritanism and the Literature of Despair* (Oxford: Clarendon Press, 1991), 172.

[11] Roger Pooley, 'The Wilderness of this World: Bunyan's *Pilgrim's Progress*', *BQ*, 27 (1978), 290–99 (295). On allegory, see, further, Chapter 21 in this volume; Brian Cummings, 'Protestant Allegory', in Rita Copeland and Peter T. Struck (eds.), *The Cambridge Companion to Allegory* (Cambridge: Cambridge University Press, 2010), 177–90; Gerald L. Bruns, 'Midrash and Allegory: The Beginnings of Scriptural Interpretation', in Robert Alter and Frank Kermode (eds.), *The Literary Guide to the Bible* (London: Collins, 1987), 625–46.

we ought to search out the spiritual meaning of them', Bunyan recommends, 'because they serve to confirm and illustrate matters to our understandings' (*MW*, 7: 5–9).[12] As a preacher and pastor, it was his duty to help others do just that. Just as the '*Prophets*' once '*set forth Truth*' through '*Metaphors*', Bunyan writes, and given that even '*grave* Paul', he notes, '*no where doth forbid / The use of Parables*', because parables—instructive fictions constructed out of extended metaphors and similes—offer nothing less than '*wonderful realities*' (*MW*, 1: 246–47), so too can Bunyan employ '*Dark Figures*' and '*Allegories*' legitimately in *The Pilgrim's Progress*: in order, that is, to '*Seek the advance of Truth*' (*PP*, 4–5).

For Bunyan, then, allegory and metaphor, types and parables, are the power tools of biblical interpretation: they allow '*Truth*' to '*be free / To make her Salleys upon Thee, and Me*' (*PP*, 6). However, the reason why metaphor and allegory, similitude and parable are ideal vehicles for instruction in matters of '*Truth*' is not because they are mechanically decodable or can simply be transferred from one realm of signification to another, like switching labels on boxes, in the merely substitutive way of *allegoresis*.[13] Rather, as Christian recognizes in Interpreter's House, it is because they work to have an experiential effect: they can affect, perhaps even transform, our 'perceptual habits'.[14] Because in allegory, as we have seen in Christian's battle with Apollyon, the metaphorical becomes realized literally and the literal becomes defined figuratively—with these two categories of signification continually changing place before our eyes—allegory makes available a perceptual space in which it becomes possible to experience in a different way what it might mean to be burdened by sin and imprisoned in despair, or to resist the devil and be saved by grace. To read things allegorically, in other words, is to begin to see them, as Bunyan describes it in his spiritual autobiography (echoing Ephesians 1:18), through the eyes of one's understanding (*GA*, 10).

What we are invited to learn from the allegorical '*Method*' of *The Pilgrim's Progress*, then, is that faith itself is something that requires us to perceive a reality based, in a Pauline sense, in things 'unseen'. Like Christian in his tour of Interpreter's House, Bunyan's pilgrim-readers too are asked to privilege in *The Pilgrim's Progress* an unseen world of spiritual realities: '*For the things that are seen, are* Temporal', Interpreter informs Christian (and us), quoting 2 Corinthians 4:18, '*but the things that are not seen, are* Eternal' (*PP*, 32). Figurative types and similitudes, metaphors and allegories, perform such a valuable function for Bunyan because, in the end, they become the means of transforming the 'perceptual habits' that are required of faith in the first place, replicating on the page something of the experience of faith itself: allowing us to see that which is unseen, making visible that which is immaterial. Keeping before our eyes that which is invisible thus becomes the key business of Bunyan's imaginative '*mode*'

---

[12] On Bunyan and typology, see *MW*, 7: xv–li; 12: xxxviii–xlvii; Greaves, *Glimpses*, 179–80; and Chapter 20 in this volume.

[13] Carolyn Van Dyke, *The Fiction of Truth: Structures of Meaning in Narrative and Dramatic Allegory* (Ithaca, NY, and London: Cornell University Press, 1985), 42–6.

[14] Stanley Fish, *Self-Consuming Artifacts: The Experience of Seventeenth-Century Literature* (Berkeley, Los Angeles, CA, and London: University of California Press, 1972), 224–64 (237).

(*PP*, 1). No wonder Bunyan defends allegory and metaphor so vigorously in his prefatory 'Apology'. For, in Bunyan's hands, *The Pilgrim's Progress* becomes a vehicle through which his reader's understanding in spiritual things can be prepared and tested, exercised and developed. *The Pilgrim's Progress* is not just an allegorical 'fable': it is a simulator for the mind's flight into Gospel '*Truth*', and into the realm of things unseen.[15]

'Let Truth Be Free'

It is easy to see why, in these terms, allegory is a model form for the story of a '*Graceless*' man transformed into a more faithful and hopeful 'Christian' by reading (*PP*, 46). It is also ideal for a text that aims to convert its readers. As Bunyan claims, '*This book will make a Traveller of thee, / If by its Counsel thou wilt ruled be*' (*PP*, 6). In the first edition of *The Pilgrim's Progress*, the word was printed as '*Travailer*', suggesting not just a fellow 'traveller', that is, but one who travails, working steadily towards '*Truth*' and thereby labouring, in the seventeenth-century sense too of child-bearing, to undergo the 'travails' of a 'new birth'. The reader of *The Pilgrim's Progress* stands, in this respect, as its principal 'character', with interpretation—as well as misinterpretation—proving to be a primary and repeated site of action throughout the narrative.[16] Famously opening with a man brought to book by the Bible in his hand, *The Pilgrim's Progress* concludes, we must not forget, with a scene of reading no less important. Having put his faith in 'a good heart that has good thoughts' and in living 'a good life […] according to Gods commandments', when that 'good Liver', Mr Ignorance, reaches the Celestial City, he does so 'supposing' that the words inscribed in 'Letters of Gold' above its portal must apply to him: '*Blessed are they that do his commandments, that they may have right to the Tree of Life; and may enter in through the Gates into the City*' (Revelation 22:14) (*PP*, 145, 123, 161–62).

Unlike Christian, however, Ignorance has not learned to read. Having held all along an erroneous (indeed, ignorant) notion of what saving faith actually is—the conviction, contrary to his own rational moralism, that salvation is offered by grace alone, not reached through one's own good deeds—he cannot understand what is meant by doing God's '*commandments*': to hold, that is, that we are justified by faith, not by a willingness simply to 'Pray, Fast, pay Tithes, and give Alms' (*PP*, 123–24).[17]

---

[15] See, further, Michael Davies, 'Bunyan and Religious Allegory', in Tom Keymer (ed.), *The Oxford History of the Novel in English, Volume I* (Oxford: Oxford University Press, 2017), 310–26.

[16] Maureen Quilligan, *The Language of Allegory: Defining the Genre* (Ithaca, NY, and London: Cornell University Press, 1979), 21, 24, 225–26.

[17] Mr Ignorance's rational moralist creed—which, for Bunyan, is damnably 'legalistic', as it proposes a false idea of salvation through adherence to the Law, not grace—can be read in the context of Bunyan's opposition to Restoration Latitudinarianism, especially given his dispute with Edward Fowler in 1672 over justification by faith. See *MW*, 4: xx–xxv; Greaves, *Glimpses*, 278–86; Isabel Rivers, *Reason, Grace, and Sentiment: Studies in the Language of Religion and Ethics in England, 1660–1780* (Cambridge: Cambridge University Press, 1991), 89–163; and Chapter 13 in this volume.

Mr Ignorance is denied admission to eternal life at the very end of *The Pilgrim's Progress* not just because he lacks the necessary credentials—he has no 'Certificate' of faith (*PP*, 163) to credit his acceptance—but because he is soteriologically illiterate. Misinterpreting the text emblazoned above the gates of the Celestial City, he assumes his guaranteed 'entrance' will be 'quickly administred' (*PP*, 162). Poor Mr Ignorance, despite being socially responsible and indeed thoroughly likable, pays dearly for failing this final interpretative test. Through his fatal misunderstanding we learn that there is indeed 'a way to Hell, even from the Gates of Heaven, as well as from the City of *Destruction*' (*PP*, 163).

Yet Bunyan's choice of allegory as the basis for *The Pilgrim's Progress* may well have a significance beyond its capacity to train its readers to experience that which is unseen or to warn us, as Mr Ignorance demonstrates, that '*By mis-interpreting evil insues*' (*PP*, 164). If we were to assume, as most Bunyan scholars do, that *The Pilgrim's Progress* was drafted around 1668–72—that is, towards the latter end of Bunyan's longest period in prison and up to ten years before it was first published—then it would have been composed at a crucial point in the ongoing Restoration debate over the toleration of Nonconformists: those religious Dissenters, like Bunyan, whose insistence on worshipping outside the Church of England met with ferocious opposition, both socially and politically, almost as soon as Charles II returned as king in 1660. As a Nonconformist preacher who refused to cease serving in his vocation, Bunyan faced a period of persecution which would last, in varying degrees of intensity, for almost thirty years.[18]

Bunyan's sudden 'fall' into allegory in *The Pilgrim's Progress*, and in particular his defence of metaphors, types, and shadows as vehicles conveying Gospel '*Truth*', take on a distinctly polemical resonance in this context. Dissenters were vilified by their antagonists, we should remember, as 'enthusiastic' extremists and as 'seditious' plotters. Evidence for this could be seen, it was purported, not only in their willingness to defy the law by meeting to worship in secret 'conventicles' but also in their very language: in, that is, their adoption of a 'Gospel' style full of 'clownish and slovenly Similitudes', 'wanton and lascivious Allegories', and 'gaudy' and 'childish Metaphors'. So wrote the intolerant Church of England divine, Samuel Parker, when deriding the '*Fanatique Tempers and Principles*' of Dissenters in *A Discourse of Ecclesiastical Politie* (1670). How could toleration be granted, Parker asks, to '*the rudest and most barbarous people in the world*' who threaten to '*blow up the very Foundations of Government*', and who 'will not talk of Religions but in barbarous and uncouth Similitudes'? For the likes of Parker, with whom Andrew Marvell famously locked horns in *The Rehearsal Transpros'd* (1672), the solution was simple: 'an Act of Parliament', he cried, should 'abridge Preachers the use of fulsom and lushious Metaphors' as 'an effectual Cure of all our present Distempers', after which

---

[18] See, further, Chapters 2 and 8 in this volume. See also Michael R. Watts, *The Dissenters: From the Reformation to the French Revolution* (Oxford: Clarendon Press, 1978); Richard L. Greaves, *John Bunyan and English Nonconformity* (London: Hambledon Press, 1992); and Greaves, *Glimpses*.

'all the swelling Mysteries of Fanaticism would immediately sink into flat and empty Nonsense'.[19]

If *The Pilgrim's Progress* were to find its compositional genesis during the Restoration Crisis of 1667–73, as Richard Greaves has argued,[20] and when Parker was putting his vitriolic views on Dissent into print, then we could see how Bunyan's defence of the very kinds of religious expression under attack by opponents of Nonconformity—allegory, metaphor, typology—engages in something more directly political. In these terms, the writing of *The Pilgrim's Progress* becomes an act of defiance: a defence of Bunyan's religion and of the '*Gospel-strains*' (*PP*, 7) in which it is expressed, as well as a bid for toleration and liberty of conscience; for peaceable Nonconformists to be freed, that is, from the legal compulsion to worship in the Church of England, and to remain unmolested by harassment, persecution, or imprisonment. Let '*Truth be free*' indeed (*PP*, 6). Yet this is a context imprinted upon the allegory in other obvious ways: in the marginal gloss that converts the dreamer's 'Denn' into Bunyan's 'Gaol' at the very beginning, for instance, and of course in the pilgrims' hostile reception at Vanity Fair, where they are tried and imprisoned, and where Faithful is murdered in a style distinctly reminiscent of John Foxe's *Acts and Monuments* or *Book of Martyrs* (first published in 1563).[21]

We can also read this history of persecution in the memorable tale we have been chasing throughout this chapter: Christian's encounter with Apollyon. Although, on one level, Christian's struggle with this particular 'devil' is the allegorical counterpart to the kind of wrestling with 'the Tempter' that Bunyan describes in such compelling detail in *Grace Abounding* (for example, *GA*, 18), on another, Christian's argument with Apollyon is about 'service' in undeniably political terms. Apollyon is Christian's '*King*', the monster claims, and Christian one of his rebellious '*Subjects*' (*PP*, 56–7). Refusing this particular master's 'wages'—'*for the wages of Sin is death*', Christian states, quoting Romans 6:23—the pilgrim's terms remain uncompromising:

> I have let my self to another, even to the King of Princes […]. I have given him my faith, and sworn my Allegiance to him; how then can I go back from this, and not be hanged as a Traitor? […] I like his Service, his Wages, his Servants, his Government, his Company, and Countrey better than thine: and therefore leave off to perswade me further, I am his Servant, and I will follow him. (*PP*, 57)

When Apollyon's powers of persuasion fail to dislodge these convictions, he resorts to more violent means of coercion. In a 'grievous rage', he reveals in no uncertain terms his enmity towards the '*Prince*' whom Christian serves: '*I hate his Person, his Laws, and People: I am come out on purpose to withstand thee*' (*PP*, 59). And so the battle begins.

---

[19] Samuel Parker, *A Discourse of Ecclesiastical Politie* (1670), xii–xxii; 65–6; 71–7; and see, further, Davies, *Graceful Reading*, 200–07.

[20] Greaves, *Glimpses*, 201–27.

[21] See, further, John R. Knott, Jr, *Discourses of Martyrdom in English Literature, 1563–1694* (Cambridge: Cambridge University Press, 1993), 179–215; and Chapter 6 this volume.

Apollyon may well be a version of 'the Tempter' who seeks to work inwardly on the new convert in order to corrode his spiritual resolve—to wound him internally, as Christian suffers, '*in his understanding, faith and conversation*' (*PP*, 59)—but he is also the embodiment of the religious persecution that Bunyan suffered throughout the 1660s and early 1670s, and that both he and his fellow Nonconformists would continue to face well into the 1680s. The nature of Christian's dispute over 'service' thus becomes clearer. This is a contest over what is owed to a king such as Apollyon, and how far being '*Subject*' to a '*Prince and God*' of such worldly '*Dominions*' may be reconciled to the '*Allegiance*' owed by Christian 'to the King of Princes' (*PP*, 56–7). As Bunyan himself recognized all too well, the mode of this struggle is primarily inward: a question of how far one can suffer for one's beliefs, and for how long. Is the prisoner of conscience, as Bunyan found himself asking when in prison, willing to face 'perpetual banishment' or even execution for the sake of his faith, like the 'Saints of old' who would not be deterred by '*Fire* and *Faggot, Sword* or *Halter*' or 'stinking *Dungeons*' (*GA*, 95, 97; *MW*, 5: 164)? How could Bunyan continue to remain in prison, he would ask of himself, when his conscientious objection required him to leave his wife and children to fend for themselves, 'parting' from whom was 'as the pulling of flesh from my bones' (*GA*, 98)?

It is precisely such doubts that Apollyon brings forward in his psychological assaults on Christian, reminding him that other '*transgressors against me*' have already '*been put to shameful deaths!*' and that only Apollyon himself can guarantee safe '*deliverance*' from such a fate (*PP*, 58). Indeed, it is by pressing on Christian's interior doubts, flaws, and 'infirmities'—of which Apollyon has a terrifyingly intimate and comprehensive knowledge, as if able, like O'Brien in George Orwell's *Nineteen Eighty-Four* (1949), to read into Christian's mind and heart his worst failures and most potent fears—that Apollyon seeks to break him down: evidence, should we ever have needed it, that the struggle between persecution and its resistance is fought most fiercely on the interior battlefields of the mind and spirit. That it is a warfare that must be waged, however, is Bunyan's point. As he concludes in *An Exposition on the Ten First Chapters of Genesis* (1692), 'the way to weary out God's Enemies' is

> to maintain, and make good the Front against them: *Resist the devil, and he will flie*. Now if the Captain, their king *Apollion*, be made to yield, how can his Followers stand their ground? The *Dragon*, the Devil, Satan, he was *cast out into the earth* [Revelation 12:9], and his Angels were cast out with him. But how? It was by fighting: *Michael and his Angels fought with the Dragon*, and overcame him [...] by *not loving of their lives unto the death* [Revelation 12:7, 11]. Let this [...] serve for Persecutors. (*MW*, 12: 179–80)

No wonder Christian offers thanks to '*blessed* Michael' for having '*helped*' him in this Apocalyptic 'Battel' to vanquish Apollyon, and for being 'delivered' from 'out of the mouth of the Lion' (*PP*, 60): from the persecution, that is, that left Bunyan, and others like him, to '*stick between the Teeth of the Lions in the Wilderness*' (*GA*, 1).

'Apollyon's Talons'

This chapter began with a claim, prompted by Christian Creswell Carver's letter of 14 March 1917, that one of the reasons why *The Pilgrim's Progress* has endured is because it is about endurance. If this is so, then it is, in no small part, because its author knew first-hand what resources were required to prevail against trial and imprisonment, harassment and humiliation, especially in the absence, as Christian puts it, of any 'present deliverance' (*PP*, 58). Yet, although the persecution experienced by Bunyan and his church in the years leading up to and also following the publication of *The Pilgrim's Progress, Part I* informs directly the terms of Christian's contention with Apollyon, it hardly limits or restricts the availability of Bunyan's allegory to readers in other contexts, who will recognize within its pages something equally resourceful when it comes to the trials of the self in conflict. George Eliot, for example, would present the painful story of Maggie Tulliver's 'inward strife' in *The Mill on the Floss* (1860)—a struggle over individual fulfilment versus the love and loyalty owed to others—with Bunyan's 'Valley of Humiliation' (the title of the novel's fourth 'book') firmly in mind. Maggie's own 'spiritual conflict', like Christian's interior wrestling with Apollyon—a tale known to her from childhood through 'a shabby old copy' of *The Pilgrim's Progress*—turns on an agonizing crisis over how best to act—what to do?—in conscience.[22]

Christian's confrontation with the 'devil' Apollyon facilitates for Eliot the expression of her heroine's traumatic inner contest. Likewise, for Lieutenant Carver, writing from the Western Front over half a century later, Apollyon is not just the Great War itself—the ever-present threat of death—but also its inward effect upon mind and spirit: the sapping of the soldier's conviction, 'when you are struggling along, through foot-deep sticky mud, and there are shells bursting on the path in front of you, and corpses lying about', that such a war has any purpose, yet which leaves little choice other than to go 'on and on from desolation to desolation'. 'I sometimes think that war is *all* criminal folly', Carver wrote tellingly in another letter home, 'and that the excuse that we were forced into it does not excuse us.'[23] What can an officer fighting in the trenches do with such a thought? What shall he do?

For many readers now, the capacity of *The Pilgrim's Progress* to endure may well lie less obviously in some of the aspects addressed in this chapter: in its remarkably resourceful biblicism, for example, or its narrative and allegorical sophistication, or even in the way it speaks vitally to its own historical and religious contexts. Its relevance may be regarded instead as lying in the questions it raises presently about conscience: how to act, when to resist, and why to fight for what we believe with relentless conviction, whether peace, justice, or liberty of conscience itself. To this end, the first words that Christian

---

[22] George Eliot, *The Mill on the Floss*, ed. Gordon S. Haight; intro. Juliette Atkinson (Oxford: Oxford University Press, 2015), 402, 460, 18. For references to *The Pilgrim's Progress*, see 18, 101, 105–06, 223, 251.
[23] *War Letters*, 65–9.

utters in *The Pilgrim's Progress*—'What shall I do?'—could be read not just as a declamation of spiritual paralysis or as evidence, as Christian's family sees it, of mental collapse: 'some frenzy distemper' (*PP*, 9). Rather, this could be heard as the fugitive outcry for action in any moment of crisis. This single phrase—'What shall I do?'—could be the always-needed call of conscience, the interior driver that compels something to be done, and a reminder too that we might still read *The Pilgrim's Progress* now in order to know what to do, how to act, before those forces that threaten to humiliate, oppress, persecute. If so, then *The Pilgrim's Progress* will continue to endure, continue to run, sustaining the human spirit through despair, injustice, and suffering, however near Apollyon's talons may be.

Suggested Reading

Collmer, Robert (ed.), *Bunyan in Our Time* (Ohio and London: Kent State University Press, 1989).
Kaufmann, U. Milo, *The Pilgrim's Progress and Traditions in Puritan Meditation* (New Haven, CT, and London: Yale University Press, 1966).
Keeble, N. H., *The Literary Culture of Nonconformity in Later Seventeenth Century England* (Leicester: Leicester University Press, 1987).
Keeble, N. H. (ed.), *John Bunyan: Conventicle and Parnassus* (Oxford: Clarendon Press, 1988).
Knott, Jr, John R., *The Sword of the Spirit: Puritan Responses to the Bible* (Chicago and London: University of Chicago Press, 1980).
Laurence, Anne, W. R. Owens, and Stuart Sim (eds.), *John Bunyan and his England, 1628–1688* (London: Hambledon Press, 1990).
Luxon, Thomas H., *Literal Figures: Puritan Allegory and the Reformation Crisis in Representation* (Chicago and London: University of Chicago Press, 1995).
Newey, Vincent (ed.), *The Pilgrim's Progress: Critical and Historical Views* (Liverpool: Liverpool University Press, 1980).
Owens, W. R. and Stuart Sim (eds.), *Reception, Appropriation, Recollection: Bunyan's* Pilgrim's Progress (Bern: Peter Lang, 2007).
Swaim, Kathleen, *Pilgrim's Progress, Puritan Progress: Discourses and Contexts* (Urbana and Chicago, IL: University of Illinois Press, 1993).

CHAPTER 15

THE LIFE AND DEATH OF MR. BADMAN (1680)

KATSUHIRO ENGETSU

The Life and Death of Mr. Badman appeared in 1680: that is, after the publication of *The Pilgrim's Progress* (1678), and before *The Holy War* (1682) and *The Pilgrim's Progress, Part II* (1684). Both the publication date and the allegorical name of the title character suggest that it may resemble quite closely these other major narrative works. However, the style of *The Life and Death of Mr. Badman* is markedly different. For the author's '*ease*' and the reader's '*pleasure*', Bunyan explains, it is written entirely in '*the form of a Dialogue*' between two godly Christians, Wiseman and Attentive, who relate and discuss as eye-witnesses the eponymous hero's '*wicked* life', from his childhood through to his horribly '*fearful*', and much-anticipated, death (*MB*, 1, 16). As Chapter 6 in this volume illustrates, the dialogue format was used by Arthur Dent in *The Plaine Mans Path-Way to Heaven* (1601), a popular Puritan manual and one of the two books Bunyan's first wife brought to him as her dowry (*GA*, 8). Behind *The Life and Death of Mr. Badman* there also lies *The Pilgrim's Progress*, written '*Dialogue-wise*' too (*PP*, 6), but which had also taught Bunyan the literary skill of employing narrative allegory in a sustained way. There is also *Grace Abounding to the Chief of Sinners* (1666), central to which stands the personal significance of conversation in Bunyan's own spiritual conversion. As a very different form of fiction—one that shows not '*the* Progress *of the* Pilgrim *from this World to Glory*' but '*the Life and Death of the Ungodly*' in '*their travel from this world to* Hell' (*MB*, 1)—we thus find in *The Life and Death of Mr. Badman* a uniquely effective combination of elements to be found throughout Bunyan's previously published writings: those of traditional devotional literature and works of religious instruction, as well as of allegory and spiritual autobiography.

If we look beyond *The Life and Death of Mr. Badman*, however, we also find some important aspects of modern literature newly emerging in Bunyan's work. 'Mr. Badman is Bunyan's nearest approach to the novel: it has in flashes both the realism—the cult of verisimilitude for its own sake—and the secular view of life which were to be the great instruments of the eighteenth century', notes Roger Sharrock, one of the greatest

Bunyan scholars of the twentieth century.[1] Anne Dunan-Page, a leading figure in twenty-first-century Bunyan studies where historical interests are often connected with literary criticism, discovers a forgotten secular 'story of Bunyan the taverner' in a nineteenth-century journal in order to interrogate the established image of Bunyan as a respectable Christian author.[2] This chapter discusses *The Life and Death of Mr. Badman* as a historical text in which traditional devotional literature is about to transform itself into modern secular writing. Prompted by Dunan-Page's provocative finding, my argument will start with a biographical and historical examination of the relationship between Bunyan and what I am calling a late seventeenth-century 'alehouse culture', which will lead us on to a consideration of the wider implications of blasphemy, Sabbath-breaking, and domestic violence in Bunyan's local community, as reflected in *The Life and Death of Mr. Badman*.[3] The aim of the chapter will be to show just how bad Badman is.

Alehouse Culture

In *The Life and Death of Mr. Badman*, the main character is represented as 'a Frequenter of *Taverns* and *Tippling-houses*' (*MB*, 45), and the alehouse is thus established at the outset as a key cultural signifier of his 'badness'. Near the beginning of the narrative, Attentive relates a horrible episode of '*Cursing and Swearing*' in '*a blind Ale-house*' located only '*a bow-shoot from*' Wiseman's former house (*MB*, 33–7).[4] We are told that the alehouse keeper had 'an half-fool' son, called Edward, but known as 'Ned', whom his father would provoke to curse and swear for the amusement of the customers (*MB*, 35). We will return to this episode later, but here I want to draw attention to an intriguing autobiographical link with Bunyan himself. A little further on, Wiseman reports having rebuked a young man for his wicked behaviour, to which the man, in a 'great huff' had replied, '*What would the Devil do for company, if it was not for such as I*.' This young man, says Wiseman, 'was my Play-fellow when I was solacing my self in my sins: I [...] make mention of him to my shame' (*MB*, 41–2). In a marginal note against this passage, Bunyan identifies this young man as 'one H. S. who once was my Companion. He was own brother to Ned, of whom you read before.'

---

[1] Roger Sharrock, *John Bunyan*, 2nd edn (London: Macmillan, 1968), 116.

[2] 'Introduction', in Anne Dunan-Page (ed.), *The Cambridge Companion to Bunyan* (Cambridge: Cambridge University Press, 2010), 1–9 (1). She found the story in *The Ladies' Monthly Museum*, 1 November 1817, p. 249.

[3] On the early modern alehouse, see, further, Peter Clark, *The English Alehouse: A Social History, 1200–1830* (London: Longmans, 1983); Keith Wrightson, 'Alehouses, Order and Reformation in Rural England, 1590–1660', in Eileen Yeo and Stephen Yeo (eds.), *Popular Culture and Class Conflict 1590–1914* (Brighton: Harvester, 1981), 1–27; and Mark Hailwood, *Alehouses and Good Fellowship in Early Modern England* (Woodbridge: Boydell & Brewer, 2014).

[4] A 'blind' alehouse was one 'out of sight, out of the way, secret, obscure': *OED*, blind *adj.*, III. 8a.

This 'H. S.' is evidently Bunyan's friend 'Harry' in *Grace Abounding to the Chief of Sinners*, 'a young man' in Bedford, who, when Bunyan rebuked his wickedness, replied 'in a great chafe, *What would the Devil do for company if it were not for such as I am?*' Bunyan later 'forsook [Harry's] company' because the 'young man' was 'a most wicked Creature for cursing and swearing, and whoring' (*GA*, 16). So, too, Wiseman, when called by God's 'Grace', parted company with the young man he had rebuked, 'still leaving him in his sins' (*MB*, 42). When we closely read *The Life and Death of Mr. Badman* in reference to *Grace Abounding to the Chief of Sinners*, we find a glimpse of the relationship between Bunyan and those who frequented an alehouse in his local community. By his own admission, in his youth he had evidently been an intimate friend of the son of the keeper of a 'blind Ale-house' in Bedford. It was not Bunyan, then, but his friend's father who was a 'taverner' in Bedford.

The local details of the 'blind Ale-house' also offer us a good case study to disentangle some threads of the literary genres that interweave *The Life and Death of Mr. Badman*. The narrative framework is a dialogue drawing on the example of Dent's *Plaine Mans Path-Way to Heaven*, while the narrative mode mixes generic features of Bunyan's own preceding literary masterpieces: the spiritual autobiography of *Grace Abounding* and the allegory of *The Pilgrim's Progress*. 'H. S.' is, as we have seen, modelled on 'Harry', an actual acquaintance in *Grace Abounding*. It is significant, then, that the alehouse keeper's son is one of only two Bedford inhabitants whose proper names appear in Bunyan's spiritual autobiography (while even Bunyan's parents and his first wife are left unnamed), the other being John Gifford, his invaluable mentor (*GA*, 25). Harry and Gifford thus occupy diametrically opposite spiritual positions in Bunyan's local world; Harry represents the old 'bad' alehouse centre of the local community to which Bunyan had been strongly attached but from which he would eventually separate himself, whereas Gifford stands at the new 'good' Nonconformist centre of a section of the local community to which Bunyan became connected and from which he would never separate himself. Harry and the '*Young* Badman' in *The Life and Death of Mr. Badman* are, moreover, defined by Attentive as '*obstinate sinners*' (*MB*, 42), reminding us of Obstinate, the character in *The Pilgrim's Progress* who appears as one of Christian's 'Neighbours' at the beginning of the allegory. Christian has made up his mind to leave his neighbourhood and to follow Evangelist's teaching, but Harry-like Obstinate tries to persuade him to come back to his '*Friends*' and '*Comforts*' (*PP*, 9–12). Badman the fictional character and 'H. S.' his companion in wickedness may thus be seen as the literary offspring of Harry the real-life figure of *Grace Abounding* and Obstinate, the allegorical figure of *The Pilgrim's Progress*.

This localized setting with real, as opposed to allegorical, locations and geographical points of reference, from Wimbledon and Wellingborough to Bedford and St Neots, is key to the construction of *The Life and Death of Mr. Badman*, and why it is, in the end, so different in style and technique from Bunyan's other allegories (*MB*, 32, 44, 48, 82). Badman lives in a recognizably real place: 'our Town', as Attentive and Wiseman put it, set in an 'English world', the sins of which are 'swallowing up a Nation' and 'sinking it' (*MB*, 69, 81, 7–8). Within this framework, the local presence of alehouse culture in *The Life and Death of Mr. Badman* is crucial: it gives a sustained sense of fictional unity to Badman's character and actions as they develop throughout the narrative. The young Badman's ungodliness, as we have seen, is characterized from the beginning by his acquaintance with the world of the 'blind Ale-house'. Similarly, the grown-up Badman's impenitence is assured by another significant alehouse episode related by Wiseman to Attentive:

> Upon a time [Badman] was at an Ale-house, that wicked house, about two or three miles from home, and having there drank hard the greatest part of the day, when night was come, he would stay no longer, but calls for his horse, gets up, and like a Mad-man (as drunken persons usually ride) away he goes, as hard as horse could lay legs to the ground. Thus he rid, till coming to a dirty place, where his horse flouncing in, fell, threw his master, and with his fall broke his legg: so there he lay. But you would not think how he swore at first. (*MB*, 131)

Wiseman's storytelling here, typical of *The Life and Death of Mr. Badman* as a whole, is both as didactic as traditional devotional literature and as realistic as the modern novel. Specifying the location of the 'Ale-house' as well as the time of the day, he begins the realistic narrative in the past tense with a set phrase to begin a story ('upon a time'). However, he switches the tense into the dramatic present when he talks of Badman's 'horse' and, drawing our attention to its 'legs', foreshadows Badman's breaking of his 'legg'. In a new sentence restored again into the past tense, Wiseman gives theological significance to the story of Badman's accident in 'a dirty place' by repeating the image of the fall: 'his horse [...] *fell* [...] and with his *fall* broke his legg' (italics added). The realistic style of narration is then transformed back into a kind of traditional devotional literature: a judgement story. Wiseman does not fail to remind us that Badman embodies this text's blasphemous alehouse culture: 'how he swore at first'. Attentive is keenly aware of his partner's homiletic message at this point because he understands '*the breaking of Mr. Badmans legg*' providentially as '*a stroak from heaven*' (*MB*, 134).

Wiseman confirms this generic feature of his own story further, again in a way characteristic of how *The Life and Death of Mr. Badman* unfolds from the outset, by drawing a parallel between his story of Badman breaking his leg and three examples from Samuel Clarke's *A Mirrour or Looking-Glass both for Saints, and Sinners* (first published in 1646 and reprinted and enlarged in many editions thereafter): a popular compilation of judgement stories in later seventeenth-century England (*MB*, 134–35). Towards the end of *The Life and Death of Mr. Badman*, Wiseman cites two more episodes from Clarke's work in order to underline 'the hand and Judgment of God' upon the old Badman in the shape of his second wife (*MB*, 146). She is 'a very Whore' who has 'companions', like Badman, 'at the Tavern and Ale-house' and gives him 'Oath for Oath, and Curse for Curse' (*MB*, 145). A marginal note summarizes the story of Badman's last years as follows: 'He is punished in his last wife for his bad carriages towards his first' (*MB*, 147). Badman's ungodliness is thus characterized by his constant acquaintance with the disreputable world of the alehouse during every stage of his life: his youth ruined by the 'blind Ale-house', his manhood humiliated by the fall from a horse on the way from an alehouse, and his old age disquieted by his remarriage to an alehouse whore.

The importance of alehouse culture in *The Life and Death of Mr. Badman* was noticed by its printer, Nathaniel Ponder. Well known for his association with Nonconformist writers like John Owen, who played an important role in procuring Bunyan's release from prison in 1677, Ponder published, among many others of Bunyan's works, *The Pilgrim's Progress*, and he knew well what readers expected from the Bedford author.[5] When Ponder reissued *The Life and Death of Mr. Badman* in 1688, the text of its first edition was newly illustrated by five woodcuts: (1) 'a Bad-man' followed by Death and the devil; (2) the horrible judgement on Dorothy Mately, who used 'to Curse and Swear;' (3) an alehouse where 'Parents take delight in Childrens Evil'; (4) an 'Informer' who reports on 'A Protestants Meeting'; and (5) Badman breaking his leg on the way back from an alehouse (*MB*, 12, 34, 36, 80, 133). The third and fifth woodcuts highlight the alehouse, which is anticipated by the first and second images of ungodliness and blasphemy. The fourth woodcut of an 'Informer' accompanies an account by Wiseman of 'W. S. a man of a very wicked life', who is compared to 'a man that was drunk' (*MB*, 81). The representation of alehouse culture and the image of the 'Informer' in these woodcuts announce the deep cultural divisions that Bunyan is both presenting and exploring in the world of *The Life and Death of Mr. Badman*.

There was in fact persistent antagonism in Bunyan's lifetime between a local alehouse culture and the Independent church at Bedford. The minutes of the Bedford congregation in 1673, for example, record the excommunication of a church member for his drunkenness at a tavern in the town. Bunyan must have been chiefly responsible for the decision because he had been appointed pastor to the congregation and released from prison in the previous year:

> *At a full assembly of the congregation* was with joynt consent of the whole body, cast out of the Church, John Rush of Bedford for being drunke after a very beastly and filthy maner, that is above the ordinery rate of drunkenness for he could not be carried home from the Swan to his own house without the help of no less then three persons, who when they had brought him home could not present him as one alive to his family, he was so dead [drunk]. (*CB*, 75)

'*'Tis a sad thing to dye drunk*', says Attentive when Wiseman reports the real case of a man in his town who 'drunk himself dead' (*MB*, 132). Like the Bedford congregation and its pastor, Bunyan, Wiseman believes that drunkenness can lead to damnation:

> For considering the hainousness of that sin, and with how many other sins it is accompanied, as with oaths, blasphemies, lyes, revellings, whoreings, brawlings, *&c.*

---

[5] Greaves, *Glimpses*, 344–47. For Ponder, see Beth Lynch, 'Nathaniel Ponder', *ODNB*; and also Chapter 9 in this volume.

it is a wonder to me, that any that live in that sin should escape such a blow from heaven that should tumble them into their graves. (*MB*, 132)

The representation of the heinous sin of drunkenness in *The Life and Death of Mr. Badman* is, then, inseparably entangled with the social reality of Bedford in Bunyan's age, and explains a great deal, perhaps, about why he was so critical of alehouse culture in his local community.[6]

This antagonism between alehouse culture and Nonconformity is allegorically developed by Bunyan in *The Holy War* (1682), Bunyan's next major literary work after *The Life and Death of Mr. Badman*. The first battle of the holy war begins with 'a notable slaughter' of six of Diabolus' Aldermen by 'one only shot' of a sling from the camp of Shaddai, the King of Mansoul: 'To wit, Mr. *Swearing*, Mr. *Whoring*, Mr. *Fury*, Mr. *Stand-to lies*, Mr. *Drunkenness*, and Mr. *Cheating*' (*HW*, 53). The reference to Drunkenness makes it clear that the six Satanic allegorical figures, slain by 'one only shot', inseparably stand for alehouse culture which, according to Wiseman, should be punished by 'a blow from heaven'. We note, too, that in the town of Mansoul there is '*Drunkards*-row, just at *Raskal*-lanes-end' where 'Mr. *Impiety* lived' (*HW*, 121). Bunyan's holy war is, in part, a spiritual battle against sins such as drunkenness and the 'many other sins' with which 'it is accompanied' and, significantly, it begins with the 'notable slaughter' of allegorical figures associated in Bunyan's writings with alehouse culture. However, the fact that the leading figure among the slaughtered Aldermen is Swearing, while Drunkenness only appears in the penultimate position, suggests that the primary concern of *The Holy War* is not so much the act of drinking but blasphemy: a consequence, for Bunyan, of the licentious condition of the early modern drinking place.

Blasphemy

Bunyan's grave concern with blasphemy around the period of the publications of *The Life and Death of Mr. Badman* and *The Holy War* is anticipated in *A Treatise of the Fear of God* (1679), a sermon in which he expounds on a plain but apocalyptic phrase from the Revelation (14:7): 'Fear God'. Insisting on the importance of 'great soberness' in making mention of the name of God, Bunyan quotes one biblical passage after another in order to warn against blasphemy:

> This therefore sheweth you the dreadful state of those that lightly, vainly, lyingly, and profanely make use of the name, this fearful name of God; either by their blasphemous cursing and oaths, or by their fraudulent dealing with their neighbour; (for some men have no way to prevail with their neighbour to bow under a cheat, but by calling falsly upon the name of the Lord to be witness that the wickedness is good and honest:) but

---

[6] See Hill, *Bunyan*, 235.

how these men will escape (when they shall be judged) devouring fire, and everlasting burnings, for their profaning and blaspheming of the name of the Lord, becomes them betimes to consider of *Jer.* 14. 14, 15. *Ezek.* 20. 39. *Exod.* 20. 7. (*MW*, 9: 12–13)

The name of God is of ineffable spiritual significance to Bunyan. In the apocalyptic vision of the Last Judgement, 'blasphemous cursing' is closely connected with the act of cheating, which is personified as one of the slaughtered members of alehouse culture in *The Holy War*. It is noteworthy that the victim of cheating is repeatedly referred to as a 'neighbour'. In talking about the apocalyptic vision of the judgement on blasphemy, Bunyan never forgets his local community in Bedford, where the alehouse threatens to challenge the neighbourhood of 'great soberness'.

Bunyan's hostility to the blasphemy that he perceived as being encouraged within local alehouses, anticipated in *The Fear of God* and reconfirmed in *The Holy War*, culminates in *The Life and Death of Mr. Badman*. Badman is clearly defined as the most irreverent troublemaker in his local community: 'Swearing and Cursing a badge of Mr. Badmans honour', we are told in a marginal note (*MB*, 27). Bunyan believes, when underlining the young Badman's sinful character, that '*Children*'—far from being innocent, as Romantics would later have it—'*come polluted with sin into the World, and* […] *oft-times the sins of their youth, especially while they are very young, are rather by vertue of Indwelling sin, than by examples that are set before them by others*' (*MB*, 17). Badman's original sin appeared at first in the form of 'Lying' (*MB*, 18). His perverse habit of 'Lying' in his 'ordinary discourse' with his 'Neighbours' (*MB*, 20), reminding us of the ninth commandment of the Decalogue ('Thou shalt not bear false witness against thy neighbour' (Exodus 20:16)), reveals its theological implication of law-breaking more clearly when it leads on to the sins of stealing and Sabbath-breaking that violate the eighth and fourth commandments respectively: '*Thou shalt not steal*' and '*Remember that thou keep holy the Sabbath day*' (*MB*, 21, 25). The image of Badman the law-breaker finally results in 'a sin against the Third Commandment, which says, *Thou shalt not take the Name of the Lord thy God in vain*' (*MB*, 27). Bunyan regards the Law of Moses as identical with that of nature because he adds that 'To curse another, and to swear vainly and falsly, are sins against the Light of Nature' (*MB*, 32). Badman's antinomian blasphemy is the most abominable threat to Bunyan's orthodox faith in the perpetual morality of the Decalogue.[7]

Bunyan's notion of profanity is based not only on theology but also on popular magic, which is associated with 'Witchcraft' (*MB*, 31), because he does not have the least doubt about the efficacy of swearing and cursing.[8] Wiseman affirms that 'Things that we swear, are, or shall be done' (*MB*, 27). Cautiously distinguishing swearing from cursing, he says

---

[7] For a more extensive discussion on the complicated relationship between Bunyan and antinomianism, see Roger Pooley, 'Bunyan and the Antinomians', in Vera Camden (ed.), *Trauma and Transformation: The Political Progress of John Bunyan* (Stanford, CA: Stanford University Press, 2008), 120–34.

[8] The popular belief in the efficacy of blasphemy as well as its relation to witchcraft in seventeenth-century England is extensively discussed in Keith Thomas, *Religion and the Decline of Magic*

that swearing 'hath immediately to do with the Name of God' while cursing is *'to wish that some evil might happen to the person or thing under the Curse, unjustly'* (*MB*, 29). However, in a further explanation he seems to dissolve the distinction between swearing and cursing, because, he says, 'Man is Gods Image, and to curse wickedly the Image of God, is to curse God himself', and 'when men wickedly swear, they rend and tare Gods Name' (*MB*, 31). He goes on to list, in the fashion typical of Wiseman and Attentive's didactically digressive dialogue, 'Examples of Gods anger against them that Swear and Curse' (*MB*, 32) in order to illustrate the efficacy of both swearing and cursing.

The most striking of these 'Examples' is the 'Dreadful Story of *Dorothy Mately* an Inhabitant of *Ashover* in the County of *Darby*' on 'the 23. of *March*, 1660' (*MB*, 32–3). Bunyan does not forget to draw a direct parallel between Mately and Badman: 'This *Dorothy Mately*, saith the Relator, was noted by the people of Town to be a great Swearer, and Curser, and Lier, and Thief; (just like Mr. *Badman*).' Mately picked two pence out of a boy's pocket and, when coming under suspicion, denied it, wishing that *'the ground might swallow her up if she had them'*. She was then swallowed suddenly into the earth and 'afterwards digged up, and found about four yards within ground, with the Boys two single Pence in her pocket' (*MB*, 33). The story of Mately, to which one of the six woodcuts in the 1688 edition of *The Life and Death of Mr. Badman* draws our special attention, shockingly conveys the popular belief in the providential dangers of blasphemy that Bunyan shares with his local audience.

The most vivid and extended representation of blasphemy and the survival of magic in *The Life and Death of Mr. Badman* appears in the interpolated episode of the 'blind Ale-house', which was also to be highlighted by a woodcut in the 1688 edition (*MB*, 35–7). Unlike the Mately episode, which took place in Ashover in Derbyshire, that of the 'blind Ale-house' took place in Bunyan's hometown because, as we have seen, a son of the alehouse keeper, H. S., is Harry, 'a young man' in Bunyan's 'Town', in *Grace Abounding*. Whereas the story of Mately is told at second hand by Wiseman, who heard it from a 'Relator', that of the 'blind Ale-house' is told at first hand by Attentive, who evidently bore witness to the horrible efficacy of blasphemy on the alehouse keeper: '*I was an ear and eye witness of what I here say*' (*MB*, 35). The immediacy and reality of the magical power of blasphemy are thus intensified in the story of the 'blind Ale-house' in Bedford over that of Mately in Ashover, in part because it is delivered—following the mode of *The Life and Death of Mr. Badman* generally—as an eyewitness account that relates 'True Stories, that are neither *Lye*, nor *Romance*' (*MB*, 82). We are asked to believe such stories, in other words, as actual, rather than just allegorical.

As we recall, the *'blind Ale-house'* was kept by an old man who was the father of 'H. S.', and Edward (or 'Ned'), 'an half-fool'. The alehouse keeper would *'entertain his guests'* by provoking the latter son to curse his father: 'The Devil take you' or 'The Devil fetch you.' One day, while *'provoking of* Ned *to curse'*, Attentive saw the alehouse keeper's *'flesh (as 'twas thought) by the Devil, gathered up on an heap, about the bigness of half an Egge; to*

(London: Weidenfeld & Nicolson, 1971), 502–19. For an interesting psychoanalytical approach to Bunyan's blasphemy, see Vera J. Camden, 'Blasphemy and the Problem of the Self', *BS*, 1 (1989), 5–21.

the unutterable torture and affliction of the old man'. The guests send for 'one *Freeman*', who '*was more than an ordinary Doctor*', to cast out the devil:

> *They had the possessed into an out-room, and laid him on his belly upon a Form, with his head hanging over the Forms end; then they bound him down thereto; which done, they set a pan of Coals under his mouth, and put something therein which made a great smoak* [...] but no Devil came out of him; at which Freeman *was somewhat abashed, the man greatly afflicted, and* I *made to go away wondering and fearing. In a little time therefore that which possessed the man, carried him out of the World*, according to the cursed Wishes of his Son. (*MB*, 35–7)

The vividly described process of the alehouse keeper's horrible death—which might be regarded as a case of murder in modern courts—suggests that Bunyan was also 'trained up', like Badman, in the ways of a superstitious local world. The presence of the witch-like 'Doctor'—called 'Freeman' here—in the rite of exorcism represents the magical element of alehouse culture in Bedford. Keenly aware of the helplessness of Freeman's medical sorcery, Bunyan never doubts the supernatural efficacy of blasphemy because he finds evidence for it in the 'Text' of the Bible, such as Psalm 109:17: '*As he loved cursing, so let it come unto him*' (*MB*, 37). Magic and biblicism are thus curiously connected in Bunyan's notion of blasphemy, being threaded together throughout both Badman's tale and *Badman's* tales.

The magical world of the 'blind Ale-house' is the pivotal place from which Bunyan converts by leaving his old companions like Harry in *Grace Abounding*, out of which Christian escapes by refusing his neighbours like Obstinate in *The Pilgrim's Progress*, and on which the forces of Shaddai make the first assault by shooting Diabolus' Aldermen, such as Swearing and Drunkenness, in *The Holy War*. In *I Will Pray with the Spirit*, first published in 1662 when the revised version of the Book of Common Prayer was issued, Bunyan resists the enforcement of the Act of Uniformity in the same year and concludes his argument as follows: 'look into the Goals in *England*, and into the Alehouses of the same: and I believe, you will find those that plead for the Spirit of Prayer in the Goal, and them that look after the Form of mens Inventions only, in the Alehouse' (*MW*, 2: 284). 'Alehouses' are thus situated by Bunyan, at the very start of the Restoration, in opposition to the meeting houses of Nonconformists, whose leaders and members were, like Bunyan, now languishing in the prisons of Bedford and elsewhere.

The local antagonism between alehouse culture and Nonconformity in *The Life and Death of Mr. Badman* elucidates something of the cultural origins of Bunyan's literary works as well as of his theological writings. In the mid-seventeenth century, at the time of the passing of the Blasphemy Act by Parliament in 1650, 'the offence of blasphemy was closely linked with heresy and seemed horrifying to godly Puritans who feared religious division and radical sectarianism'.[9] Bunyan the godly Puritan was no exception to this

---

[9] David Loewenstein, 'Treason against God and State: Blasphemy in Milton's Culture and *Paradise Lost*', in Stephen Dobranski and John P. Rumrich (eds.), *Milton and Heresy* (Cambridge: Cambridge University Press, 1998), 195.

general fear. As such, *The Life and Death of Mr. Badman* can be said to present a cultural clash in which the religious believers, such as Mr Badman's godly first wife, are sharply distinguished from a sacrilegious local community represented by her husband, much to this good woman's eventual pain and suffering.

Sabbath-Breaking

The most typical example of Bunyan's 'didactic' narrative in which Badman is differentiated from 'Godly Puritans' is Wiseman's retrospective discovery of a sign of Sabbath-breaking in Badman's childhood:

> He could not endure the *Lords Day*, because of the Holiness that did attend it; the beginning of that Day was to him as if he was going to Prison [...]. Reading the Scriptures, hearing Sermons, godly Conference, repeating of Sermons, and Prayer, were things that he could not away with. (*MB*, 24)

Sabbath-breaking must have been one of the most habitual problems in the religious life of Bunyan's local community, including that of its Nonconformist congregations. So, for example, it is recorded in the Bedford Church Book that at a church meeting held on 14 November 1676 'brother Oliver Thodye made acknoledgement of summe miscarages the Church had charged him with, as namely breaking the Saboth and brawleing with neighbors' (*CB*, 81). Although it may not be surprising to us that a young child cannot put up with 'Reading the Scriptures' and 'hearing Sermons' at church on Sunday mornings, Wiseman (or Bunyan) does not fail to accuse the young Badman of displaying from a very early age an antinomian character that violates the fourth commandment of the Law of Moses. After all, Sabbatarianism was a distinctive feature of Puritanism. Lewis Bayly's Calvinistic devotional manual, *The Practise of Pietie* (3rd edn, 1613), one of the two books brought to Bunyan by his first wife, has long sections on the right manner of Sabbath-keeping.[10] The political importance of Sabbatarianism was particularly enhanced after the controversy over the 1633 reissue of *The Book of Sports* that sharply divided Puritans and Anglicans, preparing the way for the Civil War in the 1640s.[11]

Bunyan was all the more sensitive to the problem of Sabbath-keeping because he was concerned with the conflict not only between Nonconformists and Anglicans but also between the Seventh Day and First Day Baptists. In *Questions about the Nature*

---

[10] Lewis Bayly, *The Practice of Piety: Directing a Christian how to Walk, that he May Please God* (Morgan, PA: Soli Deo Gloria, 1995), 159–207.

[11] Kenneth L. Parker, *The English Sabbath: A Study of Doctrine and Discipline from the Reformation to the Civil War* (Cambridge: Cambridge University Press, 1988), 178–216.

and Perpetuity of the Seventh-Day-Sabbath (1685), Bunyan disputes with the Seventh Day Baptists about the relationship between nature, law, and revelation: 'If the Law of Nature […] is universal in every individual man in the world, what need is there of particular Prophets, or of their holy writings? (and indeed here the Quakers and others split themselves)' (*MW*, 4: 338). The Quakers' greatest error, according to Bunyan, is their belief that 'the holy Scriptures were not the Word of God' (*GA*, 39). Badman—who, in his childhood could not endure 'Reading the Scriptures' at church on Sundays—shares with 'the Quakers and others' this emerging anti-scriptural heresy. He too rejects 'the authority, harmony, and wisdom of the Scriptures'. 'How do you know them to be the Word of God?' Badman asks: 'one Scripture says one thing, and another sayes the quite contrary', and so 'they are the cause of all dissensions and discords that are in the Land' (*MB*, 127–28). Badman is right, if only in his keen awareness of the multiplication of 'dissensions and discords' in his local community.

Bunyan sees in Badman what he himself might have been—at least concerning Sabbatarianism. He had once found himself convicted of being a Sabbath-breaker when, following his marriage to his first wife, he began 'to go to Church' regularly and heard a sermon on the subject:

> But one day, (amongst all the Sermons our Parson made) his subject was, to treat of the Sabbath day, and of the evil of breaking that, either with labour, sports, or otherwise: (now I was, notwithstanding my Religion, one that took much delight in all manner of vice, and especially that was the Day that I did solace my self therewith.) Wherefore I fell in my conscience under his Sermon, thinking and believing that he made that Sermon on purpose to shew me my evil-doing […] and so went home when the Sermon was ended, with a great burden upon my spirit. (*GA*, 9–10)

Bunyan confesses that the Sabbath had been 'the Day' to 'solace' himself with 'labour, sports, or otherwise'. He repented bitterly, but only for a short while. After he finished his meal at home, he returned to his 'old custom of sports and gaming' and started 'a game at Cat' (*GA*, 10). Just as Bunyan left his first wife at home and went out of his house again after his meal to play sport, so, too, Badman does not remain in the company of his first godly wife, but is away from home on the day of 'the Service and Worship of God' to be 'among his drunken companions' (*MB*, 71).

Antilegon, in Arthur Dent's *The Plaine Mans Path-Way to Heaven*, assumes that people usually play games at alehouses: 'If neighbours meet together, now and then, at the ale-house, and play a game at maw, for a pot of ale, meaning no hurt, I take it to be good fellowship, and a good means to increase love amongst neighbours.'[12] Although Bunyan usually avoids specifying details when writing about his own life in *Grace Abounding*, he is quite specific about this occasion when he went out on the Sabbath to play 'a game at Cat'. Unlike Badman, however, Bunyan heard 'a voice […] suddenly dart from Heaven into my Soul, which said, *Wilt thou leave thy sins, and go to Heaven?*

---

[12] Arthur Dent, *The Plain Man's Path-way to Heaven* (Pittsburgh, PA: Soli Deo Gloria, 1994), 134.

or have thy sins, and go to Hell?' Throwing down his 'cat', Bunyan felt that he could see 'the Lord Jesus looking down upon' him, and he could no longer enjoy the local 'fellowship': 'I stood in the midst of my play, before all that then were present; but yet I told them nothing' (*GA*, 10–11). This newly discovered sense of loneliness after the revelation of God only thinly distinguishes Bunyan from Badman in their Sabbath-breaking.

Unlike Bunyan, however, Badman is an unrepentant Sabbath-breaker throughout his life. When he was a young apprentice, 'His Master indeed would make him go with him to Sermons.' However, in order to 'hinder himself of hearing' sermons at church, the 'ungodly young man' used to 'sit down in some corner' and 'fall asleep', or he would 'fix his adulterous eyes upon some beautifull Object that was in the place', or would 'be whispering, gigling, and playing' with those who 'would fit his humour' (*MB*, 41). Sabbath-breaking, unsurprisingly perhaps, is also associated with the alehouse in *The Life and Death of Mr. Badman*. It is in this context, for example, that Wiseman abruptly mentions the young man whom he rebuked, who, Bunyan tells us, was 'H. S.', the other son of the alehouse keeper: 'That young man was my Play-fellow when I was solacing myself in my sins' (*MB*, 42). Wiseman's wording here—'Play-fellow', 'solacing myself'—suggest that Bunyan may be remembering once again the episode of the 'game at Cat' in *Grace Abounding*, with which he 'solace[d] my self', and how he 'stood in the midst of my play, before all that then were present' (*GA*, 9–11). Indeed, Harry ('H. S.') might have been among those who 'then were present'.

The narrative of Badman's apprenticeship goes on to expound on the 'sin of Drunkenness' and how it 'is often times attended with abundance of other evils' (*MB*, 46). Attentive wonders how Badman could afford to indulge in this '*very costly sin*' while he was only an apprentice, but Wiseman explains that the 'ungodly young man' would 'pilfer and steal from his Master' (*MB*, 47). Badman's Sabbath-breaking therefore led to the further 'sin of Drunkenness' that in turn led, chain-like, to the sin of stealing, only to produce religious division between the godly master and the ungodly apprentice: 'Young *Badmans* wayes were odious to his Master, and his Masters wayes were such as young *Badman* could not endure' (*MB*, 56). Badman, who 'could not endure the Lords Day' in his childhood, 'could not endure' his apprenticeship under the 'Godliness' of the master, either: 'He could not abide this *praying*, this *reading* of *Scriptures*, and *hearing*, and *repeating* of Sermons: he could not abide to be told of his transgressions in a sober and Godly manner' (*MB*, 60).

Badman's Sabbath-breaking subverts the social order of his local community by undermining the mutual trust not only between master and apprentice but also between husband and wife. *The Life and Death of Mr. Badman* satirically represents 'the burgeoning market economy' of mid-seventeenth-century England and its disastrous effect upon family life.[13] After setting up his own shop, Badman became bankrupt because

---

[13] David Hawkes, 'Master of his Ways? Determinism and the Market in *The Life and Death of Mr. Badman*', in N. H. Keeble (ed.), *John Bunyan: Reading Dissenting Writing* (Bern: Peter Lang, 2002), 211–30 (223).

his 'new companions' would 'commonly egg him to the Ale-house, but yet make him Jack-pay-for-all' (*MB*, 64). He successfully got a 'godly' wife 'with a good Portion' by pretending to respect 'Sermons' and 'Scriptures' (*MB*, 66). No sooner was he married than he put off the 'Vizzard of Religion' and 'would not suffer [his wife] to go out to the Preaching of the Word of Christ […] for the health and salvation of her Soul' (*MB*, 66, 70).

Badman, we are told, imposed his sin of Sabbath-breaking on his family not only by breaking the Sabbath himself but by also preventing his wife from keeping it: '*Keep at home, keep at home, and look to your business, we cannot live by hearing of Sermons*' (*MB*, 71). His concern was exclusively confined to the economic principle of 'business'. One of the reasons he hated her 'godly' life was her benefaction of money to 'her Ministers', although he 'spent it on his vain Companions' and enjoyed the 'sin of Drunkenness' to annoy his 'godly' wife: 'Now she scarce durst go to an honest Neighbours house, or have a good Book in her hand; specially when he had his companions in his house, or had got a little drink in his head' (*MB*, 70–1). It is worth noting that his 'godly' wife would go to 'an honest Neighbours house' rather than to church. She was a Nonconformist. Thus, there emerged a new division between the two houses within Badman's family life: the Sabbath-keeping 'honest Neighbours house', where 'good company' (*MB*, 70) got together, and the Sabbath-breaking 'house', the tavern, where Badman's 'companions' got together. Bunyan reveals how the problem of Sabbath-breaking, as part of an alehouse culture, leads to religious division not only in the apprenticeship system but also within Badman's own household.

Domestic Violence

'I have an Husband, but also a God'—so Badman's Sabbatarian wife challenges her anti-Sabbatarian husband once and for all when he tries to prevent her going to hear a sermon 'on a Lords day' (*MB*, 78–9). She finds herself trapped between 'an Husband' and 'a God' who 'has commanded me … upon pain of damnation, to be a continual Worshipper of him, and that in the way of his own Appointments'. Badman's reaction to her defiance is described, as ever, with eyewitness detail by Wiseman:

> At this, first, he gave her an ugly wish, and then fell into a fearfull rage, and sware moreover that if she did go, he would make both her, and all her damnable Brotherhood (for so he was pleased to call them) to repent their coming thither.
>
> Atten.   But what should he mean by that?
> Wise.   You may easily guess what he meant: he meant, he would turn Informer, and so either weary out those that she loved, from meeting together to Worship God; or make them pay dearly for their so doing. (*MB*, 79)

The image of the 'Informer' would have been of great significance to Bunyan's contemporary readers, and it was illustrated by a woodcut in the 1688 edition of *The Life and Death of Mr. Badman*. Mention of the very word revives Wiseman's sombre memory of the period of the great persecution, especially after the Conventicle Act of 1670, when Nonconformists 'were forced to meet in the Fields' (*MB*, 81).[14] The presence of the 'Informer' once again points to the insidious antagonism between a Sabbath-breaking alehouse culture and a Sabbath-keeping Nonconformity.

Bunyan's marginal note to the passage reads: 'With what weapons *Badman* did deal with his wife' (*MB*, 79). His use of the term 'weapons' suggests that he is concerned with what is now called domestic violence. The Bedford church was troubled with cases of such violence among its own members. Not long before *The Life and Death of Mr. Badman* was published, we read the following entry in the Church Book:

> *Att a Church meteing at Cotten End the beginning of October 1679*, John Stanton [...] being divers times admonished of his sine and wickednes in beateing his wife often, and other abuses towards hir, he being impenitent, not heareing the Church, but after Church admonishing perseveareing still in his sine, the Church did then cast him out of ther fellowshipe and deliver him up to Sattan for the destruction of the flesh, that the sperit might be saved in the day of the Lord Jesus. (*CB*, 84)

This agent of domestic violence was excommunicated from the Nonconformist congregation and delivered 'up to Sattan'. The grave punishment suggests that the church members regarded the case of a husband beating 'his wife' not only as a matter of individual physical abuse but also as a chronic threat to the church's standing in the community.

In his early work, *A Few Sighs from Hell* (1658), Bunyan makes clear the distinction between the realm of the alehouse and the culture of Nonconformists. Noting that the Bible is full of 'threatnings' against 'drunkards, swearers, liars, proud persons, strumpets, whoremongers, covetous railers, extortioners, theeves, lazy persons', he goes on:

> Do but go into the Alehouses & you shall see almost every room besprinkled with them [...] it is enough to make the heart of a Saint to tremble, in so much that they would not be bound to have society with them any long while for all the world. For as the wayes of the godly are not liked of by the wicked, even *so the wayes of the wicked are an abomination to the just*, Prov. 29. 27. Psal. 120. 5, 6. (*MW*, 1: 335)

The sins listed here are all incorporated into Badman's allegorical character if we regard 'strumpets' as inseparably connected with 'whoremongers'. By the likes of Bunyan, 'Alehouses' could be seen as ideologically promiscuous sites in the local community where the power of property and that of patriarchy converged to corrupt and oppress wives as well as servants. In *A Few Sighs from Hell* Bunyan thunders against all those

---

[14] See G. R. Cragg, *Puritanism in the Period of the Great Persecution 1660–1688* (Cambridge: Cambridge University Press, 1957), 60–4.

who would 'keep souls from heaven' by preventing them from attending religious services, warning that they would end up in the 'place of torment':

> Think on this you drunken proud, rich, and scornful Landlords, think on this you mad-brain'd blasphemous Husbands, that are against the godly and chaste conversation of your Wives; also you that hold your Servants so hard to it, that you will not spare them time to hear the word, unless it be where, and when your lusts will let you. (*MW*, 1: 315–16)

Equally, however, he laments the case of those 'poor souls' who 'stand in so much aw, and dread of man' that 'they will rather venture their souls in the hands of the devil […] then they will fly to Jesus Christ for the salvation of their soul'. He imagines a wife explaining why she could not go to a meeting: 'I dare not […] for my Husband, for he will be a railing, and tells me, he will turn me out of doors, he will beat me, and cut off my legs' (*MW*, 1: 336). Recapitulating Bunyan's long ministerial career in Bedford after the Protectorate, *The Life and Death of Mr. Badman* continues to suggest that domestic violence endangers not only the female body but also the administration and witness of the Nonconformist church.

Badman's domestic violence was inflicted on his children, too, to prevent them from observing the Sabbath. He himself had been beaten before 'he was pretty well grown up' by his second master, who would also 'swear, and curse' and 'laugh at and make merry with the sins of his servant *Badman*' (*MB*, 61). Badman had seven children. One of them 'loved its Mother dearly' and followed her instruction in 'the Principles of Christian Religion'. Badman 'could not abide' this child. He 'would scowl and frown upon it, speak churlishly and doggedly to it, and though as to Nature it was the most feeble of the seven, yet it oftenest felt the weight of its Fathers fingers' (*MB*, 75). Wiseman tells Attentive that 'ungodly Parents' like Badman 'let their children break the Sabbath, swear, lye, be wicked and vain' (*MB*, 78). By discouraging his children from Sabbath-keeping, Badman was inculcating his reprobate errors in his offspring.

Alehouse culture and child abuse are tightly combined in *The Life and Death of Mr. Badman*. The woodcut that illustrates the episode of the 'blind Ale-house' defines the alehouse keeper's death primarily as a family problem: 'When Parents take delight in Childrens Evil, / The Children send their Parents to the Devil' (*MB*, 36). As a result, three of Badman's children 'did directly follow his steps' and the other three 'became a kind of mongrel Professors, not so *bad* as their Father, nor so *good* as their Mother' (*MB*, 75). With the 'ungodly' father and 'godly' mother, the household became a battlefield where alehouse culture and Nonconformity contend against each other for their children's souls. As seen in the proportion of the moral division of Badman's seven children, the result is more often a victory for the 'ungodly' father. One of the greatest concerns of *The Life and Death of Mr. Badman* is how to protect children from domestic violence and thus to assure the survival of the Nonconformist church.[15]

---

[15] Anne Dunan-Page, '*The Life and Death of Mr. Badman* as a "Compassionate Counsel to all Young Men": John Bunyan and Nonconformist Writings', *BS*, 9 (1999/2000), 50–68.

Badman's domestic violence towards his wife and children rebounds on himself in his last years. His second wife was, as we have seen in the first section, 'a very Whore' who has 'companions', like him, 'at the Tavern and Ale-house' (*MB*, 145). She was so violent and profane, we are told, that she 'would give him word for word, blow for blow, curse for curse' (*MB*, 147). His house becomes a place of verbal and physical conflict: 'their railing, and cursing and swearing ended not in words: They would fight and fly at each other, and that like Cats and Dogs' (*MB*, 146). Badman's family life in his last years is daily disquieted by blasphemy and domestic violence because '*that* measure that he meted to his first wife, this last did mete to him again' (*MB*, 147). Bunyan thus highlights in the figure of Badman the irony of the unrepentant offender, an agent of sin who is also its most miserable victim. *The Life and Death of Mr. Badman* is the story of a blasphemous, violent whoremonger whose life is finally wrecked by a blasphemous, violent harridan.

It is the great trick of this book's tale to have Mr Badman die, unlike almost all of the other sinners whose gruesome deaths have been recounted by Attentive and Wiseman in the course of their long godly conversation, 'very stilly and quietly […] and as they call it, like a Lamb'. Despite the peacefulness of his ending, however, there is no doubt in Wiseman's mind that the dead 'Mr. *Badman* is gone to Hell': 'his quiet dying', he tells us, 'is so far off from being a sign of his being saved, that it is an uncontrollable proof of his damnation'. He has, without doubt, gone 'to the Devil' (*MB*, 161, 158). By contrast, Badman's first 'godly' wife died in full confidence that she would go to heaven, where she would be 'among the Saints', and would now, at last, be able to worship freely 'without Temptation or other impediment' (*MB*, 141). Her last wish was to escape from the 'impediment' of domestic violence in her home and local community and go to her congregation in 'Heaven'. She says on her deathbed to the child who had 'followed her ways', 'thou shalt follow after', just as Christiana says at the beginning of *The Pilgrim's Progress, Part II* (1684), '*my Children shall go with me*' (*PP*, 181).

The Life and Death of Mr. Badman, though generally an awful story of the damnable life and death of its unredeemed anti-hero and a conduct book that establishes instruction through its protagonist's hopelessly reprobate ways, points nevertheless to a glimpse of hope that a new generation of believers brings to the Nonconformist church in Bedford. The penultimate paragraph of *The Pilgrim's Progress, Part II* shows that 'the four boys that Christiana brought with her […] were yet alive, and so would be for the Increase of the Church in that Place where they were for a time' (*PP*, 311). At the end of the local and historical narrative of *The Life and Death of Mr. Badman*, then, we find the beginning of the much more delocalized and timeless allegory of *The Pilgrim's Progress, Part II*, the conclusion of which returns again to Bunyan's lifelong wish 'for the Increase of the Church in that Place where' he was 'for a time'. Bunyan's fidelity to his own local, godly community would be delocalized in this later allegory of collective wayfaring in order to be inscribed in the mind of each reader beyond time and place.

Suggested Reading

Camden, Vera, 'Blasphemy and the Problem of the Self', *BS*, 1 (1989), 5–21.
Clark, Peter, *The English Alehouse: A Social History, 1200–1830* (London: Longmans, 1983).
Davies, Michael, *Graceful Reading: Theology and Narrative in the Works of John Bunyan* (Oxford: Oxford University Press, 2002).
Dunan-Page, Anne, '*The Life and Death of Mr. Badman* as a "Compassionate Counsel to all Young Men": John Bunyan and Nonconformist Writings', *BS*, 9 (1999/2000), 50–68.
Greaves, Richard L., *Glimpses of Glory: John Bunyan and English Dissent* (Stanford, CA: Stanford University Press, 2002).
Hawkes, David, 'Master of his Ways? Determinism and the Market in *The Life and Death of Mr. Badman*', in N. H. Keeble (ed.), *John Bunyan: Reading Dissenting Writing* (Bern: Peter Lang, 2002), 211–30.
Hill, Christopher, *A Turbulent, Seditious, and Factious People: John Bunyan and his Church* (Oxford: Clarendon Press, 1988).
Parker, Kenneth L., *The English Sabbath: A Study of Doctrine and Discipline from the Reformation to the Civil War* (Cambridge: Cambridge University Press, 1988).
Pooley, Roger, 'Bunyan and the Antinomians', in Vera Camden (ed.), *Trauma and Transformation: The Political Progress of John Bunyan* (Stanford, CA: Stanford University Press, 2008), 120–34.
Sim, Stuart, 'Bunyan and the Early Novel: *The Life and Death of Mr Badman*', in Anne Dunan-Page (ed.), *The Cambridge Companion to Bunyan* (Cambridge: Cambridge University Press, 2010).
Wrightson, Keith, 'Alehouses, Order and Reformation in Rural England, 1590–1660', in Eileen Yeo and Stephen Yeo (eds.), *Popular Culture and Class Conflict 1590–1914* (Brighton: Harvester, 1981), 1–27.

CHAPTER 16

THE HOLY WAR (1682)

NANCY ROSENFELD

BECAUSE of the great popularity of *The Pilgrim's Progress* both during John Bunyan's lifetime and in the course of the centuries to follow, and the comparatively limited interest in *The Holy War* (1682), scholars have on occasion thought it necessary to include an *apologia* in their discussions of what E. M. W. Tillyard called 'England's Puritan epic'.[1] Stuart Sim notes that 'the text has traditionally been regarded as the least successful of Bunyan's fictions, and has tended to inspire even less enthusiasm among critics than [*The Life and Death of Mr.*] *Badman*'. Yet Sim has also suggested that a case can be made for viewing *The Holy War* as Bunyan's 'most dramatic, and certainly his most ambitious text'.[2]

The plot of *The Holy War* is summed up in the epic's full title: *The Holy War, Made by Shaddai upon Diabolus, for the Regaining of the Metropolis of the World: Or, The Losing and Taking Again of the Town of Mansoul*. It is a complex plot, in which the allegory is working on four levels: the history of the Christian scheme of salvation; the conversion process of the individual Christian; contemporary English history; and events that are to happen in the future, at the end of the world, as described in the final book of the Bible, Revelation. The scene is set by a first-person narrator:

> In my Travels, as I walked through many Regions and Countries, it was my chance to happen into that famous *Continent* of *Universe*; a very large and spacious Countrey [wherein lies] a *fair* and *delicate* Town, a Corporation, called *Mansoul*: a Town for its Building so curious, for its Situation so commodious, for its Priviledges so advantagious [...] that I may say of it, as was said before, of the *Continent* in which it is placed, *There is not its equal under the whole Heaven.* (HW, 7–8)

---

[1] E. M. W. Tillyard, *The English Epic and its Background* (New York: Oxford University Press, 1966), 406.
[2] Stuart Sim, *Negotiations with Paradox: Narrative Practice and Narrative Form in Bunyan and Defoe* (New York: Harvester-Wheatsheaf, 1990), 90.

This town is protected by five gates—Ear-gate, Eye-gate, Mouth-gate, Nose-gate, Feel-gate—representing as they do the five senses. At its centre is a castle (the heart) intended as the residence of King Shaddai (God the Father). In its original state, Mansoul was a 'goodly' town: 'It had always a sufficiency of provision within its Walls; it had the best, most wholesome, and excellent Law that then was extant in the world. There was not a Rascal, Rogue, or Traiterous person then within its Walls' (*HW*, 9). This golden age did not last, of course. When Diabolus (Satan) and his army of angels are expelled from heaven for rising up in rebellion against Shaddai, they resolve to 'revenge' themselves by 'spoiling' the town of Mansoul, since it is 'one of the chief works, and delights of King Shaddai' (*HW*, 10–11). Diabolus is depicted as 'a mighty *Gyant* [. . .] King of the *Blacks* or *Negroes* [i.e. the fallen angels], and a most raving Prince' (*HW*, 9). He leads his followers in an assault on Mansoul, and by a trick persuades them to open the gates of the town to him (alluding to the temptation and fall of Adam and Eve in Eden). Diabolus then occupies Mansoul, and puts his own men in charge. Lord Lustings becomes Lord Mayor, in place of Mr Understanding, and Mr Forget-good takes over as the Recorder, in the place of Mr Conscience.

Shaddai sends an army to recapture Mansoul (representing the moral Law of the Old Testament), but the town is only fully retaken when Emanuel (the Son of Shaddai) arrives at the head of another army and delivers Mansoul from the tyranny of the Diabolonians. However, when Emanuel leaves Mansoul, Diabolus and an army of Doubters once again take control of Mansoul. Lord Wilbewill (representing human free will) holds out against Diabolus, and sends petitions to Emanuel to return to relieve the town. Emanuel eventually returns, and takes control of Mansoul for a second time, but yet again, Diabolus returns with an army of Doubters and Bloodmen (persecutors). This time, however, he is defeated and expelled from Mansoul.

Although most of the Diabolonians are slain during this last great battle, some of them survive (a reminder that sin remains ever present). The narrative ends with Emanuel making a triumphant entry into Mansoul, and giving a set of instructions to his people on how to behave before his return at the end of the world:

> Love me against temptation, and I will love thee notwithstanding thine infirmities. [. . .] Nor must thou think always to live by sense, thou must live upon my Word. Thou must believe, O my Mansoul, when I am from thee, that yet I love thee, and bear thee upon my heart for ever.

There is, however, no returning to the Garden of Eden for Mansoul, who will need to remain vigilant:

> And dost thou know why I at first, and do still suffer Diabolonians to dwell in thy walls, O Mansoul? It is to keep thee wakening, to try thy love, to make thee watchful, and to cause thee yet to prize my noble Captains, their Souldiers, and my mercy. (*HW*, 250, 249)

The main settings of the narrative's action are the town itself, within its walls; the area outside the town where the armies of Diabolus and Emanuel make camp; and the Pit, where Diabolus and his followers hold their Great Consult. As befits an allegory—the epigraph on the title page is, as for both parts of *The Pilgrim's Progress*, 'I have used Similitudes', Hosea 12:10—most of the characters bear names representing qualities: Lord Wilbewill, Captain Patience, Mr Carnal Security, to list but a few. Others are named for their roles: the most important of these being Mr Conscience, who becomes the Recorder of Mansoul. As is the case in John Milton's *Paradise Lost* (1667; 1674), much of the action in Bunyan's epic is verbal; long sections of the work are composed of dialogue. One critic has defined *The Holy War* as 'a sustained reflection on language as it operates in a range of modes and contexts. These include petition, litigation, temptation, oration, persuasion, proclamation, and various instruments of government.'[3]

Possible Sources

The main literary source for all Bunyan's fictional texts was the Bible; indeed, one would not wish to argue with the perceived centrality of Holy Scripture in his writings. As far as is known the preacher had little formal schooling, never travelled outside the British Isles, and read no language other than English. Yet the common picture of a largely uneducated 'Tinker, and [...] poor man' (*GA*, 128) is misleading. Bunyan's reading may have been much broader than was once generally acknowledged, and his response to literary texts, whether Scripture, sermons, or tracts, is more sophisticated than was once assumed. He read widely in biblical exegesis, both canonical works, such as Martin Luther's *Commentarie* [...] *upon the Epistle of S. Paule to the Galathians* (*GA*, 40–1) and tracts on burning theological issues so popular during the revolutionary period. In addition, a variety of literary works would have been available to him from the libraries of neighbours and colleagues.[4]

A clear generic influence is the morality play. Indeed, J. B. Wharey made a cogent argument for viewing *The Holy War* itself as a morality play of sorts:

> The wresting of Mansoul by Emanuel after the town's defection to Diabolus marks but the half-way point of the story. [...] Bunyan continues to picture the contest between the devils in hell, aided by the Diabolonians still lurking in Mansoul, and the inhabitants of Mansoul aided by Emanuel. The theme, then, is not so much the epic of man's fall and redemption as the conflict between good and evil for possession of man's soul; in other words, the theme of a typical Morality play.[5]

---

[3] David Gay, 'The Nameless Instrument: Bunyan's Representation of Prayer in *The Holy War*', *BS*, 12 (2006/07), 88–104 (99).

[4] See Chapter 6 in this volume.

[5] J. B. Wharey, 'Bunyan's *Holy War* and the Conflict-Type of Morality Play', *Modern Language Notes*, 34 (1919), 65–73 (65–6).

The conflict-theme morality play, as Wharey notes, bears a seven-stage structure which can be traced in the plot of *The Holy War*: (1) state of innocence; (2) temptation; (3) life in sin; (4) repentance; (5) temptation; (6) life in sin; (7) repentance. We may, however, look to another of Wharey's insights for a source of readers' difficulty with *The Holy War*: it 'has no central hero'. As Wharey notes, 'Bunyan's marginal gloss for the phrase *the natives of Mansoul* is *Powers of the Soul*, from which it would seem that the native inhabitants of Mansoul are to be considered as representing Man.'[6] In other words, readers accustomed to empathizing with an individuated hero—even if allegorically named Christian or Christiana—may find it less than exciting to enter into the spiritual struggles of Everyman. And yet Bunyan's epic generates an excitement whose source is the reality of the setting: Mansoul is also Bedford, a vibrant market town during a revolutionary period in which disagreements about theology, rather than leading to yawns, may end in bloodshed.

Bunyan did not have the Latin which would have enabled him to read Prudentius' fifth-century *Psychomachia* in the original; but the allegorical poem was one of the most popular in the Middle Ages, and Bunyan could easily have known of it through his general reading. Either way, it provides a valuable point of comparison. The poem opens with the retelling of the story of Abraham's victory over Lot's captors (Genesis 14:10–16) as predictive of the body of the poem—a martial epic in which desirable traits do battle with, and ultimately defeat, unwanted traits: Modesty overcomes Voluptuousness, Mercy conquers Avarice.[7] Bunyan's characters, on the other hand, number in the hundreds and do not face off one-to-one with an opponent. Although this may insert an element of confusion into the storyline, it serves to create a more genuine battle scene, one which the reader may find reflective of the disorder and confusion accompanying his or her own spiritual struggles.

It has been suggested that Milton's *Paradise Lost* was familiar to Bunyan. The nineteenth-century Bunyan editor Henry Stebbing notes that 'it is almost impossible to read the beginning of *The Holy War* without feeling assured that Bunyan was well acquainted with Milton, and derived the general idea of this work from the poems of his great contemporary'. Stebbing then adds a caveat: 'in all considerations of literature, and even in some religious points', Milton is 'immeasurably the superior' of the two.[8] Yet whether one agrees with Clement H. Wyke that 'Even when Emanuel gets the stage and embattles Diabolus and his army, we get nothing like Milton's war in heaven, although some of the speeches are proportionately as long as Milton's';[9] or whether one feels, as does Sim, that the 'drama of salvation' with its 'stirring battle' and 'huge cast, cannot fail

---

[6] Wharey, 'Bunyan's *Holy War*', 67–9, 70.

[7] Sister M. Clement Eagan, 'Introduction', in *The Poems of Prudentius* (Washington: Catholic University of America Press, 1962), ix–xxv.

[8] Henry Stebbing, 'Prefatory Remarks on *The Holy War*', in *The Entire Works of John Bunyan*, 4 vols (London: J. S. Virtue, 1859), 3: 1.

[9] Clement H. Wyke, 'Distanced Experience and Faded Vision in *The Holy War*', *Humanities Association Review*, 26 (1975), 21–32 (23).

to put one in mind of *Paradise Lost*,[10] the presence of Miltonic influences in *The Holy War* is undoubted.

In addition to *Paradise Lost*, scholars have pointed out other specific contemporary sources for *The Holy War*. Bunyan was certainly familiar with Arthur Dent's *The Plaine Mans Path-Way to Heaven* (1601), and he may also have known Benjamin Keach's *War with the Devil* (1673), and John Canne's *Emanuel, or, God with Us* (1650). These texts all contain elements resembling some of those appearing in *The Holy War*. Many other seventeenth-century writers used warfare as a central metaphor. For example, in *The Christian Warfare against the Devill World and Flesh* (1634 edition), John Downame describes the Christian warriors' 'nature, the maner of their fight and meanes to obtain victorye'.[11] There may also be echoes of Richard Bernard's very popular *The Isle of Man* (1626, and reprinted throughout the seventeenth century), which tells of 'The Legal Proceeding in Man-shire against sinne, Wherein, by way of a continued Allegory, the chief Malefactors disturbing both Church and Commonwealth are Detected.' Bernard includes at the end a section on 'the spiritual use thereof, with an Apology for the manner of handling, most necessary to be first read for direction in the right use of the Allegory throughout'.[12] It is clear that in choosing to compose an allegorical war epic Bunyan was working within traditions familiar to his intended readership.

Reception

Discussing the ways in which a work of literature (or indeed any work of art) produced over three centuries ago has been received by its readers and viewed by potential readers poses a challenge: the work's reception should be seen in the framework of the literary culture of the period in which the scholar is interested. Bunyan would arguably not have defined 'success' in terms of what is now viewed as commercial or literary critical success, and may not even have seen 'popularity', however defined, as an aim. Moreover, the importance of academic, critical acclaim for one's writings was not part of the religious culture of his time. Therefore, when considering ways in which readers received, and indeed are still receiving, *The Holy War*, we need to keep a sense of the differences in the surrounding literary culture from one time and place to another.

The point most often made vis-à-vis the reception of Bunyan's epic is that throughout the centuries it has been much less popular than *The Pilgrim's Progress*. According to Tillyard, 'the Puritan phase of thought, which gave [Bunyan] his material, was past its zenith when he began to write [*The Holy War*] and could provide him with only a part of the inspiration it had commanded earlier'. Although *The Holy War* 'embodies Bunyan's authentic experience as surely as *Grace Abounding* and *The Pilgrim's Progress*', by the

---

[10] Sim, *Negotiations*, 92.
[11] John Downame, *The Christian Warfare* (1634 edn).
[12] Richard Bernard, *The Isle of Man* ('thirteenth edition', 1658).

time he set out to compose his epic the millenarian hopes, which were so pervasive an influence on the preacher-author, were 'forlorn, anachronistic, unable to mould the great shape of his mind and experience'.[13] *The Holy War*, in other words, may be less appealing to readers than Bunyan's great crowd-pleasers precisely because of its distance in time from the seminal experiences of its author's youth: both his military service during the Civil War and the religious conversion that culminated in his decision to preach God's Word, first from the pulpit and later via the printing press.

This common scholarly view of *The Holy War* is conveniently summed up in the title of Clement H. Wyke's article 'Distanced Experience and Faded Vision in *The Holy War*', cited in the first section of this chapter. Due to the distance in time between the writing of *The Holy War* and *Grace Abounding*, the preacher's sense of his own conversion experience may have been attenuated. Yet for Bunyan salvation was an ongoing process. In her discussion of *Grace Abounding*, Anne Hawkins details the *lysis* model of conversion, wherein salvation is articulated 'in the language and metaphor of education, as a gradual process of error and relearning, or fall and recovery, or wrong-doing and punishment whereby the soul matures into a regenerative state'. Thus Puritan spiritual autobiographies often evince a 'pattern of conversion, relapse, and reconversion'.[14] This repetitive pattern, clearly present in *Grace Abounding*, is reflected in the plot of *The Holy War*: the town of Mansoul falls, is redeemed, falls again, is redeemed. As with *The Pilgrim's Progress, Part I*, so too *The Holy War* may be seen as a reimagining of the process of Bunyan's own conversion as described in *Grace Abounding*.

While *The Pilgrim's Progress* was and remains Bunyan's greatest commercial success, the eighteenth century, as Anne Page-Dunan argues, was 'surprisingly kind to *The Holy War*'. Indeed, the eighteenth century saw the publication of over fifty British editions.[15] Beth Lynch also points out that while Bunyan's 'plain-speaking was an affront to polite Augustan taste, it was whole-heartedly embraced by proponents of the Evangelical revival'. It is true that in order to eliminate 'unavoidable elements of Bunyan's predestinarian theology', John Wesley systematically shortened *The Holy War* before including it in his *Christian Library*, but during the following centuries the epic continued to be reissued as part of Bunyan's collected works.[16]

The later twentieth and twenty-first centuries have seen a renewed critical and academic interest in Bunyan's oeuvre. There is also an ongoing interest on the part of Christian evangelicals in Bunyan's sermons, tracts, and fictional writings. A random search of online sites for the purchase of books yields the following posting of a

---

[13] Tillyard, *Epic*, 386, 404, 391.

[14] Anne Hawkins, 'The Double-Conversion in Bunyan's *Grace Abounding*', *Philological Quarterly*, 61 (1982), 259–76 (273, 268).

[15] Anne Dunan-Page, 'Posthumous Bunyan: Early Lives and the Development of the Canon', in Anne Dunan-Page (ed.), *The Cambridge Companion to Bunyan* (Cambridge: Cambridge University Press, 2010), 137–49 (144).

[16] Beth Lynch, '"Rather Dark to Readers in General": Some Critical Casualties of John Bunyan's *Holy War*', BS, 9 (1999/2000), 25–49 (20).

popular recommendation for *The Holy War*: 'Lively battle scenes and profound theological truths, all wrapped up into one fascinating and engaging package. Dive into John Bunyan's long-form allegory *The Holy War* for a glimpse into timeless insights about Christianity, faith, purity, and perseverance.'[17] For twenty-first-century readers, who have seen religious and cultural conflicts morph into wars even more bloody than any imagined by Bunyan, *The Holy War* may in some respects speak a familiar, often disturbing, language.

ALLEGORY AND INDIVIDUATION

Bunyan's approach to allegory in *The Holy War* may be understood by comparing his practice with that of John Milton. Both *Paradise Lost* and *The Holy War* tell of humankind's fall and ultimate redemption through the intercession of Jesus Christ. The major difference between the two epics is thus not thematic, but rather generic. Milton wrote a dramatic epic, peopled with characters who play themselves—with the exception of the Sin and Death allegory of Book 2—while Bunyan couched his prose narrative in allegory. Victoria Kahn has delineated those traditional objections to allegory which may have led Milton to give the genre a wide berth:

> Traditional allegory was seen both as the representation of what is by nature obscure to human understanding and as itself an obscure form of representation […]. Allegory could thus be said to pander to the reader, to commodify truth and thus to obstruct the kind of rational exercise of the will which is the precondition of right reading and of virtue. In not leaving room for the reader's own activity, this pandering might just as easily be described as a kind of violence or coercion. The allegory [of Sin and Death] is thus one of force, of forced signification.[18]

For Bunyan, however, writing not for a 'fit audience though few' but for a wide readership, the perceived spoon-feeding of which the genre stood accused would not have been a drawback. As he puts it in his preface to *Grace Abounding*,

> *I could* […] *have stepped into a stile much higher then this in which I have here discoursed, and could have adorned all things more then here I have seemed to do: but I dare not:* God *did not play in convincing of me; the* Devil *did not play in tempting of me; neither did I play when I sunk as into a bottomless pit, when* the pangs of hell caught hold upon me: *wherefore I may not play in my relating of them, but be plain and simple, and lay down the thing as it was.* (GA, 3–4)

---

[17] See: http://www.torontopubliclibrary.ca/detail.jsp?R=2895038, accessed 26 May 2017.
[18] Victoria Kahn, 'Allegory and the Sublime in *Paradise Lost*', in Annabel Patterson (ed.), *John Milton* (London: Longman, 1992), 185–201 (198, 191).

The preacher, in other words, saw no contradiction between his allegorical practice and the composition of plain, simple, unadorned narratives.

While Martin Luther's spiritual influences on Bunyan have received extensive documentation, Daniel V. Runyon has noted that much less work has been invested in demonstrating

> the profound impact of Luther on Bunyan's literary style, especially concerning the effective use of allegory. A study of references to allegory in Luther's commentary on Galatians gives a sense of the ways in which Luther may have shaped Bunyan's understanding of allegory and how to use it.[19]

Building on Bunyan's familiarity with Luther's discussion of Paul's use of Hagar and Sarah as representing slavery and freedom (Galatians 4:8–21), Runyon suggests that the preacher took from Luther the conclusion that allegory is only out of place when Scripture expresses itself plainly. Moreover, Bunyan learned from Luther's discussion of Paul's allegorical use of Isaac and Ishmael: 'Bunyan's preaching imitated Luther's use of allegory as illustration, and as he perfected the technique, he found extended allegory equally useful.'[20]

Louis Martz has claimed that 'the essential and unique appeal of [*The Pilgrim's Progress*] does not lie in Bunyan's ability to present common things realistically. It lies in his startling ability to convey abstract ideas through the medium of vivid, concrete details and direct, plain language.' For Martz this blending of abstract and concrete is what constitutes allegory.[21] Yet while the basic allegorical structure of *The Holy War* is clear, the three central characters—Shaddai, Emanuel, and Diabolus (God the Father, the Son, and Satan)—are not allegorical; for Bunyan they do not represent forces within the human psyche, or kinds of behaviour, but are themselves.

When comparing *The Pilgrim's Progress, Part I* (1678) with its sequel, *Part II* (1684), published some six years later, we may trace a development away from allegory and towards realism. In *Part II*, for example, Old Honest introduces himself as 'not Honesty in the *Abstract*, but *Honest* is my name' (*PP*, 247). Similarly, Mercie does not merely represent the quality of mercy, but is a pleasant young woman named Mercie, a fairly common girl's name at the time, particularly among the godly.[22] *The Holy War* may also be seen as part of Bunyan's movement towards what came to be defined as fiction. As Donald Mackenzie suggests: 'In *The Holy War* apocalypse is displaced by the mundane and the development of the latter is the work's chief strength.'[23] Margaret Olofson Thickstun has

---

[19] Daniel V. Runyon, 'Luther's Influence on Bunyan's Use of Allegory', *BS*, 14 (2010), 76–84 (77).

[20] Runyon, 'Luther's Influence', 77–8.

[21] Louis Martz, 'Introduction', in John Bunyan, *The Pilgrim's Progress*, ed. Louis Martz (New York: Holt, Rinehart & Winston, 1967), vi, vii.

[22] See Charles W. Bardsley, *Curiosities of Puritan Nomenclature* (London: Chatto & Windus, 1880), 110, 142, 198–201, 209.

[23] Donald Mackenzie, 'Rhetoric *versus* Apocalypse: The Oratory of *The Holy War*', *BS*, 2 (1990), 33–45 (38).

also drawn attention to the potential for 'realism' in the form of allegory used by Puritan writers to embody their human characters, both male and female:

> In order to offer believers a viable model for their own conduct in this world, Puritan authors present their positive characters not as abstract embodiments of ideas but as individuals capable of growing toward those virtues. In Puritan allegory, characters do not represent a Virtue or a Vice, they act virtuously or viciously […]. When Bunyan presents his allegory of spiritual quest, he chooses his characters and episodes from working-class English life; when Milton offers an allegory of the willful self-destruction of sinfulness, he has Sin discuss her conflicting responsibilities to God and to Satan as if she were an ordinary Puritan housewife.[24]

No less than *The Pilgrim's Progress*, *The Holy War* is characterized by a blurring of boundaries between allegorical characters and places on the one hand, and realistic, individual nature on the other, both vis-à-vis the individual characters and the town as a whole. Old Mr Incredulity is first of all himself, an individuated personality, and only secondarily a personification of disbelief. The town of Mansoul is a figure for the human soul at the same time as it is the Bedford of mid- to late seventeenth-century England. If one envisions a continuum with allegorical characters at one end and individuated characters at the other, it would not be far-fetched to claim that the citizens of Mansoul are marching along somewhere in the middle, but facing in the direction of individuation. Much of the reader's enjoyment comes from making the acquaintance of the more individuated characters.

A Battle Epic

Dating back to ancient times, rousing tales of battle have been popular. Much of the interest of classical epic, however, comes from readers' appreciation of the reality of the setting: the town or city, as well as the social community, in which the war takes place. This is true of *The Iliad*, with its besieged city, the besiegers' vast army camp and navy, which are depicted in all their mundane vitality: markets, courts, common soldiers, the complex relationships of the military commanders, and the political leadership of the city. While a detailed analysis of the setting of *The Holy War* is beyond the scope of this chapter, it is worth noting that much of the reader's sense of the epic's 'reality' comes from the points—and there are many—at which the reader forgets the allegorical nature of the town and feels that Mansoul has become a town very like Bedford. On the political level, Roger Sharrock and James F. Forrest discuss parallels between events in Mansoul and in Bedford, pointing out that changes in the government of Mansoul resulting from

---

[24] Margaret Olofson Thickstun, *Fictions of the Feminine: Puritan Doctrine and the Representation of Women* (Ithaca, NY: Cornell University Press, 1988), 23.

Diabolus's usurpation of political power reflect a revolution in local government which was occurring during the years when Bunyan was composing his great fictional works (*HW*, xxi). Michael A. Mullett has also argued, convincingly, that one of the strands of allegory in *The Holy War* is based on 'the political battle in Restoration England for the control of the nation's cities and boroughs and especially for their key role as parliamentary constituencies'.[25]

The high definition of the description of the social and political life of Mansoul does not, admittedly, reach that found in depictions of commercial practice as found in *The Life and Death of Mr. Badman* (1680). The eponymous anti-hero of the latter work is a haberdasher who sells undefined goods in a burgeoning market economy; his practices are described in all their ugly detail, whether he is overcharging a widow or enriching himself by carrying out what has come to be known as a Ponzi scheme. Mr Badman is a corrupt retailer, however, while Diabolus is the political leader of a whole town; he is therefore painted with a broader brush than that used to depict an individual businessman.

Having noted the setting of Bunyan's 'brief epic', let us look at the war itself. It can be claimed that the fighting which constitutes the central allegorical action of *The Holy War* is much less violent than might be expected in a tale written by a former soldier—although Bunyan may have seen comparatively little military action during some two and a half years in the Parliamentary army. Either way, *The Holy War* often appears to be characterized by a calm, an acceptance, quieter than the excitement and thrills which might be expected of a war epic. Indicative of the comparative non-violence often prevailing in Bunyan's macrocosm of the soul is the admission made by Lord Understanding, Mr Conscience, and Lord Wilbewill in their trial: they did not suffer while living under the devil's rule, and indeed 'chose it of our own mind'. Acting as prosecutor, Emanuel asks the three, '*Could you have been content that your slavery should have continued under his tyranny as long as you had lived?*' They reply '*Yes, Lord, yes*; for his ways were *pleasing* to our flesh, and we were grown aliens to a better state.' Bunyan's point is that the unregenerate soul would not suffer from the unrelenting feelings of guilt which were often the portion of the redeemed; but the soul's willing choice of the corruption of carnality, as the three note in their testimony, seems to have resulted in a simple, pleasing enjoyment of the delights of the flesh (*HW*, 104–05).

Diabolus was, of course, aware of the role played by the pleasures of daily life in misleading the soul. Towards the end of the narrative he suggests to a conclave of his supporters, '*let* Mansoul *be taken up in much business, and let them grow full and rich, and this is the way to get ground of them* […] *when they begin to grow full, they will forget their misery*'. The devil's followers see this advice as 'the very masterpiece of Hell, to wit, to choak *Mansoul* with a fulness of this world, and to surfeit her heart with the good things thereof' (*HW*, 216, 217). The idea that the good things of the earth are a

---

[25] Michael A. Mullett, *John Bunyan in Context* (Keele: Keele University Press, 1996), 229. See also Mullett's article '"Deprived of our Former Place": The Internal Politics of Bedford, 1660–1688', *Proceedings of the Bedfordshire Historical Record Society*, 59 (1989), 1–42, and Greaves, *Glimpses*, 411–14.

snare for the soul was a Puritan commonplace; the very enjoyableness of the fullness of the earth could not be denied. Bunyan's emphasis on the pleasure of 'earthly delights' would thus be traditional. At the same time the very act of recalling the fullness of the earth and the myriad possibilities of enjoying the latter adds a sense of comfort, perhaps even of relaxation, which runs the risk of drawing attention away from the struggle.

The idea of peace of mind as a sign of possible reprobation is developed in Bunyan's picture of the Mansoulians and their enjoyment of the simple pleasures of everyday life, including watching a good show. The narrator describes at one point the obvious enthusiasm with which the inhabitants of Mansoul watch the soldiers perform those military exercises which constitute a snappy display for an admiring citizenry: '*They marched, they counter-marched, they opened to the right and left, they divided and subdivided, they closed, they wheeled, made good their front and reer with their right and left wings* [...] *they took, yea, ravished the hearts that were in Mansoul, to behold it*' (HW, 110–11). Emanuel's army, in other words, spends comparatively little time fighting. In order to keep the men occupied and maintain high morale, the troops show off for the townspeople, thus affording enjoyment to the soldiers and entertainment to the public.

The Holy War does, of course, have its share of descriptions of violence, the most horrifying of which is the Doubters' massacre of women and children (the civilian menfolk are apparently beaten, though not killed):

> They made great havock of whatever they laid their hands on; yea, they fired the Town in several places; many young children also were by them dashed in pieces; yea, those that were yet unborn they destroyed in their mothers wombs [...] *women*, both young and old, they forced, ravished, and beastlike abused, so that they swooned, miscarried, and many of them died [...] these *Diabolonian* Doubters turned the men of *Mansoul* out of their Beds, and [...] they wounded them, they mauled them, yea, and almost brained many of them. (*HW*, 204–05)

In the twenty-first century, scenes of children being dashed in pieces and unborn babies torn from their mothers' wombs are viewed as war crimes. Bunyan, however, was drawing upon Scripture for these scenes, alluding to verses such as Isaiah 13:16—'their infants will be dashed in pieces before their eyes'—and Psalm 137:9—'happy shall he be who takes your little ones and dashes them against the rock!'

Actual descriptions of battles in *The Holy War* are not usually massive in scale; the narrator rather tends to concentrate on vignettes of individual characters representing individual human qualities, which forward the purpose of allegory. Captain Execution, for example, one of Emanuel's loyal generals, is kept busy in securing the backstreets and the walls of the town. Only after learning the details of his killing of Mr Prejudice, Mr Backward-to-all-but-naught, and Captain Treacherous are we told almost as an afterthought that he 'also made a very great slaughter among my Lord *Wilbewils* souldiers'. The narrator then treats us to a laconic, shoulder-shrugging summary of the victory of Emanuel's forces in what must have been a bloody conflict: 'What shall I say, the *Diabolonians* in these days lay dead in every corner, though too many yet were alive in *Mansoul*' (HW, 89–90).

The allegorical structure of *The Holy War* makes large-scale battle scenes largely unnecessary, thus putting the author of the epic in a paradoxical situation. War epics such as the *Iliad*, the *Aeneid*, and *Paradise Lost* traditionally contain long, heroic, presumably stirring descriptions of battles. Yet undesirable human qualities are probably defeated, or rooted out of the soul, more efficiently one by one; and it is in vain that we search Bunyan's epic for broad-ranging descriptions of battles of the type found in Book 6 of *Paradise Lost*.

An Antidote to Despair

The Holy War was composed well after Bunyan had been released from his long imprisonment, returned to preaching, and published his greatest popular success, *The Pilgrim's Progress, Part I*. Tillyard suggests that:

> It was Bunyan's misfortune that he began writing too late to be able to use for his art those positive hopes of a holy community in England that had earlier held men's minds. These hopes, had Bunyan been able to embrace them, would have forced him to be political and to share in the responsibility that a man incurs through advocating definite lines of political action.[26]

While Tillyard appears to be criticizing Bunyan for a lack of political awareness in his fictional works, N. H. Keeble notes that:

> The shared experience of disillusion and chastened optimism [which accompanied the Restoration], though it took men off from social and political revolution, bred a new understanding of, and sympathy for, the complexities of human psychology, and a clear-sighted address to the actual conditions of fallen man.

The necessity of subjecting oneself to persecution—the portion of many Nonconformists—was not perceived as the act of a coward, but rather as a sign of strength. According to Keeble, 'Christian patience was not presented [by Nonconformist preachers and writers] as an abject capitulation to circumstances [...]. On the contrary, it was carefully distinguished from the stagnant quiescence of hopelessness, the indifference of helplessness and the resigned stoicism of pessimism.'[27]

---

[26] Tillyard, *Epic*, 391.
[27] N. H. Keeble, *The Literary Culture of Nonconformity in Later Seventeenth-Century England* (Leicester: Leicester University Press, 1987), 24, 198.

Such pessimism, or even despair, was common among Nonconformists during the Restoration. Donald A. Bloom has defined Christian despair as

> the continuance of belief in eternal life and Christ's redemptive sacrifice, with a concomitant belief that it does not apply to oneself. [...] But because in Protestantism the individual finds his own salvation, and only through the inner working of the Spirit, the collapse of hope is essentially damnation itself, a sure sign that you are not finally of the elect.[28]

By the 1680s over two decades had passed since Charles II's Declaration of Breda (issued just before his return, in April 1660) promised religious toleration for Protestant Dissenters, and his Declaration of Indulgence (1672) was a short-lived attempt at suspending all penal laws in matters ecclesiastical. John Spurr notes the monarch's pragmatic insight that years of persecution had not created religious harmony.[29] Although it was only in 1686, four years after *The Holy War*'s first publication, that James II began to encourage Nonconformist support for repeal of the Test Acts, thus leading the public to believe that Nonconformists were gaining a modicum of royal favour, the distance in time from the persecutions and disappointments of the 1660s and 1670s might have led even the most despairing Nonconformist to conclude that survival, and even a minimal prosperity, were possible. This insight may have encouraged Bunyan to compose an epic of salvation in which a Satan character bears human, perhaps even endearing, frailties.

The reader's hearty laughs while perusing *The Holy War* are usually engendered by Diabolus. The latter is characterized by a sense of humour, by the ability to evoke laughter when poking fun at familiar types: preachers, ministers, generals. The first hint of Diabolus's sense of humour is in a short letter which he sends to one of his supporters, Captain Anything, requesting that the latter receive into his company three new recruits; the letter begins: 'Anything, *my Darling (HW*, 52)'. This friendly, casual form of address indicates a high level of informality among the Diabolonian armed forces, and again contradicts the ubiquitous epithet *tyrant* so often attached to Diabolus's name.

Unlike his Miltonic predecessor, Diabolus attempts to engage the Son in bargaining, the goal of which is to convince the Prince to allow the forces of evil to remain within the soul. Diabolus's speech to Emanuel, in which the fiend pleads for a chance to remain in Mansoul, displays his considerable abilities as a parodist. Presenting a brief of which any lawyer would be proud, Diabolus offers to cooperate with Emanuel by turning reformer and serving as the Son's deputy. In order to assure the success of these honest efforts Diabolus makes what seems to be a generous offer: he will establish and maintain both a ministry and support preachers in Mansoul (*HW*, 84). Given Diabolus's awareness of Emanuel's understanding and ability to recognize deceit, even when couched

---

[28] Donald A. Bloom, 'The Idea of Despair in Four Protestant Authors: Spenser, Milton, Bunyan, and Richardson', *Shakespeare and Renaissance Association of West Virginia Selected Papers*, 13 (1988), 66–72 (66).

[29] John Spurr, *England in the 1670s: 'This Masquerading Age'* (Oxford: Blackwell, 2000), 29.

in lawyerly terminology, we can assume that the devil is again appealing to the reader's sense of humour in making the Son 'an offer he can't refuse'. The offer itself, hinting broadly as it does at those ministries which Bunyan apparently viewed as hypocritical, is comic in its very seriousness.

Much of Diabolus's communication with his supporters in Mansoul is carried on by means of letters. In answer to an appeal from the Diabolonians he sends them a lengthy, parodic epistle beginning '*Beloved children and disciples, my Lord* Fornication, Adultery, *and the rest, we have here in our desolate den received to our highest joy and content, your welcome Letter by the hand of our trusty Mr. Profane.*' The latter is reminiscent of the addresses with which the various Epistles of Paul the Apostle begin. Diabolus continues, moreover, addressing his followers as '*right horribly beloved*' and signs off with '*all the blessings of the Pit be upon you, and so we close up our Letter*' (HW, 165–66).

Diabolus's epistolary style appears once again in a communiqué sent to his Diabolonian supporters after a consultation of the devils held in hell. This opens with a hinted sense of horror, but quickly falls into a childlike, not to say childish, humour:

> From the dark and horrible Dungeon of Hell, *Diabolus* with all the Society of the Princes of Darkness, sends to our trusty ones, in and about the walls of the Town of *Mansoul*, now impatiently waiting for our most Devillish answer to their venomous, and most poysonous design against the Town of *Mansoul*. [...] *We received your welcome, because highly esteemed Letter, at the hand of our trusty and greatly beloved the old Gentleman,* Mr. Profane. (*HW*, 176).

The humour evinced by Diabolus as he composes his letters to his followers can legitimately be called childlike both because of its repetitiveness and because of the obviousness of the parody; children love to tell jokes, but their humour tends to involve much repetition and to lack subtlety. There is little subtlety in the *right horribly beloved* or in the repeated references to all that is diabolically 'Devillish', 'venomous', and 'poysonous'. Yet one senses the enjoyment with which Bunyan must have penned these words; and in giving Diabolus such lines Bunyan may have been anticipating the joy to be felt—in the future—by those who witness the devil's final downfall.

Monica Furlong argues that for delight Puritans looked to the world yet to come because they felt themselves to be oppressed by persecution from without and demands from within for hard work and constant self-monitoring: 'Joy is never *now*, but always in some future state.'[30] Bunyan's decision to endow Diabolus with the desire and ability to poke fun at the lawyer, the minister, the politician, as well as at his satanic precursor from *Paradise Lost*, may be taken as an engagement with dangers inherent in spontaneous enjoyment, similar to the use made in *Grace Abounding* of tipcat and bell-ringing, both of which, harmless amusements in themselves, represent the danger to the believer of the enjoyments of this world. At the same time the very presence of a Satan character

---

[30] Monica Furlong, *Puritan's Progress* (London: Hodder & Stoughton, 1975), 41.

with a sense of humour indicates the possibility that the epicist wished to temper the fire and brimstone, as it were, with a draught of refreshingly cool water.

Although Diabolus should not be reduced to a genial, bumbling stand-up comedian, he is characterized by the ability to cope with approaching defeat by poking fun at the pompousness often associated with the powers-that-be, including himself. By endowing Diabolus with this particular quality Bunyan gives expression to an acceptance of the existence of human weakness, both on the wider social level and on the individual level. He could not approve of those frailties which might be a sign of reprobation; but in ascribing to his Satan a quintessential humanity he appears to be hinting that the passage of time has taught him to accept the very weaknesses which define the human heart; and as Diabolus himself points out, 'without the heart things are little worth' (*HW*, 174).

Suggested Reading

Davies, Michael, *Graceful Reading: Theology and Narrative in the Works of John Bunyan* (Oxford: Oxford University Press, 2002).

Greaves, Richard L., *Glimpses of Glory: John Bunyan and English Dissent* (Stanford, CA: Stanford University Press, 2002).

Hill, Christopher, *A Turbulent, Seditious, and Factious People: John Bunyan and his Church* (Oxford: Clarendon Press, 1989).

Keeble, N. H., *The Literary Culture of Nonconformity in Later Seventeenth-Century England* (Leicester: Leicester University Press, 1987).

Mackenzie, Donald, 'Rhetoric *versus* Apocalypse: The Oratory of *The Holy War*', BS, 2,1 (1990), 33–45.

Rosenfeld, Nancy, *The Human Satan in Seventeenth-Century English Literature: From Milton to Rochester* (Aldershot: Ashgate, 2008).

Thickstun, Margaret Olofson, *Fictions of the Feminine: Puritan Doctrine and the Representation of Women* (Ithaca, NY: Cornell University Press, 1988).

Tillyard, E. M. W., *The English Epic and its Background* (New York: Oxford University Press, 1966).

Wharey, J. B., 'Bunyan's *Holy War* and the Conflict-Type of Morality Play', *Modern Language Notes*, 34 (1919), 65–73.

Wyke, Clement H., 'Distanced Experience and Faded Vision in The Holy War', *Humanities Association Review*, 26 (1975), 21–32.

CHAPTER 17

PIETY AND RADICALISM

Bunyan's Writings of the 1680s

ARLETTE ZINCK

SPIRITUAL saint or political radical: who was John Bunyan? As Michael Mullett points out at the close of *John Bunyan in Context*, Victorian critics like George Offor and John Brown painted a picture of Bunyan as a spiritual giant largely unmarked by the soot of worldly affairs. Scholarship of the twentieth century, by contrast, shows less interest in the piety of the tinker and preacher. Instead the focus shifts to Bunyan the political radical whose deep sympathy with the working class and whose staunch advocacy for Nonconformist worship animate his writing.[1] So which is the real Bunyan? In what follows I will address this question through the history of Bunyan's last eight years of life and the tracts and treatises he wrote and published during this period. Taken at a broad sweep these works show the breadth and depth of Bunyan's mature thinking on a variety of topics, and they lend particular insight to this question of 'social radicalism' and 'political quiescence'.[2] The question is an important one because it invariably informs a view of Bunyan's potential for political violence.

Throughout the 1680s Bunyan was deeply engaged with issues of personal and communal piety, and social and political radicalism. I will attempt to demonstrate, however, that Bunyan was not tempted himself, or likely to have encouraged his followers, to engage in any militancy of the sword. Bunyan's understanding of radicalism is shaped by what Hans Frei describes as a 'pre-critical biblical hermeneutic'. This literal approach to the Bible understands Scripture as realistic narrative. Its various stories are seen as an integrated, continuous narrative wherein types and figures connect the spiritual trajectories of the old dispensation with the new. The object of this literal reading is to see the

---

[1] Michael A. Mullett, *John Bunyan in Context* (Keele: Keele University Press, 1996), 284.
[2] Mullett, *Bunyan in Context*, 284.

unity of the biblical story, and then to fit oneself into it.³ It is a style of reading deeply informed by both Calvin and Luther's approach to text, and its net effect is to collapse the distinctions between biblical history, the present, and biblical visions of the future. As Frei argues, for a pre-critical biblical reader like Bunyan:

> since the world truly rendered by combining biblical narratives into one was indeed the one and only real world, it must in principle embrace the experience of any present age and reader. Not only was it possible for him, it was also his duty to fit himself into that world in which he was in any case a member, and he too did so in part by figural interpretation and in part of course by his mode of life. He was to see his disposition, his actions and passions, the shape of his own life as well as that of his era's events as figures of that storied world.⁴

Throughout most of the prose works written and published during the last eight years of Bunyan's life we see him working to interpret the events and circumstances faced by his congregation into the biblical story. He knits events of the present into the scriptural narrative either by way of a direct comparison, or through the use of the types and figures that translate Old Testament issues and concerns into New Testament understandings and contemporary applications. This rational and systematic exposition of Scripture maintains a clear line of argument for Bunyan's readers, especially where the issues of social reform, political radicalism, and violence are concerned. Throughout, Bunyan argues that one changes the world by making it holy. Social and political justice is produced by personal and communal sanctification. The justice not only happens in eternity through the promised fulfilment of the eschatological vision, but also in the here and now. In reading his contemporary history into the biblical narrative, Bunyan outlines for his readers a way of living on the margin of society, of being empowered but also blameless in the eyes of God.

In these final eight years Bunyan ministers to individual readers and to the church as a corporate body. He teaches an 'ethic of suffering'⁵ and issues a call to holiness. He writes several works directed towards the personal sanctification of individual believers once the persecution of the early 1680s abates. He weighs into a variety of debates on church policy, including the role of women in the church, and in his last years he examines the nature of communal worship itself and provides words of advice directed towards his fellow ministers. The picture of John Bunyan that emerges from this survey is something of an amalgam of the two earlier representations of the quietist saint and the political radical. Bunyan is revealed to be a deeply radical preacher who calls his readers towards

---

³ Frei distinguishes carefully between a 'literal reading' of Scripture and 'literalism'. See *The Eclipse of Biblical Narrative: A Study in Eighteenth and Nineteenth Century Hermeneutics* (New Haven, CT, and London: Yale University Press, 1974), 1–16.

⁴ Frei, *Eclipse of Biblical Narrative*, 3.

⁵ This term is coined by Richard Greaves in his chapter 'Amid *The Holy War*: Bunyan and the Ethic of Suffering', in Richard Greaves, *John Bunyan and English Nonconformity* (London: Hambledon Press, 1992), 169–83; and see also Greaves, *Glimpses*, 485–98.

a new way of life rooted in a biblically sanctioned activism and profound pacifism modelled on the life of Christ. It is a spiritual call that is fully calculated to produce political and social change in current affairs. In the prose and poetry written and published during his last years Bunyan focuses his attentions on the mechanisms for this orthodox Christian view of radicalism by showing the reciprocal influences that connect individual piety to corporate change, while also calling his readers' attention to the spiritual solace that acts as an emollient to the stresses produced by persecution.

Ethics of Suffering and the Call to Holiness

The Greatness of the Soul (1682), *A Holy Life* (1684), *Seasonable Counsel* (1684), and the poem, *A Caution to Stir up to Watch against Sin* (1684), as well as *A Discourse upon the Pharisee and the Publicane* (1685), all fit within the broad category of works written to inculcate personal piety as a response to the renewed persecution that beset Nonconformists in the early 1680s. In the wake of Popish Plot hysteria, a holdover from the previous decade, and in the immediate context of the Exclusion Crisis, Nonconformists found many good reasons to be fearful. The exclusion debate arose during the last years of Charles II's reign. Without a legitimate son to succeed him, Charles's Catholic brother James, Duke of York, was heir to the throne. Few Britons were pleased with the prospect of a Catholic monarch, but amid the jockeying for position that went on during this era, when Parliament made successive efforts to exclude James from the royal succession, Nonconformists were particularly hard hit by policies designed by Royalist interests to secure the throne for the next Stuart monarch.[6] Affairs of church and affairs of state were assumed to be interdependent in Bunyan's England. The suffering of Nonconformists was the direct result of the assumption that citizens' theological convictions and their worship practices were directly connected to their political motivation and actions. The botched Rye House Plot of 1683 and the failed Monmouth Rebellion of 1685 also helped to underscore these connections. In Bunyan's England what one believed, whether about the afterlife or practices in worship, did have a material effect upon one's circumstances in the here and now. Bunyan's twelve years in the Bedford prison underscore this fact. Each of the works written in response to this era of renewed persecution confront, to some lesser or greater degree, the real political circumstances facing readers. But the advice spoken into that context is decidedly inwardly focused and personal, leading many commentators to assert the apolitical nature of Bunyan's engagement.

---

[6] For the history of this period, see Tim Harris, *Restoration: Charles II and his Kingdoms 1660–1685* (London: Allen Lane, 2005) and *Revolution: The Great Crisis of the British Monarchy, 1685–1720* (London: Allen Lane, 2006).

The Greatness of the Soul originated in a sermon Bunyan preached at Pinner's Hall, London, in the spring of 1682. *A Holy Life* was likely written during the following year and published by Benjamin Alsop in 1684. These two works are also directed to an audience of spiritual enquirers or believers. If one is to have recourse to one's faith for the courage to resist powerful and ungodly political administrations, it makes perfect sense that the demand for a detailed and robust understanding of that faith would be high. The instructions Bunyan provides for the personal sanctification of the faithful serve as scaffolding to buttress the weaknesses of the flesh that might otherwise collapse under the weight of trial and pain. In *The Greatness of the Soul* Bunyan takes care to make the abstractions of the soul concrete to his readers. There are few philosophical phantasms here. On the contrary, Bunyan employs his literary wisdom systematically to render the soul familiar. He compares its functions to those of the body. It 'hears the Language of things invisible' and enjoys the '*sweet smelling Myrrh*'. It has affections that are like arms and legs that allow the soul to 'take hold of, receive and imbrace what is liked by the Soul'. The soul of a saint can 'Tast and Relish God's word' (*MW*, 9: 147–50). The poet's gift for making the abstract concrete is apparent too in the poetry with which Bunyan concludes his section on 'the Loss of the Soul': "*'tis the damned's wo / To live and yet be dead*', he argues. Here again the connections are underscored between personal piety and material circumstances in this life and the next. Those who have lost their souls may think they 'live' in these prosecutorial times, but they will discover later that they are not really living at all. '*They would be rid of present pain, / Yet set themselves on fire*' (*MW*, 9: 186). By contrast, the godly folks suffering under present difficulties with a lively and healthy soul have access to otherworldly comforts of faith.

The case for the interconnectedness of the material and the spiritual is made with precise vigour in *A Holy Life*, where the Reformed doctrine underscores the all-sufficient nature of Christ's grace for salvation and the insufficiency of even the best works to replace it. The tract also argues that 'true faith' will manifest itself in a variety of tangible fruits:

> *There are Works that cost nothing, and Works that are chargeable: And observe it, The unsound Faith will chuse to it self the most easie works it can find. For example, there is Reading, Praying, hearing of Sermons, Baptism, Breaking of Bread, Church fellowship, Preaching, and the like: and there is mortification of Lusts, Charity, Simplicity, open-Heartedness, with a liberal Hand to the Poor, and their like also. Now the unsound Faith picks and chuses, and takes and leaves, but the true Faith does not so.* (*MW*, 9: 254)

An implicit political slight against both dreaded Catholics and Anglicans is apparent here in the tract's focus on the sacraments of the church, but the social implications of the Nonconformist doctrine are also obvious. The faithful not only participate in church services and personal disciplines, but also attend to the disadvantaged and provide material assistance to the poor. The point is sharpened. '*The Gospel*', argues Bunyan, '*comes to some in Word only, and the Faith of such stands but in a verbal sound: but the Apostle was resolved not to know, or take notice of such a Faith.*' His marginal notations direct readers to 1 Thessalonians 1:4, 5 and to 1 Corinthians 4:18, 19, 20, and his argument is clarified: 'For the Kingdom of God, *saith he*, is not in Word, but in Power.' The outcome of this power is decidedly tangible and immediate:

> If a Brother or a Sister be naked or destitute of daily Food, And one of you say unto them, Depart in peace, be you warmed and filled: notwithstanding you give them not those things which are needful to the body, what doth it profit? Even so Faith, if it hath not Works is dead, being alone. (*MW*, 9: 255)

Hence the Word cannot be an 'empty sound' to the true faithful. The righteous must embody the sound, quite literally become agents of the Word and, in so doing, produce life-giving changes in the world. Bunyan also argues that a holy life guards against persecutions in the here and now. A holy life ensures that the faithful become active agents of social justice in their own spheres and provides the spiritual safeguard to ensure God's protection from persecution. If the righteous suffer, as well they may, they will do so with the comfort that their suffering is God-sanctioned and for their good.

This theme is developed again in the poem *A Caution to Stir up to Watch against Sin*, the first edition of which was printed on a broadside sheet, and was likely composed earlier in 1684, the same year it appeared in print (*MW*, 6: 177). The present material circumstances of suffering and difficulty are registered in the imagery and metaphors of the poem, which direct the conversation overtly to the spiritual domain. The means of release from present suffering is reiterated here in verse: personal sanctity. History and eternal futures are collapsed into the present moment as Bunyan reminds his readers that 'No Match has SIN save God in all the World' (*MW*, 6: 181). The spiritual cure is effective in the world, and the poem makes the abstract concept of sin more concrete through a series of earthy comparators. As Graham Midgley notes, Bunyan's topic is developed with 'dramatic invention in the different character-guises of Sin, as a beggar, a briber, an importunate visitor, a flatterer, a deceiver, and a tyrant' (*MW*, 6: lv). The richness of the imagery and the accessibility of the poem's line of argument serve to clarify a theology of sin, and to draw the connection between individuals' fallen-ness and Christ's ability both to save the individual's soul for eternity and provide release from worldly enemies. The argument for the poem is summarized in the final stanza:

> Now let the God that is above,
> That hath for Sinners so much Love;
> These Lines so help thee to improve,
> That towards him thy heart may move.
>   Keep thee from Enemies external,
>   Help thee to fight with those internal;
>   Deliver thee from them Infernal,
>   And bring thee safe to Life eternal. (*MW*, 6: 182)

The faithful will be kept from 'Enemies external': the statement is passive, underscoring that none but God can intervene in this way. The next statement, however, is active. The site of the conflict is moved from the exterior to the interior. Readers must 'fight with those internal' enemies who stand between believers and access to God's protection in this life and the next.

The fact is, of course, that God did allow 'enemies external' quite a bit of room to operate during this period. The issue of unmerited suffering and a correct response to it is approached directly in *Seasonable Counsel*. Written sometime during the winter of 1684, and published later that year, *Seasonable Counsel* directs believers in their response to suffering. The thesis of the work is that sins take the faithful away from God and stunt spiritual growth. Suffering, by contrast, draws the faithful to God and corrects the deviations of spirit. In a time of suffering the faithful are exhorted to be patient. The advice is specific and practical. It addresses the concerns faced by readers with sensitivity and openness to both the certainties of the faith and the places where general rules must remain ambiguous and be interpreted in the context of specific circumstances. Bunyan ranges between the Old Testament and the New, searching for examples to make concrete the spirit and intent of principles that must remain fluid enough to adjust to the unknowable specifics of uncertain times. The diversity of examples draws readers' attention away from a rule-governed understanding of correct conduct and towards a more nuanced and spiritual understanding of the range of appropriate responses that have occurred within biblical history. Readers are left to face the ambiguities of their own particulars, but with the assurance provided by the biblical exemplars.

Bunyan's instructions cut against any instinct for unnecessary martyrdom while also cautioning against cowardice:

> Do not fly out of a slavish fear, but rather because flying is an ordinance of God, opening a door for the escape of some, which door is opened by Gods providence, and the escape countenanced by Gods word (*Matt.* 10. 23). (*MW*, 10: 74)

Here, as elsewhere, Bunyan's consolations and instructions come laced with cautions for the wicked: '*if thou be guilty, look to thy self, I am no comforter of such*' (*MW*, 10: 75). Bunyan continually holds the need for personal sanctification before his readers. No comfort can be accorded to those who are not first seeking to fear God, value their own soul, and live a holy life. The seasonable counsel that helps mitigate the stresses and sorrows of the world is deeply contingent, and only the believer and his or her God know for sure the state of his or her soul. The final instruction crosses all lines as Bunyan openly addresses each category of potential reader:

> Wherefore, my brethren, my Friends, my enemies, and all men, what Religion, Profession, or Opinion so ever you hold; Fear God, honour the King, and do that duty to both, which is required of you by the Word and Law of Christ: and then, to say no more, you shall not suffer by the Power for evil-doing. (*MW*, 10: 104)

The experience of suffering cannot be eliminated, but the manner in which one suffers can be made more comfortable. Suffering that afflicts the flesh is a lesser evil than suffering that affects the conscience, and control of that latter form of suffering is well within the reach of each believer. Vengeance, when it comes, must come from God alone. The instruction to 'honour the King' must be understood in that context, but the clear implication of Bunyan's text is that vengeance *will* come:

> Wherefore he saith to his Saints, and to all that are forward to revenge themselves: *Give place*, stand back, let me come, leave such an one to be handled by me. *Dearly beloved, avenge not your selves, but rather give place unto wrath, for it is written, Vengeance is mine, I will repay, saith the Lord* (Rom. 12. 19). (*MW*, 10: 100)

On the basis of passages like this, Owen Watkins stresses the apolitical nature of Bunyan's views, arguing that he is 'at pains to urge that all Christians should be loyal to the king, not meddle in state affairs nor even aspire to positions of power' (*MW*, 10: xvii):

> He had little to say about toleration as a principle, and it was consistent with his membership of a persecuted minority and his passive approach to politics that he never seems to have felt the need to explain how he would have the government treat those expressing unacceptable opinions. (*MW*, 10: xx)

In our own post-critical era of biblical hermeneutic and analysis, the need for a pluralistic statement about toleration is self-evident, but it was not so for a thinker of Bunyan's training and disposition. It was typical of Bunyan to believe that the only way to achieve a tolerant and peaceful state was to ensure the citizenry's conversion to the biblical norms he identifies. This acknowledgement, however, does not detract from the sincerity or the power of Bunyan's social and political radicalism. He was wholeheartedly working towards the transformation of the world around him, but he literally could not imagine that change being possible outside of the population's wholesale adoption of Christian principles and piety. Nor, however, does Bunyan's wholehearted Christian radicalism imply that he would support the use of violence or civil unrest to accomplish his goal. His pacifistic instructions to the suffering are clarified and underscored in the firm commands to obedience and patience articulated in *Seasonable Counsel*.

For all of Bunyan's injunctions against violence in these prose works, the imaginative fictions that he pens during this period—*The Life and Death of Mr. Badman* (1680), *The Pilgrim's Progress, Part II* (1684), and, most especially, *The Holy War* (1682)—are full of graphic violence, and the otherwise pious-seeming characters seem to relish the brutality. This disjuncture between the 'ethic of suffering' that Bunyan articulates so carefully in the prose works and the lusty violence included in the fictional allegories have left many scholars puzzled, if not disturbed.[7] If critics understand Bunyan's writings to

---

[7] See John R. Knott, 'Bunyan and the Cry of Blood', in David Gay, James G. Randall, and Arlette Zinck (eds.), *Awakening Words: John Bunyan and the Language of Community* (Newark, DE: University

be engaged with the political and social issues of his day, then it is tempting to see evidence of Bunyan's willingness to countenance a militant response in works like *The Holy War*, especially during the renewed oppression that he and his countrymen faced in the early 1680s. If, on the other hand, critics understand Bunyan as an apolitical pietist, the violence of the allegories is often explained by the requirements of narrative plot, or excused as a literalization of that which is clearly intended to be understood in purely spiritual terms. The militaristic imagery of *The Pilgrim's Progress, Part II* and *The Holy War* are understood to be entirely consistent with a view of the world that sees the spiritual life as a battleground where the barbarous externals of physical militarism stand as types for the bloodless battles of the spirit.

But this spiritual reading cannot satisfy scholars looking to square Bunyan's prose injunctions to patient suffering with his promises of societal reform. The prayerful turning of one's heart to God does not regularly produce swift or compelling evidence of social and political change in present struggles. Interestingly, Marxist critic Terry Eagleton observes a similar problem for those wishing to see Jesus of Nazareth as a social revolutionary. In his introduction to the New Testament Gospels, published as part of the Verso series on revolutionary texts, Eagleton argues that the life and influence of Jesus of Nazareth as they are represented in the Gospels are substantively different from the life and influence of other revolutionary leaders such as, for example, Lenin. Their differences lie in the manner in which both men regard history. Jesus was 'not a Leninist because he would have had no conception of historical self-determination', argues Eagleton. 'The only kind of history which mattered was *Heilsgeschichte* or salvation history.' Eagleton notes, however, that the church that arose in Jesus's wake developed 'a theology for which human efforts to transform the world are part of the coming of the New Jerusalem, and prefigurative of it. Working to bring about peace and justice on earth is a necessary pre-condition of the coming of the reign of God.'[8]

It is exactly here, in this understanding about how one works 'to bring about peace and justice on earth', that the nature of Bunyan's radicalism must be understood. Frei's theory of the pre-critical biblical hermeneutic provides further helpful insight. In the pre-critical understanding of history, the ending of the human drama is already in place, and all present-day history fits somewhere between the conclusion of biblical times and the symbolic rendering of end times provided in Revelation. Actions in the current era are to be performed as a sort of theatrical improvisation, directed towards that forgone conclusion.[9] The immediate effect of this understanding is to relieve the pre-critical reader of any need to manufacture a happily-ever-after conclusion to the human drama.

---

of Delaware Press, 2000), 51–67 (51), and Sharon Achinstein, 'Honey from the Lion's Carcass: Bunyan, Allegory, and the Samsonian Moment', in Gay, Randall, and Zinck (eds.), *Awakening Words*, 68–80 (78).

[8] Terry Eagleton, 'Introduction', in *Terry Eagleton Presents Jesus Christ: The Gospels* (London and New York: Verso, 2007), i–xxxii (xxii).

[9] This theatrical analogy which works out of the key assumptions of the pre-critical biblical hermeneutic described by Frei, is developed by theologian N.T. Wright in *The New Testament and the People of God* (Minneapolis, MN: Fortress Press, 1992), 139–43.

That ending is already in place. Since the biblical narrative is the 'real world' into which one's own story is to be inserted, stress is placed on the reading strategies that connect the Old Testament to the New and which must direct action in the present if the promised end is to be achieved sooner rather than later.

In the meantime, the violent actions of the allegories do provide tangible comfort of another variety. Sharon Achinstein's conclusion about Bunyan's identification with the biblical figure of Samson illuminates how this comfort works.[10] As the faithful wait for God's actions, Bunyan may have reasoned that there would be little harm in providing sanctified readers well trained in the art of interpreting allegory with the emotionally satisfying experience of a little end-times payback. The biblical Book of Revelation includes more than a little of this, and the apocalyptic mode of writing has long served as a means of speaking to distressed communities about promised release from suffering in a coded language that only insiders can understand.[11] Bunyan never stoops to argue that the godly will be redeemed by human-initiated violence. The allegories always provide the necessary buffers of ambiguity, but he is not above the enjoyment of an imagined scene in which humans become the agents of God's violence, and where violence itself stands as a crude biblical type for the kind of divine action that will eventually bring about humanity's release from suffering, once and for all.

In the twenty-first century we may be accustomed to seeing fundamentalism and violence as co-conspirators in causing pain in the world, but to impose this assumption backwards and allow it to override Bunyan's own clear statements actively distorts his message. In Bunyan's view, the faithful can no more bring about their salvation from physical sufferings than they can achieve spiritual salvation by their own works. What they can do, however, is sanctify their own souls by repentance, and trust God to act. By linking responsibility and power for societal change to the piety of individual believers, Bunyan tries to soothe the anxieties and stresses of a political and social world well outside of Nonconformist control. By resituating the locus of meaningful action within the hearts and souls of the believers themselves, Bunyan makes manageable, in a very real, material sort of way, the step-by-step structural changes required to achieve enduring societal and political change.

By the time that *A Discourse upon the Pharisee and the Publicane* appeared in early 1685, change had indeed come, but not the sort for which Nonconformists had hoped. England was under the governance of a Catholic ruler. With the death of Charles II on 6 February that year, James II ascended the throne. Eventually, James's policies of toleration made life easier for Nonconformists, but throughout 1685 and 1686 times continued to be tough for Bunyan and his fellow churchmen and women. Criminal proceedings related to the Monmouth Rebellion were underway, and Nonconformist communities continued to feel the heat generated by civil unrest. Accordingly, this tract promises comfort for the afflicted and renews the promise of God's vengeance on their enemies:

---

[10] Achinstein, 'Honey from the Lion's Carcass', 68–80.

[11] For a definition of the apocalyptic form, see J. J. Collins, *The Apocalyptic Imagination: An Introduction to Jewish Apocalyptic Literature* (New York: Crossroad, 1984), 280–83.

This is therefore a very comfortable Parable to such of the Saints, that are under hard usages, by reason of evil Men, their *Might*, and *Tyranny*. For by it we are taught to believe and expect, that God, though for a while he seemeth not to regard, yet will, in due time, and season, *arise and set such in safety from them that puff at them*, Psal. 12. 5. [...] *I tell you*, says Christ, *he will avenge them speedily*. (MW, 10: 113–14)

A Discourse upon the Pharisee and the Publicane is an extended meditation on Luke 18:10–13, which tells the story of subverted behavioural expectations in the worldly Publican, the officer of state whose conduct puts him at a remove from the spiritual laws of the temple, and the religious Pharisee, whose membership of the most zealous of the Jewish sects builds an expectation for behaviour of exceptional piety. As the biblical story unfolds, however, the expectations are overturned as the Publican displays deep humility before God, and the Pharisee proves to be blinded by pride to his own spiritual flaws. Throughout the work Bunyan calls his readers to assess whether they are Publicans or Pharisees, and he broadens his readers' understanding of each. The label Pharisee is defined beyond the narrow and negative connotation. Bunyan points out that the Apostle Paul was a Pharisee, and that the sect was among the most zealous. Bunyan also reminds readers that Paul was called out of his narrow legalism into a new life animated by Christ's mercy. The injunction to self-scrutiny, while applicable to all readers, may have been calculated to hit a particular nerve with Anglican churchmen whose outward signs of piety outran, at least in Bunyan's opinion, their inward motions of true faith.[12] The Publican, meanwhile, is defined as a 'possessor of the land' who was among 'a generation of men that were very injurious in the execution of their Office'. They were, Bunyan argues, 'reckoned among the worst of men, even as our Informers and Bum-bailiffs are with us at this day' (*MW*, 10: 118). The tract continues the pattern established elsewhere by knitting past and present together into one continuous story, and challenging readers to see their own stories within the biblical narrative. Readers are exhorted to ask tough questions, refine their own spiritual vision, and grow in personal holiness. Bunyan's argument is that the growing goodness of the world depends upon the growing goodness of individuals, and he concludes with a lengthy reflection on the value of prayer and the characteristics of sincere and honest petition.

Preaching Sanctification and Reform in an Era of Relative Peace

In April 1687 James II signed the Declaration of Indulgence and his policies of toleration soon began to make a significant difference in the daily lives of Nonconformists. The

---

[12] See Greaves, *Glimpses*, 531.

fact that toleration had been extended towards the Nonconformist community did not mean, however, that all were content with the situation. Tory Anglicans were incensed by the new liberties extended to Nonconformists, and viewed them as a direct assault against the interests of the national church. There was also considerable debate within the Nonconformist communities themselves about whether toleration should be accepted from a Catholic king. Bunyan argues consistently throughout this period against the practices of both the Catholic and the Anglican Church, but he accepted the release from suffering that James's policy of toleration allowed.[13] He also projects his readers into a reflection on a perfected future rendered symbolically in Revelation, and teaches them to see evidence of this heaven in their current circumstances.

The first edition of *The Water of Life*, which was likely composed between September and October of 1687, was published by Nathaniel Ponder in 1688. Like other prose works penned during this period, this tract exhorts readers to personal holiness and connects personal sanctity to promises of eternity and to experiences of comfort in the present. The biblical text under discussion is Revelation 22:1: 'And he shewed me a pure River of Water of Life, clear as Crystal, proceeding out of the Throne of God, and of the Lamb.' Bunyan takes up the poetic and symbolic pattern established by the primary text and carries this through a systematic meditation on the matter, quantity, and source of the 'water of life'. Throughout this work the connection between civic and national political affairs and the greater biblical pattern of reality into which they fit is worked out, while the twin messages of grace and damnation are preached together. Even though toleration makes life somewhat easier for the Nonconformists, Bunyan maintains pressure on the need for continual reform at both the personal and congregational level. The imagery throughout the tract maps for readers the connections that bind the ways and practices of the present to those of the yet-to-be fulfilled vision of the heavenly reality. Bunyan reaches forward into the symbolism of the apocalypse for the figure of the river and projects it backward to the present day. In doing so, he provides his readers with a glimpse into that heavenly realm, which he regards as underlying current circumstances. Bunyan uses the present tense whenever he discusses the water, the river, and its source in 'the Throne of Grace' (*MW*, 7: 193). This is a statement about how things both are, and could be, now.

By contrast, in *The Advocateship of Jesus Christ* the metaphor of Christ as legal counsel knits together the grand spiritual abstractions of salvation theology with the sensory details of judicial life in the 1680s. The work was published in 1688 for Dorman Newman, and likely written between late October of 1687 and February of 1688. Like *The Water of Life*, it was composed during the period of relative ease from persecution, and like the majority of tracts mentioned here, *The Advocateship* is directed to the hearts and minds of those to whom Bunyan might speak from the pulpit. In this work, and in his next, *Good News for the Vilest of Men* (1688), Bunyan speaks specifically to the unregenerate. The message in both tracts is that Jesus Christ will save the worst. Bunyan confronts

---

[13] Greaves, *Glimpses*, 572.

directly the popular notion that if one is not behaving well Christ will not advocate on one's behalf. The idea is roundly defeated with an assertion of the doctrine of grace worked through a meditation on 1 John 2:1: 'if any man sin, we have an advocate with the Father, Jesus Christ the righteous'. The discussion is meticulously laid out and systematically discussed, from broad principles to ever increasing subcategories of analysis on the particulars. It concludes with a series of questions and answers.

In *Good News to the Vilest of Men* Bunyan offers an exposition of Luke 24:47. The core message is that mercy will be offered to the greatest and most egregious of sinners first. Renewal, reconciliation, restoration: this is the work of the kingdom that Bunyan preaches, and the good word is extended from this self-styled 'Chief of Sinners' to others in this condition. One edition of the work was published during Bunyan's lifetime by George Larkin in 1688, and it was reprinted frequently thereafter. The thesis of the work is that Christ seeks to redeem the worst sinners first because they are the ringleaders in Satan's army. While he uses a similitude of military rank to describe the 'greatest sinners', Bunyan is not making a specific case about heads of state or those in authority. Rather, he is arguing that the growing good of the land is dependent upon the conversion of those who are most evil. Their worldly estate or rank is a less powerful consideration than their estate or rank as a member of Satan's legions. Although the message is overtly spiritual, the social and political implications of the message are also apparent. The reformation of the wicked will make a discernible positive change in the present circumstances. Bunyan consistently suspends discussion about spectacular moments of divine intervention and dwells instead on the mystery of why God permits evil, and the slow and careful progress that may be made towards its correction.

Preaching Congregational Reform

The majority of Bunyan's writing during the 1680s is directed towards individual readers and the acts of personal reformation that are required to survive the slings and arrows of the outrageous fortunes that beset Nonconformists during this era of renewed persecution. However, during the last eight years of his life Bunyan was also busy both with congregational life at Bedford and preaching to congregations elsewhere. The larger argument of these works bends in the same direction as those written during the same period but is directed to individuals: events of the current day are woven into the seamless biblical narrative of salvation; reformation of the world is the object of spiritual work, and any labouring to change the world for good must begin with the reformation of individuals, families, and churches.

A Case of Conscience Resolved was written and published at the height of persecution in 1683. The context for this work is explained succinctly by Bunyan at the beginning of the tract. Women of the Bedford congregation had been meeting together separately from men for prayer and worship. Bunyan heard of this, and called the women into question on the practice which, Bunyan argues, had no warrant in Scripture. According to Bunyan the women were content with his explanation and desisted in their single-sex meetings. One 'Mr. K', who is often assumed to be William Kiffin, a minister from a London congregation with ties to and interests in the Bedford church, heard of Bunyan's response and called him to account for it with a tract that he authored and circulated among the Bedford congregants (*MW*, 4: xliii). Bunyan's scriptural approach and its implications for his understanding of history are showcased in this treatise, as the logical disputation presented by Mr K is brushed aside and replaced by Bunyan's own recontextualization of the question into biblical history. Where Mr K argues for the logic of women's prayers and worship in the broader context of church doctrine, Bunyan seeks to discover specific biblical injunction for the practice, or biblical precedent for it, and, finding none, dismisses the idea as dangerous.

While Bunyan is unflinching in delivering what he fears will be an unpopular judgement on a contentious issue, and while he accuses Mr K of flattering the women of Bedford, he is at pains to make known his respect and admiration for the local women and women more generally. He acknowledges the doctrinal equality of male and female. He admits women's superior record for piety, and concedes that he and the rest of his male brethren '*come behinde*' the women in faith and holiness (*MW*, 4: 295). Nevertheless, the relation of the present to the biblical past and future that Bunyan's hermeneutic entails makes it impossible for him to approve of a practice that could otherwise be seen as the logical outcome of his stated beliefs about women's piety in general, and of the women of the Bedford church in particular.

Bunyan has been justly taken to task by a number of critics who point out that in his doctrine 'The least male is to be preferred to the best female.'[14] However, the imaginative fictions written by Bunyan around this time also provide opportunity for more positive aspects of his beliefs about the capacities of women to shine through. Just as *The Holy War* provides an emotionally satisfying experience of imaginative vengeance within the context of many prose injunctions against violence, so too *The Pilgrim's Progress, Part II* provides Bunyan with the imaginative scope to celebrate women's particular strengths, and to outline his symbolic understanding of the Church itself as gendered female. The story of Christiana and her train, while replete with examples of women's supposed physical and spiritual frailty, is also the story of the reformed and reforming church. It is a generative vision of community birthed from the isolating journey of the lone masculine figure, a community which, as Melissa Aaron has argued, poses a considerable threat to the Stuart state:

> While it is tacitly acknowledged that pilgrims will have to continue to live 'in the Fair' for some time to come, by marriage and propagation, education, community of goods, and a secure alternative society, the pilgrims will not only be safe, but slowly

---

[14] Aileen Ross, '"Baffled and Befooled": Misogyny in the Works of John Bunyan', in Gay, Randall, and Zinck (eds.), *Awakening Words*, 153–68 (167).

transform the threatening Vanity Fair into Beulah. Christiana's train will become the Church Triumphant, and the meek, many of them women, will literally inherit the earth.[15]

Here too Bunyan manages to pitch his grand argument: the turn to personal piety really does make changes, not only in the eternal scope of time but in the particular—the homely and the present issues that confront his church. Since the matter of reformation both personal and communal is the foundation upon which all of these envisioned forms are being built, Bunyan is zealous in his efforts to read current events and issues into biblical narrative and to derive a practice that is in accord with his findings, no matter if these findings offend either his emotional sensibilities or those of women in his congregation. In this context, Bunyan's sexism is most apparent in *the manner* in which he reads the women of Bedford and their meetings into the biblical narrative. He might have seen the New Testament examples of Priscilla and Aquila as evidence for a new dispensation concerning women, but he chooses instead to emphasize what he sees as a consistent arc of interpretation that connects Old and New Testament cultural prohibitions against women's leadership. He sees biblical stories that contradict these prohibitions as 'exceptions' to the rules. While the manner in which he applies his pre-critical hermeneutic betrays Bunyan's own acculturated bigotries and biases, his insistence upon this hermeneutic can be understood in a more charitable way. In this issue, and others, Bunyan insists upon an approach to Scripture that was quite literally saving to his sanity and his soul.[16]

A similarly specific issue of communal worship is taken up in a tract published by Nathaniel Ponder in 1685, and estimated to have been written between October and November of 1684. *Questions about the Nature and Perpetuity of the Seventh-Day-Sabbath* debates the issue of Saturday or Sunday worship which, as T. L. Underwood notes, was in dispute during the decades leading up to Bunyan's addressing of the issue (*MW*, 4: xlvii–lii). As Bunyan explains at the outset, arguments for a first day (that is, Sunday) Christian Sabbath had already been well articulated by others. He provides the layperson's version of these arguments, then, for those who formed his primary readership, those '*as have but* shallow *Purses,* short *Memories, and but* little *Time to spare, which usually is the lot of the mean and the poorest sort of men*' (*MW*, 4: 335). In this dispute, over the Jewish practice of the seventh-day Sabbath and the New Testament introduction of Christ's resurrection day as the new order of practice, Bunyan follows the New Testament paradigm. The ordinances signalled in the Old Testament must give way to the perfected forms ushered in by Christ. The manner and practice of Bunyan's pre-critical biblical reading practice are once again in evidence here, as he deftly connects

---

[15] Melissa Aaron, '"Christiana and her Train": Bunyan and the Alternative Society in the Second Part of *The Pilgrim's Progress*', in Gay, Randall, and Zinck (eds.), *Awakening Words*, 169–85 (183–84).

[16] Although Bunyan does not make this point himself, his concern about women meeting alone could also be informed by real fears about the threat of physical violence that attended any Nonconformist meeting in 1683, when persecution was at its height.

the themes and practices of the biblical past with the new procedures of Christ's reign and, finally, with an application for present circumstances. The biblical narrative is proven once more to be continuous, coherent, single, and one into which Bunyan is able to situate present-day concerns.

Solomon's Temple Spiritualized, likely composed in the summer of 1687 and published the following year, takes up the issues of communal worship again, but in a more general manner than the very specific tracts that Bunyan published on women's meetings and Sabbath practices allow. It is addressed to individual believers, but also to fellow ministers:

> A man may be a servant and a Son; a *servant* as he is imployed by Christ in his house for the good of others: And a *Son*, as he is a partaker of the Grace of Adoption: But all servants are not sons, and let this be for a *Caution*, and a *Call* to Ministers to do all acts of service for God, and in his house, with Reverence and godly Fear. And with all Humility, let us desire to be partakers our selves *of that Grace we preach to others*. I *Cor.* 9. 23. (*MW*, 7: 16)

The minister himself must be fit for the work of church building before any construction can begin. From here the tract explores the various types, figures, and similitudes that connect the physical attributes of the temple to contemporary 'gathered' church practice. In the introduction, Bunyan lays out the assumptions of his interpretative theory. We ought to 'search out the spiritual meaning' of the Old Testament ways of worship, 'because they serve to confirm and illustrate matters to our understandings':

> Yea, they shew us the more exactly how the *New* and *Old Testament*, as to the spiritualness of the worship, was as one and the same; only the *Old* was clouded with Shadows, but ours is with more open Face. (*MW*, 7: 8)

The types, those 'shadows' in the Old Testament, point to their New Testament antitypes by way of the common spiritual thread that joins the two. Minute details of the historical temple are given precise meaning in the New Testament understanding of church. The pragmatics of church administration and operations are linked concretely to the history of the literal building of the biblical temple. The biblical 'Word' becomes the material reality out of which the New Testament corporate body of 'church' is to be built, both literally and spiritually. Present circumstances are knitted tightly into biblical history and its projected future. 'The *New Jerusalem*', says Bunyan, 'is still the New Testament-Church on Earth, and so the same in substance with what is now' (*MW*, 7: 19).

A Discourse of the Building, Nature, Excellency, and Government of the House of God (1688) is the last poem Bunyan composed. It was written at about the same time as *Solomon's Temple Spiritualized*, and it develops a similar theme, setting out the purpose, the beauty, and the governance of the house of God. Throughout the poem evidence of what Richard Greaves calls Bunyan's 'pastoral Arminianism' abounds.[17] Jesus is the healer and the church-as-hospital dominates the imagery. The message is one of grace, and all are eligible: 'we are told there's no rebellion can / Prevent, or hinder him from being sav'd, / That Mercy heartily of God hath crav'd' (*MW*, 6: 281). Even the conclusion of the poem, where Bunyan addresses the unregenerate, as he so often does at the conclusion of his works, finishes with a message of comfort and grace rather than with the visions of hell so common in earlier works: if the sinner will turn, '*the Lord Jesus will not cast*' him out (*MW*, 6: 317).

The poem also systematically examines and comments upon the offices and duties of the house, drawing out the responsibilities of each, and the socially radical implications of Bunyan's gospel show up everywhere. The house, for example, is '*Rent-free*' for the man who '*Loves his Landlord, Rules his Passions well*'. 'This place, as *Hospitals*, will entertain / Those which the lofty of this World *disdain*.' The sufferings of an earlier period are brought to mind, with the church offered as a solution to them:

> Art thou bound over to the *great Assize*,
> For harkning to the Devil and his Lyes;
> Art thou *affraid* thereat to shew thy head,
> For fear thou then be sent unto the dead?
> Thou may'st come hither here is room and place
> For such as willingly would live by Grace. (*MW*, 6: 279, 280)

The comfort promised is not strictly of the imaginative kind. In this final poem Bunyan charts the realities of the doctrine for which he has argued for many years. The living church can indeed provide solace. Those who gather as a true church, in Bedford and elsewhere, act as safe refuge for one another. The land they inhabit together, the ground they tend as a community, can become the Beulah in which Christiana and her train reside before crossing the river. In every real, material sense many of the radical promises of the Gospel were enacted among Bunyan's congregants. The Bedford Church Book records some of these communal gestures alongside the rebukes meted out to ensure the continuation of the ideal.[18] In 1688, before the bloodless 'Glorious Revolution' that would guarantee England's release from Catholic rule and free Dissenters permanently from persecution through the Toleration Act of 1689, both of which Bunyan himself would not live to see, he could speak with confidence of sins being forgiven, as well as of prisoners being set free, all effected without the intervention of physical violence. He knew both from personal experience.

---

[17] Greaves, *Glimpses*, 583.
[18] See *The Church Book of Bunyan Meeting, 1650–1821*, intro. G. B. Harrison (London: J. M. Dent, 1928), and *CB*.

Conclusion

The prose and poetry that Bunyan both wrote and published during the 1680s—the last eight years of his life—demonstrate the deep connections that he perceived between spiritual and physical domains, and they help to reconcile competing views of the man that have lingered in the background of Bunyan scholarship for generations. John Bunyan, it turns out, is every inch the social and political radical, and in precisely the manner and style of his model, Jesus of Nazareth, who similarly confounded contemporaries with his call to societal restructuring while continually rejecting violent means for effecting such change. Bunyan, like Jesus, sees his own times within the context of salvation history, and like his Reformed mentors in scriptural interpretation, Luther and Calvin, he is oblivious to the historical separations and dislocations that are about to emerge in the following century with the advent of the German Higher Criticism and other strands of Enlightenment debate that will erase forever the reading of history, both scriptural and contemporary, upon which his hermeneutic depends. In our own decidedly post-critical age of biblical interpretation, it may require a variety of reading strategies to allow the pre-suppositions of Bunyan's radicalism to be appreciated.[19] As these late works make clear, Bunyan believed that God would and could intervene on behalf of the godly to effect change in present circumstances. He maintains that the way to bring about the final victory, which by his reading of Scripture has already been accomplished, is to look to one's own soul and make radical changes there. He believed the world would be changed forever and for the good, one believer at a time.

Suggested Reading

Cavanaugh, William T., *The Myth of Religious Violence: Secular Ideology and the Roots of Modern Conflict* (Oxford: Oxford University Press, 2009).

Comstock, Gary L., 'Two Types of Narrative Theology', *Journal of the American Academy of Religion*, 55 (1987), 687–717.

Downey, Martha Elias, 'A Perspective on Narrative Theology: Its Purpose, Particularity and Centrality', *Theoforum*, 43 (2012), 291–307.

Frei, Hans W., *The Eclipse of Biblical Narrative: A Study in Eighteenth and Nineteenth Century Hermeneutics* (New Haven, CT, and London: Yale University Press, 1974).

Frei, Hans W., *Theology and Narrative: Selected Essays*, ed. George Hunsinger and William C. Placher (New York: Oxford University Press, 1993).

Greaves, Richard L., 'John Bunyan and the Fifth Monarchists', *Albion*, 13 (1981), 83–95.

---

[19] Frei's 'plain sense' approach offers one reading strategy while Paul Ricoeur's notion of a 'second naiveté' offers another. See the final chapter in Paul Ricoeur, *The Symbolism of Evil*, trans. Emerson Buchanan (Boston, MA: Beacon Press, 1969).

Greaves, Richard L., '"Let Truth Be Free": John Bunyan and the Restoration Crisis of 1667–1673', *Albion*, 28 (1996), 587–605.

Juergensmeyer, Mark, Margo Kitts, and Michael Jerryson (eds.), *The Oxford Handbook of Religion and Violence* (Oxford: Oxford University Press, 2013).

Lynch, Kathleen, 'Into Jail and into Print: John Bunyan Writes the Godly Self', *Huntington Library Quarterly*, 72 (2009), 273–90.

CHAPTER 18

THE PILGRIM'S PROGRESS, PART II (1684)

MARGARET OLOFSON THICKSTUN

BUNYAN wrote *The Pilgrim's Progress, Part II* (1684) in an effort to silence unauthorized sequels. He had already provided a complement to Christian's journey with *The Life and Death of Mr. Badman* (1680). The story of Christian's representative experience does not require—in fact, it ought to forestall—sequels. In the original book Faithful's and Hopeful's stories already communicate the truth that there are varieties of religious experience within the way and they model the correct response to Christian's story: each man sets out on pilgrimage inspired by Christian's conduct (*PP*, 66–7; 137–38). Bunyan's decision to continue this narrative, then, arose from ministerial, not artistic, concerns: he needed to refute and displace the spurious, and theologically dangerous, sequel by one 'T. S.'.[1]

Most critics today, though, see *Part II* as not simply a continuation but also a reworking of the original text. The prefatory poem with which it opens promises that '*what* Christian *left locked up and went his way / Sweet* Christiana *opens with her key*' (*PP*, 171). As Betty Schellenberg points out, 'the complex of first work and established audience within which the sequel is written places its author in the role of authoritative mediator, writing the sequel as a kind of interpretive guide to the first work'.[2] The proem confirms this relationship, assuming readers who have already 'entertained' the story of Christian and so will respond positively to Christiana's 'calling' on them, especially when they are assured of this sequel's authenticity (*PP*, 167). Bunyan develops this metaphor of his books as visitors whom readers invite into their homes, bragging that

---

[1] See T. S., *The Second Part of The Pilgrim's Progress* (1682). 'T. S.' has often been identified as Thomas Sherman, but this has been called into question by Christopher E. Garrett, 'How T. S. became Known as Thomas Sherman: An Attribution Narrative', *Papers of the Bibliographical Society of America*, 108 (2014), 191–216.

[2] Betty Schellenberg, 'Sociability and the Sequel: Rewriting Hero and Journey in *The Pilgrim's Progress*, Part II', *Studies in the Novel*, 23 (1991), 312–24 (312).

his 'Pilgrims *book*' was not '*turned out of Door / By any Kingdom*' (PP, 169). In doing so, he conflates both Christiana with her story and her pilgrimage with the book's passage among readers. This metaphor introduces a new emphasis on domesticity and community in *Part II*.

The authorized sequel allows Bunyan to control his readers' interpretation of the initial story and to model the right way of reading. However, it is not simply Bunyan's readership that knows in advance the path of the journey this book will take: each of the pilgrims in *Part II* also carries a mental map of its landscape in the form of Christian's experiences, while having in addition an experienced guide in Great-heart to direct them. Throughout their progress, they discuss the plaques that explicate the significance of the dangerous places they visit, the monuments that commemorate heroic events, and the individuals who took wrong paths, which are now clearly marked and even blocked off with '*Chains, Posts*, and a *Ditch*' (PP, 215). Michael Davies argues that the pilgrims of *Part II* constitute 'an idealized readership of *The Pilgrim's Progress, Part I* itself', a group that Bunyan invites his actual readers to join.[3]

In writing a sequel, Bunyan saw the opportunity to clarify, to expand, and in some instances to revise the meaning of events in Christian's journey. In *Part I*, Apollyon confronts Christian in the Valley of Humiliation because Christian had once lived in his territory and was his subject; in *Part II*, Great-heart explains instead that Christian had trouble there because he had had 'slips' in coming down the hill (PP, 236). In *Part I*, Evangelist instructs Christian to fly from the wrath to come and makes no offer to come with him; solitary pilgrimage is the only way to heaven. In *Part II*, Great-heart marvels at his audacity: 'poor *Christian*, it was a wonder that he here escaped, but he was beloved of his God, also he had a good heart of his own, or else he could never a-done it' (PP, 244). Christian's success appears to derive from his singularity: other pilgrims, both the wiser and the weaker, would do well to join a convoy. Most strikingly, Bunyan reworks the lesson of Christian's initial departure. What appears to be a wrenching sacrifice *of* his family in *Part I* becomes a gracious sacrifice *for* them in *Part II*: 'Christian has quite literally saved his family by abandoning it.'[4] Clearly writing the story anew allowed Bunyan to explore areas of Christian experience, especially communal experience, that *Part I* did not address: he replaces Evangelist with the minister Great-heart; allows his pilgrims to linger in a series of house-churches where he can represent the workings of an ideal godly community; and includes women and children among the travellers. The idea of the book as visitor, introduced in the proem, continues in a narrative that emphasizes the church community as extended family.

---

[3] Michael Davies, *Graceful Reading: Theology and Narrative in the Works of John Bunyan* (Oxford: Oxford University Press, 2002), 341.

[4] N. H. Keeble, 'Christiana's Key: The Unity of *The Pilgrim's Progress*', in Vincent Newey (ed.), *The Pilgrim's Progress: Critical and Historical Views* (Totowa, NJ: Barnes & Noble, 1980), 1–20 (11).

Great-Heart and the Idea of the Minister

Although it is tempting to imagine that Bunyan intended Christiana to represent the true church, this is not the case. It is not Christiana 'who possesses the power to "bruise the head" of the enemy'—it is Great-heart, the fulfilment of Christian and of the (male) church community.[5] Christiana is a member of a travelling gathered church that interacts with other congregations: the communities at the Interpreter's House, at House Beautiful, and at Mnason's house in Vanity Fair. In recounting their experiences to Mr Contrite, Great-heart refers to spending 'some time at the House of *Gaius, mine Host, and of the whole Church*' (*PP*, 276). With the exception of Mercie, whom Gaius identifies as an appropriate spouse for Matthew, Christiana's daughters-in-law—Gaius's daughter, Phoebe, and Mr Mnason's daughters, Grace and Martha—are already members of house-churches: they do not join the church by marrying into Christiana's family. In introducing the company to the shepherds in the Delectable Mountains, Great-heart sings, '*First here's* Christiana *and her train, / Her Sons, and her Sons Wives*', and then introduces the other pilgrims separately—Honest, Ready-to-halt, Feeble-mind, Despondency, and Much-afraid (*PP*, 284). Although Christiana and these pilgrims travel in one large group, Great-heart does not perceive the others as part of 'her train': only her family fits that label. She is a member of the group, not its embodiment, and a subordinate and fairly silent member at that.

Bethany Joy Bear argues that Christiana represents instead the imagination, and that Bunyan uses the action of *Part II* to address 'the ongoing process of the fancy's transformation from a barrier against faith to a faculty of faith'.[6] Acknowledging the gendered nature of this story, she argues that Bunyan uses Christiana herself to represent fancy because women and fancy were understood to be weak, so her tendency to fall prey to fancy, often in the form of dreams, and her willingness to be instructed by the Interpreter (a figure of the Holy Spirit) and Great-heart (a minister mediating between the Holy Spirit and his congregation) model both appropriate female subordination to authority and the role of the faith community in supporting individuals in the interpretation of Scripture and of experience. If *Part I*, she proposes, dramatizes 'the anxiety of uncertain election', then *Part II* elaborates the process of sanctification within the gathered church.[7]

It is Great-heart who creates this particular church community: he is its minister, protecting the congregation both from external dangers, embodied in his frequent

---

[5] Michael Austin, 'The Figural Logic of the Sequel and the Unity of *The Pilgrim's Progress*', *SP*, 102 (2005), 484–509 (507).

[6] Bethany Joy Bear, 'Fantastical Faith: John Bunyan and the Sanctification of Fancy', *SP*, 109 (2012), 671–701 (673).

[7] Bear, 'Fantastical Faith', 672.

sword-fights with giants, and from personal frailty, as he guides them safely in the way. He offers spiritual instruction, explaining not only theological concepts, such as the nature of justification by faith, but also the significance of particular events in both Christian's and their own lives. In *Part II*, Great-heart replaces Evangelist as the source of spiritual authority and Christian as the active centre of the narrative. Michael Austin argues persuasively that Great-heart's relationship to Christian should be understood typologically, as he fulfils the promises that Christian's journey foreshadowed. In explicating the scene where Great-heart leads his band against Doubting Castle, Austin writes, 'Christian *escaped* despair, but his four sons, as part of a spiritual community, *destroyed* it.'[8] Although it is possible for an individual to remember that he has a key 'called *Promise*' (*PP*, 118), the minister carries such keys as part of his spiritual arsenal and wields them daily on behalf of others.

Because of his focus on church community and the role of the minister, Bunyan creates in *Part II* a world that is safer for and friendlier to Christians than that of *Part I*. This company of pilgrims does not travel with any sense of urgency. Lodgings appear at easy stages; they are always welcomed, feasted, and encouraged to remain in these homes for instruction and fellowship; and when they do set out again, their hosts often walk with them 'so far as was convenient' (*PP*, 279). A good Christian like Mr Mnason can live in Vanity Fair and host pilgrims without causing a hubbub. In fact, Mr Holyman, Mr Love-saint, and Mr Dare-not-lie talk rather sanctimoniously about the qualifications required of pilgrims even though, apparently, not one considers budging from the comfort and safety of the now-reformed Vanity Fair (*PP*, 276–77). Except for the episode in which Mercie, having wisely sought guidance from the church community at House Beautiful, discourages Mr Brisk's attention, the women do not interact with false pilgrims. The group does collect new members—Honest, Ready-to-halt, Feeble-mind, Despondency, Much-afraid, Valiant-for-truth, and Stand-fast—each of whom has his own tale (and often stories about others) to tell. Conversation and instruction, rather than conflict, fill this book's pages, although the group does encounter (and even seek out) giants who require killing. These episodes in which the minister protects his congregation from dangerous spiritual influences provide brief bursts of action in an otherwise sedentary text.

The pilgrims Great-heart collects satisfy Bunyan's stated intent in the proem to provide alternative models to the men of *Part I* for an expanded range of readers: '*for Young, for Old, for Stag'ring and for stable*' (*PP*, 170). Fearing and Despondency are, then, weak in spirit; Feeble-mind, in intelligence; Ready-to-halt, in body. Honest may appeal to '*some gray Head*', Mercie to 'Tripping *Maidens*' (*PP*, 172). But Valiant-for-truth and Stand-fast don't quite fit that mould: Valiant-for-truth is a strong, active young man with a '*right* Jerusalem *Blade*', who has fought his spiritual battles until 'my Sword did cleave to my Hand' (*PP*, 290–91); Stand-fast is middle-aged, married, and able-bodied. Both men have relationships that they have sacrificed to go on

---

[8] Austin, 'Figural Logic', 499, 507.

pilgrimage. Valiant-for-truth reports that, upon hearing of Christian's example, 'my Heart fell into a burning hast to be gone after him, nor could Father or Mother stay me' (*PP*, 292); Stand-fast, on his deathbed, begs Great-heart to tell his wife and children of his own and Christiana's family's pilgrimage, that they might follow his example as she and the boys have followed Christian's. Their stories reiterate the initial message of *The Pilgrim's Progress, Part I*, that a male believer must sacrifice his family in his commitment to his spiritual calling. The stories of Christiana and Mercie communicate a different message.

Christiana's Journey

Bunyan presents Christiana's salvation as mediated through her relationship to her husband. This is not at all surprising. In her book *Pilgrim's Progress, Puritan Progress*, Kathleen Swaim draws on the work of historians Laurel Thatcher Ulrich and Amanda Porterfield on Puritan womanhood to connect Bunyan's vision in *Part II* to cultural ideals about both women's spiritual role within the community—overseeing the home, their own children, and extending their mothering more widely to the church—and their necessary subordination to male guidance.[9] Christiana's sinfulness manifests itself in her failings as a wife and as a mother. What 'clogs' her conscience is not reading the Bible but recalling 'all her unkind, unnatural, and ungodly Carriages to her dear Friend [i.e. Christian]' (*PP*, 177). The messenger Secret acknowledges her penitence: 'thou art aware of the evil thou hast formerly done to thy Husband in hardening of thy Heart against his way, and in keeping of these thy Babes in their Ignorance' (*PP*, 179). Indeed, as she had told the children earlier, 'we are all undone. I have sinned away your Father, and he is gone' (*PP*, 178). What she longs for is reunion with her husband and the resumption of her appropriate wifely role: in the midst of a troubled night, she dreams that she sees '*Christian* her Husband in a place of Bliss among many *Immortals*' (*PP*, 179). Her call, in the form of a perfumed invitation, comes 'from thy Husbands King' (*PP*, 180). She encourages her children to join her on pilgrimage 'that we may see your Father, and be with him and his Companions' (*PP*, 181). Even her 'decision' to go on pilgrimage is mediated by and authorized by men. As N. H. Keeble asserts, 'Christiana's progress is, then, a return. She is in the process of becoming again the wife that everyone she meets says she in fact is.'[10]

What happens to Christiana on her journey happens because she is female, and the narrative locates Christiana's sinfulness in her unsupervised sexuality. The traumatic

---

[9] See Kathleen M. Swaim, *Pilgrim's Progress, Puritan Progress: Discourses and Contexts* (Urbana and Chicago, IL: University of Illinois Press, 1993).

[10] N. H. Keeble, ' "Here is her Glory, even to be under Him": The Feminine in the Thought and Work of John Bunyan', in Anne Laurence, W. R. Owens, and Stuart Sim (eds.), *John Bunyan and his England, 1628–88* (London: Hambledon Press, 1990), 131–48 (144).

sexual assault she endures early in the journey at the hands of two '*ill-favoured ones*' (*PP*, 194–95) occurs as a direct result of her failure to ask for guidance at the Wicket Gate (although earlier she had asked Secret for such assistance). Rescued from that attack, she is bathed, adorned, and put under the care of Great-heart, who, as both spiritual guide and chaperon, stands in for Christian during the remainder of her journey. She confesses her sense of guilt and responsibility for the attack first to Mercie and then to the Interpreter. In fact, at every community Christiana enters she is not only reminded of her wifely status, but also must confess her failings in that role—'I am that Woman that was so hard-hearted as to slight my Husbands Troubles' (*PP*, 198). She must subordinate herself to her husband or, in his absence, to another man's authority. As a 'sexed' pilgrim, Christiana must accept that she is incapable of independent action.[11]

Unlike her husband, Christiana has no external burden and so does not lose that burden when approaching the cross. Instead, Christiana and Mercie receive their new garments and seals after the Bath Sanctification. Critics are divided about the significance of this moment. Some suggest that the Bath represents baptism, although most would agree with Richard Greaves that, for Bunyan, 'ritual is not at the heart of communal experience'.[12] Whatever his opinions about baptism, Bunyan clearly marks this moment as a gendered experience: a damsel explains that 'so her Master would have the *Women* to do that called at his House as they were going on *Pilgrimage*' (*PP*, 207; first emphasis added). Elsewhere, I have explored associations with the Jewish purification practice of *mikvah*.[13] Margaret Breen associates the Bath with reproduction more generally: 'Women's travel, as the Interpreter reminds Christiana when he orders the Bath of Sanctification, entails the travail of her sex: childbearing and, by extension, childrearing.' As she points out, after the Bath Great-heart leads the group to Calvary—and explains its significance—so 'Christiana experiences spiritual cleansing twice; both times purification covers rather than rids her of her burden.'[14] Kevin Seidel sums up the situation succinctly: Christiana's 'burden' is 'her combined sense of religious and familial obligation'.[15] That is not a burden that Christiana, or any woman in Bunyan's universe, can leave behind. Christian may have saved his family by abandoning it, and may even have been '*clear of their blood*' (*PP*, 52), but Christiana serves God and her family by fulfilling her maternal responsibilities.

Some critics try to explain *Part II*'s emphasis on the need for guidance in terms of Bunyan's interest in the church community. It is true that Great-heart speaks disparagingly of men who 'are so foolishly venturous, as to set out lightly on Pilgrimage, and to

---

[11] Margaret Sönser Breen, 'The Sexed Pilgrim's Progress', *SEL*, 32 (1992), 443–60 (448).

[12] Greaves, *Glimpses*, 509.

[13] Margaret Thickstun, *Fictions of the Feminine: Puritan Doctrine and the Representation of Women* (Ithaca, NY: Cornell University Press, 1988), 98–9.

[14] Breen, 'Sexed Pilgrim's Progress', 446, 456.

[15] Kevin Seidel, '*Pilgrim's Progress* and the Book', *ELH*, 77 (2010), 509–34 (522).

come without a *Guide*' (*PP*, 244), even implying that Christian may have been slightly foolhardy. But the group repeatedly encounters solitary male pilgrims, not one of whom receives a reprimand for having attempted the journey alone or who expresses any sense of guilt over the nature of the assault he subsequently experiences. Mr Feeble-mind even asserts that

> since I went not with him [Giant Despair] *willingly*, I believed I should come out alive again. For I have heard, that not any Pilgrim that is taken Captive by violent Hands, if he keeps Heart-whole towards his Master, is by the Laws of Providence to die by the Hand of the Enemy. (*PP*, 268)

Great-heart does ask Mr Valiant-for-truth, '*Why did you not call out, that some might a came in for your Succour?*' But Valiant-for-truth defends his actions: 'So I did, to my King, who I knew could hear, and afford invisible Help, and that was sufficient for me' (*PP*, 290). Although Mr Stand-fast experiences an explicitly sexual temptation occasioned by his being 'both a weary, and sleepy' (*PP*, 300), the conversation focuses on the character of his temptress, Madam Bubble—that 'bold and impudent Slut' (*PP*, 302)—not on Stand-fast's culpability. Not once does Great-heart suggest that any male pilgrim the group collects has erred in travelling alone. But although Christiana and Mercie cry out and resist their would-be rapists, keeping their hearts 'whole' towards their Master, invisible help is not sufficient. They are held responsible for having occasioned the sexual assault by travelling without male protection. The rape if accomplished would have made 'Women of you for ever' (*PP*, 195). In order to avoid that fate, the women in *The Pilgrim's Progress, Part II* must not only submit to male guidance, they must also become the right kind of women: literal brides and mothers.

As '*Mother[s] in Israel*' (*PP*, 219), Christiana, Mercie, and the young women in the various house-churches they visit are, in Thomas Luxon's words, 'saved for the peculiarly this-worldly labor of generating sons, the raw material for new birth'.[16] The action in *Part II* suggests that 'generational growth in the true Church' requires reproduction within the church.[17] As Edmund Morgan explains in *Visible Saints*, gathered, separating churches, such as Bunyan's and the congregations described in *Part II*, assume that children of believers will grow up to become full church members, even though they understand that the new covenant creates a spiritual, not a biological, family, because a person cannot 'inherit' grace.[18] Scholars of colonial American Puritanism call this phenomenon 'tribal sainthood'. Where Christian had to abandon his family in order to save

---

[16] Thomas Luxon, *Literal Figures: Puritan Allegory and the Reformation Crisis in Representation* (Chicago and London: University of Chicago Press, 1995), 207.
[17] Davies, *Graceful Reading*, 335.
[18] See Edmund S. Morgan, *Visible Saints: The History of a Puritan Idea* (New York: New York University Press, 1963).

himself, Christiana is praised for bringing the children with her on pilgrimage. They are admitted at the Wicket-gate under their mother's auspices, even though they are quite small: too small to count as protectors during the sexual assault. The boys are still receiving religious instruction and have yet to experience a conviction of sin, but Greatheart asserts that they 'take all after their Father, and covet to tread in his Steps' (*PP*, 259). Although Gaius's catalogue of Christian's 'ancestors' is clearly metaphorical, he encourages Christiana to 'look out some Damsels for her Sons […] that the name of their Father, and the House of his Progenitors may never be forgotten in the World' (*PP*, 260). The community may expand by recruiting adult members, but the community thrives through marriages among members, who then produce and rear up the next generation of believers.

Gaius's sermon 'on the behalf of Women, to take away their Reproach' (*PP*, 261) fits neatly within the context of tribal sainthood. As Keeble points out, this 'defence of women itself follows immediately upon a recommendation that women should marry […] and conceives woman's place in terms of I Timothy 5. 14 ("I will therefore that the younger women marry") on the grounds of I Timothy 2. 15 ("she shall be saved in childbearing")'.[19] In Gaius's speech, Bunyan rehearses what were already by 1684 common points about women's greater devotion to Jesus during his life. They can be found in print as early as Amelia Lanier's prefatory epistle to her poem *Salve Deus Rex Judaeorum* (1611). The writings of Quaker women—such as *Women's Speaking Justified* (1667) by Margaret Fell (Fox) and Elizabeth Bathurst's *The Sayings of Women* (1683)—show that this perspective on the scriptural record could be and was expanded to identify not only women's physical ministry towards Jesus but their full spiritual discipleship. Gaius praises women who 'ministred to him of their Substance […] washed his Feet with Tears […] anointed his Body to the Burial […] and that sat by his Sepulcher when he was buried' (*PP*, 261). But the women writers place these physical actions in the context of prophecy and discipleship: instead of pointing to Hebrew women who 'coveted Children' (*PP*, 261), they enumerate those who prophesied and served as judges. They list the woman who anoints Jesus' head with oil, a declaration that she knows him to be the Messiah; the woman at the well in Samaria, to whom Jesus reveals that he *is* the Messiah; and the women to whom he reveals himself after his resurrection. Although Gaius concedes that it was 'Women that brought Tidings first to his Disciples that he was risen from the Dead' (*PP*, 261), neither he nor Bunyan interprets that testimony as preaching, nor do they consider the record of women's activity in Acts and in Paul's epistles, where Bunyan's female contemporaries found examples of and authorization for women's preaching and leadership within the church. Gaius does not conclude that women are spiritual equals, but rather 'sharers with *us* in the Grace of Life' (*PP*, 261; emphasis added). Their biological function defines them and constrains their participation in that fellowship.

---

[19] Keeble, '"Here is her Glory, even to be under Him,"' 144–45.

Mercie's Journey

Bunyan modelled Mercie's story on Ruth's in the Old Testament: like Ruth, Mercie will be rewarded for her devotion to her friend by being formally included among God's chosen people (Ruth 1:14–17). But, as in Ruth's case, in order to join the church 'family', Mercie must marry into it. That she has been travelling with Christiana under Greatheart's guidance does not grant her full membership. As a woman, she achieves that status by becoming herself '*a Mother in* Israel' (*PP*, 219)—not a prophetess like Deborah, but an ordinary woman, like the one in 2 Samuel 20, who may act on behalf of her community but does not hold a leadership position within it. Just as Christiana does not symbolize the Church but represents instead an ideal female member of a church community, likewise Mercie does not embody divine mercy, but rather the Christian upheld by God's forgiveness. Bunyan's good male characters possess names that are adjectives—Faithful, Hopeful, Honest—not nouns. Mercie might more appropriately have been named 'Merciful'. As she constantly knits and sews for the poor, Mercie demonstrates that she is moved to express her appreciation for divine mercy through her behaviour towards others and that she desires, like the character Honest, 'that my *Nature* shall agree to what I am called' (*PP*, 247). That Mercie does not earn anything from her efforts underscores Bunyan's belief in justification by faith alone, but Mercie also models an attitude of industrious charity. As Michael Mullett points out, 'whatever the efficacy of works, the support of the church is essential'.[20]

That Mercie arrives at the Wicket-gate uninvited and is received by the Keeper (identified in *Part II* as Christ) with these words of assurance—'I pray for all them that believe on me, by what means soever they come unto me' (*PP*, 190)—has led some critics to suggest that Bunyan's commitment to predestination had softened during the years between the writing of *Part I* and *Part II*. His theological writings belie such a claim, but Mercie's experience, and Matthew's response to Prudence's catechism—'*Who are they that must be saved?* Those that accept of his Salvation' (*PP*, 225)—seem to suggest an open call. Still, it seems important that Mercie begins her journey, as does Christiana, through a personal relationship: Christiana's departure prompts Mercie's, just as Christian's does Christiana's. When she learns of her friend's intentions, 'her Bowels yearned over *Christiana*' and 'her Bowels yearned over her own Soul' (*PP*, 183). In the light of this reaction, Seidel suggests that Bunyan 'appropriates the story of Ruth and Naomi [...] to figure as feminine the indirect encounter with God, through his people, in ties of human affection'.[21] I would argue, however, that it is more specifically the female encounter with God that Bunyan figures as indirect. After all, Christiana receives her call within the context of her marriage to Christian. It is within the familial relationship of daughter-in-law that Mercie receives specific sanctions for her journey: Christiana promises her 'nor

---

[20] Michael A. Mullett, *John Bunyan in Context* (Duquesne, PA: Duquesne University Press, 1997), 253.
[21] Seidel, '*Pilgrim's Progress* and the Book', 524.

shalt thou be rejected, tho thou goest but upon my *Invitation*. The King who hath sent for me and my Children, is one that delighteth in *Mercie*' (*PP*, 185). More importantly, at House Beautiful Mercie dreams of a winged being interrupting her solitary lamentations, wiping her eyes, and decking her with jewellery, including a crown. She then reports being led to 'a golden Gate', admitted, and welcomed from the throne. She ends her account by telling Christiana, 'I thought that I saw your Husband there' (*PP*, 223). If, as Christiana asserts in response to this account and as Milton's Eve attests at the close of *Paradise Lost*, 'God is also in sleep, and dreams advise',[22] then this dream confirms Mercie's call and affirms her place as a daughter and mother within the gathered church.

As I have argued elsewhere, Stand-fast displaces Christiana and Mercie as an embodiment of the believer as bride of Christ.[23] His temptation, which he resists without taint, is figured sexually: Madam Bubble tempts him with 'her *Body*, her *Purse*, and her *Bed*', but to no avail (*PP*, 300). In his final speech, delivered 'to his Companions' while crossing the River of Death, he appropriates the language of the bride from the Song of Solomon to express his passionate devotion to Christ: 'His Name has been to me as a *Civet-Box*, yea, sweeter then all Perfumes. [...] His Word I did use to gather for my Food, and for Antidotes against my Faintings.' His final exclamation, '*Take me, for I come unto thee*' expresses surrender to God in death as an explicitly sexual surrender: Stand-fast is ready to enter the Celestial City and to attend the marriage feast as a bride. But Stand-fast also usurps Christiana's role as model parent: in sending a message to his wife and children, Stand-fast shows that he can both sacrifice his family for his family, as Christian has done, and guide them on their pilgrimage, as Christiana has tried to do. Finally, in his love language Stand-fast asserts, 'I have seen the print of his Shooe in the Earth, there I have coveted to set my Foot too' (*PP*, 310–11). In speaking at length about his spiritual experience, both during his journey and at his death, Stand-fast assumes the role of preacher: a role not available to women in Bunyan's world. A male believer, Stand-fast is able to 'see himself' as bride, as a reflection of Christ, and as an individual who can pattern his own life on his Saviour's.

Stand-fast's closing speech captured the imagination of early biographers and critics. In his *Life of Bunyan* (1871), D. A. Harsha includes an appendix on Bunyan's style that singles out from *The Pilgrim's Progress* only the account of Christian and Hopeful entering the Celestial City and Stand-fast's soliloquy. W. Hale White in his 1904 overview *John Bunyan* quotes the speech in its entirety, asserting that 'there is nothing in the first part of *The Pilgrim's Progress* greater than the closing paragraphs of the second'. For these readers, Christiana is eclipsed by active male figures—Great-heart, Stand-fast, Valiant-for-truth, even Mr Fearing, whom White considers 'the principal figure in the Second Part of the *Pilgrim's Progress*, and perhaps the whole of it'.[24] Valiant-for-truth's song about the qualities of a true pilgrim quickly became a standard in Protestant hymnody.

---

[22] *Paradise Lost*, Book 12, line 611.
[23] Thickstun, *Fictions of the Feminine*, 103–04.
[24] W. Hale White, *John Bunyan* (New York: Charles Scribner's Sons, 1904), 150, 137.

On the other hand, Christiana and the boys, James Anthony Froude suggests, 'are tolerated for the pilgrim's sake to whom they belong'.[25]

Aesthetic and Didactic Issues

The expanded, younger, more feminine audience that Bunyan anticipates in *Part II*'s prefatory verses—'*Young Ladys, and young Gentle-women*', '*The very Children that do walk the street*' (*PP*, 169, 170)—occasions in a more realistic representation of life and a more didactic style. As Swaim points out, the sequel is populated not only by a variety of believers but by all the details of domestic life that *Part I* leaves out: 'diet, clothing, sleeping arrangements, health and sickness, childcare, dirt and house-cleaning, menus and table-settings, herbs, letters, gossip, and—surprisingly—coach travel'.[26] This attention to material culture locates the story within the everyday experience of readers, making it easier to apply the lessons of the text to their lives. The pilgrims view more emblems at the Interpreter's House than Christian did and have more extensive conversations with the women at House Beautiful. The newly added emblems—the man raking muck, the spider holding tight to the wall, the thankful chick, the hen with her different calls—appear explicitly because the pilgrims 'are Women, and they are easie for you' (*PP*, 202). Emblems appear in aural as well as visual form, as when Matthew asks Prudence a long series of questions about the spiritual significance of natural phenomena (*PP*, 231–32). Everywhere the text signals its educational agenda: as the pilgrims leave House Beautiful, Piety runs back to fetch 'a *Scheme*' of what they have seen in the house, to 'call those things again to remembrance for thy Edification, and comfort' (*PP*, 236).

Where conversation in *Part I* focused on explaining one's spiritual experience and testing other pilgrims' theological positions, the conversation in *Part II* presents more straightforward instances of catechizing. The women of House Beautiful ask Christian questions about his own experience—the specifics of his journey, his motivations for pilgrimage, his efforts to save his family—and expect him to answer from his heart, 'experimentally'. In *Part II*, Prudence asks the boys general doctrinal questions—'*who made thee?*'; '*how doth God the Father save thee?*'; '*How doth God the Son save thee?*' (*PP*, 224)—and seems perfectly satisfied with learned or 'notional' responses. That session ends with Prudence outlining the appropriate attitude of novices: the boys should continue to learn from their mother, pay attention to 'good talk', and meditate on Scripture. They should also consider 'what the Heavens and the Earth do teach you' (*PP*, 226). Frequently, conversation in *Part II* turns to drawing spiritual lessons from everyday experience. When the servants lay the tablecloth at Gaius's inn, Matthew remarks that watching the preparations makes him more hungry; Gaius develops the lesson:

---

[25] James Anthony Froude, *Bunyan* (New York: Harper & Brothers, 1880), 169.
[26] Swaim, *Pilgrim's Progress, Puritan's Progress*, 174.

> so let all ministering Doctrines *to* thee in this Life, beget *in* thee a greater desire to sit at the Supper of the great King in his Kingdom; for all Preaching, Books, and Ordinances here, are but as the laying of the Trenshers, and as setting of Salt upon the Board. (*PP*, 262)

Everything a person encounters is potentially a text that will yield spiritual truth.

Even the character and purpose of the poetry have changed. In *Part I*, Bunyan uses short—typically four- or six-line—poems in iambic pentameter couplets to sum up the narrative. Many of the poems in *Part II*, however, are multi-stanzaic lyrics in ballad metre. Modelled on the metrical psalms, these poems are often sung within the text—by the pilgrims themselves, by birds, by minstrels, by voices overheard—and could be sung by Bunyan's readers to tunes they already knew. They typically express spiritual wisdom—'*Let the most blessed be my guide*' (*PP*, 187)—and voice gratitude through a generic first-person voice—'*I am content with what I have*' (*PP*, 238). The poems that summarize narrative—such as the one following the visit to the Interpreter's House—are often presented as memory aids for the characters and could function as mnemonics for Bunyan's readers as well. Remembering the different emblems at the Interpreter's House, their meaning, and their application to the reader's life, should '*move me for to watch and pray, / To strive to be sincere, / To take my Cross up day by day, / And serve the Lord with fear*' (*PP*, 209).

Literacy

Part of Prudence's catechizing addresses how to approach the Bible and how to manage difficult biblical passages; Matthew's response—'I think God is wiser then I' (*PP*, 226)—epitomizes a new relation between characters and Scripture. In *Part I*, reading his book provokes in Christian a conviction of sin and, with brief interventions from Evangelist, textual study reveals the solution to his painful predicament at the start of the allegory. Christian carries the Bible with him on his journey, urges others to read it for incentive and encouragement, as he does, and uses scriptural quotations to document the orthodoxy of his theological positions in debates with false pilgrims. In *Part II*, characters use Scripture in a more ad hoc fashion. Great-heart does cite Paul's Letter to the Romans when he explains the significance of the cross, but he also uses a quotation from Proverbs to reassure the pilgrims as they traverse the Valley of the Shadow of Death, and another to praise James when he properly interprets the role of fear in conversion. The Keeper of the Wicket-gate offers a verse from Mark in response to the arrival of the boys; the Interpreter uses a proverb to explicate the significance of the spider in the otherwise empty room. Christiana and Mercie use scriptural passages as proof texts or 'places'. Christiana quotes Psalm 126 when she invites Mercie to join her on pilgrimage. Once the women are inside the Wicket-gate, Mercie explains her fear at being left behind by analogy to Jesus' warning: 'now thought I, 'tis fulfilled which is Written, *Two*

Women shall be Grinding together; the one shall be taken, and the other left' (PP, 191). When the Interpreter meets Christiana, he invokes the parable of the two sons, to which Christiana replies, 'God make it a true saying upon me' (PP, 199). Biblical material permeates the culture of *Part II*, but actual reading of Scripture seems less common.

Recent criticism suggests that this change in emphasis may be related to Bunyan's awareness that many of his readers, particularly female readers, would be newly and perhaps only marginally literate. Christiana dreams of 'a broad Parchment [...] in which were recorded the sum of her ways' (PP, 178), but it is not clear that in this dream she actually reads its words. She receives a written invitation to go on pilgrimage, but she is encouraged to study it 'until you have got it by root-of-Heart' (PP, 180). Breen argues that this command locates the letter in 'oral rather than print culture' and 'suggests her tentative relation to literacy'.[27] Maxine Hancock, on the other hand, observes in *Part II* overlapping literate and oral cultures: Christiana is not only supposed to read the letter, she is to share it with her children. Prudence tests the boys not to evaluate their spiritual status, but to 'see how *Christiana* had brought up her children' (PP, 224). Because women supervise the education of children, their experience of reading will remain necessarily more connected to oral culture, to rudimentary and supervised reading. That is not to say that women cannot read Scripture or difficult religious material. The feast at Gaius's house presents Christiana, Mercie, and Gaius's daughters 'in a community of readers who think about and discuss text, who "feast" on the Scriptures and who attempt to "crack hard nuts", that is, to find a hermeneutic method for resolving difficult texts'. But Hancock also points to a telling moment at the close of the pilgrims' stay there: Christiana asks James to read from Isaiah as part of the community's morning worship (PP, 265). As Hancock explains, 'womanly reading, consideration and teaching of the sacred text, and her teaching of reading within the home, were intended to be subsumed into male voicing of the biblical texts'.[28] With her boys now grown, Christiana relinquishes to them the role of reader and teacher.

The connection between gender and emergent literacy illuminates the episode in which Mercie desires the shepherd's mirror. This mirror, held one way, reveals 'the very Face and Similitude of the Prince of Pilgrims himself' (PP, 287). It also, turned slightly, reflects the reader's own image. It is clearly a metaphor for the Bible, and Hancock identifies Mercie in this moment as 'a reader who yearns to go beyond elementary "laying of letters together" to a full literacy'. Both Breen and Luxon, on the other hand, express frustration because the narrative connects Mercie's desire for the mirror with her physical situation—she is 'a young, and breeding Woman'; she seems to long for the mirror the way pregnant women theoretically crave ice cream or pickles. In fact, Mercie's conversation with Christiana about the mirror encourages this attention to biology: Mercie fears that 'if therefore I have it not, I think I shall Miscarry' (PP, 287). Hancock argues

---

[27] Margaret Sönser Breen, 'Christiana's Rudeness: Spiritual Authority in *The Pilgrim's Progress*', BS, 7 (1997), 96–111 (101).

[28] Maxine Hancock, 'Identity, Agency and Community: Intimations and Implications of Emerging Literacy for Women in *The Pilgrim's Progress*, The Second Part', BS, 11 (2003/04), 74–93 (84).

that this expression communicates Mercie's 'awareness that her full sense of identity in solidarity with the community will be unattainable without an adequate reading ability to enable her to engage the scriptures for herself'.[29] I would like to press that suggestion a bit farther.

Bunyan and his contemporaries appropriated the language of gestation and childbirth as a metaphor for ministry. When Christian in the Interpreter's House is first shown 'a Picture of a very grave Person'—a portrait perhaps of Evangelist—the Interpreter explains that this man 'can beget Children, Travel in birth with Children, and Nurse them himself when they are born' (*PP*, 28–9). Clergymen also mapped the process of conversion and deliverance on to literal pregnancies: in becoming pregnant, a woman may have conceived her death. Instead of focusing on the imminent literal birth, she ought to consider her spiritual rebirth. To do so, she must examine herself thoroughly and repent completely. One minister warns, 'you should be as much afraid of Leaving any Sin unconfessed, as you would be of having the *After-birth left in you*, after your Travail'.[30] Labour pains embody the pains of repentance and foreshadow the pains of hell. The clergyman becomes the spiritual midwife who can deliver the new soul safely. Once the new birth has occurred, the literal birth becomes irrelevant, 'for whether they live or die their souls cannot miscarry'.[31]

In this context, Mercie's longing for her mirror may have more serious implications than a sense that she is not yet a full member of the church community. Without individual access to Scripture, Mercie is in spiritual danger, and her soul may very well 'miscarry'. Christiana reassures her that 'it is no Shame, but a Virtue, to long for such a thing as that' (*PP*, 287), and the shepherds readily assent to the gift. Bunyan's play on the word 'miscarry' recalls his willingness to exploit parallels between literal and spiritual states at the beginning of *Part II*, where Christiana responds to the messenger bringing the perfumed letter with blushes and trembling, and Mercie is said 'to fall in love with her own Salvation' (*PP*, 186). It also reinforces Bunyan's belief that male and female experiences of pilgrimage differ dramatically. At the same time, this moment complicates Bunyan's insistence that a woman will always require spiritual supervision. As Breen points out, the description of Scripture as mirror 'gains its power from its sustained use of masculine pronouns, which invites the correspondence between individual worshipper ("a man") and Christ'.[32] This insistence on the male as normative raises the question of how well Mercie (or any other female believer) will be able to see 'herself' reflected in the text and to identify with Christ. Pursuing further Bunyan's metaphor, where a man might see in the text 'his own Feature exactly' (*PP*, 287)—a model for his own action in the world—the female worshipper is more likely to see not herself but her heavenly bridegroom.

---

[29] Hancock, 'Identity, Agency and Community', 87.
[30] Cotton Mather, *Elizabeth in her Holy Retirement: An Essay to Prepare a Woman for her Lying-in* (Boston, MA, 1710), 9.
[31] John Oliver, *A Present for Teeming Women* (1669), preface.
[32] Breen, 'Sexed Pilgrim's Progress', 444–45.

Reception

As Bunyan brags in the proem to *Part II*, within a few years of its publication the original *Pilgrim's Progress* had been translated into several other European languages. It had also found its way to New England, and not simply as cargo in a ship's hold: the first edition of *The Pilgrim's Progress* to be printed in North America appeared in Boston in 1681, an astonishing fact, considering that its potential readership was extremely small and that the only other texts of such length produced in New England during the seventeenth century were *The Bay Psalm Book* (1640, 296 pages; there were three later editions); translations of Genesis, the Bible, a primer, and Lewis Bayly's *The Practise of Pietie* into Algonquin (128, 1208, 128, and 208 pages respectively); and the meditations or sermon collections of New England divines.

Part II, however, was not printed in North America until 1744 and was not widely available there until the nineteenth century, when editions of the three-part *Pilgrim's Progress* competed for readers with adaptations and revisions were sold. Isaiah Thomas's highly successful adaptation, *The Christian Pilgrim*, appeared first in Massachusetts in 1798: it went through multiple printings at his own press in Worcester, Massachusetts, with other editions from printing houses in Hartford, Connecticut, Boston, Massachusetts, and Montpelier, Vermont, appearing over a twenty-year span. In adapting *The Pilgrim's Progress* for a young audience—precisely the audience Bunyan targets in the proem to *Part II*—Thomas omitted Christiana, Mercie, and the boys altogether. His text closes with Christian and Hopeful entering the Celestial City in triumph, leaving out not only all of the events in *Part II*, but Ignorance's ignominious end as well. An 1803 versification of *The Pilgrim's Progress*, printed in Hanover, New Hampshire, went through five editions and, like *The Christian Pilgrim*, concludes with Christian and Hopeful's safe arrival.

That most editions of *The Pilgrim's Progress* generally include *Part II* may not be conclusive evidence of its influence. Louisa May Alcott, for example, clearly knew of Bunyan's sequel. For the epigraph to *Little Women* (1868) she revises a selection from its proem: 'Tell them of Mercie [...] / For little tripping maids may follow God / Along the ways which saintly feet have trod.' Yet Alcott clearly expected her young readers to be thoroughly versed in Christian's adventures, rather than Mercie's: in the story of *Part I*, that is, rather than of *Part II*. *Little Women* opens with Marmee reminding the girls:

> how you used to play *Pilgrim's Progress* when you were little things? Nothing delighted you more than to have me tie my piece-bags on your backs for burdens, give you hats and sticks and rolls of paper, and let you travel through the house from the cellar, which was the City of Destruction, up, up, to the housetop, where you had all the lovely things you could collect to make a Celestial City.

Alcott then models the girls' experiences explicitly on Christian's journey, with chapters titled 'Burdens', 'Beth Finds the Palace Beautiful', 'Amy's Valley of Humiliation', 'Jo Meets

Apollyon', and 'Meg Goes to Vanity Fair'. Early in the story one daughter remarks, 'I was thinking about our Pilgrim's Progress. [...] How we got out of the Slough and through the Wicket Gate by resolving to be good, and up the steep hill by trying, and that maybe the house over there, full of splendid things, is going to be our Palace Beautiful'; later as the girls sew outdoors at a site they have named 'the Delectable Mountains', the narrator compares the far hills to the Celestial City and the girls discuss their desire to get to the real Celestial City at last. If Alcott had truly valued Mercie's story as a model for young women, she might have included some evidence from *Part II*, especially when her little women become wives and mothers themselves. But the only trace of *The Pilgrim's Progress* in Alcott's sequel, *Good Wives* (1869), is the title of the chapter in which Beth dies, 'The Valley of the Shadow', an inconclusive allusion.[33] Any direct reference to *Part II* remains notably absent.

In *The Portable Bunyan*, Isabel Hofmeyr documents how nineteenth- and early twentieth-century Nonconformists found *The Pilgrim's Progress* a fruitful source for education and inspiration. But Hofmeyr's research reveals Great-heart to be the salient role model from *Part II*, for women as well as for men. If male readers found Great-heart a refreshing antidote to a possibly effeminate Christian,

> through Great-heart, unmarried women could see themselves as heroic figures, aided rather than hampered by their singleness. Likewise, his celibacy could be put to good symbolic use. Not only could it denote purity and single-minded dedication to a cause, but it could also elevate women above the sphere of the physical body, ever a zone of potential contamination.

Hofmeyr points to a play, *The Pageant of the Woman Greatheart*, written and performed in the 1930s, in which a character explains, 'the armour is only a symbol of inward strength and resolution—that's all. The "Greatheart" spirit can use either sex, and equally well both.'[34] If *The Pilgrim's Progress*, like the Bible, can serve as a mirror in which a reader may see reflected back an image of the self's potential, these female readers preferred to see themselves as possible Great-hearts, as agents of action, not as 'mothers in Israel': the only role that Bunyan offers his female readers.

Suggested Reading

Austin, Michael, 'The Figural Logic of the Sequel and the Unity of *The Pilgrim's Progress*', *SP*, 102 (2005), 484–509.
Bear, Bethany Joy, 'Fantastical Faith: John Bunyan and the Sanctification of Fancy', *SP*, 109 (2012), 671–701.
Breen, Margaret Sönser, 'The Sexed Pilgrim's Progress', *SEL*, 32 (1992), 443–60.

---

[33] Louisa May Alcott, *Little Women*, ed. Elaine Showalter (New York: Penguin Books, 1989), 9–10, 57.
[34] Isabel Hofmeyr, *The Portable Bunyan: A Transnational History of The Pilgrim's Progress* (Princeton, NJ: Princeton University Press, 2004), 163, 160.

Hancock, Maxine, 'Identity, Agency and Community: Intimations and Implications of Emerging Literacy for Women in *The Pilgrim's Progress*, The Second Part', *BS*, 11 (2003/04), 74–93.

Keeble, N. H., 'Christiana's Key: The Unity of *The Pilgrim's Progress*', in Vincent Newey (ed.), *The Pilgrim's Progress: Critical and Historical Views* (Totowa, NJ: Barnes & Noble, 1980), 1–20.

Keeble, N. H., '"Here is her Glory, even to be under Him": The Feminine in the Thought and Work of John Bunyan', in Anne Laurence, W. R. Owens, and Stuart Sim (eds.), *John Bunyan and his England, 1628–88* (London: Hambledon Press, 1990), 131–48.

Schellenberg, Betty, 'Sociability and the Sequel: Rewriting Hero and Journey in *The Pilgrim's Progress*, Part II', *Studies in the Novel*, 23 (1991), 312–24.

Seidel, Kevin, '*Pilgrim's Progress* and the Book', *ELH*, 77 (2010), 509–34.

Thickstun, Margaret, *Fictions of the Feminine: Puritan Doctrine and the Representation of Women* (Ithaca, NY: Cornell University Press, 1988).

CHAPTER 19

'TRUTH IN METER'

Bunyan's Poetry and Dissenting Poetics

ELIZABETH CLARKE

THE critical terms in which John Bunyan's poetry is often discussed are double-edged, to say the least. The editor of *The Cambridge Companion to Bunyan* calls him 'an indifferent poet'.[1] Shannon Murray, writing on *A Book for Boys and Girls* (1686), says that 'the poems themselves do not reveal a laureate poet and most leave no doubt that Bunyan's genius was for prose'.[2] Even the Oxford editor of Bunyan's poetry, Graham Midgley, quotes several pages of negative criticism of the work and can offer in its defence nothing but a change of context, suggesting the poetry should be judged against 'godly ballads' rather than in the same breath as Herbert or Crashaw (*MW*, 6: xxv–xxx). It is certainly true that some of Bunyan's poetry, such as *A Caution to Stir up to Watch against Sin* (1684) was printed as ballad poetry, in its broadside form. Much of Bunyan's verse, as Midgley points out, is in the dialogue form so beloved of ballad poets; the prose too is often in dialogue form, perhaps because it dramatizes arguments which could otherwise be abstract and theoretical. There is much talk by critics of 'plodding' and 'thud' to describe metre, and all praise of Bunyan's poetry has a peculiarly backhanded quality, as if sophisticated use of poetic convention is hardly to be expected from one of such lowly origins. I would only comment that in Bunyan criticism Renaissance English poetry's highly elitist origins are blatantly exposed. I think the entry of Nonconformists into the literary arena, finally being celebrated in George Southcombe's pioneering anthology *English Nonconformist Poetry, 1660–1700*, is to be welcomed.[3] It reveals different strategies taken by Dissenting writers. While some

---

[1] Anne Dunan-Page, 'Introduction', in Anne Dunan-Page (ed.), *The Cambridge Companion to Bunyan* (Cambridge: Cambridge University Press, 2010), 1–9 (7).

[2] Shannon Murray, '*A Book for Boys and Girls: Or, Country Rhimes for Children*: Bunyan and Literature for Children', in Dunan-Page (ed.), *Cambridge Companion to Bunyan*, 120–34 (121).

[3] George Southcombe (ed.), *English Nonconformist Poetry, 1660–1700*, 3 vols (London: Pickering & Chatto, 2012).

tried to write in the literary tradition, others found that too elitist and secular, and so created their own poetic values.

Problems with Courtly Poetry

In this chapter I will take it for granted that Bunyan did not wish to be enlisted in the English literary tradition, and will focus on what he thought he was doing when he was writing in verse. For a start, recent literary history had largely co-opted poetry into the Royalist cause, and so as a phenomenon it was unlikely to be welcomed by Dissenters. Richard Baxter, with whose poetry Bunyan's is unfavourably compared by Midgley, does mention among his preferred reading the poetry of Katherine Philips, Abraham Cowley, and Samuel Woodford but he could hardly have agreed with them politically (*MW*, 6: xxix). Moreover, Bunyan himself is aware that there is a substantial contemporary criticism of the very use of poetry. Ironically, it is often in a verse opening to a work that he defends his use of poetic techniques. At the very start of his career as a poet, in 1661, Bunyan begs the reader of *Profitable Meditations* to 'Take none offence' at the versified nature of the work (*MW*, 6: 4). Echoing this preface over twenty years later in *A Caution to Stir up to Watch against Sin*, Bunyan warns 'With Rhimes *nor* Lines, but Truths, affected be' (*MW*, 6: 177). The famous verse preface to *The Pilgrim's Progress* (1678) surveys all the objections to his 'Method'—not primarily poetry here, of course, but allegory—and points out three answers to the 'Carper'. The first is that Scripture itself uses metaphor and allegory:

> Am I afraid to say that holy Writ,
> Which for its Stile, and Phrase, puts down all Wit,
> Is every where so full of all these things ... (*MW*, 6: 139; *PP*, 4)

Bunyan also points out that nobody raises objections to using the dialogue form, also a rhetorical fiction (*MW*, 6: 140). However, the longest defence of his literary method here is simply that it is effective; there are twenty-five lines in which the metaphors of hunting and catching are deployed to illustrate the power of a style not just allegorical but also essentially poetic:

> You see the Ways the Fisher-man doth take
> To catch the Fish; what Engins doth he make?
> Behold! how he ingageth all his Wits;
> Also his Snares, Lines, Angles, Hooks and Nets. (*MW*, 6: 137; *PP*, 3)

The fishing equipment is clearly meant to figure rhetorical techniques. The whole point of both is to 'catch' the prey: to convince the reader, despite, as Bunyan admits, the lack of illustrations, or 'those paintings' that make other books attractive (*MW*, 6: 138; *PP*, 3).

We are in a very different world from that of most canonical poetry of Bunyan's century, which tends to be court poetry. George Herbert, a big seller outside of the court, was Richard Baxter's favourite writer, but not because of his rhetorical skill; indeed, 'in Wit and accurate composure' Baxter thinks that many, including Cowley, exceeded him. Baxter is very careful to spell out his criteria for judgement, however. Excellence, although very important to him personally, is not the only standard by which he judges poetry:

> I have long thought, that a *Painter*, a *Musician* and a *Poet*, are contemptible, if they be not Excellent: And that I am not Excellent, I am satisfied: But I am more patient of contempt than many are. Common Painters serve for poor men's work: And a Fidler may serve at a Country-Wedding: Such cannot aspire to the Attainments of the higher sort: And the Vulgar are the greater number.[4]

Here, Baxter seems to value a kind of 'democracy' in poetic appreciation, surely not a common judgement in an age when 'dregs of a democracy' was a well-known derogatory phrase.[5] As Sharon Achinstein has pointed out, although she also calls it 'accessibility', such a demotic quality in poetry was very important to Dissenters.[6] Baxter is not afraid to pass judgement on any poet: Francis Quarles he labels 'competent' and George Wither he calls 'rustick' (Wither, however, is also 'honest', which is one of Baxter's favourite compliments).[7] Most radical of all, Baxter is not sure whether excellence in poetry is a worthy ambition. Some of his friends said that the very aspiration to be skilful as a poet was beneath him.[8] What qualities then remain to which the Dissenting poet should aspire?

In 1682 a more radical Dissenter than Baxter, the Independent John Reeve, made clear his criteria for good poetry.[9] He dismisses other religious poets with a stake in literary history, such as Richard Crashaw, George Herbert, Francis Quarles. They write 'bare Poems', 'the ornature being human'.[10] This concept of a distinction between 'human' rhetoric and 'divine' inspiration was the foundation of much of the criticism of the hymn, emerging in Dissenting worship in the seventeenth century.[11] In 1678, the Baptist Thomas Grantham attacked the use of hymn singing in church services, which he saw as a 'humane innovation'. He makes an absolute distinction between the production of

---

[4] Richard Baxter, *Poetical Fragments* (1681), A4v.

[5] Keith Walker (ed.), *John Dryden: A Critical Edition of the Major Works* (Oxford: Oxford University Press, 1987), 184.

[6] Sharon Achinstein, *Literature and Dissent in Milton's England* (Cambridge: Cambridge University Press, 2003), 208.

[7] Baxter, *Poetical Fragments*, A5v.

[8] Baxter, *Poetical Fragments*, A4r.

[9] See Elizabeth Clarke, 'Hymns, Psalms, and Controversy in the Seventeenth Century', in Isabel Rivers and David Wykes (eds.), *Dissenting Praise: Religious Dissent and the Hymn in England and Wales* (Oxford: Oxford University Press, 2011), 13–32 (15, 20–1).

[10] John Reeve, *Hymns and Spiritual Songs Extracted from Scripture* (1682), A3r.

[11] See, further, Clarke, 'Hymns, Psalms, and Controversy'.

art and the motions of the Spirit. Those 'who only speak what another puts into their mouths' are using 'meer Art', 'an empty sound of words, no Spiritual Song'. Anyone singing this type of hymn 'is a meer Stranger to the motions of the Spirit of truth in the holy Operation of it'.[12] This radical criticism of poetic art goes much further than a contrast between sacred subject matter and rhetorical ornament, a distinction that Dissenting criticism of poetry could otherwise look as if it is making.

Baxter, however, was not claiming divine inspiration for his work. He looked for a different quality in religious poetry, one that would appeal to the aristocratic and the vulgar alike, and would make distinctions between style and content irrelevant. That quality was passion. Archetypally a human experience, Baxter sees passion as one of God's most powerful instruments in dealing with the salvation and sanctification of human beings:

> I confess that Passion is oft such a hinderance of Judgment, that a man should be very suspicious of himself till it be laid: But I am assured that God made it not in vain; and that Reason is a sleepy half-useless thing, till some Passion excite it; and Learning to a man asleep is no better for that time than Ignorance. And God usually beginneth the awakening of Reason, and the conversion of Sinners, by the awakening of their useful Passions, their Fear, their Grief, Repentance, Desire, &c. I confess, when God awakeneth in me those Passions which I account rational and holy, I am so far from condemning them, that I think I was half a Fool before, and have small comfort in sleepy Reason. Lay by all the passionate part of Love and Joy, and it will be hard to have any pleasant thoughts of Heaven.[13]

The arousal of passion, then, can be of divine instigation: and it is this appeal to passion that poetry has always been considered so good at. At the start of *Ebal and Gerizzim* (?1665) Bunyan confesses: 'I shall lay out that poor help I have, / Thee to entice; that thou would'st dearly fall / In love with thy salvation' (*MW*, 6: 105). It is clearly his poetic resources that Bunyan is hoping will help to 'move' the reader. Echoing Baxter's praise of Herbert's poetry—that '*Heart-work* and *Heaven-work* make up his Books'[14]—Bunyan claims that his method in *The Pilgrim's Progress* is to unite head and heart: 'lay my Book, thy Head and Heart together' (*MW*, 6: 141; *PP*, 7).

It should not be surprising, then, that Bunyan's short, controversial pamphlet, *Peaceable Principles and True* (1674) ends with a forty-five-line poem entitled 'Of the Love of Christ' (*MW*, 4: 289–90). Similarly, in some of the most powerful episodes of *The Pilgrim's Progress*, Bunyan moves out of prose and into poetry; indeed, this may be one of the reasons for the amazing popularity of the book. The use of poetry in *The Pilgrim's Progress* signifies the arousal of intense emotion in the speaker, so that passionate poetry conveys 'the motions of the Spirit of truth', as Thomas Grantham might have put it. When Christian knocks at the Wicket Gate he expresses his longings in

---

[12] Thomas Grantham, *Christianismus Primitivus* (1678), 99–100.
[13] Baxter, *Poetical Fragments*, A3v–A4r.
[14] Baxter, *Poetical Fragments*, A7v.

poetry (*MW*, 6: 142; *PP*, 24–5). His joyful emotions are expressed in poetry when he awakes in the House Beautiful:

> Where am I now? Is this the love and care
> Of Jesus, for the men that Pilgrims are?
> Thus to provide! That I should be forgiven!
> And dwell already the next door to Heaven. (*MW*, 6: 143; *PP*, 53)

After the death of Faithful, Christian sings an emotional celebration of his life and death. (*MW*, 6: 144; *PP*, 97–8). It is not surprising that some of the lyrics within *The Pilgrim's Progress* have migrated into the hymn book, although the most famous ones—the song of the shepherd in the Valley of Humiliation and the song of Valiant-for-truth—come from *Part II* (*MW*, 6: 157, 160; *PP*, 238, 295).

Midgley notes the metrical advance in Bunyan's work in the later poems (*MW*, 6: xxv). He attributes this improvement to a diminishing of the influence of the Sternhold and Hopkins psalter, and it is true that by 1684 when *Part II* is published more models for divine songs were available, although, as Midgley also points out, psalms were not sung in the Bedford congregation until 1690 (*MW*, 6: xvii). The dominant hymn-writer by 1684 was William Barton, whose *Four Centuries of Select Hymns* had come out in 1668, and was augmented to 600 hymns by his son in 1688. Barton's hymns tended to be less personal and more directly biblical that Bunyan's songs. In his readiness to describe the personal response to both tragic and joyful events of the Christian life Bunyan's songs anticipate the hymns of Isaac Watts. By the same token, a Dissenting spirituality based on the emotional relationship with a deity who takes the form of the man Jesus Christ, as encapsulated in the type of poetry found in *The Pilgrim's Progress*, would have seemed sentimental and downright incorrect to Anglican theologians of the 1670s, such as Samuel Parker and William Sherlock.[15]

'Truth' in 'Meeter'

In many of Bunyan's publications, poetry is used to dramatize the events of the Christian life in a similar manner to sermons. The lengthy 1661 poem, *Profitable Meditations, Fitted to Mans Different Condition*, could be seen as a rendering of many key Reformed doctrines into poetic terms which increase their emotional impact. The poem begins by illustrating how total depravity, the first tenet of Calvinism, feels to an unredeemed human being before going on to illustrate the saving work of Christ. This is how it renders the results of justification by faith:

---

[15] See Elizabeth Clarke, *Politics, Religion and the Song of Songs in Seventeenth-Century England* (Basingstoke: Palgrave Macmillan, 2011), 187.

> Now then, if Jesus Christ stands, so shall I:
> For he is my Compleatness all the day:
> I'le look no further, here I'le live and dye;
> Come Death or judgement, CHRIST will nev'r decay. (*MW*, 6: 11)

It is not that these sentiments are extra-biblical—indeed, nearly every line has a scriptural reference in the margin—but they are translating the Bible into a different kind of discourse, one that is direct, simple, and personal. Elsewhere, this text uses the dialogue form to illustrate temptation through a conversation between Death and a sinner (*MW*, 6: 21–4), and it finishes with a dialogue between a saint in heaven and a sinner in hell, apparently '*alluding to the* 16th *of* Luke', but actually there is no mention of the rich man in hell or Lazarus the beggar in heaven (*MW*, 6: 31–5). The whole situation is transposed and modernized, not only into poetry but into the terms of Nonconformist spirituality. The following two stanzas are from the end of the sinner's lament:

> *Sin.* Oh heavie heart! The more I think of life,
> And how I lost, it doth encrease my Wo;
> Time was when I enjoy'd convincing Light;
> But I did slight it, and my Soul undo.
> […]
> Oh sad! that I had clos'd with Christ; or would
> I had not heard of Him at all, then I
> Had either saved been, or else I should
> Have had less torment to Eternity. (*MW*, 6: 35)

Clearly Bunyan wants to convey the regret and despair of the sinner in hell, but this is less biblical than typical of Nonconformist preaching. There are phrases here redolent of Nonconformist jargon; 'clos'd with Christ' means 'begun a relationship with Christ' and 'convincing' in the third line is presumably what Bunyan hopes his poetry will do, 'convicting' those who read it of the truth. (Thomas Wilson's *Christian Dictionary* defines 'convince' as 'by good reason and argument to put to silence', something the Bible could do.[16])

Three years previously, in 1658, Bunyan had published a prose pamphlet entitled *A Few Sighs from Hell, or, The Groans of a Damned Soul*. It is made clear in the lengthy subtitle that the point is to dramatize the events and emotions described:

> *Wherein is Discovered the Lamentable State of the Damned: Their Cries, Their Desires in their Distresses, with the Determination of God upon them. A Good Warning Word to Sinners, both Old and Young, to take into Consideration Betimes, and to Seek by Faith in Jesus Christ to Avoid, Lest they Come into the Same Place of Torment.*

---

[16] Thomas Wilson, *A Complete Christian Dictionary* (1661), 123.

This pamphlet, an exposition of the parable of Dives and Lazarus in Luke 16, is more biblical than the section of *Profitable Meditations* and much longer. In its prefatory epistle to the reader Bunyan spells out what he hopes will be the effect of the pamphlet on non-believers: '*know for certain, that the things signified by Parables, are wonderful realities*' (*MW*, 1: 246). Bunyan wants his poetry to make discourse realistic: to make the sounds and sights of the stories in the Bible more vivid. It is clearly this effect of making credible, and easy to grasp, the certainties of Reformed doctrine—supernatural entities like hell or theological concepts like forgiveness—that Bunyan is aiming for in his poetic version.

At the start of *Profitable Meditations* Bunyan makes an appeal to the reader:

> '*Tis not the Method, but the Truth alone*
> *Should please a Saint, and mollifie his heart:*
> *Truth in or out of Meeter is but one;*
> *And this thou knowst, if thou a Christian art.* (*MW*, 6: 4)

Bunyan is making the claim that his translation of the biblical text into the terms of modern poetry is still true to the Bible. I would argue that 'Truth' in this stanza is not the prosaic details of the biblical story, but something else. Sometimes Bunyan is describing details of hell that are not in the Bible. It is nowhere stated in the Bible, for instance, that it would be better for unbelievers that they had not heard about Christ, something Bunyan states here and repeats in *One Thing is Needful* (?1665) when the sinner wishes he had been incapable of understanding the Gospel (*MW*, 6: 100). This is a Nonconformist commonplace about the emotional effects—condensed and intensified by poetry—that the original biblical story as interpreted by preachers should have on its reader. There is very little detail about hell in the Bible, but Bunyan clearly feels that describing in vivid terms the experience of being in hell is a necessary part of his gospel message, and one that he needs to stress, in poetry. 'Meeter', or poetic convention, is one way of intensifying the message of a story that may be biblical but perhaps not intense enough for the effect Bunyan wants to have on his readers. The Presbyterian minister John Flavel says something very similar:

> I have also here set before the Reader an *Idea* or representation of the state and case of damned Souls, that if it be the Will of God, a seasonable discovery of Hell may be the means of some mens recovery out of the danger of it, and closed up the whole with a Demonstration of the invaluable preciousness of Souls, and the several dangerous snares and artifices of *Satan* their professed Enemy to destroy and cast them away for ever.[17]

According to Ian Green, there were thirteen early editions of *A Few Sighs from Hell*, and although the poetic works, unlike the huge-selling prose narratives, did not become bestsellers, Bunyan clearly thought hell a good subject for poetry.[18] Much of his poetry

---

[17] John Flavel, *Pneumatologia* (1685), A3v.
[18] Ian Green, *Print and Protestantism* (Oxford: Oxford University Press, 2000), 605.

dramatizes the plight of the sinful man facing hell. In *Ebal and Gerizzim, or, The Blessing and the Curse* we are given a reason for this literary tactic:

> Indeed the holy Scriptures do make use
> Of many Metaphors, that do conduce
> Much to the symbolizing of the place [hell],
> Unto our apprehension. (*MW*, 6: 125)

Poetic discourse is needed to convince the reader of the awfulness of hell and, it seems, there is scriptural precedent for this. What this means is that there is considerably more material on hell in John Bunyan's works than in the Bible.

Particularly grisly is *One Thing is Needful*, a representation of the four last things. This lengthy poem in quatrains was probably printed first in 1665 (though no copy appears to have survived), and again in an undated edition of about 1672, and then in a 'third edition' published by Nathaniel Ponder in 1683. The 'Introduction' states Bunyan's purpose, which is to persuade readers of the reality of death, judgement, heaven, and hell. In the first section, '*Of Death*', he describes the effect of death on the human being:

> 33. He feels his very Vitals die,
>   All waxeth pale and wan;
>   Nay worse he fears, to misery
>   He shortly must be gone.
>   […]
>
> 37. Still pulling of him from his place
>   Full sore against his Mind;
>   Death like a sprite stares in his face,
>   And doth with links him bind.
>
> 38. And carries him into his den,
>   In darkness there to lie
>   Among the swarms of wicked men,
>   In grief eternally. (*MW*, 6: 69–70)

There are no Bible references in the margin here, and indeed this account reads like an amalgam of popular culture and nightmares. By contrast, heaven is disappointingly biblical, in that human imagination does not seem to have been used. In the longest of the four sections, ninety-seven stanzas on hell, Bunyan uses all his imaginative resources to recreate the emotional and physical torment of sinners, which is, of course, supposed to be unbearable. At times the reader feels that Bunyan is supplying what he feels are the omissions in the biblical account, such as when he turns into verse the concept of eternity:

> 88. So that whatever they do know,
>   Or see, or think, or feel:
>   *For ever* still doth strike them throw,
>   As with a bar of steel.

> 89. For ever, shineth in the fire,
>   Ever, is on the chains;
>   'Tis also in the pit of Ire,
>   And tasts in all their pains. (*MW*, 6: 101)

The Nonconformist preacher, then, seems to see in poetic tactics and their concrete detail a chance to reach an audience which has already heard the gospel, if only in prose. In the prefatory poem to *The Holy War* (1682) Bunyan seems to represent a kind of truth of the imagination. Although he is using allegory, he claims to have 'seen' the story he is telling, so that it is an 'eye-witness' account, if only of his own fictional experience:

> What shall I say, I heard the *people*'s cries,
> And saw the Prince wipe tears from *Mansouls* eyes.
> I heard the groans, and saw the joy of many:
> Tell you of all, I neither will, nor can I.
> But by what here I say, you well may see
> That *Mansouls* matchless Wars no Fables be. (*MW*, 6: 168; *HW*, 4)

Poetry Conveys Passion

Bunyan's defence of rhetorical tactics is, then, consistently pragmatic. He does not claim superior inspiration, merely effectiveness. The claims he makes for poetry are modest human-centred ones: poetic techniques, including metaphor and allegory, have more effect on the reader. St Augustine's *On Christian Doctrine*, which investigates the use of rhetoric in religious enterprises, comes to much the same conclusion. Like Bunyan, who in the prefatory poem to *The Holy War* talks about his allegorical method as 'my Key' (*MW*, 6: 169; *HW*, 5), Augustine uses the metaphor of a key to describe rhetoric: 'Of what use is a gold key if it will not open what we wish?' The point both of them are making is that a key is primarily functional: sometimes it is necessary to make a point using rhetoric. But that is not to praise poetic skill. Augustine points out, using a metaphor of taste, 'that on account of the fastidiousness of many even that food without which life is impossible must be seasoned'.[19] The need for poetic or rhetorical technique is a necessity occasioned by the weakness of mankind.

It may be this sense that poetry is a sop to mankind's frailty that makes seventeenth-century authors write verse when they want to reach children. Baptists seem to have pioneered children's literature, as we can see from a compilation by one H. P., *A Looking-Glass for Children*, first published in about 1672. This opens with a collection of Henry Jessey's rather morbid tales of the deaths of children, but much the longest section of

---

[19] St Augustine, *On Christian Doctrine*, tr. D. W. Robertson, Jr (New York: Macmillan, 1958), 136.

the book is made up of poems by the Particular Baptist Abraham Cheare. These seem to have been written while Cheare was in prison, and although some are addressed to adults, most are for children. In one entitled 'To my Cousin T. H. at School', Cheare includes a stanza explaining the effect of poetry:

> kindly to attract your eye,
> From vanity to things on high,
> My thoughts to Meeter were inclin'd,
> As thinking on a Schollars mind,
> It might at first with fansie take,
> And after deep impressions make:
> Which Oh! If God would but inspire,
> Convince of folly, raise desire;
> Discover Beauty, kindle Love,
> Fix your delight on things Above;
> These weak endeavours then may stand
> As Christ's remembrances at hand.[20]

Here again is the linking of poetry with passion, this time with the plea for divine inspiration in order for useful emotions to be stirred. Cheare uses the word 'take' in the sense 'to excite a passion in (a person); to captivate, delight, charm', a common seventeenth-century usage, leading to the use of 'taking' to mean 'appealing, engaging, pleasing, charming, captivating'.[21] It is this quality that poetry is supposed to arouse in readers.

THE PROTESTANT TUTOR

Many early books of poems for children, including Bunyan's own collection, *A Book for Girls and Boys*, offer to teach children how to read first. One of the best known of these early books was *The Protestant Tutor, Instructing Children to Spel and Read English, and Grounding them in the True Protestant Religion and Discovering the Errors and Deceits of the Papists*, first published in 1679 by an opposition hero of the Exclusion Crisis, the Baptist printer, Benjamin Harris, who also seems to have compiled it. The project of teaching children to read and spell using passages from the Bible and catechisms is designed also '*to strengthen and confirm this young Generation in* Protestant *Principles*', as Harris promises the eldest son of the Duke of Monmouth in the dedication.[22] Protestant history features largely in this volume: there are narratives, illustrated by woodcuts, in which the providential events of the Reformation, 'confirmed' by God's intervention in the Armada and the Gunpowder Plot, have been annexed from an earlier rhetoric

---

[20] H. P., *A Looking-Glass for Children*, 3rd edn (1673), 28.
[21] See *OED*, 'take', *v*, 8b; 'taking', *adj.*, 2.
[22] Benjamin Harris, *The Protestant Tutor* (1679), A3v.

employed to unify English Protestants before the Civil War. An abbreviated Foxean discourse of martyrology, another genre important to the Reformation, is included: 'A Little Book of Martyrs', in verse, together with a poetic rendition of the parable of Dives and Lazarus in Luke 16.[23] A poetic version of the Ten Commandments—'Renounce all other Gods but only me / Unto no Image bow thy heart or knee'—is very similar to Bunyan's in *A Book for Boys and Girls*: 'Thou shalt not have another God than me: / Thou shalt not to an Image bow thy Knee' (*MW*, 6: 197).

The Protestant Tutor is also sometimes attributed to another Nonconformist poet, Benjamin Keach, a Baptist from Buckinghamshire. In 1664 Keach was pilloried for the publication of 1,500 copies of *The Child's Instructor*, ostensibly a primer in reading, arithmetic, and catechism, on the basis of which the Lord Chief Justice denoted Keach a dangerous Fifth Monarchist.[24] Although all copies of this edition were burned in front of his face, Keach rewrote and republished this volume at several points later in his career; at least two different versions of subsequent publications, *The Child's Delight* and *Instructions for Children*, survive and appeared in many editions.

Keach is more famous for long narrative poems which sold very well, as his publisher John Dunton noted, with a touch of literary snobbery:

> *This War-like Author* is much admir'd amongst the *Anabaptists* and, to do him right, his Thoughts are easy, just and pertinent—He's a popular Preacher and (as appears by his awakening Sermons) understands the *Humour and Necessity of his Audience*—His Practical Books have met with a kind Reception; and I believe his *War with the Devil,* and *Travels of True Godliness* (of which I printed Ten Thousand) will sell to the end of Time.[25]

Keach's poetical *War with the Devil* was published in nineteen editions by 1728, and by comparison, the first part of *The Pilgrim's Progress* was issued in twenty-two editions by 1727.[26] The link with Keach's preaching and his poetry that Dunton makes is relevant to Bunyan as well: poetry is part of the preacher's project of reaching his audience, in the process known as 'awakening'. *War with the Devil* is advertised on its title page as 'chiefly intended for the Instruction of the Younger sort'. In a commendatory poem, W. B., though admitting that Keach's verses cannot be described as 'elegant Scholastick strains', argues nevertheless that they are 'fill'd with choice Divinity'. He expands on the deceptively educative powers of verse for a potential reader, who would rather choose 'to read ten lines in Verse, than one in Prose', and:

---

[23] Harris, *The Protestant Tutor*, 98–117, 94–8.

[24] Thomas Crosby, *The History of the English Baptists, from the Reformation to the Beginning of the Reign of George I*, 4 vols (1738–40), 2: 199.

[25] John Dunton, *The Life and Errors of John Dunton* (1705), 237 (misprinted as 732 in a serially misnumbered section), sig. R2.

[26] Green, *Print and Protestantism*, 605, 635.

> as the nimble *Fly, that lightly springs,*
> Against the Flame, until she burn her wings;
> Is taken Captive with that sulphurous flame,
> With which she only sought to sport and game.

Here, the unsuspecting reader is the fly, the bright attractive powers of the flame the poetic form, and the heat of the fire the divine truth of the allegory.

Poetry, then, is everywhere apologized for, as a necessary evil: its practitioners are aware of its power, but wary of it at the same time. Rhetoric is seen as second-rate simply because it does not move the passions. As W. B. puts it: 'Rhetorick, and curious Art / Strive to affect the Fancy, not the Heart.'[27] However, verse was admitted to be a legitimate tactic in didactic writing, especially for children. George Herbert's 'The Church-Porch' was often quoted by Baptists, including someone pretending to be Bunyan in the prefatory poem to a volume of 1700 entitled *Scriptural Poems*: 'A Verse may find him, whom a Sermon flies, / And turn Delight into a Sacrifice.'[28] As we shall see, Bunyan himself, in a prefatory poem to *A Book for Girls and Boys*, displays a similarly ambivalent attitude to his choice of 'Homely Rhimes' for conveying religious truths. Instead of a 'fit audience' he claims a 'foolish' one, at which, for both egalitarian and scriptural reasons, he is aiming. He seems to be using poetry only out of necessity.

An Emblem Book?

A Book for Boys and Girls is the only poetry of Bunyan's to be given best-seller status by Ian Green, who points out that it went into nine early editions.[29] The first edition retains the structure of an educational work to teach children to read; with the characteristic division of syllables, the first page is headed 'An help to Chil-dren to learn to read English', followed by 'To learn Chil-dren to spell a-right their names', and '*To learn Children to know Figures, and Numeral Letters*' (*MW*, 6: 194–96). The first edition had no illustrations at all, which means that the text as it appears in the Oxford *Miscellaneous Works* volume is a kind of hybrid, because it reproduces the text of 1686 with woodcuts that appeared only in later editions. This means that some poems have no illustrations, because later editions included only forty-seven out of the seventy-four original poems. It also raises the interesting possibility that some poems might have been omitted from the second edition onwards because they were difficult to illustrate. Poems such as 'Upon a Stinking Breath', or 'Upon Fly-Blows' might have been left out for this reason, or

---

[27] Benjamin Keach, *War with the Devil* (1675), 1–3.
[28] John Bunyan (?), *Scriptural Poems being Several Portions of Scripture Digested into English Verse* (1700), A3v. For arguments against the ascription to Bunyan, see *MW*, 6: xx–xxiii.
[29] Green, *Print and Protestantism*, 605.

perhaps because they were just thought to be too revolting for eighteenth-century taste (*MW*, 6: 255, 260).

Shannon Murray's comment that *A Book for Boys and Girls* is not really an emblem book because of the original lack of illustration does not hold up.[30] Bunyan consistently uses the word 'emblem' in the 'Comparison' section of the poems when he explains the meaning of his chosen symbol. So, for example, the 'Comparison' section of both 'Upon the Flint in the Water' and 'Upon the Bee' begin 'This Flint an Emblem is' and 'This Bee an Emblem is' (*MW*, 6: 206, 208). The authors of manuscript emblem books, which tended not to have illustrations, did not seem to feel that the lack of an illustration was fundamental to the 'emblem' project. The origins of the emblem are multiple, in discourses ranging from esoteric symbol to commonplace proverbs. These are two figures of speech that would seem to require very different interpretive strategies, but Michael Bath argues that it is actually impossible to distinguish hieroglyphic theories from rhetorical theory about figures: they are all seen as ways of communicating, like the simile.[31] He concludes that there was a stock of material for Renaissance emblematists that included humanist commonplaces, proverbs, and hieroglyphics: the Bible, which could be seen as an emblem book in its own right, added to this stock. That the religious emblem was not completely alien to Puritans, at least in the 1590s, is shown by the fact that in 1592 Andrew Willet, the Calvinist chaplain to Prince Henry, produced one of the first emblem books, in English and in Latin, dedicated to that 'best patron', the Earl of Essex. His emblems are of three types: allegories, histories, and natural symbols such as animals. He insists that all of them are grounded in Scripture. There are no visual illustrations but that is because of the cost rather than any ideological objection to images.[32]

By the time that *A Book for Boys and Girls* was published, the emblem was well established as one genre which could be used for educational purposes and had been employed as such by Puritans. The best-selling *Emblemes* by Francis Quarles (first published in 1635) had gone into many editions in the seventeenth century. In fact, it had been reissued in 1684 and 1685, and must have helped to constitute what an emblem could possibly mean in 1686.[33] Quarles suggested an equivalence between the emblem project as a whole and the task of interpreting Scripture. He equated the emblem with the specifically biblical literary form of the parable, and also with the mystical esoteric form of the hieroglyphic:

> An Embleme is but a silent Parable. Let not the tender Eye checke, to see the allusion to our blessed SAVIOUR figured, in these Types. In holy Scripture, he is sometimes called a Sower; sometimes, a Fisher; sometimes, a Physician: And why not presented

---

[30] Murray, '*A Book for Boys and Girls*', 123.

[31] Michael Bath, *Speaking Pictures: English Emblem Books and Renaissance Culture* (London: Longman, 1994), 47.

[32] Andrew Willet, *Sacrorum emblematum centuria una* (1592), sig. A3r. On Bunyan's use of the emblem, see Jeremy Tambling, 'Bunyan and Things: *A Book for Boys and Girls*', *BS*, 16 (2012), 7–31.

[33] Green, *Print and Protestantism*, 393–95, 652.

so, as well to the eye, as to the eare? Before the knowledge of letters GOD was knowne by *Hieroglyphicks*; And, indeed, what are the Heavens, the Earth, nay every Creature, but *Hieroglyphicks* and *Emblemes* of His Glory?[34]

The application of this biblical, word-centred technique of literary criticism is suddenly broadened by Quarles to include the secular, non-verbal text of nature—earth, sky, animals, the world of *A Book for Boys and Girls*. These are described by Quarles as a different kind of language, as hieroglyphics. Although by the 1630s this word could already designate incomprehensible nonsense, Quarles, like a good Protestant, presents breaking God's code as an unproblematic task. The second edition of *A Book for Boys and Girls* was subtitled *Temporal Things Spiritualized* with the same sense of easy translation from one discourse to another.

Murray notes that *A Book for Boys and Girls* shares the faults of Bunyan's other poetry: he sometimes rhymes words with themselves, and often inverts sentences for the sake of rhyme.[35] However, there is no doubt that the increased variety of metre adds to enjoyment of the verses, and sometimes both basic conceit and its execution are moving, as in 'Meditations upon Day before Sun-Rising':

> But all this while, where's he whose Golden rays
> Drives night away, and beautifies our days?
> Where's he whose goodly face doth warm and heal,
> And shew us what the darksome nights conceal?
> Where's he that thaws our Ice, drives Cold away?
> Let's have him, or we care not for the day.
>   Thus 'tis with who partakers are of Grace,
> There's nought to them like their Redeemers face. (*MW*, 6: 221)

This volume shows us far more variety of subject matter than other books of poetry by Bunyan. A good example is a long meditation 'Of the Spouse of Christ', which is very interesting when placed alongside other contemporary uses of the biblical metaphor of the bride.[36] This poem dwells not on the anti-Catholic use of the trope, but on the supposed pedigree of the bride as spelt out in Ezekiel 16. It also draws heavily on the Song of Songs to express both the beauty of the bride, and the desirability of Jesus, the Spouse. The grace of God and the humble origins of the Church are emphasized: 'Now made the Darling, though before forsaken, / Bare-foot, but now, as Princes Daughters, shod' (*MW*, 6: 258). The use of the trope of the bride to describe the true church is characteristic of Dissenting writing of the later part of the seventeenth century, and the egalitarian

---

[34] Francis Quarles, *Emblemes* (1635), A3r.
[35] Murray, 'A Book for Boys and Girls', 122.
[36] See, further, Elizabeth Clarke, ' "*The Glorious Lover*": Baptist Literature of the 1680s and the Bride of Christ', *BQ*, 43 (2010), 452–72.

use of the trope is used to express a Dissenting sense that Christ was able to communicate his riches to the believer, no matter how humble.[37]

Another poem, 'The Sinner and the Spider', employs a long dialogue form to communicate the same egalitarian concept. The Spider insists that he is as good as the human sinner: 'I am a Spider, yet I can possess / The Palace of a King, where Happiness / So much abounds' (*MW*, 6: 219). Bunyan clearly enjoys both the comparison between human beings and the spider, and elsewhere, in 'Of Man by Nature', a poem that must have been intended as amusing to some extent, he revels in the repetition of unstressed rhymes which that comparison makes possible:

> From God he's a Back slider,
> Of Ways, he loves the wider;
> With Wickedness a Sider,
> More Venom than a Spider.
>   In Sin he's a Confider,
> A Make-bate, and Divider;
> Blind Reason is his Guider,
> The Devil is his Rider. (*MW*, 6: 261)

There are other poems which are typical of Nonconformist culture, some of which express opposition to the dominant church. The 'Formalist', who is clearly the Anglican, is described frequently as the cuckoo, as in 'Of the Cuckow', which ends with an accusation of pluralism: 'The Formalist we may compare her to, / For he doth suck our Eggs and sing Cuckow' (*MW*, 6: 223). The poem 'Upon the Sacraments', points out carefully that there are only two in Reformed Christianity, and that they have no efficacy in themselves:

> But shall they be my God? or shall I have
> Of them so foul and impious a Thought,
> To think that from the Curse they can me save?
> Bread, Wine, nor Water me no ransom bought. (*MW*, 6: 213)

In common with much Dissenting writing of the 1680s, a poem entitled 'Of the Going Down of the Sun' laments what is perceived, in the reign of a Catholic king, to be the passing of the golden age of the gospel in England: 'Our Gospel has had here a Summers day; / But in its Sun-shine we, like fools, did play' (*MW*, 6: 239).

However, in keeping with the book's intended readership, there is an emphasis on the phenomenon of 'awakening', defined in Wilson's *Christian Dictionary* as 'the minde brought to a serious consideration of that it should think upon, Joel 1. 5. Spiritually, to leave sin, Rom. 13. 11.' As noted, John Dunton regarded the poetry of Benjamin Keach as

---

[37] Clarke, *Politics, Religion and the Song of Songs*, 194.

comparable to his 'awakening Sermons'. The second poem in *The Book for Boys and Girls* is 'The Awakened Childs Lamentation', and it seems that 'awakening' is not a pleasant experience:

> Had I in God delighted,
> And my wrong doings righted;
> I had not been thus frighted,
> Nor as I am benighted. (*MW*, 6: 199)

'Awakening' is not salvation, but the uneasy prelude to it: it is what Christian is experiencing at the very start of *The Pilgrim's Progress* when, burdened and desperate, he utters his 'lamentable cry; saying, *what shall I do?*' (*PP*, 8). In 'Meditation upon Peep of Day' this 'awakening' is emblematized as that period between night and day, when it is so early that it is not yet clear what kind of day it is going to be: 'Thus 'tis with such, who Grace but now possest, / They know not yet, if they are curst or blest' (*MW*, 6: 205).

'Awakening' is clearly something poetry can do in the great scheme of salvation. It cannot save—only God can do that—but it can fulfil the function of alerting the sinner to important issues, of explaining and clarifying spiritual things. As such it has an important function, which is why Bunyan uses it. However, as he makes clear in the long poem addressed to the 'Courteous Reader' which begins the volume, this function of poetry is a very limited one:

> *Nor do I blush, although I think some may*
> *Call me a Baby, 'cause I with them play:*
> *I do't to shew them how each* Fingle-fangle,
> *On which they doting are, their Souls entangle,*
> *As with a Web, a Trap, a Ginn, or Snare:*
> *And will destroy them, have they not a Care.* (*MW*, 6: 191)

Bunyan is comparing himself with St Paul in 1 Corinthians 4:10 where he calls himself and his co-workers 'fools for Christ's sake'. The goal is that which is expressed in 1 Corinthians 9: 22: 'To the weak became I as weak, that I might gain the weak: I am made all things to all men, that I might by all means save some.' Similarly, in using poetry, Bunyan presents himself as foolish, particularly as his 'Homely Rhimes' are open to criticism on purely rhetorical grounds:

> *Some, I perswade me, will be finding Fault,*
> *Concluding, here I trip, and there I halt,*
> *No doubt some could these groveling Notions raise*
> *By fine-spun Terms that challenge might the Bays.* (*MW*, 6: 191)

Bunyan, however, is not interested in winning prizes for his poetry, and he has a truly democratic goal, an interest in everyone, no matter how young or stupid, which he believes God shares:

> *I think the wiser sort my Rhimes may slight*
> *But what care I! The foolish will delight*
> *To read them, and the Foolish, God has chose,*
> *And doth by Foolish Things, their minds compose.* (MW, 6: 192)

In fact, Bunyan implies that his simple poetic style is a choice: he could if he wanted write using a much more complex rhetoric. His criterion is not to impress his readership, but to alert them, or 'awaken' them:

> *I could, were I so pleas'd, use higher Strains,*
> *And for Applause, on Tenters stretch my Brains,*
> *But what needs that? The Arrow out of Sight,*
> *Does not the Sleeper, nor the Watchman fright.*
> *To shoot too high doth but make Children gaze,*
> *'Tis that which hits the man, doth him amaze.* (MW, 6: 192)

This is a poetry in which the readership is more than usually crucial; the judgement of literary critics is not being considered. The priority is to 'hit' or 'catch' the reader, whose eternal destiny depends on it. Thus Bunyan, who is usually expecting a poor or young readership, tempers his poetic style accordingly. As Dunton says of Bunyan's fellow Baptist Keach, he 'understands the *humour and necessity of his Audience*'. Bunyan notes that the audience for *A Book for Boys and Girls* may well be not real children but '*Boys with Beards, and Girls that be / Big as Old Women*' (MW, 6: 190)—in other words, men and women, no matter how sophisticated or unsophisticated they may be as readers. Bunyan uses poetry, then, to do what it has always been good at: engaging the emotions of the reader and bringing home the impact of truths that are salvific. The fact that his envisaged reader is little educated probably explains the uncomplimentary terms in which Bunyan's poetry is often described. Bunyan, however, expects such a response from literary critics. Rather than '*the Bays*' (MW, 6: 191) he would be more pleased with the substantial sales achieved by his volumes of prose and poetry, because more people would thereby be 'awakened'.

Suggested Reading

Achinstein, Sharon, *Literature and Dissent in Milton's England* (Cambridge: Cambridge University Press, 2003).
Bath, Michael, *Speaking Pictures: English Emblem Books and Renaissance Culture* (London: Longman, 1994).
Clarke, Elizabeth, 'Hymns, Psalms, and Controversy in the Seventeenth Century', in Isabel Rivers and David Wykes (eds.), *Dissenting Praise: Religious Dissent and the Hymn in England and Wales* (Oxford: Oxford University Press, 2011), 13–32.
Freeman, Rosemary, *English Emblem Books* (London: Chatto & Windus, 1970).
Hill, Christopher, *A Turbulent, Seditious, and Factious People: John Bunyan and his Church 1628–1688* (Oxford: Clarendon Press, 1988), chs 21 and 22.

Murray, Shannon, '*A Book for Boys and Girls: Or, Country Rhimes for Children*: Bunyan and Literature for Children', in Anne Dunan-Page (ed.), *The Cambridge Companion to Bunyan* (Cambridge: Cambridge University Press, 2010), 120–34.

Sharrock, Roger, 'Bunyan and the English Emblem Writers', *RES*, 21 (1945), 105–16.

Spargo, Tamsin, *John Bunyan* (Tavistock: Northcote House, 2016), ch. 8, '*A Book for Boys and Girls*'.

Tambling, Jeremy, 'Bunyan and Things: *A Book for Boys and Girls*', *BS*, 16 (2012), 7–31.

CHAPTER 20

BUNYAN'S POSTHUMOUSLY PUBLISHED WORKS

W. R. OWENS

By the time of his death, in August 1688, Bunyan had become a famous author, known throughout the British Isles and well beyond. Although his fame rested largely upon the enormous popularity of *The Pilgrim's Progress* (1678; 1684), he had also published some forty other books. Given his remarkable success as a published writer, it comes as something of a surprise to discover that he left behind a large collection of unpublished manuscripts, most of them in a complete state and ready for the press. There were sixteen in all, including sermons, pastoral and doctrinal treatises, millenarian writings, and lengthy commentaries on parts of the Bible. These works are of interest from many points of view. They demonstrate Bunyan's formidable powers of rhetoric as a preacher, thus helping us to understand why great numbers of people would flock to hear his sermons. They significantly enlarge our knowledge of his methods of reading and interpreting the Bible, and they illuminate in various ways his other writings, including his allegorical fictions. In some of them he discusses matters such as the state persecution of religious Dissent and the extent and nature of the obedience owed by subjects to monarchs. It has even been argued that on these political questions Bunyan 'revealed more of his mind in his posthumous treatises than in those which he published himself'.[1]

The first of his works to be published posthumously was one Bunyan had delivered to the publisher just before he died. This was *The Acceptable Sacrifice: Or, The Excellency of a Broken Heart*, an exposition of Psalm 51:17, 'The sacrifices of God are a broken spirit: a broken and a contrite heart, O God, thou wilt not despise.' It appeared in 1689, having been seen through the press by George Cokayne, a prominent Dissenting preacher in London and a long-standing friend of Bunyan's. In his 'Preface', Cokayne explains that the 'whole Book was not only *prepared* for, but also *put unto the Press* by the Author himself, whom the Lord was pleased to Remove (to the great Loss, and unexpressible

---

[1] Hill, *Bunyan*, 333.

Grief of many precious Souls) before the sheets could be all *wrought off* (*MW*, 12: 11). Also published in 1689 was *Mr. John Bunyan's Last Sermon*, which he preached at John Gammon's meeting house in Whitechapel on 19 August 1688, a couple of weeks before he died. It is very short, and may have been based on notes taken by someone present at the meeting.

It was not until late in 1692 that the main body of Bunyan's unpublished writings appeared in print, in a folio collection entitled *The Works of that Eminent Servant of Christ, Mr. John Bunyan, Late Minister of the Gospel, and Pastor of the Congregation at Bedford*. This contained twenty-two works: twelve previously unpublished manuscripts and ten works published in Bunyan's lifetime (though not including any of his best-sellers). It was edited by Charles Doe, a comb-maker from Southwark and a great disciple of Bunyan. It seems that Doe took over the task of putting the folio together following the death of Bunyan's widow Elizabeth in early 1691 (see *MW*, 12: xv–xxiv).[2] The previously unpublished works are, in the order in which they appeared in the folio:

> *An Exposition on the Ten First Chapters of Genesis*
> *Of Justification by an Imputed Righteousness*
> *Paul's Departure and Crown*
> *Of the Trinity and a Christian*
> *Of the Law and a Christian*
> *Israel's Hope Encouraged*
> *The Desire of the Righteous Granted*
> *The Saints Privilege and Profit*
> *Christ a Compleat Saviour*
> *The Saints Knowledge of Christ's Love*
> *The House of the Forest of Lebanon*
> *Of Antichrist, and his Ruine*

After the appearance of the 1692 folio, only two of Bunyan's known works remained unpublished. According to his own account, Doe had purchased the manuscript of *The Heavenly Foot-man* from Bunyan's eldest son in 1691 (*MW*, 5: 133). It is not clear why he did not include it in the folio collection, but he subsequently published it as a separate work in 1698, and it was frequently reprinted. One remaining manuscript was preserved by Bunyan's descendants until 1765, when it was sold and published that year under the title *A Relation of the Imprisonment of Mr. John Bunyan*. It comprised a series of letters or reports by Bunyan giving an account of his arrest and imprisonment in November 1660, his trial in Bedford in early January 1661, his subsequent interviews with prison officials, and his wife's courageous petitioning on his behalf at the summer assizes in 1661. It is easy to see why Bunyan never published this document in his lifetime, because

---

[2] See, further, W. R. Owens, 'Reading the Bibliographical Codes: Bunyan's Publication in Folio', in N. H. Keeble (ed.), *John Bunyan: Reading Dissenting Writing* (Bern: Peter Lang, 2002), 59–77; Anne Dunan-Page, 'Charles Doe and the Publication of John Bunyan's Folio (1692)', *Notes and Queries*, 57 (2010), 508–11. See also Chapter 9 in this volume.

it includes, in reported speech, vivid details of the exchanges between him and the magistrates. It is now usually published together with his spiritual autobiography, *Grace Abounding to the Chief of Sinners*.[3]

Dates and Context of Composition

That so many of Bunyan's works were published posthumously—sixteen out of a total of fifty-eight—raises intriguing questions. The first concerns their dates of composition: when were they written? In some cases the answer is fairly obvious. We can safely assume that *The Acceptable Sacrifice* and the *Last Sermon* were written in the months before Bunyan's death. Similarly, we can be certain that *A Relation of the Imprisonment of Mr. John Bunyan* was written very soon after the events recounted, between November 1660 and March 1662. There is strong reason to think that *The Heavenly Foot-man* is the work referred to in the preface to *The Pilgrim's Progress*, where Bunyan describes how, 'writing of the Way / And Race of Saints', he 'Fell suddenly into an Allegory / About their Journey, and the way to Glory' (PP, 1). *The Heavenly Foot-man* is an exploration of the 'way and race of saints', based on St Paul's metaphor of the Christian life as a race to obtain salvation, 'so run, that ye may obtain' (1 Corinthians 9:24). If, as is generally believed, *The Pilgrim's Progress* was begun in the late 1660s, while Bunyan was in prison, we can assume that he was writing (or had at least begun) *The Heavenly Foot-man* at this time. Richard L. Greaves dates it to the period between December 1667 and February 1668.[4]

Of the twelve works first published by Doe in the 1692 folio, none can be dated with certainty. The earliest was probably *Of Justification by an Imputed Righteousness*, which Greaves places between about July and November 1676. In 1672 Bunyan had published *A Defence of the Doctrine of Justification, by Faith*, a vigorously argued rejoinder to Edward Fowler's *The Design of Christianity* (1671). The fact that *Of Justification* offers a more comprehensive and systematic account of this key doctrine would suggest that it was written after the more polemical work. The subject matter of *Paul's Departure and Crown*, a call for Christians to be prepared to suffer for their faith 'even unto blood' (MW, 12: 359), suggests that it may have been composed during the winter of 1678–79 when much alarm had been generated by an alleged 'Popish Plot' to assassinate the king and massacre Protestants.[5] *Israel's Hope Encouraged* may be dated fairly securely to the winter of 1680–81, because it praises the efforts of 'brave Parliaments' in bringing in 'substantial Laws' for the protection of Protestants following 'the discovery of the Popish Plot' (MW, 13: 21). This seems to refer to the Parliaments of 1679 and 1680–81, in which Whigs introduced bills designed to exclude James, Duke of York, a confessed Roman Catholic,

---

[3] See Roger Sharrock, 'The Origin of *A Relation of the Imprisonment of Mr. John Bunyan*', RES, n.s. 39 (1959), 250–56.

[4] See 'Appendix: Provisional Dating of Bunyan's Publications', in Greaves, *Glimpses*, 637–41.

[5] Greaves, *Glimpses*, 361–65.

from succeeding to the throne. There is much evidence to suggest that *Of Antichrist, and his Ruine* was also written in the early 1680s. It refers to the plight of the Huguenots in France during the years leading up to the Revocation of the Edict of Nantes in 1685 (*MW*, 13: 426), and there are thematic links with other works which Bunyan published in 1682 and 1684.[6] The first half of the 1680s saw particularly fierce persecution of Dissenters, and repeated references to their sufferings in *An Exposition on the Ten First Chapters of Genesis* may suggest that Bunyan was also writing it during these years—perhaps, as Greaves argues, between the end of 1682 and the middle of 1683.[7] The fact that it is unfinished may indicate that Bunyan set it aside, or he may have been working on it right up to the end of his life.

Of the remaining seven works, two—*Of the Trinity and a Christian* and *Of the Law and a Christian*—are so short that they are impossible to date. They may have been designed for publication as broadsheets. Greaves assigns them, respectively, to the winter of 1686–87 and the early months of 1688, but on admittedly slender evidence.[8] *The Desire of the Righteous Granted* may be dated to the spring or summer of 1685, because Charles Doe writes of having heard Bunyan preach it in London that year (*MW*, 12: xviii). Greaves suggests that *The Saints Knowledge of Christ's Love* was probably begun in September 1685 and finished before the end of the year, arguing that its references to the oppression of the ancient Israelites may be read as coded allusions to the savage punishment meted out to supporters of the Duke of Monmouth's failed attempt to overthrow James II in the summer of 1685.[9] Two more sermon treatises may be placed, tentatively, in 1686: *Christ a Compleat Saviour* in the spring or summer, and *The Saints Privilege and Profit* towards the end of the summer or the autumn of that year. They are each based on texts from Hebrews, and deal with the still relevant topic of endurance under persecution. *The House of the Forest of Lebanon* is closely related to *Solomon's Temple Spiritualized*, which was published in 1688. Greaves argues, convincingly, that *The House of the Forest of Lebanon* was composed in the winter of 1686–87, when its theme of endurance under persecution would have been uppermost in Bunyan's mind, and that by the time of *Solomon's Temple Spiritualized* hopes of a relaxation of persecution were rising, following the Declaration of Indulgence issued by James II in April 1687.[10]

Another obvious question raised by the existence of so many apparently completed manuscripts is why Bunyan left them unpublished. Part of the answer must lie in the context of severe persecution of Dissent in the early 1680s, when any publication deemed offensive by the authorities could lead to arrest and imprisonment. Although the Licensing Act introduced in June 1662 (which prohibited the printing of books without a licence from a government censor) had lapsed in March 1679 and was

---

[6] See W. R. Owens, 'The Date of Bunyan's Treatise *Of Antichrist*', *The Seventeenth Century*, 1 (1986), 153–57.
[7] Greaves, *Glimpses*, 463.
[8] Greaves, *Glimpses*, 562, 587–88.
[9] See Greaves, *Glimpses*, 536–38.
[10] Greaves, *Glimpses*, 550, 555–56.

not renewed until 1685, a formidable body of statute and common law existed under which the press could be controlled. As N. H. Keeble has argued, the laws on defamation, slander, libel, and sedition were in some ways more effective than the Licensing Act. In 1684, for example, the Baptist Thomas Delaune published a tract explaining why Dissenters felt that they could not conform to the Church of England. Charged with seditious libel, he was convicted, heavily fined, and his book was burned by the hangman. Unable to pay his fine, he had to remain in prison along with his wife and two young children, who were unable to support themselves. In the foul, unsanitary conditions in Newgate, he watched first his children and then his wife die, and within fifteen months Delaune himself was dead.[11]

The savage renewal of persecution in the 1680s came about largely as a result of the extraordinary political and religious conflicts of these years. Following the discovery in the summer of 1678 of the 'Popish Plot', which precipitated an anti-Catholic frenzy, Whigs in Parliament, backed by Dissenters, redoubled their attempts to bring in legislation to exclude James, Duke of York, from succession to the throne, on the grounds that he was a confessed Roman Catholic. Charles regarded these attempts as a direct threat to royal authority, and in March 1681 he dissolved Parliament. He and his Tory supporters were henceforth determined to exact revenge on the Dissenters and their Whig allies, and the penal laws against Nonconformity, brought in after the Restoration in 1660, were applied with full force. Government spies and informers were active, and meetings of Dissenters were brutally suppressed. Officers sent to break up a religious gathering in Salisbury in December 1681, for example, 'beat many of the Persons Assembled', dragging them out 'by the Hair' and throwing them down stairs. Hundreds of Dissenters were imprisoned for non-attendance at the Church of England, and many more suffered financial ruin as a consequence of the imposition of heavy fines.[12]

The situation of Dissenters was made particularly difficult because of their association with plots against the government. Although it is difficult to know the full truth, there is evidence that a number of Dissenters and radical Whigs were prepared to resort to arms to force the exclusion of James and even to overthrow the government. In the most serious of these attempts, the Rye House Plot of 1683, the king and the Duke of York were to be assassinated on their way back from the races at Newmarket. The conspirators were betrayed and the plot came to nothing, but a number of high-profile Whigs were executed. Bunyan had links with some of those suspected of conspiracy during this period, including John Owen, Matthew Meade, and William Kiffin.[13] There is no evidence that he was involved in their activities, and indeed in published works such as *Seasonable Counsel* (1684) he forcefully condemned armed resistance and claimed not to know

---

[11] See N. H. Keeble, *The Literary Culture of Nonconformity in Later Seventeenth-Century England* (Leicester: Leicester University Press, 1987), 93–126; Keith E. Durso, *No Armor for the Back: Baptist Prison Writings, 1600s–1700s* (Macon, GA: Mercer University Press, 2007), 106–11.

[12] See Tim Harris, *Restoration: Charles II and his Kingdoms, 1660–1685* (London: Allen Lane, 2005), 301. For details of persecution in Bedfordshire, see Greaves, *Glimpses*, 487–88.

[13] See Greaves, *Glimpses*, 470–74.

'any that are dissaffected to the Government' (*MW*, 10: 40). In that work, as Richard L. Greaves has argued, Bunyan espoused an 'ethic of suffering', urging Dissenters to embrace persecution willingly as a badge of faith: 'a man when he suffereth for Christ, is set upon an *Hill*, upon a *Stage*, as in a *Theatre*, to play a part for God in the World' (*MW*, 10: 62).[14]

Matters came to a head following the death of Charles and the accession of James in February 1685. In the summer of that year, the Protestant Duke of Monmouth rose in rebellion, declaring himself king and promising toleration for Dissenters. His small army, which included many Dissenters, was defeated within days. Monmouth himself was executed, along with about 250 of the captured rebels, while around 850 were transported to the West Indies. It seems that Bunyan was acquainted with some Dissenting ministers who took part in the rebellion, though, again, there is no evidence that he approved of their actions.[15] Charles Doe described this as a time of 'severe Persecution', when Bunyan's enemies '*often searched and laid wait for him, and sometimes narrowly miss'd him*' (*MW*, 12: 454). His fears for his personal safety may be indicated by the fact that in 1685 Bunyan drew up a deed of gift making over all his possessions to his wife.[16] In such highly volatile and dangerous circumstances, when Dissenters were branded as seditious opponents of the state, it would not be surprising if Bunyan felt that he needed to exercise extreme caution in what he allowed to be published.

STYLE AND RHETORIC

Many of the posthumously published works seem to have originated as sermons, subsequently enlarged into full-scale treatises for publication. Bunyan mentions that he kept 'notes of all my sermons' (*GA*, 124), and, according to two of his friends, it was his custom to 'commit his Sermons to Writing after he had Preached them'.[17] *The Greatness of the Soul*, we are told, was a sermon 'First Preached at *Pinners Hall*, and now enlarged, and Published for Good' (*MW*, 9: 135). Although direct evidence is sparse, there is good reason to believe that Bunyan was an extraordinarily gifted and powerful preacher. Charles Doe writes of the emotional effect of hearing Bunyan deliver his sermons:

> Mr. *Bunyan* […] Preached so *New-Testament*-like that he made me admire and weep for Joy, and give him my Affections. […] me thought all his Sermons were

---

[14] Greaves, *Glimpses*, 493.

[15] Greaves, *Glimpses*, 527.

[16] See John Brown, *John Bunyan (1628–1688): His Life, Times, and Work*, ed. and rev. Frank Mott Harrison (London: Hulbert, 1928), 338–39.

[17] Ebenezer Chandler and John Wilson, 'Epistle to the Reader', in *The Works of that Eminent Servant of Christ, Mr. John Bunyan* (1692), sig. A1v. On the practice of turning sermons into treatises, see Rosemary Dixon, 'Sermons in Print, 1660–1700', in Peter McCullough, Hugh Adlington, and Emma Rhatigan (eds.), *The Oxford Handbook of the Early Modern Sermon* (Oxford: Oxford University Press, 2011), 460–79.

adapted to my Condition, and had apt Similitudes, being full of the Love of God, and the manner of its secret working upon the Soul, and of the Soul under the sense of it, that I could weep for Joy most part of his Sermons.[18]

Doe also provides evidence of Bunyan's considerable reputation as a preacher, claiming to have heard him preach in London to congregations of twelve hundred on a weekday morning, and three thousand on a Sunday (*MW*, 12: 456). Bunyan himself writes of 'hundreds' of people from 'all parts' coming to hear him preach 'that blessed Gospel that God had shewed me' (*GA*, 84).

The marks of their sermon origin are observable in the structure of many of these posthumously published works, with their numbered divisions and subdivisions in which scriptural texts are 'opened', individual words and phrases have their doctrinal significance enumerated, and 'uses' or 'applications' are drawn out. This structure was very much in line with that laid down in manuals of preaching by William Perkins, Richard Bernard, John Wilkins, and others. Perkins's influential work, *The Arte of Prophecying*, first published in Latin in 1592 and translated into English in 1607, set out three main divisions of sermons: 'explication' of the meaning of the scriptural text; 'collection' of points of doctrine from it; and 'application' of the doctrine 'to the life and manners of men, in a simple and plaine speech'.[19] Wilkins, in his *Ecclesiastes: Or, A Discourse Concerning the Gift of Preaching* (1646) described the role of the preacher as being to 'Teach clearly, Convince strongly, Perswade powerfully', and so a sermon should be made up of 'Explication, Confirmation, Application'.[20] Whether or not he had read works such as these, Bunyan would certainly have absorbed how sermons should be structured and delivered by listening to other preachers. He writes in *Grace Abounding* of having heard a sermon on Song of Solomon, 4:1, 'Behold thou art fair, my love', in which the preacher had 'made these two words, *My Love*, his chief and subject matter; from which after he had a little opened the text, he observed these several conclusions […]. [W]hen he came to the application of the fourth particular, this was the word he said […]' (*GA*, 29). We can observe traces of this sermon style in *The Pilgrim's Progress*, where the pilgrims sometimes resort to numbered points in their theological discussions (see, for example, *PP*, 152–54).

This widely followed tripartite structure was by no means a rigid formula, and there was plenty of scope for variation in the amount of time spent on the various sections. Holding the attention of audiences and helping them remember what they heard was the primary concern. As Bunyan put it, 'The heads […] and hearts of most hearers are to the *Word*, as the *Sieve* is to *Water*, they can hold no Sermons, remember no Texts, bring home no proofs; produce none of the Sermon to the edification and profit of others' (*MW*, 13: 280). A repetitious method of exposition was widely favoured, on the grounds

---

[18] Charles Doe, *A Collection of Experience* (1700), 52.

[19] See Greg Kneidel, '*Ars Prædicandi*: Theories and Practice', in McCullough, Adlington, and Rhatigan (eds.), *Oxford Handbook of the Early Modern Sermon*, 13–14, 17–18.

[20] John Wilkins, *Ecclesiastes* (1646), 5.

that it would enable listeners to follow the thread of the discourse and remember the main points more easily. According to Richard Baxter, if preachers 'do not purposely draw out the matter into such a length of words, and use some repetition of it, that they [the auditors] may hear it inculcated on them again, we do but over-run their understandings, and they presently lose us'.[21] Bunyan was aware too of the need to use language that would communicate effectively with his audience. In *The Saints Knowledge of Christ's Love*, he declares that he will speak 'not in a way of nice distinction of words, but in a plain and familiar Discourse' (*MW*, 13: 366). As he put it in an earlier work, *The Holy City* (1665), 'Words easie to be understood do often *hit the Mark*; when high and learned ones do only *pierce the Air*' (*MW*, 3: 71).

One way of helping listeners understand the doctrinal issues being expounded was for the preacher to enliven his sermon with apt similes and allegorical or metaphorical comparisons. These were referred to collectively as 'similitudes', and Richard Bernard strongly recommended them as being 'of excellent use even to teach, move and delight the hearer'.[22] Bunyan likewise thought that 'Similitudes, if fitly spoke and applyed, do much set off, and out, any point that either in the Doctrines of Faith or Manners, is handled in the Churches' (*MW*, 3: 95–6), and it is noteworthy that the epigraph on the title pages of both *The Pilgrim's Progress* and *The Holy War* (1682) is 'I have used similitudes' (Hosea 12:10). Many 'similitudes' are to be found in the posthumous works, as elsewhere in Bunyan's writing. In *Of Justification by an Imputed Righteousness*, we are told, the righteousness of Christ, by which the believer is justified, 'is still *in Him*, not *in us* [...] even as the Wing and Feathers still abide in the Hen, when the Chickens are covered, kept, and warmed thereby' (*MW*, 12: 285). The same comparison is found in *The Desire of the Righteous Granted*: 'the Righteousness of Christ covereth his [people] [...] as the Child is lapped up in its Fathers Skirt, or as the Chicken is covered with the Feathers of the Hen' (*MW*, 13: 109).

A particular feature of Bunyan's sermon style is his inclusion of little anecdotes, often related in colloquial speech patterns. In *The Acceptable Sacrifice*, for example, in a passage where he is describing what a truly heartfelt desire for salvation in Christ is like, he recounts the story of a woman who exemplified this longing:

> Once being at an honest Woman's House, I after some Pause, asked her how she did, she said, *Very badly*; I asked her if she was sick, she answered, *No*; [. . .] What, said I, is your Husband amiss, or do you go back into the World? *No, no*, said she, *But I am afraid I shall not be saved. And brake out with heavy Heart*, saying, Ah Goodman Bunyan! *Christ and a PITCHER; if I had Christ, though I went and begged my Bread with a Pitcher, 'twould be better with me, than I think it is now.*
>
> This Woman had her Heart broken, this Woman wanted Christ, this Woman was concerned for her Soul: There are but few Women, rich Women, that count Christ

---

[21] Cited in N. H. Keeble, *Richard Baxter: Puritan Man of Letters* (Oxford: Oxford University Press, 1982), 49–50.

[22] Richard Bernard, *The Faithfull Shepheard* (1607), 66.

and a *Pitcher*, better than the World, their Pride and Pleasures. This Woman's Cries are worthy to be Recorded: 'Twas a Cry that carried in it, not only a sence of the want, but also of the worth of Christ. *This Cry, Christ and a Pitcher, made a melodious Noise in the Ears of the very Angels.* (*MW*, 12: 40)

Throughout the posthumous works, Bunyan displays a wide range of rhetorical devices. We find, for example, masterful use of rhythmically balanced clauses:

Suppose a Man when he dieth should go to Heaven, that Golden place, what good would this do him, if he was not possessed of the God of it? It would be, as to sweetness, but a thing unsavoury; as to durableness, but a thing uncertain; as to society, as a thing forlorn; and as to life, but a place of death. (*MW*, 13: 22)

He is fond of challenging his listener or reader with lists of questions, as in the following example from *Israel's Hope Encouraged*, where a sense of the oral delivery of the preacher comes across strongly even in print:

What sayest thou, Child of God? Has Sin wounded, bruised thy Soul, and broken thy Bones? Why, with the Lord there is *Tender* Mercy. Art thou a sinner of the first Rate, of the biggest Size? Why, with the Lord there is *Great* Mercy for thee. [. . .] Dost thou see thy self surrounded with Enemies? Why, with the Lord there is Mercy to *Compass* thee about withal. Is the way dangerous in which thou art to go? Surely *Goodness* and *Mercy* shall *follow* thee, all the days of thy Life. [. . .] What shall I say? There is Mercy from everlasting to everlasting upon thee. What wouldest thou have? There is Mercy underneath, Mercy above, and Mercy for thee on every side; therefore, *Let Israel hope in the Lord.* (*MW*, 13: 59)

In *The Saints Knowledge of Christ's Love* there is a rhetorically effective listing of all the ways in which Christians can take comfort in the promise that Christ loves them (*MW*, 13: 402). In that work, too, there is a good example of the question-and-answer formula, as exploited here by Satan:

Says Satan, dost thou not know that thou hast horribly sinned? Yes, says the soul, I do. Says Satan, Dost thou not know, That thou art one of the vilest in all the pack of Professors? Yes, says the soul, I do. [. . .] Well, saith Satan, now will I come upon thee with my appeals. Art thou not a graceless wretch? Yes. Hast thou an heart to be sorry for this wickedness? No, not as I should. And albeit, saith Satan, thou praiest sometimes: yet is not thy heart possessed with a belief that God will not regard thee? Yes, says the sinner. Why then despair, and go hang thy self, saith the Devil. (*MW*, 13: 409)

In these posthumous works Bunyan expresses, often with great eloquence, his conviction that living the Christian life is a strenuous matter, calling for constant vigilance, self-examination, and courage. It is, we are told repeatedly, a journey or pilgrimage in which there are dangers, temptations, and fears to be faced. 'Thou must Run a long and tedious Journey, thorow the wast howling Wilderness, before thou come to the Land of Promise. […] Beware of by-paths […]. There are crooked Paths, Paths in which Men go astray […] take heed of all those' (*MW*, 5: 150, 155). 'The way of Man to the next World, is like the way from *Egypt* to *Canaan* […]. Thou shalt guide me from the first step to the last, that I shall take in this my Pilgrimage' (*MW*, 13: 49).

Typology

The posthumously published works are especially notable as rich examples of Bunyan's extraordinary skill and ingenuity in typological interpretation of the Bible. Typology as a mode of interpretation is based on the belief that, despite its apparent diversity, the Bible is a single, unified work in which the Old Testament everywhere points forward to the revelation of Jesus Christ in the New Testament. According to this way of reading, events, persons, and things in the Old Testament are to be understood not only historically, but also as 'figures' or 'types' of events, persons, and things in the Christian dispensation, which are referred to as 'antitypes' or fulfilments of the types. Examples of typological interpretation are found in the New Testament itself, as when St Paul speaks of Adam as a 'figure' of Christ (Romans 5:14). Typology formed part of the more elaborate allegorical system of exegesis developed by the early Church Fathers. Origen, for example, interpreted Noah's Ark as a 'type' of the Church, but saw it also as an allegorical representation of 'the faithful soul' which should be 'coated with bitumen within and without, that is perfect in knowledge and works'.[23] In the sixteenth century, Protestant reformers rejected such allegorical interpretations as moving too far from the 'literal' sense, which they regarded as paramount. Later exponents of typology, however, were willing to use the term in a much broader sense. According to George Lawson, in his *Exposition of the Epistle to the Hebrewes* (1662):

> The words understood both of the Type and the Anti-type make but one literal sense: For that I call the literal sense which is intended by the Spirit. And this is the excellency of the Scripture, that by the same word it signifies not onely one but several things, and that as the words signify things immediately, at first hand, so these things signify other things—things past, or present, or things to come.[24]

This understanding of Scripture as signifying things past, present, and future was widely shared, and during the seventeenth century typology became a standard method

---

[23] Cited in Thomas M. Davis, 'The Traditions of Puritan Typology', in Sacvan Bercovitch (ed.), *Typology and Early American Literature* (Amherst, MA: University of Massachusetts Press, 1972), 11–45 (21).

[24] George Lawson, *An Exposition of the Epistle to the Hebrewes* (1662), 9. Lawson was a Church of England clergyman, and a friend of Richard Baxter; see Conal Condren, 'George Lawson', *ODNB*.

of applying the Bible stories to the lives and experiences of individual readers. As Thomas Taylor put it, there was no situation a believer could find himself in where he would not be able to 'parallel his Estate in some of the Saints; he shall see his own case in some of them, and so shall obtain instruction, direction, and consolation by them'.[25] The Bible came to be seen as a guide to the understanding of contemporary events. The Old Testament, it was believed, contained many 'Prophetique Types' referring not only to the New Testament, but to happenings in this present 'time of the Gospel'.[26] As Hezekiah Woodward put it in 1643, 'I thank God that I did search the Scriptures; for now I can give a full and cleare account of all the affairs now a days.'[27]

Throughout the posthumous works we find Bunyan reading the Bible in this spirit, searching out the 'typological' significance of every word and passage, and giving these a personal or contemporary application. The 'whole History of the Bible', he says, 'with the relation of the wonderful works of God with his People [...] are written for this very purpose, that we by considering and comparing, by patience and comfort of them might have hope' (*MW*, 13: 34). So, for example, the 'house of the forest of Lebanon' in 1 Kings 7 is '*a Type of the Church in the Wilderness*', and the great wooden pillars supporting it are types of heroic saints who endure persecution: '*no* Prince, *no* King, *no* Threat, *no* Terror, *no* Torment, could make them yield [...]. They have laughed their Enemies in the Face, they have triumphed in the Flames' (*MW*, 7: 122, 130).

The most sustained, intricate, and impressive example of this kind of typological reading is found in Bunyan's unfinished commentary on the first ten chapters of Genesis. This is the longest of his works to have been left in manuscript, and it is also one of his most ambitious. No book of the Bible had attracted more interest from commentators than Genesis.[28] Bunyan, however, makes little mention of questions that had exercised these earlier commentators, such as where the Garden of Eden was located, or how the serpent managed to speak to Eve, or what the exact measurements of Noah's Ark were. His chief interest is in drawing out the typological significance of each detail of the Genesis story. So, for example, the rejection of Cain's offering and the acceptance of Abel's shows that 'they worshipped the same God after a diverse manner: The one *in Faith*, the other *without*; the one as *righteous*, the other as *wicked*'. The same distinction, Bunyan says, applies 'between Us and our Adversaries' at the present day: 'We worship [...] according to *Faith*; and They according to their *own Inventions*' (*MW*, 12: 160). Similarly, Noah's Ark is a type of Christ, 'in whom the Church is preserved from the Wrath of God', but it is also a type of 'the Works of Faith of the Godly [...] by which the Followers of Christ are preserved from the rage and tyranny of the World' (*MW*, 12: 201). The Flood is a type of the great Day of Judgement, when God will destroy the ungodly,

---

[25] Thomas Taylor, *David's Learning, or The Way to True Happinesse* (1659), 93.

[26] Thomas Goodwin, *Zerubbabels Encouragement to Finish the Temple* (1642), 53–4.

[27] Hezekiah Woodward, *The Kings Chronicle* (1643), 'Epistle Dedicatory'; cited in Kevin Killeen, *The Political Bible in Early Modern England* (Cambridge: Cambridge University Press, 2017), 2–3.

[28] See Arnold Williams, *The Common Expositor: An Account of the Commentaries on Genesis 1527–1633* (Chapel Hill, NC: University of North Carolina Press, 1948).

but its waters also have a contemporary relevance: they signify 'those Afflictions and Persecutions that attend the Church' (*MW*, 12: 218–19).

As these quotations indicate, Bunyan regarded words and passages in the Bible as capable of multiple and differing typological interpretations. He displays great confidence in his method, but is careful also to indicate where he is expressing his own opinions, which may differ from those of others (see, for example, *MW*, 12: 105–06, 121, 194, 214, 241, 274). Sometimes, though, he admits defeat; of the reference to the 'second month, the seventeenth day of the month' in Genesis 7:11, he says, 'I have but little to say; […] a Mystery is in it, but my darkness sees it not' (*MW*, 12: 214).

No part of the Bible is of less importance for Bunyan than any other, and in *Christ a Compleat Saviour* he urges his readers not to be put off by even the most seemingly recondite passages:

> I advise that you read the five books of *Moses* often; yea read and read again, and do not despair of help to understand something of the Will and Mind of God therein, though you think they are fast lockt up from you. Neither trouble your heads though you have not Commentaries and Expositions, pray and read, and read and pray. For a little from God is better than a great deal from men. (*MW*, 13: 331–32)

This is advice drawn directly from personal experience. In *Grace Abounding*, he described how he had come to understand that the 'clean' and 'unclean' animals of Deuteronomy represented varieties of men, 'the *clean* types of them that were the People of God', and 'the *unclean* types of such as were the children of the wicked One' (*GA*, 23). Similarly, in *The Pilgrim's Progress*, Faithful interprets the 'unclean' hare of Leviticus 11:6 as a 'type' of Talkative. The hare '*cheweth the Cud*' like other 'clean' animals, but unlike them it '*parteth not the Hoof*'. In the same way, Talkative '*cheweth upon the Word, but he divideth not the Hoof, he parteth not with the way of sinners*' (*PP*, 80).[29]

Millenarianism and Politics

A prominent theme running throughout many of the posthumously published works is Bunyan's expectation of a coming glorious millennium, that period of a thousand years described in Revelation 20, when Antichrist (whom he identified as the papacy) would be overthrown, the devil would be bound in the bottomless pit, and the saints making up the true church would reign on earth. During the seventeenth century, many English Protestants became convinced that these events would happen in the near future.[30]

---

[29] See, further, W. R. Owens, 'John Bunyan and the Bible', in Anne Dunan-Page (ed.), *The Cambridge Companion to Bunyan* (Cambridge: Cambridge University Press, 2010), 39–50.

[30] See Christopher Hill, *Antichrist in Seventeenth-Century England* (Oxford: Oxford University Press, 1971); B. S. Capp, *The Fifth Monarchy Men: A Study in Seventeenth-Century Millenarianism*

Political developments in England and throughout Europe seemed to support this belief. According to Joseph Mede, one of the most influential millenarian writers, the pouring out of seven vials of wrath described in Revelation 16 represented stages in the destruction of the Roman Antichrist. Three had already been poured out: Waldensians and Hussites had renounced the authority of the Pope, the Reformation had begun under Luther, and English monarchs such as Elizabeth I had enacted laws against Roman Catholicism. The fourth vial, Mede believed, was being poured out as he was writing: he predicted that the Swedish Protestant champion Gustavus Adolphus would wrest the German Empire from the control of Rome. The fifth vial would be the destruction of Rome itself, the sixth the conversion of the Jews to Christianity, and the seventh would be the final overthrow of Satan, clearing the way for the commencement of the millennium.[31] Mede's work was first published in Latin in 1627, but was translated into English in 1643. During the Civil Wars of the 1640s the idea that Antichrist's downfall was imminent became widespread. Soldiers in the Parliamentarian army told Edward Symmons they were fighting 'against Antichrist and Popery': ''tis prophesied in the Revelation, that the Whore of Babylon shall be destroyed with fire and sword, and what doe you know, but this is the time of her ruine, and that we are the men that must help to pull her down'.[32]

It is clear from Bunyan's writings that he shared the millenarian hopes current during the 1640s and 1650s. In the 1650s he was associated for a time with a group known as the Fifth Monarchists—so named because they expected that the four great kingdoms (or 'monarchies') described in Daniel 7 would be followed by a millennial 'fifth monarchy', when King Jesus would return to earth in person to rule the world with the saints for a thousand years.[33] Even after the restoration of Charles II, and his own imprisonment in 1660, Bunyan's hopes for the imminent defeat of Antichrist and the establishment of the millennium remained high. In 1665 he published *The Holy City, or, The New Jerusalem*, a commentary on the heavenly city described in Revelation 21. Bunyan interpreted this as representing the glorious state of the true church of Christ when delivered from the tyranny of Antichrist. He now thought that Christ would not return to earth until *after* the millennium, and had come to regard the establishment of the millennium not as a dramatic, supernatural intervention, but as a gradual process: a continuation of the work begun during the Protestant Reformation. Nevertheless, he painted a glowing picture of life during the millennium, when divisions and disputes among the saints would

---

(London: Faber, 1972); William M. Lamont, *Richard Baxter and the Millennium* (London: Croom Helm, 1979).

[31] Joseph Mede, *The Key of the Revelation*, tr. Richard More, 2nd edn (1650), Part 2 (separately paginated), 112–21.

[32] Edward Symmons, *Scripture Vindicated* (Oxford, 1644), sig. A3r-v.

[33] See Richard L. Greaves, 'John Bunyan and the Fifth Monarchists', *Albion*, 13 (1981), 83–95.

disappear, multitudes of Jews and Gentiles would enter the church, and rulers would either join with or be subjected to her.[34]

The political excitement surrounding the Popish Plot and the Exclusion Crisis in England, together with events such as the increasing persecution of Huguenots in France, all served to keep millenarian hopes alive. Bunyan returned to the theme in the early 1680s, and in *Of Antichrist, and his Ruine* he offers his most elaborate discussion of the subject. By contrast with *The Holy City*, which had presented an inspiring vision of the glory of the church during the shortly-to-be-expected millennium, the later work is sombre in tone. Bunyan's purpose is now to convince his fellow Dissenters that despite seemingly unending persecution they could still be confident that the destruction of Antichrist would happen and indeed was already under way. Unlike other commentators, he refuses to speculate about specific dates, concentrating instead on the signs by which the saints could tell that the fall of Antichrist was drawing near. By a grim paradox, the most important of these signs would be renewed persecution of the church, more terrible than anything ever seen before. His evidence for this is the account in Revelation 11 of the slaying and resurrection of two 'witnesses'. According to Bunyan, these represent the whole succession of Christian believers who have borne witness for God against Antichrist. They will be killed by Antichrist, not in a corporeal sense, but in a 'mystical' sense: 'there will be such Ruines brought both upon the Spirit of Christianity, and the True Christian Church State […] that there will for a time scarce be found a Christian Spirit, or a true Visible Living Church of Christ in the World' (*MW*, 13: 473).

For all his warnings of a time of great tribulation, Bunyan remained certain that Antichrist would be 'pulled down, down Stick and Stone; and then they that live to see it, will behold the *New Jerusalem* come down from Heaven' (*MW*, 13: 499). The most striking and intriguing aspect of his account of the destruction of Antichrist, however, is Bunyan's emphasis on the role of kings in bringing it about: '*Antichrist shall not down but by the Hand of Kings*'; '*Kings*, I say, must be the Men that must down with *Antichrist*' (*MW*, 13: 462, 488). He is emphatic that Dissenters should not take up the sword on their own behalf, citing the example of the Israelites who, held captive in Babylon, did not attempt to 'fight their way through their Foes', but 'waited in their captivated state with patience', until the Kings of the *Medes* and *Persians* came to deliver them' (*MW*, 13: 485). Bunyan urges his persecuted brethren to put their trust in the king: 'Let the King have verily a place in your Hearts, and with Heart and Mouth give God Thanks for him; he is a better Saviour of us than we may be aware of.' They should 'Pray for the long Life of the King' and that 'God would discover all Plots and Conspiracies against his Person and Government'. For his own part, he says, 'I do confess my self one of the old-fashion Professors, that *covet to fear God, and honour the King*', adding that he says these things

---

[34] See, further, W. R. Owens, 'John Bunyan and English Millenarianism', in David Gay, James G. Randall, and Arlette Zinck (eds.), *Awakening Words: John Bunyan and the Language of Community* (Newark, DE: University of Delaware Press, 2000), 81–96 (85–7).

'to set them right that have wrong Thoughts of me as to so weighty Matters as these' (*MW*, 13: 488–89).

Such repeated protestations of loyalty to the monarch have been central to discussions of Bunyan's political views. Some scholars have taken them in good faith. His Victorian biographer described *Of Antichrist, and his Ruine* as 'a manifesto of [Bunyan's] loyalty to his Prince'.[35] More recent scholars have been less ready to take his words at face value. William York Tindall thinks that 'professions of loyalty' are cynical attempts to cover up the 'hatred of both king and government' that can be discerned elsewhere in Bunyan's writings.[36] Christopher Hill reads them as evidence that Bunyan is far from 'excluding all possibility of revolution', and Stuart Sim and David Walker find Bunyan's comments on Stuart monarchs 'at best lukewarm in their enthusiasm'.[37]

The idea that Bunyan's repeated expressions of loyalty to the king were cynically dishonest does not fit with anything that we know about his character. A much more likely explanation is that his political views changed over the course of his lifetime. He seems to have been a supporter of the Cromwellian republic during the 1650s and would no doubt have regretted the return of Charles II.[38] Like Dissenters generally at this time, he had a dubious reputation, and was accused by his enemies of treasonable disloyalty. His jailer at Bedford got into trouble for allowing him out on parole to go to London, it being alleged that he 'went thither to plot and raise division, and make insurrection' (*GA*, 130). Nevertheless, after 1660, like many other Dissenters and former Cromwellians, Bunyan seems to have accepted the king as the legitimate ruler, to whom obedience was owed, demanding only that Dissenters be allowed freedom to worship as their conscience dictated. In *Of Antichrist, and his Ruine* he makes effective use of the example of King Artaxerxes as a model king who grants religious toleration to his subjects, even though he may not share their beliefs (*MW*, 13: 423–26). When Charles II issued his Declaration of Indulgence in 1672, Bunyan and his congregation were quick to take advantage of the liberty it granted them.[39] In the context of the Restoration period, it was perfectly reasonable to regard the king as more likely than Parliament to offer religious freedom to subjects.

It is worth noting in conclusion that trust in monarchs had been a prominent feature of earlier Protestant millenarian thinking. The Antichrist, it had been said in 1603, would be destroyed 'by the tenne kings of *Europe* [. . .] which some very learned doe reckon up to bee these, *England, Scotland, Germany, France, Spaine, Denmarke, Sweueland, Poland, Russia,* and *Hungary*'.[40] Such ideas were still current in the 1680s, and Bunyan

---

[35] Brown, *John Bunyan*, 428.

[36] William York Tindall, *John Bunyan: Mechanick Preacher* (New York: Columbia University Press, 1934), 136–37.

[37] Hill, *Bunyan*, 153, 334; Stuart Sim and David Walker, *Bunyan and Authority: The Rhetoric of Dissent and the Legitimation Crisis in Seventeenth-Century England* (Bern: Peter Lang, 2000), 117.

[38] See W. R. Owens, '"Antichrist must be Pulled Down": Bunyan and the Millennium', in Anne Laurence, W. R. Owens, and Stuart Sim (eds.), *John Bunyan and his England, 1628–88* (London: Hambledon Press, 1990), 77–94 (90–1).

[39] See Greaves, *Glimpses*, 287–89.

[40] Arthur Dent, *The Ruine of Rome* (1603), 234, 256.

was by no means alone in looking forward to the day when the king of England would 'joyn with those other Kings of the Earth, that then shall hate the Whore'.[41] For all its expressions of loyalty to the monarch, however, it is easy to understand why Bunyan came to feel that *Of Antichrist, and his Ruine* could not be published. His outspoken attacks on the Popish Antichrist, and his appeal to readers to pray that Charles would 'drive away all Evil and evil Men from his presence' (*MW*, 13: 489), could easily have been seen as coded references to James, Duke of York, a confessed Roman Catholic. With the accession of James to the throne, and the crushing defeat of the Monmouth Rising in 1685, it is not surprising that Bunyan should have decided to leave such a potentially dangerous work in the safety of manuscript.

Suggested Reading

Achinstein, Sharon, *Literature and Dissent in Milton's England* (Cambridge: Cambridge University Press, 2003).
Camden, Vera J. (ed.), *Trauma and Transformation: The Political Progress of John Bunyan* (Stanford, CA: Stanford University Press, 2008).
Greaves, Richard L., *Glimpses of Glory: John Bunyan and English Dissent* (Stanford, CA: Stanford University Press, 2002).
Hill, Christopher, *A Turbulent, Seditious, and Factious People: John Bunyan and his Church* (Oxford: Oxford University Press, 1988).
Johnson, Galen, *Prisoner of Conscience: John Bunyan on Self, Community and Christian Faith* (Carlisle and Waynesboro, GA: Paternoster Press, 2003).
Killeen, Kevin, *The Political Bible in Early Modern England* (Cambridge: Cambridge University Press, 2017).
Lamont, William, 'Bunyan and Baxter: Millennium and Magistrate', in N. H. Keeble (ed.), *John Bunyan: Reading Dissenting Writing* (Bern: Peter Lang, 2002), 39–58.
McCullough, Peter, Hugh Adlington, and Emma Rhatigan (eds.), *The Oxford Handbook of the Early Modern Sermon* (Oxford: Oxford University Press, 2011).
Mullett, Michael A., *John Bunyan in Context* (Keele: Keele University Press, 1996).
Owens, W. R., 'John Bunyan and English Millenarianism', in David Gay, James G. Randall, and Arlette Zinck (eds.), *Awakening Words: John Bunyan and the Language of Community* (Newark, DE: University of Delaware Press, 2000), 81–96.
Sim, Stuart and David Walker, *Bunyan and Authority: The Rhetoric of Dissent and the Legitimation Crisis in Seventeenth-Century England* (Bern: Peter Lang, 2000).

---

[41] Hanserd Knollys, *An Exposition of the Eleventh Chapter of the Revelation* (1679), 35–6.

PART III
DIRECTIONS IN CRITICISM

NEW
DIRECTIONS
IN CLOTHING

CHAPTER 21

BUNYAN, EMBLEM, AND ALLEGORY

JEREMY TAMBLING

At its simplest, allegory is a way of saying one thing and meaning another. The term is derived from the Greek word *allegoreo*, formed from *allos* (other) and *agoreuo* (to speak in a place of assembly, the *agora*, the marketplace). The idea of 'speaking other' suggests that allegory is a secret speech needing deciphering. In this definition, to speak of any subject necessitates speaking in another mode, or finding another way of discussing what is to be said, perhaps for political reasons, perhaps to preserve secrecy. Or, as for Paul de Man, on whom more will be said later in this chapter, it means that allegory is not so much a specific literary form that the writer opts for, but that language itself is 'other'. Speaking is to be in the sphere of the other, and therefore is already inside allegory. Because speech is 'other', all utterance is allegorical, and the subject has not the command of what is said and its meaning.

As a term in literary practice, or recommendation that rhetorical arts of persuasion should proceed as if saying something other—as understatement, litotes, sarcasm, and irony are forceful means of conveying a point while apparently making another—'allegory' dates from Roman times. The common definition appears in the Roman rhetorician Quintilian (*c*.35–*c*.90 CE), whose *Institutio oratoria*, a handbook of rhetoric, considered it an effective technique in speaking, making a point, making the listener guess at the meaning of what was said indirectly, as if in irony. Quintilian called allegory 'sustained metaphor'.[1] This requires thinking of metaphor as the practice which describes A in terms of B, saying B is A, assuming there is an analogue between two normally unrelated things, or concepts; it is not saying B is like A, which is simile. For Quintilian, allegory was a mode where the intended sense was phrased in a different mode, disguising the meaning, giving more rhetorical punch.

---

[1] For Quintillian, see Philip Rollinson, *Classical Theories of Allegory and Christian Culture* (Pittsburgh: Duquesne University Press, 1981), 16–17.

Allegory is often claimed as dualist, subordinating a literal perceptible meaning to another, invisible one. Historically, this corresponds to a Platonism characterizing early commentators on Homer and, through the Jewish Philo of Alexandria (first century CE) and Origen (184–c.254), the Bible. When interpreted allegorically, both biblical and classical texts (such as Calcidius' fourth-century commentary on Plato's *Timaeus*, for example, or Servius on Virgil) give events a moral meaning. Several figures of the late Roman Empire sealed these matters: Chrysostom (347–407) in the Eastern Church, interpreting the Bible non-literally, and in the Western Church, Jerome (c.347–420), Augustine (354–430), Prudentius (348–405, whose *Psychomachia* initiates personification allegory, describing a range of virtues and vices fighting for possession of the human soul), and Cassian (c.360–c.435). A 'persona' is a mask, or face conferred on an abstract quality; Latin personification corresponds to the Greek *prosopopoeia*.[2] Allegorization was how Christianity absorbed and removed the threat to it posed by the pagan world and pagan gods: one difference between the Renaissance poet Edmund Spenser and Bunyan—who here is more like the medieval allegorist, William Langland, in *Piers Plowman* (c.1370)—is that while Spenser's allegory is Christian, his figures and events are pagan, following a Renaissance confidence that pagan mysteries were absorbable into a Christian Renaissance.[3]

Personification

I will discuss five forms of allegory. In the first, *personification allegory*, a character epitomizes a quality, which fixes character. So, with Bunyan's Mr Badman, 'at the theological level he acts badly because he is predestined to reprobation, and on the generic level he acts badly because he is an allegorical personification of badness'.[4] Personification risks naming the 'other', so demonizing him or her, in a form of exclusion, or, in a 'mad drive to force heterogeneities together', erasing differences and otherness.[5] In *allegorical narrative*, often including personification, a series of events must be taken as meaning something specific, whose details can be read off and discussed. These two forms combined in the most significant medieval text, *Le Roman de la Rose*, by Guillaume de Lorris (writing c.1225–30) and Jean de Meun (writing c.1270–80). This, an allegory set within a dream, is followed in Langland's *Piers Plowman* and in the *Pearl* poem (c.1380).

---

[2] C. S. Lewis, *The Allegory of Love* (Oxford: Oxford University Press, 1938), discusses personification allegory, 44–111.

[3] See James F. Forrest, 'Allegory as Sacred Sport: Manipulation of the Reader in Spenser and Bunyan', in Robert G. Collmer (ed.), *Bunyan in our Time* (Kent, OH: Kent State University Press, 1989), 93–112.

[4] David Hawkes, '"Master of his Ways": Determinism and the Market in *The Life and Death of Mr. Badman*', in N. H. Keeble (ed.), *John Bunyan: Reading Dissenting Writing* (New York: Peter Lang, 2002), 211–30 (213).

[5] Gordon Teskey, *Allegory and Violence* (Ithaca, NY: Cornell University Press, 1996), 76.

Le Roman de la Rose begins with the dreamer (Amant, the lover) asleep, and imagining himself outside a walled garden. The little wicket gate opens and he is admitted by Oiseuse (Idleness) into the garden belonging to Deduit (Diversion).[6] Christian in *The Pilgrim's Progress* (1678) has the wicket gate opened to him by Good Will who directs him towards the 'narrow way' (*PP*, 25–7). Bunyan probably had not read *Le Roman de la Rose*, but draws on a continuing tradition. *Le Roman de la Rose* opens by discussing dreams:

> Many men say that there is nothing in dreams but fables and lies, but one may have dreams which are not deceitful, whose import becomes quite clear afterward. We may take as witness an author named Macrobius, who did not take dreams as trifles, for he wrote of the vision which came to King Scipio. Whoever thinks or says that to believe in a dream's coming true is folly or stupidity may, if he wishes, think me a fool, but for my part, I am convinced that a dream signifies the good and evil that may come to men, for most men at night dream many things in a hidden way which may afterward be seen openly.[7]

Macrobius was contemporary with Augustine and Cassian, dying a century before the inception of authoritative allegorical readings of the Bible by Gregory the Great (540–604). The *Roman* alludes to the *Commentary on the Dream of Scipio* (*c*.400), the dream recorded in Cicero's *De Re Publica*, which drew on the Greek authority Artemidorus of Daldis (mid-first century). In *The Interpretation of Dreams*, Artemidorus declared dreams allegorical. Macrobius' *Commentary* reviews five types of dreams, three being important here: *somnium*, or 'enigmatic dream, one that conceals with strange shapes and veils with ambiguity the true meaning of the information being offered, and requires an interpretation for its understanding', and which is therefore ambiguous, true or false; the *visio*, which is prophetic; and the *oraculum*, where a figure appears to offer advice.[8] Macrobius insists that the dream is a fabulous (fictive) narrative, but it is to be interpreted, making the justifications behind dreaming and writing narrative the same. Both are productive of truth, but it seems an uncertainty hangs over dream and fiction: either of them may be deceptive, a problem that Chaucer, influenced by *Le Roman de la Rose*, exploits in his dream-poem, *The House of Fame* (*c*.1380) lines 1–65, discussing the worth of the dream that he has experienced.[9]

Personification allegory plays virtually no part in Dante (1265–1321), the most significant allegorist of either the medieval or the early modern periods, nor, though he includes dreams, does the dream vision: Dante wants no ambiguity about the status of the poem's events, such as the *somnium* would give. Dante wakes to find that he has been lost

---

[6] Guillaume de Lorris and Jean de Meun, *The Romance of the Rose*, tr. Charles Dahlberg (Hanover, NH: University Press of New England, 1971), 37–8.

[7] De Lorris and de Meun, *The Romance of the Rose*, 31.

[8] A. C. Spearing, *Medieval Dream-Poetry* (Cambridge: Cambridge University Press, 1976), 8–11.

[9] Geoffrey Chaucer, *The House of Fame*, in *The Riverside Chaucer*, ed. Larry D. Benson (Oxford: Oxford University Press, 1987), 347–74; see notes 978–79, 995, 937.

in a dark wood, and *La Divina Commedia* (*c*.1308–20) records his progression towards Paradise, and the vision of God. Instead of working with people given abstract names, like Idleness, the people that Dante encounters in the Inferno, Purgatory, and Paradise, are historical or mythological figures who might have been real. It has been argued that Dante works with the principle which Cassian initiates: the fourfold interpretation of the Bible, according to its literal, allegorical, moral, and anagogical senses. That method became famous with Dante's prose work, *Convivio*, subdividing it into the 'allegory of the poets' and the 'allegory of the theologians'. In 'the allegory of poets', the text has a literal level, while its second level is 'a truth disguised under a beautiful lie'; it is the 'hidden sense'. The third level gives the lesson to be drawn from the text. The fourth is the 'sense beyond', which 'occurs when a spiritual interpretation is to be given a text which, even though it is true on the literal level, represents the supreme things belonging to eternal glory by means of the things it represents'.[10] Dante concedes that the allegory of the theologians, which applies to such a text as the Bible, differs from that of the poets in that the second sense is not a truth hidden under a lie. Whereas with poets the literal level is a fiction, with the Bible the literal events are true and meaningful (though how far Origen or Chrysostom might have said that remains controversial) and the point is expanded in the 'Letter to Cangrande'. This interprets the *Commedia*, Dante's major work, as if it was the allegory of theologians, so as a sacred text.[11] The influential work of Charles Singleton made the 'allegory of theologians' reading of Dante almost hegemonic, but it remains debatable whether this text was authored by Dante, as it is also questionable whether in practice a text such as the *Commedia* yields to fourfold interpretation.[12]

Two points emerge. First, the practice of allegorical interpretation, *allegoresis*, preceded the writing of allegories. The interpretive models which saw in texts meanings beneath the surface, the *hyponoia* (Greek: 'under-meaning', 'other meaning'), generated in their turn forms of writing which directed readers to allegorize, looking below the text's surface, as happens in Dante (e.g. at *Inferno*, 9: 61–3, and *Purgatorio*, 8: 19–21). Second, Dante regards all his work, from the youthful *La Vita Nuova* (*c*.1293) onwards, as texts to be interpreted, and reinterpreted, in a revisionary mode: *allegoresis* and the writing of allegory go together, and the significance of a text is to be arrived at the further the temporal distance from it. Thus Dante becomes a theorist of allegory, unlike the writers of the earlier, more secular, *Roman de la Rose*.

Renaissance allegory finds its apogee in Spenser. *The Faerie Queene* (1590; 1596), while not using the dream framework, employs personification allegory, and so associates, like *Le Roman de la Rose*, 'romance' with allegory (and with dream). Spenser's allegory

---

[10] Dante Alighieri, *Literary Criticism of Dante Alighieri*, tr. and ed. Robert S. Haller (Lincoln, NE: University of Nebraska Press, 1973), 112–13.

[11] See Alighieri, *Literary Criticism of Dante Alighieri*, 95–111.

[12] See Charles Singleton, *Dante Studies I: Elements of Structure* (Cambridge, MA: Harvard University Press, 1954), and Singleton's translations of the *Commedia*, 3 vols (Cambridge, MA: Harvard University Press, 1970–74); see also Robert Hollander, *Allegory in Dante's Commedia* (Princeton, NJ: Princeton University Press, 1969) and John Freccero, *Dante: The Poetics of Conversion* (Cambridge MA: Harvard University Press, 1986), especially 119–35.

involves moral qualities, and allegorizes nature, landscapes, and history: for instance, Book I 'involves the conflict between Una as the "true Church" or Church of England, and Duessa as the "false Church" or Church of Rome'.[13] So it addresses inside and outside conditions at once, intending in this an 'epic' quality, also present in Bunyan. Yet Spenser is possessed of another sense which makes his thinking and writing necessarily allegorical. He perceives reality as *already* allegorical, deceptive, riddling, ambiguous, like a series of 'pageants', such as those which greeted Queen Elizabeth on her state travels, simultaneously dramatic presentations and allegorical spectacles:

> So tickle be the termes of mortall state
> And full of subtile sophismes, which doe play
> With double senses, and with false debate
> T'approve the unknowen purpose of eternall fate.[14]

Yet if writing must become allegorical, the ambiguity doubles: ambiguous reality cannot be discussed through writing which doubles ambiguity. Allegory is thus problematic in being as illusionistic as reality may be. In this sense, allegory entails the refusal of unequivocal 'meaning', which, as a concept, it makes problematic. This point remains central to Walter Benjamin's thinking; in a major twentieth-century study of allegory, he associates it with melancholy, and with the breakdown of signification.[15]

Dreaming

Bunyan's *The Pilgrim's Progress* uses the allegorical framework of the dream, which, therefore, however ambiguously, gives the narrative a traditional authority:

> As I walk'd through the wilderness of this world, I lighted on a certain place, where was a Denn; And I laid me down in that place to sleep: And as I slept I dreamed a dream. I dreamed, and behold *I saw a Man cloathed with Raggs, standing in a certain place* [...]. (*PP*, 8)

'Walked' is already implicitly allegorical, suggesting the traveller or pilgrim. The 'wilderness' is like Dante's dark wood, and though the qualification 'of this world' makes the

---

[13] John Erskine Hankins, *Source and Meaning in Spenser's Allegory* (Oxford: Clarendon Press, 1971), 205.

[14] Book III, Canto iv, stanza 28, in Edmund Spenser, *The Faerie Queene*, ed. A. C. Hamilton (London: Longman, 1977), 341. See A. Bartlett Giamatti, *Play of Double Senses: Spenser's Faerie Queene* (Englewood Cliffs, NJ: Prentice Hall, 1975), 78–93.

[15] Walter Benjamin, *The Origin of German Tragic Drama*, tr. John Osborne (London: Verso, 1977), 175. On Benjamin, see Charles Rosen, 'The Ruins of Walter Benjamin', in Gary Smith (ed.), *Walter Benjamin: Critical Essays and Recollections* (Cambridge, MA: MIT Press, 1988), 129–75.

wilderness more simile-like than allegorical. Yet 'this world' must be interpreted. It is the world as actively opposed to God's kingdom (perhaps even more so in the Restoration period): a sphere of moral corruption, and what the Bible means by 'this age', which is finite, and will be removed, and so is not ultimately real. This quality aligns it to allegory, which likewise seems real but is illusionary.

So 'the wilderness of this world' fuses different allegorical modes, while the 'wilderness' adds the sphere of temptation, as in Matthew 3:1: 'then was Jesus led up of the Spirit into the wilderness to be tempted of the Devil'. Angus Fletcher quotes C. S. Lewis, that 'allegory's natural theme is temptation', thinking of allegory as being, so often, directed to freeing the soul from passions, as in *The Faerie Queene*.[16] Temptation, in both its modern and seventeenth-century sense of 'testing', is essential to this narrative, and requires the allegorical mode, which implies the subject surrounded by impersonal and personal forces, which must be named, and which may be seen as outward projections of what is internal. The 'Denn', meaning the jail, is a further allegorization. It reappears with Apollyon (*PP*, 59) and with Giant Despair (*PP*, 117). If it suggests a den of lions (Daniel 6:7), it evokes the lions Christian encounters, and Apollyon, whose 'mouth was as the mouth of a Lion' (*PP*, 45, 56). Such repetitions of images suggest that, as though in a *mise en abîme*, Christian's experience in pilgrimage replicates Bunyan's, making both the dream and the allegory specular: a mirror for showing Bunyan what his experience is. The man in rags is not his 'other', more a projection of himself.

The idea of the dream and the allegory as both mirror-like is basic to Langland and to Bunyan, who will 'trace' the life of and death of Mr Badman *'that thou mayest, as in a Glass, behold with thine own eyes, the steps that take hold of Hell'* (*MB*, 1). 'For now we see through a glass, darkly' (1 Corinthians 13:12).[17] Allegory is the enigmatic mirror showing something other to the viewing subject, while actually the self's specular image.[18] Allegory works on several layers, implying not just a one-to-one relationship (Denn = Jail), but allowing other episodes which seem far from this one to possess its presence. The dream is the allegory Bunyan is permitted to witness, while the word 'behold', employed by Bunyan at the beginning of both *The Pilgrim's Progress, Part I* and *The Life and Death of Mr. Badman* (1680), claims for it the power of a vision.

When Bunyan is released from prison, he no longer dreams (*PP*, 123 and n. 333). Perhaps the period of imprisonment allows for insight, and so dreaming. Christian's

---

[16] Angus Fletcher, *Allegory: The Theory of a Symbolic Mode* (Ithaca, NY: Cornell University Press, 1966), 20.

[17] In the Authorized (King James) Version of the Bible (1611), the margin glosses 'darkly' as 'in a riddle'; literally 'in an enigma'.

[18] Steven Kruger, *Dreaming in the Middle Ages* (Cambridge: Cambridge University Press, 1992), 136–39, discusses allegory and the mirror in Langland; see my *Allegory and the Work of Melancholy: The Late Medieval and Shakespeare* (Amsterdam: Rodopi, 2004), 9 and 42–4. See also David Mills, 'The Dreams of Bunyan and Langland', in Vincent Newey (ed.), *The Pilgrim's Progress: Critical and Historical Views* (Liverpool: Liverpool University Press, 1980), 154–81 (and, in the same volume, Brian Nellist, 'The Pilgrim's Progress and Allegory', 132–53).

literal journey sets forth in the present what the lives of the Old Testament patriarchs were like, as interpreted in the New Testament:

> These all died in faith, not having received the promises, but having seen them afar off, and were persuaded of them, and embraced them, and confessed that they were strangers and pilgrims on the earth. For they that say such things declare plainly that they seek a country. And truly, if they had been mindful of that country from whence they came out, they might have had opportunity to have returned. But now they desire a better country, that is, an heavenly, wherefore God is not ashamed to be called their God, for he hath prepared for them a city. (Hebrews 11:13–16)

But the journey in *The Pilgrim's Progress* continues and completes that pilgrimage of faith, since Christian reaches the city these Old Testament saints could not attain. In Vanity Fair, Christian and Faithful are aliens because 'they […] spoke the Language of *Canaan*', making them literally allegorists, speaking other, outside the language of the *agora*, the marketplace: Vanity Fair. 'The men told them, that they were Pilgrims and Strangers in the world, and that they were going to their own Countrey, which was the Heavenly *Jerusalem*' (*PP*, 90). This is similar to the souls purging their sins in Dante, who describe themselves in terms of pilgrimage (*Purgatorio*, 13: 94–6). There is, indeed, enough in Dante (to say nothing of the context of Chaucer's *Canterbury Tales* and the conclusion of *Piers Plowman*, which likewise shows a determination to go on pilgrimage) to link pilgrimage and allegory, perhaps because both states, however different, imply rootlessness: a state of not being at home, being an exile.[19]

Allegory now seems anachronistically out of place, exiled itself, since Romantic criticism, weighted by Goethe and Coleridge, has preferred symbolism, saying allegory depends on arbitrarily chosen images, representing qualities or states with which they are only mechanically associated. Allegory has no images possessing 'natural' meanings which bring together the symbolic image and its meaning.[20] Symbolism replaces allegory within Romanticism, in giving an intuitional sense of concept and image being united in an instant, as with those Keatsian symbols the Nightingale or the Grecian Urn. By contrast, for Walter Benjamin, in allegory, 'any person, any object, any relationship can mean absolutely anything else'.[21] Benjamin argues for allegory, against symbolism, and against the idea of a 'natural' fit between word/image and concept.

Hebrews, quoted earlier in this section, not only provides a text for Bunyan's allegory, it *necessitates* allegory in describing people living 'by faith', outside literal possession of what they live for, who must 'live a life of allegory'. So Keats said Shakespeare lived, adding: 'his works are the comments on it', as if suggesting his plays were more

---

[19] Jeremy Tambling, 'Thinking Melancholy: Allegory and the "*Vita Nuova*"', *Romanic Review*, 96 (2005), 85–105.

[20] Edwin Honig, *Dark Conceit: The Making of Allegory* (Oxford: Oxford University Press, 1959), 44–50; Paul de Man, 'The Rhetoric of Temporality', in Paul de Man, *Blindness and Insight: Essays in the Rhetoric of Contemporary Criticism*, 2nd edn (London: Routledge, 1983), 187–228.

[21] Benjamin, *Origin of German Tragic Drama*, 125.

real than his life.[22] Literalists in *The Pilgrim's Progress* are shown up as wrong. The language of the text has been called by Stanley Fish a 'self-consuming artifact': that is, the apparent premises and realities of the text, which make it apparently like real life, all disappear. 'Perceiving correctly in spiritual terms means ignoring what is plainly there and responding, instead, to a reality that is not verifiable by the light of an unilluminated reason.'[23] Fish does not refer to allegory, but that is a 'self-consuming artifact', since, through it, the text removes the reality that the language establishes, shows that the people who read literally are those out of 'the way', a concept in itself needing to be understood allegorically and not literally, for the way is not simply the literal road which is travelled, as both Fish and, similarly, Kathleen Swaim, discuss in their respective works.[24] The point is that Bunyan not only writes allegorically; the text is also about needing to understand allegorically.

FIGURA

Apart from this narrative allegory, the text works, as seen already, with personification allegory to express people's qualities and states of existence. Its two parts, of 1678 and 1684, comprise, also, two forms of allegory. Christian in *Part I* undertakes his progress alone, save for his meetings with Faithful and Hopeful. Christiana in *Part II* undertakes hers in the company of others, as though Bunyan was describing a church and thinking of its progress, which is also one within time, for her children grow up and marry during the course of the narrative. Christian's journey and the events which occurred to him are remembered constantly, by allusions, by references to the places where things happened to him, and by memorials to him. He thus becomes not only an example, but an allegory to the people in *Part II*: he becomes a *figura*. This term, implying a third form of allegory, comes from Erich Auerbach on Dante, drawing on the practice of the New Testament, which makes the events of the Old Testament a foreshadowing of events which in the New Testament happen in new clarity.[25] So St Paul speaks of what happened in the Exodus, and uses what took place then as a warning to the Corinthian Christian church: 'Now these things were our examples' and then, 'Now all these things happened unto them for ensamples: and they are written for our admonition, upon whom the ends

---

[22] Keats, letter of 18 February 1819, in *Letters of John Keats*, ed. Frederick Page (Oxford: Oxford University Press, 1954), 241.

[23] Stanley Fish, *Self-Consuming Artifacts: The Experience of Seventeenth-Century Literature* (Berkeley, CA: University of California Press, 1972), 245.

[24] See Fish, *Self-Consuming Artifacts*, 224-64 and Kathleen M. Swaim, *Pilgrim's Progress: Puritan Progress* (Urbana, IL: University of Illinois Press, 1993), 33-7. Fish is critiqued by Valentine Cunningham, 'Glossing and Glozing: Bunyan and Allegory', in N. H. Keeble (ed.), *John Bunyan: Conventicle and Parnassus* (Oxford: Clarendon Press, 1988), 217-40.

[25] Erich Auerbach, 'Figura', in Erich Auerbach, *Scenes from the Drama of European Literature: Six Essays*, tr. Ralph Manheim (New York: Meridian Books, 1959), 11-76.

of the world are come' (1 Corinthians 10:6, 11).[26] The events which befell Christian are interpreted in *Part II*, increasing their significance: they become examples, types, and are subject to *allegoresis*. *Part II* allows for a new, further allegorical reading: interpretation of allegory cannot be arrested, but continues, gathering momentum.

But it is not that *Part I*'s Christian resembles the Old Testament in relation to *Part II*'s New Testament. Rather, Christian now becomes, in a shadowy partial way, a figure of Christ, having the same power of victory, *after* the New Testament events of Christ. The events of the past, that is, in the New Testament, cast their shadows before them. They mean that Christian in *Part I* and then the Church in *Part II*, partake of their afterlife.[27] The pilgrims in *Part II* look back on *two* allegories: those unfolding in the New Testament, which draws on the Old, and the events of *Part I*. So Mr Great-heart points out to the pilgrims in *Part II* the site of Christian's battle with Apollyon, and the 'Monument, on which is Engraven this Battle, and *Christian*'s Victory to his Fame throughout all Ages':

> *The Man so bravely play'd the Man,*
> *He made the* Fiend *to fly:*
> *Of which a Monument I stand,*
> *The same to testifie.* (PP, 240)

The monument, a scriptural document, authenticates itself: no one, except itself, has written it. It directs the reader back to *Part I*, suggesting that the product of the events there is further writing, which, by demanding interpretation, becomes allegorical; riddling, though it seems simple and literal. If 'the man' 'played the man', then naming and identity are not the same.

Similarly, a few pages further on, 'they found an old *Pilgrim* fast asleep; they knew that he was a *Pilgrim* by his *Cloths*, and his *Staff*, and his *Girdle*'. Mr Great-heart wakes him, and the text calls him Mr Honest; as such he can tell that they are themselves honest people. He declines to name himself but says he came from 'the Town of *Stupidity*', and Great-heart guesses that his name is 'old Honesty'. 'So the old Gentleman blushed, and said, Not Honesty in the *Abstract*, but *Honest* is my Name, and I wish that my *Nature* shall agree to what I am called' (*PP*, 246–47). In one sense, explored by Maureen Quilligan, the text plays with language which Quilligan thinks generates personification, arguing that allegory is particularly attracted to puns and ambiguities within language, and rises out of interest in that: she speaks of 'the generation of narrative structure [in allegory] out of word-play'.[28]

---

[26] In the Authorized (King James) Version (1611), 'our examples' is glossed in the margin as 'our figures', and 'ensamples' is glossed as 'types'.

[27] See Alan Charity, *Events and their Afterlife: The Dialectics of Christian Typology in the Bible and Dante* (Cambridge: Cambridge University Press, 1966).

[28] Maureen Quilligan, *The Language of Allegory: Defining the Genre* (Ithaca, NY: Cornell University Press, 1979), 22; see 121–31 for Bunyan.

Quilligan, citing Coleridge, notes how many names—Faithful, Hopeful, Honest—are adjectives, not nouns: not characters, but their characteristics, as Honest aspires to be the man of honesty. Other names are ambiguous. Mr By-ends of Fair-speech denies that is his name: 'it is a Nick-name that is given me by some that cannot abide me, and I must be content to bear it as a reproach, as other good men have born theirs before me' (*PP*, 99–100). The irony is patent: the classic name of 'reproach' would be to be called Christian. By-ends' real name is never given, but asked why he has been called By-ends, he says that 'the worst that ever I did to give them an occasion to give me this name, was that I had always the luck to jump in my Judgement with the present way of the times, whatever it was, and my chance was to get thereby' (*PP*, 100). The character explicates the allegory of his name, but that is not simply allegorical, because of the rationale behind it, which he perfectly, and unconsciously expounds. Mercie, in *Part II*, is less characterized by mercy than its receiver: the name expresses not the character's condition, but the opposite state, and her desire for that state. The text both uses and withdraws from the nominalizations of personification allegory, especially in *Part II*, distinguishing between the abstract quality and a person who aspires towards the quality, but who can never quite have that singleness. The pilgrim must '*labour Night and Day,* / To be a Pilgrim' (*PP*, 295): the allegorical clothes designating the pilgrim are insufficient. Significantly, Christiana's sons, Matthew, Samuel, Joseph, and James, while having biblical names, which imply qualities, are not allegorically named. *Part II* thus becomes a different kind of allegorical work from the first. Allegory—and *allegoresis*—accumulate.

Emblems

Both *Parts I and II* use emblematic allegory, a fourth type. Emblems were, typically, visual images surrounded by a motto and verses explicating the image in a riddling mode. The whole is a device, or an *impresa*, setting out an intention, or a determination, which the bearer or possessor of the emblem had. It might be carried heraldically as an image, or become part of a book of emblems, as with Alciati's *Book of Emblems* (1531), setting forth pictures of the world or illustrating moral qualities. Bunyan's *A Book for Boys and Girls, or Country Rhimes for Children* (1686) illustrates this Renaissance type: here, emblems adorn moral instructions.[29] Bunyan's poems used no pictures, but the 1724 edition renamed it *Divine Emblems, or Temporal Things Spiritualized, Fitted for the Use of Boys and Girls*, adding woodcuts.

The arbitrariness of emblems increases their deliberate obscurity, indicating that images can be interpreted in diverse ways: a serpent may be an image of evil or of wisdom. That, again, differentiates allegory from symbolism. Bunyan uses emblems in the House

---

[29] See Rosemary Freeman, *English Emblem Books* (London: Chatto & Windus, 1948), who discusses Bunyan, and Michael Bath, *Speaking Pictures: English Emblem Books and Renaissance Culture* (London: Longman, 1994).

of the Interpreter in *The Pilgrim's Progress, Part I*, and doubly so in *Part II*, which, in its concern for the education of Christiana's children is similar to the *A Book for Boys and Girls*. Here, speaking pictures are essential, as in the House of the Interpreter, when the Interpreter shows Christiana and her company a room:

> where was a man that could look no way but downwards, with a Muck-rake in his hand. There stood also one over his head with a Celestial Crown in his Hand, and proffered to give him that Crown for his Muck-rake; but the man did neither look up, nor regard; but raked to himself the Straws, the small Sticks, and Dust of the Floar. (PP, 199)

The image as emblematic asks for interpretation: Christiana concludes that '*this is a Figure of a man of this World*'. The Auerbachian word 'figure' is relevant: Christiana could simply have said 'This is a man of this world.' 'Figure' makes the man an allegorical type, which needs to be decoded, but 'a man of this world' is also allegorical, being an abstraction, expressing a moral idea which is also being explained: this world is, allegorically, a place of straws, sticks, and dust.

The Interpreter agrees that his Muck-rake shows 'his Carnal mind', as emblematic of it. Interpreter says that the image:

> is to show, That Heaven is but as a Fable to some, and that things here are counted the only things substantial. Now whereas it was also shewed thee, that the man could look no way but downwards: It is to let thee know that earthly things when they are with Power upon Mens minds, quite carry their hearts away from God. (*PP*, 200)

Christiana prays to be delivered from this Muck-rake, and the Interpreter says that the prayer is virtually rusty: '*Give me not Riches*, is scarce the Prayer of one of ten thousand. Straws, and Sticks, and Dust, with most, are the great things now looked after' (*PP*, 200). This derives from Proverbs 30:8, 'Give me neither poverty or riches.' Bunyan's image and its explication lift this passage into an independent, riddling existence, which also illuminates allegory's purpose: the Muck-raker's failure to look upwards suggests the forgetting of allegory altogether, which was indeed happening at the time of Bunyan's writing.

ALLEGORY WITHIN ALLEGORY

Emblems suggest a fifth type of allegory: awareness of language as allegorical. Near the end of *The Pilgrim's Progress, Part II*, the pilgrims, arrived at the Land of Beulah, wait for death, which will take them to the Celestial City. The Post comes for Christiana with a letter, a message that she must stand before the Master (Christ) within ten days:

> When he had read this Letter to her, he gave her therewith a *sure* Token that he was a true Messenger, and was come to bid her make hast to be gone. The Token was,

An Arrow with a Point sharpened with Love, let easily into her Heart, which by degrees wrought so effectually with her, that at the time appointed she must be gone. (PP, 304–05)

The Post is allegorical of the state of dying, with the assurance that death means union with Christ; the 'token', the arrow, is emblematic. The token becomes an action: the arrow has been sharpened with love and it kills her over ten days. After Christiana's death, the Post returns to the town, this time for Mr Ready-to-halt. 'Then he also gave him a Token that he was a true Messenger, saying, *I have broken thy golden Bowl,* and loosed *thy silver Cord*' (PP, 307). The quotations come from Ecclesiastes 12:6, 'or ever the silver cord be loosed, or the golden bowl be broken', but we note the elision of the token, as emblematic image, with the language of Ecclesiastes: the token, as allegory, becomes text, disappearing as something discrete. The text is allegorical (perhaps the cord as the spine, the bowl as the skull), and riddling.

Christiana speaks about the dream that Mercie has had:

God speaks once, yea twice, yet man perceiveth it not. In a Dream, in a Vision of the Night, when deep sleep falleth upon men, in slumbering upon the Bed. *We need not, when a-Bed, lie awake to talk with God; he can visit us while we sleep, and cause us then to hear his Voice. Our Heart oft times wakes when we sleep, and God can speak to that, either by Words, by Proverbs, by Signs, and Similitudes, as well as if one was awake.* (PP, 223)

Christiana has quoted Job 35:14–15, but, within the italicized section, she has also glossed it, explaining Job by making not just dreams but proverbs too, allegorical modes, like signs and 'similitudes'. Bunyan's title page for both parts of *The Pilgrim's Progress* and for *The Holy War* (1682) quotes Hosea 12:10, 'I have used similitudes.' But proverbs are commonplace, and perhaps deceptive, as with '*A Bird in the hand is worth two in the Bush*' (PP, 30), or ambiguously true, as when Mercie quotes the proverb that '*To go down the Hill is easie*', and James qualifies it by saying '*the day is coming when in my Opinion, going down Hill will be the hardest of all*'. Mr Great-heart says that he has given her a right answer (PP, 216). No gloss is given for that; it is left as a riddle, as perhaps all proverbs are.[30] The proverb always needs another gloss. Two points follow, the first from the elision of token with language: there is no separation between allegory and other writing, for language is at all times allegorical. Hence Bunyan's texts can leap from one level of reality to another, one reference point to another. Second, the significance of a token, or a proverb, is another proverb: more riddling writing.

Bunyan declares in 'The Author's Apology for his Book', which opens *The Pilgrim's Progress, Part I*, that he '*fell suddenly into an Allegory*', as if into a particular mental or physical state. The Apology wishes to justify this procedure, doing so by reference to figuralism, saying that God's '*Gospel-laws*', meaning the laws of Moses, were set forth '*by*

---

[30] George W. Walton, 'Bunyan's Proverbial Language', in Collmer (ed.), *Bunyan in our Time*, 7–34.

Types, Shadows and Metaphors', that the prophets '*used much by Metaphors / To set forth Truth*', and that Holy Writ itself is full of '*Dark figures, Allegories*'. The Apology encourages the reader, therefore, to '*see a Truth within a Fable*', '*Riddles and their Explanation*' (*PP*, 1–7).[31] 'The Conclusion' to *The Pilgrim's Progress, Part I* tells the reader to interpret the dream, but warns against '*playing with the* out-side *of my Dream*' (*PP*, 164), which suggests not interpreting it literally. But if the interpretation of anything in the allegory is another riddling interpretation, there may not be any outside of the dream, just as Derrida says '*there is nothing outside of the text*', which his translator glosses as 'there is no outside-text; *il n'y a pas de hors-texte*'.[32] What Derrida offers here is a theory of allegory, as this is also understood by Paul de Man, using him and Benjamin: standing outside allegory would mean standing outside the text, in a unique position of truth which is not textual.

The impossibility of this is conveyed by allegory, which recognizes language as already 'other', different from the self, which cannot interpret without moving further away from allegory's own premises. This happens at several points in *The Pilgrim's Progress*:

> About the midst of this Valley, I perceived the mouth of Hell to be, and it stood also hard by the way side: Now thought *Christian*, what shall I do? (*PP*, 63)

The gap between Bunyan and Christian has virtually gone. The man outside the dream is the man inside, who 'was so confounded, that he did not know his own voice' (*PP*, 63). While the dream is presented as teaching the reader, it imposes meaning on Bunyan, who must intervene in his own dream. After the Slough of Despond:

> I stepped to him [Help] that pluckt him [Christian] out, and said; Sir, Wherefore (since over this place is the way from the City of *Destruction* to yonder *Gate*,) is it, that *this* Plat is not mended, that poor Travellers might go thither with more security? (*PP*, 15)

Help answers Bunyan, now depicted as *inside* his own dream, as 'yonder' suggests. In *Part II*, the guide, Mr Great-heart, produces a map:

> and had he not here been careful to look in his Map, they had all, in probability, been smuthered in the Mud, for just a little before them, and that at the end of the cleanest Way too, was a Pit, none knows how deep, full of nothing but Mud. (*PP*, 297)

Upon which Bunyan writes: 'Then thought I with my self, who, that goeth on Pilgrimage, but would have one of these Maps about him, that he may look, when he is at a *stand*,

---

[31] See discussion of Bunyan's use of the biblical Samson as a riddler in Sharon Achinstein, *Literature and Dissent in Milton's England* (Cambridge: Cambridge University Press, 2003), 107–14.

[32] Jacques Derrida, *Of Grammatology*, tr. Gayatri Chakravorty Spivak (Baltimore, MD: Johns Hopkins University Press, 1976), 158.

which is the way he must take?' (*PP*, 297). No distance separates dream and dreamer, who is constructed by the dream, not just using it to teach.

The Slough of Despond ghosts this pit; both being points in the allegory where a supplementary form of interpretation is required: the work of Help, or a map. It is as though the allegory itself was no longer something to be used to teach with, but was rather constructing, even overwhelming, the pilgrim. The '*Man cloathed with Raggs*' becomes not what Bunyan dreams, but what addresses him from the dream, which seems, like the 'progress'—which can be halted, as by Giant Despair—to make Bunyan Bunyan. Similarly, *Grace Abounding to the Chief of Sinners* (1666) records a life before and after conversion, but is actually the text where such a conversion happens, allegory being therefore the way where the self is changed, made 'other'. Bunyan says he 'fell into an allegory': it is not the author who makes the allegorical vision, but allegory which makes the subject. And there is no getting out of allegory: certainly not into the safety of the realist novel, which tries to fix language as either describing something real or as merely figurative. Allegory works on many levels, but does not distinguish them. All forms of expression seem real, with the biblical text becoming as concrete as everyday experience, creating in this non-differentiation a mad form of writing.

Allegory and Irony

If Bunyan's 'Apology' seems defensive in justifying allegory, this is because he was writing at a time when what he describes in *Grace Abounding* as his '*plain and simple*' style (*GA*, 3) was, under the Royal Society, becoming hegemonic: one assuming the possibility of standing outside metaphor and allegory.[33] Thus, Samuel Parker stated:

> And herein lies the most material difference between the sober Christians of the Church of England, and our modern sectaries, that we express the Precepts and Duties of the Gospel in plain and intelligent terms, whilst they trifle them away by childish Metaphors and Allegories, and will not talk of religion, but in barbarous and uncouth similitudes.[34]

Earlier, Hobbes's *Leviathan* (1651) had considered one absurdity of reasoning to come from:

---

[33] For the 'plain' style, and its impossibility in *Grace Abounding*, see my *Confession: Sexuality, Sin, the Subject* (Manchester: Manchester University Press, 1990), 88–96, and L. C. Knights, *Explorations: Essays in Criticism Mainly on the Literature of the Seventeenth Century* (Harmondsworth: Penguin, 1964), 101–19.

[34] Samuel Parker, *A Discourse of Ecclesiastical Politie* (1670), quoted in Roger Pooley, 'Plain and Simple: Bunyan and Style', in Keeble (ed.), *Bunyan: Conventicle and Parnassus*, 91–110 (94).

the use of Metaphors, Tropes, and other Rhetoricall figures, in stead of words proper. For though it be lawfull to say (for example) in common speech *the way goeth, or leadeth hither, or thither, The Proverb sayes this or that* (whereas wayes cannot go nor Proverbs speak;) yet in reckoning, and seeking of truth, such speeches are not to be admitted.[35]

This describes a turn within seventeenth-century writing inseparable from the politics of the Civil War. Metaphysical poetry works with a dramatic sharpness of phrase, which seems plain and immediate, like Bunyan's tangy and proverbial phrases throughout *The Pilgrim's Progress*, but Donne's *Devotions upon Emergent Occasions* (1624) argued:

> Thou art a *direct God*, may I not say a *literall God*, a *God* that wouldest bee understood *literally* and according to the *plaine sense* of all that thou saest? But thou art also (*Lord* I intend it to thy *glory*, and let no *prophane misinterpreter* abuse it to thy *diminution*), thou art a *figurative*, a *metaphoricall God too*: A *God* in whose words there is such a height of *figures*, such *voyages*, such *peregrinations* to fetch remote and precious *metaphors*, such *extentions*, such *spreadings*, such *Curtaines* of *Allegories*, such *third Heavens* of *Hyperboles*, so *harmonious perswasions*, so *retired* and so *reserved expressions*, so *commanding perswasions*, so *perswading commandments*, such *sinews* even in thy *milke* and such *things* in thy *words*, as all *prophane Authors*, seem of the seed of the *Serpent* that *creepes*, thou art the *Dove* that flies.[36]

Donne's writing is both plain and baroque, which Benjamin associates with allegory, if 'baroque' implies excess: continuing and developing an idea beyond its need, that is, and involving ostentatious wordplay, as with 'commanding persuasions', which forms a chiasmus with 'persuading commandments'. God would be understood literally, and plainly, but he is also figurative, metaphorical, with 'curtains of allegories'. Bunyan would have approved: the emblems, and Apollyon, and Vanity Fair, are examples of excess; and his Conclusion tells the reader to '*Put by the curtains, look within my veil; / Turn up my metaphors, and do not fail*' (*PP*, 164), where '*Turn up*' implies looking within the Bible to find the source of those metaphors, but also, learning to read 'otherwise', allegorically, turning things upside down. So, Mr Badman's peaceful death (*MB*, 157), recorded in a dialogue between Wiseman and Attentive, is not what is expected, because it is peaceful and needing Wiseman's explanation. Read in reverse, it becomes the surer indication of his damnation. For in Benjamin, allegory indicates the non-reality of what we see empirically, and is the mode allowing for reversibility: for example, Golgotha becomes the allegory of resurrection.[37]

Yet there are problems. Mr Badman's death could also be regarded as irony, which classical rhetoric called a subcategory of allegory. Allegory maintains a sense of what is

---

[35] Thomas Hobbes, *Leviathan*, ed. C. B. MacPherson (Harmondsworth: Penguin, 1968), 114–15.
[36] John Donne, *The Complete Poetry and Selected Prose of John Donne*, ed. Charles M. Coffin (New York: The Modern Library, 2001), 450.
[37] Benjamin, *Origin of German Tragic Drama*, 232.

said underneath the literal sense, which Bunyan controls through biblical phrasing and references throughout the text, marginal glosses, and doctrinal passages. Allegory seems to need the author's intention, yet de Man shows how one image can never coincide with its meaning because of the temporal lapse imposed by narrative, which means that these, image and meaning, can never coincide punctually. He calls allegory recognition of that failure of coincidence between signifier and signified, 'establishing its language in the void of this temporal difference'.[38] But the move to the novel form from allegory shifts, for de Man, into irony: now there is no longer a directional voice stabilizing meaning. I can make ironic statements, but cannot control the point that my statement may also ironize me. The subject cannot control his/her discourse; hence de Man compares writing in the conditions of irony to madness. Mr Badman's death may be ironic in relationship to the dying man's experience; or ironic in relation to how Wiseman speaks; or subversively ironic in relation to Bunyan's project. Fear of that underpins Bunyan's instruction not to play with the outside of the dream: if every statement has an outside, which the writer neither controls nor knows (a de Manian definition of allegory) then anxiety ensues, and the need to enforce interpretation.

St Paul says he uses 'plainness of speech' (2 Corinthians 3:12), and some Protestant commentators insisted on this, in partial rejection of allegory.[39] But plainness excludes neither allegory nor irony. The New Testament is full of parables, and mysteries, like Christ's metaphorical statements: 'I am the door' (John 10:9); 'I am the way, the truth and the life' (John 14:6), which as a definition suggests that Christ is a further sign, or progress, as a 'way'. Bunyan's image in his Conclusion of the curtain, or veil, evokes St Paul, who uses 'allegory' when comparing Abraham's two sons, one by Hagar (Ishmael) and one by Sarah (Isaac) to the children of the Law, associated with Sinai, and the children of promise, associated with the Grace of the Gospel. The historical events of Genesis are an allegory of the opposition of Law and Grace (Galatians 4:21–31). Paul distinguishes between the literal state of those under a written law, and those under the spiritual law of Christ, making the Old Testament events figure a now spiritually discerned condition. This Galatians passage is cited with reference to legality and Mr Worldly-Wiseman, who is not 'just' a bourgeois figure of religious hypocrisy, wonderfully socially observed in his sense of class superiority, but the illustration of a doctrinal position: of the legalist, who is a literalist, who disdains everything of spiritual reality and grace (*PP*, 23). In 2 Corinthians 3:6–18, the 'new testament', or covenant, is 'not of the letter but of the spirit, for the letter killeth, but the spirit giveth life'. The old covenant came from Moses, who had a veil over his face. Paul thinks that this veil was literal, but, allegorically, it was, he says, upon the hearts of Israel, which, as a nation, would not see that the old testament was temporary. The veil is done away in Christ, but 'even to this day, when Moses is read, the veil is upon their heart. Nonetheless, when it [Israel] shall turn to the Lord, the veil shall be taken away.' Israel will one day read the law of Moses in a mode which sees that

---

[38] De Man, 'The Rhetoric of Temporality', 207.

[39] See Thomas H. Luxon, *Literal Figures: Puritan Allegory and the Reformation Crisis in Representation* (Chicago: University of Chicago Press, 1995).

what it considered permanent was only allegorical, not fixed at the point of reference, but indicating the future, what was to come, that is, Christ.

This makes an allegorical reading ambiguous; unable to be taken in one way only, its two senses opposing each other. Sense (a) suggests that reading allegorically misses the literal sense of what is to be seen: inviting the kind of misunderstanding Hobbes speaks about, and accounting for hostility to allegory, which persists within current critical discourse that opposes allegory to 'realism'. But sense (b) suggests that to read allegorically means seeing that what is to be read must not be taken literally; the law of Moses indeed proclaimed, allegorically, its own demise, its passing away. The literal text speaks differently from how it must be read.

Whichever sense is chosen, the other remains as a troubling 'other' sense threatening to disallow the one chosen. This is de Man's point, but finishing more positively, in *The Holy War* (1682), Emanuel entertains the town of Mansoul with 'curious riddles of secrets drawn up by his Fathers Secretary', 'riddles' about the King, Shaddai, Emanuel, his son, his wars, and doings with Mansoul:

> *Emanuel* also expounded unto them some of those Riddles himself, but Oh how they were lightned! they saw what they never saw, they could not have thought that such rarities could have been couched in so few and such ordinary words. I told you before whom these *Riddles* did concern; and as they were opened, the people did evidently *see* 'twas so. Yea, they did gather that the things themselves were a kind of a *Pourtraicture*, and that of *Emanuel* himself; for when they read in the *Scheme* where the Riddles were writ, and looked in the face of the Prince, things looked so like the *one* to the *other*, that *Mansoul* could not forbear but say, This is the *Lamb*, this is the *Sacrifice*, this is the *Rock*, this is the *Red-Cow*, this is the *Door* and this is the *Way*. (*HW*, 116)

The sight of Emanuel makes these allegories readable, not the other way round. The *Oxford English Dictionary* notes the ambiguities in 'pourtraicture'. To 'portray' means to 'protract', to draw out, delay, and 'extend (an action or event) in time; to cause to continue or last longer; to prolong' and 'to draw, esp. accurately or to scale; *spec.* to mark or plot out (an area, a ground plan)'. The portrait contains the trait, or trace, of the subject: Old Testament images continue, and survive, as the figure of Christ, who appears figurally in Emanuel, since his allegorical name ('God with us'—Isaiah 7:14) puts distance between him and Christ, makes him Christ's portrait. The types or riddles in the Old Testament, find their analogue in another portrait which also defers from giving the full Christ, who exists as a trace in the riddle and in the figure of Emanuel. Allegory becomes the art of the trace which, for Derrida, questions the idea of an original or full meaning from which things come or towards which they move.[40] It disallows the duality within traditional concepts of allegory: that there is a meaning, and there is its figurative/allegorical expression. Bunyan's distinctiveness is to describe pilgrimage as ongoing, showing always

---

[40] Derrida, *Of Grammatology*, 70–1.

the trace at work even in what seems clear: one trait delays and draws on another delay and trace. Thinking of what the face implies in portraiture, we can return to 'For now we see through a glass darkly, but then face to face' (1 Corinthians 13:12). But it may not be possible to know anything further beyond the allegorical seeing in the mirror. More complete knowledge is still withheld: the face remains figural, a mask, a *persona*. The trace precedes the allegorical image, like land plotted out, and exceeds the face-to-face portrait, making for a potential for allegory in the most literal writing.

Suggested Reading

Baskins, Cristelle and Lisa Rosenthal, *Early Modern Visual Allegory* (Aldershot: Ashgate, 2007).

Boys-Stones, G. R., *Metaphor, Allegory, and the Classical Tradition: Ancient Thought and Modern Revisions* (Oxford: Oxford University Press, 2003).

Brittan, Simon, *Poetry, Symbol, and Allegory: Interpreting Metaphorical Language from Plato to the Present* (Charlottesville, VA: University of Virginia Press, 2003).

Copeland, Rita and Peter T. Struck, *The Cambridge Companion to Allegory* (Cambridge: Cambridge University Press, 2010).

Tambling, Jeremy, *Allegory* (London: Routledge, 2010).

Whitman, Jon, *Allegory: The Dynamics of an Ancient and Medieval Technique* (Oxford: Clarendon Press, 1987).

Whitman, Jon (ed.), *Interpretation and Allegory: Antiquity to the Modern Period* (Leiden: Brill, 2000).

CHAPTER 22

BUNYAN AND ROMANCE

NICK DAVIS

JUDITH WEISS characterizes romances as 'narratives of adventure that combine the real and the improbable', a definition broad enough to cover most of what we might wish to call romance as composed in any period.[1] Most of the romance texts known to Bunyan and his audience were chivalric romances, linked in with the medieval to early modern ethos of knighthood. The genre originated in the twelfth century, and became, over the following five hundred-odd years, Europe's most widely read (or heard, or seen) genre of secular narrative, developing in many forms. There were, inter alia, courtly narratives offering intricate reflection on the nature and significance of chivalric experience, especially in the area of love, but also popular plays of St George and the Dragon, chap-book abridgements of extended stories about knight-heroes, extempore storytellings of similar tenor which by their nature went unrecorded, and allegorical treatments of chivalric adventure like the early thirteenth-century French *Quest of the Holy Grail*, incorporated into Sir Thomas Malory's Arthurian cycle, or, exploring both Christian and secular ethical thought, Edmund Spenser's *The Faerie Queene* (1590; 1596). In a passage from one of his early works, *A Few Sighs from Hell* (1658), Bunyan, adopting the persona of a damned soul recalling earthly life, evokes a mentality that goes with devotion to the period's commonly available secular reading. The passage mentions two widely circulated romances:

> Alas, what is the Scripture, give me a Ballad, a Newsbook, *George* on Horseback, or *Bevis* of *Southampton*, give me some book that teaches curious arts, that tells of old fables; but for the holy Scriptures I cared not. And as it was with me then, so it is with my brethren now. (*MW*, 1: 333)

In view of Bunyan's description of his youthful life in *Grace Abounding to the Chief of Sinners* (1666), where he mentions periods in which 'the thoughts of Religion was very

---

[1] Judith Weiss (ed.), *The Birth of Romance, an Anthology: Four Twelfth-Century Anglo-Norman Romances* (London: J. M. Dent, 1992), ix.

grievous to me' (*GA*, 7), it seems reasonable to assume that the passage has some autobiographical content. Bunyan does, however, draw attention to his good fortune in having been taught to read, unusual for one of his background (see *GA*, 5). He would have been in a position to explore the field of romance storytelling, balladry, and the like with greater freedom than his fellows, who were confined to the oral medium.[2]

From the later fifteenth century, and with particularly noticeable effect by c.1600, printing had greatly increased the flow of romance narrative material through the culture. The '*George* on Horseback' which Bunyan mentions—Richard Johnson's *The Seven Champions of Christendom* (1596)—was, for example, a very popular as well as substantial work composed in the late sixteenth century specifically for printed sale. These altered circumstances of romance's production and reception worked to modify social perceptions of the genre. Lori Newcomb points out that, in an era when elite and non-elite readers were jointly accessing the productions of a print culture undergoing a phase of rapid expansion, members of the elite sometimes felt impelled to differentiate their own practices and experiences of reading from those of their social inferiors. Robert Greene was particularly well known for penning texts in popular distribution, of which the most widely circulated was probably the romance *Pandosto* (1588), and the generic chambermaid of a 1615 Overburian characterization is mocked for liking to 'read *Greenes* works over and over'.[3] But on the other hand *Pandosto* is the major narrative source for *The Winter's Tale* of c.1611, a debt which Shakespeare's play is scarcely at pains to conceal, and favourable reception of Greene's romance was far from being confined to the lower social strata; which is to say that attempts made by the era's elite to distinguish generically between culturally 'high' and culturally 'low' romance were not at this time very well founded, or secure. It was not until the practical establishment and rise to prominence of the empirical realism-oriented novel, a sort of mutation of romance (which, one might argue, *The Pilgrim's Progress* (1678; 1684) helped to bring about),[4] that romance narrative in the medieval traditions became decisively marginalized and consigned to the 'low' cultural sphere, in a way that continues to distort critical perception of it.

I shall argue that *The Pilgrim's Progress*, widely taken up by members of its period's elite but not specifically a projection of their values or snobberies, adopts no attitude of self-distancing from traditional romance in its major forms, but that it thoughtfully explores and develops further some of romance narrative's characteristic properties. The quoted passage from *A Few Sighs from Hell* is not, in the assessment of Bunyan work that I am offering, a condemnation of romance narrative, or of popular, down-market romance

---

[2] See Margaret Spufford, *Small Books and Pleasant Histories: Popular Fiction and its Readership in Seventeenth-Century England* (Athens, GA: University of Georgia Press, 1981), 6–7.

[3] See Lori Humphrey Newcomb, '"Social things": The Production of Popular Culture in the Reception of Greene's *Pandosto*', *ELH*, 61 (1994), 753–81, and W. J. Paylor (ed.), *The Overburian Characters* (Oxford: Blackwell, 1936), 43.

[4] See the conclusion of this chapter and the discussion in Chapter 5 of my *Early Modern Writing and the Privatization of Experience* (London: Continuum, 2013).

narrative, or for that matter of newsbooks,[5] but one of secular reading in a representative sampling, as prized in place of the Scriptures which uniquely point the way to salvation. The burden of the pages which follow is that Bunyan in *The Pilgrim's Progress* makes creative use of romance, in his time the most socially inclusive of narrative genres, in a way which signals allegiance to the procedures of romance writing, and which is at the same time far from betraying the convictions that animate his other works;[6] rather, it makes for their communication—at least as good communication, he seems to have found by experiment, as their more straightforwardly homiletic statement. The final section of this chapter offers some comments on Bunyan's treatment of the Scriptures in a narrative of romance adventure.

THE ROMANCE GENRE

The chivalric romances to which Bunyan alludes in *A Few Sighs from Hell* had, like others of their kind, a wide demographic. Helen Cooper has pointed out that, in introducing into his 'mad' discourse a couplet from *Bevis* ('Rats, and cats, and such small deer / Have been Tom's food for many a long year'), Edgar's 'Tom' in Shakespeare's *King Lear* is referencing a narrative, and kind of narrative, which would have been equally familiar to serving men and to members of the aristocracy.[7] The early fourteenth-century *Bevis of Southampton* (or *Hampton*), Anglo-Norman in origin, is one of the generic stories of a knight-hero's exploits, often overcoming adversity, often demonstrative of moral as much as martial excellence. '*George* on Horseback' or *The Seven Champions of Christendom*, which shows some debt to the very popular *Bevis*, is an ambitious composition centred on the nationally iconic St George,[8] one which spills over into genres abutting on romance. The title page of the first part cues the reader thus. Naming its seven titular champions, Saints George, Denis, James, Anthony, Andrew, Patrick, and

---

[5] The *OED* defines 'newsbook' as 'a small newspaper', noting that the term was in common use from about 1650 to 1700. The major English development of newsbooks occurred in the period of the Civil War.

[6] Harold Golder seems to have been the first to put forward the view that Bunyan *qua* committed Puritan ought to have held romance narrative in contempt; see 'John Bunyan's Hypocrisy', *North American Review*, 223 (1926), 323–32.

[7] See Helen Cooper, *The English Romance in Time: Transforming Motifs from Geoffrey of Monmouth to the Death of Shakespeare* (Oxford: Oxford University Press, 2004), 31, and for the lines referenced, Eugen Kölbing (ed.), *The Romance of Sir Bevis of Hampton* (London: Early English Text Society e.s. 46, 48, 65, 1885–94), 74, ll. 85–6. In a paper delivered at the conference of the International Shakespeare Association in Prague 2011, Helen Cooper pointed to the wide social catchment of *Bevis* which establishes the suitability of the reference.

[8] See John Simons (ed.), *Guy of Warwick and Other Chapbook Romances* (Exeter: University of Exeter Press, 1998), 26–30. Johnson was a pioneer in the writing of new romance narratives for printed circulation.

David, linked respectively to England, France, Spain, Italy, Scotland, Ireland, and Wales, it explains that the book will show:

> their Honourable Battels by Sea and Land: their Tilts, Iusts, Turnaments for Ladies: their combats with Giants, Monsters and Dragons: their adventures in forraine Nations: their Inchantments in the *Holy Land*: their Knight-hoods Prowess and Chivalrie, in *Europe*, *Africa*, and *Asia*, with their Victories against the enemies of *Christ*. Whereunto is added […] the true manner of their deaths, being seaven famous Tragedies: and how they came to be called the seaven Saints of CHRISTENDOM.⁹

Johnson's narrative material is diverse, more so than we find, for example, in Malory's already compendious *Morte D'Arthur* (c.1470), and the work's interest as chivalric romance abuts on that of saint's life, historical chronicle, Renaissance 'romance epic',¹⁰ wonder tale, and pre-modern travel narrative, as instanced by the widely circulated and highly regarded *Travels* of Sir John Mandeville (c.1356). The kind of generic mixing that we find in *The Seven Champions* has a bearing of its own on the conception of *The Pilgrim's Progress*.¹¹

The focus of the present discussion is, however, the genre of romance and Bunyan's working relationship with it. Defining romance primarily by reference to its formal features, I wish to put forward the view that romance structurally resembles narrative in general, but that it does hyperactively what narrative in general does more reticently or sedately. Every narrative possesses the reception quality of narrativity—which is to say that it sets its material in a state of transformation, where this transformation takes certain classifiable forms (to be identified shortly). But what we regard as romance possesses particularly high narrativity: it commands the attention of its reader or hearer or spectator by offering what narrative in general offers, but more dedicatedly and in greater measure. Judith Weiss is right to say that romance typically deals in the improbable, since the driving of narrativity to high levels in any representation of actions more or less of itself generates improbability. Among the very typical properties of discourse exhibiting high narrativity, aka romance, is that it casts its materials—virtual people, places, objects, situations—by expeditious means into a state of transformation, including openness to transformation. This transformation of materials—virtual people, places, objects, situations—that makes for narrativity can be assigned to two basic forms: (A) morphing or mutating, amounting to altering ('othering') of their substance, of the category under which they are to be understood; and (B) cognitive

---

⁹ [Richard Johnson], *The Famous Historie of the Seaven Champions of Christendom* (London: William Stansby, [1636]). The work was much reprinted during the seventeenth century, turned into a play in 1634, and, later, presented in chapbook abridgement.

¹⁰ See Colin Burrow, *Epic Romance: Homer to Milton* (Oxford: Clarendon Press, 1993).

¹¹ For *The Pilgrim's Progress*'s particular relation to *Mandeville's Travels*, see Nick Davis, 'Bunyan with Mandeville: Allegory, Originality, and the Superseding of Collective Experience in *The Pilgrim's Progress*', BS, 14 (2010), 9–33.

dislocation in their treatment.[12] Within the framework of the second the reader is led to conceptualize certain narrative materials simultaneously in more than one way: where these concepts are not compatible, for instance, or where a bivalent, either/or logic becomes inoperable. Before turning to *The Pilgrim's Progress* it will be helpful to consider characteristic examples of these transformational procedures as we find them in precedent chivalric romance.

Transformation in Romance

(A) Here we are primarily considering the development of a romance as narrative *adventure*, where the principle might be said to be embraced simultaneously by the main narrative agent and by the narrator. In *Tom a Lincolne* (written by Johnson shortly after the *Seven Champions*, published in two parts (1599; 1607), and kept in wide circulation throughout the seventeenth century) a significant confrontation takes place between the knight-hero and Caelia, the Fairy Queen. Here Fairyland is a country peopled exclusively by women found by chance in a voyage towards the West, and Caelia figures in the story as a kind of Dido. She proposes that they wed, or become lovers, on which Tom states his own position thus:

> [K]now (most excellent Princess) that there is no aduenture so dangerous, yet at your commandment would I practice to accomplish: yet for to tye my selfe in Wedlockes bonds, there is no woman in the world shall procure mee: for till I haue finished an Aduenture which in my heart I haue vowed, I will not linke my affection to any Lady in the world.[13]

To embrace chivalric adventure is to entrust oneself and one's identity exclusively to what will happen *in* a chosen adventure: one will become what occurrence along a certain chosen trajectory has been delegated to arbitrate. A tournament in chivalric romance is a small adventure in this sense: it is a collision between knights where much occurs by chance, but its outcome is nevertheless a generally accepted evaluation of its participants in which they win or lose measurable esteem ('worship', 'honour'). Within aristocratic ideology, romance adventure, despite its ostensible contingency and unpredictability—often exceeding that of a tournament—discloses what a noble individual genuinely is: Malory's Gareth, in the narrative character of the 'Fair Unknown',[14]

---

[12] For this distinction and the conception of narrative which underpins it, see Nick Davis, 'Rethinking Narrativity: A Return to Aristotle and Some Consequences', *StoryWorlds*, 4 (2012), 1–24, and 'Inside/Outside the Klein Bottle: Music in Narrative Film, Intrusive and Assimilated', *Music, Sound and the Moving Image*, 4 (2012), 9–19.

[13] Richard Johnson, *The Most Pleasant History of Tom a Lincolne*, ed. Richard S. M. Hirsch (Columbia, SC: University of South Carolina Press, 1978), 25–6.

[14] The motif is named after a French romance of *c.*1200, *Le Bel Inconnu*.

goes on adventure while concealing his rights of birth as the son of a king and nephew of Arthur, thereby demonstrating inherent personal excellence on a more convincing basis. Outside the pale of aristocratic ideology the arbitrational procedures are, however, less teleologically certain: popular storytelling may ask us to accept the genuine contingency of a narrative outcome where the lowly third brother has, in undertaking some quest, emerged as the luckiest and therefore best of all.

But, as Erich Auerbach brilliantly demonstrates,[15] to entrust one's identity in some degree to the arbitration of adventure is to find oneself making certain decisive *transitions*, sometimes defined concretely enough by a non-uniformity in the terrain through which one has passed. A narrative agent coming into proximity with some zone or moment of narrative transit, in this sense, has her/his identity opened up to redefinition and even actively redefined by the simple act of having crossed it. In the late twelfth-century *Yvain* of Chrétien de Troyes, one of the earliest chivalric romances and formative of the genre, a member of Arthur's court describes himself as having entered the terrain of adventure itself by making such a transition:

> I was travelling in quest of adventures, fully equipped as a knight should be, when on the right hand I found a way [*et trouvai un chemin a destre*] leading through a dense forest. It was a very difficult track, full of briars and thorns. Not without trouble and hardship I made my way by this path. Almost the whole day I rode on like that until I came out of the forest, which was in *Broceliande*.[16]

As Auerbach points out, it is odd to speak of finding a rightwards-leading path when no other orientation within the landscape is supplied, but clearly this is the 'right' path in an absolute sense: the necessarily arduous and testing one of chivalric adventure. In negotiating it and traversing a forest Chrétien's knight makes the transition from a relatively ordinary world to a strange one where he will find himself doing qualitatively different things: *Broceliande* as it figures in this account is a fabled region associated with inexplicable occurrence and magic.[17] In a modern romance fiction, C. S. Lewis's *The Chronicles of Narnia* (1950–56), the wardrobe through which the central figures pass is a generically aware, somewhat parodic version of much the same threshold: traversing it is adventure, and here too adventure begins. Generically aware but not remotely parodic is Bunyan's autobiographical account, in *Grace Abounding*, of having had presented to him, 'in a kind of Vision', a small doorway through the wall which he experiences as separating him from the 'poor people of *Bedford*' whom he has heard speaking 'with such pleasantness of Scripture language', and through which he finds that he can pass at the cost of 'great striving' (*GA*, 15, 19).

---

[15] Erich Auerbach, 'The Knight Sets Forth', in Erich Auerbach, *Mimesis: The Representation of Reality in Western Literature*, tr. Willard R. Trask (1946; Princeton, NJ: Princeton University Press, 1953), 123–42.

[16] Chrétien de Troyes, *Arthurian Romances*, ed. and tr. D. D. R. Owen (London: Dent, 1993), 281.

[17] See also Auerbach, *Mimesis*, 128–29. Geography also becomes anomalous in this episode of transition: the knight has left Arthur's court, which is presumably in Britain, but without having made a sea-crossing now finds himself in a region of Brittany.

Narrative thresholds of this kind are also frequently defined by the receiving of a gift or gifts, by the making of some material exchange (even blows exchanged in fighting), or by some drastic shifting of vision, as may occur, for example, in the conventionally defined experience of falling in love. In passing through such a threshold, the action, along with its main agent, is in some way, and decisively, 'othered'. In characteristic romance narrative, such alteration is particularly recurrent. More will be said about this kind of narrative transition, but I shall return to it by way of another trope of narrative which is characteristic of romance.

Cognitive Dislocation in Romance

(B) The world of a romance narrative or certain of its components, especially its people, may be offered to the reader's knowledge in more than one fashion, and thus as more than one kind of thing. Medieval romance and historiography often explore the idea that the world as we have it developed in discrepant forms out of two separate foundations.[18] There is a world which we are well equipped to understand since it is one that human beings have created through constructing civilization, and subordinating to it or eradicating other forms of life. But there is also a world of monstrous and aberrant life, very difficult to conceptualize and never finally co-opted or destroyed in the establishment of an order shaped to human purposes.[19] St George's most famous act is, of course, the slaying of a monstrous dragon which is devastating a country and on the verge of devouring a princess, in respect of which he is a modified Perseus. As represented in the opening sequence of *The Seven Champions* this act constitutes a logical outcome of his people's foundation of Britain, as Brutus, descended from Aeneas,

> first made conquest of this Land of Britaine, then inhabited with Monsters, Gyants, and a kind of wild people without government, but by pollicie [wise political action], he overcame them and established good Lawes: where he founded the first foundation of new Troy [London].[20]

Britain exports this achievement when, soon after in narrational (*récit*) time, the youthful George exterminates the dragon which has been troubling Egypt.[21] It is in the character of chivalric romance that its heroes should determinedly destroy monsters, giants, and those practices of ruthless, uncourtly warrior-leaders which constitute

---

[18] This was not necessarily an impious proposition as considered from an orthodox Christian standpoint, since these originations were taken to have been subsequent to the creation of the world described in Genesis.

[19] See Walter Stephens, *Giants in those Days: Folklore, Ancient History, and Nationalism* (Lincoln, NE: University of Nebraska Press, 1989), 58–138.

[20] Johnson, *Seaven Champions*, sig. A3v.

[21] Johnson, *Seaven Champions*, sigs C1r–C2v.

'evil customs'. Narrative here seems to be representing the progressive, ineluctable overwhelming and suppression by the civilizing order of the wayward and chaotic one. But for *The Seven Champions*, like other romances narrating what purports to be a collective history, matters are not as straightforward as this, and its George is also the Knight of the Dragon in a very disconcerting fashion.

This knight-hero has what amounts to a monstrous birth, which is, among other things, the mark of his exceptionality. Carrying him in her womb, his mother is troubled by dreams which she relates to her husband: 'me thought I was conceived with a dreadful Dragon, which would bee the cause of his Parents death'. He duly consults an oracle, which proclaims:

> Sir Knight from whence thou cam'st returne,
> Thou hast a Sonne most strangely borne:
> A Dragon that shall split in twaine,
> Thy Ladies wombe with extreame paine:
> A Champion bold from thence shall spring,
> And practise many a wondrous thing.

What is terrible in these predictions is fulfilled. In giving birth to George his mother dies, 'dismembred of her wombe', his father dies of grief produced by both this loss and the subsequent unexplained disappearance of his son. But then again, the prediction of the final couplet is also fulfilled across the rest of the narrative, in that 'Dragon' in the oracle's pronouncement evidently refers to the valiant 'Champion'. When George is born, he is found already to bear skin markings in 'the lively forme of a Dragon', as well as a red cross on his right hand and a golden garter on his left leg (he was considered to have founded the Order of the Garter).[22] This is a signal departure from nature's ordinary ways and encapsulates the future form of George's achievement, further linking him to the dragon which is his destined antagonist.

This crossing of categories between 'human' and 'monstrous' seems to me to be logically inexplicable. And this, I am trying to suggest, defines its narrative function: what George the pre-eminent hero is in certain respects resists uniform conceptualization, or conceptualization from one standpoint. Johnson's narrative contains a character who presumably *is* capable of thinking these contradictions, but she is Kalib, the Medea-like witch or magician, medium of the oracular pronouncement, and abductor of the infant George. Kalib's is not a knowledge that we can have, or probably would want, given that the narration fashions her as repugnant. But she also presides over and in some sense guards, as secret, a future which we are to accept as good. Her cave contains not only George (whom she detains there during his childhood, regaling him with pleasures and eventually falling in love with him in a reversal of the Stockholm syndrome) but also, still more bizarrely, the six other champions, their horses, and their weapons,

---

[22] Johnson, *Seaven Champions*, sigs A2r, A2v, B1r.

with armour. George obtains the secret by a trick and releases them all, trapping Kalib in her cave.

This is what I mean by conceptual dislocation, and the Kalib episode is an important part of George's narrative establishment as the romance's central figure. It also affects our conception of this romance's virtual world, which is not as purged of strangeness by these good foundational acts and their consequences as we might otherwise wish to believe. I should also note that the opening narrative sequence of Johnson's romance, which extends for these purposes from his mother's conception of George and prophetic dreaming to his killing of the dragon in Egypt, produces an exemplary sequence of threshold transitions, among the more conspicuous of which are the turning of an ordinary birth to horror, introduction of supernatural commentary on what have seemed to be natural events via the dreams and, more insistently, the oracle, and George's removal to a cave which also contains the compelling secret, and so, much like George's birthmarks, encapsulates what will happen on the larger narrative scale. Transitions implying some alteration of 'world' and conceptual dislocations, (A) and (B) will, for the time being, cue our assessment of what is romance-like in Bunyan's writing.

ROMANCE CONVENTIONS IN *THE PILGRIM'S PROGRESS*

The Pilgrim's Progress defines, by virtue of being a journey narrative, numerous significant transitions which are often signalled through the landscape which the pilgrims traverse; as for example when Christian and Hopeful leave the way for the apparently easier going of By-Path-Meadow, exiting by a stile. This use of the narrative's virtual terrain is often, for the reader, self-evident and self-explanatory, as well as evocative of romance. It is, however, worth noting that the qualitative characteristics of the way, once Christian has reached it in passing through the '*Wicket-gate*' (*PP*, 10), do not necessarily alter with changes of its physical setting. As the By-Path-Meadow episode helps to show, the option of deviating from it is as fully available at the end as it is at the beginning: observing Ignorance's fate, the Dreamer comments, 'Then I saw that there was a way to Hell, even from the Gates of Heaven, as well as from the City of *Destruction*' (*PP*, 163). It is a shocking perception, but one supported by the narrative's whole snakes-and-ladders-like manner of unfolding.

This is one of several respects in which Bunyan invokes, but also provocatively manipulates, romance narrative conventions. Negotiation of the way and its difficulties, though involving some clear transitions, is not as transformatory as it sometimes looks; or rather it *is* transformatory, but in ways that are not straightforwardly apparent. It is worth considering some of the text's other transitions in this light. What happens to Christian between passing through the wicket gate and successfully fighting Apollyon is, surely, a large-scale, major transition and strong 'othering' of what has gone before, signalled in the most obvious manner by virtual terrain as the reader follows Christian's arduous crossing of the Hill Difficulty (says Christian as he begins the ascent, '*Better, tho difficult, th' right way to go, / Then wrong, though easie, where the end is woe*'; *PP*, 42). It encompasses several more transitions of smaller narrational span: passage through the initiatory experiences of the House of Interpreter (more on these shortly); confrontation and survival of the lions' threat; sojourn at the House Beautiful where Christian receives instruction, while gaining armour and a sword;[23] and, prior to this but also most emotionally charged and connotative of salvation, the mysterious releasing of Christian from his burden which goes with the bestowal on him, by 'three shining ones', of forgiveness for sin, new clothing, a mark on his forehead, and 'a Roll with a Seal upon it' (*PP*, 38). But, in a way that seems characteristic of Bunyan's narratorial procedures, the absolute or once-and-for-all transitionality of the second and fourth of these features is immediately qualified: as Christian does not know, but as the Dreamer perceives, the lions of which he is so afraid are in fact chained, and passing them is no great feat; and Christian, of course, inadvertently drops the roll which should be 'his Pass into the Cœlestial City' (*PP*, 43), obliging him to make an anguished retracing of the way by which he came in order to retrieve it.

The arming of Christian at the House Beautiful is Bunyan's clearest evocation of chivalric romance, cueing the reader for what follows quickly upon it: a large-scale, potentially mortal or otherwise decisive combat. Christian for the time being has the physical aspect of a knight, connotatively different from that of one whose '*Raggs*', symbolic of sin, have already been replaced supernaturally, before the Cross, by a 'change of Raiment', marking his conversion (*PP*, 8, 38, 55). Christian's temporary 'knighthood' opens up or makes available certain distinctive romance perspectives on the episodic sequence to which it belongs: Christian is a Fair Unknown, not least to himself, latently capable of achievement, though this is not necessarily a foregone conclusion. His trials, in their succession, resemble the trials which an unfledged knight meets 'on adventure' and which, if adroitly met—the genre, of course, encourages us to anticipate this with at least some confidence—become stages in his knightly initiation (Malory's *Tale of Gareth* culminates in his formal reception into the court as one of unimpeachably high status). Nevertheless, Bunyan's handling of these motifs also distances the text to some extent from the ethos of chivalry. As Christian approaches Apollyon, a terrible adversary, he considers flight but, on recalling that his back lacks armour and is therefore vulnerable should he turn, goes forward 'resolv[ing] to venture' (*PP*, 56). This is a sensible way of addressing the situation, but also a pragmatic and non-noble one: the *Morte D'Arthur*, for example, in its projection of conventional chivalric values would not accommodate the thought of turning back. Christian's weaponry is irrelevant, moreover, to his passage through the Valley of the Shadow of Death, which immediately follows his survival of the battle, where he meets 'things that cared not for [his] Sword, as did

---

[23] Its closest precedent in romance narrative accessible to Bunyan is the House of Holiness where Redcross sojourns in *The Faerie Queene*, Book 1, Canto 10.

Apollyon before' (*PP*, 63). From now on Christian's arming is narratorially ignored or forgotten, and Evangelist, on meeting him and Faithful prior to their arrival at the town of Vanity, encourages them to embrace the differently-centred fortitude which goes with martyrdom.

REINVENTION OF ROMANCE IN *THE PILGRIM'S PROGRESS*

I shall, however, turn to another section of what may be provisionally termed the 'transitions' sequence to consider what is probably the most innovatory narrative transition of all. I have spoken of romance as moving characteristically from a relatively ordinary ('like ours') world to one which is stranger, and which seems to hold out special possibilities of 'adventure', as in the case Chrétien's *Broceliande*. The entry of the narrative into this world—which offers more scope for fantasy, as closer to the stuff of dreams—is often signalled/effected by encounter with what Slavoj Žižek characterizes as 'some incomprehensible or ambiguous signifying fragment—a message in a bottle, a scrap of burned paper, or the babbling of some madman hinting that beyond a certain frontier, wonderful and/or horrible things are taking place'.[24] In *Sir Gawain and the Green Knight* the piece of anomalous signification is the semi-monstrous green challenger who erupts into Arthur's court, huge axe in one hand and peaceful holly branch in the other, not straightforwardly classifiable as 'knight' in spite of this romance's supplied modern title. In *The Faerie Queene* it is Arthur's dream of (or, possibly, physical encounter with) the Faerie Queene herself (see Book 1, Canto 9, stanzas 13–15), a numinous event which is also baffling and of undetermined ontological status, which has drawn him into the poem's Faeryland. But in *The Pilgrim's Progress* it is Bunyan's very ingenious co-option of the emblem-book tradition, the living (mainly) tableaux encountered in the House of Interpreter.

The instructive meaning of these tableaux is usually clear, or becomes clear (though perhaps least so in the case of the Man in the Iron Cage of Despair), but the scenes of knowledge presented in both *Part I* and *Part II* are so constructed as to provide a continuous epistemological wrong-footing of their would-be understander, whether considered in sequence or individually. A powerful psychological frisson is produced, for example, by the arrival of Christiana and Mercie, as directed by Interpreter, in an otherwise empty room containing a spider. Mercie's first response is '*Sir, I see nothing*' (*PP*, 200), while Christiana, deciding that the spider must be significant, constructs reasoned comparisons between it and her group in their present condition. But the radical act of recognition occurs in Mercie's sudden blush and the children's covering of their faces: in

---

[24] Slavoj Žižek, 'How to Give Body to a Deadlock?', in Juliet Flower MacCannell and Laura Zakarin (eds.), *Thinking Bodies* (Stanford, CA: Stanford University Press, 1994), 63–77 (63).

some sense each person present *is* the venomous and ugly spider, in a manner beyond conceptual specification—horror occasioned by it converts directly into horror occasioned by oneself. The tableaux in both parts, then, do not straightforwardly deliver statements but, as riddling and sometimes uncanny, induce a mind-set of heightened vigilance, intelligence, and intuitive openness; they are the text's distinctive initiation and mode of transition into *this* distinctive world of arduous adventure and discovery.

Here Bunyan has reinvented a romance narrative structure. There is also considerable intellectual and imaginative drive, I would claim, in his reinvention of certain romance motifs. The Enchanted Ground is at first sight difficult to source, though the manner of the pilgrims' testing resonates with some other narratives: they must stay awake, or they are lost; Orpheus must not look back as he leads Eurydice out of the Underworld; Spenser's Guyon in Mammon's Cave will be torn to pieces by a fiend if, impelled by tiredness, he sits on the silver stool which his host has offered (see Book 2, Canto 7, stanzas 63–4). As Michael Davies points out, *Part I*'s way of addressing the Enchanted Ground's seductive powers is to distract the reader by means of an instructive dialogue which has nothing to do with the romance matter in hand: here, the Ground is not encountered and negotiated, so much as narratorially avoided.[25] Matters are different, however, in *Part II*, which opens up a vista of obstructive, uninviting muddy land which is also contradictorily laid out with arbours, 'Warm, and promising much refreshing to the Pilgrims; [...] beautified with *Greens*, furnished with *Benches*, and *Settles*' (*PP*, 296–97). As diabolic, and inimical to human welfare in its physical attractions, the Enchanted Ground is the antitype of Beulah, laid out with comparable 'Orchards and Vineyards' (*PP*, 303), with which it is strangely contiguous.

Nevertheless, I would suggest that it is possible to find a further intertextual correlate for Bunyan's Ground in Spenser's Faeryland. With the latter, we have among other things a telescoped and admonitory rereading of *The Faerie Queene* itself, whose numerous representations of 'the delightful place' (*locus amoenus*), ethically charged in varying ways, are, in this perspective, better avoided altogether. The imaginative charms of *The Faerie Queene*'s Faeryland would thus be ones to which, in a *Pilgrim's Progress* perspective, its narrative processes excessively submit. Consider, for example, Spenser's narrator's celebration of simply being 'in' this other feigned world:

> The waies, through which my weary steps I guyde,
>   In this delightfull land of Faery,
>   Are so exceeding spacious and wyde,
>   And sprinckled with such sweet variety,
>   Of all that pleasant is to eare or eye,
>   That I nigh rauisht with rare thoughts delight,
>   My tedious trauell doe forget thereby [...] (Book 6, Proem, stanza 1)

---

[25] Michael Davies, '"Stout and Valiant Champions for God": The Radical Reformation of Romance in *The Pilgrim's Progress*', in N. H. Keeble (ed.), *John Bunyan: Reading Dissenting Writing* (Bern: Peter Lang, 2002), 103–32 (111–13).

One supposes that Bunyan would have read this and the passages which contextualize it, on the hypothesis that he did read them, with mounting irritation: surely these *should* be symbolic journeys which get somewhere or demonstrate something, not wanderings in a gratuitously invented landscape of 'delight'. The Bunyan who made creative use of romance conventions was also a critically engaged reader of romances, possibly including Spenser's, the allegorical fable circulating in his era whose purposes—especially in its first book—most closely resemble his own. From *Part II*'s Enchanted Ground sequence we can perhaps infer something of the nature of his criticism.

The Interpreter episodes, as romance-initiatory sequences, contain elements of cognitive dissonance as well as enacting narrative transition. I turn now more fully to matter (B): *The Pilgrim's Progress*'s establishment of conceptual dislocation and crossings between explanatory categories, conspicuous in its representation of monsters. Apollyon is one of those composite story creatures who violate natural form in assembling features of different species, some fabulous in themselves:

> [H]e was cloathed with scales like a Fish (and they are his pride) he had Wings like a Dragon, feet like a Bear, and out of his belly came Fire and Smoak, and his mouth was as the mouth of a Lion. (*PP*, 56)

Nevertheless, this nightmare creature also has some of the characteristics of a human being, and even of a particular type of human being: 'When he was come up to *Christian*, he beheld him with a disdainful countenance, and thus began to question with him.' As is generally recognized, the encounter between Apollyon, the pretended lord ('*Prince and God*' of the City of Destruction and its '*Countrey*'; *PP*, 56), and Christian, whom he treats as his errant retainer and servant, drips class feeling and has strong contemporary resonance. There is much to recommend Michael Davies's suggestion that Apollyon's language references 'Restoration Anglican polemics [justifying] the coercion of separatists', like the members of Bunyan's community, 'into the established church'.[26] It is a series of smoothly articulated cajolings and threats; in context, intransigent, potentially violent resistance is appropriate, and even obligatory.

But the episode also focuses on the nature of such resistance and its mental–moral requirements. Bullied verbally by his would-be oppressor, Christian develops an intransigent counter-rhetoric: 'to speak truth, I like his [my Prince's] Service, his Wages, his Servants, his Government, his Company, and Countrey better then thine' (*PP*, 57). This is Christian's impressive moment of fierce, absolutely committed resistance: some of the rights of the case may in fact be Apollyon's, Christian did indeed give him fealty in the earthly city, but Christian is not going to let this evil, sneering toff carry the argument, and is spoiling for the fight which obviously impends. It may be said, then, that in order to fight Apollyon, one has to become, temporarily, somewhat like him. The situation is anomalous and produces a transgression of accepted moral boundaries, a willed

---

[26] Davies, '"Stout and Valiant Champions for God"', 122; and see Chapter 14 in this volume.

disposition to violence, different from Christian's ordinary soldier's or potential martyr's resoluteness, in those who meet its requirements. When Christian finally contrives to stab Apollyon in his vitals, the smile of triumph is his (see *PP*, 60).

Giant Despair is, similarly, a fabled monster, this time a distension and distortion of the human, but a figure endowed with the doltishness which typifies the giant of fable (one might compare Homer's Polyphemos). The episode is shot through with dark humour: Despair's wife wants him to finish off the prisoners more quickly, apparently in the spirit of tidying the house; Despair also has fits, or *absences*—it is bad to be cudgelled, but bad in a different way to be physically maltreated by someone who tends to lose the thread of what he is doing. My central point, however, is that, incarcerated by Despair and envisaging suicide, which Despair recommends as the obvious way out, Christian takes on a giant-redolent mental inertia and borderline stupidity, the state out of which he has to be dragged by Hopeful. It is in recalling that he has possessed all along the key which can unlock the prison's doors that Christian recovers ordinary, functional intelligence. All of this is convincing enough with regard to the mentally lowering effects of despair and melancholia. The presence of monsters in romance can accompany partial alignment of other narrative agents with the monstrous or denatured, exploring aspects of mental life otherwise less amenable to reflection.

'Adventure' in *The Pilgrim's Progress*

In the House of Interpreter Christian is shown 'a man of a very stout countenance' who, finding himself barred from the palace before him by a group of armed men, fights his way in, 'cutting and hacking most fiercely', and is received by figures clad in gold who clothe him with the same garments. In construing this tableau Christian is neither given nor, it seems, in need of Interpreter's assistance. What he has seen emblematizes the winning of salvation, and is an actual display of valour; his comment is, 'I think verily I know the meaning of this' (*PP*, 33–4). The reader can say much the same: the passage is without irony, and is one of several which straightforwardly enjoin mental or, where called for, physical fortitude. Such are the attributes of an effective soldier and, in higher social styling, of a chivalric knight. It is in this spirit, for example, that Hopeful, seeing Christian inclining to defeatism when in the giant's clutches, calls on him to '*remember how thou playedst the man at* Vanity-Fair' (*PP*, 117). Mr Feeble-mind is also *Part II*'s salutary reminder that lack of fortitude does not necessarily prevent an individual from being a follower of Christ. More simply and less exclusively, fortitude is both beneficial to have and—as projected, say, in Great-heart—of major potential use to others, the perception of which can again form part of romance storytelling in the chivalric convention. In *Part II* the successful fight with Apollyon is recalled as one of Christian's most illustrious achievements; 'here', remarks Great-heart, '*Christian* did […] play the Man', becoming comparable to '*Hercules*' (*PP*, 240). Bunyan does not typically reference classical mythology, and the compliment stands out.

But, shortly before paying this tribute, as it were soldier-to-soldier, Great-heart has produced a comment which might support a very different assessment of Christian's victory as accomplished in battle: it was unnecessary! The fight need not have occurred, but was the consequence of a prior, and not even in itself very grievous, moral lapse: the 'slips', implying small failures of humility, which Christian 'took' in descending towards the Valley of Humiliation, 'For they that get *slips there*, must look for *Combats here*' (*PP*, 236). Can the overcoming of Apollyon be both an illustrious achievement, potentially exemplary for all, and an action in which someone better or wiser would simply not have become involved, avoiding it, moreover, through the taking of minimal precautions?

I would suggest, however, that this question does not properly apply to the text, because it does not correspond to the way in which the reader is being invited to construe it. To explain why this is so, I'll examine a different episode. As the pilgrims of *Part II* negotiate the Enchanted Ground, night falls, and their experienced guide, temporarily losing the way, is 'put to a stand'. Reaching into his pocket, however, Great-heart produces 'a Map of all ways leading to, or from the Celestial City', striking a light to consult it. The Dreamer comments, 'had he not here been careful to look in his Map, [the pilgrims] had all, in probability, been smuthered in the Mud', given that an unfathomed pit of mud lies just before them. This observation triggers the further thought, 'who, that goeth on Pilgrimage, but would have one of these Maps about him?' This map signifies, as the marginal gloss informs us, the Bible, '*God's Book*' (*PP*, 297). But it does not, of course, look like a book within the purview of the fable, it looks like a map; and the Bible which exists externally to the fable is not, conversely, much like a piece of cartography. *Grace Abounding* describes the mode of encounter with scriptural texts which formed the major part of Bunyan's experience of conversion: a mode of encounter that continues in later spiritual experiences as his writings describe and enact them. It is freer in its approach than the reading for interpretation within controlled parameters enforced by the Anglican Church, and the more establishment-oriented or more socially conservative Dissenting churches. The sequence in which texts accrue meaning vital to the reader is determined neither by their scriptural ordering nor by that of an already accepted controlling argument, such that reading expounds an already identified doctrine. Rather, reading of the Scriptures here is 'in adventure'. What accrues in this adventure is both an essentially unpredictable self-discovery—in the sense of a discovery of individual orientation towards truth, valid at a particular juncture in life—and reflection upon it, which makes for self-understanding and a wise taking of action, perhaps in a searching for the next truth which will necessarily involve further perusal of the Scriptures. This is not much like consulting a map, but it *functions* like consulting a map, in that an individual taking of the way emerges from it as an action in progress. It resembles dealings with a map in the broad sense that a set of significations there for everyone in the same form and in collective possession—a regional map, the vernacular Scriptures—is also the means by which an entirely individual route can be determined: a single provision of information as equally relevant at a personal level to Great-heart and Feeble-mind, let us say, as it is to Faithful and to Hopeful.

I am not suggesting that Bunyan read the Bible as if it were predominantly a romance.[27] Yet, from Bunyan's standpoint, the individual's reading of the Bible is indeed 'in adventure', and a vital matter of personal discovery. This is the condition under which it has unconditional pertinence to every reader whatsoever and, returning to the metaphorics of the just-cited passage, unlimited capacity to define an individual, rightful path. The marginal glosses to *The Pilgrim's Progress* remind the reader, if this were not already evident, that its armature as action and statement is the Bible, and the Bible in the form in which the fable of a journey cues readings from it or memories of it, often individual verses or phrases or even isolated words. Its pilgrims are individually 'in adventure'—moving towards the Celestial City, losing the path to it—against a background of allusive reference to the Scriptures which is itself 'in adventure'. This is the Scriptures considered as an extremely large corpus of statements (in traditional commentary, *sententiae*) to which the reader does not have entirely organized and systematized access, of the kinds that might be provided by very exceptional memory or sophisticated computer software. It is there, in principle, to be accessed freely and with some degree of contingency, at any point of or level in its textual formation.

The Pilgrim's Progress plainly cannot provide separate threads of narrative development for every reader or every type of reader—although a considerable gallery of human types does accrue across its two parts. But it does engage simultaneously the human capacities to signify and handle signification, and to interpret what has been signified. Its mimetic-interpretative 'literal level' accrues for the reader as a coalescence of both activities: understanding of what happens to the narrative agents, projected into the narrative scene as continuously hazardous and rewarding (or admonitory) adventure, is conditioned by the scriptural text and what we construe in it as having application to them. Great-heart's account of what operates causally in Christian's fight with Apollyon, offered to Christiana's group as they reach the scene of the battle, is valid in itself while being different in important essentials from Christian's experience at the time, and our own too, in that Christian's perspective is one of those which yields our own interpretation of the fight when it occurs. To put it another way, the fight and what it signifies pertain to Christian in the same way as does the armour which he is given and puts on in the House Beautiful—this becomes for the time being *his* armour: an appurtenance which defines him. In this same aspect the fight which ensues is specifically his, in the context of this particular action of reading. The principle becomes familiar in the narrative's retellings of literal-level (*histoire*) event sequences: Faithful's passage through the Valley of the Shadow of

---

[27] Harold Golder claims with disparaging intent that the Bible 'became a sort of romance to him': 'John Bunyan's Hypocrisy', 331. But evaluation of such a claim partly depends, of course, on one's underlying conception of romance. I take the view that, as a heightening of ordinary narrativity, romance is always a potentiality latent in the making of narrative, and not one that does narrative invention itself a discredit. Numerous biblical narratives have the formal characteristics of romance, for example, the story of Joseph in Genesis.

Death differs considerably from Christian's, Christiana and her group's experience of the Valley of Humiliation has a fairly different shape from Christian's, crossing Jordan is probably different for every pilgrim, and so on.

Since in *The Pilgrim's Progress* interpretation of the Scriptures is 'in adventure', the interpretation of what it offers as lived experience, for which the Scriptures are the touchstone, is also 'in adventure'. As has been said, the literal action of the narrative is in many respects a tissue of reference to scriptural texts. But what, therefore, *is* the narrative's 'literal action?' Here Bunyan's mode of allegorical invention departs from those of Chaucer and Spenser—is so to speak 'de-Renaissancized'—and is more closely aligned with Langland's. Chaucer, influenced by French dream visions, and Spenser, influenced by Italian romance epics, establish an aesthetically pleasing and informationally self-sufficient 'literal level' of scene and action for their allegorical narratives: it is the dream which Chaucer's narrator is having, and in which he can participate at times like one narrative agent among others; it is the visual–verbal action which Spenser elaborates, and that his impersonated narrator witnesses in a spirit of fascination. Spenser's narrative agents themselves respond vividly, generally in the ways that romance characters would, to the impressions and demands made by the virtual world of which they form a part; and it is generally for the reader to work out, with cues from the dazzled narrator's commentary and some camouflaged decoding of information (often through naming or punning), what the action in hand might convey as allegorical communication.

Bunyan's 'literal level' of action, on the other hand, is, for both the participating narrative agents and the reader, a composite of what is available through signification (the shown, the offered for hearing) and what has to be accessed through interpretation, initiation into which as 'adventure' is, as has been pointed out, passage through the House of Interpreter with its epistemological puzzle tableaux, functioning as a narrative portal. Reading *The Pilgrim's Progress*, like being one of its committed pilgrims, thus inculcates an attitude to lived experience which is both responsively direct and interpretatively open. One of the models for Bunyan's narrational practice seems to be the more semiotically troubled 'literal level' of *Piers Plowman*, a quasi-surreal, Boschian composite of idea and terrain, statements of universal import, and irreducibly individual perceptions. At the same time, there is an instructive contrast between Bunyan's narrative agents and Spenser's, who act but do not at the same time actively puzzle, thereby setting interpretative conundrums which exist primarily for the reader to solve. This is a way of saying that for both readers and narrative agents, their delegates, the crucial within-fable instructors are Evangelist—the Scriptures as interpreted from the standpoint of the Gospels—and Interpreter; which implies that every individual reader, cued to acts of interpretation by this semiotic-interpretative interplay, acts with the perception of discovering her/his own 'plain sense' of what is happening in the adventure of traversing the text. The meta-romance of *The Pilgrim's Progress*, in a highly innovatory conception which much affected the development of the novel, is what flows from entrustment of oneself to the adventure of individualized reading.

Suggested Reading

Cooper, Helen, *The English Romance in Time: Transforming Motifs from Geoffrey of Monmouth to the Death of Shakespeare* (Oxford: Oxford University Press, 2004).

Davies, Michael, '"Stout and Valiant Champions for God": The Radical Reformation of Romance in *The Pilgrim's Progress*', in N. H. Keeble (ed.), *John Bunyan: Reading Dissenting Writing* (Bern: Peter Lang, 2002), 103–32.

Davis, Nick, 'Rethinking Narrativity: A Return to Aristotle and Some Consequences', *StoryWorlds*, 4 (2012), 1–24.

Golder, Harold, 'John Bunyan's Hypocrisy', *North American Review*, 223 (1926), 323–32.

Newcomb, Lori Humphrey, '"Social Things": The Production of Popular Culture in the Reception of Robert Greene's *Pandosto*', *ELH*, 61 (1994), 753–81.

Pooley, Roger, 'The Structure of *The Pilgrim's Progress*', *Essays in Poetics*, 4 (1979), 59–70.

Sharrock, Roger, 'Life and Story in *The Pilgrim's Progress*', in Vincent Newey (ed.), *The Pilgrim's Progress: Critical and Historical Views* (Liverpool: Liverpool University Press, 1980), 49–60.

Simons, John (ed.), *Guy of Warwick and Other Chapbook Romances: Six Tales from the Popular Literature of Pre-Industrial England* (Exeter: University of Exeter Press, 1998).

Spufford, Margaret, *Small Books and Pleasant Histories: Popular Fiction and its Readership in Seventeenth-Century England* (Athens, GA: University of Georgia Press, 1982).

CHAPTER 23

THE PROSE STYLE OF JOHN BUNYAN

MARY ANN LUND

And immediately the King sent an Executioner, and commanded his head to be brought, Mark 6. 27. The story is concerning *Herod* and *John the Baptist*. *Herod's* dancing girl had begged *John Baptist's* head: and nothing but his head must serve her turn; well girl, thou shalt have it. Have it? I, but it will be long first. No, thou shalt have it now, just now, immediately, *And immediately he sent an executioner, and commanded his head to be brought*.

Here is sudden work for sufferers; here is no intimation beforehand. The executioner comes to *John*; now, whether he was at dinner or asleep, or whatever he was about, the bloody man bolts in upon him, and the first word he salutes him with, is, Sir, strip, lay down your neck; *For I come to take away your head*. But hold, stay, wherefore? pray, let me commit my Soul to God. No, I must stay, I am in hast; slap, says his sword, and off falls the good mans head. This is sudden work, work that stays for no man: work that must be done by and by, immediately or 'tis not worth a rush. *I will*, said she, *that thou give me by and by in a charger, the head of John the Baptist*. Yes, she came in hast, and as hastily the commandment went forth, and immediately his head was brought. (*MW*, 10: 25–6)

BUNYAN's retelling of John the Baptist's death, in the late work *Seasonable Counsel* (1684), epitomizes the energetic and arresting narrative style which he developed during a writing life of over thirty years. He begins with the bare statement of action from the Gospel account, using the word 'immediately' as a prompt for his own version. With the efficiency of the practised storyteller, Bunyan conjures character in a few short phrases: the dancing girl, Herod's wife's daughter, is pettish, wilful ('nothing but his head must serve her turn'), and swift to complain, while Herod is the indulgent stepfather whose attempts to placate her are captured in his soothing repetitions: 'thou shalt have it [. . .] thou shalt have it now, just now, immediately'. Bunyan cuts out the wider features of the story—the reasons for John's imprisonment, the influence of Herodias over her daughter—to create a tight family drama, evoked particularly through the rhythms of colloquial speech.

The imaginative expansion of the Gospel continues as Bunyan depicts a scene not in the Bible accounts (Mark 6:27 merely notes that the executioner 'went and beheaded him in the prison'). Again, speech provides the nexus of dramatic incident, conveying both its rapidity and John's surprised reaction through the abrupt, choppy exchange. There is no time allowed for reflection, argument, or pleading, no articulation of remorse or doubt, as there is in Shakespeare's executioner scenes (such as the murder of Clarence in *Richard III*, 1.4; even the hastily ordered beheading of Hastings in the same play, 3.4, allows the condemned a moment first to prophesy). In Bunyan's text the sword joins in as another speaker, almost interrupting its owner with its vocal 'slap'. Unusually, Bunyan strikes a comic note, here at odds with the gospel narrative. His John is not the inspired prophet who baptized Jesus but a bewildered man ('hold, stay, wherefore?'), taken off guard. Bunyan's wider argument is that suffering can come without warning, and every sentence of this extract adds force to his point. The devices of repetition are used thickly here—anadiplosis ('sudden work, work'), anaphora ('work that stays for no man: work that must be done'), polyptoton ('in hast, […] hastily')—along with multiple synonyms for speed, one of which ('by and by') ties the extract's colloquialisms in with the Authorized Version's language. The style of this passage is by no means sparse; indeed, it is expansive compared to the Bible version. Yet it achieves its effects economically, and moreover matches narrative pace to content: implicitly, the gap between Herod's command and its execution is little more than the time it takes to read these two paragraphs.

This passage demonstrates in miniature the peerless and distinctive nature of Bunyan's stylistic achievement, which this chapter will further explore through an analysis of *Grace Abounding to the Chief of Sinners* (1666) and *The Pilgrim's Progress* (1678). Two features I have highlighted—his use of dialogue and his control of pace as part of the experience of the text—will form focal points of the discussion, which, given the breadth of this topic, can only be suggestive, not comprehensive.[1] In what follows, I aim to demonstrate the conscious decision-making and control Bunyan exerts over his style: despite the characterization of his writing as homely and simple, he is adept at moving across multiple registers and voices. Like the exchanges between Herod and his stepdaughter, and John and the executioner, the dialogue in *The Pilgrim's Progress* reveals Bunyan's skill in creating memorable characters, but moreover posits speech as a dimension of one's inner state. The correct interpretation of that language becomes a training in spiritual discernment. Then again, even the experienced believer in that text fails through misinterpretation, and Bunyan suggests the entangled—and entangling—nature of seemingly fine language. Another means by which he shapes his writing to reinforce spiritual lessons is through narrative pacing. The punctuation of dramatic

---

[1] For further discussion of other important facets of Bunyan's style, see Chapters 5, 20, and 21 in this volume.

incident with reflection and discussion, the intercutting of swift action with lengthier, more complex trials makes for variety and a compelling story, while also allowing the reader to enter into thought processes and imaginative experiences paralleling those of the pilgrim: *'This Book will make a Traveller of thee'* (*PP*, 6). Before analysing these features, though, I will consider Bunyan's reputation as a prose stylist, and his own conception of the act of writing.

BUNYAN THE STYLIST

'It is always dangerous to talk too long about style': so warned C. S. Lewis in his essay on Bunyan, and many commentators would seem to endorse this attitude.[2] For much of literary history, Bunyan's prose style has typically been characterized through a few brief epithets: it is in 'the lowest style of English' (Samuel Taylor Coleridge); 'a homespun style, not a manufactured one' (Robert Southey); a 'homely dialect, the dialect of plain working men' (Thomas Babington Macaulay); 'admired by all who prefer the force of plain speech to the devices of rhetoric' (Robert Bridges, who tellingly continues, 'I need describe it no further than to say that it is as direct as possible').[3] Although his writing has become a byword for plainness, homeliness, directness, and popular vigour, attention to Bunyan's style has rarely been sustained; it is almost as if, to follow Lewis's remarks, serious critical scrutiny might shatter the effects created through natural energy rather than conscious artistry.

Bunyan is recognized to have a distinctive style, but is not often considered as a stylist, at least until relatively recently. The highly influential stylistic analyses of Renaissance prose by Morris Croll, George Williamson, and Robert Adolph found their protagonists in Bacon, Andrewes, Browne, Milton, and Tillotson but had little to say about Bunyan, whose prose does not fit into models of Ciceronianism and Senecanism, or the rise of the new science.[4] Over the last half-century, the growing interest in Nonconformist literary voices has cast more light on Bunyan's style, especially in the context of Restoration debates over reason and revelation, and the language in which spiritual truths should be expressed.[5] Yet the subject has still received markedly less critical attention than it has

---

[2] C. S. Lewis, 'The Vision of John Bunyan', in Walter Hooper (ed.), *C. S. Lewis: Selected Literary Essays* (Cambridge: Cambridge University Press, 1969), 146–53 (151).

[3] These critical assessments are gathered in Roger Sharrock (ed.), *The Pilgrim's Progress: A Casebook* (London: Macmillan, 1976), 53, 57, 76, 112.

[4] Bunyan is absent from Max Patrick, Robert O. Evans, and John M. Wallace (eds.), *Style, Rhetoric, and Rhythm: Essays by Morris W. Croll* (Princeton, NJ: Princeton University Press, 1966), and from George Williamson, *The Senecan Amble: A Study in Prose Form from Bacon to Collier* (London: Faber, 1951). He receives brief commentary in Robert Adolph, *The Rise of Modern Prose Style* (Cambridge, MA: MIT Press, 1968), 273–76.

[5] See N. H. Keeble, *The Literary Culture of Nonconformity in Later Seventeenth-Century England* (Leicester: Leicester University Press, 1987), 240–62; Roger Pooley, 'Plain and Simple: Bunyan and Style', in N. H. Keeble (ed.), *John Bunyan: Conventicle and Parnassus* (Oxford: Clarendon Press, 1988), 91–110.

with writers such as Bacon and Browne, whose stylistic artistry is seen as a high-water mark of seventeenth-century prose.

The general reluctance to think about Bunyan as a stylist—epitomized by Robert Bridges's assessment—stems partly from the author's own claims about his approach to writing. In his preface to *Grace Abounding*, Bunyan declares that:

> *I could also have stept into a stile much higher then this in which I have here discoursed, and could have adorned all things more then here I have seemed to do: but I dare not:* God *did not play in convincing of me; the* Devil *did not play in tempting of me; neither did I play when I sunk as into a bottomless pit, when* the pangs of hell caught hold upon me: *wherefore I may not play in my relating of them, but be plain and simple, and lay down the thing as it was.* (GA, 3–4)

A cursory reading of this passage can be misleading, since Bunyan is not saying that he eschews stylistic considerations altogether. Instead, he carefully discriminates between his own, serious-minded, 'plain and simple' method and one which is ornate, high, and consequently frivolous, appealing to the long-rooted (and originally classical) conception of the three 'genera dicendi': low/plain, middle, and grand/high.[6] In arguing that the weightiness of his subject precludes the use of a higher style, he rejects a tradition which considered those two eminently suitable for each other. For George Puttenham, 'the matters […] that concern the Gods and divine things are highest of all other to be couched in writing' and demand a grand style, whereas 'the base and low matters be the doings of the common artificer, serving man, yeoman, groome, husbandman, day-labourer, sailer, shepheard, swynard, and such like of homely calling, degree and bringing up' and should be expressed in the lowest.[7] This division, based upon and reinforcing social 'degree', did not account for the common artificer being concerned with divine things, nor for God being concerned with the common artificer. Yet the tinker who urged his readers to remember '*the Close, the Milk-house, the Stable, the Barn, and the like, where* God *did visit your Soul*' (GA, 3), saw stylistic ornamentation as not only superfluous, but a barrier to communicating the truth.

But is Bunyan's claim to be 'plain and simple' accurate? The beginning of *Grace Abounding* might suggest otherwise:

> In this my relation of the merciful working of God upon my Soul, it will not be amiss, if in the first place, I do, in a few words, give you a hint of my pedigree, and manner of bringing up; that thereby the goodness and bounty of God towards me, may be the more advanced and magnified before the sons of men.
>
> For my descent then, it was, as is well known by many, of a low and inconsiderable generation; my fathers house being of that rank that is meanest, and most despised of all the families in the Land. (*GA*, 5)

---

[6] See Debora Shuger, 'Conceptions of Style', in Glyn P. Norton (ed.), *The Cambridge History of Literary Criticism, Vol. 3* (Cambridge: Cambridge University Press, 1999), 176–86.

[7] George Puttenham, *The Arte of English Poesie* (1589), 127.

The slightly stiff formality of this opening is in marked contrast to the extract from *Seasonable Counsel*. Its sentences are formal, periodic, and hypotactic, the first using notably complex syntax to usher in its ideas: the main verb—'give'—is delayed until well into the sentence, separated from its subject and appearing via the periphrastic 'it will not be amiss, if'. Bunyan employs hendiadys repeatedly in a dense array of synonymic or near-synonymic pairings: 'goodness and bounty', 'advanced and magnified', 'low and inconsiderable', 'meanest, and most despised'. These couplings highlight the distinctly biblical sound of this passage: 'goodness and bounty'—a widely used phrase in early modern religious writing—is not a direct scriptural quotation but calls to mind other such combinations: 'goodnes and mercie' (Psalm 23:6), 'goodnesse, and trueth' (Exodus 34:6); 'sons of men' echoes a phrase used of Christ, but also of humankind (e.g. Ezekiel 2:1).[8] Finally, the vocabulary mixes polysyllabic, Latinate, or Anglo-Norman words ('pedegree', 'magnified', 'inconsiderable') with a simpler Old English lexis ('goodness', 'low', 'meanest').

The two sentences are thus by no means unshaped, and their stylistic register is fairly high. Notably, though, Bunyan does not sustain this level throughout his narrative, and in many ways this opening is uncharacteristic of *Grace Abounding*. The following passage (on his reaction to a sermon about Sabbath-breaking) seems more representative:

> This, for that instant, did benum the sinews of my best delights, and did imbitter my former pleasures to me: but behold, it lasted not; for before I had well dined, the trouble began to go off my minde, and my heart returned to its old course: but Oh how glad was I, that this trouble was gone from me, and that the fire was put out, that I might sin again without controul! (*GA*, 10)

Here the clauses are nearly all connected paratactically, following both the temporal sequence and Bunyan's change of heart. The rhythm is looser and the clauses shorter than those earlier sentences, giving the impression of speech rather than a rhetorical sequence of formally balanced cola. The corporeal quality of his writing, often remarked upon by critics, is in evidence in the image of benumbed sinews (in the first edition, the experience is imagined to 'cut' the sinews, a far more violent picture).[9] References to specific times ('for that instant', 'before I had well dined') tie emotional and spiritual experiences to the immediate moment, to the doings of the common artificer. As he continues, 'when I had satisfied nature with my food, I shook the Sermon out of my mind' (*GA*, 10), bodily repletion is clearly connected to his renewed inward complacency.

---

[8] All Bible quotations are taken from *Holy Bible: 1611 King James Version* (Grand Rapids, MI: Zondervan, 2011). This is a facsimile of the original 1611 Bible (omitting the Apocrypha).

[9] See Nigel Smith, 'Bunyan and the Language of the Body in Seventeenth-Century England', in Anne Laurence, W. R. Owens, and Stuart Sim (eds.), *John Bunyan and his England, 1628–88* (London: Hambledon Press, 1990), 161–74; Michael Davies, *Graceful Reading: Theology and Narrative in the Works of John Bunyan* (Oxford: Oxford University Press, 2002), 81–116.

Bunyan is hence in control of a number of linguistic registers, and if he uses a more ornate style only rarely, he is nonetheless capable of employing it (as he says, he '*could also have stept into a stile much higher then this*'). His language may be characteristically 'plain and simple', paratactic, colloquial, biblical, corporeal, immediate, emotionally arresting, as so many generations of readers have found it, yet each one of those descriptions needs some qualification to be fully accurate. In the passage just quoted, for instance, there is a striking example of how Bunyan uses 'but' to signal repeated changes of direction and heart. This paratactic mode seems characteristic of *Grace Abounding* as a whole where, again and again, a conclusion is reassessed, an emotional state reversed, a conviction undermined: 'then I chose to stand under a main Beam that lay over thwart the Steeple from side to side, thinking there I might stand sure: But then I should think again' (*GA*, 13); 'But before many weeks were over I began to dispond again' (*GA*, 61); 'But, notwithstanding all these helps and blessed words of grace, yet that of *Esaus* selling of his birthright would still at times distress my Conscience' (*GA*, 68). One reason that his use of the word 'but' is so prominent in *Grace Abounding* is that it often begins a paragraph (see, for example, the sequence on pages 60–1), along with other common words such as 'Yet', 'Then', 'Now', reinforcing a sense of both conflicting impulses and temporal immediacy. However, a statistical comparison of Bunyan's text with two other autobiographical writings of similar lengths—John Donne's *Devotions upon Emergent Occasions* (1624) and Sir Thomas Browne's *Religio Medici* (1642/43)—reveals that Bunyan uses the word 'but' no more frequently than either of these stylistically more elevated writers.[10] Caution should thus be exercised in claiming that Bunyan uses parataxis more often than other writers; it is the specific way he employs it which is distinctive.

Turning to another feature, Bunyan's prose undeniably has strong biblical overtones, yet the ways in which Scripture surfaces in his texts are tremendously varied: from the Bible quotations in *Grace Abounding* which 'made me sick' (*GA*, 24) or 'darted in upon me' (*GA*, 64), forming points of obsessive self-focus, to subtle and sometimes even seemingly unconscious echoes throughout his writing, as when Christian 'was come to the *Arbour* again, where for a while he sat down and wept' (*PP*, 44), an echo of the Israelites' lament in Psalm 137:1 in the Prayer Book Psalter ('By the waters of Babylon we sate downe and wept: when we remembred (thee) O Sion').[11] Moreover, as I have already remarked and as has long been a point of debate, Bunyan can often give the impression of scripturalism when he is not directly quoting from or alluding to the Bible.[12]

---

[10] According to my search using online texts on Project Gutenberg, www.gutenberg.org, accessed 19 August 2011, the word 'but' appears in the following frequency: *Grace Abounding*, 1.06% (460 of 43,313 words); *Devotions*, 1.11% (563 of 50,706 words); *Religio Medici*, 1.16% (383 of 32,885).

[11] *The Booke of Common Prayer, with the Psalter or Psalmes of David* (1611), G5v.

[12] See C. S. Lewis, 'The Literary Impact of the Authorised Version', in Hooper (ed.), *C. S. Lewis: Selected Literary Essays*, 126–45 (139–40); Pooley, 'Plain and Simple', 97–101. See also Chapter 24 in this volume.

Style and Speech

As these remarks have suggested, for Bunyan, style is far more than ornament: it is an index of the salvific process. When Christian and Faithful enter Vanity Fair, they cause wonder among the residents at 'their Speech; for few could understand what they said; they naturally spoke the language of *Canaan*; But they that kept the *fair*, were the men of this World: So that from one end of the *fair* to the other, they seemed *Barbarians* each to the other' (*PP*, 90). Their language indicates both their origin (as sinners from the City of Destruction) and their destination: 'In that day shall five cities in the land of Egypt speak the language of Canaan, and sweare to the Lord of hostes: one shalbe called the citie of destruction' (Isaiah 19:18). In demarcating them from the people of Vanity Fair, their speech forms a gesture of dissent from the town's values as strident as their refusal to buy its wares. The clash of languages mirrors major cultural conflicts over the stylistic identities of Anglicanism and Nonconformity, and ownership of the plain style in the years following the Restoration.[13] Christian and Faithful's linguistic alienation may be a source of confusion, but it is also a matter of pride.

Speech good and bad permeates Bunyan's writings. While *Grace Abounding* may have little direct dialogue, its language is resoundingly vocal as Bunyan wrestles with Scripture and with temptation: 'methinks I hear still with what a loud voice these words, *Simon, Simon*, sounded in my ears' (*GA*, 30); 'still answering, as fast as the destroyer said, *Sell him*; I will not, I will not, I will not, I will not' (*GA*, 42). In *The Pilgrim's Progress*, speech not only dramatizes the debates and crises experienced internally in *Grace Abounding*, but also provides a crucial means of rehearsing earlier experiences and endorsing spiritual lessons, as when Christian recounts his adventures so far to Piety, Prudence, and Charity (*PP*, 47–52). As David Seed notes, retelling is a test of Christian's 'memory, motivation and powers of assimilation'.[14] It is also an educational tool, reinforcing messages for readers in catechistical style (and various dialogues take the form of catechism, most explicitly the quizzing of Christiana's children; *PP*, 224–26).

The use of dialogue as a mode of instruction was long known to Christian writers. In Bunyan's time, among the most popular examples was Arthur Dent's *The Plaine Mans Path-Way to Heaven* (1601), one of two books Bunyan's first wife brought with her as dowry. Dent's work is entirely written in dialogue 'for the better understanding of the simple', between Theologus ('a Divine'), Philagathus ('an honest man'), Asunetus ('an ignorant man'), and Antilegon ('a caviller').[15] Much of the work is a lecture from Theologus, punctuated by requests for elucidation from Philagathus and, less often, by

---

[13] See Roger Pooley, 'Language and Loyalty: Plain Style at the Restoration', *Literature & History*, 6 (1980), 2–18; Keeble, *Literary Culture of Nonconformity*; and Chapter 14 in this volume.

[14] David Seed, 'Dialogue and Debate in *The Pilgrim's Progress*', in Vincent Newey (ed.), *The Pilgrim's Progress: Critical and Historical Views* (Liverpool: Liverpool University Press, 1980), 69–90 (74).

[15] Arthur Dent, *The Plaine Mans Path-Way to Heaven* (1601), title page, 1. For more on Dent, see Chapter 6 in this volume.

challenges from the other two; Dent is not at pains to absorb his reader into a readily believable dramatic situation. There are, however, dashes of the realism we find later in Bunyan: the opening conversation about the price of cattle, for instance; or Asunetus's reply to Theologus, 'Tush, tush: what needes all this adoe?' which might remind us of a similarly dismissive response to Christian: '*Tush*, said *Obstinate, away with your Book; will you go back with us, or no?*' (*PP*, 11).[16] Yet Bunyan transforms the expository style of Dent's dialogue by placing his speakers in an imaginative landscape. Obstinate does not merely dismiss the evidence of Christian's book: he tries to take him back to the City of Destruction. Unlike his counterpart Antilegon (who remains for the full 400 pages of Dent's dialogue), Obstinate soon decides to 'go back to my place', after a few memorably aggressive remarks about '*these Craz'd-headed Coxcombs, that when they take a fancy by the end, are wiser in their own eyes then seven men that can render a reason*' (*PP*, 11–12). The mixture of insult, colloquialism, and mangled biblical allusion (to Proverbs 26:16) gives flesh in Bunyan's text to what, in Dent, is merely the voicing of an antagonistic attitude.

In his representation of speech, Bunyan's ear is carefully attuned not only to the rhythms of English speech, but also to the differences language can expose: between personality types, social classes, levels of education, genders, and, most importantly for him, spiritual states. He conveys key qualities in minor characters swiftly and precisely through their styles of conversation, using very little visual description (see, for example, *PP*, 81–4). Mr Worldly-Wiseman is evidently a 'Gentleman' from his speech: he greets Christian jovially with '*How now, good fellow* [...]?' and addresses him with the more familiar '*thou*'—thus signalling his social superiority—while Christian responds using the more formal and respectful 'you' and calls him 'Sir'.[17] Worldly-Wiseman is full of breezy confidence in his own opinion:

> *I beshrow him* [Evangelist] *for his counsel; there is not a more dangerous and troublesome way in the world* [...] *hear me, I am older than thou! thou art like to meet with in the way which thou goest, Wearisomness, Painfulness, Hunger,* [...] *and in a word, death, and what not?.* (*PP*, 17–18)

His blustering tone persuades Christian to seek relief from his burden in the town of Morality, instead of following Evangelist's directions: a near fatal mistake. It is significant, then, that Christian's first serious error of his journey comes at the hands of a social superior who misleads him through speech that appears to be authoritative.

Colloquialisms are another way in which Bunyan creates different textures of speech, with the reprobate characters tending to be far more colloquial than the pilgrims. Compare the repentant Christiana and Mrs Timorous:

---

[16] Dent, *Plaine Mans Path-Way*, 25.
[17] On Bunyan's use of *thou* forms and *you* forms, see Julie Coleman, 'The Manufactured Homespun Style of John Bunyan's Prose', *BS*, 18 (2014), 107–37 (127–32), and Chapter 24 in this volume.

Then *Christiana* reply'd, I have been sorely afflicted since my Husbands departure from me; but specially since he went *over the River*. But that which troubleth me most, is, my churlish Carriages to him when he was under his distress. [...]

Timo. Well, I see you have a mind to go a fooling too; but take heed in time, and be wise: while we are out of danger we are out; but when we are in, we are in. (*PP*, 182–84)

The degenerate citizens are characterized by their loose tongues: idiomatic expressions, platitudes, insults: 'a good riddance, for my part I say, of her' says Mrs Inconsiderate (*PP*, 184–85). By contrast, Christian, Faithful, and Hopeful, and in *Part II* Christiana and her travelling companions, tend to speak in a higher register. Their tone can certainly be conversational, as Christian's exchanges with Hopeful show: 'Thou talkest like one, upon whose head is the Shell to this very day' (*PP*, 127). Yet they avoid the relaxed over-confidence and dismissiveness of the reprobate characters, and are able to express both complex doctrine eloquently and personal conviction sincerely through the language they use.

In both parts of *The Pilgrim's Progress*, this link between style of speech and spiritual state is established early on. A subtler exploration of this connection, and a more contextually contingent one, is reserved for later in *Part I*, when Christian and Faithful meet the epitome of wordiness: Talkative. The appearance of this character marks an important development in Bunyan's analysis of 'good' and 'bad' style. C. S. Lewis considered the episode no more than 'dead wood' in *The Pilgrim's Progress*; for him, the conversation is 'bogged down in sheer doctrine' and slips out of the allegorical mode by talking directly about the spiritual life.[18] This accusation ignores, however, the many conversations in the text where characters rehearse previous experiences and draw lessons from them. On a broader level, moreover, Lewis's reading does not recognize the precise way in which Bunyan is puncturing the rhetoric of godly treatises, or rather the pat repetition of pieties gleaned from such treatises, as a substitute for authentic spiritual conviction. At first appearance, of course, it is not at all obvious that Talkative is a sinful degenerate like Obstinate or Worldly-Wiseman. Faithful is initially fooled by him, in fact, and declares that he '*will make a very excellent Pilgrim*', until Christian sets him right by revealing that 'all he hath lieth in his *tongue*' (*PP*, 77–8). He is a talker, not a doer, and the more he sounds like a religious treatise, the more Talkative reveals his true colours. He has a great fondness for lists, and knows the correct terminology: through talking, he says, 'a man may learn the necessity of the New-birth, the insufficiency of our works, the need of Christs righteousness, *&c.*' (*PP*, 76), the '*&c.*' here working to underline his glibness. Later, he even embarks on an enumeration of his points:

> I perceive then that our talk must be *about the power of things*; Well, 'tis a very good question, and I shall be willing to answer you. And take my answer in brief thus.

---

[18] Lewis, 'The Vision of John Bunyan', 146.

> First, *Where the Grace of God is in the heart, it causeth* there *a great out-cry against sin.* Secondly— (*PP*, 81)

Vincent Newey argues that 'Talkative exists for Christian and Faithful, as he does for us, as a text to be read and understood.'[19] It could be added further that Talkative's distinctiveness lies in the fact that he is so very 'textual', that he talks like a book. His approach is typical of myriad Puritan writers who divide and subdivide their subjects in Ramist fashion. A specialist in this method was William Ames, of whose writing the following is typical:

> *Quest.* The first question is, Whether an erroneous Conscience doth bind?
> *Answ.* To unfold this question rightly, these five things are briefly to be opened: 1. What an erroneous Conscience is. 2. About what things it is conversant. 3. Whence the errour of Conscience commeth. 4. The generall differences of these errors. 5. The severall waies of binding.
> 1. An erroneous Conscience is either opposed *privatively* to a good Conscience [...] or *positively*, so it signifieth onely that Conscience, that judgeth otherwise then the thing is.[20]

Talkative is by no means the only person to enumerate and divide theological topics: Faithful does it in his debate with Talkative, and Christian and Hopeful do it at much greater length during their conversation on the Inchanted Ground, as does Bunyan himself in his numerous doctrinal and controversial works. Yet there is something more automatic in the way that Talkative does this. Crucially, he never supports his learning with personal examples, or with evidence of thoughtful reading of the Bible.

Talkative's danger lies in his linguistic flexibility. Clearly, he has read the right guides to godly living and can imitate their style, but their effects go no further than his mouth: 'He *talketh* of Prayer, of Repentance, of Faith, and of the New-birth: but he knows but only to *talk* of them.' He can as easily change his mode of speech to another, depending on circumstance, being 'for any company, and for any *talk*; as he *talketh* now with you, so will he *talk* when he is on the *Ale-bench*' (*PP*, 78). He might remind us of Shakespeare's Prince Hal, the gifted mimic of different linguistic registers and modes who is 'so good a proficient in one quarter of an hour that I can drink with any tinker in his own language during my life'.[21] But this verbal slipperiness, in which language seemingly does not (as Ben Jonson would have it) most show the man, but rather forms his most effective disguise, poses a real threat to the unwary pilgrim. Fortunately for Christian and Faithful, the former has prior experience of Talkative: 'I have been in his Family, and have observed him both at home and abroad; and I know what I say of him

---

[19] Vincent Newey, '"With the Eyes of my Understanding": Bunyan, Experience, and Acts of Interpretation', in Keeble (ed.), *Bunyan: Conventicle and Parnassus*, 189–216 (190).

[20] William Ames, *Conscience with the Power and Cases Thereof* ([Leiden and London], 1639), Book 1, 9.

[21] Shakespeare, *King Henry IV Part 1*, 2.4.16–19.

is the truth' (*PP*, 78). Christian knows the truth because he has observed him, not simply through hearing him speak. But Faithful, the more experienced believer, has been deceived by Talkative's plausible patter.

Given this slip, the question raises itself: How can readers avoid falling into the same trap as Faithful, especially without the benefit of previous knowledge? The answer lies partly in making informed judgements, rather than those based on an immediate impression, and partly in developing a more discerning response to style. While Talkative appears authentic at first, the cracks in his verbal veneer start to show as Faithful (under Christian's instruction) draws out his conversation and subjects it to more rigorous analysis. Talkative's linguistic facility is more limited than he realizes, because he cannot apply generalized pieties to his own life. As Gordon Campbell notes, Talkative is 'the only good systematic theologian' in the book.[22] Yet his thinking remains at the level of system, and this is noticeable in the way he speaks. He avoids any specific reference to individuals, including himself, in his theological discussion: '*Where the Grace of God is in the heart, it causeth* there *a great out-cry against sin*', he pronounces, before querying the difference 'between crying out against, and abhoring of sin', and remarks that 'You come now to Experience, to Conscience, and God: and to appeals to him for justification of what is spoken' (*PP*, 81, 84). His attempts to remain scrupulously abstract result in notably inelegant phrasing, as he refuses to acknowledge a subject who cries out, abhors, experiences, or appeals.

By contrast, Faithful's language continually expresses the '*experimental*' nature of faith. In exploring the work of grace, he immediately talks of '*him that hath it*', and this man—typical but still individual—frames the whole of his explanation: he '*findeth* [...] *revealed in him the Saviour of the world*', has '*his joy and peace*', '*his love*', '*his desires*', '*his mind*', and, of course, '*his sin*' (*PP*, 82–3). The difference between his and Talkative's theological approaches is all the more pronounced since, when Talkative is not discussing doctrine, his language becomes crammed with first- and second-person pronouns:

> This kind of discourse I did not expect, nor am I disposed to give an answer to such questions, because, I count not my self bound thereto, unless you take upon you to be a *Catechizer*; and, though you should so do, yet I may refuse to make you my Judge: But I pray will you tell me, why you ask me such questions? (*PP*, 84)

Talkative's language revolves around personal relations, except when he talks about God; then, his conversation is made up of the 'sheer doctrine' to which Lewis objects.

Along with his failure to apply a true understanding of salvation either to others or to himself, Talkative's speech is in other ways fatally imprecise. Just as he says that he 'could give you an hundred Scriptures for the confirmation' (*PP*, 77) of grace's priority over good works, but never does, so his language gestures towards ideas which he never fully explores. One of his favourite words is 'thing': in this short episode, he uses the word in

---

[22] Gordon Campbell, 'The Theology of *The Pilgrim's Progress*', in Newey (ed.), *The Pilgrim's Progress*, 251–62 (258).

singular or plural forms twenty-five times. Faithful has started him off on this path by proposing that they discourse '*of things that are profitable*' (*PP*, 75), but Talkative takes the instruction to an extreme of Polonius-like copiousness:

> I will talk of things heavenly, or things earthly; things Moral, or things Evangelical; things Sacred, or things Prophane; things past, or things to come; things forraign, or things at home; things more Essential, or things Circumstantial. (*PP*, 77)

The nature of these 'things' is of little interest to the speaker, who is prepared to demonstrate his prowess equally in any of these fields.

Another linguistic marker of his theological imprecision is his use of 'this'. Talkative asks at one point, 'What thing so pleasant, and what so profitable, as to talk of the things of God?' and goes on to answer his own question at length:

> to talk of such things is most profitable, for by so doing, a Man may get knowledge of many things […]. By this a man may learn […]. Besides, by this a man may learn […]: by this also a Man may learn […]. Further, by this a Man may learn […]. Alas! The want of this is the cause that so few understand the need of faith. (*PP*, 76)

Here, 'this' refers to the act of talking itself. As a result, the rhetorical division Talkative employs to build the steps of his speech makes the reader's tasks harder, since we must keep referring back in order to decipher the meaning of the full speech: the fivefold repetition of 'this' takes us further and further away from that which it denotes ('to talk of such things'). Moreover, when we do look back to that phrase, it is only to find further lack of clarity about what 'such things' are: they are the 'things of God' he has mentioned earlier, but what these might actually be, he does not specify. At the root of his grand speech is, typically, 'things'. Talkative's language is thus misleading in its very vagueness: his 'by this' clauses entangle the listener or reader like the Flatterer's nets, creating the impression of formal order and logical progression to hide a total insubstantiality of conviction.

Modes of speech thus form an important locus for Bunyan's exploration of what stylistic expression can indicate about the state of the soul. Language is frequently the source of deception and danger for the pilgrims: even when Christian and Hopeful have been warned, they fall prey to Flatterer, and afterwards explain that they did not realize that 'this fine-spoken man' (*PP*, 134) could be a deceiver. Interestingly, in this instance Bunyan makes no attempt to represent the seductions of fine speech—all Flatterer says is 'Follow me […] it is thither that I am going' (*PP*, 133)—perhaps because he has already done so with Worldly-Wiseman and Talkative. Through these and other characters Bunyan provides multiple perspectives on the threats posed not just by what they say, but the manner in which they say it. The believer must train him- or herself not just in the interpretation of the good words of the Bible, but also in recognizing the deceiving words of false prophets, whose linguistic sophistication or talents at mimicry may give the impression of true piety.

Style, Pace, and Journey

Although speech makes up a significant proportion of *The Pilgrim's Progress*, it is not the only means by which style is linked to spiritual progress (or the lack of it). Through the framing allegory of pilgrimage, the experience of the text itself aims to mirror the trials that the pilgrims undergo. As James Turner has noticed, space in this text does not conform to modern ideas of consistency and accuracy in mapping. Values such as height have specific social meanings, while the dimensions of space vary 'according to the frame of mind of the pilgrim; so that the journey is long or short, easy or rough depending on Grace'.[23] Nowhere is this more evident than in Christian's experience of the Hill Difficulty, where the narrative not only describes his journey, but also recreates through its pacing the changes in his emotions and their effect on how he, and we as readers, perceive the landscape.

In this episode, Bunyan moves from a brisk, economical narrative style, focusing on external description of movement, to longer, more rhetorically loaded sentences, and a more expansive recounting of Christian's thought processes, as he becomes disheartened and the hill becomes correspondingly more difficult. Christian chooses the 'narrow way [...] right up the Hill' (*PP*, 41), avoiding the two easy paths which run on either side. As he starts his ascent, his pace slows: 'I looked then after *Christian*, to see him go up the Hill, where I perceived he fell from running to going, and from going to clambering upon his hands and his knees, because of the steepness of the place' (*PP*, 42). Although the challenging nature of his climb is communicated through anadiplosis in these movement clauses, the prose does not do much more at this point to convey a sense of arduousness: the single sentence just quoted gets Christian 'about the midway to the top of the Hill'. There Christian finds an arbour 'for the refreshing of weary Travailers' (*PP*, 42) and rests, but falls fast asleep and drops his roll. He hears a voice reproving him for laziness, 'and with that *Christian* suddenly started up, and sped him on his way, and went a pace till he came to the top of the hill' (*PP*, 43). The challenge of the first half of the hill disappears in this description: clambering is no longer needed. The triple emphasis on speed in the three paratactic clauses—'suddenly [...] sped [...] a pace'—seems to contradict or undermine the hill's name, since it poses so little difficulty to the pilgrim.

As soon as he realizes he has lost his roll, though, the narrative style changes:

> he asked God forgiveness for that his foolish Fact, and then went back to look for his Roll. But all the way he went back, who can sufficiently set forth the sorrow of *Christians* heart? somtimes he sighed, somtimes he wept, and often times he chid himself, for being so foolish to fall asleep in that place which was erected only for a little refreshment from his weariness. Thus therefore he went back, carefully looking

---

[23] James Turner, 'Bunyan's Sense of Place', in Newey (ed.), *The Pilgrim's Progress*, 91–110 (97–8, 105).

on this side, and on that, all the way as he went, if happily he might find his Roll, that had been his comfort so many times in his Journey. (*PP*, 43–4)

This journey down the hill is less physically demanding than the initial journey up it, but it takes much longer to narrate. From the time he turns back 'to look for his Roll', until he finally 'espied his Roll', absorbs 334 words, whereas the previous journey, covering the same distance, requires a mere 26. As we see in the extract just quoted, Bunyan's sentence structure reinforces the tedium of the descent: the sequence 'somtimes […] somtimes […] often times', and the repetition too of 'he went back […] therefore he went back' and 'as he went', suggests a much longer journey than the swiftly efficient original climb, while the multiple clauses of the final sentence, hypotactic but fairly loosely connected to one another, convey the painstakingly slow hunt for a lost beloved object. Descriptions of what Christian is doing are mixed with his self-addressed recriminations, which themselves comment on the time and effort being wasted:

How many steps have I took in vain! (Thus it happened to *Israel* for their sin, they were sent back again by the way of the Red-Sea) and I am made to tread those steps with sorrow, which I might have trod with delight, had it not been for this sinful sleep. How far might I have been on my way by this time! I am made to tread those steps thrice over, which I needed not to have trod but once. (*PP*, 44)

As the word count here testifies, the reader is forced to follow those steps more than 'thrice'. The protracted narrative, the self-lacerating expressions of irritation and remorse, the repetitive emphasis on drudgery of movement ('steps' appears three times in the above quotation, along with the verb sequence 'took', 'tread', 'trod', 'tread', 'trod'), all accentuate Christian's frustration. When he finds his roll and gives tearful thanks to God, the pace immediately picks up again—'But Oh how nimbly now did he go up the rest of the Hill!'—but the after-effects of his wasted journey linger: 'Yet before he got up, the Sun went down upon *Christian*' (*PP*, 45). The qualifier shows that he cannot quite recover the zealous energy of the first ascent.

In *Part II*, the hill does not pose the same challenge, although it is not without difficulties. Christiana and her companions 'set forward and began to go up the Hill, and up the Hill they went; but before they got to the top, *Christiana* began to *Pant*, and said, I dare say this is a breathing Hill' (*PP*, 215). Initially, the hill is seen to be relatively undemanding, but the picture is adjusted by Christiana's physical reaction, transplanted onto the hill through the fine transferred epithet 'a breathing hill'. The group rests at the arbour, and their conversation revisits Christian's plight as they discuss '*Which is hardest up Hill or down Hill?*' (*PP*, 216). Christiana's son James gives the 'right answer' to Mercie's query, that 'The day is coming when in my Opinion, *going down Hill will be the hardest of all*' (*PP*, 216). As I have shown, the narration of Christian's experience has already helped us to reach that conclusion. Here, as throughout *Part II*, dialogue replaces much of the demanding physical activity of *Part I*, and Mercie and James's exchange underlines the lesson of Christian's lengthy doubling-back. Even these later pilgrims experience obstacles though, as Christiana forgets the bottle of spirits given to her by Mr Interpreter and James is forced to go back for it. Visited a third time, in the story of Mr Fearing's journey, the hill's challenges are neutralized: 'When we came at the Hill *Difficulty*, he made no stick at that' (*PP*, 251). It is noticeable that, while repetition of individual episodes is an ingrained part of Bunyan's narrative style, repetition of experiences from one character to another is something he tends to avoid. The second visit to the Hill Difficulty reminds us of Christian's original, self-inflicted test of endurance through the lesson that Christiana and her group explicitly learn there—that going downhill is harder, the arbour is a '*losing* place' (*PP*, 217)—but it does not replicate it through narrative description, while Fearing, as reported by Great-heart, surmounts the hill in the briefest of colloquialisms: 'he made no stick at that'.

Conclusion

Bunyan's prose style is tightly connected to the moral and spiritual dimensions of his texts. His reported dialogue reveals not just the differences between personalities, but the linguistic textures of belief and non-belief, of authentic spiritual conviction and its deceptive counterfeit. His carefully controlled variations of pace draw the reader into the experience of the text, as in the hurried execution of John the Baptist, or Christian's pained descent of the Hill Difficulty. In the preface to *The Pilgrim's Progress, Part I* Bunyan figures language as a vessel: '*My dark and cloudy words they do but hold / The Truth, as Cabinets inclose the Gold*' (*PP*, 4). Yet this does not mean that stylistic effects produced by '*dark and cloudy words*' are superfluous, or can be cast aside: *res* and *verba* are far more intimately associated than that. At the same time, it is perhaps too easy to accept Bunyan's claim in *Grace Abounding* that '*I may not play* [...] *but be plain and simple*' as a global approach to his writing, or to characterize it by 'gravity', 'sobriety', or 'straightforward[ness]'.[24] There is playfulness in the grim 'slap' of the executioner's sword. There is even sexual wordplay in Bunyan's writing which most of his readers have chosen to ignore.[25] The energetic qualities of his texts—their intensity, corporeality, rapid changes of perspective, lively dialogue—all contribute to a prose style which may strike us as 'homespun', but is by no means transparent or inconspicuous or unsophisticated. Bunyan the stylist deserves our attention, as a writer whose command of linguistic range is broader than we may at first realize, and whose awareness of the dangers of entangling rhetoric is all the greater for it.

---

[24] Joan Webber, *The Eloquent 'I': Style and Self in Seventeenth-Century Prose* (Madison, WI: University of Wisconsin Press, 1968), 9, 48, 51.

[25] Michael Davies, 'Sex and Sexual Wordplay in the Writings of John Bunyan', in Vera J. Camden (ed.), *Trauma and Transformation: The Political Progress of John Bunyan* (Stanford, CA: Stanford University Press, 2008), 100–19.

Suggested Reading

Coleman, Julie, 'The Manufactured Homespun Style of John Bunyan's Prose', *BS*, 18 (2014), 107–37.
Graham, Jean, '"Tell All Men": Bunyan and the Gendering of Discourse', *BS*, 11 (2003/04), 8–22.
Keeble, N. H., *The Literary Culture of Nonconformity in Seventeenth-Century England* (Leicester: Leicester University Press, 1987), ch. 8.
Pooley, Roger, 'Language and Loyalty: Plain Style at the Restoration', *Literature & History*, 6 (1980), 2–18.
Pooley, Roger, 'Plain and Simple: Bunyan and Style', in N. H. Keeble (ed.), *John Bunyan: Conventicle and Parnassus* (Oxford: Clarendon Press, 1988), 91–110.
Seed, David, 'Dialogue and Debate in *The Pilgrim's Progress*', in Vincent Newey (ed.), *The Pilgrim's Progress: Critical and Historical Views* (Liverpool: Liverpool University Press, 1980), 69–90.
Shuger, Debora, 'Conceptions of Style', in Glyn P. Norton (ed.), *The Cambridge History of Literary Criticism, Vol. 3* (Cambridge: Cambridge University Press, 1999), 176–86.
Turner, James, 'Bunyan's Sense of Place', in Vincent Newey (ed.), *The Pilgrim's Progress: Critical and Historical Views* (Liverpool: Liverpool University Press, 1980), 91–110.
Webber, Joan, *The Eloquent 'I': Style and Self in Seventeenth-Century Prose* (Madison, WI: University of Wisconsin Press, 1968), ch. 2.

CHAPTER 24

THE LANGUAGE OF *THE PILGRIM'S PROGRESS*

JULIE COLEMAN

This chapter focuses on the language of *The Pilgrim's Progress* and on readers' and editors' responses to it over time.[1] While comparison between Bunyan's and his contemporaries' language, alongside that of the Bible, makes it possible to evaluate his use of archaism,[2] this chapter will also analyse differences between the language used in both parts of *The Pilgrim's Progress* to identify developments in Bunyan's written style. Doing so allows us to speculate about his intended readership and the ways in which Bunyan envisaged his redemptive allegory influencing their spiritual lives. The aim here is to demonstrate that the artful simplicity of *The Pilgrim's Progress* depends upon thoughtful consideration of its pedagogical functions and upon a sophisticated command of the English language. Although *The Pilgrim's Progress* cannot be considered representative of Bunyan's language as a whole, because it reflects only one facet of his repertoire of written styles, the broad and enduring popular appeal of this work indicates the effectiveness of Bunyan's linguistic artistry.

In recognition of the unusual prominence of direct speech, the language of *The Pilgrim's Progress* has been characterized as *idiomatic, colloquial, dialectal*, and *proverbial*. Commentators have described it as *homespun, natural, unpolluted, simple, plain, direct*, and *masculine*, and have assumed that *The Pilgrim's Progress* reflected the contemporary speech of Bunyan's uneducated readers. Less sympathetic critics have made the same assumption, but condemned Bunyan's language as *low, vulgar, rustic*, and *coarse*. Although early editors emphasized the influence of biblical language, later critics, such as Roger Sharrock and F. R. Leavis, focused on Bunyan's use of everyday language and

---

[1] I am very grateful to Michael Davies, Sarah Knight, and Mary Ann Lund for their comments on earlier drafts of this chapter.

[2] Brainerd P. Stranahan, 'Bunyan and the Epistle to the Hebrews: His Source for the Idea of Pilgrimage in *The Pilgrim's Progress*', SP, 79 (1982), 279–96, demonstrates that Bunyan relied almost exclusively on the King James translation of the Bible (also known as the Authorized Version), first published in 1611.

of his skill as a Dissenting preacher.³ C. S. Lewis downplayed the biblical influence, remarking that 'any unlearned author of Bunyan's time would be bound to remind us of the Bible whether he had read it or not'.⁴ More recent work on Bunyan's language has concentrated on his use of metaphor and allegory, a topic discussed in Chapters 14, 21 and 23, and an early Arabic translator pithily observed the apparent contrast between the simple style and layered meaning of *The Pilgrim's Progress*, in describing it as 'a book of easy expressions and fine significations'.⁵

The numerical analyses in this chapter are based on the earliest available editions of *Part I* and *Part II* of *The Pilgrim's Progress* (published by Nathaniel Ponder in 1678 and 1684 respectively). Text files were downloaded from *Early English Books Online* (http://eebo.chadwyck.com) and corrected against the site's document images. Alan Reed's *Simple Concordance Program* 4.0.7 (www.textworld.com/scp) also facilitated the analysis. Introductory verses were excluded to ensure comparability, but verses integral to the narrative in both parts of the allegory were included.

Puritan Language

Readers of seventeenth-century literature will be familiar with distinctive satirical representations of Puritan language motivated by religious and political tensions.⁶ Barber notes that fictional Puritans are characterized by their nasal voices, their opposition to swearing, and their distinctively unadorned religious vocabulary, drawing particularly upon the language of the Bible. He warns against assuming that these caricatures are reliable and finds that many Puritan writers 'have no obviously Puritan linguistic features at all'.⁷

Bunyan's language can be characterized as Puritan or more broadly Protestant, in its use of simple vocabulary to reach a general audience. Including the names of people and places, and grouping inflected and derived forms together, *The Pilgrim's Progress* employs approximately 3,200 root forms (which assumes that a reader knowing the word *slow* would be able to deduce the meanings of forms such as *to slow* and *slower*).

---

[3] This brief survey of commentary on the language of *The Pilgrim's Progress* is based on texts excerpted from Roger Sharrock (ed.), *The Pilgrim's Progress: A Casebook* (London: Macmillan, 1976).

[4] C. S. Lewis, 'The Literary Impact of the Authorised Version', in Walter Hooper (ed.), *C. S. Lewis: Selected Literary Essays* (Cambridge: Cambridge University Press, 1969), 126–45 (139).

[5] Buṭrus al-Bustānī (tr.), *Siyāḥat al-masīḥī* (Beirut: American Press, 1844), 2. Cited and translated in Peter Hill, 'Early Translations of English Fiction into Arabic: *The Pilgrim's Progress* and *Robinson Crusoe*', *Journal of Semitic Studies*, 60 (2015), 177–212 (188).

[6] See Abigail Williams, *Poetry and the Creation of a Whig Literary Culture, 1681–1714* (Oxford: Oxford University Press, 2005), ch. 1.

[7] Charles Barber, *Early Modern English*, 2nd edn (Edinburgh: Edinburgh University Press, 1997), 23–6.

The number of roots might be reduced further if compound words (such as *slow-pace*) were counted as additional examples of their elements. The 150 most common roots account for 75 per cent of the entire text, and a reader or listener would only have to know 521 roots to understand 90 per cent of *The Pilgrim's Progress*. As a point of comparison, Ogden's *Basic English* vocabulary, designed to give a functional competence in English for non-native speakers, listed 850 words, which many teachers and learners found to be too restrictive. Modern school-age English-speaking children are estimated to increase their vocabulary by approximately one thousand words each year.[8]

Of the 521 most commonly used roots in *The Pilgrim's Progress*, 62 per cent are monosyllabic; only 5 per cent have three or more syllables. Seventy-six per cent, accounting for 84 per cent of the text, had been in English since before the Conquest, including some early loans from Latin. By using such a limited range of terms, Bunyan was acting in opposition to the deliberate expansion of lexis that was characteristic of the early modern English period. His contemporaries' confidence in the possibilities of English eloquence was dependent on a continued process of adoption since the previous century, particularly of terms from the classical languages. Latin played a central part in formal education at all levels in this period, but *Gaius*, *despond*, and *conclude* are the only high-frequency post-Conquest Latin loans found in *The Pilgrim's Progress*.

The 118 frequently used roots ultimately from French had all been borrowed at least two centuries before, during which time they had become unremarkable features of everyday English. Bunyan's avoidance of loan-words is a stylistic choice, not an accidental revelation of his limited vocabulary: the first few paragraphs of *The Holy War* include *situate* (1523, from Latin), *advantageous* (c.1485, from French), *reference* (1579, from French), and *compact* (1530, ultimately from Latin).[9] His avoidance of loan-words did not require detailed etymological knowledge, however: Bunyan preferred well-established terms because they were easy to understand. The only frequently used root that might have troubled contemporary readers was the noun *despond*, apparently Bunyan's own creation from *to despond*: 'to lose heart or resolution; to become depressed or dejected in mind by loss of confidence or hope' (*OED*). The *Oxford English Dictionary*'s first citation for the verb is from an address to Parliament made by Cromwell in 1655, suggesting that the term originated among Dissenters wishing to create a grey area around religious uncertainty. This permitted scrupulous self-inquisitors, like Bunyan himself, to distinguish between doubt, fear, and the irretrievable state of despair.

---

[8] C. K. Ogden, *Basic English: A General Introduction with Rules and Grammar* (London: Kegan Paul, Trench, Trubner, & Co., 1930); Jeremy M. Anglin, *Vocabulary Development: A Morphological Analysis* (Chicago: University of Chicago Press, 1993), 9–10.

[9] Citation dates are taken from *OED*, http://www.oed.com (accessed 22 December 2016).

Typical Early Modern English Features in *The Pilgrim's Progress*

In many respects, the language of *The Pilgrim's Progress* is typical of its period. For example, the original spelling, probably the printer's rather than Bunyan's own, differs from present-day English (PDE) spelling in predictable ways. Following normal practice for early modern English (eMnE) texts for a popular audience, editors have often modernized the spelling according to contemporary and national norms. Modern readers may assume that the sounds of *The Pilgrim's Progress* have remained unchanged, and this will sometimes be correct. For example, Bunyan probably made no distinction between *knot* and *not*, though speakers of English only a generation or two before would generally have pronounced the initial /k/. However, pronunciation continued (and continues) to change, and familiar spellings can sometimes conceal differences between Bunyan's language and PDE.[10] For example, most accents of British English do not articulate the /r/ preserved in the spelling of words like *arm* and *far*, but Bunyan's contemporaries generally would have done. Bunyan would probably also have pronounced *whether* and *weather* with different initial sounds (/hw/ and /w/, respectively). A few marked differences between seventeenth-century and modern pronunciation are revealed by Bunyan's rhymes, which may seem forced to modern readers. For example, *profitable* was stressed to rhyme with *fable*:

> *Art thou for something rare, and profitable?*
> *Wouldest thou see a Truth within a Fable?* (PP, 7)

Are would have rhymed with *care* and *bugbears* with *fears*:

> *Let them acquainted be, too, how they are*
> *Beloved of their King, under his care.* (PP, 168)
> *Fright not thy self my Book, for such* Bugbears
> *Are nothing else but ground for groundless fears.* (PP, 169)

Bunyan's contemporaries would also have pronounced *was* to rhyme with *cross*:

> *Yea, tell them how plain hearted* this *man was,*
> *How after his good Lord he bare his Cross.* (PP, 172)

---

[10] For a detailed account of the phonology of early modern English, see Roger Lass, 'Phonology and Morphology', in Roger Lass (ed.), *The Cambridge History of the English Language*, vol. 3: *1476–1776* (Cambridge: Cambridge University Press, 1999), 56–185, upon which this analysis is largely reliant.

In PDE, weak verbs are generally marked for tense by the addition of <ed>. The inflection is sometimes unvoiced, particularly in British English, but under the influence of American spelling it is becoming increasingly rare to represent this graphically (e.g. *spelled* is replacing *spelt*). Bunyan (or his printer) represents the unvoiced pronunciation more frequently than PDE (e.g. *jumpt, walkt, bless't*). The insertion of apostrophes in past tense inflections (e.g. *pav'd, stun'd, pluck'd*) indicates that they were not always syllabic, even where the consonant was voiced. However, syllabic pronunciations (preserved in PDE verbs like *fitted, netted, lifted*) remained available as unmarked alternatives for many verbs, and this was particularly useful in writing verse:

> *Whereas some say a Cloud is in his Head,*
> *That doth but shew how Wisdom's covered.* (PP, 170)

Elision of <e> in past tense inflections became increasingly frequent during the sixteenth century, reaching 'more or less modern' distribution by the mid-eighteenth century.[11]

Oxford English Dictionary citation dates demonstrate that many of Bunyan's lexical choices would also have been unproblematic for contemporary readers. Examples include: *comfortable* 'encouraging; inspiring' (c.1460–1869); *congee* 'a bow' (1587–1880); *cumbred* 'encumbered; hindered' (1590–1867); *glad* 'to make glad' (Old English (OE)–1870); *hardly* 'with severity or rigour' (OE–1940); *item* 'a hint' (1561–*ante* 1860); *lumber* 'to rumble' (?1527–1904); *pelting* 'violent; passionate' (1570–1876); and *round up* 'to rebuke' (1653–1893). Bunyan's grammar is also typical of his period in many respects. In PDE, we generally form perfect and pluperfect tenses with the verb *have* (e.g. *I have kissed her, he had come*), though Old English tended to use *have* for transitive verbs and *be* for intransitives (e.g. *I have kissed her, he was come*). Bunyan usually preserves the historic *be* formations in verbs of motion: 90 per cent of (plu)perfects for *come* are formed with *be*. Here is an example: 'When he *was* entred the room, and *had* a little observed the Boy' (*PP*, 228). Bunyan's usage was not unusual in this respect. The transition to *have* in the (plu)perfect was not complete until the early nineteenth century.[12]

Dialect and Colloquial Features in *The Pilgrim's Progress*

Although the language of *The Pilgrim's Progress* is typical of its period in many respects, Bunyan offers a closer representation of speech than the rhetorically polished style favoured by many English writers for over a century. A small number of Bunyan's

---

[11] Lass, 'Phonology and Morphology', 174.
[12] Matti Rissanen, 'Syntax', in Lass (ed.), *Cambridge History of the English Language*, 187–331 (215).

terms appear to have been restricted to dialect usage, although some had been more widely employed earlier in their history. With dates from the *Oxford English Dictionary* and indications of geographical distribution from Wright's *English Dialect Dictionary*,[13] these include *brast* 'to burst' (ante 1400–1865) (Scotland to Cheshire); *checkle* 'to chuckle' (1627 + 1684) (not listed); *howlet* 'an owl' (c.1450–1828) (Scotland to Somerset); *slabbiness* 'wetness; sloppiness' (1555–1684) (*slabbey*: Scotland to Hampshire); *a good/ long stitch* 'a considerable distance' (1684 + 1901) (Lancashire and Cheshire); *stroddle* 'to straddle' (1607–1702) (Lancashire to Somerset); *stound* 'to stun; to astound' (ante 1400–ante 1825) (Scotland to Cornwall); and *wag along* 'to travel; to make one's way' (1684–1903) (Scotland to Devon). The wide geographical distribution of these examples suggests that Bunyan was representing general non-standard usage rather than the dialect of Bedfordshire.

The language of courtiers and educated men might have been held in higher regard than provincial speech, which was certainly a source of humour for playwrights in this period, but nobody would have expected or wanted people from the provinces to sound like courtiers or scholars: 'Until the end of the eighteenth century, everyone in England spoke a local dialect.'[14] Bunyan may have been unusual in representing the speech of unfashionable people, but it is unlikely that his contemporaries thought of him as a dialect writer. Stein observes that:

> we do not find explicit comments on and a branding of forms as vulgarisms, 'low' and dialectal […] until the later eighteenth century. Whatever explicit comment is made in earlier periods comes from a vantage point of older, more aristocracy-orientated bases of a politeness ideal.[15]

Given the wide distribution of the few terms that might be labelled as dialect, it is difficult to distinguish them from Bunyan's colloquialisms, which would have been equally 'rude' linguistically, including *at it* 'busy' (1609–1884); *chicken-hearted* 'cowardly' (1681–1883); and *a deal* 'to an undefined but considerable extent' (1756–1857). We might also assume that in using words that are not otherwise well documented in this period, Bunyan was reflecting spoken usage. These include *beckon* 'a gesture' (ante 1718–1871); *comfortably* 'encouragingly' (ante 1513 + 1678); *kidnapper* 'an abductor of people, particularly children' (1678–1973); and *opinionative* 'relating to belief; doctrinal' (ante 1638–1869). The *plat* at the Slough of Despond may be 'a plot of land' (n^3: 1435–1991) or 'a small bridge' (n^2: 1652–1985, chiefly English North-West). It is unlikely to mean 'an expanse of open land' (n^2: 1788–1979), though this gloss is sometimes given by Bunyan's editors.

---

[13] Joseph Wright, *English Dialect Dictionary* (London: Henry Froude, 1898–1905).

[14] John H. Fisher, *The Emergence of Standard English* (Lexington, KY: University Press of Kentucky, 1996), 147.

[15] Dieter Stein, 'Sorting out the Variants: Standardization and Social Factors in the English Language 1600–1800', in Dieter Stein and Ingrid Tieken-Boon van Ostade (eds.), *Towards a Standard English 1600–1800* (The Hague: Mouton de Gruyter, 1994), 1–17 (9).

Some grammatical features of Bunyan's writing are also typical of his period. The place of the historic present tense in the Giant Despair episode of *Part I* has been examined, for example, by Roy Pascal:

> So when he arose, he *getteth* him a grievous Crab-tree Cudgel, and *goes* down into the Dungeon to them; and there, first *falls* to rateing of them as if they were dogs, although they gave him never a word of distaste; then he *falls* upon them, and *beats* them fearfully [...]. (*PP*, 114)

Pascal notes that the present tenses here are used only for Giant Despair, and argues that they are a remnant of folktale usage in describing 'a ritual, typical, recurrent case'.[16] He remarks that *Part II* uses the historic present sparingly, but although it is true that there are no passages comparable with *Part I*'s treatment of Giant Despair, examples of the present tense are scattered throughout *Part II*, as, for instance: 'When the Interpreter had shewed them this, he *has* them into the very best Room in the house' (*PP*, 200). Although Pascal is adamant that Bunyan does not strictly use the historic present in either part of *The Pilgrim's Progress*, Rissanen notes that it dates back to the Middle English (ME) period and was commonplace in eMnE, as it is today.[17] There is no good reason, then, to invoke a folktale influence to explain this widespread and vivid feature of spoken English, which was also an accepted rhetorical technique.

ANACHRONISTIC JUDGEMENTS OF THE LANGUAGE OF *THE PILGRIM'S PROGRESS*

Although prescriptive linguists were beginning to devise rules for English in the seventeenth century, there was still considerable toleration of variation.[18] Several features of Bunyan's language that were not stigmatized among his contemporaries will have jarred for later readers. For example, the choice of determiners (*mine/thine*, but also *an*) before words beginning with <h> provides an indication of Bunyan's pronunciation. In keeping with modern practice, we find *an honest fellow* and *an hour* unproblematic, but baulk at *an helmet, an house*, and *an hand*. An /h/ deletion is also implied by Bunyan's rather dated interpretation of possessive <s> as *his*, as in: 'Then he gave me a Book of Jesus his inditing' (*PP*, 141). Bunyan's pronunciation or omission of /h/ would not have indicated a 'clownish and vulgar education'[19] to contemporary readers. Lass notes that

---

[16] Roy Pascal, 'The Present Tense in *The Pilgrim's Progress*', *Modern Language Review*, 60 (1965), 13–16 (14).

[17] Rissanen, 'Syntax', 227.

[18] See Linda C. Mitchell, *Grammar Wars: Language as Cultural Battlefield in 17th and 18th Century England* (Aldershot: Ashgate, 2001).

[19] Walter Scott, '*The Pilgrim's Progress, with a Life of John Bunyan*: By Robert Southey, Esq., LL.D.', *Quarterly Review*, 43 (1830), 469–94 (469).

'Dropping of /h/ was not stigmatized until the eighteenth century; there is little comment before the 1750s.'[20]

The eMnE period saw an unprecedented increase in vocabulary, with loan-words accounting for around half of all new terms.[21] The lexis available to writers in English quickly exceeded the vocabulary of the uneducated, and dictionaries of English for native speakers began to appear at the beginning of the seventeenth century. It was not until the eighteenth century, however, that dictionaries began to dictate that *refreshment, deterrence, innocence,* and *incoherence* were superior to Bunyan's *refreshing, determent, innocency,* and *incoherency*. Where similarly formed synonyms existed, only one tended to survive the eMnE period, but it would be unreasonable to expect Bunyan or any of his contemporaries to have foreseen which one it would be. Another usage that was later stigmatized is *learn* 'to teach' (ante 1382–1974), considered incorrect from the mid-eighteenth century. *Up* 'to rise to one's feet' (1643–1915) and *right* 'very' (?c.1200–1998) appear to have become non-standard by the nineteenth century.

An unfortunate result of Bunyan's general preference for well-established terms is that his already conservative language became markedly more dated in the period of rapid change that followed. The neoclassical revival of the early eighteenth century saw a fresh wave of borrowing from Latin and Greek, and many pre-existing English synonyms were downgraded or fell from use. By the time Southey published his edition of *The Pilgrim's Progress* in 1830, some of Bunyan's vocabulary would have seemed dated, including *amuse* 'to bewilder' (1606–1741); *come at* 'to approach' (OE–1737); *comfortable* 'sustaining (of food)' (c.1440–1816); *convenient* 'morally or ethically proper' (ante 1400–1726); *dung* 'to manure' (OE–1770/74); *fat* 'a vessel' (OE–1571), specifically 'a large vessel' (c.1400–1755); *go* 'to walk' (OE–1836); *harken* 'to listen' (OE–1832); *hosen* 'breeches' (c.1460–1650); *lade* 'to load with gifts' (1481–1878, though *laden* is the only form cited after 1820); *large* 'at length' (1395–1676); *mainly* 'considerably; very' (c.1450–1849); *merry* 'merrily' (OE–1908); *plash* 'to bend down (a branch or plant)' (?1615–1792); *smother* (*up*) 'to hush up' (1579–1752); and *sunshine* 'sunny' (1579–1894). Other terms that were also unremarkable for Bunyan's contemporaries later became restricted to dialect or poetic use, including *breed* 'to be pregnant' (1629–1885); *conceit* 'to imagine; to think' (various constructions c.1589–1935); *doubt* 'to fear' (ante 1400–1897); *fright* 'to frighten' (OE–1970); *matter* 'to regard as important' (1652–1956); *whitely* 'pale' (ante 1387–1901); and *wonderful* 'in a manner that causes wonder' (c.1400–1885).

Bunyan also fell foul of later grammatical rules, not least in his occasional use of singular verbs with plural subjects, as in: 'Now the Women and Children being weakly, they *was* forced to go as they could bear.'[22] This usage, now heavily stigmatized, is still frequently heard in many regions of Britain. For Bunyan's original readers, it would

---

[20] Lass, 'Phonology and Morphology', 118.

[21] This and other figures relating to lexis are from Terttu Nevalainen, 'Early Modern English Lexis and Semantics', in Lass (ed.), *Cambridge History of the English Language*, 332–458.

[22] This is the reading in the first edition of 1678 (175); the editor of *PP* has (silently) emended *was* to *were* (279).

probably have been unremarkable in speech, though grammarians were beginning to comment on it. As the eighteenth century progressed, educated readers would have been increasing likely to recoil when they encountered it in writing.

Strong verbs were in flux in the seventeenth century, sometimes retaining their OE three-way distinction (e.g. I *drink*, I *drank*, I have *drunk*), sometimes using the same form for both past tense and past participle (e.g. I *drink*, I *drank/drunk*, I have *drank/drunk*), and sometimes switching the historical past tense and past participle around (e.g. I *drink*, I *drunk*, I have *drank*).[23] Based on an analysis of 473 examples of the past tenses and past participles of ten frequently found strong verbs in *The Pilgrim's Progress* (see Table 24.1), it is possible to affirm that historic past tenses are sometimes also used as past participles, and vice versa, but *-en* past participles are never used as past tenses. Beyond that, it is difficult to generalize, and historic verb classes do not offer a key to the distribution of forms:

> [H]er thoughts *began* [past tense] to work in her mind. (*PP*, 177)
> In what I have *began* [past participle] to take in hand. (*PP*, 37)
> [Y]ou have *begun* [past participle] to find the first part true. (*PP*, 223)
> [T]his is the Spring that Christian *drank* [past tense] of. (*PP*, 214)
> [W]hen they had eaten and *drank* [past participle]. (*PP*, 217)

Bunyan's usage is typical of his period, except that he was conservative in retaining *gat* and *spake*, presumably under the influence of biblical language (see following section).[24] By the mid-eighteenth century, the use of past tense forms for the past participle had been stigmatized as inelegant.[25]

Bunyan's formation of comparative and superlative adjectives is similar to PDE, in that monosyllabic adjectives tend to be inflected (e.g. *higher*, *highest*) while polysyllabic adjectives use periphrasis (e.g. *more wonderful*, *most wonderful*). As now, there is some variation in disyllabic adjectives (e.g. *hungrier*, *hungriest*, *more hungry*, *most hungry*). There are only a few examples in *The Pilgrim's Progress* which do not conform to modern conventions:

> [T]was the *dreadfullest* sight that ever I saw. (*PP*, 60)
> His Voice to me has been *most sweet*. (*PP*, 311)

Although it is the very few deviations from current practice that stand out for modern readers, in this respect Bunyan's usage was modern for his time.[26]

---

[23] Lass, 'Phonology and Morphology', 167–71.
[24] They were still listed as acceptable forms in Robert Lowth's *A Short Introduction to English Grammar* (1763), ed. David A. Reibel (London: Routledge/Thoemmes, 1995), 77.
[25] See Lass, 'Phonology and Morphology', 166–71, and Jenny Cheshire, 'Standardization and the English Irregular Verbs', in Stein and Tieken-Boon van Ostade (eds.), *Towards a Standard English*, 115–33.
[26] See Lass, 'Phonology and Morphology', 156–57.

Table 24.1 Strong verb paradigms in *The Pilgrim's Progress*

	OE class	Past tense		Past participle	
		Number	(%)	Number	(%)
drank	III	9	82	2	18
drunk		0	0	0	0
beat	VII	3	50	3	50
beaten		0	0	0	0
began	III	96	97	3	3
begun		0	0	2	100
gave	V	62	98	1	2
given		0	0	43	100
took	follows VI	58	94	4	6
taken		0	0	39	100
forgot	V	2	33	4	67
forgat		1	100	0	0
forgotten		0	0	4	100
got	V	45	53	40	47
gat		3	100	0	0
gotten		0	0	6	100
wrote	I	2	100	0	0
writ		1	33	2	67
written		0	0	19	100
eat	V	7	88	1	12
ate		0	0	0	0
eaten		0	0	4	100
sang	III	5	100	0	0
sung		2	100	0	0
Total		296		177	

Later grammarians, including Lowth and Murray, objected to double negatives and double genitives on the grounds of efficiency and logic.[27] Neither of these is found with any great frequency in Bunyan's writing, but the few examples would have been unremarkable for contemporary readers:

---

[27] See Lowth, *Short Introduction to the English Grammar*, 139–40, and Lindley Murray, *An English Grammar*, new edn, 2 vols (York: Longman et al., 1808), 1: 246.

[A]fter that, came the Troubles [. . .] *of my Husbands* into my mind.²⁸ (*PP*, 205)
[Y]ou would *not neither* so have bewailed that oversight of yours. (*PP*, 196)

Archaism in *The Pilgrim's Progress*

Bunyan employs several linguistic features that were no longer in common written usage. These have two contrary effects: of elevating his written style and of making it seem provincial or unadorned.²⁹ As we have seen, later readers have been able to read Bunyan as progressively more provincial even when he was not using archaisms. This section seeks to identify linguistic features that were archaic at the time of writing. These reside more in grammar and syntax than in lexis and pronunciation. A few archaic pronunciations persisted as useful variants in writing poetry. For example, *key* could be pronounced to rhyme with *way* where required:

> *What* Christian *left lock't up and went his way,*
> *Sweet* Christiana *opens with her Key.* (*PP*, 171)

Although Bunyan's lexis was conservative, he does not tend to use archaic vocabulary, which might have impeded comprehension, but he did use archaic grammatical constructions to elevate the tone. For example, he uses *mine* and *thine* as possessive determiners before vowels in almost 50 per cent of possible occurrences (see Table 24.2). For instance:

> [H]e also wiped *mine* Eyes with his Handkerchief, and clad me in Silver and Gold; he put a Chain about *my* Neck, and Ear-rings in *mine* Ears, and a beautiful Crown upon *my* Head. (*PP*, 222–23)

This archaic usage was preserved in religious discourse under the influence of the King James Bible and the earlier translations on which it was based, as, for example, in '*my* sleep departed from *mine* eyes' (Genesis 31:40).

Old English *þu* (singular) and *ge* (plural) developed into *thou* and *ye*, with the object form (*you*) generally replacing *ye* even for the subject by about 1600. The plural forms had begun to be used respectfully to singular addressees during the thirteenth century, and by the time Bunyan was writing, *you* had almost entirely replaced *thou*. By the eighteenth century, *thou* forms were 'not really a living option in ordinary usage',³⁰ though they survived longer in some dialects than others and were more likely to be

---

[28] This is the reading in the first edition of 1678 (47); the editor of *PP* has emended to *Husband* (205).
[29] Mary Catherine Davidson discusses different types of literary archaism from this period in 'Did Shakespeare Consciously Use Archaic English?', *Early Modern Literary Studies*, 1 (1997), 1–14.
[30] Lass, 'Phonology and Morphology', 153.

Table 24.2 Bunyan's use of *my/mine* and *thy/thine* as possessive determiners

Before a consonant		Before <h>		Before a vowel	
my/thy	mine/thine	my/thy	mine/thine	my/thy	mine/thine
727	0	89	6	36	31
100%	0%	94%	6%	54%	46%

used for inferiors and intimates. The continued use of *thou* in religious discourse is under the influence of the archaic language of the Bible: there is no reason to think that Bunyan, who denounced Quaker teachings, would have adopted this linguistic mannerism from them.[31]

Because it was based on earlier translations, the King James Bible largely preserves the historical distinction between singular and plural second-person pronouns as well as the subject/object distinction between *ye* and *you*, though both were already archaic by 1611. For example:

> But John forbad him, saying, I have need to be baptized of *thee* [object], and comest *thou* [subject] to me. (Matthew 1:14)

> For if *ye* [subject] forgive men their trespasses, *your* [determiner] heavenly Father will also forgive *you* [object]. (Matthew 6:3)

Bunyan's use of second-person forms is more mixed. Sometimes he observes the singular/plural distinction. For example:

> Also I advise that *thou* put this letter in *thy* Bosome, that *thou* read therein to *thy* self and to *thy* Children, until *you* have got it by root-of-Heart. (PP, 180)

Here the switch from singular to plural serves a grammatical function, indicating that Christiana's children have also to learn the letter by rote. However, when Mrs Timorous tries to dissuade Christiana from her pilgrimage, this distinction is not observed:

> Oh the madness that has possessed *thee* [object] and *thy* [determiner] Husband, to run *your* [determiner] selves upon such difficulties! *You* [subject] have heard, I am sure, what *your* [determiner] Husband did meet with. (PP, 182)

---

[31] See T. L. Underwood, '"For Then I Should Be a Ranter or a Quaker": John Bunyan and Radical Religion', in David Gay, James G. Randall, and Arlette Zinck (eds.), *Awakening Words: John Bunyan and the Language of Community* (Newark, DE: University of Delaware Press, 2000), 127–40, and Barber, *Early Modern English*, 155–56.

Here *thou* forms are replaced by *you* forms to include Christian, but although the second sentence is clearly addressed to Christiana alone, it does not revert to *thou*. Thus *The Pilgrim's Progress* mixes the singular/plural use of the Bible and contemporary religious discourse with the colloquial preference for *you*.

The use of *you* for singular addressees was originally a mark of respect, but it would be difficult to argue that Bunyan's use is conditioned by differences in status. For example, Evangelist uses a mixture of forms in addressing Christian: 'Keep that light in *your* eye, and go up directly thereto, so shalt *thou* see the Gate' (*PP*, 10). *Thou* may sometimes retain some of its affective function, operating in the same way that a pet name might.[32] For example, despite their higher status, the Physician and Christiana initially both address Matthew as *you*: 'Come, come, said the Physician, *you* must take it. [...] I must have *you* take it, said his Mother' (*PP*, 229). However, in her attempt to overcome Matthew's reluctance, Christiana then appeals to his emotions: 'If *thou* lovest thy Mother, if *thou* lovest thy Brothers, if *thou* lovest Mercie, if *thou* lovest thy Life, take it' (*PP*, 230).

Some studies have found that *you* was preferred as the subject of lexical verbs and *thou* as the subject of auxiliaries in the sixteenth and early seventeenth centuries.[33] This trend is not apparent in *The Pilgrim's Progress* (see Table 24.3), where *you* is preferred as the subject of the auxiliaries *must, should, would,* and *could*. This may be influenced, in part, by ease of pronunciation: the selection of *thou* dictates the use of the forms *wouldst, shouldst,* and *couldst* (*must* remains unchanged). The difficulty of pronouncing these consonant clusters is suggested by the occurrence of infrequent but highly archaic forms like *wouldest*. Bunyan preserves the grammatical distinction between *thou* and *thee* but usually uses *you* for both objects and subjects. The archaic *ye* is only occasionally used for plural subjects. For example, after saving Christiana and Mercie from their attackers, the Reliever says:

> I marvelled much when *you* [subject] was entertained at the Gate above, being *ye* [subject] knew that *ye* [subject] were but weak Women, that *you* [subject] petitioned not the Lord there for a Conductor. (*PP*, 196)

There are only eighteen examples of *ye* in *The Pilgrim's Progress*, largely in biblical allusions and quotations, and particularly often in imperatives.

Historically, as we have seen, the singular second-person pronoun had been followed by a distinctive form of present tense verbs, which were generally replaced by uninflected forms during the course of the seventeenth century, although *hast, do(e)st, art,* and *shalt* remained commonplace for longer. However, Bunyan almost always employs

---

[32] See Lass, 'Phonology and Morphology', 151–52.
[33] Lass, 'Phonology and Morphology', 149.

Table 24.3 Bunyan's use of *thou* and *you* as singular subjects before selected auxiliary verbs

	Part I		*Part II*		Total	
	Number	(%)	Number	(%)	Number	(%)
thou+would	0	0	4	57	4	29
you+would	7	100	3	43	10	71
Subtotal	7		7		14	
thou+should	1	20	4	44	5	36
you+should	4	80	5	56	9	64
Subtotal	5		9		14	
thou+could	n/a		0	0	0	0
you+could			4	100	4	100
Subtotal	0		4		4	
thou+must	4	40	6	55	10	48
you+must	6	60	5	45	11	52
Subtotal	10		11		21	
thou+these auxiliaries	5	23	14	45	19	36
you+these auxiliaries	17	77	17	55	34	64
Total	22		31		53	

the conservative *-est* inflection following *thou*, as seen above. In the following conversation *art* is unremarkable, but *wast* is old-fashioned:

> Christian. What *wast* thou once?
> Man. The Man said, I was once a fair and flourishing Professor [...].
> Christian. Well, but what *art* thou now? (*PP*, 34)

PDE requires that every clause should have a grammatical subject even if it has no lexical meaning (e.g. *it is raining, there are too many people*). Subjectless clauses had been commonplace in the earlier history of English, however, and Bunyan provides a few examples, such as: 'that place was all grown over with Bryers and Thorns; excepting here and there where [] was an inchanted Arbor' (*PP*, 295–96). Similarly, relative pronouns are occasionally missing where we would expect to see them in PDE:

> There is a Looking-glass [ ] hangs up in the Dining-room. (*PP*, 287)
> There was a foul Fiend [ ] haunted the Valley of Humiliation. (*PP*, 293)

These constructions would have seemed archaic to Bunyan's contemporaries.[34]

---

[34] Rissanen, 'Syntax', 249–53.

Differences between the Language of *Part I* and *Part II*

There are a number of statistically significant differences between the language of *Part I* and *Part II* of *The Pilgrim's Progress*. These might be considered the result of Bunyan's growing confidence and reputation: an indication that *Part II* was not subject to the same anxious process of feedback and revision as *Part I*.[35] If we were to accept this explanation, *Part II* could be seen as offering a better reflection of Bunyan's own language which had not, in itself, changed in the intervening period. However, I will argue that these linguistic changes reflect Bunyan's development as a writer.

Many of the differences between *Part I* and *Part II* represent a move towards the language of the Bible. For example, *before* 'earlier' is always used in *Part I*, but *afore* occurs seven times in *Part II* ($p = 0.01$):[36] 'But met you with no opposition afore you set out of Doors?' (*PP*, 205). The *Oxford English Dictionary* cites *afore* from OE onwards, but by the late seventeenth century it was largely nautical, though also persisting in regional and archaic usage. Thus while later readers may perceive it as dialectal, contemporary readers would have been familiar with its biblical usage.

Grammatical variation offers more convincing evidence yet. For instance, Bunyan occasionally uses object pronouns in reflexive contexts. For example:

> So when they were within, they were bidden sit down and rest *them*. (*PP*, 199)
> Then he turned *him* to the Boys, and asked them of their names. (*PP*, 248)

This use of object pronouns had become infrequent by the seventeenth century,[37] but was preserved in the King James Bible, as in: 'they have made them a molten calf' (Exodus 32:8). There is only one example of this construction in *Part I*, but there are five in *Part II* ($p = 0.01$).

Returning to second-person pronouns, where the addressee is clearly singular, *Part I* has a preference for *you* forms, while *Part II* has a preference for *thou* forms ($p = 0.01$; see Table 24.4). Again, this is a feature of language preserved, for Bunyan's contemporaries, in the Bible and religious discourse.

OE and ME had more flexible syntax than PDE, but subject-verb constructions had always been common, and by the end of the ME period they predominated everywhere except in questions. Verb-subject inversions were commonplace into the sixteenth century after a restricted range of subordinating conjunctions, such as *therefore*, *yet*, and *so*, as in: 'therefore came they under the shadow of my roof' (Genesis 19:8). By the

---

[35] See Robert Southey (ed.), *The Pilgrim's Progress: With a Life of John Bunyan* (London: J. Murray & J. Major, 1830), lxxxvii.
[36] There is a probability of less than 1 per cent that this change is caused by random variation.
[37] Rissanen, 'Syntax', 255–58.

Table 24.4 Bunyan's use of *thou* and *you* forms for singular addressees

	Part I		Part II		Total	
	Number	(%)	Number	(%)	Number	(%)
thou forms	284	41	309	52	593	46
you forms	408	59	280	48	688	54
Total	692		589		1,281	

Table 24.5 Subject–verb inversion after *then*

	Part I		Part II		Total	
	Number	(%)	Number	(%)	Number	(%)
then+S+V	134	59	138	49	272	53
then+V+S	93	41	144	51	237	47
Total	227		282		509	
then+S+*to say*	7	50	74	36	81	37
then+*to say*+S	7	50	129	64	136	63
Total	14		203		217	

seventeenth century, inversion had become considerably rarer, but Bunyan makes frequent use of it. For example:

> Then *said By-ends*, I shall never desert my old Principles. (*PP*, 100)
> Then *had it* fared well with us beyond what 'tis like to do now. (*PP*, 178)

Subject and verb are inverted in almost half of the 508 clauses beginning with *then*, particularly frequently for the verb *say* (see Table 24.5). This rate was characteristic of the period 1350–1500, the era of Wyclif's Bible, one of the translations on which the King James Bible was based. By contrast, seventeenth-century writers on average inverted only about 7 per cent of this type of clause.[38] Table 24.5 demonstrates that *Part II* inverts subject and verb significantly more frequently than *Part I* ($p = 0.01$).

This pattern, by which *Part II* uses more biblicized language than *Part I*, allows us to interpret an otherwise ambiguous feature of Bunyan's syntax. Bunyan uses *do* in various constructions also found in PDE, including:

- as a lexical verb e.g. the evil thou hast formerly *done* to thy Husband. (*PP*, 179)
- to avoid repetition e.g. they […] bid him look South; so he *did*. (*PP*, 55)

---

[38] Rissanen, 'Syntax', 264–67.

Table 24.6 The use of *did* (only) in *The Pilgrim's Progress*

	Part I		Part II	
	Number	(%)	Number	(%)
Lexical or in substitution	54	31	36	20
In negative statements	20	11	12	7
In questions (positive or negative)	45	25	22	12
Periphrastic or emphatic	58	33	113	62
Total	177		183	

- in questions e.g. What *do* you think of the Bible? (*PP*, 226)
- in negatives e.g. I *do* not know. (*PP*, 14)
- in negative imperatives e.g. Remember man in time, stoop, *do* not fear. (*PP*, 149)

PDE can use *do* for emphasis in affirmative imperatives (e.g. *Do answer the question*), but Bunyan sometimes includes the pronoun, in keeping with contemporary usage: '*do* you answer that question' (*PP*, 150). None of these constructions can be considered emphatic in *The Pilgrim's Progress*.

Periphrastic *do* is commonly found in the eMnE period, though it is recorded from early ME onwards. For example, when Matthew is taken ill, Samuel remarks that 'some of the Trees hung over the Wall, and my Brother *did* plash and *did* eat' (*PP*, 229). Periphrastic *do* was in decline in affirmative statements by the seventeenth century, reaching more or less modern distributions by the eighteenth.[39] This suggests that Bunyan's uses are largely periphrastic echoes of biblical language and should not, on the whole, be read as emphatic. For example, the phrasing 'True my Child, said Christiana, he *did* take thereof and *did* eat' (*PP*, 229) is decidedly redolent of 'she took of the fruit thereof, and did eat, and gave also unto her husband with her; and he did eat' (Genesis 3:6). However, Christiana goes on to use what could be understood as an emphatic *do*: 'I *did* chide him, and yet he would eat thereof' (*PP*, 229). Although it is impossible to disentangle periphrastic, emphatic, and biblical *do* in Bunyan's writing, the higher frequency of these constructions in *Part II* ($p = 0.01$; see Table 24.6) is in keeping with the increased influence of biblical language as discussed.

Apparently in opposition with the increasing influence of biblical language, some differences between *Part I* and *Part II* suggest a closer representation of spoken idiom. For example, *yes* and *yea* had both been widely used since the OE period, but *yea* was archaic and restricted to dialect by this period. *Aye* 'appears suddenly about 1575, and is exceedingly common about 1600' (*OED*). Its origins are uncertain, but it has always been more common in nautical language and dialect. In *Part I*, the unmarked

---

[39] Rissanen, 'Syntax', 239–48.

Table 24.7 *Have* contraction

	Part I		Part II		Total	
	Number	(%)	Number	(%)	Number	(%)
would a	1	50	12	36	13	37
could a	0	0	7	21	7	20
should a	1	50	2	6	3	9
had/would like to a	0	0	3	9	3	9
might a	0	0	7	21	7	20
Other examples	0	0	2	6	2	6
Total	2		33		35	

yes accounts for 50 per cent of all occurrences, with archaic *yea* used for 41 per cent. *Aye* accounts for only 9 per cent of examples. In *Part II*, uses of *aye* increase to 17 per cent ($p = 0.05$),[40] more at the expense of *yes* (44 per cent) than *yea* (40 per cent), representing a balance between the Bible and contemporary speech in terms of their influence on Bunyan's language.

In his review of Southey's edition, Walter Scott remarked on Bunyan's use of <a> for *have*, as in: 'But it would *a* made you *a* wondered to *have* seen the dead Bodies' (*PP*, 282). Scott implied that this was a widespread spoken variant and regarded it as a matter more of spelling than grammar.[41] Indeed, forms such as *coulda* (1925–) and *woulda* (1913–) are sometimes found in representations of non-standard speech today. Bunyan's use of this variant is conditioned by grammatical context (see Table 24.7) though there is no reason to assume that he was alert to its distributional pattern. In the example given, the first contraction is typical and the second, where it is the first auxiliary, very unusual. Lexical *have* is never contracted.

Ninety-four per cent of *have* contractions occur after *would, should, could, might*, or *had/would like to*. There are significantly more examples in *Part II* than *Part I* ($p = 0.01$), indicating that this was another respect in which Bunyan was moving towards the closer representation of everyday speech.

PDE forms progressives with *be* followed by the present participle, a construction also used by Bunyan: 'I *am preparing* for a Journey' (*PP*, 181). He also indicates progressive tenses by the insertion of *a*, sometimes alongside *be*:

They found the good Woman *a preparing* to be gon. (*PP*, 181)
I *was a dreaming* last night.[42]

---

[40] There is a probability of less than 5 per cent that this change is caused by random variation.
[41] Scott, 'The Pilgrim's Progress', 489.
[42] This is the reading in the first edition of 1678 (13); the editor of *PP* has emended to *a dreamed* (182).

Less frequently, Bunyan uses *a* with past participles and adjectives. For example:

> I was *a* Dreamed that I sat all alone. (*PP*, 222)
> I was both *a* weary, and sleepy. (*PP*, 300)

These constructions were still common in speech at this time, but their use in writing reduced during the eighteenth century.[43] Although there is only one example in *Part I*, there are eight in *Part II* ($p = 0.01$), again suggesting a movement towards the closer representation of contemporary spoken idiom.

There is one grammatical difference between *Part I* and *Part II* in which spoken idiom trumps biblical influence: a shift from *-eth* to *-s* third-person singular present tenses. A northern construction in ME, found occasionally in London texts by the fourteenth century, *-s* had become normal in most contexts by the sixteenth century, though *-eth* forms offered a metrically useful extra syllable for writers of verse. Bunyan is unusual for his period in using a mixture of the two forms in prose. For example:

> [H]e *walketh* the Streets. (*PP*, 100)
> [H]e now *walks* in White. (*PP*, 176)

By the time Bunyan was writing, *-eth* forms were largely restricted to religious discourse. A few commonly used forms, including *hath* and *doth*, survived for longer, but *-eth* forms were not widely used in conversation at this period. Although earlier writers had sometimes written <walketh> to represent *walks*, it is unlikely that Bunyan was observing this archaic spelling convention: his *-eth* verbs are to be pronounced as such. Bunyan uses *-eth* forms for 74 per cent of third-person singular present tenses of a selection of common verbs in *Part I* (see Table 24.8). *Saith* and *doth* continue to be used markedly more frequently than the corresponding *-s* forms in *Part II*, but there is an overall reduction in *-eth* forms to 30 per cent ($p = 0.01$).

Conclusions

This analysis of Bunyan's language has demonstrated that although he wrote *The Pilgrim's Progress* in a simple style accessible to relatively uneducated readers, his control of the English language was far from unsophisticated. *The Pilgrim's Progress* is written in an archaic version of conservative seventeenth-century speech. It combines archaic grammatical features with simple, colloquial vocabulary that eschews recent and learned loans, thereby ensuring that the literal level of Bunyan's narrative was comprehensible even to inexperienced readers and listeners, making it ideal for family reading.

---

[43] Rissanen, 'Syntax', 217.

Table 24.8 Third-person singular present tenses in *The Pilgrim's Progress*

	Part I		Part II		Total	
	Number	(%)	Number	(%)	Number	(%)
talks	1	33	0	0	1	25
talketh	2	67	1	100	3	75
Subtotal	3		1		4	
walks	1	25	2	50	3	38
walketh	3	75	2	50	5	63
Subtotal	4		4		8	
gives	4	80	6	67	6	43
giveth	1	20	3	33	4	29
Subtotal	5		9		14	
comes	11	61	16	100	27	79
cometh	7	39	0	0	7	21
Subtotal	18		16		34	
says	3	18	2	20	5	19
saith	14	82	8	80	22	81
Subtotal	17		10		27	
does	3	10	5	11	5	7
doth	27	90	39	89	66	89
Subtotal	30		44		74	
has	19	23	136	86	155	64
hath	63	77	23	14	86	36
Subtotal	82		159		241	
-s	42	26	167	69	209	52
-eth	117	74	76	31	193	48
Total	159		243		402	

The longevity of its appeal can, then, be attributed, in part, to the avoidance of linguistic modernity, and comparison between *Part I* and *Part II* demonstrates that *The Pilgrim's Progress* became both more colloquial and more biblical when Bunyan recreated his earlier written style for the sequel to Christian's journey. Bunyan sums up the tension between these two impulses in his 'Apology' in *Part I*:

> *This Book is writ in such a Dialect,*
> *As may the minds of listless men affect:*
> *It seems a Novelty, and yet contains*
> *Nothing but sound and honest Gospel-strains.* (PP, 7)

An individual as well versed in the Bible as Bunyan would inevitably infuse his own writing with 'Biblical references, phrases and idioms'.[44] Disentangling normal features of contemporary language from stylistic archaism reveals just how the Bible speaks through Bunyan's work. His biblicized language would have sounded familiar to his contemporaries, imbuing his texts with solemn authority, but it would also have rendered the language of the Bible itself more accessible, and perhaps Bunyan developed this function of his style in response to the popularity of *Part I* amongst inexperienced readers.[45] Using biblical language not only raised the tone of *The Pilgrim's Progress*, but also allowed Bunyan to habituate his readers to linguistic features that might otherwise have been off-putting when they turned to the Bible for themselves. Linguistically as well as in its subject matter, *The Pilgrim's Progress* acts as an introduction to the Scriptures.

Bunyan's preference for well-established terms served his uneducated contemporaries well, but some of them were later marginalized by more recent loans. As a result, Bunyan's text seemed progressively more undignified and dialectal as time passed. Similarly, several grammatical features that would have been inoffensive to Bunyan's contemporaries were stigmatized by later grammarians, and readers and editors have sometimes judged Bunyan's language against these anachronistic criteria. Contemporary readers would generally not have considered Bunyan's grammar or pronunciation to be indicative of low birth or lack of education. For them, the language of *The Pilgrim's Progress* would have been characterized by its biblicized grammar and restricted vocabulary: deliberate stylistic choices for this work which demonstrate Bunyan's confident command of the language.

Suggested Reading

Barber, Charles, *Early Modern English*, 2nd edn (Edinburgh: Edinburgh University Press, 1997).

Coleman, Julie, 'The Manufactured Homespun Style of John Bunyan's Prose', *BS*, 18 (2014), 107–37.

Lass, Roger (ed.), *The Cambridge History of the English Language*, vol. 3: *1476–1776* (Cambridge: Cambridge University Press, 1999).

Mitchell, Linda C., *Grammar Wars: Language as Cultural Battlefield in 17th and 18th Century England* (Aldershot: Ashgate, 2001).

Stein, Dieter and Ingrid Tieken-Boon van Ostade (eds.), *Towards a Standard English 1600–1800* (The Hague: Mouton de Gruyter, 1994).

---

[44] W. R. Owens, 'John Bunyan and the Bible', in Anne Dunan-Page (ed.), *The Cambridge Companion to Bunyan* (Cambridge: Cambridge University Press, 2010), 39–50 (49).

[45] See Shannon Murray, '*A Book for Boys and Girls: Or, Country Rhimes for Children*: Bunyan and Literature for Children', in Dunan-Page (ed.), *Cambridge Companion to Bunyan*, 120–34.

CHAPTER 25

'NOR DO THOU GO TO WORK WITHOUT MY KEY'

Reading Bunyan Out to the Edges

MAXINE HANCOCK

WHILE it is now generally accepted that the marginal notes which elaborate Bunyan's narrative works are an important and integral aspect of his art, this has not always been the case. From the early eighteenth century on, editors and publishers took liberties with Bunyan's marginal notes. Editions appeared with them entirely omitted, or inset into the text as blocks of reduced-size print rather than as side notes flanking it, or vastly expanded by further editorial footnote commentary. During the eighteenth and nineteenth centuries, many of these interferences with the notes were aimed at deepening the didactic impact of Bunyan's narratives. In the twentieth century, however, editorial liberties taken with the marginal notes served quite a different purpose. By the 1960s, standard popular editions of *The Pilgrim's Progress* appeared with the biblical references stripped away from the original marginal notes, on the basis that such marginal notes, while perhaps helpful to the original audience, were, for the modern reader, merely a distraction.[1] This pragmatic argument was, however, actually shorthand for other, more serious objections to Bunyan's works. Modern readers were, U. Milo Kaufmann observed, 'troubled by suspicions about the originality and wholeness of a work that so persistently points beyond itself'.[2] The marginal notes were conspicuous evidence of the effort of the author to control the interpretation of the work, and were therefore contributors to what Northrop Frye identified as resistance to allegory on the part of readers who were 'offended by the author's encroachment on their freedom of interpretation'.[3]

---

[1] See, for example, editions of *The Pilgrim's Progress* by Roger Sharrock (Harmondsworth: Penguin Books, 1965) and by James Thorpe (Boston, MA: Houghton Mifflin Company, 1969).

[2] U. Milo Kaufmann, *The Pilgrim's Progress and Traditions in Puritan Meditation* (New Haven, CT: Yale University Press, 1966), 25.

[3] Northrop Frye, *Anatomy of Criticism: Four Essays* (1957; Princeton, NJ: Princeton University Press, 1973), 90.

Reduction of the marginal notes, especially of their biblical content, was seen as a way of reducing what amounted to 'religious static', which interfered with the reception of the artistic work.

However, by the second half of the twentieth century, several developments favoured renewed attention to Bunyan's print margination. The publication of the Oxford English Texts edition of Bunyan's works standardized the inclusion of the marginal notes as originally published and as augmented or corrected in early editions. Concurrent with the publication of this edition, critical attention turned to the material aspects of early modern book production and consumption, and to the book-buying and reading habits of Nonconformist readers, a newly literate and socially marginalized underclass. A confluence of this historicizing impulse with reader-response theory and, later, with poststructuralist theory, encouraged further attention to aspects of the graphic representation of language which had hitherto been largely neglected.

All of these trends, taken together, have had the outcome that the marginal notes are now understood to be integral to Bunyan's works, and can neither be ignored nor dismissed in critical discussion of them. In the last decades of the twentieth century, this renewed critical attention to early modern print marginalia was heralded by seminal articles by Lawrence Lipking, who drew attention to 'notes and asides' from Coleridge to James Joyce; by Valentine Cunningham, who dealt specifically with Bunyan's margins; and by William Slights, who drew attention to the margins of Renaissance texts across genres.[4] The study of Bunyan's marginal notes has since then been enriched by major historically and theoretically informed studies of annotation and documentation, of paratexts in general and of marginal notes in particular, as well as in refined and expanded understandings of early modern print culture and reading.[5]

Reader-generated autographic marginalia have also been the object of considerable bibliographic and theoretical interest, as a result of the same general critical interests outlined.[6] These, however, are a phenomenon quite different from printed marginalia both in intent and in impact. While both printed marginalia and handwritten marginalia are forms of additional commentary or supplementation to the central text, the latter represent the ad hoc responses of readers, whereas printed marginalia are the

---

[4] Lawrence Lipking, 'The Marginal Gloss', *Critical Inquiry*, 3 (1977), 609–55; Valentine Cunningham, 'Glossing and Glozing: Bunyan and Allegory', in N. H. Keeble (ed.), *John Bunyan: Conventicle and Parnassus* (Oxford: Clarendon Press, 1988), 217–40; William Slights, 'The Edifying Margins of Renaissance Books', *Renaissance Quarterly*, 42 (1989), 682–716, ' "Marginal Notes That Spoile the Text": Scriptural Annotation in the English Renaissance', *Huntington Library Quarterly*, 55 (1992), 255–78, and 'Bunyan on the Edge', *BS*, 10 (2001/02), 29–45.

[5] See especially Evelyn Tribble, *Margins and Marginality: The Printed Page in Early Modern England* (Charlottesville, VA: University Press of Virginia, 1993); William Slights, *Managing Readers: Printed Marginalia in English Renaissance Books* (Ann Arbor, MI: University of Michigan Press, 2001); Heidi Brayman Hackel, *Reading Material in Early Modern England: Print, Gender, and Literacy* (Cambridge: Cambridge University Press, 2005), 69–136.

[6] For more on reader-written marginalia, see H. J. Jackson, *Marginalia: Readers Writing in Books* (New Haven, CT, and London: Yale University Press, 2001); William H. Sherman, *Used Books: Marking Readers in Renaissance England* (Philadelphia, PA: University of Pennsylvania Press, 2008).

result of pre-publication decisions made to augment the central text and guide the reader's interpretation of it. Whereas handwritten marginalia use the white space around the block of print on a page to bear witness to the individual reading and personalization of the text, printed marginalia attest to the guidance towards shared meanings within an implicitly or explicitly defined community of readers. While both kinds of marginalia are of interest as we continue to explore the relationships of readers, authors, books, and meaning, they are best distinguished from each other rather than merged in discussion. This chapter will concern itself with print margination.

Alongside the general interest in book and reading history, a broadening and deepening understanding of Bunyan and his readership has allowed for an increasingly nuanced discussion regarding the significance of the margins both to Bunyan as author and to his intended audience. N. H. Keeble and Michael Davies, for example, pay attention to the particularities of the social and economic placement, together with more respectful treatments of the theological assumptions of Bunyan and his original audience of English Nonconformist readers than have often been accorded.[7] They each give careful attention to the margins, Keeble discussing the construction of the 'implied reader' and 'implied author' as revealed in them, and Davies drawing attention to the role of the marginal notes in guiding the reader towards a 'graceful', or reassuring, reading of Bunyan's works, particularly of *The Pilgrim's Progress*.

Marginal Notes as Received Convention

Marginated texts are a familiar feature of seventeenth-century books. In adding marginal notes to his works, Bunyan followed an established convention, although in his own characteristic style. Until the mid-seventeenth century, print margination was primarily used for citing references from classical and patristic sources, or for adding quotations from Latin, Greek, or Hebrew texts which were relevant to the central text. W. Speed Hill, twentieth-century editor of Richard Hooker's works, describes the 'familiar pattern' by which Hooker marginates his works: 'the base text is to be intelligible to "even the simplest"; controverted texts appear there in English, the original Latin or Greek in [marginal] notes, to satisfy "those which are learned" '. In this use of marginal notes, 'the argument proceeds simultaneously on two levels: in the vernacular for the lay reader; in the language of scholarly citation [in the margins] for the linguistically

---

[7] N. H. Keeble, *The Literary Culture of Nonconformity in Later Seventeenth-Century England* (Leicester: Leicester University Press, 1987); Michael Davies, *Graceful Reading: Theology and Narrative in the Works of John Bunyan* (Oxford: Oxford University Press, 2002).

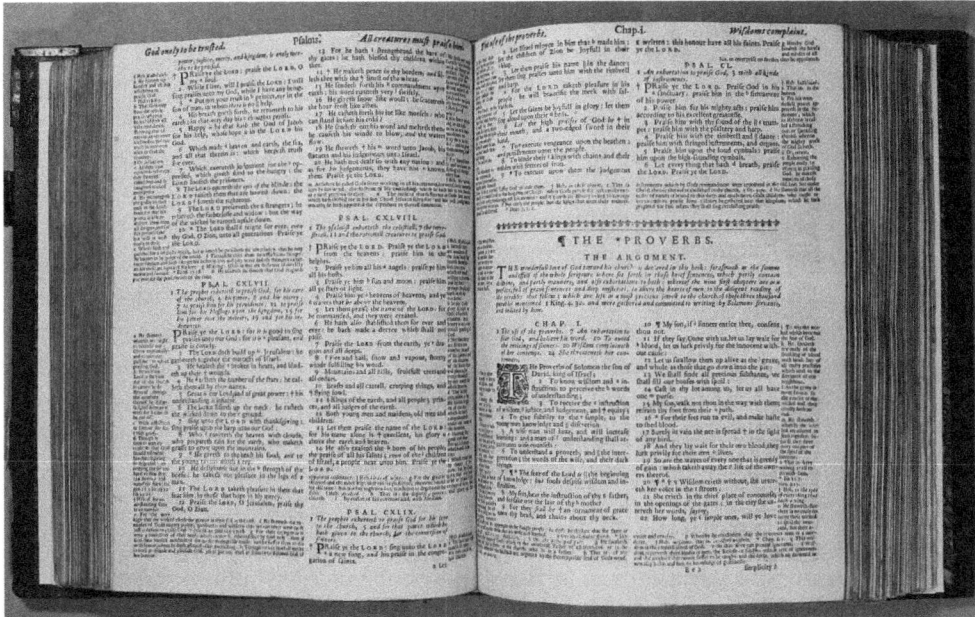

FIGURE 25.1 Opening page of Proverbs, in a 1649 edition of *The Holy Bible*.
(Image courtesy of Bruce Peel Special Collections, University of Alberta.)

adept, university-trained reader'.[8] This standard and accepted use was, however, changed with the advent and widespread reading of the Geneva Bible, in which the margins, in addition to offering textual information, gave detailed commentary for the guidance of the unlearned and 'simple' reader (see Figure 25.1, showing Authorized Version text with Geneva notes). In this use, the marginal notes became a territory for educating the relatively uninitiated reader of Scriptures rather than a place of scholarly dialogue with antecedent literature, reversing the flow of explication so that the margin now explained the text, rather than the text explaining the margin.

The printed page was best suited to margination when produced in large formats. Heidi Brayman Hackel generalizes:

> Marginal annotations occur more often in larger and hence more expensive books; the smallest books only rarely contain annotations [...]. A scholar reading primarily theology and law [...] would encounter printed marginalia in nearly all his books, whereas a contemporary reading verse in cheap small formats would seldom handle a book with printed marginalia.[9]

---

[8] W. Speed Hill, 'Commentary upon Commentary upon Commentary: Three Historicisms Annotating Richard Hooker', in D. C. Greetham (ed.), *The Margins of the Text* (Ann Arbor, MI: University of Michigan Press, 1997), 323–52 (340).

[9] Hackel, *Reading Material*, 89.

When Bunyan adds his extensive margination to often very small-paged volumes, produced for a readership from a lower income and educational level than had previously been book-buyers, he is—if quite unwittingly—participating in the democratization of the printed page. While a few of Bunyan's minor pastoral or polemical works were published in pamphlet formats with page sizes as large as 7¼" × 5¼" (for example, *A Case of Conscience*, 1683), the great majority of his works were published in very small formats, with the page size of *The Pilgrim's Progress* (1678) being 5⅝" × 3½" and other major works having similar diminutive size. The largest page size of the major works, *The Holy War* (1682), commanded a capacious 6½" × 3¾". Not until the posthumous publication of many of Bunyan's works in Charles Doe's folio edition of 1692 were his works presented on large, double-columned pages, 13½" × 8½".[10] This posthumous elevation of the 'tinker' to the status of the authors he had denigrated—that is, those who adorned their work with citations demonstrating their wide humanistic knowledge happened, ironically enough, at the very time when print margination was starting to be seen as 'old and antiquated'.[11]

Noting the frequent occurrence of printers' notices advertising marginal notes as a selling feature of books, Hackel argues that printers encouraged authors to supply marginal notes, apparently to satisfy readers' demands for the additional guidance given by the notes.[12] Bunyan's habits of writing seem to have responded to that demand, whether the impulse arose from his printers' requests, from his own remembered reading experience with his struggle towards achieving hermeneutic balance, or directly from those readers who responded to his works. At any rate, the marginal notes in Bunyan's works demonstrate both a sense of conventional use and a fresh appropriation of the white space at the edges of the central text for expressive and didactic purposes.

Authorial Responsibility for Marginal Notes

The degree to which Bunyan was the author or source of the print margination in his books is open to some debate. Roger Sharrock comments: 'Whether Bunyan was responsible for all the marginal glosses or for only some of them, seems impossible of determination. Some of these glosses are so colourless that they might very easily have been added by another hand; others are very distinctly tinged with the Bunyan flavour' (*PP*, lxxxiii). Hackel says that annotations 'could be provided by any of the many different people involved in the production of a book—authors, translators, editors,

---

[10] All measurements are as given by Frank Mott Harrison, *A Bibliography of the Works of John Bunyan* (Oxford: Oxford University Press, for the Bibliographical Society, 1932).
[11] Evelyn Tribble, '"Like a Looking-Glass"', in Greetham (ed.), *Margins of the Text*, 229–44.
[12] Hackel, *Reading Material*, 89.

friends, acquaintances'.[13] Establishing authorial integrity does, however, add significance to Bunyan's notes, and a strong case for Bunyan's authorship of the notes to his works can be made. Internal evidence indicates authorial consciousness of the margins and claims for responsibility. A consistent decorum seems to dictate the use of marginal notes across his corpus of works, with variations apparently dependent upon Bunyan's concept of genre, rather than upon the printer. While the printer may have urged Bunyan to supply marginal notes, it appears that even the 'dull' and 'ubiquitous' biblical references were, at least in the main, written by Bunyan himself.

Evidence for Bunyan's self-consciousness in his authorship of the margins is quite striking. Perhaps the best-known statement of this awareness is in his verse preface 'To the Reader' in *The Holy War*, in which the reader is given the final admonition: '*Nor do thou go to work without my Key* [...]. *It lies there in the* window' (*HW*, 5). The word 'window' is glossed with its own unambiguous marginal note: 'The margent'. But Bunyan has demonstrated his conscious use of the margins as an author much earlier. In writing to his imagined audiences in the preface to *The Holy City* (1665), he composes a set of four prefatory epistles, including one '*To the Learned Reader*', in which he says, defiantly:

> I have not given you, either in the Line, or in the Margent, a Cloud of Sentences from the Learned FATHERS, that have according to their Wisdom (possibly) handled these matters long before me. (*MW*, 3: 70–1)

The seriousness with which Bunyan takes the writing of his own marginal expansions and clarifications can also be deduced from the care with which he approaches the marginal notes that accompany the biblical texts to which habitually he refers his reader. In *The Life and Death of Mr. Badman* (1680), for example, Bunyan's narrator, Mr Worldly-Wiseman, comments on Mr Badman's broken leg as 'an open stroak' of judgement: 'And it looks much like to that in *Job* [...] *He striketh them as wicked men in the open sight of others*: Or as the Margent reads it, *in the place of beholders*' (*MB*, 134). In offering here the alternative marginal reading given in the Authorized Version (1611) as part of the scriptural quotation, Bunyan grants an insight into the significance of marginal readings to interpreting the sacred text, and, by extension, to the writing and reading of religious texts. In *A Holy Life* (1684), by contrast, Bunyan indicates the importance he gives to the marginal biblical references adjacent to his own texts, telling the reader to 'See these Scriptures in the Margent, and take heed' (*MW*, 9: 304). This direct command to the reader suggests the conscious deliberation with which Bunyan placed references in the margins; it is also clear that, in this case at least, Bunyan wrote the marginal references concurrent with the central text, with the clear intention that his reader should either recognize or take the trouble to look up and reflect upon the biblical texts noted.

In the prologues to several of his narratives, we find direct statements by Bunyan which describe the marginal notes and the relationship he intends them to bear to the

---

[13] Hackel, *Reading Material*, 127–28.

reading of the story. In 'The Author to the Reader' in *The Life and Death of Mr. Badman*, for example, Bunyan explicitly defines the marginal device of the pointing finger ('sign manual' or '*maniculum*') as indicating

> *things either fully known by me, as being eye and ear-witness thereto, or that I have received from such hands, whose relation as to this, I am bound to believe. And that the Reader may know them from other things and passages herin contained, I have pointed at them in the Margent, as with a finger thus:*☞ (*MB*, 4)

And in 'The Conclusion' to *The Pilgrim's Progress*, the reader is instructed, '*Put by the Curtains, look within my Vail; / Turn up my Metaphors and not fail*' (*PP*, 164), surely an instruction to follow the leads offered by the marginal notes.

The decorum with which Bunyan uses marginal notes as adjunct to the central text is remarkable across the many years of his career as a writer and the different printers who published his works. It is noticeable, for instance, that across the decades from 1656 onward, major works are significantly more generously marginated than minor works. Early theological treatises, *Some Gospel-Truths Opened* (1656) and *The Doctrine of the Law and Grace Unfolded* (1659) are fully marginated, as are all his major fictive and allegorical works. Polemical exchanges, by contrast, are scantly marginated, and even then mostly by references only to page numbers in the works under attack. Printed sermons are marginated mainly by chapter and or verse number, or occasional headings, as the sermon proceeds through the biblical text. Works written in rhyme are not marginated at all.

During Bunyan's lifetime, marginal notes were added to or amended in later editions of some of his works, the many additions to the early editions of *The Pilgrim's Progress*, for instance, being of considerable interest as they appear not only to reflect a changing political situation, but also to provide further explanations to prevent possible misreadings of the story. An interesting, if not easily explained, inversion of this pattern of adding notes to later editions occurs with *The Doctrine of the Law and Grace Unfolded*. A second edition printed in 1685 (and a derivative edition, also called 'second edition', in 1701) were printed with the extensive and expansive marginal notes of the first edition almost entirely omitted. Particularly interesting is the deletion of some lengthy personal marginal notes, among them one describing Bunyan's experience of conviction while playing a Sabbath game of cat (*MW*, 2: 157), a story developed more fully in his spiritual autobiography, *Grace Abounding to the Chief of Sinners* (1666). Why such signal marginal notes are omitted in the later printing is obscure, though Greaves notes that the absence of additional margination in the second edition may indicate that Bunyan 'lacked the time to make alterations', as in 1685 he was 'occupied [. . .] with other writing' (*MW*, 2: 6–7). Perhaps there was less demand from readers for marginal notes by the date of the second edition, although *The Holy War*, published only a few years earlier, was abundantly marginated. Perhaps Bunyan felt that many marginal notes could be omitted because he had more fully developed the discussion elsewhere; or perhaps the printer simply did not have a typesetter skilled enough to set the long marginal notes that had appeared in the first edition.

Of Bunyan's major narrative works, only *Grace Abounding* is unmarginated. As a personal confessional work in which Bunyan speaks in his own voice throughout, it does not seem to have called for the additional authorial voice in the margins. The fictive and allegorical works, on the other hand, allow the author to assume a narratorial persona in the central text while retaining his pastoral role of offering 'alongside' guidance in the margins, with the lively margination remaining a vital and interesting aspect of these works. Many of the marginal notes demonstrate Bunyan's sure command of idiom, proverb, and aphorism. An example of Bunyan's use of each of these modes drawn almost at random from *The Pilgrim's Progress* will serve to illustrate: 'Christian *snibbeth his fellow for unadvised speaking*'; '*The Worldly Man for a Bird in the Hand*'; 'Good discourse prevents drowsiness' (PP, 127, 31, 137).

THE CONVENTION APPROPRIATED AND ADAPTED

In adopting and adapting the convention of marginal notes, Bunyan and some of his fellow Nonconformist writers made both traditional and new uses of space that had been exploited largely for demonstrating scholarship. Bunyan's practice both imitates and subverts the convention. The very appearance of the marginated page made certain demands upon, and set up certain expectations in, the reader. Religious texts with annotations resembled the then-current editions of the English Bible, for example, and so for newly literate readers, perhaps like Bunyan himself coming to the fare of 'godly' reading from broadsheets and chapbooks, the appearance of the page signalled the requirement of intense and serious reading. Bunyan's marginal notes were, then, a place for him both to demonstrate knowledge of his own authenticating sources (the English Bible, of course, as well as a few select works well known to his own readers, such as John Foxe's *Book of Martyrs*) and to declare his ignorance of humanistic scholarly sources. By the time he writes *The Pilgrim's Progress, Part II*, Bunyan is confident enough to satirize those who claim authority through the knowledge of classical languages, glossing the Latin phrase, '*ex Carne & Sanguine Christi*' with the wry marginal comment: '*The Lattine I borrow*' (PP, 229).

For an author urgent to guide the interpretation and to link the fictive narrative to the text of the Bible as the ground of the spiritual meaning of his stories, the convention of marginal notes is an obviously useful device. In addition to the didactic and mimetic functions of the margins, Bunyan is conscious of the ability of the margins to add depth by reflecting, intensifying, or ameliorating the adjacent central text by direct comment or by juxtaposition with the biblical intertext. Since this intertext was itself marginated, Bunyan's citations have a quality of creating a hall-of-mirrors effect: intensifying and multiplying the routes by which readers might 'arrive at the desired haven' of the intended meaning.

Hackel argues that 'printed marginalia [...] served [...] to define an audience, protect the author's meaning, and forward particular habits of reading'.[14] Bunyan's works were read, quite apparently, right out to the edges, by a newly literate and intensely biblically oriented readership, the readers themselves experiencing, through the process of reading and relating what they were reading both to life and to referenced intertexts, a new sense of personal agency.[15] The implied audience of Bunyan's works is delineated by Keeble as a substantial and definable readership of people with committed Nonconformist religious views who were 'not only able but diligent readers' but financially able to avail themselves of 'books primarily directed to the consolation and encouragement of believers, and particularly Nonconformists'.[16]

Yet exactly how marginal notes were read is still an unrecovered—and perhaps irrecoverable—'black box'. Hackel sees the habits of reading encouraged by printed marginal notes to include slowed and attentive reading, with the mental habits of reviewing and rereading aided by the indexing of the marginal notes. In Bunyan's narratives, the marginal notes seem intentionally to slow the reading of the narrative, to demand that the reader reflect on the spiritual lesson inscribed in the story, forge connections to a web of scriptural references, and take time to consider how the story should apply to one's own life. Furthermore, the splitting of the page and the bifurcating of reading through the use of marginal notes reflects habits of thought based on a dual vision of reality in which 'the real' is comprised of two parts: that which is seen and that which is unseen. The dual text of Bunyan's narratives, then, both relied upon and encouraged the habit of thinking beyond the temporal or material reality to the spiritual reality seen to lie beyond it. Such intense reading as Bunyan's texts required no doubt played a significant role in the gradual internalization of the reading experience, and thus in the process of internalizing and individuating religious experience.

No doubt the attention paid to the printed marginalia varied from reader to reader, and from reading to reading. A reader who was using *The Pilgrim's Progress* as a devotional or Bible study guide, for instance, might well read it with a Bible at hand and actually stop to look up the references. A family oral reading around a table might include a mnemonic game in which family members would be challenged to quote the Scriptures indicated by the references, such memorizing of the Bible's texts by chapter and verse being encouraged and valued. Other readers might use the margins simply as a convenient way of remembering where they left off in the story, ignoring the counter-narrative pull of many of the reference notes, or only checking their own interpretation against the author's intention. In whatever ways they were read, Bunyan's marginal notes served as a device that continually tugged the eye past the edges of the central text on the page to the margins, which, in turn, signalled a fuller level of meaning to be gained

---

[14] Hackel, *Reading Material*, 127.
[15] See Charles Taylor, *Sources of the Self* (Cambridge, MA: Harvard University Press, 1989), 177–233; see also Maxine Hancock, 'Identity, Agency and Community: Intimations and Implications of Emerging Literacy for Women in *The Pilgrim's Progress, The Second Part*', BS, 11 (2003/04), 74–93.
[16] Keeble, *Literary Culture of Nonconformity*, 139.

through rereading or reinterpreting a passage, fitting it to a scriptural intertext and within a theological framework, and finally applying it to one's own lived reality beyond the page.

Taxonomies of Form, Function, and Effect

Once the significance of the margins both to the author and to the reader of Bunyan's works is granted, a rich territory of exploration is staked out for further consideration. The possible interactions between authorial design and readers' purposes and practices across time make the effects of the marginal notes on the reception of the central text extremely complex. Nonetheless, several attempts have been made to classify those effects for the purpose of further discussion, particularly with regard to 'local effects'—that is, in attempting to describe how a particular marginal note affects the interpretation of a particular pericope within the central text.

Keeble examines the functions the marginal notes perform relative to the 'implied author' and 'implied reader'. In his analysis, the author implied by the marginal notes is an active participant in the hermeneutic task, taking on a number of roles: as interpretive guide, as preacher, and as author, in his own proper person. In the persona of interpretive guide, the implied author supplies biblical texts (either to serve as interpretive key or to add commentary), provides a gloss, draws out themes, or sharpens satire; in the persona of preacher, the implied author directs a passage to a particular sector of his audience, admonishing, encouraging, and exhorting; in his own persona as author, he establishes his integrity by identifying outside sources, draws attention to his art by summarizing or signposting the plot, or indicates to the reader an appropriate response.

Another function of the marginal notes is to define audience: the 'implied reader', often described on title pages and in authorial prefaces, was also inscribed in the marginal notes. As Keeble notes, material written primarily by and for Nonconformists also extended its readership to the early modern equivalent of 'everyman'.[17] In Bunyan's works, paratexts and marginal comments indicate the author's awareness of readers ranging all the way from the anxious seeker reading to know whether she is '*blest or not*' (*PP*, 7), long seen as the primary reader of Bunyan's *The Pilgrim's Progress*,[18] through to believers making their pilgrimage towards eternal life secure within a company of like-minded travellers and, in expanding circles, to outsiders who might be reading curiously or contentiously. Occasional asides to those whose behaviour might be deemed offensive—'*Mark this, you that are Churles to your godly Relations*' (*PP*, 177)—and other

---

[17] Keeble, *Literary Culture of Nonconformity*, 148–51.
[18] Wolfgang Iser, *The Implied Reader: Patterns of Communication in Prose Fiction from Bunyan to Beckett* (Baltimore, MD: Johns Hopkins University Press, 1974), 1–28.

outsiders—'That's false Satan' (*HW*, 39)—suggest that Bunyan saw himself as having very wide readership indeed. In his prefatory letters to his readers in *The Holy City* he categorizes these readers as '*the Godly Reader*', '*the Learned Reader*', '*the Captious Reader*', and '*the Mother of Harlots*, &c.' (*MW*, 3: 69–73).

While Keeble has categorized the ways in which the marginal notes inscribe the author and the audience, other critics have attempted to classify marginal notes based on their function relative to the central text. Slights's classification, based on a broad survey of Renaissance texts of many genres, is comprehensive, listing fifteen functions (amplification, annotation, appropriation, correction, emphasis, evaluation, exhortation, explication, justification, organization, parody, pre-emption, rhetorical gloss, simplification, and translation). In a later development of his work, he helpfully simplifies this list by grouping these functions under four main headings: providing additional information or judgements on the referring text; aiding the reader in locating and remembering what is important; altering something in the centred text; and referring the reader to another text.[19] Hackel identifies kinds of notes (finding notes; notes that provide cross-references or that gloss foreign words and classical names; notes defining particular audiences; notes that indicate the intent of a passage or buttress the authority and integrity of the author; notes that suggest or aid effective reading) rather than functions.[20] Neither Slights nor Hackel see the items in their lists as representing discrete operations, Slights stating that 'this list of functions for marginalia is not intended to be complete, and some items in it overlap others. Indeed, many of the more significant contributions of marginalia to particular texts result from subtle combinations of these purposes.'[21]

The taxonomy I suggest attempts, by contrast, both to simplify and to complicate the discussion of the varied ways in which the marginal notes operate in the reading process.[22] This classification suggests that notes can be considered in terms of both function and effect. The four functions of marginal notes identified are these: to refer; to index; to interpret; and to generalize. Any particular marginal note may perform one or more of these functions in its position adjacent to the central text. In its effect on the narrative to which it is juxtaposed, the marginal note may be text-reflexive (that is, directing the reader back into the text for further reflection), or text-extensive (that is, directing the reader's attention outward from the text to the referred-to intertext, or to his or her own life). A single note may operate both text-extensively, connecting the central text to an intertext, an event, or the reader's life, and also text-reflexively, directing the reader's attention back to the text with a renewed understanding of its intent.

---

[19] Slights, *Managing Readers*, 63–4.
[20] Hackel, *Reading Material*, 131–32.
[21] Slights, *Managing Readers*, 25–6.
[22] For full discussion, see Maxine Hancock, *The Key in the Window: Marginal Notes in Bunyan's Narratives* (Vancouver: Regent College Publishing, 2000), 87–99.

The two effects of marginal notes on the adjacent text (text-reflexive and text-extensive) reflect the inherent duality of the act of reading. 'Whenever we read anything', Frye points out,

> We find our attention moving in two directions at once. One direction is outward or centrifugal, in which we keep going outside our reading, from the individual words to the things they mean [...]. The other direction is inward or centripetal, in which we try to develop from the words a sense of the larger verbal pattern they make.[23]

In Bunyan's texts, as the reader recreates the links between episodes and engages with the adventures of the characters, the ongoing narrative of the central text carries the centripetal impulse. This centripetal impulse is aided by text-reflexive marginal notes which continuously force the reader back into the central text, emphasizing elements within the narrative and aiding interpretation of it. Text-extensive marginal notes, on the other hand, are related to the centrifugal pattern of reading by which the story is linked to larger patterns of meaning, with the signification of the story being forged into an association with concepts, doctrines, and the personal experiences of the reader (see Figure 25.2).

Taxonomies such as those that have been proposed may be helpful to our understanding of Bunyan by providing a vocabulary for analysis and discussion of the marginal notes in their creation of particular local effects: that is, the effect of particular marginal notes on particular portions of the central narrative or expository texts.

In order to illustrate how they might serve, we will take two examples of text-extensive referring notes, choosing these because the 'ubiquitous' biblical notes have been often either overlooked or dismissed from discussion. A referring marginal note substantially alters the effect of the narrative at the point of Christian's fleeing from the City of Destruction at the opening of *The Pilgrim's Progress*. This passage has, of course, been seen as problematic by many—if not most—readers, as indeed it seems intended to be. The narrative description of the pilgrim setting out, blocking his ears to the cries of his wife and children and crying 'Life, Life, Eternal Life', is glossed with the biblical reference 'Luke 14. 26' (*PP*, 10): a referring marginal note which has both a text-extensive and text-reflexive action. The first effect is to draw the reader away from the story—Davies describes this directing of attention away from the narrative as 'anti-narrative'—forcing the reader's attention away from the literal level to the spiritual.[24] When the referenced Scripture is brought into juxtaposition to the narrative passage, it effects a spiral-like deepening of the text. It explains the depicted struggle in spiritual terms, transforming the plane of the action from literal to spiritual: the pilgrim must, in order to undertake the pilgrimage, reorder his affections, changing his primary attachment from his family to Christ. At the same time, the gospel text operates against

---

[23] Frye, *Anatomy*, 73.
[24] Davies, *Graceful Reading*, 276–78.

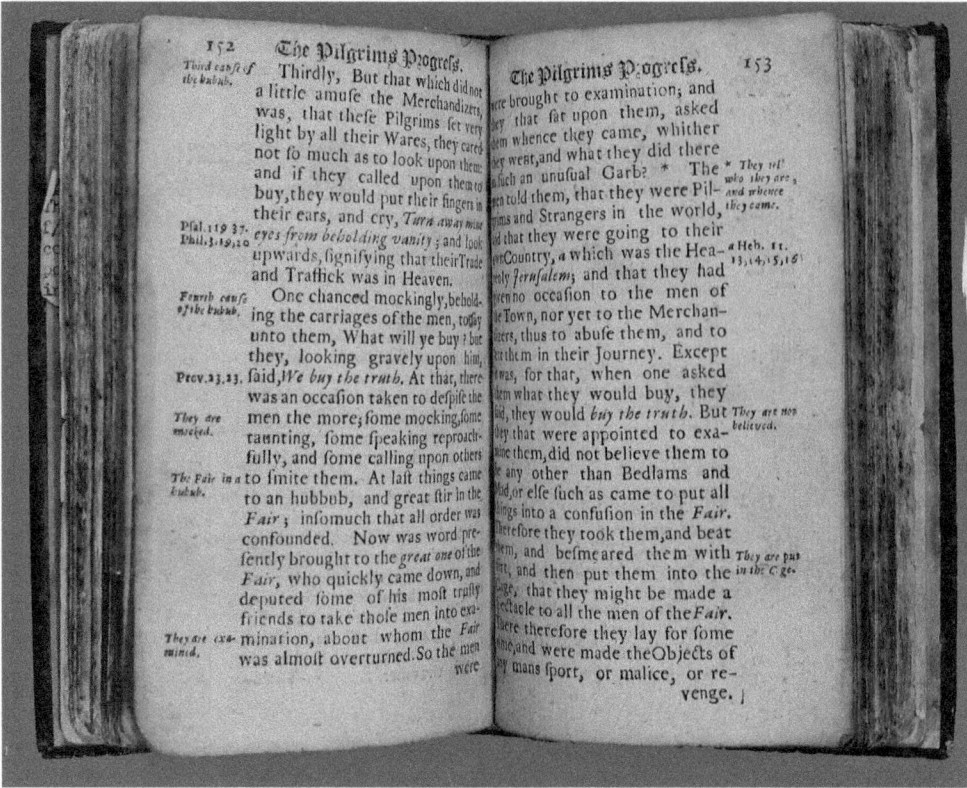

FIGURE 25.2 Pages from the 1679 edition of *The Pilgrim's Progress*.

(Image courtesy of Bruce Peel Special Collections, University of Alberta.)

an emotional rejection of the action describes: the pilgrim is doing neither more nor less than Christ's claim clearly demands.[25] The radically reorienting claims of Christ are perhaps nowhere in English literature more starkly 'chaulked' before our eyes (*PP*, 6).

If, in the passage just discussed, the text-extensive referring marginal note tends to ameliorate the effect of the central narrative text, in another passage a similar type of marginal note functions to intensify or even to supply what may seem otherwise to be an affect absent from the central text. When Bunyan's pilgrim finally comes to the cross where he will be relieved of his burden, the scene is, to any reader familiar with the tradition of meditation on the cross and the wounds of Christ, extremely sparse. '[Christian] ran thus till he came at a place somewhat ascending; and upon that place stood a *Cross*, and a little below in the bottom, a Sepulcher.' In the subsequent paragraph, the disburdened pilgrim's emotions are described rather than felt:

---

[25] For more extended discussions, see Davies, *Graceful Reading*, 277–78; Hancock, *Key*, 142–45.

> Then was *Christian* glad *and lightsom, and said with a merry heart, *He hath given me rest, by his sorrow; and life, by his death.* Then he stood still a while, to look and wonder; for it was very surprising to him, that the sight of the Cross should thus ease him of his burden. He looked therefore and looked again, even till springs that were in his head sent the *waters down his cheeks. (*PP*, 38)

The description of the pilgrim's emotional response is reinforced by a generalizing text-reflexive marginal note to the phrase 'and lightsom': '**When God releases us of our guilt and burden, we are as those that leap for joy.*' But we are still in the realm of description and explanation. It is only with the text-extensive referring marginal note that we are finally taken into the emotional aspect of the scene at an affective level. The biblical text to which Bunyan turns the reader's attention reads: 'they shall looke upon me whom they have pearced, and they shal mourne for him, as one mourneth for his onely sonne' (Zechariah 12:10).[26] When refracted through its New Testament citation (John 19:34–7), the reference in the margin offers a vignette of the crucified Christ, inviting the reader to an affective meditation upon the cross.

In each of these cases, the reading of the central narrative text is demonstrably affected by the referring marginal notes. Taxonomies are meant to keep both the sheer abundance of marginal notes and their richly complex interactions with the central texts from overwhelming the critic or commentator. There is clearly a need, then, for careful consideration and explication of many marginated sites within Bunyan's narratives. Mapping specific interactions between text and margins has really only just begun.

Theories of Margination

In the face of such overwhelming complexity, some attempts have been made to go beyond taxonomies derived from inductive analysis of marginal notes, to the rather grander project of constructing theories of margination. Until the last decades of the twentieth century, most theories of literature assumed authorial presence. Thus, in Keeble's discussion, the margins are seen as the place in which Bunyan, as Nonconformist pastor, is most directly present to the reader:

> [Bunyan] is, like all Nonconformist writers [...] intrusive, constantly watching and guiding his reader's responses. That is why he is so persistently and conscientiously present in the margins of his texts. [...] As we read, some one is there with us, looking over our shoulder. It is this awareness which ensures that we remain conscious as we read that we *are* reading, alive to our obligation to seek out the '*Truth*' within this '*Fable*'.[27]

---

[26] Quoted from the 1611 first edition of the Authorized (King James) Bible, which was the Bible most often cited by Bunyan.

[27] Keeble, *Literary Culture of Nonconformity*, 146, 149.

But Valentine Cunningham suggests another kind of authorial presence in the margins, a presence characterized by a particular kind of authorial anxiety. Cunningham points out that Bunyan's marginal notes, while certainly intended by the author to assure a 'correct' reading of text, can also be seen to represent the writer's anxiety about the possible proliferation of meanings, the writer filling the margins with additional material to attempt to stabilize meaning in recognition of the inability to control interpretation given the fundamental instability of language. Cunningham thus presciently points in the direction that poststructuralist theory would subsequently take.[28]

It is this potential for endless proliferation of meaning that Slights emphasizes in his theory of margination, with the text of the marginal notes, although bearing traces of authorial or editorial intentions, taking on something of a life of its own. He claims, 'the referential residue that might be offered in the margins to augment the hermeneutic picture tends itself always to suggest potential new links to the world beyond the text—new, rationally uncontrolled directions for readers to take'. By contrast, Evelyn Tribble argues that authors engaged in a struggle to exert their control over the whole of the page, a shift which she claims is behind the way in which, historically, marginal notes quite suddenly gave way to footnotes, with references and qualifying comments banished to the bottom of the page in the eighteenth century, and later pushed to the back of the book as endnotes.[29]

Elegant and well argued as they certainly are, these theories do not seem to be very helpful in reading Bunyan's works. Since Tribble's imagined triumphant monologic author does not emerge until the eighteenth century, her theory cannot account for Bunyan, whose marginal notes are stubbornly dialogical in nature: not only in continual dialogue with his own text and its reader, but also with his great source text and the complex tradition of its interpretation. The many battles that Bunyan fought throughout his life as Nonconformist preacher and controversialist seem to be of quite a different order than the attempt to control the surface of the page. Regarding poststructuralist theoretical approaches, Davies writes:

> Understanding Bunyan's margins in terms of Derridean *dé-bordement* (in which the edges of the printed page become 'a locus of reproductive energy, creating endless opportunities for further interpretation which infinitely defer meaning') is inappropriate in Bunyan's case not only because it ignores the overtly anti-narrative function of his marginal notes but because it fails to acknowledge that, like Interpreter, they actually attempt [...] to contain 'excess signification' in guiding the reader towards a graceful reading. [...] Bunyan's margins act as guards against the hermeneutic angst of limitless and grace-less meaning.[30]

---

[28] Cunningham, 'Glossing and Glozing', passim.
[29] Slights, *Managing Readers*, 67; Tribble, *Margins and Marginality*, passim.
[30] Davies, *Graceful Reading*, 275.

Theory-making will, of course, go on. As Cunningham helpfully pointed out early in the 'theoretical turn' in literary studies, any complete theory of literature—and certainly any theory that accounts for Bunyan's marginal notes—must be able to deal both with the centripetal and with the centrifugal tendencies of language: that is, both with its potentially endlessly deferrals and multiplying possibilities of meaning and with its structures for restraining such proliferation and for indicating the direction of interpretation. It must take into account both the approximations that are as close as language comes to indicating meaning (which Cunningham terms *kenosis*) and its adequacy, nonetheless, actually to convey meaning (which Cunningham terms *pleroma*).[31] The ability of language to signify is, after all, completed only in a context of a dialogue between reader and the textual representation of the author: a dialogue in which the author's direction of thought is acknowledged and the reader is willing to recognize the intended and inscribed meaning, to read with the grain of the text instead of across or against it.

Marginal Notes as Mimetic and Dialogic

I would like to point out two possible directions in which we might look to find a way of dealing with the 'general effect' of Bunyan's margins. The first is to take fully into account the mimetic aspects of the marginal notes to Bunyan's narratives. The second is to explore more fully the dialogic aspects of the marginal notes. Both of these aspects have been considered in earlier theories, but neither in a way which is fully satisfactory.

A mimetic theory of margination would consider the ways in which the dual text of print plus margination reflects and shapes a view of reality held by both the author and the intended readers of Bunyan's works. Whatever the use of the white space around the central print text may mean to the twenty-first-century reader, it clearly created a visual counterpart to the dualistic worldview of Bunyan and his readers. The dual text of expository or narrative central text flanked by supplementary notes, unified by the edges of the page itself, conforms to a vision of reality which sees the visible world connected to an invisible reality, the material-temporal world experienced by the senses linked to the spiritual-eternal world grasped by spiritual understanding, with both writer and reader operating in a realm of ideas made accessible through a system of correspondences between the seen and unseen realities. Allegory is, of course, a literary convention exceptionally well suited to this dual world vision of reality.[32] The format of text plus notes is, then, mimetic of the analogical mode of thought in which final meaning is located beyond the reach of human experience in the realm of revealed truth, the

---

[31] Valentine Cunningham, 'Renoving that Bible: The Absolute Text of (Post)Modernism', in Frank Gloversmith (ed.), *The Theory of Reading* (Brighton: Harvester Press, 1984), 1–51.

[32] See, further, Chapters 14 and 21 in this volume.

marginal notes serving both to signal the larger reality and to link it to its analogical, allegorical, or expository representation in the central text. As the clear sense of a dual and analogically connected cosmos gradually passed away, the dual presentation of text and the allegorical mode also passed out of use. While other factors certainly played a role in this change in print presentation, it would seem to be more than mere historical coincidence that a pervasive conceptual construction of reality, and a form of textual presentation which so accurately reflects it, should have thrived and faded away together.

There are other mimetic aspects of the marginal notes to be considered as well. The relationship of the Scriptures to the life of the Christian believer is mirrored by the use Bunyan makes of marginal notes. As Barbara Lewalski has pointed out, the Protestant meditative tradition called for a continuous application of the biblical text to the meditating subject:

> Essentially, the Protestant concern [...] is to trace the interrelation between the biblical text and the Christian's own experience, so that one is seen to be the reflection or manifestation of the other. [...] The Christian's experience is to comment upon the biblical text and the text upon his experience.[33]

The marginal notes, especially the biblical references adjacent to the central narrative, are mimetic of this meditative practice. The representative spiritual experiences described in the narrative or expository texts are to be reflected upon in the light of Scripture. The reading of the text plus notes not only reflects this method of meditation, but also provides a further training of the mind for the process.

We have already noted the way in which the marginal notes are mimetic of the interpretive guidance offered by the Nonconformist pastor. Another mimetic aspect of the marginal notes is related to the oral quality of Bunyan's works. His narratives have many qualities of oral folk storytelling.[34] A distinctive quality of oral narration lies in the use of asides both to add supplementary information and to heighten anticipation. This effect is an aid not so much to the comprehension of the story as it is to the spiritual apprehension of the truths underlying the narrative text, and of training the mind in the habits of patient hope. The text-plus-notes format may also bear similarities to the Nonconformist preacher's prepared text and to the oral delivery of the sermon, with extemporaneous comments or additional references offered as asides or supplementation.

The notes are, above all else, mimetic of the Puritan understanding of the work of the Holy Spirit in aiding the spiritual apprehension of the Scriptures. The Protestant conviction was that one does not need to rely on the Church and its traditions in interpreting

---

[33] Barbara Kiefer Lewalski, *Protestant Poetics and the Seventeenth-Century Religious Lyric* (Princeton, NJ: Princeton University Press, 1979), 154–55.

[34] On orality in Bunyan, see Maxine Hancock, 'Folklore and Theology in the Structure and Narrative Strategies of *The Pilgrim's Progress*', BS, 9 (1999/2000), 7–24.

the sacred text, but is enabled by the 'secret testimony of the Spirit' to apprehend spiritual truth.[35] Jesus had promised his disciples the *parakletos* (John 14:26), literally, one who is 'called to one's side'. The marginal notes, in their alongside position and elucidating function, can be seen to be mimetic of this teaching action of the Holy Spirit in aiding the understanding of spiritual concepts, as understood by the English Protestant mind.

The writing and reading of marginal notes both encapsulate and energize the inherently dialogic activity of language. For this reason, the various attempts to categorize and analyse the use of marginal notes can be enriched by a consideration of the dialogical nature of literature as a whole, an approach much enhanced in recent decades by an increasing understanding of the work of Mikhail Bakhtin, especially in the essays published in *The Dialogic Imagination*. Bakhtin argues that literature is continuously engaged in a process of 'dialogue' with both the dominant tradition of received conventions and the new genres that are in the process of developing as minority voices emerge to engage with them. The early modern period in which Bunyan writes falls clearly into the time which Bakhtin terms 'prenovelistic': a period in which Bakhtin sees the grip of a unified vision of the past, a unified language, and fixed genres loosened by the emergence of 'low' or 'vulgar forms' into 'high' or 'literary forms', with a range of 'sociolects' and sublanguages given voice. Dialogism, as applied to Bunyan's works as a whole and to his use of marginal notes in particular, has the potential to open up new and more comprehensive theoretical frames of reference that encompass both the centrifugal and centripetal impulses represented there, and the mimetic as well as the didactic and referential aspects of his marginal notes.[36]

Suggested Reading

Bakhtin, M. M., *The Dialogic Imagination: Four Essays*, ed. Michael Holquist, tr. Caryl Emerson and Michael Holquist (Austin, TX: University of Texas Press, 1981).

Davies, Michael, *Graceful Reading: Theology and Narrative in the Works of John Bunyan* (Oxford: Oxford University Press, 2002).

Greetham, D. C. (ed.), *The Margins of the Text* (Ann Arbor, MI: University of Michigan Press, 1997).

Hackel, Heidi Brayman, *Reading Material in Early Modern England: Print, Gender, and Literacy* (Cambridge: Cambridge University Press, 2005).

Hancock, Maxine, *The Key in the Window: Marginal Notes in Bunyan's Narratives* (Vancouver: Regent College Publishing, 2000).

Hauptman, Robert, *Documentation: A History and Critique of Attribution, Commentary, Glosses, Marginalia, Notes, etc.* (Jefferson, NC, and London: McFarland & Company, 2008).

---

[35] John Calvin, *Institutes of Christian Religion*, tr. Henry Beveridge, 2 vols (Grand Rapids, MI: William B. Eerdmans Publishing, 1975), 1: 71.

[36] See M. M. Bakhtin, *The Dialogic Imagination: Four Essays*, ed. Michael Holquist, tr. Caryl Emerson and Michael Holquist (Austin, TX: University of Texas Press, 1981), esp. 3–40 and 41–83. See also Michael Holquist, *Dialogism: Bakhtin and his World* (London and New York: Routledge, 1990).

Sherman, William H., *Used Books: Marking Readers in Renaissance England* (Philadelphia, PA: University of Pennsylvania Press, 2008).

Slights, William, *Managing Readers: Printed Marginalia in English Renaissance Books* (Ann Arbor, MI: University of Michigan Press, 2001).

Tribble, Evelyn, *Margins and Marginality: The Printed Page in Early Modern England* (Charlottesville, VA, and London: University Press of Virginia, 1993).

CHAPTER 26

BUNYAN AND THE HISTORIANS

TAMSIN SPARGO

My dear Children, call to mind the former days, the years of ancient times; remember also your songs in the night, and commune with your own heart, Psal. 77. 5, 6, 7, 8, 9, 10, 11, 12. (*GA*, 5)

IN *Grace Abounding to the Chief of Sinners* (1666) we read that under the influence of 'one poor man, that made profession of Religion', the young Bunyan 'betook me to my Bible, and began to take great pleasure in reading, but especially with the historical part thereof: for, as for *Pauls* Epistles, and Scriptures of that nature, I could not away with them' (*GA*, 12). So, the young Bunyan was interested in the past, or perhaps the stories of the past in the Bible. How gratifying for those of us whose early interest in the Bible was similarly piqued by the opportunity to read about other times, or to be carried away by narratives of the past, to see that the seventeenth-century writer shared our reading pleasures. There is, of course, a sting in this tale of historical reading and it is one that should be remembered by anyone whose pleasure, or interest, in Bunyan and his writings is primarily as records of the past, or, indeed, as vibrant, compelling narratives or treatises.

When he recalls his early reading of the Bible, Bunyan is describing his period of outward reformation and obedience to the Law, as encapsulated in the Commandments, and his delight in the 'historical part' of the Scriptures is symptomatic of superficial or, to turn a phrase from a fellow Bunyan scholar's work, graceless reading.[1] Bunyan has yet to move through the stages of the conversion process that will see his rebirth into the community of believers, and at this early stage his understanding of the Bible

---

[1] Michael Davies, *Graceful Reading: Theology and Narrative in the Works of John Bunyan* (Oxford: Oxford University Press, 2002).

might be described as worldly, or perhaps historical. It is only when he is able to perceive the transcendent message or meaning of the Scriptures rather than dwelling on the exciting narrative or glimpses of the past that Bunyan can be saved. At the heart of John Bunyan's mission as a writer lies a commitment that must frustrate any historian who seeks to use his writings as simple sources. Bunyan's much-celebrated depiction of the everyday, of the ordinary world of seventeenth-century England, is always in the service of helping the reader to understand and have faith in the supremacy of the unseen world of God's grace.

Clearly those of us studying the writing of John Bunyan, in both senses, must acknowledge that we are reading, for the most part, against the grain. We may or may not share his religious position and belief in a reading process guided by divine grace, but by the fact of working with the material of his texts, by taking them, and the world in which they were written, as our objects of study, we are inevitably marking our difference from him. But as I will argue in the final section of this chapter, when I consider the impact of the philosophical theories that underpin writing on historical research and historiography, an encounter with the radical alterity of Bunyan's life and writing can only sharpen the critical edge of a historicist reading by forcing the historian to confront his or her own views and position.

Coleridge famously asserted that 'the Bunyan of Parnassus had the better of the Bunyan of the Conventicle', a phrase often casually used to signal the literary merits that were deemed to distinguish at least some of his texts from commonplace religious discourse.[2] Yet, as other chapters in this *Handbook* show, there has been a growing, if not uninterrupted, recognition of the significance, and interconnection, of all of Bunyan's works, from the most apparently literary to the sermons and treatises, and of their involvement in the complex network of discourses and relationships of their original moment. There have been literary-critical analyses and appreciations as well as theological and devotional studies that have eschewed the need to situate Bunyan and his texts within their first, or any, historical moment but, like the popular nineteenth-century editions presenting the 'timeless' tale of the Pilgrim, critical texts that elide or efface historical difference are, explicitly or not, still working within the discursive parameters of their own time.

In the twenty-first century, even Bunyan's relatively accessible *The Pilgrim's Progress* (1678; 1684) withholds much of its richness from those who are ignorant of the theology, culture, and social conflicts that inform it. So, at even the most basic level, a degree of historical knowledge is needed to unlock Bunyan's writing, which then in turn helps to build our knowledge of the period in which it was produced. This might be seen to be the case for a majority of earlier literary texts and does indeed describe a 'commonsense' approach to reading texts in context. Historicist Bunyan studies, however, have

---

[2] *The Collected Works of Samuel Taylor Coleridge*, vol. 12: *Marginalia*, ed. George Whalley (London: Routledge & Kegan Paul, 1971–2002), Part 1, 801.

demanded a particularly explicit and energetic engagement both with the past and, inevitably, with the challenges to our understanding of it posed by radical difference.

This is not the place for a full exploration of the development of competing models of historical research and the writing of history, or historiography. But the differing approaches to Bunyan may be seen as case studies that reflect, or reveal, some of the changes that have taken place within the discipline and also in the historical and historicist work that has emerged in other contexts, notably in literary studies. This chapter presents a broadly linear narrative of some of the key historical and historicist approaches to Bunyan up to the present day and, like all such accounts, is inevitably partial in both senses. I have done my best to be even-handed, and to avoid any Whiggish, or indeed Marxist, assumption that this is a history of progress, but it is inevitably informed by my own priorities. The categories and modes to which I refer can be only a broad representation of the diversity of historians' and historicist approaches to Bunyan, and are intended to serve as guides rather than definitions.

Early Sources and Studies

Biographical and, to a certain extent, historical interest in Bunyan was evident in his lifetime and burgeoned after his death, and studies from the late seventeenth and eighteenth centuries contributed both to the preservation of material by, and on, the author. In 1692 the bookseller and comb-maker, Charles Doe, who had known Bunyan in his last years and had been given some of the writer's manuscripts by his widow, published in folio a collection of some of Bunyan's works, including a number never before published.[3] Doe's edition included the first catalogue of Bunyan's many books, which proved to be an invaluable resource for later scholars trying to establish the range and chronology of his writing, although it has, of course, been subsequently extended and revised. The volume was considerably more costly than the cheapest pamphlet editions of the single texts and Doe raised funds by advertising a year earlier in his circular *The Struggler* for subscribers (*MW*, 12: 453–60). In both the 1691 call and the folio edition, Doe presents some biographical material about Bunyan's life, and an anonymous biography was published in the same year as the folio. Doe's main purpose was to continue Bunyan's Christian mission, as his comments in the 1691 and 1692 publications and in his later account of his own career testify—and he was not alone in producing hagiographic testimonials to the author's exemplary life—but his efforts both to catalogue Bunyan's work and to summarize his life proved to be pivotal in helping to establish both as fields of study.

While it would be misleading to suggest that Bunyan and his writing have been, or are, only of interest to those with Nonconformist or similar religious views, it is notable

---

[3] See, further, Chapters 9 and 20 in this volume.

that the combination, in different proportions, of Dissenting religion and political radicalism has been a common background, albeit sometimes a rejected one, for many Bunyan scholars to the present day. It was certainly the case in the eighteenth and nineteenth centuries when his popularity in Dissenting religious circles, notably through the evangelical revival led by Wesley and Whitefield, helped to sustain the standing of Bunyan and his work at times when the literary elite viewed it as vulgar and homespun. In the literary world, after Augustan disdain and neglect, Bunyan found favour with the Romantics, whose emphasis on inspiration and social radicalism made him an attractive figure even to those who had followed Wordsworth's path from revolutionary fervour to organicist conservatism. In 1830, the once radical, but by now Tory, Poet Laureate and historian, Robert Southey wrote a life of Bunyan that was included with a lavishly illustrated edition of *The Pilgrim's Progress*. The biography initiated two debates that would fuel ongoing historical and critical research and comment through the century and beyond, namely the extent to which Bunyan exaggerated his depravity and sinfulness in *Grace Abounding* and the influences on his writing.[4] Both questions would demand that Bunyan be examined within a broader social and cultural context than had hitherto been the norm.

Nineteenth-Century Studies

The tradition of committed Christian studies of Bunyan continued in the nineteenth century, and one in particular merits attention as contributing to the historical archive. In 1885, the Reverend John Brown, one of Bunyan's successors as minister of what had become known as Bunyan Meeting in Bedford, wrote an extensive biography of Bunyan that was republished in a number of editions, culminating in a revised version edited by Frank Mott Harrison to commemorate the tercentenary of Bunyan's birth in 1928. Like so many biographers, Brown echoes Bunyan's preface to *The Pilgrim's Progress* in his own introduction to the life, noting that he 'drifted' into writing the biography rather than acting on a plan, and stressing his redemptive project: 'it is pleasant to me to think that renewed intercourse with the spirit of Bunyan in these pages may deepen the religious life in the hearts of some of my readers, bringing them into a closer, diviner fellowship with his Lord and theirs'.[5]

Yet, accompanying this double process of facilitating biographical communion and religious improvement, the text is presented with details of the many sources that have been consulted, and a list of Brown's publications included in the 1928 edition indicates his interest in broader matters of church history. Harrison notes that in revising Brown's

---

[4] *The Pilgrim's Progress, with a Life of John Bunyan by* Robert Southey (London: John Murray & John Major, 1830).

[5] John Brown, *John Bunyan (1628–1688): His Life, Times, and Work*, rev. Frank Mott Harrison (London: Hulbert, 1928), xxii, xxiv.

text, he has paid 'attention' to many details 'biographical, bibliographical, and topographical, as well as historical and antiquarian'.⁶ While this is partly a diplomatic reference to the correction of some errors, it also describes what might be called accretionary historical work, as research uncovers and offers to others ever more material for future study or, depending on the context, neglect. In this case, Harrison's appendices, listing foreign-language, children's, and other editions of *The Pilgrim's Progress* would prove of use only much later when scholarly interest turned to the texts' reception and their impact upon different social groups.

While Brown's religious motivation was paramount in his biographical study, sympathy with the broadly understood Nonconformist elements of Bunyan's work, filtered through the lens of nineteenth-century liberalism, informed the work of other historians of the period who turned their attentions to Bunyan. This approach to Bunyan also reveals something of the assumptions and operations of historiography in the period. Thomas Babington Macaulay is regarded as the foremost exponent of the Whig view that saw British history as a progression towards a more enlightened society characterized by the institutions of liberal democracy with constitutional monarchy. In his best-known narrative histories, notably his *History of England* (published in five volumes, 1848–61), Macaulay offers a dramatic and broadly optimistic representation of a society moving away from autocracy and superstition towards individual freedom and enlightenment. His short essay 'The Life of Bunyan', originally written for the eighth edition of the *Encyclopaedia Britannica* (1852–60) and reprinted in 1914 in the Oxford Plain Texts series, and his earlier, lengthy review of Southey's edition and biography reveal, however, some of the tensions in the liberal position at the time.

Macaulay's biography includes some evidence of detailed historical research, such as his observation that, despite his antipathy towards the Quakers, Bunyan shared 'one of their peculiar fashions', namely writing 'not November or December, but eleventh month and twelfth month'. Yet Macaulay's biographical approach involves as much literary-critical analysis as contextual exploration. He fleshes out the bare bones of his subject's life by focusing initially on Bunyan's self-analysis in *Grace Abounding* before moving on to the second text that forms the foundation for his assessment, *The Pilgrim's Progress*. Tellingly, he also observes that 'much of Bunyan's time was spent in controversy' and offers a summary of the author's textual battles. In this section, Macaulay notes that one of Bunyan's arguments, in disputes with Kiffin and Danvers, had been made 'in our own time' by Robert Hall, reminding the reader that religious conflicts were living, not simply historical, issues. In his survey of adaptations of *The Pilgrim's Progress* that ends the essay, Macaulay's own position in the religious conflicts of his day is evident.⁷

After a description of the original publication and subsequent popularity of *The Pilgrim's Progress* and an account of Bunyan's last years and posthumous fame, Macaulay

---

⁶ Brown, *John Bunyan*, ii.
⁷ Thomas Babington Macaulay, *Life of John Bunyan* (Oxford: Clarendon Press, 1914), 12–13.

lists and describes some of the allegory's many adaptations, sometimes with amusement, but also with evident disdain for those which attempted to turn the text to religious ends other than those intended by the author. His particular scorn is reserved for an adaptation that sought to accommodate *The Pilgrim's Progress* within a Tractarian reading he assumes to be by 'an Anglo-Catholic divine' and which he describes as 'the most extraordinary of all the acts of Vandalism by which a fine work of art was ever defaced'.[8] Macaulay's passionate and combative denunciation of this 1853 edition, described in terms of blunders and mutilation, stands as an unusual climax to what is ostensibly a biography. It also makes apparent the historian's far from objective position on matters of religion, as he employs the author and his texts to pursue the contemporary struggle between the evangelical and Anglo-Catholic wings of the Church of England that dominated mid-nineteenth-century religious and, to some extent, political life.

Along with John Milton, Macaulay celebrated Bunyan as an outstanding creative figure who could be made to serve the historian's ends by lending the energy of seventeenth-century Nonconformity to the nineteenth-century religious combatant. The work of another nineteenth-century historian, James Anthony Froude, places Bunyan within a different and, some have argued, nostalgic, even melancholic, narrative.[9] In 1880, Froude was invited to contribute to the English Men of Letters series, and chose to write on Bunyan after reconsidering his original choice, Giraldus Cambrensis, the medieval historian.[10] By the time he turned to Bunyan, the historian had undergone a spiritual journey that had been almost as personally demanding as his subject's. Froude's brother had been a founder member of the Tractarian, or Oxford, Movement, so decried by Macaulay, and Froude himself had espoused the cause as a young man but was swiftly beset by religious doubts that went beyond a reappraisal of the merits of evangelical Protestantism and struck at the core of his faith. As C. Stephen Finley notes, for Froude, Bunyan comes to stand for a lost religious certainty and intensity that acquire a particular poignancy in contrast to the state of the Church in the late nineteenth century.[11]

If the nineteenth century witnessed what some saw as the declining vigour of religious culture in Europe, it also saw the 'birth' of History as a formal academic discipline in the modern sense. It is a commonplace that as the discipline of History established its objective, and in some cases quasi-scientific, credentials, the narrative and literary underpinning of historiography, understood as the writing of history, was frequently overlooked. Yet nineteenth-century historiography was dominated by the production of either sweeping or dramatic narratives that implicitly ascribed meanings to the

---

[8] Macaulay, *Life of John Bunyan*, 19. The edition is identified as the work of J. M. Neale in Richard L. Greaves, 'Bunyan through the Centuries: Some Reflections', *English Studies*, 64 (1983), 113–21 (115).

[9] See C. Stephen Finley, 'Bunyan among the Victorians: Macaulay, Froude, Ruskin', *Journal of Literature & Theology*, 3 (1989), 77–94; Vincent Newey, 'Centring Bunyan: Macaulay, Froude, Hale White', *BS*, 17 (2013), 68–97.

[10] James Anthony Froude, *John Bunyan* (London: Macmillan, 1880).

[11] Finley, 'Bunyan among the Victorians'.

events they described and that were profoundly affected by the literary forms and tropes adopted by the historians. The 'plots' of such narrative histories have been succinctly, if a touch reductively, categorized by the contemporary historian Hayden White in terms of literary genres that he identified as having an affinity with particular ideological positions and types of argument.[12] White's model is too detailed to summarize here but the central point about ideology is worth remembering when we consider the place of Bunyan within the work of Macaulay and Froude. It is hard to overlook the contrast in the emotionally charged narratives of their historiographical treatments of Bunyan and his era, as both nineteenth-century historians address the conflicts of their own age through engagement with the struggles of the past.

The history of History in the nineteenth century also reveals another, possibly more far-reaching connection than the unacknowledged dependence on literary methods, namely the providentialist or teleological foundation of many models of the relationship between past, present, and future. For while Bunyan may have rejected his own historical reading pleasures, at least one of the early, and most influential, models of the working of history might not have been incompatible with his belief in time as a divinely controlled dimension. The model of history or of the development of the world and human society in time that underpins Bunyan's thinking is both teleological and providential, working towards a divinely ordained end. So while Bunyan's delight in the stories of the 'historical part' of the Scriptures was a sign of his spiritual immaturity, the study of the events and figures in the Old Testament did have a place in the Nonconformist Christian's spiritually profitable reading. In the relationship between Old and New Testaments we may see a dynamic model of historical understanding, shared among their seventeenth-century readers, that rivals any twenty-first-century approach. On one level the Old Testament offers narratives of the world from creation onwards, the time before the birth of Christ. But when read through the lens of the New Testament, its events and figures, understood as types, are seen to prefigure or shadow forth those of the New.[13]

Although the fact causes some embarrassment among those historians who cling to the model of scientific objectivity, the nineteenth-century German historian, Leopold von Ranke, generally viewed as the founder of the discipline, kept God in the equation. Ranke, a Lutheran who studied theology, argued for history as an empirical study of primary sources faithfully recorded in narrative form, but had a providentialist understanding of the status of the past that would fit better with Bunyan's beliefs than with those of the majority of modern historians. While Ranke famously insisted that the historian's task was to record the past *wie es eigentlich gewesen* (as it really was), focusing on the primary sources of a given period, and opposed the Whig notion of history as a

---

[12] Hayden White, *Metahistory: The Historical Imagination in Nineteenth-Century Europe* (Baltimore, MD: Johns Hopkins University Press, 1973).

[13] See Thomas H. Luxon, *Literal Figures: Puritan Allegory and the Reformation Crisis in Representation* (Chicago: University of Chicago Press, 1995).

progress with each age improving on the last, he was equally sure that the facts of history are aspects of a divine order that must be rationally comprehended.[14]

It is tempting to see Ranke's view as bridging the static disclosed world of Bunyan's *A Book for Boys and Girls* (1686) whose objects are divinely created as signs, and Hegel's teleological view in which the events of human history are part of the unfolding of the one true essence, Reason. If historical scholarship, like other forms of critical or hermeneutical practice, has depended in part on what the philosopher Jean-François Lyotard described as grand narratives or metanarratives—these being the far-reaching explanations of how the world works—then it is necessarily caught up in the logic and values of those narratives, whether acknowledged or not.[15] A similar, if historically understandable, disavowal of the religious origins of an underpinning teleological structure to historical thinking can be seen in the approach of the next, very different, school of historians and critics who turned their attentions to Bunyan to further their own cause.

EARLY TO MID-TWENTIETH-CENTURY APPROACHES

While many nineteenth-century appreciations of Bunyan had focused on the 'timeless' qualities of his writing, in 1934, a few years after the tercentenary of Bunyan's birth, the literary critic William York Tindall's *John Bunyan: Mechanick Preacher* placed Bunyan firmly within the Nonconformist culture of his own day.[16] Although what one later scholar has called Tindall's 'sneering superiority to his subject' marks his study out from the hagiographic tone of many of the publications attending the 1928 tercentenary, it is now generally accepted that Tindall made a vital contribution in situating Bunyan among other writers and preachers in the sectaries and within the millenarian religious tradition of the period.[17] In so doing, Tindall established a tradition that has extended to the present day and that acts as a counterbalance to studies that are keener to isolate Bunyan or to map onto his world the coordinates of a later political vision. Yet it was scholars committed to such a vision who would be the most energetic champions of Bunyan as a subject for historical and historicist study as the twentieth century progressed.

Tindall had been unusual as a critic who turned his attention both to modernist literature and to Bunyan. Although the 1928 tercentenary had seen a revival of interest in

---

[14] Leopold von Ranke, 'Introduction', in Leopold von Ranke, *History of the Latin and Teutonic Nations* (London: George Bell & Sons, 1909).

[15] Jean-François Lyotard, *The Postmodern Condition: A Report on Knowledge*, tr. Geoff Bennington and Brian Massumi (Manchester: Manchester University Press, 1987).

[16] William York Tindall, *John Bunyan: Mechanick Preacher* (New York: Columbia University Press, 1934).

[17] Isabel Rivers, 'Review of Richard L. Greaves, *Glimpses of Glory*', *Albion*, 35 (2003), 648–50 (648).

Bunyan in literary or elite circles, his writings had settled into a marginal, if honourable, position in the accepted canon of the discipline of English. *The Pilgrim's Progress*, however, had continued to be popular with working-class readers through the nineteenth century, although their preferences would seem of little significance in mainstream literary circles.[18] This aspect of the texts' circulation would prove to be the catalyst for the next influential tradition in historical study of Bunyan: the Marxist analysis of author and texts within the broader history of economic, political, and social struggle. In the period between the First and Second World Wars, Marxist historians and literary critics turned to the lives, writing, and cultural habits of the working class as part of a historical and historiographical project to recover a neglected past. In so doing, successive generations of Marxist critics approached Bunyan from a variety of perspectives. From Jack Lindsay in 1937, Arnold Kettle in 1951, and Alick West in 1958, to Christopher Hill throughout the second half of the century, Marxist scholars found in his life and writings material for critical and historiographical work in the service of revolutionary political and social change.

In common with fellow Marxist historians, British historians were keen to explore the development of capitalism and the transition from feudalism to the market economy. Unlike the Whig historians who would chart a similar narrative but see it as reaching a happy ending in the checks and balances of constitutional monarchy and liberal democracy, the Marxist historians were tracing a story that should end with an egalitarian society after the overthrow of capitalism. Marx denounced Macaulay as a systematic falsifier, and Marxist historical research and historiography were positioned as an alternative to dominant or mainstream practices. Yet it is instructive to note the parallels in these models of history, as well as the unacknowledged indebtedness that they may have to a religious, teleological understanding of history. In each case—that is, in both the liberal and the Marxist stories—the past and, indeed, the present may be read as meaningful only by reference to a founding, or preordained, narrative structure that connects past, present, and future.

If Marxist historians' commitment to charting a linear narrative of change brought them to the mid- and later seventeenth century as an obvious period of political and economic change, it was the particular character of the British tradition that facilitated the productive engagement with the social and cultural aspects of the past. It has long been accepted that the British Marxist intellectual tradition has been less restricted than other Marxist schools by the theory of economic determinism that would subordinate the significance of the social and cultural superstructure to the economic base. Marx's assertion that 'it is not the consciousness of men that determines their existence, but their social existence that determines their consciousness' was still a guiding tenet, but historians working in the British context found a productive seam of evidence of working-class cultural practice that would test the limits of the political philosophy's

---

[18] See Jonathan Rose, *The Intellectual Life of the British Working Classes* (New Haven, CT, and London: Yale University Press, 2001).

model of history and of the relationship between the subject and society.[19] This would, in due course and under the influence of the Marxist literary critic Raymond Williams, give rise to the development of a new discipline, Cultural Studies, but it also determined the character and scope of Marxist historical and historiographical study.

It is reductive, but not unfair, to suggest that Marxist critics approached Bunyan from two main angles. One was as a facet of the long history of working-class culture and the other was as a part of a key era of political change: the English Revolution. E. P. Thompson's influential *The Making of the English Working Class* (first published in 1963) confidently asserted that *The Pilgrim's Progress* was, with Thomas Paine's *Rights of Man*, 'one of the two foundation texts of the English working-class movement'.[20] As is shown in chapters elsewhere in this *Handbook*, Thompson's comment was a fair one, reflecting the book's evident popularity in the successive generations who constituted the working-class movement in its various forms, and the vital role played by Nonconformist and Dissenting religion in socio-political activism. Both would make Bunyan a suitable case for the attentions of the Marxist critics who challenged the liberal and conservative orthodoxies of History and historiography in the mid-twentieth century. But the differing approaches taken by the best known of those historians perhaps reveal more about the changing practice of historiography than about Bunyan.

The best known of the early Marxist studies of Bunyan was by the radical writer, publisher, and member of the British Communist Party, Jack Lindsay. *John Bunyan: Maker of Myths*, published in 1937, combines Marxist and Freudian analysis to explore the 'personal and social bedrock on which he raised his superstructure of anxiety, terror and hope, despair and reconciliation', and speculates that his family's social and economic decline played a central part in Bunyan's sense of a lost inheritance. Lindsay's study situates Bunyan's work within what he sees as the central historical process of class war and, most problematically from a modern perspective, treats the radical religion of the period not in its own terms but, if not quite as false consciousness, then as a necessary replacement for 'socially-constructive self-expression'. The radical writer is keen to identify in the earlier author and his texts a commitment to revolutionary action and change that demands that a secular meaning be uncovered below the religious surface of Bunyan's discourse. So *The Pilgrim's Progress* is interpreted as a narrative that envisions an egalitarian society that Bunyan cannot articulate in political terms. Lindsay sees the progress Bunyan depicts leading to the Celestial City as 'the dream of all England, all the world, united in Fellowship', and the older Bunyan is deemed to long for 'the active revolutionary struggle'.[21] While Lindsay's textual analysis in the service of his political interpretation did suggest some productive lines of further enquiry, its emphasis on locating Bunyan within an overarching secular narrative overwhelms and overlooks the historical specificity of both man and texts.

---

[19] Karl Marx, *A Contribution to the Critique of Political Economy* (1859), quoted in Harvey J. Kaye, *The British Marxist Historians* (New York: St. Martins, 1995), 4.
[20] E. P. Thompson, *The Making of the English Working Class* (Harmondsworth: Penguin, 1968), 34.
[21] Jack Lindsay, *John Bunyan: Maker of Myths* (London: Methuen, 1937), 8, 105, 194, 221.

Subtler analyses by other Marxist literary critics such as Alick West and Arnold Kettle redressed the balance somewhat, reading Bunyan partly on seventeenth-century terms and partly through a less determined secularization. But it was one of the most influential Marxist historians who would revolutionize the way in which Bunyan could be read and make the greatest contribution to our historical knowledge and understanding. Christopher Hill, founder of the Communist Party Historians Group, was described at his death in 2003 as the historian who 'created the way in which the people of late twentieth-century Britain—and the left in particular—looked at the history of seventeenth-century England'.[22] By this time, Roger Sharrock had championed Bunyan's writing within the discipline of English and, with others, had started the gradual process of restoring the neglected traditions of Nonconformist writing to a significant, if not central, position within literary criticism and history. But it was Hill's exceptional work on the history and culture of mid- and late seventeenth-century England that revealed Bunyan as an important part of a vibrant, complex, and revolutionary era that has since commanded the attention of generations of historians.

Hill's work placed Bunyan's writings not within the literary canon of great works, nor within a linear narrative of good Christian authors or even of working-class reading, but within the tumultuous context of a society experiencing civil war, revolution, unprecedented political and religious radicalism, persecution, and change. In a series of influential studies, to play on the title of one of his best-known books, he turned the world of seventeenth-century studies upside down, and started the exploration of a complex network of radical religious and political groups that continues today. His research on Bunyan, developed throughout his long career, focused on the extent to which the latter's writing connected with the radical ideas of the 1650s as they were subject to the changed political and social orders of the later seventeenth century.

In contrast to Lindsay, Hill did not treat the religious beliefs and priorities of the author as an example of limited historical consciousness or as manifestations of a politics that could not be articulated directly, nor did he try to 'recruit' him to the Marxist cause. It is possible to identify a preference in Hill's work for the more politically radical of the seventeenth-century movements, such as the Levellers, and individuals, such as Winstanley, but this can hardly surprise given his explicit commitment to revolutionary social change. Hill's own political position places Bunyan and the men and women of the seventeenth century within an overarching linear narrative, but his detailed research into the ideas, texts, and relationships of the period resembles the work of the Annales School of historians, or of historians influenced by Lucien Febvre's emphasis on 'history from below'.

Hill recalled that the period he studied lost its conventional label, the 'Puritan Revolution', when 'Marx, Weber, Tawney and others taught us that religion was not a self-sufficient motivating factor, but was mixed up with economic and social matters, with the rise of capitalism.'[23] While a number of historians and scholars have, rightly,

---

[22] Martin Kettle, 'Obituary: Christopher Hill', *The Guardian*, 26 February 2003.
[23] Christopher Hill, 'God and the English Revolution', *History Workshop*, 17 (1984), 19–31.

identified some limitations to Hill's treatment of religion, the impact of his work in shaping contemporary understandings of the seventeenth century cannot be overestimated.[24] It is intriguing that Hill's work on Bunyan culminated in 1988 in a biography of Bunyan, given that some Marxist historians view this genre as a bourgeois celebration of the individual. But Hill's biography might be seen as adapting the genre to suit a different purpose. As its title—*A Turbulent, Seditious, and Factious People: John Bunyan and his Church*—indicates, it is as much a cultural history of a section of seventeenth-century society as the story of one man. It is equally stimulating to think that the sustaining of interest in Bunyan's work has been, in part, because of a commitment to, or belief in, a prime mover in history very different to the divine hand that the author understood to shape the past, the present, and the future. The irony was not lost on one, avowedly non-Marxist, Bunyanist, who commented: 'If the world should be turned upside down by Marxists, would Bunyan once again rise as a prominent writer?'[25]

Contemporary Approaches

The work of the historians, literary and cultural commentators, and historicist critics of the generation who have dominated Bunyan studies from, to pick a date that means something in this narrative, 1988, the tercentenary of Bunyan's death, has been less sweeping in its assertions and, perhaps, less confident of its grounds. It is not possible, at least without the distance that a further few decades may offer a future commentator, to identify a single movement or school that has had the greatest impact on, or been most occupied with, the historical or historicist study of Bunyan. The later twentieth century and the start of the twenty-first have, however, seen some of the most detailed and thoughtful historicist analysis of Bunyan's writings, a widening of the scope of such work to include hitherto marginalized or ignored contexts, and a growing attention to the connections between Bunyan's theology and some current concerns about culture, society, and meaning.

Viewed from an empiricist perspective, the steady growth in the number of scholars working on Bunyan may be attributed to the impact of, among other things the International John Bunyan Society, formed in 1992, whose members connect the working lives of the modern founding figures of Bunyan studies including Roger Sharrock, Christopher Hill, and James Forrest, with those of the new generation of postgraduates. The publication, from 1988 to the present day, of an academic journal, *Bunyan Studies: John Bunyan and his Times* (now *Bunyan Studies: A Journal of Reformation and*

---

[24] There is a useful appraisal of some of Hill's methodological strengths and weaknesses in Richard L. Greaves's review article, 'Revolutionary Ideology in Stuart England: The Essays of Christopher Hill', *Church History*, 56 (1987), 93–101.

[25] Robert Collmer, quoted by David Herreshoff, 'Marxist Perspectives on Bunyan', in Robert G. Collmer (ed.), *Bunyan in Our Time* (Kent, OH: Kent State University Press, 1989), 161–85 (161).

Nonconformist Culture), founded by W. R. Owens and Stuart Sim, created a vital context for international, and interdisciplinary, scholarly exchange. In the work of current scholars, of whom only a few can be listed here, review and analysis of the research and historiography of earlier generations of Bunyan scholars have become an important focus for attention, though analysis of Bunyan's writings within their original context is still of paramount importance to most.

An academic whose prodigious output has been described as building on the historical work begun by figures as disparate in belief and approach as Tindall and Hill, Richard L. Greaves is possibly the only historian, in the disciplinary sense, to have achieved a pre-eminent position as a Bunyan scholar since Hill's death. The literary critic Nigel Smith built on Hill's work on radical writing in the English Revolution, studying the theological differences and textual strategies of the radical religious culture of 1640–60 in which the younger Bunyan participated, analysing the texts and discourses that formed the fabric of Hill's society in tumult.[26] A number of scholars related Bunyan's work to the ever-more popular topics of conversion narrative, female prophetic writing, and other facets of the revolutionary era.[27] But it was the historian Greaves who began a detailed exploration of the period from 1660 that formed the context for many of Bunyan's writings.

Greaves, who, as Christopher Hill acknowledged, 'transformed our understanding of Nonconformity in the Restoration period',[28] asserted that 'the Bunyan of history was a more sophisticated, shrewd, and politically concerned minister than has generally been recognized'.[29] Through meticulous and detailed research, including into the dating of publications, Greaves uncovered the material for revising many assumptions about Bunyan and about the wider context of Restoration Nonconformity, building a picture of determined resistance in the face of savage persecution. While the bulk of his work was primary-source-based research, Greaves also explored some of the historiographical challenges posed by the seventeenth century, notably the diverse and changing understandings of the terms Puritan and Puritanism.[30] His work on Bunyan culminated, as did Hill's, in a biographical study entitled *Glimpses of Glory: John Bunyan and English Dissent* (2002) that wove together research into Bunyan's life, the historical context, and textual analysis. But it was the meticulous piecing together of the evidence of Nonconformist thought and activities that has proved of greatest benefit to other scholars.

---

[26] See Nigel Smith, *Perfection Proclaimed: Language and Literature in English Radical Religion 1640–1660* (Oxford: Oxford University Press, 1989) and *Literature and Revolution in England, 1640–1660* (New Haven, CT, and London: Yale University Press, 1994).

[27] See essays collected in Anne Laurence, W. R. Owens, and Stuart Sim (eds.), *John Bunyan and his England, 1628–88* (London: Hambledon Press, 1990).

[28] Christopher Hill, 'Review of Richard L. Greaves, *John Bunyan and English Nonconformity*', *Albion*, 25 (1993), 694.

[29] Richard L. Greaves, *John Bunyan and English Nonconformity* (London: Hambledon, 1993), 205.

[30] Richard L. Greaves, 'The Puritan-Nonconformist Tradition in England, 1560–1700', *Albion*, 17 (1985), 449–86.

It could be argued that one characteristic of a majority of contemporary historicist readings of Bunyan's work has been a greater emphasis on the post-1660 context. Here the work of a number of literary and cultural historians working outside the discipline of History has been notable. Paramount in terms of its impact on the field of Bunyan studies and wider analysis of the period has been N. H. Keeble's *The Literary Culture of Nonconformity in Later Seventeenth-Century England*. This study, published in 1987, revealed, again through detailed historical research and historicist textual analysis, a vital culture that had been overlooked both through the concentration on the revolutionary era and through the traditional focus on the secular literature of the Restoration. Published not long after, the first volume of Isabel Rivers's study of religion and ethics in England 1660–1780—*Reason, Grace, and Sentiment* (1991)—contributed further to the building of a cultural history of this hitherto neglected dimension of the period.[31]

Keeble's study explored literary form and style in Nonconformist writing but also treated the texts as material objects, considering the ways in which they were produced, circulated, and read within the social structures of the period. The work of W. R. Owens, who has done much to inform and develop debates on publication, and, more recently, reading habits within Nonconformist and Dissenting cultures, similarly combines methods that sit well within an empirical research study and those of historically situated textual analysis. This historical and historicist scholarship is rarely accompanied by sweeping theoretical or philosophical statements of intent, but Owens's broader work on the history of the book and of reading experiences is one of the most significant contributions to cultural history research in recent years.[32] In 1989 the cultural historian Robert Darnton, noting 'how often reading has changed the course' of history, citing Luther's reading of St Paul and Marx's reading of Hegel, called for a history of reading to enable us to 'come closer to understanding' how the men and women of the past 'made sense of life' and 'even satisfy some of our own craving for meaning'.[33]

Darnton's comment on our 'craving for meaning' raises the question of the theoretical 'revolution' that transformed, or revised, some academic approaches to the relationship between texts, people, and society from the late 1970s onwards. In the context of this chapter, it is the impact of poststructuralist theory on understandings of the past and our relationship to it, whether as historians, as literary critics, or as human beings *tout court* that is most pertinent. The key tenet of contemporary theoretical thinking on the subject can be summarized as the historicity of texts and the textuality of history, explained as follows by Louis Montrose:

---

[31] Isabel Rivers, *Reason, Grace, and Sentiment: A Study of the Language of Religion and Ethics in England, 1660–1780*, vol. 1: *From Whichcote to Wesley* (Cambridge: Cambridge University Press, 1991).

[32] See, especially, W. R. Owens, 'Modes of Bible Reading in Early Modern England', in Shafquat Towheed and W. R. Owens (eds.), *The History of Reading*, vol. 1: *International Perspectives, c.1590–1990* (Basingstoke: Palgrave Macmillan, 2011), 32–45. See also www.open.ac.uk/Arts/reading/UK/ for details of The Reading Experience Database project, of which Owens was director 2006–11.

[33] Robert Darnton, 'Toward a History of Reading', *The Wilson Quarterly*, 13 (1989), 87–102 (102).

By the *historicity of texts* I mean to suggest the historical, social and material embedding of all modes of *writing* including not only the texts that critics study but also the texts in which we study them; thus, I also mean to suggest the historical, social and material embedding of all modes of reading. By the *textuality of histories*, I mean to suggest, in the first place, that we can have no access to a full and authentic past, to a material existence that is unmediated by the textual traces of the society in question; and furthermore, that the survival of those traces rather than others cannot be assumed to be merely contingent but must rather be presumed to be at least partially consequent on subtle processes of preservation and effacement.[34]

It is tempting to argue that the point had been understood and put into practice for some time by many Bunyan scholars, occasioned by the particular challenges of the texts and historical period/s with which they worked. Certainly the ahistorical approaches of New Criticism within English literary studies had limited currency for Bunyan scholarship. But there are implications in the application of the fullest interpretation of both the historicity of texts and the textuality of history that go beyond counselling against ahistorical reading.

While the 'linguistic turn', as the impact of poststructuralist theories of language and the relationship of texts to the real was known in history departments, undoubtedly has had a bearing on some historians' approaches to the past and to its written materials, it is notable, and perhaps to be expected, that much of the detailed work on seventeenth-century culture has been carried out by scholars in literature departments. Here, parallel critical movements, Cultural Materialism, largely in the UK, and New Historicism, mainly in North America, reread literary and non-literary texts in the light (whether directly or dimly) of the work of poststructuralist theories, from Jacques Derrida's work on language and meaning to Michel Foucault's explorations of the epistemic and discursive dimensions of history.[35] In both schools, critics explore the play of possible meanings in a historically situated text, and, while it is an oversimplified opposition, there is some truth to the assertion that while New Historicists have tended to stress the ultimate containment of subversive or radical elements, Cultural Materialists have focused on texts' potential to destabilize. While the religious as well as political works of the mid-seventeenth century and the English revolutionary period drew the attention of mid-twentieth-century Marxist critics and of those cultural historians and literary critics who succeeded them, they have never been a priority for the most well-known exponents of New Historicism and Cultural Materialism, who have famously focused on drama.

While some might argue, if a touch cynically, that greater cultural capital may still be obtained by the academic working on Shakespeare rather than on Bunyan, the demands

---

[34] Louis Montrose, 'New Historicisms', in Stephen Greenblatt and Giles Gunn (eds.), *Redrawing the Boundaries: The Transformation of English and American Literary Studies* (New York: Modern Language Association, 1992), 410.

[35] Tamsin Spargo, 'Introduction: Past, Present, and Future Pasts', in Tamsin Spargo (ed.), *Reading the Past: Literature and History* (New York: Palgrave, 2000), 1–11.

of negotiating early modern theology and Nonconformist social and cultural structures and processes may also have a troubling impact on the historicist scholar's reading. The researcher working on Bunyan's texts is constantly confronted with material that does not easily fit into the 'subvert or contain' opposition evident in some cruder historicist studies, and while the early Marxists may have easily dismissed religious discourse as false consciousness, the contemporary or 'new' historicist must acknowledge its discursive significance.

Bunyan scholarship had, indeed, been fully engaged with the mutual implication of texts and contexts for some time before this view started to permeate departments of literary studies and, to a lesser extent, other disciplines in the humanities. While a small number of literary critics may have been content with referring to a simple historical backdrop, the contested status of the mid- and late seventeenth century in rival historical accounts means that a majority of scholars have been all too aware that the meanings of the past are as multiple and contingent as those of the literary text. Thomas Luxon's historicist analysis of the relationship between textual figures and theology, Isobel Hofmeyr's post-colonial history of the publication and translation of *The Pilgrim's Progress*, Stuart Sim's and David Walker's Lyotardian reading of Bunyan, and my own exploration of constructions of authority in and through Bunyan, are just a few examples of the diverse ways in which contemporary theoretical understandings of history have been explicitly applied in Bunyan studies.[36] Yet historicist readings such as Roger Pooley's explorations of emerging notions of subjectivity and of religious discourse and John Stachniewski's analysis of the impact of Calvinism on writers in the seventeenth century are fully attentive, albeit differently, to the contingency of their subjects and methods.[37]

The History to Come

The story of the historical study of the writings of John Bunyan has, then, much to reveal about the changing discursive contexts of academic work in the humanities. But what of the present condition and future prospects? Certainly, as discussed, a broadly cultural-materialist, historicist approach is taken by many contemporary Bunyan

---

[36] See Luxon, *Literal Figures*; Isobel Hofmeyr, *The Portable Bunyan: A Transnational History of The Pilgrim's Progress* (Princeton, NJ: Princeton University Press, 2003); Stuart Sim and David Walker, *Bunyan and Authority: The Rhetoric of Dissent and the Legitimation Crisis in Seventeenth-Century England* (Bern: Peter Lang, 2000); Tamsin Spargo, *The Writing of John Bunyan* (Aldershot: Ashgate, 1997).

[37] Roger Pooley, 'Grace Abounding and the New Sense of Self', in Laurence, Owens, and Sim (eds.), *John Bunyan and his England*, 105–114, and '*The Life and Death of Mr Badman* and Seventeenth-Century Discourses of Atheism', in N. H. Keeble (ed.), *John Bunyan: Reading Dissenting Writing* (Bern: Peter Lang, 2002), 199–210; John Stachniewski, *The Persecutory Imagination: English Puritanism and the Literature of Religious Despair* (Oxford: Clarendon Press, 1991).

scholars, especially in Europe, as in most English departments, which continue to be the primary context for Bunyan studies. But there are hints of a challenge to the predominance of historicism in the post-secular criticism and thinking that are influenced by a review of continental philosophy and poststructuralist theory, especially the work of Derrida, Vattimo, and Žižek.[38] Much of this work is predicated on connections drawn between the anti-foundationalist thinking of such theorists and the challenges posed by religious thinking to the dominant secularist and rationalist assumptions of contemporary Western society. Some of the implications of such work may point to models of transcendence that make many historians uneasy. Yet if viewed within a historicist reading of our age, and with reference to the history of teleological understandings of historical process, its potential contribution may look rather different. As religious fundamentalism and evangelical atheism seem set in deadly opposition, an anti-foundationalist exploration of the non-materialist understandings of the place and meaning of human existence in time that underpinned Bunyan's writings, and influenced, unacknowledged, the development of our understanding of history, may yet have real historical value.

Suggested Reading

Greaves, Richard L., *John Bunyan and English Nonconformity* (London and Rio Grande, OH: Hambledon, 1993).

Greaves, Richard L., *Glimpses of Glory: John Bunyan and English Dissent* (Stanford, CA: Stanford University Press, 2002).

Hill, Christopher, *A Turbulent, Seditious, and Factious People: John Bunyan and his Church* (Oxford: Clarendon Press, 1988).

Knott, John R., *The Sword of the Spirit: Puritan Responses to the Bible* (Chicago: University of Chicago Press, 1980).

Laurence, Anne, W. R Owens, and Stuart Sim (eds.), *John Bunyan and his England, 1628–88* (London: Hambledon, 1990).

Owens, W. R., 'John Bunyan and the Bible', in Anne Dunan-Page (ed.), *The Cambridge Companion to Bunyan* (Cambridge: Cambridge University Press, 2010), 39–50.

Spargo, Tamsin, *The Writing of John Bunyan* (Aldershot: Ashgate, 1997).

Spargo, Tamsin (ed.), *Reading the Past: Literature and History* (New York: Palgrave, 2000).

Spargo, Tamsin, *John Bunyan: Writers and their Work* (Tavistock: Northcote House/British Council, 2016)

Underwood, Ted L., '"It pleased me much to contend": John Bunyan as Controversialist', *Church History*, 57 (1988), 456–69.

---

[38] An early example of this challenge was Lori Branch, *Rituals of Spontaneity: Sentiment and Secularism from Free Prayer to Wordsworth* (Waco, TX: Baylor University Press, 2006); see also Chapter 29 in this volume. See also Jacques Derrida and Gianni Vattimo (eds.), *Religion* (Stanford, CA: Stanford University Press, 1996), and Slavoj Žižek and John Milbank, *The Monstrosity of Christ: Paradox or Dialectic?*, ed. Creston Davies (Cambridge, MA: MIT Press, 2009).

CHAPTER 27

BUNYAN UNBOUND

Prison and the Place of Creativity

VERA J. CAMDEN

> This raving bedlam, that once was so, is he that now says, *I laboured more than them all, more for Christ then them all.* (*MW*, 11: 40)

IN a letter to the *British Medical Journal* in December 1945, D. W. Winnicott protests about research into procedures such as electroconvulsive therapy and leucotomy, in which surgeons are 'cutting brains about', without recognizing the 'shot-in-the-dark' science behind such methods. He remarks:

> I realize that the correct procedure is for us to speed up research into the psychology of insanity and so to provide a scientific basis for mental hospital work, but in the meantime are we to see our countryside littered with 'cured' mental hospital patients with permanently deformed brains? And what happens if these physical therapy methods spread to the treatment of criminals? What guarantee have we that a Bunyan in prison will be allowed to keep his brain intact and his imagination free, or, to take a more ordinary case, that a political prisoner should be allowed to maintain his political convictions and his brain? A new habeas corpus is needed now, a 'habeus cerebrum', and very quickly.[1]

Winnicott points to the unethical social and political coercion of mental patients, and by implication, of prisoners, invoking the revered name of John Bunyan: a figure emblazoned upon the literate imagination of the English people as an example both of nonconformity under religious and political persecution, and of untutored genius—a writer whose imagination actually flourished in prison. Bunyan was, according to William James's *The Varieties of Religious Experience* (1902), a 'sick soul', tormented by doubt,

---

[1] F. Robert Rodman (ed.), *The Spontaneous Gesture: Selected Letters of D. W. Winnicott* (London: Karnac Books, 1987), 12.

despair, and fear of damnation.² He may be said to have been not just a political prisoner, but a 'case' of mental illness, as well. Yet, as Winnicott's caveat allows, Bunyan keeps his brain intact, his imagination free. In this chapter, in a kind of homage to Freud's claim that psychoanalysis is a cure through love, I want to offer the case of John Bunyan in prison as a cure through creativity.³

Freud chose the image of a prisoner for the frontispiece to his *Introductory Lectures on Psychoanalysis* (1916–17) to illustrate the dynamics of wish fulfilment in dreams. Moritz von Schwind's *The Prisoner's Dream* depicts a man languishing in a medieval dungeon, while gnomes attempt to remove the bars of his cell's sun-drenched windows. This choice of image is not fortuitous, says Lionel Trilling: 'Freud's general conception of the mind does indeed make prison the image particularly appropriate' to capture the 'organization of the internal life [...] in the form, often fantastically parodic, of a criminal process in which the mind is at once the criminal, the victim, the police, the judge, and the executioner'.⁴ Bunyan's own description of the mind in despair similarly divides the sufferer: '*Despair!* it drives a man to the study of his own ruine, and brings him at last to be his own Executioner' (*MW*, 11: 66). Yet, cautions Trilling, prison is 'an actuality before it is ever a symbol; its connection with the will is real, it is the practical instrument for the negation of man's will which the will of society has contrived'.⁵ Fearing such actuality, Winnicott describes circumstances that are 'the negative of civilization'. 'But when one reads of individuals dominated at home, spending their lives in concentration camps, or under lifelong persecution because of a cruel political regime, one first of all feels that it is only a few of the victims that remain creative. These, of course, are the ones that suffer.'⁶ Bunyan in prison is such a one who thus impressed Winnicott early in his career. He suffered unjustly for his belief, yet during his long confinement the containment of the prison walls became the scene of his famous dream of *The Pilgrim's Progress* (1678).

In this chapter, I want to discuss what happened to Bunyan in prison. I will briefly highlight the chronicle in *Grace Abounding to the Chief of Sinners* (1666) of Bunyan's intense mental, physical, and spiritual suffering from which he is delivered by God's grace. Noting that by the time he is imprisoned Bunyan is over the worst of the suffering that characterized those conversion years, I will then look closely at the portions of his narrative that conclude *Grace Abounding*, in which Bunyan very explicitly

---

² William James, *The Varieties of Religious Experience*, ed. Martin E. Marty (London: Penguin Books, 1985), 157.

³ Freud writes to Jung in 1906, 'Essentially, one might say, the cure is effected by love.' See *The Freud–Jung Letters: The Correspondence between Sigmund Freud and C. G. Jung*, ed. William McGuire, tr. Ralph Manheim and Richard Francis Carrington Hull, abridged Alan McGlashan (Princeton, NJ: Princeton University Press, 1994), 10.

⁴ Lionel Trilling, *The Liberal Imagination: Essays on Literature and Society* (1950; New York: New York Review of Books, 2008), 73.

⁵ Trilling, *Liberal Imagination*, 74.

⁶ D. W. Winnicott, *Playing and Reality* (New York: Routledge, 2005), 91.

describes how his calling to preach fulfils his conversion while, at the same time, it leads to his imprisonment. I take these latter sections of *Grace Abounding* to be central to understanding Bunyan's acceptance, even embracement, of imprisonment. Bunyan's refusal to avoid his arrest, and his defiance during his trial, bespoke the 'tenacity to the point of stubbornness'—an 'obliviousness' to everything but preaching and 'saving souls'—that made it 'inevitable that he would suffer the protracted imprisonment which became for him both a refuge and a renaissance'.[7] Sir Walter Scott remarks that Bunyan 'was, of course, sent to prison, resigned and contented with his captivity', discovering there a 'peace of mind [...] such as in his lifetime he had not hitherto enjoyed'.[8] My discussion of Bunyan's imprisonment will take up the resignation and contentment, the refuge and renaissance that characterize Bunyan's protracted imprisonment. Bunyan's incarceration is, I will conclude, not only politically but psychically inexorable.[9] It consolidates his identity in every way as pastor, poet, and pilgrim. Such an understanding will then open up a deeper description of Bunyan's 'cure through creativity' while in prison.

In Bunyan's Case

The autobiographical structure that Bunyan retains through some five editions of *Grace Abounding* (published between 1666 and 1680) takes him from childhood through the early years of his imprisonment. What little we know of what he calls his 'natural' life—his birth, parenting, education, military service, marriage, work, children, and friendships—is, according to the conventions of conversion narratives, eclipsed in favour of his writing about the sufferings and providences of his conversion years in the late 1640s and the 1650s, before he begins preaching and is arrested.[10] There is a desperate, even cruel, quality to Bunyan's case. In his brief but powerful record of his tormented youth, he notes, for instance, that

---

[7] Ola Elizabeth Winslow, *John Bunyan* (New York: Macmillan, 1961), 104.

[8] Sir Walter Scott, Bart., *Critical and Miscellaneous Essays*, 3 vols (Philadelphia, PA: Carey and Hart, 1841), 1: 327. See also William York Tindall, who notes that Bunyan 'could have easily avoided arrest as he did in his later years'; *John Bunyan, Mechanick Preacher* (New York: Columbia University Press, 1964), 227, n.27.

[9] Bunyan scholars of every generation concur that, given Bunyan's refusal to give up preaching, his arrest and imprisonment were inevitable under the raft of penal legislation sometimes referred to as the 'Clarendon Code'. Yet, according to C. E. Whiting, Bunyan's 'mild confinement' 'strained the law in his favour' insofar as he might have been transported or executed in 1662; see *Studies in English Puritanism from the Restoration to the Revolution 1660–1688* (1931; London: Frank Cass, 1968), 106–07. Richard Greaves remarks that Bunyan's opposition to the Book of Common Prayer was 'more radical' than that of other Dissenters, and that this 'confrontational attitude toward the government' helps to explain 'why he, unlike his London colleagues, found himself in prison'; *Glimpses*, 159.

[10] See Dean Ebner, *Autobiography in Seventeenth-Century England: Theology and the Self* (The Hague: Mouton, 1971).

even in my childhood [the Lord] did scare and affright me with fearful dreams, and did terrifie me with dreadful visions. For often [...] I have in my bed been greatly afflicted, while asleep, with the apprehensions of Devils, and wicked spirits [...] of which I could never be rid. (*GA*, 6)

Richard Greaves avers that Bunyan's nightmares are 'key to understanding the great drama that dominates *Grace Abounding*'.[11] The torments of temptations, the Scriptures that fly at him from heaven, and the blasphemies from hell, personify these childhood nightmares. As a child he wishes he were a devil—'supposing they were onely tormentors; that if it must needs be, that I indeed went thither [to hell], I might be rather a tormentor, then tormented my self'(*GA*, 6).

Bunyan's enlistment in the Parliamentary army, most biographers have speculated, was perhaps in response to his mother's and sister's deaths when he was sixteen, and his father's 'o'er hasty' remarriage three months later. What we know from his account is only that his time in the military was one of desperate daring, captured by his story about how he plucked the sting from the mouth of an adder (*GA*, 8). When he gets out of military service, Bunyan becomes a self-proclaimed 'ring-leader' of all the town rakes (*GA*, 7). But following the reproach of a tavern keeper's wife for his terrifyingly wicked speech, coupled with a contrasting encounter with the women of the Bedford church who speak of God's tender mercies, the young profligate abandons his wild ways. Despite entering this period of 'outward' reformation (*GA*, 11–12), Bunyan now is tortured within, as if on the rack, by a guilty conscience. His early tract, *A Few Sighs from Hell* (1658) draws a direct line from childhood play to adult misery:

But the time is coming, that these rattles that now they play with, will make such a noise in their ears and consciences one day, that they shall find, that if all the devils in hell were yelling at their heels, the noise would not be comparable to it. [...] O friend, thy sins [...] will gripe thee and gnaw thee as if thou hadst a nest of poisonous Serpents in thy bowels. (*MW*, 1: 302)

The sadism in such scenes feels very much like the young preacher has indeed turned tormenter as he threatens the sinner in his audience.

This dynamic of tormenting and being tormented threads through Bunyan's writing and provides the kernel for psychoanalyst Otto Fenichel's diagnosis of Bunyan's 'anal-sadistic' character. The 'constant inner anal-sadistic attitude is counteracted by an equally constant extreme feeling of guilt. Obsessive thoughts which tell Bunyan that he would have to repeat the sin of Judas are finally overcome by a "salvation", which is based on an identification with Christ.'[12] Fenichel's diagnosis derives from an article by W. N. Evans in which he deduces from Bunyan's case that 'the

---

[11] Greaves, *Glimpses*, 6.
[12] Otto Fenichel, 'Notes on the Conversion of John Bunyan: A Study in English Puritanism', *Psychoanalytic Quarterly*, 15 (1946), 130–31 (131).

Puritan character may be regarded as an integrated system of reaction-formations'.[13] Other more recent approaches to Bunyan's 'case' have been less dependent on the Freudian models of character development, but all have sought to interpret Bunyan's obsessive guilt, despair, and punitive imagination. John Stachniewski, sounding a great deal like Erich Fromm, who felt sure that Calvinism and Lutheranism had created the authoritarian personality in our time, has rather notoriously pilloried Bunyan's Calvinism as causing a kind of psychosis of uncertainty in Bunyan and in his whole generation.[14] With less global ambitions, Arlette Zinck and John Sneep crisply diagnose Bunyan with an obsessive-compulsive disorder, as does Christian psychiatrist Ian Osborn, who extracts from Bunyan's account clinical insights into cognitive behavioural mechanisms of coping and recovery from obsessive-compulsive disorder through the sufferer's surrender to grace.[15] Greaves organizes his biography of Bunyan according to a DSM-IV diagnosis of 'major depression and dysthymia' that pervades Bunyan's early years and recurs throughout his life.[16] That Bunyan suffered from mental disturbances is, as Anne Dunan-Page puts it, a 'foregone' conclusion.[17]

Bunyan himself, as my epigraph captures, describes his conversion years as possessed by a kind of madness, for he often felt like '*Tom* of *Bethlem*' (*GA*, 13). But as the epigraph also proclaims, he emerges from these conversion years triumphant. His narrative is, precisely, a progress. 'The narrative of Bunyan's progress in his conversion is, without exception, the most astonishing of any that has been published', says his Victorian editor, George Offor.[18] Bunyan's account of his afflictions in *Grace Abounding* shows the reader

---

[13] W. N. Evans, 'Notes on the Conversion of John Bunyan: A Study in English Puritanism', *International Journal of Psychoanalysis*, 24 (1943), 176–85 (183). A 'reaction formation' is defined by Anna Freud as follows: 'In obsessional neurosis the obsession is secured by means of a reaction formation, which contains the reverse of the repressed instinctual impulse (sympathy instead of cruelty, bashfulness instead of exhibitionism).' Anna Freud, *The Ego and the Mechanisms of Defense* (London: Karnac Books, 1992), 89.

[14] John Stachniewski, *The Persecutory Imagination: English Puritanism and the Literature of Religious Despair* (Oxford: Clarendon Press, 1991). For Fromm, Calvinism as a doctrine creates the religious and existential insecurity of the 'compulsive neurotic'. 'The Puritan conscience is a slave driver that makes one's whole life an atonement for some mysterious sin [...] self-humiliation and a self-negating "conscience" are only one side of an hostility, the other side of which is contempt for and hatred against others.' Erich Fromm, *Escape from Freedom* (London: Macmillan, 1994), 92, 98.

[15] See John Sneep and Arlette Zinck, 'Spiritual and Psychic Transformation: Understanding the Psychological Dimensions of John Bunyan's Mental Illness and Healing', *Journal of Psychology & Christianity*, 24 (2005), 156–64. Ian Osborn, *Can Christianity Cure Obsessive-Compulsive Disorder? A Psychiatrist Explores the Role of Faith in Treatment* (Grand Rapids, MI: Brazos Press, 2008).

[16] Greaves, *Glimpses*, 38. See *Diagnostic and Statistical Manual of Mental Disorders: DSM-IV*, 4th edn (Washington, DC: American Psychiatric Association, 1994), 345–49.

[17] Anne Dunan-Page, *John Bunyan, The Pilgrim's Progress and the Extremes of the Baptist Mind* (New York: Peter Lang, 2006), 152. For an alternative view, however, see Michael Davies, *Graceful Reading: Theology and Narrative in the Works of John Bunyan* (Oxford: Oxford University Press, 2002), 81–116.

[18] *The Works of John Bunyan*, ed. George Offor, 3 vols (Glasgow, Edinburgh, and London: Blackie & Son, 1856), 3: ix.

what he suffered, the cycles of his struggles during his conversion years, and the ultimate resolution of these terrifying times through his surrender to grace. There are differing opinions as to the precise moment of his recovery in this narrative, with its treadmill cycling of repetition between despair and elation, even as there is a general consensus that the final cause of Bunyan's clear feeling of resolution is so hard to pin down that it almost feels anticlimactic after such dramatic vacillation. Most critics and biographers frankly admit that both his depression and obsessive-compulsive disorder lift at the end of his long conversion ordeal, 'though not for any discernible reason'.[19] It is here that the sheer power of Bunyan's narrative resides, however it may mystify his modern reader. Bunyan's chronicle of his conversion testifies to his recovery from the worst of his afflictions, and ends with the description of his gradual awakening—rather like a newborn learns gradually—to a new way of thinking, talking, and even moving in the world. This is not for Bunyan mere figuration—though he was, of course, in many ways to live in and through such figuration—but, as Vincent Newey phrases it, a recovery and rendering, in 'concrete and imagined' form, the experience of his mind and soul.[20]

At the end of his narrative, Bunyan devotes two short but significant final sections of his autobiography to '*A brief Account of the Author's Call to the Work of the Ministry*' (*GA*, 82) and '*A brief Account of the Authors Imprisonment*' (*GA*, 95) just before he comes to 'The CONCLUSION' of his spiritual autobiography (*GA*, 102). These final, explanatory sections provide a platform for his reborn identity. In these sections he details how he had in fact predicted the imprisonment for which, he feels, he was predestined. In this regard, the forces of his unconscious converge with the pressures of his conscience. Destiny offers him prison, and the time and place that will facilitate the conditions of his creative awakening.

The Call to Preach

Bunyan becomes less solitary, more communal as he matures, begins to testify, and gains admission into the Bedford congregation. Here he sustains the healing that his surrender to Christ in faith had set in motion. His explanation of this process bears our attention. Bunyan's gift for preaching was only uncovered for him through the appreciation of the Bedford congregation. His calling by the Bedford congregation is important to any consideration of the meaning of Bunyan's imprisonment: he has a God-given vocation to preach and his entire conversion was designed to prepare him for the business of 'preaching the Word' (*GA*, 83). He thus describes the process

---

[19] Greaves, *Glimpses*, 241.
[20] Vincent Newey, 'Bunyan and the Confines of the Mind', in Vincent Newey (ed.), *The Pilgrim's Progress: Critical and Historical Views* (Totowa, NJ: Barnes & Noble Books, 1980), 21–48 (35).

of his ascent to this position in the church and the power of his ministry, and how it has affected him, repeatedly stressing, for instance, how his discovery of that gift for preaching and converting souls (who quickly flock to his public sermons by the hundreds, even in these early years) leads him to a 'secret pricking forward' in his heart for this calling: 'I could not be content unless I was found in the exercise of my Gift' (*GA*, 84). Indeed, at first, he finds increased freedom from his mental afflictions through being prodded into 'public' speech, and then, recognizing his efficacy as a preacher, he discovers his personal need to keep performing in this capacity. His mental trouble, which he experienced as a death ('Indeed I have been as one sent to them from the dead'; *GA*, 85) leaves him when he preaches. He insists he is neither exaggerating nor embroidering what he went through in this initial discovery of his gift:

> I can truly say, and that without dissembling, that when I have been to preach, I have gone full of guilt and terrour even to the Pulpit-Door, and there it hath been taken off, and I have been at liberty in my mind until I have done my work, and then immediately, even before I could get down the Pulpit-Stairs, have been as bad as I was before. Yet God carried me on, but surely with a strong hand: for neither guilt nor hell could take me off my Work. (*GA*, 86)

Bunyan's dramatization of being given relief only for the period when he is in the pulpit is garnered from the first two years of his ministry. While he is growing into his identity as preacher, this is the process of his education. Bunyan's recovery from his debilitating obsessions in this sense culminates in his evolution into his calling as a minister of the Word.

Bunyan's conviction that God himself intends him to preach becomes an 'argument' in these paragraphs of his narrative: he proves his 'license' to preach through an appeal to a higher law. 'These things therefore were as another argument unto me that God had called me to and stood by me in this Work' (*GA*, 85). God is behind him in a very literal way, as he will later describe the sensation of being supported on either side, even when he famously reports feeling like his head is in a bag at the pulpit (*GA*, 90). What Bunyan is making very clear in these passages is precisely why he cannot stop preaching: he would fall back into mental anguish if he did so. This anguish was part and parcel of his obsessional doubt and ambivalence—what Greaves calls his depression—but from Bunyan's standpoint it was like an experience of death. For him to leave off preaching would be to fly in the face of this carefully chronicled evolution of himself from one who was 'dashed and abashed' at the mere mention of preaching, to one who was 'greatly animated […] by the continual desires of the Godly', like the members of the '*household of Stephanas*' described by Paul, who '*have addicted themselves to the ministery of the Saints*' (*GA*, 83, 84). To renege on this calling would be to betray Christ and the nascent, true self *in Christ* that he has only recently uncovered and enjoyed in the congregation of Bedford.

THE CALL TO PRISON

There can be no doubt that Bunyan's arrest solidifies an exalted sense of his own place within the pantheon of the Christian godly, starting, of course, with Jesus himself and going forward to the most directly applicable instance of Paul who, as emulated by Bunyan, wrote letters from prison and suffered for his proselytizing of the good news of the gospel:

> Before I came to Prison, I saw what was a coming, and had especially two Considerations warm upon my heart; the first was How to be able to endure, should my imprisonment be long and tedious; the second was, How to be able to encounter death, should that be here my portion; for the first of these, that Scripture, *Col.* 1. 11, was great information to me, namely, to pray to God *to be strengthened with all might, according to his glorious power, unto all patience and long-suffering with joyfulness.* (*GA*, 97).

Following his meditation upon the consolation of this Scripture, Bunyan explains its providence: this Scripture visited him every time he prayed, for a solid year before his imprisonment. Bunyan now considers his reflections upon the years prior to his imprisonment a kind of spiritual preparation for what inevitably was to come:

> I could seldom go to prayer before I was imprisoned, but [...] this Sentence, or sweet Petition, would as it were thrust it self into my mind, and perswade me that if ever I would go thorow long-suffering, I must have all patience, especially if I would endure it joyfully. (*GA*, 97)

Though he obviously suffers sadness and doubts during all phases of his imprisonment, it is wrong-headed, even anachronistic, to deny Bunyan his emphatic, even joyful recognition that in prison he meets Providence and experiences genuine joy and liberation unlike anything he had ever enjoyed before. In the same way that his account of his call to preaching implicitly shows that to stop preaching would be a betrayal of God, so too this emphasis on the special dispensation of the Lord's grace and spiritual revelation implicitly tells the reader that Bunyan was 'meant' to suffer for Christ (like Paul) 'in this place' of prison, which for him is a kind of palace. Key Scriptures are refreshing to him 'in this my imprisoned condition' (*GA*, 96) but, more than anything else, his description of the special dispensation he experiences in prison emphasizes *place*:

> I never had in all my life so great an inlet into the Word of God as now; them Scriptures that I saw nothing in before, are made *in this place* and state to shine upon me; Jesus Christ also was never more real and apparent then now; here I have seen him and felt him indeed [...]. I have had sweet sights of the forgiveness of my sins *in this place*, and of my being with Jesus in another world. (*GA*, 96; emphasis added)

The verses that then come to him are the same verses with which he concluded the first part of his autobiography, from Hebrews 12:22–4 (*GA*, 82). Now in prison, these verses, describing the glory of the saints' communion on Mount Zion, return to him to reveal unutterable truth: they have become 'sweet unto me in this place: I have seen that here, that I am perswaded I shall never, while in this world, be able to express' (*GA*, 96). Time and place in prison become specially sanctified as the incarcerated Bunyan experiences God's presence and help in unprecedented ways: 'I never knew what it was for God to stand by me at all turns [. . .] as I have found him since I came in hither.' He concludes, daringly, 'I have often said, *Were it lawful, I could pray for greater trouble, for the greater comforts sake*, Eccles. 7. 14; 2 Cor. 1. 5' (*GA*, 96–7).

Such paradoxes of the Christian life for Bunyan and his fellow martyrs past, present, and future—with whom he so strongly identifies and whose company he finds so emboldening—again make his sacrifice seem both searing and yet sweet.[21] His description, on the one side, of the torturous separation from wife and children ('the parting with my Wife and poor Children hath oft been to me in this place as the pulling the flesh from my bones'; *GA*, 98), and, on the other, the biblical mandate that he must 'pass a sentence of death upon everything that can properly be called a thing of this life, even to reckon my Self, my Wife, my Children [. . .] as dead to me, and my self as dead to them' (*GA*, 97) captures the cost of discipleship. His political persecution revives the raging debate over the cost of Dissent in English history, over church government and toleration. 'Bunyan's heart had been kindled by The Book of Martyrs', notes Robert Southey, and his excitement, exaltation, and triumph in following his conscience into the Bedford jail are 'akin to pride'.[22] Yet rather than doubt the convictions that kept Bunyan in prison, let us persist in understanding how these convictions worked through him, and especially his imagination. Undeniably prison became a precious place to Bunyan, despite the hardships of his actual circumstances and the human cost such otherworldly providences took on his life.

Bunyan concludes his account of imprisonment with a scene that parallels the portrayal of his conflict at the pulpit discussed earlier in this chapter. In this scene, he stages his doubts about having the fortitude to face death:

> I was [. . .] in a very sad and low condition for many weeks, at which time also I being but a young Prisoner, and not acquainted with the Laws, had this lay much upon my spirit, That my imprisonment might end at the Gallows for ought that I could tell. (*GA*, 100)

---

[21] See Greaves, *Glimpses*, 159: 'The more his enemies raged, the greater his spiritual comfort, or so he claimed'; and Henri Talon: 'We could say of him what he said of St. Paul—that he was ready to die before his enemies were ready to kill him'; *John Bunyan: The Man and his Works*, tr. Barbara Wall (London: Rockliff, 1951), 78.

[22] See *The Pilgrim's Progress with A Life of John Bunyan by* Robert Southey (London: John Murray & John Major, 1830), lxvii.

He is 'low' because he is afraid of death itself as well as of how he will handle those fears when he makes a final performance, as it were, on the stage of the gallows. The mounting of the gallows provides a parallel or sequence to the mounting of the pulpit, for both situations will challenge his capacity to endure. In the gallows scene—as at the pulpit—it is God who holds him up and takes him through the ordeal. While he is afraid of collapsing under the weight of his own doubt and terror, it is through transferring the weight to God that he not only gets through the confrontation with death but also emerges transformed by God's 'rescue':

> I thought with myself, if I should make a scrabling shift to clamber up the Ladder, yet I should either with quaking or other symptoms of faintings, give occasion to the enemy to reproach the way of God and his People, for their timerousness: this therefore lay with great trouble upon me, for methought I was ashamed to die with a pale face, and tottering knees, for such a Cause as this. [...] I was also at this time so really possessed with the thought of death, that oft I was as if I was on the Ladder, with a Rope about my neck. (*GA*, 100)

With his trembling body now a theatre of timorousness, Bunyan can resolve the obsessive image of himself on the ladder with the rope about his neck only when he counter-images, as it were, God's control of his fate and his own strength in surrender. Notable here is that Bunyan does not even presume that God will save him 'at the last': rather, he finds relief in surrendering control and responsibility. His depiction of himself moves away from the pale, trembling criminal and concludes in something daringly courageous once he can imagine the saving authority of Christ: 'I am for going on, and venturing my eternal state with Christ [...] I will leap off the Ladder even blindfold into Eternitie, sink or swim, come heaven, come hell; Lord Jesus, if thou wilt catch me, do; if not, I will venture for thy Name' (*GA*, 101).

Bunyan collects Scriptures to bolster the lesson of this experience, and ends by proclaiming: 'Now was my heart full of comfort [...] I would not have been without this trial for much; I am comforted everie time I think of it.' As he draws the main body of his narrative to a close, he notes that such experiences and such lessons are but a sample of what he could 'relate': he dedicates only 'the spoils won in Battel' to maintain the edification of his congregation and his reader (*GA*, 101). This dramatic depiction of the author's powerful victory over obsession and doubt provides finality to this narrative. To some extent the conclusion is '*in medias res*'. We cannot know precisely when this described episode occurs in Bunyan's first imprisonment, but it is probable that it occurred sometime in the early period when he began writing poetry.[23] His capacity to surrender, even to death, allows an opening up of himself that ironically nurtures his creative life.

---

[23] Greaves, *Glimpses*, xx.

The Pale Criminal

Freud's study of Dostoyevsky's 'mental economy of masochism' provides an analogy to Bunyan's experience of imprisonment. Freud notes that Dostoyevsky enjoyed productivity following the punishment of a prolonged imprisonment:

> Does this necessity for punishment on the part of Dostoyevky's mental economy explain the fact that he passed unbroken [in prison] through these years of misery and humiliation? Dostoyevsky's condemnation as a political prisoner was unjust […] but he accepted the undeserved punishment at the hands of the Little Father, the Tsar, as a substitute for the punishment he deserved for his sin against his real father.[24]

Later Freud describes the criminal who suffers 'from an oppressive feeling of guilt, of which he did not know the origin, and after which he had committed a misdeed this oppression was mitigated'. He further notes:

> A friend has directed my attention to the fact that the 'criminal out of a sense of guilt' was also known to Nietzsche. The preexistence of the sense of guilt and the deployment of the actual deed in order to rationalize this sense of guilt glimmer over toward us from Zarathustra's speeches 'On the Pale Criminal'. Let us leave to future research to decide how many criminals should count among these so-called pale ones.[25]

Freud further suggests that in such characters the guilt exists before the crime, and in fact propels it: 'It is as if it was a relief to be able to fasten the unconscious sense of guilt onto something real and immediate.'[26] Thus it is that Bunyan finds in prison the real and immediate expression of the '*pit*' and the 'slaughter-shop' of conscience that had depicted his mental state in his conversion years (*GA*, 3; *MW*, 6: 94).

Furthermore, in prison Bunyan is 'punished' for his unlawful speech, which, however unjust according to the laws and politics of the day, nevertheless satisfies a self-disciplinary conviction that he recounts as being richly deserved since his youth, when his blasphemy and cursing were uncontrolled and unrivalled.[27] Bunyan's enforced inhibitions in his early adult years derive from a conflict with the Puritan condemnation of the kinds of sport he once enjoyed: his cat-playing, dancing, bell-ringing, along with the crescendos of cursing and swearing which so impressed the shopkeeper's wife, all signal ungodly profligacy. The young man Bunyan who is trying to seek redemption

---

[24] Freud, 'Dostoevsky and Parricide', in James Strachey (gen. ed.), *The Standard Edition of the Complete Psychological Works of Sigmund Freud*, 24 vols (London: The Hogarth Press and the Institute of Psycho-Analysis, 1956–74), 21: 186.

[25] Freud, 'Some Character-Types Met with in Psycho-Analytic Work: Criminals from a Sense of Guilt', in *Standard Edition*, 14: 332.

[26] Freud, 'The Ego and the Id', in *Standard Edition*, 19: 51.

[27] See Vera J. Camden, 'Blasphemy and the Problem of the Self in *Grace Abounding*', *BS*, 1 (1989), 5–22.

whether 'legally' or in his inner man, must give up these direct, rhythmic, repetitive activities, which obviously express bodily urges. When he does let go of these carnal outlets, he lapses into passivity, and even paralysis: he cannot stoop to pick up a pin and goes moping into the field, his head filled with torments. The 'body-ego' which had expressed itself in Bunyan's youthful activities (during a period when he has just returned from the particular strains of war) is thus transferred into the highly regimented memorization of scriptural verse, sermons, religious talk of the Bedford congregation, all of which now fill his head, follow him around, find him out.[28] By contrast, when Bunyan is in prison, confined externally in very limited and close quarters and forced to submit to a very great extent (despite certain liberties that are granted him at various times by generous guards and the circumstances of the Bedford county jail), he finds his spirits consoled by the creation of verse which owes much to the incantation of his youthful prayer and song at Elstow Parish Church.

It is thus striking that Bunyan's first writing in prison is poetry. His autobiographical verse meditation, *One Thing is Needful* (1665), written earlier in his incarceration than *Grace Abounding*, reflects upon the author's own depressed state, dramatizing in poetry 'what the damned undergo eternally'.[29] The familiar images we recognize from *Grace Abounding* of being stretched upon the rack and held in chains, here indirectly unite Bunyan's internal and external states through the extended metaphor of the soul's imprisonment in sin:

> Thus without stay they alwayes sink,
> Thus fainting still they fail,
> Dispair they up like water drink,
> These Prisoners have no bail.
>
> Here meets them now that worm that gnaws,
> And plucks their bowels out [...]
>
> This ghastly worm is guilt for sin,
> Which on the Conscience feeds,
> With Vipers teeth both sharp and keen,
> Whereat it sorely bleeds.
> [...]
> Oh Conscience is the slaughter-shop,
> There hangs the Ax, and Knife,
> 'Tis there the worm makes all things hot,
> And wearies out the life.
>
> Here, then, is execution done,
> On body and on soul;
> For Conscience will be brib'd of none,
> But gives to all their doul. (*MW* 6: 94–5)

---

[28] See Vera J. Camden, '"That of Esau": The Place of Hebrews xii.16, 17 in *Grace Abounding*', in N. H. Keeble (ed.), *John Bunyan: Reading Dissenting Writing* (Bern: Peter Lang, 2002), 133–63.

[29] Greaves, *Glimpses*, 201.

Bunyan's prison poetry emerges at once from the conscious and unconscious aspects of being persecuted and imprisoned, while communicating also a more affective expressive range, rhythmically attuned to a different kind of language from that used when ranting in the village pubs and shops in former days. Children manage their instinctual urges through psycho-motoric communication passed down through generations. Psychoanalyst Elizabeth Bremner Kaplan writes, 'Later in life, the repetitive, rhythmical movement [of childhood] is expressed psychomotorically […] in learning, in all forms of art, and in genitality and love and creative living.' She cites, for instance, Beethoven's zestful and urgent exclamation that he grasped the ideas of his music 'with my hands out amid the freedom of nature in the woods, on walks, in the silence of the night, early in the morning'. The notes that were called forth before him, like poetry, would 'ring, roar, storm'.[30] Bunyan's experience in the fields of his youth afford similar transport, yet not until prison do they reach their apogee in the lyricism of his prose masterpieces which resound with the cadence of Scripture, sermon, and hymn, along with the rhythms of his native, plain speech.

The containment of prison also allows Bunyan to assume, in a compromise position, a passive stance that allows for the experience of rebirth that is so embedded in the Christian doctrine and imagination. Julia Kristeva identifies the power and place of forgiveness in Dostoevsky's works as a means to traverse, name, and expend abjection in order to reach the point of 'psychic rebirth' necessary for sublimation and the ultimate embrace of life itself. This is the trajectory shared by many artists who, in various ways, go 'down into the deep' in order to find a way into a creative flourishing.[31] To come back briefly to Freud's frontispiece, *The Prisoner's Dream*, as Alexander Grinstein points out in his analysis of the painting, 'The prison with its high ceiling, arches and passages are strongly suggestive of such anatomic considerations—that he is in the womb. The wish to be reborn often carries with it the counter-wish or the reverse of this wish, namely, the desire to be back in the womb once more.'[32]

The doctrine of rebirth likewise depends upon an extended birth metaphor whereby the believer's heart becomes a kind of 'uterus' that is filled with the Holy Spirit, nurturing new life.[33] Bunyan's imaginative appropriation of this metaphor provides him with a resolution of the Oedipal struggle with his father, allowing him to submit to the active workings of the Holy Spirit in the open space of his heart. His treatise *I Will Pray with the Spirit* (1662) explores with passion how true prayer is so emotionally penetrating that it cannot even be captured in words, but must find its

---

[30] Elizabeth Bremner Kaplan, 'Reflections regarding Psychomotor Activities during the Latency Period', *Psychoanalytic Study of the Child*, 20 (1965), 220–38 (236, 237).

[31] Julia Kristeva, *Black Sun: Depression and Melancholia* (New York: Columbia University Press, 1989), 190–91.

[32] Alexander Grinstein, 'A Psychoanalytic Study of Schwind's "The Dream of a Prisoner"', *American Imago*, 8 (1951), 65–91 (86).

[33] Greaves, *Glimpses*, 137.

truest expression in groans and wordless utterances that feel, at times, like the cries both of the newborn child and of the woman labouring to give birth to it (*MW*, 2: 263). A painfully absolute repudiation of all formal prayers such as are required by the Book of Common Prayer, this treatise insists on heartfelt expression of longing that finds utterance beyond, or perhaps before, words: '*A man that truly prayes one Prayer, shall after that never be able to express with his mouth or pen, the unutterable desires, sence, affection and longing, that went to God in that Prayer*' (*MW*, 2: 257–58). Bridging the affective regions now opening up in the prison meditations, Bunyan's early prison poetry shows a 'mellowness' not seen in the bitterness of his early sermons published before he was imprisoned.[34] Thus, the writing that Bunyan inaugurates during the early years of his imprisonment marks a positive burst of creativity, deeply imbedded in his bodily memory of the lyrics and melodies of his youth, while integrating his contemporary sense of his calling as a preacher, having relinquished some of the sadism that had so characterized his early sermons.[35]

If Bunyan's first forays into poetry provide for the prisoner an experimental and liberating return to a language of early memory and feeling, by the time he turns to the more organized presentation of the same material in his spiritual autobiography (for which, as Greaves states, the early poetry is a prolegomenon), he has discovered a way to contain his life in prose. Prison, therefore, offers Bunyan a transitional space for the reflection of an emerging self in the narrative, forged in the crucible of solitude and physical deprivation; going to prison and suffering the conditions of his punishment fulfilled certain unconscious desires in Bunyan that served, in the end, to foster his personal authority, literally allowing him to author an identity through the written testimony of his conversion.

We have seen, then, that the Winnicottian theories of containment offer a psychoanalytic formulation of the mechanism by which Bunyan enjoys, paradoxically, a special liberation in jail. In prison, Bunyan's pastoral mission becomes the way to progress through and beyond the 'mental illness' of personal despair to the acceptance of God's grace and one's own salvation, and on towards an active acceptance of his calling to creative work. As a consequence, he spent much of his life constructing maps, allegories, homilies, poems, and parables, all with the aim of guiding others through the maze of a fallen and confusing world. Bunyan acknowledges, moreover, the growth that his solitary suffering fostered: afflictions are beneficial, he writes, because they 'make the heart more deep, more experimentall, more knowing, and profound' (*MW*, 3: 239).

---

[34] Greaves, *Glimpses*, 101.

[35] Bunyan never lets go of his violent indignation or imagination as preacher, polemicist, or prose-poet. See John Knott, 'John Bunyan and the Cry of Blood', in David Gay, James G. Randall, and Arlette Zinck (eds.), *Awakening Words: John Bunyan and the Language of Community* (Newark, DE: University of Delaware Press, 2000), 51–67.

The Self-Analysis of *Grace Abounding*

For Bunyan, writing *Grace Abounding* 'contributed to his sense of spiritual and psychological well-being': it became a 'vehicle for him to revisit his previous trials and find comfort in triumph over them'.[36] Going further than Greaves here I would suggest that the production of this narrative further consolidated Bunyan's very sense of self. He accomplished something like that to which Virginia Woolf attests, in having composed *To the Lighthouse* (1927), the writing of which allowed her to recover from the haunting preoccupation with her mother, enabling a process not unlike that achieved in analysis: 'I suppose that I did for myself', she writes, 'what psycho-analysts do for their patients.'[37] It is the silent yet pervasively attentive God of Bunyan's *Prison Meditations*, however, who allows him to hear himself and listen to the Scriptures whose capacity to contain his projections, identifications, passions, and beckoning serves in a guardian function to his emerging imagination and artistry.

In Charles Doe's concise tribute to Bunyan, published with his edition of Bunyan's *Works* in 1692, he emphasizes the very process I have tried in this chapter to underscore: that Bunyan's change was great and effected by God's grace alone; that his long imprisonment brought him maturity in grace and preaching; that this progression was foreordained; and that it forged his greatness—not just to his community, but to the world. Doe observes:

> And lastly [...] all things considered [...] the great change made by Grace, and his long Imprisonment, and the great maturity in Grace and Preaching he attained to; I say, our deceased Bunyan hath not left in England, or the World, his Equal behind him, that I know of.[38]

Bunyan is heir to the Apostles: '*certain I am* [...] *that our Author* Bunyan *was really, sincerely, and effectually, a lawful successor of the Apostles* [...]. *Nay, may I say he was as a second* Paul' (*MW*, 12: 455).

If *Grace Abounding* functions therapeutically, as even his most chaste critics will allow, then his early texts, especially the *different* poetic productions that put him in touch with an earlier, less rationalistic discourse through which he finds a personal voice, form a core source for his autobiographical prose narrative. These poetic strains show us what he was thinking and struggling with before the finely crafted, breakthrough spiritual autobiography of the 'prose poet' finally emerges. Bunyan's conviction that he saw what was coming in his imprisonment suggests that in some ways he knew he needed

---

[36] Greaves, *Glimpses*, 208.
[37] Virginia Woolf, *Moments of Being* (New York: Mariner Books, 1985), 81.
[38] Charles Doe, *Reasons why Christian People should Promote by Subscriptions the Printing in Folio the Labours of Mr. John Bunyan*, in *The Works of that Eminent Servant of Christ, Mr. John Bunyan* (1692), 5T1v. See also Doe's account, 'The Struggler' (1692), reprinted in *MW*, 12: 453–60.

to experience persecution in order to be true both to his conscience and to his nascent self. *Grace Abounding* takes us up to the point of his imprisonment so that he is writing in the 1660s about the events of the later 1640s and 1650s. We can talk, then, about the breakthroughs of his narrative while suggesting that in his end is also his beginning: he is able to write this account because of a burst of creativity afforded by prison. The actual experience of writing and re-experiencing events which become fresh and remembered in the telling itself brings a self-knowledge which frees him ultimately to portray in allegory a version of this story that offers a universal vision of assured redemption: *The Pilgrim's Progress*.

For Greaves, Christian's release from Doubting Castle and the Giant Despair—his discovery that he had held the key in his bosom all along—constitutes just such liberation:

> In psychological terms, the Doubting Castle episode represents psychic confinement followed by psychic release, the experience of which Bunyan managed to capture so effectively in allegory because he had lived it. This is more than what Leo Damrosch has called release from 'an unexpected shift of mood, a sudden recovery of one's better self rather than a gradual process of introspection', for in Bunyan's experience relief was a process rather than a momentary event.[39]

Greaves has stressed a correlation between Bunyan's personal experience both of years of recurrent and cyclical depression and of a process of finding relief or a breakthrough from this otherwise chronic imprisonment in the dungeon of despair. The image of the dungeon in the castle, of incarceration, and, as Greaves points out, ultimately of release is precisely geared to Bunyan's own personal and physical condition while he is writing this allegory, even as he had previously written his own narrative in *Grace Abounding* from which, as many have claimed, *The Pilgrim's Progress* springs as an allegorical embodiment. There is, in the Doubting Castle episode, a perfect confluence of carceral images that both predicates Bunyan's imprisoned fate and, from the vantage point of his imagination, emancipated now that his body is enchained, encapsulates the very tortured state which unconsciously led him to his actual incarceration in 1660: a confinement that, paradoxically, set him psychologically free.

Suggested Reading

Adamson, Sylvia, 'From Empathetic Deixis to Empathetic Narrative: Stylisation and (De-)Subjectivisation as Processes of Language Change', *Transactions of the Philological Society*, 92 (1994), 55–88.
Carlton, Peter J., 'Bunyan: Language, Convention, Authority', *ELH*, 51 (1984), 17–32.
Damrosch, Leopold, *God's Plot and Man's Stories: Studies in the Fictional Imagination from Milton to Fielding* (Chicago and London: University of Chicago Press, 1985).

---

[39] Greaves, *Glimpses*, 240, citing Leopold Damrosch, *God's Plot and Man's Stories: Studies in the Fictional Imagination from Milton to Fielding* (Chicago: University of Chicago Press, 1985), 165.

Drummond, Christopher Q., *In Defence of Adam: Essays on Bunyan, Milton and Others* (Harleston: Edgeways, 2004).

Greaves, Richard L., *Glimpses of Glory: John Bunyan and English Dissent* (Stanford, CA: Stanford University Press, 2002).

Hudson, Brett A., 'John Bunyan, Pilgrim's Progress, and Nonconformist Prison Literature', in Philip Edward Phillips (ed.), *Prison Narratives from Boethius to Zana* (New York: Palgrave Macmillan, 2014), 79–96.

Lynch, Kathleen, 'Into Jail and into Print: John Bunyan Writes the Godly Self', *Huntington Library Quarterly*, 72 (2009), 273–90.

Milne, Kirsty, *At Vanity Fair: From Bunyan to Thackeray* (Cambridge: Cambridge University Press, 2015).

Norvig, Gerda S., *Dark Figures in the Desired Country: Blake's Illustrations to The Pilgrim's Progress* (Berkeley, CA: University of California Press, 1993).

Tindall, William York, *John Bunyan: Mechanick Preacher* (New York: Columbia University Press, 1934).

CHAPTER 28

BUNYAN, POSTSTRUCTURALISM, AND POSTMODERNISM

STUART SIM

POSTSTRUCTURALISM and postmodernism have come to play an increasingly important role in theoretical discourse in recent decades, and readings of classic authors based on those theories have become common in the critical literature. Bunyan has not gone untouched by this trend although it is fair to say that as yet his work has not been subjected to a huge amount of such attention. Other theories have been applied, however, and it is easy to work out why Bunyan's fiction would attract Marxist critics—even feminist ones if we restrict ourselves to *The Pilgrim's Progress* (taking in both parts, obviously). Marxist critics can see Christian, for example, as a rebel against a politically oppressive society; feminists can ponder on the patriarchal implications of Christian's desertion of his wife and children in order to save himself in *Part I* (1678), and then consider the shift to the feminine perspective on life as a spiritual journey that occurs in *Part II* (1684), where Christiana and her children undertake the same adventure as Christian before them.

But we might well ask, what is it about Bunyan that would attract a poststructuralist or a postmodernist reading? I will argue that there is an underlying instability in Bunyan's fiction which invites such readings, a lack of definite closure to his narrative aims that suggests a world more chaotic than the author's belief system would want to contemplate, and indeed that he is struggling to come to terms with on a personal basis. It is an instability that is also present in *Grace Abounding to the Chief of Sinners* (1666). Poststructuralism and postmodernism are theories which insistently draw attention to instability, arguing that this is more prevalent and deep-seated in our lives and characters than we would like to imagine; hence, I will argue, their applicability to Bunyan's oeuvre. In this chapter, I will survey some of the main readings of Bunyan prompted by a poststructuralist–postmodernist perspective before moving on to consider the wider implications of such theory for critical analyses of Bunyan's work. First, however,

I will run through the primary concerns of this school of thought to bring out its agenda more fully.

The Poststructuralist and Postmodernist Ethos

Both poststructuralism and postmodernism are wide-ranging cultural movements which involve thinkers across the discipline spectrum, and neither can be considered homogeneous or unified in approach. But all the same there are certain key concerns that keep cropping up, such as a commitment to plurality and difference; a generalized scepticism of institutional authority and the power of human reason; and a focus on individual experience. It has been my practice in recent years to regard poststructuralism as a subset of the postmodern, and I will continue to follow that principle here. My rationale for this judgement is that postmodernism has the wider remit and takes on an entire cultural tradition in its critique, while poststructuralism tends to have more specific, albeit still very much related, targets.

Postmodernism represents a rejection of the whole project of modernity, the dominant cultural formation in Western history from the Enlightenment period onwards. Modernity places great store in the power of human reason and regards it as the means to improve the human lot by the systematic exploitation of the environment. Rising living standards are to be achieved through the systematic development of science and technology, and these are the province of reason, freed from the constraints imposed by religious mysticism and authoritarian political rule—precisely the targets of the leading thinkers of the eighteenth-century Enlightenment. Modernity is an uncompromisingly forward-looking system committed to progress in human affairs, and although religions still survive, and thrive, around the globe, it has become the major driving force of the modern world order: it is an essentially secular phenomenon, and in theory recognizes no barriers to human development.

Postmodernism, on the other hand, emphasizes the limitations of human reason (hence the obsession of thinkers like Jean-François Lyotard with the notion of the sublime, that area lying forever beyond the reach of human knowledge[1]), and is highly critical of universal theories, or 'grand narratives', that claim to hold the answer to all human problems and therefore to be emancipatory in character. Modernity's cult of progress is just such a narrative of emancipation, and all postmodernists treat its claims with suspicion, down to those made by modernism in the artistic realm to be the only acceptable aesthetic (as in the realm of architecture, where its dominance was memorably challenged by Charles Jencks, the great champion of the architectural

---

[1] See Jean-François Lyotard, *Lessons on the Analytic of the Sublime*, tr. Elizabeth Rottenberg (1991; Stanford, CA: Stanford University Press, 1994).

postmodern²). Thus we have Lyotard's famous pronouncement that 'we no longer have recourse to the grand narratives—we can resort neither to the dialectic of Spirit nor even to the emancipation of humanity as a validation for postmodern scientific discourse'.[3] As Lyotard then goes on to say, it is to 'little narratives' that we must look instead if we want to effect change in the world, and these are to be seen as having no pretensions to universality, but to be focused instead on particular issues at particular times and to be pragmatic in their approach to these issues. This is what, for Lyotard, is the 'postmodern condition', and it is marked by 'differends', the conflicts arising between irreconcilable positions where the parties can find no common ground for negotiation and end up in a power struggle.[4] Differends almost invariably involve a marked imbalance in power, with one party resorting to its superior strength to suppress the other.

Poststructuralist theories such as deconstruction attack the notion of texts lending themselves to authoritative readings (by critics, for example), arguing that language, and therefore meaning, are too unstable to allow that. At best, we can talk about a plurality of meanings that are in a constant process of change, never fully 'present' to us at any one point. The kinds of claims that structuralists make about pinning down the grammar of texts to make them reveal their deeper meanings are rejected as illusory by thinkers like Jacques Derrida.[5] Deconstructionists insist that language will always let you down. It is endlessly being exposed to subtle shifts of meaning in its transmission down the chain of communication (from author to reader, for example); that is, to the effects of what Derrida named '*différance*', language's inability to be pinned down to mean one thing only at any given point, to be 'logocentric'. Whereas logocentricity is one of the founding assumptions of discourse in Western culture, for Derrida all linguistic communication inevitably carries ambiguity along with it.

Michel Foucault's highly influential brand of poststructuralism takes history to be a series of 'discourses', systems of belief that are used to exert power over societies, and that in consequence become a focus of conflict over who wields them and to what end. These can change, often radically, over time: the discourse of homosexuality, as a case in point, means something very different in our day than it did in the Greek classical period.[6] There is no transcendental value to a discourse therefore; it can be, and regularly is, adapted to the purposes of whatever social group holds power.

---

[2] See Charles Jencks, *The Language of Post-Modern Architecture*, 6th edn (1975; London: Academy Editions, 1991).

[3] Jean-François Lyotard, *The Postmodern Condition: A Report on Knowledge*, tr. Geoff Bennington and Brian Massumi (1979; Manchester: Manchester University Press, 1984), 60.

[4] For the differend, see Jean-François Lyotard, *The Differend: Phrases in Dispute*, tr. Georges Van Den Abbeele (1983; Manchester: Manchester University Press, 1988).

[5] See Jacques Derrida, *Writing and Difference*, tr. Alan Bass (1967; Chicago: University of Chicago Press, 1978).

[6] See Michel Foucault, *The History of Sexuality*, vol. 1: *An Introduction*, tr. Robert Hurley (1976; Harmondsworth: Penguin, 1979).

Bunyan through Poststructuralist and Postmodernist Theory

Amongst the critics who have explored Bunyan's work in terms of poststructuralist and postmodernist theory are Tamsin Spargo, Thomas H. Luxon, Alan Michie, and myself and David Walker working jointly. Spargo gives us a poststructuralist reading of Bunyan which sets out to:

> prise open the name of John Bunyan, not in order to reveal the man behind the name, but to examine the operations of that name, to explore the discursive techniques which produced the figure of the author, both in the seventeenth century and later, and to identify the different meanings which have been ascribed to it in the history of its production.[7]

In other words, Bunyan has become a 'discourse' in the Foucauldian sense, and Spargo's concern is with how that discourse has operated, with how Bunyan has been 'reproduced' as 'a particular figure of authority [...] within specific historical formations at different historical moments'. Bunyan has been appropriated for many different purposes over the course of the years, which prompts Spargo to investigate a selection of the 'instances of the operations of power in the production, reception and dissemination of Bunyan's writings'. Power is not a monolithic entity in this reading, rather something that is always being contested, and the discourse of 'Bunyan' has certainly been a site of considerable contestation from the publication of *The Pilgrim's Progress* in 1678 onwards (as can be readily seen from his reception in the contemporary academic world, where there is a notably wide diversity of interpretations on offer). What is essentially religious to some, is essentially political to others; a figure who is a religious zealot to some, is an icon for Christianity as a whole for others. Bunyan the hero of Nonconformity becomes Bunyan the ideal of Victorian rectitude becomes Bunyan the proto-Marxist. As Spargo neatly summarizes it, 'In this context as in those of the seventeenth and nineteenth centuries the writing of John Bunyan will continue to be deployed both on behalf of oppressive or restrictive knowledges and as material for their resistance.'[8]

Stanley Fish's reading of Bunyan in *Self-Consuming Artifacts* (first published in 1972) has long been a subject of controversy amongst Bunyan scholars. As Thomas H. Luxon has put it, many feel that it turns the author into 'some kind of ur-poststructuralist, deeply skeptical, as Fish appears to be, of language's capacity for articulating the truth'.[9] Luxon's suggestion, however, is that this is not necessarily a case of backdating attitudes

---

[7] Tamsin Spargo, *The Writing of John Bunyan* (Aldershot and Brookfield, VT: Ashgate, 1997), 1.
[8] Spargo, *Writing of John Bunyan*, 1, 3, 136.
[9] Thomas H. Luxon, *Literal Figures: Puritan Allegory and the Reformation Crisis in Representation* (Chicago and London: University of Chicago Press, 1995), 130. For Stanley Fish, see *Self-Consuming*

on to Bunyan in an unhistorical manner (which is a criticism that can often be made of poststructuralist readings of classic texts), but that Bunyan shares an 'anxiety about the authority of words' that is all too common in the seventeenth-century Nonconformist community. There is what amounts to a discourse of anxiety about language amongst sectarians, and Bunyan is to be seen 'as one deeply troubled by what he called the problem of "words in general", by the intractability of language as an instrument for even the simplest kinds of communication, let alone for truth-telling'. For Luxon, this anxiety about the relationship between language and truth helps to explain Bunyan's turn to allegory in *The Pilgrim's Progress*, because this enables him 'to substitute spiritual "experience" for reality' and that is where his main interest lies. This spiritual world was in effect more real to Bunyan than the world of his daily life, and as Luxon notes, Christian, Faithful, and Hopeful consistently run into difficulty when they fail to recognize this on their travels, that true reality lies in the world to come. So *The Pilgrim's Progress* is of a piece with what Luxon insists is 'a deeper commitment to allegory' in Puritanism (and indeed, in Protestantism in general) than is often acknowledged.[10]

Allen Michie argues that *The Pilgrim's Progress* can be considered a work of metafiction, much in the style of the postmodern, and that, in fact, the text 'has as much to offer postmodernism as postmodernism has to offer *The Pilgrim's Progress*' in that respect. Michie's interest lies in *The Pilgrim's Progress*'s postmodernist qualities as revealed in its formal properties, and a good case can be made for this. Given 'the play of fact and fiction', the self-conscious questioning of its narrative structure, and the veritable 'funhouse of narrative levels' to be found throughout both parts of the work, Michie feels justified in claiming Bunyan for the postmodern.[11] My own interest, however, is in the postmodernist quality of the author's cultural context and how he responds to this in his narrative fiction and autobiographical writings. It is through this latter approach that I would argue we can best appreciate the value to be gained by applying postmodernist theory to the literary activity of the period; that is, by concentrating on postmodernism as a socio-political theory rather than as an aesthetic.

Post-colonialism is often included under the heading of the postmodern in that it represents a sustained critique of a Western ideology based on the ideals of modernity, so it is worth mentioning Isabel Hofmeyr's important work on the reception and appropriation of Bunyan in the context of places like Africa, her focus being on Bunyan the 'transnational' and 'transcultural' author.[12] The various appropriations of *The Pilgrim's Progress* in what was the colonial world are intriguing. Here we have a text introduced to

---

Artifacts: The Experience of Seventeenth-Century Literature (Berkeley, CA: University of California Press, 1972).

[10] Luxon, *Literal Figures*, 130–31, 159, x.

[11] Allen Michie, 'Between Calvin and Calvino: Postmodernism and Bunyan's *The Pilgrim's Progress*', in Greg Clingham (ed.), *Questioning History: The Postmodern Turn to the Eighteenth Century* (Cranbury, NJ, and London: Associated University Presses, 1998), 37–56 (38, 47).

[12] Isabel Hofmeyr, *The Portable Bunyan: A Transcultural History of The Pilgrim's Progress* (Princeton, NJ: Princeton University Press, 2004).

those cultures by the colonizing power of the British Empire, which, rather than merely spreading an approved Christian message to local populations in a propagandistic manner, could also be turned back against that power of the colonizers by emphasizing the factor of resistance to the ruling class that is such a notable feature of the narrative. When it came to the colonial world, Bunyan's work could not avoid having a strong political dimension. The complex interactions that the text could generate are still, Hofmeyr insists, very much relevant to us nowadays: 'As the world becomes more globalized and integrated, questions of a postcolonial Bunyan will continue to loom larger. The field of postcolonial Bunyan studies seems set to expand.'[13]

Arguably, however, the most sustained dialogue with Bunyan from a postmodernist position is to be found in a book by David Walker and myself entitled *Bunyan and Authority: The Rhetoric of Dissent and the Legitimation Crisis in Seventeenth-Century England*. The thesis of the work is that seventeenth-century England, particularly from the Civil War onwards, was in a state analogous to that of the postmodern as postulated by Lyotard in *The Postmodern Condition*, in that there were radically opposed ideologies in contention to such an extent that traditional authority had all but collapsed, leading to 'a full-scale crisis of sovereignty'.[14] There was, we argue, no overall grand narrative in Bunyan's time that could command unequivocal general support, but rather a disparate collection of little narratives all jostling with each other for public attention, most of them stemming from the insistent fragmentation of the Nonconformist movement over the course of the seventeenth century. The more sects that there were in existence, the less likelihood there was of any grand narrative able to exert its domination in the manner that grand narratives traditionally aspired to do. That was why the Restoration settlement was so determined to reinstitute the power of the Anglican Church, in order to induce a sense of national conformity and unity that would make England easier to rule. Sectarianism, however, presented a very considerable barrier to the attainment of this objective, and Bunyan played a key role in this process of resistance, both through his imprisonment and then his writings. The former turned him into a highly symbolic martyr figure for the Nonconformist cause, while the latter brought the Nonconformist worldview to a much wider audience and would eventually lead to the emergence of a 'transnational' Bunyan, as Hofmeyr terms it, and the many Bunyan discourses that Spargo's study is addressing.

Throughout *Grace Abounding*, and his works of fiction too, Bunyan is fighting a grand narrative from within an opposed little narrative, which, in itself, is within yet another grand narrative framework. One politically resonant version of Christianity,

---

[13] Isabel Hofmeyr, 'Bunyan: Colonial, Postcolonial', in Anne Dunan-Page (ed.), *The Cambridge Companion to Bunyan* (Cambridge: Cambridge University Press, 2010), 162–76 (174).

[14] Stuart Sim and David Walker, *Bunyan and Authority: The Rhetoric of Dissent and the Legitimation Crisis in Seventeenth-Century England* (Bern: Peter Lang, 2000), 21. For a more extended historical analysis of this crisis, see the same authors' *The Discourse of Sovereignty, Hobbes to Fielding: The State of Nature and the Nature of the State* (Aldershot: Ashgate, 2003). The implications of postmodernism for Bunyan's writings are also explored in my 'Bunyan, Lyotard and the Conflict of Narratives: Or, Postmodernising Bunyan', *BS*, 8 (1998), 67–81.

Anglicanism, is being countered at a personal level by yet another version of the same creed, Bunyan's Independent ecclesiology (and so on throughout all the various other sects of seventeenth-century England, who are themselves in open competition with each other[15]). Yet this is in many ways a self-defeating position for someone like Bunyan to find himself in: his own grand narrative of Nonconformist belief can never really work if it is fought on a little narrative terrain which is perpetually subject to the psychological mood swings of the individual—particularly an individual as prone to such violent and disorienting episodes of these as Bunyan clearly was:

> For about the space of a month after, a very great storm came down upon me, which handled me twenty times worse than all I had met with before: it came stealing upon me, now by one piece, then by another; first all my comfort was taken from me, then darkness seized upon me; after which whole floods of Blasphemies, both against God, Christ, and the Scriptures, was poured upon my spirit, to my great confusion and astonishment.[16]

It is the intervention of such factors that has led Barry Hall to argue that there is in fact no conclusive conversion experience to be found in *Grace Abounding*. Hall's line is that Bunyan fails to overcome not just the differends at play within his society, the impasse between official Anglicanism and Nonconformity most obviously, but also the differends lurking within his own system of belief, and perhaps even, most provocatively, within his own character from the effort of trying to live up to that system's ideals. For Hall, *Grace Abounding* signals 'the failure of the spiritual autobiography as a genre' to provide the kind of spiritual assurance that radical Nonconformists are so desperately seeking.[17]

All would-be grand narratives in the period come down to readings by particular individuals, and that in effect means they are constantly being subverted: they never really have the power that they think they have or may feel is their due. Perhaps there is a need to reinvestigate what counts as a grand narrative in any given period, to ask if there ever is the unanimity within a belief system that its adherents are wont to assume and never cease to seek. Dissent and difference are always there under the surface, and those are what the postmodernism-inclined critic will always want to home in on. In Bunyan's case, these factors can be found in both his works and his life.

The question arises as to the nature of Bunyan's work/life relationship, and whether we can read his works in isolation from his life and historical context. Few critics nowadays

---

[15] For an indication as to how rancorous the intersectarian debates of the time could become, see Chapter 10 in this volume, where David Walker discusses Bunyan's early anti-Quaker writings.

[16] *GA*, 31. On Bunyan's tendencies towards bipolarity, see Vera J. Camden, 'Blasphemy and the Problem of Self in *Grace Abounding*', *BS*, 1 (1989), 5–21.

[17] Barry Hall, 'Conflict, Closure, Dilemma: Bunyan's *Grace Abounding*', *BS*, 16 (2012), 103–20 (105–06). Thomas H. Luxon comes close to this position when he remarks of Bunyan's temptation to doubt the truth of the Bible, that he 'never fully shook off this temptation or replaced it with the certainty of salvation that all his wrestlings with the Scriptures were supposed to have won him' (*Literal Figures*, 136).

are disposed to do so (although theoretical readings can approach that condition if one is not careful), but marked differences can come to light between those who emphasize either the theological or the political context in which Bunyan was working. The tone for the latter was set most famously in the modern era by Christopher Hill, who saw Bunyan's work as a product of the 'English Revolution'.[18] Nonconformism of Bunyan's type becomes symbolic for Hill of a wider struggle against class-based exploitation, with Bunyan turning into something akin to a working-class hero bravely standing up to the overbearing establishment. E. P. Thompson reminds us of the influence that Bunyan had on the Chartists and other working-class movements in nineteenth-century England:

> *Pilgrim's Progress* is, with *Rights of Man*, one of the two foundation texts of the English working-class movement [...]. Many thousands of youths found in *Pilgrim's Progress* their first adventure story, and would have agreed with Thomas Cooper, the Chartist, that it was their 'book of books'.[19]

Postmodern readings such as Sim's and Walker's continue that strongly political line, if with a less partisan ideological agenda than Marxist-influenced commentators like Hill and Thompson.

Poststructuralist and postmodernist interpretations can represent a challenge to theologically oriented readings of Bunyan, such as those put forward by commentators like Michael Davies.[20] Davies reveals himself to be sympathetic to postmodernist readings to the extent of stating that his study 'shares something of a growing interest in the "post-modern" Bunyan', but he emphasizes that his primary concern is with 'how we respond as readers to the complex narrative strategies that Bunyan presents in works such as *Grace Abounding* and *The Pilgrim's Progress*' rather than with the politics of the works as such.[21] He takes a lead from Brian McHale's pioneering work on postmodernist fiction, as well as, to some extent, Stanley Fish's reader-response method.[22] Allen Michie displays a similar interest in the implications of postmodernist reading strategies for our engagement with Bunyan. The more overtly postmodernist readings, however, see politics everywhere in Bunyan's fiction, from the protagonist's encounters, and even pitched battles, with figures of authority like Worldly-Wiseman and Apollyon in

---

[18] See Christopher Hill, *The English Revolution 1640*, 3rd edn (1940; London: Lawrence & Wishart, 1955), and his award-winning biography of Bunyan, *A Turbulent, Seditious, and Factious People: John Bunyan and his Church 1628–1688* (Oxford: Clarendon Press, 1988).

[19] E. P. Thompson, *The Making of the English Working Class* (1963; Harmondsworth: Penguin, 1968), 34. The influence of *The Pilgrim's Progress* on working-class readers is also demonstrated and discussed in Jonathan Rose, *The Intellectual Life of the British Working Classes* (New Haven, CT, and London: Yale University Press, 2001), esp. 29–31, 33–4, 93–6, 104–07, 117, 372.

[20] Michael Davies, *Graceful Reading: Theology and Narrative in the Works of John Bunyan* (Oxford: Oxford University Press, 2002). For an even stronger insistence on the primacy of the theological in Bunyan's fiction, see Daniel Runyon, *Bunyan's Master Story: The Holy War as Battle Allegory in Religious and Biblical Context* (Lewiston, NY: Mellen, 2007).

[21] Davies, *Graceful Reading*, viii.

[22] See, in particular, Brian McHale, *Postmodernist Fiction* (New York and London: Methuen, 1987).

The Pilgrim's Progress; through the condemnation of the debauched lifestyle of the reprobate Mr Badman, a figure only too representative of everything that is wrong with Restoration worldliness and pragmatism; to the bitter war being fought incessantly between Mansoul and the forces of Diabolus in *The Holy War* (1682).

Both Christian and Mansoul are perpetually beset by enemies who want them to conform to their belief system and submit to their socio-political authority, and who will resort to force in order to realize those aims and ensure the triumph of their particular discourse if that proves to be necessary. The protagonists' position is, as R. H. Tawney described the Nonconformist experience in general, analogous to that of being 'a soldier in hostile territory'.[23] The judges of Badman's life, Wiseman and Attentive, feel themselves similarly surrounded by enemies, marooned in a society which is clearly going to the bad, dominated as it is by figures like Badman. As the author pointedly puts it in his preface: '*Mr. Badman has left many of his Relations behind him; yea, the very World is overspread with his Kindred*' (*MB*, 1). How postmodern thought can help us better to understand the Restoration period and its ideological turmoil forms the next topic for consideration.

Reconsidering Postmodernism: Reconsidering Bunyan

I would argue that we should be interpreting postmodernism as a theory about the conflicting narratives and ideologies present in any society, past or present, and how these interact. It has to be conceded that poststructuralist readings do run the risk of being ahistorical, of backdating modern debates on language and meaning onto previous societies (although deconstructionists would claim that language always contains an intrinsic ambiguity, regardless of whether users believe otherwise), but postmodernist readings have to engage with historical context. Postmodernism is a theory which insists that the idea of a homogeneous society is a myth, demonstrating that what we shall discover when we analyse any culture in depth is, instead, a network of differences—and indeed differends—between competing systems and individuals. Its concern in the first instance is to outline those networks and the tensions and conflicts to which they could give rise in their cultures.

Looking back, it is all too easy to assume a homogeneity about almost any society that in reality may never have been there, or was never felt as such by its members. There are always dissenting voices in even the apparently most closed, or rigidly structured, of societies. Medieval Europe can appear homogeneous to us from a twenty-first-century vantage point, a Catholic theocracy in effect. But medieval Catholicism was riven by heresies such as Catharism and Anabaptist millenarianism, and, of course, it eventually

---

[23] R. H. Tawney, *Religion and the Rise of Capitalism* (London: John Murray, 1926), 229.

generated the Reformation, thereby initiating a viable alternative interpretation of Christianity which was highly successful in drawing in adherents. In addition, the feudal settlement had more than its share of peasant revolts, as well as perpetual power struggles between monarchs and their ambitious nobility. That is what lends credibility to the use of postmodern theory in relation to Bunyan, someone living through one of the most turbulent periods in British history, striving as best he can to articulate his own, in many ways internally conflicted, beliefs within a context of ideological turmoil and social upheaval.

From that perspective it is a mistake to look for complete consistency in the work of Bunyan, in that he was having to negotiate his individual way through a keenly fought battle between antithetical ideologies in the Restoration period. His fictional output brings out the strain this causes in attempting to reconcile the internal contradictions of his theology's belief system and present it as the holistic grand narrative that he believes it is. Davies, however, disagrees, finding instead a consistency of line in Bunyan's religious beliefs (based on his commitment to the doctrine of grace) and taking issue with readings of Bunyan, such as those offered by John Stachniewski, as well as Sim and Walker, which subordinate the theological dimension to the political and the psychological.[24] For Davies, this is to misrepresent Bunyan as a 'harsh doctrinarian' above all, and he stands opposed to what is for him 'a demonization' of the author's belief system. Bunyan is a far less conflicted individual in Davies's reading than he tends to be in works by the more politically inflected commentators:

> Bunyan's doctrine is [...] essentially accommodating and consoling [...]. [R]eading doctrinal works such as *Saved by Grace* and *The Water of Life* [and] exploring Bunyan's metaphors for grace, I was struck immediately by the medicinal, curative, and restorative images that Bunyan uses throughout his works to describe the process of salvation.[25]

Davies's argument can be persuasive and it is certainly valid to remind commentators that the political and the psychological can be overemphasized with such a figure, to the extent of losing sight of what Bunyan himself took to be most important in his life and his relations with others. Bunyan did not see himself as a politician after all, but as a preacher, and Davies very usefully directs our attention to the complexities and subtleties of the doctrines that Bunyan is engaging with throughout his writings as a whole. Nevertheless, I would argue that to concentrate too much on the theological side of Bunyan's thought is to lose sight of him in another way, by giving too little weight to the political implications that theology manifestly had in the period. The Bible was, as Christopher Hill emphasizes, a site of intense ideological conflict in the seventeenth century. It was a text that 'could mean different things to different people at different

---

[24] See John Stachniewski, *The Persecutory Imagination: English Puritanism and the Literature of Despair* (Oxford: Clarendon Press, 1991).

[25] Davies, *Graceful Reading*, 19, vii.

times, in different circumstances. It was a huge bran-tub from which anything might be drawn'; so it is little surprise that people were able to draw political conclusions from it in a society where it played such a pivotal role.[26] One might say that, in seventeenth-century England, the biblical was the political.

Bunyan's fiction is clearly full of conflict, and it fails to conceal all the contradictions of his own set of beliefs (although, fairly enough, Davies reminds us that there are also regular instances of 'recuperation' and 'healing' to be found in works like *The Pilgrim's Progress* that politically based readings often fail to acknowledge[27]). The resolutions to the narratives can sound very forced, as if the author were trying to convince himself as much as his readers that he has a coherent belief system that will eventually overcome its enemies—even if the latter appear to be in overall social control at present (the dilemma also faced by John Milton, of course). Christian may reach the Celestial City but only at the expense of others like Ignorance, summarily conveyed to hell from the City's very gates (a fate likely to befall the majority of the characters whom Christian encounters along his way, one has to assume). Badman's life may on the face of it appear to signal his reprobate nature as clearly as any Nonconformist could wish for, but the nature of his death still leaves awkward unanswered questions. Mansoul may be assured constantly that Emanuel will save him from the Diabolonian hordes, but that desired end has not yet come to pass at the narrative's end and has to be taken on trust: a difficult thing to do as attacks from outside keep mounting up. Wherever one looks closure seems less than satisfactory and loose ends tantalizingly invite analysis.

The author's own internal struggles in *Grace Abounding* may be strangely de-socialized, but Christian's are pictured within a world that, although allegorical, is very much a social one in which relationships have to be negotiated and renegotiated constantly with one's fellow men and women on the arduous journey through life. Interior life is exteriorized here into a world which features all the everyday problems that any polity involves: problems that demand decisions and actions which carry a strong political resonance (backed up by appropriate biblical allusions in the marginalia). The harsh treatment meted out to Christian and Faithful in Vanity Fair is clearly politically motivated. The pair refuse to abide by the laws and customs of the land they are in (unfair and intolerant though these may be) and thus become political rebels standing up for the cause of difference: difference being exactly what such a society cannot allow as it represents a direct threat to its authority, its dominant grand narrative. Difference can only be interpreted by the authorities as a loss of socio-political power and control, which is effectively how the Restoration rulers viewed the continued nagging presence of Nonconformism in its midst, and therefore tried their best to eradicate it through the penal legislation often described as the 'Clarendon Code'. In the words of one of Faithful's accusers before the bar of Vanity Fair:

---

[26] Christopher Hill, *The English Bible and the Seventeenth-Century Revolution* (London: Allen Lane, 1993), 5. See also Kevin Killeen, *The Political Bible in Early Modern England* (Cambridge: Cambridge University Press, 2017).

[27] Davies, *Graceful Reading*, 231.

> [T]his man [...] is one of the vilest men in our Countrey; He neither regardeth Prince nor People, Law nor Custom; but doth all that he can to possess all men with certain of his disloyal notions, which he in the general calls Principles of Faith and Holiness. And in particular, I heard him once my self affirm, *That Christianity, and the Customs of our Town of Vanity, were Diametrically opposite, and could not be reconciled*. By which saying, my Lord, he doth at once, not only condemn all our laudable doings, but us in the doing of them. (*PP*, 93)

Christian is in a constant battle with the 'diametrically opposite' establishment throughout *The Pilgrim's Progress*, fending off the attention of a string of figures determined to deflect him from his quest to reach the Celestial City. In the main, they advise him to return to the normal social round, immersing himself in daily life and not becoming a maverick challenging his society's ethos, as in the counsel delivered by Worldly-Wiseman:

> *[I]t is happened unto thee as to other weak men, who meddling with things too high for them, do suddenly fall into thy distractions; which distractions do not only unman men, (as thine I perceive has done thee) but they run them upon desperate ventures, to obtain they know not what.* (*PP*, 18)

The solution Worldly-Wiseman offers is to settle down in the village of Morality, where he promises Christian will '*meet with much safety, friendship, and content*' and will live alongside '*honest neighbors, in credit and good fashion*' (*PP*, 19). That is precisely the lifestyle that Ignorance has chosen, keeping a low public profile and offering no threat to the established order: 'I know my Lords will, and I have been a good Liver, I pay every man his own; I Pray, Fast, pay Tithes, and give Alms' (*PP*, 123). Ignorance is apparently the archetypal good citizen, uncomplainingly adhering to the rules of his society's grand narrative and following the conventions laid down by his social betters. By contrast, Christian's career follows the dictates of the little narrative, in this instance supported by an ally in the person of Hopeful, one of only two close companions that he meets over the course of his journey engaged on the same quest. Christian and Hopeful are the ultimate winners in this ideological dispute, but only at the expense of a life of endless confrontation, personal anguish, and the threat of sudden death (as does in fact happen in Vanity Fair to Faithful, Christian's earlier like-minded travelling companion).

Badman is in many ways a strikingly modern character, a reckless and self-seeking capitalist of the kind that we have become all too familiar with in recent years thanks to the global credit crisis: someone interested only in his own financial gains, no matter how illicitly they may have been achieved or how much suffering their accumulation has caused others.[28] Postmodernists would see him as only too representative of a grand narrative that regards other human beings largely as objects for commercial

---

[28] A point I expand upon in 'Bunyan and the Early Novel: *The Life and Death of Mr Badman*', in Dunan-Page (ed.), *Cambridge Companion to Bunyan*, 95–106.

exploitation. Wiseman delivers a damning judgement on him from the standpoint of a Nonconformist narrative, treating each and every detail of his life as a sign of his reprobate nature, and refusing to see anything of merit in him at all: 'the man that I am concerned for now, was one that never was good, therefore such an one who is not dead only, but damned. He died that he might die, he went from Life to Death, and then from Death to Death, from Death Natural to Death Eternal' (*MB*, 14).

Yet doubts remain even in Wiseman's mind about Badman's eventual fate, indicating that there are aspects of his own grand narrative that he can never completely fathom; a sublime that cannot be understood by mere humans, no matter how strong their commitment to their narrative. The signs attending Badman's death—he '*went from a sinfull life so quietly, so peaceably, and so like a Lamb*' (*MB*, 168)—cannot be unambiguously interpreted even by such a skilled reader as Wiseman; they are subject to the actions of the *différance* that runs through religious discourse, especially when it is filtered through the individual psychology. Like the Bible itself, Badman's death is capable of meaning different things to different people depending on their circumstances. Even Wiseman feels compelled to admit that 'this is enough to puzzle the wisest man' (*MB*, 167), and we are left to ponder on the realization that faith, rather like reason for the postmodernist, has its limits. To put this in deconstructionist terms, there is always an aporia putting in an appearance in any system of thought, a gap that resists being bridged and that leaves the individual in a state of psychological insecurity, vainly trying to work out the latest 'puzzle' to come to light—and puzzles there are aplenty in the world of Restoration England for Nonconformists.

The Holy War pictures a world in which the individual, and by extension the Nonconformist community in general, is under constant siege and can never really relax and live as it wants. The attacks are even more hostile than they are in *The Pilgrim's Progress*, collapsing on occasion into scenes of carnage that recall the Civil War in their gory violence: 'I told you before, how that these *Diabolonian* Doubters turned the men of *Mansoul* out of their Beds, and now I will add, they wounded them, they mauled them, yea, and almost brained many of them. Many, did I say, yea most, if not all of them' (*HW*, 205). Life for the Nonconformist is a matter of being on a permanent war footing, always at risk from attack, either by one's own religious grand narrative acting through one's conscience, or the political authorities committed to suppressing difference wherever it raises its head. This is precisely what Lyotard conceives of as a differend. Bunyan's grand narrative and that of the Restoration regime can 'not be reconciled': there is no real compromise possible between two such widely divergent worldviews.

The most that Bunyan and his fictional characters can hope for is a brief respite from the struggle, because the forces of Diabolus will always regroup and come back at them. Again, this is a severe test of the individual's faith: a faith that ebbs and flows according to his current state of mind, and as we know from *Grace Abounding*, that is rarely less than very troubled in Bunyan's case—a trait that he passes on to his fictional protagonists in *The Holy War* and *The Pilgrim's Progress*. The sheer volume of the rescues and assurances that Mansoul receives is testament as to just how fragile the state of the

Nonconformist psyche can be when it is faced by a life full of 'puzzles'. As the work's preface tells us:

> *The Town of* Mansoul *is well known to many,*
> *Nor are her troubles doubted of by any*
> *That are acquainted with those* Histories
> *That* Mansoul, *and her Wars* Anatomise. (*HW*, 1)

There is no hiding place safe from the attentions of the Diabolonian grand narrative. Equally, Bunyan cannot hide from the demands of his own grand narrative, which will keep returning to worry away at his conscience. It is a conflict which can never be over until the Celestial City is reached, and the final decision on whether you will be successful in that respect belongs to the realm of the sublime—as Ignorance discovers to his cost.

Grace Abounding has a similar sense of a character being perpetually harried and never left in peace as he wrestles with his personal interpretation of the Christian grand narrative: a narrative that demands specific, and incontrovertible, evidence from him that he can ever be justified in considering himself to be one of the elect. Each item of evidence that he can cite, however, invariably comes accompanied by a subsequent plummet from grace, as crushing doubt at the likelihood of his salvation returns to assail the author in a series of falls that are painfully remembered: 'down I fell, as a Bird that is shot from the top of a Tree, into great guilt and fearful despair' (*GA*, 43). Even after he appears to have reached a state of relative security concerning his spiritual prospects, doubts can still insidiously creep back into his thoughts and he is left to reflect on the fact that even 'when I have been preaching, I have been violently assaulted with thoughts of blasphemy, and strongly tempted to speak them with my mouth before the Congregation' (*GA*, 90). The sublime keeps one forever guessing, never entirely sure what one's fate is going to be, and even what might come into one's mind the next minute—preachers being no less susceptible to this than anyone.

The conflict of little and grand narrative in Bunyan's own life is arguably at its starkest in *A Relation of the Imprisonment of Mr. John Bunyan* (a series of letters written by Bunyan from prison in 1660–62, but unpublished until 1765), where the author is subjected to hostile questioning by local figures of authority determined to impose religious conformity on their community as directed by the Restoration government. Despite being sternly warned that 'the King then commands you, that you should not have any private meetings; because it is against his law, and he is ordained of God, therefore you should not have any' (*GA*, 124), Bunyan still refuses to give up preaching. It is a refusal which ultimately sees him consigned to jail over a period of twelve years. Ignorance would no doubt have submitted to this greater political power, but Bunyan just cannot; to the extent that when he finds, as he puts it, 'some liberty granted' by his jailer before his final sentencing, he promptly returns to 'my wonted course of preaching' (*GA*, 129), a move which can only make him appear all the more dangerous in the authorities' eyes. This is the situation in which Christian is placed in Vanity Fair, of course, a vulnerable individual faced by the power of the state, and it is an image which recurs throughout

Bunyan's fiction: Christian when confronted by the might of Apollyon physically barring his way; the town of Mansoul by the numerically superior, and ever-persistent, Diabolonian forces massing at its gates.

Conclusion

A common feature of poststructuralist and postmodernist readings of Bunyan is that they all see him as struggling against difference, *différance*, and differends throughout his fiction, and, as we have seen, these do seem to be significant factors throughout his life as well. It is this aspect above all that makes Bunyan's work lend itself to such readings and makes him such an attractive prospect for critics of that persuasion. This is not to say that a postmodernist approach is the only valid one (or even *the* most valid one), but for those whose interests lie in the politics of the period, and the complex interaction occurring between the literature and the politics then, it does offer a very fruitful analytical method. The instability and sense of insecurity that pervade so much of Bunyan's fictional writings speak volumes for the author's historical context, and form a natural terrain for the postmodern critic to go to work upon.

Suggested Reading

Davies, Michael, *Graceful Reading: Theology and Narrative in the Works of John Bunyan* (Oxford: Oxford University Press, 2002).

Fish, Stanley, *Self-Consuming Artifacts: The Experience of Seventeenth-Century Literature* (Berkeley, CA: University of California Press, 1972).

Hofmeyr, Isabel, 'Bunyan: Colonial, Postcolonial', in Anne Dunan-Page (ed.), *The Cambridge Companion to Bunyan* (Cambridge: Cambridge University Press, 2010), 162–76.

Luxon, Thomas H., *Literal Figures: Puritan Allegory and the Reformation Crisis in Representation* (Chicago and London: University of Chicago Press, 1995).

Lyotard, Jean-François, *The Postmodern Condition: A Report on Knowledge*, tr. Geoff Bennington and Brian Massumi (1979; Manchester: Manchester University Press, 1984).

Lyotard, Jean-François, *The Differend: Phrases in Dispute*, tr. Georges Van Den Abbeele (1983; Manchester: Manchester University Press, 1988).

Michie, Allen, 'Between Calvin and Calvino: Postmodernism and Bunyan's *The Pilgrim's Progress*', in Greg Clingham (ed.), *Questioning History: The Postmodern Turn to the Eighteenth Century* (Cranbury, NJ, and London: Associated University Presses, 1998), 37–56.

Sim, Stuart, 'Bunyan, Lyotard and the Conflict of Narratives: Or, Postmodernising Bunyan', BS, 8 (1998), 67–81.

Sim, Stuart and David Walker, *Bunyan and Authority: The Rhetoric of Dissent and the Legitimation Crisis in Seventeenth-Century England* (Bern: Peter Lang, 2000).

Spargo, Tamsin, *The Writing of John Bunyan* (Aldershot: Ashgate, 1997).

CHAPTER 29

BUNYAN, THEORY, AND THEOLOGY
A Case for Post-Secular Criticism

LORI BRANCH

An abiding premise of Bunyan studies is the relationship between *Grace Abounding to the Chief of Sinners* (1666), Bunyan's spiritual autobiography, and his first and most famous allegory, *The Pilgrim's Progress* (1678). Most scholars follow Roger Sharrock in understanding that crucial linkage as a 'creative reworking', a sense many readers over the last 300 years would share.[1] For clearly, as different as these works are in form and content, there are deep correlations between the two. But the task of pinpointing the precise mode of that creative reworking is particularly promising, for complicating any notion of simple correlation between the life-writing and the fictional account prompts us to draw on the language and tools of both historical theology and literary theory and then draw those languages together. In the discipline of English, speakers of these dialects rarely converse, and engagement with critical theory is generally taken to be inimical to a historically specific, theologically sound scholarship on Bunyan, as on a host of other religious authors.

In this chapter, I hope to demonstrate that the reverse is true, showing the benefit of reading Bunyan in simultaneously theological and theoretical registers, without letting one foreclose the other. The potential and promise of such an approach are that of a genuinely post-secular literary practice, growing out of the emerging contours of post-secular reason more broadly.[2] My wager is that in laying our heads, hearts, and

---

[1] Roger Sharrock, *John Bunyan* (London: Macmillan, 1968), 157; see also Hill, *Bunyan*, 206–07; Kathleen M. Swaim, *Pilgrim's Progress, Puritan Progress: Discourses and Contexts* (Urbana, IL: University of Illinois Press, 1993), 14.

[2] For helpful accounts of post-secular criticism, see the special issue of the journal *Religion and Literature*, 41 (summer 2009), 'What is Religion and Literature?', and a forum, 'Locating the Postsecular', in the same volume (autumn, 2009). See also Lori Branch, 'Postsecular Studies', in Mark Knight (ed.), *The Routledge Companion to Literature and Religion* (London: Routledge, 2016), 91–101.

Bunyan's books together (to paraphrase the tinker), we can read Bunyan in ways that, to historico-theological and theoretical readers alike, are legible yet surprising, even salubriously disconcerting. This sort of reading is genuinely but not exclusively critical, in that it recognizes critical suspicion as only one side of the coin of the uncertainty of the linguistic condition. Faith is the other side: a believing from within uncertainty from which even the most sceptical reader can never finally extricate himself. The promise of a way of reading that owns up to the trace of belief on every inscription of knowledge is not just a way of reading that might be loving in addition to sceptical and self-critical in addition to critical, but also a scholarly subject position which does not amputate faith, hope, or love from its conception of human reason. As a scholar and person, I am interested in this way of reading and being in the world, for, by refusing to divide human experience and thought along secularist lines, it holds the benefit of moving beyond the soul-killing dryness of critical thought as it is most generally practised in the humanities at present.[3] The most direct route to try this experiment is to read Bunyan's works with an eye towards faith, theologically and theoretically conceived.

'THAT RARE AND CURIOUS PIECE OF ART': FAITH IN *GRACE ABOUNDING*

One of the most fruitful points of departure for interpreting the significance of Bunyan's spiritual experience in its cultural milieu and its representation in his works lies in a crucial sequence of events in Bunyan's spiritual awakening related early in *Grace Abounding*. 'But upon a day', writes Bunyan, in well-known and moving lines,

> the good Providence of God did cast me to *Bedford*, to work on my calling; and in one of the streets of that town, I came where there was three or four poor women sitting at a door in the Sun, and talking about the things of God; [...] their talk was about a new birth, the work of God on their hearts [...] they talked how God had visited their souls with his love in the Lord Jesus [...] And me thought they spake as if joy did make them speak [...] as if they had found a new world. (*GA*, 14–15)

Hearing these women, Bunyan was overcome, in his words, with 'a very great softness and tenderness of heart, which caused [him] to fall under the conviction of what by Scripture they asserted', and he began to hope that the spiritual Eden of communion with Jesus was true (*GA*, 15). But by their words he was also 'convinced that [he] wanted the true tokens of a truly godly man'; his mind now 'lay like a Horseleach at the vein [...] fixed on Eternity', and he 'began to look into the Bible with new eyes [...] that [he]

---

[3] See the forum on the post-secular and the post-critical in response to Rita Felski's *The Limits of Critique* (Chicago: University of Chicago Press, 2015), in *Religion and Literature*, 48 (2016), 156–95.

might know the truth, and way to Heaven and Glory' (*GA*, 15, 17). That way is faith, and Bunyan fears he is not following it. That mind like a 'Horseleach' soon cannot release this vein of thought, 'until I did now come to some certain knowledge whether I had Faith or no; this always running in my minde, *But how if you want Faith indeed? But how can you tell you have faith?*' (*GA*, 18). For pages and months and years Bunyan sucks at this vein a seemingly bottomless well of doubts: Does he have faith, is he elected, is he converted?

In this opening sequence, faith becomes an epistemological question: 'I could not rest content until I did now come to certain knowledge whether I had Faith or no' (*GA*, 18). What we must grasp here is the essential transmutation of the Christian category of faith into knowledge, into propositional certainty, a shift indicative, certainly, not of spiritual inclinations peculiar to Bunyan, but of the transformation of Christian theology and spirituality in those rival sibling movements: medieval Scholasticism and the Reformation. In a characteristically earnest moment, Bunyan declares:

> I […] was willing to put myself upon the tryal, whether I had Faith or no. But alas, poor Wretch! so ignorant and brutish was I, that I knew to this day no more how to do it, than I know how to begin and accomplish that rare and curious piece of Art, which I never yet saw nor considered. (*GA*, 18)

Bunyan's confession of his ignorance, his lack of knowledge, compares experimental, covenant theology, the empirical method, and their ways to truth, to the creation or construction of a beautiful 'piece of Art', the technique for which Bunyan has never learned and the model for which he has never seen. Like so many sentences in Bunyan, this one intimates that knowledge—'certain knowledge [of] faith' which he hopes to discover by 'tryal' like a law or fact of the material world—is bound up not so much in our objective, 'scientific' discovery as in our artistic creation and participatory co-creation with God, with others, with the spiritual artisans who have gone before us. The knowledge of faith which Bunyan seeks reveals itself in Bunyan's language as *faith's* knowledge: a work of art and construction that Bunyan realizes, in a deep moment of truth-telling, he does not know how to create or perform.

It is on the heels of this missed recognition of the status of faith and knowledge that temptation comes: 'while I was thus considering […] the Tempter came in with this delusion, That there was no way for me to know I had Faith, but by trying to work some miracle', a trial which leaves him so 'tossed betwixt the Devil and my own ignorance, […] that I could not tell what to doe' (*GA*, 18–19). Just as in Genesis 3, the temptation for Bunyan is to that tree of the knowledge of good and evil, which brings death and cuts us off from the tree of life: of trusting, life-giving relation with God. Though Bunyan at the time felt that it was spiritual prudence that prompted him thus to interrogate the condition of his soul, he later indicates that it is Satan who poses the epistemological question and fuels its ceaseless repetition (*GA*, 21), but the ramifications of this insight are not fully explored. As is also characteristic in Bunyan, the epistemological impasse climaxes and becomes spatialized in a dream in which Bunyan sees Christ as the narrow gap in the barrier-wall of the Scriptures through which one must leave the world to become a Christian (*GA*, 20). This spatialization serves to tame the uncertainties of language that coat and mediate all reality, transforming words and the Word into a barrier in space that can be fully mapped and finally passed through. Salvation in Bunyan's dream is to move through the barrier of language to the reality or certain knowledge of faith, beyond language. And yet Bunyan is honest enough to admit after this dream that, still, 'I knew not where I was' (*GA*, 20).

One of the most amazing aspects of this account is the way that, by Bunyan's own reckoning, God helps him in ways that *should* serve subtly to break up his rigid textual literalism and spiritual experientialism. This is especially true of his first relief from this relentless questioning, the comforting word from Ecclesiasticus 2:10, '*Look at the generations of old, and see, did ever any trust in God and were confounded?*' (*GA*, 21). In the first occasion of the Word 'coming upon' Bunyan, the word that comes upon him is not from the Word but from the Apocrypha: that body of deutero-canonical books that, from most Protestant viewpoints, marks the Latin West's infidelity to the doctrine of *sola scriptura*.[4] It is as though God's comfort of Bunyan with this text, outside the Reformed canon of Scripture, was meant to remedy the latter's problematic penchant for making the Bible into a proof text of systematic salvation-knowledge, a roadmap to a spiritual world on the physical model. God's comfort of Bunyan through an unscriptural Scripture, evoking a youth in the established church which he has renounced (for Ecclesiasticus was read in the seventeenth-century lectionary), indicates that God's love and care are more capacious than the text fixed and fixated upon by the Reformers, and that *sola scriptura*, held out as the remedy for papist ills, may cause at least as many spiritual maladies as it cures.

Bunyan's acceptance of help from Ecclesiasticus is therefore carefully handled: he cannot discover the source of the quotation for over a year, and when he does, it 'at the first did somewhat daunt' him that it was from 'the Apocrypha-Books', but 'it troubled [him] the less' when he considered that 'this sentence was the sum and substance of many of the promises', and 'by this time [he] had got more experience of the love and kindness of God' (*GA*, 22). What is remarkable here is Bunyan's trusting heart: one that can believe even an apocryphal text can, like *The Pilgrim's Progress*, '*hold / The truth, as Cabinets inclose the Gold*' (*PP*, 4). Alongside the excruciating epistemological pressure that transmutes Christian faith into a quest for both propositional truths and an evidentiary knowledge that provides more scepticism than answers, abides an amazing hope that eventually, in the latter years of Bunyan's ministry, gathers to a gentleness, as many have noted, mitigating the full severity of Calvinist doctrines of predestination for Bunyan and his congregants. But the reverse formulation is also true, for Bunyan holds both strands to the end: shadowing this hope is the vision of God as judge and giver of

---

[4] In an essay in which theory shuts down theology, Peter Carlton diagnoses such incidents of the Word 'coming upon' Bunyan as 'disclaiming locutions'. See Peter Carlton, 'Bunyan: Language, Convention, Authority', *ELH*, 51 (1984), 17–32.

election and reprobation, a vision that so undeniably troubles, for Bunyan, that sweet love of the Bedford women talking in the sun.

This is the crucial paradox: how the privilege proclaimed by the Reformers to examine the Scriptures in search of salvation is related to the paralyzing self-scrutiny that pervades Bunyan's autobiography—and how, in spite of that, hope for love and salvation remains. In the early portion of *Grace Abounding*, Bunyan imagines God *forcing* him to believe in love: 'If now I should have burned at a stake, I could not believe that Christ had love for me' (*GA*, 26). This is an incredibly rich formulation, not only because it points towards the violence from which this ideal of certainty cannot extricate itself, but because forcing Bunyan to believe in his love is precisely what God will not do, in *Grace Abounding* or elsewhere. Bunyan's language bespeaks some recognition that this epistemology is torturing him, but we also cannot escape how it perversely, if longingly, imagines God as burning him at the stake to force him to believe in his love. Later in the narrative, Bunyan seems to feel 'a kind of threatning me if I did not [...] venture my Salvation upon the Son of God' (*GA*, 53). In imaging God's coercion of him—a coercion which God in the text forever resists—Bunyan's writings sound a deep homology with his fellow Dissenter and co-pioneer of the English novel, Daniel Defoe, in *Robinson Crusoe* (1719), in which the central, unanswered theological conundrum comes from the childlike mouth of Friday: '*If God much strong, much might as the Devil, why God no kill the Devil, so make him no more do wicked?*'[5] Both writers continually imagine violent coercion from God, abstracted as a principle of omniscience and omnipotence, *alongside* a silent, potent recognition that God is there and yet silently resists relating to humanity in this way. In Bunyan, this fantasy of violence forcing knowledge, to which God never answers, points to a quiet gentleness of God and a corollary, circumscribed but no less majestic, human freedom. God's silent refusal of the violence of forced certainty and the ineradicable trace of human freedom remain throughout *Grace Abounding* as a great chasm, in which echo Bunyan's 'tumultuous thoughts': 'masterless hellhounds' that 'roar and bellow, and make a hideous noise within me' (*GA*, 53).

In this tumult of thoughts, the Scripture that comes upon Bunyan is never so loud that the dogs of spiritual war tuck tail and run once and for all. 'When comforting time was come'—the time when that rapturous experience of the phrase '*My Love*' from Song of Songs 4:1 fills him with such joy that he would speak of it 'even to the very Crows that sat upon the plow'd lands before me'—Bunyan writes, within forty days of even this experience, 'I began to question all again' (*GA*, 29, 30). This passage points to the softening effect of time on memory and also embodies one of the lingering ambiguities of *Grace Abounding*: whether this or any experience in the autobiography can be pinpointed as Bunyan's conversion.[6] Perhaps the integrity of *Grace Abounding* is best shown in that,

---

[5] Daniel Defoe, *Robinson Crusoe*, ed. Thomas Keymer (Oxford: Oxford University Press, 2007), 184.

[6] Roger Pooley, '*Grace Abounding* and the New Sense of Self', in Anne Laurence, W. R. Owens, and Stuart Sim (eds.), *John Bunyan and his England, 1628–1688* (London: Hambledon Press, 1990), 105–14 (109). On conversion in Bunyan, see also Anne Hawkins, *Archetypes of Conversion: The Autobiographies of Augustine, Bunyan, and Merton* (London: Wipf & Stock, 2014), and Barry Hall, 'Conflict, Closure, Dilemma: Bunyan's *Grace Abounding*', *BS*, 16 (2012), 103–20.

for all its certainty-seeking, it does not shirk the uncertainty of conversion. Teaching and reading *Grace Abounding* and *The Pilgrim's Progress* again and again, I find myself unable to escape the sense that their greatest assurance of love and faith lies not in evidence such as Bunyan desires. Rather, if there is any assurance of love and proof of faith in the Bunyan corpus—and I think its popularity declares undeniably that in some sense there is—it is mainly in the form of the very heart which, by related motions, accepts the apocryphal text as divine comfort on the one hand and, on the other, imagines that *The Pilgrim's Progress* might likewise be an apocryphal conduit of genuine grace and truth. This is the heart that hopes for the roll, the certificate of assurance, the contract of salvation economically imagined, but more importantly for the Celestial City too, and to share that comfort with others: the heart that *loves*, creates, and plays, as Bunyan exemplifies in *The Pilgrim's Progress*.

FAITH IN *THE PILGRIM'S PROGRESS*: 'SET DOWN MY NAME'

The paradox and the glory of *The Pilgrim's Progress*, in this understanding, are the way that it supplies knowledge of faith—in the roll Christian receives certifying his conversion, in his spatialized journey to the Celestial City, in his crossing the River of Death—alongside its literary reconfiguration of that evidence and the quest for certainty.[7] Reading *The Pilgrim's Progress* on the heels of *Grace Abounding*, we can appreciate both the pains Bunyan goes to in 'The Author's Apology for his Book' to defend it as a '*Dream*' and as a container for '*Nothing but sound and honest Gospel-strains*' (PP, 7), and how funny and free he seems here. Sprightly humour that never appears in *Grace Abounding* dances through this prefatory poem. To friends who are uncertain if he should print this dangerously fictional, allegorical tale, he replies with nearly cavalier wit that he can put it to the test by printing the book and seeing if it does good. This at least is an uncertainty he can resolve quite simply, without apparent risk of harm. One can feel the breeze blowing freely in Bunyan's creative spirits, and as a reader I can believe him when he says he wrote this for his own satisfaction. It has the feel of a relieving activity, a distraction from the epistemological pressures that otherwise so consumed him. The quest for certainty that remade faith into knowledge in *Grace Abounding* is, in *The Pilgrim's Progress*, outshone by the construction and creation that were only hinted at in the autobiography: precisely if unintentionally as that 'rare and curious piece of art' Bunyan previously could not imagine crafting.

---

[7] I develop a psychoanalytic reading of this connection, not incompatible with this interpretation, in Lori Branch, '"As blood is forced out of flesh": Spontaneity and the Wounds of Exchange in *Grace Abounding* and *The Pilgrim's Progress*', ELH, 74 (2007), 271–99.

Acknowledging how this construction frees Bunyan, we likewise cannot deny how he must denigrate it as only a cabinet enclosing the gold, and the opening sequence in *The Pilgrim's Progress* confirms Bunyan in the trenchant problem of his spirituality. The narrative makes an early threefold progression—from the description of the desired heaven,[8] to the Slough of Despond, to Worldly-Wiseman (who circumvents despond by trusting in Morality)—that confirms Christian in his epistemology and recuperates the misery of uncertainty in its favour, suggesting that any system that would relieve this suffering more effectively must be false. In the logic of the text, a Christian is right to feel despair in his universe of textual truths, never perfectly confirmed. And yet, with good readers' hearts, other Christians are right, too, to feel that there is something abject about this insistence on tormenting uncertainty and the idea that any other Christian theology offering better spiritual medicines is untrue.

The Pilgrim's Progress, then, not unlike *Grace Abounding*, also makes faith into knowledge, with despondency as its necessary basis. And yet its very status as a creative work allows Bunyan to capture the possibilities that remain inexpressible in the theology and epistemology he professes. This is nowhere clearer than in the horrific spectacle of the Man in the Iron Cage, shown to Christian by the Interpreter, and whose condition of despair is distinctly reminiscent of Francis Spira's: the apostate whose 'dreadful story' Bunyan encounters at one point in *Grace Abounding* (*PP*, 34–5; *GA*, 49–50). Recounting this image from the House of the Interpreter, Christian later declares, 'the Man had sinned himself quite out of hopes of Gods mercy' (*PP*, 53), suggesting both Spira's and Bunyan's great fear that he has committed the so-called unpardonable sin and is not one of the elect. But the tableau of the Man in the Iron Cage immediately follows that of the Valiant Man, the 'man of a very stout countenance' who approaches the recorder of the names of those who will enter the heavenly palace, and says, in one of the most heartening lines of the story, '*Set down my Name Sir*'—which the bookkeeper does; the Valiant Man proceeds to do battle with the forces of darkness and to make his way into the heavenly kingdom (*PP*, 33–4). The conjunction of the parables of the Valiant Man and the Man in the Iron Cage suggests that it is *despair* that 'sins the man out of God's mercy', first and foremost when he blasphemously claims, 'God hath denied me repentance' (*PP*, 35). It is not that sins cannot be forgiven, but that one believes they won't be that is the problem; thus, closing that door by accusing God of lack of mercy is a sin against the Holy Ghost. Similarly, in battle with Apollyon, Christian bravely argues preference against the monster: I 'like [Christ's] Service [...] better than thine', so don't try to persuade me further (*PP*, 57). The effect of the narrative is, as critics have noted of much of Bunyan's work, to mitigate the most vicious psychological effects of the Calvinist doctrine of double predestination by encouraging readers to hope, to imitate the Valiant Man and bravely say, 'Set down my name.'

In both *Grace Abounding* and *The Pilgrim's Progress*, Bunyan's insomniac questioning 'whether I had Faith or no' (*GA*, 18) is answered, then, not through the sort of proof

---

[8] By Christian to Pliable and again at the House of the Interpreter (*PP*, 13–14, 33).

Bunyan teaches us to expect—through the Scripture coming upon him or the assurance offered by the roll—but through the gradual accumulation of Bunyan's experience of his desire for faith and salvation. We might well tally the times Bunyan and Christian say 'I was for going on': 'so he resolved to go on' (*PP*, 63); 'I am for going on and venturing my eternal state with Christ, whether I have comfort here or no' (*GA*, 101). Without the evidence of comfort or final assurance, he is for venturing—and this 'being for' undoes the paralyzing horrors of Calvinist doctrines of election and reprobation: it becomes the experience of hope and faith, without external certification that that is what they are, for faith itself is 'the evidence of things not seen' (Hebrews 11:1).

These two great pillars of the Bunyan corpus, so loved and read across the subsequent three centuries, show how, for Protestantism on the cusp of modernity, the *agon* between faith and knowledge is itself the resounding battle and animating tension. Bunyan's surface anxiety is for certain knowledge of correct biblical doctrine and of the state of his soul in the legal terms of salvation, but the victory that overcomes the world is not knowledge but faith (1 John 5:4): faith that maintains hope for life and for goodness in the face of the determinisms of both predestination and the material and economic forces of the century to come. In this sense, *The Pilgrim's Progress* is, and is not, Bunyan's roll: the imaginative, creative profession of the heart that is 'for going on'—for venturing, for going on pilgrimage, for holding out hope to others. Seeking for the certain knowledge of faith in *Grace Abounding*, Bunyan arrives in *The Pilgrim's Progress* at that 'rare and curious piece of Art which I never yet saw or considered' that does confirm that he has faith, but in a mode appropriate to faith and freedom: that is, fiction, albeit fiction at pains to claim its status as knowledge-on-deposit, as cabinets enclose the gold.

Towards the end of *The Pilgrim's Progress* both hope and epistemological anxiety intensify. As Christian and Hopeful approach the Celestial City, a Shining One soberly reminds them: 'you must obtain [the Celestial City] by your own faith' (*PP*, 156). Reaching its gates, Christian is back where Bunyan started, so to speak, and the question approaching the River of Death is whether he has faith of his own or no.[9] Christian has his roll; but in the story, the faith that takes one across the River of Death is different from the roll that certifies it. Moreover, it is hard to classify this faith, strictly speaking, as his own: the roll doesn't help him across, but Hopeful does. When the pilgrims enter the water, Christian begins to sink, and 'a great darkness and horror' falls upon him:

> *Hopeful* therefore here had much adoe to keep his Brothers head above water, yea sometimes he would be quite gone down, and then ere a while he would rise up again half dead. *Hopeful* also would endeavour to comfort him, saying, Brother, I see the Gate, and Men standing by it to receive us; but *Christian* would answer, 'Tis you, 'tis you they wait for [...]. *Hopeful* added this word, *Be of good cheer, Jesus Christ maketh thee whole*: And with that *Christian* brake out with a loud voice, Oh I see him again!

---

[9] On death and anxiety of death among Nonconformists at this time, see Abram Steen, '"Over this Jordan": Dying and the Nonconformist Community in Bunyan's *Pilgrim's Progress*', *Modern Philology*, 110 (2012), 49–73.

and he tells me, *When thou passest through the waters, I will be with thee; and through the Rivers, they shall not overflow thee.* Then they both took courage, and the enemy was after that as still as a stone, until they were gone over. (*PP*, 157–58)

The personal faith unto salvation that cannot be the object of certified knowledge in *Grace Abounding*, which is compared to a work of artistry and placed in the Apocrypha, is manifested most vividly in Bunyan's most precarious moments of hope, and confesses itself, by the end of *The Pilgrim's Progress*, to be a work of art, a miracle of fellowship and brotherly love, of speaking and listening to another, barely one's own at all.

Poststructuralist Faiths and the Linguistic Condition

In his 1998 essay 'Faith and Knowledge: The Two Sources of Religion at the Limits of Reason Alone', which has since become a touchstone for post-secular studies, Jacques Derrida explores the vicissitudes of faith in modernity in terms strikingly resonant with Bunyan's, distinguishing between two different sorts of faith. The first is Kantian reflective faith that, not unlike Bunyan's, is formed in relation to reason and the law, 'bound to [them] by the band of their opposition'.[10] This sort of faith, however inadvertently, guarantees a radical dissociation between God and the moral self, who, in Kant's scheme, by virtue of pure practical reason must ultimately act not in personal relation to God, hoping for reward, but precisely as though God does not exist[11]—as Bunyan does at the end of *Grace Abounding*, imagining jumping off the ladder blindfold into eternity. Derrida shows that this rationalized faith ends in ontotheology, which 'determines knowledge as the truth of religion', which crucially is 'distinct from faith, prayer, or from sacrifice' per se and actually 'destroys religion'.[12] Derrida's second sort of faith, aligned with prayer and sacrifice, resists the comforts of abstraction, mastery, and the mechanisms of the law, by passing through them without stopping at false certainty, towards what he calls the 'desert in the desert' where, beyond rational outbidding in the quest for knowledge, the aporias of law and knowledge appear, and where belief and the experience of the sacredness of the other might take place.[13] This desert in the desert may resemble a destitution of the possibility of goodness, truth, or ethics, but it can also 'render possible precisely what it appears to threaten'—or, as he put it elsewhere, it is 'the

---

[10] Jacques Derrida, 'Faith and Knowledge: Two Sources of Religion at the Limits of Reason Alone', in Jacques Derrida and Gianni Vattimo (eds.), *Religion* (Stanford, CA: Stanford University Press, 1998), 1–78 (2).
[11] Derrida, 'Faith and Knowledge', 11.
[12] Derrida, 'Faith and Knowledge', 15.
[13] Derrida, 'Faith and Knowledge', 21, 33.

principle of indeterminism' that 'makes the conscious freedom of man fathomable'.[14] In other words, the uncertain destitution of the desert in the desert allows for the possibility of faith that remains faith and is not subsumed into knowledge. Such a fundamental, radical experience of faith may be related, Derrida goes on to explain, to that other fundamental religious experience, 'the experience of *sacredness* or of *holiness*'.[15]

The experience of alterity, freedom, and responsibility related to the uncertainties of faith is, for Derrida, like Bunyan, and since his earliest works, rooted in the nature of language. Building on Saussure's notion of the differential nature of the sign, Derrida's 1968 essay 'Différance' shows that thought and our perception of reality are governed by the same structure: the work of *différance* that produces presence as an effect of temporal and spatial displacement which leaves a perpetual trace of alterity on each idea and concept. This does not mean that there is no knowledge or meaning, but that there is no knowledge or meaning in isolation, as Bunyan or virtually any modern epistemologist imagines it. '*Il n'y a pas de hors-texte*' then really means that all human reality is textual, which is to say that everything in it is relationally connected as in language. At the origin of thought is what Derrida calls 'archi-writing', the process he describes as the spatio-temporal movement of *difference*, and in our examination of this linguistic process, he claims, 'we shall no doubt catch sight of something like a primordial *différance*'.[16] Or, perhaps, in gospel terms more friendly to Bunyan, 'in the beginning was the Word' (John 1:1). 'We cannot refrain here from going by way of a written text', Derrida writes with a gleam in his eye, 'from ordering ourselves by the disorder that is produced therein—and this is what matters to me first of all.'[17]

In Christian theological terms, we might gloss this by saying that the Trinity, understood as three-in-one and one-in-three—Father, Word, and Spirit—bears witness that 'language' or signification is not secondary and that *différance* as distinction-with-unity is primary: perhaps even that *being qua* personhood has the nature of speech. In one of the most overlooked sentences in the whole Derridean corpus, Derrida affirms that *différance* also means that 'we question the authority of presence *or* its simple symmetrical contrary, absence or lack'.[18] The challenge, to his mind, is to 'question the absolute privilege of [...] consciousness as meaning in self-presence', and to imagine the profound truth of the presence of Being (that existential cipher for God) *at the same time* that we comprehend the absence or gap that remains in language between beings, that allows for their perpetual responsibility and freedom.[19] For *différance*, as Derrida

---

[14] Derrida, 'Faith and Knowledge', 17; Jacques Derrida, 'My Chances/*Mes Chances*', in J. H. Smith and William Kerrigan (eds.), *Taking Chances: Derrida, Psychoanalysis, Literature* (Baltimore, MD: Johns Hopkins University Press, 1984), 1–32 (8).

[15] Derrida, 'Faith and Knowledge', 33.

[16] Jacques Derrida, '*Différance*', in *Speech and Phenomena* (Evanston, IL: Northwestern University Press, 1973), 129–60 (138).

[17] Derrida, '*Différance*', 133.

[18] Derrida, '*Différance*', 139; emphasis added.

[19] Derrida, '*Différance*', 147. Derrida addresses freedom and responsibility in works of the early 1990s; see Jacques Derrida, ' "Eating Well", or the Calculation of the Subject: An Interview with Jacques Derrida',

describes it, is gentle, founding without force, like Bunyan's quiet God in some respects, making possible our freedom. *Différance*:

> commands nothing, rules over nothing, and nowhere does it exercise any authority. [...] Not only is there no realm of *différance*, but *différance* is even the subversion of every realm. This is obviously what makes it threatening and necessarily dreaded by everything in us that desires a realm, the past or future presence of a realm.[20]

Différance is no 'unique word, a master name'; we must perceive its 'reduction to a lower-case letter' and conceive of it 'without *nostalgia*'; 'we must *affirm* it with a certain laughter and with a certain dance', and with what he admits is more shocking, 'hope'.[21]

Rereading '*Différance*', one can see why, thirty years later, Derrida was still writing in 'Faith and Knowledge' about 'the act of faith in the appeal to faith that inhabits every act of language and every address to the other'.[22] Faith, for Derrida, is inherent in the linguistic condition. Echoing Lyotard's language in *The Differend*, Derrida describes this desert of uncertainty as the very structure of the 'link' itself: that moment when, not from a condition of knowledge or of certainty, but in contingency and faith, we link words and ideas together—we interpret, construct, respond, and act—in the ever incomplete gesture of doing justice to the other.[23] To draw Bunyan and Derrida even closer together, the question that Bunyan's texts raise from Derrida's perspective would be, not whether Christian has faith, but what kind of faith he has; not whether Christian has faith that is his own, but whether faith is ever truly one's own. In Derridean ears, and despite his desire to know whether he has faith, Bunyan's texts whisper faith's knowledge that faith is always contingent and constructed, in relation to others and to the faith of others, who, in the fragile ether of language, do not block our way to God like the wall of Scripture in *Grace Abounding* but, like Hopeful at the end of *The Pilgrim's Progress*, miraculously urge us on to believe in good things to come—since faith itself, to paraphrase Hebrews 11:1, is the Christian's 'evidence of things hoped for'.

It is equally in light of reading Bunyan on his own spiritual, theological terms, and of reading him alongside Derrida, that I would argue here, as I have elsewhere, for the peculiar secularism of Bunyan's works. In his proto-Kantian reflective faith, Bunyan confirms as much as Derrida the way this faith silences prayer and by its despair of faith-as-knowledge 'destroys religion'. The effect of this secularism within religious thought is to advance secularist modes of thought *and*, equally, at one and the same time, to retain

---

tr. Peter Connor and Avital Ronell, in Eduardo Cadava, Peter Connor, and Jean-Luc Nancy (eds.), *Who Comes after the Subject?* (New York: Routledge, 1991), 96–119; Jacques Derrida, 'Force of Law: The "Mystical Foundation of Authority"', in Drucilla Cornell, Michael Rosenfeld, and David Gray Carlson (eds.), *Deconstruction and the Possibility of Justice* (New York: Routledge, 1992), 3–67.

[20] Derrida, '*Différance*', 153.
[21] Derrida, '*Différance*', 159.
[22] Derrida, 'Faith and Knowledge', 18.
[23] Derrida, 'Faith and Knowledge', 16. Jean-François Lyotard, *The Differend: Phrases in Dispute*, tr. Georges Van Den Abbele (Minneapolis, MN: University of Minnesota Press, 1989).

faith and hope, in the forms of symptom and of fantasy fiction.[24] By secularism, I do not mean secularization, but secularism as a modern ideology, as Talal Asad and others teach us to identify it. Arguing the particular form of secularism that attends Bunyan's texts differs from supporting or countering the secularization thesis itself, which has by and large come unravelled. I am suggesting rather that we follow Asad, Danièle Hervieu-Léger, and Peter Berger in tracking not the decline but the transformation of religion in modernity.[25]

The transformation of Christianity in modernity takes place to no small degree via its internalizations of forms of thought inimical to it by virtue of their secularism: that is, the extent to which they imagine the world of reason and language, of commerce and the nation-state, and eventually of global capitalism, as given, knowable realities purged of faith as illusion. In Graham Ward's telling, in the sixteenth and seventeenth centuries in Western Europe, God takes flight into the heavens; faith as belief from within uncertainty has no meaning, and is cashed out as knowledge of faith; God and grace are meaningful only in the terms of propositional truths.[26] Pushed out from the realm of the material world, inaccessible through either sacrament or (after fears of enthusiasm) direct spiritual experience,[27] God becomes knowable only at the arm's reach of reason, in an infinity and transcendence that are pushed further and further from human life in the world, a genealogy that continues up to the present day, in which we have theorists and philosophers in the early twenty-first century speaking of the 'demise of metaphysics'.[28]

Put another way, by secularism, I mean what our contemporary theoretical moment has come to understand as the fantasy of a world without belief, inhabited by the Lacanian subject, a subject of illusory wholeness.[29] That is, we may see secularism in its economic-Marxist, linguistic-Derridean, and psychoanalytic-Lacanian aspects; it trades in commodity fetishisms, and it bears deconstructive traces and psychoanalytic symptoms. The ultimate commodity and the fantasy of language that Derrida was forever showing to deconstruct itself are an imagined sphere of knowledge directly present and possessable in language and unmediated by faith, a sphere in which one could have knowledge of whether he has faith, for instance. And the subject that Lacan never tired of analysing is the subject whose fantasy this is: who, in the quest to shore up the ego

---

[24] On *Grace Abounding* and the Lacanian symptom, see Branch, '"As blood is forced out of flesh"'.

[25] Talal Asad, *Formations of the Secular: Christianity, Islam, Modernity* (Stanford, CA: Stanford University Press, 2003); Danièle Hervieu-Léger, *Religion as a Chain of Memory*, tr. Simon Lee (New Brunswick, NJ: Rutgers University Press, 2001); Peter Berger (ed.), *The Desecularization of the World: Resurgent Religion and World Politics* (Grand Rapids, MI: Wm. B. Eerdmans Publishing, 1999).

[26] Graham Ward, *True Religion* (Oxford: Blackwell, 2003).

[27] Regina M. Schwartz, *Sacramental Poetics at the Dawn of Secularization: When God Left the World* (Stanford, CA: Stanford University Press, 2008).

[28] John Caputo, 'Introduction: Who Comes after the God of Metaphysics?', in John Caputo (ed.), *The Religious* (Oxford: Blackwell, 2002), 1–19 (2).

[29] For an expanded account of the secular subject position encouraged in academia, see portions of the introduction and conclusion of Lori Branch, *Rituals of Spontaneity: Sentiment and Secularism from Free Prayer to Wordsworth* (Waco, TX: Baylor University Press, 2006), namely 'Spontaneous, Secular Subjects', 29–33, and 'On the Religiousness of Criticism', 211–25.

in its illusory wholeness, subjects itself to the symbolic order and the law, and by this succumbing to the temptation of knowledge promised in the symbolic order is trapped in binaries of egotism and desire that seek to master all it encounters.[30] This subject, as Bunyan can also tell us, is painfully bereft of love—for love does not let us remain master and, as Lacan tells us, may live only beyond the law, its threats of punishment, and its transgressive desire.[31]

FAITH AND POST-SECULAR READING

The particular secularism of Bunyan's works, together with the symptoms of faith that in some ways are their finest moments, is best registered by a fully theological and theoretical reading, by scholarship informed by the humanities' 'religious turn' and the coming of age of what is being called post-secular studies. Certainly, not all scholarship in the religious turn is properly post-secular; in fact, much of it simply reboots the secular/religious binary the post-secular criticizes, restaging a modern desire for certainty and disavowal of faith. Terry Eagleton's *Reason, Faith, and Revolution* and Simon During's *Exit Capitalism: Literary Culture, Theory, and Post-Secular Modernity* are two cases in point. Eagleton prefaces his critique of the New Atheism by assuring us on the second page that he does not 'believe in the archangel Gabriel, the infallibility of the pope, the idea that Jesus walked on water, or the claim that he rose up into heaven before the eyes of his disciples'.[32] In his only use of the word 'post-secular' outside the book's title, During is likewise quick to assure readers that though 'new post-secular occasions for leaps of faith' are appearing in 'endgame capitalism', 'revealed religion cannot be revived in any intellectually respectable way'.[33] Both writers situate themselves, then, not at the beginning of a genuinely post-secular criticism but within the last vestiges of the modernist epistemological project, disavowing belief in a quest for certainty and a defensible subject position in an intellectual climate that, several decades in, still has not come to grips with the implications of the linguistic turn for our understanding of faith's workings in language.

In John Caputo's more vital rendering, 'The "post-" in "post-secular" should not be understood to mean "over and done with" but rather *after having passed through*

---

[30] Jacques Lacan, 'The Mirror Stage as Formative of the Function of the I as Revealed in Psychoanalytic Experience', in Jacques Lacan, *Écrits: A Selection*, tr. Alan Sheridan (New York and London: Norton, 1977), 1–7. For the devaluing of love under the secular logic of certainty, see Daniel Boscaljon, 'Secularization and the Loss of Love in Bunyan's *Pilgrim's Progress*', *Religions*, 4 (2013), 669–86.

[31] Jacques Lacan, *The Four Fundamental Concepts of Psychoanalysis*, ed. Jacques-Alain Miller, tr. Alan Sheridan (New York: Norton, 1981), 276.

[32] Terry Eagleton, *Reason, Faith, and Revolution: Reflections on the God Debate* (New Haven, CT: Yale University Press, 2009), xii.

[33] Simon During, *Exit Capitalism: Literary Culture, Theory, and Post-Secular Modernity* (London: Routledge, 2009), ix.

modernity'. For Caputo, one of the most important things 'postmodern' might have meant 'had it not been ground senseless by overuse' is post-secular. For what is most distinctive about postmodernity, Caputo claims, is not its unreason but its embrace of a humbler epistemology and chastened reason: a post-secular reason that recognizes that no thinking is devoid of belief and that deconstructs the idea of 'rigid borders between faith and reason, public and private, subject and object, politics and science or religion' as 'an artifice'.[34] Postmodernity thus represents not a rejection of Enlightenment reason but, according to Caputo, a 'more enlightened Enlightenment [that] is no longer taken in by the dream of Pure Objectivity[;] […] it deploys a new idea of reason that is no longer taken in by the illusion of Pure Reason'.[35] Like Derrida, Caputo helps us to see how the disavowal of belief and the claim to rational certainty in modernity have been the basis of all manner of fundamentalisms and violences, of the mass murders and re-education camps of materialist regimes in the century preceding our own, and in this one, of gross militarism in the name of religions that have forgotten they are faiths. 'At the core of fundamentalism', Caputo maintains, 'there lies a repressed fear that faith is only faith and as such a risk with no guarantee of anything, which is the truth about religion to which it testifies in the mode of repressing it'.[36] This is a formulation apropos of the reading I am here advancing of Bunyan: that his works documenting the quest for certain knowledge of faith end up testifying to the faith of faith in the symptomatic, fantasy mode of literary fiction.[37]

A vibrantly post-secular criticism would thus spring from a recognition of the inevitability of faith, based in the structure of language itself, with a corollary humility and lack of violence. In this sense, it is astounding to think of exactly how Christian a place contemporary literary theory has come to, even when it seems most secularist. For Christianity is the religion that has the distinction of making a cardinal virtue of faith: of imagining that uncertainty—something besides the binary certainties of the 'tree of the knowledge of good and evil'—might be the grounds of freedom and loving relation, the tree of life itself. The question from this perspective is not whether to have faith, but what kind of faith to have—one owned up to, in humility and contingency, or one disavowed and repressed in submitting to an ideology as a system of knowledge, to uphold the illusory wholeness of the ego? To paraphrase Derrida in 'Eating Well', the question

---

[34] John Caputo, *On Religion* (London and New York: Routledge, 2001), 37, 60, 65.

[35] Caputo, *On Religion*, 37, 61, 64. Recent works of Jürgen Habermas, Susan Neiman, and Tamsin Spargo, for instance, enact precisely this reconceiving of human reason to incorporate faith and hope. See Jürgen Habermas, 'Notes on a Post-Secular Society', *Sign and Sight*, 18 June 2008, available at http://www.signandsight.com/features/1714.html, accessed 26 January 2011; Susan Neiman, *Evil in Modern Thought: An Alternative History of Philosophy* (Princeton, NJ: Princeton University Press, 2002); and Tamsin Spargo, 'Have You Never a Hill Mizar to Remember? Some Thoughts on Agnosticism and Meaning', *International Journal of Religion and Spirituality*, 1 (2011), 15–24.

[36] Caputo, *On Religion*, 124.

[37] For other analyses of Bunyan's intertwined religious and secular logics, see Kevin Seidel, '*Pilgrim's Progress* and the Book', *ELH*, 77 (2010), 509–34, and Jason Crawford, 'Bunyan's Secular Allegory', *Religion and Literature*, 44 (2012), 45–72.

is not to believe or not to believe, but how to believe well—which amounts to the same thing: a gentle appropriation of and by the other in and as our shared life. In searching out how to believe well, post-secular criticism usefully attends to what we might call the difficulties of believing badly: of repressing belief, displacing it, only to have it return in the form of symptoms that it enjoys and desires in the mode of their impossibility.

Religion, specifically Christianity in all its multiformity over the last thousand years, saturating so much of Anglophone literature, and so illegible to most contemporary criticism except as either the handmaid or nemesis of various class, racial, national, or sexual ideologies, comes to life within our discussions of literature if we have ears to hear the ways that it is engaged, all sails to the wind, in the very issues of language, epistemology, and subjectivity that grip us too—not least of all in the ways its writers, like us, either disavow or own up to faith or try to recast it as knowledge, and never without symptoms. This assumption that the religious exists, not necessarily as false consciousness but as something indicative of human life and language, is freeing in every sense and opens vistas onto precisely those things in literature which are most often neglected, particularly prayer. Moreover, it beckons to us with the excitement of reading with a theological mindset that is historically specific and accurate, but which also understands that historical specificity against the widest backdrop of Christian history (what I call to my students 'the Jaroslav Pelikan history of Christianity'), so that we are able to see not just particular Reformation and Counter-Reformation arguments in careful detail, but also the grounding assumptions and 'simple abstractions' that enable those debates, and so that we can see too what is accumulated and what is lost as different discourses are abandoned and adopted, as new economic and intellectual contexts dawn, as Bunyan moves from admiring those humble women who talk lovingly in the sun, to seeking 'certain knowledge whether he had faith or no'.

Besides the compelling readings of individual literary works which it opens, and alongside a critical understanding of the transformation of religion in modernity more generally, a post-secular approach to literary criticism helps us more broadly to understand the relationship of religion and literature in and after the Enlightenment. Following *The Pilgrim's Progress* we can trace the logic whereby Christianity in the world of emerging capitalism and modern epistemologies becomes increasingly a faith that produces commodities—especially novels and films—equally as a way of preserving hope *and* as a symptom of its imbrication in the symbolic order. A post-secular perspective helps us understand one of the most sweeping and least explicated currents of Anglophone literature in modernity, the post-Restoration, English Christian love for and eventually principled insistence upon fantasy literature. With Spenser and Cavendish its prophets, Bunyan its father, and C. S. Lewis its most venerable proponent, its practitioners range from Wordsworth to J. R. R. Tolkien, J. K. Rowling, and even Stephenie Meyer, and its passionate readership is immense.[38]

---

[38] On Bunyan and Christian imagination, see Bethany Joy Bear, 'Fantastical Faith: John Bunyan and the Sanctification of Fancy', *SP*, 109 (2012), 671–701; and on nineteenth-century Christian fantasy more generally, Stephen Prickett, *Victorian Fantasy*, 2nd edn (Waco, TX: Baylor University Press, 2005).

In Lewis's classic account in 'On Stories', for instance, we hear echoes of Bunyan's texts and the sensibility which they helped to shape. For Lewis, good fiction takes us beyond the realm of 'theorems' and reason's knowledge into the 'more central region' where the reader finds an 'intrinsic surprisingness'—something one doesn't encounter in the world of theorems but which one desires and enjoys in both reading and fiction-making, where the realities of active faith and hope are at work.[39] Lewis even has something like his own version of *différance* when he postulates an ineluctable 'something' which we only partially catch in a plot's net of space and time. And Lewis, with Bunyan, places his hopes for spiritual transformation in our acquiring a taste for this eerie presence of faith only symptomatically expressed in stories.[40] We can gain fertile critical perspectives on the role of imaginative literature within Western Christianity in modernity and particularly in Protestantism without making any single great theory or theorist its final word. For belief may be repressed or engaged in a multitude of ways, and there is room for much work on the function and contours of both belief and believing in literature.

A post-secular approach enables us to understand John Bunyan, even after three and a half centuries, in new lights. A martyr not to the Restoration Church or monarchy, as he long feared, Bunyan appears rather as a sufferer at the hands of a modern rationality *avant la lettre*; a saint to whose grave (literary and literal) believers across the next three centuries of rationalization and industrialization will make pilgrimage; a confessor of sorts, testifying to and preserving for them an essential experience of faith, in the form of faith as hope, as symptom, and as irreducible kernel of Christianity within and over and against that fantasy of certainty. He is a martyr of a sort, that is, for modernity, whose great appeal and comfort lie in his showing how, in the deathly shade of the tree of the knowledge of good and evil and its binary, deterministic framing of the world, one may hope—for freedom from egotism, for love, for life.

At the climax of his fantasy of religious certainty, Bunyan shows that it is in dying to one's own self, the solitary subject and knower who must possess her own faith in order to be accepted at the Celestial City, that the way lies to life and resurrection. Faith, dying to self, and resurrection are certainly the ancient heart of the Gospel, but this particular experience of hope as shadowing symptom of modern epistemology and as fantastic fiction, bound to that reason 'by the bands of its opposition', is particular to modernity and its conceptions of knowledge and language, of the symbolic order and the subject. This newly vivid picture of Christianity and of historically specific Christianities is what a post-secular, fully critical, fully theoretical, vibrantly theological understanding of Bunyan has to offer us, and it has never been more important than at our own historical moment, when so much hinges on our ability to understand the sources of violence and the sources of solid, lively hope in our world, to muster the courage to choose between them, and to venture on.

---

[39] C. S. Lewis, 'On Stories', in C. S. Lewis, *On Stories and Other Essays on Literature*, ed. Walter Hooper (New York: Mariner Books, 2002), 3–20 (15, 16).

[40] Lewis, 'On Stories', 19–20.

Suggested Reading

Branch, Lori, 'Postsecular Studies', in Mark Knight (ed.), *The Routledge Companion to Literature and Religion* (London: Routledge, 2016), 91–101.

Iser, Wolfgang, 'Bunyan's *Pilgrim's Progress*: The Doctrine of Predestination and the Shaping of the Novel', in *The Implied Reader: Patterns of Communication from Bunyan to Beckett* (Baltimore, MD: Johns Hopkins University Press, 1974), ch. 1.

'Locating the Postsecular' [forum], *Religion and Literature*, 41 (autumn 2009), 68–126.

Ward, Graham, 'To Be a Reader: Bunyan's Struggle with the Language of Scripture in *Grace Abounding to the Chief of Sinners*', *Journal of Literature and Theology*, 4 (1990), 29–49.

Ward, Graham, 'Theology and the Crisis of Representation', in Gregory Salyer and Robert Detweiler (eds.), *Literature and Theology at Century's End*, American Academy of Religion Studies in Religion, vol. 72 (Atlanta, GA: Scholar's Press, 1995), 131–58.

'What is Religion and Literature?' special issue *Religion and Literature*, 41 (summer 2009).

PART IV
JOURNEYS

CHAPTER 30

BUNYAN AND THE EARLY NOVEL

CYNTHIA WALL

[W]ith the same illusion as we read any tale known to be fictitious, as a novel, we go on with the characters as real persons, who had been nicknamed by their neighbours.[1]

THE PILGRIM'S PROGRESS is not quite a novel. The term barely existed in 1678, when Bunyan published what would be his most famous work, and at that time it referred primarily to what we would now call romances. Yet Bunyan's allegory comes from the same cultural swirl that produced the early novel, and in many ways it behaves like a novel, and recognizes itself as '*a Novelty*' (*PP*, 7). That, of course, was one of the worries for a conscientious Puritan. 'But it is feigned', objects the hypothetical reader in 'The Author's Apology for his Book' (*PP*, 3), to which Bunyan replies: '[W]*hat of that, I tro? / Some men by feigning words as dark as mine, / Make truth to spangle, and its rayes to shine*' (*PP*, 3–4). Jesus, for example, employed '*Types, Shadows and Metaphors*', and even '*grave* Paul [. . .] *no where doth forbid / The use of Parables*' (*PP*, 4, 5). So Bunyan is jolly well going to '*find out* [. . .] *by pins and loops*', by the everyday things of this world, '*By Calves, and Sheep; by Heifers, and by Rams; / By Birds and Herbs*', and '*Dialogue-wise*' just how the Pilgrim Christian '*seeks the everlasting Prize*'—'*whence he comes, whither he goes, / What he leaves undone; also what he does: / It also shews you how he runs, and runs*' (*PP*, 4, 6). Bunyan constructs a religious allegory that, in its vivid characters, pungent dialogue, energetic adventures, familiar landscapes, homely objects, and self-referentialities, bursts its self-inscribed boundaries, and spills into something that centuries of readers have responded to as if it were a novel, 'forget[ting]', as Henri Talon

---

[1] Samuel Taylor Coleridge, writing in 1830; cited in Roger Sharrock (ed.), *The Pilgrim's Progress: A Casebook* (London: Macmillan, 1976), 53.

observes, 'the allegory over and over again'.[2] *The Pilgrim's Progress*, notes N. H. Keeble, is 'not only our first novel, but our last allegory, a bridge between two worlds, the medieval and the modern'.[3]

Although Bunyan warns us not to be '*extream*' and to play too much with '*the* out-side *of* [his] *Dream*' (*PP*, 164), that is exactly what I intend to do in this chapter. I will look primarily at *The Pilgrim's Progress*—both parts (1678; 1684)—but also at Bunyan's other 'fictional' work, *The Life and Death of Mr. Badman* (1680), and his literarily evocative spiritual autobiography, *Grace Abounding to the Chief of Sinners* (1666), to pull out the novelistic bits, highlighting along the way both Bunyan's influence *on* the early novel, and the varieties of lumber in the seventeenth-century English cultural warehouse that influenced Bunyan *alongside* the early novelists. A fascination with *things*, for example: Christian's roll, his burden, the objects in the dusty parlour, the Giant's grievous crabtree cudgel, all the pomegranates and honeycombs, milk and apples, not to mention the pearls and crowns and gold-paved streets of the Celestial City, find their match in Robinson Crusoe's umbrella and earthenware pot, his raisins and limes, and his country bower. Things in the early novel seem almost to hang suspended in a rather blank, lightly evocative landscape; and yet the early reader was able to fill in those blanks, to see what was implied.

Similarly, spaces in Bunyan's works—rooms and inns, towns and fairs, hills and rivers—emerge *within* the narrative track rather than in a descriptive pool alongside it, just as they do for Moll Flanders and Roxana, Fantomina and Count D'Elmont, Joseph Andrews and Tom Jones, Pamela and Clarissa. Characters, too, share genealogies: Bunyan's Giant Despair and his wife Mrs Diffidence indulge in comfortable bedroom chats (albeit about beating their prisoners to death), as intimate and colloquial as the conversations between Moll and her Jemy. The emblematic names—Pliable, By-ends, Lord Hategood, Pickthank, Worldly-Wiseman—also inhabit contemporary Restoration drama (Horner, Pinchwife, Squeamish, Fidget) as well as the early novels (Thwackum, Square, Mrs Slipslop, Lady Tattle, Friday). And why not dramatic dialogue as well, since even '*men (as high as Trees)*' (philosophers and religious writers such as Robert Boyle and poet-critics such as John Dryden) '*will write / Dialogue-wise*' (*PP*, 6). Finally, the matters of textuality itself—metanarratives, interpolated narratives, self-reflexivity—suggest overlapping narrative interests between Bunyan and the early novelists. The marginalia, the dream framework, the multiple voices, the songs, the constant retelling of stories in *The Pilgrim's Progress*, all find descendants—direct or collateral or cultural—in the patterned repetitions of Defoe, the interrupting narrators of Fielding, the bits and bobs of every other literary genre (newspapers, histories, poems, drama) digested by the early novel. *The Pilgrim's Progress* emerged from the same cultural landscape as the early novel, and in many cases inflected its neighbours.

---

[2] Henri Talon, *John Bunyan: The Man and his Works* (1948), tr. Barbara Wall (London: Rockliff, 1951), 162.

[3] John Bunyan, *The Pilgrim's Progress*, ed. N. H. Keeble (Oxford: Oxford University Press, 1984), xxi.

Things

Virginia Woolf asserts that in *Robinson Crusoe* 'there are no sunsets and no sunrises; there is no solitude and no soul. There is, on the contrary, staring us full in the face nothing but a large earthenware pot.'[4] The early novel is full of earthenware pots, almost untidy in its scattering of objects, its littering of landscapes. Those material objects, in Virginia Woolf's opening (and disingenuous) premise, take the place of soul, crowd it out of the textual room. Bunyan himself urges: '*Do thou the substance of my matter see*' (*PP*, 164). This is almost too obvious to point out: Bunyan's things are superfreighted with emblematic force, and as if the point weren't self-evident within the text, there are usually one or two more explanations to hand (the explanations themselves acquire a certain thinginess). The moment Christian enters the House of the Interpreter, he says to its master: 'I was told [...] that if I called here, you would shew me excellent things, such as would be an help to me in my Journey' (*PP*, 28). Yes indeed, says the Interpreter, and leads him immediately to a room in which 'a Picture of a very grave Person hang[s] up against the wall' (*PP*, 29). The picture is described; Christian asks what it means; the Interpreter tells him first the meaning and then the reason he showed the picture first. The marginalia chime in: '*Christian *sees a brave Picture*', '**The fashion of the Picture*', '**The meaning of the Picture*', '**Why he shewed him the Picture first*.' Every object must be read for its meaning, yet every object also projects its meaning almost without waiting to be read. In that sense, the objects can seem to lie lumpenly around, too obvious to be interesting. I do understand that when the candle is lit, there is '*Illumination' (*PP*, 28). And, of course, we know that '*the things that are seen, are* Temporal; *but the things that are not seen, are* Eternal' and so we agree ''*tis not best to covet things that are* now; *but to wait for things to come*' (*PP*, 32).

And yet things in the early novel, very much including *The Pilgrim's Progress*, also remain just too thingy to be too overtaken by their emblematic meanings. As J. Paul Hunter reminds us, the literary 'by-products' of Puritan allegorical writing spring from a world 'where secular activity is meaningful, where history (even the history of every man's trivialities) is somehow the record of divine activity'.[5] The formula works just as well in the other direction: the objects that represent divine messages are also the record of human activity, of human experience. Defoe's Robinson Crusoe describes

> the many Hours which for want of Tools, want of Help, and want of Skill, every Thing I did, took up out of my Time: For Example, I was full two and forty Days making me

---

[4] Virginia Woolf, 'Robinson Crusoe', in Virginia Woolf, *The Common Reader, Second Series*, ed. Andrew McNeillie (London: The Hogarth Press, 1986), 54.

[5] J. Paul Hunter, *The Reluctant Pilgrim: Defoe's Emblematic Method and Quest for Form in Robinson Crusoe* (Baltimore, MD: Johns Hopkins University Press, 1966), 115, 123.

a Board for a long Shelf, which I wanted in my Cave; whereas two Sawyers with their Tools, and a Saw-Pit, would have cut six of them out of the same Tree in half a Day.[6]

Crusoe's shelf is one of those many objects filling up his island, but like most of them, that material point is the intersection of a great deal of time and energy and desire and frustration. As we will see with spaces in the early novel, things are larger than they appear, bulging with their own creation inwards, casting long emblematic shadows outwards.

In their use of and love for their novelistic things, the novelists employ the ancient practice of pragmatographia, or 'description of thinges', which Henry Peacham defined in 1577 as the ability to 'open and set abroade those thinges whiche were included within one word'.[7] Christian's burden and roll are the two most immediate and heavily laden one-word things, and one drops off and the other is dropped along their immortal and mortal trajectories (*PP*, 8, 10; 38, 42). But burdens and rolls do not have quite the same afterlife in later early novels as clothes and ornaments, so the ways that the pilgrims pay attention to their attire—I should say raiment—gives purchase for connections.

The Three Shining Ones give Christian 'change of Raiment' when his burden drops at the sight of the cross (*PP*, 38); very shortly he muses happily on his new clothes—'a *Coat*' that the Lord of the Celestial City 'gave me freely in the day that he stript me of my rags' (*PP*, 41). The margin whispers: '**Christian has got his Lords Coat on his back, and is comforted therewith*.' Clothes that comfort: Crusoe is deeply satisfied with his locally sourced, organic outfit—a cap made of tanned goatskin, 'with the Hair on the out Side to shoor off the Rain', along with 'a Wastcoat, and Breeches open at Knees'—although he admits that, 'if I was a bad *Carpenter*, I was a worse *Tayler*'. However, 'they were such as I made very good shift with; and when I was abroad, if it happen'd to rain, the Hair of my Wastcoat and Cap being outermost, I was kept very dry'.[8] Richardson's Pamela could hardly be more pleased with her three bundles, when she sorts her various items of clothing according to history, meaning, and value, preparatory to leaving Mr B once and for all (really, she means it this time). The third bundle in particular—the combination of what she brought with her and what she's made and what she thinks she really deserves—gets its own whole detailed paragraph, stuffed with 'a Calicoe Night-gown, that I used to wear o' Mornings'; 'a quilted Callimancoe Coat, and a Pair of Stockens I bought of the Pedlar, and my Straw-hat with blue Strings'; 'a Remanant of *Scots* Cloth'; and 'an old Shoe-buckle or two'.[9] The amount of attention paid in describing an object is a mark of how dear it is to the heart of the character (or the novelist, usually for different reasons).

---

[6] Daniel Defoe, *Robinson Crusoe* (1719), ed. Thomas Keymer (Oxford: Oxford University Press, 2007), 98.

[7] Henry Peacham, *The Garden of Eloquence* (1577), O4ᵛ.

[8] Defoe, *Robinson Crusoe*, 114–15.

[9] Samuel Richardson, *Pamela* (1740), ed. Thomas Keymer and Alice Wakely (Oxford: Oxford University Press, 2001), 78.

Clothing as ornament is a case in point. The amount of white raiment and gold and pearls bestrewing *The Pilgrim's Progress* almost equals the attention Pamela pays to her third bundle. Pliable is very excited about the crowns and cloths of gold (*PP*, 13); the people back home 'talk strangely about' Christian, saying 'he *now walks in White*, that he has a Chain of Gold about his Neck, that he has a Crown of Gold, beset with Pearls upon his Head' (*PP*, 176). At the House of the Interpreter, the 'Damsel that waited upon these Women' goes and fetches 'white Rayment' for Christiana and Mercie, who then argue: 'For, You are fairer then I am, said one, and, You are more comely then I am, said another' (*PP*, 208). Mercie laughs in her dream in the House Beautiful, when 'one coming with Wings' wipes her weeping eyes with his handkerchief, then '*clad* [her] in *Silver* and *Gold*; he put a Chain about [her] Neck, and Ear-rings in [her] Ears, and a beautiful Crown upon [her] Head' (*PP*, 222–23). And, of course, at the end, on the other side of the river, are 'many men, with Crowns on their heads, Palms in their hands, and golden Harps to sing praises withall' (*PP*, 162).

This is, of course, divine ornament, and as physical beauty has often represented a natural or psychological connection to spiritual beauty, the metaphorical transference glides more easily. For Bunyan, the heaps of gold crowns, pearls, and fine white linen throughout both parts of *The Pilgrim's Progress* (along with the gold-paved streets of the Celestial City), all help push the imagination of the local Bedfordshire villager—probably tired, probably poor, and virtually illiterate—into an unfamiliar realm, perhaps glimpsed behind the doors of the local gentry, or seen in a painting or a stained-glass window, echoed from the Bible. The physical beauty slants upward for Bunyan. For other early novelists, the fairness and comeliness that Mercie and Christiana see in each other in their new clothes could be spelled out even more precisely and dazzlingly, as in Eliza Haywood's description of the exotic Bellraizia in *Idalia: Or, The Unfortunate Mistress* (1725), or Roxana's description of her Turkish dress in Defoe's *The Fortunate Mistress* (1724), or Lovelace's detailed description of Clarissa's hair, skin, and embroidered dress as they flee Harlowe Place in Samuel Richardson's *Clarissa* (1747–48). The allegorical beauty becomes worldly beauty; it represents only itself, and in most cases slants downward towards trouble (envy, abuse, lust, kidnapping, rape), the descriptive detail part of the netting of darker plot rather than the reward for escape from the earthly nets.

One way to arrange all these novelistic things within the text is through lists, which became popular in a variety of seventeenth-century genres. Lists gather things together to create a visual heap capable of structural meaning. They can make grammatical and conceptual connections between objects, which we generally find between their commas and within their formal order. Bunyan shares with the early novelists a fascination with the idea of cluster, with the power of cumulative repetition, and like Swift fifty years later, is capable of composing a ringing, reverberating, devastating collection of nouns.

The Pilgrim's Progress itself, as a journey narrative, a sequence of adventures, is a sort of list or collection of episodes: '*My dark and cloudy words they do but hold / The Truth, as Cabinets inclose the Gold*' (*PP*, 4). The seventeenth-century curiosity cabinet was partly a by-product of and partly a temporal companion to the new interest in natural philosophy and experimental science made both professional and popular by the Royal Society. Both parts of *The Pilgrim's Progress* start with comfortingly instructive collections. Christian is ushered into the armoury of House Beautiful, 'where they shewed him all manner of Furniture, which their Lord had provided for Pilgrims, as Sword, Shield, Helmet, Brest plate, *All-Prayer*, and Shooes that would not wear out' (*PP*, 54). The layering of nouns confirms the layers of protection. In a similar way, when Christiana and Mercie are welcomed into the House of the Interpreter, they bide their time waiting for supper by exploring the significant rooms, and the margins keep a list of the notables, a little like labels on the drawers of the cabinet: '*Of the Spider*', '*Of the Hen and Chickens*', '*Of the Butcher and the Sheep*', '*Of the Garden*', '*Of the Field*', '*Of the* Robbin *and the* Spider', '*Of the Tree that is rotten at heart*', '*They are at Supper*' (*PP*, 200–04). The margins list the titles of stories, of lessons learnt, of emblematic curiosities that can be returned to, reopened, retold. They preserve the collections: cabinets holding truths.

In Vanity Fair, the lusts and sins of daily life pile up into a pyre:

> [A]t *this Fair* are all such Merchandize sold, as Houses, Lands, Trades, Places, Honours, Preferments, Titles, Countreys, Kingdoms, Lusts, Pleasures, and Delights of all sorts, as Whores, Bauds, Wives, Husbands, Children, Masters, Servants, Lives, Blood, Bodies, Souls, Silver, Gold, Pearls, Precious Stones, and what not.
>
> And moreover, at this Fair there is at all times to be seen Juglings, Cheats, Games, Plays, Fools, Apes, Knaves, and Rogues, and that of all sorts.
>
> Here are to be seen too, and that for nothing, Thefts, Murders, Adultries, False-swearers, and that of a blood-red colour. (*PP*, 88)

To my mind, the only literary list in English that meets if not surpasses this in terms of accumulated narrative power is from Jonathan Swift's *Gulliver's Travels* (1726), where Gulliver triumphantly corrects his Houyhnhnm master on the violent capabilities of humans, their 'Cannons, Culverins, Muskets, Carabines, Pistols, Bullets, Powder, Swords, Bayonets, Sieges, Retreats, Attacks, Undermines, Countermines, Bombardments, Sea-fights [. . .]'.[10]

The things of novelistic narrative are thus hardly static lumpen objects, but bites of immediacy and longing, scattered apart or chained together, looking homely and meaning heavenly. 'And is there any reason', Virginia Woolf demands, 'why the perspective that a plain earthenware pot exacts should not satisfy us as completely, once we grasp it, as man himself in all his sublimity standing against a background of broken mountains and tumbling oceans with stars flaming in the sky?'[11]

---

[10] Jonathan Swift, *Gulliver's Travels*, in *The Prose Works of Jonathan Swift*, ed. Herbert Davis, 14 vols (Oxford: Blackwell, 1939–68), 11: 231.

[11] Woolf, 'Robinson Crusoe', 58.

SPACES

The spaces between things—their settings (landscapes, buildings, rooms)—are as notoriously vague in seventeenth- and early eighteenth-century literature as the objects themselves are brightly specific.[12] Certainly this seems to be the case with *The Pilgrim's Progress*. We first see Christian (or Graceless, as he is then), through the Dreamer's eyes, '*cloathed with Raggs, standing in a certain place*' (*PP*, 8)—*what* certain place? He walks 'solitarily in the Fields' (*PP*, 9); he wallows in 'a very *Miry Slow*' (*PP*, 14); he rather extraordinarily notices a 'wide field full of dark Mountains' (*PP*, 42) and later joins the shepherds in the Delectable Mountains where they all 'walked together towards the end of the Mountains' (*PP*, 122). The Delectable Mountains, first seen from afar, are 'beautified with Woods, Vinyards, Fruits of all sorts; Flowers also, with Springs and Fountains, very delectable to behold' (*PP*, 55). After the trials of Vanity Fair, Christian and Hopeful come to a 'pleasant River', on the banks of which were '*green Trees*, that bore all manner of Fruit [...]. On either side of the River was also a Meadow, curiously beautified with Lilies; And it was green all the year long' (*PP*, 110–11). These are all vivid images, but they are not particularly detailed—a basic combination of recognizable adjective plus familiar noun. And yet almost from the moment of publication, the readers of *The Pilgrim's Progress* have been filling in the spaces, either imaginatively or textually. In 1682 one T. S. wanted to correct 'a fourfold Defect' in Bunyan's work, including the lack of descriptive detail about 'the *State of Man* in his first Creation', and so he offers the following priceless paragraph as the introduction to his *The Second Part of The Pilgrim's Progress*:

> The Spring being far advanced, the Meadows being Covered with a Curious Carpet of delightful Green, and the Earth Cloathed in Rich and Glorious Attire, to Rejoyce and Triumph for the Return of her Shining Bridegroom: The Healthful Air rendred more Pleasing and delightful by the gentle Winds then breathed from the *South*, impregnated with the Exhilerating Fragrancy of the Variety of Flowers and odoriferous Plants over which they had passed[.][13]

In 1832 Thomas Babington Macaulay had no need of T. S.'s interpolated picturesque; he sees it all already:

> There is no ascent, no declivity, no resting-place, no turn-stile, with which we are not perfectly acquainted. The wicket-gate, and the desolate swamp which separates

---

[12] For claims about the paucity of detail in early novels, see Dorothy Van Ghent, *The English Novel: Form and Function* (1953; New York: Harper & Row, 1967), 49–50; Max Byrd, *London Transform'd: Images of the City in the Eighteenth Century* (New Haven, CT: Yale University Press, 1978), 13; Daniel Defoe, *Robinson Crusoe*, ed. J. Donald Crowley (Oxford: Oxford University Press, 1972), xv; Daniel Defoe, *Moll Flanders*, ed. George Starr (Oxford: Oxford University Press, 1971), xx; Simon Varey, *Space and the Eighteenth-Century English Novel* (Cambridge: Cambridge University Press, 1990), 138.

[13] T. S., *The Second Part of the Pilgrims Progress* (1682), 1.

it from the City of Destruction, the long line of road, as straight as a rule can make it, the Interpreter's house and all its fair shows, the prisoner in the iron cage, the palace, at the doors of which armed men kept guard, and on the battlements of which walked persons clothed all in gold, the cross and the sepulchre, the steep hill and the pleasant arbour, the stately front of the House Beautiful by the wayside, the chained lions crouching in the porch, the low green valley of Humiliation, rich with grass and covered with flocks, all are as well known to us as the sights of our own street.[14]

And in 1890 John Brown, a minister in Bunyan's chapel in Bedford and one of his most important biographers, also seems to see the Bunyan landscape opening richly before him, prompted only by the thought of that well-known journey:

Let us suppose that it is early Summer. The foliage on lime tree and elm is still soft and green; the birds make music from hedgerow and copse; the flowers brighten the meadows; and in cheerful sunlight nature seems to be putting forth all her witchery to tempt us into the open. [...] The quiet fields reaching from Elstow Green to Harrowden Hill are classic ground. They are, with the neighboring town, the Land of Bunyan[.][15]

These latter-day descriptive infills suggest a sense in which the spaces in *The Pilgrim's Progress* are larger on the inside than they seem from the outside. That is the literal case in some instances, such as the 'wide field full of dark Mountains', or in the strange rooms of the House of the Interpreter, which can hold whole countries: Christian's tour begins with the room that seems to hold only a picture; then moves to the dusty parlour; then to the room with the two children, Patience and Passion; then to the room with the fire burning against the wall; and then to the 'pleasant place, where was builded a stately Palace' (*PP*, 33). But in a sense *all* the scenes are like that, or were like that for the contemporary reader. The simple equation of adjective + noun was, in Bunyan's vivid economy of phrase, powerful enough to open in the reader's imagination the scene in full: landscapes, like objects, would, upon the lightest touch, 'open and set abroade those things which were included in one word', to borrow Peacham's account of his pragmatographia.

Bunyan had predicted that '*This Book will make a Traveller of thee*' (*PP*, 6), and Henri Talon claims that 'In walking beside Bunyan's pilgrim we walk beside ourselves.' Talon continues: 'If space and horizons and free air are to be conjured up before us, landmarks on a road such as a gate, a slough, a cross and a palace are not enough. No, a feeling of muscular exertion must be induced in the reader by the movement of the prose.' That, he concludes, is why '*The Pilgrim's Progress* conveys so well the idea of space'.[16] Our reading experience swings us from gate to slough to cross to palace with the concentrated energy of adjective plus noun: the gesture of inflection doubles the motion of the pilgrims. 'The first lines' of the work, Dorothy Van Ghent shows us, 'launch us with great swift

---

[14] Thomas Babington Macaulay, cited in Sharrock (ed.), *The Pilgrim's Progress: A Casebook*, 67.
[15] John Brown, *Bunyan's Home* (London: E. Nister, 1890), n. p.
[16] Talon, *John Bunyan*, 218.

strides' into its world: 'the brief past-tense forms of the verbs, with their clear Anglo-Saxon vowels and serried ranks of consonants—"I walked", "I lighted", "I dreamed", "I looked"—have the energy and hard feel of reality, and hurry us to that cry, "What shall I do?".'[17] And that is a cry for the reader as well as the traveller. As J. Paul Hunter has argued for Fielding, 'the essence of movement through space has as much to do with readers as with travelers [...]. [R]eaders do not travel at speeds altogether predetermined, and their relationship to an incident or a place may be more or less intense than that of any given character.'[18] (This may explain why Stanley Fish encounters *The Pilgrim's Progress* as 'antiprogressive, both as a narrative and as a reading experience', and I don't.[19]) The spaces of the early novel are Bunyan's spaces: fluid, interpretable, shaped as much in the reader's mind by response to the semi-descriptive prose.

CHARACTERS

As the epigraph from Coleridge at the beginning of this chapter attests, the characters in *The Pilgrim's Progress* have always seemed novelistic to readers—'real persons, who had been nicknamed by their neighbours'. Although their names seem relentlessly emblematic, the characters keep finding ways to escape that confinement. The vernacular pungency of their dialogue and the psychological complexity of their personalities spill over the edges of emblem. Early novelistic characters were regularly criticized by early twentieth-century critics as 'flat' rather than 'round', in E. M. Forster's terminology.[20] But much later twentieth- and twenty-first-century work, by Deidre Shauna Lynch, J. Paul Hunter, Michael McKeon, David Brewer, and others, has satisfactorily readjusted our ideas of their complexity. As with things and spaces in the early novel, characters which have a sort of dehydrated feel to the modern reader just need a bit of saturation in the contemporary perspective—the richness of gesture, the fullness of implication—to leap out as vividly to us as to Coleridge, Macaulay, and Brown.

Christian, Faithful, Hopeful; Christiana, Mercie, Great-heart; Apollyon, Giant Despair, Worldly-Wiseman; Pliable, By-ends, Ignorance: such emblematic names in a religious allegory make perfect sense. And yet such names are not limited to allegory: plays, poems, novels, literary criticism, and philosophical essays of the seventeenth and eighteenth centuries (and well before and well after: think Shakespeare and Dickens) abound with names that seem to pin their characters to a piece of carefully cut cardboard. For drama, think Pinchwife and Horner in William Wycherley's *The Country*

---

[17] Van Ghent, *English Novel*, 45–6.
[18] J. Paul Hunter, *Occasional Form: Henry Fielding and the Chains of Circumstance* (Baltimore, MD, and London: Johns Hopkins University Press, 1975), 143.
[19] Stanley Fish, *Self-Consuming Artifacts: The Experience of Seventeenth-Century Literature* (Berkeley, Los Angeles, CA, and London: University of California Press, 1972), 229.
[20] E. M. Forster, *Aspects of the Novel*, ed. Oliver Stallybrass (London: Penguin, 2000), 73–81.

Wife (1675), Sir Fopling Flutter and Mrs Loveit in George Etherege's *The Man of Mode* (1676), Willmore and Angellica Bianca in Aphra Behn's *The Rover* (1677); for novels, Lemuel Gulliver, Moll Flanders, Pamela, Lovelace, Thwackum and Blifil; for criticism, Eugenius, Crites, Lisideius, and Neander in John Dryden's *Essay of Dramatick Poesie* (1668). Defoe's *The Complete English Tradesman* (1725) features a Lady Tattle; Robert Boyle populates his *Occasional Meditations* (1665) with his pseudonymously named friends Eugenius, Eusebius, Genorio, and Lindamor. U. Milo Kaufmann has argued that the names in *The Pilgrim's Progress* 'are adjectival in nature rather than substantival, and hence hint at attribute rather than essence'.[21] There is a sense in which that is true of all these early modern fictional names—they point to things—but there is also a sense in which the early modern period believed that the act of naming was an act of creating, of characterizing. Hence Walter Shandy's agony when the maid Susannah ('a leaky vessel') spills the 'good' name 'Trismegistus' somewhere on the staircase and arrives for the baptism with 'Tristram', thus dooming Walter's son to a life of mishap, because Walter believes that 'there never was a great or heroic action performed since the world began by one called *Tristram—*'.[22]

It is obvious enough how the characters in *The Pilgrim's Progress* fit into their names; it is more interesting when they don't, or when the characters themselves play metanominally. Faithful says of Shame, for example: 'of all the Men that I met with in my Pilgrimage, he, I think, bears the wrong name: the other [Discontent] would be said nay, after a little argumentation (and some what else) but this bold faced *Shame* would never have done' (*PP*, 72). Talkative, 'notwithstanding his fine tongue, [. . .] is but a sorry fellow' (*PP*, 77). At the trial in Vanity Fair, Envy turns that trick against Faithful: 'My Lord, this man, notwithstanding his plausible name, is one of the vilest men in our Countrey' (*PP*, 93). Envy both asserts the name as an identifier, and then slices into it, arguing the possibility of misnomer. (Of course, that's what envy does: in the transitive sense of the verb, Envy envies Faithful his name—he 'refuses to give' him his own meaning (*OED*).) And in one of the more interesting unfoldings, we have By-ends: 'He told them, That he came from the Town of *Fair-speech*, and he was going to the Cœlestial City, (but told them not his name)' (*PP*, 98). The margin whispers: 'By-ends *loth to tell his name*.' Hopeful says to Christian (who suspects this man to be By-ends): '*Ask him; methinks he should not be ashamed of his name*' and as it turns out, it is not his name, but his nickname (*PP*, 99–100). The term means: 'An object lying aside from the main one; a subordinate end or aim; *esp.* a secret selfish purpose, a covert purpose of private advantage' (*OED*). Obviously, By-ends' neighbours nicknamed him well. As Christian concludes: '*I fear this name belongs to you more properly then you are willing we should think it doth*' (*PP*, 100).

---

[21] U. Milo Kaufmann, *The Pilgrim's Progress and Traditions in Puritan Meditation* (New Haven, CT: Yale University Press, 1966), 90.

[22] Laurence Sterne, *The Life and Opinions of Tristram Shandy, Gent.* (1759–67), ed. Howard Anderson (New York: W. W. Norton, 1980), 4, xiii; 214.

In *The Pilgrim's Progress* names are used for self-analysis. Old Honesty, for example, is modest about the contributory virtues of his name: 'Not Honesty in the *Abstract*, but *Honest* is my Name' (*PP*, 247). And characters can agree on the descriptiveness of a name for another; as Honesty says of Mr Self-will, 'he would always be like himself, *self-willed*' (*PP*, 255). The names are fluid and admit slippage, and they can be self-reflexive as much as determinative. Yet there is room for change—Fearing and Feeble-mind can gain strength from each other and make it through the journey, when on their own their weaknesses, like Pliable's, could strike them down. And at the same time, some things fundamental to a character—to character—refuse to remain long hidden. And yet, even without these spillages and idiosyncrasies, if we remember that every one of these characters is living inside the Dreamer's head, we have yet another version of psychological complexity—an overarching character who on his pilgrimage experiences hope and despair, battles with his internal demons, hunts down his own hypocrisies and self-delusions, and tests his faith in the fire.

Dialogue and diction are other ways that the characters of Bunyan anticipate those of the early novel. The format of *The Pilgrim's Progress* looks in many places something like a play in the middle of transforming itself into a novel:

> Now I saw in my Dream, that just as they had ended this talk, they drew near to a very *Miry Slow* that was in the midst of the Plain, and they being heedless, did both fall suddenly into the bogg. The name of the Slow was *Dispond*. Here therefore they wallowed for a time, being grieviously bedaubed with the dirt; And *Christian*, because of the burden that was on his back, began to sink in the Mire.
>
> Pli.   *Then said* Pliable, *Ah, Neighbour* Christian, *where are you now?*
> Chr.   Truly, said *Christian*, I do not know.
> Pli.   At that *Pliable* began to be offended; and angrily, said to his Fellow, *Is this the happiness you have told me all this while of? if we have such ill speed at our first setting out, what may we expect, 'twixt this, and our Journeys end? May I get out again with my life, you shall possess the brave Country alone for me.* (*PP*, 14)

The stage directions are given and then the novelistic narrative, complete with recorded dialogue, fills the interior spaces. In Bunyan's *The Life and Death of Mr. Badman* (1680), the dialogue is steadfastly dramatic in form (the subtitle of the work being *A Familiar Dialogue between Mr. Wiseman and Mr. Attentive*):

> Wiseman.   Good morrow, my good Neighbour, Mr. *Attentive*; whither are you walking so early this morning? methinks you look as if you were concerned about something more than ordinary. Have you lost any of your Cattel, or what is the matter?
> ATTENTIVE.   *Good Sir, Good morrow to you, I have not as yet lost ought, but yet you give a right ghess of me, for I am, as you say, concerned in my heart, but 'tis because of the badness of the times.* (*MB*, 13)

Yet dialogue in fictionalized texts increasingly wobbled between dramatic and novelistic form (playing with the idea of quotation marks along the way) until it finally settled down around the mid-eighteenth century into a more consistently narrativized format. In the First Dialogue of Part I of Defoe's *The Family Instructor* (1715), for example, the dialogue is straightforwardly in dialogue/drama format:

I was looking up there, *says the Child*, pointing up in the Air.

Fath. Well, and what did you point *thither* for, and then point *to the Ground*, and then to your self afterwards, what was that about?
Child. I was *a wondring*, Father.
Fath. *At what*, my Dear?
Child. I was a wondring what Place that is.
Fath. That is the *Air*, the *Sky*.
Child. And what is beyond that, Father?
Fath. Beyond! *my Dear*; why above it all, *there is Heaven*.[23]

But a few years later, in the Third Dialogue of Part II of *The Family Instructor* (1718), the format is intriguingly mixed. An unhappy wife has a 'subtil Deceiver' (a quite tenacious Bunyanesque devil) following her around suggesting a solution to her problem (a husband who gets in the way of her social life with his prayers): '*Poison him, poison him*: At first she started at the Suggestion, and seem'd frighted at the Thoughts of such a horrid Thing; but he that set it at Work, ply'd it so close, that she thought she heard no other Sound for some time, but that, *Poison him, poison him*.' And the drama—or the novella—unfolds in different typographical directions:

Susan, who sat in the next Room before, but had come in while she was on the Bed, run and took her up, and lay'd her on the Bed again; but it was long e're they brought her to her self: When she began to come to her self, she asked *Susan* if she heard the Thunder?
Yes, Madam, says *Susan*, it was a dreadful Thunder; and the Lightning was so terrible, Madam, *said she*, it frighted me out of my Wits.
Mistress. But did you hear nothing but Thunder, *Susan*?
Susan. No, Madam; what shou'd I hear?[24]

Although by the time of *A Journal of the Plague Year* (1722) Defoe has internalized almost all his dialogue inside narrative ('The Watchman [...heard] a Voice of one that was crying, *What d'ye want, that ye make such a knocking?* He answer'd, *I am the Watchman!*

---

[23] P. N. Furbank (ed.), Daniel Defoe, *The Family Instructor, Volume I* (1715), in *Religious and Didactic Writings of Daniel Defoe*, gen. eds. W. R. Owens and P. N. Furbank, 10 vols (London: Pickering & Chatto, 2006), 1: 48.

[24] P. N. Furbank (ed.), *Daniel Defoe, The Family Instructor, Volume II* (1718), in *Religious and Didactic Writings of Daniel Defoe*, 2: 102, 105.

how do you do? What is the Matter? The Person answered, *What is that to you? Stop the Dead-Cart*'), there was still room for the dramatic form in the story of the three men who flee London and successfully outwit the plague (and the villagers) in the countryside: John the Biscuit-Maker and his brother Thomas the Sailmaker have a three-page dramatic dialogue embedded in their longer, well-shaped narrative.[25]

Each character in Bunyan has his or her own idiolect, a manner of speaking that is a manner of behaving, of being in the world. Even the Giant has an unexpectedly cosy domestic side:

> Now *Giant Despair* had a Wife, and her name was *Diffidence*: so when he was gone to bed, he told his Wife what he had done, to wit, that he had taken a couple of Prisoners, and cast them into his *Dungeon*, for trespassing on his grounds. Then he asked her also what he had best to do further to them. So she asked him what they were, whence they came, and whither they were bound; and he told her; Then she counselled him, that when he arose in the morning, he should beat them without any mercy. (*PP*, 114)

Notwithstanding her name in one sense (although 'diffidence' as 'lack of faith' matches up in another), Mrs Diffidence is a woman of strong opinions, and her husband respects her advice. They have other counsels as the stakes get higher and Christian and Hopeful remain stubbornly alive: 'I fear', says Mrs Diffidence, 'that they live in hope that some will come to relieve them, or that they have pick-locks about them; by the means of which they hope to escape. And, sayest thou so, my dear, said the *Giant*, I will therefore search them in the morning' (*PP*, 117). It's a good marriage when partners share interests and advice.

'Mercie *has a sweet heart*', we're told (*PP*, 226), and the whole episode of Mr Brisk's courtship is, according to Sir Charles Firth, 'simply an incident in the life of a fair Puritan described with absolute fidelity to nature: the actors are ordinary men and women of the time, and the fact that their names have a moral significance makes no difference to the story'. Mr Brisk decides that Mercie spends too much energy 'making of Hose and Garments for others' (*PP*, 227) and loses interest. Mercie says rather defensively, '*I might a had Husbands afore now, tho' I spake not of it to any; but they were such as did not like my Conditions, though never did any of them find fault with my Person: So they and I could not agree*' (*PP*, 227–28). Firth notes: 'We are passing, in fact, from allegory to the novel with an improving tendency.'[26]

This is the language of 'lightness and laughter' that T. S. disapproved of, a bit lax in 'grammatical precision' and of 'extreme coarseness', according to Joshua Gilpin in

---

[25] Daniel Defoe, *A Journal of the Plague Year* (1722), ed. Cynthia Wall (London: Penguin, 2003), 49, 118–21.

[26] C. H. Firth (1898), cited in Sharrock (ed.), *The Pilgrim's Progress: A Casebook*, 102. See also Roger Sharrock, *John Bunyan* (London: Macmillan and New York: St. Martin's Press, 1968), 145; Talon, *John Bunyan*, 161–62, 202; Van Ghent, *English Novel*, 42–5.

1811[27]—and yet, though the 'lowest style of English', according to Coleridge, it is 'without slang or false grammar', and in fact 'if you were to polish it, you would at once destroy the reality of the vision'.[28] This dialogue, this language, is what makes the characters recognizable and distinctly themselves, and what makes *The Pilgrim's Progress* something much like a novel.

TEXTUALITIES

'Metafiction' is defined in *The Encyclopedia of the Novel* as writing 'which self-consciously and systematically draws attention to its status as an artefact in order to pose questions about the relationship between fiction and reality'. Although the term is rather unsatisfactorily assigned to '*avant-garde* works by American and British writers published from the 1960s up to the early 1990s, and is considered an important component of postmodernist literary style', it is recognized that the practice can be found earlier—Cervantes and Sterne are mentioned.[29] But it's a sad book in any century that doesn't point at its own bookish boundaries ('Reader, I married him'; 'the tell-tale compression of the pages'). It is hard to think of an early novel that does *not* play with the metafictional. In *A Journal of the Plague Year*, right smack in the middle of H. F.'s description of the burial ground in Moorfields, we get the note: 'N.B. The Author of this Journal, lyes buried in that very Ground, being at his own Desire, his Sister having been buried there a few Years before.'[30] Crusoe's daily memoranda of his time on the island are inserted in his narrative of his time on the island. Pamela's letters are bedewed with tears; Clarissa's letters are torn into bits. Eliza Haywood's narrator in *Fantomina* (1725) steps in just at the moment when disbelief is about to lose its suspension to assert in the first person that this is, in fact, the case. Fielding; well, *Fielding!* Wayne Booth wrote a whole book on that one. And so, too, with Bunyan: metanarrative itself, along with a series of other metatextual practices, make *The Pilgrim's Progress* a true literary cousin to its contemporary novels.

The most immediate aspect of metafiction (after the elaborate Author's Apology) is the double-frame narrative in both parts: 'And as I slept I dreamed a Dream.' Throughout, the Dreamer will assert himself, sometimes even entering the drama of the pages he is writing, moving in and out of his own text: 'Now I saw'; 'Now I also saw'; 'So I saw in my dream' (*PP*, 8, 9, 10, and throughout). The Dreamer occasionally comments inside the narrative: the battle with Apollyon was 'the dreadfullest sight that ever

---

[27] Joshua Gilpin, *The Pilgrim's Progress* [...] *A New and Corrected Edition, in which the Phraseology of the Author is Somewhat Improved* (1811), xv.

[28] Coleridge (1830), cited in Sharrock (ed.), *The Pilgrim's Progress: A Casebook*, 53.

[29] Weihsin Gui, 'Metafiction', in Peter Logan (gen. ed.), *The Encyclopedia of the Novel*, 2 vols (Oxford: Wiley-Blackwell, 2011), 2: 514.

[30] Defoe, *Journal of the Plague Year*, 223.

I saw' (*PP*, 60); in the Valley of the Shadow of Death, the Dreamer's vision seems almost as clouded and uncertain as Christian's: 'About the midst of this Valley, I perceived the mouth of Hell to be'; and 'One thing I would not let slip, I took notice that now poor *Christian* was so confounded, that he did not know his own voice: and thus I perceived it' (*PP*, 63); and he watches Christian and Faithful go 'very lovingly on together' after Christian's fall (*PP*, 66). The dream surrounds but does not interrupt the stay, trial, and execution at Vanity Fair (*PP*, 88, 98). Suddenly, the Dreamer wakes up—and just as suddenly goes back to sleep (*PP*, 123). Most critics and biographers gloss this interruption as Bunyan's first release from prison in 1672. Even so, it's an odd moment, where 'real' life is interrupting a dream life which is narrating a story, and the 'real' interruption is no more than the fluttering of an eyelid. While the Dreamer watches Christian and Hopeful talk in their sleep, the Gardener talks to the Dreamer in the Delectable Mountains (*PP*, 155–56). And at the very end, as he's gazing on all the things going on at once, he also 'turned [his] head to look back', just before his final awakening to 'behold it was a Dream' (*PP*, 162–63). The Dreamer carries the story in his head—and in his sleep—and he also enters his own story, not as its creator (like Fielding's Narrator) but as a beholder.

The marginal notes are themselves another level of metanarrative, most of the time behaving as quiet little signposts to biblical reference, but quite frequently hopping in with a point of view, or even sarcasm: 'Talkatives *fine discourse*'; '*O brave* Talkative'; 'Talkative *flings away from* Faithful'; '*A good riddance*' (*PP*, 76–7, 84–5). Towards the end, the marginal note glosses the Dreamer, rather than the other way around—with a printer's pointer, no less: '☞ *The Dreamers note*' (*PP*, 137).[31] And just as the marginal lists described in the second section of this chapter act as a cabinet of story titles that can be returned to, reopened, retold, so within the narrative stories are re-emphasized and preserved by many retellings. In narrative loops not unlike those of Defoe's narrators incessantly returning to their stories, Bunyan's pilgrims happily recount their adventures in just about every new place where they arrive and to every new person they meet. So, Evangelist demands that Christian tell him all about his meeting with Mr Worldly-Wiseman; he does (*PP*, 21). When Christian meets Good Will, he retells his story: 'my Wife and Children saw me at the first; and called after me to turn again: Also some of my Neighbours stood crying, and calling after me to return; but I put my Fingers in mine Ears, and so came on my way' (*PP*, 26). The damsel named Discretion at the House Beautiful 'asked him whence he was, and whither he was going, and he told her. She asked him also, how he got into the way, and he told her' (*PP*, 47). And so on. In *Part II*, Christiana retells her husband's story numerous times, to numerous audiences (*PP*, 184, 197, 205, 206, 271–73)—even though everyone already knows it (*PP*, 293). (And just retelling a story is never enough—Christian and his friends need to sing about it as well.) The narrative is internally dialogic, weaving itself stronger and stronger in its answers to itself.

---

[31] See, further, Chapter 25 in this volume.

The Pilgrim's Progress speaks to so many because it has so many voices itself. The Author's Apology and Conclusion, the Dreamer's framework and intrusions, the chirping in the margins, the reiterated discourse, the many voices of the characters, their debates and squabbles and songs, and even the ambiguity of the ending—which does not leave us with Christian in the Celestial City, but with Ignorance fumbling in his bosom for the certificate he well knows he doesn't have, and being shoved into the hole at the side of the hill ('Then I saw that there was a way to Hell, even from the Gates of Heaven'; *PP*, 163)—all are part of an almost Bakhtinian chorus that, with an inside larger than its outside, has managed to absorb the world by creating one. I expect Bunyan would resist being categorized in the same breath as Eliza Haywood, Daniel Defoe, and Henry Fielding. Yet *The Pilgrim's Progress* was itself bedaubed by the 'Miry Slow' of a late seventeenth-century English landscape and culture: Bunyan's pungent vernacular, homely details, and crisply slippery characterization all emerge from the same contexts as the very early novel and powerfully influenced its descendants, indeed becoming the stuff *of* novels in subsequent centuries.

Suggested Reading

Brewer, David A., *The Afterlife of Character, 1726–1825* (Philadelphia, PA: University of Pennsylvania Press, 2005).

Hancock, Maxine, *The Key in the Window: Marginal Notes in Bunyan's Narratives* (Vancouver: Regent College Publishing, 2000).

Hunter, J. Paul, *Before Novels: The Cultural Contexts of Eighteenth-Century English Fiction* (New York: W. W. Norton, 1990).

Keeble, N. H., *The Literary Culture of Nonconformity in Later Seventeenth-Century England* (Leicester: Leicester University Press, 1987).

Keen, Suzanne, 'Interior Description and Perspective in Deloney and Bunyan', *Style*, 48 (2014), 496–512.

Lynch, Deidre Shauna, *The Economy of Character: Novels, Market Culture, and the Business of Inner Meaning* (Chicago: University of Chicago Press, 1998).

McKeon, Michael, *The Origins of the English Novel 1600–1740* (Baltimore, MD: Johns Hopkins University Press, 1987).

Newey, Vincent (ed.), *The Pilgrim's Progress: Critical and Historical Views* (Liverpool: Liverpool University Press, 1980).

Sills, Adam, 'Mr. Bunyan's Neighborhood and the Geography of Dissent', *ELH*, 70 (2003), 67–87.

Smith, Nigel, 'John Bunyan and Restoration Literature', in Anne Dunan-Page (ed.), *The Cambridge Companion to John Bunyan* (Cambridge: Cambridge University Press, 2010), 26–38.

CHAPTER 31

THE PILGRIM'S PROGRESS IN THE EVANGELICAL REVIVAL

ISABEL RIVERS

THIS chapter is concerned with the ways in which evangelicals of various persuasions in the later eighteenth century—Methodists (both Arminian and Calvinist), Church of England evangelicals, and evangelical Dissenters (both Congregationalist and Baptist)—adopted *The Pilgrim's Progress* as one of their key texts and made it speak to their own situations. It is important to stress the point—which may seem a surprising one, given Bunyan's status in the 1660s and 1670s as a proscribed Nonconformist—that much of the active interpretation and commentary at this time was made by members of the Church of England. It is, of course, the case that most eighteenth-century readers and buyers of *The Pilgrim's Progress* must have been members of the Church of England, given the huge numbers of copies in circulation and the numbers of new editions published, as compared with the small proportion of Protestant Dissenters in the population. The substantial increase in the number of Dissenters by the mid-nineteenth century was owing to the impact of evangelicalism, in its origins a movement within the Church of England (the standard estimate for the proportion of Dissenters in England is just over 6 per cent in 1715–18 and 17 per cent in 1851).[1] *The Pilgrim's Progress* was particularly important as a book that transcended denominational boundaries and united people who embraced the doctrines of grace, particularly as understood in a Calvinist sense. It proved an invaluable guide to how to lead the religious life, not so much as an individual but as a member of a religious society, and this emphasis on society membership as something different from and additional to church membership is one of the significant features of the evangelical revival. The chapter focuses on three main topics: first, how, in the hands of its editors, *The Pilgrim's Progress* became a polemical text, especially from the 1770s onwards, one hundred years after the book's publication;

---

[1] Michael Watts, *The Dissenters: From the Reformation to the French Revolution* (Oxford: Clarendon Press, 1978), 269–70; vol. 2: *The Expansion of Evangelical Nonconformity* (Oxford: Oxford University Press, 1995), 28–9.

second, how it was used as a guide to Christian experience as lived by evangelicals; and third, how it became a means of writing the history of Dissent and evangelicalism.

POLEMICAL EDITIONS OF *THE PILGRIM'S PROGRESS*, 1743–95

Why was the 1770s a key decade for *The Pilgrim's Progress*? Between 1775 and 1795 there were six separate annotated editions, all reissued many times, plus an adaptation and a commentary, with further editions and another adaptation in the early nineteenth century. To understand this we have to go back to the early days of Methodism and John Wesley's abridgement of the first part of *The Pilgrim's Progress*, published in 1743.[2] Wesley's early reading at Oxford and in Georgia from 1725 to 1738 was drawn from a wide variety of sources, but it did not include Puritan writers until the main features of Methodism had been established in 1739 and his colleague, George Whitefield, had embraced Calvinist predestinarian doctrine. In this year Wesley read Bunyan's *The Pilgrim's Progress, Grace Abounding to the Chief of Sinners*, and *The Doctrine of the Law and Grace Unfolded*.[3] Four years later he published his abridgement of *The Pilgrim's Progress* as an important component of his burgeoning publishing enterprise, alongside works of a very different tendency, such as *The Christian's Pattern* of Thomas à Kempis and William Law's *Serious Call*.[4] Wesley abridged a large number of works over the course of his career in order to make them short and cheap and accessible, but he also excised doctrines of which he disapproved. His own defining doctrine of Christian perfection and his detestation of the doctrines of predestination and the imputed righteousness of Christ brought him into sharp conflict with former friends and associates, such as Whitefield and James Hervey.

Wesley made a number of changes to his text of *The Pilgrim's Progress* that undoubtedly altered the meaning, one of the most significant being Christian and Hopeful's dialogue with Ignorance.[5] Hervey warned Wesley in a posthumously published apologia of 1765 to beware the fate of Ignorance: 'I must then caution you to take heed lest you cross, or attempt to cross the *River*, in the boat of *vain Confidence*. You have abridged, if I mistake not, *The Pilgrim's Progress*, therefore can be at no loss to understand my Meaning.'[6] Richard Hill, in his *Review of all the Doctrines Taught by [...] John Wesley*,

---

[2] John Bunyan, *The Pilgrim's Progress* [...] *Abridged by John Wesley* (Newcastle upon Tyne, 1743).

[3] John Wesley, *Journal and Diaries II (1738–43)*, ed. W. Reginald Ward and Richard P. Heitzenrater, The Bicentennial Edition of the Works of John Wesley (Nashville, TN: Abingdon Press, 1984–), 19 (1990): 410, 414.

[4] Isabel Rivers, 'John Wesley as Editor and Publisher', in Randy L. Maddox and Jason E. Vickers (eds.), *The Cambridge Companion to John Wesley* (Cambridge: Cambridge University Press, 2009), 144–59.

[5] Isabel Rivers, *Reason, Grace, and Sentiment: A Study of the Language of Religion and Ethics in England, 1660–1780*, 2 vols (Cambridge: Cambridge University Press, 1991–2000), 1: 219.

[6] James Hervey, *Eleven Letters from the Late Rev. Mr. Hervey, to the Rev. Mr. John Wesley* (1765), 204.

published in 1772, at a time when hostilities between the Calvinist and Arminian wings of Methodism were at their height, similarly linked Wesley with Ignorance, and warned Wesley's followers that the book they were reading was not Bunyan's. Wesley, said Hill,

> has had the great disingenuity not only to leave out the principal part of the conversation between *Ignorance* and *Christian*, concerning Justification through the personal imputed righteousness of Christ; but absolutely to alter Bunyan's words for several lines together, and thereby to make both *Ignorance* and *Christian* speak quite another language from what the evangelical author of the piece puts into their mouths. Mr. Wesley's reason for this is clear. He did not choose to have his followers see the exact harmony between his own faith and that of *Ignorance*; but I am sorry that the purchasers of the book should be so imposed upon as to have that palmed upon them for the Pilgrim's Progress which in reality is no such thing; and therefore hope they will compare the true Bunyan with the false one.[7]

Readers with access to booksellers could readily have found copies of unabridged versions of *The Pilgrim's Progress* (though not at the bargain price of fourpence, the cost of Wesley's abridgement of *Part I*, distributed through his very efficient publishing network). What we find is a surge from the mid-1770s of *annotated* editions which stressed Bunyan's theology of grace in uncompromising terms. Those responsible either moved in the circles of Whitefield and the Countess of Huntingdon, or expressed their admiration for both, especially for Whitefield, whose importance in the spread of Calvinist evangelicalism cannot be overemphasized. Some of these people had had good relations with Wesley to start with and shared his Arminian views, as had Lady Huntingdon, but they then moved in the Whitefieldian direction. Whitefield had himself contributed a preface to the third edition of Bunyan's *Works* in folio, published in 1767, in which he stressed the link between Puritans, particularly those driven out by the 'black Bartholomew-act' of 1662, and the evangelical revival: 'for these thirty years past I have remarked, that the more true and vital religion hath revived, either at home or abroad, the more the good old Puritanical writings, or authors of a like stamp, who liv'd and died in communion of the church of England, have been called for'. He drew attention to the increasing demand for the writings of Bunyan, Matthew Henry, John Flavel, and John Owen, and particularly praised Bunyan's catholic spirit.[8] Whitefield is prominently identified on the title page as chaplain to the Countess of Huntingdon.

Although the disagreements between the Arminian and Calvinist wings of Methodism had been rumbling for thirty years, they came to a head in the early 1770s, after Whitefield's death, because of the controversy resulting from the minutes of the Wesleyan Conference of 1770. The minutes reiterated the dangers of leaning too much toward Calvinism (this meant Wesley's attempt in the 1740s to find a compromise

---

[7] Richard Hill, *A Review of all the Doctrines Taught by the Rev. Mr. John Wesley* (1772), 19.
[8] *The Works of that Eminent Servant of Christ Mr. John Bunyan* [...] *with a Recommendatory Preface, by the Reverend George Whitefield*, 2 vols (1767–68), 1: iii–iv. The preface is dated 3 January 1767.

with Whitefield's position) and emphasized the importance of repentance and works as a condition of salvation, while insisting that this did not signify salvation by the merit of works.[9] Members of Lady Huntingdon's circle were horrified. One could say that this conflict between the two wings of Methodism reflects similar conflicts in the Restoration period as epitomized in the dispute between Bunyan and Edward Fowler,[10] but the gap was now actually much larger, because of the daring implications of Wesley's doctrine of perfection or holiness, even though this had antecedents in Restoration Anglican theology, among other sources, and because the debate about human nature had changed radically as a result of eighteenth-century philosophical enquiry into the foundation of morals.[11] Ranged against Wesley were a number of writers, including A. M. Toplady, Richard Hill, and William Mason; the key supporter on Wesley's side was John William Fletcher. From the Wesleyan perspective the danger of the Calvinist emphasis on free grace, election, predestination, and human incapacity was that its tenets led to antinomianism (i.e. indifference to moral law)—hence the title of Fletcher's series of pamphlets, *Checks to Antinomianism* (1771–75). From the perspective of the Huntingdon circle the danger was that the Arminian or Wesleyan emphasis on salvation offered to all—along with free will, cooperation with grace, and the attainment of holiness or perfection in this life—led to denial both of human depravity and of the essential function of Christ as redeemer. This was often summed up as a fundamental distinction between inherent righteousness in mankind and righteousness imputed to sinners by Christ.

Editions of *The Pilgrim's Progress* by those on the Calvinist side played an important part in this debate. United in their belief in human depravity and in the transformation effected in the elect by free grace, the commentators also attacked antinomianism and stressed that the recipient's grace-enabled response was holiness, though they carefully distinguished it from the Wesleyan meaning. There are evident links between some of these editions in terms of their recommenders and subscribers. Their aims, doctrinal emphases, and assumed audiences are, however, by no means uniform.

The first annotated edition of *The Pilgrim's Progress*, whose editor is as yet unidentified, was published in 1775 and was dedicated to Lady Huntingdon; the recommendatory preface was by John Edwards, a Methodist preacher turned Congregational minister, so the edition itself advertises the fluid relationships at this date between Anglican and Dissenting Calvinists. This is a handsomely produced illustrated edition in octavo priced at 4s. or 5s. bound in leather: it clearly has a wealthy audience in view, rather like that of Law's *Serious Call*. The editor, in a note to the episode in *Part II* in which Mercy

---

[9] John Wesley, *The Methodist Societies: The Minutes of Conference*, ed. Henry D. Rack, Bicentennial Edition, 10 (2011): 392–94; Henry D. Rack, *Reasonable Enthusiast: John Wesley and the Rise of Methodism* (London: Epworth Press, 1989), 198–201 (the 1740s dispute); 391–92, 450–61 (the 1770s dispute).

[10] Isabel Rivers, 'Grace, Holiness, and the Pursuit of Happiness: Bunyan and Restoration Latitudinarianism', in N. H. Keeble (ed.), *John Bunyan: Conventicle and Parnassus* (Oxford: Oxford University Press, 1988), 45–69 (55–62).

[11] See Rivers, *Reason, Grace, and Sentiment*, vol. 2: *Shaftesbury to Hume*.

listens to the souls' lament in the by-way to hell shown by the Shepherds, castigates parents for allowing their children 'the joys of the assembly, the wit of the stage, or the pleasing anxieties of the card-table [...] the intoxicating pleasures of gay company, and [...] the irresistible charms of the *beau monde*', while neglecting their souls. The editor notes of Faithful's encounter with Shame that nowadays there are thousands who brand the advocates of religion 'with the nick-names of enthusiast, or methodist'. In his note to Gaius's account of the family of Christian in *Part II* he makes his own high Calvinist views on election and predestination explicit: 'The Lord chose a people from all eternity, who, in the fulness of time, were to be redeemed unto himself'.[12]

The Lady Huntingdon edition was followed the next year by an anonymous annotated edition of *Part I* only in duodecimo; the second edition of 1782 was advertised at 1s. 6d.[13] In 1803, when it was published together with an annotated edition of *Part II* by a Church of England clergyman, Robert Hawker, the editors of *Part I* were identified as John Newton and others.[14] It is very likely that one of the others was another Church of England clergyman, Richard Conyers, identified in a bookseller's catalogue of 1788 as author of the notes of the 1782 edition of *Part I*.[15] Newton, the most famous of the Bunyan editors of this period, had had friendly relations with Wesley when he was unsuccessfully seeking ordination, but the relationship cooled; he exchanged letters with Wesley in 1765, after he had become curate of Olney, objecting to Wesley's doctrine of perfection.[16] Conyers, who is much less well known, fits a similar pattern: a friend of both Lady Huntingdon and Wesley, like Newton he resisted Wesley's attempt in 1764 to unite the gospel clergy of the Church of England.[17] However, Wesley, having had an agreeable meeting with Conyers in early 1777, described him in his *Journal* as 'a deeply serious man, who would fain reconcile the Arminians and Calvinists'.[18]

The Newton/Conyers edition of *Part I* of *The Pilgrim's Progress* is very attractive for several reasons. The notes are clearly and engagingly written, and they include several of Newton's and William Cowper's *Olney Hymns*, three years before they appeared as a volume. The preface spells out (as do several other editions) that many readers do not

---

[12] John Bunyan, *The Pilgrim's Progress* [...] *Complete in Two Parts*. [...] *A New Edition, Carefully Revised and Corrected* [...]. *To which is now First Added, Practical and Explanatory Notes* [...] *Dedicated* [...] *to the Right Honorable the Countess of Huntingdon; and Recommended by the Rev. Mr. Edwards* (1775): Part II, 139, n. x; Part I, 93–4, n. u; Part II, 106, n. o. Prices are given in the *London Evening Post*, 16 May 1775.

[13] John Bunyan, *The Pilgrim's Progress* (1776).

[14] John Bunyan, *The Pilgrim's Progress* [...] *with Notes on the First Part, by the Rev. J. Newton, and Others. On the Second Part, by the Rev. Dr. Hawker* (1803).

[15] *W. Ash's Divinity Catalogue, for 1788* (1788), 32.

[16] D. Bruce Hindmarsh, *John Newton and the English Evangelical Tradition between the Conversions of Wesley and Wilberforce* (Oxford: Clarendon Press, 1996), 126–35.

[17] Wesley, *Journal and Diaries IV (1755–65)*, ed. Ward and Heitzenrater, Bicentennial Edition, 21 (1992): 444, 452–53, 458; Frank Baker, *John Wesley and the Church of England* (London: Epworth Press, 1970), ch. 11.

[18] Wesley, *Journal and Diaries VI (1776–86)*, ed. Ward and Heitzenrater, Bicentennial Edition, 23 (1995): 43.

know how to read *The Pilgrim's Progress*, and that only those enlightened by the Spirit can do so: 'If you are not convinced of sin, and led by the Spirit to seek JESUS, notwithstanding the Notes, the PILGRIM will still be a riddle to you.' Formalists and hypocrites do not see the necessity of the imputation of Christ's righteousness; the doctrine voiced by Ignorance is that of modern pulpits: 'They do not in words reject the Redeemer's righteousness; but by the terms and conditions which they enjoin, in reality they make it of none effect.'[19]

In 1776, the same year as the Newton/Conyers edition, the Congregational minister William Shrubsole published *Christian Memoirs*, his extraordinary adaptation of Bunyan's allegory to the present state of religion, which will be discussed in the final section. Here Shrubsole's links with other Calvinists and Bunyan editors are worth noting. The book—published in octavo and sold for 3*s*. 6*d*.—has a list of over 400 subscribers: Shrubsole's church was in Sheerness, Kent, and the vast majority of subscribers are laypeople from Kentish ports and towns. But some names stand out: Dr Conyers of Deptford; the Rev. John Edwards of Leeds; the Rt. Hon. Countess Dowager of Huntingdon, who subscribed twelve copies; Mr J. W. Piercy, Printer, Coventry, who sold the 1775 edition; and Mr William Mason, of Rotherhithe, the editor of the next edition of *The Pilgrim's Progress*.[20] Shrubsole's address 'To the Reader' includes a recommendatory letter from Mason, who read and corrected the work in manuscript. Mason, an Anglican layman and magistrate, appears in Shrubsole's allegory as Mr Knowself, Recorder of the City of Hephzibah, who for two years followed Duplex (Shrubsole's name for Wesley) and contended for perfection, but then came to accept the doctrine of imputed righteousness.

Mason's edition had a very long life and must have been extremely popular, but it is the most polemical in tone of the annotated versions, and the one that most clearly relates the narrative to contemporary disputes. Mason explained that he was asked to write notes at a time when no one had yet done so, and that, at the request of friends, he had increased the number of notes to *Part II* and made them longer.[21] The early publishing history is quite complicated; in 1778 it was published in octavo in eight parts at 6*d*. each, and in boards at 4*s*. and bound at 5*s*., and was also circulated with *The Gospel Magazine*.[22] Mason's edition has engravings by George Burder, a trained engraver who became a Congregational minister, and who was himself the next person to annotate *The Pilgrim's Progress*.

Mason addresses the reader in his notes with insistence and sometimes with ferocity. Only the spiritually quickened reader overwhelmed with 'a sense of sin, a fear of

---

[19] Bunyan, *Pilgrim's Progress* (1776), notes by Newton and Conyers, A4; 249, n. y.

[20] William Shrubsole, *Christian Memoirs: Or, A Review of the Present State of Religion in England; in the Form of a New Pilgrimage to the Heavenly Jerusalem* (Rochester, 1776), xiii–xix.

[21] John Bunyan, *The Pilgrim's Progress* [...] *A New Edition* [...] *with* [...] *Notes, Explanatory, Experimental, and Practical, by W. Mason* (1778); see Preface, *Part I*; Advertisement, *Part II*, dated 8 March 1776.

[22] *Westminster Journal and London Political Miscellany*, 14 March 1778; 'Memoirs of William Mason, Esq.', *The Evangelical Magazine*, 2 (1794), 3–11 (8).

destruction, and dread of damnation' will be able to understand the text.[23] Mason takes plenty of opportunities to attack Arminianism and perfectionism. 'It is plain Mr. Bunyan was no Arminian', he says in a note on the tableau of the oil of grace in the House of the Interpreter.[24] On Christian losing his roll, he notes: 'Happy for Christian that he did not fall into the dream of his own *sinless perfection*, so as to take up with a fool's paradise'; in the Plain called Ease, 'some fall asleep and dream of SINLESS PERFECTION'; crossing the style into By-Path-Meadow means 'you must quit Christ's imputed righteousness, and trust in your own inherent righteousness'.[25] In his note on Ignorance's objection that Christian's account of Christ's righteousness loosens the reins of lust, Mason lambasts the current use of this argument: 'Under this plausible pretence for holiness, Christ's righteousness is rejected [...]. This is a spreading heresy of the flesh, which most dreadfully prevails at this day.'[26] Mason values Great-heart's account of Christ's righteousness in *Part II* highly, and in a note on Great-heart's quotation in the Valley of Humiliation, 'that trembles at the word' (Isaiah 66:2), he makes a direct attack on Wesley's abridgement. 'Trembling' in Mason's reading means not picking and choosing doctrines:

> I believe, says one, the doctrine of the atonement and salvation of Christ; but I set my face against the doctrine of his imputed righteousness, God's electing love, and the final perseverance of his saints. Do you so? No wonder, then, that we find an extract from the Pilgrim's Progress, with these precious truths left out.[27]

The remaining editions and commentaries were published after the contentious 1770s, but they were nonetheless marked by those debates. We know from the *Memoir of George Burder* by his son that Burder refused to go to a Dissenting academy as a young man because of the pride and self-importance he saw in the tutors, and that he was much more impressed by the evangelical clergy and the Calvinistic Methodists. As a Congregational minister in Lancaster he heard Wesley preach several times in 1781, and commented (much more generously than some other Calvinists): 'He preached much of love. In whatever he is wrong, he is surely right in preaching up that.'[28] Burder is a very important figure in the spread of popular religious literature in the late eighteenth and early nineteenth centuries. His 1786 duodecimo edition of *The Pilgrim's Progress* sold at 3s. 6d., and was designed to be very user-friendly. He had given classes on *The Pilgrim's Progress*, as had Newton and Conyers, and the object of his edition was partly to help other ministers to do so.

Burder explains that his edition is in an entirely new form: it is divided into chapters, 'the design of which is to oblige the reader to make a frequent pause: for so entertaining

---

[23] Bunyan, *Pilgrim's Progress* (1778), notes by Mason, *Part I*, 2, n. b.
[24] Bunyan, *Pilgrim's Progress* (1778), notes by Mason, 31, n. g.
[25] Bunyan, *Pilgrim's Progress* (1778), notes by Mason, 44, n. n; 123, n. i; 129, n. p.
[26] Bunyan, *Pilgrim's Progress* (1778), notes by Mason, 176, n. b.
[27] Bunyan, *Pilgrim's Progress* (1778), notes by Mason, *Part II*, 89, n. d.
[28] Henry Forster Burder, *Memoir of the Rev. George Burder* (London: Frederick Westley & A. H. Davis, 1833), 99.

is the narrative, that the heart becomes interested in the event of every transaction, and is tempted to proceed with a precipitation that excludes proper reflections'.[29] The explanatory notes that follow each chapter are not footnotes. Burder indicates that the kind of reader he wants to reach might not know how to use footnotes, or might just pass over them. He acknowledges his debt to earlier commentators, but points out that he sometimes differs from them. Like Mason, he attacks doctrinal Arminians and antinomians, but he also has a broader target. In his notes on the pilgrims' dialogue with Ignorance, he stresses the irony of the work's popularity:

> It is somewhat surprizing that the *Pilgrim's Progress* should be universally esteemed, seeing that it condemns the far greater part of those who read it [...] Does not *Ignorance* speak the language of most nominal christians? [...] Their dependence is on what they *do*, or (which is nearly the same) on what is done *in* them. They despise christian experience as enthusiasm, and think that trusting to the righteousness of Christ, leads to licentiousness. Such is the language both of the parlour and the pulpit in this day; and yet, though it is here so justly exposed, every body admires the *Pilgrim's Progress*!

In his notes on the Shepherds of the Delectable Mountains, Burder criticizes destructive modern errors, presumably the development of liberal attitudes among Dissenters: 'a false moderation, and unscriptural charity now prevail, and the grossest heresies are by some held to be harmless sentiments, while all zeal for truth is accounted bigotry'.[30]

The next commentator, 'Andronicus', the anonymous author of *A Key to The Pilgrim's Progress* (1790), appears from internal evidence to have been an evangelical Dissenter, probably a Congregational minister. However, he reaches beyond this constituency. The reader is assumed not to know that 'the System of Christianity alluded to throughout the Allegory, is the Calvinistic, or, as it is denominated in the present Day, Evangelic: and the Modes of Religion alluded to, are those of Nonconformity'.[31] He acknowledges his debt to the 1776 edition (the one with notes by Newton and Conyers) and to Mason's of 1778, but he is doing something rather different. His *Key*, published without Bunyan's text, sold for 2s. 6d. or in twelve weekly numbers for 3d.[32] It is cast in the well-worn form of letters to a friend, but it effectively combines the Pauline with the polite. Andronicus writes to Syntyche (the names are mentioned briefly in Romans 16:7 and Philippians 4:2) elucidating episodes, and in one letter gives a number of vignettes of inhabitants of Vanity Fair such as Avaro, Martius, and Philologus, in the style of William Law or James Hervey. Andronicus imagines Syntyche objecting: 'Did these Ideas ever enter the Head of JOHN BUNYAN?', to which Andronicus replies, 'I know not that they did: but I know that were he living [...] he would acknowledge the Gentry I have named to be eminent

---

[29] John Bunyan, *The Pilgrim's Progress* [...] *A New Edition, Divided into Chapters: To which are Added, Explanatory and Practical Notes* [...] *by G. Burder* (Coventry, 1786), v.
[30] Bunyan, *Pilgrim's Progress* (1786), notes by Burder, *Part I*, 188; *Part I*, 149.
[31] Andronicus, *A Key to the Pilgrim's Progress* (1790), vi.
[32] *General Evening Post*, 6 January 1791; *Public Advertiser*, 28 December 1791.

and capital Traffickers in this Fair.' Later, with reference to the Flatterer, Andronicus devotes two pages to telling the story of Artabanes, 'a lovely, lively, and affectionate Disciple', who is led astray by an antinomian preacher but is torn between the extremes of antinomianism and legality: 'though he had embraced Antinomian Principles with Fondness, he dreaded the Spirit and Practice of them: and he was equally afraid that if he verged toward his former Sentiments, his Mind would sink into Legality and Bondage'.[33] Eventually he returns to his former brethren.

Andronicus makes his preference for Whitefieldian evangelicalism clear by portraying Whitefield as Euodias (also named in Philippians 4:2) holding forth the torch of truth from which the revival catches fire. With reference to the Mountain of Error he obliquely criticizes Wesley's attempt to differentiate opinion from doctrine: 'Opinions, say some, are harmless, and to make a Noise about them, savours of Bigotry and narrowness of Soul; I say so too of some Opinions, but while I read of Heresies and damnable Errors, I must distinguish between Opinion and Opinion'; that is, that do and do not have pernicious consequences.[34] Knowing readers would have recognized this as a rejection of Wesley's recurrent emphasis on 'opinion' as something that should not be allowed to divide adherents of real religion.[35]

One might imagine that by the 1790s there were enough annotated editions and commentaries to satisfy the market, but this was evidently not the case. John Bradford—who advertised himself as an Oxford BA, although his career change from Church of England curate to Congregational minister via the Countess of Huntingdon's Connexion was an unconventional one—produced in 1792 a handsomely printed and relatively expensive octavo edition with plates, advertised in 1795 at 7s. It has the advantage of including an index: not alphabetical, but a summary of topics in order of appearance. Bradford makes clear his high Calvinist views, emphasizing depravity and imputed righteousness, and his opposition to Wesleyan perfection and holiness. Fletcher's anti-Calvinist tracts are dismissed out of hand: 'there is no other check to Antinomianism but faith'. He significantly alters the wording of Great-heart's criticism of the antinomian figure of Self-will, and goes to some lengths to show that Bunyan cannot be understood 'to favour man's free-will and merit'.[36] The problem here seems to be the word 'condition', with all that it had come to imply. Bunyan's Great-heart says: '*For indeed we are exempted from no Vice absolutely, but on condition that we Watch and Strive*' (PP, 255). However, Bradford's Great-heart says: 'For, indeed, we are exempted from no vice absolutely; and such is our condition, in order that we may watch and strive.' In his attacks on perfection Bradford goes much further than other critics: he suggests gratuitously that Bunyan's Atheist might once have professed to be perfect, and in a note on Great-heart's comforting of Feeble-mind he launches into a fierce attack on those 'who profess a great zeal

---

[33] Andronicus, *Key*, 194, 276–78.
[34] Andronicus, *Key*, 241.
[35] Rivers, *Reason, Grace, and Sentiment*, vol. 1, 225–26.
[36] John Bunyan, *The Pilgrim's Progress* [...] *with Notes, by a Bachelor of Arts, of the University of Oxford* [John Bradford] (1792), 149, n. h.; 356, n. x.

for inherent holiness and good works', comparing them with 'their brother Judas': 'Many such professors we have, who, with all their pretended zeal for holiness, can grind the faces of the poor, exact upon their servants, reduce their wages, and practise the most wretched extortion.'[37]

The last of the eighteenth-century annotated editions of *The Pilgrim's Progress*, that of the Church of England clergyman Thomas Scott, was the most often reprinted in the nineteenth century, alongside Mason's.[38] This is surprising for three reasons: the upmarket nature of the edition, the intellectual demands made by the commentary, and the critical view that Scott takes of various manifestations of evangelicalism. In the 1770s Scott had read and reasoned his way from Socinianism to Calvinism, arguing with Newton along the way, a process he described in his fascinating autobiography, *The Force of Truth* (1779). He makes clear in his preface to *The Pilgrim's Progress* that the publishers wanted the edition to be characterized by its elegance, a term he repeats several times. Their commercial ambitions and Scott's intense admiration for the book coalesced. Neither side was put off by the existing annotated editions. Scott told the reader it was now the practice 'to publish every approved work, in such a style of elegance, and with such decorations, as may recommend it to a place in the collections of the curious and affluent; and thus attract the notice of those who would perhaps otherwise have overlooked it'.[39] He clearly saw himself as writing for a different audience from those served by previous annotators.

Scott's edition was beautifully designed, printed from a new type by Caslon, with eight engraved plates, and it was extremely expensive by comparison with the earlier editions: it was initially advertised for sale in eight parts at 1s. 6d. per number, and then as a royal octavo at £1 1s. or a demy at 12s.[40] The copies of the rare first edition of 1795 in the Bodleian and the British Library both have the subscription list bound in. The subscribers were mostly laypeople with London addresses, among them Lady Austen, Cowper's former friend, who had been Scott's lodger when he succeeded Newton as curate at Olney, plus a sprinkling of clergy, of whom the best known is John Venn of Clapham. Scott explained that having notes placed separately at the end of each part 'is deemed conducive to elegance in printing'. From the point of view of the reader he thought it an advantage, as the reader would unriddle the allegory first and then consult the notes. Scott kept all Bunyan's biblical references, placing them at the foot; he omitted the marginal notes, because these would encumber the page and 'preclude elegance', substituting a running title at the top of each page.[41] He was a conscientious

---

[37] Bunyan, *Pilgrim's Progress* (1792), notes by Bradford, 356, 378, n. e.
[38] John Bunyan, *The Pilgrim's Progress* […] *with Notes, and the Life of the Author: By Thomas Scott* (1795).
[39] Bunyan, *Pilgrim's Progress* (1795), notes by Scott, iv.
[40] *Morning Chronicle*, 9 December 1794; *General Evening Post*, 19 April 1796; *Hints for the Consideration of Patients in Hospitals: By Thomas Scott* (1797), 'Published by the same Author', n. p.
[41] Bunyan, *Pilgrim's Progress* (1795), notes by Scott, vi–vii.

editor, comparing modern editions with old ones, and restoring to the text words that modern editors had altered.

Scott had a firm view of the strenuousness of the Christian life and the many errors held about it at the time among different religious groupings. In his notes he targets in various places the dangers of evangelical enthusiasm and the political ambitions of Dissenters, and he defends his own difficult position as a Calvinist who emphasized the importance of moral effort. In a note on the torments of the Valley of the Shadow he points out that the trials of Christians are made worse by a range of falsely gratifying doctrines:

> These experiences, sufficiently painful in themselves, are often rendered more distressing, by erroneous expectations of uninterrupted comfort, or by reading books, or hearkening to instructions, which state things unscripturally; representing comfort as the evidence of acceptance, assurance as the essence of faith, impressions or visions as the witness of the Spirit; or perfection as attainable in this life, nay actually attained by all the regenerate;—as if this were the church triumphant, and not the church militant.[42]

The trial of Faithful gives Scott the opportunity to berate those, he claims, who 'make religion the pretext for intermeddling *out of their place* in political matters' and thus 'strengthen men's prejudices against the doctrines of the gospel, and the whole body of those who profess them'.[43] This kind of attack on Dissenters is not to be found in the earlier editions. In his comment on the worsening condition of the Slough of Despond in *Part II*, Scott imagines Bunyan's views about the state of religion in the 1680s, but he is obviously giving his own interpretation of the 1790s:

> The author seems to have observed a declension of evangelical religion, subsequent to the publication of his original pilgrim. Probably he was grieved to find many renounce or adulterate the gospel, by substituting plausible speculations, or moral lectures in its stead [this is clearly aimed at much Anglican writing]; by narrowing and confining it within the limits of a nice system, which prevents the preacher from freely inviting sinners to come unto CHRIST [this is aimed at contemporary arguments by high Calvinists among the Baptists]; by representing the preparation of heart requisite to a sincere acceptation of free salvation, as a *legal condition* of being received by him; or by condemning all diligence, repentance, and tenderness of conscience, as interfering with an evangelical frame of spirit [Scott is here defending his own emphasis on repentance against charges of legalism].

In general, what Scott found most dangerous in contemporary evangelical religion was opinions arising 'from a false and flattering estimate of human nature'.[44]

---

[42] Bunyan, *Pilgrim's Progress* (1795), notes by Scott, Part I, 251.
[43] Bunyan, *Pilgrim's Progress* (1795), notes by Scott, Part I, 276.
[44] Bunyan, *Pilgrim's Progress* (1795), notes by Scott, Part II, 190, 201.

THE PILGRIM'S PROGRESS AND EVANGELICAL EXPERIENCE

Although *The Pilgrim's Progress* is undoubtedly a polemical work in which Bunyan damns his enemies, this is, of course, not the main focus of the book, nor of its eighteenth-century editors. Their commentaries tell us a great deal about how the book was used in the particular circumstances of the revival. Bunyan's editors all praised his skill in illustrating the varieties of Christian experience, and agreed, as Bradford said, that 'the true end of reading is a practical improvement of what we read'.[45] Scott warned readers to 'beware, lest they be fascinated, as it were, into a persuasion, that they actually accompany the pilgrims in the life of faith, and walking with GOD, in the same measure, as they keep pace with the author, in discovering and approving the grand outlines of his plan'.[46] How did the editors help their readers to improve the text, in the sense of turning it to their spiritual advantage, and enable them to accompany the pilgrims in the life of faith? Three aspects are particularly illuminating: the use of the book in society meetings; the emphasis on the House Beautiful; and the incorporation of hymns into the commentary.

Several ministers expounded *The Pilgrim's Progress* at society meetings, and the editions of Newton and Burder grew out of this process. Newton did this at his Tuesday prayer meetings in Olney in the late 1760s, and there are accounts in his letters published during and after his life of how carefully and slowly he took the members through the book. He wrote to Alexander Clunie on 26 July 1766:

> We reached the wicket-gate last Tuesday, and shall perhaps stay there a fortnight. There is such a fulness and depth in the Pilgrim's Progress, that a small portion of it affords a sufficient text for an evening; and I see more in it, now I come to examine it closely, than I ever observed before, though I have read it so often that I have it in a manner by heart.[47]

Similarly, he wrote to Miss Medhurst on 20 July 1768:

> [T]hough we have been almost seven months travelling with the pilgrim, we have not yet left the house Beautiful; but I believe shall set off for the Valley of Humiliation in about three weeks. I find this book so full of matter, that I can seldom go through more than a page, or half a page, at a time. I hope the attempt has been greatly blessed amongst us; and for myself, it has perhaps given me a deeper insight into John

---

[45] Bunyan, *Pilgrim's Progress* (1792), notes by Bradford, x.
[46] Bunyan, *Pilgrim's Progress* (1795), notes by Scott, *Part II*, 238.
[47] John Newton, *The Christian Correspondent; or a Series of Religious Letters, Written by the Rev. John Newton [...] to Captain Alexr. Clunie* (Hull, 1790), 129.

Bunyan's knowledge, judgement, and experience in the Christian life, than I should ever have had without it.[48]

Burder noted in his memoirs for 1784: 'Began a series of observations, at the Monday evening prayer-meetings, on the Pilgrim's Progress. These were remarkably well attended, three or four hundred people, perhaps, being present.'[49] In his edition published two years later, Burder implied that this was now a common practice: 'Several ministers have thought it a pleasing and profitable exercise, to read and explain the PILGRIM to their people in private meetings.'[50] He hoped his book, with its organization into chapters, would be useful for the purpose. Other expounders of Bunyan are known. One was Conyers (described by Shrubsole, who knew him when he was the incumbent at Deptford, as 'the *venerable lecturer on Mr. Bunyan's Progress*').[51] Another was David Simpson, Church of England clergyman at Macclesfield, an Arminian and close friend of Wesley, who gave a course of lectures in his schoolroom in the 1770s, and then, many years later, to the senior scholars of his Sunday School.[52]

Thus, *The Pilgrim's Progress* was perceived as a book to be read and applied in group meetings, and, as Burder suggested, in families. The commentaries place a strong emphasis on social religion, some of them stressing how much both toleration and revival have changed things for the better, others with warnings about the difficulties involved. The House Beautiful in both parts, and the houses of Gaius and Mnason in *Part II*, occasion significant comments about church and society membership, sometimes blurring the distinction, and sometimes with an interdenominational emphasis. Burder provides a contentious definition: 'THE house called *Beautiful*, signifies a visible church of Christ, or a society of regenerate persons, who voluntarily associate to enjoy the means of grace, for the glory of God, and their mutual edification.'[53] He insists, as a Congregationalist, on strict terms of admission. Bradford, however, citing this definition, warns that 'a society of regenerate persons', 'all wheat and no tares', is not to be found on earth.[54] Scott, in a characteristically cautious and thoughtful note on the House Beautiful, considers Bunyan's own position as 'a protestant dissenter, an *Independent* in respect of church government and discipline, and an *Anti-paedo-baptist* [...] who held open communion with *Paedo-baptists*', and concludes that Bunyan's portrayal 'may suit the admission of new members into the society of professed christians, in any communion, where a serious regard to spiritual religion is in this respect maintained', though Scott questions 'how far, in the present state of things, this is practicable.'[55]

---

[48] John Newton, *The Works of the Rev. John Newton*, 6 vols (1808), 6: 37–8. I owe this reference to Bruce Hindmarsh.
[49] Burder, *Memoir*, 131.
[50] Bunyan, *Pilgrim's Progress* (1786), notes by Burder, v.
[51] Shrubsole, *Christian Memoirs*, 53.
[52] 'A Memoir of the Late Rev. David Simpson, M.A.', *Methodist Magazine*, 36 (1813), 3–12, 81–92 (82–4).
[53] Bunyan, *Pilgrim's Progress* (1786), notes by Burder, 63.
[54] Bunyan, *Pilgrim's Progress* (1792), notes by Bradford, 56, n. y.
[55] Bunyan, *Pilgrim's Progress* (1795), notes by Scott, Part I, 238–39.

Other commentators are more optimistic. Piety in Shrubsole's allegory explains that the House Beautiful 'is now become the resort of warm-hearted unprejudiced souls, both of the *City of Establishment* [i.e. the Church of England], and its suburbs'. Charity adds:

> This house was never so pleasant to me as it now is. I think myself in the *Celestial city*, when I behold persons of the adjacent city and its suburbs, of different denominations, unite here to sing, pray, hear, and discourse together about the best things, without one word of contention.[56]

Andronicus sees 'the great Number of religious Societies established of late Years' as a consequence of civil liberty under the Toleration Act, and devotes a whole letter to the House Beautiful, celebrating the way love 'unites different Societies of Christians, of different Modes of Worship in one Spirit of Amity […]. It anticipates that State where Persons of very different Sentiments in some Particulars here, shall dwell together in everlasting Harmony.'[57]

A striking aspect of the commentaries is the part played by hymns. The change in the status of hymns and the huge increase in hymn publication over a hundred years are crucial here. Hymn-singing was contentious in the seventeenth century, but it informed all aspects of eighteenth-century evangelical culture. Hymns were used in worship, in society meetings, and in families; they were edited and revised in different collections that went through multiple editions; they were used in private devotion and learned by heart, and quoted in journals and letters, and on deathbeds.[58] Several of the commentators—Newton, Burder, and Bradford—wrote hymns and edited hymn collections. By including hymns in commentaries on *The Pilgrim's Progress* the authors were following Bunyan's example, but also extending the book's range and function. Of the popular eighteenth-century hymn-writers and editors, Isaac Watts and Charles Wesley are quoted by both Shrubsole and Andronicus; Whitefield by Shrubsole, Andronicus, and Burder; and Joseph Hart by Shrubsole, Andronicus, Burder, Mason, and Bradford. (Scott thought the attractions of Joseph Hart were particularly dangerous.)[59]

Shrubsole, whose allegory is full of hymns, often portrays his pilgrims singing at the end of a chapter as they march on to the next stage of their journey. Bradford quotes himself, anonymously, with reference to Hopeful's wish to sleep on the Enchanted Ground:

---

[56] Shrubsole, *Christian Memoirs*, 63, 65.
[57] Andronicus, *Key*, 84, 91.
[58] See Isabel Rivers and David L. Wykes (eds.), *Dissenting Praise: Religious Dissent and the Hymn in England and Wales* (Oxford: Oxford University Press, 2011); Isabel Rivers, *Vanity Fair and the Celestial City: Dissenting, Methodist, and Evangelical Literary Culture in England, 1720–1800* (Oxford: Oxford University Press, 2018), ch. 11.
[59] John Scott, *The Life of the Rev. Thomas Scott*, 5th edn (London: L. B. Seeley & Son, 1823), 339, 341.

I doubt not but the author of the following lines wrote them from his own experience:

> Whene'er becalmed I lie,
> And all my fears subside,
> Then to my succour fly,
> And keep me near thy side;
> For more the treacherous calm I dread,
> Than tempests bursting o'er my head.[60]

The Newton/Conyers edition included two hymns by Cowper and two by Newton, subsequently published in Books 2 and 3 of *Olney Hymns*.[61] Just as Newton expounded *The Pilgrim's Progress*, so he expounded his own hymns in his prayer meetings. The hymns in his edition are specifically linked to Bunyan's narrative: 'The Shining Light' by Cowper; 'A Welcome to the House Beautiful' by Newton (entitled 'A Welcome to Christian Friends' in *Olney Hymns*), 'The Lord of the Hill' (unidentified, not in *Olney Hymns*), 'Christian in the Valley of the Shadow of Death' by Cowper, and, at the very end of *Part I*, 'The Pilgrim's Song' by Newton.[62]

The Pilgrim's Progress as a Means of Writing History

In the hands of its editors and adapters *The Pilgrim's Progress* became more than a way of defining doctrine and of experiencing the Christian life. It was also a means of writing the history of Dissent and evangelicalism from the Calvinist point of view, which is, of course, not the whole story. Joseph Ivimey, writing as a Baptist and thus, he thought, better able to interpret Bunyan than members of other denominations, edited *The Pilgrim's Progress* in 1821 as an allegory of Bunyan's own life and of what happened to Nonconformists from 1650 to 1688.[63] In his sequel, *Pilgrims of the Nineteenth Century*, published in 1827, he wrote a new third part in Bunyan's format to take the history of Dissent in the period of toleration up to the present day, when the possible repeal of the Test and Corporation Acts was in the balance (they were repealed the following year).[64]

Fifty years earlier, Shrubsole offered a much more striking reading of evangelical history in *Christian Memoirs: Or, A Review of the Present State of Religion in England*. For

---

[60] Bunyan, *Pilgrim's Progress* (1792), notes by Bradford, 188, n. a; and see *A Collection of Hymns, by John Bradford* (1792), 201.

[61] [John Newton and William Cowper], *Olney Hymns, in Three Books* (1779), Book 2, hymn 70; Book 3, hymns 8, 20, 42.

[62] Bunyan, *Pilgrim's Progress* (1776), notes by Newton and Conyers, 6–7, 72, 81, 99, 279–80.

[63] John Bunyan, *The Pilgrim's Progress* [...] *A New Edition* [...] *with Historical and other Notes; by Joseph Ivimey* (1821).

[64] Joseph Ivimey, *Pilgrims of the Nineteenth Century; a Continuation of The Pilgrim's Progress, upon the Plan Projected by Mr. Bunyan: Comprising the History of a Visit to the Town of Toleration* (1827).

Shrubsole, as for Andronicus and perhaps for Mason, the principal agent of the revival was Whitefield, elevated after his death to the status of Protestant saint.[65] Shrubsole dedicated his book

TO

THOSE PROTESTANTS OF EVERY DENOMINATION

WHO, IN THEIR FAITH AND PRACTICE,

RECEIVE AND ADORN

THE DOCTRINAL ARTICLES OF

THE ESTABLISHED CHURCH OF ENGLAND

The dedication thus takes his readers back to the terms of the Toleration Act, but it also stresses the reciprocity of Anglican and Dissenting evangelicalism, and excludes liberal or rational Dissent, which in Shrubsole's view is closely allied with deism and infidelity. Shrubsole has much to say about the whole spectrum of religion in his day, but his account of Methodism from the perspective of an evangelical Dissenter is particularly interesting. In his portrait of the City of Establishment, his hero, George Fervidus (Whitefield), stirred up by Providence, did much to renovate Arminian Row, but John Duplex (Wesley), formerly Fervidus's associate, failed to reform Methodist-lane. Much later in the narrative, Shrubsole contrasts the different routes by which Fervidus and Duplex lead their followers to the City of God. Fervidus captains the vessel called the Covenant Transport on the River of Life, but Duplex always leads his followers by land alongside the river, through the perils of Arminian-wood, Free-will forest, Goodwin's sand, and Baxter's heath, where they are beset by banditti called Aphorisms. (Shrubsole is alluding to Wesley's abridgements of anti-Calvinist works by John Goodwin and Richard Baxter.)

Fervidus allows no 'merit-monger, or self-justifier' on his vessel, but he is generous in his judgement of Duplex:

> In our juvenile days, we had many disputes about our different ways of travelling, and I still believe him to be in the wrong; but I perceive that he makes use of this river, and am sure that he is made useful to souls; therefore I honour him as a laborious servant of our *Immanuel*.

Shrubsole concludes his lengthy and complicated narrative with Fervidus crossing the river to the Celestial City, where he is congratulated by Immanuel for bringing in so many pilgrims. Shrubsole was well aware that his allegorical history might look strange to Dissenters, and in his preface he grants that 'The character of *Fervidus*, both on this

---

[65] Isabel Rivers, 'Whitefield's Reception in England, 1770–1839', in Geordan Hammond and David Ceri Jones (eds.), *George Whitefield: Life, Context, and Legacy* (Oxford: Oxford University Press, 2016), 261–77.

and the other side the *River of Death*, may be thought too much strained and exalted.'[66] In his second revised edition of 1790, however, he firmly defended his approach:

> The Author has been censured for favouring and exalting *Methodism* too much: but it should be remembered, that this work is a Review of the *Present State of Religion*. It cannot be denied, that there hath been a great revival of Religion among us, within the last fifty years. This Revival originated, and was continued, under the ministry of those called *Methodists*. Other religious sects have but little pretence to any share of the honour of this work. [67]

He capped this by concluding this edition with his elegy on Whitefield's death, which he had first published in 1771.

It is sometimes assumed that the crucial distinction to be made with regard to the change in Bunyan's standing in the eighteenth century is between literary and religious readings of *The Pilgrim's Progress*.[68] This chapter attempts to provide, through an account of these editions and versions, a fuller and more complicated picture. *The Pilgrim's Progress* in the hands of its editors, commentators, and adaptors was a polemical work, a guide for members of religious societies to how to live Christian lives, and a way of describing how English religion was transformed in the second half of the eighteenth century in ways that were thought, perhaps implausibly, to be consonant with Bunyan's vision.

Suggested Reading

Forrest, James F. and Richard Lee Greaves, *John Bunyan: A Reference Guide* (Boston, MA: G. K. Hall, 1982). [Note: some of the items covered in this chapter are missing from this *Reference Guide*; William Mason is also misidentified.]

Hindmarsh, D. Bruce, *John Newton and the English Evangelical Tradition between the Conversions of Wesley and Wilberforce* (Oxford: Clarendon Press, 1996).

Hofmeyr, Isabel, *The Portable Bunyan: A Transnational History of The Pilgrim's Progress* (Princeton, NJ, and Oxford: Princeton University Press, 2004).

Johnson, Barbara A., *Reading Piers Plowman and The Pilgrim's Progress: Reception and the Protestant Reader* (Carbondale and Edwardsville, IL: Southern Illinois University Press, 1992).

Noll, Mark A., *The Rise of Evangelicalism: The Age of Edwards, Whitefield and the Wesleys* (Leicester: Inter-Varsity Press, 2004).

---

[66] Shrubsole, *Christian Memoirs*, 226, 234, x.

[67] Shrubsole, *Christian Memoirs* [. . .] *A New Edition* (Rochester, 1790), xix.

[68] Barbara A. Johnson, *Reading Piers Plowman and The Pilgrim's Progress: Reception and the Protestant Reader* (Carbondale and Edwardsville, IL: Southern Illinois University Press, 1992), 217, posits three kinds of reader, Protestant, lettered, and ordinary, but does not differentiate kinds of Protestant reader.

Rivers, Isabel, *Reason, Grace, and Sentiment: A Study of the Language of Religion and Ethics in England, 1660–1780*, vol. 1: *Whichcote to Wesley* (Cambridge: Cambridge University Press, 1991).

Rivers, Isabel, *Vanity Fair and the Celestial City: Dissenting, Methodist, and Evangelical Literary Culture in England, 1720–1800* (Oxford: Oxford University Press, 2018).

Smith, David E., *John Bunyan in America* (Bloomington, IN: Indiana University Press, 1966).

van Os, M., and G. J. Schutte (eds.), *Bunyan in England and Abroad* (Amsterdam: VU University Press, 1990).

CHAPTER 32

BUNYAN AND THE ROMANTICS

JONATHON SHEARS

Robert Southey, the 1830 *Pilgrim's Progress*, and the Literary Context

As with Shakespeare, Milton, and Dante, it is commonly acknowledged that the end of the eighteenth century marks a discernible transition in the way that Bunyan's writings, particularly *The Pilgrim's Progress* (1678; 1684), were received, read, and understood. Two significant markers stand out, corresponding roughly to the beginning and the end of the Romantic period. The first belongs to William Cowper: a poet whom Vincent Newey, Gerda S. Norvig, and others have placed in a direct line of descent from the brand of radical Protestant self-interrogation for which Bunyan became famous.[1] Cowper's is a tentative eulogy, so much so as to suggest that, in the 1780s at least, Bunyan's was a name which had fallen into darkness, with attendant dangers compassed round:

> I name thee not, lest so despised a name
> Should move a sneer at thy deserved fame,
> Yet e'en in transitory life's late day,
> That mingles all my brown with sober gray,
> Revere the man whose PILGRIM marks the road,
> And guides the PROGRESS of the soul to God.[2]

---

[1] Vincent Newey, 'Bunyan's Afterlives: Case Studies', in W. R. Owens and Stuart Sim (eds.), *Reception, Appropriation, Recollection: Bunyan's Pilgrim's Progress* (Bern: Peter Lang, 2007), 25–48; Gerda S. Norvig, *Dark Figures in the Desired Country: Blake's Illustrations to The Pilgrim's Progress* (Berkeley and Los Angeles, CA: University of California Press, 1993), 86–96.

[2] William Cowper, *Tirocinium, or, a Review of Schools* (1784), lines 141–46; cited in Roger Sharrock (ed.), *The Pilgrim's Progress: A Casebook* (London and Basingstoke: Macmillan, 1976), 51–2.

The second marker comes almost fifty years later in the decision of Robert Southey—Poet Laureate from 1813 to 1843—to publish in 1830 a new edition of *The Pilgrim's Progress, with a Life of John Bunyan*. According to Barbara A. Johnson, Southey's was in all senses an edition produced for the literary establishment, bearing 'the signs of a serious literary endeavor' including prefaces and a title page on which Southey's name and laureateship feature prominently.[3] The image of Bunyan dreaming, by Robert White, that ordinarily accompanied an edition of *The Pilgrim's Progress* throughout the eighteenth century was replaced by an engraving after the Thomas Sadler portrait of Bunyan, depicting him with a book (presumably the Bible) in his hand: a deliberate attempt to foreground the author's literacy and inspiration. Bernard Barton supplied a tub-thumping verse to endorse the inclusion of the Sadler portrait, which couldn't be further removed from Cowper's cagey tone. He singles out Bunyan's 'Shrewdness of intellect, strength of mind, / Devout though lively, acute though grave' that in 'fiction sought the soul to save'.[4]

What kind of shift has occurred in the intervening years to allow Barton to praise *The Pilgrim's Progress* in such unqualified terms? The answer to this question forms the substantial part of what follows in this chapter.[5] The commentary of Barbara Johnson provides us with a starting point, particularly her belief that 'the Southey edition [...] represents the first full-scale attempt to turn *The Pilgrim's Progress* into literature'.[6] For those unfamiliar with the reception history of *The Pilgrim's Progress*, this sounds initially like an odd claim. It should be understood firstly in the context of the vast number of poor-quality, cheap, abridged, or bastardized editions of Bunyan's work that circulated throughout the eighteenth century, along with Bunyan's enduring reputation as an unlearned and unlettered writer whose talent shone despite his poor education. Here, instead, was Robert Southey's *Pilgrim's Progress*: an edition that looked good enough to enter the canon, ready to be established as a bona fide classic. Sir Walter Scott wrote approvingly: 'it might seem certain that the established favourite of the common people should be well received among the upper classes'.[7]

Johnson's observation needs equally to be understood in terms of the historicity of what she is calling 'literature'. As she rightly notes, 'the category of the literary is an historical construct, and its contours can be traced in the changing reputation of *The Pilgrim's Progress*'.[8] The elision of the historical and ideological determinants that enable the attribution of a term like 'literary' to a text like Bunyan's allegory is an issue that

---

[3] Barbara A. Johnson, *Reading Piers Plowman and The Pilgrim's Progress: Reception and the Protestant Reader* (Carbondale and Edwardsville, IL: Southern Illinois University Press, 1992), 168.
[4] Johnson, *Reading Piers Plowman and The Pilgrim's Progress*, 170.
[5] See also Chapter 31 in this volume.
[6] Johnson, *Reading Piers Plowman and The Pilgrim's Progress*, 165.
[7] Cited in Sharrock (ed.), *Pilgrim's Progress: A Casebook*, 64–5. Norvig argues that the perceived 'humble, evangelical roots' of *The Pilgrim's Progress* were the main reason why, until the later eighteenth century, it was not considered suitable subject matter for creative illustration; see *Dark Figures*, 120. See also Chapter 36 in this volume.
[8] Johnson, *Reading Piers Plowman and The Pilgrim's Progress*, 163.

has occupied other critics in recent times. In summing up the 'literary' reputation of *The Pilgrim's Progress* Michael Davies has, for example, argued that the conferral of aesthetic merit on to Bunyan's writing has meant that literary criticism has often tended to 'universalise' and 'decontextualise' the specific theological content, sidestepping in particular the Calvinist discourses of election and reprobation, in order to make Christian's journey more palatable to a broadly liberal and secular readership.[9] For Davies the necessity of this ahistoricism is arrived at through false terms: the content of Bunyan's message emphasizing a forbidding Calvinist doctrine of predestination less than a more amenable covenant theology.[10] It is, in Davies's words, a common error to view Bunyan 'somewhat simplistically as a proponent of a grim and psychologically terrorizing divinity at the heart of which lies a wrathful Creator […] forgiving to but a helpless (and severely limited) few'. Rather, *The Pilgrim's Progress* offers an education in the accommodation of one's sinfulness to faith in Christ: a reading of Bunyan's belief that underwrites most of the discussion that follows in this chapter.[11]

The historically untethered approach to reading Bunyan 'reaches its apogee', to borrow Vincent Newey's phrase, with F. R. Leavis's afterword to the Signet Classics edition of 1964, in which Leavis makes the case for reading *The Pilgrim's Progress* 'without any thought for its theological intention'.[12] Whilst not denying its historical place, Leavis prefers to describe *The Pilgrim's Progress* as 'a classic produced by English Puritanism of the seventeenth century' but not residing there. 'It is', according to Leavis, 'hard to think of that relation to the sectarian exclusiveness of his polemical and damnation-dispensing theology as conducive to a generous creative power.' A high-water mark Leavis may well provide, but to locate the origins of the critical discourse that enables him to identify *The Pilgrim's Progress* as a 'humane classic', and in doing so to distinguish it from a document 'of sectarian controversy', we need to go back to, and inspect in more detail, the Romantic period.[13]

What we find there is not only a deviation from, and a distortion of, Bunyan's theological message that has, perhaps too hurriedly in the past, been seen as the sum total of comments made by Romantic heavyweights such as Coleridge and Scott, but also the sustenance of a particular type of 'creative power' manifested in the kind of radical self-inspection that we associate, first, in the period with Wordsworth's *The Prelude* (1805; published 1850). Perhaps more surprisingly, we also find, particularly in William Blake's prophetic visions, Coleridge's marginalia to *The Pilgrim's Progress*, and in Scott's account of the Cameronian community in *The Heart of Midlothian* (1818), an abiding interest

---

[9] Michael Davies, *Graceful Reading: Theology and Narrative in the Works of John Bunyan* (Oxford: Oxford University Press, 2002), 351.

[10] See also Chapter 4 in this volume.

[11] Davies, *Graceful Reading*, 18.

[12] Vincent Newey, '"With the eyes of my understanding": Bunyan, Experience, and Acts of Interpretation', in N. H. Keeble (ed.), *John Bunyan: Conventicle and Parnassus* (Oxford: Clarendon Press, 1988), 190n. Leavis's Signet Classics afterword is reprinted in Sharrock (ed.), *Pilgrim's Progress: A Casebook*, 204–20 (204).

[13] Sharrock (ed.), *Pilgrim's Progress: A Casebook*, 205 and 208.

in some of the specific details of Bunyan's soteriology. *Grace Abounding to the Chief of Sinners* (1666) and *The Pilgrim's Progress* provide, according to Newey, 'a telling perspective from which to explain and interpret emphases' within the writing of Wordsworth, and the same holds true, as we will see, for Blake, Coleridge, and Scott to different degrees.[14] Yet that key separation of theological content from literary technique, important as it is, does not, I would suggest, exhaust or entirely explain the Romantic response to Bunyan and the discrete ways in which he influenced a group of writers as remarkable for their differences as they are for their similarities.

WALTER SCOTT, S. T. COLERIDGE, AND ALLEGORY

We do not have to go far to find documents that attest to Bunyan's imaginative powers despite his perceived Calvinist belief in predestination and justification by faith alone. This is the tenet of Walter Scott's review of the 1830 edition of *The Pilgrim's Progress*, which begins on the defensive, excusing Bunyan's decision to confine Ignorance to hell for his inability to produce a certificate for his calling, right at the point of admittance to the Celestial City. Scott seemingly writes this off as an aberrant moment in an otherwise uncontroversial work, which 'might be perused without offence by sober-minded Christians of all persuasions'.[15] Scott's understanding of *The Pilgrim's Progress* stresses inclusivity in the reading process, even whilst he navigates the perceived exclusivity of the 'discomfiting creedal context' that later occupied Leavis and was more deeply embedded in critical responses to Bunyan by Donald Davie, Gordon Campbell, and John Stachniewski.[16] Scott delights in the 'simple and captivating tales', the sympathy aroused by the experiences of Christiana, her children, and Mercie in *Part II*, and the character Great-heart whose strength and valour support 'the natural feebleness and timidity' of the female pilgrims.[17] For David Walker, however, Scott's review is pernicious because it depoliticizes Bunyan, attempting to 'whitewash the radicalism' and political dissent from *The Pilgrim's Progress*. Walker sees in Scott a wilful blindness arising from 'his determination not to hold up to the radicals of the present the political theology of the

---

[14] Vincent Newey, 'Wordsworth, Bunyan, and the Puritan Mind', in Vincent Newey, *Centring the Self: Subjectivity, Society and Reading from Thomas Gray to Thomas Hardy* (Aldershot: Scolar Press, 1995), 69–86 (69).

[15] See Sharrock (ed.), *Pilgrim's Progress: A Casebook*, 58.

[16] See Davies, *Graceful Reading*, 20. See also Donald Davie, *A Gathered Church: The Literature of Dissenting Interest 1700–1930* (London: Routledge & Kegan Paul, 1978); Gordon Campbell, 'Fishing in Other Men's Waters: Bunyan and the Theologians', in Keeble (ed.), *Bunyan: Conventicle and Parnassus*; and John Stachniewski, *The Persecutory Imagination: English Puritanism and the Literature of Despair* (Oxford: Clarendon Press, 1991).

[17] Sharrock (ed.), *Pilgrim's Progress: A Casebook*, 60.

revolutionaries of the past'.[18] In 1830, the question of religious toleration and hostility towards Catholics and evangelicals was a live issue, even allowing for the fact that a lull was felt in political radicalism during the succession of William IV.

That Scott is thinking primarily in aesthetic rather than in soteriological terms is underlined by his comments on Bunyan's use of character names, which 'saves the author the trouble of tagging his characters with descriptions, always somewhat awkward, of person and disposition'. He raises two points regarding verisimilitude. One considers the way that names such as 'Fair-speech' and 'By-ends' have the advantage of being probable enough to approach reality whilst still 'maintaining the reader's attention on the author's meaning'. The other is drawn from his memory of reading *The Pilgrim's Progress* as a child when imagination took hold as 'we stumbled betwixt the literal story and metaphorical explanation'.[19] In both cases an interesting tension is disclosed in Scott's view of figurative language: the implication is that the story, the vehicle, of *The Pilgrim's Progress* needs to be read carefully in order for it not to become divided from its tenor or meaning. Interpretively, this gap is more pronounced in Coleridge's often maligned distinction between the Bunyan he associated with Parnassus—the site of the Muses in Greek mythology—and the Bunyan of the conventicle, of Nonconformist seventeenth-century religious assemblies.

The comments can be found in Lecture 3 of the 1818 Literary Lectures, in which Coleridge makes, for him, some crucial distinctions about the effectiveness of the allegorical mode in Spenser, Milton, and Bunyan:

> The dullest and most defective parts of Spenser are those in which we are compelled to think of his agents as allegories [. . .] but in that admirable Allegory, the first Part of Pilgrim's Progress, which delights every one, the interest is so great that [in] spite of all the writer's attempts to force the allegoric purpose on the Reader's mind by his strange names—Old Stupidity of the Tower of Honesty, &c &c—his piety was baffled by his Genius, and the Bunyan of Parnassus had the better of Bunyan of the conventicle—and with the same illusion as we read any tale known to be fictitious, as a Novel—we go on with his characters as real persons, who had been nicknamed by their neighbours.[20]

Here Coleridge attributes to *The Pilgrim's Progress* a doubleness whereby literary 'realism', for want of a better expression, is opposed to allegory. The message contained in the latter is felt to interfere with the trajectory of the story of Christian and, as with Scott, Bunyan's use of proper names is seen as somewhat artificial. Coleridge's logic is that the theological meaning, when too overtly stressed, puts pressure on Bunyan to neglect his characters' emotional responses to joy and suffering. Davies, following Janet

---

[18] David Walker, 'Bunyan's Reception in the Romantic Period', in Owens and Sim (eds.), *Reception, Appropriation, Recollection*, 49–67 (55, 59).

[19] Sharrock (ed.), *Pilgrim's Progress: A Casebook*, 61, 63, and 65.

[20] *The Collected Works of Samuel Taylor Coleridge*, vol. 5: *Lectures 1808–1819 On Literature*, Part 2, ed. R. A. Foakes (London: Routledge & Kegan Paul, 1987), 103.

Martin Soskice, has demonstrated that the distinction is a false one, because it implies that metaphor is used to replace a 'literal' biblical meaning. This ignores the fact that what Bunyan teaches is a way of reading the Word: a 'shared Scripture-centred interpretive and descriptive tradition' that belongs *to* Scripture.[21] It mistakenly views *logos* or doctrine as something qualitatively different from imaginative or metaphorical language, rather than perceiving that scriptural exegesis is of a piece with Bunyan's allegorical method.

In reading *The Pilgrim's Progress* we are, then, faced with a profound distinction between the thoughts of Coleridge about literary merit and those of Bunyan about Christianity. Two points require some explication, and are best seen in close analysis of Bunyan's prose style. The first involves the experience of reading Bunyan for realistic content; the second involves addressing in more detail the specific way in which Coleridge conceived of allegory. In the first case, evidence for the kind of genius that results in a reader's desire to suspend disbelief and pursue the stories of Christian and Christiana as though they were 'real persons' can be found by looking at the opening to *Part II*. There is an ease with which Bunyan returns us to the scene of his first dream and introduces Mr Sagacity to the company of his dreamer. Their mutual recollections about the prior journey of Christian, the Dreamer's enquiries about his wife and family, and the shared conclusions about the gossip circulating in the City of Destruction suggest the freshness of new acquaintance, endorsing the Dreamer's comment that the two travellers simply 'fell into discourse' (*PP*, 175). The prose is scuffed here and there with simple idiomatic turns of phrase such as 'Too true' (*PP*, 175) and 'I dare say' (*PP*, 176) that direct the conversation without ostentation. A switch in style follows as the Dreamer turns to consider the 'heavy Cogitation' of Christiana's regret and grief at the memory of her husband's 'restless Groans, brinish Tears and self-bemoanings' (*PP*, 177). The anguish of Christiana's exclamation 'Lord have mercy upon me a Sinner' (*PP*, 178), while her young sons stand helpless by, is deeply moving, while in her dream of Christian, the sense of fear and bodily paralysis as 'two very ill favoured ones' (*PP*, 178) debate their ability to wrest her soul for themselves is palpably real.

The manner in which the Dreamer picks over Christiana's torment, embellishing and strengthening its purchase on the reader at each turn, lies at the heart of Coleridge's attribution of 'genius' to Bunyan. However, any exclusive focus on the way that technique informs verisimilitude comes without the specific theological exposition offered by Bunyan in the marginal notations and elsewhere. This returns us to the second key point concerning Coleridge's conceptualization of allegory. The example of Christiana's grief demonstrates that her experience should properly be seen as reminding the reader of the repeated motif of the tears of the righteous shed in despair, a point that the Dreamer makes to Mr Sagacity in the discussion of Christian's journey to salvation immediately prior to the introduction of Christiana (*PP*, 176). As Valentine Cunningham points out, such experiences 'are offered as readable signs [...] because they're modelled on biblical

---

[21] Davies, *Graceful Reading*, 222.

examples which are held to function with a ready legibility'.²² We might compare the tears that Mercie sheds for the 'poor Relations' (*PP*, 186) that she leaves behind, which is elucidated by Christiana through her remembrance of Psalm 126:

> I hope, *Mercie*, these Tears of thine will not be lost, for the truth hath said, *That they that sow in Tears shall reap in Joy, in singing. And he that goeth forth and weepeth, bearing precious seed, shall doubtless come again with rejoicing, bringing his Sheaves with him.* (*PP*, 186)

Allegory in a Coleridgean sense is perceived to be functional and mechanical, foregrounding a hermeneutic 'process of recognizing double references': on the one hand, the literal story of Christian or Christiana, on the other, the theological meaning that is attributed to their experiences.²³ Bunyan is at his best as a writer of fiction, according to Coleridge, when he stops thinking about his larger design and attends to the details before him: 'for if the allegoric personage be strongly individualized so as to interest us, we cease to think of it as allegory'.²⁴ In *The Statesman's Manual* (1816), Coleridge elucidates this viewpoint, and his preference for the Symbol:

> On the other hand a Symbol [...] is characterized by a translucence of the Special in the Individual or of the General in the Especial or of the Universal in the General [...]. It always partakes of the reality which it renders intelligible; and while it enunciates the whole, abides itself as a living part in that Unity, of which it is the representative.²⁵

In Coleridge's terms, allegorical meaning fails to partake of the 'reality which it renders intelligible' as it is drawn from a different order of meaning: an abstract truth revealed elsewhere. The Symbol, in contrast, is characterized as an organic form of revelation, wherein the general or abstract is discovered within the visible world for those privileged enough to see it. The pattern is part of a larger historical movement in which the Romantic period is usually viewed as a watershed: according to Seamus Perry, 'before the Romantics, truth [...] was deeply one and universal and general; after, it becomes reconceived as particular and local and individual—precisely that which is beyond any successful generalization'.²⁶ While Romantic writers may, then, be seen to 'universalize' Bunyan's meaning, there is a corresponding particularization in their method through

---

²² Valentine Cunningham, 'Glossing and Glozing: Bunyan and Allegory', in Keeble (ed.), *Bunyan: Conventicle and Parnassus*, 217–40 (223).
²³ Davies, *Graceful Reading*, 221.
²⁴ *Collected Works of Samuel Taylor Coleridge*, vol. 5: *Lectures 1808–1819*, Part 2, 102.
²⁵ *Collected Works of Samuel Taylor Coleridge*, vol. 6: *Lay Sermons*, ed. R. J. White (London: Routledge & Kegan Paul, 1972), 30.
²⁶ Seamus Perry, 'Coleridge, Bunyan, and the Arts of Bafflement', *The Wordsworth Circle*, 32 (2001), 89–95 (94).

which invocations of Bunyan's soteriology can be seen to contain as much difference as similarity.

WORDSWORTH, *THE PRELUDE*, AND WILLIAM BLAKE

The test case is Wordsworth's narrative verse, specifically *The Prelude*, in which allusions to *The Pilgrim's Progress* abound, and to which, unsurprisingly, Coleridge's observations apply most readily. Like Bunyan, Wordsworth's conversion narrative sees the poet wavering between intense experiences of joy and despair, bound up with guilt and self-reprobation, but as Lucy Newlyn observes, Wordsworth's inheritance from Bunyan of the issues of election, justification, and predestination 'is as much a process of revision as of absorption'.[27] Bunyan argues throughout *Grace Abounding*, for example, that the guilt of sin, which causes him to despair, can only be taken off by belief in Christ's sacrifice as recorded in the Word of the Gospel: 'the guilt of sin did help me much, for still as that would come upon me, the blood of Christ did take it off again' (*GA*, 40). A characteristic point of biblical authority can be found in Galatians 2:16: 'even we have believed in Christ Jesus, in order to be justified by faith in Christ, and not by works of the law, because by works of the law shall no one be justified'. Wordsworth too can be seen to owe something to the Lutheran exposition of Scripture, and when we hear of Wordsworth operating in a Protestant 'tradition',[28] a source can be found in Luther's rejection of the Law as a source of justification in *Colloquia Mensalia*: 'Therefore let us leave Moses to his laws [. . .] *which God hath planted in nature* [. . .] which concern God's true worshipping and service, and a civil life.'[29] In *The Prelude* we find, however, that this Protestant emphasis on the morality embedded within human nature is blended with the influence of David Hartley, Joseph Priestley, and, above all, Jean-Jacques Rousseau, which manifests itself as a belief in a God who can 'be perceived in the patterns of nature', not the Word of the Gospel, evincing the language of late eighteenth-century radicalism and not of Bunyan.[30]

It becomes apparent in the opening sequence of *The Prelude*, for example, that Wordsworth maps out the terms of his quest to understand the poet's calling in ways that directly recall Bunyan, but that the similarities operate within a context of difference.

---

[27] Lucy Newlyn, '"The noble living and the noble dead": Community in *The Prelude*', in Stephen Gill (ed.), *The Cambridge Companion to Wordsworth* (Cambridge: Cambridge University Press, 2003), 55–69 (60).

[28] See, for example, Newey, 'Wordsworth, Bunyan, and the Puritan Mind', and Newlyn '"The noble living and the noble dead"'.

[29] Martin Luther, *Colloquia Mensalia; or the Familiar Discourses*, 2 vols (London: W. Bennett, 1840), 1: 282; emphasis added.

[30] Newlyn, '"The noble living and the noble dead"', 58.

The poem begins with a sign of grace—'Oh there is blessing in this gentle breeze'—and throws the reader into the present tense to share this blessing with the poet: '*Now* I am free, enfranchised and at large.' The spirit of relaxed community is the same as that through which Mr Sagacity and the Dreamer 'fell into discourse', but the poet's guide is drawn from the natural world:

> The earth is all before me: with a heart
> Joyous, nor scared at its own liberty,
> I look about, and should the guide I chuse
> Be nothing better than a wandering cloud,
> I cannot miss my way.[31]

Similarity comes in the ability to choose 'the way', but also in the swiftness with which the right way might be lost or missed. So while Wordsworth looks back in order to invoke the potential for new beginnings—referencing the culmination of John Milton's *Paradise Lost* (1667; 1674)—his strong declaration of purpose—'I *cannot* miss my way'—is more conditional than it would initially appear. Just as 'the way' for Christian signifies an inner spiritual journey that is manifested in the literal act of travelling, so Wordsworth's 'way' lies underfoot but also within the poet's heart and in the growth of the poet's mind.

Judging and keeping to the correct path become a matter of individual responsibility and interpretation; the dangers in leaving this path have already been suggested in the lines immediately prior to these when Wordsworth indicates the poet's recent escape from 'City walls […] / A prison where he hath been long immured'.[32] Placed at the opening of the poem, these lines recall Christian's escape from the City of Destruction, but also from the town of Vanity Fair. For Christian, the way of the righteous is the 'narrow way' (*PP*, 41). This is the way that lies right up the Hill called 'Difficulty' (*PP*, 41), the way from which Worldly-Wiseman attempts to steer Christian ('His turning thee out of the way'; *PP*, 23). As in *The Pilgrim's Progress*, so too in *The Prelude*, falling from 'the way' is a spiritual anxiety and both authors fear 'the precariousness of the […] sense of calling […] which compels them to establish their credentials through revaluation of the past and, in the process, make trial of their ability to meet the challenge of doubt'.[33] Bunyan records that 'there are in our Lives, gross Sins; many horrible Backslidings; also we oft-times suck and drink in many abominable Errors and deceitful Opinions' (*MW*, 11: 179). Wordsworth's signs of grace or blessing are also countered by doubts and backslidings, but in the case of *The Prelude*, the poet's inability to make these signs fully legible suggest that they lie too far within the particularity of his experience.

---

[31] William Wordsworth, *The Prelude*, Book 1, ll. 15–19, in *The Major Works*, ed. Stephen Gill, rev. edn (1984; Oxford: Oxford University Press, 2000), 375; emphasis added. All references to *The Prelude* are taken from this edition.

[32] Wordsworth, *The Prelude*, Book 1, ll. 7–8.

[33] Newey, 'Wordsworth, Bunyan, and the Puritan Mind', 73.

In Book 7, Wordsworth remembers and revaluates in great detail his sojourn in London prior to returning to the Lake District. While the structure clearly owes much to Bunyan's Vanity Fair, the emphasis is entirely different. Gone is the sense that pattern can be discerned through the relationship between experience and the Word. This is replaced by Wordsworth's establishment of what Newlyn calls 'the deep patterning of consciousness' through 'sights, sounds and sensations (not through abstract ideas)'.[34] Idly wandering the city's urban maze, for example, the poet, who is occupied in deep inward reflection, suddenly encounters a blind beggar with a sign around his neck. As Coleridge put it in *The Statesman's Manual*, Wordsworth discovers in the apparently chance occurrence a translucent meaningful centre:

> And once, far-travelled in such mood, beyond
> The reach of common indications, lost
> Amid the moving pageant, 'twas my chance
> Abruptly to be smitten with the view
> Of a blind Beggar, who, with upright face,
> Stood propped against a Wall, upon his Chest
> Wearing a written paper, to explain
> The story of the Man, and who he was.
> My mind did at this spectacle turn round
> As with the might of waters, and it seemed
> To me that in this Label was a type,
> Or emblem, of the utmost that we know,
> Both of ourselves and of the universe;
> And, on the shape of the unmoving man,
> His fixèd face and sightless eyes, I looked
> As if admonished from another world.
>
>   Though reared upon the base of outward things,
> These, chiefly, are such structures as the mind
> Builds for itself.[35]

Noticeably, Wordsworth's language partakes of Bunyan's emblematic force. Above 'common indications', the recollection implies a level of privileged insight, a blessing or a sign of grace that returns the poet to the rightful 'way', having been 'lost' in doubt. The passage is structured to suggest a caution against the gloom brought on by introspection and against pondering too deeply on matters unintelligible to human comprehension. The emphasis lies not in the universal, however, but very pointedly in the individual, particular, and conditional: 'My mind', 'to me', 'as if'.

Wordsworth's evaluation of the scene affirms the shaping role of the imagination, the 'structures of the mind' or patterning of consciousness, which, discerned in the

---

[34] Newlyn, '"The noble living and the noble dead"', 64.
[35] Wordsworth, *The Prelude*, Book 7, ll. 608–26.

apparent 'chance' of sense impressions, bespeaks a larger design. Rather than being a Bunyanesque emblem in which belief in Christ's sacrifice is reaffirmed after a period of doubt, the passage is a self-conscious debate about the relationship between chance and intention. Is the conjunction of the blind beggar and the poet an arbitrary occurrence or a designation of purposeful design? The anxiety for Wordsworth, reformulated by Harold Bloom, arises from 'an uneasy alternation of two opposing superstitions: either everything that happens to us is arbitrary and haphazard or everything that happens to us is determined or even overdetermined by fate'.[36] *The Pilgrim's Progress* does not come to us with this kind of metaphysical question, as it resides wholly within what Edward Bostetter called a 'Christian syntax'.[37] Wordsworth's terms and language choice are close to—and emerge from—those of Bunyan, in terms of their experimental enquiry into redemptive possibilities, but the encounter with the blind beggar demonstrates that their substance and intention are massively different. The dormant pattern of the everyday is revealed to hold symbolic content for the imagination attuned to the language of nature. A conversion narrative in the Protestant tradition of Bunyan? Yes. But symbol replaces allegory and nature replaces the Word.

The motif of revising the Protestant tradition of meditation and self-questioning can also be seen as an organizing force in William Blake's prophetic writing. Unlike Wordsworth and Coleridge, however, Blake eschews the Romantic discourse of the symbolic content inherent in the everyday and constructs his own version of allegory through a visionary poetics. As Jonathan Roberts and Christopher Rowland argue, Blake follows Bunyan in the way that he repeatedly contests Calvinist exegesis, 'insofar as it promotes division' and 'disintegration' leading to 'a world fractured by the elevation of some and the rejection of others'.[38] Far from avoiding the discomfiture of Bunyan's creedal context, Blake shares a vocabulary with his precursor and works through precisely the same difficulties involving the proper recognition of belief and salvation.

If we take a characteristic extract from the epic poem *Milton* (c.1800–04), we find that Blake exploits the language of the conventicle to overturn the notion of justification by law alone:

> Glory! Glory! Glory to the Holy Lamb of God!
> I touch the heavens as an instrument to glorify the Lord.
> The Elect shall meet the Redeemed: on Albion's rocks they shall meet,
> Astonished at the transgressor, in him beholding the Saviour.
> And the Elect shall say to the Redeemed, 'We behold it is of divine

---

[36] Harold Bloom, *Kabbalah and Criticism* (New York: Seabury Press, 1975), 49.

[37] Edward Bostetter, *The Romantic Ventriloquists: Wordsworth, Coleridge, Keats, Shelley, Byron*, rev. edn (1963; Seattle and London: University of Washington Press, 1975), 4.

[38] Jonathan Roberts and Christopher Rowland, 'William Blake', in Rebecca Lemon, Emma Mason, Jonathan Roberts, and Christopher Rowland (eds.), *The Blackwell Companion to the Bible* (Oxford: Wiley-Blackwell, 2009), 373–82 (373).

> Mercy alone, of free gift & election that we live.
> Our virtues & cruel goodnesses have deserved eternal death.'
> Thus they weep upon the fatal brook of Albion's river.[39]

The immediate context for Blake's epic is a personal vision of Milton's return from heaven to revitalize the poet's flagging inspiration and allow him to conjure a universe wherein the actions of Satan can properly be judged. The idiosyncrasies of the mythology are held together and made legible by the language and structure of Protestant thought, particularly the Calvinist emphasis on election and reprobation. In a typical moment of Blakean revelation, the race called the 'Elect' undergo a paradigm shift in their encounter with Christ 'the Saviour', becoming aware that 'Divine / Mercy alone' holds the route to salvation. The 'Virtues' and 'Cruel Goodnesses' are patently actions undertaken in a mistaken aim to gain salvation through the law.

Both 'Saviour' and 'Transgressor', Blake believed that Christ deliberately flouted the legal aspects of the Old Testament. In *The Marriage of Heaven and Hell* (1790), he describes the manner in which Christ broke the Ten Commandments, arguing that 'no virtue can exist without breaking these ten commandments. Jesus was all virtue, and acted from impulse, not from rules.'[40] Blake's sometimes obscure soteriological path meets with Bunyan's here: for a while the two walk the same way. Where difference arises is in Blake's stress upon the free reign of the imagination and his inward sense—moving into the territory of seventeenth-century Quakerism—that Christ's resurrection is an action repeatable within all men (not only the so-called Calvinist elect).[41] As Robert Rix puts it, 'Christ's Resurrection was', for Blake, 'not only an historical event, but also a model for every man's potential for eternal life in the spirit.'[42] Roberts and Rowland make it clear that this 'inner' resurrection of spirit is achievable for Blake only through the imagination. Blake distinguishes imagination from the rational faculties of the mind and so comes close again to Bunyan's insistence that belief in Christ must come through the heart or instinct rather than the reason. Preoccupation with 'Old Testament emphasis on morality, Law, and separation of the sacred from the profane'—or indeed the elect from the reprobate—concern both Bunyan and Blake equally.[43]

Blake's imagination catches fire in debating Protestant exegesis. In 1824 he produced twenty-eight illustrations of *The Pilgrim's Progress* that further demonstrate the fact. Thirty years earlier, in an illustration called *The Man Sweeping the Interpreter's Parlour*, the pattern for the larger work was laid down. Interestingly, the illustration entirely circumvents

---

[39] *The Poems of William Blake*, ed. W. H. Stevenson, text by David V. Erdman (London: Longman, 1971), 503–04.
[40] *The Poems of William Blake*, ed. Stevenson, 121.
[41] For discussion of Bunyan's perception of the Quaker 'Light within', see Davies, *Graceful Reading*, 76.
[42] Robert Rix, *William Blake and the Cultures of Radical Christianity* (Aldershot: Ashgate, 2007), 18.
[43] Roberts and Rowland, 'William Blake', 380.

the literal or realistic content of the emblem in Interpreter's House and goes straight for a visionary interpretation of Bunyan's meaning. The man sweeping is given devil's wings, while the 'Damsel' of Bunyan's text is no recognizable housemaid but rather an angel who enters with a glow of light from the left-hand side. The parlour in which the scene occurs is replaced by a backdrop of spectral light effects. The endorsement of Bunyan's explication is visually striking: 'He that began to sweep at first, is the Law; but She that brought water, and did sprinkle it, is the Gospel' (*PP*, 30). Equally, the illustrations chosen for the 1824 sequence suggest a continual engagement with Christian's emergence from self-division brought on by legalism. Gerda S. Norvig sees Blake emphasizing the internal psychological development of the Dreamer in the sequence. In the second plate, for example, Blake depicts Christian's burden, which 'is figured as itself an emblem of self-division, as if it were both growing from and striving with Christian's bodily form'. In the next illustration, Christian meets Evangelist; Norvig explains that the third plate develops pictorially out of the second as the book or Old Testament, positioned to the right, is structurally replaced by the figure of Evangelist, an embodiment of the Gospel, 'the inner life of the Christian Word come suddenly to life'.[44] While the notion of Christian being self-divided is communicated in terms of the Romantic imagination, the psychodrama of the sequence and its terms are drawn directly from the theological content of Bunyan's work.

The manner in which he dissociates true salvation from justification by the Law can be explained, as with Wordsworth, through Blake's allusions to Bunyan, but the explanation needs also to recognize that a shared conceptual context does not equal shared beliefs. The logical extension of Blake's antinomianism actually moves him closer to a seventeenth-century sect, despised by Bunyan, known as the Ranters. Throughout Bunyan's writings, including *The Pilgrim's Progress*, Ranters are depicted as opportunists, extreme antinomians who might, as Ignorance tells Christian, 'loosen the reines of our lust, and tollerate us to live as we list' (*PP*, 148). Although they placed emphasis on human unrighteousness and the impossibility of living by the Law, they advocated that, though sinful, the elect could, in effect, never be damned. Conviction of sin, then, was not seen to lead to righteousness in Christ: instead it led to the wholesale embrace of carnal pleasure for its own sake. At the opening of Blake's *Songs of Experience* (1794), Earth bemoans its 'free love with bondage bound', linking sexual to seasonal regeneration: 'Does spring hide its joy, / When buds and blossoms grow?' This is balanced with the kind of sentiment we read in 'To Tirzah': 'The death of Jesus set me free.'[45] Blake's debt to the traditions of Protestant exegesis in the seventeenth century is, then, a complex blend of ingredients, including the free expression of sexual love linked to faith in Christ and the poetic faculties that arise from the contraries of legalism. His interest in Protestant soteriology is not, however, a cosmetic addition to an otherwise opaque personal vision: it is the foundation of nearly all of his religious and poetic thought.

[44] Norvig, *Dark Figures*, 142–43.
[45] *The Poems of William Blake*, ed. Stevenson, 210–11, 591.

Coleridge's Marginalia to *The Pilgrim's Progress* and Scott's *The Heart of Midlothian*

Attending to Romantic allusions to Bunyan, and the inheritance of some of the tropes of the Protestant conversion narrative, in the work of writers like Wordsworth and Blake helps us better to understand the way that *The Pilgrim's Progress* became a so-called 'literary' artefact in the early nineteenth century and to determine of what this literariness consisted. Key points include the rejection of allegory for symbolism, the rescription of the pilgrim's salvation into an inner psychodrama, the consequent privileging of self-reliance over accommodation to Christ, and the focus on realistic human suffering to the exclusion of theological meaning. Blake's illustrations to *The Pilgrim's Progress* suggest that he believed the essence of Bunyan's vision to be Lutheran and not Calvinist. So far I've presented Coleridge and Walter Scott as antagonists and misreaders, responsible for splitting *The Pilgrim's Progress* between a seventeenth-century 'damnation dispensing' Bunyan and a Romantic literary Bunyan. But that is in itself a conclusion lacking in contextualization. A brief overview of Coleridge's marginalia to *The Pilgrim's Progress* provides some emendation.

Coleridge owned two copies of *The Pilgrim's Progress*, including the 1830 edition with which I began, and it was Southey's 100-page introduction that seems to have prompted him to annotate both. As N. H. Keeble comments, 'Coleridge's chief interest in both these later sets of marginalia (and particularly in the first) was theological rather than literary.'[46] Coleridge's eye is initially drawn to defending Bunyan against Southey's historical misjudgements concerning Bunyan's persecution for his faith, berating his 'partizanship for Laud, Sheldon, and the Stuarts'. When Southey notes that Bunyan has been 'most wrongfully represented as having been the victim of intolerant laws, and prelatical opposition' on one hand, and on the other that 'He remained a prisoner for twelve years', Coleridge is scandalized, adding 'O S! S!—would I had the couching needle—tho' verily this is a very *Niagara* of a Cataract! No *gutta* serena, but a *mare* furiosum.' Coleridge turns on Southey the accusations of wilful blindness that David Walker levels at Scott. Coleridge also sees in Southey the hypocrisy of one who can side with Stuart authority in breaking up the conventicles, when as a younger man he espoused their shared radical notions of Pantisocracy: '*Then* you saw clearly the difference of the occasional *religious* persecutions under the Republic and the Protectorate—& the foul cruelties enacted by the Prelates for *State & Church* interests under the first and 2^d Charles!'[47]

---

[46] N. H. Keeble, '"Of him thousands daily Sing and talk": Bunyan and his Reputation', in Keeble (ed.), *Bunyan: Conventicle and Parnassus*, 241–63 (255–56).

[47] *Collected Works of Samuel Taylor Coleridge*, vol. 12: *Marginalia*, Part 1, ed. George Whalley (London: Routledge & Kegan Paul, 1984), 808, 810, 807.

Instead of bypassing Bunyan's politics and faith, the *Marginalia* see Coleridge engaging in the kind of graceful reading that Michael Davies so carefully depicts. Coleridge marks the Dreamer's vision of Christian in self-doubt at the burning pit where 'one of the Wicked ones got behind him, and stepped up softly to him, and, whisperingly suggested many grievous blasphemies to him, which he verily thought had proceeded from his own mind'. Coleridge's thoughts turn immediately to Luther, 'ever reminding the individual, that *not* he but Christ is to redeem him—and that the way to be redeemed is to think with will, mind and affections of Christ, and not on HIMSELF'. Coleridge had previously produced fifteen marginalia on Luther's *Colloquia Mensalia*, and everywhere in Bunyan he saw the thought of Luther. His note appended to one of Bunyan's sermons, included in the Southey edition, makes the point clear:

> It is the fashion of the day to call every man, who in his writings or discourses gives a prominence to the doctrines on which beyond all others the first Reformers separated from the Romish Communion, a Calvinist. Bunyan *may* have been one; but *I* have met with nothing in his Writings (with the exception of his Anti-paedobaptism, to which he lays no *saving* importance) that is more characteristically *Lutheran*.

Ironically, considering Coleridge's reputation in initiating a 'secular' *Pilgrim's Progress*, he then turns to a brand of mini-allegory to explain Bunyan's distinction between 'doers' and 'talkers':

> It is indeed Faith alone that saves us; but such a Faith, as cannot be alone. Purity and Beneficence are the Epidermis, Faith=Love the Cutis vera of Christianity—Morality is the outward Cloth, Faith the Lining—both together form the Wedding-garment, given to the true Believer by Christ—even his own Garment of Righteousness, which like the Loaves & Fishes he mysteriously multiplies. The images of the Sun in the earthly dew-drops are unsubstantial phantoms; but God's Thoughts are Things; the Images of God, of the Sun of Righteousness, in the spiritual Dew-drops are Substances, imperishable Substances.

The parable of the loaves and fishes is recorded in all four Gospels (Matthew 14:17, 15:32ff; Mark 6:35ff; Luke 9:12ff; John 6:5ff); the points of authority for Coleridge's image of reflection and the dewdrops can be found in Psalm 19 and Deuteronomy 32:2.[48]

The *Marginalia* don't, of course, discount the potency and extensive influence of the comments on allegory, but they do demonstrate that Coleridge found literary inspiration in the drama of Christian's faith and they complicate some of the lines in the debate about unhistoricized generalizations in Romantic literary criticism. This is also the suggestion behind the note that Coleridge adds to his copy of Scott's novel *The Heart of Midlothian* (1818): 'Calvinism never put on a less rigid form, never smoothed its brow & softened its voice more winningly than in the Pilgrim's Progress.'[49] For his part, Scott

---

[48] *Collected Works of Samuel Taylor Coleridge*, vol. 12: *Marginalia*, Part 1, 813, 810, 814–15.
[49] *Collected Works of Samuel Taylor Coleridge*, vol. 12: *Marginalia*, Part 1, 801.

directly labels Bunyan a 'Calvinist' in the *Quarterly Review*, and the story of Jeanie Deans in *The Heart of Midlothian* underlines this view. What, then, sends Coleridge back to *The Pilgrim's Progress* feeling a soft and winning voice? The answer is probably Scott's hero of conservative moderation, the Duke of Argyle, but it is undeniable that large sections of Scott's novel draw drama out of a spiritual crisis that invokes Bunyan's pilgrims.

The action of *The Heart of Midlothian* is initially embedded in the doctrine of the lowland Cameronian community still extant in Edinburgh during the Porteous Riots of 1736. It is represented most forcefully in the novel by the character of Davie Deans, father to Jeanie and Effie. Scott's city is one of Old Testament values and Presbyterian caricatures: Davie believes in 'an eye for an eye, a tooth for a tooth, life for life, blood for blood'. The intractability of the law, and the despair it provokes, are satirized by Scott in the plot of Effie Deans's imprisonment on suspicion of child murder. The narrator leaves us in no doubt that her father's religion has played a large part in her demise. Fear of damnation 'created a division of feelings in Effie's bosom, and deterred her from her intended confidence in her sister'. Legally, if Effie confided her pregnancy in her sister she would escape imprisonment. The moral steadfastness of Jeanie—her adherence to the letter of the law—prevents her from providing false testimony during the dramatic scenes of Effie's trial. At every step Scott's language is drawn from *Grace Abounding* and *The Pilgrim's Progress*. Ratcliffe offers to take the 'crazed' Madge Wildfire in hand 'and gar her haud the straight path'. Jeanie resigns herself to the fact that her marriage to Reuben Butler is now impossible due to the stigma attached to her sister: 'No, Reuben, I'll bring disgrace to nay man's hearth [...] I will bear my load alone; the back is made for the burden.' The same sense of despair comes to dominate her father's outlook as he turns inward to nurse his own burden: 'Leave me, sirs—leave me; I maun warstle wi' this trial in privacy and on my knees', while George Staunton, the father of Effie's child, embraces his role as villain declaiming, 'You see before you a wretch predestined to evil here and hereafter.'[50]

As with Wordsworth, Scott blends his observations on Presbyterianism with a Rousseauesque discourse, in which Effie is characterized as an 'untaught child of nature' whose virtuous impulses clash with the rigorous tenets of the Cameronian sect. This contrasts with Bunyan's insistence on 'original and inward pollution' (*GA*, 28) in *Grace Abounding*. But the journey out of Presbyterian Edinburgh—and the corresponding symbolic journey of Jeanie—is noticeably conducted with reference to Bunyan and not Rousseau. The legend of Jeanie around which Scott builds his story involves her walking barefoot to London to seek the Duke of Argyle, whose merciful intervention grants her an interview with Queen Caroline, who promises to overturn Effie's death sentence. Jeanie is, for a time, accompanied on her 'pilgrimage' by Madge Wildfire, through which Scott invokes the companionship of Christiana and Mercie. Madge's knowledge of *The Pilgrim's Progress* is expert and she sings 'John Bunyan's ditties'. The narrator tells us

---

[50] Sir Walter Scott, *The Heart of Midlothian* (London: A. & C. Black, 1945), 105, 99, 307, 176, 119, 105, 154.

that Jeanie, in contrast, 'had never read the fanciful and delightful parable' because 'he [Bunyan] was [...] a member of a Baptist congregation'. These references to Bunyan are not just ornamental: they provide the structure of hope and backsliding familiar to us from the Protestant conversion narrative. In interview with Mrs Balchristie on her departure, for example, Jeanie fails to 'find words to justify herself': it is an eloquence she learns by the time she reaches London. Her doubts nearly prompt her to 'turn back and solicit money from, her father', while Madge asks her to 'teach me to find out the narrow way and the strait path'. Like Christian, Jeanie is rewarded for her adherence to the narrow way. Unlike Christian she achieves this through a refusal to relinquish her burden and perjure herself by lying under oath on behalf of Effie (so breaking the ninth commandment).[51]

It is important to stress that the ultimate solution to the plot does not, for Scott, lie within Jeanie's adherence to the law. While she is rewarded for her steadfastness and while Scott depicts the drama of her crisis of faith with sensitivity, Staunton's father, an Anglican clergyman, advises her 'to recollect that the same divine grace dispenses its streams in other kingdoms as well as Scotland'.[52] Such moderate Protestantism is mirrored in the virtues of liberal rule embodied by the Duke of Argyle and Queen Caroline. As in the *Quarterly Review*, Scott adheres to his belief in the judicious capacity of moderate British government. The pilgrimage of Jeanie Deans can be seen, then, as both an idealization of her endurance and a satire on the inflexibility of Presbyterianism. It can also be seen as a product of the brand of Romantic-period 'literariness' with which we began. While I have argued that it would be wrong to whitewash the differences in the responses of individual authors to the work of Bunyan, the trajectory towards secularizing and humanizing *The Pilgrim's Progress* can be seen in miniature in the plot of *The Heart of Midlothian*. If we wanted a 'humane classic' that engages with, but ultimately overturns, sectarian controversy, then *The Heart of Midlothian*, rather than *The Pilgrim's Progress*, would be it. Barbara Johnson is right: the category of the 'literary' is indeed an historical construct. In the Romantic period the development of a literary Bunyan is, however, not as uniform or as bifurcated as the simple division of 'conventicle' and 'Parnassus' would lead us to believe.

Suggested Reading

Coleridge, Samuel Taylor, 'Marginalia to *The Pilgrim's Progress*', in *Collected Works of Samuel Taylor Coleridge*, vol. 12: *Marginalia*, Part 1, ed. George Whalley (London: Routledge & Kegan Paul, 1984), 801–27.
Coleridge, Samuel Taylor, '1818 Literary Lecture 3', in *Collected Works of Samuel Taylor Coleridge*, vol. 5: *Lectures 1808-1819 On Literature*, Part 2, ed. R. A. Foakes (London: Routledge & Kegan Paul, 1987).

---

[51] Scott, *Heart of Midlothian*, 97, 258, 318, 319, 265, 390–91, 270, 313.
[52] Scott, *Heart of Midlothian*, 356.

Davies, Michael, *Graceful Reading: Theology and Narrative in the Works of John Bunyan* (Oxford: Oxford University Press, 2002).

Keeble, N. H., '"Of him thousands daily Sing and talk": Bunyan and his Reputation', in N. H. Keeble (ed.), *John Bunyan: Conventicle and Parnassus* (Oxford: Clarendon Press, 1988), 241–63.

Newlyn, Lucy, '"The noble living and the noble dead": Community in *The Prelude*', in Stephen Gill (ed.), *The Cambridge Companion to Wordsworth* (Cambridge: Cambridge University Press, 2003), 55–69.

Newey, Vincent, 'Wordsworth, Bunyan, and the Puritan Mind', in Vincent Newey, *Centring the Self: Subjectivity, Society and Reading from Thomas Gray to Thomas Hardy* (Aldershot: Scolar Press, 1995), 69–86.

Norvig, Gerda S., *Dark Figures in the Desired Country: Blake's Illustrations to 'The Pilgrim's Progress'* (Berkeley and Los Angeles, CA: University of California Press, 1993).

Scott, Sir Walter, *The Heart of Midlothian* (London: A. & C. Black, 1945).

Sharrock, Roger (ed.), *The Pilgrim's Progress: A Casebook* (London and Basingstoke: Macmillan, 1976).

Walker, David, 'Bunyan's Reception in the Romantic Period', in W. R. Owens and Stuart Sim (eds.), *Reception, Appropriation, Recollection: Bunyan's Pilgrim's Progress* (Bern: Peter Lang, 2007), 49–67.

Wordsworth, William, *The Prelude* (1805), in Stephen Gill (ed.), *The Major Works*, rev. edn (1984; Oxford: Oxford University Press, 2000).

CHAPTER 33

BUNYAN AND THE VICTORIANS

VINCENT NEWEY

The Victorian period was by common consent a secularizing age. This does not necessarily mean that it saw a general decline in religious faith and observance. Indeed, statistics suggest that attendance at Nonconformist places of worship increased steadily throughout the nineteenth century,[1] and it is worth noting in this regard that the Metropolitan Tabernacle built for C. H. Spurgeon, the Baptist preacher, which opened in 1861, held congregations of around six thousand.[2] What Carlyle termed 'the religious classes' supplied at this time a substantial readership for *The Pilgrim's Progress* (1678; 1684), of which, as Mary Hammond has shown, there appeared a stream of didactic editions, including a cheap reissue by Nelsons in 1857 of William Mason's 1813 volume, heavily annotated with doctrinal comment and exhortation.[3]

Nevertheless, as the century progressed, Bunyan's classic became a variable commodity in an increasingly diverse cultural milieu. Hammond describes editorial treatments of the work as a guide to the pioneering spirit (appropriate for an era of imperialist expansion), a gallery of 'characters', an antiquarian text, a coffee-table book, and a shorthand primer. In all these approaches or applications the appeal of *The Pilgrim's Progress* depends on, or is at least significantly underpinned by, Bunyan's creative genius, the quality famously recognized in Coleridge's elevation of 'Bunyan of Parnassus' over 'Bunyan of the Conventicle', the proto-novelist over the theological writer, and in Walter Scott's comparable highlighting of his 'warm imagination and clear and forcible

---

[1] Valentine Cunningham, *Everywhere Spoken Against: Dissent in the Victorian Novel* (Oxford: Clarendon Press, 1975), 106.

[2] Donald Davie, *A Gathered Church: The Literature of the English Dissenting Interest, 1700–1930* (London: Routledge & Kegan Paul, 1978), 88.

[3] Mary Hammond, '*The Pilgrim's Progress* and its Nineteenth-Century Publishers', in W. R. Owens and Stuart Sim (eds.), *Reception, Appropriation, Recollection: Bunyan's Pilgrim's Progress* (Bern: Peter Lang, 2007), 99–118 (104–14). See also Chapter 31 in this volume.

expression'.[4] This same attraction is acknowledged even in the extreme doctrinaire discourse of William Mason, who takes pains to rearm 'spiritually quickened souls' against its perilous seductions:

> Did you ever see your sins, and feel the burden of them, so as to cry out […]? If not, you will look on this precious book as a romance or history which in no way concerns you; you can no more understand the meaning of it, than if it were written in an unknown tongue; for you are yet carnal.[5]

Whatever the strength of orthodox religion in Victorian England, though, the sceptics and apostates were prominent in creative and intellectual circles. Among the writers who responded to or were influenced by Bunyan, they had the initiative and laid secure claim on the future. The period saw important literary-critical reappraisals, most notably Lord Macaulay's seminal appreciation in his review of Robert Southey's 1830 edition of *The Pilgrim's Progress* and James Anthony Froude's landmark study of 1880 for the 'English Men of Letters' series, a work which, combining biography with explication of major and minor texts, consolidated both Bunyan's reputation and the canon.[6] Our focus will nonetheless be drawn mainly to authors whose interest in Bunyan falls within the context of their renunciation of conventional religion—though not Christian morality—and pursuit of alternative philosophies of being. This situation applies in some measure to Froude himself, a man who lost not only his belief but also, when his agnostic novel *The Nemesis of Faith* appeared in 1848, his Oxford fellowship. Throughout his monograph he keeps eloquent watch over a process where, as he views it, the 'fire' of Bunyan's religion, which was that of 'the best and strongest minds in Europe', has become 'but smoke and ashes'. All the same, the Puritans' moral discipline, their 'conviction of sin' resting on obedience to supernatural authority, does remain, for Froude, a compelling reference point, problematically so, in an age of scientific advance and widespread freethinking that excites him for its promise of human progress but disturbs him by its lack of stable values and clear direction. As a whole, moreover, *Bunyan* presents its eponymous subject as an author with an undoubted afterlife in and beyond the present with its 'decomposing theology' because of his personal and literary qualities, which Froude identifies in a range from his 'masculine sense and strong, modest intellect' to the Shakespearean 'sympathy' informing his creation of 'flesh and blood' characters.[7] This is a fair argument and brings Bunyan in from the periphery. For his greater

---

[4] *Coleridge on the Seventeenth Century*, ed. Roberta Florence Brinkley (Durham, NC: Duke University Press, 1955), 475–76. Walter Scott, 'Review of Robert Southey's 1830 Edition of *The Pilgrim's Progress*', *Quarterly Review*, 43 (1830), 469–94 (489).

[5] *The Pilgrim's Progress*, with explanatory notes by William Mason (London: T. Nelson & Sons, 1857), 11–12.

[6] For extended discussion of Macaulay and Froude on Bunyan, see my 'Centring Bunyan: Macaulay, Froude, Hale White', *BS*, 17 (2013), 68–96; also C. Stephen Finley, 'Bunyan among the Victorians: Macaulay, Froude, Ruskin', *Journal of Literature and Theology*, 3 (1989), 77–94. See also Chapter 26 in this volume.

[7] James Anthony Froude, *Bunyan* (London: Macmillan, 1880), 55–6, 181, 180, 40, 91, 95.

and deeper relevance and impact among the Victorians, however, we must go to places where, as we shall discover, they are woven somehow into the very fabric of the writer's vision or practices.

Along such lines Stephen Finley makes an adroit analysis of Ruskin's debt as an art theorist to the reading of emblematic scenes that is taught to Christian at the House of the Interpreter.[8] Carlyle's blending of this same tradition in Puritan meditation with Romantic 'natural supernaturalism' supplies the opening strand of Barry Qualls's *The Secular Pilgrims of Victorian Fiction* (1982). It is with nineteenth-century fiction itself, however, that we find Bunyan in the mainstream, being adopted, adapted, or challenged in the service of particular artistic and ideological purposes. In a way the genre in general continues *The Pilgrim's Progress*, for many of its exponents considered their works more or less consciously to be a source of revelation, albeit at a further remove from the Bible than was the case with Bunyan and his allegory. Carlyle understood this trend to be what we might call a religio-literary culture, believing that novels should deliver 'doctrine', 'reproof', 'edification', 'healing', 'guidance', and a 'divine awakening voice' for 'the Heroic that is in all men'.[9] Qualls reminds us that on another occasion Carlyle insists that, although we may no longer have the Celestial City as the end point of our existence, 'Art also and Literature' remain 'intimately blended with Religion' since their subject is 'our inward world' and the ways it connects with the life around us.[10] I shall concentrate my attention, in contrast to Qualls, on works with some direct relation to Bunyan.

Charles Dickens

Dickens's well-documented dislike of evangelical religion, whether Anglican or Nonconformist, is amply exemplified in such characters as the hypocritical ranters Stiggins (*Pickwick Papers* (1836–37)) and Chadband (*Bleak House* (1852–53)) or the destructive self-righteousness of Mrs Clennam (*Little Dorrit* (1855–57)). Yet *The Pilgrim's Progress*, which he may first have read as a child in Chatham under the tutelage of the Baptist William Giles, claimed a productive and lifelong place in his imagination. The several references in his novels underline the importance and appeal of two particular aspects of the work: the motif of pilgrimage itself and the great experiential dramas such as the fight with Apollyon, the Valley of the Shadow of Death, Vanity Fair, Doubting Castle, and the River of Death. The impact of these episodes in the nineteenth century was enhanced by the flow of illustrations, which included a series by John Martin for Southey's 1830 edition. They were surely to the fore of Macaulay's thinking when,

---

[8] Finley, 'Bunyan among the Victorians', 83–8.
[9] Thomas Carlyle, 'Sir Walter Scott' (1838), in *The Works of Thomas Carlyle*, ed. H. D. Traill, 30 vols (London: Chapman & Hall, 1896–99), 29: 76.
[10] Thomas Carlyle, 'On History' (1830), in *Works*, ed. Traill, vol. 27; quoted in Barry V. Qualls, *The Secular Pilgrims of Victorian Fiction* (Cambridge: Cambridge University Press, 1982), 1–2.

in his review of this volume, he identified as the 'highest miracle of genius' in Bunyan that 'things which are not should be as though they were—that the imaginations of one mind should become the personal recollections of another'.[11] Bunyan's fictions, in other words, have assumed in the psyches of individuals—and by implication the collective consciousness—the force of truth.

Little Nell in *The Old Curiosity Shop* (1841) proves Macaulay's point. As she and her grandfather leave London, she remembers 'an old copy of the Pilgrim's Progress, with strange plates, [...] over which she had often pored whole evenings', and, though thinking the present scene 'prettier and a great deal better than the real one', tells her fellow refugee, ' "I feel as if we were both Christian, and laid down on this grass all the cares and troubles we brought with us." '[12] For Nell the 'real' scene is the one in the book. Her direct allusion to Bunyan makes it the more likely that readers will recognize subsequent implicit ones. Among these, for example, Christian's passage through the 'flame and smoke', 'rushings too and fro', and 'hideous noises' of the Valley of the Shadow of Death, where '*Fiends*' reach out to drag him into the mouth of hell (*PP*, 63), lies behind Nell's perilous journey across the Midlands with its factories of 'strange unearthly noises' and figures 'moving like demons among the flame and smoke [...] flushed and tormented'. Dickens draws from Bunyan a mythic aura, which spreads over the modern industrial landscape, making of it something rich and strange. Yet repetition can also highlight difference. Even in this novel Dickens's core values are humanitarian rather than spiritual. When Nell reflects upon her goal, her concern is not with the salvation of her soul but with the safety and well-being of her grandfather: ' "I have saved him," she thought. "In all dangers and distresses, I will remember that." ' Her pilgrimage ends, not with a place in heaven, but in the 'profound repose' of a 'beautiful' death.[13]

Artistic debt, divergent vision. As I have shown in detail elsewhere,[14] this formulation holds good for the range of Dickens's retrievals of Bunyan. Bill Sikes in *Oliver Twist* (1837–39) also does battle in the Valley of the Shadow of Death, when interrupting his flight from the city to join men fighting a fire, but emerges as the antitype of the heroic Christian, finding at daybreak only the unrelenting demons of a murderer's guilty conscience. Pip's public display of loyalty towards Magwitch at the latter's trial in *Great Expectations* (1860–61) recalls Christian's support of Faithful at Vanity Fair but in a context which questions the sincerity of his action and thus complicates the process of reading the narrative as moral fable mooted by Q. D. Leavis when uncovering this connection with Bunyan.[15] Christian's combat with Apollyon, the sinful shadow side of his nature, becomes in Dickens a psychodrama in which Pip cathartically works through

---

[11] Thomas Babington Macaulay, 'Review of Southey's 1830 Edition of *The Pilgrim's Progress*', *Edinburgh Review*, 54 (December 1831), 450–61 (452).

[12] Charles Dickens, *The Old Curiosity Shop*, ed. Angus Easson (London: Penguin Books, 1985), 175.

[13] Dickens, *Old Curiosity Shop*, 417, 406, 652, 654.

[14] Vincent Newey, *The Scriptures of Charles Dickens: Novels of Ideology, Novels of the Self* (Aldershot: Ashgate, 2004), passim.

[15] F. R. and Q. D. Leavis, *Dickens the Novelist* (1970; London: Penguin Books, 1994), 417–18.

repressed feelings of guilt in an account of his struggle with his own dark double, Orlick. In a telling inversion of the Wicket Gate and 'yonder shining light' (*PP*, 10) that fix Christian's course to the Celestial City, Bradley Headstone, the murderous schoolmaster in *Our Mutual Friend* (1864–65), draws near to the Lock House that marks the threshold of his last few steps to self-destruction, 'keeping his eyes upon the light with strange intensity, as if he were aiming at it'.[16] Headstone, who dies writhing in the ooze of the river, is a man past all redemption. Yet neither is there any suggestion of his damnation beyond the earthly torment of mental disintegration. Dickens, it seems, has no place for eternity, whether gloriously bright or abysmally dark.

Dickens's most sustained use of Bunyan, or rather of the genres in which he excelled, is *A Christmas Carol* (1843), the story of Scrooge's conversion. Scrooge is described at the outset as an 'old sinner'.[17] The instruments of his 'reclamation' are strongly evocative of meditative practices at work in *The Pilgrim's Progress* and in Bunyan's spiritual autobiography, *Grace Abounding to the Chief of Sinners* (1666). Marley's ghost, fettered with 'cashboxes, keys, […] and heavy purses wrought in steel', is at once an allegorical figure and a cautionary spectacle reminiscent of the 'Man in an Iron Cage' of everlasting despair exhibited as a warning to pilgrims at Interpreter's House (*PP*, 34–5). The deciphering of emblems and signs is as necessary to Scrooge's progress as to Christian's: no one who has read the *Carol* forgets his reaction to the sight of Tiny Tim's empty stool or the tombstone that foretells the end of his own barren life. Most important of all in the process of Scrooge's transformation, perhaps, is the effect of memory as a source of self-knowledge and future direction. To move forward Scrooge has first to turn back, reliving in his imagination times of dereliction and happiness, recovering 'his forgotten self as he had used to be'.[18] The equivalent of this is the spiritual autobiographer's habitual observance of the summons to 'call to mind the former days, […] look diligently, and leave no corner therein unsearched, for there is treasure hid' (*GA*, 3).

This last point then returns us at once to the fact that Dickens's concept of sin and redemption is very different from Bunyan's. Bunyan explores his past above all for evidences of the working of the 'Grace of God toward me' (*GA*, 3). Scrooge must rediscover there his own humanity—his capacity for giving and receiving love. There is more to this than the substitution of a New Testament ethos for a strict traditional theology. Dickens offers a new ideology. Scrooge offends at the beginning of the *Carol* against the claims of family by refusing his nephew's invitation to Christmas dinner, against charity by refusing to donate to the annual collection for the poor, and against his responsibility as an employer by refusing his clerk a proper holiday. The change that comes to him, when he has atoned for these and similar transgressions, is from introverted and acquisitive businessman to an outgoing and generous one, 'as good a master, and as good a man, as the good old city knew'. In Dickens's Victorian order, which foretells the modern liberal-humanist dispensation, capitalism is crucially tempered by benevolence. If

---

[16] Charles Dickens, *Our Mutual Friend*, ed. Stephen Gill (London: Penguin Books, 1971), 868.
[17] Charles Dickens, *A Christmas Carol*, ed. Michael Slater (London: Penguin Books, 1985), 46.
[18] Dickens, *Christmas Carol*, 69, 57, 72.

Dickens subscribes to any religion, it is to the Religion of Humanity, the creed developed by Ludwig Feuerbach in *The Essence of Christianity* (1841), which proposed that humankind was ready to cast off the supernatural forms into which it had projected its own needs and potentialities and move from the rule of 'God is Love' to that of 'Love is God'. The only afterlife in Dickens is accordingly that of a good or ill reputation, as the unregenerate Scrooge is brought to understand when presented with a vivid emblematic contrast between his own status as hate figure and that of the 'loved, revered, and honoured head' with 'good deeds springing from the ground, to sow the world with life immortal'.[19] Barry Qualls makes the telling point that Dickens's 'good "Christian" ' often speaks like Ignorance, the character Bunyan casts down to hell:[20]

> Chr. [T]he Word of God saith of persons in a natural condition, [. . .] every imagination of the heart of man is only evil, and that continually.
> Ignor. I will never believe that my heart is thus bad. (*PP*, 146)

GEORGE ELIOT

The main exponent in England of Feuerbach's ideas was George Eliot, who in 1854 published what is still the definitive translation of *The Essence of Christianity*. In 1859 she records in a journal that she has been rereading 'old Bunyan' after a lapse of years and remarks on 'the true genius manifested in the simple, vigorous, rhythmic style'.[21] This warm yet business-like response comes from one who had long left behind the Evangelical attachments of her early years. Bunyan remained present to Eliot as a link with her youth but also as a reference point against which she could define her mature humanistic beliefs. Her position is made explicit in the celebrated ending of Chapter 14 of *Silas Marner* (1861):

> In old days there were angels who came and took men by the hand and led them away from the city of destruction. We see no white-winged angels now. But yet men are led away from threatening destruction: a hand is put into theirs, which leads them forth gently towards a calm and bright land, so that they look no more backward; and the hand may be a little child's.[22]

Silas Marner begins by throwing *The Pilgrim's Progress* into reverse: its protagonist leaves the city, turning his back on religion, embittered at being expelled from his sect through

---

[19] Dickens, *Christmas Carol*, 133, 118.
[20] Qualls, *Secular Pilgrims*, 136.
[21] *The Journals of George Eliot*, ed. Margaret Harris and Judith Johnston (Cambridge: Cambridge University Press, 1998), 82.
[22] George Eliot, *Silas Marner*, ed. David Carroll (London: Penguin Books, 1996), 131.

a friend's treachery. He bears a twofold burden, the physical one of his weaver's loom and the inner one of the loss of faith and community—the latter representing, as Q. D. Leavis points out, a characteristic Victorian condition.[23] As the quoted coda with its citing of the destinies of Lot and Christian brings home, Eliot then reinstates the affirmative soteriology of the Bible and Bunyan, but makes the agent of redemption emphatically human: a 'little child', the golden-haired Eppie who wanders into Marner's cottage and rescues him from avarice and isolation.

Eliot's clearest lesson in the Religion of Humanity comes with Dorothea Brooke's awakening from egotism to the life beyond self in *Middlemarch* (1871–72). Details from *The Pilgrim's Progress* are reprocessed as Dorothea enters 'a new condition' and recognizes her responsibility to help the three people with whose lives her own has become entangled—Ladislaw, Rosamond, and Lydgate:

> And what sort of crisis might not this be in three lives whose contact with hers laid an obligation on her as if they had been suppliants bearing the sacred branch? [...] She yearned towards the perfect Right, that it might make a throne within her, and rule her errant will. 'What should I do—how should I act now, this very day if I could clutch my own pain, and compel it to silence, and think of those three!'
>
> It had taken her long to come to that question, and there was light piercing into the room. She opened her curtains, and looked out towards the bit of road that lay in view, with fields beyond, outside the entrance-gates. On the road there was a man with a bundle on his back and a woman carrying her baby; in the field she could see figures moving—perhaps the shepherd with his dog. Far off in the bending sky was the pearly light; and she felt the largeness of the world and the manifold wakings of men to labour and endurance.[24]

Supreme authority has passed to 'the perfect Right' of duty. The question is not now Christian's '*What shall I do to be saved?*' or to inherit 'Eternal Life' (*PP*, 9, 10) but how to 'act now' from 'vivid sympathetic experience' of others. While Christian, fleeing the City of Destruction, must shut his ears to the wife and children that 'cry after him to return' (*PP*, 10), here the figures of the 'man with a bundle' and woman with her baby centre the claims of family. The far-off 'pearly light', though reminiscent of the Celestial City 'builded of Pearls' (*PP*, 155), is no heavenly kingdom but a setting for an enlightened awareness of 'the largeness of the world' and its 'palpitating life'. When Dorothea then symbolically changes her clothes, as Christian and Hopeful do theirs at the Celestial City, it is to journey forth to liberate Rosamond from self-absorption, as she has been liberated from hers.

Bunyan does in a way make a positive contribution to the texture of this passage. The old idiom of spiritual struggle and transformation allows Eliot to raise Dorothea's

---

[23] Q. D. Leavis, Introduction to Penguin Classics edition (1967); reprinted in *Silas Marner*, ed. Carroll, 208–34 (214).

[24] George Eliot, *Middlemarch*, ed. Rosemary Ashton (London: Penguin Books, 1994), 788.

experience and the knowledge it yields to the level of a sacred call. She achieves the 'special sense of dignity in ourselves' which W. H. Mallock in *Is Life Worth Living?* (1880), a widely noticed attack on Positivism, feared would be at risk from a dedication exclusively to this-worldly values.[25] Eliot comes nonetheless to bury Bunyan and his religion: not by proclamation, as Froude had once done,[26] but within the discourse of her own secular humanism as she maps out confidently the route to a brave new world.

Yet Bunyan is not so easily tied down or seen off. Eliot's passage brings to mind, as an unintended consequence, a part of the nineteenth-century topography where his footprint was newly established and highly visible. The 'man with a bundle on his back' bearing the demands of 'labour and endurance' (a simulacrum perhaps of Christian himself and of Eliot's own Silas Marner) triggers thoughts of Bunyan and his protagonist as heroes of the working class. The description of Dorothea looking out from her manorial home through a window that frames a landscape she in large part owns, with figures that might belong to a picturesque painting, reflects and reinforces the existing social hierarchy, whatever her feelings of human kinship with those beneath her.

Neither does Macaulay's review of Southey's edition of *The Pilgrim's Progress* fundamentally challenge the status quo, but it at least foregrounds Bunyan's working-class identity, designating him 'the tinker', dwelling on the details of his humble background, and above all paying extended tribute to the 'miracle' he has wrought in 'the vocabulary of the common people' and 'the dialect of plain working men': a medium sufficient 'for every purpose of the poet, the orator, and the divine'. When the essay then talks about this triumph of 'the old unpolluted English language' we glimpse stirrings of the interest in Bunyan's Englishness and the nation's folk culture that became a prominent aspect of Bunyan's popularity in the next century. As Whig historian, moreover, Macaulay does not miss the potential for political advantage in Bunyan's allegory, for he considers it certain that the proceedings against Faithful under Lord Hategood and the rest at Vanity Fair are a satire on the 'shameless partiality' and 'odious mummeries' of state trials under Charles II, while 'stout old' Great-heart is taken to be based on the devout Parliamentary commanders at Naseby and Worcester.[27] We may note that Eliot, by contrast, uses the same segment of the Vanity Fair episode as the source of an epigraph for Chapter 85 of *Middlemarch*, which underscores a moral distinction between the self-contempt of Bulstrode, the exposed hypocrite, and the self-assurance of the man of integrity like Faithful.

---

[25] W. H. Mallock, *Is Life Worth Living?* (London: Chatto & Windus, 1880), 136.

[26] James Anthony Froude, 'The Philosophy of Christianity' (1851), in James Anthony Froude, *Essays in Literature and History* (London: J. M. Dent, n.d.), 185–86: 'The promised land is smiling before us, but we may not pass over into possession of it while the bones of our fathers […] lie […] a prey to unclean birds; we must gather them and bury them.'

[27] Macaulay, 'Review of Southey', 452, 459–60.

HALE WHITE/MARK RUTHERFORD

It is a short step from Macaulay's emphases to voices below: reformers for whom *The Pilgrim's Progress* was an iconic text. For the Chartist leader, Thomas Cooper, it was the 'book of books', in which Lord Hategood and Giant Despair represent the oppressive power of the landowning classes while Christian exemplifies the merit and valour of the upright lowly born.[28] Emma Mason points out that the radical weaver Samuel Bamford, who in his memoirs wrote of the early impact of *The Pilgrim's Progress* on the 'exercise of my feelings and imagination', directly associated Bunyan with the militancy he came to adopt in his struggle for working-class rights.[29] In 1839 a socialist *Political Pilgrim's Progress* by an anonymous author was serialized in the Chartist magazine *The Northern Liberator*, recounting a journey from the City of Plunder to the City of Reform.[30]

The radical publisher John Chapman employed the young Marian Evans as an assistant at his London office in the days before she became George Eliot. There she worked for a time alongside William Hale White, who later wrote novels as Mark Rutherford. Hale White, who lived from 1831 to 1913, was another of the Victorians whose faith fell away, but he remained deeply sympathetic towards Bunyan and his legacy. This is hardly surprising, for he was a child of Bedford Old Meeting, where Bunyan is number 27 in the records of church membership and he is 1,936.[31] In *John Bunyan,* his book of 1905, Hale White lets Bunyan's works speak mostly for themselves through paraphrase and quotation, 'so that it may be seen how little translation they need'. This approach reflects perhaps not only the customary respect of critics for the force and clarity of Bunyan's writing but also a survival in Hale White himself of the Puritan commitment to unmediated contact with the Word. *John Bunyan* nevertheless contains at least one notable intervention, which, as a summary appraisal of Bunyan's achievement in *The Pilgrim's Progress*, comes close to rivalling Macaulay's grasp of his genius for structuring the imagination of readers and therefore their view of reality. Free at this stage of both personal anxiety and the swell of public controversy on religious questions, Hale White can salute Bunyan as a 'theological' writer, for two centuries the 'beloved interpreter of their religion to common folk', but then affirm that his lasting appeal rests pre-eminently on his communication of the fundamentals of existence—'the experience of life, with its hopes and fears, bright day and black night'. Even Calvinism itself was, for the Puritans, never 'mere speculation' but a reaching for 'a theory of the world and its government […]

---

[28] Cooper's phrase is quoted in E. P. Thompson, *The Making of the English Working Class*, rev. edn (Harmondsworth: Penguin Books, 1972), 34.

[29] Emma Mason, 'The Victorians and Bunyan's Legacy', in Anne Dunan-Page (ed.), *The Cambridge Companion to Bunyan* (Cambridge: Cambridge University Press, 2010), 152–53.

[30] Norman Vance, 'Pilgrims Abounding: Bunyan and the Victorian Novel', in Owens and Sim (eds.), *Reception, Appropriation, Recollection*, 73.

[31] My fuller account of Bunyan and Hale White appears as 'Mark Rutherford and John Bunyan: A Study in Relationship', *BS*, 16 (2012), 53–70.

by which we can live'. *The Pilgrim's Progress* itself is 'almost entirely the story of the pilgrimage of man, not of Puritan man especially, but man in all ages'.[32]

Thus, Hale White not only accounts for the work's popularity on many fronts in the nineteenth century, religious and secular, but also uncovers its potential for being constantly reinterpreted in future generations. He affirms what is implicit in his own novels and the creative writing of others—that Bunyan can and should be consistently read, not for doctrine, but for ontological and psychological truth. It is no coincidence that he made his statement on the threshold of the new century and at roughly the same time that, in another intellectual field, William James (in America) claimed Bunyan as a subject for extended analysis in his pioneering study of the psychology of religion.[33]

'Bright day and black night.' Suffering and the strength to win through constitute a recurrent theme in Hale White's own writing. A 'hue of resolution', the quality William James found at the heart of *Grace Abounding*,[34] colours the lives of many of his fictional characters. Heroism permeates ordinary and extraordinary circumstance alike. A 'diviner heroism' than the sacrifice of 'a martyr and saint', for example, is that of the printer Zachariah Coleman in Hale White's novel *The Revolution in Tanner's Lane* (1887) who, trapped in a loveless marriage with forty years before him, 'determined to live through them, as far as he could, without a murmur'. Later, when Zachariah, made fugitive by his radical politics, faces the 'infinite abyss' of despair, Bunyan's 'immortal *Progress*' becomes an actual element in his story, supplying the tried and trusty weapons of memory and the Word:

> He remembered that gloom so profound [. . .]; he remembered the flame and smoke, the sparks and hideous noises, the things that cared not for Christian's sword [. . .]; he remembered the voice of a man going before, saying, '*Though I walk through the valley of the shadow of death I will fear none ill, for Thou art with me*.'[35]

The demons neither of hell nor of hell-on-earth care for the *sword* but *words* keep them at bay. Hale White also wrote, on the other side of the issue of faith, one of the headline texts of Victorian doubt and unbelief, rivalled in depth and intimacy only by Edmund Gosse's *Father and Son* (1907). A semi-fictional elaboration of his own experience, *The Autobiography of Mark Rutherford* (1881) is a perfect mirroring of *Grace Abounding*—a deconversion narrative.

The action of Bunyan's spiritual autobiography turns on the long battle of the biblical verses, where that about Esau finding 'no place of repentance' fights it out for supremacy in the protagonist's head with that about 'the arms of grace' being open. There is a similar

---

[32] [William Hale White], *John Bunyan*, By the Author of 'Mark Rutherford', Etc. (London: Hodder & Stoughton, 1905), 120–21, 21, 76, 120.

[33] William James, *The Varieties of Religious Experience* (1902), ed. Martine Marty (Harmondsworth: Penguin Books, 1985).

[34] James, *Varieties of Religious Experience*, 188.

[35] [William Hale White], *The Revolution in Tanner's Lane*, [By] Mark Rutherford (London: Hogarth Press, 1984), 24, 115.

harrowing episode of monomania in the *Autobiography*, complete with physical shock and verbal automatism. Mark, for example, recalls his obsession with the threat of futility attendant on the evaporation of his belief in immortality—'Why this ceaseless struggle, if in a few short years I was to be asleep for ever?'—as among the 'ideas that would frequently lay hold of *me* with such relentless tenacity that I was passive in their grasp'. The impression of violent assault redoubles as Mark's unsettled being becomes more and more a microcosm of the tremors of an epoch in cataclysmic transition. We read notably of the 'sledgehammer' blow that leaves him 'stunned, bewildered' when he realizes that he can no longer hold on to the 'Christ-idea' irrespective of whether or not it was ever made flesh. Even more terrifying is the unremitting 'process of excavation'—a painful hollowing out from within—that is Mark's longer-term destiny.[36]

This turmoil owes much to the influence of Mark's intellectual companion, Edward Gibbon Mardon, rationalist and non-believer. Some of the characters of *The Pilgrim's Progress* are Christian's helpers or role models (Evangelist, Faithful) and some are his adversaries or seducers, representing attitudes he must somehow overcome (Worldly-Wiseman, Talkative). Mardon is both Mark's friend and his enemy: a double, embodying inclinations in himself that he can neither readily acknowledge nor ultimately resist. In Bunyan's allegory names signify nature and function. Mardon's forenames plainly associate him with the anti-religious scepticism of the author of *The Decline and Fall of the Roman Empire*, while, more subtly, his last name suggests 'spoiling' ('mar') and is an anagram of 'random', deepening the picture of Mark's descent into chaos as his long-held beliefs are hewn away.

The nadir comes for Mark when, shortly after abandoning a soulless refuge as a Unitarian minister, he looks out at night from his small garret:

> There were scattered lights here and there marking roads, but as they crossed one another, and now and then stopped where building had ceased, the effect they produced was that of bewilderment with no clue to it. Further off was the great light of London, like some unnatural dawn, or the illumination from a fire which could not itself be seen. I was overcome with the most dreadful sense of loneliness.

The distant trace of Christian's sighting of the Celestial City merges with echoes of Dorothea's epiphany in the 'pearly light' of a new dawn. Mark's desolate vision is the inverse of both Bunyan's understanding of spiritual triumph and Eliot's secular usurpation of it. The criss-cross lines, going nowhere, symbolize the meaningless spread of urban civilization, but they seem also to be a projection of the bars of the prison house—or iron cage—of the despairing self. The *Autobiography* has no heaven and two hells: the 'infinite abyss' of madness into which Mark stares with 'nameless dread' and the city sprawl whose fiery 'illumination' from some hidden source has more than a hint of the infernal region bordering the Valley of the Shadow of Death.[37] The work signals a key

---

[36] [William Hale White], *The Autobiography of Mark Rutherford, Dissenting Minister*, ed. William S. Peterson (Oxford: Oxford University Press, 1990), 90, 60–1, 65.

[37] [White], *The Autobiography*, 133–34; 134.

change in the Victorian frame of mind. The sound is no longer either a lament or a cheer for the coming of non-belief but rather the dull throb of a bemused and directionless modernity.

Later in the *Autobiography* and in its sequel, *Mark Rutherford's Deliverance* (1885), Hale White does identify ways beyond this impasse. Above all, through the pantheism of Spinoza and Wordsworth, with its immanent deity, he restores value to the universe and our interaction with it. There is something of this philosophy in the conclusion of the *Deliverance*, where Mark describes an excursion in the countryside with his wife and daughter: '[W]e beheld the plain spread all out before us, bounded by the heights of Sussex and Hampshire. It was veiled with the most tender blue, and above it was spread a sky that was white on the horizon […]. We were all completely happy.'[38] The allusion here is not to Bunyan but to the other giant of the Puritan imagination, John Milton, whose Adam and Eve, expelled from Eden, have the world 'all before them'.[39] The late Victorian descendants of our first parents find a residual prelapsarian happiness in the presence of nature and in their own company.

Thomas Hardy

Married love itself often emerges among the Victorians as a crucial source of stability against a background of spreading uncertainty, the classic instance being Matthew Arnold's 'Ah, love, let us be true / To one another' in his poem 'Dover Beach' (first published in 1867). The same mutuality also holds sway at the climax of Mary Ward's *Robert Elsmere* (1888), as Robert, having rejected conventional Christianity for a vaguely Unitarian position and devotion to social regeneration, is ecstatically reconciled on his deathbed with his fiercely orthodox wife. Before that, he is visited in a dream by 'that old familiar image of the river of Death'—familiar no doubt, as Norman Vance says, from Bunyan.[40] Robert sees old friends on the other side but feels 'no pang of separation, of pain' since he knows he is 'about to cross and join them'.[41] Whether Robert's ill-defined creed allows for immortality or whether the joining is simply a sharing in death is impossible to say. Whatever the case, the emphasis of these closing scenes is squarely on the surpassing worth of affection and fellowship. Our final text also closes with a marriage and the River of Death firmly in evidence, but to dramatically different effect.

Thomas Hardy had contact with and an interest in Dissent throughout his career. He went to the Nonconformist school at Dorchester. Bastow, his fellow pupil at the

---

[38] [William Hale White], *Mark Rutherford's Deliverance* (Oxford: Oxford University Press, 1936), 132–33.

[39] *Paradise Lost*, Book 12: 646.

[40] Vance, 'Pilgrims', 78.

[41] Mrs Humphry Ward, *Robert Elsmere*, ed. Rosemary Ashton (Oxford: Oxford University Press, 1987), 565.

office of Hicks the architect, was a committed Baptist who almost persuaded him to undergo a second baptism, an experience that came to inform the insightful account of Paula Power's dilemma in the second chapter of *A Laodicean* (1881). The richly sympathetic portrait of Woodwell, the Baptist pastor in the same novel, matches Hardy's high opinion of Perkins, Dorchester's Baptist minister. *Tess of the d'Urbervilles* (1891) has the less straightforward figure of the itinerant evangelist who daubs the countryside with monitory texts and also Alec d'Urberville's equally ambiguous conversion, which, though not lasting, may or may not be sincere. Near the end of his life Hardy's wife, Florence, noted that he was 'evidently thinking a great deal' about Bastow and giving the impression that 'he would like to meet this man again more than anyone'.[42] The mixture of intimacy and distance that Hardy displays across these various contexts is exactly the relation he has to Bunyan in his last novel, *Jude the Obscure* (1895).

Hardy certainly knew *The Pilgrim's Progress*. His biographers record that he was terrified at the age of ten by an illustration of Apollyon assailing Christian.[43] In a notebook of 1867 he copied an extract of a very different tenor: 'There, said they, is the Mount Zion, the heavenly Jerusalem, the innumerable company of angels, and the spirits of just men, made perfect.'[44] Both episodes feature among the several allusions to *The Pilgrim's Progress* in the early pages of *Jude the Obscure*. Running home after his first glimpse of the distant Christminster, Jude is troubled by thoughts of 'Apollyon lying in wait for Christian'. He calls the city 'the heavenly Jerusalem'; in the fading sunlight it 'like the topaz gleamed'; it is the home of 'shining ones', the 'city of light'. We may remember that Christian approaches the Celestial City through a landscape in which 'shining Ones commonly walked' and the City, built of 'Pearls and Precious Stones', so shone in the 'Sunbeams' that he 'with desire fell sick' (*PP*, 154–55). As the festive bells welcome Christian, so does the wind carry a message to Jude which 'surely […] was the sound of bells, the voice of the city, faint and musical, calling to him, "We are happy here."'[45]

In a sense *Jude the Obscure* supplies an appendix to our study of Bunyan and the Victorians, for it enters new, if not altogether unheralded, territory. The issue around Jude's bid to find a place in Christminster, the Oxford of Hardy's Wessex, is one of educational opportunity, which was of course a preoccupation of the working-class radicals that lionized Bunyan. Moreover, Hardy's interest at the beginning of the novel lies specifically with the power of imaginative illusion. Macaulay's insight into the genius that can make 'things which are not […] as though they were' shifts over in Hardy to a concern with obsession: 'the fancied place [Jude] had likened to the New Jerusalem'

---

[42] Florence Emily Hardy, *The Later Years of Thomas Hardy, 1892–1928* (London: Macmillan, 1930), 237. See also Cunningham, *Everywhere Spoken Against*, 110–12.

[43] See, for example, Robert Gittings, *Young Thomas Hardy*, rev. edn (Harmondsworth: Penguin Books, 1978), 45.

[44] *The Literary Notebooks of Thomas Hardy*, ed. L. A. Björk, 2 vols (London: Macmillan, 1985), 2: 463–64.

[45] Thomas Hardy, *Jude the Obscure*, ed. Dennis Taylor (London: Penguin Books, 1998), 21–5. The present discussion is based on my 'The Disinherited Pilgrim: *Jude the Obscure* and *The Pilgrim's Progress*', *Durham University Journal*, 75 (1987), 59–61.

acquired 'a permanence, a hold on his life'.[46] Yet this does in turn reconnect us to a sense of relationship between Hardy and Bunyan's text. When Christian follows Evangelist's 'yonder shining light'—the way of Christ's 'I am the way'—to the Celestial City, he seeks an end which, though inward, exists objectively as part of the given scheme of salvation. Jude, on the other hand, pursues only a fantastical image, a 'mis-taking'. With Hardy it is not a question of embracing Bunyan's vision (the devout), or rejecting it (the non-believer), or adapting it (the secular humanist), but of treating it seriously yet with ironic detachment.

At least this is Hardy's stance at stages throughout *Jude the Obscure*, which, whether he intends it or not, reproduces many of the conventions of Bunyan's model of soul journey but with a negative or sardonic twist. We may, for example, contrast the parchment roll given to Christian by Evangelist, which will be his passport to the Celestial City, with the books Jude receives from Phillotson the schoolmaster, which he expects will supply him with a 'secret cipher' but simply convince him of the inevitability of 'years of plodding'. For Jude there is nothing 'therein to his comfort' (*PP*, 42), only crushing disenchantment. Neither is there any wayside helper or intervention of Providence to lift him from his slough of despond as he realizes his 'gigantic error', for 'nobody did come, because nobody does'.[47] At such points Jude's journey seems almost a parody of Christian's pilgrimage.

The same impression arises when Jude later arms himself with a biblical text, taking us back to the moment when Christian puts Apollyon to flight with the words '*Rejoice not against me, O mine Enemy*' (*PP*, 60). Learning from the Master of Biblioll's cuttingly brief letter of rejection that 'the gates were shut' against him, Jude regains momentum by writing defiantly on the college wall the cry of self-assertion from Job, 'I have understanding as well as you; I am not inferior to you.'[48] Thus Jude finds a way through his Vale of Humiliation. There is, however, an overarching irony. That he makes his mark in chalk signalizes the provisional nature of his stand. Christian's passage through the Wicket Gate, where he raises a song of thanksgiving before the welcoming legend of '*Knock and it shall be opened*' (*PP*, 25), foreshadows his entry into the Celestial City. Jude's fundamentally ineffectual gesture before closed doors is in keeping with his destiny as the eternal outsider.

Hardy's protagonist, like Bunyan's, proceeds by a pattern of repeated arrest and recovery, but for both there comes a time to stand back and take stock. Christian reaches this point when, on the approach to the Enchanted Ground, reviewing his own close-run victories over Faint-heart and Mistrust, he concludes that we must learn to live with uncertainty and trust to God for final outcomes, since 'no man can tell what in [the] Combat attends us' and all is ultimately as He 'would have it' (*PP*, 129–30). The equivalent in Hardy is Jude's extempore address to the crowd awaiting the Remembrance Day procession in Christminster, in which, looking back over his history of failed aspiration,

---

[46] Hardy, *Jude the Obscure*, 22.
[47] Hardy, *Jude the Obscure*, 31.
[48] Hardy, *Jude the Obscure*, 118.

he concedes the limitations of human endeavour and understanding, for 'who knoweth what is good for man in this life?—and who can tell a man what shall be after him under the sun?' Jude's is the more unstable condition, for he has neither any assurance of an overarching order in the affairs of men nor any set of established convictions to guide him in thought and action. In presenting himself as an *exemplum* of a widespread 'spirit of mental and social restlessness', he refers specifically to his attempt at scaling the barriers of class and privilege. His complaint of being 'too early', a pioneer before his time, however, conjures up the larger picture of a society in which old frameworks of belief were under pressure and new ones were struggling to mature. In Jude's memorable phrases, this meant for many being 'in a chaos of principles—groping in the dark'. It is against this backdrop of a world unsettled and in flux that we must in the final analysis view the death of Jude Fawley.

Sounds of Remembrance Day festivities reach Jude's 'deserted room' from the concert hall and from the river, as he calls for water:

> No water came, and the organ notes, faint as a bee's hum, rolled in as before.
> While he remained, his face changing, shouts and hurrahs came from somewhere in the direction of the river.
> 'Ah—yes! The Remembrance games', he murmured. 'And I here. And Sue defiled!'
> The hurrahs were repeated, drowning the faint organ notes. Jude's face changed more: he whispered slowly, his lips scarcely moving:
> '*Let the day perish wherein I was born* [...].'
> ('Hurrah!')
> '*Let that day be darkness* [...]. *Lo, let that night be solitary, let no joyful voice come therein.*'
> ('Hurrah!') [...]
> '*There the prisoners rest together* [...]. *Wherefore is light given to him that is in misery, and life unto the bitter in soul?*'[49]

The darkness of Jude's last hours is unrelieved by any glimpse of hope, either on his part or Hardy's. Jude is given on his deathbed a religious language in which to deny the consolations of religion. The effect of the immediate festive background is to intensify the impression of dereliction, the passage being so orchestrated that we take the 'Hurrahs' that punctuate his incantation as the sign of a world oblivious to his misery and bitterness of soul, or, yet more painful, as cheers of derision and good riddance as he prays for his whole existence to be erased.

This scene has echoes of the endings of both parts of *The Pilgrim's Progress*: the River (of Death); the 'much refreshing' of pilgrims in Beulah (*PP*, 154–56, 303); the 'great shout' and 'melodious noise' announcing Christian's arrival (*PP*, 160); the 'ceremonies of joy' that accompany Christiana and her companions as they cross over (*PP*, 303, 306); their 'Celestial Visions' and 'Chambers [that] were perfumed' (*PP*, 304); how Stand-fast's

---

[49] Hardy, *Jude the Obscure*, 327, 403.

'Countenance changed' (*PP*, 311); the pilgrims' last words, among them Valiant's '*Death where is thy sting?*' and Stand-fast's 'I see my self now at the end of my Journey […] I am going now to see […] *that* Face […] in whose company I delight' (*PP*, 309, 311); how in general they join the typology of the chosen, the pilgrims of old, Abraham, Isaac, Jacob. These details form a palimpsest or buried fragments of a consummation of which Jude's end and the ending of *Jude* are the negation. Jude calls in vain for refreshment, is mocked by 'shouts and hurrahs' (his 'face changing'), and is brought to a sharp sense of his separation from the one in whom *he* delights. His parting words link him typologically to the anguished Job, from whose verses they are taken, and frame a wish that his journey had never even begun. The reminders of the rapture of Bunyan's pilgrims as they reach the 'heavenly Jerusalem' fuel the supreme irony that our final sight of the place Jude thought was the 'city of light', the abode of happy souls, reveals, as we move from his desolate room to the crowd gathering at the riverside, a Vanity Fair of 'fun' and 'nosegays', a 'hot mass' of hedonistic frivolity.[50]

The pessimism of *Jude the Obscure* has always drawn comment. An early critique by Thomas Selby likens the novel's 'morbid ingenuity' to the 'woebegone signs […] which stamp Bunyan's pilgrim when he is first presented to our notice'. For Selby, Hardy has no proper regard for man's 'poor soul' and, when condemning Jude to 'the eclipse of sackcloth darkness', offends against 'faith and […] sober-minded optimism'.[51] Driven by a Christian theology that privileges redemptive process, this reaction underlines the distance between Hardy and Bunyan even as it makes a connection between them. Yet Selby misses something important in Hardy. For one thing, his approach blinds him to the force of Hardy's creativity, which, not least through the reprise of Job, makes, out of Jude's suffering, a notation that grants the character a kind of immortality as the archetypal spiritual exile. More to the immediate point, Selby fails to see that, though faithless in a narrow sense, Hardy's vision is intimately bound up with faith. W. H. Mallock offers a relevant insight during his analysis of the contemporary deprecation of supernatural religion, arguing that rejection can itself be a form of longing, 'like the bitterness of a woman against her lover, which has not been the cause of her resolving to leave him, but which has been caused by his leaving her'. 'Deep feeling often expresses itself by contradicting itself.'[52] The subtext of references to *The Pilgrim's Progress* and especially its twin climaxes pays respect to an order of beauty and coherence to which the late Victorian present is indeed 'a chaos of principles'. More sympathetic in response than Eliot with her secularizing strategy, as deeply if less visibly in touch than Hale White, Hardy felt and preserved in a unique way the undertow of the dispensation over against which his last fiction was in no small measure set. Though the spirit of John Bunyan and his religion was unavailable to Hardy as a guiding light, and yielded gloom rather than glory, it persisted for him as a compelling point of attraction and source of creative impetus.

[50] Hardy, *Jude the Obscure*, 405–06.
[51] Thomas G. Selby, *The Theology of Modern Fiction* (London: Charles H. Kelly, 1896), 89–90, 100, 130.
[52] Mallock, *Is Life Worth Living?*, 152.

SUGGESTED READING

Cunningham, Valentine, *Everywhere Spoken Against: Dissent in the Victorian Novel* (Oxford: Clarendon Press, 1975).

Finley, C. Stephen, 'Bunyan among the Victorians: Macaulay, Froude, Ruskin', *Journal of Literature and Theology*, 3 (1989), 77–94.

Froude, James Anthony, *Bunyan* (London: Macmillan, 1880).

Hammond, Mary, '*The Pilgrim's Progress* and its Nineteenth-Century Publishers', in W. R. Owens and Stuart Sim (eds.), *Reception, Appropriation, Recollection: Bunyan's Pilgrim's Progress* (Bern: Peter Lang, 2007), 99–118.

Keeble, N. H., '"Of him thousands daily Sing and talk": Bunyan and his Reputation', in N. H. Keeble (ed.), *John Bunyan: Conventicle and Parnassus* (Oxford: Clarendon Press, 1988), 241–63.

Macaulay, Thomas Babington, 'Review of Robert Southey's 1830 Edition of *The Pilgrim's Progress*', *Edinburgh Review*, 54 (December 1831), 450–61; repr. in Thomas Babington Macaulay, *Critical and Historical Essays*, arranged A. J. Grieve, 2 vols (London: J. M. Dent & Sons, 1961), 2: 399–410.

Mason, Emma, 'The Victorians and Bunyan's Legacy', in Anne Dunan-Page (ed.), *The Cambridge Companion to Bunyan* (Cambridge: Cambridge University Press, 2010), 150–61.

Newey, Vincent, 'Centring Bunyan: Macaulay, Froude, Hale White', *BS*, 17 (2013), 68–97.

Qualls, Barry V., *The Secular Pilgrims of Victorian Fiction* (Cambridge: Cambridge University Press, 1982).

Vance, Norman, 'Pilgrims Abounding: Bunyan and the Victorian Novel', in W. R. Owens and Stuart Sim (eds.), *Reception, Appropriation, Recollection: Bunyan's Pilgrim's Progress* (Bern: Peter Lang, 2007), 69–79.

CHAPTER 34

BUNYAN AND AMERICA

JOEL D. S. RASMUSSEN

At the close of the twentieth century the political philosopher Jean Bethke Elshtain remarked, 'The progress of *Pilgrim's Progress* tells us a good bit about the American story.'[1] She was undoubtedly correct. Yet anyone unfamiliar with John Bunyan's classic—easily his most important work as far as his reception in the United States goes—could probably barely imagine the extent to which it encodes some of the literature that is today regarded as distinctively American. Bunyan's influence in this respect is perhaps second only to the Bible (alongside which *The Pilgrim's Progress* often had its place in early American homes), and in varying ways and degrees provides substance and structure to some of the works of, among others, Benjamin Franklin in the eighteenth century, Nathaniel Hawthorne and Louisa May Alcott in the nineteenth, and Frank Baum, Robert Lowell, Kurt Vonnegut, and, arguably, the entire genre of 'road' literature in the twentieth. The present chapter explores the different ways in which, through a series of politically, theologically, and artistically motivated realignments, American adaptations of the English classic helped to shape key features both of American Protestantism and a distinctively American literary tradition. By fleshing out just some of the various respects in which Elshtain's pregnant claim is true, it seeks to enable clearer insight into this important strand of modern religious history and literary culture, along with a fuller understanding of one of Bunyan's own most significant 'journeys'.

THE PILGRIMS AND THE IRONY OF AMERICAN 'PROGRESS'

Due to the transatlantic character, Puritan ethos, and high literacy of the Massachusetts Bay Colony, individual copies of Bunyan's writings—including *The Pilgrim's*

---

[1] Jean Bethke Elshtain, 'Jane Addams: A Pilgrim's Progress', *Journal of Religion*, 78 (1998), 347.

Progress—were carried to New England's shores almost immediately upon publication in England. By the time Bunyan's *The Pilgrim's Progress, Part II* was published in 1684, the first part was so well known in New England as to have received there, in Bunyan's words, '*So much loving Countenance, / As to be Trim'd, new Cloth'd & Deckt with Gems*' (*PP*, 169). Bunyan's imagination embellishes the work somewhat more than the Massachusetts printer would have done, but he refers here to the first American edition of *The Pilgrim's Progress*, handsomely printed, bound, and published in Boston in 1681, just three years after its publication in London in 1678.

It is a peculiar feature of the American colonial literature that, despite the extensive readership of Bunyan's work—one among only a handful of books whose sales topped a thousand copies prior to 1690—it receives scant comment from the most prominent and prolific colonial divines. We search in vain for obvious references to Bunyan by Increase Mather, for example, or even among the near four hundred publications authored by his son, Cotton Mather. Given the shared millenarian concerns of Bunyan and these divines, along with the immense popularity of Bunyan's work in New England, this initial silence seems odd. David E. Smith has speculated that the most likely reason for this silence is that Bunyan's writings were 'beneath the notice of gentlemen'.[2] But since one of Cotton Mather's associates was largely responsible for the Boston publication of *The Pilgrim's Progress*, it beggars belief to conclude that the principal intellectuals had not privately and purposefully read the work.[3] After all, the conception of life as a pilgrimage in Christian faith shaped the ethos of New England Puritan culture from its founding, and in *The Pilgrim's Progress* the colonists would find their prototypical figure for this journey.

There were certain features of Bunyan's work, however, that did not neatly conform to the experience of the colonists' errand into the wilderness. Since, in the first instance, a spiritual allegory deploys a set of specific and familiar referents to communicate its theological meaning, the lack of such referents in a different context means that reading the allegory requires an additional imaginative stage in the process of interpretation. So, for example, because the vast forests of New England were so dissimilar to the landscape features of seventeenth-century England, we might well imagine that the significance of keeping to the narrow path, or of entering into the path by the wicket gate, entailed an imaginative transposition by the colonists that it did not for Bunyan's readers in England. Moreover, since in the American wilderness no Jerusalem substitute of, say, Canterbury or Walsingham waited as the symbolic destination at the end of a difficult pilgrimage, the holy city, in order to symbolize the journey's end, needed to be *built*. However, this requirement fitted nicely with the theopolitical aspirations of Bunyan's New England readers, for the notion of building the holy city was already an important part of their narrative. In 1630, Governor John Winthrop—spun out from the

---

[2] David E. Smith, *John Bunyan in America* (Bloomington, IN: Indiana University Press, 1966), 122. This work remains the indispensable point of departure for any study of Bunyan's influence in American religious history and literary culture.

[3] Smith, *John Bunyan in America*, 122.

millenarian foment that would a dozen years later erupt into the English Civil War—had delivered his famous sermon aboard the *Arbella* envisioning a New England that was to be, after Matthew 5:14, 'as a City upon a Hill'. His successors continuously elaborated on this theme, depicting the true vocation of the New England colonists as one of ushering in what Cotton Mather evocatively called a 'New Jerusalem', an 'American Zion'.[4]

In this vein, the first in a long string of American variants on Bunyan's model appeared in 1715 upon the publication of Joseph Morgan's *The History of the Kingdom of Basaruah*, arguably the first American novel. Composed as an allegorical primer in New England covenant theology, the work reproves the complacency of the sojourners who pursue their satisfactions in 'the imaginary pleasures of the wilderness', and thereby neglect their true vocation of 'seeking a *better Country*, which was the end for which the King sent them hither'.[5] Despite its setting in a physical wilderness, *The Kingdom of Basaruah* clearly echoes *The Pilgrim's Progress* in the way it allegorizes pilgrimage as a means of summarizing Puritan teaching. In doing so, Morgan's variant offers what one might suppose would be attractive to colonial readers, namely, a commentary keyed specifically to the physical experience of seeking a 'better country' through a hostile wilderness. Nonetheless, however one judges the merits of Morgan's allegory, Bunyan's original remained considerably more popular with colonial readers. The years between 1789 and 1800 alone saw the publication of thirty American editions of *The Pilgrim's Progress*, while by that same decade Morgan's work had already fallen into obscurity.[6]

Notably, the steady popularity of *The Pilgrim's Progress* attends the decreasing influence of American Puritanism more generally. Orthodox piety in the strict sense was increasingly eclipsed by the homespun moralism of Yankee ingenuity. Benjamin Franklin, early America's first internationally celebrated polymath, became the type and foremost proponent of this Yankee wisdom: frugality, industry, and temperance—'early to bed and early to rise makes a man healthy, wealthy, and wise'. He was also, as a boy, a Bunyan enthusiast, and in his *Autobiography* (begun in 1771 but left uncompleted at his death in 1790), he recounts that he used whatever little money came his way to purchase books: 'Pleas'd with the Pilgrim's Progress, my first collection was of John Bunyan's Works'.[7] Franklin's parents had hoped he would enter the Christian ministry, but in time it became clear that this would entail too great a financial expense for the family. This realization suited Franklin. Granted, Bunyan's works made a strong impression on him. But so did other authors, and later, upon reading works by Lord Shaftesbury and Anthony Collins, he became 'a real Doubter in many Points of our Religious Doctrine'.

---

[4] See, for example, Cotton Mather, *Theopolis Americana, an Essay on the Golden Street of the Holy City* (Boston, MA: B. Green, 1710), 3, 27.

[5] Joseph Morgan, *The History of the Kingdom of Basaruah*, ed. Richard Schlatter (Cambridge, MA: Harvard University Press, 1946), 57.

[6] David E. Smith, 'Publication of John Bunyan's Works in America', *New York Public Library Bulletin*, 66 (1962), 630–52 (632).

[7] Benjamin Franklin, *Autobiography and Other Writings*, ed. Ormond Seavey (Oxford: Oxford University Press, 1993), 13. Subsequent serial quotations refer to Franklin, *Autobiography*, 18 and 23, respectively.

Despite his conversion to Deism, however, Franklin's plan for moral regeneration, his own personal worldly asceticism, and his witty but solemn aphorisms all attest to his Puritan inheritance. Indeed, the structure and some of the images of Franklin's *Autobiography* suggest he patterned that work after 'my old favourite Author Bunyan's *Pilgrim's Progress*', and Franklin's own mixture of narration and dialogue reflects a technique he reports first learning from 'Honest John'. The similarities are striking enough to have prompted one scholar to call Franklin an 'American Bunyan', and his *Autobiography* an 'American *Pilgrim's Progress*'.[8]

Insofar as this is an apt characterization, it is equally important to observe how, for Franklin, the Puritan virtues no longer serve doctrinal commitments and celestial aspirations. Rather, although Franklin no longer regards the old principles as salvific, he still recognizes that they are nonetheless useful, and he redirects frugality, industry, and temperance to worldly advantage: financial success and nation-building on the international scene. As one of the leading diplomats and statesmen in the founding period of the United States of America, Franklin's mission came to be that of fostering the growth of a new society among the rank of nations. And he composed his *Autobiography* in order to depict how he 'emerg'd from the Poverty & Obscurity in which [he] was born & bred, to a State of Affluence & some Degree of Reputation in the World', so as to commend his principles of conduct to posterity as 'fit to be imitated'.[9] With Franklin and his successors, the vision of America as a beacon and example to Europe takes a new form. Following the birth of the new nation, America was marked out not because of its puritanical piety, but because of the way it increasingly tilted the economic balance in its favour through the generalized habits of frugality, industry, and temperance. Franklin's conception of progress—the conception that by and large fired the popular imagination of the young nation—was an ironic misprision of Bunyan's *The Pilgrim's Progress*: an imaginatively transformed redeployment of the Puritan prototype charting a path to international esteem and prosperity.

In the nineteenth century, the westering spirit of a new nation with imperial ambitions would itself take on the theopolitical language of 'manifest destiny', and frontier resourcefulness and commercial success came to be identified by many with moral regeneration and the spread of civilization—in a word: 'progress'. Compared to this new sense of progress, however, the Puritan covenantal vision of America as a New Zion was a far cry in the wilderness. When John Winthrop envisioned a settlement that would become 'as a City upon a Hill', he glossed this to mean its inhabitants would model 'Christian Charity' to the world, and not 'be seduced and worship other gods, our pleasures and profits, and serve them'.[10] Moreover, so long as Puritanism held sway in the American consciousness, the new country was only ever conceived to be a *reflection* of the Celestial City, provisional to 'crossing over'. Even while Franklin was still a child,

---

[8] Charles Sanford, 'An American *Pilgrim's Progress*', *American Quarterly*, 6 (1954), 297–310 (303).

[9] Franklin, *Autobiography*, 3.

[10] John Winthrop, 'A Model of Christian Charity', in Amanda Porterfield (ed.), *American Religious History* (Malden, MA: Wiley-Blackwell, 2002), 171–74 (173).

Morgan's *History of the Kingdom of Basaruah* had warned of reconceiving the Puritan errand into the wilderness as an imperialistic venture (much as Bunyan warned of mistaking the Hill Lucre for the Delectable Mountains):

> The people were no sooner come into this Country, but they fell to digging up the imaginary Riches of it, as if they thought to abide there forever; [...] the loss of the *Celestial Country* was little regarded, and many would not believe that the King would deprive them of it for so small an offence, as they thought their Rebellion was.[11]

In this vein, Morgan's eighteenth-century *History* portended a succession of mid-nineteenth-century American adaptations of Bunyan's *The Pilgrim's Progress*, almost all of which, in one way or another, denounced the spreading secularized conception of 'progress'.

The Nineteenth-Century 'School of Progress'

If Franklin's *Autobiography* first adumbrated the secularized ideal of the American pilgrim for the eighteenth century, then John Gast's 1872 painting entitled *American Progress* gave it a definitive pictorial representation for the nineteenth. The painting depicts a monumental Columbia striding westward across the American continent with a star of destiny on her tiara. In the left-hand margin of the painting, Native Americans and wild animals steal an apprehensive look back over their shoulders while beating a retreat before the advancing figure. With her left hand, Columbia effortlessly strings telegraph wire across the posts that lead back to a great port city in the East. In her right, she carries a 'School Book' (helpfully labelled as such for the viewer) with which to civilize the wilderness. Just ahead of Columbia, an advance guard of frontiersmen and prospectors rush across the mountains to seek their personal fortune, with covered wagons transporting settlers to their homesteads following them closely. Just behind her, three new railway lines fan out from the eastern seaboard through newly tilled farmland, carrying adventurous Yankees and recent European émigrés towards a golden future in the western expanse. In aspiration if not also in actuality, Gast's *American Progress* completes the transformation of the notion of 'progress' in America from the Puritan conception of a difficult journey in personal and social holiness towards the Celestial City, into the popular conception of inevitable western expansion triumphing over the wilderness and rolling the frontier into the Pacific Ocean.

---

[11] Morgan, *Basaruah*, 57.

In a variety of ways this secularized vision, so effective generally in creating a national myth of American exceptionalism, entailed a conception of 'progress' that a conservative minority found deeply unsettling. Although by the nineteenth century America had entered a decidedly post-Puritan age, in some quarters the piety of the forebears still gave the culture what Nathaniel Hawthorne called its 'prevailing tint', no matter how 'diversified with later patchwork' the nation as a whole had become.[12] And the strictest among this evangelical Calvinist remnant met the modernized conception of 'progress' with a considerable deal of anxious antipathy. Among them were several Bunyan enthusiasts who in the middle of the century composed Bunyan-inspired allegories to denounce what they took to be the pernicious consequences of modern optimism, imperial expansionism, and liberalization. Between 1826 and 1855—the years immediately following the period during which *The Pilgrim's Progress* enjoyed its greatest popularity in America[13]—a cluster of works appeared with the common mission of correcting the waywardness of the contemporary generation, and of promulgating the expectation of the imminent millennium, as the very title of the anonymously published *The Pilgrim's Progress in the Last Days* (1843) makes clear. Together with that work, William R. Weeks's *The Pilgrim's Progress in the Nineteenth Century* (serialized in 1826, and published in an enlarged edition in 1849), George B. Cheever's *A Reel in a Bottle* (1852), Joseph A. Benton's *The California Pilgrim* (1853), and George Wood's *Modern Pilgrims* (1855) also take up the cause of holding the hard Calvinistic line, while popularizing the invective by redeploying Bunyanesque allegory.[14] As the publisher for one of these works advertises it: 'so much discriminating evangelical truth, in so pleasing a style, was perhaps never before published before in our world'.[15]

George Cheever was, without doubt, the most prominent of these authors, and this was due not simply to his *A Reel in a Bottle* (republished in at least four editions between the 1850s and the 1880s), but also to works such as *The Hill Difficulty* (1849) and *Waymarks of the Pilgrimage* (1851), and especially to the remarkably popular series of lectures on Bunyan he delivered in New York in 1843–44.[16] Additionally, Cheever was

---

[12] Nathaniel Hawthorne, *The Blithedale Romance*, in *Nathaniel Hawthorne: Novels*, ed. Millicent Bell (New York: The Library of America, 1983), 629–848 (803).

[13] Smith, 'Publication of John Bunyan's Works in America', 632.

[14] Anon., *The Pilgrim's Progress in the Last Days* (New England: Published for the Author, 1843); William R. Weeks, *The Pilgrim's Progress in the Nineteenth Century* (New York: M. W. Dodd, 1849); George B. Cheever (publishing under the name the Rev. Henry T. Cheever), *A Reel in a Bottle, for Jack in the Doldrums: The Adventures of Two of the King's Seamen in a Voyage to the Celestial Country* (New York: Charles Scribner, 1852); Joseph A. Benton, *The California Pilgrim: A Series of Lectures* (Sacramento, CA: Solomon Alter, 1853); George Wood, *Modern Pilgrims: Showing the Improvements in Travel, and the Newest Methods of Reaching the Celestial City*, 2 vols (Boston, MA: Phillips, Sampson, & Co., 1855).

[15] Weeks, *Pilgrim's Progress in the Nineteenth Century*, 'Publisher's Advertisement', iii.

[16] George B. Cheever, *The Hill Difficulty, and Some Experiences of Life in the Plains of Ease* (New York: John Wiley, 1849); George B. Cheever, *Waymarks of the Pilgrimage; or Teaching by Trials* (Boston, MA: American Tract Society, 1851); George B. Cheever, *Lectures on the Pilgrim's Progress and on the Life and Times of John Bunyan*, 3rd edn (New York: Wiley & Putnam, 1845).

well known for his impassioned support of the abolition of slavery, for his outspoken opposition to the forced removal of Native Americans, for his temperance activism, and, not least, for his crusade against the violation of the Sabbath by the railways. For present purposes, Cheever's *A Reel in a Bottle* can stand as exemplary for all the authors named, since (apart from the conceit of its nautical setting) it targets the same 'liberal' and 'worldly' excesses as the other works do, and *mutatis mutandis*, seeks to draw the same moral.

In *A Reel in a Bottle*, Cheever recontextualizes Bunyanesque allegory by casting two sailors—Peter and John—in the role of millenarian pilgrims facing a series of trials as they sail for the Celestial City across the sea from the modern City of Destruction. Upon a break in their journey in one 'Country of Self-Deceit', they discover that residents there are not indifferent to the Celestial City, but that they 'transcendentalized' their religion, and regarded the pilgrim notion of fleeing from 'the burning of the world' to be 'quite antiquated'. Such language really only means:

> a transfiguration into a purer state, into which they themselves were already passing, so that every pound of guano which they put upon their fields and gardens to quicken vegetation, and every moral virtue which they cultivated, was a part of the flame of that threatened conflagration, and thus earth was to be transformed into heaven. They said, moreover, that a railroad was in process of construction, and had been carried already as far as the Delectable Mountains, and from there to the Celestial City a joint-stock company had prepared a line of aerial steamers and balloons.[17]

Along with such moral and technological progress, the inhabitants of Self-Deceit were making great strides in the sciences as well, especially in geology. 'A new geological survey of the world had just been ordered', Peter and John are told, and 'the Mosaic account of the creation must either be renounced or spiritualized, and that, to save the credit of the Bible, they were pretty generally transcendentalizing the whole thing, or regarding it but as the beginning of a higher revelation.' Needless to say, the pilgrims are relieved when finally they escaped this land of 'progress', with its self-deceptive immanentalizing of the religious message, and were again on the open sea.

But even under sail the pilgrims must combat new and liberal doctrines. When they encounter a pleasure yacht with streamers, they allow it to come alongside and engage in conversation with the crew. They learn that the ship—captained by a man named Glib, and crewed by Mr Man's Wisdom, Deism, Plausible, Surface, Shallow, Pick-flaw, Anything, and Nothing, among others—was built in the Country of Liberal Christianity, and had at its stern a propeller called Philosophy. In the ship's library one finds titles such as *Salvation made Easy* and *Every Man his own Redeemer*, while the ship's cargo and

---

[17] Cheever, *A Reel in a Bottle*, 36–7. Subsequent serial quotations refer to *A Reel in a Bottle*, 32–3, 93–4, 94, 98, and 98, respectively.

ballast together are called the Dignity of Human Nature. When Peter tells Glib they are on pilgrimage, and speaks of fidelity to the Word of God, the captain responds:

> Well, you may take *your* course, and we'll take ours. We are bound now to Cape Transcendental, to carry our wares, and get the latest notions [...]. I thank God the world is no longer in leading strings to a squad of Calvinistic Theologians. One man has *his* way, and another man *his*; in the end all will come out right. God is good.

When Peter insists that the different ways an individual may travel lead either to heaven or to hell, and that God's Word is given so that one might choose eternal life in the Celestial City rather than the fire of perdition, Glib retorts, 'We don't want any of your fire and brimstone preaching.' Steersman Deism is also offended, and asks incredulously, 'Who talks about the Celestial City, as if Heaven were a place? We shall have heaven on earth when society is reconstructed.'

Cheever's satire of the American 'School of Progress', as represented both by the inhabitants of Self-Deceit, and by Glib and his crew, is representative of the whole cluster of mid-nineteenth-century 'pilgrim's progresses' mentioned, as David Smith has shown. These versions shared the millenarian Christianity of the seventeenth-century Puritans, and sought to recover Bunyan's conception of pilgrimage not as general worldly improvement, but as passage from a corrupt world to eternal life in heaven. While never eclipsing the popularity of Bunyan's original, nonetheless they contemporized Bunyan's allegory with respect to the suspicions they and their traditional co-religionists had about modern science, modern technology, and theological liberalism. They anticipate by almost a century H. Richard Niebuhr's critique of nineteenth-century Protestant Liberalism as professing faith in 'A God without wrath [who] brought men without sin into a kingdom without judgment through the ministrations of a Christ without a cross.'[18] And yet, although these modern pilgrims get in some trenchant digs at the optimistic presumptions of modern science, technocracy, and theological liberalism, nonetheless their millenarianism does not fare any better unless one already shares the prejudices of their conception of Christian faith. Moreover, while this conservative appropriation and adaptation of Bunyan are largely typical of American authors in the nineteenth century, it is not true, as Smith claims, that 'one would search in vain for any nineteenth-century American adaptations which did not attack liberalism in church and state.'[19] Religious conservatives were not alone in admiring Bunyan. There were some outside the strict Calvinist tradition who also availed themselves of Bunyanesque allegory in order to come to terms with the quickly modernizing world, and among these the very first book—entitled *The Adventures of Search for Life*—was squarely in the liberalizing stream of American religion.

---

[18] H. Richard Niebuhr, *The Kingdom of God in America*, 2nd edn (New York: Harper & Row, 1937), 193.
[19] Smith, *John Bunyan in America*, 124.

Non-Dogmatic Pilgrims in Nineteenth-Century America

In many ways, D. J. Mandell's *The Adventures of Search for Life, a Bunyanic Narrative* (1838) presents a sympathetic view of the very theological liberalism that Cheever and his co-religionists ridicule. Notably, the work was published more than a decade earlier than any of the theologically conservative works of Cheever and company and, moreover, it can hardly be considered 'glib'. Its author was the pastor of a Universalist congregation in Maine, and the form of Christian Universalism he represented emerged expressly over and against the doctrine of eternal reprobation that features so prominently in orthodox Calvinism. Mandell's *Bunyanic Narrative* is thus an imaginative inversion of Bunyan's own allegory. It tells the story of one Mr Search for Life and his pilgrimage from his native City of Partialism in the domain of Error, through many hazards of prejudice and the Wilderness of Doubt, across the Bridge of Reason, and ultimately into the City of Universalism, situated on the Mountain of God's Mercy. Mandell depicts Partialism as a grim city walled by 'eternal misery':

> Above the place hangs a large cloud, called *the wrath of God*. There is a legend among the inhabitants of the city of Partialism, that this cloud, though large and threatening, will not break upon the city, but, that the Sun will burst through ultimately in noontide grandeur, and concentrate upon the place all its glory; while the clouds above will pour their gathered torrents upon those who dwell without the walls and sweep them into a bottomless abyss which yawns near by.[20]

Another feature of Partialism is that the names of its inhabitants do not agree with their natures. Gospel Charity Esq., for example, established an institution of learning, but then 'required the young men to believe just as *he* did'. Another, the Rev. Mr Preach Truth, DD, was educated in the theological institution of which Dr Hold-fast to Election is professor, and is so well educated that he reassures his congregation that 'even if he *believed* the doctrine of universal salvation, he *would not preach it*'. But Search for Life cannot abide such hypocrisy, and he eventually escapes Partialism. He encounters numerous difficulties (the Road Infidelity, the Wilderness of Doubt, the Highway of Denial of God, and the Mountains of Despair, and so on), but at last stumbles upon the Bridge of Reason. It is this bridge that brings Search for Life into the 'territory of ancient Christianity', from which professedly all-embracing perspective he discovers that 'the diversion of Scripture into Partialism, *was the most foolish and fatal thing which its inhabitants could have done* for its prosperity'. Arriving finally atop the Mountain of God's

---

[20] D. J. Mandell, *The Adventures of Search for Life, a Bunyanic Narrative, as Detailed by Himself* (Portland, ME: S. H. Colesworthy, 1838), 6. Subsequent serial quotations refer to *Adventures*, 8, 14, 28, 85, and 70–1, respectively.

Mercy, Search for Life is welcomed into Universalism, where he encounters inhabitants 'utterly devoid of hypocrisy, and incapable of self-righteousness. They walked arm in arm together, and conversed familiarly with each other, as though there existed between them the strictest brotherhood.'

Whatever the literary merits of the work might be, *The Adventures of Search for Life* is historically and theologically significant for the fact that Mandell emplots his story of pilgrimage in a 'Bunyanic' way, even while critiquing the sectarian commitments of Bunyan and his fellow Puritans. Although he could hardly have been familiar with Coleridge's claim that 'the Bunyan of Parnassus had the better of the Bunyan of the Conventicle',[21] Mandell would certainly have agreed with him. Mandell's own narrative aims to recast Bunyan's sectarian Christian as a nineteenth-century spiritual seeker. In doing so, he inaugurates what we might call the meta-allegorical reading of *The Pilgrim's Progress* in America. That is to say, while *The Pilgrim's Progress* itself is a specifically Puritan allegory about the path the elect walk to eternal life (and not to reprobation), the Universalist reading allegorizes the Puritan allegory itself, abstracting it to another level so it speaks symbolically about the toils and snares all human beings face in their journey through life. It is surely along such lines that the post-Christian Transcendentalist Henry David Thoreau speaks when, in his first book, he insists that although 'there is no infidelity, nowadays, so great as that which prays, and keeps Sabbath, and rebuilds the churches', nonetheless 'The New Testament is an invaluable book [and] I think that Pilgrim's Progress is the best sermon which has been preached from this text.'[22]

But it is two of Thoreau's Concord neighbours—Nathaniel Hawthorne and Louisa May Alcott—who are probably best known among contemporary readers for their adaptations of Bunyan's work. Since it is Alcott's use of Bunyan that is most in line with the liberalizing trend, let us consider her work first, and then return to Hawthorne. Alcott was born in 1832 into a family very much at the centre of experimental utopian Transcendentalism, associated especially with her father's short-lived attempt at communal living at 'Fruitlands' in Harvard, Massachusetts. Both of her parents, Bronson and Abby, were educational reformers and friends of such New England notables as Thoreau, Ralph Waldo Emerson, and Margaret Fuller, all of whom combined the anti-Puritan sensibilities of their childhood Unitarianism with deep feeling, prodigious conscientiousness, and an enduring conception of life as a spiritual quest. Fuller, for instance, referred to herself as a 'pilgrim and a sojourner on earth',[23] and would resonate with Bronson Alcott's claim that Bunyan's *The Pilgrim's Progress* was one of the few books that 'gave me to myself' in that one did not merely read it, but could take

---

[21] Quoted in Roger Sharrock (ed.), *The Pilgrim's Progress: A Casebook* (London and Basingstoke: Macmillan, 1976), 53.

[22] Henry David Thoreau, *A Week on the Concord and Merrimac Rivers* (Boston, MA: Houghton Mifflin, 1961), 72, 77.

[23] Quoted in Shaun O'Connell, *Imagining Boston: A Literary Landscape* (Boston, MA: Beacon Press, 1990), 68.

it on and in a sense *live* it through playing it.²⁴ Alcott combined this sense of life-as-pilgrimage with the Romantic educational philosophy he developed out of Coleridge's *Aids to Reflection* (1825), employing Bunyan's allegory in his parenting and teaching, to cultivate what he believed was the child's innate divinity, and so direct a sojourner's appetites from carnality to spirituality. The mark of her father's educational philosophy on Louisa May Alcott is apparent as early as the first page of her most famous work, the semi-autobiographical *Little Women* (1868), whose preface overtly adapts lines from Bunyan's 'way of sending forth his second part of the Pilgrim' as follows:

> Go then, my little Book, and show to all
> That entertain, and bid thee welcome shall,
> What thou dost keep close shut up in thy breast;
> And wish that thou dost show them may be blest
> To them for good, may make them choose to be
> Pilgrims better, by far, than thee or me [...].
> For little tripping maids may follow God
> Along the ways which saintly feet have trod.²⁵

Little Women charts the progress of the four March girls—Meg, Jo, Beth, and Amy—and their story proved popular enough for Alcott to subsequently follow the March family through three further novels: *Good Wives* (1869), *Little Men* (1871), and *Jo's Boys* (1886). By contrast with the earlier adaptations already discussed, Alcott does not employ *The Pilgrim's Progress* allegorically, but rather draws upon it as a framing device, and as a rich reservoir of apt allusions for characterizing the challenges of her protagonists. Several chapter titles give this away at a glance: 'Playing Pilgrims', 'Burdens', 'Beth Finds the Palace Beautiful', 'Amy's Valley of Humiliation', 'Jo Meets Apollyon', 'Meg Goes to Vanity Fair', and so on. The first of these opens on the domestic scene in which the girls are discontentedly making Christmas preparations, grumbling over their relative poverty and paucity of presents, while lamenting the absence of their father, who is away serving as a chaplain in the Union Army during the Civil War. In order to cheer them and give them purpose, Mrs March (Marmee) reminds her daughters of how they used to 'play Pilgrim's Progress' when they were younger:

> Nothing delighted you more than to have me tie my piece-bags on your backs for burdens, give you hats and sticks, and rolls of paper, and let you travel through the house from the cellar, which was the City of Destruction, up, up, to the house-top, where you had all the lovely things you could collect to make a Celestial City.

---

²⁴ Bronson Alcott, *The Journals of Bronson Alcott*, ed. Odell Shepard (Boston, MA: Little, Brown, & Company, 1938), 111.

²⁵ Louisa May Alcott, *Little Women*, ed. Valerie Alderson (New York: Oxford University Press, 1994), 4. Subsequent serial quotations refer to *Little Women*, 14, 14, and 15, respectively.

When the girls happily recall this role play, Marmee encourages them to enter into the game once again, only in a deeper way:

> We are never too old for this, my dears, because it is a play we are playing all the time in one way or another. Our burdens are here, our road is before us, and the longing for goodness and happiness is the guide that leads us through many troubles and mistakes to the peace which is a true Celestial City. Now, my little pilgrims, suppose you begin again, not in play, but in earnest, and see how far on you can get before father comes home.

The girls agree to the plan, although Jo identifies one further difficulty. 'We were in the Slough of Despond tonight', she reflects, 'and mother came and pulled us out as Help did in the book. We ought to have a roll of directions, like Christian. What shall we do about that?' To which Marmee answers, 'Look under your pillows, Christmas morning, and you will find your guide book.' And in the grey Christmas dawn the pilgrims discover under their pillows a little copy of the New Testament. In this way, *Little Women* takes *The Pilgrim's Progress* as its framing device, and like Bunyan's work, identifies its manual as the New Testament. In order to endure their father's absence during the war and find their separate peace, the March girls adapt the model of Bunyan's Christian to their domestic drama. And even after their father's return, when frail Beth goes to her death, both her New Testament and *The Pilgrim's Progress* rest on her bedside table.

Despite Alcott's indebtedness to Bunyan, however, the differences between Bunyan's Christian and Alcott's pilgrims are equally striking. As Elshtain notes, although the world of Bunyan's pilgrim was 'indispensable and inescapable' to the March girls, 'their pitfalls and villains were less clear than Christian's, whose instructions by the nineteenth century had become just a bit blurred'.[26] The principal 'blurring' in this particular instance is the thoroughgoing domestication of the concept of pilgrimage. Smith's judgement on the work is for this reason censorious: 'It was inevitable that a society for whom the medieval Christian concept of a spiritual quest had lost all meaning would translate it into the banal and mediocre language of middle-class sentimental piety.'[27] But even granting that Alcott develops her theme under the similitude of juvenilia, one can read *Little Women* more charitably than Smith does. Its subtle pedagogy of gender equality, its message of the importance of character formation, and its exemplification of moral responsibility to family, friends, and community, contributed importantly to the domestic reform movement of the late nineteenth century. Still, in *Little Women* the personal sacrifice entailed in pilgrimage is notably dissimilar to the self-dispossession modelled by

---

[26] Elshtain, 'Jane Addams: A Pilgrim's Progress', 346–47.

[27] Smith, *John Bunyan in America*, 102. It should be noted that *Little Women* was by no means the only such sentimental 'domestication' of *The Pilgrim's Progress* in this period. As Ruth K. MacDonald has shown, other now-forgotten titles include Martha Finley Farquharson's *Elsie Dinsmore* (1867), and Susan Warner's *The Wide, Wide World* (1878), among others. See MacDonald, *Christian's Children: The Influence of John Bunyan's The Pilgrim's Progress on American Children's Literature* (Bern: Peter Lang, 1989), 46–68.

Bunyan's Christian and Christiana. And it is in this respect telling that when in the final sentence of *Jo's Boys* Alcott lets 'the music stop, the lights die out, and the curtain fall for ever on the March family', the family has not by grace and with difficulty entered the Celestial City, but has instead built a home of sweetness and light called 'Parnassus' on the hill next to the school and college they have founded, and 'endeavoured to suit everyone by many weddings, few deaths, and as much prosperity as the eternal fitness of things will permit'.[28] Thus, Alcott's classic quartet makes in earnest the very point the evangelical Cheever parodies when he has the Steersman Deism declare: 'We shall have heaven on earth when society is reconstructed.'[29] No matter how high-minded, this progressive universalization of the conception of pilgrimage nonetheless fails to recognize the fundamental incongruity between progress to Parnassus and the paradoxical New Testament dictum that one must lose one's life in order to gain it.

Nathaniel Hawthorne was considerably less sanguine about the authenticity of this modern conversion of the concept of pilgrimage. Due perhaps in part to his own failed experiment in communal utopianism at Brook Farm, just west of Boston, Hawthorne was not a liberal progressive like the Alcotts (he was Bronson's contemporary), but neither was he a latter-day Puritan like George Cheever, his former classmate at Bowdoin College in Maine. He saw more clearly than progressive Americans like Franklin, Mandell, and Alcott, on one hand, and evangelical Americans like Cheever and company, on the other, the outrageous implication that, if Christianity is true, then authentic progress entails a self-dispossession so thoroughgoing that very few indeed genuinely walk that path. His faith was idiosyncratic and non-institutional. He very rarely attended worship services, but in 'Sunday at Home' (1837) claims that although his 'form be absent' from the services he finds frigid, still his 'inner man goes constantly to church'.[30]

There is ample reason to believe, however, that *The Pilgrim's Progress* retained the old earnest warmth Hawthorne encountered in his early reading, and indeed that Bunyan remained among his primary influences.[31] In 'The Hall of Fantasy' (1843) Hawthorne characterizes Bunyan as 'moulded of homeliest clay, but instinct with celestial fire',[32] and in 'The Celestial Rail-Road' (1843) he rekindles Bunyan's classic with his penetrating ironic imagination. In common with Cheever and company, Hawthorne's parody mocks the nineteenth-century concept of 'progress' conceived as liberalization and technological modernization. Unlike the evangelicals, however, Hawthorne's dreaming

---

[28] Louisa May Alcott, *Jo's Boys* (London: Puffin Books, 1994), 350.

[29] Cheever, *A Reel in a Bottle*, 98.

[30] Nathaniel Hawthorne, 'Sunday at Home', in *Selected Tales and Sketches*, ed. Michael J. Colacurcio (New York: Penguin Books, 1987), 200–07 (202).

[31] Austin Warren writes, 'At six, Hawthorne made the acquaintance of *Pilgrim's Progress*. [He] was accustomed to take the old family copy to a large chair in a corner of the room near a window, and, without speaking, to read it by the hour. The early impression was ineffaceable: *Pilgrim's Progress* is the one book to which the unallusive Hawthorne constantly alludes in his own writing'; 'Hawthorne's Reading', *New England Quarterly*, 8 (1935), 480–97 (482).

[32] Nathaniel Hawthorne, 'The Hall of Fantasy', in *Selected Tales and Sketches*, ed. Colacurcio, 246–58 (247).

narrator does not extol the ostensible sincerity of modern-day surrogates for Christian and Faithful, but rather describes his own journey on a newly built railway running from the City of Destruction towards the Celestial City, which he undertakes merely as a diversion: 'Having a little time upon my hands', he says, 'I resolved to gratify a liberal curiosity by making a trip thither.'[33]

In this respect, the protagonist of 'The Celestial Rail-Road' is, as Smith suggests, a latter-day incarnation of Bunyan's character 'Ignorance'.[34] It is through the eyes of this disingenuous tourist that readers encounter the conflict between residual Puritanism, on one side, and the progressive idealism of Protestant Liberalism and American Transcendentalism, on the other. His guide on the outing is a Mr Smooth-it-away, one of the largest stockholders in the railway corporation. As they cross the 'convenient bridge' over the 'the famous Slough of Despond', Smooth-it-away boasts that they 'obtained a sufficient foundation for it by throwing into the slough some editions of books of morality, volumes of French philosophy and German rationalism, tracts, sermons, [etc.]'.[35] Another convenience is the introduction of a baggage-car on the train, so that passengers need not bear their burdens, but instead reclaim them at journey's end. Mr Greatheart, having grown 'preposterously stiff and narrow' in later years, no longer champions pilgrims on their way, but Christian's old enemy Apollyon has been persuaded to become chief engineer, and this reconciliation, together with the considerable number of passengers of the most respectable sort, is reckoned a great advance: 'It would have done Bunyan's heart good to see it.' Along the way, the train rolls by the cave that the Giants Pagan and Pope used to inhabit. The name of the new resident is Giant Transcendentalism, a vague figure of 'fog and duskiness' who calls after them 'in so strange a phraseology that [the passengers] knew not what he meant, nor whether to be encouraged or frightened'. Next they arrive at Vanity Fair, a place full of Unitarian ministers and Transcendentalist lecturers, and which 'the Christian reader, if he have had no accounts of the city later than Bunyan's time, will be surprised to hear that almost every street has its church, and that the reverend clergy are nowhere held in higher respect'.

Clearly, this Vanity Fair is a dig at Hawthorne's contemporary New England—'such are the charms of the place, that people often affirm it to be the true and only heaven', and Tophet (hell) is 'denied even a metaphorical existence'. Here Hawthorne's tourist also meets two anachronistic pilgrims who spurn the easy way to paradise symbolized by new technologies and liberal religious philosophies. These 'worthy simpletons' exhort listeners to choose the traditional way of pilgrimage. But, despite the fact that his conscience is stirred to sympathy and almost to admiration for them, still Hawthorne's Ignorance is not so simple as to forgo his 'original plan of gliding along easily and commodiously by rail-road'. And the tale ends with the two 'worthy simpletons' crossing

---

[33] Nathaniel Hawthorne, 'The Celestial Rail-Road', in *Selected Tales and Sketches*, ed. Colacurcio, 316–35 (316).

[34] Smith, *John Bunyan in America*, 61.

[35] Hawthorne, 'The Celestial Rail-Road', 317. Subsequent serial quotations refer to 'The Celestial Rail-Road', 318, 326, 327, 327, 324, 330, and 331, respectively.

through the river and being welcomed into the Celestial City, while the rail passengers are transferred to a steamboat and ferried down the river towards a fiery destination. At this, Hawthorne's narrator awakens to find that it was a dream, but also a caveat: the seductive manifestations of modern progress—both technological and philosophical—foster spiritual laziness, superficiality, and, in a word, sin.

Hawthorne shares with his narrator the characteristic that he too is personally unable to side firmly with Bunyan's pilgrims. But unlike his narrator Hawthorne does not complacently succumb to the temptations of modernism. Rather, one finds in 'The Celestial Rail-Road' (as in Hawthorne's writings generally) the juxtaposition of multiple intellectual alignments held together ironically, yet hopefully, through a distinctively modern form of sceptical theism. As a key component of this symbolist project, Bunyan's allegory enables Hawthorne to indict the bankruptcy of liberal optimism and the ubiquity of sin in a way that prefigures developments in twentieth-century Protestantism articulated by such American 'theologians of crisis' as Reinhold Niebuhr and H. Richard Niebuhr.

SECULARIZATION AND THE PROGRESS OF MR LITTLE-FAITH

From its zenith in the middle of the nineteenth century, the popularity of *The Pilgrim's Progress* in America gradually receded, along with its role as a cultural and religious touchstone. Granted, the work remained a reservoir of eulogistic phrases for political discourse, as Galen Johnson has recently shown.[36] But Bunyan's theological and literary influence became so thematically diluted in the twentieth century there were few readers and even fewer authors of whom one could say *The Pilgrim's Progress* served as their *primary* inspiration. Occasionally Frank Baum's *The Wonderful Wizard of Oz* (1900) is cited as an exception. But if so, it proves the rule since, in John Updike's words, it is 'a *Pilgrim's Progress* emptied of religion'.[37] Baum puts a happy but vacuous face on a human condition that increasing numbers viewed as profoundly meaningless. In a century of wars—hot, cold, and proxy—perceptions that the country (indeed, 'civilization') had lost its way grew pervasive. Concomitant with this new sense was the general assumption that the Puritanical worldview of Bunyan and his co-religionists in America could no longer speak to a secularized humanity come of age, even when the old sectarian allegory was 'transcendentalized' to address the journey of life universally. It simply failed to capture the imagination of readers as it had done. And not *voluntary* readers only: in

---

[36] See Galen K. Johnson, '*The Pilgrim's Progress* in the History of American Public Discourse', *LATCH*, 4 (2011), 1–31.

[37] John Updike, 'Oz is Us', in John Updike, *Due Considerations: Essays and Criticism* (London: Hamish Hamilton, 2007), 212–20 (220).

1916 one writer fretted that *The Pilgrim's Progress* was 'being slowly but surely withdrawn from the lists of required reading in our secondary schools'.[38] Then in 1950, it secured the top spot as 'most boring' classic in a Columbia University Press poll.[39] No doubt this relegation was due in part to increased secularization, with the attendant assumption that the path Christian travels leads nowhere.

This is not to deny that Bunyan sometimes figures in the literature of the so-called 'American Century', even if in a more attenuated fashion than in previous generations. Updike occasionally seasoned his narratives with allusions to *The Pilgrim's Progress*, and readers have ascertained hints of Bunyan in, among other places, Jack Kerouac's *On the Road* (1957), the poetry of Elizabeth Bishop, and the lyrics of Bob Dylan.[40] The list could be extended. But twentieth-century American authors rarely evoked Bunyan to narrate the path to the Celestial City. Rather, where allusions prove substantive, they tend to be dialectical appropriations aimed at accepting the perceived absurdity of the human condition, as in Robert Lowell's profession that 'Faith is trying to do without / faith.'[41] By and large, with the spread of secularization, American writers appropriated *The Pilgrim's Progress* typically either to 'storify' atrocities, as in E. E. Cummings's *The Enormous Room* (1922) and Kurt Vonnegut's *Slaughterhouse-Five* (1969), or to lament lost faith in an age where the threat of nuclear apocalypse has eclipsed Puritan millenarianism, as in Lowell's *For the Union Dead* (1964): '[W]e wish the river had another shore, / some further range of delectable mountains.'[42]

This eclipse, however, does not necessarily signal the end of Bunyan's influence on American religious history and literary culture. For one notable and explicitly theological exception both to earlier partisan appropriations of Bunyan and to the twentieth-century elegiac form is Richard R. Niebuhr's *Experiential Religion* (1972). Due to his

---

[38] Martha Hale Shackford, 'Shall we Study "The Pilgrim's Progress"?' *English Journal*, 5 (1916), 647–58 (647).

[39] '10 "Boring Classics" Voted by Readers: Editors, Authors, Librarians in Poll—Bunyan Wins First Place, "Moby Dick" Second', *New York Times* (3 July 1950), 23.

[40] See George W. Hunt, *John Updike and the Three Great Secret Things: Sex, Religion, and Art* (Grand Rapids, MI: Eerdmans, 1980), 31, 35, 38, 43; Tim Hunt, *Kerouac's Crooked Road: The Development of a Fiction* (Carbondale, IL: Southern Illinois University Press, 2010), 89–90; Zachariah Pickard, *Elizabeth Bishop's Poetics of Description* (Montreal: McGill-Queens University Press, 2009), 28, 119–20; and Michael Gray, *The Art of Bob Dylan*, new edn (London: Hamlyn, 1981), 48–9. It should be noted that although Bunyan's influence on these authors is clear, it is also comparatively diluted. Kerouac's 'road' theme, especially, might just as well be affiliated with Mark Twain's work, whose own writings bear little substantive comparison with Bunyan's classic, notwithstanding the title of his first book, *The Innocents Abroad, or The New Pilgrims' Progress* (1869), or for that matter, Huckleberry Finn's remark that he 'read considerable in [*The Pilgrim's Progress*] now and then. The statements was interesting, but tough': *The Adventures of Huckleberry Finn* (New York: Harper, 1912), 140.

[41] Robert Lowell, *For the Union Dead* (New York: Farrar, 1964), 40.

[42] E. E. Cummings, *The Enormous Room* (New York: The Modern Library, 1949). See also Smith, *John Bunyan in America*, 105–19; Kurt Vonnegut, *Slaughterhouse-Five* (New York: Dell Publishing Company, 1969), and see also Peter Freese, 'Kurt Vonnegut's *Slaughterhouse-Five* or, How to Storify an Atrocity', in *Kurt Vonnegut's Slaughterhouse-Five: New Edition*, ed. Harold Bloom (New York: Infobase Publishing, 2009), 19; Lowell, *For the Union Dead*, 59.

late modern juxtaposition of various intellectual alignments, Niebuhr shares much with Hawthorne's appropriation of Bunyan. The key difference, apart from genre, is that whereas Hawthorne explores the incongruity of different alignments by recasting the figure of Ignorance, Niebuhr does so through 'the present-day counterpart of Mr. Little-Faith, of whom Christian and Hopeful once talked rather charitably as they made their way roundabout toward the Celestial City'.[43] Niebuhr explores Little-faith's strife with doubt as emblematic of the modern-day crisis of being both in and out of faith, bombarded as individuals are by the sheer welter of experience, the boon and bane of new technologies, and the overlapping variety of ways of being human in the world. In such a context, progress in the experience of 'God-ruling' (Niebuhr's rendering of the Kingdom of God) comes from relinquishing dogmatic certainty, and making do with 'the homely virtues of courage, wisdom, justness, and temperance, leavened perhaps by a little faith, hope, and love'.[44] In the tradition of Bunyan, Niebuhr's own way of reflecting on recognizable faith within the world exemplifies Marilynne Robinson's insight that 'great theology is always a kind of giant and intricate poetry, like epic or saga'.[45] It also demonstrates why, even a century after schoolteachers began to worry that *The Pilgrim's Progress* was being removed from the required reading lists of American schools, we cannot regard it as just another unread classic. For, again citing Robinson (whose love of Puritan literature and theology might also suggest a subterranean indebtedness to Bunyan), 'Who can imagine how the things we call ideas live in the world, or how they can change, or how they perish, or how they can be renewed?'[46]

Suggested Reading

Buell, Lawrence, *New England Literary Culture: From Revolution through Renaissance* (Cambridge: Cambridge University Press, 1989).

Caldwell, Patricia, *The Puritan Conversion Narrative: The Beginnings of American Expression* (Cambridge: Cambridge University Press, 1983).

Covey, Cyclone, *The American Pilgrimage: The Roots of American History, Religion, and Culture* (New York: Collier Books, 1964).

Johnson, Galen K., '*The Pilgrim's Progress* in the History of American Public Discourse', *LATCH*, 4 (2011), 1–31.

MacDonald, Ruth K., *Christian's Children: The Influence of John Bunyan's The Pilgrim's Progress on American Children's Literature* (Bern: Peter Lang, 1989).

Miller, Perry and Thomas H. Johnson, *The Puritans* (New York: American Book Company, 1938).

Pahl, Jon, *Empire of Sacrifice: The Religious Origins of American Violence* (New York: New York University Press, 2010).

---

[43] Richard R. Niebuhr, *Experiential Religion* (New York: Harper & Row, 1972), xi.
[44] Niebuhr, *Experiential Religion*, 5.
[45] Marilynne Robinson, *The Death of Adam: Essays on Modern Thought* (New York: Picador, 2005), 117.
[46] Robinson, *The Death of Adam*, 226.

Sanford, Charles L., *The Quest for Paradise: Europe and the American Moral Imagination* (Urbana, IL: University of Illinois Press, 1961).
Smith, David E., *John Bunyan in America* (Bloomington, IN: Indiana University Press, 1966).
Smith, David E., 'Publication of John Bunyan's Works in America', *New York Public Library Bulletin*, 66 (1962), 630–52.

CHAPTER 35

BUNYAN: CLASS AND ENGLISHNESS

GARY DAY

IN some ways it is quite easy to talk about Bunyan and class. He attacks the rich in *A Few Sighs from Hell* (1658), accusing them of being ungodly and of oppressing the poor. The antagonism between the two is evident even after death when the poor delight in watching the torments of the rich in hell. The profit motive is denounced in *The Life and Death of Mr. Badman* (1680) and Bunyan himself was sufficiently conscious of his origins to write, at the beginning of *Grace Abounding to the Chief of Sinners* (1666), that his father's house was 'of that rank that is meanest and most despised' (*GA*, 5). Equally, it is not difficult to talk about Bunyan and Englishness. Mr Wiseman, one of our narrators in *The Life and Death of Mr. Badman*, complains of the English love of 'cursing' (*MB*, 29–30), which seemed to be as much a part of the national character as, according to Daniel Defoe, was drink, another vice which Mr Wiseman roundly condemns (*MB*, 45–7).[1] Other supposedly English traits such as the plain style and an awkwardness or even downright hostility to the flesh can also be found in Bunyan's writing.[2] Moreover, we can detect in works like *A Few Sighs from Hell* and *Grace Abounding* versions of that melancholy which was a key component of the early modern English temperament.[3] We move, for example, from a state of 'sadness' in the former publication to black despair in the latter one. But it is perhaps the place of *The Pilgrim's Progress* (1678; 1684) in the literary canon that most seems to secure Bunyan's status as a representative of Englishness. In his preface to *A Dictionary of the English Language* (1755), Samuel Johnson declared

---

[1] See Daniel Defoe, 'The True-Born Englishman', in W. R. Owens (ed.), *The True-Born Englishman and Other Poems* (London: Pickering & Chatto, 2003), 98.

[2] See Michael Davies, 'Bunyan's Bawdy: Sex and Sexual Wordplay in the Writings of John Bunyan', in Vera J. Camden (ed.), *Trauma and Transformation: The Political Progress of John Bunyan* (Stanford, CA: Stanford University Press, 2008), 100–19.

[3] See, for example, Douglas Trevor, *The Poetics of Melancholy in Early Modern England* (Ann Arbor, MI: University of Michigan Press, 2004).

that 'the chief glory of every people arises from its authors',[4] and the sturdy individualism of Christian, his independence of mind and determination to succeed, embodied the ideals of the English character.

CLASS, ENGLISHNESS, AND CRITICISM

But if it is so simple to talk about Bunyan and class and Bunyan and Englishness, then why, in the burgeoning field of Bunyan studies, has comparatively little been written on either of these topics, at least in recent times?[5] The short answer is that class has gone out of fashion in criticism. The topic of class was much discussed in the 1930s and that is where we find some key studies of Bunyan and class, the two most important of which are William York Tindall, *John Bunyan: Mechanick Preacher* (1934) and Jack Lindsay *John: Bunyan: Maker of Myths* (1937).[6] The rise in unemployment following the Wall Street Crash in 1929 and the British financial crisis of 1931 seemed to indicate that capitalism was near to collapse and the literature of the time, in England at least, was notoriously divided along class lines. Probably not since the English Civil War was writing so partisan. The sense of class conflict in this period coloured perceptions of the past. 'For the saints,' wrote Tindall, 'the class struggle needed the dignity of divine auspices, and as the miserable of today look for their sanction to Karl Marx and *The Communist Manifesto*, their seventeenth-century predecessors looked to Jesus and the Bible.'[7] Lindsay viewed the Civil War as a class war. It was a struggle between the crown, the middle classes, and 'the masses'. 'Communism', he declares, was 'the social aim behind the whole struggle.'[8] In *John Bunyan: Maker of Myths*, he makes a direct link between Bunyan's struggle to earn a living with that of the unemployed in 1930s Britain.[9] Lindsay also explains Bunyan's crisis of faith in *Grace Abounding* in terms of the economic upheaval of seventeenth-century England. Why, he asks, does Bunyan's temptation come to him in the form that he should 'sell Christ' (GA, 42)? His answer is that the metaphor

---

[4] Samuel Johnson, 'Preface' to *A Dictionary of the English Language*, in Donald Greene (ed.), *Samuel Johnson: A Critical Edition of the Major Works* (Oxford: Oxford University Press, 1984), 307–28 (327).

[5] There seems to be very little recent research published on Bunyan and class. Two exceptions are Paul Creelan and Robert Granfield, 'The Polish Peasant and *The Pilgrim's Progress*: Morality and Mythology in W. I. Thomas' Social Theory', *Journal for the Scientific Study of Religion*, 25 (1986), 162–79, and Paul Stevens, 'Bunyan, the Great War and the Political Ways of Grace', *RES*, 59 (2008), 701–21. There seems to be even less currently available on Bunyan and Englishness.

[6] William York Tindall, *John Bunyan: Mechanick Preacher* (1934; New York: Russell & Russell, 1964). Jack Lindsay, *John Bunyan: Maker of Myths* (1937; London: Methuen, 1969). See also Chapter 26 in this volume.

[7] Tindall, *John Bunyan*, 94.

[8] Jack Lindsay, *England my England: A Pageant of the People* (London: Fore Publications, n.d.), 29, 33.

[9] Lindsay, *John Bunyan*, 49–50.

'is the basis on which society is organized'. Men had no choice but to sell their labour because their own small plots of lands had been enclosed.[10]

Aside from E. P. Thompson's classic account of *The Making of the English Working Class* (first published in 1963), which identifies *The Pilgrim's Progress* as one of the 'foundation texts of the English working-class movement', there is no other full-length study of Bunyan and class until Christopher Hill's *A Turbulent, Seditious, and Factious People: John Bunyan and his Church 1628–1688* (1988).[11] Among other things, Hill stresses the economic causes of the Civil War; locates Bunyan's prose style in the tradition of popular protest; details the radical ideas that Bunyan would have been exposed to in the New Model Army; and highlights the class dimension of religious groups.[12] The pronounced class analysis of Hill's book is partly explained by the social unrest in Britain in the 1980s. Privatization, the deregulation of finance, deep cuts in welfare, the stripping away of union power, and the defeat of the miners in 1985 were all means by which Mrs Thatcher's government weakened the working class. Hill's book was a reminder that, contrary to what the Prime Minister said, there was an alternative to her economic policy and it honoured the radical tradition she was trying to extinguish.

But what of Englishness? Isabel Hofmeyr argues that the successful use of *The Pilgrim's Progress* to spread Christianity, particularly in Africa, excited pride in Bunyan as an icon of 'Englishness' back home. But after the decline in the number of missionaries in the late nineteenth century, this aspect of Bunyan's work gradually became the preserve of the academic establishment.[13] There is, however, some evidence of a more general interest in Bunyan and Englishness in the interwar years. This was no doubt prompted by the tercentenary of his birth in 1928, but it also owes something to the mood of the nation at this time. Revulsion at the horrors of the First World War and fear about the effects of the Russian Revolution (1917), combined with anxiety about strikes and working-class unrest, made many long for a return to an older, rural, more tranquil England.[14]

This longing was reflected in a number of activities such as hiking, rambling, and cycling, and also by a constant stream of guidebooks and magazines devoted to recovering the true spirit of the countryside. Among the most popular publications were John Betjeman's *Shell Guides*, Batsford's Face of Britain series, and J. Robertson Scott's *The*

---

[10] Lindsay, *John Bunyan*, 66. According to Lindsay, '8.45 per cent. of Bedfordshire was enclosed between 1455 and 1607': *John Bunyan*, 79. Christopher Hill claims that 'one quarter of the land of England was enclosed in the seventeenth century' and he also quotes, with approval, part of James Turner's argument about Christian in *The Pilgrim's Progress* that, as a displaced person, he is seen as a trespasser on the lands of others, for example, Giant Despair. See Hill, *Bunyan*, 17, 219, and James Turner, 'Bunyan's Sense of Place', in Vincent Newey (ed.), *The Pilgrim's Progress: Critical and Historical Views* (Liverpool: Liverpool University Press, 1980), 91–110.

[11] E. P. Thompson, *The Making of the English Working Class* (London: Penguin, 1980), 34. See also Chapter 26 in this volume.

[12] Hill, *Bunyan*, 16–27, 28–38, 45–60, 92–9.

[13] Isabel Hofmeyr, *The Portable Bunyan: A Transnational History of The Pilgrim's Progress* (Princeton, NJ: Princeton University Press, 2004).

[14] See, for example, Alison Light, *Forever England: Femininity, Literature and Conservatism between the Wars* (London and New York: Routledge, 1991).

Countryman, which, as Krishan Kumar has argued, made explicit links between the English heritage and the English national character.[15] The Homeland Association performed a similar operation. Its aim, according to Prescott Row, the founder and general editor, was to 'help our fellow countrymen to travel in, to appreciate intelligently, and to study their own country and its story, in other words to encourage knowledge of and love of our native Britain'.[16] Each of its booklets contained a foreword on the inside cover followed by a series of photographs accompanied by one or two lines of text, the whole being bound between two cardboard sheets.

C. Bernard Cockett's *John Bunyan's England: A Tour with a Camera in the Footsteps of the Immortal Dreamer* (1928) was published in the Homeland series of publications in Bunyan's tercentenary year. The 'Foreword' gives a very brief account of Bunyan's life. He is hailed (erroneously) as 'the Father of the Novel' and presented as 'a wild flower' in England's 'garden'. The photographs, and the short descriptions which accompany them, are intended to make the reader not just 'love England the better' or 'know Bunyan the more', but to 'turn tourists into pilgrims'. The majority of pictures are of places associated with Bunyan's life: his birthplace, his cottage, the village green where he played 'tipcat', spots where he preached, and so on. There are also a few photographs of locations associated with *The Pilgrim's Progress*, for example, the ruins of Houghton House, believed to be the original of the House Beautiful, and the view of the 'Delectable Mountains' from 'Hill Difficulty in Ampthill'.[17]

The photographs carry several meanings. First, they evoke a strong sense of place, and, second, they suggest a continuity between the countryside in Bunyan's time and the countryside now—a continuity that acts as a reassuring contrast to the experience of rapid change which characterizes the modern world. Third, the photographs define the landscape in both literary and historical terms. *The Pilgrim's Progress* animates the locality around Bedford, marking it as a scene both of Christian's adventure—of his struggles, temptations, and eventual triumph—and of Bunyan's own persecution, imprisonment, and ultimate liberty. The hill outside Ampthill is not just a hump of ground: it is also, as the 'Hill of Difficulty', a symbol of Christian effort and endurance. Such markers in the Pilgrim's journey reinforce the spiritual nature of his struggle against temptation and the forces of evil. The idea of the country that emerges from *John Bunyan's England* is of a land whose identity, defined in largely literary and Christian terms, persists through time. A key aspect of this identity is inwardness. Cockett describes Bunyan's work as the 'epic of an inner life'. The implication is that the English, as represented by Bunyan, are partly characterized by the drama of their inner life, which is a rich blend of literature and Christianity.

---

[15] See Krishan Kumar, *The Making of English National Identity* (Cambridge: Cambridge University Press, 2003), 229–33.

[16] Prescott Row, quoted on the back cover of C. Bernard Cockett, *John Bunyan's England: A Tour with a Camera in the Footsteps of the Immortal Dreamer* (London: The Homeland Association, 1928).

[17] Cockett, Foreword to *John Bunyan's England*, n.p.

But Cockett doesn't just see Bunyan as the embodiment of Englishness. He is an 'apostle for Christian unity' for the whole world: 'Visitors from the Dominions coming "Home", Americans of British Ancestry, and pilgrims of all nationalities long to drink at the ancient springs of life and literature in these sea-girt isles.'[18] That Bunyan could be both a national and international figure was the result of a particular conception of empire, one which saw subject nations almost as a mirror of England itself. In the words of John Seeley, Professor of Modern History at Cambridge in the nineteenth century, the empire was primarily a union of English-speaking peoples: 'When we have accustomed ourselves to contemplate the whole Empire together and call it all England, we shall see that [it] is a great homogeneous people, one in blood, language, religion and laws, but dispersed over boundless space.'[19] This idea that the empire was simply England writ large appears to have influenced Cockett's view of Bunyan as a representative of both England and the world.

Charles G. Harper, whose book *The Bunyan Country* was also published for the 1928 tercentenary, makes Bunyan's Christianity a unifying force solely for the English. Downplaying Bunyan's Puritanism, whose 'excesses meant republicanism, violence and destruction', he instead emphasizes how Bunyan 'counselled meekness towards all magistrates and obedience to them and the King'.[20] Harper dismisses descriptions of Bunyan as a Baptist, Congregationalist, or even a Dissenter. Bunyan himself, he notes, refused all titles but that of 'a Christian', saying that all the others 'came neither from Jerusalem nor Antioch but rather from Hell and Babylon, for they naturally tend to divisions'.[21] Harper's sense of Bunyan's Englishness, then, is similar to Cockett's. Both link it with his Christianity and both identify him closely with the landscape, but Harper also locates Bunyan's Englishness in his paradigmatic use of the language: 'He is eloquent because he is so absolutely sincere, and his style achieves grace because of its direct, effortless simplicity.' Bunyan, indeed, belongs to that 'pure English' which had its 'beginnings in Chaucer and Gower'. This honesty and directness of speech are used to further distance Bunyan from the Puritan tradition whose 'hypocrisy and self-righteousness […] laid England under a yoke of sadness for years'.[22]

There is a class element to Harper's conception of Bunyan's Englishness. Harper is dismissive of 'the average ploughman and the villager' who take no delight in 'the speculative mind'. Their lack of interest in ideas or in the work of imagination is what sets them apart from Bunyan, whose work can only be appreciated by the educated man or woman. This sentiment is reinforced when Harper visits Bedford. Despite knowing the location of the Bunyan meeting house, he asks for directions 'from curiosity to find out

---

[18] Cockett, Foreword to *John Bunyan's England*, n.p.
[19] John Robert Seeley, *The Expansion of England* (1883; Chicago: Chicago University Press, 1971), 126.
[20] Charles Harper, *The Bunyan Country* (Oxford: Fox, Jones & Co., Kemp Hall Press, 1928), 18, 19. On the point about submission to kings, see also W. R. Owens, ' "Antichrist Must Be Pulled Down": Bunyan and the Millennium', in Anne Laurence, W. R. Owens, and Stuart Sim (eds.), *John Bunyan and his England, 1628–88* (London: Hambledon Press, 1990), 77–94, esp. 89–94.
[21] Cited in Harper, *Bunyan Country*, 20. See *MW*, 4: 270.
[22] Harper, *Bunyan Country*, xvii, x, 18.

what would be the answers'. He is particularly scathing about a 'shop girl in the High Street [who] hesitated and fumbled so long about it that her complete ignorance was quite evident'. Immediately after this incident, Harper himself is asked if he knows where 'the Billiards Hall was'. Now it is his turn to be unable to answer though, to be fair, he is only a visitor to the town. But his tone is decidedly lofty: '[I] surmised it might be in the High Street, where the public houses and the kinema palaces and all the other vanities are mostly gathered together.' He mentally dismisses his enquirer with the thought that 'Bunyan would not have approved of billiards.'[23]

Bunyan is used to mark a cultural boundary. He is recruited to the ranks of 'high culture' by virtue of his Christian integrity and literary achievements, which are implicitly contrasted with the supposed vanities and distractions of the new mass culture. There is a certain irony here. Bunyan, like many 'mechanick' preachers, would actually have been quite hostile to the conception of culture that Harper upholds. Baptists, Quakers, and other sectarians responded to the charge that they lacked learning by claiming that divine inspiration was far superior to a knowledge of the classics and the Church Fathers.[24] Pressing Bunyan into service on behalf of a cultured minority creates problems, then, for Bunyan as an icon of Englishness. His Christianity may, once it has been purged of its Puritan element, act as a binding force on the nation, but his literary qualities serve to divide it along cultural lines. And since there is a close connection between class and cultural pursuits, it is not too great a leap to say that Bunyan figures in Harper's argument as a symbol of class division. This point highlights one of the problems that bedevils the discussion of class and Englishness. How can people who share the same national identity be separated by a different class identity unless, of course, a sense of class is intrinsic to the very notion of what it means to be English?

F. R. Leavis's review article, 'Bunyan through Modern Eyes', brings together the issues of class and Englishness, though he prefers the phrase 'life of the people'. Leavis dismisses Lindsay's analysis in magisterial fashion: 'like most Marxist critics who undertake to explain art and culture, he produces the effect of having emptied life of content and everything of meaning'. He has more sympathy with Tindall, who is praised for acknowledging that Bunyan was one of a host of preachers, which tells us something 'about the genius of the English people in that age', but Tindall is also criticized for failing to grasp the nature of Bunyan's achievement, which is rooted in 'the life of the people'. This consists not merely of 'an idiomatic raciness of speech, expressing a strong vitality, but an art of social living, with its mature habits of valuation'. *The Pilgrim's Progress* grows out of this tradition. What makes it a great book, for Leavis, is 'its rich, poised and mature humanity' which transcends 'the uglier and pettier aspects of the intolerant creed, the narrow Calvinistic scheme of personal salvation, that Bunyan sets out explicitly to allegorize'.[25]

---

[23] Harper, *Bunyan Country*, 94, 218–19.
[24] See Tindall, *John Bunyan*, chs 4 and 5.
[25] F. R. Leavis, 'Bunyan through Modern Eyes', in F. R. Leavis, *The Common Pursuit* (Harmondsworth: Penguin, 1993), 204–10. This article first appeared in *Scrutiny*, 6 (1937–38), 461–68,

Leavis is the only critic, to my knowledge, who confronts the problem of hierarchy and Englishness in Bunyan together, though he prefers idioms like 'popular culture', 'traditional art', and 'the life of the people', which avoid what he considers to be the simplifying tendency of 'class'. These terms imply the existence of a coherent nation, one that finds its expression through literature. Moreover, this literature is created in part by the people themselves. Their earthy idioms, vivid sayings, and homely metaphors are the raw material from which the writer will shape his or her art: 'The same people that created the English language for Shakespeare's use speaks in Bunyan, though now it is a people that knows its Authorised Version.'[26] The idea that the people are the creators, and indeed the curators, of the language also gives a continuity to English history. However, the means of understanding that history are weakened by sidelining the notion of class. Whatever conceptual or empirical limitations it may have, the term class does at least draw attention to questions of wealth, power, ideology, and institutions: questions which Leavis believes have no bearing on the question of artistic merit, but which do throw some light on who controls the language.

Wider Cultural Trends Affecting Bunyan, Class, and Englishness

With Leavis's essay, we effectively come to the end of critical interest in both Bunyan and class and Bunyan and Englishness. There are many reasons for this abrupt terminus, but two stand out. First: the rise of literary theory, one of whose effects was to call into question the traditional canon of which *The Pilgrim's Progress* was a part. However, given theorists' interest in signification, it is surprising more attention wasn't paid to Bunyan, whose work often foregrounds the problem of meaning.[27] The second reason for the apparent lack of interest in the question of Bunyan and class, was that, from the mid-1980s the term 'class' itself almost vanished from literary studies, where it was displaced by an interest in feminism, ethnicity, and sexuality: a development that was in itself a reflection of wider social changes. The decline of heavy industry, the rise of mass culture, and the repeated claims in the media both that 'we are all middle class now' and (paradoxically) that Britain is a 'classless' society, all played a part in the demise of 'class' as a tool for literary and social analysis.

---

and was reprinted in *The Common Pursuit* (originally published in 1952). For further comments on Bunyan, see also Leavis's essay 'Literature and Society' in the same volume, 182–94, and his 'Afterword' to the Signet Classics/New American Library edition of *The Pilgrim's Progress*, ed. Catharine Stimpson (New York and London: Signet/New American Library, 1964), 284–300, reprinted in *Anna Karenina and Other Essays* (London: Chatto & Windus, 1967), 32–48.

[26] Leavis, 'Bunyan through Modern Eyes', 207–08.
[27] A notable exception is Tamsin Spargo, *The Writing of John Bunyan* (Farnham: Ashgate, 1997).

But the situation was different with 'Englishness'. From the end of the 1990s there have been numerous books about this subject and it continues to be hotly debated in the media, particularly now that Britain is poised to withdraw from Europe. If criticism really does reflect the concerns of the age, then surely there ought to be an abundance of material on Bunyan and Englishness. But there isn't. Here it may be useful to draw on the German historian Friedrich Meinecke's distinction between the political and the cultural nation.[28] The former refers to laws and institutions such as the monarchy and Parliament, while the latter refers to a common language, literature, and religion, though there is considerable overlap between the two. In the 1920s, Englishness was considered broadly a cultural matter. And, as Bunyan was linked, generally speaking, to the literature, the land, and the Christian heritage, he could be considered in these terms a representative of the 'cultural nation'.

But the phrase 'cultural nation' seems somewhat outmoded in our increasingly globalized and homogeneous world. It is difficult now to see Bunyan as a representative of Englishness in terms of either his Christianity, his attachment to place, or, indeed, his literary achievement. In general, these three elements, which were bound together in the views of writers such as Cockett and Harper in the late 1920s, have been separated out and consequently diminished. Arguably, this is particularly true of Bunyan's literary achievement since the very idea of the 'canon' has been regarded with intense scepticism since the late 1970s. Moreover, Bunyan's religious beliefs have little relevance to British society where Christianity, if not other faiths, has suffered a sharp decline since the 1960s. While Bunyan's faith is still mentioned and even promoted as a key to understanding 'our British roots', the subtitle of Woodrow Kroll's *Faith of Our Fathers*,[29] it is now of minor importance. Kroll's small book is an attempt to show the continuity of Christian thought and how it shaped not just British but also American society. But the specialist nature of this particular publication simply illustrates the decline of Christianity as a shaping force in modern society. If it thrives at all, it does so on the margins: in the evangelical churches whose spirit Bunyan would probably recognize.

It is a similar story with Bunyan and place. Writing in 1972, Ethel Mannin could point out of places of biographical interest in Bedford and Elstow. But there is no attempt here, as with previous writers, to link *The Pilgrim's Progress* to specific locations. Indeed, she declares that 'this kind of allegory is not readable in the late twentieth century'. Consequently, Bedford and its environs no longer carry the spiritual charge that they did in the work of Cockett or Harper, who made the landscape an integral part of understanding the allegory, and vice versa. It was that 'charge' which connected the past with the present but, since Mannin downplays *The Pilgrim's Progress*, she has to find other ways to show that the town is 'inescapably Bunyan's Bedford'. And she has a hard job. The places where Bunyan lived have vanished, as has the jail where he was imprisoned,

---

[28] Friedrich Meinecke, *Cosmopolitanism and the National State*, tr. Robert B. Kimber (1907; Princeton, NJ: Princeton University Press, 1970).

[29] Woodrow Kroll, *Faith of Our Fathers: Tracing Our British Roots* (Lincoln: The Good News Broadcasting Association, 1992).

though there is a plaque marking the spot on which it stood. The town has lost 'most of the outward and visible signs of its history'. The streets are dense with traffic but the town is 'thoroughly alive' thanks to 'the numerous Italians and the coloured immigrants with their bright clothes and their lovely children'. In the end, Mannin is reduced to asserting that the town 'is, nevertheless, very much Bunyan's Bedford'.[30]

But if Bunyan can no longer be deemed relevant in a cultural or topographical sense, then perhaps we should focus on his political legacy. He belongs to a tradition of Dissent which espoused liberty of conscience and developed habits of self-government and local autonomy. Such a tradition is not to be dismissed lightly in our increasingly corporate and conformist world. If this aspect of Bunyan's work has, to an extent, been overshadowed by his connections with literature and landscape it may be because it is politically divisive. It may be thought by some to associate him with 'republican' opposition to the monarchy: one of the most cherished institutions of British political society. Similarly, his particular brand of Christianity may be seen as an earlier, if less extreme, manifestation of the religious fundamentalism of our own day.[31] It would appear, then, that Bunyan, as both an expression of Englishness and as a figure of political opposition, is in danger of disappearing. He and his work have ceased to be part of 'common' experience and 'popular' memory. Instead they have become the subject of specialist study. The difficult challenge for experts will be to find a way of making Bunyan relevant to the new order that will emerge in a post-Brexit society.

The Pilgrim's Progress, Tourism, and *England, England*

Mannin unwittingly offers one possible way forward. She gives the reader a tourist's guide to Bedford, as does a more recent work, John Pestell's *Exploring the World of John Bunyan, Author of The Pilgrim's Progress* (2002).[32] Using Bunyan to advertise Bedford and its surrounding countryside is nothing new. Brown, Cockett, and Harper did the same, though their work was part of a much larger programme devoted to the promotion of Englishness. What is less remarked is that a rudimentary sense of tourism is integral to *The Pilgrim's Progress* itself.

The word 'tourism' did not enter the English language until the eighteenth century but the activity of sightseeing or visiting famous places goes back at least to Roman

---

[30] Ethel Mannin, *England: My Adventure* (London: Hutchinson, 1973), 50, 56.
[31] A point explored in Stuart Sim, 'Bunyan and his Fundamentalist Readers', in W. R. Owens and Stuart Sim (eds.), *Reception, Appropriation, Recollection: Bunyan's Pilgrim's Progress* (Bern: Peter Lang, 2007), 213–28.
[32] John Pestell, *Exploring the World of John Bunyan, Author of The Pilgrim's Progress* (Epsom: Day One, 2002). See also John Nicholson, *An Illustrated Guide to Bunyan's Bedford* (London: Bozo, 1989).

times.[33] One of the many interesting things about *The Pilgrim's Progress* is that it anticipates its own place in the leisure industry. Christian's visit to Interpreter's House, for example, takes the form of a guided tour. He is shown, among other things, a picture of a man who is holding a Bible and whose eyes look up to heaven; a 'live' piece of theatre in the form of a man sweeping a room and a woman sprinkling it with water; and a tableau of two children, Passion and Patience, sitting in chairs (*PP*, 30–1). He is also shown 'Records of the greatest Antiquity' at the Palace Beautiful (*PP*, 53), and both he and Hopeful are intrigued by 'an old Monument' whose 'strangeness of form' appears to be that of 'a *Woman* transformed into the shape of a Pillar': an inscription explains that the figure represents Lot's wife (*PP*, 108).

Travel, visits, and sightseeing are more pronounced in *The Pilgrim's Progress, Part II*, mainly because Christiana is following in her husband's footsteps. She sees many of the things he saw, and also novel ones. In Interpreter's House, for instance, Christiana views what Christian 'had seen sometime before' as well as new displays like the man with the Muck-rake who can only look down (*PP*, 199). Led by Mr Great-heart, the party then continues the route taken by Christian, with Great-heart providing a commentary on the passing scenery. At the Hill of Difficulty, for example, their guide 'again took an occasion to tell them of what happened there when Christian came by' (*PP*, 214). When they stay at Palace Beautiful, Christiana, her children, and Mercie are taken into a closet and shown one of the apples eaten by Eve, Jacob's Ladder, and the altar, wood, fire, and knife that would have been used in Abraham's sacrifice of Isaac. Piety, one of the women of the Palace, also shows Christiana the place 'where *Christian*, your Husband, met with the foul Fiend *Apollyon*' (*PP*, 233, 236). Great-heart expands on this encounter by pointing to Christian's blood on the stones, shards from Apollyon's darts, and the monument commemorating Christian's victory (*PP*, 240).

Visitors to the newly refurbished Bunyan Museum in Bedford don't see anything as didactic or, indeed, exciting as Christiana and her group, but they do share their 'tourist gaze'. On entry they encounter a life-size wax model of Bunyan. A curved linear feature runs round the centre of the room showing scenes from *The Pilgrim's Progress*, a timeline of events and of key episodes in Bunyan's life. Along the walls are reconstructions of seventeenth-century interiors, including part of a kitchen, and there are more life-size figures, including one of a tinker. Bunyan's time in the army is depicted by a barrack room complete with furniture, while the representation of the 'day-room' in Bedford jail gives a sense of what his life was like in prison. There are also facsimiles of certain documents, such as Bunyan's arrest warrant, a panel detailing the lack of political and religious rights, and a number of artefacts. A guide is always on hand to give more information should the visitor require. And, of course, there is a shop where tourists can purchase books, mugs, pens, and tea towels to commemorate their visit.

---

[33] See, for example, Loykie Lomine, 'Tourism in Augustan Society (44 BC–AD 69)', in John K. Wilson (ed.), *Histories of Tourism: Representation, Identity and Conflict* (Clevedon: Channel View Publications, 2005), 71–87.

Bunyan's allegorical journey narrative anticipates the tourist nature of Bunyan Museum to the extent that it presents history as spectacle. Simplifying drastically, Christian makes history, and Christiana revisits the scene of its making. *The Pilgrim's Progress* shows that history, to adapt Marx's famous saying, does indeed occur twice: the first time as struggle, the second time as tourism. As such, it could be said that the allegory's two parts contain the germ for the development of England's heritage industry.[34] This is characterized, in part, by a commodified view of the past. Institutions and episodes in English history can be packaged for touristic consumption rather than historical understanding. Or rather they can be presented in such a manner as to reinforce a particular view of the past: one that celebrates national unity while covering over inequalities of wealth and power. By these means, they prevent the past from making a contribution to the present, thereby implying that history, as well as God, is dead.

Julian Barnes satirizes this process in his novel *England, England* (1998), which tells the story of entrepreneur Sir Jack Pitman's audacious scheme to relocate all of England's major tourist attractions to the Isle of Wight.[35] Although Barnes's novel and Bunyan's allegory are obviously very different, it is a possible to see an affinity between Christiana's gaze and that of the tourists who flock to Sir Jack's theme park to see re-enactments of the great moments of English history. In *The Pilgrim's Progress*, 'history' is used didactically. When Christiana's party come to the place where Christian met Mistrust and Timorous, they see a stage with verses underneath recording how those two miscreants were punished '*for endeavouring to hinder* Christian *in his Journey*' (*PP*, 218). Their fate is a warning to show what will happen to those who do not see their journey through to the end. The treatment of history in *England, England* is more complex. It is a form of instruction to the extent that performances of the Battle of Hastings or the Battle of Britain are used to bolster a mythic view of national identity. At the same time, Barnes is constantly drawing our attention to how history is constructed, how it is related to national identity, and whether either of these entities can be regarded in any way as authentic. In short, the difference between the two works is that in Bunyan 'history' serves a clear purpose, while in Barnes the very notion of what history means comes under scrutiny. Moreover, Bunyan's sense of history is conceived entirely in Christian terms: it has nothing to do with England or Englishness, whereas for Barnes history is intimately connected to the notion of national identity.

And there is one further difference. The encounter with monuments, stages, and scenes of combat in *The Pilgrim's Progress* is designed to make the pilgrim cast off the comforts of this life so that he or she can enter the kingdom of heaven. To that end, he or she can expect to be chastised if they step out of their way. This is what happens to Christian and Hopeful, for example, when they are whipped by the 'shining One' for allowing themselves to be trapped in a net by a flatterer (*PP*, 133–34). In Barnes's novel,

---

[34] For a good introduction to the complex relations between history and heritage, see Dallen J. Timothy, *Cultural Heritage and Tourism: An Introduction* (Clevedon: Channel View Publications, 2011).

[35] Julian Barnes, *England, England* (London: Jonathan Cape, 1998).

by contrast, the point of history as a tourist attraction is to make people 'feel better'.[36] But, despite these differences, what *The Pilgrim's Progress* and *England, England* share is a sense of history as heritage: in one it is fledgling, in the other it is fully developed. Interestingly, this is precisely the conception of history enacted in both *The Pilgrim's Progress* and *The Life and Death of Mr. Badman*, in which the events of the present are seen as fulfilments of the past. At the House Beautiful, for example, Christian learns of 'Prophecies and Predictions of things that have their certain accomplishment, both to the dread and amazement of enemies, and the comfort and solace of Pilgrims' (*PP*, 54), while Mr Badman's love of flattery is seen as 'the saying of the wise man fulfilled' (*MB*, 64). But what *The Pilgrim's Progress* fulfils is, for better or for worse, its own unconscious prophecy of the rise of 'heritage'.

Class

If, as Marx and Engels claimed, 'The history of all hitherto existing society is the history of class struggles',[37] then the concept of class potentially becomes a way of restoring to history that continuity which the heritage industry could be seen as having broken. How, though, do we define class? And is the term applicable to mid- to late seventeenth-century England? The traditional Marxist definition of class distinguishes between those who own the means of production—a term that includes land, factories, raw materials, and tools—and those who do not. This definition applies to seventeenth-century England to the extent that land ownership was concentrated in a few hands.[38] There were objections to this arrangement from the Diggers, who believed that land should be held in common; from the Levellers, who wanted to reverse enclosures; and from the Fifth Monarchists, who advocated the redistribution of land so that 'no poor man shall have too little, nor the rich too much';[39] and all were united in their opposition to the system of tithes (the parishioners' annual payment of a tenth of their yearly produce to the local church).

The question of property ownership was at the heart of the Putney Debates (1647). Colonel Thomas Rainsborough argued that everyone should 'have an equal voice in the election of the representatives', while Commissary-General Henry Ireton countered that only those who had a 'permanent fixed interest in the kingdom', by which he meant

---

[36] Barnes, *England, England*, 70.

[37] Karl Marx and Friedrich Engels, 'Manifesto of the Communist Party', in Karl Marx and Frederick Engels, *Selected Works* (London: Lawrence & Wishart, 1968), 35.

[38] See Kevin Cahill, *Who Owns Britain: The Hidden Facts behind Land Ownership in the UK and Ireland* (Edinburgh: Canongate Books, 2002).

[39] Cited by Helen Hayward, 'Attitudes to the Ownership and Distribution of Land 1500–1930: A Survey with Particular Reference to Old Testament Paradigm and the Role of the Church' (Jubilee Research Paper, Cambridge, 1992), 8.

property, had a right to vote.[40] At times, the discussion touched indirectly on national identity. Is what makes an Englishman (not an Englishwoman) the fact that he owns property or that, along with every other Englishman, he has the right to frame the laws under which he should live? The fight against Charles was also a fight against a system of laws imposed by the Normans which had held the English in subjection. Now, by overthrowing those laws and establishing new ones there was an opportunity to express a specifically English identity.[41] The English had acquired their religious identity, Protestantism, during the Reformation; the Civil War was a chance to acquire a political one. But it was not to be. There was no universal suffrage and no redistribution of land, simply a sale of crown and church property to a mostly aristocratic class: class, not Englishness, triumphed.

As Hill has argued, Bunyan cannot have been unaware of these and other debates,[42] but it is difficult to talk about Bunyan's work in class terms for at least two reasons. The first is that there is an ongoing debate about the part played by class, in the Marxist sense, in the English Civil War.[43] There were multiple causes for that conflict, political and religious as well as economic, and the terms status or rank may be more appropriate in analysing the social structure of that period. Nevertheless, an embryonic awareness of class seems present in Gregory King's *Naturall and Political Observations* (1696), which not only differentiated people according to their income, but also according to their productive capacity: an idea that would become central to Marx's conception of class.

The second reason why it is difficult to talk about class in Bunyan is that his spiritual idiom militates against a social and economic analysis of his society, even as it allows him to protest against its inequalities. At the same time, there is an overlap between the imagery of Christianity and that of feudalism. The terms 'master', 'lord', and king have as much currency in one system as they do in the other, while frequent references to '*Immanuel's land*' in *The Pilgrim's Progress* (*PP*, 55) serve to validate the notion of property ownership on which feudalism was based. Equally, Christian's character appears to be the prototype of the bourgeois, who, in the pursuit of his own self-interest, is prepared to sacrifice all other ties, including those of his family. In the words of Marx and Engels, the bourgeois 'has put an end to all feudal, patriarchal, idyllic relations' and has 'pitilessly torn asunder the motley feudal ties that bound man to his "natural superiors"'. Christian may not 'have torn away from the family its sentimental value and reduced the family relation to a mere money relation', but, by running away from his wife and children and putting his fingers so he cannot hear their cries, he does show that he is prepared to dismiss them for the sake of his own salvation.[44] And, indeed, the relationship with God is conceived here partly in monetary terms. Faithful sounds like a speculator

---

[40] Andrew Sharp (ed.), *The English Levellers: Cambridge Texts in the History of Political Thought* (Cambridge: Cambridge University Press, 1998), 102, 103.
[41] Sharp (ed.), *English Levellers*, 116, 118.
[42] Hill, *Bunyan*, 52–8.
[43] For an overview of this problem see my *Class* (London: Routledge, 2001), 64–88.
[44] Marx and Engels, *Selected Works*, 38.

when he implies that one should 'venture the loss of all' for the reward of heaven, while Hopeful employs the language of accounting when he says, 'I have by my sins run a great way into God's Book and [...] my now reforming will not pay off that score' (*PP*, 72, 140).

The conflation of imagery from two different economic systems in *The Pilgrim's Progress* suggests that, in part, it reflects the transition from a feudal to a capitalist order. Its ideological sympathies lie with the former because there is a much greater fit between the feudal imagery and the allegory's spiritual project than there is between that project and the capitalist imagery. For example, the doctrine that 'all is of Grace, not of works' (*PP*, 77) is contrary to the bourgeois value of self-reliance. The attack on Vanity Fair, together with the episode of the silver mine (*PP*, 88–9, 106–08), makes it very clear that money and commerce destroy the soul because they lead to all manner of sin such as 'Rioting, Revelling, Drinking, Swearing, Lying, Uncleanness, Sabbath-breaking, and what not' (*PP*, 137). This largely moral critique is also evident in *The Life and Death of Mr. Badman*, but one of the things which distinguishes that work from *The Pilgrim's Progress* is its rudimentary analysis of capitalism: how, for example, the rich make their money by impoverishing the rest. One example given by Mr Wiseman is that of 'Hucksters, that buy up the poor man's Victuals by whole-sale, and sell it to him again for unreasonable gains' (*MB*, 109). There is also a recognition that capitalism uses advertising to create a desire for commodities that people do not really need. There are those, for instance, who inflate the value of their goods, thereby showing they have 'a wicked and covetous mind' (*MB*, 116): goods which in most cases only serve 'to feed the lusts of the eyes' (*MB*, 115).

In addition to the accumulation of profit, and partly as a consequence of the production of 'Fangles and Toyes' (*MB*, 122), capitalism also seems to generate a fantasy world. Mr Wiseman remarks on how trade itself is seen as a form of delusion (*MB*, 40) and how people are more ruled by 'Fancy' than by the Bible (*MB*, 125). Being in business requires a talent for acting. Mr Badman pretends to be pious in order to marry a woman for her money, which he needs for the debts he incurred on his shop (*MB*, 65–9). More fundamentally, there is something in the nature of trade that seems to dissolve the very substance of the self. Mr Badman studied 'to please all men and to suit himself to any company' with the aim of making them 'his Customers or Creditors for his Commodities' (*MB*, 83–4). In effect Mr Badman becomes a mirror, reflecting those around him: 'I can be *religious*, and irreligious, I can be anything or nothing; I can swear and speak against swearing; I can lye and speak against lying' (*MB*, 84). This, of course, is part of what makes him 'bad', but at moments like this *The Life and Death of Mr. Badman* seems to transcend its moral framework to give an insight into the working of capitalism itself, and how it strips away identity and substance, leaving only acting and performance.[45]

---

[45] On this point, see Richard Sennett, *The Corrosion of Character: The Personal Consequences of Work in the New Capitalism* (New York: Norton, 1998).

Conclusion: Bunyan, Class, and Englishness

How, then, do we bring class and Englishness together in Bunyan? They seem to be very different. Class refers to economic divisions, Englishness to cultural characteristics which transcend those divisions. But we can relate the two if we examine the nature of the exchange relation which, along with production, is the 'foundation on which the bourgeoisie built itself up'.[46] According to Marx, money provides a common measure by which commodities can be exchanged. It does so by representing commodities not as they are, but by what they have in common, and what they have in common is the human labour power used to produce them. The difference in price between commodities reflects the different amounts of labour used to produce them. In order for money to represent what commodities have in common, it must ignore what is individual about them. Money, we might say, takes no account of the fact that one commodity is a car and another is a laptop: it is simply a measure of the different amount of labour time necessary to produce these different items. Neither does money differentiate between different kinds of labour, but views the variety of work purely in terms of time. It is therefore an abstract system of representation dealing in quantities not qualities. This system, incidentally, is mirrored in Bunyan's characters. Their allegorical nature is every bit as abstract as the operation of exchange itself. But to make good this claim requires more space than is available here.

What we can say with a little more certainty is that anxiety about the effects of money registered both in *The Pilgrim's Progress* and *Mr. Badman* and in Bunyan's constant use of the word of 'selling' to convey the temptation he experiences to abandon Christ in *Grace Abounding* (GA, 41–4, 71–2) hint not only at the growing dominance of commercial values but also that the thinking characteristic of exchange has started to penetrate the innermost recesses of the self. To put this in another way: although Bunyan criticizes commercial values from a spiritual and partly feudal perspective, his very criticism of them testifies to the ascendancy of those values. The very logic of exchange is crucial to his thinking. His mind displays the contours of the bourgeois, one who breaks all ties with the past: an action that is analogous to the operation of grace since it cancels out all former sins.

The dominance of the bourgeois mindset in the form of exchange has implications for understanding the problem of Englishness. If it is the nature of exchange to ignore what is individual about a commodity, then it is implicated in the erosion of identity. The anxiety about Englishness, in other words, is partly the result of a system of commerce that hollows out all substantial being. We saw how, in *Mr. Badman*, business demanded a talent for acting, and the same process is at work in Julian Barnes's *England, England*

---

[46] Marx and Engels, *Selected Works*, 40.

where actors are hired to impersonate both mythical and historical figures, for example Robin Hood and Dr Johnson. The turning of history into entertainment, rather than into the spiritual lesson it is in *The Pilgrim's Progress*, is accompanied by a narrowing of thought in the wider culture. For anything that does not submit to the logic of exchange, anything that is not measurable or transparent, is deemed not to exist. Bunyan, it appears, saw more deeply into the nature of capitalism, and had a clearer view of how it would turn out, than Marx.

Suggested Reading

Anderson, Benedict, *Imagined Communities: Reflections on the Origin and Spread of Nationalism* (London: Verso, 2016).

Camden, Vera J., *Trauma and Transformation: The Political Progress of John Bunyan* (Stanford, CA: Stanford University Press, 2008).

Gay, David, James G. Randall, and Arlette Zinck (eds.), *Awakening Words: John Bunyan and the Language of Community* (Newark, DE: University of Delaware Press, 2000).

Greaves, Richard, *John Bunyan and English Nonconformity* (London: Hambledon Press, 1992).

Jackson, Leonard, *The Dematerialisation of Karl Marx: Literature and Marxist Theory* (London: Routledge, 1994).

Johnson, Barbara A., *Reading Piers Plowman and The Pilgrim's Progress: Reception and the Protestant Reader* (Carbondale and Edwardsville, IL: Southern Illinois University Press, 1992).

Kumar, Krishan, *The Making of English National Identity* (Cambridge: Cambridge University Press, 2003).

Laurence, Anne, W. R. Owens, and Stuart Sim (eds.), *John Bunyan and his England, 1628–1688* (London: Hambledon Press, 1990).

Rutherford, Jonathan, 'The Art of Life', in Jonathan Rutherford (ed.), *The Art of Life*, (London: Lawrence & Wishart, 2000), 63–78.

Watson, Shelia (ed.), *Museums and their Communities: Leicester Readers in Museum Studies* (London: Routledge, 2007).

Wilson, John K. (ed.), *Histories of Tourism: Representation, Identity and Conflict* (Clevedon: Channel View Publications, 2005).

CHAPTER 36

WAYFARING IMAGES

The Pilgrim's Pictorial Progress

NATHALIE COLLÉ

In his foundational biography of Bunyan (1885), John Brown commented on the evolution of the text and paratext of Bunyan's most famous allegory in these terms:

> After the first three editions of the First Part, when [...] the book was practically complete, there were only a few unimportant subsequent additions, consisting of Scripture passages and marginal references. The interest of succeeding editions lies therefore mainly in the question of illustrations.[1]

A number of Bunyan scholars followed Brown's lead, and have focused on the significance of the history of illustrations in both parts of *The Pilgrim's Progress* (originally published in 1678 and 1684). For example, in the introduction to his 1928 Clarendon Press edition, James Blanton Wharey traced the development of the corpus of visual images in editions published in England from 1678 to 1688, notably the famous *Sleeping Portrait* by Robert White, as well as the early copper engravings and woodcuts which accompanied the text. Less than a decade later, Frank Mott Harrison began examining the sets of pictorial representations which appeared over the centuries alongside the text.[2] Their research prompted other scholars to look at more specific cases, notably the illuminated editions published in North America up to 1870,[3]

---

[1] John Brown, *John Bunyan: His Life, Times, and Work* (1885), rev. Frank Mott Harrison (London: Hulbert Publishing, 1928), 441.

[2] Frank Mott Harrison, 'Some Illustrators of *The Pilgrim's Progress* (Part One)', *The Library*, 3 (1936), 241–63.

[3] David E. Smith, 'Illustrations of American Editions of *The Pilgrim's Progress* to 1870', *Princeton University Library Chronicle*, 26 (1964), 16–25.

John Flaxman's drawings,[4] William Blake's watercolours,[5] and Dutch artist Jan Luyken's engravings.[6] More recently, Bunyan scholars have appraised the origins of the earliest illustrations of *The Pilgrim's Progress*,[7] the portraiture of Bunyan,[8] and the significance of 'indigenized' depictions in the mission translations of *The Pilgrim's Progress*.[9]

My own interest both in the issue of pictorialization and in book history has led me to explore the genealogy of the thousands of illustrated editions of *The Pilgrim's Progress* published in Great Britain and abroad, and to analyse them in light of the development of the book market and evolving publishing practices. My research has also taken me from a purely bibliographical and descriptive approach to book illustration towards a more interpretative and theoretical appraisal of it as an artistic form: not just as a component of the published work, but also as an agent of its production and reception, wherever it has been circulated and read—or seen.[10]

A further unexplored avenue of research into the history of visual depictions of *The Pilgrim's Progress* remains the many other forms that 'illustration' has taken, beyond the printed book. These include bronze door panels, stained-glass windows, postcards, murals, panoramas, card and board games. These 'illustrations', in the broad sense of the term, have extended the life of the text materially and interpretatively, with many of them offering varied and, at times, contradictory readings of it. This chapter will trace some of the near-countless extra-textual lives of *The Pilgrim's Progress*, showing how the journeys of these 'wayfaring images' have extended the book's reach to Christians and non-Christians worldwide. I will begin with a brief account of the history of illustrations to Bunyan's most famous allegory, before moving on to discuss examples of images which have developed 'beyond' the book, including 'three-dimensional' artwork born of the text and of its iconographic tradition. I will then consider 'transitional' depictions and products, and, finally, what I have called 'back to the book' representations.

---

[4] G. E. Bentley, Jr, 'Flaxman's Drawings for *Pilgrim's Progress*', in Paul Fritz and Richard Morton (eds.), *Woman in the Eighteenth Century and Other Essays* (Toronto: Samuel Stevens Hakkert, 1976), 245–78.

[5] Gerda S. Norvig, *Dark Figures in the Desired Country: Blake's Illustrations to The Pilgrim's Progress* (Berkeley, CA: University of California Press, 1993).

[6] Hendrick van't Veld, *Beminde broeder die ik vand op 's werelts pelgrims wegen: Jan Luyken (1649–1712) als illustrator en medereiziger van John Bunyan (1628–1688)* (Utrecht: De Banier, 2000).

[7] Roger Pooley, 'The Earliest Illustrations of *The Pilgrim's Progress*: Notes and Queries', *The Recorder*, 6 (2000), 10–15.

[8] Anne Dunan-Page, '"The Portraiture of John Bunyan" Revisited: Robert White and Images of the Author', *BS*, 13 (2008/09), 7–39.

[9] Isabel Hofmeyr, *The Portable Bunyan: A Transnational History of The Pilgrim's Progress* (Princeton, NJ: Princeton University Press, 2004).

[10] See works by Nathalie Collé-Bak listed in the Suggested Reading section.

From This Text to All Those Images to Come

The history of the accompanying artwork for *The Pilgrim's Progress* starts with Nathaniel Ponder, the allegory's first publisher, and is still in the making more than three centuries later. It was Ponder who, in the third edition (1679), placed White's famous *Sleeping Portrait* of Bunyan as a frontispiece to the text (see Figure 36.1), and who included

FIGURE 36.1 *The Sleeping Portrait*, frontispiece, Robert White engraver, *The Pilgrim's Progress*, 3rd edn (London: Nathaniel Ponder, 1679).

(© The British Library Board. All Rights Reserved (C.70.aa.3).)

FIGURE 36.2 *The Death of Faithful at Vanity Fair*, woodcut reproduction of one of the original illustrations for *The Pilgrim's Progress*, anonymous engraver, *The Pilgrim's Progress*, 7th edn (London: Nathaniel Ponder, 1681).

(© The British Library Board. All Rights Reserved (C.59.a.32).)

copper engravings in the fifth edition of 1680 (see Figure 36.2).[11] These engravings were repeatedly reprinted in subsequent editions, and were copied in pirate editions, imitated, and altered up until today.[12]

---

[11] These early illustrations are included in recent paperback editions of *The Pilgrim's Progress*, edited by W. R. Owens (Oxford: Oxford University Press, 2003), and by Roger Pooley (London: Penguin Classics, 2008).

[12] See Nathalie Collé-Bak, 'La Destinée éditoriale et iconographique de *The Pilgrim's Progress* de John Bunyan, de 1678 à 1850: les enjeux d'une mise en images' (Doctoral thesis, Université Nancy 2, 2002); and 'La Destinée iconographique de *The Pilgrim's Progress* de John Bunyan du XVIIe siècle au début du XIXe

Jan Luyken was the first identified illustrator of Dutch and Franco-Dutch editions of *The Pilgrim's Progress*. Having been commissioned by Amsterdam publisher and bookseller Johannes Boekholt to illustrate the fourth edition of his Dutch translation of the work (*Eens Christens Reyse na de Eeuwigheyt*, 1684), this renowned Dutch engraver produced eight etchings which supplemented the frontispiece he had already provided for the first edition of *Eens Christens Reyse*, published by Boekholt in 1682, and which replaced the twelve anonymous half-page engravings originally supplied there. Luyken's etchings were also used in Boekholt's French-Flemish translation of the work, *Le Voyage d'un Chréstien vers l'Eternité*, which appeared in Amsterdam in 1685.[13] Until 1728, the dominant set of pictures found in British editions of the work consists of a compound made of seven of the thirteen anonymous engravings announced in the advertisement to the fifth edition of 1680 and the set of nine etchings designed by Luyken for the 1685 Franco-Dutch edition, all copied from the originals and re-engraved on wood or on copper. This nationally and stylistically mixed set, instituted in the fourteenth London edition of 1695 (no doubt by its publisher, Robert Ponder, Nathaniel's son), became the established set of illustrations for *The Pilgrim's Progress* and remained so for several decades.

In 1728, a new set of images was commissioned by John Clarke and engraved by John Sturt for the Queen Caroline edition, published by subscription on the occasion of Bunyan's centenary anniversary.[14] From that date onward, and until the end of the century, this new set replaced the old pictures and reappeared numerous times in subsequent editions of the work, either as reproduced from the original plates, copied more or less skilfully, or simply vaguely imitated. Throughout the eighteenth century new editions of *The Pilgrim's Progress* were appearing regularly, with many more pictures—on average, there were thirteen to twenty or so per edition in the seventeenth and early eighteenth centuries, and up to several hundred per edition by the nineteenth century—some of which were of a more prestigious pedigree. Originally cut by engravers who have remained anonymous to this day, these later illustrations of *The Pilgrim's Progress* began, from the middle of the eighteenth century onward, to be drawn and engraved by artists of renown whose work was itself valuable, independent of Bunyan's allegory. Thomas Stothard in the eighteenth century, and then Richard Westall, Harold Copping, John Martin, the Dalziel brothers, David and William Scott, John Gilbert, J. D. Watson, C. H. Bennett, Frederick Barnard, W. Small, the Rhead brothers, William Strang, Robert Anning Bell, and also William Blake in the nineteenth century, are just

---

siècle: Répétitions, variations en chaîne et mutations', *Bulletin de la Société d'Études Anglo-Américaines des XVIIe et XVIIIe siècles*, 53 (November 2001), 201–32.

[13] See Jacques B. H. Alblas, 'The Bunyan Collection of the Vrije Universiteit, Amsterdam', *BS*, 6 (1995–96), 78–84, and *Johannes Boekholt (1656–1693): The First Dutch Publisher of John Bunyan and Other English Authors* (Nieuwkoop: De Graaf, 1987).

[14] *The Pilgrim's Progress* [...]. *The Two and Twentieth Edition. With Plates by J. Sturt* (London: Printed for J. Clarke, 1728).

FIGURE 36.3 Title page of a chapbook version of *The Pilgrim's Progress* (Glasgow: Orr and Sons, n.d.).

(© The British Library Board. All Rights Reserved (4408.bb.25.12).)

some of those who contributed to the visual decoration of Bunyan's text, and to its amazing afterlife.

Illustrated chapbook versions of the work from the nineteenth century, a number of them dating back to the 1830s, provide an interesting instance of the gradual transformation of the corpus of Bunyan-inspired images, and particularly of the changing nature of the relationship between text and artwork, both within the book and, later, beyond its pages. These chapbooks are of two types: those which present only one illustration, usually on the title page (traditionally, the *Sleeping Portrait*, engraved on wood and inserted between the title and the imprint (see Figure 36.3)), and those which are profusely illustrated. Another interesting feature of these chapbooks is that their pictures are typically crude copies of others originally dating back to the 1780s and 1790s. Iconographic repetition and imitation, rather than invention, are at stake with such formulaic publications.[15] For in these chapbooks, the pictures are of primary importance, and the text secondary not only in the sense that they take precedence over it, but also because the text is a dramatically reduced version of the original in any case.[16] In some of these chapbooks the text has even become a kind of caption to the images. It might even be argued that, in most cases, the few accompanying lines of text have been written about a pre-existing illustration, to 'explain' it and to relate it to the distant original and authorial text (see Figure 36.4).

From the 1830s through to the 1860s we see the birth of new types of iconographic renderings of *The Pilgrim's Progress* within illustrated editions as well as in the more derivative form of chapbooks, and in portfolios of prints too, published either with short extracts of the text,[17] or with no text at all.[18] Thomas Stothard initiated this trend when he produced sixteen stand-alone designs engraved on copper by Joseph Strutt, reproduced as sepia prints, and first issued independently from Bunyan's text, loose in portfolio, in 1788 by John Thane (see Figure 36.5). A few years later, these designs were used in different editions of the work, notably one published in 1792, which also included work by other artists. Following Stothard, artists such as John Flaxman in 1792, William Blake around 1824, George Townsend in 1840, Claude Reignier Conder in 1869, William Strang in 1895, Ambrose Dudley in 1908, W. Stanley Martin in 1923, and Edward Ardizzone in 1957, all designed illustrations which were not originally meant to be published in any edition of the work. Also noteworthy is a remarkable series of postcards issued by the Religious Tract Society in London, reproducing original drawings by Harold Copping in permanent bromide photographs (see Figure 36.6), thus allowing the text to travel to wherever their senders had determined.[19]

With its increasing popularity, and through the initiative of publishers and artists, *The Pilgrim's Progress* became a pre(-)text for illustrations, not only in the traditional sense, but also in more unexpected ones. One of the most significant aspects of the

---

[15] See Collé-Bak, 'La Destinée iconographique'.

[16] Kirsty Milne, '"The Miracles They Wrought": A Chapbook Reading of *The Pilgrim's Progress*, with an Edited Transcript of *The Pilgrims Progress to the Other World* (1684)', *BS*, 13 (2008–09), 47.

[17] For instance, Frederick James Sheilds, *Illustrations of The Pilgrim's Progress, with Excerpts from the Text by Frederick J. Sheilds* (London: Simpkin & Co., 1864), and Bernard Barton and Josiah Conder, *Illustrations of the Pilgrim's Progress: Accompanied with Extracts from the Work, and Descriptions of the Plates, by Bernard Barton. And a Biographical Sketch of the Life and Writings of Bunyan by Josiah Conder* (London: Fisher, Son & Co. Newgate Street; Paris: Quai des Grands Augustins, n.d.).

[18] Henry C. Selous, *Portfolio of Outline Drawings, Illustrations of The Pilgrim's Progress, Prepared for the Edition Issued to the Subscribers of the Art Union of London* (London: H. M. Holloway, 1844), and Claude Reignier Conder, *Pictorial Scenes from Pilgrim's Progress: Drawn by C. R. Conder* (London: Hodder & Stoughton, 1869). On all of these, see Nathalie Collé-Bak, 'L'Ur-texte et son double? De l'autre côté du miroir des illustrations, avec *The Pilgrim's Progress* de John Bunyan', in Nathalie Collé-Bak, Monica Latham, and David Ten Eyck (eds.), *Left Out: Texts and Ur-Texts* (Nancy: Presses Universitaires de Nancy, 2009), 193–217.

[19] The Copping images can also be found in several illustrated editions of the work published at the beginning of the twentieth century.

FIGURE 36.4 Illustrated page of a chapbook version of *The Pilgrim's Progress* (Glasgow: Orr and Sons, n.d.).

(© The British Library Board. All Rights Reserved (4408.bb.25.12).)

iconographic tradition engendered by Bunyan's allegory is perhaps indeed its organic and transformative nature, to which we now turn.[20]

Images beyond Book and Text

Illustrations in the traditional sense were only one of many forms chosen, first by the publishers, and then by the artists, amateur or professional, who resolved to represent

[20] Collé-Bak, 'La Destinée iconographique'.

FIGURE 36.5 *Christian and Hopeful Reaching the Celestial City*, portfolio illustration of *The Pilgrim's Progress* by Thomas Stothard, engraver, and Joseph Strutt, printmaker (sepia print) (London: John Thane, [1788]).

(© John Bunyan Library, Bedford Central Library, Bedford, England.)

Bunyan's text in other—complementary or independent—media. *The Pilgrim's Progress* has indeed been interpreted—embodied even—in a variety of ways, and not only iconographically. It has been visualized in still pictures produced on different materials, and also through moving pictures of various types. It has also been turned into theatrical, as well as cinematographic, productions. What started out as a text, and more specifically a religious allegory in prose, was—and is still being—gradually and literally transformed: that is, altered in its very form, substance, and nature.

The *Moving Panorama of Pilgrim's Progress*, also known as the *Bunyan Tableaux*, is just one example of how print or visual culture and its agents have seized upon Bunyan's text and found ways of reinterpreting it within changing contexts of public reception. Conceived in the winter of 1848 by National Academicians Edward Harrison May and Joseph Kyle, the giant painting features over fifty scenes from the allegory. It was designed by May and Kyle, but also featured work by other renowned artists of the time, notably Daniel Huntington, Frederic Edwin Church, and Jasper Cropsey, alongside eminent illustrators Felix O. C. Darley and Henry Courtney Selous. May, Kyle, and Jacob Dallas painted the finished scenes onto a canvas about 8 feet tall and 1,200 feet

FIGURE 36.6 *Evangelist Points the Way*, postcard illustration of *The Pilgrim's Progress* by Harold Copping (London: The Religious Tract Society, [c.1903]).

(From the author's private collection.)

long, mounted on wooden rollers or spools that allowed it to be unfolded using a crank to transfer the canvas from one spool to another, to the accompaniment of music.[21] The *Bunyan Tableaux* 'opened at Washington Hall in New York in November of 1850 and was a tremendous critical and financial success, grossing nearly $100,000 in its first six months'. This 'prompted the artists to produce a second version. Finished in April 1851,

---

[21] For more information on the panorama, see Nathalie Collé-Bak, 'Bunyan's Pilgrims on Canvas, on Stage, in the Cellar, and in the Art Gallery: The History, Loss and Renaissance of the *Moving Panorama of Pilgrim's Progress*', BS, 15 (2011), 112–28, and Jessica Skwire Routhier, Kevin J. Avery, and Thomas Hardiman, Jr, *The Painters' Panorama: Narrative, Art, and Faith in the Moving Panorama of Pilgrim's Progress* (Lebanon, NH: University Press of New England, 2015).

FIGURE 36.7 'Slough of Despond', *The Moving Panorama of Pilgrim's Progress*, 1851.
(© Collection of the Dyer Library/Saco Museum, Saco, Maine, USA.)

the "revised edition" was executed by Kyle and Dallas and, after traveling nationwide for decades, was ultimately given to the Saco Museum in 1896.[22] It was, according to a *New York Times* journalist, 'one of the more successful productions' of the 1850s, and 'reviews of the panorama were ecstatic'.[23]

The panorama (see Figures 36.7 and 36.8) remains a curiosity within the history of the manifold depictions of *The Pilgrim's Progress* for many reasons. Its circulation and display by stagehands in theatres, meeting houses, and barns across the United States throughout the latter half of the nineteenth century recall the extensive travels of Bunyan's text in the hands of its publishers. The Religious Tract Society, the American Tract Society, and the Society for Promoting Christian Knowledge, for instance, all ensured the transnational distribution and use of *The Pilgrim's Progress* via missionary channels, while the Bible Society, the Presbyterian Mission Press, and the Pacific Christian Literature Society, among others, fostered its international dissemination to other countries and cultures. To a certain extent, the history of the *Bunyan Tableaux* also encapsulates the iconographic tradition of the allegory: its transcontinental migration reflects the work's universal appeal across languages and cultural barriers; and its artistic production mirrors the processes which numerous illustrators undertook in reconsidering and reinterpreting its earlier pictorialization. Like the many deluxe editions containing refined images by famous painters and engravers which appeared throughout the nineteenth century, the *Moving Panorama* provides 'a rare existing example of this genre of painting which bridged high art and

---

[22] See http://www.sacomuseum.org/panorama/, accessed 1 February 2017.
[23] Eve M. Kahn, 'Back when Theatre was Simply Unrolled', *New York Times*, 'Antiques' section (3 December 2010), C32.

FIGURE 36.8 'Christiana, her Children and Secret', *The Moving Panorama of Pilgrim's* Progress, 1851.

(© Collection of the Dyer Library/Saco Museum, Saco, Maine, USA.)

popular culture'.[24] From the perspective of the whole iconographic tradition born of *The Pilgrim's Progress*, then, the idea of the panorama as a single, nationally unifying object translates into that of a single, transnationally unifying production which bridges apparently irreconcilable eras as well as continents, faiths, cultures, and both reading and viewing publics.

Apart from the sheer scale of its format and medium, and the impact that this must have had upon its 'readers', the *Moving Panorama* is very much like the iconographic renderings of the text supplied by more traditional versions: it consists of a series of pictures which tell the story both sequentially (following the original narrative and its order) and selectively (offering a choice of 'close-up' moments and motifs from the story). What distinguishes the panorama from an illustrated edition—its material form aside—is the absence of the text. The text is obviously there, but abstractly (in the reader's mind, or in some sort of collective memory, perhaps) rather than either physically or verbally. In a way, then, the panorama is a hybrid of traditional depictions and of later, more modern renderings of the text. It combines the fixed, pictorial dimension of book images and the 'moving' feature of cinematographic and dramatic adaptations. The history of the *Moving Panorama* thus reflects what I see as the mutual development of the popularity of the text and its expanding body of

---

[24] See http://www.sacomuseum.org/panorama/, accessed 1 February 2017. This idea is also expressed by Kevin J. Avery in 'The Panorama and its Manifestation in American Landscape Painting, 1795–1870' (PhD dissertation, Columbia University, 1995), 235.

illustrations.[25] From a transnational point of view, it replicates, on a smaller scale, the physical and metaphorical 'transportability' of the text: that is to say, its ability both to travel and to adapt to—or rather perhaps, to be adapted to—different historical and geographical contexts, or what Isabel Hofmeyr calls its 'translatability'.[26]

Aside from straightforward book illustrations, several other pictorial types of interpretation might also be mentioned for their ability to represent Bunyan's original text in forms different from either the usual text-and-picture or the image-without-text formulas discussed so far. Creations such as lantern slide shows, murals, stained-glass windows, or sculptures mark emancipation from the materiality of the page, paper, or canvas, and anticipate or recall *Pilgrim's Progress*-related productions which are further removed from book images. They are all noteworthy in the sense that they offer new ways of presenting and approaching the text and its relationship to changing contexts of production.

For example, the lantern slide series now held by the Museum Victoria in Melbourne, Australia—composed of twelve circular hand-coloured prints on glass, with black masks, mounted in rectangular wooden frames—depicts the pilgrimage of Christiana and her family and friends in a form visibly suited to the public of the time: that is, one fascinated by all things precursory to the moving (i.e. cinematic) image. Produced in England between 1830 and 1880, and acquired by the Australian and Victorian governments in 1975 through a loan and subsequent donation from the Australian Film Institute, these magic lantern slides are now part of the Francis collection of pre-cinematic apparatus and ephemera at the Museum Victoria. They stand out within the iconographic tradition born of *The Pilgrim's Progress* in that they are devoted exclusively to the second part of the allegory—a fact rare enough to be underlined. These slides represent, then, a new phase in the customization of the text both in a new medium and for a new epoch—one captivated by moving pictures and their potential for storytelling.

Like the moving panorama, the lantern slide show is remarkable for its peculiar combination of fixity (the pictures in the round frames) and relative mobility (their materialization through projection), as well for the interplay of darkness and light upon which it relies. Both are pictorial and artistic in nature—being made of individually painted tableaux—as well as theatrical, the panorama having to be presented on a stage, the slide show on a screen. What the slide show adds to the iconographic and dramatic aspects it has in common with the panorama is a sense of transparency: one that can be found in stained-glass window interpretations of Bunyan's text, as we shall see. The images born

---

[25] Nathalie Collé-Bak, 'The Role of Illustrations in the Reception of *The Pilgrim's Progress*', in W. R. Owens and Stuart Sim (eds.), *Reception, Appropriation, Recollection: Bunyan's Pilgrim's Progress* (Bern: Peter Lang, 2007), 81–98, and 'The *Pilgrim's Progress*es of John Bunyan's Publishers and Illustrators, or the Role of Illustrations in the Life of a Text/Book', in Nathalie Collé-Bak, Monica Latham, and David Ten Eyck (eds.), *Book Practices and Textual Itineraries, Vol I: Tracing the Contours of Literary Works* (Nancy: Presses Universitaires de Nancy, 2011), 157–82.

[26] Hofmeyr, *The Portable Bunyan*, 11–41.

of *The Pilgrim's Progress* indeed first appeared on paper, yet they were developed in innovative and engaging ways on materials as diverse as canvas, photographic film, glass panes, and walls, their creators generating each time varying approaches to, and artistic handlings of, the text.

A good example of this innovation can be seen in Hans Feibusch's murals depicting *The Pilgrim's Progress*, designed during 1944 for the crypt of St Elisabeth's Anglican Church, Eastbourne. Ken Simpson has argued that these murals 'offer rare opportunities to study the process of interpretation and the transformation of narratives'.[27] Indeed, he draws attention to the relationship between the original text and its intended physical medium of representation: 'Feibusch adapted Bunyan's episodes to the three-part structure of the room and its long walls, integrating form and function as much as possible.' His 'plan to depict *Pilgrim's Progress* as a continuous flow of "life-size" murals, "like a very large tapestry along the walls", was affected not only by the length of the room but also by its height'.[28]

In referring repeatedly to 'Feibusch's version of Bunyan's story', or 'Feibusch's *Pilgrim's Progress*', Simpson highlights the fact that the *Pilgrim's Progress* we encounter in these murals is not just Feibusch's as much as it is Bunyan's, but more the artist's almost than the original author's. Perhaps unsurprisingly, as a Jewish refugee in England fleeing Nazi Germany, Feibusch's rendition offers a strongly patriotic reading of *The Pilgrim's Progress*. Simpson notes, for example, that Great-heart is depicted holding the national flag of England, the St George's Cross, although no such flag appears in Bunyan's text, inviting the viewer to feel a sense of 'solidarity, resilience, and pride in England and all things English—and there was no better way to celebrate these values in 1944 than by painting scenes from what was considered at the time to be a quintessentially English text'. With these murals, as with any other type of representation of the work, pictorial or otherwise, the process of creation implies an act of interpretation which both adapts and transforms the original, and which recasts it in a new medium and for a new audience. Simpson claims that '[t]hese extraordinary appropriations of *The Pilgrim's Progress* by the Church of England were made possible by the institutionalization of Bunyan as a writer of the English nation and as a writer of broad Christian appeal, whose works could be enjoyed in spite of the author's theological views and devotional practices'.[29]

In a similar way, the various Bunyan or *Pilgrim's Progress* stained-glass windows found in churches in various parts of the world are also examples of the text's emancipation from the materiality of the printed book. They too provide testimonies to the critical encounter between the text, its interpreters, and the media they have chosen in its changing contexts of reception. The most famous of these windows are certainly

---

[27] Ken Simpson, 'Toward a New Monumentality: Hans Feibusch's Pilgrim's Progress Murals', *BS* 13 (2008–09), 82–106 (82). There are also murals based on *The Pilgrim's Progress* in St John's Primary School at Redhill, Surrey, dating back to 1939–41.

[28] Simpson, 'Toward a New Monumentality', 96.

[29] Simpson, 'Toward a New Monumentality', 96, 88, 88–9, 100.

those of the Bunyan Meeting Church on Mill Street in Bedford.[30] Designed and installed between 1927 and 2000, the series represents Bunyan himself alongside scenes from Christian's pilgrimage. The window picturing Bunyan in jail, which is famous for having been sent in postcard form to Terry Waite in 1988 while held captive in Beirut, was designed to commemorate the tercentenary of the publication of *The Pilgrim's Progress* (see Figure 36.9). Its history—like the history of all the other commemorative windows—therefore combines that of the work with its ongoing worldwide circulation and reception.

What is remarkable about the windows based specifically on *The Pilgrim's Progress* at Bedford is their capacity not just to retell the story but also to rework in coloured glass, held together by strips of lead and supported by a rigid frame, previous visual representations of the text. 'Evangelist Points the Way' (see Figure 36.10), for instance, is clearly based on Harold Copping's version of the scene, which appeared both as book illustration (see Figure 36.11) and individual print. With such arts-and-craft types of representation, *The Pilgrim's Progress* comes even closer to being 'illustrated' in the primary sense of the term: that is, brought to light. Like murals, stained-glass windows are wall decoration or art, but of an illuminated type, using not just the material structure of a place (its walls), but also the light behind it. One of their functions is to induce contemplation in the viewer while telling a story in light and colour; one of their points is to make him or her see beyond the scenes pictured into another dimension. To some extent, then, ecclesial stained-glass windows are akin to allegory, or at least Bunyan's view of it, in the sense that they provide 'outsides' of stories, or 'curtains', or 'vails', which point to a reality behind and beyond themselves (*PP*, 1–7, 164).

THREE-DIMENSIONAL IMAGES

The mystical dimension, as well as the sense of relief produced by the glass and lead structure of stained-glass windows, are also present in artistic creations such as sculptures, be they individual or serial. Examples of the first type would include *Christian's Repentance*, by Edward J. Kuntze (1876), or *Christian's Fight with Apollyon*, carved in pear-wood by Joseph Parker (see Figure 36.12), which was based on H. C. Selous and M. Paolo Priolo's iconographic interpretation of the scene in the 1850s (see Figure 36.13). The bronze doors at the entrance of Bunyan Meeting in Bedford are an example of the second type (see Figure 36.14). These were carved by sculptor Frederick Thrupp (who modelled them on Lorenzo Ghiberti's early fifteenth-century design for the doors of the Battistero di San Giovanni (St John's Baptistery) in Florence), and donated to the church in 1876 by the ninth Duke of Bedford. With the first or individual type, the same process of selection and amplification involved in traditional book or print illustration is at

---

[30] See http://www.bunyanmeeting.co.uk/history/windows-and-church-doors/, accessed 1 February 2017.

FIGURE 36.9 'John Bunyan in Prison', stained-glass window, Bunyan Meeting Church, Bedford. Photograph by David Stubbs.

(© By kind permission of the Trustees of Bunyan Meeting, Bedford, England.)

stake. With the second or serial type, the process and effect are much the same as with a sequence of pictures for a book or a portfolio: a series of scenes from the original text have been selected and interpreted in the chosen medium—ten in the case of the bronze doors. To some extent, carving is akin to engraving: the intended image being carved into wood or metal or stone, and given more or less relief or depth depending on both the projected effect and the material being worked.

FIGURE 36.10 'Evangelist Points the Way', stained-glass window, Bunyan Meeting Church, Bedford. Photograph by David Stubbs.

(© By kind permission of the Trustees of Bunyan Meeting, Bedford, England.)

Where sculptures provide three-dimensional illustrations of the text, a more animated form of such representation can be found in the puppet show designed by professional puppeteer David Simpich, and performed at Bob Jones University in Greenville, South Carolina, in 2006. In an interview with *The Collegian*, the Bob Jones University's weekly newspaper, Laura Stapp reports that, for Simpich, the puppet show is live theatre: 'an audience and a performer connecting with a story'. Simpich works the marionettes and

EVANGELIST POINTS THE WAY
'Do you see yonder shining light?'

[see p. 19.

FIGURE 36.11 *Evangelist Points the Way*, illustration by Harold Copping in *The Pilgrim's Progress* (London: The Religious Tract Society, [c.1903–1904]).

(From the author's private collection.)

does the voices, providing an interpretation of *The Pilgrim's Progress* which is both a type of performance and an art form since he uses thirty or so handcrafted marionettes (about twenty inches tall and made from plastic clay) dressed in costumes made from scraps of fabric and trim. 'His attention to detail helps reflect the subtleties of the specific characters', Stapp writes. For him, 'it's a different way of presenting the story, but the story lends itself well to marionette theater because the characters are "bigger than life" characters'.[31] Bringing the story to life through the art of puppetry is yet another way of

---

[31] Laura Stapp, 'Professional Puppeteer to Perform *The Pilgrim's Progress*', *The Collegian*, 20:5 (12 October 2006).

FIGURE 36.12 *Christian's Fight with Apollyon*, pear-wood sculpture by Joseph Parker.
(© By kind permission of the Trustees of Bunyan Meeting, Bedford, England.)

helping an audience to 'connect' with the story—one based on visual and auditory perception. With this marionette show, we are only one step away from the stage performances of *The Pilgrim's Progress*, and only a few more from film adaptations, professional as well as amateur, all too numerous and varied to be treated here.

Transitional Images

The Pilgrim's Progress has been interpreted in yet other ways and other media. Sometimes, one form of representation has brought another into being, thereby

FIGURE 36.13 *Christian's Combat with Apollyon*, illustration drawn by H. C. Selous and M. Paolo Priolo and engraved by L. Chapon, in *The Pilgrim's Progress* (London, Paris, New York, & Melbourne: Cassell & Company, 1902).

(From the author's private collection.)

evidencing the potential for transformation, not simply of the text, but also of its derived forms. A good example of this process is a postcard representing 'Bunyan's Dream/*The Pilgrim's Progress*' which reproduces a watercolour on paper by award-winning painter, printmaker, draughtsman, and graphic designer Edward Bawden. His watercolour was itself a study for a tapestry he designed in 1977 to commemorate the tercentenary of the publication of *The Pilgrim's Progress*, the 350th anniversary of Bunyan's birth, and the Queen's Silver Jubilee. The tapestry was commissioned by the Higgins Gallery, Bedford, where it is now on permanent display (see Figures 36.15 and 36.16).

Another religious-commercial product based on *The Pilgrim's Progress* is a piece entitled *Triumphant Journey* by American artist Phyllis F. Sweeney. Issued in 2005, it is available in two forms: a 'brilliantly colored' digitized poster, and an 'attractively packaged' 1,000-piece puzzle, each accompanied with a twelve-page booklet providing a paragraph-long description of the events illustrated, with biblical references to expand further on them, and intended for all ages. Produced by Ultimate Achievements, LLC, a Florida-based company, this dual piece is 'designed for your spiritual encouragement'. It is presented on the website of the company as 'an artistic rendition of John Bunyan's *The Pilgrim's Progress*' which 'creatively portrays this timeless spiritual allegory on canvas'.

FIGURE 36.14 Bronze doors representing scenes from *The Pilgrim's Progress* at the entrance of the Bunyan Meeting Church, Bedford.

(© By kind permission of the Trustees of Bunyan Meeting, Bedford, England.)

Artistic rendition and creative portrayal are put to the fore, in addition to the fact that '[e]ach product is uniquely designed for suitable framing and display'.[32] Instruction through entertainment, as well as artistry and artistic use, are presented as the basis and outcome of this creative enterprise. Like the postcards already discussed, *Triumphant Journey* marks a significant step away from purely artistic renderings of the work towards partially or entirely marketable and profitable ones.

The same marriage of derivation to commercialization motivates the various board games that have been produced based on *The Pilgrim's Progress*, such as the 1994 Family

---

[32] See http://www.pilgrimsprogresspuzzle.com/nr.htm, accessed 22 September 2011.

FIGURE 36.15 'Bunyan's Dream/*The Pilgrim's Progress*', needlework/tapestry by Edward Bawden.

(© By kind permission of the Trustees, Cecil Higgins Art Gallery, Bedford, England, and the Estate of Edward Bawden.)

FIGURE 36.16 'Bunyan's Dream/*The Pilgrim's Progress*', watercolour by Edward Bawden.

(© By kind permission of the Trustees, Cecil Higgins Art Gallery, Bedford, England, and the Estate of Edward Bawden.)

Time edition designed by Marla Hershberger, and the 2008 Candle Books version by Tim Dowley. Presented as 'educational and fun', they make the players step into the pilgrims' shoes (via small plastic or metal stands representing the characters, some with detachable burdens) and travel from the City of Destruction to the Celestial City. In these games, the original text has been turned into a board game accompanied by a series of cards and retold through an illustrated storybook. In such recreational and educational interpretations of the work, the text is still present, albeit abridged, and still visually depicted, while portions of it get acted out by the players. From book illustrations to portfolios of designs and individual prints, and from still images on different types of materials to those animated in various ways, all designed for special uses and effects, visual and material representations of *The Pilgrim's Progress* have thus taken multiple book and non-book forms, and have touched a remarkably wide-ranging public for over three hundred years.

Back to the Book

As we have seen, visual representations of *The Pilgrim's Progress* were originally supplementary elements which gradually superseded both the written text and the published book as the media in which Bunyan's allegory was at first transmitted. In different forms and formats, and through different types of publishing enterprises and artistic initiatives, the images have at times seceded from the text and book entirely to enjoy a life of their own. Recently, however, they have found yet new forms of expression, both in relation to the book-as-object and alongside the printed text. A remarkable example of this is the book sculpture created in March 2010 by Justin Rowe, bookseller and paper artist from Cambridge (see Figure 36.17). Entitled *Hopeful Had Much Ado to Keep his Brother's Head Above Water*, it uses what Rowe calls 'the source book itself, with no additions', and tries 'to simulate waves engulfing Hopeful and his brother with the paper cutting'.[33] With such a creation, the image literally comes not just from the text but also from the book, and the scene takes on a three-dimensional aspect thanks to yet within the book-object. Both the text and the book have been used as bases for interpretation and turned into a piece of book art worthy to be displayed in a glass case (see Figure 36.18).

This work of art in turn became the basis for yet another form of representation of the text and book, inasmuch as greeting cards were made from a photograph of this creation and are now available for purchase on the Internet. What this multiple creation, like so many others, testifies to, is the potential offered by Bunyan's text for what is known today as customization. Among instances of the many customizable Bunyan images that can

---

[33] See http://daysfalllikeleaves.blogspot.com/2011/03/hopeful-had-much-ado-to-keep-his.html, accessed 28 September 2011.

FIGURE 36.17 *Hopeful Had Much Ado to Keep his Brother's Head Above Water*, book sculpture by Justin Rowe.

(© By kind permission of Justin Rowe, Cambridge, England.)

FIGURE 36.18 *Hopeful Had Much Ado to Keep his Brother's Head Above Water*, book sculpture by Justin Rowe, showcased.

(© By kind permission of Justin Rowe, Cambridge, England.)

be found on the Internet (such as individual prints or posters which can be framed, or greeting cards which can be personalized, all reproducing old or new illustrations of *The Pilgrim's Progress*), some stand out as ultimate examples of the legacy of Bunyan, and of his interpreters'—or exploiters'—willingness to perpetuate his work. Customizable iPhone cases featuring Thomas Sadler's famous portrait of Bunyan, or White's no less famous *Sleeping Portrait*, are the latest and most remarkable manifestations of this trend. To be sure, then, Bunyan and *The Pilgrim's Progress* continue to be represented and circulated in new forms, and adapted to new publics, even today.

Conclusion

For over three hundred years, *The Pilgrim's Progress* has fascinated and inspired publishers, engravers and painters, sculptors, playwrights and performers, photographers, puppeteers, composers and musicians, comic strip authors, film producers, and directors and actors, among other artists. Their work has been aimed at an impressive number and variety of receptors: readers, viewers, spectators, and listeners—a whole range of addressees who have been offered, since the 1680s, a full array of *Pilgrim's Progress*-based extra-textual paraphernalia. In their different forms both within and beyond the book-object, the images generated by the work have ensured its continuing circulation and dissemination through time and around the globe. They have made travellers of Bunyan's words and message, of his name, and of his admirers. As such, they should perhaps encourage his critics to expand their idea of Bunyan's *reader*ship to that of an actual *audience*, and compel us to reconsider the dominant idea of illustrations as artefacts of secondary importance in the life of a literary work. After all, the various artistic renderings of *The Pilgrim's Progress* have undeniably contributed to its production, promotion, circulation, and reception.

What this (necessarily non-exhaustive) survey of the pictorial and visual traditions of illustration born of Bunyan's allegory is suggesting is that these graphic and material representations have played an essential role in the work's journey through changing historical, geographical, and cultural milieus. These traditions all have in common a capacity to retell Bunyan's story extra-literarily: that is, beyond the need for or the presence of the original text. Like Faithful and then Hopeful with Christian, or like Mercie and Great-heart with Christiana, the artwork that *The Pilgrim's Progress* has inspired has escorted it not only in and around its birthplace, but also across seas and oceans and over unpredictable terrains. For generations it has acted as guide, interpreter, and even motivator on the way towards the reading and interpretation of Bunyan's allegory.

The variety of media in which Bunyan's allegory has been interpreted certainly testifies to its appeal and popularity. Perhaps one of this chapter's most controversial proposals, however, is that these interpretations have not only provided an extended life to *The Pilgrim's Progress* but have also found a life of their own, independent of the text from which they initially sprang. Another, perhaps even more controversial, intimation is that more than merely retelling the text, the representations of *The Pilgrim's Progress* have always been a driving force in its dissemination, serving as a key instrument in its reception. Their variety reflects perhaps not so much the text's adaptability to various times, places, and publics as the desire and ability of these publics to adapt the text to their own interests. Such sundry representations are, finally, precious evidence of the text's own journeying, and they provide, consequently, a valuable indication of its multiple modes of diffusion and its sometimes surprising forms of production. As D. F. McKenzie's approach suggests, they invite us to understand that the pictorial materiality of *The Pilgrim's Progress* can in itself tell the compelling story of its historicity.[34]

Suggested Reading

Collé-Bak, Nathalie, 'Spiritual Transfers: William Blake's Iconographic Treatment of John Bunyan's *The Pilgrim's Progress*', *BS*, 16 (2012), 32–51.

Collé-Bak, Nathalie, '*The Pilgrim's Progress*, Print Culture and the Dissenting Tradition', in Sandro Jung (ed.), *British Literature and Print Culture* (Cambridge: D. S. Brewer, 2013), 33–57.

Hofmeyr, Isabel, *The Portable Bunyan: A Transnational History of The Pilgrim's Progress* (Princeton, NJ: Princeton University Press, 2004).

Hofmeyr, Isabel, 'Evangelical Realism: The Transnational Making of Genre in *The Pilgrim's Progress*', in W. R. Owens and Stuart Sim (eds.), *Reception, Appropriation, Recollection: Bunyan's Pilgrim's Progress* (Bern: Peter Lang, 2007), 119–45.

Hofmeyr, Isabel, 'Bunyan: Colonial, Postcolonial', in Anne Dunan-Page (ed.), *The Cambridge Companion to Bunyan* (Cambridge: Cambridge University Press, 2010), 162–76.

Kilpatrick, Shirley and M. Howard Mattsson-Bozé, *Pilgrim's Progress Windows: A Story of Grace in Glass* (Geneva: Fern Cliffe House Publishers, 2011).

Routhier, Jessica Skwire, 'The Painters' Panorama: Narrative, Art, and Faith in the *Moving Panorama of Pilgrim's Progress*', *The Recorder*, 20 (2014), 13–15.

The Grand Moving Panorama of Pilgrim's Progress [exhibition catalogue] (Montclair, NJ: Montclair Art Museum, 1999), available at http://www.tfaoi.com/newsm1/n1m487.htm, accessed 24 January 2018.

---

[34] D. F. McKenzie, *Bibliography and the Sociology of Texts* (Cambridge: Cambridge University Press, 1999).

CHAPTER 37

BUNYAN FOR CHILDREN

SHANNON MURRAY

The *Pilgrim's Progress* (1678; 1684) is, among other things, a children's book, and an extraordinarily important one.[1] To get a sense of how profound the influence of *The Pilgrim's Progress* has been on children's literature in English, we need only look at that American children's classic, Louisa May Alcott's *Little Women* (1868). Early in the novel, as the four March girls wallow in self-pity, their mother reminds them of the game they played when they were younger:

> Do you remember how you used to play Pilgrim's Progress when you were little things? Nothing delighted you more than to have me tie my piece-bags on your backs for burdens, give you hats and sticks and rolls of paper, and let you travel through the house from the cellar, which was the City of Destruction, up, up, to the housetop, where you had all the lovely things you could collect to make a Celestial City.[2]

Each of the four girls then remembers pretending to be Bunyan's Christian. Jo remembers adventure, danger, and action; Meg, the moment when the 'burden' fell off her back and tumbled down the stairs; Amy, what was beautiful; Beth, what was morally good. Alcott early on defines her little women by how they read Bunyan.[3] As the novel unfolds, chapter by chapter, often with explicit references to characters like Apollyon or episodes like the House Beautiful, Alcott structures her novel to follow the course of Christian's journey; and she relies on her young reader to know Bunyan well enough to parallel the journey of the March girls with that of Christian.

---

[1] In *The Hidden Adult: Defining Children's Literature* (Baltimore, MD: Johns Hopkins University Press, 2008), Perry Nodelman suggests the three ways that a book could be considered children's literature: if it is written for children, if it has at its core a child protagonist, or if it is read by children. *The Pilgrim's Progress* is the last.

[2] Louisa May Alcott, *Little Women* (Boston, MA: Roberts Bros., 1868), 11.

[3] In fact, even the idea of girls playing pilgrims is lifted from Alcott's own experience. Her father, the innovative educator and philosopher Bronson Alcott, encouraged his own four daughters to re-enact Christian's journey. See, further, Chapter 34 in this volume.

She was right to do so. We know from first-hand accounts of children's reading practices that it was not the religious allegory or dialogue that tended to draw young people to the book; rather, it was the journey of its hero and the dangers and adventures he encounters. Samuel Bamford, for example, recounts his early experience of reading in his memoirs:

> The first book which attracted my particular notice was 'The Pilgrim's Progress' with rude woodcuts; it excited my curiosity in an extraordinary degree. There was 'Christian knocking at the strait gate', his 'fight with Apollyon', his 'passing near the lions', his escape from Giant Despair', his 'perils at Vanity Fair', his arrival in the 'land of Beulah', and his final passage to 'Eternal Rest'; all these were matters for the exercise of my feeling and imagination.[4]

And in the early days of children's literature, *The Pilgrim's Progress* was considerably more exciting than those stories that were written specifically for young readers. Because of its godly content, though, *The Pilgrim's Progress* also was palatable to book-buying adults, and so through the eighteenth, nineteenth, and into the beginning of the twentieth century, it became one of the few books that all literate Protestant English children could be expected to have read.

The allegory was not written specifically for a young audience, although Bunyan did write one volume for children, a collection of poems entitled *A Book for Boys and Girls* (1686). The place of *The Pilgrim's Progress* in the canon of children's literature comes more from an accidental confluence of the preferences of the audience, the changing ideas held by parents and educators, and the interests of booksellers than from any intention on Bunyan's part. Children from Great Britain, America, and beyond encountered Christian's journey through specialized editions, through dozens of adaptations, and through significant allusions in other children's books. If, as Northrop Frye suggests, the Bible is the 'great code' for English literature,[5] *The Pilgrim's Progress* became its 'little code', ubiquitous in the history of children's literature but also shaping the landscape of generations of young minds.

The Beginnings of Children's Literature

Bunyan's place in the history of children's literature results partly from timing. As Seth Lerer suggests, there has always been some kind of writing for children, but before the

---

[4] Quoted in Natalie Collé-Bak, 'The Role of Illustrations in the Reception of *Pilgrim's Progress*', in W. R. Owens and Stuart Sim (eds.), *Reception, Appropriation, Recollection: Bunyan's Pilgrim's Progress* (Bern: Peter Lang, 2007), 81–97 (91).

[5] Northrop Frye, *The Great Code: The Bible and Literature* (London: Routledge & Kegan Paul, 1982).

seventeenth century, that writing largely consisted of alphabets, battledores (cardboard booklets with illustrations of words), and early readers, all with the aim of bringing young people to reading and then to the world of adult books.[6] Even the folk and fairy tales that one now associates with children came to the nursery shelf only in the nineteenth century. The idea of writing stories for the moral education of children arose in the seventeenth century; stories for their pleasure would come considerably later.

Three writers can provide a sense of the attitude towards children and children's literature in Bunyan's time and immediately after: John Locke, Isaac Watts, and James Janeway. Locke's *Some Thoughts Concerning Education* (1693) covers a wide range of ideas about how children should both learn and be raised, but when he turns to what they should read, he determines that the fables of Aesop are 'the only book almost as I know fit for children'.[7] That statement suggests how scarce such books are, but his choice of moral fables also points to the assumption throughout this period that writing for children ought to be in some way instructive. Isaac Watts and James Janeway, both writing a little after Bunyan, are among the earliest strong influences on the direction of children's literature in English. Watts's *Divine Songs Attempted in Easy Language for the Use of Children* (1715) focuses on addressing and correcting vice, and although, as F. J. Harvey Darton points out, the voice in some of these songs is gentle and tolerant, most present-day readers would, I think, be shocked by the threats and downright violence by which Watts means children to be frightened onto the right path.[8] Think of the lyric 'Obedience to Parents', for example, in which inattentive children will have ravens pick out their eyes and eagles eat them; or the more representative 'Against Evil Company', in which the child speaker wishes not to be 'sent to hell, / Where none but sinners are'.[9] The way to a good young life for Watts is always balanced with the threat of justice in this world and hellfire in the next.

James Janeway's *A Token for Children: Being an Exact Account of the Conversion, Holy and Exemplary Lives, and Joyful Deaths of Several Young Children* (1691) delivers precisely what its title promises: thirteen stories of young death intended as models of behaviour. Like Watts, Janeway had a very serious, even urgent, purpose in mind: saving children's souls. It has been argued that the rise of Puritanism in England in the seventeenth century actually necessitated the creation of a literature for children precisely because of that urgency. If the individual Christian is responsible for the state of his or her own soul, and if the soul's salvation depends on a personal relationship to the Bible, then every man, woman, and child must be able to access the Bible him or herself—and as early as possible. To read the Bible, one must first know how to read; and because child mortality rates were so high, it was imperative for a child to learn that skill as soon as possible. The earlier one could read, the safer one's soul would be. And so this new body

---

[6] Seth Lerer, *Children's Literature: A Reader's History from Aesop to Harry Potter* (Chicago: Chicago University Press, 2009).
[7] John Locke, *Some Thoughts Concerning Education* (1693), 141.
[8] F. J. Harvey Darton, *Children's Books in England* (Cambridge: Cambridge University Press, 1932).
[9] Isaac Watts, *Divine Songs Attempted in Easy Language for the Use of Children* (1715), 74, 68.

of literature aimed at young people became a kind of intermediate step between the basic alphabets or battledores and the Bible itself. Given the morbid if well-intentioned fare from Janeway and others, it is perhaps not surprising that Bunyan's *The Pilgrim's Progress* and even other adult fiction like Jonathan Swift's *Gulliver's Travels* (1726) or Daniel Defoe's *Robinson Crusoe* (1719) were adopted by children seeking adventurous rather than cautionary tales.

A Book for Boys and Girls, or, Country Rhimes for Children

Although Bunyan's largest contribution to the history of English children's literature was *The Pilgrim's Progress*, he did write one book for a child audience. First published in 1686, *A Book for Boys and Girls* is a collection of seventy-four short poems, perhaps the first such collection in English for children. Helping young readers learn to read is clearly part of the purpose—the collection opens with an alphabet, numbers, and the spelling and pronunciation of typical children's names—but the majority of the book is, like Watts's *Divine Songs*, invested in a child's spiritual development.

The poems show Bunyan to be a competent rhymer with some sense of rhythm, but I cannot claim that their value lies in those artistic elements.[10] Instead, his tone and attitude to his audience are what seem so extraordinary, particularly when compared with his contemporary writers for children. Unlike either Watts's or Janeway's, Bunyan's approach involves more enticement than scare tactic, and there is a complexity that Jeremy Tambling describes as 'more knowing, less simple than is usually said'.[11] The poems help children read the book of the world with a pattern that resembles that of an emblem book without the pictures; an everyday, natural event or object is described and then turned into a metaphor. Many of the poems focus on something that most ordinary English seventeenth-century children would have had experience of: tops, horses, fish, bees, birds, spiders, or sunrise, for example. Here is an example, one of six poems meditating on a time of the day:

> *Meditation upon Peep of day*
> I oft, though it be peep of day, don't know,
> Whether 'tis Night, whether 'tis Day or no.
> I fancy that I see a little light;
> But cannot yet distinguish day from night.
> I hope, I doubt, but steddy yet I be not,
> I am not at a point, the Sun I see not.

---

[10] See, further, Chapter 19, on Bunyan's poetry, in this volume.
[11] Jeremy Tambling, 'Bunyan and Things: *A Book for Boys and Girls*', BS, 16 (2012), 7–31 (21).

> Thus 'tis with such, who Grace but now possest,
> They know not yet, if they are curst or blest. (*MW*, 6: 205)

Here, Bunyan chooses the common experience of daybreak and through the first six lines speaks in the first person, telling the child reader the difficulty he has in distinguishing night from day. This emphasis on the speaker's own experience highlights the connection between child and speaker. The style here is all Bunyan: simple diction, nice parallelism, repetition. The most striking element is that it is descriptive and not prescriptive: this is how people new to grace *do* feel, not how they ought to feel. There is a gentle humanity here, an experience of the world that Bunyan is choosing to share with children, and a reassurance that doubt is not a sign of failure or of reprobation but something that all true recipients of grace will feel.

Here is another example, this time a meditation on a bird's flight:

> *Upon the Swallow*
> This Pretty Bird, Oh! how she flies and sings!
> But could she do so if she had not Wings?
> Her Wings, bespeak my Faith, her Songs my Peace,
> When I believe and sing, my Doubtings cease. (*MW*, 6: 207)

Again, a common experience of the natural world is expressed in plain language, along with a delight in the movement and song of the swallow. This poem also feels personal; it is not about when *others* believe or should believe, but about 'when *I* believe and sing'. The speaker guides the reader to understand the meaning of the analogy: wings mean faith, songs mean peace. No threats of hellfire here, no eyeball-eating ravens. Instead the poems help children see how the book of the world can help them to understand their own experience and their own relationship to God.

The introductory poem in this collection shows that Bunyan was intentional in his tone and approach to children. He means to entice them, by using their playthings and the natural world to bring them to thoughts of heaven: '*I seek*', he writes, '*to please*' and '*thus I would be catching Girls and Boys*'(*MW*, 6: 191). He will lure them towards the good rather than scaring them away from the bad. And he clearly has other contemporary writers in mind, accusing them of misunderstanding their audience: of aiming 'Thunder-bolts' at children but missing the mark (*MW*, 6: 190). This approach of appealing to children with what is attractive to them, like a spoonful of sugar to help the medicine go down, may not seem strange to a twentieth-century reader. Yet compared to the Puritan hellfire of his contemporaries, Bunyan is delightfully ahead of his time. Although only one edition of *A Book for Boys and Girls* appeared in Bunyan's lifetime, this collection of poems went on to enjoy a healthy readership, being 'read by more generations, and reprinted more often than any other of his poetic volumes', as Graham Midgley has noted (*MW*, 6: 185). However, subsequent editions both changed its title and presented considerably abbreviated collections. A second edition published in 1701, for example, was entitled *A Book for Boys and Girls: Or Temporal Things Spiritualized*, and contained just forty-nine poems: twenty-five fewer than the original (see *MW*, 6: 185–89). For whatever reason, *A Book for Boys and Girls*, despite its enticements, seems to have had less of an afterlife than, say, Isaac Watts's songs did. In fact, far more important in the history of English children's literature is a book that Bunyan did not write for children. That book was *The Pilgrim's Progress*, published at about the time a true literature for children was first beginning to appear in English.

The Pilgrim's Progress: Editions and Adaptations for Children

Over the two hundred years following its original publication, *The Pilgrim's Progress* became one of three books written for an adult audience that found their way to nursery shelves, and, because of its godly content, it was the one book many households would permit their children to read on Sundays. As Ruth MacDonald points out, 'Compared to the adult works they might read, and even the children's literature from the Sunday School, *The Pilgrim's Progress* was much more readable. And if one tired of religion, one could simply skip over it.'[12] And so the imaginative landscape of generations of young minds was shaped by the hills, the gates, the sloughs, and the houses of Bunyan's allegory.

Through much of the eighteenth century, however, both children and adults were reading *The Pilgrim's Progress* in the same editions, some of which included illustrations. Into the nineteenth century, some of these editions were attractively bound—like the American Tract Society's colourful, leather-bound illustrated editions from the 1820s— or increasingly affordable, like the American Sunday School Union's editions. While neither was particularly aimed at a child audience, those same things that would make a text more attractive to a child, like large print or illustrations, would also attract newly literate readers.[13] In the nineteenth and twentieth centuries, editions of Bunyan's allegory with the original text intact were clearly being packaged for a young readership— and for the people who bought books for children.

Early in the nineteenth century, though, merely having a child read Bunyan's book seems not to have been enough—at least not for editors and for book-buying parents— and so began the process of adapting *The Pilgrim's Progress* for the young reader. There are dozens of examples in the nineteenth century alone, even more in the twentieth century. The sheer number and variety of these adaptations suggest interesting things about attitudes not only towards Bunyan's work but also towards children and the nature of children's literature. Adaptations of *The Pilgrim's Progress*, of course, start remarkably

---

[12] Ruth K. MacDonald, *Christian's Children: The Influence of John Bunyan's The Pilgrim's Progress on American Children's Literature* (Bern: Peter Lang, 1989), 32.

[13] Ruth K. MacDonald, 'The Case for the Pilgrim's Progress', *Children's Literature Association Quarterly*, 10 (1985), 29–30.

early: with sequels and unacknowledged revisions at the end of the seventeenth and beginning of the eighteenth centuries. What is most remarkable about many of those attempts is their concern for improving the homely, Saxon language of the original. By the nineteenth century, when the adaptations for children begin, the emphasis is on simplifying the language for a young readership.

One of the most intriguing examples of such simplified language is Mrs Edward Ashley Walker's *The Pilgrim's Progress* […] *in Words of One Syllable* (1869). It is, as the title suggests, completely monosyllabic except for the proper names, and here is an example of how it sounds: 'So I saw in my dream that the man set out to run. Now he had not run far from his own door when his wife saw him and cried to him to come back; but he would not hear, and cried as he ran, "Life! Life! Life that shall not end!"' Despite some contortions to avoid polysyllables, it is a remarkably readable adaptation. Walker's purpose is to make the book available to new readers, both young and old. She writes, 'If this book can help little children in busy households, and adults to whom a disyllable is still a burden, to know the Immortal Pilgrim earlier than they could otherwise have done, the writer will be glad.'[14] A concern for simpler or for less archaic language increases into the twentieth century.

It is in the nineteenth century, though, that some adaptors object not to Bunyan's language but to his 'experimental theology', in the words of the Reverend J. M. Neale. His 1853 adaptation makes it clear how important *The Pilgrim's Progress* has become as a religious text but also how potentially dangerous the peculiarities of Bunyan's theology could be for young Anglo-Catholics. Neale's *The Pilgrim's Progress of John Bunyan* is subtitled *For the Use of Children in the English Church*, and his introduction argues that children will—and must—read *The Pilgrim's Progress*, both because they delight in it and because their grandparents have admired it, which establishes a kind of literary cross-generational community. But because of the 'fascination which it exercises over the minds of Children,'[15] *The Pilgrim's Progress* could, he argues, encourage the uncorrected child to believe, for example, that communion is of little importance or that confirmation does not exist. Neale claims in his introduction that parents regularly omit what is unclear or heretical when they read the allegory to their children, a claim that offers some evidence, if not wholly reliable, of a pattern of reception by children. All that his adaptation does, Neale writes, is watch for where those expurgations naturally occur already and ensure that even those who have hitherto avoided Bunyan because of his heresy may now read him with pleasure and good conscience. In Neale's version, for example, Christian encounters a triple baptism at the Wicket Gate and experiences both confirmation and communion at the House Beautiful. He also repeatedly substitutes Bunyan's word 'faith' with his own 'acts'. Neale was not alone in his perhaps overzealous bowdlerizing: as Marion J. Phillips argues, both evangelicals and Anglo-Catholics

---

[14] Mrs Edward Ashley Walker, *The Pilgrim's Progress* […] *in Words of One Syllable* (New York: Geo. A. Leavitt, 1869), 14, 6.

[15] J. M. Neale, *The Pilgrim's Progress of John Bunyan: For the Use of Children in the English Church* (Oxford: John Henry Parker, 1853), x.

attempted to control Bunyan's narrative for their own ends.[16] For the purposes of tracing the children's reading patterns, though, Neale's introduction is even more interesting than his edition, suggesting as it does both the extent of the child audience and the habits of worried parents as they read the theologically suspect Bunyan aloud to their children.

Some other adaptors for children worry not about language and theology but about attention spans and frightening episodes. But while many of the adaptations, especially in the first quarter of the twentieth century, set out to edit what they think will be dull or difficult for young readers, some others are concerned that children will be tempted *only* to read for the adventure, as Alcott's Jo March did. A. L. O. E.'s *The Young Pilgrim* (1869), for example, was, in her words, 'written as a CHILD'S COMPANION TO THE PILGRIM'S PROGRESS'. She writes in her preface that

> That invaluable work is frequently put into youthful hands long before the mind can unravel the deep allegory which it contains, and thus its precious lessons are lost, and it is only perused as an amusing tale. I would offer my humble work as a kind of translation [...] a translation of ideas beyond youthful comprehension into the common language of daily life.[17]

Most of the adaptations, though, are eager to give children what they want, like Isaac Taylor's *Bunyan Explained to a Child, being Pictures and Poems Founded upon the Pilgrim's Progress, Part I. or Christian's Journey* (1824). Taylor argues that children love the story before they can grasp the allegory, and he is reluctant to 'deny them so great a gratification': a simpler version approached early may, he suggests, 'prepare the mind to understand the detail, by having some previous acquaintance with the great outline of the story'.[18] J. C.'s 1858 abridgement, *The Story of the Pilgrim's Progress Told for Young People*, is defended in similar terms:

> The Allegory contained in John Bunyan's *Pilgrim's Progress* is certainly one of the most beautiful that ever was written. It is, however, so overlaid with repetition and conversations about questions of doctrine which no child can possibly understand, that I am constrained to believe no young people can ever read the whole book through without being wearied. It is for them that I have printed the present edition, in which all the story of the allegory is given in the author's own words (with occasional exceptions) and in which the long conversations I refer to are omitted.[19]

By far, this is the most commonly cited reason for undertaking an adaptation: children read for pleasure, for adventure; give them that and spare the rest.

---

[16] Marion J. Phillips, 'Inimitable Bunyan Stands his Ground', BS, 2 (1990), 26–31 (28).

[17] A. L. O. E. [Miss C. Tucker], *The Young Pilgrim: A Tale Illustrative of The Pilgrim's Progress* (New York: Robert Carter & Brothers, 1860), iv–v.

[18] Isaac Taylor, *Bunyan Explained to a Child* (London: Frances Westley, 1824), iii.

[19] J. C., *The Story of the Pilgrim's Progress Told for Young People* (London: Sampson Low, Son, & Co., 1858), iii.

In reading these adaptations one can also guess at other principles at work, especially when the episodes in the adventure turn to distress, danger, or violence. Faithful, for example, is sometimes still beaten, stabbed, and burned, but just as often in children's versions his torments are streamlined or shortened; he is only burned or only beaten to death. While the experience in Doubting Castle is usually pretty faithful to the original—occasionally the pilgrims are just given poison or not encouraged to kill themselves at all—one version explicitly sets out to leave out all such episodes, for a really interesting reason. The 1860 *The Young Pilgrim* omits both the Valley of the Shadow of Death and the Slough of Despond because, the author argues rather hopefully:

> of fearful inward struggles and temptations, such as befell the author of that work, the gloom and horrors of the valley of the shadow of death, the little ones who set out early on the path, know but little. They find the stepping stones across the Slough of Despond, and are rarely seized by Giant Despair.[20]

So in these adaptations, we have variously no burning, no despair, or no halters, depending upon the sensibilities of the adaptor. In each case, clues are left suggestive of the dominant attitude not just to *The Pilgrim's Progress* but also to the child as a reader.

Some of the most inventive adapting tackles Christian's initial flight from the City of Destruction. Fewer than half the adaptations are faithful to Bunyan's own description of the pilgrim running away, fingers in ears, while wife and children run after him. Perhaps the adaptors might imagine that their audience would identify more readily with the abandoned child than with the fleeing parent. In some, wife and children are simply not mentioned at all, as in John Warner Barber's delightful *Metamorphosis*. Published in America in 1821, the *Metamorphosis* is essentially just one large sheet of paper, ingeniously folded and cut so that each scene offers three possible views and some text. Lift the top, and a new view appears; lower the bottom half, and a third picture is made.[21] The tiny, sweet *Little Pilgrim's Progress*, on the other hand, published in Philadelphia in 1844, makes Christian's wife a scold: 'he was derided and despised by his friends and neighbours, and even his wife'. In this version, children are never mentioned. So when he does leave, he does not run, fingers in ears: 'Christian no sooner heard this [...] than he set forth most earnestly to find his way to the gate; and one of his neighbours, Pliable by name, resolved to go with him.'[22] So here there are no children and no neighbours following and fussing at Christian's departure.

The most common solution to the problem is simply to make the pilgrim a child, as in the illustrated pop-up book *Go with Christian!* (1996), or in Enid Blyton's popular *Land of Far-Beyond* (1942). In H. L. Taylor's *Little Christian's Pilgrimage: The Story of the Pilgrim's Progress, Simply Told* (1889), the City of Destruction has many adults, but all

---

[20] A. L. O. E., *The Young Pilgrim*, vi.
[21] J. W. Barber, *Bunyan's The Pilgrim's Progress [...] Exhibited in a Metamorphosis, or a Transformation of Pictures* (Hartford: P. B. Goodsell, 1821).
[22] *The Little Pilgrim's Progress* (Philadelphia, PA: H. C. Peck & Theo Bliss, 1844), 5, 9.

the pilgrims are children. One of the more disturbing examples of the 'child-as-pilgrim' group is Mrs Sherwood's *The Infant Pilgrim's Progress, from the Valley of Destruction to Everlasting Glory* (1821). In this version, we follow the pilgrimage of three children who set on their road only after they are abandoned by their parents. They live in the ironically named City of Family Love, which has been afflicted with earthquakes. Evangelist comes to the house and urges both parents to run, and to leave their three children (all under the age of ten) behind. These three— Humble Mind and his two sisters, Playful and Peace—are left alone, their clothes fall to rags, and they almost starve to death before setting out on the road to Beulah. Sherwood deals with parental abandonment first by including it—making it even worse than in the original, in fact, because here both parents flee—and then by focusing on the children left behind, and on how they fashion their own journeys.

Perhaps the most remarkable solution to the problem of child abandonment is hit upon by 'A Lady' in her *Explanation of The Pilgrim's Progress: Abridged and Adapted to the Capacities of Children, in Dialogue, between a Child and his Mother* (1818). This tiny book takes the child 'Charles' through *The Pilgrim's Progress* with his mother, as she explains its events to him. When he asks, 'But why did Christian leave his wife and children behind?' she blames Christiana:

> Because his wife at that time, was like many unthinking women at this present day: she was so delighted with the vanities and follies of the world, that she would not listen to her husband, or take his advice, though for her own good; but she treated him as a madman, so he was obliged to leave her. This was his first severe trial on his pilgrimage, for he loved her with true affection.

Here, responsibility for the abandonment gets left squarely on Christiana's shoulders— 'because, if he had been an entire *stranger* to her, she ought to have been more liberal than to hurt his feelings and censure his conduct, as she did'.[23] In all these changes to Bunyan's 'flight' scene, there is the implicit suggestion not only that the presentation of a father running away from his children, fingers in ears, needs explanation, but also that children will find it difficult to accept such apparently inexplicable behaviour, and might even see themselves as the child being left behind rather than as the pilgrim setting out on his journey.

All these adaptations of *The Pilgrim's Progress* for children suggest changing attitudes towards childhood and child reading as well as about the reception of Bunyan. The fear that children might miss the improving nature of the dialogue and allegory—and so an impulse towards explanation and expansion—gives way to the belief that children should be allowed, even helped, to avoid both allegory and theological dialogue. The erasure of Bunyan's 'experimental theology' to which Neale refers in his edition is made orthodox. Various adaptors see the episodes in Vanity Fair, in Doubting Castle, and especially in the parting of Christian from his family as too violent, too disturbing, or even

---

[23] A Lady, *Explanation of The Pilgrim's Progress* (London: J. Barfield, 1818), 9–10.

just unnecessary to the interests and experiences of a child. And Bunyan's language goes from too low—a nervous specimen of homely Saxon, in Neale's words—to too difficult and in need of simplification.

Through all these decisions, the underlying assumption is that Bunyan must be accessible to young readers. Children *do* read Bunyan for pleasure even without adult intervention, and so, the argument goes, they *must*, and versions altered with them in mind hope for an even larger and more approving audience. An entry into the story early in life might encourage a later, fuller reading. Some of these ideas about adapting for children could extend as easily to Shakespeare or Dickens or any other canonical writer, but two things set Bunyan apart from such authors, and may account for both the high number and the surprising variety of adaptations to have emerged. The first is simply that, as a godly and improving book, *The Pilgrim's Progress* could be read without guilt on the Sabbath, the way L. M. Montgomery and Louisa Alcott and Nathaniel Hawthorne and so many other children encountered the story. Secondly, this is a book that also invites readers to see themselves as the main character, as Christians following Christian's journey, and so to rewrite the book with themselves as the hero.

Bunyan as Subtext in Children's Literature

This leads us to the other way in which Bunyan finds himself so firmly a figure in the history of children's literature: read and imitated by the child protagonists. I have already mentioned the example of *Little Women*, in which Alcott models her structure on *The Pilgrim's Progress* and which signals in other ways that the March girls' lives are to be seen as imitating Christian's journey. David Smith and Ruth K. MacDonald list dozens of examples of children's books that either allude to *The Pilgrim's Progress*, or show children reading the allegory, or that mirror Christian's journey: from *What Katy Did* (1872) and *Rebecca of Sunnybrook Farm* (1903) to *The Wizard of Oz* (1900) and *The Phantom Tollbooth* (1958). Two other children's writers from the golden age of children's books, however, illustrate how central *The Pilgrim's Progress* had become in children's reading: Frances Hodgson Burnett in her *Two Little Pilgrims' Progress* (1895) and L. M. Montgomery in both *A Tangled Web* (1938) and *Emily of New Moon* (1925).

Burnett, best known for *Little Lord Fauntleroy* (1885–86), *The Little Princess* (1905), and *The Secret Garden* (1911), was commissioned to write *Two Little Pilgrims' Progress* by the directors of the Columbian World's Exposition of 1893 as part of the celebration of the Chicago World's Fair. Like so many of Burnett's other heroes and heroines, the children at the centre of the story are orphans searching for a home. Meg and Robin have been sent to live with their hard-working farm-bound aunt, who takes little interest in them. Meg, a great reader, finds a copy of *The Pilgrim's Progress*, which she reads and rereads in the barn loft, eventually declaring to her brother, 'oh Robin! [...] I don't want to hear of the people down there. I've been reading the *Pilgrim's Progress*, and I do wish—I do wish there was a city beautiful.' Robin's response is, 'there is going to be one'. He tells her about the World's Fair in Chicago, which they both immediately imagine is a Celestial City on earth, and from there the two plot how to travel to this promised western land on their own. They collect money, make plans, and as they do, they imagine what stage in Christian's journey they have reached. From then on, *The Pilgrim's Progress* becomes their personal roadmap in the journey from Boston to Chicago. Yet even before they leave, they see their own difficulties and obstacles as types of Bunyan's metaphorical landscape. The narrator tells us that 'They had never read that old, worn *Pilgrim's Progress* as they did in those days. They kept it in the trough near the treasure and always had it on hand to refer to. In it they seem to find parallels for everything.' Meg's great revelation comes just as they leave home:

> 'Robin,' said Meg suddenly, shutting the book and giving it a little thump on the back, 'it's not only Christian's city that is like our city. We are like Christian. *We* are pilgrims, and our way to that place is our Pilgrim's Progress.'[24]

What is even more interesting in their journey, though, is the fact that they are so self-aware as readers. They know explicitly how they are reading *The Pilgrim's Progress*. As the narrator says, 'somehow one could scarcely tell where one ended and the others began, they were so much alike, the three cities—Christian's, Meg's, and the fair, ephemeral one that the ending of the nineteenth century had built upon the blue lake's side.'[25] But at no point do the children—nor does Burnett, I think—recognize the irony of superimposing Bunyan's Celestial City onto that most worldly of things, a World's Fair. And while Bunyan's Celestial City is one from which Christian doesn't return, these children do go home. They have remapped *The Pilgrim's Progress* as a worldly rather than as a spiritual journey.

The Pilgrim's Progress also gets a secular revision in L. M. Montgomery's *A Tangled Web* (1931). Most famous for her series of novels about the heroine of *Anne of Green Gables* (1908), in this novel, she writes about two rival families, the Penhallows and the Darks. Aunt Becky, one of Montgomery's many allusions to William Makepeace Thackeray's novel *Vanity Fair* (1847–48), decides that she will publish the contents of her will before she dies. Every one of her possessions is promised to one member of the family or another, all but the one thing that everyone desperately wants: a jug. Much of the rest of the novel involves the various members of the Penhallow and Dark clans plotting and bribing and lobbying to get that jug. In this severely dysfunctional family, Margaret stands out as one of the few good people, and one who gets what appears to be the least valuable bequest:

---

[24] Francis Hodgson Burnett, *Two Little Pilgrims' Progress* (New York: Scribners, 1895), 9, 54, 71.
[25] Burnett, *Two Little Pilgrims' Progress*, 53.

> She got Aunt Becky's *Pilgrim's Progress*, a very old, battered book. The covers had been sewed on, the leaves were yellow with age. One was afraid to touch it lest it might fall to pieces. It was the most disreputable old volume which Theodore Dark, for some unknown reason, had prized when alive. Since his death, Aunt Becky had kept it in an old box in the garret, where it had got musty and dusty.[26]

Margaret was not disappointed, we're told, but neither does she value the gift: 'As for the old *Pilgrim's Progress*, it could lie on in the Pinery attic for all she cared.'[27] It does, though, turn out to be the most valuable part of the estate, though for financial rather than spiritual or moral reasons, when the copy turns out to be a first edition, sold to allow her to buy a home of her own with the local orphan boy. This first edition of *The Pilgrim's Progress* allows her, then, to live her life the way she wishes: not married to a man she doesn't love, nor living with other female relatives, but able to take in an unloved boy, Brian Dark. Hers is an unconventional choice, and though it involves having someone who needs to be loved, it is not quite Christiana's community on the road.

So Montgomery's novel ends by looking at what has real rather than false value. The jug itself was a fragile and empty vessel, yet everyone wanted it—making it a perfect example of the vain wares sold in Bunyan's Vanity Fair. That copy of *The Pilgrim's Progress* is the only thing of true value, it seems, yet no one sees it. In fact, Montgomery's greatest joke on her clans is that not one of her characters has a moment of true revelation: a moment in which they think that there could be some spiritual truths contained within its musty covers—not even Margaret. Whereas in *The Two Little Pilgrims' Progress* Bunyan's work becomes a physical, not a spiritual, map to follow, here, its value is purely as a commodity.

Although no one in *A Tangled Web* actually reads *The Pilgrim's Progress*, Montgomery certainly did, and her journals give us yet another example of a real child's experience of Bunyan, this time from a nineteenth-century Canadian girl:

> *Pilgrim's Progress* was read and reread with never failing delight. Many a time did I walk the straight and narrow path with Christian and Christiana—although I never liked Christiana's adventures half so well as Christian's. For one thing there was such a crowd with Christiana; she had not half the fascination of that solitary intrepid figure who faced all alone the shadows of the dark valley and the encounter with Apollyon.[28]

Emily Byrd Starr, the central character in Montgomery's trilogy of novels—*Emily of New Moon* (1923), *Emily's Climb* (1925), and *Emily's Quest* (1927)—comes closest to Montgomery's own picture of herself as a girl. The first of these novels, *Emily of New*

---

[26] L. M. Montgomery, *A Tangled Web* (Toronto: Bantam, 1982), 52.
[27] Montgomery, *Tangled Web*, 73.
[28] L. M. Montgomery, *The Selected Journals of L. M. Montgomery*, ed. Mary Rubio and Elizabeth Waterston, 3 vols (Oxford: Oxford University Press, 1985–92), 1: 394.

Moon, begins with Emily's reading of *The Pilgrim's Progress* and a judgement of the book almost identical to that of her creator:

> So Emily curled herself up in the ragged, comfortable old wing-chair and read *The Pilgrim's Progress* all the afternoon. Emily loved *The Pilgrim's Progress*. Many a time had she walked the straight and narrow path with Christian and Christiana—although she never liked Christiana's adventures half so well as Christian's. For one thing, there was such a crowd with Christiana. She had not the fascination of that solitary intrepid figure who faced all alone the shadows if the Dark Valley and the encounter with Apollyon. Darkness and hobgoblins were nothing when you had plenty of company. But to be *alone*—ah, Emily shivered with the delicious horror of it![29]

She goes on to write that Emily, like her creator, was 'proud of liking *The Pilgrim's Progress*', and when Emily is later fostered by her strict Presbyterian aunts, *The Pilgrim's Progress* is the only book she is permitted to read on Sunday. These three novels make an interesting contrast, then, to *Little Women*, in which *The Pilgrim's Progress* is again a central text, but where the March sisters really do structure a moral and spiritual life for themselves based on Bunyan. Here, *The Pilgrim's Progress* functions as a shared narrative, a journey metaphor, and whether used seriously or satirically, it becomes a way to the rewards of this world.

In these three examples of children's fiction, as in *Little Women*, *The Pilgrim's Progress* is a common text, one that their authors expect audiences to know well and which the authors themselves have read in their own youth, as an individual pleasure in Montgomery's case or as a communal re-enactment in Alcott's. If the many illustrated editions and children's adaptations that have appeared over the last two centuries suggest a market for *The Pilgrim's Progress*—with both publishers and parents believing that children would and should read the book—then writers like Alcott, Montgomery, and Burnett could rely on it to provide a common thread between themselves and their audiences.

Conclusion

In *The Adventures of Huckleberry Finn* (first published in 1884), Mark Twain's young hero finds some books in one of the homes he visits. Appropriately for a boy on a journey, one is *The Pilgrim's Progress*, 'about a man that left his family, it didn't say why. I read considerable in it now and then. The statements was interesting, but tough.'[30] Twain knew that his readers would get the joke, would recognize the book and be amused by Huck's innocent judgement. While in the later twentieth century one could count on children

---

[29] L. M. Montgomery, *Emily of New Moon* (Toronto: Seal, 1983), 2–3.
[30] Mark Twain, *The Adventures of Huckleberry Finn* (New York: Harper & Brothers, 1912), 134–35.

reading *The Pilgrim's Progress* less and less often in its original form (or on English-speaking children sharing, in fact, a knowledge of any single book), copies of Enid Blyton's *The Land of Far-Beyond* and even Helen L. Taylor's *Little Pilgrim's Progress* are still easily available, as are large-format illustrated retellings for even younger children, like Geraldine McCaughrean's prize-winning *John Bunyan's A Pilgrim's Progress* (1999). There is even a graphic novel, with a very muscular-looking Christian, and a pop-up version that allows young readers to re-enact the young Christian's journey by pulling tabs to make Apollyon jump up or by shining a flashlight through the darkened Valley of the Shadow of Death.

So while at the end of the twentieth century one could no longer claim, as one could at the end of the nineteenth, that *The Pilgrim's Progress* was a story most young English-speaking readers would surely know, there remains enough of a sense of its importance, as one of those books one ought to read (or, in some cases, a religious guidebook that ought to be followed) to encourage more children's editions and adaptations. Though its place in a contemporary children's canon may be supplanted by Winnie the Poohs and Harry Potters, for some two hundred years in the history of English children's literature Christian's journey from the City of Destruction to the Celestial City helped form the landscape of young minds, and the imaginations of the adults who wrote for them.

Suggested Reading

Collé-Bak, Natalie, 'The Role of Illustrations in the Reception of *Pilgrim's Progress*', in W. R. Owens and Stuart Sim (eds.), *Reception, Appropriation, Recollection: Bunyan's Pilgrim's Progress* (Bern: Peter Lang, 2007), 81–97.

Darton, F. J. Harvey, *Children's Books in England* (Cambridge: Cambridge University Press, 1932).

Lerer, Seth, *Children's Literature: A Reader's History from Aesop to Harry Potter* (Chicago: Chicago University Press, 2009).

MacDonald, Ruth K., *Christian's Children: The Influence of John Bunyan's The Pilgrim's Progress on American Children's Literature* (Bern: Peter Lang, 1989).

Murray, Shannon, 'A *Book for Boys and Girls: Or, Country Rhimes for Children*: Bunyan and Literature for Children', in Anne Dunan-Page (ed.), *The Cambridge Companion to Bunyan* (Cambridge: Cambridge University Press, 2010), 120–36.

Murray, Shannon, 'Playing Pilgrims: Adapting Bunyan for Children', *BS*, 18 (2014), 78–106.

Nodelman, Perry, *The Hidden Adult: Defining Children's Literature* (Baltimore, MD: Johns Hopkins University Press, 2008).

Smith, David E., *John Bunyan in America* (Bloomington, IN: Indiana University Press, 1966).

Wooden, Warren, *Children's Literature of the English Renaissance*, ed. Jeannie Watson (Lexington, KY: University Press of Kentucky, 1986).

CHAPTER 38

BUNYAN AND EMPIRE

SYLVIA BROWN

NOT long after its first appearance in 1678, *The Pilgrim's Progress* replicated itself in new forms that circulated around the globe. A Dutch translation appeared as early as 1683, and, two years later, the first edition in French issued from the same Amsterdam press. Even before these first translations, *The Pilgrim's Progress* had already crossed the Atlantic to be printed in New England in 1681.[1] Bunyan himself acknowledged his allegory's 'travels' to France, Flanders, Holland, Scotland, Ireland, and New England in his preface to *Part II*, first published in 1684 (*PP*, 169). Almost from the beginning, then, *The Pilgrim's Progress* not only remained constantly in print, in multiple editions and adaptations, it also travelled across linguistic, cultural, and national boundaries. Other works by Bunyan were also translated and circulated, but none enjoyed the early and wide dissemination of *The Pilgrim's Progress*. By 1793, the first non-European translation had appeared: missionaries in Vepery near Madras (now Chennai) produced a bilingual edition with English on the left and Tamil on the facing (right) page of each opening, the first in a tradition of South Asian editions and adaptations that continues to the present.[2]

The Pilgrim's Progress was thus already a text of the world by the time that Britain was becoming a world empire. It is tempting to connect the astonishing domination of a small island nation with the equally surprising global spread of a text by a modest preacher from Bedford. Yet what exactly is the nature of the connection? In her book exploring the authority (in multiple senses) of John Bunyan, Tamsin Spargo has argued that the aggressive global circulation of Bunyan by missionary and imperial interests cemented his canonization as a simultaneously universal and essentially English author, an argument developed by Isabel Hofmeyr's various writings on the transnational

---

[1] *Eens Christens Reyse na de Eeuwigheyt* (Amsterdam: Joannes Boekholt, 1683), the publication date is incorrectly listed as 1682 on the title page; *Voyage d'un Chrestien vers l'Eternité* (Amsterdam: Jean Boekholt, 1685); John Bunyan, *The Pilgrim's Progress* (Boston, MA: Samuel Green, 1681).

[2] *The Pilgrim's Progress, Text in English and Tamil* ('Printed in the Office of the Mission at Vepery near Madras', 1793).

Bunyan.[3] If Bunyan benefited from his imperial associations in terms of canonical authority, was there also a way in which imperialism made use of Bunyan? Was there an aesthetic or cultural ingredient in Bunyan's allegory that contributed to the developing ideology of imperialism? The American theologian Jon Pahl has recently argued for just such a colonizing power intrinsic to Bunyan's text. In 'its heavy-handed metaphors and literalizing analogies', he writes, '*The Pilgrim's Progress* clears the way for the taking of land that became the epitome of a wide variety of European (and eventually American) empires'. Pahl sees in Bunyan's 'antipilgrimage pilgrimage' an evacuation of the material and the experiential from place, and the promotion, instead, of a transcendent realm of meaning and spiritual experience which facilitates empire. For Pahl, then, *The Pilgrim's Progress* is not only an example of this procedure but, by the very 'fact' of its popularity among the Puritan founders, one of the instigators of an American culture of violence whose logic connects religious sacrifice with imperial expansion.[4]

Whether one wishes to cast Bunyan's text as actively promoting empire or as merely seconded to imperialist or colonizing projects—or, as a third alternative, which will be pursued in this chapter, as having also the potential to work against such projects—it seems clear that, as a book, *The Pilgrim's Progress* has historically had a quality of mobility and adaptability comparable to the Christian Scriptures. This dynamic quality has resulted from a combination of the formal, the material, and the cultural. The allegorical, episodic form of *The Pilgrim's Progress* has its own adaptive and generative possibilities. More contingently, historically and sometimes personally specific imaginings of how this text has been understood to work in the world in addition to the material and pragmatic conditions of its production and transmission have resulted in an astonishing proliferation of editions and adaptations. Any appreciation of Bunyan's global career alongside the rise and decline of empire must therefore take into account the particular, often contingent routes travelled by specific editions, translations, and adaptations of his writings: sometimes as forerunners, sometimes as accomplices, sometimes as enemies to colonial ambitions and authority.

'To Enlighten the Habitable Globe': Universal Claims and Particular Agents

We need to begin our assessment of such matters in the nineteenth century: the age of empire. For it was in 1853, while David Livingstone was crossing Africa, that the Baptist

---

[3] Tamsin Spargo, *The Writing of John Bunyan* (Aldershot: Ashgate, 1997), 103–04. Isabel Hofmeyr, 'Bunyan: Colonial, Postcolonial', in Anne Dunan-Page (ed.), *The Cambridge Companion to Bunyan* (Cambridge: Cambridge University Press, 2010), 162–76; 'How Bunyan Became English: Missionaries, Translation, and the Discipline of English Literature', *Journal of British Studies*, 41 (2002), 84–119; and *The Portable Bunyan: A Transnational History of The Pilgrim's Progress* (Princeton, NJ: Princeton University Press, 2004).

[4] Jon Pahl, *Empire of Sacrifice: The Religious Origins of American Violence* (New York: New York University Press, 2010), 146.

book collector George Offor gave the public what he hoped would become the 'Standard Edition' of Bunyan's writings, to 'be extensively used wherever the English language is known' but also to help spread the 'benign influence' of the Gospel to 'all kindreds, and tongues, and nations that dwell upon the earth'.[5] The tension here between Bunyan as a specifically English author, to be given the same treatment as Shakespeare or Milton, but also as global evangelizing force with the potential to influence 'all kindreds, and tongues' will, as we shall see, be maintained across different phases of Bunyan's imperial career. Offor also published a 'new' and 'correct' edition of *The Pilgrim's Progress*, where he asserted the world's indebtedness both to Bunyan's 'surprising narrative of a new birth', *Grace Abounding to the Chief of Sinners* (1666), and to his even more famous allegory, a book which had, in his view, 'proved a most important blessing, not only to this nation, but to the whole world'.[6]

Offor felt that Bunyan had captured, in both his general allegory and in his personal conversion narrative, the essence of Christian experience. This, according to Offor, showed Bunyan's writings not only to be divinely inspired (and thus indisputably authoritative) but also irresistibly mobile, proliferating across the globe in multiple languages for peoples at all points on the road to Christian enlightenment:

> Thus, by an irresistible impulse from heaven upon the mind of a prisoner for Christ's sake, did a light shine forth from the dungeon on Bedford bridge which has largely contributed to enlighten the habitable globe [...]. Even the Caffrarian and Hottentot, the enlightened Greek and Hindoo, the remnant of the Hebrew race, the savage Malay, and the voluptuous Chinese—all have the wondrous narrative in their own languages.[7]

Offor's image of a heavenly beam emanating from homely Bedford, searching into and lighting up the dark heathen corners of the world, is a colonialist image of the civilizing power of English 'enlightenment' over the 'habitable globe': 'habitable' suggesting 'ours for the inhabiting'. The light shines from the metropole to the benighted peripheries, without suggesting that any reflection returns to the point of origin—except the light of international renown which authorizes the production of yet another new edition of *The Pilgrim's Progress* for Britain.

Furthermore, Offor's emphasis on the 'irresistible impulse from heaven' leaves out the primary agents of this global dissemination. These were the missionaries and translators of a Nonconformist or Evangelical bent, as well as their even less visible helpers recruited from the 'heathen' themselves. The motives of these missionary translators were complex, sometimes conflicted, and the difficulties they faced in producing, funding, and distributing Bunyan for 'all kindreds, and tongues' contribute to a more laboured story

---

[5] See Gordon Goodwin, 'George Offor', rev. Alan Bell, *ODNB*. George Offor, 'Preface' [dated 1853], in *The Works of John Bunyan*, ed. George Offor, 3 vols (Glasgow, Edinburgh, and London: Blackie & Son, 1855), 1: viii.

[6] George Offor (ed.), *The Pilgrim's Progress* [...] *A New Edition, with a Memoir and Notes* (London: Routledge, Warne, & Routledge, 1861), x, xii.

[7] Offor (ed.), *The Pilgrim's Progress*, xxv.

of textual transmission than Offor's metaphor of an inexorable force beaming like light around the world. Missionary translations and adaptations often reflected local and personal needs, moreover, refracting rather than just receiving the light from Bedford. The traces of the complicated labour and interests that effected the distribution of Bunyan all over the world can be read on the surviving title pages of the missionary presses, and in what can be recovered of the production and reception of texts like the 1850 translation of *The Pilgrim's Progress* into Telugu, printed at the Mission Press in Vizagapatam, India, or the 1900 Cree translation by John Sinclair, a part-native Anglican minister, printed for the 'Methodist Mission Rooms' in Toronto. Analysis of the material forms of these translations can provide evidence not only of attempts at assimilation, but also of creative re-appropriation or even outright resistance on the part of would-be readers and users. The American Tract Society's publication of *The Pilgrim's Progress* in Hawaiian in 1842, for example, failed to become the instant classic its translators had promised and ended as remaindered unbound sheets, sold to Chinese vegetable peddlers to wrap their produce.[8]

Just as Bunyan travelled the routes of empire, so too did the missionaries who translated, promoted, and sought solace in him. In neither case, however, is the relationship to empire straightforward. Hofmeyr notes that there 'is a tendency in talking about Bunyan in empire to conflate the colonial state, white settler interest and missions and treat these as identical'.[9] Missionaries, however, might precede and cooperate with imperial expansion; they also came into conflict with colonial interests. Adaptable Bunyan entered in a variety of guises into this complicated dynamic between Christian evangelization and the establishment of European (and later American) economic and political hegemony over parts of Asia and Africa, as well as over indigenous populations in the Americas and the Pacific. Because the dominance of the 'West' coincided with the global expansion of Christianity, it has often been assumed, as Norman Etherington points out in his introduction to *Missions and Empire*, that the latter was simply 'a reflex of imperialism'. Yet as the contributions to Etherington's collection and the growing historiography on missions and empire make clear, 'the precise connections between religion and Empire have yet to be fully delineated by historians'. The popular redaction of the causal chain—'first the missionary, then the trader, then the gunboat'—is not borne out by numerous local studies.[10] Like the image of the beam of light originating from Bedford, then, this perspective is static, imagining only a single channel of imperial purpose and power emanating from the purported 'centre' of the map.

Without a doubt, missionaries who looked to Bunyan as part of their heritage and to *The Pilgrim's Progress* as an essential in their toolkit for evangelization were the primary agents in the propagation of his authority and his texts. Their key targets were

---

[8] David W. Forbes, *Buniana* (San Francisco, CA: Paul Markham Kahn, 1984), 10.
[9] Hofmeyr, 'Bunyan: Colonial, Postcolonial', 168.
[10] Norman Etherington, 'Introduction', in Norman Etherington (ed.), *Missions and Empire* (Oxford: Oxford University Press, 2005), 1–2.

those peoples and places subject to colonization. Yet those same people and places transformed Bunyan, adding adapted renditions to their own toolkits, bringing him out as needed in the service of their own developing identities and resistance. As English Nonconformity's most influential global text, *The Pilgrim's Progress* has, over the last two centuries, proved a remarkably capacious and flexible container for a range of imperial as well as anti-imperializing strategies directed at, and sometimes coming from within, colonial populations, both indigenous and settler.

MISSIONARY BUNYAN AT HOME AND AWAY

Isabel Hofmeyr has written the authoritative account of the transnational circulation of Bunyan's books, particularly *The Pilgrim's Progress*. At the centre of her work is the question of why this particular text became so phenomenally 'portable'. Although a small selection of Bunyan's other writings were translated and distributed worldwide, particularly *The Holy War* (1682) and *Grace Abounding*, it was *The Pilgrim's Progress* that, by the nineteenth century and well into the twentieth, enjoyed a global reach and reputation across languages, locations, and cultures. Second only to Scripture, it was an 'early example of a translingual mass text'.[11] Part of the explanation of the portability of *The Pilgrim's Progress* during the time of global imperial expansion lies in its already established utility 'at home' as one of the fundamental guides for religious experience. After the Evangelical Revival of the eighteenth and early nineteenth centuries, Nonconformists in particular seized on *The Pilgrim's Progress* as an accessible and arresting model of the believer's journey from sin through conversion to redemption. In Hofmeyr's summary: 'its riveting plot, memorable tableaux, and powerful images […] provided readers with a language to talk about the emotional and personal experience of religion'.[12]

As Nonconformists in Britain and evangelical Christians in other countries began to send missions around the world, they turned to a work already prominent on their evangelizing bookshelf. Sending 'The Pilgrim' into the wider world, however, was itself confirmation of its significance at home, generating a paradox thoroughly elaborated by Hofmeyr: the further it was carried across the globe, the more thoroughly *The Pilgrim's Progress* became entrenched as a local text, the quintessence of vernacular English religion, particularly that of the more evangelical temper and language. Bunyan's most widely circulated work, therefore, did not merely carry the culture of evangelizing Christianity 'abroad'. The very fact of its global circulation, witnessed in the proliferation of missionary translations and adaptations, became a constituent element of that culture at 'home'. Mission exhibitions, for instance, routinely displayed the most recent crop of

---

[11] Hofmeyr, *Portable Bunyan*, 3, 12–13.
[12] Hofmeyr, 'How Bunyan became English', 89.

foreign translations; missionary magazines and annual reports, analogously, listed the many languages into which *The Pilgrim's Progress* had been translated.[13] These inventories served multiple purposes. A tangible proof of missionary success, they made the far-flung places of missionary endeavour more real to potential supporters at home. They also served to boost Nonconformist pride. Translations of *The Pilgrim's Progress* were conceived as a tribute to one of 'their own', an author loved by Nonconformists but still generally undervalued. As marginalized Nonconformists sought to gain more prestige and influence at home, the translation of Bunyan into the 'exotic' languages of the mission field intensified.[14] Nonconformist success in promoting Bunyan might be measured by the adoption of *The Pilgrim's Progress* as a 'universal' Christian text, circulated by the London-based Religious Tract Society, the American Tract Society, and even adapted by Roman Catholics.[15] On a more abstract level, the very proliferation of translations reinforced assumptions about the text's mobility and universality.

For all these reasons, *The Pilgrim's Progress* was typically the first work after Scripture to be translated by missionaries into the local language. Hofmeyr has counted translations into nearly two hundred languages, the majority non-European.[16] Translators did not even wait for the Word of God to be complete before they put the word of Bunyan into potential converts' hands. In their letters and reports, missionaries often reported working simultaneously on the production of these 'two gospels' in the local vernacular, as in a bulletin from a New Zealand mission to Maori of 1835, which sandwiched an announcement of the near completion of a translation of *The Pilgrim's Progress* between news of progress on the Gospels and Epistles. Because of difficulties of funding, or of just managing the production and distribution of books for small remote populations, missionaries might decide to focus their attention on *The Pilgrim's Progress* first, as in the production of an abridgement of *Part I* in Aneityum, a language spoken only on the southernmost island of the New Hebrides (now Vanuatu), even before the first half of the Old Testament.[17]

---

[13] On translations of *The Pilgrim's Progress* displayed at missionary exhibitions, see Hofmeyr, *Portable Bunyan*, 65–6. For printed inventories of translations, see John Brown, 'Appendix II: Languages and Dialects into which the "Pilgrim's Progress" has been Translated', in John Brown, *John Bunyan: His Life, Times, and Work*, 2nd edn (Boston, MA, and New York: Houghton, Mifflin & Company; Cambridge: The Riverside Press, 1886), 489–92; *The Pilgrim in Many Lands* (Philadelphia, PA: American Sunday-School Union, 1848), 7.

[14] Hofmeyr, 'How Bunyan became English', 87–8.

[15] For a discussion of two Roman Catholic adaptations into French, see Robert G. Collmer, 'Roman Catholic Versions of *The Pilgrim's Progress*', 1650–1850: Ideas, Aesthetics, and Inquiries in the Early Modern Era, 13 (2006), 225–44.

[16] Hofmeyr, 'How Bunyan became English', 93. See also Hofmeyr, *Portable Bunyan*, 1 and appendix 1 (which lists translations into eighty African languages).

[17] Report of George Clarke, 'Australasia Mission: New Zealand', *Church Missionary Record, Detailing the Proceedings of the Church Missionary Society for the Year 1836*, VII (London: Richard Watts, 1836), 164. 'New Hebrides', *The Sixty-Sixth Report of the British and Foreign Bible Society* (London: Spottiswoode, 1870), 245. The abridged translation into Aneityum was *Intas va Natga u Kristian. Par apan an pece Upene* [tr. John and Charlotte Geddie] (Aneiteum: Mission Press, 1868). Another edition was printed at 'Luntun' (London) in 1880.

At a time of expansion in British missionary endeavour and British colonial ambitions abroad—the two operating in tandem although not always cooperatively or with the same objectives—the uncultivated 'heathen' ripe for conversion were added to the classes of unsophisticated readers for whom Bunyan's allegory was supposed to hold particular appeal. John Brown, Congregationalist pastor of Bunyan Meeting in Bedford from 1864, noted in his biography of Bunyan that while *The Pilgrim's Progress* was 'written specially for no one class, it has found its way to the affections of every class, and secured the homage of cultured and uncultured alike'. Everyone knows, wrote Brown, 'what a charm it has for children' and 'the mighty hold it has always had upon the toiling poor'. It is also 'one of the first books translated by the missionary who seeks to give true thoughts of God and life to heathen men, because it is one of the few books that can easily make themselves at home among nations the most diverse'.[18]

Brown thought that a combination of demotic language, lending itself 'so readily to idiomatic thought and dialectic variety', and a less definable quality of affect, that 'so livingly touches the universal heart beating under all nationalities', gave to *The Pilgrim's Progress* a power like that of enchantment: the magical power to fly effortlessly across borders of cultural and historical difference. Brown harnessed the purportedly universal appeal of Bunyan to Christian universalism. For Brown, Bunyan belonged, like Christianity itself, to no one nation or class of persons, but rather to 'that region where men are neither of Paul, nor Apollos, nor Cephas, but of Christ'.[19] Equally, the assumed appeal of Bunyan's text to paraliterate readers made it a good textbook for the evangelical pedagogy of missionaries keen to bring the 'childlike' heathen, still connected as they were to a world of superstition and oral culture, into the ambit of Christian enlightenment. *The Pilgrim's Progress*, especially in simple adaptations, thus became a primer not only of the gospel message but also of the basics of Western subjectivity as constituted by literacy, numeracy, and the clock. The Aneityum abridgement was, for instance, bound together with a 'First Catechism' as well as the Westminster Shorter Catechism, a list of the ordinal numbers, and the times of sunrise and sunset on Aneityum.[20]

The almost magical power of Bunyan's book to transcend all cultural divides was expressed by the recurring personification of the travelling Pilgrim, able to take on the dress of any nation and to speak in any local idiom. A late example may be drawn from the Canadian Arctic where Maurice Flint, a missionary to Inuit, made quasi-liturgical use of parts of *The Pilgrim's Progress* at 'alternative evening services' at the Anglican Mission at Pond's Inlet in 1939. A decade later, writing impersonally for a recruitment pamphlet published by the Bible Churchmen's Missionary Society, Flint recreated the scene:

> When the missionary was preparing the first manuscript of the syllabic edition of *Pilgrim's Progress*, he read instalments to the natives each evening. As he enlarged

---

[18] Brown, *John Bunyan*, 299–300.
[19] Brown, *John Bunyan*, 299.
[20] Brown, *John Bunyan*, 492. 'Apparent Time of the Sun's Rising and Setting on Aneityum', *Intas va Natga*, 139–40.

upon the Slough of Despond, one old Eskimo man suddenly saw himself weighed down by his own sins and slowly sinking in the 'soft snow of evil' all around.

Flint went on to describe the old man's exemplary death, implicitly the result of the transformative encounter with Bunyan's text. He then reflected more generally on the condition of these 'poor children of the dark and icy wilderness', some of whom he observed had responded to the 'joyful news of salvation' with 'clean igloos and bright faces'.[21]

These accounts assumed that *The Pilgrim's Progress* could be carried across cultures with seamless ease. (The 'soft snow of evil' sounds rather too good to be true.) They were, moreover, founded on the heathen convert's emotional, seemingly childlike response to its storied quality. Offor, noting that *The Pilgrim's Progress* 'has proved an invaluable aid to the Sunday School Teacher, and to the Missionary', told the story of a 'Pundit […] engaged to translate it into Singhalese' who, upon reading of Christian's burden dropping from his shoulders, 'laughed, wept, clapped his hands, danced, and shouted, "delightful, delightful!"'[22] In the accounts of both Offor and Flint, it is a specific episode in *The Pilgrim's Progress*—the Slough of Despond or the burden dropping from Christian's back—that activates the enchantment. The episodic journey narrative spoke, then, both to uneducated Europeans and to non-Europeans with analogous story forms in their own cultures, while its modular quality made Bunyan's text highly adaptable for missionaries seeking to address particular audiences or occasions. Yet Flint and Offor also invoke something less tangible. Both describe *The Pilgrim's Progress* establishing its hold over readers and making connections across cultures through affect; or, in the language Nonconformists might have used, through 'heartwork'. Such stories from the mission field affirmed the superiority of *The Pilgrim's Progress* in catalysing the thorough conversion of heart by which evangelically minded Protestants distinguished themselves. Like the missionary exhibitions and catalogues of translations, these narratives of Bunyan abroad gave added strength to a Nonconformist identity at home.

Isabel Hofmeyr has argued that Bunyan's global circulation helped Nonconformists to think of themselves and their ambitions as international.[23] As stories of the heathen converts returned home and became a Sunday School staple, the rising generation were themselves initiated into a globally inflected subjectivity which could work both for and against imperialism. The story of the delighted Malay, for example, was repeated in *The Pilgrim in Many Lands*, a brief pamphlet published by the American Sunday-School Union in 1848 to encourage children to read Bunyan's allegory because it was prized all around the world. They were told of Chinese schoolgirls who willingly left their play to delight in it, and of schoolchildren in Ceylon who carried home copies bound in marble papers with gilt edges 'as the best prize they could obtain in the missionary school'.

---

[21] Maurice S. Flint, *The Arctic: Land of Snowmen*, Field Survey No. 2 (London: Bible Churchmen's Missionary Society, 1948), 36.

[22] George Offor, 'Introduction', in *The Pilgrim's Progress* (London: J. Haddon for the Hanserd Knollys Society, 1847), cxlvi.

[23] Hofmeyr, *Portable Bunyan*, 31.

This pamphlet rationalized the attraction Bunyan's book held for 'the east' by citing an oriental fondness 'for hearing and telling stories'. Yet the 'native converts also need guides, who can teach and encourage them on their way, and they find in the Pilgrim just such a friend as they want'.[24]

The play of personification on the title of Bunyan's book was another assertion of its affective hold over readers and its seemingly autonomous agency as text. In addition to *The Pilgrim in Many Lands*, the American Sunday-School Union printed colourful editions of *The Pilgrim's Progress* for children in the United States and presented these offerings alongside pamphlets redacting Bunyan for the potential converts of foreign missions. The American Tract Society pursued a similar marketing strategy. As in England, the association of foreign converts and home-grown children perpetuated not only a culture-bound narrative about children, and especially working-class children, as little heathens in need of conversion but also a parallel narrative about infantilized foreigners 'naturally' suited to the paternal care of a superior imperializing power.[25] The worldwide distribution of this guide for childlike heathen converts confirmed them in their nonage rather than allowing them to progress through it, as when Maurice Flint reflected further on the 'poor children of the dark and icy wilderness'. He, like other Anglican missionaries contemplating the belated contact of Inuit with secular modernity, was concerned to preserve among them 'the innocence and purity of childhood'.[26] By this chain of associations, the text of a seventeenth-century religious Dissenter was understood to be one of the best means to preserve the childlike innocence of Inuit in the mid-twentieth century.

The 'home heathen', the benighted working classes who received missionary attention at home, were similarly to be saved from degradation by Bunyan's magical, transformative texts. The traffic between home and away ran in both directions, for the perceived effectiveness of Bunyan's allegory as a global evangelizer was conditioned by its use at home, as both exemplar and textbook, in the hierarchical settings of the nursery and the slum missions in the East End of London.[27] The fluidity of *The Pilgrim's Progress*, its adaptability to multiple audiences global and local, was partly due to its liminality, as a text for the nearly literate, a printed book grounded in orality. This was the common ground between children, the illiterate working classes, and the heathen to be converted and brought into the ambit of advanced Christian nations like England and the United States. Although the mobility of *The Pilgrim's Progress* across these paraliterate worlds did not necessarily serve colonial interests, and could even be ranged against them, it did reinforce a hegemonically organized imperial world, one in which the heathen at home were kept in place by means of the heathen abroad, and vice versa.

---

[24] *Pilgrim in Many Lands*, 8–11.
[25] Ruth K. MacDonald, *Christian's Children: The Influence of John Bunyan's The Pilgrim's Progress on American Children's Literature* (Bern: Peter Lang, 1989), 149, 151–52.
[26] Flint, *The Arctic*, 36.
[27] Hofmeyr, 'How Bunyan became English', 92.

Bunyan in Imperial Africa and India: Assimilation, Appropriations, and Resistances

Although *The Pilgrim's Progress* travelled with English Protestant missionaries to colonial outposts, the transnational movement of Bunyan's text cannot simply be read as the spread of an English hegemony—whether of religion, culture, or politics—writ small. Bunyan's allegory certainly could be used as a conveyance for cultural value and authority, to be used to signify and propagate 'Englishness' through a colonial hierarchy. In the British colonies of Africa, for instance, both translated and English versions of *The Pilgrim's Progress* were mandated for school syllabuses. In the nineteenth century, Bunyan's prose also became one of the set texts for the Indian civil service examinations; he received state canonization as one of 'the greatest English writers' whose thought and style were to be mastered by the men, both Anglo and Indian, who were to run the machinery of the British Raj.[28] In these cases, Bunyan's text was drafted for service to empire, occupying a shifting ground between an English-inflected evangelical Christianity and the newly born discipline of English Literature.

Bunyan could also be appropriated, however, for other, local purposes. Indeed, as it circulated in imperial contexts, *The Pilgrim's Progress* was a notable shape-shifter: anything but a static container of 'English' colonialist ideology. While white settler populations within the British Empire tended to read the book as imperial allegory (as will be discussed later in this chapter, in examples from 'The Empire Club of Canada'), a very different 'Bunyan' emerged from the translation and adaptation efforts of the missionaries who were the prime disseminators of *The Pilgrim's Progress*. As Hofmeyr observes, mission translations 'bore the imprint of converts' ideas and opinions and were seldom, if ever, straightforwardly imperial'.[29] Like the Scriptures in Africa, Bunyan could be stolen. Instead of serving imperialism, he could be wrested away from those who had brought him as part of the project 'of conversion and civilisation, of colonisation and conquest'. His writings could be contested, appropriated, or turned to indigenous purposes.[30]

In some cases, Bunyan was appropriated overtly for anti-imperial and anti-colonial purposes. In 1930s colonial Nyasaland (now Malawi), George Simeon Mwase drew on *The Pilgrim's Progress* to frame his own account of the anti-colonialist uprising of John

---

[28] Hofmeyr, 'How Bunyan became English', 95. *The India List and India Office List for 1905* (London: Harrison & Sons, 1905), 199. For the place of Bunyan and the new discipline of 'English' in the colonial service, see Hofmeyr, *Portable Bunyan*, 218, and Gauri Viswanathan, *Masks of Conquest: Literary Study and British Rule in India* (New York: Columbia University Press, 1989), 54, 198.

[29] Hofmeyr, 'Bunyan: Colonial, Postcolonial', 168.

[30] Gerald O. West, *The Stolen Bible: From Tool of Imperialism to African Icon* (Leiden: Brill, 2016), 2.

Chilembwe earlier in the century. Mwase wrote his account, titled 'Strike a Blow and Die', from jail (like Bunyan) and clearly invoked Bunyan's 'Apology for his Book', which he may have known by heart from his mission education. Yet, as Hofmeyr points out in her study of Bunyan in Nyasaland, the story here is not as simple as that of mission or 'English' influence over African writing. Mwase equally drew on adaptations from indigenous African and African-American Christian milieux, in which Chilembwe was also immersed. For both men, seventeenth-century Protestant radicalism hybridized with African traditions, identities, and crises. Mwase (who idealized William Prynne as a champion of free speech) wrote of the Baptist pastor Chilembwe and his followers decapitating a neighbouring white settler: a 'tyrannicide' which recalled the fate of both Charles I as well as the many enemies of Chilembwe's ancestor, Kalonga Mphiri, whose name (meaning 'packer') alluded to his practice of packing enemies' heads into baskets.[31] This is an especially dramatic appropriation of Bunyan, but the range of African Bunyans is wide and richly populated, from Africanized illustrations (including photographs where members of the local African mission elite posed for particular scenes) to the deployment of material copies of *The Pilgrim's Progress* as fetish. The latter appropriation mapped African beliefs about the powers of magical objects onto both a Protestant tradition of fetishizing the evangelizing 'Word'—a tradition to which Bunyan powerfully contributed—as well as onto the documents required and circulated by colonial authorities, for which Christian and Hopeful's 'certificates' for heaven provided a useful analogue.[32]

The decision of missionaries to teach and translate in the vernaculars of the peoples they were evangelizing facilitated appropriation and resistance. The Anglican missionary Henry Venn was instrumental in establishing the policy pursued by the Church Missionary Society, for instance, in organizing the Vernacular Education Society for India in 1858: a policy opposed to the thinking of a secular-minded imperialist like Thomas Babington Macaulay. In his infamous 'Minute' on education, Macaulay argued against funding the teaching of native languages in India as he considered Indian languages 'poor' in literary and scientific terminology and so without the linguistic resources for any 'valuable' translations.[33] While Macaulay made an unapologetic case for the superiority of English as the repository of knowledge of all kinds, he notably did not mention religious knowledge. The many contemporary missionaries and native catechists, busily translating the knowledge they considered most valuable of all into local

---

[31] Isabel Hofmeyr, '*The Pilgrim's Progress* as World Literature: John Bunyan and George Simeon Mwase in Nyasaland', *1650–1850: Ideas, Aesthetics, and Inquiries in the Early Modern Era*, 13 (2006), 175–99.

[32] See Hofmeyr, *Portable Bunyan*, for extensive discussion of Bunyan in Africa. For photographs from the Kongo Baptist mission in northern Angola, see Isabel Hofmeyr, 'Bunyan in Africa: Text and Transition', *Interventions: International Journal of Postcolonial Studies*, 3 (2001), 322–35 (331–34). For fetishization, see Hofmeyr, *Portable Bunyan*, 137–50.

[33] Thomas Babington Macaulay, 'Minute [. . .] Dated the 2nd February 1835', in *Selections from Educational Records, Part I (1781–1839)*, ed. H. Sharp (Calcutta: Superintendent, Government Printing, 1920; repr. Delhi: National Archives of India, 1965), 107–17.

vernaculars, were therefore positioning themselves directly against Macaulay and linguistic colonization. Indeed, in India, the interests and aims of missionaries often came into conflict with colonial governors. Moreover, mission translations of *The Pilgrim's Progress* were generally collaborative undertakings between second-language missionaries and their first-language native assistants. The latter had plenty of opportunity to adapt Bunyan selectively for local purposes. The pragmatic missionary strategy of disseminating Bunyan in 'bits-and-pieces'—from brief adaptations to magic lantern slides—also allowed local audiences considerable liberty in deciding which 'bits' of Bunyan they would adopt and which they might choose to disregard.[34]

The case of *The Pilgrim's Progress* in Tamil shows the range of possible accommodations between Bunyan's text and indigenous language and culture. English Protestant missionaries at Vepery issued a translation from the SPCK Press in 1793. This was the very first translation into a non-European language and was bilingual, presenting English on the left and Tamil on the right side of the page. A second edition appeared from the same press in 1826.[35] Further Tamil editions were published in 1848, 1861, 1872, and 1882. These translations were apparently well received, one missionary reporting that it was read aloud to large groups of people.[36] In fact, Tamil versions of *The Pilgrim's Progress* have remained continuously in print up to the present, seeming to enjoy an exceptional popularity. Tamil-speakers might have been especially prepared to accommodate Bunyan's allegory through their familiarity with analogous narrative forms in their own literary and religious traditions, like the 'purana'. Tamil religious communities each had their own signature epic or 'purana'. One early eighteenth-century Jesuit missionary tried to imitate this native genre with his own life of St Joseph in Tamil, but the adaptation of the Bunyan 'purana' seems to have been more enduring.[37] An 1861 edition printed at Jaffna notes that it is 'a free translation—in some places slightly condensed; in others a little is added; so as to make the work really Tamul in its character'.[38]

As in other mission fields, native Tamil readers and users of the translated *Pilgrim's Progress* adapted and appropriated it to their own ends, sometimes reinforcing and sometimes diverging from missionary or colonial agendas. P. D. Dewsagaim, for

---

[34] Hofmeyr, 'Bunyan in Africa', 325–26.

[35] *Oru Parateci, Jon Paniyan Carittiram* [Pilgrim's Progress], 2nd edn (Vepery: SPCK, 1826). See Stuart Blackburn, *Print, Folklore, and Nationalism in Colonial South India* (Delhi: Permanent Black, 2006), 58, 65, 194.

[36] Brown, *John Bunyan*, 491. Brown lists editions of 1793, 1848 (printed by the American Mission Press in Madras), and 1882 ('A new translation by the Rev. S. Paul, C. M. S.'). The Day Missions Library at Yale holds a copy of *The Pilgrim's Progress*, 2nd edn (Jaffna: Ripley & Strong, 1861). *The Pilgrim's Progress* [. . .] *with a Life of the Author*, ed. P. D. Dewsagaim (Nagercoil: London Mission Press, 1872). Blackburn, *Print, Folklore, and Nationalism*, 65.

[37] Indira Viswanathan Peterson, 'Between Print and Performance: The Tamil Christian Poems of Vedanayaka Sastri and the Literary Cultures of Nineteenth-Century South India', in Stuart Blackburn and Vasudha Dalmia (eds.), *India's Literary History: Essays on the Nineteenth Century* (Delhi: Permanent Black, 2004), 25–59 (45).

[38] *The Pilgrim's Progress by John Bunyan* [Tamil, 1861], verso of title page.

instance, though a native minister of the Nagercoil Church, took the colonialist position in his 1872 edition of *The Pilgrim's Progress* in Tamil, using Bunyan to separate and 'raise' himself from his cultural roots. Although he noted the 'great taste which the people of this country have for interesting narratives and allegories', he also hoped that the footnotes he had added would help his 'less intelligent' countrymen and that his version would 'produce true religion and heavenly-mindedness among the native Christians in this heathen land'. As one of the legion of native ministers recruited by the London Missionary Society as part of a commitment to offer the Christian Gospel in the vernacular, Dewsagaim nonetheless took on the voice of the colonizer as he also donned the trappings of the scholarly editor. Both he and his edition functioned as instruments of empire, a function ironically reflected in the notice of his death, written by P. C. Joseph, his nephew and collaborator on *The Pilgrim's Progress*, where he was described as 'a trophy of the London Missionary Society in this land'.[39]

Historically, Dewsagaim's 1872 preface to *The Pilgrim's Progress* adumbrates an increasingly racialized ideology of empire permeating the work of missions in India—a development that corresponded with the increasing emphasis on Bunyan not as an author of the world but as an author of England, as Hofmeyr puts it. The ability to read Bunyan's 'similitudes' was the test of a higher intelligence and, implicitly, a higher humanity. Such elevation came with the gift of a civilizing Christianity that seemed to emanate not from Bethlehem, Nazareth, Jerusalem, or any of the places associated with Christ, but rather from England and from the text of an Englishman, John Bunyan.

Henry Albert Krishnapillai, roughly contemporary with Dewsagaim, was also moved by Bunyan's 'wonderful book' to adapt it for Tamil readers. It had been instrumental in his own conversion from Hinduism to Protestant Christianity. He, however, published an original Tamil poem, 'Rakshanya Yatrikam' ('The journey of salvation') in 1894, which was modelled both on *The Pilgrim's Progress* and on the Ramayana, an ancient epic from his own tradition. The Bunyan-inspired 'Rakshanya Yatrikam' has itself become part of the canon of literature in Tamil.[40] Against Macaulay's colonialist denigration of Indian languages and knowledge, this hybridized assimilation of *The Pilgrim's Progress* realized the rich possibilities of the Tamil language and literary inheritance but it was hardly the anti-colonial adaptation of Bunyan that George Simeon Mwase's 'Strike a Blow and Die' was to be forty years later. By the end of the nineteenth century in India, as in Africa, *The Pilgrim's Progress* was circulating as a vigorous, diverse, and contradictory world text, fragmented and reassembled for new uses and new readers. Although it travelled the routes of empire, both the authority and adaptability of Bunyan's text made it useful for, against, and alongside empire.

---

[39] Letter of 'P. C. Joseph, Deacon', *Chronicle of the London Missionary Society* (April 1885), 105.
[40] Robert Eric Frykenberg, 'Christians and Religious Traditions in the Indian Empire', in Sheridan Gilley and Brian Stanley (eds.), *The Cambridge History of Christianity: World Christianities c.1815–c.1914* (Cambridge: Cambridge University Press, 2006), 473–92 (483).

The Pilgrim's Progress 'Englished' and the Claims of Universality

Paradoxically, arguments for Bunyan's universality intensified and took on a new life just as global translations of *The Pilgrim's Progress* became particular, local, diversified, and abundant at a late stage of empire. Isabel Hofmeyr notes that most translations of Bunyan's allegory into languages other than English actually took place in the mid-twentieth century. It was at this point that Bunyan became simultaneously the quintessential English and the quintessential universal author, in a new secular career that reclassified his evangelizing text as one of the central titles of the canon of English literature. The stage for these developments, though, was set in an earlier period: within the context of Christian universalism. Many evangelical Protestants treated *The Pilgrim's Progress* as a substitute Bible. Like Scripture, it transcended human nations, belonging to the 'universal heart' in its 'comprehensive Christ-like spirit'.[41] This universalism had pragmatic value for missionary societies and publishers, like the Religious Tract Society, who solicited donations and justified their existence by citing the 'evidence' of *The Pilgrim's Progress*'s universal appeal and efficacy as an instrument to touch the hearts of potential converts.

The message of universality, however, could work both for and against the hegemonic structures which supported and were in turn perpetuated by empire. On the one hand, translating *The Pilgrim's Progress* into all languages, like providing the Christian Bible in all vernaculars, gave a textual basis to the argument for the universal brotherhood of all men: all men could read, understand, and form themselves according to the seminal Christian texts. Differences of culture or skin colour were simply a matter of dress, of outsides, so the 'Pilgrim' could dress in, for instance, sealskin parka and sun goggles among Inuit. One message subscribers back 'home' could take from this was that differences of dress or skin colour did not matter as much as shared Christianity; under the different 'outsides' was the familiar. Pushed to its liberalizing limit, such thinking can work against the differentials of entitlement upon which colonization depends.

On the other hand, the erasure of differences under a myth of universal intelligibility could work to support an invisible hegemony of all things 'English'. Thus Edmund Venables, writing in the widely distributed 'Great Writers' series in 1888, asserted that the 'charm' of Bunyan's works, especially *The Pilgrim's Progress*, 'lies in the pure Saxon English in which they are written'.[42] While 'pure Saxon' could be regarded

---

[41] Brown, *John Bunyan*, 299.
[42] Edmund Venables, *Life of John Bunyan* (London: Walter Scott; New York: Thomas Whittaker; Toronto: W. J. Gage, 1888), 168–69. See also Brown, *John Bunyan*, 299, 450.

as a simple stylistic judgement, for some, Bunyan came to represent a pure Englishness that was distinct from and innately superior to anything foreign as evinced by its universal, magical 'charm'—an account that conveniently overrode the pragmatic, even subversive operations that non-English readers themselves performed on Bunyan. Macaulay celebrated Bunyan's use of 'the old unpolluted English language', offering him as an example of 'how little it has been improved by all that it has borrowed'. The 1865 edition of *The Pilgrim's Progress* which reprinted Macaulay's essay placed it firmly at the centre of the canon of English Literature, 'in the first rank of genius, along with Shakespeare and Milton'. Further, in a move that would come to dominate both popular and scholarly assessments of *The Pilgrim's Progress*, the book's quintessential Englishness was paradoxically linked to its universal hold over all ages, classes, and races of humanity: 'It charms our childhood and cheers our mature age; it is the favourite alike of the peasant and the philosopher; and it kindles enthusiasm as much on the banks of the Orinoco or the Ganges as by the side of its native Ouse.'[43] The diverse citizens of a British Empire were brought together by an emerging canon of English literature.

In the context of examining the commodification of 'Bunyan' more generally as a flexible source of cultural authority, Tamsin Spargo was the first scholar to suggest that the global dissemination of Bunyan by missionary and imperial interests prepared for his somewhat belated recognition as an author 'essentially English'.[44] It was only after he had become 'essentially English', however, that he also became an 'imperialist'. It was as late as 1928 that Augustine Birrell, once secretary for Ireland and now man of letters, judged Bunyan 'a plain Englishman to the core, and as good an Imperialist as it is possible for any Christian man to be'. An empirical approach has shown, however, that before the twentieth century it was primarily missionaries and not 'British imperialists who packed the allegory in their trunks and transported it throughout much of the world'.[45] As the allegory travelled, it was, moreover, changed, and not always in the interests of the British imperialists. Bunyan, an inspiration for the African Baptist rebel Chilembwe, did as much to dismantle empire as to build it. As Hofmeyr has argued in her essay 'How Bunyan became English', Bunyan's association with the non-white readers of the mission field, like John Chilembwe, had to be purged in order for his 'essential Englishness' to become the dominant source of value of the text. Those non-white resistant readers who made their own anti-colonial use of Bunyan also need to be written out of the story in order for Bunyan to become a good servant of empire.

Bunyan's simultaneous recruitment to the canon of English literature and the cause of imperialism can be seen in the settler colonies of the British Empire,

---

[43] Thomas Babington Macaulay, 'Introduction', in *The Pilgrim's Progress* (London and Edinburgh: A. Fullarton & Co., 1865), ix, xxxii.

[44] Spargo, *The Writing of John Bunyan*, 102–04.

[45] Augustine Birrell, 'Links of Empire: Books (IX) *The Pilgrim's Progress*', *Empire Review*, 47 (February 1928), 79–87; Greaves, *Glimpses*, 633.

especially as they headed towards decline. The connection between canonicity and empire was also a feature of the 1928 tercentenary celebrations of Bunyan's birth at Bedford, a town once favoured, it seems, by retired colonial officers, the common thread being an 'English heritage' obscurely under threat.[46] Meanwhile, Colonel Henry C. Osborne, addressing the Empire Club of Canada in 1929 on the subject of First World War memorials, invoked Bunyan to connect the many casualties from across the empire to continuing imperial endeavour: 'There are some words which John Bunyan in his *Pilgrim's Progress* puts into the mouth of a character as he went down to the river of death. "My sword", he said, "I give to him who shall succeed me in my pilgrimage."' Major W. H. Edwards, addressing the same club in 1910, had likened the political enemies of an expanded military service in defence of the empire to Bunyan's 'Man with the Muck Rake': here Bunyan's allegory was invoked against 'a slumberous Imperialism'.[47] Finally, Alice Law, writing in the *Empire Review* in 1927, thought Bunyan not only the most 'suitable' companion for the travelling 'pilgrims' of the British Empire, but wrote of *The Pilgrim's Progress* as a kind of apotropaic fetish against imperial decay: 'Nor need anything be feared for that Empire, so long as she cherishes and practices the teaching of the immortal spiritual allegory.'[48]

The moment of Bunyan's tercentenary and Alice Law's pious pronouncement coincided, paradoxically, with the decline of *The Pilgrim's Progress* as a universal book—one that could be assumed to appeal magically to readers across differences of religion, race, and class. In her analysis of Bunyan's authority, Tamsin Spargo has observed that the cultural value assigned to the name of 'Bunyan' and associated with *The Pilgrim's Progress* in particular has had little to do with how extensively and even whether he is read, especially in the last century and especially in his old home territory of the Anglo-Protestant West. Assertions of his 'universal' appeal continue nonetheless, and he is 'still in print' in many languages, but the rhetorical purposes of such assertions and the global routes taken by versions of his famous allegory have changed. In one sense, the continuing global reach of Bunyan is a residue of the very mobility and adaptability of Bunyan's writing—by missionaries and converts, by imperialists and anti-colonialists. It is the residue, in other words, of empire. In a contemporary moment, however, in which slow, fraught, and determined efforts to decolonize meet jarringly with the persistence of empire, *The Pilgrim's Progress*'s wayward children have made their way into every corner of the globe and inhabit divergent worlds of reception and use. The vitality of Bunyan's dispersed textual

---

[46] Hofmeyr, *Portable Bunyan*, 222–23.

[47] Col. Henry C. Osborne, C.M.G., 'The Great Remembrance', in *The Empire Club of Canada Speeches 1929* (Toronto: The Empire Club of Canada, 1930), 62–77. Major W. H. Edwards, 'England's Greatest Needs', in J. Castell Hopkins (ed.), *The Empire Club of Canada Speeches 1910–1911* (Toronto: The Empire Club of Canada, 1912), 130–38.

[48] Alice Law, 'Some Aspects of *The Pilgrim's Progress*', *The Empire Review*, 46:318 (1927), 48–55; quoted in Hofmeyr, *Portable Bunyan*, 223.

legacy is not now to be referred to any magical universality, but presents rather an opportunity for the critical examination of the local and the particular, as both of and against the totalizing ideologies of nation and empire.[49]

Suggested Reading

Birrell, Augustine, 'Links of Empire—Books (IX): *The Pilgrim's Progress*', *Empire Review*, 47 (February 1928), 79–87.

Brown, Sylvia and Arlette Zinck, '*The Pilgrim's Progress* among Aboriginal Canadians: Missionary Translations of Bunyan into Cree and Inuktitut', *1650–1850: Ideas, Aesthetics, and Inquiries in the Early Modern Era*, 13 (2006), 201–23.

Hofmeyr, Isabel, 'Bunyan in Africa: Text and Transition', *Interventions: International Journal of Postcolonial Studies*, 3 (2001), 322–35.

Hofmeyr, Isabel, 'How Bunyan became English: Missionaries, Translation, and the Discipline of English Literature', *Journal of British Studies*, 41 (2002), 84–119.

Hofmeyr, Isabel, *The Portable Bunyan: A Transnational History of The Pilgrim's Progress* (Princeton, NJ: Princeton University Press, 2004).

Hofmeyr, Isabel, '*The Pilgrim's Progress* as World Literature: John Bunyan and George Simeon Mwase in Nyasaland', *1650–1850: Ideas, Aesthetics, and Inquiries in the Early Modern Era*, 13 (2006), 175–99.

Hofmeyr, Isabel, 'Bunyan: Colonial, Postcolonial', in Anne Dunan-Page (ed.), *The Cambridge Companion to Bunyan* (Cambridge: Cambridge University Press, 2010), 162–76.

Keeble, N. H., '"Of Him Thousands Daily Sing and Talk": Bunyan and his Reputation', in N. H. Keeble (ed.), *John Bunyan: Conventicle and Parnassus* (Oxford: Clarendon Press, 1988), 241–63.

Law, Alice, 'Some Aspects of *The Pilgrim's Progress*', *The Empire Review*, 46:318 (1927), 48–55.

Mignon, Laurent, 'A Pilgrim's Progress: Armenian and Kurdish literatures in Turkish and the Rewriting of Literary History', *Patterns of Prejudice*, 48 (2014), 182–200.

Spargo, Tamsin, *The Writing of John Bunyan* (Aldershot: Ashgate, 1997).

---

[49] Examples of such local studies include Sylvia Brown and Arlette Zinck, '*The Pilgrim's Progress* among Aboriginal Canadians: Missionary Translations of Bunyan into Cree and Inuktitut', *1650–1850: Ideas, Aesthetics, and Inquiries in the Early Modern Era*, 13 (2006), 201–23. More recently, Laurent Mignon has adduced the Armeno-Turkish translation of *The Pilgrim's Progress* as an example of the erasure of the literary culture of non-Muslim ethno-religious communities from national histories of 'Turkish Literature'. See his 'A Pilgrim's Progress: Armenian and Kurdish Literatures in Turkish and the Rewriting of Literary History', *Patterns of Prejudice*, 48 (2014), 182–200.

Index

A. L. O. E. (Miss C. Tucker) 657
Aaron, Melissa 302
Achinstein, Sharon 134, 191, 298, 327
Ackroyd, Peter 4
Act of Uniformity (1662) 38, 188, 266
adaptation and reception of JB's works
   academic studies 4–10
   Africa 491, 668, 674–5, 679
   America *see* United States
   British Empire *see* British Empire
   Bunyan Studies (journal) 10, 128, 464–5
   Canada 671–2, 680
   children, for *see* children's literature
   cinema 1–3, 9, 11, 13
   'common cultural resource' 11
   contradictory views 7
   controversy 5
   'cultural memory' 11, 15
   enduring relevance 13–15
   'Englishness' 4, 610–16
   Evangelical Revival *see* Pilgrim's Progress, The
   Evangelicalism 6, 8, 17, 280, 456
   everyday language 11
   fantasy literature 516
   First World War 241
   folk tradition 5
   illustration *see* illustration
   India 665, 668, 675–7
   International John Bunyan Society 10
   John Bunyan Museum 57, 103, 617–18
   memorials 12
   music 13
   New Zealand 670
   novels 13, 245, 255, 256, 322, 604
   painting *see* painting
   political radicalism 5
   popular culture 5
   popularity 4
   presence in cultural landscape 2, 10, 15
   rights of ordinary men and women 2
   'road' literature 245, 590, 605
   Romanticism *see Pilgrim's Progress, The*
   sculpture *see* sculpture
   translation 665, 670, 672, 676, 678
   'universal' writer 3
   visionary writer 4
Adolph, Robert 399
'adventure' 392–5
Africa *see* adaptation and reception
Alciati, Andrea 370
Alcott, Abby 599
Alcott, Bronson 599
Alcott, Louisa May 12, 322–3, 590, 599–602, 650, 660
alehouse culture 259–63
allegory
   awareness of language as allegorical 371–4
   definition 361
   dreaming 365–8
   emblems 370–1
   figura 368–70
   irony and 374–8
   personification 362–5
Alleine, Joseph 44
Alsop, Benjamin 293
Alsop, Vincent 41, 42
Ambrose, Isaac 112
America *see* United States
Ames, William 406
Anabaptists 29, 39, 51, 54, 63, 83, 84, 154, 173, 183, 227, 335, 495
Andrewes, Lancelot 399
'Andronicus' 544, 550

INDEX

Anglicanism
   Anglo-Catholicism 458, 656
   Book of Common Prayer *see* Book of
      Common Prayer
   Conventicle Act (1664) 204
   Dissent and 36, 40, 42, 44, 46, 540, 552
   evangelical *see* Evangelicalism
   JB's opposition to 102, 223, 224, 233, 239,
      293, 299, 391, 493, 547
   Latitudinarian 114
   Methodism and 540
   missionaries 673
   Nonconformism in opposition to 300, 329,
      339, 493
   'popish' persecution, and 42
   Restoration Settlement *see* Charles II
   Royalism and 38
   Sabbatarianism 267
   stylistic identity 403
   Tory 48
   see also Church of England; Evangelicalism
Annesley, Samuel 42, 43
Apollyon 11, 243–57
archaism in *Pilgrim's Progress* 423–6
Arminianism *see* Methodism
art *see* painting
Artaxerxes, King of Persia 287
atheism, Calvinism and 111
Auerbach, Erich 368, 384
Austen, Jane 534
Austen, Lady 546
Australia, lantern slide series of *Pilgrim's
   Progress Part II* 636
Authorised (King James) Bible 90; *see
   also* Bible
autobiography
   JB *see Grace Abounding to the Chief of
      Sinners*
   spiritual 145

Bacon, Francis 399, 400
Bacon, Nathaniel 111
Bakhtin, Mikhail 450, 536
Bale, Christian 13
ballads, JB's reading of 102–3
Bamford, Samuel 581
baptism *see* Bunyan, John, Christian faith

Baptists
   Evangelical Revival 537
   growth of 43
   JB and 63, 173
   Metropolitan Tabernacle 573
   opposition to Quakers 176
   Presbyterian opposition to 173
   Restoration suppression of 38, 40
   Sabbath-keeping 267
Barber, Charles 414
Barber, John Warner 658
Barebones Parliament (1653) 178
Barnes, Julian 618, 622
Barton, Bernard 556
Barton, William 329
Bates, William 42
Baum, L. Frank 245, 590, 604
Bawden, Edward 643, 645
Baxter, Richard 37, 38, 41, 42, 44, 45, 46, 47, 49,
   77, 134, 140, 145, 172, 326, 327, 328, 350, 552
Bayly, Lewis 71, 105, 211, 267, 322
Bear, Bethany Joy 310
Beaumont, Agnes 123, 127, 209
Beckett, Samuel 13
Bedford, Bedfordshire
   Bunyan family home 22
   Bunyan Meeting Church 638, 639, 640, 644
   churches and congregations 12, 29, 31,
      33, 37, 62
   Dissent 33
   Higgins Gallery 643
   JB remembered 12, 14, 612, 615
   John Bunyan Museum 57, 103, 617–18
   Quakers 176
   tourism 616
Bedford, Francis Russell, 9th Duke of 638
Bedford Congregation
   discipline 65, 95, 262
   domestic violence 271
   further study 68
   gathered church 53
   membership 58
   minutes ('Church Book') 57–8
   music and hymns 103
   officers 63
   White, Hale, and 581
   see also Bunyan Meeting Church

Behn, Aphra 530
Benjamin, Walter 367, 375
Benton, Joseph A. 595
Bernard, Richard 279, 349, 350
Besse, Joseph 36
Betjeman, John 610
Beukels, Jan ('John of Leyden') 173
Beza, Theodore 195
Bible
   Authorised (King James) Bible 90
   books *see* Bible, books
   Geneva Bible 90, 437
   Holy War, and 277
   JB's reading of 70, 86–90, 101
   literacy 319
   marriage imagery 91–6
   pilgrimage imagery 96–9
   Pilgrim's Progress, and 86, 247
   typology 89, 352–4
   unpardonable sin 111
   Wyclif's translation 428
Bible, books
   Genesis, JB's *Exposition see* Bunyan, John, works, prose
   Genesis 3 504; 6 and 7 92; 7:11 354; 14:10–16 278; 19:8 427; 19:17 99
   Numbers 12:6–10 118; 25:1–5 92
   Deuteronomy 354; 7:1, 2 and 6 92; 12 92; 32:2 569; 32:16 and 19 92
   Joshua 22:17 92
   Judges 14:5–8 187, 205
   Ruth 1:14–17 316
   Nehemiah 1:26 92
   Job 35:14 and 15 372; 41 247
   Psalm 19 569; 44:12 218; 51:17 343; 106:11 and 12 205; 106:30 and 40 92; 109:17 266; 120:5 and 6 271; 126 319, 561; 137:1 402; 137:9 285
   Proverbs 437; 12:4 91; 29:27 271; 30:8 371; 30:15 214; 31:10 91
   Ecclesiastes 190, 198, 349; 7:14 478
   Song of Songs 4:1 349, 506; 4:8 205
   Isaiah 7:14 377; 13:16 285; 19:18 403; 64:6 30, 247
   Daniel 6:7 366; 7 355
   Hosea 12:10 277, 372
   Joel 1: 5 339
   Micah, 7:8 246, 248
   Zechariah 3:4 247; 12:10 447
   Ecclesiasticus (Apocrypha) 2:10 88, 505
   Matthew 5:14 592; 7:13 and 14 98, 207, 243; 9:2 2; 10:23 295; 11:13 and 14 89; 14:17 569; 15:32ff 569; 18:20 53; 21:31 and 32 111; 25:10 92; 25:36 202
   Mark 3:8–9 111; 6:27 397, 398; 6:35ff 569; 10:49 2
   Luke 9:12ff 569; 12:10 111; 13:24 243; 16 180, 194, 330, 331; 16:22 and 23 181; 24:47 301
   John 1:1 511; 1:14 99; 6:5ff 569; 10:9 376; 14:6 140, 376; 18:36 139; 19:34–37 447
   Acts 9:1 and 2 96; 14:22 135; 19:23 96; 22:4 96; 23 135; 23:11 2; 24 135, 205; 24:14 96, 202; 24: 15 202; 24:22 96
   Romans 319; 3:10 30; 5:14 352; 7:1–4 91; 8:26 191; 8:37 248; 8:37–39 136, 246; 12:19 296; 13:11 339
   1 Corinthians 1:26 22; 2:1–5 139; 3:10 190; 4:10 340; 4:18–20 294; 9:22 340; 9:24 99, 244, 345; 10:6 369; 10:11 89, 369; 11:7 91; 13:12 366, 377; 14:15 189
   2 Corinthians 1:5 478; 3:6–18 376; 3:12 376; 6:17 143; 12:2–5 191; 12:4 190; 12:9 136
   Galatians, Luther's *Commentary see* Luther, Martin
   Galatians 2:16 562; 4:8–21 281; 4:21–31 376; 4:24 109; 4:28 120
   Ephesians 1:18 251; 3:1 135; 5:28 and 29 91; 6:13–18 248
   Philippians 4:2 545
   1 Thessalonians 1:4 and 5 294
   1 Timothy 134
   Titus 3:7 and 8 198
   Philemon 1:9 135
   Hebrews 134, 352; 4:12 248; 6:4–8 111; 11:1 509; 11:13–16 140, 367; 12:1 and 2 97; 12:22–24 31, 478
   James 4:7 248, 249
   1 Peter 3:7 91
   1 John 2:1 301; 5:4 509
   Revelation 200, 298; 9:1–11 247; 11 356; 13 247; 16 355; 20 354; 20:1–6 199; 21 91, 355; 21:2 92; 22:1 300; 22:14 252

Birrell, Augustine 679
Bishop, Elizabeth 605
'Black Bartholomew's Day' (1662) 188
Blake, William 557, 565–7, 568, 625, 628, 630
blasphemy 263
Blasphemy Act (1650) 266
Bloom, Harold 565
Blyton, Enid 658, 664
board games 644
bodies *see* gender
Boehm, Joseph Edgar 12
Boekholt, Johannes 628
Bolton, Major Robert 25
book history scholarship *see* Bunyan, John, publication
Book of Common Prayer
   abolition 27, 37
   conformity 38
   JB's rejection of 27, 189, 191, 192, 198, 266, 483
   opposition to 189
   reinstatement 27, 188
   revision 39
Booth, Wayne 534
Boyle, Sir Robert 46, 522
Braddyll, Thomas 160
Bradford, John 545, 550
Branch, Lori 188
Breen, Margaret Sönser 17–18, 313, 320
Bridges, Robert 399
Brightman, Thomas 199
British Empire
   Africa 674
   Bunyan's universality 678
   India 675
   missionaries 669
   nineteenth century 666
   Pilgrim's Progress 665–6
Brittain, Vera 3, 9
Brontë, Charlotte 534
Brown, John 126, 290, 357, 456–7, 528, 624, 671
Brown, Sylvia 128
Brown, T. J. 112
Browne, James 399, 400
Bunyan, Elizabeth, wife 127
Bunyan, John, biographies
   Brittain, Vera 3, 9
   Brown, John 126, 456–7, 528, 624
   Doe, Charles 22
   Greaves, Richard L. 465
   Hill, Christopher 464
   Macaulay, Thomas Babington 456–8
   Southey, Robert 126, 456
Bunyan, John, Christian faith
   baptism 37
   baptism, beliefs about 23, 29, 63, 173
   Bedford Congregation 53, 581
   Bible 86
   books, importance of 105, 211
   conversion 26, 28, 111, 172, 206, 472
   doctrine 30
   imprisonment
      conditions of 191–2
      Grace Abounding and 484–5
      ministry in relation to 475
      psychological insights 480–3
      spiritual crisis and conversion in relation to 472–5
      spiritual experience, as 477–9
      time of 2, 30, 40, 59, 133, 152, 204, 344
   ministry 30, 64, 173, 217, 475
   music and hymns 103
   political thought 33–4, 140–3, 183
   prayer 27
   preaching 31
   prison writings *see* Bunyan, John, works
   Puritanism 5, 37
   radicalism 181
   theology *see* Bunyan, John, theology
   trial 27, 188
   view of Restoration Dissent 36, 51
   writings *see* Bunyan, John, works; Dissent
Bunyan, John, life
   army service 24, 208
   death 31, 32, 343
   early life, education, and career 22, 103, 210
   first marriage (wife's name unknown) 21, 31, 105, 155, 173, 192, 210
   imprisonment *see* Bunyan, John, Christian faith
   origins 22
   portraits 164, 556, 626
   second marriage (Elizabeth Bunyan) 27, 105

tercentenary 680
timeline xxv–xxvii
Bunyan, John, publication
  book history scholarship 166–7
  Doe, Charles 149–51
  illustration 162–6
  local imprints 152
  Ponder, Nathaniel 158–62
  Smith, Francis 153–8
Bunyan, John, reading
  Ambrose, Isaac 112–13
  ballads 103
  Bayly, Lewis 105–6, 211
  Bible 70, 86–90, 101
  Dent, Arthur 105–8, 211
  early reading 102–5
  Foxe's *Acts and Monuments* 114–16
  Luther's commentary on
      Galatians 108–10, 212
  newsbooks 103–4
  popular religious books 105
  popular romances 104–5
  range of 116
  Spira, Francis 111
Bunyan, John, theology
  baptism 226–8
  Bible 86
  Calvinism 70, 83
  Christology 72
  ecclesiology 82–3
  essentials of faith 224–6
  faith and post-secular reading 514
  faith in *Grace Abounding* 503–7
  faith in *Pilgrim's Progress* 507–10
  fear 236–7
  fulfilment of Christian hope 237–9
  gender *see* gender
  godliness 211–16
  grace 229–32
  homosexuality 125
  hypocrisy 234–5
  justification 228–9
  law and covenant 74–6, 184
  marriage 91–6, 147
  martyrology 36, 115–16
  millenarianism 34, 83, 142, 176, 187, 198–201, 354–8

  opposition to Anglicanism 102, 223, 224, 233, 239, 293, 299, 391, 493, 547
  opposition to Catholicism 81, 85, 142, 147, 222, 223, 228, 293, 300, 338
  opposition to Church of England 83, 85, 133, 137, 141, 220, 221, 228, 233
  opposition to Quakers 26, 32, 176, 201, 268
  opposition to Ranters 174, 201, 567
  order of salvation 76–82
  politics and pastoral sermons 232–3
  prayer 189–91
  resurrection 119, 201–2
  sexual sin 120
  soteriology 72–4
  sources of 70
  unpardonable sin 111
  women *see* gender
  writings *see* Bunyan, John, works; Dissent
Bunyan, John, works
  adaptation and reception of *see* adaptation and reception
  allegory in *see* allegory
  children's literature *see* children's literature
  universality of 678–81
  class, and *see* class
  Dissent, writing of *see* Dissent
  early novel, in relation to *see* early novel
  early works
    opposition to Quakers in 176–80
    opposition to Ranters in 174–6
    radical religion in 1650s, and 172–4
  historical studies of *see* historical studies
  marginal notes in *see* marginal notes
  poetry
    critical disparagement of 325
    Book for Girls and Boys, A 161, 334, 336–41, 370, 371, 460, 653–5
    Caution to Stir up to Watch against Sin, A 292, 294, 326
    courtly poetry 326–7
    Discourse of the Building, Nature, Excellency and Government of the House of God, A 55, 65, 304–5
    Ebal and Gerizzim 192, 196, 328, 332
    One Thing is Needful 192, 195, 196, 331, 332, 481

Bunyan, John, works (*cont.*)
   passion 333
   Pilgrim's Progress 326, 328–9
   Pilgrim's Progress Part II 329
   Prison Meditations 134, 155, 192, 194, 484
   prison writings 191
   Profitable Meditations 155, 192, 326, 329
   truth 329–33
   'Who would true Valour see' ('To Be a Pilgrim') 11, 13
  posthumously published works
   dates of composition 345–6
   millenarianism and politics in 354–8
   non-publication by JB, reasons for 346–8
   publication in folio 344
   sermon origin, structure and style of 348–52
   typology in 352–4
  prison writings
   effect of prison experience on JB 199–200, 202–3
   poetry 191–7
   time as theme in 197–202
  prose
   Acceptable Sacrifice, The 343, 345, 350
   Advocateship of Jesus Christ, The 91, 300
   Antichrist, and his Ruine, Of 34, 142, 346, 356–8
   Barren Fig-Tree, The 111, 237
   Case of Conscience Resolved, A 118, 127, 301, 438
   Christ a Compleat Saviour 346
   Christian Behaviour 91, 106, 124, 129, 130, 134, 144, 155, 197–8
   Come, & Welcome, to Jesus Christ 79, 91, 237–9
   Confession of my Faith, and A Reason of my Practice, A 29, 59, 72, 76, 79, 92, 134
   Defence of the Doctrine of Justification, by Faith, A 114, 134, 345
   Desire of the Righteous Granted, The 346, 350
   Differences in Judgment about Water-Baptism, No Bar to Communion 29, 64
   Discourse of the House of the Forest of Lebanon, A 115
   Discourse upon the Pharisee and the Publicane, A 78, 79, 292, 298
   Doctrine of the Law and Grace Unfolded, The 32, 74, 90, 109, 144, 161, 176, 182–5, 207, 440
   Exposition on the Ten First Chapters of Genesis, An 142, 255, 346, 353
   Few Sighs from Hell, A 89, 102, 114, 156, 172, 175, 176, 180–2, 194, 271, 330, 379, 380, 381, 473, 608
   Good News for the Vilest of Men 79, 301
   Grace Abounding see *Grace Abounding to the Chief of Sinners*
   Greatness of the Soul 111, 292, 293, 348
   Heavenly Foot-man, The 98, 183, 344, 345
   Holy City, The 92, 134, 198, 199, 350, 355, 439, 444
   Holy Life, the Beauty of Christianity, A 144, 292, 293, 439
   Holy War see *Holy War, The*
   House of the Forest of Lebanon, The 346
   I Will Pray with the Spirit 27, 155, 187–91, 198, 482
   Instructions for the Ignorant 125
   Israel's Hope Encouraged 345, 351
   Justification by an Imputed Righteousness, Of 30, 345, 350
   Law and a Christian, Of the 346
   Life and Death of Mr. Badman, The see *Life and Death of Mr. Badman, The*
   Mapp Shewing the Order and Causes of Salvation and Damnation, A 77, 110, 165, 195
   Mr. John Bunyan's Last Sermon 79, 344, 345
   Paul's Departure and Crown 345
   Peaceable Principles and True 29, 82, 328
   Pilgrim's Progress see *Pilgrim's Progress, The*
   Pilgrim's Progress Part II see *Pilgrim's Progress Part II, The*
   Questions about the Nature and Perpetuity of the Seventh-Day-Sabbath 303
   Relation of the Imprisonment of Mr. John Bunyan, A 142, 344, 345, 500
   Resurrection of the Dead, The 101, 119, 201
   Saints Knowledge of Christ's Love, The 346, 350, 351
   Saints Privilege and Profit, The 346
   Saved by Grace 156, 496
   Seasonable Counsel 34, 50, 136, 292, 295, 347, 397, 401

Solomon's Temple Spiritualized 89, 101, 109, 304, 346
Some Gospel-Truths Opened 26, 32, 113, 114, 118, 119, 152, 176–9, 440
Strait Gate, The 32, 79, 98, 156, 237
Treatise of the Fear of God, A 161, 263
Trinity and a Christian, Of the 346
Vindication of the Book Called, Some Gospel-Truths Opened, A 113, 119, 177, 178–80
Water of Life, The 159, 161, 300, 496
publication *see* Bunyan, John, publication
radical writings *see* piety and radicalism in 1680s
romance *see* romance
style *see* style
theological and literary theoretical approaches combined
    faith and post-secular reading 502–3, 514
    faith and secularism 512
    faith in *Grace Abounding* 503–7
    faith in *Pilgrim's Progress* 507–10
    poststructuralism 510–14
theology *see* Bunyan, John, theology
universality 678
Works of that Eminent Servant of Christ, Mr. John Bunyan, The (Doe's edition) 149, 344, 438, 455, 484
Bunyan, Mary, daughter 192
Bunyan, Thomas, father 22
Bunyan Meeting Church
  sculpture 638, 644
  stained-glass windows 638, 639, 640
Bunyan Studies (journal) 10, 128, 464–5
Bunyan Tableaux 632–6
Burder, George 542, 543, 549
Burg, Barry 125
Burnett, Frances Hodgson 660
Burrough, Edward 41, 113, 118, 119, 177, 179, 550
Burton, John 54, 63, 71

Calvert, Elizabeth 154
Calvin, Jean 30, 56, 70, 72, 77, 89
Calvinism
  conformist 45
  heritage of 83–5
  JB's theology 70, 83
  Methodism and 539

Cambers, Andrew 102
Camden, Vera 128
Campbell, Gordon 195, 407, 558
Canada *see* adaptation and reception
Canne, John 279
Capp, Bernard 178
Caputo, John 514
Carlyle, Thomas 573, 575
Carver, Christian Creswell 241, 256
Castlemaine, Barbara Palmer, Countess of 120, 122
Catholicism
  Anglo-Catholicism 458, 656
  anti-Catholic providentialism 104
  Bible and 89
  Book of Common Prayer, and 27
  Charles II 47, 48
  Commonwealth and 178
  Exclusion Crisis (1678–81) *see* Charles II
  'Glorious Revolution', and 305
  James II *see* James II
  JB's opposition to 81, 85, 142, 147, 222, 223, 228, 293, 300, 338
  Pilgrim's Progress, adaptation and reception 670
  Popish Plot 233, 347
  Protestant martyrdom, and 115
  Protestant millenarianism, and 355
  re-catholicization in Europe 42
  Toleration Act (1689) 51
Cavalier Parliament (1661–79) 38, 48, 49, 199, 204
Cavendish, Margaret, Duchess of Newcastle 516
Cervantes, Miguel de 534
chapbooks 629
Chapman, John 581
Chapman, Livewell 154
characters in early novels 522, 529
Charles I 37, 105, 171, 188, 189
Charles II
  Catholic sympathies 47
  Council of State 48
  death 298, 348
  Declaration of Breda (1660) 38, 48, 186, 204, 287
  Declaration of Indulgence (1672) 33, 48, 287, 357

Charles II (*cont.*)
  Exclusion Crisis (1678–81) 42, 292, 345, 347, 356
  'feminine' image 124
  Fifth Monarchists 199
  Owen, John, and 47
  'Popish Plot' (1678) 292, 345, 347, 356
  portraits 124, 163
  restoration 171, 253, 355
  Restoration libertine sexuality 120, 143
  Restoration Settlement 38, 186, 492
  Rye House Plot (1683) 43, 292, 347
  suppression of Dissent 347
Chaucer, Geoffrey 363, 395
Cheare, Abraham 334
Cheever, George B. 595–7, 602
children's literature
  beginnings of 651–3
  Book for Girls and Boys, A 334, 336–41, 370, 371, 460, 653–5
  Bunyan as subtext in 660–3
  Pilgrim's Progress adapted for 655–60
Chilembwe, John 675, 679
Chrétien de Troyes 384, 389
Christian community, strength of 147
Christology *see* Bunyan, John, theology
Church of England
  Anglo-Catholicism 458
  attendance 95, 233
  comprehension 36
  conformity with 188, 254, 539
  disestablishment 25, 153
  divines 47, 74, 105, 253, 374, 541, 546, 549
  division 36
  evangelicalism 458, 537
  Latitudinarians 114, 229, 230, 231
  Pilgrim's Progress murals in 637
  primacy 34
  re-establishment 38, 185
  rites 38
  separation from 54, 253, 347
  Spenser, Edmund, and 365
  see also Anglicanism; Evangelicalism
cinema *see* film
Civil War
  class war, as 609, 620
  JB's army service 24

metaphysical poetry 375
millenarianism 355
poststructuralism and postmodernism 499
Clare, John 13
Clarendon, Edward Hyde, Earl of 38, 204
'Clarendon Code' 38, 46, 49, 156, 199, 204, 497
Clarke, John 628
Clarke, Samuel 104, 260
Clarkson, Laurence 123
class
  Civil War as class war 609, 620
  class warfare, *Pilgrim's Progress* and 5, 461, 494
  definition 619
  'Englishness', JB and 4
  Englishness and 609, 622
  JB and 620–1
  property and 619
  tourism 616–19
  wider cultural trends affecting 614–16
  working class radicalism, *Pilgrim's Progress* and 5, 461, 494, 610
clothing in early novels 524
Clunie, Alexander 548
Cockett, C. Bernard 611
Coffey, John 199
cognitive dislocation 385
Cokayne, George 343
Coleridge, Samuel Taylor 7, 69, 70, 98, 367, 370, 399, 435, 454, 521, 529, 534, 557, 559–61, 564, 568, 573, 600
Collé, Nathalie 162
College, Stephen 157
Collini, Stefan 15
colloquialism in *Pilgrim's Progress* 417
colonialism *see* British Empire
Commonwealth 178, 182
comprehension, policy of 36, 42, 46, 48, 49, 51
Congregationalists
  churches and congregations 62
  comprehension 46
  conferences 54
  conversion 206
  Evangelical Revival 537
  growth of 37, 43
  licensing 48
  Restoration suppression 39

separatism 42, 54
toleration 51
see also Bedford Congregation
Conventicle Act (1664) 39, 55, 192, 204
Conventicle Act (1670) 39, 40, 271
Convention Parliament (1689) 38
Conyers, Richard 541, 549
Cooper, Helen 381
Cooper, Thomas 581
Copping, Harold 630, 633, 638
Corporation Act (1661) 38
'Country party' 49
covenant see Bunyan, John, theology
Cowley, Abraham 326, 327
Cowley, Matthias 152
Cowper, William 541, 546, 551, 555
Craft, Ellen 12
Craft, William 12
Cragg, Gerald 36
Crashaw, Richard 325, 327
Crist, Timothy 157
Croll, Morris 399
Cromwell, Oliver 7, 37, 46, 124, 171, 178, 182, 199
Cromwell, Richard 171, 182
Crook, John 176
cultural impact see adaptation and reception
Cultural Materialism 467
'cultural nation' 615
Cummings, E. E. 605
Cunningham, Valentine 435, 448, 449, 560

Damrosch, Leo 485
Danby, Thomas Osbourne, Earl of 48, 49
Dante Alighieri 363, 368
Danvers, Henry 156, 457
Darnton, Robert 466
Davie, Donald 558
Davies, Michael 57, 89, 120, 390, 436, 448, 494, 496, 497, 557, 559, 569
de Vries, Pieter 76
Declaration of Breda (1660) 38, 48, 186, 204, 287
Declaration of Indulgence (1672) 33, 48, 287, 357
Declaration of Indulgence (1687) 299, 346
Defoe, Daniel 207, 506, 522, 523, 525, 532, 534, 535, 536, 608, 653

Delaune, Thomas 347
Denne, Henry 23
Dent, Arthur 71, 105, 106, 181, 211, 244, 258, 260, 268, 279, 403
Derrida, Jacques 373, 377, 469, 489, 510, 515
Dewsagaim, P. D. 676
dialect in *Pilgrim's Progress* 417
Dickens, Charles 575–8
difference, theme of 501, 510
Diggers 180
Directory of Worship 27, 189
Dissent
    Anglicanism and 36, 40, 42, 44, 46, 540, 552
    Evangelical Revival 537
    Great Persecution 36
    JB's writings
        heavenly focus 137–40
        impact of imprisonment 133–7
        licensing of works 141–3
        strength in community 147–8
        submissiveness not submission 140–1
    Puritan Revolution 7, 37
    radical religion in 1650s 172–4
    Restoration suppression 347
    strength 33, 51, 537
    toleration of 33
    tradition of 5, 15
    trials of 37–43
    triumphs of 43–51
    see also Nonconformism
Dixon, Edmund 161
Dod, John 24, 71
Doe, Charles 22, 149–51, 344, 345, 346, 348, 438, 455, 484
domestic violence 270–3
Donne, John 193, 375, 402
Dostoyevsky, Feodor 480
Dowley, Tim 646
Downame, John 279
Dryden, John 522, 530
Dunan-Page, Anne 163, 200, 259, 280, 325, 474
Dunton, John 335, 339, 341
During, Simon 514
Dutch editions of *Pilgrim's Progress* 628
Dutton, Richard 69
Dylan, Bob 605

Eagleton, Terry 297, 514
early life, education, and career *see* Bunyan, John, life
early novel
    characters 522, 529–34
    metafiction 534–6
    spaces 522, 527–9
    things 522, 523–6
ecclesiology *see* Bunyan, John, theology
Edict of Nantes, Revocation of (1685) 42, 346
Edward the Confessor 147
Edwards, John 539, 542
Edwards, Thomas 173, 180, 181
Edwards, W. H., Major 680
Eliot, George 12, 14, 256, 578–80, 581
Eliot, John 46
Elizabeth I 90, 188, 355, 365
Elshtain, Jean Bethke 590, 601
emblems 370–1
Emerson, Ralph Waldo 599
empire *see* British Empire
English Civil War *see* Civil War
English heritage *see* heritage
English republic 171
English Revolution 5, 16, 174, 220, 462, 465, 467, 494
Englishness *see* class
engravings *see* illustration
Etherege, George 125, 530
Etherington, Norman 668
Evangelical Revival
    hymns 550
    JB and 456
    Pilgrim's Progress, and *see Pilgrim's Progress, The*
Evangelicalism
    adaptation and reception of JB in 6, 8, 17, 280, 456
    Anglo-Catholicism, and 458
    Calvinism and 44, 83
    conversion narratives 61
    JB and 89
Exclusion Crisis (1678–81) 42, 48, 49, 157, 292, 345, 356

faith *see* Bunyan, John, Christian faith; Bunyan, John, theology
fantasy literature, adaptation and reception in 516
fashion, Nonconformism and 138
Feibusch, Hans 637
Fell, Margaret 118, 120, 127
femininity *see* gender
Fenichel, Otto 473
Fenne, Samuel 63, 64
Ferguson, Robert 43
Ferguson, Stephen 112
Feuerbach, Ludwig 577
Fielding, Henry 522, 529, 534, 536
Fifth Monarchists 38, 83, 127, 154, 199, 335, 355, 619
figura 368–70
film
    Knight of Cups 13
    Matter of Life and Death, A 1–3, 9, 11
Finley, C. Stephen 458, 574
Fire of London *see* London
First World War, *Pilgrim's Progress*, and 241, 256
Fish, Stanley 490, 529
Five Mile Act (1665) 39
Flavel(l), John 40, 44, 331, 539
Flaxman, John 625
Fletcher, Angus 366
Fletcher, John William 540, 545
Flint, Maurice 671, 673
Forrest, James F. 8, 283, 464
Forster, E. M. 529
Foucault, Michel 467, 489
Fowler, Edward 45, 71, 74, 79, 90, 102, 114, 144, 345, 540
Fox, George 41, 118, 119, 139, 176, 177, 180
Foxe, John 71, 83, 114–16, 136, 163, 254, 335, 441, 478
Franklin, Benjamin 12, 590, 592
Frei, Hans 290
Freud, Sigmund 470, 480
Fromm, Erich 474
Froude, James Anthony 458, 574
Frye, Northrop 434, 445, 651
Fuller, Margaret 599

Furlong, Monica 127, 288
Fussell, Paul 241, 242

Galatians, Luther's *Commentary see*
    Luther, Martin
Garbe, Richard 14
Gast, John 594
Gaskell, Elizabeth 12
Gauden, John 189
gender
    bodies 118–26
    roles 126–32
    women prophets 118
    women's prayer and worship 301–3
    women's role 127, 302, 312, 316
Geneva Bible 90, 437; *see also* Bible
Ghent, Dorothy Van 528
Ghiberti, Lorenzo 638
Gielgud, Sir John 13
Gifford, George 106
Gifford, John 29, 37, 54, 57, 58, 61, 63, 71, 109,
    152, 172, 260
Gilpin, Joshua 533
Giraldus Cambrensis 458
'Glorious Revolution' (1689) 305
Goethe, Johann Wolfgang von 367
Goldie, Mark 39, 44
Goodwin, John 47, 552
Goodwin, Thomas 37
Goring, Marius 1
Gosse, Edmund 582
Gouge, Thomas 140
Gouge, William 92
Grace Abounding to the Chief of Sinners
    army service, JB's experience of 24
    Bible, authority of 214–15
    Bible, reading of 71, 87, 101
    blasphemy 266
    books, importance of 211
    British Empire 667, 669
    class 608, 609, 622
    'clean' and 'unclean' animals 354
    contrast between Law and Gospel 109
    early life, education, and career 22, 103
    editions 9, 209
    faith 503, 510

godliness 211
guilt 562
historical study 453, 457
Holy War, and 279, 288
imprisonment 135, 187, 204, 345, 471
marginal notes 441
marriage imagery 98
ministry 30, 217
Mr. Badman, and 260
order of salvation, as 76
original version 207
Pilgrim's Progress, and 209, 218, 502,
    507, 508
poststructuralism and postmodernism 487,
    492, 497, 500
preaching 31
publication 21, 156, 161, 162, 204, 246, 258
Quakers 179
Ranters 174
reading of religious books 107
romance 379, 384
Romanticism and 558
sermons 349
sexual sin 123
sin 208
spiritual autobiography 145
spiritual crisis and conversion 28, 111,
    172, 206
structure 208
style 208, 400, 403
Victorian period and 577, 582
Graham, Jean 128
Grantham, Thomas 24, 327, 328
Great Fire *see* London
Greaves, Richard L. 8, 78, 81, 90, 155, 172, 181,
    187, 192, 197, 201, 254, 305, 313, 345, 346,
    348, 465, 473, 483, 485
Green, Ian 331
Greene, Robert 380
Gregory, Olinthus 112
Grinstein, Alexander 482
Gustavus Adolphus, King of Sweden 355

Hackel, Heidi Brayman 437, 438, 442, 444
Hacker, Francis 188
Haigh, Christopher 107

Hale, Sir Matthew 46
Hall, Barry 493
Hammond, Mary 573
Hancock, Maxine 320
Hardy, Thomas 12, 14, 584–8
Harper, Charles G. 612
Harrington, James 171, 182
Harris, Benjamin 334
Harrison, Frank Mott 456, 624
Harrison, G. B. 57
Harsha, D. A. 317
Hart, Joseph 550
Hartley, David 562
Hawker, Robert 541
Hawthorne, Nathaniel 590, 595, 599, 602–4, 606
Haywood, Eliza 524, 534, 536
Hazard, Thomas 153
Hegel, Georg Wilhelm Friedrich 466
Henry, Matthew 539
Henry, Prince 105, 337
Herbert, George 325, 327, 336
heritage
   Calvinist 83
   Christian 615
   'cultural nation' 615
   English 611
   English heritage industry 618
   historical 10, 619
   literary 10, 245
   Puritan 84
   shared English and American 2
Hershberger, Marla 646
Hervey, James 538
Heveningham, William 188
Higgins Gallery, Bedford 643
Hill, Christopher 10, 181, 357, 461, 463, 464, 465, 494, 496, 610, 620
Hill, Richard 538, 540
Hill, W. Speed 436
historical studies of JB and his milieu
   contemporary historical studies 464–8
   early sources and studies 455–6
   future studies 468–9
   Marxist 461–4
   nineteenth-century studies 456–60
   twentieth-century studies 460–4
Hobbes, Thomas 171, 374

Hofmeyr, Isabel 17, 162, 322, 468, 491, 492, 610, 665, 668, 669, 670, 672, 675, 677
Hogarth, William 105
Holles, Denzil 49
Holy War, The
   allegory 281–3, 377
   Bible and 277
   British Empire 669
   Christian despair 286–7
   drunkenness 263, 266
   epic form 283
   epigraph 277, 350
   Grace Abounding, and 279, 288
   Homer's *Iliad* 283
   humour 287–9
   hypocrisy 114
   language 415
   language as allegorical 372
   marginal notes 438, 439
   military metaphors 25
   Mr. Badman, and 275, 284
   poetry 333
   popularity 279
   poststructuralism and postmodernism 495, 499
   prayer 191
   publication 258
   realism 282–3
   salvation 77
   sources 277–9
   title page 277, 350
   women's role 127, 302
Homeland Association 611
Homer's *Iliad* 283
homosexuality 125
Hooker, Richard 436
House Beautiful (magazine) 11
How, Samuel 101
Howe, John 40, 44
Howgill, Francis 41
Hubberthorne, Richard 41
human rights 2
Hunter, J. Paul 523, 529
Hunter, Kim 1
Huntingdon, Selina Hastings, Countess of 539, 540, 541, 542, 545
Hutchinson, Lucy 147

Iliad 283, 362
illustration
　accompaniment to text 626–30
　board games 644–6
　Book for Girls and Boys, A 334, 370
　Bunyan Tableaux 633–6
　chapbooks 629–30
　contemporary representations of
　　text 646–8
　inspired by text 631–8
　lantern slide series 636
　Life and Death of Mr. Badman 262,
　　271, 272
　murals 637
　Pilgrim's Progress 115, 152, 162, 247, 456, 540,
　　566, 575, 585
　postcards 630, 633, 638, 640, 641
　puppetry 640
　range of 648–9
　sculpture *see* sculpture
　stained-glass windows 637, 639, 640
　three-dimensional images 638–42
　transitional images 642–6
　Triumphant Journey 643; *see also* Sweeney,
　　Phyllis F.
　woodcuts 626–8
imperialism *see* British Empire
imprisonment *see* Bunyan, John,
　Christian faith
imprisonment, writings *see* Bunyan,
　John, works
Independents *see* Congregationalists
India *see* adaptation and reception
International John Bunyan Society 10, 464
Ireton, General Henry 619
irony, allegory and 374–8
Ivimey, Joseph 551

James, William 470, 582
James I 90
James II
　accession 42, 348, 358
　Catholic conversion 47, 142
　Declaration of Indulgence (1687) 299, 346
　Exclusion Crisis *see* Charles II
　Monmouth Rebellion (1685) 43, 292, 346,
　　348, 358

Nonconformist writing, in 339
　portraits 163
　Rye House Plot *see* Charles II
　Smith, Francis, and 158
　toleration policy 46, 48, 287, 298, 299
Janeway, James 652
Jeffreys, Sir George 157
Jencks, Charles 488
Jessey, Henry 37, 71, 154
John Bunyan Museum 57, 103, 617
'John of Leyden' (Jan Beukels) 173
John the Baptist 411
Johnson, Alan 8
Johnson, Barbara A. 556, 571
Johnson, Richard 104, 245, 380, 381, 385
Johnson, Samuel 608, 623
Joseph, P. C. 677
Joyce, James 435
Joyce, Rachel 13

Kahn, Victoria 281
Kalonga Mphiri 675
Kant, Immanuel 510, 512
Kaplan, Elizabeth Bremner 482
Kaufmann, U. Milo 434, 530
Keach, Benjamin 71, 140, 279, 335, 339, 341
Keats, John 367
Keeble, N. H. 127, 188, 202, 286, 312, 347, 436,
　　442, 443, 447, 466, 522, 568
Kelyng, Sir John 27, 188
Kerouac, Jack 605
Kettle, Arnold 461, 463
Kiffin, William 347, 457
Killigrew, Henry 122
Killigrew, Thomas 121, 130
King, Gregory 620
King James (Authorised) Bible 90
Kipling, Rudyard 11
Knight of Cups (film) 13
Knoppers, Laura Lunger 186
Knott, John 115, 196
Krishnapillai, Henry Albert 677
Kristeva, Julia 482
Kroll, Woodrow 615
Kumar, Krishan 611
Kuntze, Edward J. 638
Kyle, Joseph 632

Langland, William 245, 362, 366, 395
language
   awareness as allegorical 371
   everyday language 11
   Pilgrim's Progress, in *see Pilgrim's Progress, The*
lantern slides 636
Larkin, George 156, 301
Latitudinarians 45, 114, 144
Law, Alice 680
Law, William 538
law and covenant *see* Bunyan, John, theology
Lawson, George 352
Leavis, F. R. 413, 557, 558, 613
Leavis, Q. D. 8, 576
Lely, Sir Peter 121, 124
Lerer, Seth 651
L'Estrange, Sir Roger 155
Levellers 180, 463
Lewalski, Barbara 450
Lewis, C. S. 366, 384, 399, 405, 414, 516, 517
libertine sexuality 120
Licensing Act (1662) 141, 160, 346
licensing of JB's works 143
Liebler, Naomi Conn 104
life *see* Bunyan, John, life
Life and Death of Mr. Badman, The
   alehouse culture and drunkenness 259–63
   allegory 375
   blasphemy 263–7
   characters 531
   Christian behaviour 129
   class 608, 621, 622
   death 110, 273
   domestic violence 270–3
   dreaming allegory 366
   extended dialogue 106
   fashion 138
   Grace Abounding, and 260
   Holy War, and 275
   illustration 262, 271, 272
   irony 375
   marginal notes 439, 440
   marriage 91, 92, 93
   newsbooks as source 104
   personification allegory 362
   Pilgrim's Progress, and 260
   Pilgrim's Progress Part II, and 273, 308
   poststructuralism and postmodernism 495, 497
   publication 32, 159, 161, 258, 262
   reprobation 78, 97
   Sabbath-breaking 267–70
   sexual misconduct 123
   violence 296
Lilburne, John 180
Lindale, William 188
Lindsay, Jack 461, 462, 609
literary heritage 10, 245
literary history *see* historical studies
Livesey, Roger 1
Lobb, Stephen 41
Locke, John 39, 49, 652
London
   Great Fire (1666) 44, 156, 204
   JB's ministry in 23, 31, 33, 349
   Nonconformist congregations and meeting houses 43, 62
   publishing *see* Bunyan, John, publication
   Stationers' Company *see* Stationers' Company
   suppression of Dissent 41
Lord's Day *see* Sabbath
Lorris, Guillaume de 362
Louis XIV, King of France 49, 50
Lovelace, Richard 525
Lowell, Robert 590, 605
Lowth, Robert 422
Luther, Martin
   allegory 282
   Coleridge, Samuel Taylor, and 569
   Commentary on Galatians 23, 71, 84, 90, 108–10, 183, 212, 277, 562
   social origin 22
   typology 89
Luxon, Thomas 92, 127, 320, 468, 490
Luyken, Jan 625, 628
Lynch, Beth 95, 176, 280
Lyotard, Jean-François 460, 468, 488, 492, 499, 512

Macaulay, Thomas Babington 399, 457, 527, 574, 575, 580, 581, 675, 677, 679
MacDonald, Ruth K. 655, 660

Mackenzie, Donald 282
Macrobius 363
Malick, Terrence 13
Mallock, W. H. 580
Malory, Sir Thomas 379, 381, 383, 388
Mandelbrote, Giles 161
Mandell, D. J. 598–9
Mandeville, Sir John 381
Mannin, Ethel 615
Manton, Thomas 42, 46
marginal notes
    authorial responsibility for 438–41
    dialogic aspects 451
    mimetic aspects 449–50
    received convention, as 436–8
    taxonomies of 443–7
    theories of 447–9
    usage 441–3
Marlborough, John Churchill, Duke of 122
Marlowe, Christopher 111
marriage
    imagery in the Bible 91–6
    JB see Bunyan, John, life
    virtue of 147
Marshall, William 149, 165
Martin, John 575
martyrology see Bunyan, John, theology
Martz, Louis 281
Marvell, Andrew 103, 120, 142, 171, 253
Marx, Karl 463, 466
Marxist perspectives 5, 461, 494, 619
Mary of Modena, Queen 163
Mason, Emma 581
Mason, William 540, 542, 574
Mately, Dorothy 265
Mather, Cotton 591
Mather, Increase 591
Matter of Life and Death, A (film) 1–3, 9, 11
May, Edward Harrison 632
Mayle, Edmund 50
McCarthy, Cormac 245
McCaughrean, Geraldine 664
McGee, J. Sears 192, 198
McHale, Brian 494
McKenzie, D. F. 649
Meade, Matthew 347
Mearne, Samuel 156, 157

Mede, Joseph 199, 355
Medhurst, Miss 548
Meinecke, Friedrich 615
memorials see adaptation and reception
metafiction in early novels 534
Methodism
    Arminianism and 539
    Calvinism and 539
    Evangelical Revival 538
    Wesleyan Conference (1770) 539
Metropolitan Tabernacle 573
Meun, Jean de 362
Meyer, Stephenie 516
Michie, Alan 490, 491, 494
Midgley, Graham 294, 325, 326, 329, 654
millenarianism see Bunyan, John, theology
Milne, Kirsty 11, 12, 14, 17
Milton, John 44, 136, 139, 142, 145, 182, 186, 195, 201, 277, 278, 281, 286, 288, 399, 458, 497, 559, 566
mobile phone cases 648
Monmouth Rebellion (1685) 43, 292, 346, 348, 358
Montgomery, L. M. 661–3
Montrose, Louis 466
Moore, Alan 5, 13
Moore, Steven 7, 14
Morgan, Edmund 314
Morgan, Joseph 592, 594
Moving Panorama of Pilgrim's Progress 632–5
Mullett, Michael A. 127, 188, 284, 290
Münster Anabaptists 173
murals 637
Murray, Lindley 422
Murray, Shannon 325, 337, 338
museum see John Bunyan Museum
music
    Dylan, Bob 605
    Pilgrim's Progress, The (opera, Vaughan Williams) 9, 13
    Similitude of a Dream, The (music album) 13
Mwase, George Simeon 674, 677

Neal Morse Band, The 13
Neale, J. M. 656, 659
Nedham, Marchamont 171

Netherlands, *Pilgrim's Progress* editions 628
New Criticism 467
New England *see* United States
New Historicism 467
New Model Army 25, 37, 208, 610
Newcomb, Lori 380
Newey, Vincent 10, 406, 557, 558
Newlyn, Lucy 562, 564
Newman, Dorman 300
newsbooks, JB's reading of 103–4
Newton, John 541, 546, 548, 550, 551
New Zealand *see* adaptation and reception
Nicholson, William, Bishop of Gloucester 49
Niebuhr, H. Richard 597, 605
Niven, David 1
Nonconformism
 Anglicanism in opposition to 300, 329, 339, 493
 Declaration of Indulgence (1672) 33, 48
 ejection of ministers ('Black Bartholomew's Day') 188
 evangelical *see* Evangelicalism
 fashion, and 138
 growth of 43
 literary culture 44
 'popish' persecution 41
 radical religion in 1650s 172
 stylistic identity 403
 toleration under James II 287, 298, 299
 see also Dissent
Northern Rising (1663) 43
Norvig, Gerda S. 567
novels *see* adaptation and reception; early novel
Nuttall, Geoffrey 10
Nye, Philip 44

Oates, Titus 42, 163
Offor, George 290, 474, 667, 672
Ogden, C. K. 415
O'Hara, Captain Charles 25
opera *see* music
Orwell, George 255
Osborn, Ian 474
Osborne, Henry C. 680
Overton, Richard 180
Owen, John 37, 42, 43, 44, 46, 47, 62, 71, 77, 135, 158, 262, 347, 539

Owen, Wilfrid 242
Owens, W. R. 10, 149, 199, 465, 466

Pahl, Jon 666
Paine, Thomas 462
painting
 Charles II portraits 124
 Gast, John 594
 libertine sexuality 120
 Sadler, Thomas 12
Parker, Joseph 642
Parker, Samuel 40, 253, 329
Parliament
 Barebones Parliament (1653) 178
 Cavalier Parliament (1661–79) 38, 48, 49, 199, 204
 Convention Parliament (1689) 38
 Rump Parliament (1648–53) 171
Patrick, Simon 244
Peacham, Henry 523
Penn, William 41, 120, 138
Pepys, Samuel 120, 121, 163
Perkins, William 23, 71, 110, 165, 195, 206, 349
Perry, Seamus 561
personification allegory 362–5
Pestell, John 616
Philips, Katherine 326
Phillips, Marion J. 656
pictures *see* illustration; painting
Piercy, J. W. 542
piety and radicalism in JB's works in 1680s
 congregational reform 301–5
 connection between spiritual and physical domains 306
 holiness and suffering 292–9
 reform and sanctification 299–301
pilgrimage imagery in the Bible 96–9
Pilgrim's Progress, The
 adaptation and reception
  Africa 491, 668, 674–5, 679
  America *see* United States
  Canada 671–2, 680
  Catholic Church 670
  India 665, 668, 675–7
  New Zealand 670
 allegory 248–52, 282–3
 American printing 322
 Apollyon 11, 243–8

Bible reading 319
British Empire *see* British Empire
'Calvinist tract', as 69
characters 529–34
children's editions 655–60, 663
circulation in manuscript 142
class *see* class
clothing 524
contrast between Law and Gospel 109
conversation 318
conversion 207
Dutch editions 628
editions 9, 14, 335, 538, 591, 655
emblems 371
endurance of faith 242, 256
enduring relevance 14, 242, 256
epigraph 277, 350
Evangelical Revival, and
    evangelical experience 548–51
    Pilgrim's Progress as means of writing
        history of 551–3
    polemical editions 1743–95 538–47
faith in 507–10
figura 368–70
First World War, and 241, 256
foundation for political radicalism 5
free choice in 78
gender behaviour and roles 130
Giant Despair 105
Giant Pope 104
Grace Abounding, and 209, 218, 502, 507, 508
Heavenly Foot-man, and 345
historical study 454, 456, 461, 462, 468
illustration *see* illustration
imprisonment 133, 200, 471, 485
journey metaphor 32
judgement 181
language
    anachronistic judgements of 419–23
    archaism 423–6
    characterized 413
    dialect and colloquialisms 417–19
    differences with *Part II* 427–31
    early modern English features 416–17
    Puritan language 414–15
    sophistication 431–3
language as allegorical 372

Law and Grace 197
Lord Hategood 188
male and female characteristics 126–32
marginal notes 434, 440, 442, 443, 445
marriage imagery 93–6
martyrology 114, 115
misfit with modern secular-liberal
    culture 6
Moving Panorama 632–5
Mr. Badman, and 260
novel, as 521
order of salvation, as 76
Palace Beautiful 56
personification allegory 363–5
pilgrimage imagery 96, 97, 99, 309
poetry 192, 326, 328
popular culture, in 5, 13
popularity 275, 279
poststructuralism and postmodernism 487, 491, 494, 498, 499
prayer 191
preface 86, 326
present-day readership 8
publication 158, 258
references in other works 11
reinvention of romance 389–92
remaking in other media 12
romance 'adventure' 392–5
romance conventions 387–9
romance genre 381–3
Romanticism and
    Blake, William 565–7
    Coleridge, Samuel Taylor 559, 568
    Scott, Sir Walter 558, 569, 570–1
    Southey's edition (1830) 420, 555, 558, 568, 574, 575, 580
    Wordsworth, William 562–5
sermon style 349
sexual temptation 121
spaces 527–9
style 398, 403–11
tercentenary 638, 643
textualities 534
things 523–6
title page 277, 350
titles of other works, and 11
tourism 616–19
translations 322, 665, 670, 672, 676, 678

Pilgrim's Progress, The (cont.)
    truth 252–5
    universal availability 3
    universality 678
    unpardonable sin 111
    Victorian novelists and
        Dickens, Charles 575–8
        Eliot, George 578–80
        Hardy, Thomas 584–8
        White, Hale 581–4
Pilgrim's Progress, The (opera, Vaughan Williams) 9, 13
Pilgrim's Progress Part II, The
    American printing 322
    British Empire 665–6
    Christian community 131, 147
    didactic style 318
    emblems 370–1
    Evangelical Revival, and 540, 547, 549
    figura 368–9
    gender behaviour and roles 117, 126–32
    language
        differences with *Part I* 427–31
        grammatical features 419
    language as allegorical 371
    literacy of readers 319–21
    male and female characteristics 126–32
    marginal notes 441
    marriage imagery 91, 92, 93
    martyrology 116
    ministry 217, 310
    Mr. Badman, and 273, 308
    pilgrimage imagery 96, 97
    poetry 329
    popularity 322
    preface 160
    publication 258
    realism 282, 318
    romance 389, 392
    Romanticism and 558, 560
    sexual temptation 121
    style 405, 410–11
    textualities 535
    tourism 617
    violence 296
    'Who would True Valour See' 195
    women's role 302, 312–16

political radicalism, *Pilgrim's Progress* as foundation text 5
political thought *see* Bunyan, John, Christian faith
Pomponius Algerius 115
Ponder, Nathaniel 149, 156, 158–62, 262, 300, 303, 332, 414, 626, 628
Ponder, Robert 628
Pooley, Roger 197, 468
'popish' persecution 41
'Popish Plot' (1678) 292, 345, 347, 356
popular romances, JB's reading of 104
popularity *see* adaptation and reception
Porteous Riots (1736) 570
portraits *see* painting
postcards 630, 633, 638, 640, 641
post-colonial Africa, adaptation and reception in 491
posthumously published works *see* Bunyan, John, works
poststructuralism and postmodernism
    Bunyan and difference 501
    Bunyan through 490–5
    faith and language 510–14
    postmodernist and poststructuralist ethos 488–9
    postmodernist perspective on Bunyan 495–501
Powell, Michael 1
Powell, Vavasor 189
prayer *see* Bunyan, John, theology
Prayer Book *see* Book of Common Prayer
Presbyterians
    ascendency 27
    against Baptists 173
    comprehension 46
    execution of Charles I, and 37
    licensing 48
    meetings 44
    political 49
    Restoration suppression 38, 39, 41, 42
    strength 43
    theology 47
    toleration 50
    Toleration Act 1689 51
Pressburger, Emeric 1
Priestley, Joseph 562

printing *see* Bunyan, John, publication
Printing Act (1637) 153
Printing Act (1662) 155, 157, 161
Printing Act (1695) 151
Priolo, M. Paolo 638, 643
prison *see* Bunyan, John, Christian faith
prison writings *see* Bunyan, John, works
Privy Council 153, 157
Proctor, William 161
prose style *see* style
Protectorate 171, 182
Protestant Tutor, The 334–5
Prynne, William 675
Pryor, Margaret 118
psychology of imprisonment 480–83
publication *see* Bunyan, John, publication
puppetry 640
'Puritan Whigs' 49
Puritanism
   ecclesiology 56
   and English 'folk' culture 5
   heritage 84
   language 414
   New England 590
   Puritan Revolution 7, 37
   Restoration suppression 38
   Sabbatarianism 267
   spiritual autobiography 145
   see also Bunyan, John, Christian faith;
      Presbyterians
Putney Debates (1647) 181, 619
Puttenham, George 400

Quaker Act (1662) 39
Quakers
   Baptists against 176
   books of 'Sufferings' 36, 41, 49
   corporeal and spiritual 118
   growth of 43
   integration into parish life 50
   JB's opposition to 26, 32, 176–80, 201, 268
   Restoration suppression 38, 41
   separatism 42
   toleration 51
Qualls, Barry 575
Quarles, Francis 327, 337
Quilligan, Maureen 369, 370

radical religion in 1650s 172–6
Raffles, Thomas 112
Rainsborough, Colonel Thomas 619
Ranke, Leopold von 459
Ranters 174–6, 197, 198, 201, 210, 567
Rastrick, John 45
Raymond, Joad 103
reading *see* Bunyan, John, reading
reception *see* adaptation and reception
Reed, Alan 414
Reeve, John 327
religion *see* Bunyan, John, Christian faith
Religious Tract Society 630, 634, 670
Restoration *see* Charles II
resurrection *see* Bunyan, John, theology
Richardson, Samuel 525, 534
rights *see* human rights
Rigney, Ann 9, 10, 13
Rix, Robert 566
'road' literature 245, 590, 605
Roberts, Jonathan 565
Robin Hood 623
Rochester, John Wilmot, Earl of 125
Roman Catholicism *see* Catholicism
romance
   'adventure' in *Pilgrim's Progress* 392–5
   cognitive dislocation in 385–7
   conventions in *Pilgrim's Progress* 387–9
   genre 381–3
   reinvention in *Pilgrim's Progress* 389–92
   transformation in 383–5
Romanticism, *Pilgrim's Progress* and *see*
      Pilgrim's Progress, The
Rousseau, Jean-Jacques 570
Row, Prescott 611
Rowe, Justin 646, 647
Rowland, Christopher 565
Rowling, J. K. 516
Royal Society 526
Rump Parliament (1648–53) 171
Runyon, Daniel V. 281
Ruskin, John 575
Rutherford, Mark *see* White, W. Hale
Rye House Plot (1683) 43, 292, 347

Sabbath-breaking 267–70
Sadler, Thomas 12, 556

Salmon, Joseph 175
salvation *see* Bunyan, John, theology
Saunders, Laurence 115
Savoy Confession (1658) 71, 75
Schellenberg, Betty 308
Schwind, Moritz von 471
Scott, J. Robertson 610
Scott, Sir Walter 126, 556, 557, 558, 569–71, 573
Scott, Thomas 546–8, 550
Scripture *see* Bible
Scroggs, Sir William, Lord Chief Justice 157
Scudéry, Madeleine de 144
sculpture
   Boehm, Joseph Edgar 12
   Garbe, Richard 14
   Kuntze, Edward J. 638
   Parker, Joseph 642
   Rowe, Justin 646, 647
   Thrupp, Frederick 638
secularism
   faith and 573
   Victorian 573
Sedley, Sir Charles 120
Seeley, John 612
Seidel, Kevin 313
Selous, H. C. 638, 643
sexuality, libertine 120
Shaftesbury, Anthony Ashley Cooper, first Earl of 49, 157
Shakespeare, William 194, 367, 380, 381, 398, 406
Sharrock, Roger 9, 283, 413, 438, 463, 464, 502
Sheldon, Gilbert, Archbishop of Canterbury 39
Sherlock, William 329
Sherwood, Mrs 659
Shrubsole, William 541, 550, 551
Sim, Stuart 357, 465, 468, 490, 494
Similitude of a Dream, The (music album) 13
Simpich, David 640
Simpson, David 549
Simpson, Ken 637
Sinclair, John 667
Smith, David 660
Smith, David E. 591, 597, 603
Smith, Francis 43, 149, 153–8
Smith, Nigel 10, 119, 175, 465

Sneep, John 474
Society for Promoting Christian Knowledge 634
Socinians 81, 178
sodomy 125
Somerville, C. John 105
Soskice, Janet Martin 559–60
soteriology *see* Bunyan, John, theology
Southcombe, George 172, 325
Southey, Robert 126, 399, 420, 456, 478, 556, 558, 568, 574, 575, 580
spaces in early novels 522, 527
Spargo, Tamsin 127, 490, 665, 679, 680
Spenser, Edmund 104, 245, 361, 364, 379, 390, 395, 516, 559
Spinoza, Baruch 584
Spira, Francis (Francesco Spiera) 111
spiritual autobiography 145
Spurgeon, C. H. 573
Spurr, John 45, 287
St Augustine 333
St Paul 134, 139, 183, 190, 202, 205, 281, 340, 352, 368, 376, 466, 476, 477, 484
Stachniewski, John 468, 474, 496, 558
stained-glass windows 637–8
Stapp, Laura 640
Stationers' Company 151, 152, 153, 155, 157
Stationers' Register 153, 154, 156, 159
statues *see* sculpture
Stebbing, Henry 278
Stein, Dieter 418
Sterne, Laurence 530, 534
Sterry, Peter 44
Stevenson, Bill 50
Stillingfleet, Edward 46, 47
Stoker, David 161
Stothard, Thomas 630, 632
Strutt, Joseph 630, 632
Strype, John 160
Sturt, John 164, 628
style
   Bunyan as stylist 397–402
   energetic qualities of 411
   Grace Abounding 208
   pace and journey in relation to 409–11
   sermons 348–52
   speech and 403–8

Swaim, Kathleen 312
Sweeney, Phyllis F. 643
Swift, Jonathan 526, 653
Sylvester, Matthew 41

Talon, Henri 10, 521, 528
Tambling, Jeremy 653
Tawney, R. H. 463
Taylor, Helen L. 658, 664
Taylor, Isaac 657
Taylor, Thomas 353
Test Acts 47, 287
textualities in early novels 534–6
Thackeray, William Makepeace 661
Thane, John 630
Thatcher, Margaret 610
theatre, libertine sexuality in 120
theology *see* Bunyan, John, theology
Thickstun, Margaret Olofson 128, 282
things in early novels 522, 523–6
Thomas, Isaiah 322
Thomas à Kempis 538
Thomason, George 153
Thompson, E. P. 5, 15, 462, 494, 610
Thoreau, Henry David 599
Thrupp, Frederick 638
Tibbutt, H. G. 57
Tillotson, Geoffrey 399
Tillotson, John, Archbishop of Canterbury 46, 47, 144
Tillyard, E. M. W. 275, 286
Tindall, William York 460, 465, 609
Toleration Act (1689) 50, 305, 550, 552
Tolkien, J. R. R. 516
Tombes, John 37
Toplady, Augustus Montague 540
Trapnel, Anna 127
Tribble, Evelyn 448
Trilling, Lionel 471
Triumphant Journey (multimedia) 643; *see also* Sweeny, Phyllis F.
Tucker, Miss C. ('A. L. O. E') 657
Twain, Mark 661
typology, biblical 89, 352–4

United States
    American Tract Society 634, 655, 670, 673

Pilgrim's Progress
    Bunyan Tableaux 633–5
    children's editions 655–60
    New England Puritanism 590–4, 666
    nineteenth-century liberal theology 598
    nineteenth-century 'School of Progress' 594–7
    popularity 322
    'road' literature 245, 590, 605
    secularisation 604
Pilgrim's Progress Part II
    publication in North America 322
universality
    British Empire, within 678
    JB as 'universal' writer 3
    Pilgrim's Progress 3, 678
unpardonable sin 111

Vane, Sir Henry 188
Vattimo, Gianni 469
Vaughan Williams, Ralph 9, 13
Venables, Edmund 678
Venn, John 546
Venner, Thomas 38, 42, 154, 199
Victorian period, *Pilgrim's Progress* and *see Pilgrim's Progress, The*
Vonnegut, Kurt 590, 605

Waite, Terry 630
Walker, David 357, 468, 490, 492, 494, 558
Walker, Mrs Edward Ashley 656
Walsham, Alexandra 104
Walwyn, William 180
Ward, Graham 513
Watkins, Owen 296
Watt, Tessa 165
Watts, Isaac 44, 550, 652
Weber, Max 463
Weeks, William R. 595
Weiss, Judith 379
Welles, John 244
Wesley, Charles 550
Wesley, John 280, 456, 538, 541, 542, 543, 545, 552
Wesleyan Conference (1770) 539
West, Alick 461, 463
Westminster Assembly of Divines 27

Westminster Confession of Faith 71, 75
Wharey, James Blanton 277, 624
White, Robert 162, 556, 624, 626
White, W. Hale 317, 581–4
Whitefield, George 456, 538, 545, 550, 552, 553
Wilkins, John 46, 349
Willet, Andrew 337
William III 50
William IV 559
Williams, Raymond 462
Williamson, George 399
Wilson, Thomas 330, 339
Wingate, Francis 187
Winnicott, D. W. 470
Winstanley, Gerrard 180, 463
Winthrop, John 591
Wither, George 327
Wizard of Oz, The Wonderful (book) 245, 604
Wood, George 595

woodcuts *see* illustration
Woodford, Samuel 326
Woodward, Hezekiah 353
Woolf, Virginia 484, 523
Wordsworth, William 516, 557, 562, 584
working class *see* class
works *see* Bunyan, John, works
Wright, John Michael 124
Wright, John, 'the younger' 152
Wright, Joseph 418
Wright, M. 152
Wycherley, William 529
Wyclif, John 71, 89, 428
Wyke, Clement H. 278, 280

York, James Stuart, Duke of *see* James II

Zinck, Arlette 474
Žižek, Slavoj 469